Third Edition

W9-DHY-227

PUBLIC HEALTH LEADERSHIP

PUTTING PRINCIPLES INTO PRACTICE

LOUIS ROWITZ, PHD

PROFESSOR EMERITUS, SCHOOL OF PUBLIC HEALTH
UNIVERSITY OF ILLINOIS AT CHICAGO
CHICAGO, IL

JONES & BARTLETT
LEARNING

KENT STATE UNIVERSITY LIBRARY, KENT, OHIO

World Headquarters
Jones & Bartlett Learning
5 Wall Street
Burlington, MA 01803
978-443-5000
info@jblearning.com
www.jblearning.com

Jones & Bartlett Learning books and products are available through most bookstores and online booksellers. To contact Jones & Bartlett Learning directly, call 800-832-0034, fax 978-443-8000, or visit our website, www.jblearning.com.

Substantial discounts on bulk quantities of Jones & Bartlett Learning publications are available to corporations, professional associations, and other qualified organizations. For details and specific discount information, contact the special sales department at Jones & Bartlett Learning via the above contact information or send an email to specialsales@jblearning.com.

Copyright © 2014 by Jones & Bartlett Learning, LLC, an Ascend Learning Company

All rights reserved. No part of the material protected by this copyright may be reproduced or utilized in any form, electronic or mechanical, including photocopying, recording, or by any information storage and retrieval system, without written permission from the copyright owner.

Public Health Leadership: Putting Principles into Practice, Third Edition is an independent publication and has not been authorized, sponsored, or otherwise approved by the owners of the trademarks or service marks referenced in this product.

The screenshots in this product are for educational and instructive purposes only. All trademarks displayed are the trademarks of the parties noted therein. Such use of trademarks is not an endorsement by said parties of Jones & Bartlett Learning, its products, or its services, nor should such use be deemed and endorsement by Jones & Bartlett Learning of said third party's products or services.

This publication is designed to provide accurate and authoritative information in regard to the Subject Matter covered. It is sold with the understanding that the publisher is not engaged in rendering legal, accounting, or other professional service. If legal advice or other expert assistance is required, the service of a competent professional person should be sought.

Production Credits
Publisher: Michael Brown
Managing Editor: Maro Gartside
Editorial Assistant: Chloe Falivene
Production Manager: Tracey McCrea
Production Assistant: Alyssa Lawrence
Senior Marketing Manager: Sophie Fleck Teague
Manufacturing and Inventory Control Supervisor: Amy Bacus
Composition: diacriTech
Cover Design: Michael O'Donnell
Cover Image: © Nik_Merkulov/ShutterStock, Inc. (bottom), © Mazzzur/ShutterStock, Inc. (top)
Printing and Binding: Courier Companies
Cover Printing: Courier Companies

To order this product, use ISBN: 978-1-284-02173-8

Library of Congress Cataloging-in-Publication Data
Rowitz, Louis.
   Public health leadership : putting principles into practice / Louis Rowitz.—3rd ed.
      p. ; cm.
   Includes bibliographical references and index.
   ISBN 978-1-4496-4521-2 (pbk.)
   ISBN 1-4496-4521-6 (pbk.)
   I. Title.
   [DNLM: 1. Public Health Administration.   2. Leadership. WA 525]
   362.1068—dc23
                                             2012033832

6048

Printed in the United States of America
17 16 15 14 13   10 9 8 7 6 5 4 3 2

DEDICATION

To my wife of over fifty years, Toni, who still inspires me,
makes me laugh, and is my best friend.

Table of Contents

Part V   Leadership, Evaluation, and Research   629

Part VI   The Future   681

Preface to the Third Edition

Over the past year, as I put together this third edition of my two combined leadership books, my personal life changed as well. I had my first major surgery with a fairly long recuperation. I celebrated 50 years of marriage, and shared my life with a wonderful woman, two special daughters, and four positively intriguing grandchildren. I retired after 46 years.

I now stand on the brink of an exciting new adventure, as a professor emeritus with the opportunity to return to my public health school part-time. I will be writing more, with the time to explore new areas of leadership and public health practice. I will continue to conduct leadership workshops and write my leadership blog. I also hope to do some public health systems research with friends and colleagues.

For me, retirement will just be a change of venue with winter in a warm place. Life is filled with both positives and negatives, but all these experiences aid me in the growth tied to lifelong learning. I would like to share a special lesson from this past year that I described to my blog readers (http://rowitzonleadership.wordpress.com):

> During my personal illness, I learned so much. I spent the last several years exploring leadership, management, organizational development, and the importance of connections and collaboration. I needed to understand how I have put my faith in others from the exceedingly stable 50 years of love from my wife and family. Over the past several months, they have supported me, loved me, and helped me through my turmoil. I learned to respect and trust all those around me who have kept our activities and relationships going and protected me on the days that I was not able to protect myself. The skills and expertise of my fellow public health workers on the planet cannot be underestimated. My professional friends have kept me in their hearts and texted and called me on each day of my journey.
>
> It is all about the relationships in our lives. It is about our trust and faith in each other and our

willingness to make changes in order to improve the lives of our fellow citizens. The two most important words in our language are "Thank You." The greatest lesson for me is to avoid complicating what we do. The basic human skills are the most important. Our leadership skills are about being good servants of the public's trust, doing our jobs in the most effective manner, respecting our colleagues, and resolving our conflicts in trusting ways. We can have diversity in our views but use our differences to build new levels of understanding to develop ways that we can work together more effectively and efficiently.

Our battles are not over. Fighting for the future of our nation and the necessary priorities related to improved health and quality of life in a shrinking economic environment provides challenges, but also innovative and creative solutions.

Progress requires constant change, continuous quality improvement, testing new approaches, and working toward improved health outcomes through more effective performance of our programs and activities.

We will find new partnerships as well as new ways to connect and collaborate. We cannot lose our basic skills, but must improve them and make them stronger. The secret is in our communities and our ability to make our ideas work on a foundation of trust and respect for others. It is true that it is important to stop and smell the roses and see all the wonderful connections that your life makes each morning.

I am now smelling the roses… and they smell sweet.

An Author's Vision—2001

During my career as a governmental mental health agency professional, as a researcher in a state-based research institute oriented to improving the quality of life of people with disabilities, as an associate dean in a school of public health, as a professor of public health, and as the director of the Mid-America Regional Public Health Leadership Institute for 8 years, I have found that each set of experiences has added to my knowledge of leadership in public health. Two important facts have come to the forefront of my professional beliefs. First, public health affects us all. It is not a field that can go away in the future. There will always be a need for professionals to monitor the health of the public and create programs to enhance our health. Second, public health leaders are needed to make the whole public health process work.

It is possible to train the public health leaders who will strengthen the infrastructure of public health in our society. Leadership knowledge and tools can be taught. However, public health professionals need to put the knowledge and tools into action. It is through action that skills become developed. In addition, leadership needs to occur within the context of public health and the paradigms that guide the public health field. Public health leaders need to synthesize the comprehensive approaches to leadership by the business community with the special needs of the public health field. The outcome will be training and educational approaches unique to public health. Leaders exist at all levels of the public health system. Leadership is more than a place on the top of the organization chart. It reflects a strong belief that public health leaders will influence the public health landscape. Public health leaders gain tools and skills from strong public health mentoring. Our experienced colleagues offer much knowledge and many practice experiences. Mentoring puts leadership development into the real world and allows for the continuity of leadership over time.

Public health leaders not only function within the traditional public health organization—they also function across organizations. Transorganizational skills are critical. In addition, public health leaders practice their leadership within community settings. It is often through public health leaders that the validation of our community values and our beliefs in social justice occur. Leadership development is also a way to link academic public health with the practice of public health because information integrates research knowledge with the realities of public health practice.

During the 1990s, there was increasing evidence that leadership needed to come to public health. Through the support of the Public Health Practice Program Office at the Centers for Disease Control and Prevention, a national public health leadership institute and a number of state-based or regional leadership institutes were developed. Public health professionals in 40 states now have access to a state or regional leadership institute. Almost 4,000 public health professionals have participated in a leadership development program.

Public health professionals at the top of their organization are eligible for training in a national institute. Public health leaders have taught us about practice and about the multilayered realities of leadership. Public health leadership programs need to be available to professionals in all of the nation's states and territories. The first decade of the 21st century will increasingly require the need for leadership to guide the public health agenda in an ever-changing healthcare system.

My vision is to orient public health leaders to a better understanding of who they are and how to use their public health leadership tools and skills. Leaders are committed to lifelong learning. If public health leaders take the leadership risk, they will greatly strengthen the public health system. Common paradigms of action will be blended with a flexibility that is required when change is a constant factor. Not only must the leader know what leadership is all about, but must also learn techniques that can be transferred into reality. It is important to look to the future and always be responsive to the world around us.

This book was written because I believe in the public health profession and I also believe in our ability to lead. Public health has always been oriented to solving the health problems of the present with a view to potential problems of the future.

In Part I, information is related to the knowledge associated with the theories and principles of leadership, leadership styles and practices, the public health system, and the five levels of public health leadership. The core functions model is presented and applied to public health leadership in Part II. Part III explores the leadership tools needed for the 21st-century leader. Public health leaders continually develop their skills and put their skills to work on improving the health of the public. Part IV presents information on the personal evaluation of leadership and the evaluation of leadership programs. Part V looks to the future and presents some emerging public health trends.

Throughout the book, case studies written by public health leaders are presented, and public health leadership exercises can also be found. There are also discussion questions in each chapter.

This is your chance to have a key role in defining the future of public health. *Carpe diem!* Seize the day!

Acknowledgments

I would first like to thank the 900 fellows who have graduated from the Mid-America Regional Public Health Leadership Institute. Each one of these leaders has taught me much about the challenges facing public health. I have also learned much from my colleagues, who over the years have struggled with the complex issues involved in leadership development. I especially want to thank Ann Anderson, Beth Quill, Mike Reid, Cynthia Lamberth, Magda Peck, Barney Turnock, Carol Woltring, and Kate Wright for our many discussions about leadership. I also wish to thank all the case study writers for their willingness to write the cases that help strengthen the public health leadership model presented in this book.

My colleagues and friends at the CDC, or retired from the CDC, who believed in public health leadership development over the years must be thanked: Ed Baker, the late Tom Balderson, Donna Carmichael, Steve Frederick, Joe Henderson, Stephanie Bailey, Dennis Lenaway, John Lisco, and Bud Nicola have battled to maintain a national focus on public health leadership development. During my study of public health leaders in 1996, the CDC supported my sabbatical.

I want to personally thank Gary Robinson of the Illinois Department of Public Health for supporting leadership development over the past 20 years. Kathy Weaver, Jerry King, and Sue Hancock in Indiana; Margaret Schmelzer, Larry Gilbertson, Mary Young, and Terry Brandenberg in Wisconsin; and Dina Kurz in Michigan helped me move a leadership program in Illinois to a partnership with several other states.

I also need to thank my colleagues and friends at the University of Illinois School of Public Health: Patrick Lenihan, Ramon Bonzon, Geoff Downie, Sophie Naji, Rani Mishra, and Diane Knizner. My friend and former colleague Judy Munson and I still try to push the envelope to see where public health leadership development needs to go. Special thanks must go to Shirley Randolph, who was with me at the beginning of my leadership journey. I need to thank my publisher Mike Brown for all his support from the very beginning. Finally, I need to thank Chloe Falivene and Alyssa Lawrence of Jones & Bartlett Learning for guiding me through the translation of my manuscript into a book.

Prologue

The events of September 11, 2001 changed the landscape of leadership development. We began to make a distinction between more traditional approaches to leadership development and the important area of development of leaders who need to function in crisis situations, from natural disasters to domestic terrorism situations. During the first decade of this new century, we saw the development of special leadership development programs on crisis leadership. A number of authors wrote books during this first decade to demonstrate not only that crisis needs to be looked at in detail, but that there is also a need to understand the leadership skills needed to function in all sorts of crises, including business downturns, reputational crises, legal crises generated by changes in the law, and so on. There are clearly a number of complexity issues inherent in crises as well. Distinctions have been made between risk and crisis communications. In 2006, I wrote a whole book on leadership and crisis and how leaders can make their public health organizations more prepared. It is now time to bring this book and that book together in a comprehensive approach to public health leadership.

I developed an exercise that I have used in numerous groups to distinguish between the skills of public health leaders as they work in organizations that are not in a crisis situation and leadership skills that are utilized to ameliorate the impact of a public health emergency. This exercise is included in this edition of this book. In my early experience with this exercise, groups appeared to make clear distinctions between the skills needed by leaders in traditional or normal situations and the skills needed to function in an emergency preparedness and response situation. It also became apparent during this period that there was confusion over what management was and what leadership was. Preparedness situations and the general perspectives tied to incident command seemed to reflect more of a command-and-control management and linear perspective rather than a systems-based leadership perspective. I have covered some of these issues in a number of my blog articles (http://rowitzleadership.wordpress.com). One of the interesting results of this exercise was an increasing awareness that all leaders need to know how to function in an organization on a daily basis, but not all leaders seem able to function during a crisis. In other words, crisis leaders need to function in a resilient manner in both traditional and crisis-focused organizations, but some leaders seem to function well only in noncrisis situations.

Leaders must be leaders regardless of the realities that they face each day. Leaders develop not only their personal leadership skills, but also skills for their work on teams and in other collaborative relationships, skills at the organizational level, skills at the community or systems level, and skills involved in promoting knowledge and leadership at the professional level. Leaders need to learn when to manage and when to lead. They must work on trying to develop their personal as well as their organization's resilience. They must learn that leadership is about normal times and not so normal times stimulated by a crisis. If resilience is low, an administrator needs to be able to draw on the skills of others who can lead in a crisis. What this discussion means is that the parallel development of traditional and crisis leadership skills needs to be merged. Leadership is about leadership under changing circumstances and contexts. It is time to view leadership as a lifelong learning process in which leaders explore and develop new skills and tools as they need them to address these changing situations. I have recently used the concept of synergistic leadership to define leaders as individuals who draw from many sources and resources to address all possible situations. When traditional leaders cannot deal with crises, they need to call upon others who can deal with these potential crises. However, traditional and crisis skills build upon each other to form a more comprehensive approach to leadership development. For me, this means that I have to combine my two leadership books into an integrated whole to reflect the complexities of leadership as well as the overall needs of effective leadership in a constantly changing social environment. In addition, we now need to consider the impact of health reform, with an expanding definition of public health and understanding of how our leaders will be affected by these new changes.

The field of public health in the United States is changing as you read this prologue. The profession of public health was very organization focused in the past. It was perceived through the lens of a governmental public health agency that not only concentrated its activities on clinical services into the 1990s, but also talked of prevention and a population-based focus. Being healthy is not a silo-based activity. It requires not only the involvement of each person, but also the support, collaboration, and involvement of many other people and organizations. I believe health promotion is a leadership issue, always with an eye on future behavior. Over the past several decades, we have set health goals for the nation for each decade. A new decade appears and we seem to start all over again with a new set of goals and expectations. For every step forward, we seem to take two steps backward. Unexpected health crises, a new pandemic, or a new problem to be addressed seems to shift our health priorities. Each type of event becomes tied to a specific health profession or health organizational silo. For example, the events of September 11, 2001 seemed to be a public health crisis, and much money was allocated to build public health infrastructure through the advocacy of a preparedness approach to emergencies and other public health crises. And yet subtle and not so subtle shifts occurred in which emergency preparedness and response seemed to become the domain of law enforcement and fire departments, with public health often appearing to take a back seat.

Whether we want to admit it or not, it is not only the public health professions and their organizations that define public health. Public health is defined by the economic climate of the country, politics, economics, culture, and the possibility of global pandemics. In addition, today's health issues also define what public health agencies are supposed to be doing. It is also true that these contemporary issues help define our field, although we sometimes drop the ball and some other profession or organization picks it up. For example, violence has been seen as a public health issue, and yet we did not know how to address this issue. Public health leaders often let law enforcement, schools, and other organizations pick up our dropped ball.

The field of public health is expanding in the face of health reform by governmental officials at the federal and state levels. Funded public health workforce and leadership development programs are being asked to consider the training of health professionals in preventive medicine, HIV health professions, emergency preparedness, maternal and child health professions, and community health center administration. The argument being made is that people working in health and community clinical areas are beginning to carry out public health work at the population-based community level. This expansion of the purview of public health means that we need to reevaluate our training, research, service, community engagement activities, and leadership activities in this ever-changing public health environment. We need to create alliances and other mechanisms for the discussion of these issues. It will be necessary for governmental health professionals to talk to academic and public health practice leaders in concert with their professional organizations to aid in the redefining of public health in a rational manner. Business and citizen involvement may also be necessary. Our decisions today will have an impact on the future of public health for many years to come.

Leadership Theories and Principles

CHAPTER 1

The Basics of Leadership

In a society capable of renewal, [leaders] not only welcome the future and the changes it brings but believe they can have a hand in shaping that future.

—J. W. Gardner, *Self-Renewal*

The 21st century has not unsurprisingly increased the amount of attention paid to the concept of change. Yet change has always been and always will be a fact of life. For instance, the passage of a national health reform package in the first decade of the 21st century provides evidence that accelerated change may occur in the public health field. However, the passage of this legislation in the United States has led to major turmoil among the two major political parties in the United States. With major federal deficits, this legislation may be substantially revised or appealed during the second decade of this new century. An increasing connection between primary care and public health seems to be happening as well. Public health is in constant flux and will continue to be in the future. To cite two contemporary examples where change is demanded, large segments of the U.S. population are unemployed or employed in low-paying jobs and thus remain uninsured or underinsured. Certain culturally diverse racial and ethnic groups, as well as many if not most illegal immigrants, have less access to health care than the population as a whole. The health reform legislation, if sustained, should address this for large segments of the population. *except African Americans*

Public health agencies and professionals are experiencing an identity crisis because of the recent reconfiguring of their emergency preparedness and response leadership and service roles and responsibilities since the terrorist events of September 11, 2001, and the many natural disasters during the first decade of this new century. Adding to these crisis events is the public's lack of awareness of the nature of public health and the accomplishments of the public health system. Parents and friends still ask public health professionals what they do for a living. Of course, confusion about professional identity exists elsewhere in the health professions. Physicians who work for managed care organizations resist the restrictions placed on their ability to provide the tests and services they feel their patients require, not to mention the limitations on their salaries. The traditional caregiving roles of nurses are also changing as hospital bed utilization declines and many hospitals close their doors.

In order to manage the changes that are occurring, health care and public health professionals need to become involved in advocacy at the political and policy development levels. They need to create their own vision of what personal health care and population-based health should be and to act in concert to realize that vision, and for these tasks to be accomplished, some of these professionals must acquire the full range of leadership skills and translate these skills into action. In 1988, *The Future of Public Health* made the argument that the creation of effective leaders must not be left to chance.[1] In line with this view, the report also stated a concern that schools of public health were not teaching the necessary leadership courses. This was reinforced in the 2003 report on *The Future of the Public's Health*, where a recommendation was made that leadership training needs to be a requirement for public health professionals working in the governmental public health sector.[2] In 2007, the Institute of Medicine listed leadership development as one of the 16 critical public health content areas in the training of physicians for careers in public health.[3]

The training of future leaders is critical. Public health leaders will need training not only in the specialties of public health but also in the latest management techniques and tools. To support public health activities at the local, state, and federal levels, they will require good communication, problem-solving, decision-making, and policy development skills, and skills in addressing all public health emergencies, among others. Leaders must learn how their organizations function; how to work across organizations, which has been called meta-leadership or boundary-spanning leadership; and how to integrate their organizations' activities into the communities they serve. In addition, the changing demographics of the U.S. population will lead to the need for ethnically diverse public health professionals to accept leadership positions in the governmental and primary care sectors.

There is a major difference between managing change and leading change.[4] To lead change, leaders must be able to develop a vision to partially define the future. They must then get others to share their vision and help realize it. Of course, managing change and performance management are also important, for they keep the system running smoothly.

Selling a vision to others can be especially difficult for people from ethnically diverse groups, people with disabilities, and women, for the vision they are trying to sell might well involve cultural, ethnic, community, and gender issues, and they will probably have to disseminate it to people who have a different background than they do.[5] Developing a vision that can be shared is critical in a society where diversity is the rule rather than the exception. Any vision will remain just a vision if it falls outside the belief system of the managers and the leaders.

In 1996, the Institute of Medicine released a report on the first year of its committee on public health. The report, *Healthy Communities: New Partnerships for the Future of Public Health*,[6] reviewed the 1988 *Future of Public Health* report and concluded that progress had occurred in leadership development in the 1990s. Among other signs of progress was the creation of a national public health leadership program and a number of state and regional leadership development programs. As I write this, the funding of these programs at the federal level (Centers for Disease Control and Prevention) has stopped. The training of public health leaders needs to continue, especially in this new era of health reform. Stress must be placed on the multidimensional aspects of leadership as well as the multidisciplinary approaches of the public health field as a whole. Building and strengthening the infrastructure of public health requires strong and effective leaders to address emergency situations as well as more traditional public health situations.

Note, however, that until now leadership development has been based on an industrial or agency paradigm of leadership.[7] Leaders of the 21st century must possess different skills with a systems thinking and complexity focus. They will also need to recognize that leading is a process in which they must pursue their vision through influencing others and the places they work. Leaders will find that advancing the skills of their workforce will increase the chance that their vision will become a reality. In addition, they will have to break down the barriers between organization and community to create an environment in which a shared value system and a shared vision for the future can come into being.

The remainder of the chapter comprises two short sections containing a definition of leadership and five essential skills for a public health leader and a long section that discusses 16 important principles of public health leadership. As part of their effort to understand the nature of leadership, students should do Exercise 1-1, which provides an opportunity for students to express what they believe about leadership in general and public health leadership in particular. This exercise also presents the option of developing a journal to record ideas, leadership notes on papers or books read, and personal reflections on leadership experiences.

DEFINITION OF LEADERSHIP

Leadership is creativity in action. It is the ability to see the present in terms of the future while maintaining respect for the past. Leadership is based on respect for history and the knowledge that true growth builds on existing strengths. Leading is in part a visionary endeavor, but it requires the fortitude and flexibility necessary to put vision into action and the ability to work with others and to follow when someone else is the better leader. Leaders also need resilience to function in normal and not-so-normal times.

Public health leadership includes a commitment to the community and the values for which it stands. A community perspective requires a systems thinking and complexity orientation. Community refers not only to the local community in which a person works but also to the larger global community that can affect the health of the public over time. Whatever health crises occur in other parts of the world will have an effect on what will eventually affect the health of the public in our local communities. It also includes a commitment to social justice, but public health leaders must not let this commitment undermine their ability to pursue a well-designed public health agenda. In addition, public health leaders need to act within the governing paradigms of public health, but this does not mean they cannot alter the paradigms. Leaders propose new paradigms when old ones lose their effectiveness. The major governing paradigm today relates to the core functions and essential services of public health.

LEADERSHIP ESSENTIALS

Over the past 20 years, I have read probably more than 1,000 books on leadership and management. A large number of these books present theories about what leadership is and how it works. Many leaders have embraced one theory, a combination of theories, or their own theory about leadership and how they practice it. As these theories are examined (see a sample of well-known books that present differing approaches in Case Study 1-A), it becomes useful to try to determine the essential skills of successful leaders. To simplify this task, let's limit the essentials to the five most important skills:

1. *Ability to identify the most useful information and to use it.* Leaders are bombarded with new information on a daily basis from new health data statistics,

new public health technical reports, new funding opportunities, and new demands for service based on emerging threats or program emphases. All this new information has to be translated into the context of public health and the governing paradigms that drive public health action.

2. *Ability to motivate and work with others.* Leaders have learned that the technological expertise that brought them into public health careers is secondary to their relationships with colleagues and external partners. Leaders must have the social skills necessary to collaborate with others with ease. This set of basic skills has come to be called *emotional intelligence* in recent years.

3. *Ability to take risks and follow through.* Not only do leaders need to be visionary and creative, they need to be able to take risks and to translate their ideas into action with well-defined projected outcomes. Every new vision or creative idea has a potential risk associated with it. Many people are fearful of change. Risk taking is the attempt to change the status quo and move in new directions.

4. *Ability to communicate at many different levels.* Leaders have to learn to communicate both verbally and in writing. They need to listen to others carefully. They may also have to communicate cross-culturally or to others who do not speak their native language. They need to be able to communicate through the Internet. Social networks can become critical to their work. Most leaders are excellent at using real-life events to show how their theories work. They can also be excellent storytellers.

5. *Ability to act as systems thinkers with an understanding of how complexity affects their work.* Leaders understand that they need to concentrate on the big picture. They look at their agency as a whole organization with interacting parts. They see their agency in the context of a whole community. They understand that most of their work is about upsetting the status quo in order to change things for the better. Public health leaders think about the population and how to improve the health of everyone in their geographic jurisdiction. They also understand that the best plans may still lead to unanticipated consequences.

All the other leadership skills that are described by the many leadership writers and by leaders themselves grow out of these five essential skills.

PUBLIC HEALTH LEADERSHIP PRINCIPLES

One way of filling out the definition of public health leadership in particular is to consider some of the principles that public health leaders should use to guide their actions. Following is a list of 16 such principles. In a study of 130 public health leaders in the United States, England, Scotland, and Ireland during 1996, the author conducted an hour-long conversation with each of these leaders to find out his or her view of the future role of public health agencies. The perspective of these leaders is still relevant today.

The public health leaders interviewed generally thought that they and business leaders have much in common. Good leadership is essential for the effectiveness of companies engaged in business and can increase the effectiveness of public health agencies as well. But although the leadership practices of business and public health leaders are similar, there are also important differences. For example, the social justice perspective that characterizes public health is more or less absent from the business world where a profit motive predominates. One of the leaders interviewed argued strongly that the social justice perspective is critical for public health but that public health leaders must be careful not to let this value interfere with the work that public health needs to do. One way of putting this is that social justice is only part of the leadership value system. Gardner[8] integrates that value with the values of freedom, social and ethnic equality, the worth and dignity of each individual, and the brotherhood of all human beings.

Principle 1

The public health infrastructure and the system in which it is embedded must be strengthened by utilizing the core functions of public health and its essential services as a guide to the changes that should occur. The future of public health will be determined by the way in which core functions are carried out and essential services are provided. Public health leaders must evaluate the health status of the population, evaluate the capacity of the community to address its health priorities, and implement preventive measures to reduce the effect of or even avoid public health crises. Leaders must not rely on the current assurance models (service interventions) but need to implement new assurance models built on integrated and collaborative systems of service and program delivery. Leaders must also help

to restructure the policies and laws that govern health and public health. Leaders must be policy makers who have a view of the future grounded in the realities of the present and built on the experiences of the past.

Principle 2

The goal of public health is to improve the health of each person in the community. Public health leaders believe deeply that health promotion and disease prevention are possible. In fact, a focus on prevention is intrinsic to public health. In this regard, public health contrasts with the medical care system, which places an emphasis on treatment and rehabilitation. Every citizen needs to learn about the benefits of public health and how quality of life can be greatly improved if certain rules are followed and if people take personal responsibility for their own health needs.

A public health leader who truly believes in this principle will become a teacher and mentor for the community. Education will be the prevailing program model rather than medical care. The leader will reach out to schools, churches and synagogues, businesses, physical fitness centers, households, and healthcare providers and promote the vision of good health for all throughout life. The leader will also be concerned with the quality of care. If someone becomes ill, access to the best possible care is a community requirement. A visionary leader sees the total health system existing in the community and helps to ensure that the system is integrated and comprehensive, provides the services that are necessary, and does not contain duplicate services and programs, which are a waste of valuable resources.

A public health leader can play an important role in promoting a sense of community among community members. The leader might help define the values of the community and clarify the cultural aspects of the community life. Not all geographic areas have a cohesive cultural infrastructure. In an area that lacks such an infrastructure, the public health leader can help the community to define itself.

Principle 3

Community coalitions need to be built to address the community's public health needs. Public health is both a community responsibility and a population-based activity. This means that the mission of public health is to work with all groups in a community to improve the health of all members of the public.

All communities have assets and all sorts of community resources. Unfortunately, communities, like people in general, tend to be careless with their assets.[9] Consequently, each community needs to learn how to manage its assets if it doesn't know how to do that already. In short, it needs to take responsibility for its future. It may be too dependent on those who work in human services. Promoting good health is every citizen's responsibility. Public health leaders can play a critical role in helping the community move from a value system based on dependency to one based on shared responsibility. Public health leaders and their cousins in the human services field are thus the true servant leaders.[10]

Coalition building and other forms of collaboration require knowledge and creativity. First, coalitions made up only of managers are doomed to failure.[11] Coalitions need leaders to guide the process. Second, coalitions require trust among their members. If there is no trust, change will not occur. Third, there must be positions of power in a coalition. Key players must not be excluded or the process will fail. Expertise is also necessary so that informed decision making will occur. Fourth, the coalition must have credibility so that it will be taken seriously by others (both inside and outside the community) who can affect the implementation of the change agenda. *Transparency is also needed.*

Principle 4

Local and state public health leaders must work together to protect the health of all citizens regardless of gender, race, ethnicity, or socioeconomic status. Public health leaders firmly believe in the principle that all people are created equal. Several U.S. public health leaders interviewed by the author stated that the U.S. public health system must be understood within the context of the American political tradition and that it is impossible to be an effective public health leader without knowing about that tradition.

They should feel this way or be this way introving locally

Access to service is sometimes affected by who you are. Women have found that the healthcare system does not always respond to their special medical needs. Public health leaders see that they have a responsibility to press for improvements in health care for women. They also have a responsibility to develop health promotion programs for women as well as men. For example, local health departments can take a leadership role in the development of breast examination programs for cancer prevention. Cultural and ethnic groups often have difficulty in accessing health programs because of color, language, or socioeconomic status. Diabetes-screening programs are often the first programs to go when funding cuts occur, despite the critical need for these programs in our communities. Public health leaders have important tasks to perform in protecting the rights of the unserved and underserved.

We live in a culturally diverse society. Our diversity is a strength as well as a weakness. Public health leaders must deal with their personal prejudices each day and consciously move beyond them to create a public health system that respects the needs of every citizen. State public health leaders must monitor the needs of all citizens as well as create the policies of inclusion that will lead to an improvement in the public's level of health. In addition, these leaders must make state legislators and other elected officials partners in this enterprise. The other critical partner is the local public health leader, who, in conjunction with the local board of health or county board of commissioners, is the gatekeeper for the community. What the state proclaims, the local leaders must adapt for local implementation. Local public health leaders must be extremely creative in the adaptation process. They must also speak loudly for the unique needs of their local community and take the local public health agenda to places where the state leaders do not tread.

Principle 5

Rational community health planning requires collaboration between public health agency leaders, the local board of health (if such a board exists), other local and county boards, and other external community stakeholders. The relationship between the administrator of the local health department and the chair of the board of health needs to be a close one and based on a philosophy of equality and trust. The chair and the other members of the board of health do more than approve the health department budget and select the health administrator. The board members are residents of the community. They are the protectors of the community's interests and, with the administrator, serve an important gatekeeper function. Shared leadership and a shared vision are critical here. The health department and the board of health must be partners, not adversaries, which means they must work collaboratively to achieve agreed-upon outcomes. The exchange of information is an important part of the relationship, because relevant information is essential for the making of good public health decisions.

Principle 6   Mentoring

Novice public health leaders must learn leadership techniques and practices from experienced public health leaders. Mentoring is a critical part of leadership. A mentor is a person who helps another person learn about the world and how it works.[12] Mentors also help people in their care choices. Mentors tend to be well-known individuals who help their protégés meet their major goals.[13]

Murray[14] discusses what she calls "facilitated mentoring," which is a process designed to develop effective mentoring relationships. It is also designed to guide the teaching of the person being mentored. If the mentoring experience is successful, there will be an effect on the mentor, the person mentored, and the agency promoting the mentoring experience.

Mentors are ideally not threatened by the professional progress of their protégés. They personally feel good about the mentoring experience. All of the leaders interviewed by the author said that they had been mentored at various times in their public health careers. They thought that mentoring was important and that the need for mentoring does not stop with the attainment of a leadership position. Mentoring is beneficial to leaders throughout their careers. Furthermore, leaders who have been mentored have a responsibility to pass on the gift of learning they received.

Principle 7   Money towards training

One issue of import is whether leaders are born or made. If leadership is innate, leaders wouldn't need to develop their skills, but if leaders are made, anyone has the potential to become a leader. The most defensible position is that leaders are both born and made—that some people are natural leaders with the talents necessary for successful leadership but nonetheless need to develop their leadership abilities.[15]

In fact, public health leaders must continuously work to develop their leadership skills. Leaders never stop learning. They are like detectives who pick up clue after clue in order to find the solution to a mystery. Leaders seek solutions to challenges rather than to mysteries, but the attainment of new knowledge is just as important for finding these types of solutions. Furthermore, each solution leads to new challenges and the need for additional learning.

Support for programs for lifelong learning is critical. There has been a tendency in recent years not to allocate funds for learning activities, based partly on the argument that the public does not want to pay for training programs. When the funds are available, they tend to be classified as discretionary and used for purposes other than training. Yet allowing leaders to improve their skills can lead to substantial benefits.[16] Very few public health practitioners have ever received major job-related training, to the detriment of the agencies they work for.

Over the past 20 years, a unique experiment occurred, funded by the Centers for Disease Control and Prevention and state health departments. A national public health leadership institute and a number of state and regional leadership programs were created to help state and local health department professionals, board of health members, local and state legislators, faculty members, and community leaders develop their leadership potential. The programs, which teach public health theory and practice, promote the education of public health professionals and, through them, the education of all citizens in a community. Public health leadership development, at its best, can create a partnership between public health leaders, the public health academic community, and the public health professional community in the public and private sectors. The main lesson learned from this experiment is that public health leadership development must build on the mission of public health but must orient itself to the future of public health. A second lesson is that these programs need to be experientially based and need to focus on projects that strengthen the infrastructure of the public health system. These programs also have the value-added result of increasing networking among the public health leaders who attend these programs.

Principle 8

Leaders must be committed not only to lifelong learning but to their own personal growth. Self-esteem is a key factor in personal growth and is essential to the personal competence necessary to cope with life's challenges.[17] Furthermore, the higher a leader's self-esteem, the more able the leader is to inspire others. Research on children has shown that children with high self-esteem are more willing to take risks and to assume leadership roles than children with low self-esteem.[18] Sethi has described the seven R's of self-esteem:[19]

1. *Respect.* It is necessary to respect and trust your employees.
2. *Responsibility and Resources.* Encouraging creativity among employees and delegating responsibility for tasks are essential.

3. *Risk Taking*. Only through risk taking can innovation occur.
4. *Rewards and Recognition*. People need to be recognized for their accomplishments.
5. *Relationships*. The quality and quantity of personal relationships have an effect on self-esteem.
6. *Role-Modeling*. The work practices of an organization should be consistent with its values.
7. *Renewal*. It is critical to maintain a strong belief in lifelong learning.

Self-esteem is tied to each of the seven R's. Each factor affects the self-esteem of the leaders and their associates inside the agency and in the community. Building the self-esteem of leaders and associates is a prerequisite for the building of strong organizations.[20]

Principle 9

The infrastructure of public health must be built on a foundation of health protection for all, democratic ideals and values, and respect for the social fabric of American society. The assumption underlying this principle is that physical, psychological, emotional, economic, and social health are all elements of the health of a community. By acting as role models for the community, public health leaders strengthen the infrastructure of public health in the community. This infrastructure is not just a physical building or an official agency called the department of public health; it comprises the entire community.

Principle 10

Public health leaders should think globally but act locally. Although public health professionals practice their craft primarily at the community level, they should not ignore the rest of the world. Emerging viruses know no boundaries. Disease is carried not only on the wind but even in airplanes. Public health leaders need to be vigilant in looking for potential health problems. The Centers for Disease Control and Prevention has a national center for infectious disease that monitors emerging diseases globally, and public health professionals located throughout the world are investigating potential worldwide health problems such as the possibility of a pandemic influenza outbreak. Some multiregion crises have been documented in books such as R. Preston's *The Hot Zone*,[21] L. Garrett's *The Coming Plague*,[22] and J. B. McCormick and S. Fisher-Hoch's *Level 4: Virus Hunters of the CDC*.[23] When a crisis hits, the international public health community must work together on the problem. Public health leaders thus have several overlapping communities to which they owe allegiance, and they must understand how to coordinate their multiple allegiances.

Principle 11

Public health leaders need to be good managers. In the above-mentioned interview study of public health leaders, the leaders pointed out that they, as heads of agencies, not only define their agencies' practice activities but also help to implement those activities. Managers do not have to be leaders, but tomorrow's leaders will need to possess both management and leadership skills (see **Table 1-1**). Reconciling these two sets of skills will not be easy, because they are based on two different ideological and talent perspectives. Managers are oriented toward ensuring that current systems are functioning smoothly. They tend to orient their activities to strengthening the public health agency in which they work. Leaders are change agents who are concerned with moving their agencies forward. Because change is unavoidable, today's managers will become obsolete if they cannot keep up with the ever-increasing pace of change. Leaders and dynamic managers will have to steer their organizations in new directions, and they will have to utilize cutting-edge leadership skills and managerial tools to do this.

Principle 12

Public health leaders need to walk the walk. They must not only define a vision but sell the vision and inspire others to accept it and try to realize it.[24,25] In his book on visionary leadership, Nanus[26] pointed out that there are four major types of leadership activity. First, a leader has to relate to the managers and other workers in the organization. The leader should be the guide to and motivator of action in the organization. Second, the leader has to relate to the environment or community outside the organization. A public health leader, for example, must carry the agency's vision and message into the community. Third, the leader has to influence all phases of the operation of the organization. Finally, the leader has to anticipate future events and move the organization forward in a manner that takes these events into account. If it is clear that managed care organizations will provide medical care for all members of a community, then the public health leaders of that community need to get the public health department out of the direct service business and into population-based health promotion and disease

TABLE 1-1 A Comparison of the Characteristics and Responsibilities of Practitioners, Managers, and Leaders

Practitioners	Managers	Leaders
The practitioner implements.	The manager administers.	The leader innovates.
The practitioner follows.	The manager is a copy.	The leader is an original.
The practitioner synthesizes.	The manager maintains.	The leader develops.
The practitioner focuses on programs and services.	The manager focuses on systems and structures.	The leader focuses on people.
The practitioner relies on compliance and behavior change.	The manager relies on control.	The leader inspires trust.
The practitioner has a narrow view.	The manager has a short-range view.	The leader has a long-range view.
The practitioner asks who and where.	The manager asks how and when.	The leader asks what and why.
The practitioner's eye is on the client and the community.	The manager's eye is always on the bottom line.	The leader's eye is on the horizon.
The practitioner separates programs from services.	The manager imitates.	The leader originates.
The practitioner protects the status quo.	The manager accepts the status quo.	The leader challenges the status quo.
The practitioner is in the infantry.	The manager is the classic good soldier.	The leader is his or her own person.
The practitioner is a conflicted pessimist.	The manager is a pessimist.	The leader is an optimist.
The practitioner is a reflective thinker.	The manager is a linear thinker.	The leader is a systems thinker.
The practitioner follows the agency agenda.	The manager does things right.	The leader does the right things.

Source: Modified from *On Becoming a Leader* by Warren Bennis. © 1989, 1994, 2009 by Warren Bennis, Inc. Reprinted with permission of Perseus Books Publishers, a member of Perseus Books Group.

prevention. In general, this has occurred since 1996. The deterioration of the economy since 2008 has led to some reevaluation of this argument as the community health center movement has gained prominence, with some local health departments getting back into the direct service business by opening community health centers with federal funds.

Principle 13

Public health leaders need to be proactive and not reactive. Up to the present, they have mostly tended to respond to public health crises as they occurred rather than focus on preventing crises. A reactive stance will probably always be part of the strategy of any state or local health department. However, reactivity tends

to tarnish a health department's image. Public health agencies and professionals need to develop action plans to address the health needs of the citizens in their service area. Assessment activities will help to evaluate the health status of the community and give guidance for action. Action planning is more than planning for a crisis, which is an anticipatory activity that assumes a problem is on the horizon. Action planning is essentially preventive. Its goal is to create programs to prevent the occurrence of problems rather than create programs to deal with problems after they occur.

Principle 14

Each level of the public health system has a need for leaders.[27] In fact, a leader does not need to have an official position to be a leader, and nonpositional power is likely to become more and more important. However, a defined leadership position does not hurt. Change will come from many different sources, and leaders will step forward to make sure the required tasks are accomplished. For example, if an environmental crisis occurs in a community, the environmental director from the health department, a community resident who is an engineer, a firefighter, a police officer, and others may form a leadership team to deal with the crisis. When the crisis has passed, the members of this ad hoc leadership team will step back into their normal roles. Much has been written on this issue since the tragedy of September 11, 2001. The National Incident Management System (NIMS) is one example of this team effort to address a public health emergency.

Each level of an organization also has a need for leaders.[28] And like members of a community, members of an organization often share leadership tasks by forming a team to tackle issues. These critical shared leadership experiences are often ignored in the leadership literature.

Principle 15

Public health leaders practice their craft in a community setting and must understand what a community is. Shaffer and Anundsen stated that Americans are searching for a revitalized sense of community.[29] A community is more than a place; it consists of people living together who "participate in common practices; depend upon each other; make decisions together; identify themselves as part of something larger than the sum of their individual relationships; and commit themselves for the long term to their own, one another's and the group's well-being."[30(p.10)]

Human beings have a desire to be free and independent, but those who take independence as an absolute value risk becoming profoundly lonely by not including other people in their lives.[31] Being part of the community involves inclusivity, commitment, and consensus. It also can lead to a sense of realism, because communities, through the actions of individual members, contemplate and evaluate themselves. Finally, communities tend to be safe places, which is one reason Americans, with their increasingly well-founded fear of violence, have a renewed interest in the sense of community.

In the now classic book *Habits of the Heart*,[32] Bellah and his collaborators argue that we Americans have become committed to the lexicon of individualism and have consequently lost our way morally. We are losing our sense of community and our commitment to improve society at large. Everyone from our politicians to our educators is pushing for a return to our moral roots, by which is meant a return to community.

Public health leaders have traditionally had a strong belief in community. Their focus, after all, is on improving the health of the communities they live and work in. Public health leaders also believe they can strengthen their communities by working with community leaders to bring about change. If they are to be effective in bringing about change, they need to study and learn how their communities function. In particular, they need to know how to empower the members of their communities and get them to take their share of the responsibility for improving their own health.

Leadership Tip

Read your mail or answer e-mails when your energy level is low. Do important tasks when your energy levels tend to be high.

Principle 16

Public health leaders must practice what they preach. If they are promoting family values, they must live lives that are consistent with these values. If they are promoting good health and developing programs to get people to stop smoking, they should not smoke themselves.

This principle is not always easy to abide by. Some of our most successful leaders have personal lives that are in shambles. O'Neill called this the paradox of success.[33] Leaders often become prisoners of their official position and are unable to find a workable balance between their professional commitments and their private lives. Indeed, achieving a balance between work and home is becoming more difficult, as individuals are required to work harder due to such factors as downsizing. Decisions regarding the balance between work and home must be built into the culture of the places where we are employed,[34] especially as nowadays both spouses in a marriage usually work. The costs of not achieving a proper balance are high. Conflicting pressures and stresses can have serious health consequences.

I was running a leadership program and was planning for a six-month follow-up meeting to an initial program. All trainees from the first meeting were expected to come to the second meeting. One day before the second meeting was to occur, I received a telephone call from one of the trainees. She told me that her son was ill and that she was trying to find someone to take care of him. She was worried about missing the meeting. I asked her what she thought she needed to do. She said she felt she needed to stay with her son. I told her she had made the right choice. Balancing is making the right choice.

SUMMARY

The one thing that a review of the leadership literature makes clear is that leadership is a complex series of processes affected by many factors. These factors, for public leaders in particular, include the principles described above, which apply to leadership style, leadership practices, the public health system, the core functions and essential services of public health, and leadership tools (see **Figure 1-1**).

Leading is a multidimensional activity. Every leader uses leadership skills in his or her own way, which is to say that every leader has his or her own leadership style and unique set of personal talents. Every leader engages in a set of leadership practices and uses a unique set of tools. All these elements determine whether a leader is successful. In Case Study 1-B, I interview Dr. Virginia Caine, a former president of the American Public Health Association and director of the Marion County Health Department in Indianapolis, Indiana, about leadership in public health.

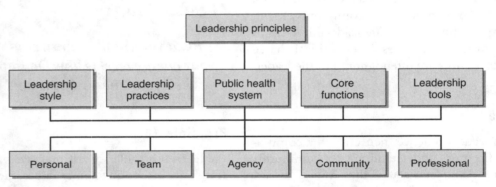

FIGURE 1-1 Conceptual Model of Public Health Leadership.

Case Study 1-A

Leadership Bookshelf
Louis Rowitz

1. Stephen Covey, **The Seven Habits of Highly Successful People**. Covey is one of the most read of the leadership authors. This book has become a classic in its discussions of the seven habits of being proactive, being oriented to end actions, dealing with important things first, having a win-win orientation, increasing understanding of other people's positions, being synergistic, and being oriented toward continuous improvement.
2. John Gardner, **On Leadership**. The complexity of modern-day events and increasing complexity of our organizations has pointed to the need for strong leadership. It is important that leaders understand the needs of the people they work with and the needs of people outside their organizations. Gardner explores these issues extensively in one of the most important leadership books in the field.
3. Peter Senge, **The Fifth Discipline**. This book lays the groundwork for the need for leaders to be systems thinkers. The archetype of systems thinking is also developed.
4. Ronald Heifetz, **Leadership Without Easy Answers**. By studying famous leaders, Heifetz explores leadership and what makes leaders succeed and sometimes fail. This book begins the exploration of adaptive behavior that Heifetz explores in later books like **Leadership on the Line**.
5. James MacGregor Burns, **Leadership**. Burns, who is a historian, has written an excellent book about the differences between transactional and transformational leaders.

6. Daniel Goleman, *Emotional Intelligence*. Goleman is credited with being a major voice in recognizing the importance of emotional intelligence (EI) skills for leaders. EI involves self-awareness and awareness of others.
7. John Kotter, *Leading Change*. This is an excellent book about change and how it works.
8. Ken Blanchard, *Leadership and the One Minute Manager*. Blanchard's books are all based on the idea that different situations require leaders to act in different ways. He uses stories to explain his leadership principles.
9. Edward De Bono, *Six Thinking Hats*. This is one of my favorites. It presents a great tool for generating new ideas and solutions to old problems.
10. Bernard Turnock, *Public Health: What It Is and How It Works*. This is the best book for leaders who want to understand how public health in the United States works.
11. James M. Kouzes and Barry Z. Posner, *The Leadership Challenge*. This is a very practical book that explores the five practices that make great leaders.
12. Max DePree, *Leadership Is an Art*. This is a wonderful little book. Leadership is about ideas. It is about relationships and drawing your personal strength from others. The art of leadership is trusting others to find the way to do things in the most effective and efficient manner. Servant leadership is very important.
13. Warren Bennis and Burt Nanus, *Leaders*. This classic book addresses such issues as the importance of character, the ability to build organizations and systems, the importance of passion for work, the need for a vision, the ability to communicate trust through positioning, and the ability to empower others. It was hard to choose between this book and Bennis's *On Becoming a Leader*.

It would be interesting to see what books you would put on your bookshelf. The only challenge for me is that when this bookshelf was completed, I wanted to add a second bookshelf with other books. Reading about leadership is always a fun activity. That may be why I wrote my books. In your comments, I hope you will add your favorite books.

Source: Reprinted from L. Rowitz (2010, February 1). A Leadership Bookshelf [Web log]. Retrieved from http://rowitzonleadership.wordpress.com/2010/02/. Accessed June 24, 2012.

Case Study 1-B

Public Health Practice Quiz for Virginia Caine

1. How would you define leadership?

Leadership is

- Creating a vision others can see
- Promoting the capacity of other people to take action on that vision
- Taking a diverse group of people with different backgrounds and ideas, focusing the group on a common goal, and motivating the group to overcome obstacles and reach the goal

2. What do you think are the critical strengths needed to be a successful public health leader?

Successful public health leaders are those who are visionary, decisive, good communicators, change agents, and risk takers. They have the conviction of their values and are deeply committed to improving the health of everyone in this country.

These leaders are also politically astute, are able to listen and hear what people are really saying, are respectful of different cultures, have emotional intelligence, are resilient and future focused, and have a love for public health.

They understand that relationship building and collaboration are the cornerstones of public health work.

3. What will be the major challenges of public health in the next 10 years?

The major challenges for public health in the next 10 years include the following: the improvement of the health of everyone in the country; the strengthening of the public health infrastructure; the aging of the public health workforce; the changing demographic populations (age distribution, cultural diversity) and their impact on disparities; chronic diseases; lack of access to health care and the uninsured; global health; health promotion and behavior change; environmental hazards and global warming; and the integration of public health and traditional medical information systems.

(Continues)

Other challenges for public health include genomics and ethical issues, credentialing and accreditation, emerging infectious diseases and drug-resistant bacteria, and the ability to convene and collaborate with people across the political and opinion spectrum.

4. What needs to be done to develop a culturally diverse leadership workforce?

We need to encourage and promote diversity in our public health leadership training across the entire public health system, not just the public health departments. Also, public health agencies in collaboration with the education system, from preschool to the academic institutions, that is, colleges, need to create opportunities for students of all cultures to gain the knowledge and skills needed. Public health agencies need to promote more recruitment where it's robust and not passive of a culturally diverse workforce.

Some of these opportunities may include partnerships with diverse populations and organizations, providing scholarships, peer counseling, internships, and outreach educational endeavors for students of all cultures to gain the knowledge and skills needed to be 21st-century public health leaders with appropriate incentives.

5. Is leadership in the private sector similar to leadership in the business sector?

Leadership is leadership no matter what system you are in.

Leadership Tip

Think and act locally with global health issues involved in your activities.

DISCUSSION QUESTIONS

1. What is your personal definition of leadership? — HOLDING onto ethical solutions and putting them into action.
2. Who is a living person whom you define as a leader and why?
3. What, in your view, are the differences between business leaders and public health leaders?
4. How does creativity play a role in leadership activities?
5. How is collaboration related to leadership?
6. What role does social justice play in public health?
7. What are the main goals of public health?
8. What does it mean to say that public health leaders should think globally but act locally?
9. Is leadership different from management?

EXERCISE 1-1:   Course Expectations

Purpose: to explore the expectations that students have at the beginning of a leadership course

Key concepts: expectations, leadership development, preconceptions

Procedure: Each student writes down initial thoughts or preconceptions about leadership and also writes down expectations for the course and for leadership training in general. The class then divides into groups of 5 to 10 members, and each group discusses the preconceptions and expectations. The students should keep the lists they have created. One way to make this a meaningful experience is for students to start a leadership journal in which their list becomes the first page of a journal.

REFERENCES

1. Institute of Medicine, *The Future of Public Health* (Washington, DC: National Academies Press, 1988).
2. Institute of Medicine, *The Future of the Public's Health* (Washington, DC: National Academies Press, 2003).
3. Institute of Medicine, *Training Physicians for Public Health Careers* (Washington, DC: National Academies Press, 2007).
4. J. P. Kotter, *Leading Change* (Boston: Harvard Business School Press, 1996).
5. S. E. Melendez, "An Outsider's View of Leadership," in *The Leader of the Future*, ed. F. Hesselbein et al. (San Francisco: Jossey-Bass, 1996).
6. Institute of Medicine, *Healthy Communities: New Partnerships for the Future of Public Health* (Washington, DC: National Academies Press, 1996).

7. S. M. Bornstein and A. F. Smith, "The Puzzles of Leadership," in *The Leader of the Future*, ed. F. Hesselbein et al. (San Francisco: Jossey-Bass, 1996).

8. J. W. Gardner, *Self-Renewal* (New York: W.W. Norton, 1981).

9. J. McKnight, *The Careless Society* (New York: Basic Books, 1995).

10. R. K. Greenleaf, *The Servant as Leader* (Indianapolis, IN: Greenleaf Center for Servant Leadership, 1970).

11. Kotter, *Leading Change*.

12. F. Wickman and T. Sjodin, *Mentoring* (Chicago: Irwin Professional Publishing, 1996).

13. L. Phillips-Jones, *The New Mentors and Proteges* (Grass Valley, CA: Coalition of Counseling Centers, 2001).

14. M. Murray, *Beyond the Myths and Magic of Mentoring*, rev. ed. (San Francisco: Jossey-Bass, 2001).

15. P. Hersey et al., *Management of Organizational Behavior*, 9th ed. (Upper Saddle River, NJ: Prentice Hall, 2007).

16. P. M. Senge et al., *The Fifth Discipline Handbook* (New York: Dell, 1994).

17. N. Brandon, "Self-Esteem in the Information Age," in *The Organization of the Future*, ed. F. Hesselbein et al. (San Francisco: Jossey-Bass, 1997).

18. D. Baumrind, "An Exploratory Study of Socialization Effects on Black Children: Some Black-White Comparisons," *Child Development* 43 (1972): 261–267.

19. D. Sethi, "The Seven R's of Self-Esteem," in *The Organization of the Future*, ed. F. Hesselbein et al. (San Francisco: Jossey-Bass, 1997).

20. K. Blanchard and N. V. Peale, *The Power of Ethical Management* (New York: Fawcett Columbine, 1988).

21. R. Preston, *The Hot Zone* (New York: Random House, 1994).

22. L. Garrett, *The Coming Plague* (New York: Farrar, Straus & Giroux, 1994).

23. J. B. McCormick and S. Fisher-Hoch, *Level 4: Virus Hunters of the CDC* (Atlanta: Turner Publishing Co., 1996).

24. J. M. Kouzes and B. Z. Posner, *The Leadership Challenge*, 4th ed. (San Francisco: Jossey-Bass, 2007).

25. P. M. Senge, *The Fifth Discipline: The Art and Practice of the Learning Organization* (New York: Doubleday, 2006).

26. B. Nanus, *Visionary Leadership* (San Francisco: Jossey-Bass, 1992).

27. S. Helgesen, "Leading from the Grass Roots," in *The Leader of the Future*, ed. F. Hesselbein et al. (San Francisco: Jossey-Bass, 1996).

28. J. W. Gardner, *On Leadership* (New York: The Free Press, 1990).

29. C. R. Shaffer and K. Anundsen, *Creating Community Anywhere* (New York: Jeremy P. Tarcher and Perigee, 1993).

30. Shaffer and Anundsen, *Creating Community Anywhere*.

31. M. S. Peck, "The Fallacy of Rugged Individualism," in *In the Company of Others*, ed. C. Whitmyer (New York: Jeremy P. Tarcher and Perigee, 1993).

32. R. N. Bellah et al., *Habits of the Heart* (Berkeley: University of California Press, 1985).

33. J. R. O'Neill, *The Paradox of Success* (New York: Jeremy P. Tarcher and Putnam, 1994).

34. J. Kofomidos, *The Balancing Act* (San Francisco: Jossey-Bass, 1993).

CHAPTER 2

Leadership Styles and Practices

But leadership in public health involves more than individual leaders or individuals in leadership positions. Public health is intimately involved in leadership as an agent of social change by identifying health problems and risks and stimulating actions toward their elimination.

—B. J. Turnock, *Public Health*

This chapter begins by examining several styles of leadership. Leadership style generally refers to the way a leader provides direction to his or her organization, how plans and programs get implemented, and how staff are motivated to do their work. The first model describes McGregor's distinction between two main leadership styles, referred to as Theory X and Theory Y. It then discusses another way of categorizing leadership styles, based on the Leadership Grid, and explores the view that a leader needs to use different styles in different situations. The next section of the chapter is devoted to an account of the characteristics that a leader must possess in order to lead effectively. The last section presents a discussion on the importance of talent as a critical component in leadership.

LEADERSHIP STYLES

Theory X and Theory Y

In a classic study, McGregor discussed two leadership styles, Theory X and Theory Y, which are appropriate for different types of organizations.[1] Theory X is more suitable for an organization in which the employees do not like their work situation and will avoid work whenever possible. In this case, the employees have to be forced, controlled, or reprimanded in order for the organization to meet its goals and objectives. The employees are looking for control because they are not willing to guide the work process themselves. The thing they are most interested in is security.

McGregor noted that a situation in which employees are unhappy and need to be controlled will push leaders toward an autocratic style of leadership. Theory X represents a mainly negative approach to leadership. I had dinner with a local public health administrator at an American Public Health Association annual meeting several years ago. During the discussion, the question of why this administrator did not send any of his staff to a leadership program was raised. His answer—that he was the leader and his staff did not need leadership development—exemplifies the Theory X style of leadership.

Theory Y is appropriate for an organization in which the employees like their jobs and feel that their work is natural and restful. Furthermore, because they accept the goals and objectives of the organization, they tend to be self-directed and even to seek higher levels of responsibility. Finally, decision making occurs at all levels of the organization. Theory Y is essentially a democratic form of leadership. A public health administrator who had completed a state public health leadership program decided that he had benefited greatly from the training. Over the following five years, he sent most of his executive staff to the program to develop their leadership skills. After 10 years passed, this director began to send his new staff through the same leadership development program. His actions exemplify the Theory Y style of leadership. His successor was an

individual whom he had sent to the leadership development program. The new director continues the practice of sending her staff through the leadership program. Exercise 2-1 is intended to help elucidate the difference between Theory X and Theory Y.

In the context of today, Theory X has more commonly been referred to as the "command and control" form of leadership. In the emergency preparedness area, the leader of the Incident Command Structure tends to be seen as this type of leader and also as more of a manager than a leader. Theory Y leaders are seen as democratic or collaborative and empower their staffs to take similar approaches to problem solving.

Managerial Grid

Blake and Moulton adapted the Managerial Grid, a tool devised by Blake and his colleagues, to form the Leadership Grid (**Figure 2-1**).[2] There are 81 positions on the grid and five different leadership styles. The vertical

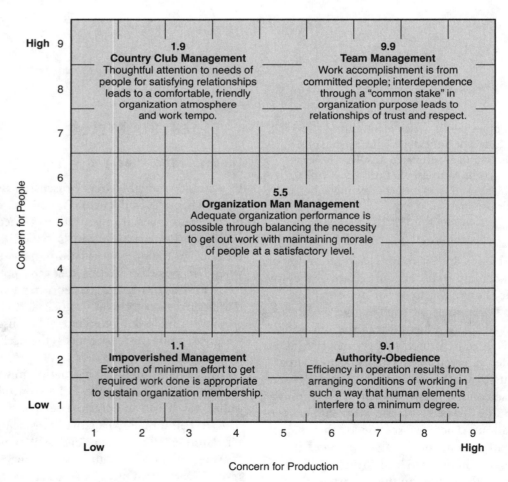

FIGURE 2-1 **The Leadership Grid**®. *Source*: Blake, R., Moulton, J. (1964). *The Managerial Grid: The Key to Leadership Excellence*. Gulf Publishing Company.

axis represents concern for people, and the horizontal axis represents concern for production (task-oriented behaviors). The location of each style on the grid is determined by where the style falls with respect to the two dimensions. For example, the *country club management* approach is characterized by a high level of concern for people and a low level of concern for production and is thus placed in the upper left-hand corner of the grid. This managerial approach creates a relaxed atmosphere and makes people happy to come to work in the morning.

If a leader is not seriously concerned about the well-being of the employees or about production, the result is *impoverished management.* In this style of leadership, the leader engages in the least amount of work necessary to solve a production problem.

The third approach is *team management,* in which the level of concern for employees and production is high. Strong, trusting relationships develop, and all or most employees feel a commitment to accomplish the tasks at hand.

In the *authority-obedience* approach, the primary concern of the leader is to control the production process and increase productivity. The leader's concern for the employees' well-being is minimal.

Organization man management tries to balance the needs of the employees and the needs of production.

Situational Leadership

Instead of using just one leadership style, leaders should use different styles for different situations, according to some authors.[3-6] The series of One Minute Manager books, by Blanchard and others, tries to integrate the needs of organizations with the needs of both employees and customers. Blanchard and his coauthors designated their approach Situational Leadership II.[7,8] As with the Managerial Grid, leadership behavior is evaluated along two dimensions: directiveness and supportiveness. The type of leadership that is relatively nonsupportive and nondirective is termed a "delegating" style of leadership. The type that is supportive but nondirective is termed a "supporting" style of leadership. Leadership behavior that is highly supportive and highly directive constitutes "coaching," and leadership behavior that is highly supportive and highly directive is called "directing."

The model is intentionally flexible. A leader will need to relate to an employee in a given situation using a specific leadership style, a style partly determined by the task and the employee's years in the organiza-

tion. There are certain assumptions here. First, there is the assumption that people want to learn and develop their skills over time. Second, Blanchard pointed out that there may be no guaranteed best leadership style to make this happen. Some people may have a better capacity for learning than others do.

There are clear overlaps between McGregor's analysis of leadership styles and Blanchard's. Theory X involves directing and some coaching. Theory Y involves some coaching, supporting, and delegating. However, the Situational Leadership II model is the more adaptive of the two. Hersey, Blanchard, and Johnson noted an overlap between McGregor's model and the Situational Leadership II model, but they thought that Theory X and Theory Y represented leaders' and managers' assumptions about leadership and that these assumptions often did not get translated into action.[9]

It is clear that leaders must use different strategies for different employees. Leadership occurs in a social context in which values and norms cannot help but influence the process of leading. One leadership approach will not work for every individual in an agency. Unfortunately, some public health leaders are inflexible and use one style predominantly. For instance, one local public health administrator believed it was necessary for him to use an authoritarian approach for managing his staff. Years later, he moved to a new public health agency that he discovered to be more democratic in form. He changed his leadership style but did not seem to learn that leadership style needs to be tied to the situation at hand and not to the agency.

Other Analyses of Leadership Style

In a classic paper, Tannenbaum and Schmidt explored how a leader-manager might be democratic in some situations and autocratic in others.[10] As can be seen in **Figure 2-2**, both leadership styles are used to carry out the activities of the organization. In fact, most leadership practices fall between the two extremes. For example, the action of presenting ideas to subordinates and inviting questions from them involves the use of authority by the manager but also gives to the subordinates a degree of freedom or power. Tannenbaum and Schmidt's analysis is similar to the work of Lewin and his colleagues at the University of Iowa.[11,12] The Lewin group distinguished three leadership styles: autocratic, democratic, and laissez-faire. Their research showed that the democratic style seemed to be especially suitable for group process-oriented activities.

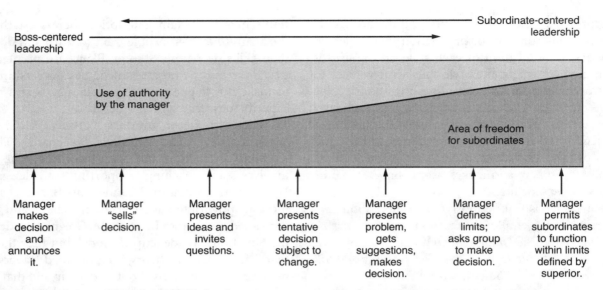

Subordinate-centered leadership

Boss-centered leadership

Use of authority by the manager

Area of freedom for subordinates

| Manager makes decision and announces it. | Manager "sells" decision. | Manager presents ideas and invites questions. | Manager presents tentative decision subject to change. | Manager presents problem, gets suggestions, makes decision. | Manager defines limits; asks group to make decision. | Manager permits subordinates to function within limits defined by superior. |

FIGURE 2-2 **Continuum of Leadership Behavior.** *Source:* Reprinted from *Harvard Business Review.* "How to Choose a Leadership Pattern" by R. Tannenbaum and W. H. Schmidt, May–June 1973. Copyright © 1973 by the President and Fellows of Harvard College; all rights reserved.

Bass found that leaders differ in the approach they take to leading their organizations, in part because of the variation in the issues they need to address.[13] Furthermore, he noted that leadership behaviors generally fall on a continuum between task-oriented and relationship-oriented behaviors.

Fiedler explored the relationship between three factors that affect leadership effectiveness: personal relationships with work associates, the structure of the task to be performed by the work group, and the power associated with the leader's position in the organization.[14] These three factors can be combined in eight ways. According to Fiedler, leaders who are task oriented tend to be more effective in very favorable or very unfavorable situations than those who are relationship oriented. Leaders who are relationship oriented, in contrast, perform better in situations that fall between the two extremes. Note that public health leaders must be both task and relationship oriented, because public health programs demand good communication between public health leaders and their constituents.

Hersey, Blanchard, and Johnson developed a typology of task- and relationship-oriented behavior: high-task and low-relationship behavior, high-task and high-relationship behavior, high-relationship and low-task behavior, and low-task and low-relationship behavior.[15] The authors added effectiveness-ineffectiveness as a third dimension. As noted above, public health leaders need to exhibit high-task and high-relationship

behavior, which is effective in groups being able to set goals, arrange work activities, and create a positive set of work relationships. It is ineffective in sometimes creating an inflexible structure and not enough solid interpersonal relationships.

In the 1940s, a series of studies was done by the Bureau of Business Research at Ohio State University.[16] The researchers defined leadership as the direction of group activities for the purpose of attaining a goal. Leadership, in their view, involved two types of behavior: initiating structure (task-oriented behavior) and showing consideration for the needs of employees (relationship-oriented behavior). The researchers hypothesized, on the basis of their data, that both types of leadership behavior are necessary, but they found little relationship between the two types of behavior.

Utilizing the Ohio State model elements, House formulated a path-goal model.[17] According to this model, a leader's task was to help followers attain their goals through appropriate direction and support. In other words, the leader points the way to the right path to enhance the ability of followers to reach their goals. In addition, House characterized leadership behaviors as directive, supportive, participative, or achievement oriented.

Researchers at the University of Michigan followed the Ohio State model by dividing leadership behaviors into those that were employee oriented (roughly equivalent to showing consideration for employees) and those that were production oriented (roughly equivalent to structure initiation activities).[18]

A recent look at leadership style presents the view that leaders are either multipliers or diminshers.[19] Multipliers are leaders who bring out the best in people, whereas diminishers do the opposite. The five disciplines of the multipliers and helping individuals develop their talents, promoting the best thinking in others, providing challenges, allowing debates to occur, and delegating accountability to others.

When leaders have an idea, a new program to develop, a cause, or a new paradigm for action, they want to see these things work. They jump in immediately and do the detail work necessary to bring these processes to life. Some of the ideas work and some do not. Even when these new directions seem to take flight, outsiders may or may not buy these processes, ideas, or techniques. These leaders need to convince people inside their agencies or organizations and external stakeholders why this innovation is useful and worth supporting. These leaders develop the style of a champion.

Champions are leaders who support causes and new ideas and who think what they are doing and developing needs a wider audience. These champions fight for the cause. They talk to politicians, foundations, government agencies, community leaders, and others to make this new thing work and become valued. They sell the ideas and programs. Champions are multipliers who allow others to move their ideas forward.

LEADERSHIP TRAITS

Those who study leadership traits usually attempt to create an interface between the way leaders think and the ways they tie their thoughts into action on a daily basis. It is these traits that are reflected in the leadership styles of individuals. Traits seem to combine some innate qualities with qualities that seem to be learned. Bass and Stogdill reviewed studies of leadership traits and abilities done between 1948 and 1970.[20] **Table 2-1** contains a list of all the traits and abilities reported in three or more of the studies. Leading the list are technical skills, social nearness and friendliness, task motivation and application, supportiveness toward group activities, social and interpersonal skills, emotional balance and control, and leadership effectiveness and achievement.

After 1970, the idea of universal leadership traits was abandoned. Bass studied the trait issue for the period from 1970 to 2006.[21] Personality and character

TABLE 2-1 Factors Appearing in 3 or More Studies of the 52 Surveyed

Factor	Number of Studies Found
Technical skills	18
Social nearness, friendliness	18
Task motivation and application	17
Supportive of the group task	17
Social and interpersonal skills	16
Emotional balance and control	15
Leadership effectiveness and achievement	15
Administrative skills	12
General impression (halo)	12
Intellectual skills	11
Ascendence, dominance, decisiveness	11
Willingness to assume responsibility	10
Ethical conduct, personal integrity	10
Maintaining a cohesive work group	9
Maintaining coordination and teamwork	7
Ability to communicate; articulativeness	6
Physical energy	6
Maintaining standards of performance	5
Creative, independent	5
Conforming	5
Courageous, daring	4
Experience and activity	4
Nurturant behavior	4
Maintaining informal control of the group	4
Mature, cultured	3
Aloof, distant	3

Source: Modified with permission of The Free Press, a Division of Simon & Schuster, Inc. From *Bass & Stogdill's Handbook of Leadership: Theory, Research, and Management Applications,* Third Edition by Bernard M. Bass. © 1974, 1981, 1990 by The Free Press. All Rights Reserved.

traits were still seen as important. Task competence and socioemotional performance were also seen as important. Verbal and nonverbal communication skills have become critical for the successful leader as well. Bass also pointed out that much research has shown that both nature and nurture are important in leadership.

Kouzes and Posner compared the traits identified in 1987 and again in 2010 as the chief characteristics of admired leaders (**Table 2-2**).[22] The five most frequently mentioned leadership traits of the most admired leaders in 1987 were honesty, forward-lookingness, the ability to inspire, competence, and intelligence. In 2010, the same five traits headed the list. Honesty was also reported as the number-one trait in Canada, Brazil, Australia, Japan (tied with forward-looking), Korea (tied with forward-looking), the Philippines, Malaysia, Mexico, South America, and United Arab Emirates. Being forward-looking was reported as the number-one trait of admired leaders in Turkey.

TABLE 2-2 Characteristics of Admired Leaders (Percentage of People Selecting Characteristic over the Years)

Characteristic	2010	2002	1987
Honest	85	88	83
Forward-looking	70	71	62
Inspiring	69	65	58
Competent	64	66	67
Intelligent	42	47	43
Broad-minded	40	40	37
Dependable	37	33	32
Supportive	36	35	32
Fair-minded	35	42	40
Straightforward	31	34	34
Determined	28	23	20
Cooperative	26	28	25
Ambitious	26	17	21
Courageous	21	20	27
Caring	20	20	26
Imaginative	18	23	34
Loyal	18	14	11
Mature	16	21	23
Self-controlled	11	8	13
Independent	6	6	10

Source: Reprinted with permission of John Wiley & Sons, Inc. From J. M. Kouzes and B. Z. Posner, *Credibility*, 2nd ed. (San Francisco: Jossey-Bass, 2011).

A determination of the traits expected of leaders is used by the military in an effort not only to designate traits but also to use these traits as indicators of those that will reflect the values and culture of the military service and the country. For example, the Marine Corps lists 14 traits for people in the military who wish to become Marine leaders. Many if not all of these traits may also reflect the expectation of a leader in public health. These 14 traits are:[23]

1. *Justice*, which is the practice of being fair and consistent;
2. *Judgment*, which is the ability to think clearly and in an orderly fashion for decision making;
3. *Dependability*, which reflects the ability to perform duties properly;
4. *Initiative*, which is taking action with or without orders;
5. *Decisiveness*, which is making good decisions expeditiously;
6. *Tact*, which is dealing with people in a way that maintains good relations;
7. *Integrity*, which is honesty and truthfulness;
8. *Enthusiasm*, which is sincere involvement and enthusiasm in work;
9. *Bearing*, which is the way the leader conducts and carries him- or herself;
10. *Unselfishness*, which is the avoidance of self-comfort at the expense of the comfort of others;
11. *Courage*, which is calmness while recognizing fear;
12. *Knowledge*, which is acquiring the knowledge necessary to carry out one's work;
13. *Loyalty*, which is devotion to one's country; and
14. *Endurance*, which is physical and mental stamina.

Leadership is dynamic, and there is probably no universal list of leadership traits that apply to all situations.[24] Nonetheless, whereas all the traits and abilities presented in Tables 2-1 and 2-2 are capable of enhancing the effectiveness of a leader, at least in certain circumstances, the 10 leadership abilities and practices described next have been singled out as especially important for successful leadership in the 21st century.

Leadership Practices

First, leaders must be *knowledge synthesizers*. They must bring intelligence to the leadership enterprise. They need to know about past events, understand the realities of the present, and have a vision of the future. They must not only be experts in their chosen field but be familiar with many other areas as well. Good leaders know how to use their knowledge to carve out a perspective and move their organization forward. Intelligence alone is not enough.[25] Self-awareness, self-control, self-confidence, commitment, integrity, the ability to foster change, and the ability to communicate with and influence others are all necessary.

Second, leaders need to be *creative*. They must not only manage large amounts of information but use it creatively to guide action. To do this successfully, they must ignore information that is not pertinent. It is hard to teach people to be creative, although most individuals tend to be creative in areas where they have high interest. When you have enthusiasm for what you are doing, there seems to be a natural flow to the process. It is possible for individuals to expand their creative abilities through practice, including through interacting with others in a social context.[26] Exercise 2-2 is designed to explore the creativity of the team members engaged in devising a solution to a public health problem.

Third, leaders need to be able to *create a vision* and get others to *share the vision* and demonstrate a *commitment to the vision* and the mission it represents. Creating a vision is not an easy thing to do, because it requires careful consideration of different scenarios that might occur if certain factors are present. Furthermore, creating a vision is next to pointless unless others can be convinced to share the vision. Pfeffer stated that a vision gets others to see beyond the obstacles of things to the important possibilities that can ensue in the future.[27] Long-term visions tend to allow people the opportunity to create many innovations, whereas short-term visions seem to be limited by the barriers that today's reality presents. Leaders also need to be flexible enough to modify the vision to better satisfy their partners in the visioning process. Finally, leaders need to fit the vision to a mission and devise an action plan to realize the vision.

Fourth, leaders need to foster and facilitate *collaboration*. No one in an organization exists in a vacuum, nor does anything get done in a vacuum. Turning a vision into reality requires the development of partnerships with external stakeholders and, in fact, the sharing of leadership. In shared leadership, each partner must respect the needs and wants of each of the other partners.

Fifth, leaders need to possess *entrepreneurial ability*. Traditional approaches to running companies and

Leadership Tip

Keep your knowledge and skills up to date.
Be committed to lifelong learning.

agencies no longer seem to be working. Leaders will increasingly need to explore alternate funding sources for their programs and learn how to use their resources in new ways.[28]

This change in perspective will increase not only program efficiency but also program effectiveness. Perhaps surprisingly, leaders in the governmental public health sector need to learn these skills.

Sixth, successful leaders are *systems thinkers* who must also address the needs of complex environments. Acting as a change agent for an organization requires mastering the techniques of systems thinking as well as looking at the organization systemically.[29]

Systems thinkers are consciously aware that everything is connected to everything else. The obvious problems plaguing an organization may be symptoms rather than root causes. A systems approach to change allows leaders to logically analyze the dimensions of the problems.

One way to put systems thinking into practice is to turn the organization into a learning organization—"an organization that is continually expanding its capacity to create its future."[30](p.14)

In a learning organization, the system becomes the guiding mechanism for change. This allows the organization to keep pace with the rapid rate of change in today's world, to function in a more interdependent manner, and to respond to the changing needs of society.[31] In a system, all the parts are interrelated, and activities that occur in one part affect all the others. The traditional linear approach to decision making is not appropriate for a true system. Systems thinkers see the big picture and are interested in the ways organizations and individuals interrelate. They are students of change and the transformational patterns that affect change. Systems thinkers also think strategically. They try to determine strategies for facilitating change as they address the challenges of the system.

Seventh, leaders must *set priorities*. They have to determine what issues will be addressed by the organization. Because of the current focus on team development and community coalition building, leaders often set priorities in concert with team or community partners. Public health places a strong emphasis on the community assessment of health and disease, which helps in setting health priorities for a community. Because the health priorities are determined with partners, subjective and objective factors tend to influence the priority-setting process. Decisions about priorities are often determined by political issues and community concerns.

Eighth, leaders need to *form coalitions and build teams*. They no longer practice the leader's craft in a vacuum, and they must be aware that their success depends on their being able to work with others. Because different individuals bring different expertise to the decision-making environment, teams are created to solve problems and make decisions. In teams, leadership is shared and different members move into the leadership position at different phases of the problem-solving process. Because of public health's strong community perspective, building coalitions to support the local public health agenda becomes critical. A community coalition is a team in which many community groups are represented, and it is a means of empowering the community to address its own problems.

Ninth, leaders, as pointed out previously, must not only bring a creative spark to the organization but also help put innovative ideas into practice. Therefore, they must become masters of the latest *management and leadership techniques*. This does not mean they should adopt all the latest management fads. Rather, they should explore new techniques and integrate into their repertoire those techniques that will likely make the organization stronger, more productive, and more customer oriented.[32] The overall objective of managing is to guide the organization toward achievement of its vision. (Note that new management techniques will occasionally have to be adapted to the systems perspective, because even now many new techniques are linear in nature.)

Tenth, a successful leader acts as *a colleague, a friend, and a humanitarian* toward everyone in the organization. Leaders must be effective communicators and be able to empathize with colleagues, peers, and customers. They should protect the values of their organizations as well as the values of the communities in which they live. In fact, they will occasionally need to help define organizational and community values.

Most leaders of the 21st century, to be fully effective, will need to possess these 10 leadership abilities and characteristics. These abilities and characteristics provide a solid foundation for the activity of leading the process of developing a vision (and a mission) and bringing that vision to fruition.

THE TALENT ISSUE

In the past several years, there has been an emergence of a new dimension of leadership that is tied to the relationship of talents of people and how these talents are reflected in the work of managers and leaders. Talent becomes a filter in which knowledge and skills

get translated into action. Thus, it is more than a series of traits in that the combination of specific talents is unique in each individual. The following formula puts these new trends into perspective:

$$\frac{Knowledge + Skills + Talent + Attitude + Personal\ Values}{Personal\ Strengths + Organizational\ Values} = Action$$

The traditional view was that knowledge, attitudes, and skills led to action. Recent research shows that the process is more complicated.

In a number of books, the Gallup Organization has investigated the critical aspect of talent and how it affects action.[33,34] What was discovered was that most organizations stressed the weaknesses of employees rather than their personal strengths. In order to address these weaknesses, individuals were often sent for training related to these weaknesses rather than training to make personal strengths stronger. In a study of 80,000 people in administrative positions, Buckingham and Coffman said that our orientation to weaknesses was incorrect.[35] Training does not substantially improve an individual's weaknesses. Our brains are wired to support our strengths rather than our weaknesses. This is the talent dimension. Thus, administrators have discovered that it is necessary to change our approaches to training and performance improvement. It is better to train people to use their personal talents more effectively.

The authors also pointed out that effective administrators have to become more expert at dealing with human capital issues. This means they need to become more ready to hire people on the basis of their talents and not just on their technical knowledge and skills. It is in the day-to-day activities that an individual's talents are displayed. The administrator needs to let his or her direct reports define process on the basis of these personal talents. If this happens, then the administrator can concentrate on helping individuals determine outcomes and then measure performance on these outcomes. Thus, performance plays out on an individual's strengths rather than on his or her weaknesses. The challenge then is to find the best fit for jobs on the basis of the combination of knowledge, skills, and talent.

In order to explore talent from the vantage point of strength, the Gallup Organization began an extensive research process to investigate what are the major talents of individuals. Buckingham and Clifton discussed this study of more than two million people.[36] They reported that this research made the assumption that all individuals have a different combination of talents and strengths. Whereas using trait approaches tries to match individuals to the traits required for a job, talent research pointed out that each individual is different and that it is important to create the best fit between these personal talents and strengths and the tasks to be performed. Because our brains are wired for our strengths, the combination of talents is unique to each of us. It is to our personal strengths that we need to move in our pursuit of knowledge and skills.

Out of the Gallup surveys was developed an instrument called Strength Finder, which is now in its second iteration.[37] This instrument measures 34 trait categories. The 34 talents are organized around four key themes, which are discussed by Coffman and Gonzalez-Molina.[38] First, there are themes involving relationships and how well we perform in these talents related to other people. The second theme involves our abilities to create impact in how we motivate people to act. Kouzes and Posner also listed enabling other people to act as a key leadership practice.[39] The third theme involves talents associated with our abilities to be action oriented. The final theme relates to our thinking talents. **Table 2-3** lists the 34 talents related to the four themes.

An important lesson from this research is that an individual can become a strong performer in a particular job category and not be a strong performer in a higher level that requires a different set of talents that the individual may not have. The other part of the formula presented at the beginning of this section relates to the attitude that a person brings to his or her performance. Rath discusses how his grandfather, Donald Clifton, who helped develop an instrument to measure strengths related to talent, also discussed the importance of positive thinking for managers and leaders.[40] The more positive reinforcement the individual gets, the better the work performance becomes. The other numerator variable relates to the values we bring to a job and to our other life activities. These values are also a guide to how we view our actions. The denominator of the formula on page 24 adds the way organizational values and our personal strengths filter the way we practice leadership and action. Our leadership style grows out of many of the factors listed in the formula, which affects the actions we take in problem solving and decision making. Experiment with the concepts in this section by doing Exercise 2-3.

SUMMARY

Traditional theories of leadership have tended to ignore situational factors that can influence which leadership style is best for a given set of circumstances. In addition, most of the leadership literature concerns leadership in the business sector, yet public and not-for-profit agencies seem to work differently than for-profit companies.

TABLE 2-3   Talent Categories of People

Relating Themes	Impacting Themes	Striving Themes	Thinking Themes
Communication	Command	Achiever	Analytical
Empathy	Competition	Activator	Arranger
Harmony	Developer	Adaptability	Connectedness
Includer*	Maximizer	Belief	Consistency†
Individualization	Positivity	Discipline	Context
Relator	Woo	Focus	Deliberative
Responsibility		Restorative	Futuristic
		Self-assurance	Ideation
		Significance	Input
			Intellection
			Learner
			Strategic

* Previously "inclusiveness"
† Previously "fairness"

Source: From *Follow This Path* by Curt Coffman and Gabriel Gonzalez-Molina PhD. Copyright © 2002 by The Gallup Organization. By permission of Grand Central Publishing. All Rights Reserved.

William Foege, a former director of the Centers for Disease Control and Prevention, has said on numerous occasions that social justice is the value that most motivates leaders in public health. Another way of saying this is that concern for people's well-being is primary. Case Study 2-A reviews some of the concerns and motivations of public health leaders.

Given this fact of a people rather than a product orientation, the most balanced type of leadership in public health should probably be called not organization man management (as it is designated in the Leadership Grid), but something like community collaboration leadership. A public health leader's concern for people encompasses many constituencies other than his or her work associates. Furthermore, production, in a public health setting, includes all sorts of programs and activities, from community assessment to the development of effective community interventions.

Case Study 2-A

Inner World to the Future: Leaders' Perspective on the Future
Louis Rowitz

We are at a crossroads. Public health agencies appear to be under attack from multiple sources, including government entities, government superagencies, managed care organizations, the mass media, community groups, and disgruntled citizens. There is confusion about what the thing called "public health" is. There is concern about the involvement of public health agencies in direct medical service activities. Perhaps, some say, it is time for government to get out of the public health service business and spin off public health agency activities to the private sector.

To these concerns must be added a strong belief that leaders make a difference. Leaders bring hope and vision and have an ability to find solutions for the challenges that face the field of public health. It is to the training of public health professionals that the public health community looks as a possible way to strengthen the infrastructure of public health in this country and to clarify the vision of public health for the 21st century. There is a strong belief in the public health community that leadership skills can be taught. There is also a strong belief that a commitment to lifelong learning is critical. For the past several years, national, regional, and state public health leadership programs have been developed. These programs have helped public health leaders increase their leadership skills and learn the latest techniques for improving and strengthening organizations. These programs have also trained public health leaders to work with communities to help define the role of public health at the community level. These programs have also stressed the importance of promoting the public health paradigm of core functions and essential public health services and of urging leaders to use their skills to build the public health system. These programs have developed unique approaches to training that promote an experiential application of all training materials back to the workplace and the community. The greatest challenge for these programs, other than the obvious one of financial sustainability, is the measurement of their long-term effect on the infrastructure of public health.

The combination of public health's challenges and the present-tense quality of our public health leadership programs, even when we talk about the future, raises an important series of issues related to where public health needs to go over the next several decades. The perspective is partly one of vision, but it is also one that goes to the very soul of the beliefs of public health leaders around the world. The experience of public health work changes us as professionals. Our inner world processes all our experiences and creates what the experimental psychologist Edward Tolman called a cognitive map. Each experience changes the topography of our lives. This includes our personal experiences and our community living experiences as well as our professional experiences.

Interviews with Public Health Leaders

During 1996, I began a personal odyssey to find out what public health leaders think about public health today and what they perceive will be public health's future. I traveled throughout the United States, England, Scotland, and Ireland conversing with public health leaders about the future of public health. I talked to more than 130 leaders in conversations that lasted about an hour. These conversations changed my cognitive map and my inner world by showing me the field of public health in ways that I had never perceived it. I talked to leaders at all levels of government. I talked to public health professionals at the federal, state, and local levels in the United States as well as to academics. I talked to foundation professionals as well as professional trainers. I also talked to public health leaders who moved to the private sector. These leaders have given me insights about ways to strengthen our training programs in the future so that we can make public health more responsive to the needs of the public. They have also taught me what we do wrong and the importance of blending our strengths in solutions of our problems.

Lessons Learned

Public health leaders live the reality of their chosen profession on a daily basis. They struggle with the crises of the day as well as with the concerns that public health faces as it progresses into the 21st century. Leaders in the United States face concerns with the impact of managed care on the public health field. Leaders in the United Kingdom and Ireland see public health within the context of a nationalized health service where managed care is a reality rather than a specter on the horizon. As I talked to U.S. leaders at the federal, state, and local levels as well as in both the public and private sectors, I found that all the leaders struggle with what that elusive field called public health is. The confusion extends to the issue of whether public health as a profession is different from public health as an organizational entity. U.S. public health is multidisciplinary as well as multisectorial in perspective. This means that we speak with many voices and do not always convey a unified message. Despite this multidisciplinary orientation, public health has a strong medical perspective and an increasingly economic one as well. One result is that the primary prevention goal of public health is sometimes lost as we pursue treatment and rehabilitation programs for underserved or unserved populations. Many leaders argue that the local public health agency must be a provider of last resort when there are limited medical services available for the people in local communities. As local public health agencies continue to act as direct service providers, leaders argue that managed care organizations' move into the local area of service is a threat to local health agencies that rely heavily on the service dollars received for direct service. However, public health needs to be seen as a partner in a total integrated health program in the community. Some leaders see public health agencies as playing the leading role in a comprehensive community-based healthcare system.

There is increasing acceptance of the core functions paradigm of assessment, policy development, and assurance, along with a lesser degree of acceptance of the essential public health services perspective. There is a concern that the core functions terminology is too abstract and confusing to people outside the public health field. U.S. leaders feel that we perform assessment activities fairly well, although we tend not to be conversant with the latest technology advances in informatics. Leaders at all government levels feel that they have a critical role in policy development but do not always exercise the policy opportunities that they have. Several leaders pointed out that public health leaders need to be students of the democratic process and understand how our political process works. The leaders are concerned that politicians and local board of health members or county board members have most of the control of the budget that drives the public health machine. They also believe that the relationship between the local health agency and its boards is often adversarial. Leaders argue that boards could become more of a voice for public health in the community than they currently are. In addition, these issues point to the question of how public health leaders can affect the decision-making process.

Most questions were raised about the assurance function and the difficulties in specifying completely our assurance role, because this is the role that underwent the most change during the last decade of the 20th century. There is agreement that public health needs to support a lifelong learning perspective and encourage and support continued educational and training opportunities for the public health workforce. However, training dollars are currently scarce.

Many leaders express concern about the future of public health in the United States and the increasing split between national public health concerns and state and local concerns. The agenda of each level of government is different and often not integrated with the issues of concern at other levels. In addition, we have not explored the possibilities of regional collaboration as a viable way to share programs across counties and other local entities and across states in different geographic areas. An added challenge concerns the absorption of public health into state human services umbrella agencies. However, some leaders feel that the umbrella agency model may increase the importance of public health agencies and leadership at the local level. Public health practice is really a local concern and needs to be protected. It must not become too parochial, because public health has a global perspective. State and local public health leaders need to think globally but act locally.

There are several other issues of concern to public health leaders. First, our assessment activities tend to ignore the important perspective of epidemiology, which provides methods for interpretation of data. Leaders often do not know how to use data for effective decision making. Second, public health needs to reclaim its primary prevention perspective and its key role in health promotion. Educational models should predominate in health promotion activities. Third, public health is developing academic and practice linkages, but not too many successful ones. Next, public health needs to do a better job in the areas of social marketing and health communications, because the public still does not know what public health is. Finally, public health needs to do a better job building community coalitions to address community public health needs. However, there is much to learn about the development of coalitions and how to keep up the interest of these coalitions over time.

In England, Scotland, and the Republic of Ireland, I saw national health systems in which public health often played a secondary role. In all three countries, public health is dominated by physicians. All other public health–related groups are in secondary support roles. Only physicians can head a public health program in a district. If other professionals want to move into a leadership role, they are often limited to roles in academic teaching settings. However, all public health physicians have received training in public health and have passed national credential examinations.

Purchasing of services becomes the primary role of the health service public health physicians. Primary prevention programs may exist in some areas, like immunization, but these programs are contracted out to local physicians or hospitals and clinics. A common complaint of the district physicians was their inability to use their public health knowledge in the health districts. They felt that a large amount of their professional energies was expended on conflicts with local managers, who are often not health trained. In England, public health physicians felt that public health is losing its foothold and becoming less visible. In the Republic of Ireland, public health offices were abolished for 20 years under the mistaken belief that all of the public health concerns of Irish society had been solved. Only in the past few years has public health been re-established in the districts. However, it is taking time for these offices to re-create public health programs. Scotland is an interesting case, in that community-based programs are being developed and supported within the Scottish office of the national health service.

The major lesson to be learned is that public health often has trouble surviving in a system in which all the citizens have access to services. However, primary prevention programs do not flourish in this environment without a vigorous struggle. Time pressure resulting from calendar overload becomes a problem. Bureaucracy and an overabundance of meetings at the local and national levels are the rule rather than the exception. In addition, each public health profession has its own organization, the agendas of these organizations conflict, and there is a consequent lack of agreement between these groups as to how to pursue a common public health agenda. However, these European countries are small, and most public health people know each other. This does offer opportunities for collaboration that are not often pursued.

The Future

Public health concerns never go away. Although it is possible to see variations in the ways public health is practiced, there will continue to be crises and issues of concern to the public health profession. There is growing anxiety about emerging infections and increasing resistance to the effects of antibiotics. Money available for health services is shrinking. Managed care and primary care organizations do not seem to hold all the answers for the healthcare needs of the American public.

The changing demographics of our population require public health interventions. The need for primary prevention activities and the development of health promotion and disease prevention initiatives remains critical. Ebbs and flows in the support for government-based public health programs will continue.

Public health leaders remain hopeful. They see growing support for leadership programs for the public health workforce. They project a growing influence of public health activities undertaken by local health departments. They are ambivalent about the movement to create superagencies at the state level, although they recognize that public health agencies need to work closely with other human services agencies. Our technology knowledge will increase significantly over the next several decades. The Centers for Disease Control and Prevention will continue to be a major public health voice in this country. Public health will work more closely with its healthcare partners to develop more integrated systems of care. Some leaders see this collaboration as occurring from within an integrated healthcare system. Other leaders believe that public health agencies will remain part of the government system, because their oversight function must not be compromised. Closer linkages will evolve between academic institutions and public health agencies. Finally, public health's emphasis on core functions and essential services will lead to increased infrastructure strength in the future.

In summary, public health leaders bring a message of hope for the future. Public health will survive.

Source: Reproduced from L. Rowitz (1997). "Inner World to the Future: Leaders' Perspective on the Future," *Journal of Public Health Management and Practice*, 3, 4, 68–71, July 1997.

DISCUSSION QUESTIONS

1. What are the differences between the Theory X and Theory Y leadership styles?
2. What are the five leadership styles defined in the Leadership Grid?
3. What is an example of high-task, low-relationship leadership behavior?
4. How would you describe your dominant leadership style?
5. How flexible are you in modifying your dominant leadership style in situations that require a different style?
6. What are two examples of how you practice leadership?
7. What are five of the most cited traits of admired leaders?
8. What do you think are the most important traits a leader needs to possess?
9. Why do leaders of public organizations need entrepreneurial ability?
10. What are the similarities and differences between traits and talents?

EXERCISE 2-1: Authoritarian and Democratic Leadership Styles

Purpose: to explore alternative approaches to decision making and to investigate how alternative leadership styles can influence program outcomes

Key concepts: authoritarian leadership style, democratic leadership style, decision making

Procedure: The class or training group should divide into two or more groups. Each group has the assignment to create a plan for developing a community's public health infrastructure using a given set of resources. The plan should address core infrastructure elements, including the local public health workforce, public health facilities and services, public health surveillance and information systems, and relationships with medical, social, community, government, and business organizations. To develop this plan, each team chooses a leader, who is given an envelope containing a note designating the leader as a supporter of the Theory X or the Theory Y leadership style. The leader guides the group through a planning process according to the characteristics of the leadership style assigned but does not inform the other team members which leadership style he or she is using. After half an hour, each team reports back to the class or training group as a whole, describing the exercise process, evaluating the leader, and describing the infrastructure plan chosen by the team and what its ramifications are.

EXERCISE 2-2: An Exercise in Creativity

Purpose: to generate solutions to a public health problem from several leadership perspectives and to learn how to use creativity to discover the best solution for a problem

Key concepts: community coalition, creativity, problem solving, team

Procedure: The class or training group should divide into small teams of five to eight people. Each member of each team should select a public health problem that concerns the particular member. The team then chooses one of the problems and tries to solve it from a personal perspective, a public health agency perspective, and a community coalition perspective. The exercise is repeated using the supposition that the mayor of the town or the governor of the state does not want public funds expended on the problem. The entire team should explore the advantages and limitations of the alternative solutions and the role that creativity plays in developing the solutions.

EXERCISE 2-3: Talent and Strength

Purpose: to become aware of when we make strong decisions and explore the underlying talents we have as leaders

Key concepts: talent, personal strengths, decision making

Procedure: Jot down in your journal or on a sheet of paper the last three decisions you made that demonstrate your effectiveness as a leader. Break down the class or training group into small teams of five to eight and discuss one example with your team where you showed your strength in making a decision. Looking at the list of talents in Table 2-3, determine what talents you displayed in your decision-making style.

REFERENCES

1. D. McGregor, *The Human Side of Enterprise* (New York: McGraw-Hill, 1985).
2. R. R. Blake et al., *The Leadership Grid* (Houston: Gulf Publishing Co., 1991).
3. K. Blanchard and S. Johnson, *The One Minute Manager* (New York: Morrow, 1982).
4. K. Blanchard and R. Lorber, *Putting the One Minute Manager to Work* (New York: Morrow, 1984).
5. K. Blanchard et al., *Leadership and the One Minute Manager* (New York: Morrow, 1985).
6. K. Blanchard et al., *The One Minute Manager Builds High Performing Teams* (New York: Morrow, 1990).
7. Blanchard et al., *Leadership and the One Minute Manager.*
8. Blanchard et al., *The One Minute Manager Builds High Performing Teams.*
9. P. Hersey et al., *Management of Organizational Behavior*, 9th ed. (Upper Saddle River, NJ: Prentice Hall, 2007).
10. R. Tannenbaum and W. H. Schmidt, "How to Choose a Leadership Pattern," *Harvard Business Review* (March–April 1958): 95–102.
11. K. Lewin and R. Lippitt, "An Experimental Approach to the Study of Autocracy and Democracy: A Preliminary Note," *Sociometry* 1 (1938): 292–300.
12. K. Lewin, "Field Theory and Experiment in Social Psychology," *American Journal of Sociology* 44 (1939): 868–896.
13. B. M. Bass, *The Bass Handbook of Leadership* (4th ed.), (New York: The Free Press, 2008).
14. F. E. Fiedler, *A Theory of Leadership Effectiveness* (New York: McGraw-Hill, 1967).
15. Hersey et al., *Management of Organizational Behavior.*
16. R. M. Stogdill and A. E. Coons, eds., *Leader Behavior: Its Description and Measurement*, Research Monograph No. 88 (Columbus: Ohio State University, Bureau of Business Research, 1951).
17. R. J. House, "A Path-Goal Theory of Leadership," *Administrative Science Quarterly* 16 (1971): 321–338.
18. R. L. Kahn and D. Katz, "Leadership Practices in Relation to Productivity and Morale," in *Group Dynamics: Research and Theory*, ed. D. Cartwright and A. Zander (Evanston, IL: Peterson & Co., 1960).
19. L. Wiseman, *Multipliers: How the Best Leaders Make Everyone Smarter* (New York: Harper Business, 2010).
20. Bass, *Bass Handbook of Leadership.*
21. Bass, *Bass Handbook of Leadership.*
22. J. M. Kouzes and B. Z. Posner, *Credibility*, 2nd ed. (San Francisco: Jossey-Bass, 2011).
23. http://www.au.af.mil/au/awc/awcgate/usmc/leadership_traits.htm
24. Hersey et al., *Management of Organizational Behavior.*
25. D. Coleman, *Working with Emotional Intelligence* (New York: Bantam, 1998).
26. M. Csikszentmihalyi, *Creativity* (New York: HarperCollins, 1996).
27. J. Pfeffer, "No Excuses Leadership," *Leader to Leader* 46 (Fall 2007): 31–34.
28. D. Osborne and T. Gaebler, *Reinventing Government* (Reading, MA: Addison-Wesley, 1992).
29. D. L. Kauffman Jr., *Systems 1: An Introduction to Systems Thinking* (Minneapolis: Future Systems, Inc., 1980).
30. P. M. Senge, *The Fifth Discipline: The Art and Practice of the Learning Organization*, rev. and updated ed. (New York: Doubleday, 2006).
31. Senge, *The Fifth Discipline.*
32. S. P. Robbins and M. Coulter, *Management*, 8th ed. (Upper Saddle River, NJ: Prentice-Hall, 2005).
33. M. Buckingham and C. Coffman, *First Break All the Rules* (New York: Simon and Schuster, 1999).
34. M. Buckingham and D. O. Clifton, *Now, Discover Your Strengths* (New York: The Free Press, 2001).
35. Buckingham and Coffman, *First Break All the Rules.*
36. Buckingham and Clifton, *Now, Discover Your Strengths.*
37. T. Rath, *Strength Finder 2.0* (New York: Gallup Press, 2007).
38. C. Coffman and G. Gonzalez-Molina, *Follow This Path* (New York: Warner Books, 2002).
39. J. M. Kouzes and B. Z. Posner, *Leadership Challenge*, 4th ed. (San Francisco: Jossey-Bass, 2007).
40. T. Rath and D. O. Clifton, *How Full Is Your Bucket?* (New York: Gallup Books, 2004).

CHAPTER 3

The Interface Between Management and Leadership

> A manager is responsible for the application and performance of knowledge.
>
> —Peter Drucker

There is an interesting training exercise called the Human Likert, which has a large group line up along an imaginary continuum.* The general instruction is to decide how each individual defines his or her professional life. On one side of the line are individuals who define themselves as public health practitioners with a major specialty, such as an environmental health professional. In the middle of the line are those who define themselves as managers or administrators, and at the end of the line are those who define themselves as public health leaders. The facilitator then goes down the line asking people why they placed themselves as they did and whether they see themselves as moving along the line as they professionally advance in their chosen public health field. What this exercise does is

demonstrate how people view their professional training, their personal definitions of management, and what they perceive as leadership. In a recent use of the Human Likert by me, one individual who defined himself as an environmental health professional said that he wanted to become an expert in his chosen field. He saw this as a demonstration of leadership without a specific designated leadership position in his organization. Those in the management position also saw that leadership could be demonstrated in a management position as well. Thus, it is possible to move horizontally as well as vertically in an organization. Horizontally, you advance by becoming the best public health practitioner that you can or the best manager or the best leader. If you want to move to a higher administrative position in your organization—a vertical move—it is necessary to move in the direction of your strengths rather than your weaknesses.[1] What the Human Likert exercise teaches the participants is that practitioners develop expertise in their disciplinary specialty; managers maintain the organization and develop people; and leaders define the system, build relationships, and create visions for the future.

---

*I learned this exercise from Dr. Magda Peck of the University of Wisconsin-Milwaukee as she did this exercise before a maternal and child health leadership group.

This chapter explores the connections between management and leadership. The following section examines the management issues and is followed by an example of matrix forms of organization that was tried by the Centers for Disease Control and Prevention (CDC) through its goals management initiative in the Gerberding administration (2002–2008). This is followed by a discussion of the starfish organizational model. Next is a discussion of some of the connections between management and leadership with a discussion of transactional and transformational leadership. A discussion of meta-leadership is then presented as one way to look at the interface between management and leadership. The final section of the chapter presents a road map that begins to demonstrate how these management and leadership functions interrelate.

MANAGERS AND MANAGEMENT

There are clear distinctions between managers and leaders. Managers are tied to the present and to the mission of the agencies they serve. Leaders tend to be less bound by their home agencies or their positions, although they need to be concerned about their vision for the agency and the support of the individuals who work in the agency to move the agency forward into the future. Leaders in public agencies allocate much of their time to building relationships with external stakeholders in the public health enterprise.[2] Although both managers and leaders tend to be tied to a specific agency position, the manager seems to be more locked into the requirements of the job than the leader does. Leaders are more oriented to their vision and the overall public health system, whereas the manager needs to concentrate on making the agency effective and efficient. The effective manager makes the dreams and visions of the leader real.

Another reality is that a specific individual may be hired into an administrative position (management) and be expected to carry out both management and leadership activities. This may not always be an easy task. People are different, and they view the world in different ways. Browning has pointed out that people have different thinking attributes.[3] There are people who tend to be linear thinkers and are intrigued with rules, regulations, and protocols. They are structured in the way they do things. They tend to be organized and to resist change. These structured thinkers can be contrasted with people who tend to be analytical in their thinking. These are the problem solvers who are very logical and like abstract thinking. They like to put facts and numbers together. If we extend this structural and analytical thinking to the organizational level, we are probably talking about many governmental agencies that like process, analyze facts, follow rules and protocols, and tend to support a status quo perspective. Many managers tend to fall into this classification of structural and analytical.

Browning stated that there are two other major thinking preferences. There are the conceptual thinkers who tend to want to view the big picture. They like change and tend to stir things up. For example, you think that you have the last draft of a technical report, and the conceptual thinker will ask if you have thought about solution X. Conceptual people tend to be creative and look at new ways to achieve their visions and goals. The fourth thinking attribute is social. Those strong in this thinking preference tend to like to work in teams and show great concern for others. They tend to be empathic. Some literature has pointed out that managers need to have strong people skills in today's environment.[4] Managers have to be able to fit people's talents into appropriate jobs that fit the needs of the organization.[5] The Browning Emergenetics Model can be seen graphically in **Figure 3-1**, where the analytical and structural half of the diagram represents left-brain thinking, and the conceptual and social half represents right-brain thinking.[6] Most people will show preference in more than one thinking attribute. All sorts of combinations are possible, from strong preference in one, two, three, or four thinking attributes. However, the thinking preferences of an individual are filtered and affected by their behavioral attributes of expressiveness, assertiveness, and flexibility.

Management takes place in the context of an agency or an organization. In 1916, Fayol defined the five elements of management as prevoyance (planning), organizing, commanding, coordinating, and controlling.[7] Planning involves a series of actions to achieve organizational goals. Organizing involves the assignment of tasks to employees, fitting assignments into the existing hierarchical structure of the organization, and tying organizational goals to these work processes. Commanding is about leadership inside the organization. Some writers discuss the issues of employee productivity, turnover and absenteeism, job satisfaction, and other human capital issues for this function.[8] Wagner and Harter of the Gallup Organization strongly argue for following a 12-step model for engaging employees that will be the orientation of great managers.[9] Part of the motivation of employees involves the

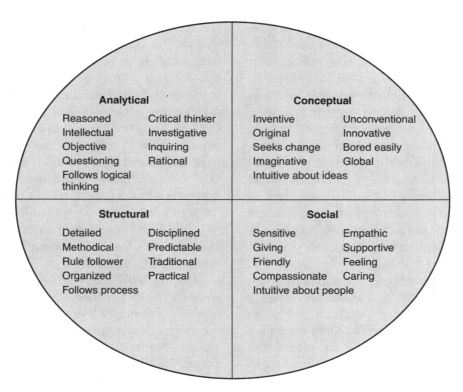

FIGURE 3-1 Your Thinking Attributes. *Source*: Reprinted with permission from G. Browning, *Emergenetics* (New York: HarperCollins, 2006). With permission of the author.

leaders in the organization sharing their vision with the managers. The coordinating and controlling elements involve the necessity for the manager to monitor activities of the agency and make corrections and realignments as necessary. Drucker defined the three tasks of management as determining the mission of the organization, creating a work environment that is productive and leads to worker achievement, and recognizing the social impact and social responsibility of the organization's activities.[10] It is interesting to note here that businesses as well as governmental public health agencies have a social impact and social responsibility dimension that for public health is related to the philosophy of social justice.

Fayol also developed a 14-principle guide for management that is as relevant today as it was when he formulated it early in the 20th century.[11] As can be seen in **Table 3-1**, the 14 principles cover all aspects of an organization's management, from a division of work to the creation of a positive environment in which people may work. A clarification regarding management needs to be made. Management activities will differ at different levels of the organization. Robbins and Coulter point out that technical skills will be necessary at the program level of the organization, with people skills

TABLE 3-1 Henri Fayol's 14 Principles of Management

1. Division of work (specialization)
2. Authority
3. Discipline
4. Unity of command (one supervisor)
5. Unity of direction
6. Subordination of individual interest
7. Remuneration
8. Centralization (or decentralization)
9. Scalar chain (organizational hierarchy)
10. Order
11. Equity
12. Stability of tenure of personnel
13. Initiative
14. Esprit de corps

Source: Data from Fayol, *General and Industrial Management* (Paris: Dunod, 1916).

becoming more important as you move up horizontally in the organization.[12] Conceptual skills become critical for the top managers and leaders in the organization. The leaders create change.

Administrators of state or local public health agencies or offices are generally appointed by elected officials or by local boards of health. New public health administrators tend to be seen as political appointees. These appointments to so-called leadership positions are in reality perceived to be high-level management positions. The job of these appointees is to manage the official public health agency. The new administrators face all types of organizational challenges during the early part of their tenure. As they accommodate to their new positions, demands from external community stakeholders need to be addressed. As community issues take precedence, the administrator may need to delegate managerial responsibilities to other people in the department.

Working in government is not the same as working in business. It is not that the tools or skills necessary to work in these two sectors are very different, but rather that the public health leader needs to adapt these tools and skills to the public sector. There are at least four challenges for leaders who work in the public sector:[13]

1. The public sector administrator has to work within the framework of laws, rules, regulations, and procedures defined by governmental entities. These laws, rules, regulations, and procedures put limits and restrictions on the public agency executive, which can affect mission, vision, performance, and progress at addressing public health issues.
2. The performance of the agency is extremely visible to the outside world through legislative oversight and media scrutiny. Moore has stated that performance is affected by the challenge of creating public value for public sector issues.[14]
3. The internal and external stakeholders that are affected by the work of public agencies are more numerous and representative of diverse value perspectives than in the business world. Each stakeholder has unique issues. There are multiple and diverse demands and levels of influence on the work of the agency.
4. The realities of bureaucracy often impede or delay the ability of administrators to carry out the public's work in an effective, efficient, and timely manner.

Even though we live in a democratic society, people who work in government often seem to feel limited in their ability to move their agency agendas forward because of external scrutiny as well as political agendas.

It is incorrect to assume that all agencies are the same. Different agencies require different types of administrators to address these differences. There are at least five different organizational settings for the new administrator. Daly and Watkins define these settings as a startup situation, turnaround, realignment or shift in priorities, accelerated growth, and maintaining a successful organizational strategy.[15,16] In startup and turnaround situations, the new administrator needs to make changes quickly and does not have the leisure to learn about the organization and its staff, as in realignment and success-sustaining situations. Accelerated growth refers to organizations going through a major growth spurt. Exercise 3-1 will allow the class or training group to experiment with Daly and Watkins's five organizational settings, utilizing a public health scenario.

During 2007, the National Association of County and City Health Officials (NACCHO) undertook a process of developing a plan for a new local health official orientation program (now called the Survive and Thrive Program). In concert with a NACCHO committee, the staff of the association began an interactive process of developing this program. The committee, NACCHO staff, and curriculum design consultants developed the curriculum.[17] It became clear early that the program needed to be strong on management issues because the committee, composed of several seasoned health administrators, strongly argued that new administrators needed to spend time on management issues. Five specific competency expectations for new health officials were determined.[18] New health officials should:

1. Clearly describe to their staff and variety of public audiences the roles and responsibilities of the new administrator within local health departments (LHDs) and the LHD's roles and responsibilities within the local health system.
2. Effectively engage elected officials, governing boards, and the state health department in carrying out the roles and responsibilities of the LHDs.
3. Effectively manage their LHDs, including providing insight and direction of strategic planning and the agency's human, financial, and information resources.

Leadership Tips

Treat your board members as supporters and not enemies.

4. Effectively engage community partners in developing local public health systems for community health improvement and community preparedness initiatives.
5. Rapidly access peer and coaching resources that may assist in developing leadership skills for addressing and resolving problems and issues that challenge local health officials.

Competency 3 clearly involves management competencies. Competencies 1 and 2 require both management and leadership activities. Competencies 4 and 5 are leadership competencies. What this means is that public health administrators have to do both management and leadership activities to carry out their jobs effectively. The cautionary consideration is that some people are great managers and some are great leaders. Bringing the two sets of talents and skills together may not always be possible.

It is clear that public health needs both excellent managers and excellent leaders. In order to address the management domain, the University of North Carolina School of Public Health and the Kenan-Flagler Business School have developed a model training program for managers. The Management Academy was created to develop teams of health professionals to address management challenges in community health.[19] The training curriculum helps individuals to improve their management skills, work in small groups on interactive management exercises, transfer new skills into action, build teams, create networks, and learn how to develop business plans. The curriculum includes information on managing people, business planning, human resources development, financial management, civic entrepreneurship, marketing, communication, partnerships, negotiation, program implementation, and team building. Steve Orton, director of the Management Academy, answers the public health practice quiz in Case Study 3-A.

A Public Health Practice Quiz for Steve Orton

Case Study 3-A

1. What types of management training do public health professionals need?

Public health professionals have widely varied skills and backgrounds, so individuals have different needs. Public health work does seem to present some specific challenges, though—and I believe that the current environment creates some challenges for managers across the board.

For public health, I think managers need training that builds skills in managing teams, because so much of the high-yield work they do involves convening teams, bridging differences, translating across disciplines and/or organizations, and sustaining effort (often without positional authority).

They need training in managing money, because so few of them have a background in finance. We have done pre-course assessments in the Management Academy for many years: too many public health managers have no confidence in their abilities to read a spreadsheet, create a budget, calculate a break-even point for a program, or understand the financial reports for the programs they manage. Few managers have taken finance in school, even those with MPH preparation. And few public health organizations have a culture of attending to finances, so managers don't have to learn money management to succeed. External pressures are building, though—I think many managers now feel the need to develop finance skills.

Managers generally, not just in public health, need training that they can quickly translate into practice. I see a need for training in managing people effectively, so that they are engaged and committed and well deployed.

Clearly, in each of these areas, it isn't sufficient to read the book or listen to the lecture about the topic: these are skills. It isn't even sufficient to have the individual ability, because in these areas the "competence" is in some sense collective: teamwide, organization-wide, even community-wide.

2. How do we evaluate the effectiveness of this type of training?

Very carefully. I think that evaluating management training for professionals should make sure the process is working (and constantly improving), and should also seek measures of impact on behaviors and ultimately organizations, where management gets enacted. Training transfer to the workplace should always be the goal.

My own experience with this process convinces me that evaluation, and evaluators, should be integrated into design and quality improvement. Don't expect to determine effectiveness by hiring an evaluator after the program runs.

(Continues)

I say "very carefully" because I worry that some people have unrealistic expectations of what an educational intervention can accomplish, when so many forces act on organizations and communities. But I also worry that other people have such low expectations.

3. How is management training different from leadership training?

Short answer: leadership training is big-picture; management training is nuts-and-bolts. At UNC, this is how we differentiate our leadership and management programs in executive education. For instance, leadership communication is about message mapping and media skills. Management communication is about communicating in a work team, writing e-mails, or crafting a good PowerPoint presentation.

4. How do we create an interface between management and leadership training?

Education is not inoculation. Workforce development isn't a one-time shot; it's an individual and organizational commitment to keep learning. The best leaders, and the best organizations, are seeking out training continually, assessing themselves, strategizing, learning new skills, practicing, stretching, staying fresh. Personally, I think the individuals and organizations that get that are already doing a good job of integrating learning from lots of different sources.

The challenge for producers of training is to stay in touch with the needs of the audience to keep training relevant. The integration, ultimately, happens at the consumer level—so those of us funding or implementing training programs need to stay tuned in.

5. What is the next level of management training for public health professionals?

I think there is plenty of need for manager development at the current level! To me, the "next level" would be to have many more public health managers developing new skills. Systemwide, we have plenty to do to make sure managers have reasons and resources to develop themselves in relevant areas.

MATRIX ORGANIZATIONS IN PUBLIC HEALTH

In recent years, there have been discussions about the difficulties of working in traditional hierarchical organizations. The concept of a silo has been used to reflect what goes on in vertical organizations when programmatic units become insulated from other programs in an organization or agency. There have also been discussions about changes in the way work is done in the public sector. Goldsmith and Eggers have discussed these issues in a governance by network model.[20] We are seeing the rise of third-party government where we contract with private firms and nonprofit organizations to do the work of government. There are also joined-up government activities where partnerships are created between two or more governmental entities to provide an integrated approach to delivering public programs. Changes in technology are also affecting our work relations in that it is possible to work

Leadership Tip

Without trust, leaders often fail.

on common projects from great distances using the Internet. Friedman described this process as evidence of a flattening world.[21] Goldsmith and Eggers also described consumer demand and the possibilities of customized service models in the future. Governmental employees involved in these new initiatives will find that the way they work will change. Instead of supervising employees in the agency, these new managers will find themselves managing portfolios of projects being done outside their home agency.

With these changes possible, it becomes necessary to change our agencies as well. One model builds on the matrix form of management with the goal of leveling the organization to be more project or goal focused with techniques for coordinating activities across projects. Robbins and Coulter have defined a horizontal matrix structure as a form of organizational model involving program specialists from various functional units in an organization to work on a multidisciplinary team to carry out a project- or goal-based program.[22] **Figure 3-2** graphically shows a sample matrix structure model. The model labels each unit as a portfolio to reflect that the project or goal approach will allow the individual unit to manage all parts of a project or projects related to the unit program. The role of the

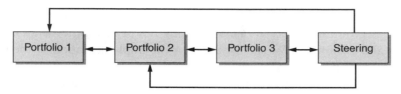

FIGURE 3-2 Mapping the Horizontal in Matrix Structure: Overall Strategic Plan.

steering committee is to be a group that includes a representative of each project or goal unit to supervise the whole project and to prioritize all the projects and goals of the organization.[23] The steering committee can also be the manager of the overall strategic plan of the organization.

On the positive side, this organizational model is flexible and allows for projects and goals to be added or subtracted as appropriate. This model also allows new projects to draw on the talents and strengths of people in the agency who will help benefit a specific project. Each unit staff also requires that both management and leadership processes happen. Creativity in the developing of new projects or subprojects will also be encouraged.

There are also difficulties with the design. First, the matrix model is often superimposed on a traditional vertical organization. What this does is complicate the processes and work of the organization. On the one hand, the programmatic silos continue to exist at the same time as the matrix units are developed. The challenge then becomes how to have the silo teams buy into the matrix units' projects and goals. Marketing within the organization needs to be done to support the matrix structures.

There may also be control and communication difficulties with the model as well as resistance to the design by the established vertical organization. Some staff of the agency sometimes believe that they have two bosses and have to report to their silo supervisor as well as the team leader of the matrix unit. There is also the issue of power and the difficulty to share power. Credibility and trust issues also have to be addressed. There are possible methods for addressing some of these silo concerns. Lencioni has delineated a four-part model for this.[24] The model, if addressed early, may prevent some of the resistance to a project- or goal-based horizontal matrix model. There needs to be a clear vision for the agency that is shared by all of the silo directors serving as a leadership team for the agency. Agency goals also need to be determined. These goals are then translated into clearly defined objectives or projects that can

TABLE 3-2 Management and Leadership Outputs

Goals aligned with customers and partners
Processes aligned with customers
Capacity in line with the strategic plan
Resources deployed effectively
Performance improvement implemented as needed
Create standards and use common methodologies
Develop teams that produce results
Promote organizational learning
Collaborative leadership
Creation of an innovative portfolio
Shared leadership
High-performing teams
Working inside the organization and with external partners

Source: Courtesy of *The New Matrix Management*, P. Martin, Cincinnati, OH: Martin Training Associates, 2005.

evolve into matrix units around these objectives or projects. These objectives then need to be aligned to standard operational requirements. Finally, there needs to be a methodology for measuring the results of the agency's activities and programs.

There are both management and leadership outputs from matrix structures. **Table 3-2**, which is adapted from the work of Paula Martin, shows these outputs.[25] The CDC provides us with an intriguing variation of the matrix model in its reorganization and goals development program. The next section will look at the CDC Health Protection Goals agenda during the Gerberding administration as an example of the application of a modified matrix management program.

CDC Futures Initiative

Dr. Julie Gerberding, director of the CDC from 2002 to 2008, announced in June 2003 the start of a Futures Initiative to restructure the CDC, prioritize its strategies for the 21st century, revamp its programs, and determine resources and needs.[26] CDC professionals assigned to the Futures group collected information from CDC partners and customers. An extensive review was made of the agency's performance, organization, and operations. From all these deliberations, six strategic directions were formulated for the agency:

1. Health Impact Focus
2. Customer-Centricity
3. Public Health Research
4. Leadership
5. Global Health Impact
6. Accountability

Dr. Gerberding and her leadership team said that it was necessary for the CDC to address the many new health and safety challenges for the 21st century in the United States and globally. These activities began with a project called the Futures Initiative. The major determination was to develop a management and strategic plan for the agency that would address many of these concerns. Gerberding had to sell the plan at a national level as well as at the agency level before many of the details of the initiative could be implemented.

There were two major changes that came about as a result of the Futures Initiative. The first was a major restructuring of the agency in April 2005 in an attempt to break down the silo model that had existed for a number of years and decrease the number of programs that reported directly to the CDC director. The second change involved the development of a number of health protection goals that would provide the direction for the CDC's work in the future. Ideally, these two changes would become integrated in a holistic manner. The new structure designated eight national centers:

1. Environmental Health
2. Injury Prevention
3. Global Health
4. Health Promotion
5. Infectious Diseases
6. Public Health Information, Health Marketing, and Health Statistics
7. Terrorism Preparedness and Emergency Response
8. Workplace Health and Safety

These national centers had a number of programmatic divisions with their own financial resources. These divisions had their own directors and tended to be resistant to many of the changes within the CDC. As can be seen in **Figure 3-3**, there were six coordinating centers and the National Institute for Occupational Safety and Health. The directors of these coordinating centers were supposed to work together to provide direction to the activities of the agency as well as provide mechanisms for the implementation of the CDC Health Protection Goals.

The Coordinating Center for Environmental Health and Injury Prevention included the National Center for Environmental Health and the National Center for Injury Prevention and Control. The Coordinating Office for Global Health included all global health initiatives. The Coordinating Center for Health Promotion included the National Center on Birth Defects and Developmental Disabilities, the National Center for Chronic Disease Prevention and Health Promotion, and the Office of Genomics and Disease Prevention. The Coordinating Center for Infectious Diseases included the National Center for HIV/AIDS, Viral Hepatitis, STD, and TB Prevention; the National Center for Immunization and Respiratory Diseases; the National Center for Zoonotic, Vector-Borne, and Enteric Diseases; and the National Center for Preparedness, Detection, and Control of Infectious Diseases. The Coordinating Center for Health Information and Service included the National Center for Health Marketing, the National Center for Health Statistics, and the National Center for Public Health Information. The Coordinating Office for Terrorism Preparedness and Emergency Response covered the preparedness initiatives for the CDC. The National Institute for Occupational Safety and Health covered the programs related to workplace safety and health. As pointed out, the national centers, with their individual directors and the divisions within centers, were to work horizontally with each other (modified matrix model) as well as vertically with their coordinating centers (a silo model). The National Centers have a leadership committee but not a steering committee, which is more traditional in matrix systems.

In addition to the coordinating centers, there were a number of offices tied to the director of the CDC. These offices include:

1. Office of the Chief Science Officer
2. Office of Chief of Public Health Practice
3. Office of Chief Operating Officer
4. CDC Washington Office
5. Office of Strategy and Innovation
6. Office of Workforce and Career Development
7. Office of Enterprise Communication
8. Office of Chief of Staff
9. Office of Dispute Resolution and Equal Employment Opportunity

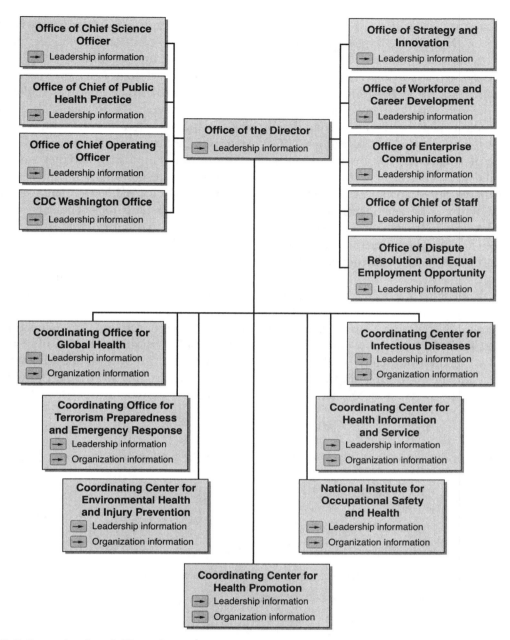

FIGURE 3-3 CDC Organizational Chart (2007). *Source:* Reproduced from the Centers for Disease Control and Prevention (2007). CDC Office for Enterprise Communications: Organizational Chart and CDC Structure under Julie Geberding.

The advantage of this new structural model was that it better programmatically represents the real program emphases of the agency as a whole. It also cut down the number of direct reports to the CDC director.

Structurally, the new organization was extremely complex. It did not do away with silos. In fact, it created silos within silos and several different matrices as well. It became structurally hard to maintain over time. The leaders at the top provided general management oversight to the agency as a whole, but communication throughout the new system was difficult in an agency oriented to both science and practice. The top leadership was insulated from the divisions in the national centers, which were embedded within the coordinating centers and affected morale and commitment to both the agency leadership and the goals and objectives of the agency programs. Each coordinating center and its national centers had the potential for creating all the negatives of a silo-based organization. Good management was definitely possible at the program level even though it is difficult for CDC leadership to get a grasp of all the activities in which the agency is engaged. Wagner and Harter stated that employees need to know what is expected of them at work.[27] The CDC structure limited communication to the front lines of the organization. There were now so many different organizational levels with managers at each level that many professionals felt removed from the decision-making activities of the agency. This could be observed by visiting and reading the entries on the blog site called CDC Chatter.[28] The site was closed down in 2010. However, it becomes critical for meta-leadership techniques to be utilized in complex organizations that will help alleviate the frustrations tied to communication difficulties. Meta-leadership concepts will be introduced later in this chapter.

The second product of the CDC had been the development of health protection goals for the future. There were four major overarching goals for these now 14 strategic goals. **Table 3-3** lists the overarching and strategic goals. Two of the overarching goals became Strategic Goals 13 and 14. At an organization level, a determination was made to create a goals action team for each of the major goals. A matrix approach was taken. A goals team leader was recruited from other organizational units within the CDC, and team members were also selected. Thus, another level of organization was created, which led to a second matrix structure within the agency. Each goals team leader and team were responsible to a steering committee. Team members were responsible to the goals leader and the supervisor from the units in which they worked. Each goals team had the responsibility for the development of an action plan for its goal. These plans were reviewed from November 2007 into 2008. The alignment of the goals to budget was to occur in 2008.

This CDC example represents the difficulty in changing a major governmental agency. Daly and Watkins would call this reorganization a turnaround model with the need for a strong leader who would need to utilize a command and control approach to create the changes necessary.[29] The director of the agency clearly had a vision for the future of the agency that is creative and innovative. She supported the organizational changes that she thought would do away with the silos of the past. She met with external stakeholders

TABLE 3-3   Centers for Disease Control and Prevention Health Protection and Strategic Goals

Overarching Goal 1: Healthy people in every stage of life
Strategic Goal 1: Start strong (0–3 years)
Strategic Goal 2: Grow safe and strong (4–11 years)
Strategic Goal 3: Achieve healthy independence (12–19 years)
Strategic Goal 4: Live a healthy, productive, and satisfying life (adults, 20–49 years)
Strategic Goal 5: Live better longer (ages 50 and over)
Overarching Goal 2: Healthy people in healthy places
Strategic Goal 6: Healthy communities
Strategic Goal 7: Healthy homes
Strategic Goal 8: Healthy schools
Strategic Goal 9: Healthy workplaces
Strategic Goal 10: Healthy healthcare settings
Strategic Goal 11: Healthy institutions
Strategic Goal 12: Healthy travel and recreation
Overarching Goal 3: People prepared for emerging health threats (Strategic Goal 13)
Overarching Goal 4: Healthy people in a healthy world (Strategic Goal 14)

Source: Reproduced from the Centers for Disease Control and Prevention (2007). CDC Health Protection Goals and Strategic Goals under Julie Geberding.

to explain the plan and gain their support. She assigned the new Office of Strategy and Innovation with the development of protocols to make the plan work. The reorganization was done, but new silos and several matrix structures came into being. The professional staff, including many researchers within divisions, resisted the changes and argued that the new organization did not reflect the work that needed to be done or the work in which they were engaged.

The new organizational structure was seen as overly complex, with elements of traditional bureaucratic hierarchies still in place as well as matrix structures that were superimposed on the organization. Changes like those that had been made do not occur overnight. There was cultural change going on. Both leadership and management relationships needed clarification. Different scenarios can be tested. Exercise 3-2 will help you experiment with different options for change that might expedite the process. From 2008 to 2012, Dr. Thomas Frieden, the successor to Dr. Gerberding, dismantled the Gerberding structure and replaced it with a new one that is in many ways as complex as its predecessor model, with several offices that replace the coordinating centers and also the continuation of a number of national centers. The deputy director of each office reports to the CDC director.

STARFISH ORGANIZATIONS IN PUBLIC HEALTH

In traditional organizations, an organization dies if its major reason for existence is gone. Brafman and Beckstrom use the analogy of a spider when you cut off its head.[30] However, when you cut off one of the limbs of a starfish, it grows a new limb. The starfish model is an example of a completely decentralized organization where no specific person is in charge. Rather, all the participants share in the leadership of the organization. Offices may exist in different places, depending on the project, which means that information and knowledge management may also be decentralized. Power is also distributed. Funding is mostly project or program based. Roles and responsibilities change as projects diversify. All people are equal in the core. Decisions about the organization as a whole are made by all participants as core members of the organization. Individuals may be hired for a specific project or program and leave when the project is over.

Figure 3-4 graphically shows the starfish model. Some public health academic units, like research,

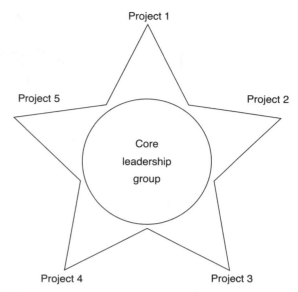

FIGURE 3-4 Starfish Organizational Model. *Source*: Adapted from O. Brafman and R. A. Beckstrom, *The Starfish and the Spider* (New York: Portfolio Books, 2007).

academic, or satellite agency centers, may use this organizational model. The core leadership group may be a group of researchers with a common multidisciplinary research perspective like public health systems research or center for public health practice. Because the center is probably funded primarily through grants and contracts, each limb represents one of these projects. The staff of the project includes several core researchers, academics, or practitioners and staff funded by the grant or contract. When the project is over, project staff leave or move to another project. The core staff stay and look for new grants or contracts.

For a comparison of the different public health organizational models presented, **Table 3-4** shows the differences in the traditional hierarchy, a transitional model not presented specifically above, the matrix model, and the starfish model. Structurally, we have looked at these models from centralized to decentralized. More centralized organizations tend to be focused operationally in more of a linear way than a systems way. The more decentralized, the more systems-based or complexity oriented. Hierarchical organizations tend to be more authoritarian and tend to move toward being more democratic as the organization begins to move toward fewer organizational levels in a transition from hierarchy to matrix. The management focus tends to concentrate on the organization and less on the people. People management becomes more important in the transition model and the other decentralized models.

TABLE 3-4 Comparison of Several Organizational Issues in Public Health

	Hierarchy	Transition	Matrix	Starfish
Leadership Style	Authoritarian	Democratic	Democratic	Shared
Leadership practice	Focus on the organization	Focus on the organization	Internal and external focus	External focus
Leadership thinking preference	Linear	Linear	Systems	Complexity
Primary administrative organization	Management focus	Management focus	Partial management and partial leadership focus	Shared leadership
Structure	Centralized	Partially centralized	Partially decentralized	Decentralized

TRANSACTIONAL AND TRANSFORMATIONAL LEADERSHIP

The CDC example above demonstrates how the line between what is leadership and what is management often becomes blurred. This relationship becomes even more complicated when we look at the issue of transactional leadership and transformational leadership, where the management role seems to vanish altogether. Most discussions about leadership concern vision and change. Burns has pointed out that leadership is about reciprocity.[31]

Through the development of relationships between partners with varying perspectives on values and motivation, the partners are often in conflict and competition in relation to the overarching goals, which should bring the leaders together to realize their goals and to work together to reach these goals. Moreover, these goals are influenced by the realities of the environment or communities in which these leaders come together.

Burns defined two critical types of leadership: transactional and transformational.[32] The transactional leader engages others in the reciprocal activity of exchanging one thing for another. Most management and leadership activities are related to the exchange of one thing for another. Transformational leadership examines and searches for the needs and motives of others while seeking a higher agenda of needs. Transformational relationships are intense and raise the participants to a higher level of mutuality and morality so that the interaction between leaders or between leaders and followers changes both parties. From these definitions, it can be argued that both transactional and transformational skills are important for leaders. They are complementary types of skill. Transformational leadership demands higher-level negotiation activities and will lead to change at both the organization and systems levels.

The attempt to put the concept of transactional leadership into action has led to a reinterpretation of this type of leadership to be a reconceptualization of management. The exchange of work for various types of rewards seems tied to the organization where there is an attempt to maintain the stability of the organization. Transformational leadership seems to be more about change. **Table 3-5** demonstrates how these two leadership concepts are viewed today and also puts managers in the leadership camp.[33] In recognizing that public health leaders need to transform the public health system in which they work and also change the understanding and commitment to the work of public health with their internal and external partners, the National Public Health Leadership Development Network had to define the characteristics and competencies of a transformational leader.[34] The three major activities of the public health transformational leader involve the skills necessary to engage in the development of mission and vision as well as the development of skills related to monitoring and facilitating the process of change.

In order to begin to clarify distinctions between management and leadership, it is possible to begin this dialogue by creating a continuum from management to leadership. **Figure 3-5** does this by putting management at the left side of the continuum and covering traditional management processes. Transactional leadership is at the center of the continuum and blends traditional management with the reciprocity concerns discussed by the Gallup Organization in its

TABLE 3-5 Transactional vs. Transformational Leadership: Differences Between Managing and Leading

	Transactional Leadership or Management Skills	Transformational Leadership or Leadership Skills
Performance:	Considered by leadership writers to produce ordinary performance	Considered by leadership writers to produce extraordinary performance
Goal:	To maintain the status quo by playing within the rules	To change the status quo by changing the rules
Goals arise out of:	Necessity, are reactive, and respond to ideas; they are deeply imbedded in the organization's history and culture	Desires; they are active, shaping ideas; may be a departure from organization's history and culture
Emphasis:	Rationality and control, limits choices, focuses on solving problems	Innovation, creativity to develop fresh approaches to long-standing problems, and open issues to new options
Attitudes toward goals:	Impersonal, if not passive, attitude	Personal and active attitude
Incentives:	Based on exchange of needs (i.e., "tit for tat")	Based on the greater good
Locus of reward:	Maximize personal benefits	Optimize systemic benefits
Requires:	Persistence, tough-mindedness, hard work, intelligence, analytical ability, tolerance, and goodwill	Genius and heroism
View work as:	Enabling processes, ideas, and people to establish strategies and make decisions	Creative, energizing, and emerging
Tactics employed:	Negotiate and bargain, use of rewards, punishment, and other forms of coercion	Inspire followers, create shared vision, motivate
	Strive to convert win-lose into win-win situations as part of the process of reconciling differences among people and maintaining balances of power	Strive to create new situations and new directions without regard to reconciling groups or power

Source: Reproduced from Robertson, T. D., Fernandez, C. S. P., and Porter, J. E., "Leadership in Public Health," in Novick, L. F., Morrow, C. B., and Mays, G. P. (eds.), *Public Health Administration*, 2nd ed. Sudbury, MA: Jones & Bartlett, 2007.

look at great managers. It is with transactional leadership that we can begin to see the interface between management and leadership. Transformational leadership and its change and vision agenda are on the extreme right side of the continuum. Most leaders need to have both transactional and transformational talents and skills.

In order to put this leadership continuum in a clearer perspective, the continuum can be viewed as a leadership change triangle in which change affects the way a leader will function. Two other forms of leadership practice need to be added to the continuum. Managerial leadership is a transitional phase in which the

public health professional blends the skills of management with the transactional skills of people development. Strategic leadership blends the needs of making transformational change work strategically in the interface between choosing the right people to help in transformational and systems change. Leaders need to learn when to use their management skills and when to use their various leadership skills. In change, leaders needs to work within their home organizations and externally with their various stakeholders. Transformational and systems change must be translated into action through transactional relationships and eventually to application at the organizational level.

FIGURE 3-5 The Leadership Change Triangle.
Source: Reproduced from L. Rowitz (2009, February 3). The Leadership Change Triangle [Web log]. Retrieved from http://rowitzonleadership.wordpress.com/2009/02/. Accessed June 26, 2012.

META-LEADERSHIP—A NEW PERSPECTIVE

In 1990, in the last edition of their now classic textbook, Pickett and Hanlon pointed out that change is inevitable in public health.[35] Public health will have to work in new ways. This will require a flexibility that is often missing in governmental organizations. This work will occur in a transorganizational environment where public health leaders will work with partners outside their home agencies. In this new environment, leaders will have to understand the values that drive the different agendas of their partners. It will be necessary to build coalitions and other forms of external alliances and partnerships. Negotiation will be an important element in these new relationships. These transorganizational activities will demonstrate transformational leadership in action.

Meta-leadership is the new terminology for working across organizations. Leaders need to move outside their organizational positions and utilize their talents, knowledge, and transactional and transformational skills to create new models for collaboration with partners. It requires a systems perspective, an understanding of how values shape action, and risk taking related to initiatives that may in part negatively affect their home organization. Henderson has defined the meta-leader as an individual who is able to connect the purposes, activities, and work of different agencies and organizations and their program components to achieve a greater good at the systems level.[36] Public health requires actions that cross agency boundaries. The meta-leader is able to align the core interests, motivations, and values of different organizations into a new synergistic value orientation (meta-values) that will create an integrated vision and set of actions to create change. Marcus and his colleagues have used the word "connectivity" to refer to this process.[37]

The traditional leader gains power from the position that he or she holds in the organization that he or she represents. This power from the home organization can be called silo power. This power is closely allied to what we called transactional leadership. Meta-leaders need to gain trust, credibility, and power in their external collaborations as well as they demonstrate their transformational leadership skills. There are five dimensions to meta-leadership (**Figure 3-6**).[38] The meta-leadership model was developed to gain a better understanding of how leaders function in crisis. Some event will affect how leaders will function. There may be challenges to defining the event from the vantage point of size and scope, scale, and the substance and understanding of what may have triggered it.

Some of the expected qualities of a leader in crisis include courage, curiosity, imagination, organizational sensibilities, persuasion, conflict management, crisis management, emotional intelligence, and persistence.[39] I have included in my discussions of crisis leaders such additional skills as systems and complexity thinking, collaboration skills, concerns for community safety, understanding of health law and ethics, understanding of risk and health communication, ability to determine tipping points and change strategies, and community building.[40] Not only do meta-leaders have to be masters of the ability to work within and between organizations, but they also have to be able to influence action inquiries and plans to make the results of the collaborations work in the real world. There may be a need to develop meta-managers as well as meta-leaders.

Leading up has challenges. The meta-leader has to learn how to deal with boards, county commissioners, other elected officials, and subject matter specialists. American public health leaders feel weakest in their policy development and advocacy roles. Henderson has pointed out that all crisis events in the United States are political. In fact, almost all public health decisions also have political implications. When the leader is not successful in advocacy and other political relationships,

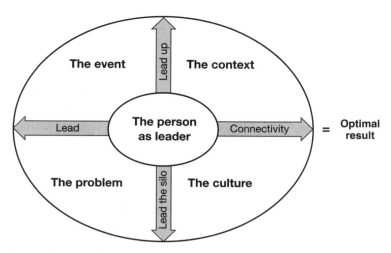

FIGURE 3-6 Dimensions of Meta-Leadership. *Source*: Reprinted with permission from L. J. Marcus, I. Askenazi, B. Dorn, and J. Henderson.

it can affect the agency in a number of ways. Staff morale may be affected and the trust in the leader may decline as a result. The credibility of many local activities (scientific findings as well as agency decisions) may be questioned. This lack of credibility and trust may make it more difficult to resolve the conflict or crisis in a timely manner. Henderson recommends that meta-leaders manage up one level at a time.

Leading within the silo is important if followers are going to have trust in their leaders and believe in the vision and strategy formulated by the leader. Gaining input from all staff during the formulation of vision and strategy is important. External stakeholders from the political and nonpolitical realms need to be involved in this process as well. Good managers are needed in the silo to carry out the vision and strategy of the leader through agency operations and execution of strategy through action and through the connection of the strategy to activities of the agency as a whole. Henderson has pointed out that after leadership and management there needs to be a third phase to the process: evaluation. The evaluation phase involves measuring impact, monitoring change, measuring productivity and performance, and ensuring that all public health systems support a continuous quality improvement process.

It is in connectivity that meta-leaders shine. It is their work to connect the purposes and activities of the many organizations with whom they partner for the good of the public health agenda in their communities. Their curiosity and need to explore many creative avenues should affect the process of collaboration. They

need to become experts in conflict leadership and how to resolve the differences in ideas that arise. The meta-leader is a risk taker and needs to be able to address the consequences of his or her actions. Meta-leaders also need to be able to determine when their shared goals have been met.

Over time, theories and practice related to a leadership perspective evolve. As a model fans out from its original development site, questions arise and further refinements of the paradigm occur. The important issue in meta-leadership relates to whether connectivity really occurs and whether the results of the collaboration are effective. In addition, when we work across organizations, networks are created. Using some form of social network analysis will help determine how leaders work together in terms of information processing, knowledge management, the resolution of differences, and the social skills of the participants.[41] Network analysis will help to determine who the meta-leaders are in the network and how they relate (connect). Second networks are composed of individuals who are interested in the issue or the problem to be addressed. This demonstrates that leaders will be involved in several networks, depending on the issue to be addressed. For example, crisis network membership will differ from non-crisis public health networks. Networks will also be involved in better understanding how a silo functions within an organization. The end result of network analysis is the ability to determine how effective the silo work is and how effective the multi-organization collaboration is working.

THE PUBLIC HEALTH MANAGEMENT AND LEADERSHIP ROAD MAP

Now it is necessary to put the management and leadership puzzle together. By adapting the Gallup Path to the governmental sector and adding the leadership dimension as well, it is possible to develop a public health management and leadership road map such as that shown in **Figure 3-7**.[42] Because public health has strong roots in the community, it is important to look at the context of public health as the starting point in our understanding of how the work of public health is accomplished. The public health agency becomes the coordinating organization from which to view the public health system and the specific activities of public health. The leader who is engaged is one who is able to work outside the agency with stakeholders from the political realm as well as from other sectors to improve the health of the public. This is meta-leadership in action. This high level of planning, negotiation, and action is tied to the role of the public health administrator leader

in the transformational leadership role. The public health leader is often engaged in these activities as a major part of the job of promoting the public's health. Because of the time-intensive nature of these activities, the leader often has to rely on engaged managers in the agency to carry out the day-to-day activities of the agency itself. In some instances and especially in smaller health departments, the leader may also have to carry out the activities of the manager as well.

The development of the public health workforce within the agency is often the responsibility of management. Following the work of the Gallup Organization on talents, the manager has to be able to identify the talents of workers and fit those talents within the system requirements of the agency and its programs.[43] In traditional management jargon, this involves the organizing function of management. The excellent and great managers also have control and coordination responsibilities. These managers also have to engage the agency employees in the work of the agency so that they understand the vision of the

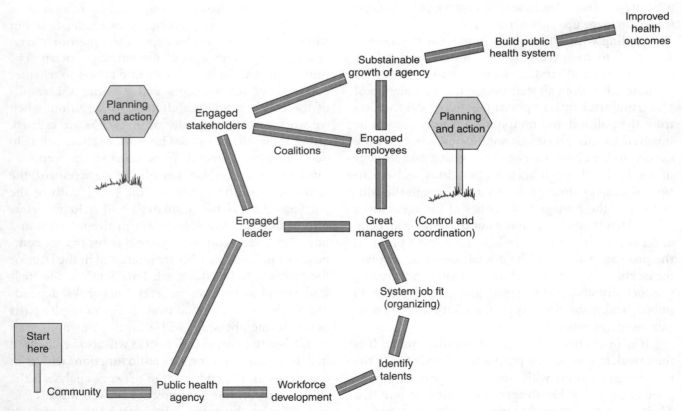

FIGURE 3-7 Management and Leadership Road Map in Public Health. *Source:* Adapted from C. Coffman and G. Gonzalez-Molina (2002). *Follow This Path.* Grand Central Publishing.

agency leadership. The management staff and the engaged employee have to interact on planning and action protocols as well because this is often a team effort.

As the leader continues to work with external stakeholders, engaged employees get to work with other staff of the engaged stakeholder groups in coalitions and other groups to carry out the specific tasks necessary to help the public improve its health status. If these leadership and management tasks are carried out well, there should be sustainable growth of both the public health agency and its community partners. With this growth, the infrastructure of public health and the public health system as a whole will be strengthened. The outcome of all these activities will be improved health outcomes in the community being served.

SUMMARY

This chapter has addressed the complex relationship between management and leadership. The functions of leaders and managers are clearly different even though it is necessary for leaders and managers to work together. In smaller jurisdictions, public health administrators will have to be both manager and leader. However, this marriage is not an easy one because the role of manager/leader requires multiple sets of skills. The individual may have the talent to carry out one set of skills better than the other. It is important for the individual to understand his or her personal strengths and fit his or her talents to the needs of the organization in its current state of development.

DISCUSSION QUESTIONS

1. What are the differences between management and leadership?
2. Do you think it is possible to be a great manager and a leader at the same time?
3. What are the differences between working in the governmental and business sectors?
4. Distinguish between hierarchy, matrix, and starfish organizations.
5. What are the relationships among traditional management, transactional leadership, and transformational leadership?
6. What is meta-leadership, and why is it an important leadership approach?
7. What are organizational silos, and how can communication between these silos be improved?
8. Give examples of how the public health management and leadership road map might work.

EXERCISE 3-1: Organizational Development and Strategic Health Priorities (Application of Daly and Watkins Model)

Adapted from P. H. Daly and M. Watkins, *The First 90 Days in Government* (Cambridge, MA: Harvard Business School Publishing, 2006).

Purpose: to see the relationship between the organizational structure of a public health agency and the way it addresses local public health priorities

Key concepts: startup, turnaround, accelerated growth, realignment, success-sustaining perspective, health priorities

Procedure: Scenario: The American County Health Department has been involved in carrying out a community health assessment in its county. American County has come up with four strategic health priorities:

1. Strengthen the public health workforce.
2. Address the needs of those who require public health services.
3. Improve health outcomes for cardiovascular diseases.
4. Create a broader sense of community connectedness.

The class or training group will be divided into four groups of 8 to 10. One group will discuss the problem from the perspective of a startup agency. The second group will address the problem from the perspective of an agency in a turnaround situation. The third group will discuss the scenario from the perspective of a realignment organization. The final group will discuss the priorities from the perspective of a success-sustaining organization. Your task as a leadership team for your county is to determine how to address these priorities when your agency is in one of the four organizational development phases discussed by Daly and Watkins. You have an hour to discuss these issues. Your team will then report to the class or training group as a whole on how you addressed these issues.

EXERCISE 3-2: Scenario Building for the CDC

Purpose: to explore different approaches to organizational development and the CDC Health Protection Goals that might have increased the chance of success for the goals program

Key Concepts: scenario building, organizational restructuring, goals alignment, health protection goals, coordinating centers, silos, leadership, management

Procedure: Utilizing the CDC example in this chapter, divide the training group or class into teams of 8 to 10. Each team is to develop two to three different scenarios for ways to integrate the Health Protection Goals into the CDC structure or to make proposals for the reorganization of the CDC in a more efficient and effective manner to make goals a part of the total CDC organization.

REFERENCES

1. M. Buckingham, *Go Put Your Strengths to Work* (New York: Free Press, 2007).

2. J. H. Fleming and J. Asplund, *Human Sigma* (New York: Gallup Press, 2007).

3. G. Browning, *Emergenetics* (New York: HarperCollins, 2006).

4. C. Cherniss and D. Goleman, *The Emotionally Intelligent Workplace* (San Francisco: Jossey-Bass, 2001).

5. M. Buckingham and D. O. Clifton, *Now, Discover Your Strengths* (New York: Free Press, 2001).

6. Browning, *Emergenetics*.

7. H. Fayol, *General and Industrial Management* (London: Pittman Publishing, 1949).

8. S. P. Robbins and M. Coulter, *Management*, 11th ed. (Upper Saddle River, NJ: Prentice-Hall, 2011).

9. R. Wagner and J. K. Harter, *12: The Elements of Great Managing* (New York: Gallup Press, 2006).

10. P. F. Drucker, *The Essential Drucker* (New York: Harper Business, 2001).

11. Fayol, *General and Industrial Management*.

12. Robbins and Coulter, *Management*, 11th ed.

13. P. H. Daly and M. Watkins, *The First 90 Days in Government* (Cambridge, MA: Harvard Business School Publishing, 2006).

14. M. H. Moore, *Creating Public Value* (Cambridge, MA: Harvard University Press, 1995).

15. Daly and Watkins, *The First 90 Days in Government*.

16. M. D. Watkins, "Picking the Right Transition Strategy," *Harvard Business Review* 87, no. 1 (2009): 49–53.

17. B. J. Turnock and L. Rowitz, *NACCHO New Local Health Official Orientation Curriculum: Final Design* (Washington, DC: National Association of County and City Health Officials, 2007).

18. Turnock and Rowitz, *NACCHO New Local Health Official Orientation Curriculum*.

19. S. Orton, K. E. Umble, B. Rosen, J. McIver, and A. J. Menkens, "Management Academy for Public Health: Program Design and Critical Success Factors," *Journal of Public Health Management and Practice* 12, no. 5 (2006): 409–418.

20. S. Goldsmith and W. D. Eggers, *Governing by Network* (Washington, DC: Brookings Institution Press, 2004).

21. T. L. Friedman, *The World Is Flat* (New York: Farrar, Straus, and Giroux, 2006).

22. Robbins and Coulter, *Management*, 11th ed.

23. P. Martin, *Quick Guide: The New Matrix Management* (Carmel, NY: Martin Training Associates, 2005).

24. P. Lencioni, *Silos, Politics, and Turf Wars* (San Francisco: Jossey-Bass, 2006).

25. Martin, *Quick Guide: The New Matrix Management*.

26. http://www.cdc.gov

27. Wagner and Harter, *12: The Elements of Great Managing*.

28. http://cdcchatter.net

29. Daly and Watkins, *The First 90 Days in Government*.

30. O. Brafman and R. A. Beckstrom. *The Starfish and the Spider* (New York: Portfolio Books, 2007).

31. J. MacGregor Burns, *Leadership* (New York: Harper and Row, 1978).

32. Burns, *Leadership*.

33. T. D. Robertson, C. S. P. Fernandez, and J. E. Porter, "Leadership in Public Health," in L. E. Novick, C. B. Morrow, and G. P. Mays (eds.), *Public Health Administration*, 2nd ed. (Sudbury, MA: Jones & Bartlett, 2007).

34. K.S. Wright, L. Rowitz, A. Merkle, et al., "Competency Development in Public Health Leadership," *American Journal of Public Health* 90 (August 2000): 1202–1207.

35. G. Pickett and J. J. Hanlon, *Public Health: Administration and Practice*, 9th ed. (St. Louis: Times Mirror/Mosby College Publishing, 1990).

36. J. M. Henderson, *Meta-Leadership and the Challenge for Public Health* (talk) (Raleigh: North Carolina State Health Director's Conference, 2007).

37. L. J. Marcus, B. C. Dorn, and J. M. Henderson, *Meta-Leadership and National Emergency Preparedness* (Cambridge, MA: Harvard Center for Public Leadership Working Papers, 2005).

38. Henderson, *Meta-Leadership and the Challenge for Public Health*.

39. L. Rowitz, *Public Health in the 21st Century: The Prepared Leader* (Sudbury, MA: Jones & Bartlett, 2006).

40. Henderson, *Meta-Leadership and the Challenge for Public Health*.

41. R. Cross and A. Parker, *The Hidden Power of Social Networks* (Boston: Harvard Business School Press, 2004).

42. C. Coffman and G. Gonzalez-Molina, *Follow This Path* (New York: Warner Business Books, 2002).

43. Buckingham and Clifton, *Now, Discover Your Strengths*.

CHAPTER 4

A Systems and Complexity Perspective

> Life was simple before World War II. After that, we had systems.
>
> —G. Hopper

All types of health-related events have effects on the community, whether the event affects one organization in the community or many organizations or residents of the community. The prepared public health leader knows that an event, whether a crisis or a non-crisis one, is the community's business and that the event needs to be addressed from the vantage point of the community. It is for this reason that systems thinking skills are so critical for successful leadership. To be a systems thinker, a leader needs to see and talk about situations in a way that helps others to better understand and carry out activities within organizations and agencies that affect the lives of people who live in the community. A prepared public health leader must see the big picture. An interesting demonstration of the complexities involved in the issue of infectious disease outbreaks related to monkeypox can be seen in Case Study 4-A. It demonstrates the systemic aspects of disease and the importance of knowing global disease trends and their potential applications at the local level. What happens in one part of the world can affect other parts of the world very quickly.

This case not only points out the issue of systems analysis but also shows the importance of collaboration at a local level in addressing the threats associated with the outbreaks of infectious disease. This latter point is extremely important because the importance of collaboration to bring about change is not directly addressed by writers in the discussion of systems thinking approaches. The systems approach becomes problematic because the systems thinker is often at odds with others within the home organization or with partners who do not think in a systems way. In addition, the tools of systems do not take into account the collaborative nature of social relationships. It is the social relationships within an organization or community that are the most important. The structure of the system is less important. If it is people who create the system, then the system will be fluid and ever changing. In actuality, people do create social structures and do collaborate, but the social structure and cultural norms and rules that guide action also are

Case Study 4-A

Monkey on Our Backs: Identifying and Containing an Outbreak of Monkeypox on a Regional Basis

Douglas Beardsley, MPH; Christine Borys, BSN, MPH; Cheryl Lee, BA, MS; Jean McMahon, MS, BSN; Heather Miller, BS; Larry Swacina, MS

Introduction

In the spring of 2003, it was discovered that prairie dogs originating from a pet distributor became infected with monkeypox (MP). The infected prairie dogs had been sold directly to distributors who in turn sold them to consumers in several neighboring states. Communicable disease personnel at various local health departments and the state department of public health began contacting pet owners to investigate possible MP cases in humans. Personnel from the state's department of agriculture and investigators from the Centers for Disease Control and Prevention were also involved in the investigation. Because this was the first time that MP had been seen in the Western Hemisphere, staff at all levels had many questions and came to the situation with a great deal of zeal and energy. All persons involved made every effort to be thorough, but this had the unintended effect of creating redundancy, uncoordinated effort, and lack of information sharing. As investigators worked with family members of infected individuals, they found that one investigator was leaving through the side door as another was coming in the front door. Pieces of information known to one agency, which potentially could have been critically important to the human investigation, had to be accidentally discovered at a later time by personnel from another agency. Fortunately, all of the persons exposed to MP made a full recovery, and the cases were not widespread.

This case study will examine the events leading up to the incidents of human cases of MP and the events surrounding the investigation, containment, and remediation of the cases. The case will present policy questions surrounding legal authority to act, when to seek legal counsel, coordinating the activities within and between agencies, and developing incident command and unified command approaches as applied to public health investigations.

The focus of this case study is to address the core function of policy development. According to the three core functions, this case study will explore the need for developing policy to address the steps needed to take action when a public health emergency arises that needs immediate and effective response.

Introduction and Background

Even before the catastrophic events of September 11, 2001, public health began to recognize the need for emergency preparedness plans related to potential bioterrorism events. For many state and local health departments, emergency preparedness and planning were neglected. Post 9-11, emergency response plans and training were accelerated. Although new funding was in the pipeline for many of these activities, policy makers tried to emphasize that preparedness for an emergency should be a process of strengthening the overall infrastructure and competency of the public health system and should not become an activity divorced from day-to-day public health functions.

The investigation of a new or unknown disease and that of a potential bioterrorism event have many parallels. Both share a number of the same assumptions, procedures, and resources. Much of the training made available to local health departments (LHDs) emphasized the need to communicate and cooperate across various agencies and jurisdictions through the use of incident command. The rationale behind this concept was that an investigation might have already been initiated before knowing if an event was related to terrorism. Consistent communication on a regular basis with other agencies will facilitate more efficient and effective action when a public health emergency occurs.

Monkeypox is a rare viral disease caused by the monkeypox virus, which belongs to the orthopoxvirus group of viruses. (Other orthopoxviruses that cause infections in humans include variola [smallpox], vaccinia [used for smallpox vaccine], and cowpox viruses.) It occurs mainly in the rainforest areas of central and west Africa. The disease was first discovered in laboratory monkeys in 1958. Blood tests of animals in Africa later found evidence of monkeypox infection in a number of African rodents. The virus that causes monkeypox was recovered from an African squirrel. Laboratory studies showed that the virus also could infect mice, rats, and rabbits. In 1970, monkeypox was reported in humans for the first time. In June 2003, monkeypox was reported in prairie dogs and humans in the United States.

In humans, monkeypox is similar to smallpox, although it is often milder. Unlike smallpox, monkeypox causes lymph nodes to swell (lymphadenopathy). The incubation period for monkeypox is about 12 days (range 7 to 17 days).

The illness begins with fever, headache, muscle aches, backache, swollen lymph nodes, a general feeling of discomfort, and exhaustion. Within 1 to 3 days (sometimes longer) after the appearance of fever, the patient develops a papular rash (i.e., raised bumps), often first on the face but sometimes initially on other parts of the body. The lesions usually develop through several stages before crusting and falling off.

Brief Description of Scenario

On June 7, Midwest State Department of Public Health (MWSDPH) informed the Simian County Health Department (SCHD) that it was investigating a potential exposure of monkeypox (MP) to customers of a pet shop in Primate County (a county in the same state, about 60 miles west of Simian County). SCHD was asked to follow up with customers in its jurisdiction. SCHD was provided with information specific to its jurisdiction and was not made aware that similar investigations would be taking place in other counties. The only information shared between all parties was that the suspected exposure was through Gambian rats and prairie dogs, which had been sold by Rod's Pox Pets in Primate County.

On June 8, Simian County Health Department (SCHD) personnel contacted a family in their jurisdiction that had bought a prairie dog at a swap meet. The prairie dog had originated from Rod's Pox Pets. The 9-week-old prairie dog appeared healthy when bought on May 18. Sonny, the 10-year-old boy in the family, was the primary caretaker of the prairie dog and regularly played with and cuddled the prairie dog, in addition to the 1-year-old prairie dog he had raised. Upon arrival at the family's house, SCHD Communicable Disease (CD) investigators learned that inspectors from the State Department of Agriculture (SDOA) had already been working with the family for more than a week. One week after purchase, the new prairie dog had become ill, showing aggressive behavior, loss of appetite, eye discharges, and lesions on its face. Three days later the new prairie dog died and the father disposed of it in the trash. SDOA personnel had instructed the family to isolate the surviving prairie dog from other animals but had not given any instructions about human contact.

CD personnel educated the family on MP and took health histories of all family members. The family was strongly advised not to travel and to limit contact with others as much as possible until the incubation period for MP had passed in two more weeks. The family was somewhat upset because of a planned vacation the following week. Investigators were unsure if they had authority to "officially quarantine" the family or otherwise restrict their movements. The SCHD contacted the State Attorney's office to get clarification on the health department's authority to quarantine.

The State Attorney's office said they would check into the matter. Ironically, this happened to be an election year. SCHD was told the State Attorney would not be taking a position on this matter.

SCHD personnel followed up with the family by phone on a daily basis to monitor the family's health. On June 11, the CDC issued its first case definition of human MP for this incident. None of the family members reported any illness.

On June 12, SCHD personnel were unable to contact the family by phone. Investigators were sent to the family's home, but no one was present. Neighbors told the investigators the family, father, mother, and their three sons, had left that morning on vacation to Montana for two weeks. When asked about the remaining prairie dog, the neighbor said the family told her that "some government agency" had taken the prairie dog and put it to sleep. SCHD personnel were not able to confirm this with SDOA until three days later.

The investigators then called the MWSDPH for recommendations on the situation, with the family away on vacation. During the course of the conversation, the MWSDPH adviser informed SCHD personnel of several cases of MP in Primate County. SCHD personnel were somewhat disturbed that they had not been informed of these cases. SCHD wanted more details on the signs and symptoms experienced to better detect a case and to provide physicians with this information. The MWSDPH adviser indicated that he thought CDC had contacted SCHD with this information because they were running the investigation.

Later that day, SCHD learned that several dead mice had been discovered at the family's residence a week earlier and were taken by the CDC for examination. SCHD environmental personnel were concerned that the mice might have been infected. The disease could potentially spread throughout the community and become permanently established in the rodent population. Results ultimately showed that the mice had died of rat poisoning and were not diseased.

In the meantime, the MWSDPH issued a press release on the monkeypox situation, including the current number of cases and the precautions being implemented. One of the cases included a 17-year-old in Primate County. The family contacted the television media, who in turn made assumptions prior to confirming facts with the Primate

(Continues)

County Health Department (PCHD). The PCHD responded with a press conference to clarify the situation and provide accurate information. Daily updates were then provided.

On June 18, the family who left the state against medical advice visited the Mountain County Health Department (MCHD) in Montana. Sonny had developed approximately 20 lesions on his trunk and complained of tender cervical lymph nodes. Sonny had pharyngeal lesions, which increased the chance of spreading the virus by air transmission whenever Sonny coughed. The MCHD strongly advised the family not to travel back to Midwest State but rather to seek medical care in Montana. The family decided to return to Midwest State, ignoring health department advice for the second time. This meant the family would spend over 24 hours in a car together, with the potential of spreading the virus to other family members by air transmission from coughing. The family also stopped frequently at fast food establishments en route.

The MCHD contacted SCHD to inform them of the contact with the family and that the family was en route to Midwest State against MCHD's recommendation. On June 19, the family called SCHD and informed them they should be arriving the next day. They mentioned Sonny had a fever and was quite uncomfortable with the lesions and would need to see a doctor right away. The family informed SCHD that their insurance would only allow them to go to Simian Community Hospital (the Hospital).

SCHD personnel immediately contacted the Hospital to prepare for an infectious patient. Although the Hospital had an infectious disease plan and had been participating in the county's emergency preparedness activities, including smallpox exercises, no personnel at the hospital had received the smallpox vaccine prophylactically. The Hospital was reluctant to admit a patient with MP. Prior to this event, the hospital had withdrawn its phase one emergency response smallpox vaccination program. After much deliberation and negotiation, the Hospital allowed a nonaffiliated physician who had received the smallpox vaccine to have temporary treatment privileges at its hospital to administer healthcare services to Sonny.

The family arrived at the Hospital, and after initial examination, the child was admitted. The mother, exhausted from the long trip, became upset when seeing her child in pain and connected to multiple tubes and monitors. The distraught mother removed the tubes from the child. She attempted to leave with the child against medical advice and without signing required release forms. Security was called and physicially blocked the exit, at which point the mother reluctantly complied with medical treatment. Four days later, the child was discharged and eventually made a full recovery without any long-term effects.

Conclusion

Even though this was a fictional account with a factual basis, the local health departments responded well and effectively within their jurisdictions. Each responding agency had a protocol for responding to such an event; however, there was an initial lack of communication and coordination within and between the agencies involved and a lack of an incident command structure. The situation was further complicated by misinformation in the media, family noncompliance with medical advice, questions on legal authority in the investigation protocols, political consideration expressed by the State Attorney's office during election year, the lack of regulation of exotic pets, the lack of a timely response to address the wild mice population as a potential reservoir for MP, and the Hospital's questionable adherence to its own emergency response plan.

affected. The leadership challenge relates to the necessity of the leader working with his collaborators to use a systems framework to better understand problems so that the solutions become more comprehensive and more likely to work to improve the functioning of the community. To paraphrase an old popular song, the system and partners need to go together "like a horse and carriage."

Public health is about the system. Medical care is more about management than leadership. Public health moves from a focus on the individual to a focus on all the people in a community. The change in focus requires a systems orientation with the need for public health leaders to understand systems and how they work. The 1998 Institute of Medicine report on public health defined the mission of public health from a systems perspective.[1] The mission involved the fact that society and thus the community have an investment in their population, and this investment involves making sure that the health of the population is protected. This assurance activity includes the utilization of most current scientific and technical expertise available. All community stakeholders need to be involved in this process. The local public health agency will usually take a lead role in these activities. Thus, leadership within a systems perspective is critical.

Public health is a clear example of a complex adaptive system, within which public health practice takes place. Public health as a complex system has several properties:[2]

1. A focus on emergent patterns related to health outcomes of the population.
2. The health of the individual is affected by the body as a complex system in itself that interacts with many environmental factors.
3. Social networks and the interactions between people in many social situations bring an additional complexity issue to the occurrence of disease events.
4. Public health has a strong, unpredictable political dimension that affects how public health issues affect communities.
5. Public health systems are affected by the array of healthcare programs in communities as well as the complex nature of insurance coverage.
6. Public health systems are affected by the education of the public health workforce as well as the location and size of the community, municipality, or county. Rural health jurisdictions are not the same as large urban ones.

In the next section, we will explore systems thinking and then introduce the archetype tools of systems. A discussion of leadership and power will be followed by the complex issue of systems relative to management inside an agency and working outside that agency. Finally, a short note discusses some new systems possibilities.

SYSTEMS AND SYSTEMS THINKING

The modern emphasis on systems and systems thinking began to occur in the years after World War II but was affected by the Macy Conferences from 1942 to 1951. These conferences involved many important thinkers of the time, including anthropologists Margaret Mead and Gregory Bateson; the early computer scientist John von Neumann; the early leader on the issues of artificial intelligence, Warren McCulloch; and Norbert Weiner, who founded the field of cybernetics.[3] In two influential books published in 1948 and 1950, Weiner discussed a new field called cybernetics and systems.[4,5] His perspective becomes clearer in his 1950 book on the human use of human beings. Cybernetics is the science of steering rather than rowing. Society can be mainly understood by the study of messages and the way these messages are communicated between man and machines. Cybernetics relates to the way systems function regardless of whether the system is mechanical or social. Weiner also discussed the importance of feedback. Feedback is tied to performance and the importance of previous information and experience guiding present performance, especially when some unexpected event occurs. Both people and modern machines thus function in a similar way.

In the 1950s, the biologist von Bertalanffy pointed out that structure was a critical component in systems.[6] In fact, structure is more important than function. These principles can be applied not only to biology but to such diverse fields as sociology and electronics. In the 1960s, Forrester studied economic and social systems using computer simulation techniques.[7] The difficulty in understanding all aspects of the systems approach is that systems tend to be viewed from different perspectives by scientists and practitioners. Churchman viewed the systems approach from the perspective of the business community.[8] All approaches seem to see the system as a set of coordinated parts that pursue the accomplishment of a series of goals. Thus, an animal is a system, as is a community. The management scientist as well as the leader attempt to define the parameters of the system. The managers and leaders also define the environment in which the system will be viewed. This translates into the need to define goals, objectives, actions, resources, management requirements, and performance measurements as they affect the parts of the system. According to Churchman, it is important to be aware that the systems approach is sometimes seen as too general for some management/leadership professionals who feel that it eliminates the specificity of problems that also need to be addressed.

Senge expanded the issue of systems to the leadership and management area in the 1990s.[9] Systems thinking was seen as important for leaders. They need to see the big picture if they are to solve organizational and community problems. A systems perspective allows us to build learning organizations where people are able to systematically understand challenges to their organizations and communities as a methodology for getting the results that will help their organizations and communities to grow. In learning organizations, people expand their thinking and learning in a nurturing way.

Senge defined five disciplines to guide the work and understanding of learning organizations.[10] These five disciplines work together. The first discipline relates to personal mastery, which involves each person in a learning organization working to expand his or her knowledge and skills over time as well as building upon personal strengths. The second discipline involves the critical cultural dimension of mental models. Each individual has an outlook on the world based on personal values and experiences. It is important that the individual learn to understand these factors if he or she is going to work in organizations and communities to create change. Values clarification is an important component of learning organization activity. The third discipline is shared vision, which involves the buy-in of all people in an organization to the vision. Commitment to the leader's vision is a requirement for successful change strategies to come into being. The fourth discipline is team learning, in which the members of a team, coalition, or partnership work together in a coordinated fashion. The fifth discipline is systems thinking, in which all need to work together and view problems and challenges from the wide perspective of the total organization or the total community. In essence, a system is composed of a purpose, its components, and the interconnectedness of its parts.[11] Exercise 4-1 looks at the differences in solving a community health issue when the perspective is limited to public health and when it expands to the community as a whole. Other exercises on the five disciplines can be found in Rowitz.[12]

In recent years, Senge and his colleagues have been exploring the effect on the individual of working in learning organizations on systems issues. They have pointed out that the core capacity needed to look at the future collectively is called presence.[13] Systems thinking involves a change in perspective. It involves looking at the world in new ways. Status quo is no longer an option. Change is the reality. This new perspective

means that our old ways of identifying ourselves and what we do must also undergo change. Our view must be forward-looking and not constantly on re-creating our past. These shifts in perspective mean that leaders will shift from a concentration on organizational hierarchies to an approach in which those leaders will work through shared social networks. This new view leads to a new model for this collective type of learning—Theory U.

Theory U is a new approach to integrating the five disciplines to these new approaches to collective learning and practice. **Figure 4-1** shows the relationship between the five disciplines and the Theory U approach.[14] Working with others requires that the team inquire in depth as to the source and understanding of their mental models to see reality more clearly ("co-sensing"), find ways to increase the connections with the mission or purpose and the vision of the problem ("co-presencing"), and translate these visionary activities into feedback-based working action models ("co-realizing"). As can be seen in Figure 4-1, mental models, team learning, and systems thinking come into play in the processes of co-sensing and co-presencing. Co-presencing also shows the disciplines of personal vision and shared vision as happening. In the move from co-presencing to co-realizing, team learning and systems thinking play critical roles in the process.

Scharmer clarifies Theory U by defining five movements toward change as the U Process evolves.[15] He first adds the movement of "co-initiating," which involves the process of engagement between people and environmental contexts with the importance of listening to

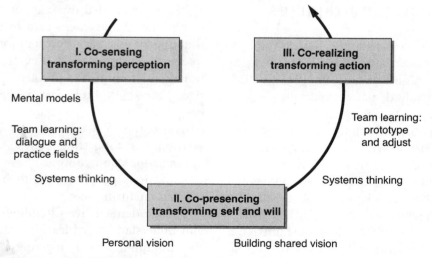

FIGURE 4-1 The U Process and the Five Disciplines. *Source*: From *The Fifth Discipline* by Peter M. Senge, copyright © 1990, 2006 by Peter M. Senge. Used by permission of Doubleday, a division of Random House, Inc.

others and what you perceive that you will need to do. This stage precedes "co-sensing" and starts the U Process. He then clarifies the movements after "co-presencing," when reflection and deep understanding need to occur. Then the movement of "co-creating" occurs when different strategies and scenarios for the future are explored. The final movement stage is "co-involving," when new models and innovations occur from the strong interrelationships between the people who are involved in the change process. This is the stage of transforming action that is shown in Figure 4-1 as "co-realizing." Scharmer points out that Theory U redefines leadership as a collective activity that will occur at all levels of the organization or community.

Leadership in a Systems Environment

The importance of systems thinking for public health leaders became extremely visible as a result of the events of September 11, 2001. A number of training programs and modules related to crisis leadership have developed with this strong systems orientation. It is not that systems thinking has been absent from traditional leadership development programs; it just has become more critical in the training of crisis leaders who need to work in a public health preparedness environment. In this section, the relationship between management and leadership will be explored in the context of a systems-based world where there are connections across organizations (meta-leadership), across jurisdictions from local to state to national, and eventually around the globe.

The traditional management approach is linear in perspective. It involves rules, regulations, and procedures to make an organization work more effectively and efficiently. Leadership in today's knowledge, skills, talents, and practice world is more of a systems set of issues. Cabrera has developed a systems organizing model that is based on the four components of vision, structure, learning, and action (VSAL).[16] **Figure 4-2** shows this model. These four components have a role in traditional linear and hierarchical organizations as well as in more systems-oriented or community-based organizations. In each of the Cabrera quadrants, there is a continuum to demonstrate this move from traditional

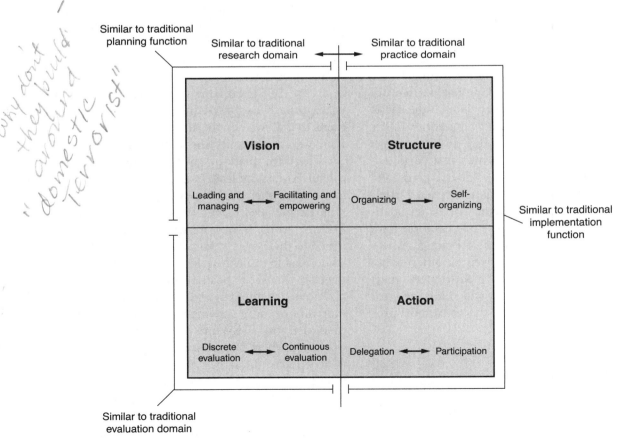

FIGURE 4-2 **Systems Organizing Model.** *Source*: Reprinted with the permission of Derek Cabrera. From Cabera, D. 2001. *Knowledge Age Operating System: Four Principles of Project Design, Version 1.0.* Loveland, CO: Project N Press.

to systems orientations. The components are shown in a two-by-two contingency table format to show that all four parts are interactive with each other. Another important aspect to the model is that it builds on a theory, research, and action interrelationships, which for us is a demonstration of public health practice in action. The National Cancer Institute has used this model to show systems thinking in tobacco control initiatives.[17]

Starting with the quadrant labeled vision, it is important to recognize that vision has generally been part of a consistent set of visioning tools tied to leadership in traditional as well as systems-oriented organizations. Vision is closely allied with the planning activities in an organization or agency. For most organizations and agencies, the top administrator as leader has set the tone for the work of the organization through defining a vision, living the vision, and inspiring others in the organization to support and take ownership of the vision.[18,19] The top administrator, as lead manager, and other organization managers have the critical role of making the organization vision work in a practical way.

In a systems organizing perspective, vision becomes a collective activity in which a leadership network approach defines a shared vision. Leadership becomes more a demonstration of empowering others and facilitating the visioning process. Here, we see the use and development of many tools to help in the process. For example, there is brainstorming where ideas get generated;[20] the six thinking hats framework for generating ideas and solving problems;[21] the use of logic models to link planning and evaluation;[22] future search techniques to define the future and how to get there;[23] the Search Conference, which is a participatory model for visioning, creating strategic goals, and developing action plans;[24] facilitation to create participation, address conflict, make effective decisions, manage meetings, and show how to use process tools for a group's work;[25] and Communities of Practice, where leaders from the community as well as other stakeholders, including public health practitioners, meet face-to-face and virtually to learn and share ideas for the possible development of resources to support programs in a special area of interest.[26]

Leadership Tip

Root your vision in reality.

The second quadrant relates to structure, which involves the movement from organizing people and activities by managers and leaders to the systems orientation of self-organizing, which is a critical component in complexity thinking.[27] In traditional organizations, the structure is fairly well defined. There are organization charts and individual performance appraisal processes, and individuals' work often seems to be defined through inflexible job descriptions. This inflexible structure often limits the problem-solving possibilities and the decisions that are made because of the rules, regulations, and protocols that define action. Traditional structure also defines who you can talk to as well as the ability to work with external stakeholders.

The structure of the system is self-organizing and encourages leaders to interact with all types of people and organizations. The structures that evolve are tied to the networks that are created to support collaboration between the partners. However, our present reality is that traditional and systems structures coexist. Systems thinkers struggle with understanding and interpreting how traditional organizations work in a systems world. A whole series of systems tools has been developed to increase this understanding. Systems archetypes are one such set of tools, where problems are viewed through a number of graphic representations to show the underlying framework for success and failure of programs and events.[28–30] These archetypes are used more in understanding why things are as they are rather than determining how to solve these problems or events. Self-organizing systems do provide a different approach to these issues by creating an environment that allows for the structure to evolve as needed to address community and systems challenges.[31]

The third quadrant involves action. In traditional organizations, the leaders and managers tend to delegate work to their staff. How delegation occurs is important. People need incentives, rewards, and recognition for their work.[32] They are willing to do the work if it is tied to their talents, knowledge, and skills. Managers who are able to fit the talents of each staff member to the tasks that are to be done are critical in today's organizations, whether these organizations are traditional in nature or more systems-based. The subtle but critical dimension here is for systems-organizing leaders to work with their organizational colleagues to connect their work to the larger collective vision of the community or system as a whole. The philosophy is more than the original belief of thinking globally and acting locally. In systems, the philosophy now becomes acting locally for the benefit of the community and society as a whole. Local work has global consequences. It is at the local level that mission leads to the goals that bring vision into reality. Social entrepreneurs are leaders who use systems solutions to address global, national, and local social problems.[33]

The final quadrant involves the differences in learning in traditional organizations in contrast to systems organizations and communities. Best and his colleagues see learning in an evaluation context.[34] In traditional organizations, this evaluation learning is tied to the linear perspective related to planning, implementing, and carrying out programs. This type of evaluation is discrete and done as required by the project but tends not to be ongoing. Systems work that is ongoing is about creating learning organizations and learning collaboratively. Whereas the researcher or leader/manager defines activities for the organization, systems research is more participatory in nature. In systems, the needs of the researcher and the practitioner must be collaborative in nature.

In their simplest form, logic models involve the process of defining inputs, throughputs, and outcomes. They are oriented more toward traditional program structures and try to simplify discussions of

cause-and-effect relationships and link them to process and outcome considerations. Best et al. see logic models as more traditional in nature and see systems dynamics with the important component of feedback as necessary to link the effects of programmatic actions as they influence factors such as those inputs in the logic model.[35] The effect of actions also affects the relationships between these actions and the outcomes that occur. The Centers for Disease Control and Prevention has developed a systems framework for evaluation. **Figure 4-3** shows the elements of a systems approach to evaluation as a series of steps.[36] The inclusion of feedback opportunities at each step of the process would make this model even more acceptable to systems thinkers.

There are two interesting examples that will allow you to see the leadership issues in systems change. In November 2007, the Commonwealth Fund released a report outlining the issues necessary for the development of a high-performance health system for the United States.[37] First, it will not be possible to create such a system without a concern for public health issues. There will need to be an alignment between the

FIGURE 4-3 Elements of Evaluation Framework for a System. *Source:* Reproduced from Framework for Program Evaluation in Public Health, *Morbidity and Mortality Weekly Report*, Vol. 48, 1999, the Centers for Disease Control and Prevention.

healthcare system and the public health system in the areas of health promotion and disease prevention. Public policy and the political structure must find ways to promote healthy lifestyles. Without these public health dimensions, a reform of the American health system cannot occur. These public health concerns need to be aligned at a systems level with affordable coverage for all people with improvements in access to care and quality, efficiency, and cost control; aligned incentives and cost control through better information systems, payment reforms, better management of high-cost and chronic conditions, transparency through public reporting, improved administrative efficiencies, and elimination of unnecessary waste; accountable coordinated care; quality control and efficiency; and accountability among health leaders.

The second example, which illustrates the application of the systems-organizing VSAL model, is presented in Case Study 4-B. This study was developed by a team of public health professionals from Quebec who attended the Mid-America Regional Public Health Leadership Institute in 2002 and 2003 and undertook a study of ways to restructure the Quebec Public Health Program. The team also was concerned with the ways that leadership works in a systemwide program change.

Case Study 4-B

Leadership Issues Associated with the Development of the Quebec Public Health Program

André Dontigny, Céline Farley, Isabelle Garon, Odette Laplante, Mariette LeBrun-Bohémier, Guy Poudrier, Jocelyne Sauvé, Lise Renaud

Once upon a time there was a program ...

In November 2002, Quebec's department of health and social services (*ministère de la Santé et des Services sociaux*, MSSS) made public its national public health program. This program defines the scope of public health action in Quebec and sets out the priorities and activities to be undertaken for the regional partners of public health departments (DSPs) and local partners (the local community service centers, or CLSCs).

Our case study focuses on the challenges involved in developing this program and the leadership exercised by various stakeholders to meet these challenges. This document is an initial assessment resulting from consultation with several key stakeholders. It will serve as a basis for a discussion of the challenges with a group of Quebec's public health leaders. This discussion will allow us to gather ideas to help implement the program and prepare and implement the action plans resulting from it.

Context and Stakeholders

Quebec's health and social services network, a deconcentrated system accessible to the whole population, is made up of several partners acting at different levels. At the provincial level, the MSSS funds this network and defines major orientations, policies, and programs, both curative and preventive. The 18 regional boards plan and coordinate services, allocate resources, monitor the budgets of the institutions in their region, and ensure that results are achieved for their region, whereas the institutions manage the care and services that they deliver. The regional boards also provide regional public health services through the mandate given to public health directors. The CLSCs provide curative and preventive services and are the local public health mandataries, whereas the medical clinics deliver care and some preventive services. Finally, several community organizations provide preventive community services.

Over the past 12 years, the MSSS has produced about 20 documents addressed to public health stakeholders and other resources of the health and social services network. They are, for example, the Policy on Health and Well-Being (1990), the Framework for the Development of the Public Health Program, and the Organization of the Public Health Network (1992), a report focusing on the development of children, literally translated as "Quebec wild about its kids" (*Un Quebec fou de ses enfants*) (1993), Quebec Priorities in Public Health (1997), the Tobacco Act (1998), followed by the National Tobacco Control Program (*Programme national sur le tabac*) and the Public Health Act (2001). The most recent document is the Quebec Public Health Program (2002). To sum up, it seems that several documents have been introduced one after the other into the network in a short period of time and had to be absorbed, but they were not all associated with a plan to integrate these into practice.

The Quebec Public Health Program hoped to be different from the documents that preceded it. While striving to achieve the same high-quality document as its predecessors, it is intended to serve as a platform for mobilizing public health stakeholders and partners around the full scope of public health actions that are common to all of Quebec. The program, just like the Public Health Act, which was developed at the same time, was seen as a structuring measure to consolidate the public health infrastructure. It was an element in a vast project to strengthen and enhance the credibility of public health. The Quebec health and social services network has just undergone a period of major change—that is, a shift to ambulatory services in the context of budgetary pressure. This indirectly caused some disinterest from the authorities toward public health actions as the attention of the media and politicians, in Quebec and elsewhere, was once more focused on the overcrowding of emergency departments and the length of waiting lists.

The aim of the MSSS was to share a common vision of public health and to provide the conditions so that public health actions would be coherent, with a strong science base and carried out by all partners—that is, the health and social services network (the regional boards' public health departments and the CLSCs) as well as community organizations and partners in other sectors. It was hoped that the program would be the product of broad-based collaboration and participation of the entire network.

The key stakeholders who influenced this process were the Assistant Deputy Minister of Public Health and the Minister for Health and Social Services, who wished to strengthen the capacity of preventive health services; the National Public Health Director, who was particularly skillful at developing structuring measures, supported by a team of dynamic professionals; several public health directors; executive directors of CLSCs convinced of the advantages of working together; as well as the institute for public health (*Institut de santé publique* [INSPQ]), which could provide high-quality expertise.

Leadership Activities Linked to Policy Development

The following activities linked to policy development have served as an analytical framework for this case study:

- Developing support, particularly by building coalitions, empowering other stakeholders, recognizing community assets, and making representations on the health challenges targeted by the policy
- Clarifying values, creating a vision, linking that vision to the mission, and using partners to establish the priorities on which this policy is to be based
- Organizing goals and translating them into action
- Organizing and seeking new resources, and making organizational changes to better meet community needs
- Emphasizing innovation, delegating responsibilities for programming, and supervising programs resulting from the policy

Initial Challenges

In the autumn of 2000, at the very beginning of the process of developing the Quebec Public Health Program, a number of challenges to be met were identified through interviews conducted with public health authorities at different levels. At the time, it was expected that the program would provide a way to strengthen the capacity of all public health teams to act effectively in partnership and to be recognized as such in the health and social service system and by other sectors. These challenges are as follows:

- The desire of the MSSS to increase the coherence and a more uniform access to public health services and interventions in Quebec's regions and local territories served by the CLSCs by defining the supply of public health services that are common to all regions and CLSC territories of Quebec
- The intention of the MSSS to use the program as a lever and a tool to mobilize all public health mandataries and support decisions on resource allocation
- The shared desire on the part of the MSSS, DSPs, and CLSCs for the program to give public health a greater role in the political space of the health and social services network and to confirm the importance of promotion and prevention, particularly in CLSCs
- The desire to conserve a degree of regional and local flexibility
- The recognition of CLSCs as public health mandataries in their own right, which is in keeping with the spirit of the public health bill being developed at the time and the need for them to assert themselves as such

(*Continues*)

- The fear on the part of a number of public health departments and CLSCs that a program would be too constraining and that it would stifle innovation and not take into account regional or local characteristics
- The choice of all public health mandataries to establish a participatory process to define the program, one in which all public health organizations would be involved under the leadership of the MSSS

Another major issue underlying the process was to reach an agreement on the content of the program, since the first attempt 10 years earlier had been transformed into seven "national priorities" in public health, because an agreement could not be reached on the content of an entire program.

On the whole, the idea of developing a national public health program, which was provided for under the act respecting health services and social services since 1993,[1] but never written, originated from the MSSS. It mainly reflected the search for coherence in public health activities, which often varied from one region and one CLSC to the next, and did not address some major health challenges. This desire also reflected a recognition of the need to make more room for public health within the health and social services system.

Although several public health departments shared this vision, others feared that their regional flexibility would be reduced because the act respecting health services and social services defined their responsibilities but not the explicit link with the central level, except in the event of a health threat. For their part, the CLSCs appeared to be happy to participate in the process but had to assert themselves as a new stakeholder in the planning of public health activities. On the other hand, they had to figure out how to restore the importance of activities that deal with the cause of health and social problems, because they had to increase their ambulatory care activities during periods of budgetary pressure, therefore often at the expense of prevention.

While the program was being written, the Public Health Act,[2] which was being developed at the same time, was used as another opportunity to provide the legal foundation on which to build the public health program and to confirm and specify the role and responsibility (and accountability) of the stakeholders in the program and its implementation.

Clarifying Its Foundations, Orientations, and Values

The task of specifying the foundations, clarifying the vision as well as the orientations and values to be conveyed by the program, was a challenge in itself because there was no consensus on vision and content. Although the values were, to a certain extent, shared and supported by professionals at all levels, several schools of thought had to be reconciled in terms of boundaries of the public health domain, philosophies, and intervention practices. The entire process of drafting the program, which took more than two years, was used in part to do this conciliation.

At the time, there was no program model from elsewhere that could simply be copied. The program was therefore written with a view to innovating and reconciling knowledge on practices that have been proven to be effective. Fairly early on in the process, the writing team, supported by the advisory committee, suggested that interventions be grouped under main areas or domains, which required that, as much as possible, actions be carried out with common partners and be based on common determinants. Although several times during the writing process doubts were raised about this "perspective," it served as the basis throughout the construction of the program.

Organizing the Process

The work structure to be used in developing the program was defined in the spring of 2000, based on a central idea—that is, a participatory process in which all levels of the public health organization would be involved[3] (MSSS, the INSPQ, DSPs, CLSCs) to ensure the highest quality product and support for the program by organizations with a public health mandate, even though the legal framework allowed the MSSS to establish the program on its own.

Partners from within[4] the health and social services sector joined these representatives to form an advisory committee with the responsibility of providing an opinion on the content of the program. For its part, the main working committee was made up of managers and professionals from different levels of the public health organizations (the MSSS, the INSPQ, public health departments). The working groups responsible for developing the contents of the program were made up mainly of public health professionals and resources at the regional and national as well as the local levels. Finally, a team of MSSS professionals supported the process and led the working groups. Partners from other sectors and community organizations were invited to participate in developing the program on only a few occasions.

The choice of this structure demonstrates the wish of the public health mandataries to, on the one hand, assess the situation "among themselves" in order to plan public health activities and, on the other hand, to promote the maximum participation of the public health mandataries without weighing down the process by broadening it to other sectors. It was agreed that the trans-sectoral partners and community organizations would be asked to participate later, during consultations on the draft program. However, the choice of this work structure was not neutral; rather, it reflected the need of public health mandataries to plan public health activities together before turning to outside partners. The stage of recognizing community assets was carried out by professionals who made up the working groups, who brought with them the concerns of their communities (based on needs assessments previously conducted by the CLSCs and DSPs), and then validated by the CLSCs; the program's authors took for granted that these assets existed without describing or examining them.

Agreeing on "What"

A crucial stage was defining the conceptual framework (see **Figure 4-4**), which represented the will to clearly define the scope of public health action by the functions exercised, to structure public health activities according to intervention areas or domains,[5] and to guide these activities based on health and social objectives aimed at enhancing health and well-being as well as reducing the major health problems through interventions known to be effective. This was done in the autumn of 2000.

Moreover, the proposal of an ethical framework and the choice of action strategies, also in the autumn of 2000, helped to identify the set of fundamental values on which the program would be based. Through this process, it was possible to identify consensus on the values that would constitute guideposts to support the ethical consideration on the choice of interventions to be carried out and to guide the interventions themselves. The key values are the public interest; beneficence and nonmaleficence; respect for confidentiality and private life; responsibility; solidarity; recognition of the potential of individuals and communities and the necessary protection of individuals, groups, and communities that are at risk; and justice.

Another crucial stage was determining the program's actions and activities, which mainly involved identifying main health and psychosocial problems as well as determining effective interventions to act on the problems and their determinants. This process was carried out in sub-groups by more than 200 public health professionals. It involved considerable work carried out intensively over four months (during the winter of 2001) and then continued for nearly a year, until January 2002. This process was supervised by the program's main working committee and the professional team of the MSSS. The latter was also responsible for determining whether the material met the criteria of inclusion of activities in the program. During this stage, the professionals attempted to influence the program content through their work and expertise (but also through representations).

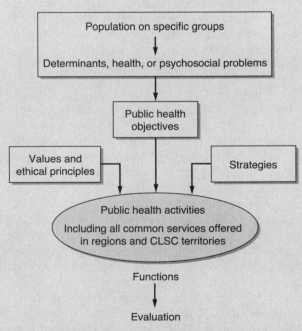

FIGURE 4-4 Components of the Quebec Public Health Program.

The sometimes poor adherence to the criteria of inclusion in the program, particularly regarding whether or not the activities belonged to the field of public health or were effective; the speed with which discussions took place between the professionals who had developed the content and the ministerial team (a speed that prevented the professionals from having the decisions validated by their working groups); the difficulty in uniformly applying the criteria of inclusion of activities; the lack of clarity about how the priorities could be determined; and the fear of seeing certain areas of expertise being left out of the program are all elements that gave rise to tensions during that period. It was at that turning point that a professional suggested conducting a strategic analysis of the issues in order to clarify the issues, expectations, fears, conditions for success, and pitfalls, and beginning to focus on "how" to manage change rather than focusing only on "what" the content of the program should be.

Which Priorities?

Furthermore, the program's advisory committee and the public health authorities met a few times to validate the proposed contents and to establish priorities. The lack of consensus on the need to use duly established criteria to determine the priorities as well as on the relative importance of the proposed activities made this operation difficult. However, an exception should be noted—that is, a meeting held at the end of the development process, in which the criteria of feasibility and opportunity made it possible to determine, on the basis of consensus, the activities to be conducted during the first stage of the program.

In general, despite efforts and good will, some deficiencies were observed in the transmission of information throughout the process of development of contents and establishment of priorities. Indeed, information was perceived to have been insufficiently communicated or was communicated too late between the different groups (MSSS-DSPs-INSPQ-CLSCs, between the authorities and the professionals or other resources), and even within the same group. Apart from a newsletter that was disseminated by the MSSS a few times and on an irregular basis and the information transmitted to the national roundtables on public health (which include the regional and central public health organizations, except for CLSCs) and to the management committee of the MSSS's General Department of Public Health (*Direction générale de santé publique*), few mechanisms had been specified and established to communicate information between members of the advisory committee and the organizations where they came from and between the authorities and professionals or other resources, except for a periodic and widely disseminated information letter and consultation meetings' reports.

The speed of the process involved in this stage and the lack of time to disseminate information by the drafting team account, but only partly, for the unsteady flow of the information transmitted, and especially received, during the program's development. The lack of information received only partly explains the tensions observed during this stage and the lack of synergy between the organizations and the different levels of the same organization during this stage of program development. Much of this perception of lack of information may have reflected the expectations of the professionals, in particular those who had been involved in the working groups, that they would participate in all stages of decision making and drafting the program.

The Writing and Consultation Stage

The writing of the program's consultation draft (first full draft of the text) began in July 2002 following an advisory committee meeting in which the majority of members agreed with the comments made. This consultation, which had been postponed for a few months in relation to the initial schedule, was to last from 8 to 10 weeks. However, this process was upset by the ministers' agenda. Although the consultation was to be launched during the Annual Public Health Days (*Journées annuelles de santé publique*) in November 2002, the ministers wished that the program be disseminated during this event instead. The consultation draft therefore had to be finished sooner than expected; and the consultation period was thus limited to around 12 days. It was intended for the public health organizations only, except for the principal intersectoral ministerial partners concerned by the program. Thus it was deemed unfeasible and inappropriate to consult the national groups of community organizations during such a short time, because the latter would not have enough time to consult their members.

Within this context, it was clear that the program could not be appropriated during such a brief consultation process, in particular by the CLSCs and the transsectoral partners, and an appropriation stage was to be planned for later. However, the matter of the minister missing the opportunity to launch the program was considered to be worse, given the risk of missing a key opportunity for appropriation by the minister and decision makers in the health and social service network. The assistant deputy minister thus decided to put his cards on the table during a teleconference with the regional and local public health partners.

Despite these difficult conditions, the responses to the consultation were most generous. Indeed, nearly all the organizations consulted sent their comments to the MSSS within the prescribed time. Moreover, the comments made were excellent and most were rapidly integrated. The regional and local public health leaders also seemed to agree that the opportunity provided by the ministers to rapidly disseminate the program should be grasped while the long-awaited synergy was present.

The Home Stretch …

The final draft of the program was thus written (including all the comments, many of which involved major rewriting), formatted, and printed in record time (four weeks).

The program was launched as planned on the Annual Public Health Days by the Minister for Health, Social Services, Youth Protection and Prevention; a rallying assistant deputy minister; and before representatives of all public health levels who seemed to enthusiastically welcome the first Quebec public health program.

What Comes Next …

The development of regional action plans followed by that of local action plans are crucial stages during which public health directors and executive directors of CLSCs will have to exercise strong leadership at their respective levels in order to formulate their action plans for implementing the program in their respective territories. Moreover, these stages are critical for program appropriation by professionals in the DSPs and workers in CLSCs as well as their partners. The development of regional and local action plans will also be a key moment to involve the community organizations and other trans-sectoral partners in the development of action plans and to seek their support for the program and the action plans.

The program's implementation has begun. The Follow-up Committee of the Quebec Public Health Program, which includes representatives of all public health organizations (MSSS, INSPQ, DSPs, CLSCs), has held its first meeting. Its members accepted the mandate to jointly follow up the program's implementation as well as its evolution based on the population's health needs and the organizational and financial contexts. This committee will be required to play a key role in supporting the program's implementation. Lastly, training activities and evaluation activities, which will make use of the services of all public health stakeholders, are essential to the successful implementation of the program.

Although the program's publication is the end of a decisive stage, other issues in the implementation of the program are just as crucial:

- Changes in practice to be reconciled, supported, and facilitated
- Changes at the organizational level to facilitate changes in practice
- Professional and management leadership at all levels to promote implementation and a dynamic evolution
- Coherent actions of public health teams that are based on effective or promising interventions relying on community assets, and that foster innovation
- Mechanisms for reconciling different perspectives with partners as well as within and between public health teams
- Obtaining funding to support implementation

Conclusion

Building alliances. Special efforts were made to ensure the development of a program that fosters a broad consensus, both within the public health network and with key partners in its implementation. However, the appropriation exercise must continue, in particular in the development of regional and local action plans because the network's people were not all closely involved in the process, particularly at the local level, but also in the regional and national organizations. Training and appropriation activities will be critical for the effective implementation of the program.

Clarifying values. The program clearly raises the ethical issues associated with public health action and makes a solid synthesis of evolving concepts and practices in public health, taking account of both the importance of public policies and the empowerment of communities, while proposing actions that are most likely to have an impact on avoidable morbidity, injuries, and mortality. In brief, this is a visionary program that will require time and sustained concerted efforts for appropriation and implementation.

Organizing goals. The prioritization of activities must nevertheless be continued in collaboration with the regional and local partners and will be reflected in the regional and local action plans, taking advantage of the strengths and minimizing the weaknesses due to the fact that the program is vast, not having reduced the proposed interventions enough through prioritization.

Additional effort will be needed to quantify certain goals and promote evaluation in order to measure and follow the degree of achievement, which could not be finalized before the release of the program. Evaluation is nevertheless a major issue of the program. The aim of improving the operation of the evaluation parameters will be to facilitate the follow-up of the program's implementation as well as the capacity to report on the degree of achievement of goals. Lastly, the periodic evaluation can also be instrumental in supporting the program's visibility and implementation.

Seeking new resources. The program's adoption seems to have further contributed to the government's intention to increase funding for prevention. A first commitment to increase existing funding for public health actions by 25% was made by the government in March 2003. Another major issue relates to the network's capacity to promote the transition from intention to action and to invest in activities considered to be priority activities in terms of their potential impact on the health of the population.

Emphasizing innovation. By the very nature of its content and mission, the program leaves necessary room for innovative approaches while promoting its implementation. In brief, through the development of the program and the resulting activities, a context that is conducive to its implementation at the political level (associated with funding) seems to be emerging. Local, regional, and national organizations can take advantage of this context to intensify their collaboration, in particular by providing the conditions that are conducive to the program's implementation (achievement of the action plan). This increased collaboration should be accompanied by the identification of other means to foster stronger public health leadership and infrastructure in this new context.

Notes

1. The act respecting health services and social services stipulated that the minister "establish the public health program, take the measures that are best suited to ensure the protection of public health, and ensure national and inter-regional coordination" (R.S.Q., c. S-4.2, s. 341.9).
2. Adopted in December 2001, the Public Health Act sets out four basic functions of public health: surveillance and monitoring, prevention, promotion, and health protection. It replaces the Public Health Protection Act, which dated back 25 years. It also defines the components of the program, the regional and local action plans, and the responsibilities of the mandataries.
3. The fact that people who were "committed" rather than "representatives" had been chosen to create a product that was based on the best expertise available rather than on the interests of the parties resulted in situations of quid pro quo, in terms of the information and the involvement of stakeholders from participating organizations at several stages of the process.
4. The advisory committee included a member of each of the following organizations: College of Physicians, Professional Association of Nurses, and several others.
5. The intervention areas are (a) development, adjustment, and social integration, (b) lifestyles and chronic diseases, (c) unintentional injuries, (d) infectious diseases, (e) environmental health, and (f) occupational health.

Note: Special thanks to Marthe Hamel, coordinator of program development, to the DSP, the MSSS, for the text's history and basis.
Source: Courtesy of the Mid-America Regional Public Health Leadership Institute.

BRIEF DISCUSSION OF THE TOOLS

Advocates of systems thinking have developed a number of tools to graphically plot out understandings of how the systems work. The tools are also used to communicate to others how these potential solutions can affect the organization or community. The tools have been developed to simplify the explanation of very complex phenomenon. Although there are many different tools for systems work, the following discussion concentrates on systems archetypes. There are three other graphic systems tool measurements: causal loop diagrams, computer simulation software packages, and microworlds.[38] *Causal loop diagrams* graphically show dynamic interrelationships in a system by tying such things as behavior of different variables over time to some systems factors.[39] *Computer simulation software* includes such things as computer modeling and learning laboratories. Jackson discussed *microworlds* as management flight simulators that were constructed from data related to computer simulation models.[40]

Leaders who are systems thinkers view their world in terms of loops and links.[41,42] In systems thinking, the leader believes that his or her tools will reflect a story.[43] These stories can be seen in a series of archetypes that are graphic models that help to explain reality in a systems way. The archetypes tell us something else. Certain structural patterns seem to occur over and over again.[44] These system archetypes thus become tools for learning and also analyzing the various social structures that seem to exist in our organizational and personal lives. Although each social situation is unique, there are still enough similarities in given cultures to allow the systems thinker as leader to classify these situations. Thus, these systems archetypes, which are few in number, can be useful tools. These system archetypes were defined and discussed by Senge and colleagues,[45–47] and also extensively by Kim.[48,49]

It all seems to be about thinking in loops. All systems archetypes are based on two processes: the reinforcing process and the balancing process. These two processes are represented by a loop with feedback built into the loop. The reinforcing loop is based on a growth and collapse model.[50,51] Using a simple public health scenario, **Figure 4-5** shows how reinforcing loops work. If you are overweight, you tend to eat more than a person of normal weight. The more you eat, the greater your weight. Reinforcing loops also show that a change in one direction dynamically increases change in that same direction.[52] Using the reinforcing loop process can give you other public health examples (**Figure 4-6**). If you already realize that obesity and other nutritional disorders are not really as simple as portrayed in Figure 4-5, then you are ready to look at balancing loops.

Balancing loops refer to processes that limit growth and generate processes of resistance.[53] Balancing loops attempt to stabilize a system or bring it into equilibrium.[54] The balancing loops also show some other things. Look at **Figure 4-7**. You are 50 pounds

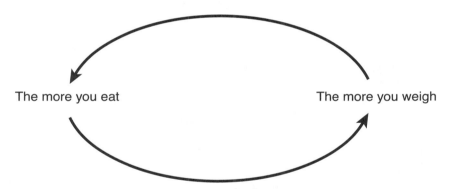

The more you eat   The more you weigh

FIGURE 4-5 Example of a Reinforcing Loop.

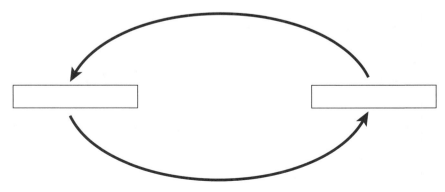

FIGURE 4-6 Reinforcing Loops.

overweight relative to your height and age. The gap then is 50 pounds that you want to lose. As you eat more, the gap between your actual and acceptable weight will increase. So what can be done? You can exercise and go on a diet (corrective action). Your weight decreases, and the gap between your actual and acceptable weight also decreases. Some diagrams make a distinction between the gap and the desired level, as can be seen in Figure 4-7. Give public health examples utilizing **Figure 4-8**. Now you can explore an archetype approach by putting together Figures 4-5 and 4-7.

Wouldn't it be great if all situations were this easy to analyze? It is important to point out that every link in a system contains a delay. A delay can affect the

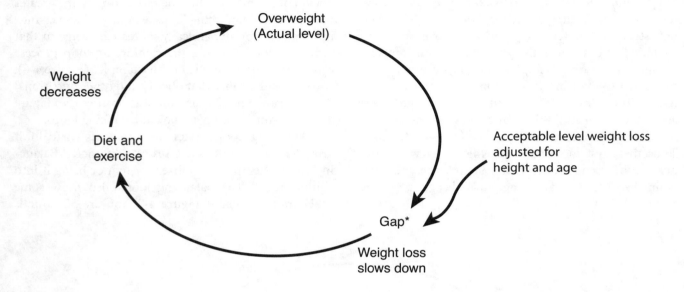

FIGURE 4-7 Balancing Loops Seek Equilibrium—Some Desired Level of Performance.

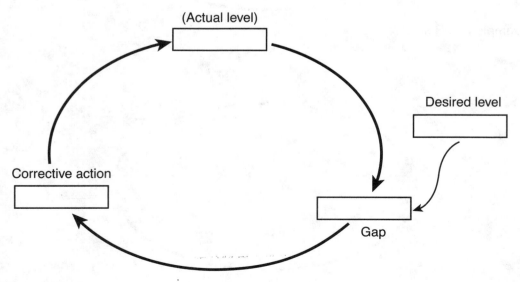

FIGURE 4-8 Balancing Loops.

The Paradox of Inside/Outside: A Complexity Concern

operation of a system or other components in a system. There are four types of delay.[55]

The first type of delay refers to delays that are physical in nature. Physical delays are time based and involve getting from here to there. For example, for some individuals, it may take three months to lose 10 pounds with exercise and diet. For other individuals, it may take six months. Thus, there is a physical delay in the time a corrective action is instituted and the desired state is actualized.

The second type of delay is transactional in that various procedural activities can slow down the change process. Using the above nutrition example, the buying of the diet products may be delayed due to delivery or production problems or even a change in price. The dieter may be affected by any of these transactional problems.

The third form of delay is informational in that there may be delays in communicating information about the physical changes that the diet and exercise may cause. The overweight person's diet may be under the supervision of a physician who is monitoring the changes through various laboratory tests or communications from a nutritionist who works for an entity that has complex procedures related to sending reports back to the doctor who has to evaluate the report before giving information to the patient or modifying the diet in light of these new results.

The final delay is perceptual in that the dieting individual may misinterpret the messages which he or she has received.

When all the above pieces are put together, we have a systems archetype. There are basically eight major systems archetypes. **Figure 4-9** shows a brief description of the eight archetypes and some guidelines for using them.[56] Exercise 4-2 will allow you to try to apply the archetypes to scenarios in a team.

LEADERSHIP AND POWER

The issue of how a leader views work within an organization or system presents an interesting view of the world through the eyes of a manager and a leader. A manager is concerned with keeping the organization or agency moving in a forward fashion within the constraints imposed on that entity from the director or from a governing or advisory board. Although the organization is a system in principle, in practice the manager is usually more linear when moving from specific problems and challenges to specific conclusions. The leader needs to see the organization as a system

that has roles and responsibilities in the context of the organization as a whole or its roles and responsibilities in the context of a community.

Systems and leadership can be viewed as power concerns.[57] Power within a system is used to transform the system and to move it in a new direction. The goal of leaders is to use power to improve the system, and in public health, the goal is to improve the quality of life of all residents of the community. The prepared public health leader wants to help all members of the system gain self-awareness and see that systems thinking is beneficial to improved organizational and community health. Position by itself does not guarantee power, but rather the leader who understands the organization or community and how to move the system forward in a courageous way defines the real meaning of power. Power is the management of the energy in the system.[58] The effective leader knows when to turn up the heat in a difficult situation and when to cool it down.[59] Heating things up brings a creative tension to the situation.

In addition, there is the critical skill of relationship building needed to improve the functioning of the system.[60] In addition, the whole process of systems change can be seen as a story, called an *archetype* in systems language. These archetypes help to monitor and better understand how systems work. As pointed out above, archetypes become critical analytical tools for the leader as a systems thinker. The problem for the average individual is that the parts are seen and the whole is lost. This has been labeled as *spatial blindness*.[61] To this can be added the concept of *temporal blindness* to refer to the fact that all systems have a history or story to tell. The blindness refers to the fact that most people live in the present but ignore the past. The goal of a successful prepared public health leader must be to see the whole world systemically.

THE PARADOX OF INSIDE/OUTSIDE: A COMPLEXITY CONCERN

In traditional public health organizations and agencies, the walls of the building that house the public health entity serve as virtual boundaries from the outside community. Within the agency, programmatic silos also become isolated from the total mission and vision of the public health enterprise. When the administrator works with the community, the other staff of the agency often remain far removed from the administrative leader's work with the community. With the increasing

Drifting goals

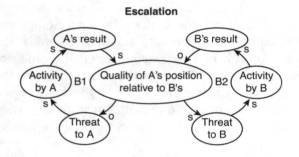

Description

In a Drifting Goals archetype, a gap between the goal and current reality can be resolved by taking corrective action (B1) or lowering the goal (B2). The critical difference is that lowering the goal immediately closes the gap, where as corrective actions usually take time.

Escalation

In the Escalation archetype, one party (A) takes actions that are perceived by the other as a threat. The other party (B) responds in a similar manner, increasing the threat to A and resulting in more threatening actions by A. The reinforcing loop is traced out by following the outline of the figure-8 produced by the two balancing loops.

Fixes that fail

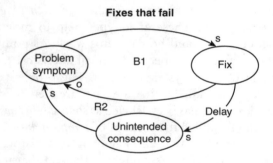

In a Fixes that Fail situation, a problem symptom cries out for resolution. A solution is quickly implemented that alleviates the symptom (B1), but the unintended consequences of the "fix" exacerbate the problem (R2). Over time, the problem symptom returns to its previous level or becomes worse.

Growth and underinvestment

In a Growth and Underinvestment archetype, growth approaches a limit that can be eliminated or pushed into the future if capacity investments are made. Instead, performance standards are lowered to justify underinvestment, leading to lower performance, which further justifies underinvestment.

FIGURE 4-9 Systems Archetypes at a Glance.

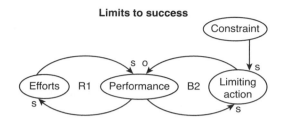

Limits to success

Description
In a Limits to Success scenario, continued efforts initially lead to improved performance. Over time, however, the system encounters a limit that causes the performance to slow down or even decline (B2), even as efforts continue to rise.

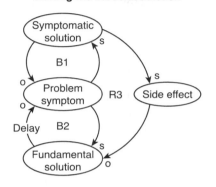

Shifting the burden/addiction

In a Shifting the Burden situation, a problem is "solved" by applying a symptomatic solution (B1), which diverts attention away from more fundamental solutions (R3), (see *The Systems Thinker*, September 1990). In an Addiction structure, a Shifting the Burden degrades into an addictive pattern in which the side effect gets so entrenched that it overwhelms the original problem symptom.

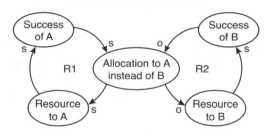

Success to the successful

In a Success to the Successful archetype, if one person or group (A) is given more resources, it has a higher likelihood of succeeding than B (assuming they are equally capable). The initial success justifies devoting more resources to A, and B's success diminishes, further justifying more resource allocations to A(R2).

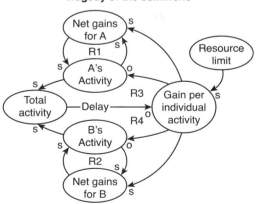

Tragedy of the commons

In a Tragedy of the Commons structure, each person pursues actions that are individually beneficial (R1 and R2). If the amount of activity grows too large for the system to support, however, the "commons" experiences diminishing benefits (B5 and B6).

FIGURE 4-9 Systems Archetypes at a Glance (*continued*).

complexity of public health as a community system, the leader struggles with these issues. Traditional agencies and organizations are like machines. These entities tend to concentrate on the individual people, parts, programs, and silos rather than on the whole organization or agency. When a part breaks, it is necessary to fix it or the whole will suffer. These organizations tend to be hierarchical in structure, with generally a command and control type of leader. The status quo tends to be the governing principle. The mission of the organization often does not align well with the activities of the organization.[62] You do not get aligned thinking or action until the vision of the leader drives the action.[63]

This machine view tends to limit the effectiveness of the work of public health. This machine view creates a world that is delimited by boundaries.[64] Wheatley believes that this machine model is extremely limiting and does not deal with organizations and communities as living systems. Systems often function in a chaotic manner and not according to the logic of the more linear mechanistic model. Systems are about chaos and change. Systems thinkers need to get away from the study of an organization or community as a machine and concentrate on the human relationships that drive the system. Wheatley and Kellner-Rogers pointed out that a system is holistic in that it is not really a sum of its parts.[65] There are no separable parts. A system is basically about relationships between people. Exercise 4-3 will give you the opportunity to explore the differences between organizational and community collaborative skills.

The complexity model of systems is clearly an innovative approach that builds on the following premises:[66]

1. The universe is a living system that is creative in nature and exists at all levels from the microbe level to the cosmos.
2. Life's energy is oriented toward organization. Life becomes more and more complex as it develops diversity and requirement for sustainability.
3. Life is oriented toward defining a self and is organized to create an identity.
4. Life self-organizes at all levels of complexity as networks, patterns, and structures emerge without external pressures.
5. People do not like to be controlled. If left alone, they will use their intelligence, talents, creativity, and ability to adapt, and they will search for meaning and organize themselves in appropriate ways.
6. Organizations are also living systems that follow all of the above premises.

In several books, Wheatley defines this new complexity paradigm in terms of the following dimensions:[67–69]

1. Focus on relationships and not facts, positions, and structure
2. Concentration on the importance of interconnectedness, which creates a web of relationships
3. Constant evolution
4. Concentration on process rather than only on outcomes
5. Different systems in different places
6. An agenda that is always on order out of chaos and a process that is always messy
7. The principle that life seeks organization and uses messes to get there

At the organization level, then, it is process and not structure that drives action. Structure needs to come out of the process. As soon as a group is brought together to address a public health issue—tobacco control, for example—a structure will evolve to address the issue. In **Figure 4-10**, Rogers shows graphically that the phenomenon of organizations starts with the interrelationship between structures and systems organized around the processes needed to carry out action.

From organizations and their processes of change, the individual and especially the leader develop identity through the organizing process, from the information collected and from the relationships as they develop to how they affect action. Rogers adds the important level of meaning, action, and trust because these activities create the capacity for change and evolving organizations. To gain clarification on Rogers, who is an international consultant on complexity in organizations, a Public Health Quiz appears in Case Study 4-C. Exercise 4-4 shows how groups change as a result of new members entering the discussion.

LEADING AND COMPLEXITY

As the events of September 11, 2001, demonstrated, unanticipated events sometimes occur. Complexity science has emerged in recent years as a new methodology for dealing with the chaos and complexity of the modern world. Chaos theory is sometimes viewed as the next iteration of systems theory, with complexity science being the next point on the continuum.

Systems theory is based on nonlinearity.[71] However, it does not seem to explore critically the process of small changes leading to large effects. This latter point was a critical aspect of chaos theory. It is chaos theory

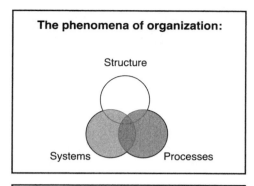

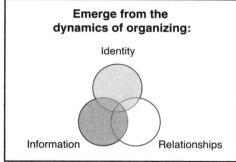

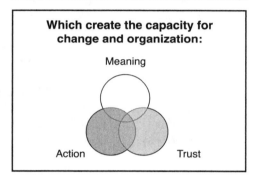

FIGURE 4-10 Complexity and Organizations.
Source: Reprinted with the permission of Myron E. Rogers.

that argued that chaotic systems seem to develop according to verifiable rules or equations. Complexity science goes the next step. There are three system states: chaotic, stable, and a zone of adaptability somewhere between these two extremes.[72] In addition, systems can change.

Another aspect of complexity thinkers is that they focus on the interactions between individual agents in the system and monitor their effects on the system as a whole. There is also a strong belief that order will arise out of chaotic times. However, it is not always possible to determine what that new order will be, but self-organization is the basic characteristic of the universe.[73] Self-organizing groups come into being during periods of bounded instability when the outcomes of a crisis or event are infinite.[74] Complexity theory

should prove useful to those leaders who struggle with the changes that the terrorist events of 2001 have brought.

The new leaders and managers will have to learn the skills of managing the unknowable.[75] When a system is undergoing dynamic change, it is not possible to study the system in terms of its parts. The dynamic system affects all the participants in it in ways that may not be predictable. It almost seems that the system is operating out of control. The traditional archetypes don't seem to apply. The public health leader needs to think in terms of whole systems and interconnections between one system and another, and also view the patterns of behavior that the disorder creates in individuals. The leader has to observe the small changes that may change the whole system. Details within the system are often distracting. With the changes that complexity brings, new leadership strategies will be needed. Seven approaches can be taken:[76]

- The first approach relates to the change in the way a prepared public health leader gets the managers in an agency or the partners in a community collaboration to change their mental model concerning control. A traditional approach to trying to deal with an organizational or community challenge is to increase awareness that these unexpected challenges often require innovative and sometimes either organization-wide or community-wide involvement in a possible solution. Old rules and approaches may not work. How does the manager or leader control a situation that may not have traditional rules and regulations to guide the process?
- The second approach is tied to the first and relates to the issue of power. In working collaboratively on a problem solution, existing power relationships may need to be changed to allow for a sharing of power and leadership in the solution. Conflict may also be critical in order to explore all possible issues related to resolving the unexpected occurrence.
- The third approach requires that problem solving and decision making be done in self-organizing learning teams. Self-organization may well involve individuals' opinions and judgments about who should be on the team relative to the skills and contributions that will be required to deal with the event.[77] These teams will have to define their goals and objectives for the crisis and its possible resolution.
- The fourth approach adds the complex issue of multidisciplinary or multiple cultural group involvement. It is often difficult to create a common culture

A Public Health Practice Quiz for Myron Rogers

1. How do systems thinking and complexity thinking differ?

Complexity theory is a subset of systems theory. When thinking about organizational life, it's most useful to consider living systems theory, as opposed to cybernetics, which is fundamentally about machines as systems. Systems thinking is a way of understanding the phenomenon of life as an interrelated, interconnected, dynamic whole. Life is a pattern of relationships, and more precisely a network of patterns of relationships. The old mechanistic view of the world was answering the question "What is a thing made of?" Systems thinking seeks to answer the question "How is a thing made?" This is a shift in thinking from things to processes; from parts to the whole; from linear, predictable steps to nonlinear, unpredictable outcomes; from analysis of substance to seeing patterns; from neat and nested hierarchies to messy and dynamic networks; from matter to relationships; from control to order.

If systems theory explores the process nature of wholes, complexity theory seeks to understand how patterns emerge from networks, and how order emerges in a system. Scientists have long noted that over time, the evolution of a living system and its environment produces more complex patterns, relationships, and networks. This creates the ability of a system to respond to complexity in its environment in a way that preserves the system, even as the system changes itself to preserve itself. The basic question in complexity theory is, "What are the simple rules that allow a system to continually self-organize into higher levels of complexity, capable of better response to an unpredictable environment over time?"

An understanding of complexity theory allows us to see how the dynamic patterns of a system come into being. I would say that complexity theory is actually a theory about simplicity. We seek to understand the simple rules that, when freely iterated over time, produce the ability to respond to complex environments and adapt successfully. The understanding of adaptation—how a system learns, grows, and thrives—is a central feature of complexity theory.

Consider for a moment the difference in applying either the mechanistic view of the world or the complexity view of the world. A mechanistic approach seeks to control the parts of the system. In organizational life, this translates into the imposition of rules, regulations, policies, procedures, micro-measurement, and micro-management. The outcome over time is complex bureaucracies with little ability to respond quickly to new information or new events in the environment. In the complexity view, the focus is on adaptation and learning, and therefore focuses on some simple rules or conditions that, iterated over time, create greater access and systemwide intelligence and enable coherent responses. In a mechanistic approach, you could look at the policy manual of an organization as the history of mistakes people have made, and each time a mistake was made, a rule was created to make sure no one else ever makes the same mistake. In a complex adaptive systems view, the essential need is to foster open networks of relationships, based on a shared sense of who we really are and what we are trying to do, and allow immediate response to whatever arises, then distributing the learning, as feedback, across the network, creating greater capacity for responsiveness in the future.

2. Why is relationship building so critical to organizational change?

It is the quality of the relationship within and across the system that determines the system's access to information, its ability to respond coherently to the challenges it faces, and its ability to learn, grow, and develop.

I worked with the U.S. Army back in the 1990s. A challenge for the Army is how to create the capacity for rapid decision making and action in local units in response to immediate conditions, while still serving the objectives of the whole. The Army recognized that traditional command and control would not serve it in a time of confusion and complexity in the battle theater—it's too slow and cumbersome and relies on limited intelligence (that of a small group of leaders). How do you create this capacity for rapid response from which emerges coordinated, systemwide action? The answer lies in the development of a coherent identity, built on a shared view of what is significant, what really matters, and how we should act. But this identity cannot be imposed. Meaning is constructed, not dictated. Individual soldiers have a local experience and make sense of it based on their own interpretation. So, we might have a shared experience in an event, but we don't make sense of it in a way that will create shared meaning of its significance. This results in fragmented learning, and therefore fragmented, incoherent action over time, and ultimately, a fragmented identity, based on where you sit.

In any experience, each person holds a different and unique view of what transpired. And each person is wrong in the sense that his or her view is incomplete. We need to tap into the range of experience people have, and construct a shared view of the event, in order to tap into the intelligence that is everywhere in the system. Our ability to tap into this intelligence is a function of the quality of our relationships. If we believe that information has a hierarchy, that the captain's experience is of greater value than the private's, we'll lose information that is critical to our learning, and therefore our ability to adapt to changing circumstances. Creating a quality of relationship that invites people's experience without judgment, evaluation, or blame is essential to creating a learning organization. When evaluation is present, learning is absent.

It is the quality of our relationships across hierarchies, roles, and divisions that determines our access to information that is within the system. Access to the information and intelligence in the system determines our ability to learn and to create the freedom to act in response to what really matters. This is the key capacity of high-performing organizations.

3. What factors cause governmental agencies to change from traditional mechanistic organizations to systems-based organizations?

One clarification here: governmental agencies are systems and operate following the dynamics of life, whether we choose to acknowledge it or not. When we are operating mechanistically, we are working against these dynamics. The dynamics of life—self-organizing, self-generating, emergent networks of relationships, fed by information—are unstoppable. When we work mechanistically, we only predictably create unintended consequences. We then spend our energy trying to fix what showed up that we did not intend, and we become focused on the unintended, rather than on what we need and what to be.

So, what would cause a governmental agency to shift its view of how to get the results it wants from a mechanistic to a systems approach? I think there are many possible answers to this question, but the one I most frequently hear from my clients, who are leaders of complex organizations, is their awareness that more is possible. That no matter how well they've done, they haven't really tapped into the potential of their people. They are seeking a better way, a simpler way, a way that results in greater service to all their stakeholders. They set off on a path of inquiry, willing to explore new possibilities and new ideas, and have a willingness to experiment.

Of course, sometimes what creates this shift is crisis or failure in the system. As the organization becomes more rule bound, over time it reaches a kind of inertia, unable to act reliably and rapidly to sudden shifts in the environment. People have two common reactions at this point—do what we've been doing with more force (use a bigger hammer), or consider what the source of problem is. Once you go beyond trying to manage and control the phenomena and ask the question "What is the source of this problem?" new options for organizing become possible.

4. Do leaders need special knowledge, talents, and skills to work in a complexity environment?

Well, yes and no. I would say leaders everywhere need to focus on certain talents and skills that they've neglected if they've been leading mechanistically, through command and control. And, they need to let go of some qualities they've been rewarded for inappropriately.

I believe most importantly that certain qualities of character are essential for leading in these times. One is humility. Another is compassion. A leader in public education once defined these for me in the most compelling way:

Compassion is when I realize you don't have the whole picture.
Humility is when I realize I don't either.

This sense that we need each other, that we each possess a piece of the picture, that none of us knows it all, creates a willingness to be curious and engage people everywhere in finding a shared understanding of what matters and why. I think great leaders possess these qualities in their DNA. They've shed the heroic ideals of leaders having all the answers and saving people. This heroic, mechanistic model leads to robbing people of their own competence. Many leaders trap themselves and limit their people by moving every problem up the hierarchy, to be solved above and far away from the problem, and then impose the solution in linear steps. Leaders who create true organizational capacity hold their people in the problem long enough and well enough for them to find their own solution, and regain their own competence. They see their role as nurturing relationships, connecting people to each other around questions and work that matters, and thereby connecting the system to more of itself.

Of course, this can require some special skills. Some knowledge of high-engagement, high-participation processes that bring the whole system into the room is useful. Some self-mastery that allows the leader to hold people in the space of exploration and chaos longer than they are comfortable being there, long enough for new ideas and insights to develop, is helpful. And finally, a willingness to hold the organization in new processes and ways of working together long enough for people to regain their sense of competence is essential.

(*Continues*)

I'd add to this a good dose of curiosity. Curiosity drives the desire to truly explore the source of a problem or challenge, and motivates the leader to seek answers everywhere in the system. This act alone is a powerful impetus for change.

5. Why are the three levels of change in your phenomena of organizational change so important?

This model of change helps people understand how change works and why it doesn't. It is a powerful tool for understanding the source of an issue or problem.

At the phenomenal level, we're dealing with the material form of organization—the stuff we can see and touch. Our mechanistic heritage says that this is where change should be made. For instance, if the organization isn't working right, it must be because the structure is wrong. So, we move chairs, create new and more or less complicated arrangements, in an attempt to align the parts of the system. If we do this right, the parts will add up to a whole that is what we want.

But is this anyone's experience? Structural, materialistic change has been the route for 50 years or more, and the pace of this kind of change is accelerating. Yet, when we examine what happens with structural change, the only predictable outcome is unintended consequences. What is the source of the unintended consequences we experience?

I suggest that the source of the unintended consequences is how a new structure is taken up by the "dynamics of organizing" in the next level of the model. When we change a structure, we are not just changing where people sit and who they report to—we are challenging their identity. What I've come to see as important, how I've learned to contribute, and what I've been valued for is now disrupted. The network of relationships I've built that helps me do work that matters is shattered, and now information that is essential is lost. This usually results in resistance. The source of the resistance is my sense of my identity being threatened or rejected. Now, I'm seen as a resistor, and additional pressure is applied to me. Leadership chants a mantra: "People resist change." But this is not so. People resist being changed.

If we are working with the dynamics of organizing, then we are seeking to engage everyone in developing a shared view of what matters and why, what works, and what doesn't. As our collective sense of what is truly significant grows, our ability to take right action in the moment expands. This shifts the work of leadership to connecting the system to more of itself. The work is about nurturing the network of relationships, accessing the intelligence and information in the system, and generating a shared sense of identity. It's about deciding how we belong together. The ability to make meaning that is coherent across the system grows, liberating intelligent action everywhere in the system. Learning thrives; adaptation is possible without command and control.

This model provides a good map for understanding what is really happening in the organization, and why. It can be a path into the source of intelligence or the cause of stupidity in our collective actions. Just work with it from where you are. Start anywhere, but follow it everywhere.

---

or a consensus solution when different groups are affected differently by the solutions proposed. If external experts are brought into the group as consultants or facilitators, the proposed solutions to these challenges will also be affected. Control, power, and decision making are all affected by the composition of the problem-solving body.

- In the fifth approach, the prepared public health leader takes a sometimes calculated risk in sharing control and power with others. Creative solutions may lead to revolutionary change. It may not be possible to determine the creativity of a solution until after the event has been managed.[78] The issue of how much risk the leader is taking is difficult to evaluate when an event and its outcome are unpredictable and when the future seems to be unknowable because the old ways of doing things have changed. The question becomes whether any sort of preparation is possible.

- The sixth strategy points to the need to improve group learning skills as a prerequisite to addressing the unknowable.[79] If we apply the learning organization perspective, then we can extend the perspective to argue that each team can determine the training and other tools that will expedite its work. Training should not be a one-shot deal. Because of the complexity of the world and the unpredictability of events, learning must be ongoing.

- The final approach involves the critical leadership concern related to the time factor.[80] It is impossible to predict how long it will take to address an unexpected event. Discussion and experimentation take time. It is necessary for a leader to give slack to the team so that it can carry out its work. The prepared public health leader has to determine how much slack time can realistically be allowed. The leader has to maintain stable equilibrium in times of complexity when the team needs learning time as well.[81]

Stacy summarized these reasons for a complexity approach to systemic problem solving as a way to better indicate how organizations and communities create conditions for spontaneous self-organization to generate emergent outcomes to crisis situations or other unpredictable events.

A SHORT NOTE ON THE FLATTENING WORLD

Collaborations are changing on a daily basis. Technology is changing the ways we expand our collective capabilities and creativity to create change, innovations, growth, and new measures of success. With the growing concern on the spread of infectious diseases around the world and the potential effect of the spread of these diseases in the United States, public health leaders have become concerned about the global nature of public health and its eventual effect on public health at the local level. It is thanks to technology and specifically the ability to collectively share information through the Internet that many of our discussions on systems and complexity are evolving to a new level of development. Friedman has discussed 10 forces that he believes are affecting our perspective on all the work done in the business and the governmental sector.[81] The first force relates to two events in 1989 that changed the world as we know it: the fall of the Berlin Wall and the development of the personal computer and the Windows 3.0 operating system. Communication between the peoples of the world changed, and by 1995, the World Wide Web expanded the connections of people in ways previously unknown (flattener 2). The other flatteners included workflow and community-developed software, uploading, outsourcing, off-shoring, supply-chaining, insourcing, informing, and numerous other types of technological development. One of my colleagues has developed an online course. Students sign up for the course and do all the work of the course online. My colleague can respond to the students on a regular basis from anywhere in the world, including a French café.

As the world shrinks, public health professionals are beginning to track diseases around the world on the Internet and with public health colleagues worldwide. The term "Wikinomics" was coined to describe how mass collaborations are possible and how these new forms of collaboration in a complex world are affecting leadership in public health.[82] In fact, the Internet now allows anyone to participate in the activities of the world in ways he or she never could before. In discussing Wikinomics, Tapscott and Williams use the term "peer production" to refer to the new possibilities for people joining together on the Web and addressing any issue of concern.[83] The online encyclopedia Wikipedia allows anyone to add or delete information from a specific entry. YouTube can be used to share videos on various subjects. Second Life allows you to test new ideas in a second-life world where you can be whoever you want to be. Many other examples can be given to demonstrate that all our institutions and organizations will be affected by these changes in technology. Leadership in a complex world will be different.

SUMMARY

The world as we know it has changed significantly since 2001. This chapter has looked at traditional organizations and the shifts that are occurring in public health as we move to a community- and systems-based view of the work that we do. Our systems perspectives are also being affected by an increasing understanding of the role of chaos and complexity in our lives. This is clearly a period of development in the conceptualization of all the elements of importance in the understanding of complexity, self-organization, and emergence.[84] Edward de Bono argues caution as these changes occur.[85] The decisions we make need to be simple even in a complex world. People have trouble understanding complex and convoluted decisions. It is important that we strive for simple explanations without much jargon if we are to be successful leaders.

DISCUSSION QUESTIONS

1. Explain public health in the context of a complex adaptive system.
2. What is a learning organization, and what is the role of a leader in it?
3. What are the five disciplines of the learning organization?
4. What are "Presence" and "Theory U"?
5. Describe the differences between traditional linear organizations and systems-based organizations.
6. What is complexity thinking, and how does it relate to systems thinking?
7. Explain the four components of the systems-organizing model of vision, structure, learning, and action.
8. What are social entrepreneurs?
9. How are systems thinking, complexity thinking, and leadership affected by a flattening world?

EXERCISE 4-1: Childhood Obesity and Systems Thinking

Purpose: to examine the difference in solving a public health issue from a public health perspective and from a community systems perspective

Key concepts: traditional linear thinking, systems thinking, meta-leadership

Procedure: Childhood obesity is becoming an epidemic in the United States. Your county has seen a 20% increase in childhood obesity cases in the past five years. Your local health department decides to create a public health intervention to address the problem. Internal staff meet to come up with a program plan for the project. Professor McDavid from the local university feels that the proposed initiative of the local health department is too narrow and that childhood obesity needs to be seen as a systems problem that needs countywide attention with many different stakeholders involved.

1. Divide the class or training group into teams of 8 to 10. Half the teams will develop a program from only a public health agency perspective, and half the teams from a systems perspective working across agencies.
2. Spend an hour devising the strategy and plan for your team.
3. Present the plan to the group as a whole.
4. Discuss the differences in the two types of plans.

EXERCISE 4-2: Systems Archetypes

Purpose: to use systems archetypes for public health issues

Key concepts: systems archetypes, drifting goals, escalation, fixes that fail, growth and underinvestment, limits to success, shifting the burden, success to be successful, tragedy of the commons

Procedures: Divide the class or training group into groups of 8 to 10. Apply each scenario to the system archetype. You can make any assumptions necessary to better understand how archetypes work.

System Archetype	Scenario
Drifting Goals	You decide to go on a diet to lose 50 pounds. After a year, you lose 25 pounds. You lower your diet goal.
Escalation	A smoking coalition talks to a local theater owner about instituting a no-smoking policy in the theater bar. The local health department tobacco control department head is threatened.
Fixes That Fail	Teenage pregnancy rates in a community are increasing. A condom distribution plan is initiated in the local high school. Rates decline for six months and then increase again.
Growth and Underinvestment	A million dollars is given to your community to build capacity to address potential disasters. Six months into the process, your budget is cut by a third.
Limits to Growth or Success	The federal government allocates funds to local public health agencies to make them prepared to handle bioterrorism events. Training occurs. A bioterrorism event occurs.
Shifting the Burden	In the community with an increasing rate of teenage pregnancy, the short-term solution of condom distribution does not alleviate the problem. The high school develops a program to increase self-esteem.
Success to Be Successful	You have been promoted to director of your local health department. The promotion means you will be away from home four nights a week. How do you balance work and family responsibilities?
Tragedy of the Commons	There is a flu vaccine shortage. You hear that 100 shots will be given at the local high school on Saturday. You go on Saturday. Everyone else has the same idea.

EXERCISE 4-3: Organizational and Community Collaborative Skills

Purpose: to explore the different types of management and leadership skills to work inside a public health agency and the skills necessary to work collaboratively with external stakeholders

Key concepts: management, leadership, meta-leadership, collaboration, talents, linear thinking, systems thinking

Procedure: Divide the training group or class into small groups of six to eight people. Each group will get a large piece of flip chart paper and a colored marker. Half the groups will create a list of the talents and skills necessary to be a manager/leader inside a public health agency. Half the groups will create a similar list for leaders working collaboratively with external stakeholders. Groups will present their list to the group or class as a whole. Comparisons of the lists will then be made.

EXERCISE 4-4: Complexity Through Rotation

Purpose: to examine how the rotation of people in a group changes its internal dynamics

Key concepts: complexity, relationships, self-organizing systems

Procedure: All people need to be organized into groups of 8 to 10. Start your work on this exercise by discussing the following question: How are these times of stress affecting you personally? After 10 to 15 minutes, have one of the people in your group move to another group and someone from another group move into your group. The next question is, "How difficult is it to work across departments in this agency [students can answer this question by talking about difficulties in working in different groups in different classes], and what can we do about it?" After 10 to 15 minutes, the rotation is done again, and the next questions are, "Do we work in ways that support interconnectedness rather than separateness? How can we break down our silos?" After another 15 minutes, rotate again and answer the question, "If public health is a system, how does our agency reflect the systems needs of our state?" After 10 to 15 minutes, there is a final rotation, with the question, "How do we improve our relationships with our community partners?" Debrief the exercise after the 15-minute discussion.

REFERENCES

1. Institute of Medicine, *The Future of Public Health* (Washington, DC: National Academies Press, 1988).
2. G. H. Eoyang, "Public Health and Human Systems Dynamics: What Can We Learn from Each Other?" *In Complexity Science in Practice: Understanding and Acting to Improve Health and Healthcare* (Allentown, PA: Plexus Institute, 2003).
3. J. O'Connor and I. McDermott, *The Art of Systems Thinking* (London: Thorsons, 1997).
4. N. Weiner, *Cybernetics* (Cambridge, MA: MIT Press, 1948).
5. N. Weiner, *The Human Use of Human Beings* (Boston: Houghton Mifflin, 1950).
6. L. von Bertalanffy, *General Systems Theory* (New York: Braziller, 1968).
7. J. W. Forrester, *Industrial Dynamics* (London: Productivity Press [Taylor and Francis], 1961).
8. C. W. Churchman, *The Systems Approach* (New York: Laurel Books, 1970).
9. P. M. Senge, *The Fifth Discipline* (New York: Doubleday, 2006).
10. Senge, *The Fifth Discipline.*
11. D. H. Meadows, *Thinking in Systems* (White River Junction, VT: Chelsea Green, 2008).
12. L. Rowitz, *Public Health in the 21st Century: The Prepared Leader* (Sudbury, MA: Jones & Bartlett, 2006).
13. P. Senge, C. O. Scharmer, J. Jaworski, and B. S. Flowers, *Presence* (Cambridge, MA: Society for Organizational Learning, 2004).
14. Senge, *The Fifth Discipline.*
15. C. O. Scharmer, *Theory U* (Cambridge, MA: Society for Organizational Learning, 2007).
16. D. Cabrera, *Knowledge Age Operating System: Four Principles of Project Design, Version 1.0 Workbook* (Loveland, CO: Project N Press, 2001).
17. A. Best, P. I. Clark, S. J. Leischow, and W. M. K. Trochim, *Greater Than the Sum: Systems Thinking in Tobacco Control* (Washington, DC: National Cancer Institute, Tobacco Control Monograph Series, 18).
18. J. M. Kouzes and B. Z. Posner, *The Leadership Challenge*, 4th ed. (San Francisco: Jossey-Bass, 2007).
19. M. Lipton, *Guided Growth* (Boston: Harvard Business School Press, 2003).
20. A. F. Osborn, *Your Creative Power: How to Use Imagination* (New York: Charles Scribner, 1948).
21. E. de Bono, *Six Thinking Hats* (New York: Little, Brown and Co., 1999).

22. W. K. Kellogg Foundation, *Logic Model Development Guide* (Battle Creek, MI: W. K. Kellogg Foundation, 2004).

23. M. R. Weisbord and S. Janoff, *Future Search* (San Francisco: Barrett-Kohler, 1995).

24. M. Emery and R. E. Purser, *The Search Conference* (San Francisco: Jossey-Bass, 1996).

25. I. Bens, *Facilitating with Ease* (New York: John Wiley & Sons, 2000).

26. E. Wenger, R. McDermott, and W. M. Synder, *Cultivating Communities of Practice* (Boston: Harvard Business School Press, 2002).

27. Best et al., *Greater Than the Sum: Systems Thinking in Tobacco Control.*

28. Senge, *The Fifth Discipline.*

29. D. H. Kim and V. Anderson, *Systems Archetype Basics* (Watham, MA: Pegasus Communications, 2007).

30. Rowitz, *Public Health in the 21st Century: The Prepared Leader.*

31. M. J. Wheatley, *Leadership and the New Science* (San Francisco: Berrett-Kohler, 1999).

32. R. Wagner and J. K. Harter, *12: The Elements of Great Managing* (New York: Gallup Press, 2006).

33. D. Bornstein, *How to Change the World: Social Entrepreneurs and the Power of New Ideas* (New York: Oxford University Press, 2007).

34. Best et al., *Greater Than the Sum: Systems Thinking in Tobacco Control.*

35. Best et al., *Greater Than the Sum: Systems Thinking in Tobacco Control.*

36. Centers for Disease Control and Prevention, "Framework for Program Evaluation in Public Health," *Morbidity and Mortality Weekly Report Recommendations and Reports*, 48, RR11, 1–40.

37. The Commonwealth Fund Commission on a High Performance Health System, *A High Performance Health System for the United States* (Washington, DC: The Commonwealth Fund, November 2007).

38. M. C. Jackson, *Systems Thinking* (London: John Wiley and Sons, 2003).

39. D. H. Kim, *Systems Archetypes I* (Waltham, MA: Pegasus Communications, 1992).

40. Jackson, *Systems Thinking.*

41. D. H. Kim, *Introduction to Systems Thinking* (Waltham, MA: Pegasus Communications, 1999).

42. Senge, *The Fifth Discipline.*

43. Jackson, *Systems Thinking.*

44. Senge, *The Fifth Discipline.*

45. Senge, *The Fifth Discipline.*

46. P. Senge, C. Roberts, R. B. Ross, B. J. Smith, and A. Kleiner, *The Fifth Discipline Fieldbook* (New York: Doubleday, 1994).

47. P. Senge, A. Kleiner, C. Roberts, R. Ross, G. Roth, and B. Smith, *The Dance of Change* (New York: Doubleday, 1999).

48. Kim, *Introduction to Systems Thinking.*

49. D. H. Kim, *Systems Thinking Tools* (Waltham, MA: Pegasus Communications, 1994).

50. Senge, *The Fifth Discipline.*

51. Kim, *Introduction to Systems Thinking.*

52. Kim, *Introduction to Systems Thinking.*

53. Senge et al., *The Dance of Change.*

54. Kim, *Introduction to Systems Thinking.*

55. Kim, *Introduction to Systems Thinking.*

56. Kim, *System Thinking Tools.*

57. B. Oshry, *Leading Systems* (San Francisco: Berrett-Kohler, 1999).

58. Oshry, *Leading Systems.*

59. R. Heifetz, A. Grashow, and M. Linsky, *The Practice of Adaptive Leadership* (Boston: Harvard Business Press, 2009).

60. B. Oshry, *Leading Systems.*

61. S. Goldsmith and W. D. Eggers, *Governing by Network* (Washington, DC: Brookings Institution Press, 2004).

62. J. Steffen, *Aligned Thinking* (San Francisco: Berrett-Kohler, 2006).

63. Wheatley, *Leadership and the New Science.*

64. M. J. Wheatley and M. Kellner-Rogers, *A Simpler Way* (San Francisco: Berrett-Kohler, 1996).

65. Wheatley and Kellner-Rogers, *A Simpler Way.*

66. Wheatley, *Leadership and the New Science.*

67. Wheatley and Kellner-Rogers, *A Simpler Way.*

68. M. J. Wheatley, *Turning to One Another* (San Francisco: Berrett-Kohler, 2002).

69. M. J. Wheatley, *Finding Our Way* (San Francisco: Berrett-Kohler, 2005).

70. R. Lewin and B. Regine, *Soul at Work* (New York: Simon and Schuster, 2000).

71. Lewin and Regine, *Soul at Work.*

72. R. Lewin, R. S. Kelly, and M. A. Allison, *The Complexity Advantage* (New York: McGraw-Hill, 1999).

73. F. Westley, B. Zimmerman, and M. Q. Patton, *Getting to Maybe* (Toronto, ON: Vintage Canada, 2006).

74. R. D. Stacy, *Managing the Unknowable* (San Francisco: Berrett-Kohler, 1992).

75. Stacy, *Managing the Unknowable.*

76. Stacy, *Managing the Unknowable.*

77. R. D. Stacy, *Complexity and Creativity in Organizations* (San Francisco: Berrett-Kohler, 1992).

78. Stacy, *Complexity and Creativity in Organizations.*

79. Stacy, *Complexity and Creativity in Organizations.*

80. Stacy, *Managing the Unknowable.*

81. T. L. Friedman, *The World Is Flat* (New York: Farrar, Straus, and Giroux, 2006).

82. D. Tapscott and A. D. Williams, *Wikinomics* (New York: Portfolio, 2010).

83. Tapscott and Williams, *Wikinomics.*

84. M. Mitchell, *Complexity: A Guided Tour* (New York: Oxford University Press, 2009).

85. E. de Bono, *Simplicity* (London: Penguin Books, 1999).

CHAPTER 5

The Leadership Wheel and Organizational Change

> Devote yourself to loving others, devote yourself to the community around you, and devote yourself to creating something that gives you purpose and meaning.
>
> —Morris Schwartz, *Morrie: In His Own Words*

Good leadership depends on systems thinking and an understanding of the effect of complexity. This type of thinking focuses on ways to implement, in the short and long term, system components necessary for meeting identified needs. To ensure that systems thinking is effective, public health agency leaders must support the systems perspective and make sure staff understand what is involved in a systems approach to change. Communication must be frequent enough to allow the staff to help manage the implementation of strategic policies. The leader is responsible for guiding the implementation activities and presenting to the community the steps being taken by the agency in response to local public health issues.

Team building is a critical part of leading a public health agency. The leader creates teams inside the agency and coalitions, alliances, and partnerships outside to address the programmatic needs of the agency. Once the members are appointed, the teams need to clarify the values that will guide their activities. Community coalitions, alliances, and partnerships have basic similarities to teams, and their development resembles team development.

Public health leaders must:

- think systemically and act strategically
- create a learning organization
- coordinate knowledge and performance management activities
- promote and support the change process
- support the values of the agency and the community
- understand the relationship between system inputs, program interventions, and outputs
- monitor and evaluate the effects of change

The remainder of this chapter covers the main stages in the systems approach to organizational change as represented by a leadership wheel (**Figure 5-1**). Strong leaders with a high level of commitment must serve as the conveners and inspirational voices for the

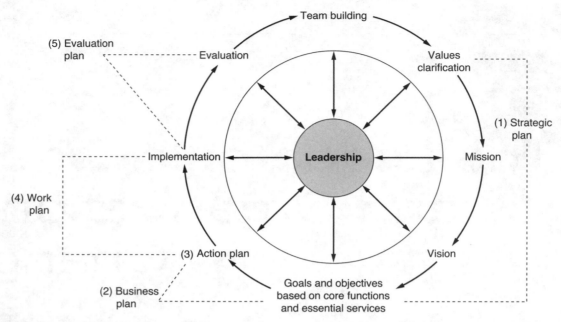

FIGURE 5-1 Systems Approach to Organizational Change (Leadership Wheel).

process. These stages include values clarification, construction or revision of the agency's mission and vision, identification of goals and objectives, development of an action plan, implementation of the action plan, and assessment of the effects of the implementation. As a systems-based working model, the leadership wheel sees the integration of planning, action, and evaluation. An important consideration in this whole process is the need to understand the assumptions that provide a foundation for all the activities that occur as part of the systems perspective for both internal and external stakeholders.[1] In actuality, we often do not have all the knowledge necessary to the understanding of a public health or programmatic need before we start to work on it. The assumptions we make will depend on whether we take a linear perspective on an issue or we take a systems perspective. This assumption approach is tied to what Churchman has called an inquiry system.[2] An inquiry system involves the process of creating a system of interrelated parts or components that provide a holistic perspective on the appropriate knowledge to address a problem or challenge.

The leadership wheel will lead to five specific products: a strategic plan, a business plan, an action plan, a work plan, and an evaluation plan. In the strategic planning phase, values, mission and vision, and goals and objectives are clarified. Moving from the formulation of goals and objectives, a business plan is developed in which the cost of programs that are developed

to implement the goals and objectives becomes critical. The goals and business plan will lead to an action plan. With implementation imminent, a work plan is devised. The evaluation plan becomes the fifth document to drive the process. Quality improvement methods and techniques are often employed as a performance measurement set of priorities. In the following sections, we will examine the stages of the leadership wheel.

VALUES CLARIFICATION

Blanchard and O'Connor make a distinction between the Fortune 500 and the Fortunate 500.[3] The latter are businesses in which management by values occurs. In the management-by-values process, which can take three years to complete, an agency goes through three stages. The first stage involves clarification of the agency's mission, values, and vision. The second stage involves communicating the agency's newly clarified mission, values, and vision to others. The final stage, which is the most complex, involves aligning the leadership and management practices of the agency with its stated values. In the case of public health leadership, the alignment of practices and values applies to the individual, team, agency, community, and professional levels.

An agency's culture is made up, in part, of the values and beliefs that the members of the agency have in common.[4] These values and beliefs guide the members' individual and collective behavior. Also part of the agency's culture are the rituals and myths that have grown out of the agency's history. For example, a myth might be created about a former administrator, who, as an avid promoter of public health in the community, might be idealized as a public health hero. Treating the administrator as a hero has its benefits, because it reaffirms the importance of health promotion. Yet it can also have a downside. For one thing, it may lead to organizational stasis, for the myth suggests that everything the administrator did, every policy decision made, is above question, and thus the current members of the agency may be more reluctant to make necessary changes than if they viewed the administrator as praiseworthy but fallible.

Agency rituals might include a special public health award given to a community organization each year at an annual luncheon. If this award is named after the former administrator, the ritual supports the myth. A new public health administrator with new ideas and a new vision for the agency will need to work with the agency staff to redefine its values, and thus the current myths and rituals—and even the agency's physical layout, which is a component of organizational culture—may need to be changed.

A value, according to Rokeach, is "an enduring belief that a specific mode of conduct or end-state of existence is personally or socially preferable to an opposite or converse mode of conduct or end-state of existence."[5(p.5)] Each community has a unique configuration and a unique set of values, and the local public health agency is a reflection of these values. Societies that are geographically and politically separated from each other tend to develop different community approaches to dealing with their particular problems.[6] For example, a county with a mostly rural population will have different public health priorities than a county with a mostly urban population. Rural health leaders often have to do more with less. They have less money, fewer staff than large urban health departments, sometimes geographic isolation, limited technical resources, lower salaries for staff, and often fewer external partners.[7] Case Study 5-A examines some of these issues as well as leadership wheel issues in a local public health response to a potential smallpox outbreak in a rural county.

Some general truths about values are worth noting. First, certain values are universal, whereas others occur only in specific locales. There is a clear recognition that there are some values that are universally

held. These universal values tend to be heterogeneous in content with some tied to our human nature and some tied to living in cultural groups. Brown has tied the study of universal value systems to both human biology and evolutionary psychology.[8] Second, values tend to be organized into value systems. Third, people generally have the values they do because of the socialization they have undergone. Fourth, values are present in every social situation.

The increasing diversification in many communities has led to changes in value systems and in some cases to a confusing diversity of values. To ensure that a system of shared values evolves, a community must undertake a process of values clarification. This type of process respects diversity but is aimed at elucidating the dominant values of the community. A vision cannot be realized unless it is built on an infrastructure of shared core values.

Credible leaders use personal values to affect their organization or community.[9] To make action activities work, leaders need to align personal values with organizational and community values. When this occurs, it is possible to push a shared values agenda. Shared values lead to finding a common ground for action. Jansen Kraemer pointed out that a values orientation enhances action.[10] The prerequisites for strong leadership from a values perspective include self-reflection, the ability to see issues from many perspectives, life balance, confidence in personal abilities, and also real humility. Twenty-four leaders from around the world and from various professions were asked to address the issue of universal values.[11] They reached a consensus that the following values were universal: love, truthfulness, fairness, freedom, unity, tolerance, responsibility, and respect for life. Some widely shared values were nonetheless not universally shared, but these were listed as well: courage, wisdom, hospitality, obedience, peace, stability, racial harmony, respect for women's place in society, and protection of the environment. In the case of American culture, two other widely shared values should be added to the list: health protection and quality of life. Americans, among others, are concerned about the effect that disease can have on quality of life. Public health leaders promote a public health agenda oriented toward improving the quality of life of people in their service communities.

Americans are also concerned about having a choice.[12] In the health reform debate in the early 1990s and again in the first decade of the 21st century, the potential for the loss of choice of medical provider (and loss of power over other aspects of medical care) was a

Case Study 5-A

Pustules Proliferate in Dairyair County—A Local Public Health Response to a Smallpox Outbreak: A Case Study in Assurance Mid-America Regional Public Health Leadership Institute, April 2003

Sue Becker, Kurt Eggebrecht, Sherry Gehl, Sue Kunferman, Jody Langfeldt, Cheryl Mazmanian, Lora Taylor

Opening/Introduction

The risk of smallpox being used by terrorists as a bio-weapon is becoming a viable threat to citizens of the United States. In the event of a smallpox outbreak, healthcare providers, emergency service personnel, and state and local governments are going to be working in a crisis mode not only to treat the victims, but to contain the outbreak and begin mass vaccination. Communities and especially individual neighborhoods may be initially left to fend for themselves during the onset of the crisis.

Ensuring that the health needs of the citizens of Dairyair County are met is the responsibility of Jo Jersey, the director/health officer of the Dairyair County Health Department. Jo is a member of Dairyair County's community response team and has been trained in the Incident Command System.

Dairyair County is located in north central Wisconsin. It has a population of 100,000 people. Farming is the main industry of the county, with eight migrant farms supplying the majority of the workforce. A number of smaller factories are located in the county, the largest of which is the Cow Pie Factory, employing 3,000 workers. The median annual income in this county is $29,000. The largest municipality in this county is the small urban center, Lodge City (40,000 population), with other surrounding rural communities making up the rest of the population. A rural newspaper, the *Dairyair Daily*, is read by most of the residents of Lodge City, with limited circulation to the rest of Dairyair County. Two local radio stations, WSPOX and WPUS, are both linked to the county emergency broadcast system.

Case Body

The county executive, Wanda Windbag, has just been notified of a $400,000 Community Preparedness Grant that has been awarded to the county to be used for bioterrorism preparedness. She is soliciting input from community leaders on how these dollars should be spent to prepare the county to respond to a bioterrorist attack. The perception of a bioterrorism event occurring in Dairyair County is believed to be so remote that most residents and local officials gave little weight to the warnings and preparations going on about them. For example, Fire Chief Blaze Arson was skeptical of the likelihood of a biological attack. He is convinced, and is working to influence county supervisors to agree, that the county's limited resources should be devoted to personal protective equipment and training for firefighters. Sheriff Sly Straightshooter believes, as a result of the training he received from the Federal Bureau of Investigation, that the likely scenario will be a car bomb at the Dairyair administration building. He is advocating for security badges for all county employees and that bomb reduction film be placed on the windows of the administration building. The executive of General Hospital, Mavis Moneypenny, has contacted the governor expressing concerns regarding the hospital's lack of sufficient decontamination equipment and negative pressure rooms and is advocating for funding to improve the situation. Although the hospital is supportive of the local health department's planning effort, the hospital's lack of resources makes it incapable of fulfilling its role. Cricket Copyright, the aggressive reporter of the *Dairyair Daily*, is pressuring County Executive Windbag to disclose how these limited resources will be used.

Jo Jersey, aware of the real risk to the community in the event of a bioterrorism event, particularly a smallpox outbreak, had been working closely with the state and the Centers for Disease Control and Prevention (CDC) on educating and vaccinating her staff. Plans were being developed to educate the other members of the Incident Command Team and the political leaders regarding the unique issues the community would face in a biological emergency. Tommy Tabletop, the Dairyair county director of emergency management, has not embraced the recommendations of Jo Jersey to sponsor a biological incident exercise due to his limited knowledge and lack of understanding regarding bioterrorism issues.

As the discussion and political wrangling continued, on January 1, 2003, a woman from Lodge City walked into the local emergency department (ED) with a four-day history of fever, malaise, headache, and severe backache. She was exhibiting a pustule-type rash covering most of her extremities and face. As usual for a holiday, the ED was very busy, with at least 45 people present. Two days following the woman's presentation in the ED, a family of four, mom, dad, and two children, walked into the local health clinic exhibiting the same symptoms. The clinic was busy, with 28 people in the waiting room and a staff of 10. After much testing and significantly more exposure, the tentative diagnosis was variola major, better known as smallpox. During the next 48 hours, 10 more people in Dairyair

County were tentatively diagnosed with smallpox. The suspect smallpox patients were either quarantined at home, or for those requiring hospitalization, placed in an isolation area in the local hospital.

The unexpected had occurred. Local health officials began working on a plan to vaccinate all the citizens of Dairyair County. The CDC had released the vaccine. With more and more cases of smallpox presenting every day, it was imperative that the entire population be vaccinated. Never had the community faced this type of emergency, a biological one.

Within 48 hours and the diagnosis of 20 cases of smallpox, the community was in a panic. Clinic and hospital staff were afraid to go to work. The school superintendent, following a recommendation from Jo Jersey, closed all schools. Absenteeism in all workplaces was at an all-time high. People were isolating themselves and their families. The shelves in the stores were emptying fast. Following the advice of Jo Jersey, Tommy Tabletop activated the Incident Command Center and delegated the leadership role to Jo Jersey. Under Jo's leadership, it became clear that this was a public health emergency that would require a nontraditional approach by the community emergency response team in Dairyair County.

Utilizing the state and the CDC mass vaccination protocols, clinics were established throughout Dairyair County. Jo assigned Tommy Tabletop the task of recruiting and organizing medical and nonmedical volunteers to assist with these clinics. Sheriff Straightshooter was assigned the role of public information officer. A community moratorium was ordered on public events. An emergency communications network was established. The CDC website was recommended as the source for information on smallpox. In addition, working with the media partners, municipal leaders assured the community that sufficient vaccine had been acquired to immunize all of the citizens of Dairyair County, and it would be made available to residents at multiple immunization clinics throughout the county. Chief Arson was assigned to work with the coroner's office and the hospitals to ensure the appropriate handling of the deceased.

Seventy-two hours after the first case of smallpox was diagnosed, the first of many vaccination clinics occurred. Clinics were set up on a daily basis at numerous sites around the county. An exhaustive public awareness campaign on the need to be vaccinated was launched throughout the county. After a 10-day vaccination effort, with no additional residents presenting for vaccination, it was determined that only 75,000 smallpox vaccinations were provided, leaving 25,000 citizens unprotected and unreached by the vaccination efforts.

Source: Courtesy of the Mid-America Regional Public Health Leadership Institute.

critical factor in the defeat of the Clinton plan but lives again in the healthcare reform legislation of this new century. It almost became more important than the potential benefits of universal health care. To partially fill out the list of American cultural values, Americans are preoccupied with the biggest and newest consumer products, pursue dreams even when the chance of success is slight, are impatient, and tend to improvise in the making of changes. All these need to be taken into account in designing public health policies. It is interesting to examine the Commonwealth Fund report on the future of the American healthcare system because many of the issues discussed in the Clinton health plan were incorporated into the Patient Protection and Affordable Care Act passed by Congress during the Obama administration in 2010.

Shared values play an important role in any reform of the public health system. Exercise 5-1 is intended to illuminate the relationships among personal, professional, organizational, and community values.

Public health leaders, as protectors of the values of the agency and the community, must emphasize the importance of maintaining high ethical standards inside the agency and in the community. One necessary task is to do an ethics check. Are the procedures used in the agency and the community legal? And even if they are legal, are they consistent with the values of the agency and the community? Leaders also need to examine the relationship between the science of public health, the facts that guide public health practice, and the explicit knowledge that comes from our formal learning.[13] As can be seen in **Figure 5-2**, which evolved from my discussion with Dr. Patrick Lenihan, the 2003 president of the National Association of County and City Health Officials, the science and explicit knowledge dimension of a public health system needs to be understood in relationship to the experiences, action activities, and tacit knowledge that grow out of practice and internal agency learning and operations. Tacit knowledge is difficult to communicate because it

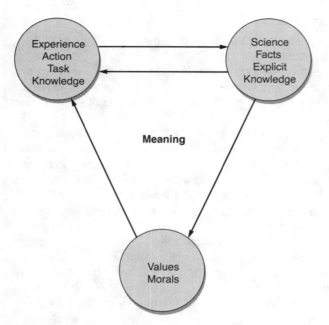

FIGURE 5-2 Leadership and Meaning.

involves the internal understandings of people to the experiences they have filtered through their personal values and beliefs. The science and experience dimensions are quite interactive but derive meaning after being screened by our values positions. It is not knowledge, experience, or values alone that are important—it is the meaning that is attached to these activities. Leaders and managers have the critical role of translating tacit knowledge into explicit knowledge so that there is meaning in these events for internal and external stakeholders. This translation helps the organization address similar problems in the future.

Public health leaders, besides identifying values, must consider how these values will affect the implementation of programs. They should be aware that the process of values clarification can simplify the solution of many local public health issues. Following is a list of strategies for leaders for clarifying values and promoting them in the agency and community:

- Learn which values are universal (or nearly universal) and promulgate them in the community.
- Learn which additional values prevail in the community and in the agency.
- In conjunction with agency members and community partners, integrate universal, community, and agency values.
- Evaluate prevailing values and revise those that need to be changed.
- Develop a shared values statement.

MISSION AND VISION

Leaders need to be oriented toward the future and help create the vision that guides the activities of the agency. They must also inspire their colleagues to share the vision and use it to guide their activities. Therefore, the next task after values clarification is to evaluate both the agency's mission and the current vision for the agency (or create a new one).

An agency's mission and the vision must reflect each other. A vision is a picture of what, according to its leaders, the agency's future should be like. The agency's mission is the role it sees itself playing in the community. If the vision and mission truly reflect each other, then the agency, in fulfilling its mission, will help realize its vision (i.e., help bring about the kind of future it desires).

In addition, public health, like other areas of society, is changing rapidly, and an agency's vision and mission must change in concert. For example, disaster preparedness and response, public–private partnerships, emerging infections, drug resistance, mental health, community violence, and health reform are issues, some newer than others, that public health must address. A public health agency's mission statement must be revised periodically to take into account new problems, changing priorities, or other developments that have occurred in the public health arena. Agencies are also affected by many different constituencies as well as a number of elected officials, which makes the development of an agency vision much more complicated than it would be in the business world.[14] However, the agency mission may be defined by state or local statutes.

An organization's mission defines its purpose—its reason for existing.[15] A standard mission for a public health agency is the promotion of health and the prevention of disease. If an agency views itself as having this mission, then it should not be primarily involved in providing direct services with a strong medical orientation. During the past two decades, health departments have stopped doing most direct service activities. Community health centers, hospitals, drug stores, and a number of big box stores like Walmart and Target have begun delivering immunizations and other primary care services.

A mission statement can be short or long. It can be a statement of the agency's general purpose, or it can detail the agency's role in several areas. According to Wall and colleagues, a mission statement needs to answer four questions:[16]

1. What is the purpose of public health?
2. How does the public health agency intend to coordinate its values and actions?
3. Who makes up the constituencies of the agency?
4. How does the agency link the present with the future?

Pearce and David claimed that a mission statement should address such things as the customer market (community), service-related issues, geographic concerns (global, national, state, or local), the level of technology, the requirements of agency survival, the personal concerns of the agency's leaders, the agency's philosophy, and the image of the agency in the community.[17] Albrecht recommended addressing the environment of competitors, economic concerns, political concerns, legal concerns, and social issues.[18] Wilson cautioned that a mission statement may leave out critical organizational activities, which sometimes shrivel financially and programmatically if not included in the mission.[19]

A mission statement should be inspiring, for the public health agency's workforce needs to embrace the mission.[20] Getting the staff members to do this could be difficult, because many of them have a minimal background in public health. Many will have been hired to perform clinical functions rather than engage in community-oriented preventive activities.

The mission is an important determinant of the agency's goals and objectives and should be closely tied to the agency's action plan. Therefore, the agency leaders must communicate the mission to community partners and constituents as well as to the agency workforce.[21] One strategy is to ask partners and constituents to read the mission statement in order to evaluate its clarity.

There is a question whether the mission or vision should be developed first. Typically, a public health agency has a clear idea of its mission but an undeveloped vision of its future. In a case like this, the mission is virtually given and the vision is what must be worked on. Sometimes an organization's mission and vision are both treated in a single statement that covers the present and the future. For example, the public health mission enunciated in *Healthy People in Healthy Communities* can also be viewed as a vision of the future.[22]

As pointed out earlier, managers are focused on protecting the integrity of their organization, whereas leaders are visionary and committed to change. Therefore, leaders can often benefit from developing their visioning skills. A vision can be likened to a blank canvas on which the leader sketches a possible future.

Although a vision statement is about the future, it is often written in the present tense, which is one method of expressing the strong connection between the "now" and the "then." Lipton has developed a vision framework for leaders.[23] The core for building the vision includes organizational and/or community values, the mission of the agency, and strategy tactics. The leader needs to carefully select an executive team for implementing the vision. There also need to be methods that will maintain a growth-oriented perspective for the agency and, finally, techniques for managing people and getting buy-in for the vision.

Two cautionary notes: First, leaders are responsible for more than creating a vision. They need to motivate others and to play a major role in the development of action plans. Second, leaders may need to give up power in order to bring the vision into reality.[24] For example, they may be required to make changes to the organizational chart.

Following is a brief description of one method for developing a vision statement. First, the visioning team lays out the values and principles that will guide the visioning process. Second, the team develops a glossary of terms to go along with the shared mission statement. Third, it includes key constituents in the visioning process. Fourth, it describes the functions of a vision statement and how the vision statement to be created will be used. Fifth, the visioning team discusses the future and where it wants public health activities to go. (The team should consider scenarios likely to occur if the agency moves in certain directions. Scenario building is an important step in the visioning process.) Next, the team redefines terms and relates them to concepts in the glossary. Then it devises a vision statement based on the work it has done. The construction is followed by general editing, which occurs in smaller teams. The final step is to reach a consensus on the vision statement. Of course, once the vision statement is agreed upon, it is necessary to audit progress toward the implementation of the vision.

Following is a summary of the steps public health leaders need to take in order to develop a mission and vision for their agencies:

- Use a mission statement to guide the daily activities of the public health agency.
- Create a vision statement to guide the activities of the agency as it moves forward in time.
- Use visioning skills to create the vision.
- Involve colleagues and community partners in the development of a shared mission and vision.

- Develop a glossary of public health terms for colleagues and community partners.
- Review the mission and vision statements yearly.

Mission and vision are also affected by whether the leader is a traditional thinker who defines public health in a narrow sense as tied to the programmatic activities of the governmental public health agency or more systemically from the perspective of the community as a whole. Because leaders often work from the inside of their agency to the outside and also recognize the possibilities and concerns of external stakeholders as an outside-to-inside approach, the practice of action inquiry needs to occur.[25] Action inquiry is a systems activity of transformational leaders that should lead to mutual approaches to addressing public health challenges. It is through action inquiry that knowledge and action will come together.

GOALS AND OBJECTIVES

The next task in the systems approach to organizational change is to translate the mission and the vision into measurable goals and objectives. The mission statement is framed in general terms and does not contain the details of how the mission is to be fulfilled. Nor does the vision statement lay out how the vision is to be realized. Goals are more specific than either the mission or vision, and objectives are more specific still. They are, so to speak, the individual steps on the way to fulfilling the mission and realizing the vision.

Goals can be classified in several ways. One distinction is between organizational goals, which the activities of the organization are intended to achieve, and order goals, which are pursued as a means of preventing certain events from happening.[26] Organizational goals can be further divided into the stated goals of an organization and the actual, sometimes hidden, goals of the organization. Creating a fit between organizational goals and systems goals is an important leadership activity. Goals can also be classified in terms of the areas of human activity to which they pertain, as seen in the division between economic, cultural, social, and political goals.

Objectives are the quantitatively and qualitatively measurable steps needed to achieve the goals of the organization. Along with the goals, they are used to guide the managerial processes for which public health agency leaders are responsible. The goals and objectives also need to reflect the vision of the agency and

community, or the vision or goals need to be revised. Specifically, the leader then has the responsibility for:

- translating the agency's mission and vision into programmatic goals and objectives
- discovering any hidden goals that may sabotage activities (action inquiry)
- considering the budgetary requirements necessary to realize the goals and objectives
- examining goals to determine if they are translatable into action

Exercise 5-2 explores the relationship between an organization's mission, vision, and goals and objectives, which are key components of a strategic plan.

THE ACTION PLAN

The next step is to develop an action plan for achieving the goals and objectives identified in the preceding stage. The action plan, which can include the key components of a business plan, consists of operational steps that, if performed, will lead to the attainment of the stated goals and objectives. In this step, the agency leaders are required to be especially creative, because the action plan will almost certainly demand innovative approaches to achieving the goals and objectives. Creativity is called for by the structural tension that exists between the vision and the current reality. A creative leader looks for ways of resolving the tension in order to move the organization forward.[27]

Brainstorming is frequently used at this stage because it is an effective way of discovering worthwhile ideas. In addition, the leaders, in creating an action plan, must take into account the environment (the agency and its community) and the resources needed to carry out the plan.[28] Another set of techniques involves scenario planning, which is the development of stories to examine variations in eventual outcomes in bringing vision into reality. Scenario planning uses many tools, including forecasting, forces for change, tabletop exercises, computer simulations, environmental changes, politics, and systems tools and techniques.[29]

Leadership Tip

Public health is about adapting to change.
There is really no status quo.

The creative process can be divided into three stages.[30] First comes the germination phase, in which the leader uses personal excitement to address the problems that need to be dealt with. In the second stage, the organization and its employees begin to adapt to the leader's agenda. In the third stage, the process is completed. At this time, the leader often starts the process over again.

Some management experts suggest that devising strategies for goal attainment is more effective than an action plan. Mintzberg, for example, argued that the action plan approach is too narrow.[31] For one thing, it separates strategic thinking from the goal-attainment process, and the separation prevents leaders from responding creatively to the changing environment. In Mintzberg's view, planning is an incremental process and is not something that can be done all at once. One way of proceeding is to create an action plan that addresses only a few important areas. If the plan is too complex, failure may result.[32] Note that if the strategic approach is used, the strategies chosen may in fact replace goals in the minds of the various constituencies.

One way of looking at an action plan is as a process of learning through action. Constant feedback is a necessary part of the process. If progress toward the goals is not occurring, revisions in the plan will need to be made. The leaders may have to go back to previous stages and repeat them. Feedback in systems is in actuality quite complex, as can be seen in **Figure 5-3**.[33] This diagram demonstrates that a critical aspect of action is to close the gap between a designated goal or set of goals and a series of action steps. Part of the reason for this gap is that there may be hidden goals in the system that come to the forefront when specific action steps are implemented. As action steps are implemented, unexpected occurrences may also happen that change the system. This fits the Wheatley argument that change is messy and chaotic.[34]

One point to mention here is that government agencies tend to be highly bureaucratic because of the legislative need for oversight and accountability. As may be expected, civil service requirements often work against organizational change, and networks are often difficult to form in bureaucratic organizations. Yet an interesting phenomenon is occurring that may help in overcoming some of the barriers caused by bureaucratization. Prior to 2012, almost all states had an in-state or regional public health leadership institute, and such institutes facilitaed the development of leadership networks. Websites, forums, blogs, social media sites, chat rooms, and other forms of electronic communication are making networking easier.

The structure of any organization is multilayered, and those devising an action plan need to take account of the hidden parts of the organization's structure.[35] Furthermore, they need to keep in mind that any stage in the implementation of the plan will be affected by all the previous stages. They also must pay attention to authority issues and the effect that the implementation of the plan will have on the workforce, because major changes can alter a staff member's sense of identity.

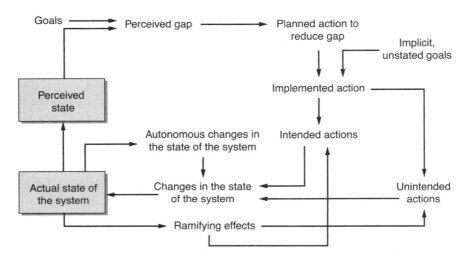

FIGURE 5-3 Feedback Loops in a System Dynamics Model. *Source*: Reproduced from A Best, PI Clark, SJ Leischow, and WM Trochim, *Greater than the Sum: Systems Thinking in Tobacco Control*. Washington, DC: National Cancer Institute Tobacco Control Monograph Series, 2007.

A number of strategies, including the following four, can be used to reduce the problems likely to arise from a major change. First, resulting changes in roles and relationships should be determined as the action plan is being created. Staff will worry about no longer having a job when the process is completed—and in fact, jobs may vanish as a result of the implementation. Second, the human resources office may have to be reorganized or its practices reformed in light of the proposed change. Third, an information system capable of monitoring the implementation process may have to be created. Finally, the financial management of the organization may have to be altered.

One way to measure the effectiveness of an action plan is to use the balanced scorecard model developed by Kaplan and Norton.[36] This model evaluates the degree of success from the financial, internal organization process, customer, and learning and growth perspectives. What the balanced scorecard demonstrates is that action planning needs to be aware of the many different dimensions to action planning activities. We need to be careful to include all the dimensions in our action activities. Oversimplification can be as much of a problem as too much complexity. For an action plan to work, according to the authors, the leaders of the organization must communicate the mission and vision, the goals and objectives, and the action plan to all the relevant constituencies. Second, the leaders must understand and be able to explain to these constituencies the linkage between the action plan goals and the rewards associated with good performance—what might be called "encouraging the heart."[37] Third, the process of developing the plan must include target setting. Fourth, the action plan must include feedback and learning components.

An action plan can usher in a new era for the organization or be its death knell. It is more likely to benefit the organization if it is created by means of a well-thought-out method and is implemented using the strategies mentioned above. Following is a list of guidelines that public health leaders should follow when engaged in action planning:

- Develop an action plan tied to the agency's mission, vision, and goals and objectives.
- Use strategic planning techniques for action planning.
- Formulate operational steps or strategies for each goal and objective.
- Know the resources that are needed and the resources that are available to implement the action plan.

- Explore existing barriers to successful action planning.
- Use the balanced scorecard model to measure the effectiveness of the action plan.

IMPLEMENTATION

The implementation of an action plan for the purpose of achieving goals and objectives and thereby realizing the agency's vision is the practice of public health, or at least part of it. During implementation, the leaders of the agency have the task of communicating the mission, vision, and goals and objectives of the agency to the staff and community constituents and doing this within the governing paradigm of the public health core functions of assessment, policy development, and assurance. In short, the leaders must become a bridge between the agency and the community.

Very little has been written about the implementation of action plans in the field of public health, although quality improvement techniques will work to make this occur. Yet it is clear that implementation of an action plan can involve many of the same activities public health leaders normally engage in as part of their responsibilities. These include:

- identifying community leaders and other external stakeholders
- delegating tasks to staff members and community partners
- establishing relationships with constituents
- communicating health information to the community
- working with the legislature
- working with the county board or local board of health

In a survey of California public health officers and executives, the respondents stated that their work encompassed budgeting, programming, disease control, staffing, environmental issues, health issues related to foreign nationals, and issues arising from undocumented care.[38] The researchers examined the lessons that the public health leaders had learned from their daily activities. These lessons included the importance of accuracy of information, flexibility, the total involvement of all stakeholders, action based on vision, patience, and providing information to the public.

EVALUATION

After an action plan and work plan are implemented, the results of the implementation need to be evaluated. The object of the evaluation is to determine to what degree the goals and objectives were achieved. Although the leaders of a public health agency will not be directly involved in gathering and analyzing the evaluation data, they will use the conclusions of the evaluation to determine what steps to take next to realize the agency's vision.

Leaders of an agency need data to foster a culture of evidence-based practice within the agency and among community constituents. For one thing, public health leaders are seen as sources of knowledge about community public health issues, and ensuring that evaluation data are gathered and publicized in some form confirms the legitimacy of their role as knowledge providers. In addition, the data will show the effects of the agency's activities on the residents of the community and, assuming they are mostly positive, will confirm the legitimacy of the agency's role as a protector of the community's health.

The evaluation process has been analyzed as consisting of six separate steps:[39]

1. posing questions about the program
2. setting effectiveness standards
3. designing the evaluation
4. collecting the data
5. analyzing the data
6. reporting the results

Not part of the evaluation process itself but an essential step nonetheless is the use of the results to determine further changes that need to be made.

Evaluation seems to frighten American health professionals, who tend to think evaluation data will jeopardize their jobs. In Great Britain, in contrast, public health leaders seem convinced that evaluation helps strengthen programs.

SUMMARY

This chapter describes the main stages in the systems approach to organizational change using the leadership wheel. The first step is for the organization to clarify its values and create a strategic plan. Once it does that, it can more easily construct a mission for itself and create a vision of its own future. The next task is to determine which goals and objectives, if achieved, will lead to the fulfilling of the organization's mission and the realization of its vision (development of a business plan). The third task is development of an action plan designed to accomplish the goals and objectives. The action plan needs to be implemented during the fourth task (creation of a work plan). The fifth step, of course, is to do an evaluation to determine whether the goals and objectives were accomplished and whether their accomplishment led to the realization of the organization's vision. Usually the evaluation uncovers changes that need to be made if the vision is to be realized. Feedback mechanisms need to be included if the integrity of the systems perspective is to be maintained.

DISCUSSION QUESTIONS

1. What are the similarities and differences between systems thinking and strategic thinking?
2. What are the values that characterize public health in the United States or in your home country?
3. How do an organization's mission and its vision differ, and how are they similar?
4. What is the relationship between goals and objectives and vision?
5. What is an action plan, and what is the typical purpose of such a plan?
6. What are four strategies for reducing the seriousness of problems resulting from major changes?
7. What are the six steps in the evaluation process?
8. What is the role of leaders in the change system defined by the leadership wheel?

EXERCISE 5-1: Shared Values Team Assignment

Purpose: to elucidate the relationships among personal values, community values, organizational values, and professional values

Key concepts: community coalition, community values, organizational values, personal values, professional values, value alignment, meaning

Procedure: The class should divide into teams of four or five members each. Each team pretends to be a community coalition charged with creating a shared values position statement intended to guide the coalition as it addresses the community's public

(Continued)

EXERCISE 5-1: Shared Values Team Assignment (*Continued*)

---

health needs. The statement should integrate personal, organizational, community, and professional values—the values that guide our personal lives, the organization we work in, the community we live in, and the profession we are members of. Each team will perform the following steps:

1. Each team member writes down on a Post-it one of his or her personal values. The member acting as "mayor" (facilitator) collects the Post-its and sticks them on a poster board in a column. The team reviews the values to see if a pattern emerges.

2. Each team member writes on a different color Post-it (one of another color than the Post-its used in step 1) a community value (the team members should choose from among the values held by the community in which they live). The mayor collects the Post-its and puts them on the poster board in a column next to the personal value Post-its. The team reviews the community values and compares them with the personal values.

3. Each team member writes on a different color Post-it a professional value held by public health practitioners. The mayor collects the Post-its and puts them on the poster board in a third column. The team reviews these values and discusses the ways in which they are consistent or inconsistent with the values previously listed.

4. Each team member writes on a different color Post-it an organizational value held by the organization in which he or she works. The mayor collects the Post-its and puts them on the poster board in a fourth column. The team reviews the values listed and discusses their relationship to the other sets of values.

5. The team reviews all the values listed and creates a values list that reflects the shared interests of all the team members (remember, the team members are pretending to be representatives of the organizations in a community coalition).

6. Each team presents its list of values to the whole group.

EXERCISE 5-2: The Vision Thing

Purpose: to elucidate the initial steps in the systems approach to organizational change; the role of a public health agency's mission, vision, and goals and objectives; and the connections between these

Key concepts: goals and objectives, mission, vision

Procedure: The class should divide into agency work teams of 5 to 10 members each. The first task is for each team to act as an ad hoc committee assigned the job of drafting a mission statement for a public health agency. If a glossary of terms is necessary, one should be drafted. After the mission statements are completed, the teams present them to the class as a whole, and the class then develops a shared mission statement.

In the second task, each team acts as a committee that has been assigned the job of developing a vision statement utilizing the shared mission statement created in the first task. Some team members should be designated as senior staff and others as front-line staff. After the vision statements are completed, the teams present them to the class as a whole, and the class then develops a shared vision statement.

In the third and final task, each team develops goals and objectives statements that indicate what actions must be achieved in order to implement the agency's mission and vision.

REFERENCES

1. I. I. Mitroff and H. A. Linstone, *The Unbounded Mind* (New York: Oxford University Press, 1993).

2. C. W. Churchman, *The Design of Inquiring Systems* (New York: Basic Books, 1971).

3. K. Blanchard and M. O'Connor, *Managing by Values* (San Francisco: Berrett-Koehler, 1997).

4. P. Hersey et al., *Management of Organizational Behavior*, 9th ed. (Upper Saddle River, NJ: Prentice Hall, 2007).

5. M. Rokeach, *The Nature of Human Values* (New York: The Free Press, 1973).

6. R. M. Williams Jr., *American Society: A Sociological Interpretation*, 3rd ed. (New York: Knopf, 1970).

7. Center for Rural Public Health Practice, *Bridging the Health Divide: The Rural Public Health Research Agenda* (Pittsburgh: University of Pittsburgh, 2004).

8. D. E. Brown, *Human Universals* (Boston: McGraw-Hill, 1991).

9. J. M. Kouzes and B.Z. Posner, *Credibility* (San Francisco: Jossey-Bass, 2011).

10. H. M. Jansen Kraemer Jr., *From Values to Action* (San Francisco: Jossey-Bass, 2011).

11. R. M. Kidder, "Universal Human Values: Findings on Ethical Common Ground," *Futurist* 28, no. 2 (1994): 8–13.

12. J. Hammond and J. Morrison, *The Stuff Americans Are Made Of* (New York: MacMillan, 1996).

13. H. Mintzberg, B. Ahlstrand, and J. Lampel, *Strategy Safari* (New York: Free Press, 1998).

14. B. Nanus, *Visionary Leadership* (San Francisco: Jossey-Bass, 1992).

15. S. P. Robbins and M. Coulter, *Management*, 11th ed. (Upper Saddle River, NJ: Prentice Hall, 2011).

16. B. Wall et al., *The Visionary Leader* (Rocklin, CA: Prima Publishing & Communication, 1992).

17. J. A. Pearce Jr. and P. R. David, "Corporate Mission Statements: The Bottom Line," *Academy of Management Executives* (May 1992): 109–116.

18. K. Albrecht, *The Northbound Train* (New York: American Management Association, 1994).

19. J. Q. Wilson, *Bureaucracy* (New York: Basic Books, 1989).

20. N. M. Tichy, *The Leadership Engine* (New York: Harper Business, 1997).

21. E. Marzalek-Gaucher and R. J. Coffey, *Transforming Healthcare Organizations* (San Francisco: Jossey-Bass, 1990).

22. T. Norris and L. Howell, *Healthy People in Healthy Communities: A Dialogue Guide* (Chicago: Coalition for Healthy Cities and Communities, 1998).

23. M. Lipton, *Guiding Growth* (Boston: Harvard Business School Press, 2003).

24. Wall et al., *The Visionary Leader*.

25. B. Torbert and Associates, *Action Inquiry* (San Francisco: Berrett-Kohler, 2004).

26. A. Etzioni, *A Comparative Analysis of Complex Organizations* (New York: The Free Press, 1971).

27. R. Fritz, *The Path of Least Resistance for Managers* (San Francisco: Berrett-Kohler, 1999).

28. E. E. Bobrow, *Ten Minute Guide to Planning* (New York: Macmillan, Spectrum, and Alpha Books, 1998).

29. G. Ringland, *Scenario Planning: Managing for the Future* (New York: John Wiley and Sons, 1998).

30. R. Fritz, *The Path of Least Resistance* (New York: Fawcett, 1984).

31. H. Mintzberg, *Mintzberg on Management* (New York: The Free Press, 1989).

32. Albrecht, *The Northbound Train*.

33. A. Best, P. I. Clark, S. J. Leischow, and W. M. Trochim, *Greater Than the Sum: Systems Thinking in Tobacco Control* (Washington, DC: National Cancer Institute Tobacco Control Monograph Series, 2007).

34. M. J. Wheatley, *Leadership and the New Science*, 2nd ed. (San Francisco: Berrett-Kohler, 1999).

35. P. M. Senge et al., *The Fifth Discipline Fieldbook* (New York: Bantam, 1994).

36. R. S. Kaplan and D. P. Norton, *The Balanced Scorecard* (Boston: Harvard Business School Press, 1996).

37. J. M. Kouzes and B. Z. Posner, *The Leadership Challenge*, 4th ed. (San Francisco: Jossey-Bass, 2007).

38. J. C. Lammers and V. Pandita, "Applying Systems Thinking to Public Health Leadership," *Journal of Public Health Management and Practice* 3, no. 4 (1997): 39–49.

39. A. Fink, *Evaluation Fundamentals* (Newbury Park, CA: Sage, 1993).

CHAPTER 6

The Five Levels of Leadership

Effective leaders are capable of reframing the thinking of those whom they guide.

—D. R. Conner, Managing at the Speed of Change

A leader is a person who inspires others to action and guides their undertakings. These others can be members of a team, employees of an agency, or heads of groups that have formed a coalition, an alliance, or a partnership, for example. In other words, leaders in public health, as in other arenas, operate on different levels. The major difficulty in conceptualizing what leadership is relates to the fact that we live in an ever-changing world that demands that leaders adapt to these changes in a continuous way. Each day leaders face new technical challenges for which solutions need to be found. These challenges require more than the usual solutions tied to an authoritative position or to the standard operating procedures of an organization or community. All we need to do is look at the events of September 11, 2001, to see that the world has changed. Heifetz and Linsky pointed out that these adaptive challenges require solutions that are innovative, perhaps experimental, and create new forms of

adjustment.[1] Adaptive change may require a change in attitude, values, and behavior, or a new interpretation of events.

Sometimes this new perspective may involve trying to see the situation from the perspective of others. I have suggested to students that simply changing their seats from one class session to another will give them a new perspective of me as professor. I recently saw this effect in a management training program. The trainees were asked to develop a new public health program during the first six months of the training. During the second six months, the trainees' task was to develop a business plan for their new program. They reported that the business plan project gave them a whole new perspective on their project and the feasibility of making the project work. Heifetz and Linsky have added a variation on this technique, which they named the balcony exercise.[2] If you are at a dance, you tend to concentrate on dancing with your partner. If you go to the balcony between dances, you can see the whole dance floor. You can see the band, and you can see all the dancers. In other words, you get the big-picture view. You can see all the interacting parts. You can see the dancers who stumble and have difficulty with the dance steps. You are a systems thinker on the balcony. The systems thinker not only sees how his or her organization is functioning, but can also see how the organization functions in the context of the community in which the organization is embedded.

Let us assume that there is a second balcony. From this balcony, events and activities appear less structured. As you add new information to the dance floor and all the activities outside the building, you begin to change information into knowledge synergistically. Your synergistic leadership approach allows you to see the mess beyond the structure. Thus, you need to expand your leadership in this complex environment beyond the dance floor or your organization. You begin to cultivate new relationships as your activities become more complex and less predictable. Lewis warns of self-organized criticality (SOC), which is the point at which the system partially or totally collapses.[3] Structures become less permanent, new structures come into being, and they seem to grow into these new cultivated relationships. Social networks expand and contract due to increasing real time and virtual social network relationships. You will notice more chaotic situations that create interventions to resolve. Wheatley has pointed out that human beings seek organization in their lives, and it takes messes to get us to organization.[4] Organization is clearly about developing new relationships and new structures that are co-evolving. Change is the organizing force. Order is about our ability to influence our organization and community to organize, reorganize, and continue to grow more complex. The second balcony can clearly be an exciting place that increases our understanding of the activities on the dance floor and the first balcony.

It is also important to understand what entices people into leadership roles. Over the past 20 years, there has been a strong belief that leadership can be taught. Many public health leadership programs have come into being with the goal of training public health professionals to be better leaders with the belief that leadership is one of the key dimensions in building a stronger public health system. Parks has stated that there are important explanations of why people want to be leaders.[5] She calls these explanations "hungers" and discusses five of them as follows:

1. hunger to contribute and make society better
2. hunger to be in an authority position
3. hunger to implement and explore systems issues
4. hunger to show others how to adapt to change
5. hunger to demonstrate moral courage on behalf of the "common good"

This chapter first discusses the abilities that public health leaders need at any level, including the personal level (i.e., when dealing with another individual one on one), then goes on to consider the particular abilities and strategies they put to use in heading a team, heading an agency, working on a community collaboration activity, or guiding their profession toward improvement. As we proceed, it is important to remember that each of the five levels of leadership provides a foundation for the next level of leadership. It is almost like going up a flight of stairs on which we need to go up the first stair before going to the second stair. Skipping a stair might trip us up.

PERSONAL LEADERSHIP DEVELOPMENT

This section considers some of the prerequisites for being an effective public health leader at any level. These prerequisites include a commitment to social justice, an understanding of democracy, an understanding of the political process, communication skills, mentoring skills, decision-making skills, and the ability to balance work and life outside work. There are at least eight learning strategies that will enhance personal leadership development activities:

1. Lifelong multidisciplinary learning
2. Systems thinking and complexity
3. Reading
4. Exploring the arts
5. Creativity
6. Family–work balance
7. Retreats and reflection
8. Experiential learning

Values

Public health leaders, to be fully effective, must be committed to the values that characterize public health, especially social justice. However, they need to be careful not to let the social justice agenda prevent them from doing the tasks that need to be done. Furthermore, social justice is a broad concept and encompasses a range of different issues. The predominant social justice issue of concern to almost all public health leaders is equity in access to care. However, no consensus exists that, for instance, there should be a radical redistribution of wealth in the society at large.

A commitment to a value such as equity in access to care entails a willingness to challenge the political status quo and act as an advocate for the public health agenda. Leaders are supporters of organizational and community values and should be on the front lines in attempts to make public health practices and policies conform to these values. Leaders also need to be at the front of the line if values need to be changed, modified, or reinterpreted.

Politics and Governance

Public health leaders need to understand the political system of the location in which their activities take place. In this country, they need to understand how the American version of democracy works at the local, state, and national levels and how to influence the political process. As an example, the author, on a visit to the office of a public health professional in a state health department, noticed *The Federalist Papers* and de Tocqueville's *Democracy in America* on the shelf. The public health leader said that he often referred to these books for guidance in making decisions.

One question that arises is whether there is a difference between government (or governance, the activity of governing) and politics. Governance, in large part, consists of administering programs and adjusting them to fit policies developed as part of the political process.[6] Unfortunately, these policies are sometimes not founded on the best available evidence but instead reflect the personal concerns (including the desire to get reelected) of the politicians who vote them into existence. Several years ago, I talked to a state legislator about having a school of public health supply data on specific health issues and social determinants of health of interest to the legislator. He refused the offer, because, according to him, he did not need data to make his decisions. (As someone has pointed out, politicians have "spin doctors," whereas government agencies have "spokespeople."[7] That says something about the difference between politics and government.)

Public health agencies are government agencies, and public health leaders are implementers of policies set by politicians. This creates interesting possibilities for a partnership between the political and governmental sectors. Leadership theories often focus exclusively on organizational tasks, such as setting organizational policies and motivating the workforce, but public health leaders need to develop the skills necessary for working with elected officials. Their role is to use the values, mission, vision, and goals and objectives of their agency to clarify public health issues and ensure that the policies created to deal with these issues will have a good chance of being effective.

Communication and Empowerment

The AIM Leadership Model is based on the idea that leaders have to learn to take action, learn how to influence the field, and be motivated by the process.[8] According to the model, the five building blocks of effective personal leadership are communication, the empowerment of followers, a focus on key issues, linkage to others, and life balance. Each of these building blocks is affected by leadership style and practices as well as the systems approach to organizational change.

Good communication skills are critical. Effective communication has several aspects, including slowing the thought processes, increasing understanding, testing conclusions, listening constructively, getting to the essence of things, and exploring areas of disagreement.[9] In addition, gender differences, racial or ethnic differences, and age differences can affect whether messages are received as intended.[10] Leaders need to understand all the factors that influence communication so they can synthesize public health information into effective messages.

Leaders, in trying to empower work and community associates, often act as their mentors. Interaction between leaders and constituents is critical,[11] and leaders need to empower "followers" in ways that give them the chance to be more effective as well as to develop their own leadership skills. Followers are themselves people with exceptional talents, and according to one study, 80% of the effectiveness of a project is due to the followers and only 20% to the leadership (80–20 rule).[12]

Leading and Following

Also, followers in one situation become leaders in another, and many public health practitioners see themselves in both leadership and follower roles. Public health practitioners who work for public health agencies see themselves as professionals first and even leaders in their profession, but those who are part of a traditional public bureaucracy are frequently expected to be less leaders than followers, which can create a contentious work environment.

Members of a board of health often see themselves as powerful individuals and therefore as natural leaders. Health administrators also see themselves as leaders rather than followers. This may lead to conflict. For example, a health administrator addressing a group of public health professionals in a leadership program said that it was his job to protect board members from gossip and controversies. A local board of health president who was in the training program said that if the health administrator kept information hidden from board members, someone in the community would give them the information instead. Board members need information and lose trust in health administrators who hold back information.

Another board of health president pointed out that the administrator of the health department was his employee, because he could fire the administrator and recommend cutting the local health department budget. This shows how important it is for the board of health members and the public health administrator to develop an understanding that they are partners. In this regard, governance has an important role to play.[13] A governance public health framework should include mechanisms for organizing values, carrying out the public health mission, formulating goals and objectives, developing realistic action plans, resolving conflicting agendas, determining the need for structural change, improving the relationship between the board and the health department, and developing mechanisms to share governance with the appropriate governmental body. As one public health leader stated:

> To create effective governing boards, we must examine our values and determine why our boards need to exist. Once we discover our common purpose, we can develop skills and processes to improve our effectiveness. Boards and administrators need a shared vision, commitment, and leadership to make goals a reality. As public health leaders, it is our job to develop boards that are a part of our leadership teams and join us in creating healthy communities.[14(p.11)]

Agenda Setting

Public health leaders should learn about and use the systems approach to organizational change and the public health core functions model to ensure that their agencies' agendas are tied to the core functions of public health. In addition, they need to master the art and science of public health. Leaders are the grand integrators of science and practice, and part of their job is to explain public health issues to health professional associates and community partners.

Leaders should acquire agenda-setting skills. An organization needs to prioritize the problems that it is

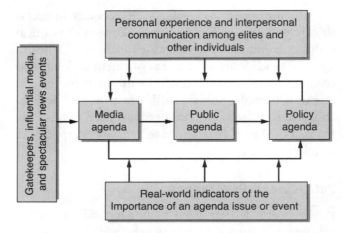

FIGURE 6-1 Three Main Components of the Agenda-Setting Process: The Media Agenda, Public Agenda, and Policy Agenda. *Source*: Reproduced from Rogers and Dearing, Agency-Setting Research: Where Has It Been? Where Is It Going? In *Communication Yearbook*, Vol. 11, J. A. Anderson, ed., p. 5, © 1988 by Sage Publications, Inc. Reprinted by permission of Sage Publications, Inc.

facing and create action plans that deal with the largest problems first.[15] **Figure 6-1** presents a model for agenda setting that includes the creation of a media agenda, a public agenda, and a policy agenda. The fact that public health leadership practice takes place in a government setting means that community and political realities affect the agenda-setting process. Also influencing the process are gatekeepers, the media, and spectacular news stories (e.g., a story about children becoming ill after eating in a fast-food restaurant).

Barriers to Effectiveness

In 1988, the Institute of Medicine issued a report stating that the public health system in the United States was in disarray.[16] The report listed a number of barriers that reduce the ability of public health leaders to be effective, including the following:

- a lack of a consensus on the content of the public health mission
- inadequate capacity to carry out the essential public health functions of assessment, policy development, and assurance of services
- disjointed decision making uninformed by the necessary data and knowledge
- inequities in the distribution of services and the benefits of public health
- disharmony between the technical and political aspects of decisions
- rapid turnover of leaders

- an inadequate relationship between public health and the medical profession
- organizational fragmentation
- problems in relationships between layers of government
- an inadequate development of necessary knowledge across the full array of public health needs
- a poor public image of public health, inhibiting necessary support
- special problems that unduly limit the financial resources available to public health

Without question, the public health system in the United States needs to become more effective, and public health leaders will be at the forefront of attempts at reform.[17] One problem is that public health agencies are dealing with more complex problems today than previously, and the complexity of problems in the areas of infectious diseases and chronic diseases will probably continue to increase. Therefore, organizational stability may not be possible to achieve. In addition, public health professionals come from different disciplines with different approaches to problem solving, which leads to professional disagreements.[18] It will be only through collaboration that effective problem solving and decision making will occur.

In a speech before the Illinois Public Health Leadership Institute in 1992, George Pickett said that public health leaders need to increase their skills transorganizationally; that is, they need to be able to understand and communicate with others in community sectors with values and priorities different from theirs. Public health leaders are often deficient in collaboration skills,[19] and consequently they are sometimes prevented from cooperating effectively with leaders from important sectors, such as the business community and the religious community. Fortunately, obstacles to cooperation are becoming less frequent.

It should be noted that, in general, leaders who are extremely effective tend to be key players in rather than reactors to the change going on around them.[20] Effective leaders, when confronted with a problem, typically consider a wide range of options and seem to know how to select the important factors first. They also think in terms of win–win and try to arrange it so all parties are winners in a dispute. They are good listeners who try to understand others and their perspectives before trying to make themselves understood. They are excellent synthesizers who try to foster cooperation and collaboration. Finally, they constantly renew themselves through training, education, exercise, values clarification, and so on.

Leadership Style

Public health leaders need to develop an appropriate leadership style. Autocratic and directive styles work best when the leader structures the tasks and the workers are willing to do what the leader asks. In public health, the democratic style seems to work better.[21] Participative forms of leadership, in which staff members are involved in the problem-solving process, facilitate the building of a consensus and the acceptance by the staff of the decisions arrived at. Collaboration should be viewed as a creative process whose goal is to discover new approaches and new solutions for old problems.[22]

Dealing with Diversity

Professional diversity in public health brings its own set of problems.[23] Practitioners from different professions view public health differently. Public health leaders need to look at public health in its totality and develop strategies for integrating the different approaches. Exercise 6-1 provides an opportunity to consider the issue of professional diversity and its effect on public health strategies.

Public health leaders need to confront not only professional diversity but gender, race, ethnic, and age diversity. For example, the so-called glass ceiling for women still exists,[24] and therefore public health leaders must conscientiously promote gender equality. The first step is to gather the data necessary to determine whether gender inequalities exist and, if so, where they exist. The next step is to hire a consultant to evaluate the agency's environment and its receptiveness to gender equality. The third step is to use a benchmarking process (comparing the agency with the best agencies, not the average ones) to identify best practices for achieving gender equality and taking full advantage of the skills that women bring into the workplace. The final step, so to speak, is to prepare oneself for a backlash. Case Study 6-A is an interview with Dr. Joyce Lashof, who has held a number of public health leadership posts over the past 50 years. The interview explores some of the gender issues that public health leaders typically confront.

Diversity encompasses gender, age, race, ethnicity, sexual orientation, work and family issues, education, work experiences, tenure within the agency or organization, personality, risk tolerance, geographic region, and religion.[25] A unified diversity enhancement program for public health professionals and clients may be difficult to construct because of the different issues that are prominent in each diversity category.

A Leadership Interview with Joyce C. Lashof, MD

Shirley F. Randolph

Joyce C. Lashof, MD, is dean emeritus, School of Public Health, University of California at Berkeley. Her most recent previous positions include president of the American Public Health Association; Dean, School of Public Health, University of California at Berkeley; president, Association of Schools of Public Health; Assistant Director, Office of Technology Assessment, U.S. Congress; Senior Scholar in Residence, Institute of Medicine, National Academy of Sciences; Deputy Assistant Secretary for Health Programs and Deputy Assistant Secretary for Population Affairs, U.S. Department of Health, Education, and Welfare; and Director, Illinois Department of Public Health.

The first name that comes to mind when one thinks of women leaders in the field of public health is Joyce C. Lashof, MD. Dr. Lashof has done it all. After five decades in public health leadership positions, she is, quite simply, the quintessential public health leader.

And she did it all while successfully integrating her workplace duties with her responsibilities as the wife of a university professor (her husband, Richard, is a well-known mathematician) and the mother of one son and two daughters—two of whom have made Joyce and Richard grandparents, and all of whom are growing as young professionals in their chosen fields. Her insights into leadership issues, particularly as they apply to women, are perceptive and fascinating.

One of the first areas Dr. Lashof and I explored during an interview several years ago dealt with the challenge women often experience when faced with men as "gatekeepers" to upward mobility.

What have been your greatest challenges when confronting the male monopoly on power and men as gatekeepers on the upward path to leadership?

There was definitely a problem early in my career. Moving up depended a good deal on having a mentor who paved the way. At the beginning of my career, after I received my MD from Woman's Medical College of Pennsylvania and completed my residency in medicine at Montefiore Hospital in New York, I went to the University of Chicago first as a physician at the Student Health Services and then as an assistant professor in the Department of Medicine.

I served year to year on a one-year appointment for three years and then asked for a regular three-year appointment. I was told by the chairman of the Department of Medicine that he would never give a married woman a tenured track appointment because she would leave and go where her husband's career took him. Needless to say, I was unhappy about the situation and told him "thanks, but no thanks" to another one-year appointment. That was in 1960. At that time, of course, there were no laws about discrimination and affirmative action.

Luckily, colleagues referred me to Dr. Mark Lepper at the University of Illinois, College of Medicine, and Presbyterian–St. Luke's Hospital, Chicago. Mark offered me a faculty appointment in the Department of Preventive Medicine at the University of Illinois and arranged an appointment as assistant attending physician at Presbyterian–St. Luke's Hospital. This led to a series of succeeding appointments and long-term collaboration.

In many ways, Mark was a mentor who opened doors for me. Most specifically, he appointed me research director of a study of health needs of poverty populations funded by the Office of Equal Opportunity (OEO). It was this study that led to recommendations that health centers to serve the disadvantaged be opened in Chicago. The study was well received by the OEO and resulted in the further development of a proposal to open a health center on Chicago's West Side. The West Side's Mile Square organization approached Presbyterian–St. Luke's about developing such a health center. We put together a proposal for an OEO-funded Mile Square health center. The proposal was successful, and Mile Square Health Center was the second OEO-funded health center in the country. I served as its director for five years.

During this same period of time, I was promoted to attending physician and director, Section of Community Medicine, at Presbyterian–St. Luke's Hospital. As the only woman to head up a section, during staff meetings I was the lone woman sitting around the table with all the men. They were more or less accepting of me, but I could sense that in their eyes I was not quite an equal. I walked a thin line between asserting myself and not being too assertive.

When Dan Walker became Illinois's governor in 1973, he said he was going to appoint women to his cabinet. He did, and I became the first woman to be named the director of a state public health department. I think I ought to thank the women's movement!

What changes in the male monopoly are occurring as we move into a new era with a new vision about women as leaders and managers?

Things are certainly changing. Obviously there are now laws against overt discrimination against women. But just as important as the legal ramifications of discriminating against women (or anyone else), the fact is that women have proved themselves capable and are accepted as leaders and managers. In addition, women are networking more. Not being the only woman sitting around a table with a group of men makes a real difference in relationships with colleagues. And the younger generation of men is much more accepting of women in peer relationships. Men who are not comfortable with women as leaders and managers and who do not accept them as colleagues are a dying breed.

How did you counteract the obstacle of discrimination in the workplace because you are a woman? Was discrimination more or less a problem as you moved from mid-level management to top leadership roles?

Of course the way I counteracted the first obstacle at the University of Chicago was by leaving. Beyond that, I think I just did the best job I knew how to do. I worked hard to be sure that I met every expectation and did not give anyone any excuses to criticize me because of my gender.

Then again, sometimes I just ignored the problems, and sometimes I took a little action. For example, at Presbyterian–St. Luke's, we would sit around the table and select interns and residents. We would come to a woman applicant and the men would make comments like, "Let's take her … she is really attractive." I would wait until we came to a likely male applicant and then I would say, "Yes, I think we should take him … he's quite a handsome fellow."

Problems related to discrimination because of my gender became less and less as I moved up. It was easier working with younger men and women. But some of the "old timers," both in terms of age and length of service in an agency, were still a problem that had to be faced.

Is it your sense that leadership opportunities are increasing or decreasing for top leadership positions for women?

In many ways, top leadership opportunities for women are increasing. For instance, more women are serving as directors of state health departments, as deans of schools of public health, and in high-level leadership positions at all levels of government. On the other hand, I look at medical school professorships and I'm not sure that the number of women professors has increased. I think people are looking for women to fill leadership roles, but it is still a problem when you look at the top jobs.

Are the opportunities for women to fill leadership positions greater or lesser in the field of public health?

There are greater opportunities for women in public health. I think one reason for this is the more liberal nature of the public health field, the result being more opportunities and less discrimination. Public health professionals have a commitment to equality, social justice, women's rights, minority rights, etc. In addition, a career in public health often gives a woman the opportunity to be a leader in politics and in government by virtue of the position she holds.

Are the attributes and characteristics of successful women leaders different than they are for successful men leaders?

Women's leadership styles tend to be different from men's to some degree. Whether those differences are the things that account for success is the question. Are women more successful as leaders because they have different values and styles? This is a research question and an issue that is currently being studied. In my experience, especially earlier on in my career, I found women to be more sympathetic, compassionate, much less aggressive, less domineering, and more inclusive … all very valuable traits when one looks at leadership. We know now that research studies regarding capable leadership indicate that those who have an inclusive leadership style are more effective. Obviously, there are always exceptions to this rule. Taken as a whole, the inclusive leadership approach is lower key; it is more sharing and more "motherly." One of the best compliments I received as assistant director of the Office of Technology Assessment was that I was good at "mothering" them, but I could also kick their rears when I needed to!

In addition to being a successful public health leader in a variety of forums, you are also a wife, mother, and grandmother. How did you integrate the workplace with your private life responsibilities and "juggle" the complexities that resulted from your various roles?

It has been a real juggling act! Of course, things got easier as my three children grew up, but at times it was wild! One of the very conscious decisions I made early on in my career was to move toward public health and research in the medical care area because it was less competitive and would result in a less intensive demand on my time,

(*Continues*)

which gave me more time to be with my family. Before I made this decision, I had been working in infectious diseases. I observed how competitive this field was and felt that with three young children at home it wasn't what I wanted to do. I wanted to be home with my husband and children at night and on the weekends, holidays, etc. When the children were all in school and busy with their individual activities, the balancing act became easier. Also, I was very fortunate in having the same full-time housekeeper for over 20 years.

My need to spend time with my family was one of the main reasons why I decided to go into public health and medical care research. It was really serendipity … opportunity knocked through Mark Lepper's mentoring, and I was there.

The present job market is very competitive for public health practitioners regardless of gender. What leadership skills are most important for women to cultivate who are currently at the lower and middle levels of a public health organization?

First and foremost, one needs to know one's field. One has to be looked at as one who is a good problem solver. My advice is to learn how to be objective and analytical and how to be fair. Other important leadership skills include developing an inclusive leadership style, learning how to be a good listener and to reflect on what you hear. One leadership skill that is absolutely essential is knowing how to relate well to other people and to be honest in those relationships.

As public health redefines its role within a new healthcare delivery system that is likely to emerge as the result of some form of healthcare reform, will there be different or "new" opportunities for women in public health leadership positions?

If the whole healthcare system becomes more and more competitive through a corporate approach, some women will be able to fit into that structure as leaders. If we move into a system that is accountable for populations (core functions included), opportunities for women to attain top leadership positions certainly should increase. As public health grows and strengthens its positions as an integral part of the healthcare delivery system, there will be increasing leadership opportunities for both women and men.

One way for public health leaders to deal with diversity issues is to empower staff so that they become advocates for themselves. It is important to understand how human beings in our society act and what needs they have. In his classic work *Motivation and Personality*, Maslow defined a hierarchy of needs.[26] At the most basic level, individuals want their physiological needs met. Second in order of importance are their safety needs. In other words, issues of job security and amount of income are critical for most people. Next come social needs, including the need for recognition by colleagues. One level up, people want to experience a sense of self-esteem. They want to take pride in their work and hence want to be empowered to do a good job. A professional who works well and without the need of much direction will usually be allowed the freedom to design his or her own activities, an almost sure way of increasing self-esteem. Finally, people have a need for self-actualization—the ability to make personal dreams become reality.

Balancing Work and Play

Work has a tendency to take up most of a leader's waking hours, and family life can suffer as a result. O'Neil called this dilemma the paradox of success.[27] In his view, the myth of success is that success offers complete fulfillment, that success is tied to how much money is made, and that success increases freedom. In fact, success causes a constant craving for more success and hence can lead to a kind of bondage. Factors that can help a leader keep a balance between work life and private life include self-knowledge, managing conflicting pressures, and maintaining a concern for how others feel.[28]

Women seem to be proficient at balancing personal and professional interests. For working women with a family, work and home are full-time jobs that they typically seem to handle equally well. At work, women, by redesigning their positions and demanding employee training and development, are helping to break traditional organizational molds.[29] They are also helping to break down the barriers between home and work by pushing for flex time, child care, and family leave.

This section raised and discussed many issues related to personal leadership development. Following is a list of leadership strategies that can be used to increase one's leadership skills and abilities:

- Be a value role model. Live the values that the community espouses.

- Understand the democratic process and how it affects the public health system.
- Translate political policy into action.
- Improve communication skills.
- Be a mentor to others.
- Learn to follow when appropriate.
- Be partners with the agency's governing board.
- Learn agenda-setting skills.
- Address barriers to effective public health practice.
- Explore community partnerships.
- Be creative in finding new funding sources.
- Balance work and family.
- Increase leadership opportunities for others.

LEADERSHIP AT THE TEAM LEVEL

Public health leaders do not work alone. Public health practice is a group activity. Therefore, among the most important skills a leader can possess are those that are necessary for building and maintaining teams and increasing their effectiveness. It almost seems that somebody always wants to take charge when even two people are in a room.

A team is a group of people who come together to pursue a common purpose.[30] The results of the team's activities are often greater than the sum total of the results that would have occurred had each team member been acting alone.

Each team member should be viewed as leader although one person will generally become the official leader. The team leader will share information in an equitable manner with other team members.[31] The leader will build trust in the team process and share authority and power with other members. The leader will also intervene when necessary to move the team forward. The expectation is that all members will be involved in the performance of the team tasks.

Team members who are also members of the public health agency may need to act as a link between the team and the agency and community constituents. These team members, in particular, will need to learn the skills of conflict resolution and negotiation. When a skilled leader guides the team process, creativity and innovation are the result.

Reasons for Creating Teams

The reasons for creating teams include the following: First, a team allows an organization to use the leadership skills and talents and the multidisciplinary and multicultural backgrounds of its staff. For example, a multidisciplinary team that includes nurses, social workers, and environmental health specialists, among others, might be assembled to address the low level of prenatal care in the community. If we add on multicultural team members, potential conflicts may arise due to different cultural orientations related to prenatal care. Second, creating a team allows the members time to get to know one another and to develop a sense of togetherness in the context of shared leadership. In general, team members find they can communicate with each other better even once they have left the team or the team has been disbanded. In addition, they learn how to cooperate and collaborate, and cooperation and collaboration increase productivity.[32] Finally, team decision making produces decisions that are supported by the majority of the team's members.

Teams that are created to lighten a supervisor's workload are often doomed to failure.[33] Teams are not a replacement for training and not a way for leaders to observe the opinions and working style of the staff. Teams do not necessarily increase the personal productivity of their members. They need leaders to clarify issues and set the parameters of their activities.[34] One of the strengths of teams is that they are flexible and can reorient themselves as roadblocks occur. Yet the freedom teams are given can be a weakness as well. Teams sometimes fail because they lack discipline and a sense of responsibility for achieving the desired outcomes. When team members realize they will be completely in charge of their activities and will have the power to make decisions, they sometimes abuse this power, with negative results for the agency. This risk can be reduced if the agency leaders make clear to each team how they expect it to proceed and what results they expect it to achieve.

Leadership teams work differently than management teams. Management teams carry out the instructions of a supervisor. Their tasks are circumscribed, and there is very little room for creativity or innovation. Leadership teams share leadership with the public health administrator, who openly delegates decision-making power to them. In some leadership teams, the health administrator becomes a team member. If given the trust of the agency administrator, leadership team members become committed to the agency and lose their fear of reprisal. They feel that they are respected for their expertise and ability to innovate. They also know that their recommendations will be seriously considered.

Facts about Teams

Katzenbach and Smith studied teams in 30 organizations, including businesses, schools, and social agencies.[35] They found that teams were critical for building quality organizations and improving customer service. The authors came up with 10 findings about teams in general.

The first finding is that teams are created to address a performance challenge, and indeed a leadership team must have a purpose (mission) if it is to succeed. The second finding is that the team's composition and its purpose need to be thought through. Not every leadership team should be of the same size or professional composition. Third, leaders need to promote team performance opportunities. As the leaders view the organization, they will find these opportunities exist throughout. Fourth, many teams composed primarily of people at the top fail because of the other demands made on these individuals' time and energy. Fifth, organizations and their leaders find it easier to work with individuals than with teams. Everything, including the hiring of people, the determination of salary, the construction of career paths, and the monitoring of performance, is oriented toward the individual. Teamwork seems to go against the structure of individual responsibility.

The sixth finding is that organizations committed to high performance standards are more likely to use teams than organizations with lower performance standards. Seventh, very few high-performance teams exist. High-performance teams can be either leadership or management teams. However, leadership teams are generally clearer on the purpose for which they were created. They take control of their activities and promote the development of relationships between their members. They build team activities on good communication. The leaders maintain their flexibility, work productively together, and recognize the accomplishments of their leader colleagues. Leadership teams also seem to have high morale. (High-performance teams can be created using the PERFORM model, propounded by Blanchard and colleagues.[36] The acronym stands for Purpose, Empowerment, Relationships and communication, Flexibility, Optimal productivity, Recognition and appreciation, and Morale.)

The eighth finding is that teams do not replace organizational hierarchies. Instead, teams enhance these hierarchies, partly because they are able to cross over structural boundaries. Because of the strong community orientation of public health agencies, leadership teams can be used to address community concerns. These teams may include community partners among their membership.

The ninth finding is that teams are small learning organizations that integrate performance and learning. Typically a team will do research on a subject related to its purpose. Team members also learn team-building and leadership skills. They often learn that each member is a leader or potential leader. The conjoining of performance and learning in teams is generally a plus, because their conjunction throughout an organization is often a prerequisite for the organization to increase its effectiveness. This applies to public health agencies as well.

The final finding is that teams are effective in addressing new issues as well as old issues. In the case of old issues or problems, they often discover new solutions. One reason teams are good at discovering solutions to problems is that they view the problems from a systems perspective rather than using the traditional cause-and-effect approach.[37] They are also experts at sharing information and coordinating actions, and members of one team frequently tie their activities to the activities of other teams working on different though related issues.

The important question is why so many teams fail when their importance to the work of public health is so important. Lencioni pointed to five major dysfunctions that affect the success of team-based activities.[38] First, teams fail when there is a lack of trust either in their organization or in their leadership. This includes the implicit leadership of the team as well. Second, team members fear conflict and contesting the decisions of other team members. Conflict is not necessarily a personal issue, but rather is often an issue related to the challenge that the group must address. The third dysfunction relates to the level or lack of commitment of team members to the process. The Leadership Wheel pointed to the important dimension of values clarification and the need to get all team members to commit to the team activities or project. If there is a lack of commitment, then the fourth dysfunction occurs. The lack of accountability will often affect the effectiveness of team activities. The fifth dysfunction relates to the problem of ignoring the results of the teamwork regardless of the reasons. If the boss had the team do busywork or did not allow the team any involvement in the decision-making process, all the dysfunctions come into play. There will be no trust, no conflict on the surface, no commitment to the process, no accountability, and obviously no attention to the results.

Teams build social capital, which brings people together in a way that individuals alone cannot do. Building social capital helps to develop trust, allows for shared leadership and creativity, expands social networks for the team members, develops shared purpose in team activities, levels the playing field for the members in terms of equity, increases collaboration and commitment, enhances knowledge sharing, and fits different talents of individuals into a comprehensive whole.[39] At the individual level, teamwork provides many benefits to the individual as well and creates satisfaction and sometimes personal rewards in the accomplishments of the team.

Team Classification

Many writers have attempted to classify teams. One helpful classification is as follows:[40] Natural work teams are made up primarily of individuals who work together as part of their regular activities. These teams, which can be either management or leadership teams, are usually given a set of designated activities to perform. Cross-functional teams, the second type, include members who have different functions within the organization. They are primarily leadership teams. Corrective action teams are management teams assigned to work on the solutions to problems that are already determined. Finally, hybrid teams address issues not addressed elsewhere in the organization. They may be either management or leadership teams, and they utilize the techniques associated with all the other types. Local public health departments use all four types of teams.

The Importance of Empowerment

Teams and their members need to be empowered by administrators to take active decision-making roles.[41] Empowerment, which gives team members the freedom to use their knowledge, experience, and skills to address important issues,[42] tends to increase their commitment to the agency and the level of their performance as well. Empowerment must come from the agency leader, and there appears to be a direct relationship between the amount of responsibility staff are given and the degree of their empowerment.[43]

The transfer of power to a team must be real and not merely nominal. A public health leadership team from a state public health leadership institute worked with a local health department to develop a lead-screening program for children. The administrator allowed the team to work on the creation of this new program because she had been told by the state to develop the program. However, the administrator viewed the team members as outsiders, and though she told them that she had respect for them and would seriously review any recommendations they made, she used the team merely to show the state that she was complying with its request and in reality had no intention of implementing the team's recommendations. This is an example of team activity subverted by a hidden agenda. The power to have an effect on the development of a program through recommendations was implied but was in fact an illusion.

As **Figure 6-2** shows, empowerment is related to organizational values, leadership activities, human resource systems, and the structure and activities of the organization. Empowerment is often used as a tool for the improvement of programs and services.

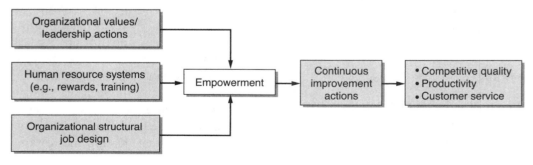

FIGURE 6-2 **Empowerment in Contemporary Organizations.** *Source*: Reprinted with permission from R. S. Wellins, W. C. Byham, and J. M. Wilson, *Empowered Teams*: *Creating Self-Directed Work Groups that Improve Quality, Productivity, and Participation.* p. 23, © 1991, Jossey-Bass Inc., Publishers.

Teams and Leadership Style

The situational leadership model identifies four leadership styles: directing, coaching, supporting, and delegating. This same classification can be applied to team-based activities.[44] When a team is first created, the leader is involved in formulating the team's purpose and determining the activities to be performed. The leader, in other words, is using a directive style. During the next phase, the leader, acting as a coach, clarifies the team's activities. The leader then begins to involve team members in decision making, a process that falls into the category of providing support. In the final phase, the leader empowers the team members, and empowerment, as pointed out above, is closely related to the delegation of responsibility.

It is also important to concentrate on the leadership activities associated with working on teams. LaFasto and Larson discussed the six tasks of team leadership.[45] First, leaders clearly need to focus and pay attention to the goals of the project that will occur during the teamwork. Second, the critical nature of collaboration within the team to get the work done is an important leadership activity. Third, team members like to think and feel that the team process builds their confidence in the way the work is progressing. Team members want to see short-term and long-term results in the work. Team leaders need to help build this confidence and need to be willing to keep team members knowledgeable about external events that affect the work of the team. Secrets defeat teamwork. The fourth leadership activity involves leaders demonstrating technical knowledge and abilities. This activity also means the leader will ask for help or technical assistance when necessary. The fifth leadership activity involves keeping the team on track by setting priorities. It is important to keep the team on task and prevent distractions if possible. When priorities change, leaders must make note of this to the team. The sixth and final task relates to the necessity of managing performance, giving feedback through the group process, and rewarding results.

Team Preparedness

Of course, teams are at different places in their involvement in and commitment to the tasks they have been assigned, and leaders need to monitor team readiness, which ranges from unable and unwilling to carry out the team assignment to able, willing, and confident. In some cases, leaders may have to utilize planning strategies for key team members as well as for the team as a whole.

One useful team technique, based on the so-called skunkworks model, is to send a team to a neutral place away from the organization to work on issues related to the team's activities.[46] The "skunkworks" is a subteam composed of experts on the topic that is the focus of the team activities. These team members tend to be transformational leaders who will move the organization forward.

Team Members

Mallory studied the characteristics of various types of team members.[47] Some members tried to take control of the activities of the team, and these he labeled *dominant members*. These individuals do well in structured situations with a well-defined purpose. The *influencers* tend to be creative and extremely talented in interpersonal relationships. They also tend to be optimistic and try to keep the team together. The *balancers* look at the big picture in an objective manner and try to reconcile the differences among the team members. The *loyalists* are committed to the status quo. Each actual team member, although mainly of one type, has at least a little of every personality characteristic associated with any of the four types. Exercise 6-2 is based on this personality typology. It is intended to get you to reflect on the type of team member you are likely to be.

Team members benefit in several ways from working on a team. First, they gain experience in working together with colleagues on a project.[48] They also learn problem-solving skills, interpersonal relationship skills, and new technological information. In addition, they learn about accountability from a personal perspective as well as a team perspective and become more committed to the team's goals and objectives.

The Life Cycle of Teams

Teams have a life cycle that is similar to the life cycle of human beings.[49] A team starts out as an infant and disbands as it ages and finishes its tasks. Organizational leaders must develop the ability to function as team leaders at each stage of the team life cycle. This is especially true in the public health field, where so many leadership activities occur in a team setting.

Following are guidelines that organizational leaders should use when creating and working with teams:

- Develop teams to address agency or community public health problems.
- Choose multidisciplinary team members for their expertise and leadership qualities.

- Allow teams to make decisions and recommendations for change. Share power and control.
- Share information.
- Intervene in the team process when necessary.
- Do not create teams to alleviate your workload.
- Use the skunkworks technique for dealing with team issues.
- Tie team development to performance standards.
- Put a time limit on the activities of the team.

LEADERSHIP AT THE AGENCY LEVEL

In a 2011 book on management in the health field, the authors claimed that managers nowadays have to integrate clinical practice skills and management skills.[50] The view propounded here is that public health leaders have to integrate public health practitioner skills, management, and leadership skills.

Currently, public health agencies typically have a management orientation. In the 21st century, they will need to become consumer and community driven.[51]

The leadership expertise of agency staff will need to be increased if the agencies are to keep up with the speed of change. **Figure 6-3** shows the relationships among management theories, the healthcare environment, clinical expertise, and consumer healthcare expectations. Most of the items listed are relevant to public health as well as medical care. Two missing items that pertain particularly to public health are building community coalitions and health promotion and disease prevention.

Public health agencies, along with other types of organizations, are undergoing many reforms but need to change further. For one thing, they have not fully incorporated the lessons of business. They are still run as traditional bureaucracies, although community groups are trying to take a role in the making of decisions about public health issues.

In a bureaucracy, the managers and leaders are often far removed from the daily activities of the staff,[52] yet they feel the need to control these activities. Perhaps this is one reason that Peters and Austin urged the importance of "managing by wandering

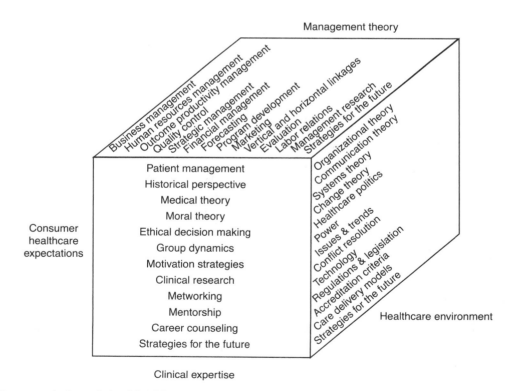

FIGURE 6-3 Characteristics of the Healthcare Management Role. *Source:* Reproduced from J. G. Liebler and C. R. McConnell, *Management Principles for Health Professionals*, 4th ed. Sudbury, MA: Jones & Bartlett, 2004.

around."[53] Of course, it is true that leaders need to monitor operations, but they also need to delegate authority to managers and staff members.[54] By doing this, they can help make the professionals in their organization excited about coming to work in the morning. Leaders need to remember that associates are customers too.

In the late 1950s, Drucker noted that traditional bureaucratic organizations were gradually becoming knowledge-based organizations.[55] Public health agencies have always been knowledge based, and in fact the business community can learn much from public health leaders about knowledge-based organizations and how they work. However, the models for knowledge management are more developed on the business side. For example, Tiwana has examined the four phases of knowledge management strategies for knowledge-based organizations.[56] First, it is necessary to evaluate the current structure for dealing with knowledge in an agency (an infrastructure issue). Second, it is important to develop the system related to knowledge in terms of the analysis dimension, the design of the system, and how it is developed. Third, the issue of deployment and how to use the results of the system becomes critical. Finally, it is necessary to determine the return on investment for the system, the performance evaluation of the system, and making refinement as necessary. Public health leaders have an important role in knowledge management. It will be important for leaders to apply these phases to public health and to modify the models to better reflect the knowledge management aspects of public health practice.

Public health leaders, in order to thrive in the ever-changing environment, need to make a commitment to change and to focus on increasing customer satisfaction, fostering innovation, empowering staff, and instituting appropriate structural reforms.[57] Leadership is not just a matter of charisma; it is hard work.[58]

Nanus identified four main leadership roles (**Figure 6-4**).[59] First, public health leaders (to keep to the focus of this discussion) are spokespeople who present the contemporary public health issues to the community. Second, they are "direction setters" and involve community leaders in prevention activities and in the search for ways to increase the level of health in the community. Third, they act as coaches or mentors for agency associates as a means of improving the agency's effectiveness. Finally, they act as organizational change agents.

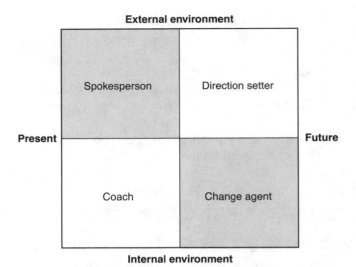

FIGURE 6-4 Leadership Roles. *Source:* Reprinted with permission from B. Nanus, *Visionary Leadership,* p. 13, © 1992, Jossey-Bass Inc., Publishers.

Looking into the Future

If public health leaders are oriented to change and want to become catalysts for change, they need to develop program scenarios for possible futures. This means that they should look for societal trends to guide agenda setting for the agency. They need to be students of change, in other words, and look closely at the predictions of futurists.

The social scientist Alvin Toffler tried to make sense of the changes that are occurring now by looking at past periods of vast social change.[60,61] Toffler identified three waves of societal and organizational change. The first wave was the agricultural revolution, the second was the industrial revolution, and the third, which is occurring now, is the information revolution.

Toffler developed what he called social wavefront analysis, by means of which a scientist can supposedly analyze the leading edge of a wave to predict its future. In *Creating a New Civilization*, he and Heidi Toffler examined the effects of the shift from the second wave to the third wave.[62] Political tensions have arisen between those whose thinking was formed during the industrial period and the new leaders of the information age. An interesting question can be framed regarding the current structure of government in this country. If government reflects its era, does this mean that the old governmental organizational structures, created prior to the industrial age but refashioned during that era, are now obsolete and need to be reworked to fit the information age?

If Alvin Toffler is correct, then public health will undergo major reforms in the 21st century. Even if he isn't, it is unimaginable that public health will remain perfectly static. The developments and trends likely to drive changes in public health agencies in the 21st century include the following:

New models of public health. The direct service activities of local public health departments will continue to decline in the next 20 years.[63] New program and service models will emerge, and community-based public health activities will increase.

Team-based problem solving. More multidisciplinary teams, both ad hoc and permanent, will be created to address public health concerns. Use of the team approach will lead to the structural leveling of organizations. Team success will empower the public health workforce and increase the self-esteem of individual health professionals.

Community health coalitions based on partnership. Public health activities take place in a community setting. Consequently, community partners as well as staff members need to be empowered. Also, partners need to have their expectations met and even exceeded.[64] If their expectations are exceeded, they will become "raving fans" of the agency.

Privatization of assurance activities. Privatization of service provision and program development will become a reality in the future. One local health department struggled with running a mental health program in its county. It also owned the building where mental health services were provided. The program was being operated at a loss, and the health department decided to contract out the delivery of mental health services. A contract was signed (although the department kept oversight responsibility), the building was sold, and the deficit vanished.

Decentralization of responsibilities. Community partners can do some of the work. If they become involved in public health, all sorts of activities will occur. Empowered communities address community issues.[65] Financial issues become less important because community volunteers will find a way to get things done even when the money is not there. Power must be shared to be effective.

Community-wide governance. Governance will need to be incorporated into the activities of the agency and the activities of the community partnerships.

Revision of values. Public health leaders not only will be protectors of the community's values but will help create new or revised value statements that reflect societal and cultural changes. It is interesting to note that politicians defend the status quo, whereas organizational leaders support the generation of new values.

Nonetheless, there seems to be a lag between the development of new values in the society and their adoption at the agency level.

New political structures. There appears to be a trend on the horizon that may affect the future activities of agencies in the public sector. A number of states and local jurisdictions have combined public health departments and human services departments into superagencies. These mergers have caused some public health professionals to wonder whether public health has a future. However, my study of public health leaders indicated that these leaders are generally very hopeful about public health. Public health problems will not go away and will still have to be addressed by agencies headed by public health leaders.

Third-wave leaders. The leaders of the new age are breaking down barriers to collaboration. These leaders know how to build their agencies using self-directed teams with high performance standards. Third-wave leaders also are expert at community building and empowerment. The goals of the agency become integrated with community goals. Third-wave leaders are innovative, creative, flexible, and adaptable to change.

Integration of individual and community goals. Public health leaders must articulate the relevance of public health initiatives to the personal life of individual citizens. In an interview, one public health leader talked about an initiative designed to respond to the nationwide increase in tuberculosis cases. The leader, who worked for a congressional representative, pointed out that tuberculosis would need to be present in the representative's jurisdiction for him to be concerned about the problem. The unfortunate fact is that the societal perspective of public health practitioners—the attitude that protection of the public's health is a matter of social justice—has yet to be accepted by our elected officials.

Complete community empowerment. Citizens as well as public health professionals need to be empowered to carry out public health activities. Empowerment leads to shared responsibility for addressing the public health needs of the local jurisdiction.

Universal access to services. The service system of the future will be comprehensive. Programs will be integrated across agencies, and community coalitions will work together to address health needs. Leadership will be shared. The passage of health reform legislation in 2010 appears to be changing the healthcare system in the United States in spite of criticisms of this legislation.

Because of the terrorist events of September 11, 2001, preparedness will take center stage in the activities of public health with new skills required of public health leaders in this new environment. Although public health will still be local in practice, it will be global in perspective and orientation.[66] The future of American society will be affected by globalization, the expanding of information technology, our chronic financial deficits, and our high energy consumption.[67] Friedman and Mandlebaum argue that it is possible to address these issues and come to positive outcomes, although these outcomes need much work to become reality. These concerns will affect what public health and its infrastructure will be like in the future.

Public Health Functions

From the 1840s to the 1940s, six basic local health agency functions evolved: the collection and interpretation of vital statistics, sanitation, communicable disease control, the provision of maternal and child health programs, health education, and the provision of laboratory services.[68] Between 1940 and 1980, other functions were added, including the provision of environmental health services, the development and provision of personal health services, the coordination of community health services, the operation of medical care and public health facilities, area-wide planning, and the assessment of the adequacy of health services. The year 1988 saw the release of the Institute of Medicine report on public health. This report promoted the use of core functions to organize the activities of public health at the community level.[69]

Public health leaders have changed as public health has changed. They have adapted to new developments and devised innovative approaches to performing the standard public health functions. Although somewhat dated, **Table 6-1** presents a comparison of the activities of a local health department in 1947 and 1995.[70] Since 1995, local health departments have continued to change. Many direct service activities have been outsourced. Local health departments have reoriented some of their activities to emergency preparedness and response activities.[71] I discussed this table with Dr. Bernard Turnock, who pointed out that the determination of which performance measures predominate at a particular point in time is somewhat subjective. Different organizations, performance management committees, and public health professional writers will often come up with different lists of measures. Thus, it is important to determine the credibility of the source.

TABLE 6-1   Comparison of Public Health Practice Performance Measures Used in 1947 and 1995

Examples of Performance Measures from Evaluation Schedule (1947)
Hospital beds: percentage in approved hospitals
Practicing physicians: population per physician
Practicing dentists: population per dentist
Water: percentage of population in communities over 2,500 served with approved water
Sewerage: percentage of population in communities over 2,500 served with approved sewerage systems
Water: percentage of rural school children served with approved water supplies
Excreta disposal: percentage of rural school children served with approved means of excreta disposal
Food: percentage of food handlers reached by group instruction program
Food: percentage of restaurants and lunch counters with satisfactory facilities
Milk: percentage of bottled milk pasteurized
Diphtheria: percentage of children under 2 years given immunizing agent
Smallpox: percentage of children under 2 years given immunizing agent
Whooping cough: percentage of children under 2 years given immunizing agent
Tuberculosis: newly reported cases per death, 5-year period
Tuberculosis: deaths per 100,000 population, 5-year period

Consolidated Panel of Core Function-Related Performance Measures (1995)

Assessment

For the jurisdiction served by your local health department, is there a community needs assessment process that systematically describes the prevailing health status in the community?

In the past three years in your jurisdiction, has the local public health agency surveyed the population for behavioral risk factors?

For the jurisdiction served by your local health agency, are timely investigations of adverse health events, including communicable disease outbreaks and environmental health hazards, conducted on an ongoing basis?

Are the necessary laboratory services available to the local public health agency to support investigations of adverse health events and meet routine diagnostic and surveillance needs?

For the jurisdiction served by your local public health agency, has an analysis been completed of the determinants and contributing factors of priority health needs, adequacy of existing health resources, and the population groups most affected?

In the past three years in your jurisdiction, has the local public health agency conducted an analysis of age-specific participation in preventive and screening services?

Policy Development

For the jurisdiction served by your local public health agency, is there a network of support and communication relationships that includes health-related organizations, the media, and the general public?

In the past year in your jurisdiction, has there been a formal attempt by the local public health agency at informing elected officials about the potential public health impact of decisions under their consideration?

For the jurisdiction served by your local public health agency, has there been a prioritization of the community health needs that have been identified from a community needs assessment?

In the past three years in your jurisdiction, has the local public health agency implemented community health initiatives consistent with established priorities?

For the jurisdiction served by your local public health agency, has a community health action plan been developed with community participation to address priority community health needs?

Examples of Performance Measures from Evaluation Schedule (1947)

Tuberculosis: percentage of cases reported by death certificate

Syphilis: percentage of cases reported in primary, secondary, and early latent stage

Syphilis: percentage of reported contacts examined

Maternal: puerperal deaths per 1,000 total births, 5-year rate

Maternal: percentage of antepartum cases under medical supervision seen before sixth month

Maternal: percentage of women delivered at home under postpartum nursing supervision

Maternal: percentage of births in hospital

Infant: deaths under 1 year of age per 1,000 live births, 5-year rate

Infant: deaths from diarrhea and enteritis under 1 year per 1,000 live births, 2-year rate

Infant: percentage of infants under nursing supervision before 1 month

School: percentage of elementary children with dental work neglected

Accidents: deaths from motor accidents per 100,000 population, 5-year rate

Health department budget: cents per capita spent by health department

(*Continues*)

TABLE 6-1 Comparison of Public Health Practice Performance Measures Used in 1947 and 1995 (*Continued*)

Consolidated Panel of Core Function-Related Performance Measures (1995)

During the past three years in your jurisdiction, has the local public health agency developed plans to allocate resources in a manner consistent with the community health action plan?

Assurance

For the jurisdiction served by your local public health agency, have resources been deployed as necessary to address the priority health needs identified in the community health needs assessment?

In the past three years in your jurisdiction, has the local public health agency conducted an organizational self-assessment?

For the jurisdiction served by your local public health agency, are age-specific priority health needs effectively addressed through the provision of or linkage to appropriate services?

In the past three years in your jurisdiction, has there been an instance in which the local public health agency has failed to implement a mandated program or service?

For the jurisdiction served by your local public health agency, have there been regular evaluations of the effect that public health services have on community health status?

In the past three years in your jurisdiction, has the local public health agency used professionally recognized process and outcome measures to monitor programs and to redirect resources as appropriate?

For the jurisdiction served by your local public health agency, is the public regularly provided with information about current health status, healthcare needs, positive health behaviors, and healthcare policy issues?

In the past year in your jurisdiction, has the local public health agency provided reports to the media on a regular basis?

Source: Reproduced from Turnock and Handler. "From Measuring to Improving Public Health Practice." *Annual Review of Public Health*, Vol. 18: 261–282 © 1997.

Not all states have local public health agencies. In states that do not, the state health department operates like a local agency. In states with local agencies, the activities of the state health department leaders are separate from the activities of the agency leaders. For example, state health departments have tended to stay away from the provision of direct services, especially in the case of services being provided by local public health agencies.[72] A state health department may provide special services that the local agencies do not offer. It is also likely to be engaged in overseeing and coordinating public health activities in the state.

State health department functions include communicable disease control, tuberculosis control, venereal disease control, acquired immune deficiency syndrome monitoring, sanitation, industrial hygiene, dental health, laboratory services provision, public health nursing, case management, maternal and child health program provision, public health education, technical assistance, public health workforce training, development of new local health departments, epidemiologic surveillance, regulation of healthcare facilities, licensure, inspection, cancer screening, and many more. The state health department also serves as the repository for state health data. Since 2001, the activities related to emergency preparedness and response have been added to the list. There clearly is still a need for inclusion of emergency mitigation and recovery dimensions for public health work as well.

State health department leaders are responsible for organizing the state public health system to reflect its mission, vision, and goals and objectives. They need courage to carry out their action plans in the face of community opposition and must know how to reform the state public health system without overstepping the boundaries of the state political system, for, among other reasons, the state is the conduit for funding for local public health agency programs.

In order to see where our performance measurement thinking is today, **Table 6-2** shows the measures determined by the United States Department of Health and Human Services in 2011. There are five major goals for public health and a number of objectives tied to each goal. The measures do provide a framework for state and local health agencies and their leaders to guide public health programs in the future.

TABLE 6-2 HHS Performance Measures, 2011

No.	Task	Most Recent Result	FY 2015 Target	Source
Goal 1: Strengthen Health Care				
Objective A: Make coverage more secure for those who have insurance, and extend affordable coverage to the uninsured				
1.A.1	Increase the proportion of legal residents under age 65 covered by health insurance by establishing healthcare insurance Exchanges and implementing Medicaid expansions	84% (FY 2008)	93% of legal residents with insurance coverage[1]	Current Population Survey
1.A.1.a *Interim Goal*	Increase the number of young adults ages 19 to 25 who are covered as a dependent on their parent's employer-sponsored insurance policy	6.8 million (FY 2008)	7.9 million (FY 2013)[2]	Current Population Survey
1.A.2	Reduce the average out-of-pocket share of prescription drug costs while in the Medicare Part D Prescription Drug Benefit coverage gap for non-Low Income Subsidy (LIS) Medicare beneficiaries who reach the gap and have no supplemental coverage in the gap	100% of cost paid out-of-pocket while in coverage gap (FY 2010)	48% of cost paid out-of-pocket while in coverage gap	Reconciled Prescription Drug Event (PDE) data
Objective B: Improve healthcare quality and patient safety				
1.B.1	Increase the number of Patient Safety Organizations (PSOs) listed by HHS Secretary	75 listed PSOs (FY 2009)	85	AHRQ PSO Web site, http://www.pso.ahrq.gov/
1.B.2	Protect the health of Medicare beneficiaries by increasing the percentage of dialysis patients with fistulas as their vascular access for hemodialysis	54% (FY 2009)	62% of Medicare dialysis patients will receive arteriovenous fistula as their vascular access for hemodialysis	Data submitted by the dialysis facilities Large dialysis facilities submit directly to CMS through a file transfer The 18 End Stage Renal Disease (ESRD) Networks collect data from independent dialysis facilities
1.B.3	Increase the number of hospitals and other selected healthcare settings that report into the National Healthcare Safety Network (NHSN)	2,619 (all types) (FY 2010)	31,000 healthcare facilities	National Healthcare Safety Network (NHSN)

(Continues)

TABLE 6-2 HHS Performance Measures, 2011 (*Continued*)

No.	Task	Most Recent Result	FY 2015 Target	Source
	Objective C: Emphasize primary and preventive care linked with community prevention services			
1.C.1.a	Increase the proportion of individuals who receive Affordable Care Act–targeted clinical preventative services			
	Proportion of privately insured children under age 18 who receive appropriate preventative services			
	Proportion of privately insured children ages 10–17 who received a well-child checkup in the past 12 months	71.4% (FY 2008)	75%	National Health Interview Survey (NHIS)
	Proportion of privately insured adults under age 65 who receive appropriate preventative services			
	Colorectal cancer screenings for privately insured adults ages 50–64	64.7%3 (FY 2010)	70%	NHIS
	Flu shot in last year for privately insured adults ages 50–64	41.9%	50%	NHIS
	Proportion of Medicare beneficiaries who receive appropriate preventative services	See Measures Below.		
	Colorectal cancer screening for Medicare enrollees ages 50–75	63.8% (FY 2007)	70%	Medicare Current Beneficiary Survey (MCBS)
1.C.2	Identify three key factors influencing the scaling up of research-tested interventions across large networks of services systems, such as primary care, specialty care, and community practice	Variables for measuring implementation include organizational culture and climate, capacity for organizational change, dimensions of supervisory adherence to treatment principles, and adherence to clinical guidelines (FY 2009)	Identify three key factors that influence the scaling up of research-tested interventions across large networks of services systems, such as primary care, specialty care, and community practice	Progress reports and publications
1.C.3	Increase percentage of pregnant women who receive prenatal care in the first trimester	70.8% (FY 2007)	72%	National Vital Statistics Reports

	Objective D: Reduce the growth of healthcare costs while promoting high-value, effective care			
1.D.1	Reduce unnecessary hospital readmission rates among Medicare beneficiaries	Reduce all-cause hospital readmission rates by 5% per year from 2012 to 2015	TBD (Hospital readmission rate of Medicare recipients in FY 2012)	Medicare claims data
1.D.2	Review and appropriately value potentially misvalued codes (i.e., high expenditure or high cost) under the Medicare Physician Fee Schedule system for analysis under misvalued code process	80%	TBD	Annual Physician Fee Schedule Regulation
1.D.3	HHS is currently working to develop meaningful performance measure(s) in support of reducing the incidence of hospital-acquired conditions in Medicare and Medicaid. New performance measure(s) for this objective will be incorporated into the HHS Strategic Plan once this work has been completed.			
1.D.4	HHS is currently working to develop meaningful performance measure(s) in support of delivery system reform in Medicare. New performance measure(s) for this objective will be incorporated into the HHS Strategic Plan once this work has been completed.			
	Objective E: Ensure access to quality, culturally competent care for vulnerable populations			
1.E.1	Broaden availability and accessibility of health insurance coverage by increasing enrollment of eligible children in CHIP and Medicaid.	TBD	CHIP: 7,717,317 (FY 2009) Medicaid: 29,943,162 (FY 2009)	Statistical Enrollment Data System (SEDS) and CMS-2082 data; targets will be developed in the near future
1.E.2	Increase the proportion of adults ages 18 and older who are screened in IHS–funded clinical facilities for depression	60%	44% (FY 2009)	Clinical Reporting System (CRS)
1.E.3	Increase the number of pilot sites administering Aging and Disability Resource Centers (ADRCs)	320	197 (FY 2008)	ADRC discretionary grant semi-annual reports
1.E.4	Increase the number of patients served by Health Centers	38.7 million	19.5 million (FY 2010)	HRSA Bureau of Primary Health Care's Uniform Data System
1.E.5	Implement recommendations from Tribes annually to improve the consultation process.	At least 3 recommendations	0 (FY 2009)	Routine IHS Tribal consultation documentation for HHS consultation report and IHS Director's Activities database

(Continues)

TABLE 6-2 HHS Performance Measures, 2011 *(Continued)*

No.	Task	Most Recent Result	FY 2015 Target	Source
Objective F: Promote the adoption and meaningful use of health information technology				
1.F.1	Increase the percentage of eligible primary care professionals participating in Medicare and Medicaid who receive meaningful use payments[4]	TBD (FY 2011)	TBD	CMS Meaningful Use Registration and Attestation System
1.F.2	Increase the percentage of office-based primary care physicians who have adopted EHRs (basic).	TBD	TBD	National Ambulatory Medical Care Survey (NAMCS)
Goal 2: Advance Scientific Knowledge and Innovation				
Objective A: Accelerate the process of scientific discovery to improve patient care				
2.A.1	Make freely available to researchers the results of 300 high-throughput biological assays screened against a library of 300,000 unique compounds, and the detailed information on the molecular probes that are developed through that screening process	The NIH Molecular Libraries Small Molecule Repository (MLSMR) contains 341,830 unique compounds (FY 2009)	Make freely available to researchers the results of 300 high-throughput biological assays screened against a library of 300,000 unique compounds, and the detailed information on the molecular probes that are developed through that screening process	NIH Molecular Libraries Small Molecule Repository (an NIH Roadmap project) http://mli.nih.gov/mli/compound-repository/
2.A.2	Increase the cumulative number of Effective Health Care (EHC) Program products available for use by clinicians, consumers, and policymakers	–6 Systematic Reviews –13 Summary Guides –16 Effective Health Care Research Reports (FY 2010)	–53 Systematic Reviews –83 Summary Guides –110 Effective Health Care Research Reports	AHRQ Effective Health Care Program Web Site: http://effectivehealthcare.ahrq.gov/
2.A.3	Identify and characterize two molecular pathways of potential clinical significance that may serve as the basis for discovering and treating asthma exacerbations	A SNP (–251) in the Interleukin-8 gene was identified and found to be associated with exacerbations of asthma in children (FY 2009)	Characterize two molecular pathways of potential clinical significance that may serve as the basis for discovering new medications for preventing and treating asthma exacerbations	Progress reports or publications

Objective B: Foster innovation to create shared solutions			
2.B.1	Increase the number of identified opportunities for public engagement and collaboration across agencies	TBD	TBD	Data collection associated with development of Open Government Plan
2.B.2	Increase the number of high-value data sets and tools that are published by HHS	TBD	TBD	HHS Data Council
2.B.3	Increase the number of participation and collaboration tools and the activities conducted by the participation and collaboration community of practice	TBD	TBD	HHS Innovation Council
Objective C: Invest in the regulatory sciences to improve food and medical product safety			
2.C.1	Promote innovation and predictability in the development of safe and effective nanotechnology-based products by establishing scientific standards and evaluation frameworks to guide nanotechnology-related regulatory decisions	TBD	Publish at least two guidances related to the safe use of nanoparticles in cosmetic products and nanotechnologies in foods	Office of the Chief Scientist systems
Objective D: Increase our understanding of what works in public health and human service practice			
2.D.1	Increase the number of annual Community Guide reviews	13 (FY 2009)	20	Program Data
Goal 3: Advance the Health, Safety, and Well-Being of the American People			
Objective A: Ensure the safety, well-being, and healthy development of children and youth			
3.A.1	Take actions to strengthen the quality of early childhood programs by advancing recompetition, implementing improved performance standards and improving training and technical assistance system in Head Start; promoting community efforts to integrate early childhood services; and expanding the number of states with QRIS that meet high quality benchmarks for Child Care and other early childhood programs developed by HHS in coordination with the Department of Education	Head Start: Convened training and strategic planning meeting with National Centers, Office of Head Start, and Training/Technical Assistance staff (Dec 2010); Notice of Proposed Rulemaking for Recompetition published (Sept 2010) Child Care/QRIS: Notice of Proposed Rulemaking submitted to the Office of Management and Budget (June 2011)	Child Care/QRIS: Targets for QRIS performance are not yet available Targets will be established once quality benchmarks are finalized and baseline data is collected	Head Start: Office of Head Start Monitoring Reviews Child Care/QRIS: QRIS data from state submissions to the ACF Office of Child Care

TABLE 6-2 HHS Performance Measures, 2011 *(Continued)*

No.	Task	Most Recent Result	FY 2015 Target	Source
3.A.2	Increase the number of low-income children receiving Federal support for access to high-quality early care and education settings, including Head Start, Early Head Start (EHS), and Child Care	12,911 additional Head Start children served 46,465 additional EHS children served (March 2011) 314,000 (estimated) children receiving child care subsidies supported by Recovery Act funds (March 2011)	Increase the number or percentage of low-income children receiving Child Care and Development Fund (CCDF) subsidies who are enrolled in high-quality care settings	The Head Start Enterprise System and the Office of Child Care Information System (OCCIS) from state monthly case-level administrative data report (ACF-801) The ACF Office of Child Care plans to revise the case level administrative data report (ACF-801) to support new reporting on the quality of care for children receiving Child Care and Development Fund subsidies
3.A.3	Improve outcomes for children with trauma-related mental health issues	76% (FY 2009)	79%	Grantee data from SAMHSA's National Child Traumatic Stress Network
Objective B: Promote economic and social well-being for individuals, families, and communities				
3.B.1	Increase the percentage of adult TANF recipients who become newly employed	34.6% (FY 2008)	1.9 percentage points over FY 2009 result	National Directory of New Hires (NDNH)
3.B.2	Maintain the collection rate for current child support orders	62% (FY 2009)	62%	Child Support Enforcement Annual Data Report (Form OCSE 157), Office of Child Support Enforcement (OCSE)
3.B.3	Increase the percentage of refugees entering employment through ACF-funded refugee employment services	40% (FY 2009)	60%	Performance Report (ORR-6)
Objective C: Improve the accessibility and quality of supportive services for people with disabilities and older adults				
3.C.1	Maintain at least 90% of Older Americans Act clients from selected home and community-based services who rate services "good" to "excellent"	>91.03% (FY 2008)	90%	National Survey
Objective D: Promote prevention and wellness				
3.D.1	Reduce the proportion of adolescents (grades 9–12) who are current cigarette smokers	19.5% (FY 2009)	17.5%	Youth Risk Behavior Surveillance (YRBS) and the National Youth Tobacco Survey
3.D.2	Reduce underage drinking in America (as measured by the percentage of youth ages 12–20 who report drinking in the past month)	26.4% (FY 2008)	23.8% (represents a 10% reduction)	National Household Survey on Drug Use and Health (NSDUH)

3.D.3	Increase the number of states with policies to improve nutritional quality of competitive foods (foods and beverages available or sold outside of the federally-reimbursed school meals programs) in schools	27 (FY 2009)	42	National Association of State Boards of Education (NASBE) policy database
3.D.4	Increase behavioral health outcomes (as measured by the SAMHSA National Outcome Measures) for military members and their families served through SAMHSA-supported programs	TBD	60%	SAMHSA Performance Measure Measurement system(s) (TRAC, SAIS, CSAMS)
3.D.5	Increase epidemiology and laboratory capacity within global health ministries through the Field Epidemiology (and Laboratory) Training Program (FELTP)	2,166 total graduates 134 active trainees (FY 2009)	3,166 total graduates 219 active trainees	Program and Administrative Data
Objective E: Reduce the occurrence of infectious diseases				
3.E.1	Reduce the rate of illness caused by Salmonella enteritidis	2.5 cases per 100,000 (3-year average, FY 2007–2009)	1.8 cases per 100,000	FoodNet system
3.E.2	Reduce the estimated number of cases of invasive MRSA infection	89,785 (FY 2008)	56,152	Active Bacterial Core Surveillance
3.E.3	Reduce the Central Line Associated Blood Stream Infection (CLABSI) standardized infection ratio	0.8 (FY 2010)	0.4	National Healthcare Safety Network
3.E.4	Increase proportion of racial and ethnic minorities served in Ryan White HIV/AIDS-funded programs	73% (FY 2009)	Proportion of racial and ethnic minorities in Ryan White HIV/AIDS-funded programs served exceeds representation in national AIDS prevalence data by 5 percentage points	HRSA HIV/AIDS Bureau's Ryan White HIV/AIDS Program Services Report
Objective F: Protect Americans' health and safety during emergencies, and foster resilience in response to emergencies				
3.F.1	Increase the percentage of state public health agencies that can convene—within 60 minutes of notification—a team of trained staff that can decide on appropriate response and interaction with partners	70% (FY 2009)	100%	Division of State and Local Readiness (DSLR)

(Continues)

TABLE 6-2 HHS Performance Measures, 2011 (*Continued*)

No.	Task	Most Recent Result	FY 2015 Target	Source
3.F.2	Increase the number of new medical countermeasures for CBRN and emerging infectious diseases under EUA or licensed	CBRN Licensed: 4 EUA: 4 EID: Licensed: 6 EUA: 1 (FY 2009)	CBRN: Licensed: Plus 4 EUA: Plus 2 EID: Licensed: Plus 5 EUA: TBD[5]	ASPR contract files
Goal 4: Increase Efficiency, Transparency, and Accountability of HHS Programs				
Objective A: Ensure program integrity and responsible stewardship of resources				
4.A.1	Ensure that ARRA Recipients submit at least 96% of expected quarterly reports required under Section 1512 of the Recovery Act	99% response rate (Quarter ending 03/31/2010) (19,874 reports submitted out of 20,079 expected)	98%	Recovery.gov
4.A.2	Maintain the average survey results from appellants reporting good customer service (on a 1–5 scale) at the ALJ Medicare Appeals level	4.30 (FY 2010)	4.30	Appellate Climate Survey
Objective B: Fight fraud and work to eliminate improper payments				
4.B.1	Prevent Medicare fraud and abuse by strengthening CMS provider enrollment actions Increase the percentage of administrative actions taken on Medicare enrollment site visits to targeted high-risk providers and suppliers	TBD	25%	Developmental[6]
4.B.2	Increase the Medicaid Integrity Program Return on Investment (ROI)	175% (FY 2009)	180%	Medicaid Integrity Contractors will compile the data on audits where overpayments are identified and recouped; Results from state system audits identifying overpayments using algorithms
4.B.3	Decrease improper payments in Title IV-E Foster Care Program by lowering the national error rate	4.7% (FY 2009)	3.7%	Regulatory IV-E Foster Care Eligibility Reviews

	Objective C: Use HHS data to improve the health and well-being of the American people		
4.C.1	Increase the electronic media reach of CDC Vital Signs through the use of mechanisms such as CDC.gov and social media outlets	250,000 (FY 2010)	509,355 (5% over FY 2014)	The data source for this measure is Omniture® web analytics, which is a software product that provides consolidated and accurate statistics about interactions with CDC.gov and social media outlets as individuals seek and access information about CDC Vital Signs.
4.C.2	Reduce the average number of field staff hours required to collect data per respondent household for the MEPS	13.0 field staff hours (FY 2009)	12.75 field staff hours	Interviewer pay reporting system
	Objective D: Improve HHS environmental, energy, and economic performance to promote sustainability			
4.D.1	Increase percentage of employees who use telework or an alternative work schedule (AWS) to reduce commuting by four days per pay period	TBD	20%	Department-wide Data Calls
4.D.2	Reduce total HHS fleet emissions by 2%	13,778 MT CO_2e (FY 2008)	13,502 MT CO_2e	PSC
4.D.3	Ensure power management is enabled in 100% of HHS computers, laptops, and monitors	32% (FY 2010)	100%	Department-wide Data Calls
Goal 5: Strengthen the National Health and Human Service Infrastructure and Workforce				
	Objective A: Invest in the HHS workforce to help meet America's health and human service needs today and tomorrow			
5.A.1	Reduce HHS-wide hiring lead times from their current levels to 65 days or less (time from receipt of the complete recruitment request in the HR Office to the date the employee enters on duty.)	130 days (FY 2009)	65 days	Capital HR
	Objective B: Ensure that the Nation's healthcare workforce can meet increased demands			
5.B.1	Expand the field strength of the National Health Service Corps (NHSC)	7,530 (FY 2010)	9,025	HRSA Bureau of Clinician Recruitment and Service's Management Information Support System
5.B.2	The number of primary care providers who complete their education through HRSA's Bureau of Health Professions-supported programs with FY 2010 Prevention and Public Health funding	0 (New program in FY 2010)	500 primary care physicians 600 physician assistants 600 nurse practitioners	HRSA grantee reporting

(Continues)

TABLE 6-2 HHS Performance Measures, 2011 *(Continued)*

No.	Task	Most Recent Result	FY 2015 Target	Source
Objective C: Enhance the ability of the public health workforce to improve public health at home and abroad				
5.C.1	Increase the number of CDC trainees in state, tribal, local, and territorial public health agencies	119 (FY 2009)	198	Program and administrative data
Objective D: Strengthen the Nation's human service workforce				
5.D.1	Increase the percentage of Head Start teachers with AAs, BAs, advanced degrees, or a degree in a field related to early childhood education	83.2% (FY 2009)	100%	Head Start Program Information Report (PIR)
5.D.2	Increase the number of individuals trained by SAMHSA's Science and Services Program (e.g., ATTCs, CAPT, Medical Residency)	48,297 (FY 2009)	49,746	Data from SAMHSA's three science and Services programs
Objective E: Improve national, state, local, and tribal surveillance and epidemiology capacity				
5.E.1	Increase the number of counties and communities that implement evidence-based policies and interventions as a result of their county health ranking	Baseline to be established in 2010	TBD	Association of State and Territorial Health Officials

[1] Target provided from Douglas W. Elmendorf, Director, Congressional Budget Office, to the Honorable Nancy Pelosi, Speaker, U.S. House of Representatives, In letter dated March 20, 2010.

[2] Cannot project beyond 2013 because young adults may prefer to get their own policies in the Exchanges once they are available.

[3] Data from first quarter 2010. Baseline will be updated with full year 2010 data when available.

[4] Includes Medicaid incentive payments for adopting, implementing, and upgrading certified EHR technology in the first year.

[5] EID (pandemic influenza) products would be eligible for use in a public health emergency under EUA in advance.

[6] During FY 2011, in coordination with CMS, the Medicare Administrative Contractors (MACs) and Zone Program Integrity Contractors (ZPICs) will develop a methodology for computing Risk Indicators for Part A and B providers and suppliers similar to the National Supplier Clearinghouse's (NSC's) Fraud Level Indicators for Durable Medical Equipment, Prosthetics, Orthotics and Supplies (DMEPOS) suppliers and utilize them to identify "high risk" providers. For this measure, Risk Indicators will be defined per the proposed regulations at 42 CFR Parts 424, 431, 438, 455, and 457 Medicare, Medicaid, and Children's Health Insurance Programs; Additional Screening, Application Fees, Temporary Enrollment Moratoria, Payment Suspensions and Compliance Plans for Providers and Suppliers; CMS-6028-P. Medicare contractors will utilize CMS-developed reporting requirements to compile the data on the numbers of targeted "high risk" enrollment site visits conducted and the percentage which resulted in an administrative action and to track and report the results of the administrative actions (eg, dollars denied as a result of prepayment review). While the goal is national, based on the aggregate number of "high risk" site enrollment site visits conducted, individual contractors will be strongly encouraged to meet and exceed the national goal to the extent appropriate for the provider population in their jurisdiction.

Source: Reproduced from U.S. Department of Health and Human Services (2011). About the Secretary: Appendix B: HHS Performance Measures. http://www.hhs.gov/secretary/about/appendixb.html. Accessed May 2, 2012.

Responsibilities of Public Health Leaders

Leaders of local public health agencies have the responsibility to promote their agencies. They make sure the agencies are viewed as repositories of public health information as well as providers of high-quality programs and services. They develop relationships with the leaders of public health agencies throughout their state and also develop partnerships with community health providers.

Funding, of course, is critical for strengthening the public health system, and there is currently intense competition in the entire health industry for additional money.[73] Public health leaders need to be involved both in the allocation of public health funds and in the funding for related health service programs. They will need to make strong arguments for public revenues. Public health leaders have become more entrepreneurial since the 1990s. They received grants from and developed contracts with public and private funding organizations to supplement their base budgets. Fund-raising needs to be tied to the mission and vision of the public health agency.

Public health leaders are concerned with excellence in public health. They act as role models for emerging public health leaders. They develop benchmarks for best practices. In their oversight role, they motivate community providers to improve their performance. They work with the leaders of other organizations to develop a comprehensive, integrative approach to improving public health in the community. Public health agencies do not want to duplicate programs or services adequately provided by others, although they might offer competing services if the quality of a community provider's services is open to question.

Public health agency leaders have important responsibilities toward agency staff. They must honestly monitor and evaluate job performance and job satisfaction.[74] If job evaluations are done fairly and regularly, staff will be able to learn their full job responsibilities and meet them more effectively. In addition, public health leaders must be enthusiastic about the task of protecting public health and be able to motivate their colleagues to be enthusiastic as well, by fostering collaboration and sharing power with them, for example.[75] They also should cheer colleagues and their progress. Einstein's formula $e = mc^2$ has been reinterpreted as enthusiasm equals mission times cash and congratulations. People have to be cheered, and they also have to be paid for their efforts.

As noted already, leaders need to empower agency staff. Empowerment must occur at the team level, the agency level, and the community level. **Table 6-3** presents a list of principles of empowerment.[76]

In summation, at the agency level public health leaders have the responsibility to:

- understand how the agency functions
- delegate authority whenever possible
- monitor client satisfaction
- develop performance measurement metrics
- make structural changes in the agency to accommodate new or emerging public health issues
- encourage knowledge management systems development
- explore alternate futures for the agency
- apply the core functions model to agency activities
- empower the agency staff and the community residents

TABLE 6-3   Ten Principles of Empowerment

1. Tell people what their responsibilities are.
2. Give them authority equal to the responsibilities assigned to them.
3. Set standards for excellence.
4. Provide them with training that will enable them to meet the standards.
5. Give them knowledge and information.
6. Provide them with feedback on their performance.
7. Recognize them for their achievements.
8. Trust them.
9. Give them permission to fail.
10. Treat them with dignity and respect.

Source: Adapted from "Ten Principles of Empowering People" from *10 Steps to Empowerment* by Diane Tracey. Copyright © 1990 by Diane Tracey.

LEADERSHIP AT THE COMMUNITY LEVEL

Leadership at the community level requires more systems-based skills than are utilized at the team and agency levels. At this level, public health leaders work to increase the visibility of the public health agency. In interviews with 100 American public health leaders, the author found consistent agreement that the public lacked in-depth knowledge about public health. Thus, public health leaders have a duty to provide public health information to the business community, the medical and health industry community, social agencies, and the general public. Public health leaders need to develop skills in community building in order to work with community groups to create an environment for positive social change.

Figure 6-5 shows the dimensions of public health leadership. Public health leaders build on the core functions model, regardless of the level of leadership, while taking into account the political and social realities that affect the agency and the community. Public health agencies must take into consideration social and political issues if they are to survive. For one thing, they are mandated by funding sources to provide certain basic services and programs. (This raises the issue of the proper balance between mandated services and community-based services and programs not included in the mandated services protocol.)

The Nature of Community

Over the past couple of decades, business discovered community.[77] Business leaders now see that community involvement needs to be part of the practice of business.

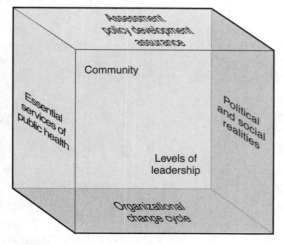

FIGURE 6-5 Dimensions of Public Health Leadership.

Public health agencies, by their nature, serve communities, but serving a group of citizens who live in a specified geographic area does not mean community issues are being addressed. My study of public health leaders found that their efforts at developing community coalitions have been uneven at best. Almost all of the respondents stated that public health agencies have not been successful in getting the public to understand public health.

Community is more than bricks and mortar. It is more than a place to live. It is the place in which our dreams and aspirations are or are not fulfilled. When we talk about improvement in our quality of life, community is part of the improvement process. Community is the place where values are put into action. Community is a complex system made up of individuals, families, politicians, health organizations, human services agencies, churches, schools, businesses, business organizations, and so on (**Figure 6-6**). It is a system that accepts challenges, and to develop the resources to deal with them it needs to be built on the strengths of its constituent parts, not on their weaknesses.[78]

One view currently prevalent is that we need to rediscover civility.[79] Civility requires that community leaders be open to the opinions of other people and other organizations. It also means that it is important to not degrade others. If civility training needs to be done, it should include a discussion of civility and its components, the relationship of civility to leadership, problem solving and decision making, conflict resolution and negotiation, levels of collaboration at the vertical and horizontal levels, systems thinking, values and ethics, and the relationship of civility to trusteeship. Furthermore, public health leaders must transfer the leadership skills they use at the team and organizational levels to the community level. Leaders build communities in all their leadership activities.

It should be noted that public health concerns are part of almost every crisis that confronts a community. Exercise 6-3 is intended to explore what is likely to occur when a community experiences a natural disaster.

Advocacy through the Media

Media advocacy is an important way to promote public health programs and services.[80] The use of social media like Facebook and Twitter is another approach. Public health leaders should learn how to use the media to create support for agency goals. For example, they should consider sending letters on a regular basis to newspapers and other sources to increase the visibility of public health.

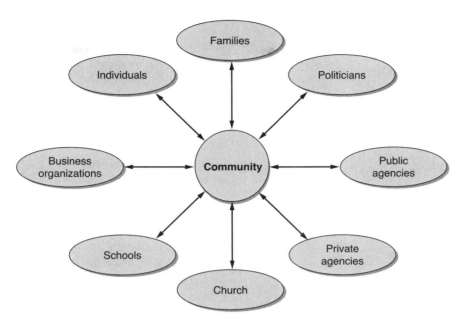

FIGURE 6-6 Community Constituents.

Think of the importance of using the media in the following situation: a public health leader in a conservative, middle-class community discovers that five cases of human immunodeficiency virus infection have recently been discovered. A statistic like this can hit the nerve center of a community. It is the public health leader who will have the skills to defuse the crisis and get community constituents to become partners in dealing with the problem.

One of the most important responsibilities of public health leaders is to promote prevention at the community level.[81] Our knowledge of health and disease is constantly growing, and new technologies and community-based prevention strategies are continually being developed to address public health concerns. The public needs to be convinced of the importance of using these technologies and strategies. It is the job of public health leaders to make the case.

Linking Programs

There is a good argument that public health programs should be linked together where possible.[82] The Centers for Disease Control and Prevention created Prevention Research Centers in a number of universities. Many, if not all, of these centers rely on community support to carry out their activities. Public health leaders, who see the future of their agencies as tied to primary prevention rather than direct services, know that linkage to academic programs will strengthen the infrastructure of public health in their communities.

Community Building

Community building is a complex process that does not occur overnight. Peck analyzed it into four stages.[83] In the first stage, various community representatives who have formed a coalition pretend to have the community's interests at heart in order to gain acceptance for their own agendas. Peck called this the pseudocommunity stage. The second stage, which begins when the coalition realizes that community concerns are not being addressed, is one of chaos. Next comes the stage of emptiness, in which the leaders have to empty themselves of all their preconceived notions about the community and its concerns. It is extremely difficult for the leaders to leave their agendas at the door. The fourth stage is when true community comes into being.

Organizations involved in building a community need leaders.[84] These leaders must be students of the community and its culture and be able to involve individuals with different power bases in community change. Because each community resident has an agenda to which he or she is committed, leaders have to find ways to reconcile the differing agendas.

Community coalitions ideally should be learning organizations.[85] The members of a coalition need to examine their predispositions and how these predispositions affect the community-building process. In addition, the scientific perspective needs to be incorporated into the group's deliberations.

Community building is best achieved through the use of collaborative leadership.[86] Following are

10 factors that can contribute to the success of collaboration and community building:

1. good timing and a clear need
2. strong stakeholder groups
3. broad-based involvement
4. credibility and openness of process
5. commitment and/or involvement of high-level leaders
6. support or acquiescence of "established" authorities or powers
7. overcoming mistrust and skepticism
8. strong leadership of the process
9. interim successes
10. a shift to broader concerns[87]

Coalition Building

Coalition building is an important part of empowering communities. Public health agencies can no longer work in isolation. Community leaders need to be involved in addressing public health issues. The major advantage of a coalition is that all voices are heard and programs can be developed that better reflect the health needs of the community. The major disadvantage is that being part of a coalition is time consuming.

Cohen and colleagues developed an eight-step model for developing community coalitions (**Table 6-4**).[88] The model is based on the experience of the Contra Costa County (California) Health Services Department Prevention Programs. The authors define a coalition as a group of interested parties (individuals and organizations) that want to influence the attempt to solve a critical problem. The coalition members need to develop strategies for each of the eight steps and know when to move to the next step.

A coalition can have many advantages. It can help to save resources. It can influence a large number of people in a community through its diversified membership. It can create an agenda that is more comprehensive than the agenda of any single community organization. It can create a network for the sharing of information, a network that could be used beneficially by the local public health agency for purposes of marketing and fostering change in the community. In addition, coalition members gain satisfaction when they see positive things happen, and a coalition can influence emerging grassroots organizations as they explore their roles in the community.

Building community through coalitions that are responsible and credible is an important goal of public health leaders. A report from the Centers for Disease Control and Prevention stated that public health should use a process called community engagement.[89] Community engagement involves collaboration between people who are in the same geographic area, share special interests, or are in similar situations. A mixture of social science and art, community engagement integrates the ideas of culture, community, coalition building, and collaboration. The report reviewed the literature for examples of successful engagement and presented a list of the principles of community engagement (**Table 6-5**).

Partnerships are collaborative relationships that involve more than minimal cooperation. They tend to evolve through the same steps outlined in the systems model of organizational change. Partnerships have a vision and a mission, they have goals and objectives, and they develop and implement action plans and evaluate their degree of success. The late Reverend Everett Hageman, who was one of the founders of the National Association of Local Boards of Health (NALBOH), was a major supporter of leadership development in public health, and I spent many hours talking to him about the importance of partnership. After Hageman's death, I put together a list of principles based on discussions with him. The principles that pertain to partnerships follow:

TABLE 6-4 Eight Steps to Building an Effective Coalition

Step 1: Analyze the program's objectives and determine whether to form a coalition.

Step 2: Recruit the right people.

Step 3: Devise a set of preliminary objectives and activities.

Step 4: Convene the coalition.

Step 5: Anticipate the necessary resources.

Step 6: Define elements of a successful coalition structure.

Step 7: Maintain coalition vitality.

Step 8: Make improvements through evaluation.

Source: Reprinted with permission of Contra Costa Health Services, *Developing Effective Coalitions: An Eight Step Guide.* © 1994, Contra Costa County Health Services Department Prevention Programs.

TABLE 6-5 Characteristics of Successful Community Engagement

- Community engagement efforts should address multiple levels of the social environment, rather than only individual behaviors, to bring about desired changes.
- Health behaviors are influenced by culture. To ensure that engagement efforts are culturally and linguistically appropriate, they must be developed from a knowledge and respect for the targeted community's culture.
- People participate when they feel a sense of community, see their involvement and the issues as relevant and worth their time, and view the process and organizational climate of participation as open and supportive of their right to have a voice in the process.
- Although it cannot be externally imposed on a community, a sense of empowerment—the ability to take action, influence, and make decisions on critical issues—is crucial to successful engagement efforts.
- Community mobilization and self-determination frequently need nurturing. Before individuals and organizations can gain control and influence and become players and partners in community health decision making and action, they may need additional knowledge, skills, and resources.
- Coalitions, when adequately supported, can be useful vehicles for mobilizing and using community assets for health decision making and action.
- Participation is influenced by whether community members believe that the benefits of participation outweigh the costs. Community leaders can use their understanding of perceived costs to develop appropriate incentives for participation.

Source: Reproduced from Centers for Disease Control and Prevention (1997). Public Health Practice Program Office, *Principles of Community Engagement*, Agency for Toxic Substances and Disease Registry.

- Leave time to get to know your community partners on a personal level.
- Partnership is part of the human condition.
- Working together is better than fighting.
- Learn by listening to your partners.
- True partnership is the gourmet approach to organization.

Each community coalition needs to be revitalized on a regular basis. A community coalition often seems to work better when a community crisis is occurring.[90] When the crisis is over, people tend to move away from the coalition back to their own personal agendas. Thus, public health leaders need to be aware of this fact and make an extra effort to keep community coalitions alive after crises are resolved.

National and International Communities

Thus far the discussion has been on leadership in local communities, but there are also national and international communities that offer an arena for action by public health leaders. National leaders, like local leaders, act as advocates for public health. They keep the public informed about health issues. They work on the construction of a national mission and vision as well as public health goals for the future. They collaborate with leaders at the state level on the creation of a coordinated nationwide approach to public health. They collaborate with national elected officials to address key

Leadership Tip

When you are given another committee assignment:
(a) Ask, why me?
(b) State that you are willing to be on this committee for the next three months, then you will come back and discuss whether you should continue on this committee.
(c) Tell the committee chair that you do not want to be on another committee for life. You want the group to decide on how long the committee will remain in existence. If more time is needed, you want to determine whether you will continue to serve.

public health concerns, including the training of the public health workforce.

On the international level, public health leaders implement public health programs in countries where public health is not a priority. These leaders need to develop skills to enhance their ability to improve the quality of life of people in these countries. Rather than reinvent public health, these leaders develop networks with public health leaders throughout the world to share model program methods for addressing specific public health problems. As already stated, public health leaders need to think globally about public health concerns while acting locally (to protect community residents from potential health crises). Building healthy communities is partially a matter of applying knowledge gained from all parts of the world to local conditions. The importance of the 2005 International Health Regulations (IHR) cannot be overestimated. These rules and regulations were agreed upon by 193 countries. These countries believe that these international rules and procedures will help to make the world safe from potential threats to global health. The IHR were approved by the World Health Organization in the summer of 2005.[91] These rules will affect every community in the world.

Most of the strategies and techniques discussed in this chapter have universal application. Following is a list of guidelines of special pertinence for public health leaders working at the community level:

- Build trust.
- Form coalitions.
- Develop partnerships.
- Teach community groups about the core public health functions.
- Do community building with partners.
- See the community as a system.
- Encourage coalitions or partnerships to continue after a public health crisis has been resolved.
- Use the media to promote best practices in public health.
- Push a prevention agenda.
- Understand the connections between public health at a global level and public health at a local community level and their connections.

LEADERSHIP AT THE PROFESSIONAL LEVEL

Despite the multidisciplinary nature of public health, its leaders need to speak with a unified voice. Public health as a profession takes precedence over the particular educational backgrounds of the public health workforce. The following situation occurs much too often. A physician with almost no background in public health was appointed the administrator of a large county health department. He made decisions from a medical viewpoint and felt that physicians were the only ones who were qualified to do the department's work. He ran the department using a direct medical service approach and totally ignored the population-based approach to public health.

Public health practitioners tend not to travel to professional meetings or for professional development. Many local health departments have a small staff and are reluctant to let employees go to meetings. Funds for professional development are generally minimal, and paying for professional development is typically considered by taxpayers to be a waste of money. Yet public health leaders know that it is important to communicate with other public health professionals. Some of these leaders go to the annual meetings held by the various public health associations and even take a leadership role in these associations. They help to create public health policy that will trickle down to the local public health programs. Leadership development training seems to be a factor here. For example, most of the presidents over the past 15 years of the Illinois Public Health Association were either faculty members or fellows of the Mid-America Regional Public Health Leadership Institute (Illinois, Indiana, Wisconsin, and Michigan).

Public health leaders need to become active participants of the American Public Health Association (APHA). This association represents all segments of the professional public health workforce. It is at the annual meetings of the APHA that national public health policy tends to be made. The National Association of County and City Health Officials (NACCHO) is a key national organization for local health leaders. The Association of State and Territorial Health Officials (ASTHO) is a similar national organization for state health leaders. Leaders should also consider taking key roles in the various associations for state and county public health directors. Board of health leaders can also become involved in a national organization for boards (NALBOH). Following is a list of guidelines for leaders who wish to make a mark in the profession of public health:

- Promote public health as a profession.
- Encourage staff to become involved in state and national public health associations.
- Be active in state and national public health associations by serving on committees or agreeing to run for an association office.
- Run for office in these associations.

SUMMARY

Leaders need to operate on five different levels. On the most basic level, they need to know how to exert their influence as leaders on other individuals person to person. To do this, they need a whole range of skills and abilities, from communication skills to the ability to balance work and private life. Regardless of the level at which the leader works, commitment and passion for the work are critical. Leaders strongly believe in what they do. Bolman and Deal believe that there is a spiritual quality to leadership that is difficult to explain or study.[92] However, it can be seen in the work and the dedication of leaders. Thus, leadership is not only about money; it is also about all the things that make us wake up in the morning with anticipation for the job we have to do today. Leadership at the personal level is about our passion in action.

Leaders also must be capable of functioning in teams, either as team leaders or as ordinary team members. Some of the leadership skills needed for teamwork are also needed on the personal level, but some are different. It is on teams that we see the mission of our work in action.[93] It is at the team level that we also see the emotional aspects of working together and creating networks of collaboration and friendship.

Public health leaders are often the heads of public health departments or agencies and thus need agency-level leadership skills as well. Their duties as agency heads include such things as mission and vision statement development, fund-raising, job performance evaluation, and role modeling. At the agency level, leaders also see systems thinking in action. It is the big picture that guides our work.

Public health is obviously community oriented, and so public health leaders need to be able to play a major role in the community by acting as advocates on public health issues and building coalitions to deal with such issues. They thus need advocacy skills and coalition-building skills, among others. At the community level, we can see the passion and commitment of our partners.

Finally, public health leaders, like other public health practitioners, have an obligation to try to improve the field of public health, by becoming involved, for instance, in professional organizations such as the APHA, NACCHO, ASTHO, and NALBOH. Many leaders have told me that the networking that occurs at the national level is important and helps leaders to sustain their strong belief that public health can make a difference. Fighting our battles legislatively becomes easier when we work with our public health colleagues. Professional friendships often become lifelong.

DISCUSSION QUESTIONS

1. What is the difference between politics and governance?
2. What is the relationship between communication and empowerment?
3. What are several of the main barriers preventing public health leaders from being as effective as they could be?
4. What is one way public health leaders can deal with the increasing cultural diversity in the public health workforce?
5. What are some of the main reasons for creating and using teams?
6. What are the main agency-related responsibilities of public health leaders?
7. What are the main community-related responsibilities of public health leaders?
8. How do partnerships differ from other types of collaborative relationships?
9. How can public health leaders further the interests of the public health profession?

EXERCISE 6-1: The Drawbacks and Benefits of Professional Diversity

Purpose: to explore how professional diversity affects public health decision making

Key concepts: decision making, diversity, professionalism

Procedure: There has been an increase in teen gang violence in Midcity over the past 10 years. The mayor and the city council have asked the Midcity Department of Health to develop a plan to address this public health problem. The class should divide into teams to discuss the problem. Each team will have a designated leader from a different profession (e.g., physician, nurse, social scientist, environmental health specialist, or business expert). In addition to discussing the issue at hand, which should be done for half an hour, each team should reserve 5 to 10 minutes to examine how the professional background of the leader influenced the process and the outcome of the discussion. Each team will then report its conclusions and observations to the class as a whole.

EXERCISE 6-2:   Leadership and Team Building

Purpose: to explore leadership behavior in team situations

Key concepts: team building, leadership in teams, leadership style

Procedure: Using the Mallory personality typology, each group member, using the worksheet (**Table 6-6**), should classify him- or herself as one personality type or as a combination of types and analyze the degree to which he or she possesses the characteristics associated with all four types. The group should then break into teams and discuss the results of the self-evaluations, focusing on issues that are critical to team development, such as team communication, discussion facilitation, consensus development, priority setting, and conflict resolution.

TABLE 6-6   Personal Worksheet for Team-Building Activities

1. Name _____

2. Leadership Personality Type

   For each personality type, determine the percent of time you spend demonstrating each type

Personality Type	Percent of This Type	
Dominant		
Influencer		Total = 100%
Balancer		
Loyalist		

3. How many years have you spent in activities related to teams?

4. Would you rather work alone or in teams?

5. How often have you chaired the team?

6. Describe any major successes on teams on which you have worked.

7. Describe your experiences on teams that have not been successful.

8. How have teams affected your job performance positively or negatively?

9. Have you felt stress while working on teams?

10. Do you find working on teams to be structured or unstructured?

11. How would you describe your people skills?

Source: Adapted from E. Mallory, *Team-Building*, pp. 17–18. © 1991, National Press Publications.

EXERCISE 6-3:   A Community in Crisis

Purpose: to explore the role public health leaders play in dealing with a natural disaster

Key concepts: collaboration, community crisis, strategic planning

Procedure: In February, California is hit by storm after storm. The town of Crisona is flooded for a two-week period, the entire town is evacuated, and mudslides eventually begin to occur in the surrounding hills.

The class should divide into teams of 6 to 10 members. In each team, half the members are assigned to play the role of Crisona City Council members, including the role of the mayor and of the head of the Crisona Department of Public Health. The remaining team members are to act as community leaders. These leaders and the head of the Department of Public Health testify about the disaster and offer suggestions for addressing it. The city council listens to the testimony and then works with the community leaders to develop a strategy for dealing with the crisis. The whole team should develop a one-page consensus statement outlining a strategy for responding to the crisis.

REFERENCES

1. R. A. Heifetz and M. Linsky, *Leadership on the Line* (Boston: Harvard Business School Press, 2002).
2. Heifetz and Linsky, *Leadership on the Line*.
3. T. G. Lewis, *Bak's Sand Pile* (Williams, CA: Agile Press, 2011).
4. M. J. Wheatley, *Leadership and the New Science*, Revised and Expanded (San Francisco: Berrett-Kohler, 1999).
5. S. D. Parks, *Leadership Can Be Taught* (Boston: Harvard Business School Press, 2005).
6. P. M. Senge et al., *The Dance of Change* (New York: Bantam, 1999).
7. A. Delaney, *Politics for Dummies* (Foster City, CA: IDG Books, 1995).
8. P. Capezio and D. Morehouse, *Secrets of Breakthrough Leadership* (Franklin Lakes, NJ: Career Press, 1997).
9. E. Tosca, *Communication Skills Profile* (San Francisco: Jossey-Bass, 1997).
10. D. Tannen, *You Just Don't Understand: Women and Men in Conversation* (New York: Morrow, 1990).
11. J. W. Gardner, *On Leadership* (New York: The Free Press, 1990).
12. R. Kelley, *The Power of Followership* (New York: Doubleday, 1992).
13. J. Carver, *Boards That Make a Difference*, 3rd ed. (San Francisco: Jossey-Bass, 2006).
14. V. Mamlin-Upshaw, "Creating Effective Boards," *Leadership* 2, no. 3 (1993): 1, 11.
15. J. W. Dearing and E. M. Rogers, "Agenda-Setting," *Communication Concepts* 6 (1992): 1–98.
16. Institute of Medicine, *The Future of Public Health* (Washington, DC: National Academies Press, 1988).
17. B. J. Turnock, *Public Health: What It Is and How It Works*, 5th ed. (Burlington, MA: Jones & Bartlett Learning, 2012).
18. Turnock, *Public Health*.
19. Turnock, *Public Health*.
20. S. R. Covey, *The Seven Habits of Highly Effective People* (New York: Simon & Schuster, 1989).
21. M. M. Chemers, "Contemporary Leadership Theory," in *The Leader's Companion*, ed. J. T. Wren (New York: The Free Press, 1995).
22. R. Hargrove, *Mastering the Art of Creative Collaboration* (New York: McGraw-Hill Business Week Books, 1998).
23. Turnock, *Public Health*.
24. S. Wellington, "Breaking the Glass Ceiling," *Leader to Leader* 6 (1997): 37–42.
25. R. R. Thomas Jr., "Diversity and Organizations of the Future," in *The Organization of the Future*, ed. P. Hesselbein et al. (San Francisco: Jossey-Bass, 1997).
26. A. H. Maslow, *Motivation and Personality* (New York: Harper & Row, 1954).
27. J. R. O'Neil, *The Paradox of Success* (New York: Jeremy P. Tarcher and Putnam, 1993).
28. Capezio and Morehouse, *Secrets of Breakthrough Leadership*.
29. S. Helgesen, "Women and the New Economy," *Leader to Leader* 4 (1997): 34–39.
30. C. Mallory, *Team-Building* (Shawnee Mission, KS: National Press Publications, 1991).
31. S. P. Robbins and M. Coulter, *Management*, 11th ed. (Upper Saddle River, NJ: Prentice Hall, 2011).
32. Mallory, *Team-Building*.
33. Mallory, *Team-Building*.
34. P. F. Drucker, *Management: Tasks, Responsibilities, Practices* (New York: Harper & Row, 1985).
35. J. R. Katzenbach and D. K. Smith, *The Wisdom of Teams* (Boston: Harvard Business School Press, 1993).
36. K. Blanchard et al., *The One Minute Manager Builds High Performance Teams* (New York: Morrow, 1990).
37. P. M. Senge, *The Fifth Discipline Fieldbook* (New York: Doubleday, 1999).
38. P. Lencioni, *The Five Dysfunctions of a Team* (San Francisco: Jossey-Bass, 2002).
39. D. Cohen and L. Prusek, *In Good Company: How Social Capital Makes Organizations Work* (Boston: Harvard Business School Press, 2001).
40. P. Capezio, *Supreme Teams: How to Make Teams Really Work* (Shawnee Mission, KS: National Press Publications, 1996).
41. Wellins et al., *Empowered Teams* (San Francisco: Jossey-Bass, 1991).
42. K. Blanchard et al., *The Three Keys to Empowerment* (San Francisco: Berrett-Koehler, 1999).
43. Wellins et al., *Empowered Teams*.
44. P. Hersey, K. H. Blanchard, and D. E. Johnson, *Management of Organizational Behavior*, 9th ed. (Upper Saddle River, NJ: Prentice-Hall, 2007).
45. F. LaFasto and C. Larson, *When Teams Work Best* (Thousand Oaks, CA: Sage Publications, 2001).
46. T. Peters and N. Austin, *A Passion for Excellence* (New York: Random House, 1985).
47. Mallory, *Team-Building*.
48. J. R. Katzenbach and D. K. Smith, *The Wisdom of Teams* (Boston: Harvard Business School Press, 1993).
49. Capezio, *Supreme Teams*.
50. J. G. Liebler and C. R. McConnell, *Management Principles for Health Professionals*, 5th ed. (Burlington, MA: Jones & Bartlett Learning, 2011).
51. Liebler and McConnell, *Management Principles for Health Professionals*.
52. J. Q. Wilson, *Bureaucracy* (New York: Basic Books, 1989).
53. Peters and Austin, *A Passion for Excellence*.
54. K. Blanchard and S. Bowles, *Gung Ho* (New York: Morrow, 1998).
55. P. F. Drucker, *Landmarks of Tomorrow* (New York: Harper & Row, 1957).
56. A. Tiwana, *The Knowledge Management Toolkit*, 2nd ed. (Upper Saddle River, NJ: Prentice-Hall, 2002).
57. T. Peters, *Thriving on Chaos* (New York: Knopf, 1987).
58. P. F. Drucker, *Managing for the Future* (New York: Truman, Talley Books, and Dutton, 1992).
59. B. Nanus, *Visionary Leadership* (San Francisco: Jossey-Bass, 1992).
60. A. Toffler, *The Third Wave* (New York: Bantam, 1980).

61. A. Toffler and H. Toffler, *Creating a New Civilization* (Atlanta: Turner Publishing Co., 1994).

62. Toffler and Toffler, *Creating a New Civilization*.

63. P. K. Halverson et al., *Managed Care and Public Health* (Gaithersburg, MD: Aspen Publishers, 1998).

64. K. Blanchard and S. Bowles, *Raving Fans* (New York: Morrow, 1993).

65. M. DePree, *Leading Without Power* (San Francisco: Jossey-Bass, 1997).

66. L. Rowitz, *Public Health in the 21st Century: The Prepared Leader* (Sudbury, MA: Jones & Bartlett, 2006).

67. T. L. Friedman and M. Mandelbaum, *That Used to Be Us* (New York: Farrar, Straus, and Giroux, 2011).

68. W. Shonick, *Government and Health Services* (New York: Oxford University Press, 1995).

69. Institute of Medicine, *The Future of Public Health*.

70. Shonick, *Government and Health Services*.

71. Rowitz, *Public Health in the 21st Century*.

72. Shonick, *Government and Health Services*.

73. Turnock, *Public Health*.

74. D. J. Breckon, *Managing Health Promotion Programs* (Gaithersburg, MD: Aspen Publishers, 1997).

75. J. M. Kouzes and B. Z. Posner, *The Leadership Challenge*, 4th ed. (San Francisco: Jossey-Bass, 2007).

76. D. Tracy, *10 Steps to Empowerment* (New York: Harper-Collins, 1992).

77. F. Hesselbein et al., eds., *The Community of the Future* (San Francisco: Jossey-Bass, 1998).

78. J. P. Kretzman and J. L. McKnight, *Building Communities from the Inside Out* (Evanston, IL: Northwestern University Center for Urban Affairs, 1993).

79. M. S. Peck, *A World Waiting to Be Born* (New York: Bantam Books, 1993).

80. L. Wallack and L. Dorfman, "Media Advocacy: A Strategy for Advancing Policy and Promoting Health," *Health Education Quarterly* 23, no. 3 (1996): 293–317.

81. R. C. Brownson and E. A. Baker, "Prevention in the Community: Taking Stock," *Journal of Public Health Management and Practice* 4, no. 2 (1998): vi–vii.

82. R. C. Brownson et al., "Demonstration Projects in Community-based Prevention," *Journal of Public Health Management and Practice* 4, no. 2 (1998): 66–77.

83. M. S. Peck, *The Different Drum* (New York: Simon & Schuster, 1987).

84. R. H. Rosen, *Leading People* (New York: Viking, 1996).

85. P. M. Senge, "Creating Quality Communities," in *Community-Building*, ed. K. Gozdz (San Francisco: New Leaders Press, 1995).

86. D. O. Chrislip and C. E. Larson, *Collaborative Leadership* (San Francisco: Jossey-Bass, 1994).

87. Chrislip and Larson, *Collaborative Leadership*.

88. L. Cohen et al., *Developing Effective Coalitions: An Eight Step Guide* (Pleasant Hill, CA: Contra Costa County Health Services Department Prevention Programs, 1994).

89. Centers for Disease Control and Prevention, Agency for Toxic Substances and Disease Registry, *Principles of Community Engagement* (Atlanta: CDC Public Health Practice Program Office, 1997).

90. Peck, *A World Waiting to Be Born*.

91. "International Health Regulations Enter Into Force," *Medical News Today*, June 16, 2007.

92. L. G. Bolman and T. E. Deal, *Leading with Soul*, 2nd ed. (San Francisco: Jossey-Bass, 2001).

93. R. Wagner and J. K. Harter, *12: The Elements of Great Managing* (New York: Gallup Books, 2006).

Leadership Applications in Public Health

CHAPTER 7

Building Infrastructure

Form follows function—that has been misunderstood. Form and function should be one, formed in a spiritual union.

—Frank Lloyd Wright, 1908

Over the past two and a half decades, public health leaders and by extension human service leaders have struggled with the need to build the infrastructure of the public health and the human services systems. Since the publication in 1988 by the Institute of Medicine of *The Future of Public Health*, the issue of the human services system and its infrastructure has been on the table.[1] This chapter will address some of the building block issues related to strengthening the infrastructure of public health and other health and human services systems, which requires effective leadership to make the changes necessary to build the public health system. First, the most important building block relates to people. Workforce development is a key building block. The education that each public health professional has before entering the human services arena is not sufficient over the long run. Lifelong learning and the ability to adapt to changing realities are critical to the future adaptability of professionals in the human services fields. Second, public health leaders have spent the past twenty-five years promoting the core functions and essential public health services paradigm and have developed its programs on the basis of these core service dimensions. Strengthening the infrastructure of public health will require support for this service paradigm and the data systems necessary to support this paradigm. This paradigm is applicable to most human services systems as well as to the emerging concerns related to emergency preparedness and response. A common language, governing paradigm, community planning systems, and organizational capacity are also critical components for building infrastructure. **Figure 7-1** shows a public health services pyramid that the Centers for Disease Control and Prevention (CDC) has named the Pyramid of Preparedness. All public health is about preparedness and hopefully prevention.

There are a number of other components that need to be considered in better understanding how to build infrastructure. First, it is important for leaders to assess the health of the people in their service areas on a regular basis so that their human services systems are more

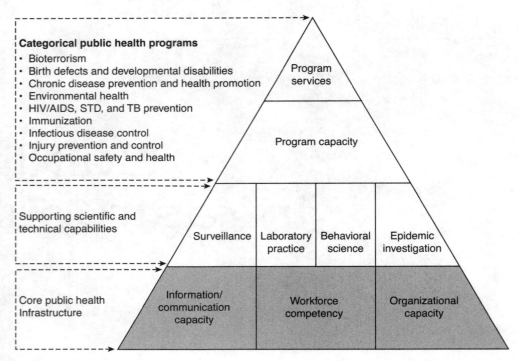

Categorical public health programs
- Bioterrorism
- Birth defects and developmental disabilities
- Chronic disease prevention and health promotion
- Environmental health
- HIV/AIDS, STD, and TB prevention
- Immunization
- Infectious disease control
- Injury prevention and control
- Occupational safety and health

Supporting scientific and technical capabilities

Core public health Infrastructure

Program services

Program capacity

Surveillance | Laboratory practice | Behavioral science | Epidemic investigation

Information/ communication capacity | Workforce competency | Organizational capacity

FIGURE 7-1 **Pyramid of Preparedness.** *Source:* Reproduced from Centers for Disease Control and Prevention (2002). *Public Health Preparedness: A Status Report.* Public Health Practice Program Office.

responsive to emerging health and mental health needs of the public. It is for this reason that the development of model service standards and assessment tools becomes important to a nimble public health and human services system. Public health leaders have pointed out over the years that assessment methods and strategies have been a real strength of the public health system. Assessment as well as other epidemiologic techniques are also strong components of the human services system and its infrastructure. The second enhancement to infrastructure building is an increasing awareness that a performance management approach to organizational effectiveness and the various tools that measure performance are also important aids in strengthening our health service systems. Closely allied to performance measurement as a third factor is the incorporation of quality improvement methodologies into the culture of our human services and public health infrastructure. Leaders need to support this cultural shift. Other techniques that are emerging as important for the improvement in quality of agency programs and services are the community balanced scorecard methodology[2] and the results-based governance approaches.[3]

Development of an accreditation system for local public health agencies creates a level of excellence as well as trust and credibility for public health. Recognition of the good work of public health raises public

awareness as well. These standards of excellence for agencies also build infrastructure. A voluntary accreditation program for local health departments was implemented in 2011.[4] The fifth building block is closely tied to accreditation, and that is certification.[5] Certification refers to the individual and standards of excellence for the work of the public health professional. Certification can be tied to the field of practice of the individual as well as to evidence of management or leadership skills in practice. Health administrator and board of health member certification would be beneficial to the successful direction of local public health and human services agencies. Accreditation informs us of the quality of the work of the agency, and certification tells us how effective these professionals are in these quality organizations.

It is impossible to build infrastructure without well-trained leaders. Most of our professional education programs do not include much, if any, management and leadership training. There are now a number of public health leadership programs to train health professionals in management and leadership. These programs explore the practice of leadership in governmental and not-for-profit agencies in contrast to that in business organizations. Leadership is a critical building block in infrastructure capacity building. Finally, all of the above concerns need to be addressed if we want to reach more positive health outcomes. The effectiveness and efficiency of the work of our organizations need to be measured against the successes of our work on health outcomes.

WORKFORCE DEVELOPMENT AND LEADERSHIP

Workforce development in public health and other human services fields is clearly important if our health professionals are to remain current, be proactive, and improve community health outcomes over the long run. Collaboration is necessary if we are to address the critical concerns of training health professionals. Workforce development does not belong to any one organization. Expertise does not exist in only one organization, in one consulting firm, or in one professional organization. Training needs to be seen as an evolving system, like building an onion layer by layer. Each set of trainers adds a layer to the onion that leads to a more comprehensive approach to training with its important practice orientation. Thus, training and workforce development specifically must be viewed as a collaborative activity. Personal organizational agendas must not predominate in these workforce discussions. I have personally seen some governmental agencies, consulting firms, and organizations claim that they are *the* workforce development organization. Professional development can occur in many venues. At the federal level, each agency clearly has a role to play in adding another layer and training orientation to the onion. At the professional organization level, an agency must work with multiple partners to make workforce development comprehensive and collaborative.

Leadership development is clearly a critical component in workforce development. As health professionals, we are educated at the technical level to be expert in our chosen health professions. We are not trained to be managers or even leaders. We look for programs to teach us these skills when we move into higher administrative positions. I cannot understand how some of my professional colleagues do not see the connection between training managers and leaders as being a workforce development issue. All training is about being better at what we do. Not only do we need to support Public Health 101 training and learning, we need to add training on Management 101 and Public Health Leadership 101. As mentioned above, training of our professional colleagues is also a collaborative activity; we all learn from each other. Our training partners teach us new skills and approaches to leadership development. They teach us about new tools and resources. They offer us insights into new books with innovative approaches. How can we be effective trainers if we do not collaborate or learn from others? The secret is in the collaboration, if training programs are to be effective in training our colleagues. Personal agendas need to be pushed to the back burner. We need to build the workforce development onion together.

THE LEADERSHIP PYRAMID

Effective leaders are lifelong learners. To put this lifelong learning approach into perspective, it is useful to look at education and learning in a sequential manner. The following discussion is based on a new approach to leadership development conceptualized by Lichtveld, Rowitz, and Cioffi.[6]

Over the past 20 years, there has been increasing interest in developing a framework for training public health professionals in management and leadership under the assumption that leaders help build a stronger public health system. Yet there is controversy about whether leaders differ in the realms of business and the governmental human services fields. Although it is true that leadership is a universal phenomenon, it takes different forms depending on the cultural and ecological context in which it takes place. There is clearly a difference between the profit motive in business and the social justice motive that drives much of the public health enterprise. As we view the public health system during the second decade of the new century with all the new challenges that public health now faces, it is necessary that the issue of leaders in public health be looked at from a new perspective. This model presents a perspective for a better understanding of leadership from the vantage points of leadership competencies, performance, capacity building, and best practices.

Public health leaders act within the core functions of public health and the essential services that drive the public health enterprise. In addition, the public health leader is prepared for any natural or abnormal crisis that might occur in the community. The leader is committed to lifelong learning and the need to develop competencies required to protect the health of the public.

Figure 7-2 presents the leadership pyramid as an inverted triangle. Each level of the pyramid requires a determination of the specific competencies necessary to master that level of the pyramid. The triangle is inverted to show that the breadth of the set of core

New leadership pyramid

FIGURE 7-2 **New Leadership Pyramid.** *Source*: Reproduced from M. Lichtveld, L. Rowitz, and J. Cioffi, "The Leadership Pyramid." *Leadership in Public Health* 6(4), 3–8.

public health skills that public health professionals need to have act as the foundation for all that follows. There are numerous approaches these days to the learning competencies needed to practice certain professional and administrative skills. The pyramid requires that we reorganize these competencies to fit each level of the leadership pyramid. As each public health workforce member masters each level of the pyramid, performance should improve and the infrastructure of public health should strengthen. Performance management systems and performance standards guided by a set of principles (e.g., essential public health services) would monitor this process.

Training is the key to mastering these skills, which are necessary to build infrastructure. If public health professionals improve their skills and become more effective as a result, they have increased their personal skills, which can then be translated into team-based and other collaborative processes. All of this would eventually improve the capacity of the total public health system. The bottom of the pyramid emphasizes the importance of best practices. The business community is not shy about discussing its best. Public health must begin to do the same. Quality assurance can then be newly defined by the following formula:

Quality improvement + leadership competency as evidenced by best practices + high-performance expectations + strategic capacity building

We can look for clues to the understanding of this quality improvement approach in the body of the pyramid. The first layer emphasizes the importance of an understanding and mastery of a set of core public health skills. Public health must have a public health workforce that is trained in public health principles and practice. Too many of the people in our existing governmental public health workforce have no formal public health training. Recent discussions on credentialing have raised some of these issues, and proponents have argued that the public health system cannot be strengthened without this training. The set of competencies required for this level of the pyramid has been developed by a number of different organizations. All of this means that these skills will be required of all public health workers in the governmental public health sector.

Public health is a profession with a workforce from many different disciplines. Doctors, nurses, dentists, lawyers, business administrators, behavioral scientists, epidemiologists, biostatisticians, and many other discipline-specific experts are required if public health is to carry out its major responsibilities. The major message in level two of the pyramid is that the successful public health practitioner must blend the competencies of public health with discipline-specific competencies if public health is to function in an effective manner. Business learned these lessons long ago and has been able to build profit enterprises through the combination of sound business practices with discipline-specific expertise in many different areas.

The skills necessary to achieve competence at the first two levels of the pyramid are somewhat technical in nature. When the public health professional moves to level three of the pyramid, the tasks to be performed relate to making an agency run effectively and efficiently. Thus, a shift occurs when an individual decides to move into a management role. New sets of skills are needed. In addition, many public health professionals find that during their professional education they were not trained to be managers. Although business schools have been involved in the development of competencies for work in commerce, adaptation of these skills to the public sector needs to become more formalized. Management competencies are quite complex and require training in such diverse topics as time management, performance appraisal, strategic planning, office management, budgeting, and so on. A few certification programs now exist for public health management that do begin to build a public health competency-based management model. Illinois, Missouri, and Iowa have tested such systems.

The move from management to leadership is not as easy as it first appears. First, there is a shift from an agency focus to a systems and community focus affected by the complexity of modern life. The manager looks inside the organization to make sure it is functioning efficiently and effectively. The leader looks outward and is concerned with how public health functions at the community and national levels. In addition, the technical skills required at levels one and two and the administrative task-oriented skills of level three become secondary to people and relational skill competencies. The core skills required to be an effective leader are also not taught in most traditional health science curricula. The national, regional, and state-based public health leadership institutes have been trying to fill this gap since the early 1990s. The National Public Health Leadership Network, in collaboration with the Centers for Disease Control and Prevention, developed a framework of core public health leadership competencies that have been integral to the training of public health leaders. Public health leaders throughout the country have gone through these training programs. The philosophy of these training programs has been that leaders exist throughout the public health system and that leadership can be taught.

Training without implementing the content of the training is nothing more than an academic exercise. Leadership development needs to be available for the practicing public health professional who can use these new leadership skills in the work and community context of their professional work. Leadership needs to be implemented to be effective. This may not be an easy task in environments that are resistant to change. Leaders need to be students of the cultural settings in which they work. Each new skill will undergo some transformation as it is applied in the work and community setting. These new challenges may require skills beyond those that occur in most leadership development programs. It is at this level that such skills as collaboration, team building, community building, assets planning and mapping, emotional intelligence, and others come to play a key role in effective leadership.

The events of September 11, 2001, changed the field of public health. Program priorities have changed. Bioterrorism and emergency preparedness specialists have become a critical component of the public health professional workforce. With these shifting priorities, it is clear that new leadership skills are needed to guide health departments. Public health preparedness and response have become a major priority for public health. Public health leaders have discovered that new skills are needed for the types of collaboration required to deal with crisis events in communities. Public health leaders need skills not only in risk management but also in health crisis communications. Forensic epidemiology has become a new specialty. Public health informatics is a new approach to the creation and use of data. Strategies are needed for working with families of the victims of a crisis event. New partnerships are required with the Federal Bureau of Investigation, police departments, fire departments, hospitals and other health facilities, crisis agencies, community partners, and elected officials. Communicating with people who use different jargon has also become a major leadership challenge. Higher levels of emotional intelligence skills have become more critical. Bioterrorism leadership competencies are different from traditional leadership skills. It is a new type of leadership with more complex skills needed for working in environments of constant change. Exercise 7-1 will put some of these issues in perspective by helping you examine public health before September 11, 2001, and today.

The leadership pyramid presents a start on the development of a complex, new approach to the training of public health leaders. Leaders themselves will need to move from level to level in the development of their personal, team, agency, community, and professional skills. Whereas technical skills are usually required to get a person a job in an agency, people skills become more critical to job performance over the long run. Leadership development becomes a lifelong learning activity that leaders must commit to if best practices are to occur and if the infrastructure of public health is to be strengthened.

PUBLIC HEALTH INFRASTRUCTURE

Underlying all discussions of public health training and education programs (much of this section of the chapter is based on the 2002 CDC report *Public Health's Infrastructure: A Status Report*) is the rationale for why these programs are important. Public health professionals perform better when they have not only the skills and competencies necessary to make an agency run effectively, but also the vision and understanding of techniques to improve the health of people who live in their jurisdiction. Public health leaders provide the vision and direction for making these things happen. On one hand, we have the people who power the public health system. On the other hand, we have the structural components that make the system run. Public health infrastructure is embedded in the community and its organizational systems, the competencies for successful performance, and the relationships that are needed to carry out the mission of public health to improve the health of the public. Finally, public health is affected by the resources that aid public health professionals to perform well in their communities.

Above, the discussion involved the first key component of infrastructure: the public health workforce. The second component of basic infrastructure relates to information and data systems. This component addresses the key issue of the need for information to guide the public health enterprise. Uniformity in the way data are collected as well as agreed-upon definitions for data elements are required. Training the public health workforce in data collection techniques as well as in the important skills related to the use of information is necessary. Up-to-date data guidelines are needed. These guidelines include recommendations, health alerts, and standards-based information and communications systems to monitor disease and enable efficient and effective communication among public and private health organizations, the media, and the public. It is clear that the more traditional approaches to data provided by epidemiological methods are no longer sufficient. It is for this reason that the new science of public health informatics is making such advances. Public health leaders must know how to use information as well as have the ability to judge the quality of the data to be used; these skills are more important than the data collection procedures. However, the prepared public health leader needs to know how to ask the appropriate questions about data. A basic background in epidemiology is thus required.

The third component of basic infrastructure relates to organizational capacity. Organizational capacity relates to the ability of public health to collaborate with others in coalitions, alliances, and partnerships to guarantee that the three core functions of assessment, policy development, and assurance, as well as all 10 essential services, are being met in every jurisdiction (**Table 7-1**). Public health leaders need to work with other professionals in public as well as private healthcare organizations to accomplish this. Organizational capability is enhanced by these relationships. Public health is a community issue, not just an agency-based one. As was pointed out above in the discussion of the leadership pyramid, public health leaders need many types of leadership skills if they are to be effective and prepared to address any health challenges in their communities.

The three components of basic infrastructure are clearly interrelated. A deficiency in one affects the other two. CDC has argued that the goal of strengthening the basic public health infrastructure means the achievement of improvements in all three. In addition, leadership is required to bring about these improvements. The public health leader is one who will see the systemic relationship between the three components of basic infrastructure and their relationship to the other two levels of the pyramid. The second level of the public health pyramid relates to the ability of the public health system to provide essential capabilities to respond more effectively to public health crises. These essential capabilities involve the knowledge, skills, and abilities related to surveillance (see Figure 7-1). Public health needs 360° vision so that its leadership can be on the watch for all potential threats to the health status of people in its jurisdictions. An occurrence of a new threat in another part of the world can affect the local community in the future. These techniques of surveillance involve quantitative as well as qualitative factors. Surveillance means listening to the stories of our colleagues at a national or local meeting. It involves an awareness of the fears and concerns of people who live in our neighborhoods. It involves news reports from other parts of the world about an outbreak of SARS;

TABLE 7-1   The 10 Essential Public Health Services

Assessment
1. Monitor health status to identify community health problems.
2. Diagnose and investigate health problems and health hazards in the community.
Policy Development
3. Inform, educate, and empower people about health issues.
4. Mobilize community partnerships to identify and solve health problems.
5. Develop policies and plans that support individual and community health efforts.
Assurance
6. Enforce laws and regulations that protect health and ensure safety.
7. Link people to needed personal health services, and ensure the provision of health care when otherwise unavailable.
8. Ensure a competent public health and personal healthcare workforce.
9. Evaluate effectiveness, accessibility, and quality of personal and population-based health services.
Serving All Functions
10. Research new insights and innovative solutions to health problems.

a major earthquake and tsunami that kills hundreds of thousands of people in southeast Asia; a major tornado in Joplin, Missouri; or some emerging infectious agent.

Our public health laboratories and the work they do to discover threats and potential threats are essential to public health. In recent years, there has been a need for public health laboratories to work with crime laboratories on potential bioterrorism activities. Communication as well as an understanding of chain-of-evidence techniques become critical. The whole new field of forensic epidemiology has developed to address these new concerns. The third essential capability involves the important role of epidemiology in public health's day-to-day activities. It is not that we don't know the importance of epidemiology in our work; it is the limited number of epidemiologists to do the necessary work. Small health departments cannot afford an epidemiologist on staff. Models for sharing this expertise are becoming important in our environment of preparedness. Part of our workforce development strategy should be to train the public health workforce in basic epidemiologic skills.

The tip of the pyramid involves the new vision of public health. Today, most of public health's work relates to responding to bioterrorism, emerging infections, and other health threats. This preparedness model needs to be expanded to include all those other concerns that public health has been addressing over the past decades. Water and air quality are still

important. Restaurant inspections are still important. Teenage pregnancy is still an issue. Many other local issues continue to need to be addressed.

There are many issues that drive our agenda relative to strengthening public health infrastructure. There never seems to be enough money to do our jobs well. Public health still seems to lack importance among the public and the policy makers. Accountability for spending taxpayers' money is always an issue. When financial deficits occur at the federal, state, and local levels, public programs are often the first things to be cut. Although public health has made many advances in the past, it is almost impossible to predict when another public health breakthrough will occur. Policy makers are often complacent about funding public health programs unless a crisis or threat appears imminent. The fear of potential terrorist acts on American soil has led to an influx of money into the public health sector. More traditional public health programs continue to be underfunded. Public health professionals need to learn the valuable lesson that our business leaders learned long ago: all money builds infrastructure regardless of source. Whining does not serve us well. There will never be enough money. It is important to do the best we can with the resources we have.

Public health is becoming an increasingly complex field. The scope and variability of the skills required to keep the public health system functional are quite extensive. Public health involves the investigation of outbreaks to questionnaire design, interviewing techniques, population-based program development, lab specimen collection techniques, standards for effective community prevention services, and many other emerging techniques. When you add all the skills necessary to be a successful manager and leader, the public health toolbox gets full. Despite the specialized competencies that are needed, many elected officials continue to believe that training programs are a frivolous expense.

Many global factors also affect infrastructure, including such things as the global movement of goods and people, antimicrobial resistance, global infrastructure gaps that prevent the containment of potentially lethal diseases, environmental and ecological changes such as deforestation and pesticide use, and the potential for bioterrorism. Public health leaders need to think globally even though they act within a local jurisdiction. The prepared public health leader is one who monitors the health issues of the world and is able to see the effect of these worldwide trends on local health conditions. Prepared leaders are visionary and always think of the future in developing local public health priorities.

Other issues of concern to public health leaders relative to building infrastructure include the necessity of building public health and emergency preparedness capacity at both the local and state levels. It is critical that any enmity between state and local public health professionals be removed. Collaboration is necessary. In addition, a strong relationship between a local or state health administrator and the board of health (if one exists) and elected officials is also a critical partnership if communities are to become prepared for all potential health threats. Another important infrastructure issue is the defining role of the public health agency in the community setting. Public health agencies need to be seen as responsive to the health needs of the entire population. If these agencies are to serve as coordinating centers for all public health concerns, then they must develop collaborations with all other health providers in the community. Although it is often a social justice philosophy that drives many public health professionals into the field, it is sound management and leadership competencies that will strengthen the public health system.

Many infrastructure discussions involve the issue of service access and the elimination of health disparities. It is important to move beyond access issues to strategies to change the existing situation. The public health leader knows that solutions need to be found in places other than the financial area. Arguments have accumulated that universal health coverage is the answer. It may be, but leaders know that universal health coverage is still a long way off. So the strategies that must be developed will require innovative approaches to health promotion and disease prevention as well as new collaborations to increase the health service coverage for the people in our communities.

New types of information are needed. Better data on the public health workforce are needed, ranging from the composition of the workforce to the movement of public health professionals through the system. Performance appraisals based on individual assessment need to be changed to team performance appraisals, as so much of public health's work occurs in the community with community partners. The views of expenditures with the concern of methods of determining costs for community-based activities also needs to be part of the public health infrastructure discussion. Public health leaders need to work with their business partners to develop new measures for this nontraditional form of activity.

A final issue of importance is tied to the program mismatch between mandated public health services and the 10 essential public health services. First, the public and the policy makers often do not understand the essential services mode. It is clearly an approach that makes sense to the public health leader in the context of the public health system. The essential services are the driving force behind much of what is done in the public health system at a community level. The local public health agency may not carry out all 10 essential services, but all the community agencies involved in public health should carry them out collaboratively. Second, public health leaders know that it is specific mandated programs that are understandable to the public. The public understands the need for clean water and inspected restaurants. The essential services provide a framework for action for public health infrastructure. The prepared public health leader knows that he or she must communicate the results of these actions in a understandable way. The leader must stop being shy about marketing public health's good deeds and best practices. In Case Study 7-A, Dr. Bernard Turnock, director of the Illinois Department of Public Health in the 1980s and now professor of community health sciences at the University of Illinois at Chicago School of Public Health, answers a public health practice quiz related to the issues raised in this chapter regarding the changes in the public health system in the past several years.

Case Study 7-A

A Public Health Practice Quiz for Bernard Turnock

1. How has public health practice changed since 2000?

Public health practice has always been about identifying and addressing threats to health. Since 2000, there has been much more attention focused on health threats attributed to terrorism, but preparing for and responding to emergencies have long been major roles for public health practitioners. Public health practice has not really changed; however, there have been significant changes in the environment in which public health practice takes place, in terms of greater public visibility, expectations, and accountability.

2. Does the essential public health service paradigm make a difference in the way public health professionals practice public health?

The essential public health services provide a framework for public health practice, allowing standards to be established for individual and collective practice. Having a more formalized set of practice standards does indeed change what individuals and organizations do. After all, what gets measured gets done.

3. Why does the discussion of public health infrastructure development dominate the emergency preparedness and response dialogues?

Preparedness and response are attributes of public health systems. Improving public health systems involves making positive changes in the structures and processes (i.e., the infrastructure) of those systems. You can't improve preparedness and response without focusing on public health infrastructure.

4. Do leadership development programs make a difference in the practice of public health?

Leadership is essential to configure and guide the resources and relationships available for public health ends. Leadership development programs bring enhanced skills and attitudes to public health professionals even before they assume leadership positions. The net result is an ever-expanding corps of current and future leaders sharing common values and skills and greater consistency in and better results from modern public health practice.

5. Are leadership skills different in emergency preparedness and response than in traditional public health practice activities?

Not really. Emergency preparedness and response are, and always have been, traditional public health practice activities. This role may not have been widely understood or appreciated prior to the events of 2001, but it is one that public health agencies have carried out since their inception.

HEALTHY PEOPLE 2020

The new *Healthy People* report demonstrates that infrastructure development is critical to all the health topic areas in the report.[7] The key goals of the new report involve objectives related to health improvement, the development of environments that promote good health, and teaching people ways to promote their good health and improve their health behaviors. The job of the public health leader is to build infrastructure to provide a framework to address the social determinants of health. The World Health Organization defined social determination of health as follows:[8]

> The complex, integrated, and overlapping social structures and economic systems responsible for most health inequities. These social structures and economic systems include the social environment, physical environment, health services, and structural and societal factors. Social determinants of health are shaped by the distribution of money, power, and resources throughout local communities, nations, and the world.

A concern about building public health infrastructure for the year 2020 has led to the development of several emerging issues, including tribal public health infrastructure, public health workforce disparities, public health agency accreditation, public health systems research, and public health law.[9] **Exhibit 7-1** presents the recommended objectives related to public health infrastructure in the *Healthy People 2020* document.[10] These infrastructure objectives provide guidance to public health leaders for some of their work and collaborative activities.

EXHIBIT 7-1 *Healthy People 2020* Summary of Public Health Infrastructure Objectives

Public Health Infrastructure

Number	Objective Short Title
Workforce	
PHI-1	Competencies for public health professionals
PHI-2	Continuing education of public health personnel
PHI-3	Integration of core competencies in public health into curricula
PHI-4	Public health majors and minors
PHI-5	Public health majors and minors consistent with core competencies
PHI-6	Associate degrees and certificate programs in public health
Data and Information Systems	
PHI-7	National data for *Healthy People 2020* objectives
PHI-8	National tracking of *Healthy People 2020* objectives
PHI-9	Timely release of national data for *Healthy People 2020* objectives
PHI-10	State vital event reporting
Public Health Organizations	
PHI-11	Public health agencies laboratory services
PHI-12	Public health laboratory systems performance of essential services
PHI-13	Epidemiology services
PHI-14	Public health system assessment
PHI-15	Health improvement plans
PHI-16	Public health agency quality improvement program
PHI-17	Accredited public health agencies

Topic Area: Public Health Infrastructure

Workforce

PHI-1: Increase the proportion of Federal, Tribal, State, and local public health agencies that incorporate Core Competencies for Public Health Professionals into job descriptions and performance evaluations.

PHI-1.1 (Developmental) Federal agencies.

Potential data source: Office of Personnel Management.

PHI-1.2 (Developmental) Tribal agencies.

Potential data source: Indian Health Service.

PHI-1.3 (Developmental) State public health agencies.

Potential data source: State and Territorial Public Health Survey, Association of State and Territorial Health Officials (ASTHO).

PHI-1.4 Local public health agencies.*

Target: 25 percent.

Baseline: 15 percent of local public health agencies incorporated Core Competencies for Public Health Professionals into job descriptions in 2008.

Target setting method: 10 percentage point improvement.

Data source: National Profile of Local Health Departments, National Association of County and City Health Officials (NACCHO). (*Data for local public health agencies include only data on job descriptions.)

PHI-2: (Developmental) Increase the proportion of Tribal, State, and local public health personnel who receive continuing education consistent with Core Competencies for Public Health Professionals.

Potential data sources: Indian Health Service, the Public Health Foundation TRAIN database, and HRSA's Public Health Training Centers.

PHI-3: Increase the proportion of Council on Education for Public Health (CEPH) accredited schools of public health, CEPH accredited academic programs, and schools of nursing (with a public health or community health component) that integrate Core Competencies for Public Health Professionals into curricula.

Target: 94 percent.

Baseline: 91 percent of Council on Education for Public Health (CEPH) accredited schools of public health, CEPH accredited academic programs, and schools of nursing (with a public health or community health component) integrated Core Competencies for Public Health Professionals into curricula for public health professionals in 2006.

Target setting method: 3 percent improvement.

Data source: Council on Linkages Study, Council on Linkages Between Academic and Public Health Practice.

PHI-4: Increase the proportion of 4-year colleges and universities that offer public health or related majors and/or minors.

　　PHI-4.1 Majors.

Target: 10 percent.

Baseline: 7 percent of 4-year colleges and universities offered public health or related majors in 2008.

Target setting method: Modeling/projection.

Data source: Catalog Scan of Undergraduate Public Health Programs, the Association of American Colleges and Universities (AAC&U).

　　PHI-4.2 Minors.

Target: 15 percent.

Baseline: 11 percent of 4-year colleges and universities offered public health or related minors in 2008.

Target setting method: Modeling/projection.

Data source: Catalog Scan of Undergraduate Public Health Programs, the Association of American Colleges and Universities (AAC&U).

PHI-5: (Developmental) Increase the proportion of 4-year colleges and universities that offer public health or related majors and/or minors which are consistent with the core competencies of undergraduate public health education.

Potential data source: Association of Schools of Public Health (ASPH) in collaboration with the American Association of Colleges and Universities (AAC&U).

PHI-6: Increase the proportion of 2-year colleges that offer public health or related associate degrees and/or certificate programs.

　　PHI-6.1 Associate degrees.

Target: 3 percent.

Baseline: 2 percent of 2-year colleges offered public health or related associate degrees in 2009.

Target setting method: Modeling/projection.

Data source: American Association of Colleges and Universities (AAC&U); American Association of Community Colleges (AACC).

　　PHI-6.2 Certificate programs.

Target: 1 percent.

Baseline: 0 percent of 2-year colleges offered public health or related associate certificate programs in 2009.

Target setting method: Modeling/projection.

Data source: American Association of Colleges and Universities (AAC&U); American Association of Community Colleges (AACC).

(Continues)

EXHIBIT 7-1 *Healthy People 2020* Summary of Public Health Infrastructure Objectives (*Continued*)

Data and Information Systems

PHI-7: (Developmental) Increase the proportion of population-based *Healthy People 2020* objectives for which national data are available for all major population groups.

Potential data source: Assessment of Objective Data Availability (AODA), CDC, NCHS.

PHI-8: Increase the proportion of *Healthy People 2020* objectives that are tracked regularly at the national level.

> **PHI-8.1** (Developmental) Increase the proportion of objectives that originally did not have baseline data but now have at least baseline data.

Potential data source: Assessment of Objective Data Availability (AODA), CDC, NCHS.

> **PHI-8.2** (Developmental) Increase the proportion of objectives that have at least a baseline and one additional data point.

Potential data source: Assessment of Objective Data Availability (AODA), CDC, NCHS.

> **PHI-8.3** (Developmental) Increase the proportion of objectives that are tracked at least every 3 years.

Potential data source: Assessment of Objective Data Availability (AODA), CDC, NCHS.

PHI-9: (Developmental) Increase the proportion of *Healthy People 2020* objectives for which national data are released within 1 year of the end of data collection.

Potential data source: Assessment of Objective Data Availability (AODA), CDC, NCHS.

PHI-10: Increase the number of States that record vital events using the latest U.S. standard certificates and report.

> **PHI-10.1** States using the standard certificate of birth.

Target: 52 (50 States, the District of Columbia, and New York City).

Baseline: 28 States used the 2003 U.S. standard birth certificate in 2008.

Target setting method: Total coverage.

Data source: National Vital Statistics System-Natality (NVSS-N), CDC, NCHS.

> **PHI-10.2** States using the standard certificate of death.

Target: 52 (50 States, the District of Columbia, and New York City).

Baseline: 30 States used the 2003 U.S. standard death certificate in 2008.

Target setting method: Total coverage.

Data source: National Vital Statistics System-Mortality (NVSS-M), CDC, NCHS.

> **PHI-10.3** States using the standard report of fetal death.

Target: 52 (50 States, the District of Columbia, and New York City).

Baseline: 22 States used the 2003 U.S. standard report of fetal death in 2008.

Target setting method: Total coverage.

Data source: National Vital Statistics System-Fetal Death (NVSS-Fetal Death), CDC, NCHS.

Public Health Organizations

PHI-11: Increase the proportion of Tribal and State public health agencies that provide or ensure comprehensive laboratory services to support essential public health services.

> **PHI-11.1** Disease prevention, control, and surveillance.

Target: 97 percent.

Baseline: 88 percent of State public health agencies provided or ensured comprehensive laboratory services to support disease prevention, control, and surveillance in 2008.

Target setting method: 10 percent improvement.

Data source: Comprehensive Laboratory Services Survey (CLSS), Association of Public Health Laboratories (APHL).

PHI-11.2 Integrated data management.

Target: 61 percent.

Baseline: 55 percent of State public health agencies provided or ensured comprehensive laboratory services that had integrated data management in 2008.

Target setting method: 10 percent improvement.

Data source: Comprehensive Laboratory Services Survey (CLSS), Association of Public Health Laboratories (APHL).

PHI-11.3 Reference and specialized testing.

Target: 86 percent.

Baseline: 78 percent of State public health agencies provided or ensured comprehensive laboratory services that had reference and specialized testing in 2008.

Target setting method: 10 percent improvement.

Data source: Comprehensive Laboratory Services Survey (CLSS), Association of Public Health Laboratories (APHL).

PHI-11.4 Environmental health and protection.

Target: 61 percent.

Baseline: 55 percent of State public health agencies provided or ensured comprehensive laboratory services for environmental health and protection in 2008.

Target setting method: 10 percent improvement.

Data source: Comprehensive Laboratory Services Survey (CLSS), Association of Public Health Laboratories (APHL).

PHI-11.5 Food safety.

Target: 34 percent.

Baseline: 31 percent of State public health agencies provided or ensured comprehensive laboratory services for food safety in 2008.

Target setting method: 10 percent improvement.

Data source: Comprehensive Laboratory Services Survey (CLSS), Association of Public Health Laboratories (APHL).

PHI-11.6 Laboratory improvement and regulation.

Target: 45 percent.

Baseline: 41 percent of State public health agencies provided or ensured comprehensive laboratory services that had laboratory improvement or regulation in 2008.

Target setting method: 10 percent improvement.

Data source: Comprehensive Laboratory Services Survey (CLSS), Association of Public Health Laboratories (APHL).

PHI-11.7 Policy development.

Target: 74 percent.

Baseline: 67 percent of State public health agencies provided or ensured comprehensive laboratory services for policy development in 2008.

Target setting method: 10 percent improvement.

Data source: Comprehensive Laboratory Services Survey (CLSS), Association of Public Health Laboratories (APHL).

PHI-11.8 Emergency response.

Target: 67 percent.

(*Continues*)

EXHIBIT 7-1 *Healthy People 2020* Summary of Public Health Infrastructure Objectives (*Continued*)

Baseline: 61 percent of State public health agencies provided or ensured comprehensive laboratory services for emergency response in 2008.

Target setting method: 10 percent improvement.

Data source: Comprehensive Laboratory Services Survey (CLSS), Association of Public Health Laboratories (APHL).

PHI-11.9 Public health-related research.

Target: 32 percent.

Baseline: 29 percent of State public health agencies provided or ensured comprehensive laboratory services for public health-related research in 2008.

Target setting method: 10 percent improvement.

Data source: Comprehensive Laboratory Services Survey (CLSS), Association of Public Health Laboratories (APHL).

PHI-11.10 Training and education.

Target: 52 percent.

Baseline: 47 percent of State public health agencies provided or ensured comprehensive laboratory services training and education in 2008.

Target setting method: 10 percent improvement.

Data source: Comprehensive Laboratory Services Survey (CLSS), Association of Public Health Laboratories (APHL).

PHI-11.11 Partnerships and communication.

Target: 67 percent.

Baseline: 61 percent of State public health agencies provided or ensured comprehensive laboratory services partnerships and communication in 2008.

Target setting method: 10 percent improvement.

Data source: Comprehensive Laboratory Services Survey (CLSS), Association of Public Health Laboratories (APHL).

PHI-12: (Developmental) Increase the proportion of public health laboratory systems (including State, Tribal, and local) which perform at a high level of quality in support of the 10 Essential Public Health Services.

Potential data source: Association of Public Health Laboratories.

PHI-13: Increase the proportion of Tribal, State, and local public health agencies that provide or ensure comprehensive epidemiology services to support essential public health services.

PHI-13.1 State epidemiologists with formal training in epidemiology.

Target: 100 percent.

Baseline: 87 percent of State epidemiologists had received formal training in epidemiology, as reported in 2009.

Target setting method: Total coverage.

Data source: Epidemiology Capacity Assessment (ECA), Council of State and Territorial Epidemiologists (CSTE).

PHI-13.2 (Developmental) Tribal public health agencies.

Potential data source: Survey of Regionally Based Public Health Services/Infrastructure in Indian Country, Tribal Epidemiology Centers (Epi Centers), CDC, and IHS.

PHI-13.3 State public health agencies.

Target: 100 percent.

Baseline: 55 percent of State public health agencies provided or ensured comprehensive epidemiology services to support essential public health services in 2009.

Target setting method: Total coverage.

Data source: Epidemiology Capacity Assessment (ECA), Council of State and Territorial Epidemiologists (CSTE).

PHI-13.4 Local public health agencies.

Target: 100 percent.

Baseline: 64 percent of local public health agencies provided or ensured comprehensive epidemiology services to support essential public health services in 2008.

Target setting method: Total coverage.

Data source: National Profile of Local Health Departments, National Association of County and City Health Officials (NACCHO).

PHI-14: Increase the proportion of State and local public health jurisdictions that conduct a public health system assessment using national performance standards.

PHI-14.1 State public health systems.

Target: 78 percent.

Baseline: 49 percent of State public health systems had ever submitted State Public Health System Performance Assessment data to the National Public Health Performance Standards Program in 2009.

Target setting method: Modeling/projection.

Data source: National Public Health Performance Standards Program, CDC, Office for State, Tribal, Local, and Territorial Support.

PHI-14.2 Local public health systems.

Target: 50 percent.

Baseline: 28 percent of local public health systems had ever submitted Local Public Health System Performance Assessment data to the National Public Health Performance Standards Program in 2009.

Target setting method: Modeling/projection.

Data source: National Public Health Performance Standards Program, CDC, Office for State, Tribal, Local, and Territorial Support.

PHI-14.3 (Developmental) Local boards of health.

Potential data source: National Public Health Performance Standards Program, CDC, Office for State, Tribal, Local, and Territorial Support.

PHI-15: Increase the proportion of Tribal, State, and local public health agencies that have implemented a health improvement plan and increase the proportion of local health jurisdictions that have implemented a health improvement plan linked with their State plan.

PHI-15.1 (Developmental) Tribal agencies.

Potential data source: Indian Health Service.

PHI-15.2 (Developmental) State public health agencies.

Potential data source: State and Territorial Public Health Survey, Association of State and Territorial Health Officials (ASTHO).

PHI-15.3 (Developmental) Local public health agencies.

Potential data source: National Profile of Local Health Departments, National Association of County and City Health Officials (NACCHO).

PHI-15.4 (Developmental) Local jurisdictions that have linked health improvement plans to the State plans.

Potential data source: National Profile of Local Health Departments, National Association of County and City Health Officials (NACCHO).

PHI-16: (Developmental) Increase the proportion of Tribal, State, and local public health agencies that have implemented an agency-wide quality improvement process.

(*Continues*)

EXHIBIT 7-1 *Healthy People 2020* Summary of Public Health Infrastructure Objectives (*Continued*)

Potential data sources: State and Territorial Public Health Survey, Association of State and Territorial Health Officials (ASTHO); National Profile of Local Health Departments, National Association of County and City Health Officials (NACCHO); and the Indian Health Service.

PHI-17: (Developmental) Increase the proportion of Tribal, State, and local public health agencies that are accredited.

Potential data source: Public Health Accreditation Board.

Source: Reproduced from Healthy People 2020. Public Health Infrastructure Objectives. http://www.healthypeople.gov/2020/topicsobjectives2020/objectiveslist.aspx?topicid=35. Page last updated: Thursday, July 26, 2012. Accessed July 30, 2012.

SUMMARY

It is important to tie concerns of lifelong learning for public health leaders with a continuing need to strengthen the infrastructure of public health in order to improve the health status of all citizens in our communities. Leaders must be prepared to address whatever situations affect the health of their constituents. It is imperative that the public health leader recognize that there is more to being prepared than creating another bookshelf plan or conducting another tabletop exercise or drill. Public health leaders need to consider the contextual issues that affect the public health system as well as specific competencies and skill sets that are needed for effective public health leaders now and in the future. The skills needed for public health in an emer-

gency preparedness and response environment mean that prepared public health leaders need to develop not only the core public health leadership skills discussed earlier in this chapter, but also new skills that work in new program environments.

Figure 7-3 presents a graphic view of the skills that are necessary to prepare our public health leaders for their new tasks. First, there are three critical dimensions to the public health infrastructure that require our attention. From a conceptual basis, strengthening the public health system is tied to our ability to build strong community relationships. Social capital concepts will be used to demonstrate this. Second, *Healthy People 2020* gives a series of recommendations to guide public health infrastructure development over the current decade. As strategies are developed to implement the

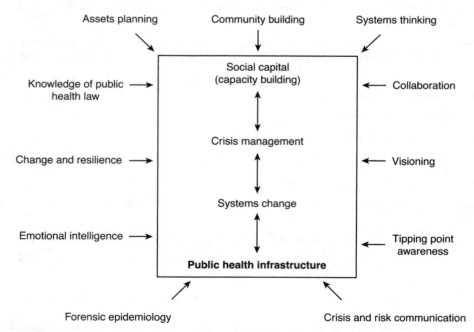

FIGURE 7-3   The Skills of the Prepared Public Health Leader in Crisis.

recommendations of this report, the public health system as a whole will undergo change. In addition, crisis management techniques become imperative to address emergency preparedness and response, as well as utilizing the principles of social capital development.

DISCUSSION QUESTIONS

1. Why is the Pyramid of Preparedness important?
2. Why is leadership and management training a critical component in workforce development?
3. Using the *Healthy People 2020* infrastructure goals and objectives, take one objective from each goal and discuss possible strategies for reaching the objective.

EXERCISE 7-1: Social Forces of Change

Purpose: to explore changes in public health since September 11, 2001

Key concepts: social forces, public health infrastructure, crisis, shifting priorities

Procedures: Divide the class or training group into smaller groups of about 10 people. Provide a flip chart for the groups.

1. Each individual fills out the worksheet below.
2. The small group discusses the lists of forces of its members and lists the different forces at work on the flip chart.
3. The small group discusses the forces and the reasons for them.
4. The small group summarizes the discussion and comes up with the five forces before and after September 11, 2001, that influenced public health priorities.
5. Small groups discuss the forces they found with the group as a whole.
6. The large group then summarizes the small group priorities and comes up with their own social forces for change in the two time periods, and then describes how these changes will affect public health in the future.

Prior to 2001	Since 9/11/2001
1.	1.
2.	2.
3.	3.
4.	4.
5.	5.

REFERENCES

1. Institute of Medicine, *The Future of Public Health* (Washington, DC: National Academies Press, 1988).
2. R. S. Kaplan and D. P. Norton, *The Balanced Scorecard* (Boston: Harvard Business School Press, 1996).
3. P. D. Epstein, P. M. Coates, and L. D. Wray, *Results That Matter* (San Francisco: Jossey-Bass, 2006).
4. Public Health Accreditation Board, www.phaboard.org
5. National Board of Public Health Examiners, www.publichealthexam.org
6. M. Lichtveld, L. Rowitz, and J. Cioffi, "The Leadership Pyramid," *Leadership in Public Health*, 6, no. 4 (2004), 3–8.
7. U.S. Department of Health and Human Services, Office of Disease Prevention and Health Promotion, *Healthy People 2020*, www.healthypeople.gov/2020. Accessed on November 20, 2011.
8. Commission on Social Determinants of Health (CSDH), *Closing the Gap in a Generation: Health Equity Through Action on the Social Determinants of Health*. Final report of the CSDH (Geneva, Switzerland: World Health Organization, 2008).
9. www.healthypeople.gov/topicsobjectives2020/overview.aspx?topicd=35. Accessed November 9, 2011.
10. *Healthy People 2020.*

CHAPTER 8

The Changing Public Health System

We must sustain our commitment to a healthier nation through education, investment, and political will.

—Jo Ivey Boufford and Christine K. Cassell, Co-Chairs
Committee on Assuring the Health of the Public
in the 21st Century, Institute of Medicine, 2003

The field of public health in the United States is changing. The profession of public health was very organization-focused in the past. It was perceived through the lens of a governmental public health agency that not only concentrated its activities on clinical services into the 1990s but also talked of prevention and a population-based focus. Being healthy is not a silo-based activity. It requires not only the involvement of each person, but also the support, collaboration, and involvement of many other people and organizations. Health promotion is a leadership issue always with an eye on future behavior. Over the past several decades, we have set health goals for the nation for each decade. A new decade appears and we seem to start all over again with a new set of goals and expectations. For every step forward, we seem to take two steps backward. Unexpected health crises, a new pandemic, or a new problem to be addressed seems to shift our health priorities. Each type of event becomes tied to a specific health profession or health organizational silo. For example, the events of September 11, 2001, seemed to be a public health crisis, and much money was allocated to build public health infrastructure through the advocacy of a preparedness approach to emergencies and other public health crises. And yet subtle and not-so-subtle shifts occurred in which emergency preparedness and response seemed to become the domain of law enforcement and fire departments, with public health often appearing to take a back seat.

Whether we want to admit it or not, it is not only the public health professions and their organizations that define public health. Public health is defined by the economic climate of the country, politics, economics, culture, and the possibility of global pandemics. In addition, today's health issues also define what public health agencies are supposed to be doing today. It is also true that these contemporary issues help define our field, although we sometimes drop the ball and some other profession or organization picks it up. For example, violence has been seen as a public health issue, and yet we did not know how to address this issue. Public health leaders often let law enforcement, schools, and other organizations pick up our dropped ball.

The field of public health is expanding in the face of health reform by governmental officials at the federal and state levels. Funded public health workforce and leadership development programs are being asked to consider the training of health professionals in preventive medicine, HIV health professions, emergency preparedness, maternal and child health professions, and community health center administration. The argument being made is that people working in health and community clinical areas are beginning to carry out public health work at the population-based community level. This expansion of the purview of public health means that we need to reevaluate our training, research, service, community engagement activities, and leadership activities in this ever-changing public health environment. We need to create alliances and other mechanisms for the discussion of these issues. It will be necessary for governmental health professionals to talk to academic and public health practice leaders in concert with their professional organizations to aid in the redefining of public health in a rational manner. Business and citizen involvement may also be necessary. Our decisions today will have an effect on the future of public health for many years to come.

A NEW PERSPECTIVE

Although everyone seems to talk about preparedness today, the talk is primarily about preparedness related to preventing and responding to bioterrorism events. A wider view of preparedness is for public health agencies to be able to address any type of crisis that may affect their communities. Preparedness also requires that public health leaders take a community-oriented approach to the challenges facing public health rather than the more traditional agency focus. If preparedness is about the entire structure of public health, then the public health leader needs to be concerned about all of public health and not just bioterrorism preparedness and response. To take this wider view, public health needs an agenda. This chapter will look at public health's agenda. The quote that started this chapter states public health's critical mission in a succinct manner.

Dilemmas of the Public Health Workforce

Building social capital is about strengthening the social relationships among people. Strengthening the public health infrastructure that forms the foundation of the public health system is also about people. The public health workforce is both aging and also lacking in the skills necessary to build public health in the 21st century. Not enough young people are entering the field. An investment in people is critical. We need to train the current workforce and try to get them to delay retirement until we can get more people to choose public health careers. The development of lifelong learning opportunities oriented to the new skills needed to address a constantly changing public health landscape needs to occur. The current trend toward investment in learning management systems is a step in the right direction. These systems can create online registration processes for both online and face-to-face courses. All such courses need to be competency based. These systems also allow for the creation of a continuous learning record for all individuals who register for any course. In addition, these systems allow for ongoing needs assessments of future course needs, as well as gaps in an individual's learning requirements.

Politicians must stop passing early retirement buyouts for the public health workforce if public health is to continue to do its work. Deficits in state and local budgets have led to this phenomenon. The governmental workforce in many places is shrinking. Early retirement programs lead to the abolition of positions. A shrinking workforce is not conducive to building public health infrastructure or the public health system. In 2011, the Association of State and Territorial Health Officials surveyed the senior health officials of the 57 states and territories as well as the District of Columbia about public health workforce trends.[1] ASTHO reported a significantly growing shortage of public health employees in a majority of the states. State budget deficits in this first decade of the 21st century have exacerbated the problem. A shrinking workforce complicates the work of public health leaders who are trying to strengthen the infrastructure of public health in their communities.

Some specific findings from the 2010 ASTHO survey included information on the aging public health workforce, whose average age is 47 years.[2] It was projected that the rate of retirements will grow steadily from 18% in fiscal year 2010 to 27% in fiscal year 2014. In some parts of the country, the public health employee turnover rate is as high as 14%. But only 15% of the vacancies are leading to recruitment. The recession of 2008 is probably a factor here. In addition, the current vacancy rates are almost 20% in some states. In fact, the governmental public health workforce is older than the workforce in other parts of the governmental sector. The governmental public health agencies reported the most significant shortages in the areas of nursing, environmental health, epidemiology, and laboratory science.[3] Low salaries complicate the process of filling the personnel shortage areas. The private health and healthcare sector pays significantly better than the public sector. These shortages also affect leadership capacity. Most states are now affiliated with a state and regional public health leadership institute in order to fill this gap. If we do not expand the public health workforce and provide training to increase the competencies of the workforce to address everyday events as well as potential natural and human-caused events, it will not be possible to be prepared for coping with these crisis events. The public health leader needs a competent, well-trained workforce if public health preparedness is to become a reality in both normal and not-so-normal times.

Reports on the workforce status of local public health agencies show that there are often more public health professionals in actual numbers working in metropolitan health departments than in state health departments.[4] The average number of full-time-equivalent employees in local public health agencies is about 13. Specifically, this translates to about 31 staff in metropolitan area local public health agencies, 18 in suburban departments, and 12 in rural health agencies.[5] Fraser[6] recognized the reality of present-day economics but saw it as an opportunity to determine the type and number of public health professionals who will be needed in the future to effectively carry out our public health preparedness activities. It is a time to review the structure of our public health system, and leadership will be needed to explore issues related to how the public health system can be structured in the future.

Public health preparedness is defined by both the governmental public health workforce and public health's community partners.[7] **Table 8-1** summarizes and reviews some of the major competencies needed by a prepared public health workforce as gleaned from a number of key public health documents released from 1988 to 2002. Sixteen competency areas are defined, ranging from

TABLE 8-1 Identified Needs for Public Health Workforce

Competency/Content	IOM 1988[a]	Healthy Communities 1996[b]	Faculty Agency Forum[c]	Competencies Developed 2001–2002, Council on Linkages[d]	Performance Standards; Core Functions; Essential Services[e, f]	The Future of the Public's Health in the 21st Century (2002)[g]	Who Will Keep the Public Healthy? (2003)[h]
Managerial skills	✓		✓		All of the above	✓	✓
Leadership skills	✓	✓		✓	All of the above	✓	✓
Technical professional skills	✓						
Citizen participation	✓	✓				Community-based participatory research	Community-based participatory research
Minority health	✓					Health disparities	Health disparities
International health	✓					Global health	Global health
Modern disease (e.g., AIDS)	✓						

(Continues)

TABLE 8-1 Identified Needs for Public Health Workforce (*Continued*)

Competency/Content	IOM 1988[a]	Healthy Communities 1996[b]	Faculty Agency Forum[c]	Competencies Developed 2001–2002, Council on Linkages[d]	Performance Standards; Core Functions; Essential Services[e,f]	The Future of the Public's Health in the 21st Century (2002)[g]	Who Will Keep the Public Healthy? (2003)[h]
Assessment skills	✓	✓	✓	✓	All of the above	✓	MPH
Policy skills	✓	✓	✓	✓	All of the above	✓	MPH
Assurance skills	✓	✓	✓	✓	All of the above	✓	MPH
Law	✓	✓		✓	Performance standards	✓	✓
Managed care		✓				Private sector	Private sector
Partnerships and interactions		✓				✓	
The ten essential services		✓		✓		✓	
Communication skills			✓				✓
Cultural skills			✓				✓

[a] Institute of Medicine, *The Future of Public Health* (Washington, DC: National Academies Press, 1988).
[b] Institute of Medicine, *Healthy Communities* (Washington, DC: National Academies Press, 1996).
[c] Faculty Agency Forum. Retrieved from http://bookstore.phf.org/prod119.htm.
[d] Council on Linkages Core Competencies. Retrieved from www.phf.org
[e] Centers for Disease Control and Prevention, *National Public Health Performance Standards Program*, Retrieved from http://www.cdc.gov/nphpsp/
[f] Centers for Disease Control and Prevention, "Core Functions—Essential Services," *National Public Health Performance Standards Program*. Retrieved from http://www.cdc.gov/nphpsp/essentialservices.html
[g] Institute of Medicine, *The Future of the Public's Health in the 21st Century* (Washington, DC: National Academy of Science, 2002). Retrieved from www.nap.edu/books/030908704X/html.
[h] Institute of Medicine, *Who Will Keep the Public Healthy?* (Washington, DC: National Academies Press, 2003). Retrieved from http://www.nap.edu/openbook.php?isbn=030908542X

Source: Reproduced from Lichtveld, M. Y., and Cioffi, J. (2003). Public Health Workforce Development: Progress, challenges, and opportunities. *Journal of Public Health Management and Practice, 9*(6), 445.

managerial and leadership skills to skills related to cultural competency. There are six strategic elements related to the development of the public health workforce:

- More detailed information needs to be collected about the composition of the public health workforce.
- The competencies necessary for public health practice today need to be clearly defined. Then the competencies need to be tied to specific educational and training materials to ensure that the competencies will be attainable.
- Integrated learning management systems need to be developed to better document the learning experiences of the public health professional workforce.
- Incentives for learning must be integrated into the lifelong learning models that are critical for public health preparedness.
- Programs must be evaluated.
- The necessary financial support must be provided.

Lichtveld and Cioffi[8] looked at these six challenges from the perspective of building a science base, of the implications to policy, and of the critical need to tie training to practice. The summary of this analysis can be found in **Table 8-2**.

TABLE 8-2 Challenges and Implications for Public Health Workforce Development

Strategic Element	Science	Policy	Implications for Practice
Monitor workforce composition and project needs	Without a scientific base upon which to develop a standard ratio of workers to area, the use of workforce target numbers is arbitrary.	New policy is needed that defines a standard ratio of workers needed per unit area.	Currently, only estimates of the number and composition of the workforce have been generated, which creates difficulty in projecting resource needs for program implementation.
Identify competencies/ Develop curriculum	Key scientific gaps still exist in many disciplines, hampering development of discipline-specific competencies.	Policy leading to national acceptance of standardized, competency-based training with built-in incentive structures (certification/cedentialing) is needed.	Competencies must be translated into integrated training to ensure that public health professionals understand each other's skills, thereby improving coordination of multidisciplinary efforts.
Integrate learning system	Only limited data exist regarding distributed learning delivery systems and adult learning performance.	Strategies should be developed to integrate the several existing federal, state, and local academic learning systems.	The infrastructure, networks, and awareness of learning systems varies significantly among agencies.
Provide incentives to ensure competency	No national system of incentives (including certification and credentialing) exists to ensure competency. Any such system should include strategies to promote lifelong learning.	Policy is needed to encourage recognition of specialized training and to allow portability of that recognition across state lines in emergency situations.	Development of models for career ladders and other incentives for staff (recognition, pay increase, promotion potential) needs to parallel implementation of new learning requirements.
Conduct evaluation and research	A knowledge base linking individual competence to organizational performance and health outcomes is not well developed.	Evaluation strategies should be based on relationships among individual competence, organizational performance, and health outcomes.	Lack of feedback from evaluation makes it difficult to determine capacity and preparedness of the workforce.
Ensure financial support	Evaluation and accountability efforts are critical to public health's demonstration of its essential worth to the nation and to achieve recognition of the cost-benefit in expenditure of resources on public health programs.	To foster dual use of the nation's public health network, DHHS must ensure that various federal programs working to enhance the nation's public health preparedness work in collaboration.	Sustainability of core funding continues to be a prime concern for the public health infrastructure. While the influx of bioterrorism funds can further the development of public health workforce capacity, it could result in a resource drain on nonbioterrorism public health programs.

Source: Reproduced from Lichtveld, M. Y., and Cioffi, J. (2003). Public Health Workforce Development: Progress, challenges, and opportunities. *Journal of Public Health Management and Practice*, 9(6), 448.

1988 Institute of Medicine Report

Many health professionals believe that most technical reports make little difference. When a report is released, there is a flurry of press coverage and sessions at annual professional meetings about the report and its recommendations. Much criticism often occurs. Is the public health system really in disarray? Some critics may argue that the recommendations are unrealistic. Then, with time, the pretty salmon-colored report goes on the shelf and is lost among the flurry of new reports that get released. The Institute of Medicine's (IOM) 1988 report, *The Future of Public Health,*[9] did make a difference and affected the direction of public health throughout the 1990s and still is affecting public health in the 21st century as the follow-up report is being discussed. Most, if not all, prepared public health leaders have a copy of this report and use it frequently as a guide to public health practice. Every page of the report has had an effect on public health. To put the report in perspective, **Table 8-3** lists 10 infrastructure effects of the report. Other writers may select other issues, but the list does point to some of the report's significant effects.

The report reviewed the history of public health in the United States in order to put into perspective the definition and contemporary mission of public health, which was to fulfill society's interests in ensuring conditions in which the American people can be healthy. It is clear from the way the mission was stated and from the report as a whole that the mission related to the community as a whole. The health of the public needed to be seen as a shared responsibility. The word *public* itself implied a community perspective. Ensuring conditions for health would also seem to have implied that public health is affected by personal health behaviors; environmental health concerns such as air quality, water quality, and potential toxic agents; economic downturns; behavioral health concerns; natural and not-so-natural crisis events; and programs and services consistent with the values that guide community life.

When public health professionals think of the 1988 report, the major idea that is most often mentioned relates to the delineation of the three public health core functions of assessment, policy development, and assurance. These three functions have become the foundation for a governing paradigm of public health. The assessment function relates to the need for information to guide the public health enterprise. This is the function that relates to data collection and analysis, issues related to how data are used, epidemiology, biostatistics, health screening and status information, laboratory analysis, and the whole new field of public health informatics, which has evolved since the 1988 report was published. The development of many new assessment tools has also occurred since 1988.

An important policy was determined when the recommendation was made: every state and territory should have a health department with a director with cabinet-level status. This is still a critical dimension of public health system development, in spite of the movement to state human service superagencies in the 1990s with public health being a component of these agencies. The superagency model has left the directors of public health without cabinet-level status in many instances. The superagency decision has often been made for political reasons and an assumption that the model will save money. This has not often been the

TABLE 8-3   1988 Institute of Medicine Top 10 Infrastructure Effects

1. Clearer mission for public health
2. Promotion of the public health core functions model
3. Why every state should have a health department
4. Creation of public health leadership institutes
5. Support for nationwide health objectives
6. Importance of public health law
7. Emphasis on improving access to care
8. Increasing importance of collaborative relationships
9. Importance of training programs for the public health workforce
10. Promotion of a systems perspective for public health—community responsibility versus agency responsibility

Source: Adapted from Institute of Medicine (1988). *The Future of Public Health*. Washington, DC: National Academies Press.

case. Public health leaders have struggled in these agencies to define the state public health mission and the state funding necessary to carry out the mission. Many American governors are resistant to raising the taxes necessary to support a strong public health system as well as a strong educational system.

The 1988 report recognized the critical issues related to public health leadership as well as the rapid turnover in the leadership of the field. Public health leaders are the major spokespeople for communicating to the public the various health risks and problems. These leaders also must make strong arguments for the expenditure of funds to address these problems. They need to build constituencies to support their work. They also need to support the continuing need for scientific research to find ways to either cure or ameliorate these public health problems and risks. The major dilemma here is that many of the individuals who are appointed to high-level governmental positions have little or no specific public health training. A medical degree is not sufficient. Public health administrators need leadership development training that introduces them to not only public health but also the skills and tools necessary to be an effective public health leader. Since 1988, the Centers for Disease Control and Prevention in concert with schools of public health have supported the development of a national public health leadership institute and a number of state and regional institutes. The CDC funding for these programs ended in fiscal year 2011. As I write this chapter, a number of these programs have found alternative funding, although this is not the case for all these programs. There has been a shift in the priorities of the CDC to fund only one applied public health leadership program oriented to the training of community teams, many of whom are the recipients of 2012 community transformation grants.

Public health professionals have tended to support a national public health agenda with national objectives. A process was implemented to develop a national set of health objectives for the years 2000, 2010, and 2020. Although public health has made strong arguments in support of these national agendas, they have been difficult to implement because of fiscal restraints. The 2000 report was discussed much during the 1990s, but there have been barriers and problems surrounding the implementation plans for the 2010 objectives. We do not as yet know the effect of the 2020 objectives. Without political and legislative support for the plans, implementation as well as follow-through are almost impossible to attain. Public health leaders have not always been successful in their advocacy for public

health agendas. It is important that leaders do not give up on a national agenda. A national agenda is critical to the strengthening of the public health system and the implementation of a national public health practice agenda.

The 1988 report made us aware of the importance of public health statutes and laws. The concern raised in 1988 was that the public health laws in the various states needed to be revised in terms of the clear delineation of the roles and responsibilities of health officers and state agencies related to public health activities. The report also noted the necessity of updating the disease control measures for contemporary healthcare problems. It has become increasingly apparent over the intervening years how important these laws and statutes are and how they affect the manner in which the public health system operates and determines its priorities. Much discussion has been occurring since September 11, 2001, on the development of a model statute related to bioterrorism events as well as statutes to revise public health laws in the states. A prepared public health leader clearly has to understand how the legal code works and also understand the nuances of public health laws and statutes.

There has been continuing concern in the United States about the inability of segments of the population to access health and public health services. Public health agencies at the local level are often providers of last resort. The 1988 report strongly argued for the assurance of high-quality services that included personal health services. These services were supposed to be available to all community residents. In the many years since the report was published, this access issue still is a challenge for the health and public health system. The failed attempt to gain support for universal health care by the Clinton administration during the 1990s only exacerbated the problems. The passage of health reform legislation in 2010 has not solved the problem yet. There is concern that the 2010 legislation may be overturned in 2013. Millions of people lack health insurance—both employed and unemployed individuals. Another interesting twist in the access issue has been the recent movement toward eliminating health disparities. This new wrinkle adds the dilemma of cultural diversity and the lack of cultural competency by many in the health professions in working with patients and clients with different racial and cultural characteristics. The prepared public health leader knows the importance of cultural awareness and works with others to improve culturally diverse relationships. There is another important dimension to the access issue: the health of the public needs to be seen in the ecological context of the community because many solutions to the access problem need to be developed at the local level by the public health leader and his or her community partners.

The above discussion leads to the eighth infrastructure effect of the 1988 report. Collaboration is critical. Public health is a shared responsibility. The major work of public health occurs outside the walls of the local or state health agency. The authors of the report stated that the goals and objectives of public health cannot be addressed by the health department alone, but need to be addressed collaboratively by private health and social organizations, health practitioners from the community, other public agencies, and the community at large. The involvement of grassroots leaders is also important if the public health agenda is to be met. An important dimension tied to collaboration involves the critical need for the state health apparatus to work with local communities to support local service capacity, especially when many of these local communities have difficulty in raising revenue to support local health initiatives. If public health is local in operation, then it is important that no resident of the community be unable to gain access to public health programs and services.

The public health workforce needs training. The skills that we learned in school in the past century are or may no longer be sufficient to help us function efficiently and effectively in the new century. To increase the capacity of the public health system, an investment in the public health workforce is important. The 1988 report pointed out that one way to provide this training would be to involve the schools of public health at various universities in these training activities. This would significantly improve academic and practice linkages. The development of educational and training opportunities for the public health workforce has been growing in recent years partly because of the terrorist events of September 11, 2001, and because of the need to prepare the workforce for its critical public health roles in emergency preparedness and response. There are also ongoing discussions about the development of a certification process for public health workers.

In many ways, one of the more significant effects is the gradual shift from an agency-based public health perspective in the 1980s to a community or systems-based approach today. The systems perspective points to a community focus for public health with responsibility shared by the public health agency, its community

partners, and every resident of the community. It is a "big picture" approach. However, many communities do not have a well-integrated public health system in operation. Many relationships between agencies are competitive. Duplication of services and programs continues to be a problem today, although shrinking budgets and deficits may require more consolidation and collaboration.

The 1988 report significantly affected the modern view of public health. There was an awareness that strong public health leadership is needed if the public health system is to become stronger and more effective. It is also clear that the public health leader needs to spend more time out in the community working with other leaders to create and implement the changes necessary to strengthen public health infrastructure and to bring about a more effective public health system for every American community.

1996 *Healthy Communities* Report

An interim report was released in 1996 to record the progress in implementing the recommendations of the 1988 report and to account for the healthcare concerns related to the growth of managed care in the 1990s.[10] Distinctions were made in the report about the differences between personal health services and community interventions. In many instances, local health departments found themselves delivering personal health services as well as community interventions when these personal health services were not available through other healthcare providers to segments of the community. In fact, at least one health department in Florida experimented with creating its own health maintenance organization to serve the poorer segments of its service area. Some local public health agencies have argued that the delivery of personal services has provided the local health agency with revenue to run its community programs. Revenue for these community programs is often hard to obtain. Public health leaders had to become quite entrepreneurial in the 1990s if their agencies were to continue functioning at a high level of efficiency. These leaders began to apply for various grants and contracts to supplement limited local revenue sources.

The relationship between managed care and public health became contentious during the 1990s. The 1996 report tried to clarify the role of public health agencies in the changing healthcare environment. First, public health agencies were and still are the primary source of information on the health status of the population, emerging disease risks, and determinants of health. Second, public health agencies can work with managed care entities in planning and policy development. Third, public health agencies can provide specialized services such as family case management and other enabling services to all residents of the service community regardless of where these residents receive their health care. Finally, managed care organizations can gain assurance and oversight assistance from local health departments. The report pointed out that the core functions perspective would strengthen the relationship between public health agencies and their local healthcare partners.

The report also clarified the increasing role of local public health agencies in community partnerships. A critical role for governmental public health agencies was seen to involve the identification and work with all organizations that might affect the health of the public. The rationale given was that the public health agency has the knowledge and skills to understand and communicate the comprehensive array of factors that affect the health of the community. Part of this knowledge relates to the governing paradigm of public health. The core functions of assessment, policy development, and assurance have been further clarified through the delineation of the 10 essential public health services. These core functions and essential services help to organize information and help public health leaders in their work with communities.

The 1996 report also recognized the importance of training public health professionals. It specifically noted the advances in training public health leaders through the Centers for Disease Control and Prevention initiatives related to public health leadership and the general training of public health workers through the Public Health Training Network. Public health leaders need to be equipped with skills necessary to carry out the core functions and essential services of public health. These skills include knowledge about communication, strategic planning and continuous quality improvement, cultural competency skills, conflict resolution and negotiation skills, and mentoring techniques.

The report also pointed out that progress in reaching the objectives of the 1988 report was slow in occurring. However, the report also stated that the recommendations of the original report were still relevant and should still guide the development of future public health programs. There was also an awareness that the core functions model was not understandable to everyone and needed to be translated into language that other partners, and even elected officials, can understand. There clearly remained the issue of limited resources to carry out the public health agenda. Public health supporters then and now still struggle to gain acceptance and revenue for the public health agenda, even though bioterrorism and other terrorist threats have increased the visibility of public health's role in prevention of these crises. Funding has increased in recent years for these initiatives.

The Future of the Public's Health in the 21st Century

At the beginning of the new report in 2003, *The Future of the Public's Health in the 21st Century*, recognition was given to the effects of the events of September 11, 2001, on the public health system.[11] It seemed clear that the governmental public health system was not prepared for dealing with terrorism or bioterrorism events. Years of political neglect, budget cuts, political agendas that were oriented toward the protection of the private sectors of the economy, the aging of the governmental public health workforce, and the lack of public health training of this workforce all added up to a lack of preparedness on the part of public health. Thus, the United States is vulnerable on many fronts: from emerging infectious disease and the lack of research to protect the public to the types of social and environmental conditions that undermine the health of the public. All these factors have drawn attention to the need for support and the strengthening of the public health system. This report addressed these priorities. Although it is true that there has been increasing support for public health in recent years related to emergency preparedness and response, many of the traditional public health programs and services still tend to be severely underfunded. It is critical to remember that there is more to public health than bioterrorism. Despite many criticisms of the recommendations of this report, the report goes a long way in addressing and creating an agenda for public health in the future. Some of these issues are discussed by Dr. Hugh Tilson, former senior advisor to the dean at the University of North Carolina School of Public Health at Chapel Hill, in Case Study 8-A. Tilson has taken a major leadership role in defining the agenda for public health in the future.

A Public Health Practice Quiz for Hugh Tilson

1. To build the public health infrastructure in the future, what strategies can be employed to get young health professionals to choose a career in public health?

We need a national public health service that permits a single civil service status for all public health employees—federal, state, and local—with transferability of benefits and suitable salaries.

2. You have served on IOM committees for both the *Future of Public Health* reports as well as the *Healthy Communities* interim reports. What do you think were the major effects of the 1988 report?

The 1996 IOM Commission and Public Health Roundtable (for which I was co-chair) held hearings and learned of dozens of remarkable strides attributed by opinion leaders and implementers. Most impressive was the alignment of the field around the construct of "assure, assess, and develop policy" as the nondelegable core functions of public health.

3. How do we go about developing strategies to implement the recommendations of the 2003 report in light of the events of September 11, 2001?

The implementation of the 2003 IOM report is already ongoing and of great importance to the future of public health. Among major steps already under way, perhaps none is more important than a strong, nationwide consensus that the "10 essential services," embodied in the public health system performance standards, and embodied in the recommendations for public health infrastructure in the IOM report, form the backbone of the health-prepared community, and that public money spent to improve preparedness should be directed to build the public health infrastructure.

4. What types of skills will the prepared public health leader need to be able to implement the recommendations of the 2003 report in light of the events of September 11, 2001?

Another fundamental recommendation of the 2003 IOM report is that the public health workforce not only must be competent, but also must organize to demonstrate and credential that competence, and then continuously train public health professionals to maintain and upgrade their competencies. Although there are many "new" competencies urged in the IOM report on education of public health professionals and many more that could be specified, the core public health practice competencies already well negotiated and widely agreed upon by the Council on Linkages will remain the essentials for the next decades.

5. How can our national public health organizations help in pushing the public health agenda?

Without concerted effort by the national associations responsible for one or more of the recommendations of the IOM reports and the public health system they reflect, we will fall short of our full potential. Whatever individual commitment each public health organization makes, it will be important for the American Public Health Association to revisit the medicine–public health link, for the Association of State and Territorial Health Organizations (ASTHO) to advocate for a National Public Health Services Corps, for the National Association for County and City Health Organizations (NACCHO) to build on the "operational definition" of a local agency, and for the Council on Linkages to advance the public health systems research agenda, to name just a few. The key will be for these organizations to all agree to meet regularly and help each other be accountable for follow-through.

The report proposed six areas of action and change:

1. The adoption of a population health approach based on the multiple determinants of health
2. Building and strengthening public health infrastructure
3. Collaboration with all segments of the community
4. Accountability related to the assurance of high-quality public health programs and the availability of these programs for all who need them
5. Building an evidence-based public health system
6. Improvements and enhancement of communication in the public health system

The report presented 34 major recommendations. **Table 8-4** presents 10 key recommendations from this report that have important implications for the prepared public health leader and for the future of public health more specifically. This report needs to be taken seriously. Although criticism and discussion are

TABLE 8-4   10 Key Recommendations of the 2003 Institute of Medicine Report of Public Health

1. Create a national commission to review public health law.

2. Expand workforce development activities to increase competencies of public health workers to carry out the core functions and essential public health services—including a possible credentialing scenario.

3. Emphasize and continue to train public health leaders to function in an emergency preparedness environment.

4. Emphasize communication skills as a core public health set of competencies.

5. Build the public health information infrastructure.

6. Develop methods for the assessment of public health infrastructure and its ability to carry out essential public health services to every American community.

7. Develop a public health practice research agenda.

8. Build collaborative relationships within communities.

9. Improve media relationships.

10. Increase prevention activities.

Source: Reproduced from the Institute of Medicine (2003). *The Future of the Public's Health in the 21st Century*. Washington, DC: National Academy of Sciences.

necessary, the next step in addressing the recommendations of the report must involve the development of strategies to bring the vision of the report to fruition. Strong public health leadership is needed if this is to occur. The logic of the report can be seen in **Figure 8-1**. The major assumption that undergirds the report is the belief that the U.S. population is not as healthy as it could be. The explanations for this can be seen both in systems problems and in societal norms and influences. To address these concerns, governmental public health agencies must work with other community partners to create the changes necessary to create a healthier society. Strong public health and community leadership is needed to make this happen. Societal norms and influences need to change. The public health system also needs to change. This will occur partly through changes in public policy. To create an outcome that promotes health in all our communities, there needs to be improvements in population health and the elimination of health disparities.

The first key recommendation is the creation of a national commission to review all existing public health laws and proposals that are being developed related to model statutes for public health and for emergency health powers. There are many inconsistencies in our laws at the federal, state, and local levels. A national commission could work to develop a framework for public health law in this country. However, it is important to listen to local public health providers and others about how law affects the day-to-day operations

of public health programs and service. There is also a need to recognize that law reform is a complex process integrally tied to the total functioning of a democratic society. A major challenge involves the fact that acts of bioterrorism often cross state boundaries. Differences in laws in different states need to be reconciled.

There has been much discussion over the aging of the public health workforce and the lack of training of the workforce. A major set of recommendations in the report involved this issue. Strong arguments were made for training that was competency based. In 2000, the Council on Linkages Between Academia and Public Health Practice came up with the following list of core public health competencies:[12]

1. Analysis and assessment
2. Policy development and program planning
3. Communication
4. Cultural competency
5. Community dimensions of practice
6. Basic public health sciences
7. Financial planning and management
8. Leadership and systems thinking

The direction of training programs is toward linking these competencies to the core public health functions as well as to essential public health services. The goal of training is to have support persons in a public health agency who understand public health at the fundamental level and also public health leaders who are experts in their fields.[13] The competency framework

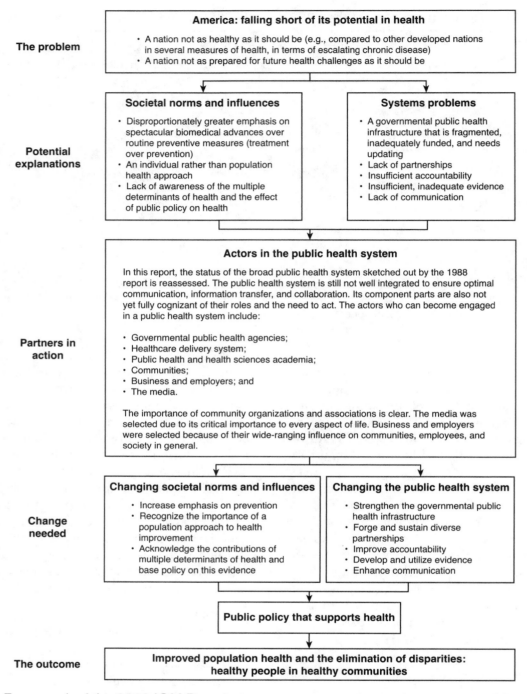

The problem

America: falling short of its potential in health

- A nation not as healthy as it should be (e.g., compared to other developed nations in several measures of health, in terms of escalating chronic disease)
- A nation not as prepared for future health challenges as it should be

Potential explanations

Societal norms and influences

- Disproportionately greater emphasis on spectacular biomedical advances over routine preventive measures (treatment over prevention)
- An individual rather than population health approach
- Lack of awareness of the multiple determinants of health and the effect of public policy on health

Systems problems

- A governmental public health infrastructure that is fragmented, inadequately funded, and needs updating
- Lack of partnerships
- Insufficient accountability
- Insufficient, inadequate evidence
- Lack of communication

Partners in action

Actors in the public health system

In this report, the status of the broad public health system sketched out by the 1988 report is reassessed. The public health system is still not well integrated to ensure optimal communication, information transfer, and collaboration. Its component parts are also not yet fully cognizant of their roles and the need to act. The actors who can become engaged in a public health system include:

- Governmental public health agencies;
- Healthcare delivery system;
- Public health and health sciences academia;
- Communities;
- Business and employers; and
- The media.

The importance of community organizations and associations is clear. The media was selected due to its critical importance to every aspect of life. Business and employers were selected because of their wide-ranging influence on communities, employees, and society in general.

Change needed

Changing societal norms and influences

- Increase emphasis on prevention
- Recognize the importance of a population approach to health improvement
- Acknowledge the contributions of multiple determinants of health and base policy on this evidence

Changing the public health system

- Strengthen the governmental public health infrastructure
- Forge and sustain diverse partnerships
- Improve accountability
- Develop and utilize evidence
- Enhance communication

Public policy that supports health

The outcome

Improved population health and the elimination of disparities: healthy people in healthy communities

FIGURE 8-1 Framework of the 2003 IOM Report. *Source*: Reproduced from the Institute of Medicine (2003). *The Future of the Public's Health in the 21st Century.* Washington, DC: National Academy of Sciences. Reprinted with permission.

has undergone revisions through the first decade of this new century.[14]

The third recommendation relates to the need to train public health leaders. The report recognized the progress made in the training of public health leaders beginning in the early 1990s. The development of leadership competencies is critical for carrying out the work of public health. The National Public Health Leadership Network has developed a public health leadership competency framework that has served as a guide for the development of public health leadership training programs around the country. The model developed by the network was created in 1996 with an awareness that competency frameworks must not be etched in stone. They must be modified and updated as new realities enter our public health agendas. The network continues to examine these competencies to make sure they represent the needs of public health practice today. Wright and her colleagues[15] presented the following list of major competency areas for public health leaders:

1. Core transformational competencies
2. Political competencies
3. Transorganizational dynamics
4. Team-building competencies

This competency framework recognized early on the importance of collaboration in public health. Transformational competencies include skills related to visioning, creating a mission, development of change strategies, and becoming a change agent. Political competencies involve skills in working within the political structure of the community, state, and federal systems. Political competencies also affect policy development, conflict resolution and negotiation skills, ethics and value-based strategies, and marketing and education skills. Transorganizational competencies include the understanding of organizational dynamics, interorganization collaboration techniques, social forecasting methods, and scenario building. Team-building competencies include skills in the development of teams, coalitions, alliances and partnerships, group facilitation techniques, mediation roles, and ability to work with others. Subcompetencies are included under all four major competency categories.

The leadership framework also recognized the importance of communication in public health. Communication skills are a core public health set of competencies. The IOM report supported the need for strong communication skills both for internal functioning of governmental public health agencies and for external relationships with community partners and the public. One of the important activities for public health professionals is the transmission of information about health issues to outside sources, including the media. Communication skills include the use of all the new information technology sources that are at our disposal today. Messages given need to be culturally appropriate and suitable for the literacy levels of the audience for whom the message is being sent. Different language is needed for different audiences. Public health leaders need to become communication experts. Communication is a complex process with mastery needed in 20 different communication skill areas. In general, the communication of public health information is important as a mechanism for getting information from the community about the health concerns that it has. It is also important as a mechanism for getting information to the public about health risks to the community from disease outbreaks and from disasters both natural and man-made.

Communication with the media is becoming more and more critical. The prepared public health leader needs to be able to communicate with the press and be the voice of public health in television and radio interviews. Public health leaders can develop trusting relationships with journalists and other media people and provide accurate information on health risks to the community as well as interpret new research findings. Most television stations, for example, now have health reporters and editors. The goal of public health communication is to provide accurate and up-to-date information during a crisis.

The fifth key recommendation involves the infrastructure of public health information. The report noted all the changes occurring in the information technology area over the past decade with the realization that public health information systems have lagged behind technology advances in other sectors. With proposed advances in technology, as well as bioterrorism grants to local health departments with the partial goal of improving information systems, it should be possible to build the information capabilities of the public health system over the next decade. These advances should also help build public health infrastructure by supporting and improving public health monitoring and disease surveillance activities. Prepared public health leaders need to learn how to use these new technologies as well as to develop competency in the use of data for program development and policy development. Specifically, the report recommended development and implementation of a national health information infrastructure. One cautionary note was discussed by the authors of the report. They warned that the public health information system needs to be as comprehensive as possible if it is to be the most useful. A silo-based bioterrorism information system would not be the most optimal information system for public health.

The next recommendation seems to be an extension of a recommendation from the 1988 IOM report, with the addition of the essential public health services component. This recommendation involved the importance of assessment as a public health function in the building of the infrastructure of public health. There is agreement that the core functions and essential public health services paradigm is an infrastructure building model. The paradigm defines the activities of public health. The model allows comparisons to be made across governmental public health agencies. It does not obliterate the fact that each community will carry out these activities in different ways, but it does say that these activities need to be carried out if public health is to be strengthened. The essential public health services model creates a structural system for public health and serves as a guide for the prepared public health leader in carrying out the public health agendas in his or her community. It is not meant to replace the need for governmental public health agencies to provide the many mandated services they routinely provide, such as maternal and child health programs and restaurant inspections. The structural framework allows public health agencies to see the big picture in their work.

The report expands the assessment function to include the following:

1. Evaluation of federal, state, and local public health funding mechanisms
2. Study of the adequacy and capacity of the system to address the health needs of the public
3. Development of a funding and technical assistance plan to ensure sustainability of public health programs and services
4. Continual evaluation at the state and local levels of public health capacity through community-wide health assessments and implementation of a performance standards review of the state and local public health system

The seventh key recommendation involves the importance of developing a public health practice research agenda. Public health practice offers many opportunities for research related to the public health system as well as the factors that will guide policy decisions for public health practice. There are a number of groups that are looking at the issue of public health practice research, including the Centers for Disease Control and Prevention, the Council on Linkages Between Academia and Public Health Practice, the Association of Schools of Public Health and its Public Health Practice Council, the National Public Health Leadership Network, and other public health professional organizations. A coordinated plan needs to be developed to address the different perspectives of each of these organizations.

Some of the specific areas to be addressed in the development of a practice research agenda include monitoring the types and levels of the public health workforce and the effectiveness of various training initiatives; studies of how to develop and evaluate public health infrastructure; financial investments necessary to sustain a comprehensive public health system; performance of the essential public health services at the state and local levels; effectiveness of governance related to public health activities; participatory research related to improvements in health status of the public; and analysis of effectiveness of prevention programs.

Building on recommendations from previous IOM reports, the 2003 report emphasized the importance of seeing public health in a community context. The eighth recommendation emphasized the importance of collaboration. Because community-based organizations are so close to the people they serve, it is imperative that public health agencies work with these organizations and other grassroots community leaders. Without collaboration, the system will not work. These community-led efforts should include such activities as developing inventories of community resources, community assessment of needs, determination of gaps in service, formulation of collaborative response to these determinations of need, evaluation of outcomes related to community health improvement programs, and programs to increase service access for all segments of the population and, of course, to eliminate any health disparities that may exist. Governmental public health agencies also need to provide technical assistance to community organizations and work collaboratively to obtain external funding to provide critical service and prevention programs for the community.

Recognizing the critical importance of leadership to collaboration, a collaborative leadership project was developed as part of the Robert Wood Johnson Turning Point Initiative. A training manual was prepared to train collaborative leaders.[16] The training program involves the following six modules:

1. Assessing the environment
2. Creating clarity
3. Building trust
4. Sharing power
5. Developing people
6. Self-reflection

The prepared public health leader must become competent in these six areas if collaborative techniques are to be mastered. Exercise 8-1 will give you the chance to self-reflect on the issue of virtue. Virtue generally refers to the important concerns related to moral excellence and living the values by which a society defines itself.

An interesting collaborative effort involves the development of a Syndemics Prevention Network through the National Center for Chronic Disease Prevention and Health Promotion at the CDC.[17] The Syndemics Prevention Network was developed to find ways to improve community health and to work toward health equity. Syndemics has been defined as two or more afflictions that interact synergistically to contribute to an excess burden of disease in a population. A syndemic orientation would require the partners in the activity to inquire extensively into the various conditions that create and sustain health. The collaborative effort would also need to question and determine how these various health conditions might differ among various groups. The goal of these activities would be to find ways to remove those conditions that perpetuate health disparities. The network specifically involves the development of a national group of partner organization and community leaders, researchers, health officials, and others to work with the CDC to find new prevention opportunities and strategies for energizing people throughout the public health workforce. The network wants to determine, using this collaborative approach, whether syndemics can alter public health science and action. The network is concerned with answering the following questions:

1. What is a syndemic?
2. What principles characterize a syndemic orientation?
3. Under what conditions is it appropriate to use this orientation?
4. What advantages and limitations are associated with this new orientation?
5. What procedures are available for planning and evaluating initiatives to prevent syndemics?
6. How can the public and the public health workforce be prepared to adopt the syndemics orientation?

Exercise 8-2 is related to the use of this model.

The ninth recommended priority of the IOM report involves the critical issue of improving media relationships. The skills associated with risk and crisis communication are associated with this recommendation. The report recognized that public health leaders have often been ineffective in working with representatives from the mass media. In addition, many public health activities do not attract media attention. Most of us have heard that when public health is successful, nothing happens. Nothing tends to lack interest for the media. One of the more interesting recommendations in the report pointed to the value of developing an evidence base related to media influences on health knowledge and behavior in addition to the promotion of healthy public policy.

The final, and probably the most important, set of recommendations is related to the need to increase our public health prevention activities. The committee behind the report felt that the majority of funded research through the various National Institutes of Health were for biomedically based research activities. There is clearly work that needs to occur on the prevention front. One specific recommendation related to an increase in funding levels for the CDC-funded Prevention Research Centers. Some of the most influential prevention research has been carried out by these centers over the past decade. The innovative Special Interest Projects (SIPs) have also added to our knowledge base. Each of the Prevention Research Centers focuses on projects related to a public health theme. Yet these programs and centers have been underfunded. Increased funding is necessary for these centers, although these centers may be unfunded beginning in fiscal year 2012.

In addition, it was strongly argued that National Institutes of Health funding should be increased for population- and community-based prevention research that does the following:

1. Identifies population-level health problems
2. Involves a definable population and also operates at the level of the whole person
3. Evaluates the application and effects of innovative programs and services as well as new discoveries on the actual health and health status of the population
4. Concentrates on the behavioral, psychological, and environmental factors associated with primary and secondary prevention of disease and disability in populations

To this latter point should be added the factors involved in tertiary prevention activities as well.

National Strategy Plan of 2011

One of the positive effects of the passage of the Affordable Care Act of 2010 was the creation of the

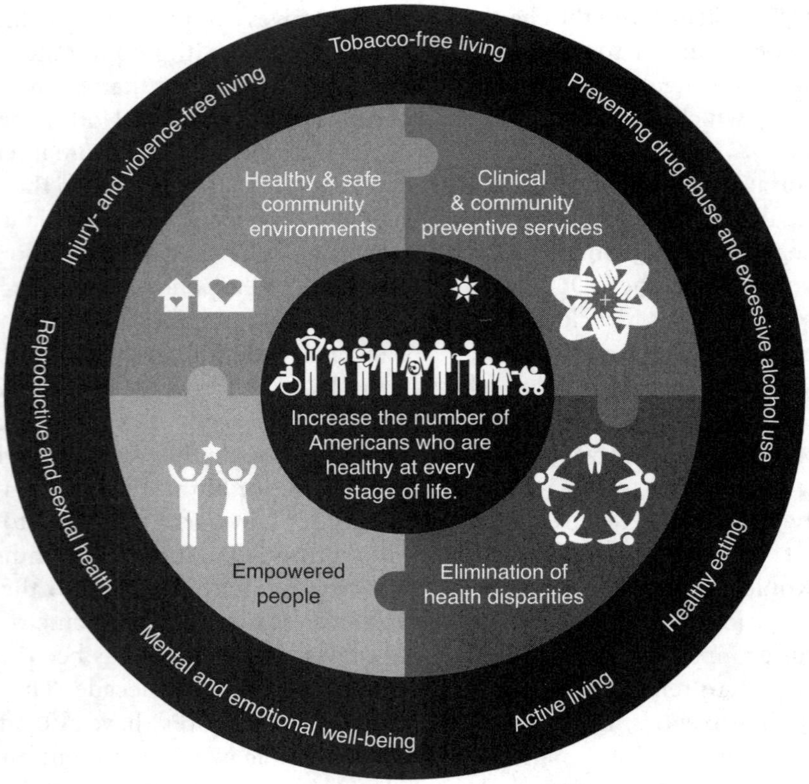

FIGURE 8-2   National Prevention Strategy: America's Plan for Better Health and Wellness. *Source*: Reproduced from National Prevention Council, National Prevention Strategy (2011). Washington, DC: U.S. Department of Health and Human Services, Office of the Surgeon General.

National Prevention Council, which was responsible for the development of the National Prevention Strategy of 2011.[18] The strategy builds on the concept of lifelong health. The vision behind the strategy is that we all need to work together to improve the life of the American people. The goal in prevention is to increase our life span by being healthy at all stages of life. Four strategic directions and seven targeted priorities were identified to realize the vision put forth in the plan. **Figure 8-2** shows these strategies and priorities in graphic form. In addition, leadership at the national level is critical if the strategy is to become reality. The Council is charged with coordinating the prevention plan and determining how federal departments, agencies, and offices will play a role under the chairmanship of the surgeon general. Specifically, the Council will engage partners, align policies and programs, use assessment methods to monitor new and emerging trends and also evolving and tested

evidence, ensure accountability, and set up a Prevention Advisory Group.

In 2011, the Office of Public Health Preparedness and Response of the Centers for Disease Control and Prevention released its national strategic plan for preparedness and response.[19] The CDC vision is "People protected—public health secured." The plan has eight strategic objectives, which can be seen in **Figure 8-3**. Leadership is critical for addressing the objectives of this plan. The plan lists the five following values that will be important to the leadership of CDC in addressing the objectives:

1. Make transparent and accountable decisions.
2. Engage partners and leverage all collaborations.
3. Promote and champion effective communication and information sharing.
4. Base decisions on evidence-based science.
5. Expand the evidence base for public health security.

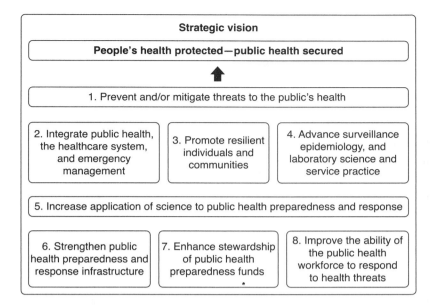

FIGURE 8-3 National Strategic Plan for Preparedness and Response. *Source:* Reproduced from the Centers for Disease Control and Prevention. *National Strategic Plan for Public Health Preparedness and Response.* Atlanta, GA: CDC Office of Public Health Preparedness and Response, 2011.

SUMMARY

This chapter has been all about leadership. Any success that the public health profession will have in accomplishing the recommendations of these various reports, particularly the National Prevention Strategy of 2011 and the National Strategic Plan for Public Health Preparedness and Response of 2011, requires not only prepared public health leaders but also a prepared public health workforce. A vision of the future of public health requires a template for guiding the agenda of public health. The various reports discussed in this chapter provide such a template. The additional requirements of emergency preparedness and response create an overlay to this agenda.

DISCUSSION QUESTIONS

1. Describe preparedness as a universal public health concept.
2. Trace the changes in public health from 1988 until the present through the several Institute of Medicine reports and other governmental documents discussed in this chapter.
3. What is syndemics? Give an example.

EXERCISE 8-1: Self-Reflection

Purpose: to better understand on a personal level the virtues that make excellent leaders

Key concepts: self-reflection, virtues (moral excellence), ethics, values

Procedures: List 10 ideal virtues for people living in the United States today. Put a checkmark by the virtues that you believe refer to you. How can you improve your leadership behavior so that all 10 virtues become virtues by which you live your life?

EXERCISE 8-2: A Problem in Syndemics

Purpose: to explore the relevance of syndemics for public health practice

Key concepts: syndemics, epidemic control, community health improvement

Procedures: A syndemic orientation implies that a key mission for public health is to move beyond epidemic control to incorporate community health improvement techniques in the process. There has been a significant increase in adolescent pregnancy in your community over the past decade. Explore some of the syndemic issues involved, and also develop strategies

EXERCISE 8-2:   A Problem in Syndemics (*Continued*)

for ways to reduce the rates. Using this new orientation might help your community coalition to better define the conditions under which categorically organized interventions can be effective, as well as the extent to which fragmented programs might themselves be a barrier to the goal of protecting the public's health.

1. Divide the class or training group into smaller groups of eight, each of which represents a community coalition

    a. Local health department administrator

    b. Director of family planning agency

    c. Principal of local family planning agency

    d. President of high school parents' organization

    e. Adolescent mother

    f. Member of county board of health

    g. Local business leader

    h. Minister, priest, rabbi, or other religious leader

2. Using a combination of procedures such as those listed below, address the problem, plan program strategies, and determine ways to document achievement:

    a. Determine differences in epidemic control (attribution) and systems change or community health improvement issues (contribution factors).

    b. Expand traditional outcome measures to include other community outcome issues based on culture and other factors.

    c. Define the conditions for a healthy community.

    d. Develop strategies for monitoring progress using a navigational model rather than a traditional steering model.

    e. Document changes in the community as a result of new strategies being implemented.

3. Develop a two-page community syndemics plan for the problem and then present it to the group facilitator to present to the mayor of the community.

REFERENCES

1. Association of State and Territorial Health Officials, *ASTHO Profile of State Public Health*, vol. 2 (Washington, DC: ASTHO, 2011).

2. ASTHO, *ASTHO Profile of State Public Health*, vol. 2.

3. Association of State and Territorial Health Officials, *State Public Health Employee Worker Shortage Report* (Washington, DC: ASTHO, 2004).

4. M. P. Fraser, "Commentary: The Local Public Health Agency Workforce: Research Needs and Practice Realities." *Journal of Public Health Management and Practice* 9, no. 6 (2003): 496–499.

5. A. Hajat, K. Stewart, and K. L. Hayes, "The Local Public Health Workforce in Rural Communities." *Journal of Public Health and Practice Management* 9, no. 6 (2003): 481–488.

6. Fraser, "Commentary."

7. M. Y. Lichtveld and J. Cioffi, "Public Health Workforce Development: Progress, Challenges, and Opportunities." *Journal of Public Health Management and Practice* 9, no. 6 (2003): 443–450.

8. Lichtveld and Cioffi, "Public Health Workforce Development."

9. Institute of Medicine, *The Future of Public Health* (Washington, DC: National Academies Press, 1988).

10. Institute of Medicine, *Healthy Communities* (Washington, DC: National Academies Press, 1996).

11. Institute of Medicine, *The Future of the Public's Health in the 21st Century* (Washington, DC: National Academy of Science, 2003).

12. Council on Linkages Between Academia and Public Health Practice, *Core Competencies for Public Health Professionals* (Washington, DC: Public Health Foundation and Health Resources and Services Administration, 2001).

13. H. Tilson and K. Gebbie, "The Public Health Workforce," pp. 341–356 in J. E. Fielding, R. C. Brownson, and N. M. Clark (eds.), *Annual Review of Public Health*, vol. 25 (Palo Alto, CA: Annual Review, Inc., 2004).

14. Council on Linkages Between Academia and Public Health Practice, *Core Competencies and Public Health Professionals—Tiers 1 Through 3* (Washington, DC: Public Health Foundation, 2009).

15. K. Wright, L. Rowitz, A. Merkle, W. M. Reid, G. Robinson, B. Herzog, et al., "Competency Development in Public Health Leadership." *American Journal of Public Health* 90, no. 8 (2000): 1202–1207.

16. Turning Point Leadership Collaborative. *Collaborative Leadership Learning Mules* (Seattle: Turning Point National Program Office, 2004).

17. Centers for Disease Control and Prevention. *Syndemics Overview* (Atlanta: CDC Syndemics Prevention Network, 2001).

18. National Prevention Council, *National Prevention Strategy* (Washington, DC: U. S. Department of Health and Human Services, Office of the Surgeon General, 2011).

19. Centers for Disease Control and Prevention, *A National Strategic Plan for Public Health Preparedness and Response* (Atlanta: Office of Public Health Preparedness and Response, 2011).

CHAPTER 9

Introduction to the Core Functions of Public Health

Healthy People 2020 is committed to the vision of a society in which all people live long, healthy lives.

—*Healthy People 2020*

In this chapter, we focus on the core functions of public health—assessment, policy development, and assurance—and the role of leadership in ensuring that these functions are carried out effectively by public health organizations. The overall mission of public health, as noted already, is to fulfill "society's interest in assuring the conditions in which people can be healthy."[1](p.4) What this means, of course, needs to be spelled out, and one way of doing this is to divide the mission into its main parts, or core functions. There are various sets of core functions one might choose, but the trio mentioned above is certainly among the most defensible. Protecting and improving the general health of people in the community (the mission of public health) must begin with an evaluation of the current level of health and the current threats to health in the community (assessment). Following the assessment comes the step of developing policies to address the health threats or problems. Then the policies are implemented to improve the public's health (assurance). This step can be viewed as the last in a three-step process, but it must be followed by an evaluation of the effectiveness of the implementation, which will start the whole process over again, for the evaluation will undoubtedly uncover further problems or show that the implementation was only partially successful, leading to further policy development and implementation (**Figure 9-1**). This latter point demonstrates again the importance of feedback as a mechanism for making change.

FIGURE 9-1   The Government Role in Health. *Source:* Reprinted with permission from Institute of Medicine, *The Future of Public Health*, p. 43, © 1988, National Academies Press.

CORE FUNCTIONS OF PUBLIC HEALTH

Many human service fields struggle with the issue of credibility. Part of the lack of credibility is due to the fact that the public often does not understand the nature of the services being provided. Developing a paradigm can help to increase public understanding. A paradigm of public health, for example, can define the structure and parameters of public health work. The core functions model of public health is such a paradigm.

A paradigm is a map with boundaries that elucidates a major area of endeavor.[2] Public health leaders, to an extent, see the world in terms of core functions (or, in other words, a core functions paradigm). They also see it in terms of a leadership paradigm and a management paradigm. Leaders will sometimes substantially revise a paradigm or replace it with another. This is called a paradigm shift.[3] A paradigm shift, which usually takes a long time to be completed, creates a new set of rules, procedures, and perspectives.

The Future of Public Health first described the core functions paradigm.[4] The functions of assessment, policy development, and assurance are tied to the phases of public health practice. Assessment involves the identification of health problems, policy development involves the identification of possible solutions, and assurance involves the implementation of the supposed solutions (usually in the form of programs and services). Public health leaders have major responsibilities associated with each core function. It can be argued that these core functions are a universal model for understanding how human services programs work. At a clinical level, this model may also make sense. For example, an individual comes to a physician complaining of certain symptoms. The physician *assesses* the situation and the symptoms. The physician then puts the symptoms together according to the general rules and protocols of the medical profession and makes a diagnosis. This grows out of medical *policy* and procedures. The physician then defines the intervention, which is *assurance* in action. Thus the core functions operate at both an individual (clinical) and a population-based level.

Policy development is seen as linking assessment to assurance. In reality, policy development is often an afterthought in the American public health system—that is, assurance activities sometimes occur before policies are developed. Many public health leaders with whom I have spoken nevertheless have pointed out that leaders need to be effective in the policy development area if they are to create a comprehensive public health system.

One limitation of the original core functions model is that it does not show the interaction between the functions. A second limitation is that "the concepts of assessment, policy development, and assurance, while useful in the public health community itself, have been difficult to translate into effective messages for key stakeholders, including elected officials and community groups. These concepts need to be translated into non-technical language that these groups understand."[5(p.50)]

It is worth viewing the core functions model as an interactive system rather than as linear. **Figure 9-2** presents the core function model as a system, with the added element of governance. Governance and public health practice are the glue that makes the entire interactive system cohere and function as it should. It is therefore a central concern for leadership at all levels of the public health system.[6] Governance in public health is a community responsibility, which means that the community needs to be empowered to become more involved in policy development. If all people involved in public health become empowered, then governance as demonstrated through sound and effective public health practice will be part of the infrastructure of the entire public health system. In fact, governance is a major component in all aspects of public health policy and practice. A governing

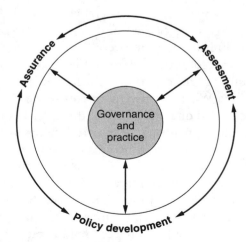

FIGURE 9-2 A Core Functions Systems Design.

body in public health can be an individual, a board of health, a council, or another entity that serves as a trustee for the community or county population.[7] Governance needs to be tied to the core functions and essential services of public health to be able to work in concert with leadership of the state or local public health system.

Figure 9-3 combines the core functions model and the leadership wheel systems model of organizational change. The assessment of need in a community starts the system cycle, allowing leaders to think and act strategically as well as tactically. Leaders then decide on the best strategies for improving health and engage in action planning, which is oriented toward developing tactics for meeting the responsibilities of public health through the practice of the public health core functions. Public health leaders also need to monitor public health activities to ensure they are effective.

This important systems view can be seen in Case Study 9-A, which was written by a group of academics and public health practitioners as part of their leadership development experience. This case, about a natural disaster, was developed from the perspective of the assurance function but clearly demonstrates the other two functions as well.

Policy development plays a role throughout the process of protecting and improving the public's health. First, mission and vision development is a form of policy development. Second, whenever an evaluation is conducted, whether of a team, a community coalition, a program, or a service, the information gathered may suggest that policy revisions or entirely new policies may need to be instituted. Obviously, though, assessment and policy development activities are pointless unless the policies chosen are implemented.

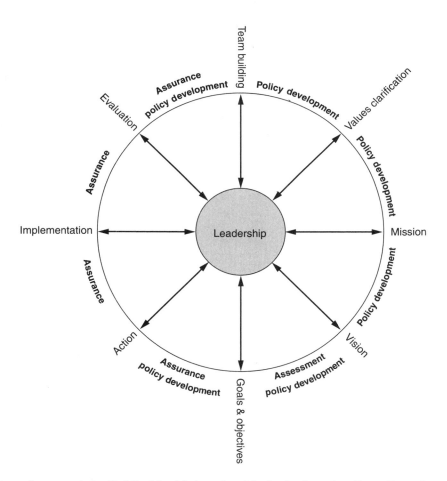

FIGURE 9-3 A System Approach to Public Health Leadership Including the Core Functions.

The Flood

A Case Study in Assurance and Leadership, Mid-America Regional Leadership Institute Year 15 Fellows: Barb MacGregor, Rashmi Ganesan, Dina Kurz, Lisa Stefanovsky, Donovan Thomas, and Lynne Doyle

The city of Robinson is located along the picturesque Muddy River. This big, beautiful river has a history of winter ice jams causing flooding of some of the adjacent low-lying areas. Two neighborhoods in Robinson, Atlantis Drive and Sunken Boulevard, which until a few years ago had been predominately summer cottages, have been affected by the floodwaters many times. These communities are constructed within the 100-year floodplain. Waterfront property in this area has been increasing in value, and it is considered a very desirable place to live. Therefore, many of the property owners in these neighborhoods have chosen to live in these homes year-round.

The Robinson City Health Department (RCHD), Environmental Health Section, has two sanitarians that have been with the department for 20 years and had an environmental health director who retired in late 2004 after 38 years of service. In early 2005, the RCHD hired a new health officer (Mr. Ivan), who was formerly a KGB agent, and a new environmental health director who had tremendous experience in mortuary science (Ms. Rigormortis). This new team had ideas for significant departmental change and immediately began declaring its authority by reorganizing. This met with resistance from staff, who had a long history of effectively carrying out the goal of the RCHD Environmental Health Division: to provide protection from environmental threats through education, collaboration, and enforcement of laws and regulations that ensure a safe and healthy future for Robinson residents.

In the first week of January 2006, a large ice dam formed on the Muddy River, causing the worst flood in 40 years. Sunken Boulevard and Atlantis Drive were the areas most severely affected. Most homes had about four feet of standing water in their main floor, and many cars were under water. Drinking water wellheads were completely submerged and the residential septic systems saturated.

The Sunken Boulevard and Atlantis Drive neighborhoods consisted of approximately 60 homes and cottages that were built in the 1940s and 1950s. The structures were built prior to public health regulations for well and septic systems and before city/township building regulations had been developed. Neither well nor septic systems met modern public health code standards for floodplain areas. However, it is important to note that the local health department's environmental health section had been routinely inspecting and passing the well and septic systems in these neighborhoods for years. The neighborhoods had been informally "grandfathered" through the system due to the extreme cost and difficulty of completely updating the well and septic systems to current standards. In some cases, costs of updates would have forced some residents to sell their properties.

Residents in the Sunken Boulevard and Atlantis Drive neighborhoods evacuated their homes voluntarily during the 2006 flood. These residents were forced to find alternative housing with family or friends or at local hotels, or they accepted emergency housing assistance from the Red Cross. These families were also expected to continue to pay their mortgages on homes that were under water and uninhabitable.

From an environmental health standpoint, the following public health issues were identified by the RCHD for the homes and property in the flooded areas:

1. The drinking water supply was threatened and exposed to surface water contamination from the Muddy River, and potentially from raw sewage from the flooded septic systems.
2. Septic systems were saturated and nonfunctioning, which meant the systems were either backing up into the homes or spilling over into the groundwater and surface water.
3. The conditions of the homes themselves were compromised due to the standing water and ice, the future drying process, and subsequent potential mold problems.
4. Structural foundations were compromised due to ice flows and the heavy forces of water.

In addition, electric power had been cut off to the neighborhoods during the flooding due to safety concerns.

Approximately one week after the flooding forced residents from their homes, a town hall meeting was held at a local elementary school as many residents began to ask what they would need to do to move back into their homes. Mr. Ivan (the health officer), representatives from law enforcement, and city officials met with residents to discuss the problems caused by the flood. Mr. Ivan chose to steadfastly uphold his interpretation of the public health code and told residents at the town hall meeting that they would not be able to move back into their homes until their wells and septic systems were brought up to the current health code. This message was delivered as an autocratic directive with little compassion for the situations the residents faced. This set the stage for the residents to become very angry and distrustful of the RCHD.

This situation presented a great number of problems for the citizens affected by the flooding, as well as challenges for the public health staff who had to contend with its aftermath. Certainly, this event offered an opportunity for the Health Department's key decision makers to exercise leadership and demonstrate good decision making while ensuring the health and safety of the community.

The environmental health team had the responsibility in this situation to investigate the effect the flooding had on private water and sewer systems; monitor the health of the citizens affected; inform and educate the public regarding health issues the flooding caused; collaborate with community partners to help identify and provide solutions for immediate and future problems; and uphold laws and regulations to protect the community's health. All tasks would have to be completed while working under public pressure in a challenging environment. The need for leadership was clear to ensure that necessary services were maintained and community needs addressed.

In the early stages of the flood, multiple agencies were involved to address the situation, including the health department, city authorities, utility companies, the county emergency services director, city police, the fire department, the Federal Emergency Management Agency (FEMA), and the State Department of Environmental Quality. Despite some very qualified individuals, no agency or individual took charge of the situation or helped residents understand how they could get back into their homes. One resident of the area was quoted in the local paper as saying, "We just want some honest answers. I thought the government was supposed to help us. Why do we pay taxes?"

It was two to three months before the ice dam melted and the floodwaters completely receded. Many residents claimed financial burden and difficulties due to the flood.

As the floodwaters slowly withdrew, Mr. Ivan declared that the septic systems had failed and therefore could not operate again. In a department meeting, Mr. Ivan said, "I don't care what it costs to fix them; nobody moves in without our approval—NOBODY." Ms. Rigormortis agreed, stating, "Although I don't really know how a septic system works, I know this isn't good."

In March 2006, in his attempt to ensure compliance with the public health code, Mr. Ivan assembled the environmental health staff to "discuss" the options for rebuilding the affected septic systems. Mr. Ivan directed that residents would have to install new systems that met current code before they could return to their homes. Options approved by Ivan the health officer included:

1. Residents could build individual sewage holding tanks on stilts. These tanks (about $5,000 per tank to install) must be pumped out every two weeks at a cost of $200 to $300 per pump.
2. Residents could construct six-foot elevated septic mounds to meet flood-level elevation requirements, which would cost each residence approximately $10,000.
3. The residents could build a community sewer system at the cost of over $1,000,000 (roughly $20,000 per residence).
4. All drinking water wells would have to be tested and replaced if not installed to current sanitary code (many were shallow wells with no construction record, and therefore did not meet current requirements).

At the same time, the City Planning and Grants Department was working with the Federal Emergency Management Agency (FEMA) to apply for a grant that would buy the flooded homes. This option failed because the governor refused to declare a state of emergency, claiming that the emergency was not large enough. Another federal grant was pursued that would buy the properties at 75% of appraised value, and the purchased properties would be deeded to Robinson City (approximately one-third of the homeowners later elected to enter into this agreement). Finally, the State Department of Transportation became involved and announced that it was interested in buying four properties in the neighborhood as part of a future highway expansion.

Unfortunately, the residents viewed this activity as a forced government land acquisition. A resident was quoted as saying, "They don't care about us; they just want our land. I don't trust any of them."

Investigation of these options stalled progress for approximately two to three months (May–June 2006) after the water had receded. The residents were still unable to move back into their homes, and many were running out of resources and temporary housing. It was suspected that a few residents had returned to their homes illegally.

After months of heated debate, mistrust, anger, and inaction, a major change in the situation came when Mr. Ivan and Ms. Rigormortis resigned together to leave the stress of local government and start an alpaca farm. Mr. Ivan was heard saying as he left, "This is the most dysfunctional city government I have ever seen. Llamas are smarter than these people." Ms. Rigormortis agreed, stating, "Although I don't really know much about llamas, I know this isn't good."

(Continues)

For the first time in the six months since the flood began, there was an opportunity for alternate opinions and direction. Critical partners in the situation began to think "outside the box" and considered potential alternatives to the interpretation of the sanitary codes that would allow residents to move back into their homes safely. The city administrator, the new health officer, the new environmental health director, and other subject matter experts met and proposed the following criteria for resettlement:

1. Wells needed to be disinfected and water samples needed to pass inspection.
2. Wells needed to be physically protected from future flood exposure by either elevating casings or using a "snorkel" system.
3. Septic tanks needed to be pumped by certified haulers and receive a certificate of inspection.
4. Contingencies were put in place so when the owners went to sell the homes, the well and septic systems would need to be brought up to code, which included installing holding tanks.
5. Homeowners would need to move out of their homes if the area flooded again. The affected water and septic systems would have to be reevaluated prior to resettlement.

Homeowners were offered these options as well as the buyout option at a second town hall meeting held in late June 2006. The goal of this meeting was to get information to the homeowners so they could make informed decisions about their properties and futures. A very different approach to assurance was used at this town hall meeting. The focus was on answering questions, listening to the concerns of the residents, problem solving, and working collaboratively with other agencies. One resident said, "They finally sent someone to listen to us and fix the problem."

The Health Department continued to hold public meetings monthly as residents considered the various options and slowly returned to their homes. Meanwhile, residents who had returned to their homes prior to the cleanup called the RCHD and local health facilities complaining of hay fever–type symptoms, running noses, itchy red eyes, and skin rashes. As these calls poured in, it was evident that there was no policy to mitigate other health hazards, such as mold. There was disconnect between environmental health functions and personal health functions to address such issues. Previous leadership had frowned upon interdepartment collaboration between both divisions and had created animosity and a lack of communication within the organization.

The new health officer and new environmental health director worked with the Health Education Division to create educational fact sheets related to mold exposure. Additionally, a 1-800 hotline number was established in collaboration with the Information Services Department to educate the community about possible mold exposure. The health officer worked with the city administrator to provide options for hiring private companies to remediate the mold problems. The cleanup and recovery phase continued over the course of several months.

There are many different styles of leadership. A good leader must remain flexible because different issues often require different strategies. Leadership is dynamic, and there is no universal list of leadership traits that apply to all situations. During this event, it was important for the public health leader to support and enable the public health staff to act, because this situation required not only leadership but more leaders. By empowering others to act, leadership responsibilities could be shared. Communication was also a key issue; it was important to communicate and build trust with the citizens affected. A good leader is able to take complex information and simplify it so it has meaning to a broad audience. Likewise, the ability to communicate difficult information while leading others forward is vital to success. In addition, it was equally important for the leader to cultivate collaboration with community partners. This situation could not be handled solely by the Health Department.

Natural disasters can cause events that lead to public health emergencies. Assurance and policy development play crucial roles in mitigating disasters. Although sheltering is not a basic function of public health, enforcing laws and regulations that protect and ensure safety is an essential public health service. This includes meeting both the environmental and personal health needs of the community. In developing solutions to community problems, a local health department must engage residents and essential community partners in a form of collaborative leadership. This leads to connectivity and creative solutions.

Connectivity also spans across other agencies to create forms of meta-leadership that link public health, law enforcement, city, and county government. The new health officer assessed the emotional and cultural intelligence of the community, presented them with options, educated residents on potential hazards, and effectively managed the public health emergency. Meta-leaders exercise good active forms of leadership in an organization and cross organizational boundaries to protect the health and welfare of community residents.

Source: Courtesy of the Mid-America Regional Public Health Leadership Institute.

CORE ORGANIZATIONAL PRACTICES

Efforts have been made since the late 1980s to further define the role of government in the U.S. public health system. In 1989, the Public Health Practice Program Office of the Centers for Disease Control and Prevention initiated a process to identify the core organizational practices necessary for governmental agencies to carry out the mission of public health.[8] Representatives from government public health agencies and related associations identified 10 organizational practices that help illuminate the three core functions, which are obviously more general in nature. The major criticism of this model, which is unfortunately not utilized today, is that it tends to be somewhat narrow in perspective and more about the public health organization than the public health system. However, this model begins the process of seeing that the public health organization needs to look outward to its community and its external stakeholders. The public health agency is part of the local public health system and needs to define the organizational practices that will make the organization an effective partner in the local system. There are still leadership activities associated with this model that are required if the local public health system is to be strengthened. **Table 9-1** does demonstrate that these 10 organizational practices begin to provide an operational definition of a functional local public health department. Do not be surprised if you later see a connection between the organizational practices, the essential public health services paradigm, and the standards for voluntary accreditation for local health departments.

Assessment Practices

Three organizational practices are tied to the core function of assessment. The first, which concerns the health needs of the community, involves establishing a

TABLE 9-1   Leadership and the Organizational Practices

Core Functions	Organization Practices	Leadership Activities
Assessment	1. Assess the health needs of the community.	Lead the community assessment process.
	2. Investigate the occurrence of health effects and health hazards in the community.	Collect and utilize information to enhance the investigation.
	3. Analyze the determinants of identified health needs.	Integrate data with decision making.
Policy development	4. Advocate for public health, build constituencies, and identify resources in the community.	Build coalitions; empower others; engage in public health advocacy; recognize community assets.
	5. Set priorities among health needs.	Clarify values; create a vision; tie vision to mission; use partners to set priorities.
	6. Develop plans and policies to address priority health needs.	Organize goals and objectives; translate goals into action.
Assurance	7. Manage resources and develop organizational structure.	Search for new resources; make organizational changes to better address community needs.
	8. Implement programs.	Stress innovation; delegate programmatic responsibility to others; oversee programs.
	9. Evaluate programs and provide quality assurance.	Support program evaluation; evaluate data collected; monitor performance.
	10. Inform and educate the public.	Use mentoring and training to educate workforce; use social marketing and health communication to educate public.

Source: Adapted from W. W. Dyal, *Public Health Infrastructure and Organizational Practice Definitions*, 1991, Public Health Practice Program Office, the Centers for Disease Control and Prevention.

systematic needs assessment process that is coordinated by the local health department and its leadership team and directed toward gathering data on the health status and health needs of the community. Although public health leaders initiate the process, community participation in the process is essential.

The second practice involves the investigation of health hazards in the community, especially timely epidemiological research to identify the magnitude of the health problems, their duration and location, health trends, and populations at risk. As obvious as the importance of epidemiological research is, it is not routinely done. A significant challenge for smaller health departments is doing investigations without an epidemiologist or behavioral scientist on staff. Another significant challenge is finding the necessary funds. Public health leaders need to understand how data are collected and used to monitor health status and uncover health hazards.

The third practice is the analysis of identified etiologic and contributing factors that place certain segments of the population at risk for adverse health outcomes. The data generated by the assessment process are used as raw material for this type of analysis. Public health leaders need to understand how to analyze data and how to use data for decision making.

Policy Development Practices

Three of the 10 organizational practices are involved in the policy development core function. The fourth organizational practice involves the following activities: acting as an advocate for public health, building community constituencies, and identifying resources in the community. These activities are important because they help generate supportive and collaborative relationships with public and private agencies as well as with potential community partners and thereby create organizational mechanisms for the effective planning, implementation, and management of public health programs and services. These activities are also essential

Leadership Tip

All leadership decisions are framed by the core functions and essential public health services.

for developing action plans in cooperation with community partners.

The fifth organizational practice is the setting of priorities. Criteria used in ranking health problems include the size and seriousness of the problems, the acceptability of the problems, the economic feasibility of solving them, and the effectiveness of the interventions developed to address them. Priority setting is not a completely objective process. For example, a concern about personal safety may exist even without a high community crime rate. If the community groups or politicians push hard enough, the community coalition in concert with the public health agency leader may designate violence as a key issue despite a lack of statistical validation. Public health leaders, in determining health priorities for the community, use value clarification skills, visioning skills, and partnership skills.

The sixth organizational practice is the development of plans and policies to address the prioritized health needs of the community. The development process involves establishing goals and objectives to be accomplished by means of a systematic plan that focuses on local community health needs and the equitable distribution of financial and nonfinancial community resources. This practice requires the participation of the community stakeholders and representatives from other related agencies. Public health leaders will guide the development of goals and objectives and help translate them into action steps.

Assurance Practices

The final four organizational practices are associated with the assurance core function. The seventh organizational practice involves managing resources and developing an organizational infrastructure to carry out the public health agenda. Critical leadership and management skills are necessary for the acquisition, allocation, and control of human, physical, cultural, and fiscal resources. Managing resources also encompasses maximizing the operational functioning of the local health system through the coordination of community agencies' efforts and the avoidance of the duplication of services. The issue of duplication is complicated by the professional protection of programs and resistance to the abolition of duplicative services. The seventh practice is unique in that it applies organizational considerations to the issue of public health agency operations. Public health leaders will search for new resources and alter their organizations to better reflect changing health priorities in the community.

The eighth organizational practice involves action plan implementation, which often involves the creation of services and programs. Plan implementation demands creativity and sound leadership, because legislative mandates must be interpreted and statutory responsibilities must be translated into programs. Public health agencies and health departments are usually given the task of providing population-based services, whereas personal services are seen as the responsibility of the medical care system. Public health leaders stress innovation in program development, delegate programmatic responsibility to others, and take an oversight role in monitoring program performance.

The ninth practice involves the evaluation of program activities. First, there is the issue of quality assurance—whether the program activities are being performed in accordance with professional and regulatory standards. Second, there is the issue of effectiveness—whether the program is achieving the intended goals and objectives. Third, there is the question of revision—whether the program needs to be reformed or resources need to be redirected. Given all the discussion in recent times on reinventing government, it makes sense for public health leaders to use evaluation data for purposes of reorganization. Leaders will need to support program evaluation, evaluate the data collected, and support performance monitoring.

The last assurance practice involves the provision of public health information to the community. Public health agencies have a responsibility to educate the residents of the community on ways to improve personal health—a responsibility they have not always fulfilled. They need to develop health education initiatives in order to increase health knowledge, change attitudes about unhealthy behaviors, and foster healthy habits. To meet their educational responsibility, public health leaders need to learn health communication skills, translate research intervention results into practice, and create linkages to academic institutions in order to develop health education strategies. They also need to use social marketing and health communication strategies to reach community residents and to use mentoring and training to educate the public health workforce. The goal is to get the entire public to view public health issues as important. People must be made to realize that public health hazards put everyone at risk, not just the poor.

As can be seen from the discussion of the 10 practices, the public health model is extremely complex and needs a committed leadership to make it work. Turnock and colleagues, who have studied the core functions and organizational practices, claimed in an article that the 10 organizational practices have been applied in the local health department system as a way to build capacity.[9] It appears that public health leaders and other public health professionals understand the model and feel that it is applicable to their work.

In a follow-up article, Turnock and colleagues reported on the use of the 10 practices.[10] In a study of health departments, 50% of 208 respondents stated that they employed the 10 practices. Use was higher for the practices associated with the policy development core function, and it was also higher for departments serving a population of 50,000 or more and for smaller local health departments organized at the city or city-county level.

In a 1995 study, Turnock, Handler, and Miller investigated the relationship between the application of the core functions paradigm and the effectiveness of public health practice activities using a random sample of local health departments stratified by population size and type of jurisdiction.[11] They found that the U.S. public health system did not reach the proposed national health objectives for the year 2000 to a significant degree. In addition, the goal of having 90% of the population served by a local health department utilizing the core public health functions was not achieved. The researchers found that there was only 54% compliance on implementation of the core functions and organizational practices, about 4% higher than in the previous survey.

Voices had been raised that the core functions model is too abstract, and it was replaced with a model that includes an emphasis on research activities in local public health systems. There seems to be general agreement about what public health does and little

Leadership Tip

Schedule your reading time, phone call time, and all other activities in your calendar. When an emergency meeting occurs, or if your supervisor calls, immediately reschedule activities that are being displaced.

agreement about what public health is. The essential public health services model approach to public health, which is discussed next, can be viewed as the systems perspective step toward a better understanding of what public health practitioners do in communities and how they do it. Public health is at a crossroads because of all the changes and proposed reforms in the health system.[12] Yet it must be kept in mind that public health, because it is population based and community oriented, is importantly different from other health professions, whether at the local, state, regional, or federal level.

ESSENTIAL PUBLIC HEALTH SERVICES

The public health system will be affected by the implementation of any proposals for a national health system (**Figure 9-4**) or indeed by any substantial changes in the medical care system. Yet what the effects will be is largely a mystery, especially because the core functions

paradigm is still confusing to policy makers and citizens, although the identification of organizational practices associated with the core functions helps to elucidate the paradigm. To offer further help, Baker and colleagues presented a list of essential public health services that are community based rather than organization based.[13] This list, unlike the models of public health discussed thus far, includes research, enforcement of laws and regulations, and the assurance of a competent health services workforce.

Table 9-2 lists not only essential services but also related leadership activities, and **Table 9-3** gives a brief description of each of the 10 services.[14] Leaders have key roles in the delivery of all of the essential services. There is a significant overlap in the leadership activities associated with the organizational practices approach and the essential services approach. The new leadership activities are associated with the three essential services not specifically covered in the organizational practices approach. With regard to enforcement of laws, public health leaders enforce laws and

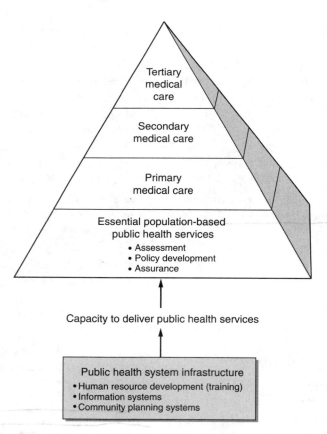

FIGURE 9-4 Public Health: The Foundation of a National Health System. *Source:* Reproduced from E. L. Baker, et al., Health Reform and the Health of the Public, *Journal of the American Medical Association,* Vol. 272, No. 18, pp. 1278–1282, 1994, American Medical Association.

TABLE 9-2 Leadership and the Essential Public Health Services

Essential Public Health Services	Leadership Activities
Monitor health status to identify community problems.	Use data for decision making.
Diagnose and investigate health problems and health hazards in the community.	Use data for decision making.
Inform and educate people about health issues and empower them to deal with the issues.	Engage in mentoring and training, social marketing, and health communication activities; empower others.
Mobilize community partnerships to identify and solve health problems.	Build partnerships; share power; create workable action plans.
Develop policies and plans that support individual and community health efforts.	Clarify values; develop mission; create a vision; develop goals and objectives.
Enforce laws and regulations that protect health and ensure safety.	Protect laws and regulations; monitor adherence to laws.
Link people to needed personal health services and ensure the provision of health care when otherwise unavailable.	Stress innovation; delegate programmatic responsibility to others; oversee programs.
Ensure a competent public health and personal healthcare workforce.	Build a learning organization; encourage training; mentor associates.
Evaluate effectiveness, accessibility, and quality of personal and population-based health services.	Support program evaluation; evaluate data collected; monitor performance.
Do research for new insights and innovative solutions to health problems.	Utilize research findings to guide program development.

Source: Adapted from J. Harrell and E. Baker, *The Essential Services of Public Health*, 1997, American Public Health Association.

TABLE 9-3 Essential Public Health Services

Monitor health status to identify and solve community health problems: This service includes accurate diagnosis of the community's health status; identification of threats to health and assessment of health service needs; timely collection, analysis, and publication of information on access, utilization, costs, and outcomes of personal health services; attention to the vital statistics and health status of specific groups that are at higher risk than the total population; and collaboration to manage integrated information systems with private providers and health benefit plans.

Diagnose and investigate health problems and health hazards in the community: This service includes epidemiologic identification of emerging health threats; public health laboratory capability using modern technology to conduct rapid screening and high-volume testing; active infectious disease epidemiology programs; and technical capacity for epidemiologic investigation of disease outbreaks and patterns of chronic disease and injury.

Inform, educate, and empower people about health issues: This service involves social marketing and targeted media public communication; providing accessible health information resources at community levels; active collaboration with personal healthcare providers to reinforce health promotion messages and programs; and joint health education programs with schools, churches, and worksites.

Mobilize community partnerships and action to identify and solve health problems: This service involves convening and facilitating community groups and associations, including those not typically considered to be health related, in undertaking defined preventive, screening, rehabilitation, and support programs; and skilled coalition-building ability in order to draw upon the full range of potential human and material resources in the cause of community health.

Develop policies and plans that support individual and community health efforts: This service requires leadership development at all levels of public health; systematic community-level and state-level planning for health improvement in all jurisdictions; development and tracking of measurable health objectives as a part of continuous quality improvement strategies; joint evaluation with the medical healthcare system to define consistent policy regarding prevention and treatment services; and development of codes, regulations, and legislation to guide the practice of public health.

(Continues)

TABLE 9-3   Essential Public Health Services (*Continued*)

Enforce laws and regulations that protect health and ensure safety: This service involves full enforcement of sanitary codes, especially in the food industry; full protection of drinking water supplies; enforcement of clean air standards; timely follow-up of hazards, preventable injuries, and exposure-related diseases identified in occupational and community settings; monitoring quality of medical services (e.g., laboratory, nursing homes, and home health care); and timely review of new drug, biologic, and medical device applications.

Link people to needed personal health services and ensure the provision of health care when otherwise unavailable: This service (often referred to as "outreach" or "enabling" services) includes ensuring effective entry for socially disadvantaged people into a coordinated system of clinical care; culturally and linguistically appropriate materials and staff to ensure linkage to services to special population groups; ongoing "care management"; transportation services; targeted health information to high-risk population groups; and technical assistance for effective worksite health promotion/disease prevention programs.

Ensure a competent public and personal healthcare workforce: This service includes education and training for personnel to meet the needs for public and personal health service; efficient processes for licensure of professionals and certification of facilities with regular verification and inspection follow-up; adoption of continuous quality improvement and lifelong learning within all licensure and certification programs; active partnerships with professional training programs to ensure community-relevant learning experiences for all students; and continuing education in management and leadership development programs for those charged with administrative/executive roles.

Evaluate effectiveness, accessibility, and quality of personal and population-based health services: This service calls for ongoing evaluation of health programs, based on analysis of health status and service utilization data, to assess program effectiveness and to provide information necessary for allocating resources and reshaping programs.

Research for new insights and innovative solutions to health problems: This service includes continuous linkage with appropriate institutions of higher learning and research and an internal capacity to mount timely epidemiologic and economic analyses and conduct needed health services research.

Source: Adapted from J. Harrell and E. Baker, *The Essential Services of Public Health*, 1997, American Public Health Association.

regulations that protect the health of the community. With regard to development of a competent workforce, they build learning organizations based on systems thinking and support continuing education opportunities for the public health workforce. With regard to research, they utilize research findings to guide program development. **Figure 9-5**, which was originally designed by the Health Resources and Services Administration, shows the relationship between the core functions and the 10 essential public health services.[15] It is presented as a circle to demonstrate that public health works in a system. Essential Service 10 is seen as research for systems management and greater understanding of how the public health system carries out its activities.

If we think of the three core functions as the trunk of a tree, organizational practices constitute one branch that lead to a dead end, and the essential public health services constitute another branch that has continued to grow. The two approaches (organizational practices and essential public health services) do have much in common, and because the essential services approach has predominated, it has been modified to include the organizational practices that are not now part of it (i.e., setting priorities among health needs, managing resources, and developing organizational structure). The National Association of County and City Health Officials (NACCHO) put the pieces together and came up with an operational definition of a functional local public health department. NACCHO was clearly aware that local health departments take many forms, but they need to support the core functions and 10 essential public health services within a public health systems approach.[16] The local public health department represents the governmental public health presence at the local level. The way they will do this is to follow a set of standards as noted in **Table 9-4**. The residents of a community will hold their local public health responsible for adhering to these standards.

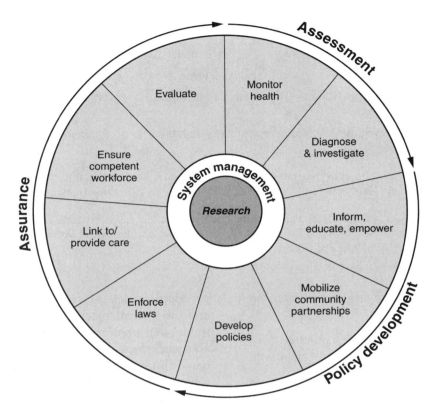

FIGURE 9-5 Core Functions and 10 Essential Services of Public Health. *Source*: Reproduced from U.S. Department of Health and Human Services (1999). *Public Health Functions Project.* http://www.health.gov/phfunctions/images/pubh_wh2.gif. Accessed July 30, 2012.

TABLE 9-4 Standards for a Functional Local Health Department

A functional local health department:

Understands the specific health issues confronting the community, and how physical, behavioral, environmental, social, and economic conditions affect them.

Investigates health problems and health threats.

Prevents, minimizes, and contains adverse health effects from communicable diseases, disease outbreaks from unsafe food and water, chronic diseases, environmental hazards, injuries, and risky health behaviors.

Leads planning and response activities for public health emergencies.

Collaborates with other local responders and with state and federal agencies to intervene in other emergencies with public health significance (e.g., natural disasters).

Implements health promotion programs.

Engages the community to address public health issues.

Develops partnerships with public and private healthcare providers and institutions, community-based organizations, and other government agencies (e.g., housing authority, criminal justice, education) engaged in services that affect health to collectively identify, alleviate, and act on the sources of public health problems.

Coordinates the public health system's efforts in an intentional, noncompetitive, and nonduplicative manner.

Addresses health disparities.

Serves as an essential resource for local governing bodies and policy makers on up-to-date public health laws and policies.

Provides science-based, timely, and culturally competent health information and health alerts to the media and to the community.

(Continues)

TABLE 9-4 Standards for a Functional Local Health Department (*Continued*)

Provides its expertise to others who treat or address issues of public health significance.
Ensures compliance with public health laws and ordinances, using enforcement authority when appropriate.
Employs well-trained staff members who have the necessary resources to implement best practices and evidence-based programs and interventions.
Facilitates research efforts, when approached by researchers, that benefit the community.
Uses and contributes to the evidence base of public health.
Strategically plans its services and activities, evaluates performance and outcomes, and makes adjustments as needed to continually improve its effectiveness, enhance the community's health status, and meet the community's expectations.

Source: Reproduced from National Association of County and City Health Officials, *Operational Definition of a Functional Local Health Department* (Washington, DC: NACCHO, 2005).

Following is a list of leadership activities related to the core functions paradigm:

- Put the core functions model into practice.
- Develop leadership skills to carry out the essential public health services approach.
- Increase commitment to the model by the public health workforce and by community partners.
- Utilize a systems perspective in implementing the essential public health services.

Exercise 9-1 is intended to help you explore the core functions paradigm and learn how the core functions are related to organizational practices, essential services, and strong public health leadership.

SUMMARY

This chapter introduced the core functions of assessment, policy development, and assurance as a paradigm for the practice of public health. Public health leaders have roles and responsibilities related to each of the functions. As a way of illuminating the three functions, the chapter described the early 10 organizational practices model associated with the three functions and the systems-based essential public health services model that predominates today. With this move from an agency-focused view of public health to a systems-based approach, an innovative operational definition of a functional local public health department has been developed by NACCHO and became an important cornerstone in the development of a national voluntary accreditation program for local health departments. The idea of accreditation will be expanded to state health departments as well.

DISCUSSION QUESTIONS

1. What are the three core functions of public health?
2. What is a paradigm, and what is a paradigm shift?
3. What are the similarities and differences between the organizational practices and the essential services of public health?
4. What leadership activities are required for priority setting?
5. What is one of the main criticisms of the core functions model of public health?
6. What are the reasons for creating an operational definition of a functional state and local health department?

EXERCISE 9-1: The Core Functions Debate

Purpose: to explore the core functions of public health and their relationship to organizational practices and essential public health services

Key concepts: assessment, assurance, core functions, essential public health services, organizational practices, policy development

Procedure: The class should divide into teams of 5 to 10 members. Each team is assigned a core function and the task of constructing an argument that purports to show why this function is the most important of the three core functions. In constructing the argument, the team should use the organizational practices and the essential services associated with the core function to clarify the nature of the function. It should also discuss the leadership issues involved. One team should be given the task of preparing an argument favoring a model in which all three core functions are treated as equally important. Each team selects a spokesperson to present its argument, and then all the teams vote on the arguments to determine which is most persuasive.

REFERENCES

1. Institute of Medicine, *The Future of Public Health* (Washington, DC: National Academies Press, 1988).
2. S. R. Covey, *The Seven Habits of Highly Effective People* (New York: Simon & Schuster, 1989).
3. J. A. Barker, *Paradigm* (New York: Harper Business, 1992).
4. Institute of Medicine, *The Future of Public Health*.
5. M. A. Stoto et al., eds., *Healthy Communities: New Partnerships for the Future of Public Health* (Washington, DC: National Academies Press, 1996).
6. P. Block, *The Empowered Manager* (San Francisco: Jossey-Bass, 1987).
7. M. Fallon and L. Rowitz, "Governance and Leadership," in L. F. Fallon, Jr. and E. J. Zgodzinski (eds.), *Essentials of Public Health Management*, 3rd ed. (Sudbury, MA: Jones & Bartlett Learning, 2012).
8. W. W. Dyal, *Public Health Infrastructure and Organizational Practice Definitions* (Atlanta: Centers for Disease Control and Prevention, Division of Public Health Systems, Public Health Practice Program Office, 1991).
9. B. Turnock et al., "Implementing and Assessing Organizational Practice in Public Health," *Public Health Reports* 109, no. 4 (1994): 478–484.
10. B. J. Turnock et al., "Local Health Department Effectiveness in Addressing the Core Functions of Public Health," *Public Health Reports* 109, no. 5 (1994): 653–658.
11. B. J. Turnock et al., "Core Function-Related Local Public Health Practice Effectiveness," *Journal of Public Health Management and Practice* 4, no. 5 (1998): 27–32.
12. E. L. Baker et al., "Health Reform and the Health of the Public," *JAMA* 272, no. 18 (1994): 1278–1282.
13. E. L. Baker, et al., "Health Reform and the Health of the Public."
14. J. Harrell and E. Baker, *The Essential Services of Public Health* (Washington, DC: American Public Health Association, 1997).
15. www.health.gov/phfunctions/images/pubh_wh2.gif. Accessed October 14, 2003.
16. National Association of County and City Health Officials, *Operational Definition of a Functional Local Health Department* (Washington, DC: NACCHO, 2005).

CHAPTER 10

Leadership and Assessment

[Assessment] involves identifying and studying important data sources.

—G. Pickett and J. J. Hanlon, *Public Health*

Assessment brings public health agencies and communities together as partners. Ideally, the leaders of a public health agency should work with a number of community groups to determine the health needs and health priorities of the community. Over the past century, public health has developed a number of methodological approaches to studying the health status of a community. One important lesson is that the determination of community health needs and strategies for dealing with these needs must take into account community boundaries, community resources, and the local culture. Otherwise, intervention strategies risk being rejected by community residents and will then wind up being largely ineffective. Another important lesson is that public health agencies must not ignore community groups and individuals in determining the community's public health priorities. The tendency of all types of human service

organizations to ignore community input may have contributed to making communities overly dependent on outside help.[1]

Public health agencies have long used epidemiological methods and demographic and social science techniques to obtain an objective picture of community needs. The difficulty with this approach is that it is based on the assumption that problems exist. According to McKnight, human service organizations need to use an anti-diagnostic approach that focuses on evaluating the capacities and strengths of the community and the flexibility of community leaders.[2] In practice, this would involve community organizations, including governmental public health agencies, increasing their connections to the assets of a community or county.[3] Investment in these assets would also be important. Finally, it is also important to strengthen community-based programs. These organizations should first do an assets assessment. Once the strengths of the community are determined, the problems of the community can be addressed from a positive perspective in which community leaders take a key role in developing connections to the community through personal gifts and talents, creating community citizen associations, and making the principles of hospitality a reality.[4]

THE ASSESSMENT PROCESS

Local health departments often view a complete community needs assessment as a burden rather than a tool for guiding their activities. The solution is for them to treat assessment as an ongoing dynamic process. If health department leaders incorporate assessment activities into everyday activities, assessment won't appear as a monumental task, because assessment data will be gathered as a matter of course.

Despite awareness on the part of public health professionals that assessment is a critical activity, they are often confused about the nature of assessment. Probably the best way to approach assessment is to focus on its basic component, which is problem identification.[5] It is with regard to this component that community research activities become especially important. Exercise 10-1 explores the issue of developing assessment strategies for an emerging gang problem in a small city.

The first step in the assessment process is to design a durable integrated public health information system.[6] The accomplishment of this step calls for a true partnership, based on public health leadership principles, among local and state health departments, national health-related agencies (including the Centers for Disease Control and Prevention [CDC]), citizen groups, and other agencies. The data systems must be designed to allow growth and the incorporation of new technologies and new databases as they become available.[7] A challenge relates to the lack of a coherent national data template for population health that can be an aid to understanding the health status of Americans.[8]

The second step is to identify community resources and evaluate their effectiveness.[9] Public health leaders need to be students of the community in which they work. They must examine the community health resources, such as health facilities, health professionals, available medicines and vaccines, and emergency medical transportation systems. They must also look at other community resources, such as sanitation programs, education programs, disaster response plans, and mental health and other counseling programs, to determine their availability and effectiveness. Their availability should be analyzed in terms of proximity, accessibility, affordability, acceptability, and appropriateness. The effectiveness measures should include such factors as population size relative to need, proportion of the population in need reached by existing community services, program effectiveness, program costs, and the cost to cover the population not covered. Finally, alternative program approaches should be evaluated.

The third step is to utilize the data that are collected.[10] These data need to be transformed into information that public health leaders can use for effective decision making. Indeed, assessment activities should lead directly to the policy development activities. Over the past two decades, there has been a shift in the use of data to drive assurance activities and now more use of data to drive policy. Public health leaders often fail to express information clearly, and they lose credibility with policy makers as a result. They should present the data simply and straightforwardly, not in a convoluted fashion. They should also orient the presentation to the specific audience receiving the information. The presentation should answer questions that have been posed. Public health leaders need to learn the art of presentation so that the recipients are educated by being given the information through knowledge management approaches.

Case Study 10-A, which describes the leadership activities of a disease surveillance group, explores obstacles that can prevent an assessment from being successful and ways of overcoming these obstacles.

Case Study 10-A

Removing Obstacles for Assessment: The MSDH Disease Surveillance System

Kate Wright, Mahree Fuller Skala, Ronald Gribbons, and Adelaide Merkle

The following case study reviews a selection of problems faced by many disease-oriented or risk factor–oriented public health surveillance systems. Some surveillance systems may not be comprehensive or may contain fragmented disease registries, holding large quantities of surveillance data not utilized to their full potential. This ultimately affects not only local public health and well-being but also state, regional, and national efforts to identify public health problems and implement interventions to control and prevent them.

Middle State Health Department

Surveillance System Problems

Surveillance for communicable diseases has been one of the most visible and critical assessment functions of the Middle State Department of Health (MSDH). Like other state health departments, MSDH reacted to the need for assessment of communicable diseases by designating for itself which diseases were necessary to track.

The department developed its own requirements for collecting data on both individual and outbreak cases and added them to the federal report list. Various reporting procedures were developed by six different MSDH programs responsible for surveillance of various reportable diseases. Program-specific procedural differences resulted in the development of different report forms, several targeted reporting sources, and six separate surveillance databases.

Required information was provided to MSDH by various health providers, who could report directly to their local health departments or to MSDH. Most reports were forwarded by local agencies intending to maintain control over "local" surveillance functions. Even if accurate data were forwarded by some local authorities in an efficient manner, this did not create a "real-time" data system available to MSDH for critical decision support when needed. The largest cities in the state were exempted from state reporting requirements, which resulted in additional complications, including the existence of different local ordinances, report forms, and procedures.

As a result of the lack of systemwide tools and procedures and policies, the problem of underreporting of communicable diseases became increasingly apparent during the late 1980s and early 1990s. Depending on the seriousness and rarity of the disease and the accessibility of the reporting system, a range of from 10% to 90% of diagnosed disease cases were reported annually. Many factors were blamed for the underreporting of communicable disease surveillance data. These included misunderstandings by providers regarding reporting requirements and confidentiality and the inconvenience of compliance given the wide range of reporting procedures and forms. Analysis of surveillance data did not present complete or accurate conclusions regarding disease trends, with the result that policy development and prevention and control measures to reduce public health risks were less than optimal.

History and Background Information

Historically, the public health system in Middle State was based on cooperation between autonomous local health departments and the state health department. The relationship was formalized through contractual arrangements that provided state general revenue funds to the local jurisdictions for core public health activities, including disease surveillance. Most local health departments received the majority of their funding from local taxes, Medicaid charges, and federal funding for nutritional and other services for mothers and children. These departments reported to local governing boards and set their priorities based on local constituent demands and funding source requirements.

Local health departments in cities with less than 75,000 residents were governed by MSDH administrative rules regarding the list of and procedures for reporting disease and health conditions. Larger cities were exempted from these rules by law but were required to establish their own reportable disease lists and submit surveillance data to MSDH. In practice, most cities used the state list along with their own versions of the report form and the processes and procedures. Over time, additional diseases were added to the state report list, but rarely were any diseases deleted. The criteria for adding a reportable disease included disease severity, the number of individuals affected by it, and the availability of public health measures to prevent or control it. In 1994, there were 49 diseases and conditions listed in the CDC list of nationally reportable diseases, of which most were included in the MSDH list of designated diseases.

The location where a disease case entered the surveillance system depended on the disease, the patient's residence, and the initial recipient of the information. State administrative rules defined those responsible for reporting requirements, although there were no penalties for failure to comply. The list included physicians, laboratories, school nurses, day-care providers, and nursing homes. Hospitals were not included on the list, although they often completed reporting requirements for physicians. In practice, laboratories were the chief source for disease reporting, followed by hospitals and physicians.

Both local and state jurisdictions were responsible for disease control activities, and the locus of responsibility depended on the disease. Local health authorities were responsible for investigating and controlling most reportable diseases, but state authorities would step in when local control was not assumed. MSDH policy specified the need for cooperation with local authorities in cases requiring state involvement. In fact, many smaller local health

(Continues)

departments did not have full-time disease control personnel, and these often requested MSDH to assist with surveillance and follow-up activities.

The complexity of the MSDH surveillance system grew over time. Within the Division of Epidemiology, six of the seven programs maintained their own disease registries. Three of these programs (sexually transmitted disease [STD]/acquired immune deficiency syndrome [AIDS], tuberculosis [TB], and Immunization) received most of their funding from categorical federal grants. Program managers and supervisory staff were CDC employees assigned to MSDH as advisers; the CDC determined most aspects of their operations, including the diseases tracked, the data reported to the CDC, and even the computer database programs and record format used. Local and district data were transmitted weekly, through computer modem transmission, to the Miscellaneous Diseases Program Office, where they were aggregated and sent to the appropriate registries, including national reportable data, which were also transmitted to the CDC.

The largest of the division's registries, the STD database, received 18,500 case reports in 1994. The TB registry added approximately 10,000 tuberculosis infections and 270 cases per year. The Immunization database added fewer than a hundred cases per year to several hundred per year, varying with the occurrence of outbreaks. The Miscellaneous Diseases and Zoonotic Diseases programs, supported by meager state general revenue funds, shared one centralized disease registry, which in 1994 received approximately 9,000 case reports. The Environmental Health program had two established registries, one for occupational fatalities and one for blood lead-screening results. Each used specialized methods and database formats mandated by federal funding agencies and entered and analyzed data in the program office. About 160 occupational fatalities and 30,000 blood lead levels were recorded annually.

MSDH distributed specialized case report forms for STDs, TB infection, TB disease, miscellaneous diseases (also used by Zoonotic Diseases and Immunization), miscellaneous diseases reported by laboratories (used by several programs), human immunodeficiency virus (HIV) infection, AIDS, occupational fatalities, and lead screening. In 1994, a new set of specialized forms was being developed by the Environmental Health program for additional reportable conditions. The major metropolitan health departments developed their own case report forms for most of the reportable diseases. A few MSDH forms were universally accepted, most notably for HIV and AIDS. As a result of the variances in report form acceptance and use, physicians, pediatricians, internists, and emergency department physicians, who initially diagnosed most reportable diseases, used at least 10 different report forms to meet surveillance obligations. In addition, each reportable disease had requirements regarding whether it should be reported immediately, by telephone or by mail, and whether the form should be sent to the local health department, district office, or directly to MSDH.

The division's largely decentralized system had positive and negative attributes. Local control allowed physicians and other sources to report to their city or county health department, which helped minimize delays in local case investigation and implementation of control measures. Each large urban and suburban health department and each MSDH district office had access to its own database to track workloads; complete investigations; analyze for local assessment and planning purposes, such as determining trends; identifying high-risk populations; and generating report source feedback reports to local agencies. Localized data entry also reduced the workload burden for MSDH disease registry clerical staff. Although local authorities with investigation resources preferred to maintain control, local control resulted in variations in local policies, procedures, and report forms. These variations affected the quality and accuracy of surveillance procedures, data analyses, report transmissions, and timely disease investigations and follow-up.

The Challenge

In July 1994, three opportunities for change created visibility for those wanting to address problems and begin reinventing the surveillance system. First, MSDH's capacity in the area of environmental epidemiology was expanded. This created an opportunity for allocation of new resources to expand the surveillance system to include environmental and occupational conditions that were not previously reported and increase the accuracy of and number of reporting sources for surveillance data. The division director, Mr. Jenkins, realized the importance of not dedicating new resources to perpetuate and further complicate the existing system. Other individuals supporting the need for change included the state epidemiologist and the program chiefs of the following programs: STDs/HIV/AIDS, TB, Immunization, Zoonotic Diseases, Environmental Epidemiology, and Miscellaneous Diseases. At the local level, the Communicable Disease directors from West City, East City, Suburban East City, and Southwest City, the largest cities in the state, expressed similar concerns.

While these needs were surfacing, the Middle State agency for licensing of physicians offered its newsletter as a forum for informing physicians about disease surveillance reporting obligations. They asked the division to provide their newsletter staff with a precise and succinct description of the state's system and reporting requirements. During the same period, the MSDH director's office identified population health measurement as a priority and created an initiative to assist local health departments in developing community assessment and strategic-planning activities. Local support for this initiative was based on increasing demand for consumable and accurate data on the health status and needs of local populations. Local departments wishing to access all data for community assessment had to request surveillance data from each MSDH program.

As a result of these developments, Mr. Jenkins became more aware of the complexity of the disease-reporting system in Middle State and identified a pressing need to expand surveillance for environmentally induced conditions, teach physicians how to use the reporting system, and make local disease data accessible for local community assessment projects. His challenge, as a leader, was to simplify the system in order to improve its efficiency, accuracy, sensitivity, and ability to have an impact on the continuous improvement of disease-preventing investigation and follow-up policies and procedures. In general, the challenges confronting the division were complicated by:

- the variety of division programs involved
- different categorical funding sources
- different federal requirements due to ties to the CDC, including different data criteria for each program
- lack of a centralized database
- the obligation of various report sources to submit disease reports, complicated by different disease-specific requirements and report forms
- the involvement of different levels of the public health system in surveillance data management and response

Postscript: Taking Action

In October 1994, Mr. Jenkins called a meeting of the program chiefs to discuss possible solutions to the problems facing the division. The following suggestions were made:

Develop a generic report form. This was supported by Immunization, Miscellaneous Diseases, and Environmental Health but rejected by STD/AIDS and TB. The program chiefs believed that specific, detailed information about clinical history and treatment was essential to determine the appropriate follow-up procedures for each case.

Utilize electronic disease-reporting methods. The Miscellaneous Diseases program advocated the use of fax and computer bulletin board technology to make reporting easier. This would require development of a simple generic form that could be faxed and scanned.

Centralize the reporting locus or "target." Some of the larger, well-funded programs advocated centralization of reporting requirements. They requested that all reports be sent directly to MSDH. Others warned that additional (unavailable) resources would be required to handle the increased workload and that centralized reporting could delay local response and investigation. There were additional concerns that transmission of all reports to MSDH would erode communication lines between local health providers and public health departments.

Next, Mr. Jenkins contacted the local communicable disease directors to solicit their input. They were supportive of the concept of a generic report form; West City and Suburban East City already had generic forms in local use and would continue to use them regardless of any changes MSDH implemented. All local directors insisted that local disease reports should be sent directly to them to prevent unacceptable delays in investigation and creation of a negative impact on local reporting relationships. Opinions on fax reporting were divided; some sites were already receiving most of their reports by fax.

A division disease surveillance work group was established that included members from each of the disease control programs, the four city communicable disease directors, and three other members from local health agencies involved in surveillance and follow-up. The committee chose simplification of reporting requirements as its first priority. Its tasks included:

- updating the disease report list
- reducing the report categories to two
- eliminating outdated report requirements
- expanding the categories of sources required to submit disease reports (it added hospitals to the list) and defining group practice requirements
- developing a generic disease report form

(*Continues*)

The committee accomplished these objectives during the spring of 1995 and received board approval the following August. In October 1995, these policy changes were published in the *Middle State Register* for public comment. It was expected that policies recommended by the committee would go into effect by April 1996.

All jurisdictions involved were in agreement over the use of the new generic report form as well as other policy-simplifying report requirements. These changes represented a major shift in collaboration at all levels to ensure meeting public health needs. However, the remaining challenges were formidable. The fundamental problem regarding the locus of responsibility for reports entering the system and local jurisdiction over local disease surveillance continued to raise concerns. Providers remained unclear as to where reports should be sent. The issue of managing disease surveillance data from customer source to an electronic system that could transmit information to the appropriate locus and ensure disease investigation and follow-up also remained a challenge. As of 2012, this system is still in operation, although modifications have occurred over the years.

Source: Courtesy of the Mid-America Regional Public Health Leadership Institute.

ESSENTIAL SERVICES ASSOCIATED WITH ASSESSMENT

Two essential services are associated with the core function of assessment. The first involves monitoring health status to assess the health needs of the community. The researchers who defined these practices also gave performance indicators for each practice. These performance indicators have been adapted to the essential services paradigm. It is important to note that the performance indicators are transferable from the organizational practice paradigm to the essential public health services paradigm, but the systems perspective of the essential services paradigm takes the activities and uses them in a total community context. In addition, the performance indicators serve as a guide to the public health agency in the community assessment process. The five organizational practice indicators show whether the essential service is actually in place:[11]

1. A community health needs assessment planning process is in place.
2. Needs assessment includes community input.
3. Morbidity and mortality data are obtained from vital records.
4. Morbidity and mortality data are obtained from other sources.
5. Behavioral risk factors are included in the community needs assessment.

The second essential service involves diagnosing and investigating the occurrence of adverse health events and health hazards in the community. This essential service has six performance indicators:

1. Epidemiological surveillance systems are functioning.
2. No preventable mortality or morbidity occurs as a result of delays in surveillance.

3. Health needs identified by the needs assessment are analyzed.
4. Determinants and contributing factors are identified.
5. Health needs of population groups are analyzed.
6. Existing health resources are analyzed.

The remainder of this chapter discusses the various approaches to needs assessment that have been developed in recent years. Public health has begun to use the community assets model in the Mobilizing for Action through Planning and Partnerships (MAPP) assessment process discussed below. As soon as needs assessment becomes a leadership partnership activity, assessment and policy development move closer together, and it is out of the marriage of these two core functions that assurance activities come into being.

ASSESSMENT METHODOLOGIES

This section presents six methodologic approaches to community and organizational assessment. Each of these approaches, despite being analyzable into a set of operational steps, requires leaders to be creative in their supervision of assessment activities. The leaders, of course, must delegate many of the activities to managers and other professional staff.

APEX*PH*

In 1987, the Assessment Protocol for Excellence in Public Health (APEX*PH*) project was started under a cooperative agreement between the American Public Health Association (APHA), the Association of State and Territorial Health Officials, the CDC, the National

Association of County and City Health Officials (NACCHO), and the National Association of County Health Officials.[12] Two major groups were established: a steering committee and an APEX*PH* working group. What eventually developed was a voluntary process for organizational and community self-assessment, a process for planned improvements, and methods for continuing evaluation and reassessment. The critical component is a set of procedures that local health departments can use to assess public health concerns. The final report and the manual created by the two working groups pointed to the differences between their approach and other approaches, some of which are indicated by the following outline of APEX*PH*:

1. APEX*PH* is a true self-assessment protocol that can be used by an agency to meet its needs and those of the community.
2. APEX*PH* leads to a practice-based plan of action.
3. APEX*PH* concentrates on a local health department's administrative and leadership capacity, the basic structure and organization of the local health department and its place in the community, and the community's actual and perceived problems instead of technical performance compliance with programmatic objectives by specific public health programs.
4. APEX*PH* offers opportunities for the local health department to assess its relationship with other local government agencies, with the community as a whole, and with state and federal agencies. The protocol can give guidance on ways to strengthen partnership relationships and obtain needed support.
5. APEX*PH* offers an approach by which the health department and its leadership will become accepted by the community as major players in the public health arena. It includes a community assessment process, health priority setting, policy development, and activities to ensure that the health needs of the public are being met.
6. APEX*PH* is adaptable to different local situations and different arrays of resources.

By following APEX*PH*, public health leaders fulfill the responsibility of the local agency to perform a community assessment. They will also increase their and the agency's credibility within the community and foster strong partnerships with community groups. The principles of APEX*PH* include these:

1. Because government has a primary responsibility to ensure the health of the public, health departments need to provide direction for their communities in assessing health problems, developing policies, and addressing community health problems.
2. Because leadership and accountability go together, health departments must establish and meet competency and practice standards that are seen by their communities as appropriate to health protection and health promotion.
3. Because public health practitioners are often placed in difficult situations in which hard choices need to be made, health department leaders have to be risk takers who shape their programs to the communities they serve in ways the communities will find acceptable.
4. Because public health problems demand a strong, coordinated, authoritative response, state and local health departments need to discover techniques for working in partnership with each other so as to strengthen each other's resources and authority.
5. In order to set health priorities utilizing scientific knowledge, health department leaders must become health information experts. They must routinely provide information to their communities and aid their communities in the development of community-based health plans.
6. Owing to the multidimensional nature of public health problems, health departments have to find creative approaches to solving local health problems using a wide variety of community resources.
7. With a strong belief that improvements in the health of the public require active community ownership and commitment, health departments need to develop and maintain partnerships with community agencies, community leaders, interest groups, and representatives of high-risk population groups.

APEX*PH* is a three-part process. Part I is an organizational capacity assessment—an eight-step internal review of the health department itself (**Figure 10-1**). The object is to evaluate the health department's administrative structure and its capacity to undertake a community assessment (Part II of APEX*PH*). The internal review is performed by the health department director and a team of key staff members. As Figure 10-1 shows, the review includes preparing for further steps, scoring indicators in regard to importance and current status, identifying strengths and weaknesses, analyzing and reporting agency strengths, analyzing weaknesses, ranking problems, developing and implementing action plans, and institutionalizing the assessment process.

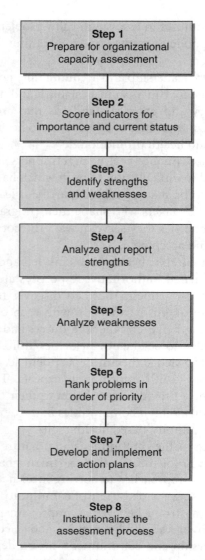

Step 1
Prepare for organizational
capacity assessment

Step 2
Score indicators for
importance and current status

Step 3
Identify strengths
and weaknesses

Step 4
Analyze and report
strengths

Step 5
Analyze weaknesses

Step 6
Rank problems in
order of priority

Step 7
Develop and implement
action plans

Step 8
Institutionalize the
assessment process

FIGURE 10-1 Flowchart of Steps in Assessing Organizational Capacity. *Source:* Reproduced from *Assessment Protocol for Excellence in Public Health*, 1991, the Centers for Disease Control and Prevention, National Association of County and City Health Officials. http://wonder.cdc.gov/wonder/prevguid/p0000089/p0000089.asp. Accessed July 13, 2012.

Part II of APEX*PH* is a community assessment. Public health leaders need to reach out and involve the community in the assessment process. The process involves evaluating the health of the community as well as identifying community strengths and the potential role of the health department in addressing health problems. (How community strengths are to be determined is not clearly laid out.) Part II also provides for the utilization of objective health data and the community's perceptions of community health problems. Those responsible for the community assessment gather demographic

data, socioeconomic data, environmental data, and data on years of potential life lost; access to primary health care; other health indices; perinatal indicators; the leading causes of mortality; the estimated prevalence of disease; and the leading causes of hospitalization. They then construct a community health problem summary, rank the top 10 contributors to years of productive life lost, and develop a community health plan.

The final part of the APEX*PH* process is called "completing the cycle." In this part, public health leaders integrate the plans developed previously into the ongoing activities of the health department and the community it serves. This part involves policy development, assurance, monitoring, and evaluation of plans developed in Parts I and II. As a result of the total APEX*PH* process, the leaders make recommendations for changes in current services or the development of new services. They also usually find ways of improving the functioning of the local health department (capacity building). The protocol guidelines are quite comprehensive and allow for assessment to be an ongoing agency process.

Beginning in the late 1990s, NACCHO, in partnership with the CDC, engaged in a revision of APEX*PH*. The new protocol, called MAPP, ties assessment to essential public health services as well as to the National Public Health Performance Standards (set by the CDC). It stresses the importance of community partnerships in the public health enterprise and the importance of measuring the outcomes of public health programs. Leadership is necessary at all levels of the assessment process.

MAPP

With the MAPP[13] process, there was a shift from the agency-based community assessment process to a systems-based process. Although some local health departments still choose the APEX*PH* approach to assessment, many are moving to the MAPP model. The tools that were developed began a process of seeing strategic planning as a set of activities tied to the community health improvement process. MAPP was developed in a partnership between NACCHO and the Public Health Practice Program Office of the CDC. As of 2012, the program was moved to a new Office for State, Tribal, Local, and Territorial Support. Between 1997 and 2000, a work group was established to develop this new approach by community representatives, CDC representatives, and academicians. The vision for MAPP is "communities achieving improved health and quality by mobilizing partnerships and taking strategic action."

Seven principles were designated to serve as the foundation for MAPP and to aid implementers in the understanding of the reasons behind the MAPP innovations. The seven principles are:

1. Systems thinking
2. Dialogue
3. Shared vision
4. Data to inform the process
5. Partnerships and collaboration
6. Strategic thinking
7. Celebration of successes

MAPP was designed by the work group to include the following elements:

1. Community-driven and community-owned approach
2. Builds on previous experiences and lessons learned
3. Utilizes traditional strategic planning concepts at a community level
4. Creates and strengthens the local public health system
5. Creates governmental public health leadership opportunities
6. Uses essential public health services to define public health and its work
7. Brings four community assessments together to provide a comprehensive strategic plan

With the seven principles and the seven elements in mind, NACCHO compared the APEX*PH* process with the new MAPP process, which can be seen in **Table 10-1**.

As can be seen in **Figure 10-2**, there are four integrated assessments that occur as a local public health system engages in the MAPP process:

1. *Community themes and strengths assessment.* Themes that engage community groups and residents as well as perceptions about quality-of-life issues. Community assets are also explored.
2. *Local public health system assessment.* Capacity of the local public health system to carry out the 10 essential public health services, which include performance standards tied to the essential services.
3. *Community health status assessment.* Analyzes data about health status of residents, quality-of-life issues, and potential risk factors.
4. *Forces of change assessment.* Forces at a local, regional, national, or international level that will affect the community and the health of the public.

As can be seen in Figure 10-2, the MAPP process involves partnership development, visioning, the assessments themselves that need to be done on an ongoing basis, identification of strategic issues, the formulation of goals and objectives, and evaluation and implementation of the results of the process.

There is also an assessment strategy tied to environmental health. PACE-EH is an assessment protocol for determining community excellence in environmental health.[14] The strategy uses a systems framework and is strongly committed to community engagement. The protocol assumes the involvement of local public health agencies that organize and facilitate the process. PACE-EH has four goals:

1. Evaluate environmental health conditions.
2. Target populations at risk.
3. Set priorities.
4. Support health equity and social justice.

TABLE 10-1   Comparison Between APEX*PH* and MAPP

APEX*PH*	MAPP
• Build local health department (LHD) leadership	• Build LHD leadership, but also promote community responsibility for the health of the public
• Assess LHD capacity for delivering public health services	• Assess capacity of entire local public health system
• Operational planning	• Strategic planning
• Focus on health status	• Focus on health status, community perceptions, forces of change, and local public health system capacities
• Develop plans to address needs	• Strategically match needs, resources, ideas, and actions

Source: Reproduced from National Association of County & City Health Officials (2012). Mobilizing for Action through Planning and Partnerships (MAPP). http://www.naccho.org/topics/infrastructure/mapp/. Accessed July 30, 2012.

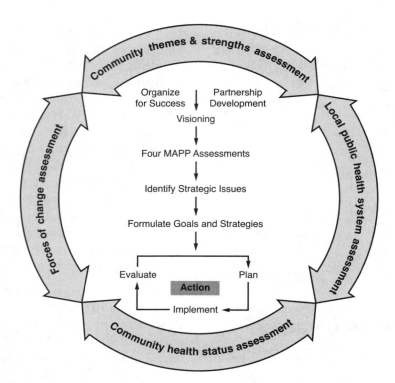

FIGURE 10-2 **MAPP Model.** *Source:* Reproduced from National Association of County & City Health Officials (2012). Mobilizing for Action through Planning and Partnerships (MAPP). http://www.naccho.org/topics/infrastructure/mapp/. Accessed July 30, 2012.

A major limitation of the assessment protocol is that it does not utilize the 10 essential public health services paradigm per se, although it can be used to operationalize these 10 services for environmental health. There is a leadership challenge in that environmental health needs to play a key role in the public health agency and in the public health system by showing other leaders how public health and environmental health need to be integrated.

PATCH

The CDC was one of the partners in the development of another assessment protocol, the Planned Approach to Community Health (PATCH). Other participants included state and local health departments and community groups. The protocol was designed in the mid-1980s to strengthen the capacity of state and local health departments to plan, implement, and evaluate community-level health promotion activities targeted at priority health problems.[15] It was developed in response to a shift in federal policy regarding categorical grants to states. Although PATCH includes strong assessment components, it has strong policy development and assurance components as well. It can be used to link local, state, and federal public health agencies, yet it is oriented toward local public health initiatives. Consumers are also essential partners in the PATCH process.

PATCH, like APEX*PH* and MAPP, has a methodology that communities can use for planning, conducting, and evaluating health promotion and disease prevention programs.[16] The methodology includes procedures for establishing a health promotion team, collecting and using local data, setting health priorities, planning and implementing programs, and evaluating the results. The promotion of PATCH was tied to the *Healthy People 2000* health objectives, and although some health departments still utilize the PATCH process, the number is shrinking.

The object of PATCH is to inculcate behaviors that are conducive to health. The process uses educational techniques, public health policy, and environmental strategies to encourage community residents to choose healthy lifestyles. Each community, in conjunction with its public health leaders, needs to do its own community assessment, set its own health priorities, formulate solutions, and take ownership of its programs.

The main principles of the PATCH process include the following:[17]

1. Community members must participate in the process.
2. Data should guide program development.
3. A comprehensive health promotion strategy must be developed.
4. The evaluation of programs should emphasize ways of improving them.

The PATCH procedures can be adapted to various health problems and communities. The whole process can be analyzed into five phases, which are summarized below.

Phase I: Mobilizing the Community

Public health leaders must use their coalition-building skills to involve the community in the PATCH process. They first need to complete a demographic profile of the community so as to identify the best community leaders and organizations to recruit. During this phase, the public health leaders must also work at informing the community about the PATCH process.

Phase II: Collecting and Organizing Data

The community work group, which includes community leaders, obtains and analyzes data on mortality and morbidity and their causes. It also collects behavioral data. Community groups may identify other sources of data that might be useful. The data are then analyzed in order to determine the leading health problems in the community.

The community work group should collect extensive data on the community and compare its community's statistics with state and national statistics. The addition of data from multiple sources will aid the group in other phases of the PATCH process. The assessment should include data on the causes of death and disability and identify ways of preventing premature death and disability (**Table 10-2**).

Both quantitative and qualitative data are collected. Among the quantitative data are mortality and morbidity data gathered from state and local health departments, state and local social service departments, the

state department of highway safety, state and local police departments, boards of education, voluntary agencies, hospitals, major employers or the chamber of commerce, and colleges and universities. Among the qualitative data are community opinion data. In order to get this type of information, it is necessary to identify community leaders, develop a series of survey questions, train interviewers, conduct interviews, collate and analyze data, and prepare a report of the results. The survey results will allow problems to be ranked according to the number of times they were mentioned. Public health leaders need to discuss the survey results report with community groups.

Phase III: Choosing Health Priorities and Target Groups

Behavioral data and other relevant data are presented to the community work group, which then analyzes the behavioral, social, economic, political, and environmental factors that affect behaviors and thereby put community residents at risk for disease, death, and injury. After reviewing all the behavioral data, the community group sets health priorities and appropriate community objectives and decides which priorities are to be addressed initially.

Phase IV: Developing a Comprehensive Intervention Strategy

In this phase, interventions are chosen, designed, and eventually implemented. Existing health resources, policies, environmental supports, and programs need to be identified before new programs are created so that duplication of services can be avoided. The work group begins to explore the assurance function of public health and develops a comprehensive health promotion intervention plan, including strategies, a timetable, and a schedule for completing tasks.

Phase V: Evaluating PATCH

In this phase, an evaluation work group is set up by the public health leaders. The work group's job is to evaluate progress, including improvements in the health of community residents, through the use of standard evaluation methods. The purpose of the evaluation is to provide feedback to program participants and public health leaders so they can enhance the effectiveness of the interventions.

TABLE 10-2 Contributors to the Leading Causes of Death

	Heart Disease	Cancers	Stroke	Injuries (nonvehicular)	Influenza Pneumonia	Injuries (vehicular)	Diabetes	Cirrhosis	Suicide	Homicide
Behavioral risk factor										
Tobacco use	•	•	•		•					
High blood pressure	•		•							
High blood cholesterol	•		P							
Diet	•	•	P				•			
Obesity	•		•				•			
Lack of exercise	•		•							
Stress	P		P							
Alcohol abuse	•	•	•	•		•		•	•	•
Drug misuse	P		P	•		•		•	•	•
Seatbelt nonuse						•				
Handgun possession				•					•	•
Nonbehavioral risk factor										
Biological factors	•	•	•				•	•	•	•
Radiation		•								
Workplace hazards		•		•						
Environmental		•			•				•	
Infectious agents	P	•			•			•		
Home hazards				•						
Auto/road design						•				
Speed limits						•				
Health care access	•	•	•	•	•	•	•	•	•	•

P = possible

Source: Reproduced from the Centers for Disease Control and Prevention (1994). PATCH: Planned Approach to Community Health: Guide for the local coordinator. http://lgreen.net/patch.pdf. Accessed July 13, 2012.

Steckler and colleagues evaluated 27 PATCH sites that had been functioning in 13 states for one to three years.[18] **Figure 10-3** shows a presumptive PATCH model containing the steps that 72% of the sites had completed. All 25 sites had completed a behavioral risk factor survey, which is discussed later in this chapter. Of the 18 sites that had completed the six CDC training workshops, 55.6% had completed most of the PATCH processes. The researchers found that PATCH was well liked by the participants. Funding for the process, however, tended to be a problem. Finally, PATCH was perceived to be effective as a community organization process by almost half of all state and local coordinators as well as by community leaders.

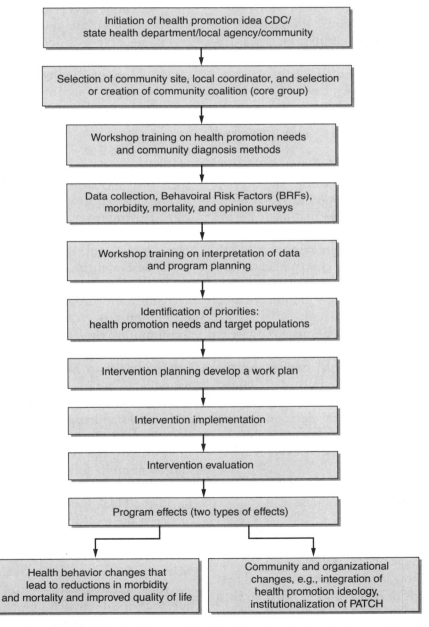

FIGURE 10-3 The Presumptive PATCH Model. *Source:* Reprinted from the Centers for Disease Control and Prevention (1994). *PATCH: Planned Approach to Community Health: Guide for the local coordinator.* http://lgreen.net/patch.pdf. Accessed July 13, 2012.

MODEL STANDARDS

A fourth major assessment methodology was based on model standards.[19] The model standards project, developed under the auspices of the APHA, was an attempt to bring together the various approaches to community assessment and apply the tools of assessment to the *Healthy People 2000* health objectives as a way of determining how and to what extent the objectives were being achieved. It was assumed that communities would adapt the national health objectives to local needs, in particular by a process in which community leaders and agencies, under the guidance of public health leaders, would set health priorities. Eventually, plans would need to be developed for programs designed to achieve the local health objectives.

The following principles are intended to guide the use of model standards:[20]

1. The health objectives should be measurable and reality based.
2. Plans should be flexible, and community coalitions should quantify their objectives and develop local strategies for addressing problems.
3. Community-wide partnerships that focus on the community as a whole should be fostered.
4. Government is the "residual guarantor" of health services, which means that a government agency provides the services directly or ensures their delivery by a public or private community-based organization.
5. Negotiation is the secret to relationships between agencies.
6. The use of the term "standards" implies that the objectives are uniform (in the interests of equity and social justice), and the use of "guidelines" suggests the existence of local decision-making discretion.
7. Assurance and accessibility to services are requirements of model standards.
8. Program development is emphasized rather than professional practice considerations.

In August 1990, a meeting was held at the CDC headquarters in Atlanta. The meeting, attended by representatives from the major U.S. public health organizations, focused on how local communities could best use planning methods in order to meet the objectives for the nation for the year 2000. Out of the discussion came the 11 steps of the model standards process:[21,22]

1. Determine and assess the role of one's health agency.

2. Assess the lead health agency's organizational capacity.
3. Develop an agency plan to build the necessary organizational capacity.
4. Assess the community's organizational and power structures.
5. Organize the community to build a stronger constituency for public health and establish a partnership for public health.
6. Assess the health needs of the community and its available resources.
7. Determine local priorities.
8. Select outcome and process objectives that are compatible with local priorities and the *Healthy People 2000* objectives.
9. Develop community-wide intervention strategies.
10. Develop and implement a plan of action.
11. Monitor and evaluate the effort on a continuing basis.

The model standards methodology can be used in conjunction with other assessment methodologies, such as APEX*PH*, PATCH, and MAPP. In *The Guide to Implemented Model Standards,* it was argued that APEX*PH* improves the public health infrastructure in the community by enhancing the community's capacity to perform the core functions of assessment, policy development, and assurance.[23] PATCH was seen more as a generic planning and implementation tool geared toward chronic diseases prevention and health promotion programs. The guide recommended that a community choose either APEX*PH* or PATCH but not both, although there are overlaps and connections between the two methodologies. Today, the advice would be to use MAPP. The model standards process is oriented toward the health priorities for the nation, and model standards are organized into four categories in each of the 22 priority areas of *Healthy People 2000*: health status, risk reduction, services and protection, and community surveillance. In essence, the model standards approach creates a blueprint (with extensive fill-in-the-blank forms) for addressing the health priorities at the local level. The integration of APEX*PH*, MAPP, or PATCH with the model standards approach would provide a comprehensive tool for discovering what a community needs to reach its goals.

An interesting extension of the model standards approach was presented in a report by Randolph and Ford.[24] A model standards work group worked with the model standards project staff to design and review community strategies for public health. The strategies were developed for the purpose of training staff to involve the community in the model standards process. A series of steps for "putting it all together" was also constructed. The first step is to choose the head of a lead agency to serve as coordinator of activities and meetings, collector and disseminator of data and information, and overall moderator and reporter for each of the various activities. The local health department head should take on this leadership role if possible. The role will allow the health department head to help improve public health in the community by:

- aiding the community in the assessment of local health problems by using health education methods
- establishing appropriate laws, regulations, and policies to protect the health of the public
- establishing and maintaining practice standards that encourage public confidence
- involving community residents in the planning of community-wide programs
- developing partnerships through linkage with the state health department and other local government agencies also involved in activities related to public health
- developing community resources to address problems
- acting as a trustee and guarantor (leadership roles) that the health needs of the public are being addressed
- encouraging flexibility in the development, adaptation, and elimination of programs based on the health needs of the community
- following the 11 steps for implementing the model standards[25]

The model standards project attempts to integrate the various assessment procedures. All three assessment methodologies are oriented toward collecting health status information about the residents of a community. They all require public health leaders to implement the assessment process. They just do it in different ways. The role of public health leaders in any kind of assessment is to:

- lead the community assessment process
- use health information data in decision making
- carry out the assessment using one of the assessment methodologies
- communicate the results of the assessment to the community

The major limitation of model standards is that it was not updated for the 21st century. This is not to say that the protocol could not be adapted for MAPP and other new assessment approaches. As new strategies develop, there is a tendency to ignore the strengths of previous approaches.

COMMUNITY HEALTH ASSESSMENT

From 2005 on, there has been an increasing move to view the process of assessment from the perspective of the community and not only public health. Major grant initiatives have occurred from the Centers for Disease Control and Prevention's Communities Putting Prevention to Work (CPPW) from 2010 to 2012 and the Community Transformation Program (CTG) beginning in 2011. The CPPW projects implemented evidence-based and practice-based approaches in policy, systems, and environmental change. The goal was to create community change through collaboration with the specific objective to reduce chronic disease morbidity and mortality associated with obesity and tobacco use.

Case Study 10-B presents a few CPPW success stories.[26]

Case Study 10-B

Success Stories
Centers for Disease Control and Prevention

Several communities are working toward interventions to combat the two leading causes of preventable disease: obesity and tobacco use. Although there are many innovative interventions relating to policy, systems, and environmental change through the 50 Communities Putting Prevention to Work (CPPW), here we will highlight six community programs from across the nation.

Bartholomew, Indiana

Establishing healthy behaviors during childhood and maintaining them is easier and more effective than trying to change unhealthy behaviors during adulthood. However, in the state of Indiana, one-third of high school students are already considered overweight or obese.

(*Continues*)

Poor eating habits, along with physical inactivity, contribute to obesity and other serious health problems. Concern has been raised about the nutritional quality of foods and beverages sold in schools outside of federally regulated meal programs. Schools play a critical role in preventing childhood obesity and in promoting the health and safety of young people and helping them establish lifelong healthy behaviors.

To improve the health of its students, the Bartholomew Consolidated School Board unanimously approved a new model school wellness policy that expands efforts in both nutrition and physical activity. The model ensures that healthy options are served in the school environment, identifies improvements in how the food will be prepared and identifies how students' physical activity opportunities can be increased, and provides improved recommendations for school events so that healthy food options can be offered. Bartholomew County has strengthened its commitment to support healthy eating and physical activity choices by creating an environment where the healthy choice is the easy choice.

Kauai, Hawaii

Although Hawaii is one of our nation's most popular travel and recreation destinations, native Hawaiians have a combined overweight and obesity rate of nearly 75% and have markedly elevated risk for chronic disease. Each year, Hawaii spends nearly $400 million in obesity-attributed medical costs. Kauai municipalities are engaging in a variety of interventions to decrease overweight and obesity and increase physical activity among its residents. In response to this alarming trend, the communities of Kauai are taking action to increase the level of physical activity—and the overall health—of their 64,000 residents.

In September 2010, Kauai established a countywide Complete Streets strategy. This strategy incorporates a set of design principles that promote safe access for pedestrians, bicyclists, motorists, and public transportation users of all ages and abilities. As a result, a Safe Routes to School program was developed that addresses deficiencies in the built environment. Bike lines have been painted, and flashing in-roadway warning lights at crosswalks are being installed to make it possible for more children and their families to safely walk or bicycle to school in Kauai school districts.

In May 2010, the Kauai community promoted and secured the expansion of an 18-mile multiuse path along its beautiful coastline, and now over six miles of that corridor is safe and accessible for biking and walking. Additionally, Kauai's mayor has established the Walking Workbus program in Lihue, which encourages people to get together one day a week for a two-mile walk—approximately 30 minutes of moderate intensity aerobic activity.

Los Angeles County, California

California and Los Angeles (LA) County have made tremendous strides in reducing the prevalence of smoking over the past generation. However, more work needs to be done to reduce tobacco use and dangerous exposure to secondhand smoke. More than 1 million adults in Los Angeles County continue to smoke. The top five causes of death in LA County—lung cancer, coronary heart disease, chronic airway obstruction, other cardiovascular diseases, and other cancers—are all associated with tobacco use. In addition, millions of LA residents are exposed to secondhand smoke every day, including more than half a million adults in LA County and 336,000 children who are regularly exposed to secondhand smoke in both single and multiunit homes, not because they live with a smoker but because they live in multiunit housing.

Infants and children exposed to secondhand smoke are inhaling many of the same cancer-causing substances as smokers, and because their bodies are developing, they are especially vulnerable to these poisons. Children exposed to secondhand smoke are at an increased risk for sudden infant death syndrome (SIDS), acute respiratory infections like bronchitis and pneumonia, ear infections, and more frequent and severe asthma attacks. Exposure can also slow lung growth in children.

Smoking continues to cost the county more than $2.3 billion in direct medical costs each year, including hospitalization costs and ambulatory care. In addition, the cost in lost productivity tops $2 billion annually.

Los Angeles County's Project TRUST (Tobacco Reduction Using Effective Strategies & Teamwork) aims to further reduce smoking prevalence among residents and decrease exposure to secondhand smoke, especially in disadvantaged communities. Project TRUST's work aims to reduce exposure to secondhand smoke among residents living in multiunit house. Smoke-free environments have also been shown to reduce the likelihood that children and youth will initiate tobacco use.

These efforts were made possible with funding through the Communities Putting Prevention to Work initiative. For more information about Los Angeles County's Public Health's Tobacco Control and Prevention Program, visit http://publichealth.lacounty.gov/tob/index.htm.

Portland, Maine

Obesity is a costly condition that can reduce quality of life and increases the risk for many serious chronic diseases and premature death. Consumers need to have access to calorie information in order to make informed decisions about what they eat when dining out. Combating obesity is a complex problem, but reducing calories is one way to start. The number of obese adults in Portland continues to increase—estimated at 20.6% in 2008 compared to 17.2% in 2004. Here are a few examples of what Portland is doing to reduce obesity:

- Portland is encouraging local, nonchain restaurants in Maine to provide nutritional information on menus.
- These restaurants are also working to provide lower-calorie options for patrons.
- The program is providing free assistance from a registered dietician to analyze menus with nutritional information.

In the fall of 2010, the first restaurant to take advantage of this service release its expanded lower-calorie menu options and new menu board with calorie counts. As more restaurants take advantage of this program, Portland families will have healthier options and access to nutritional information so they can make informed choices when dining out at their favorite locally owned restaurant.

Santa Clara County, California

While there have been great strides in reducing tobacco use in counties across California, about one in ten adults and youth in Santa Clara County still smoke. Tobacco-related health care costs the County an estimated $380 million each year.

In addition, until recently, Santa Clara County had no protection from secondhand smoke exposure for its residents living in multiunit housing. More than two out of every five households living in multiunit housing in Santa Clara County have children six years of age or younger. Infants and children exposed to secondhand smoke are inhaling many of the same cancer-causing substances as smokers, and because their bodies are developing, they are especially vulnerable to these poisons. Children exposed to secondhand smoke are at an increased risk for sudden infant death syndrome (SIDS), acute respiratory infections like bronchitis and pneumonia, ear infections, and more frequent and severe asthma attacks. Exposure can also slow lung growth in children.

To improve the health of adults and children, a 100% smoke-free policy for apartments, townhouses, and condominiums, as well as their common areas, in unincorporated Santa Clara County has been put in place. Smoking inside multiunit residences is now limited and exposure to secondhand smoke is reduced in approximately 300 multifamily complexes with 1,100 individual housing units.

For more information about Santa Clara County's tobacco prevention initiatives, visit http://www.sccphd.org/tobacco-prevention.

San Antonio, Texas

San Antonio has seen a dramatic rise in obesity and is now one of the heaviest cities in the country in which 31% of adults are obese. Because of the high obesity rates, more San Antonians have diabetes, heart disease, hypertension, asthma, and many other illnesses.

To combat this issue, the City of San Antonio recently launched three initiatives to encourage residents to improve nutrition and increase physical activity. The first focuses on e-health: www.sabalance.org enables residents to create customized nutrition and physical activity plans to improve their health and wellness. Second, San Antonio's Mayor Julian Castro created a Fitness Council to unite public, private, and nonprofit sector partners to engage residents in local fitness, sports, and nutrition programs. Lastly, select San Antonio restaurants are participating in the "Por Vida!" healthy menu initiative. Through this initiative, restaurants will display a special logo next to healthy items on their menus to assist families in making healthier options when dining out.

The obesity rates in Texas are expected to triple medical and economic costs to $39 billion by 2014, a number that is expected to grow without action. In addition, projections show that the number of overweight or obese adult Texans is expected to increase to three out of every four adults by 2040. This staggering increase will certainly have a negative impact on San Antonio's children who are already suffering from obesity-related health problems.

If you want to join San Antonio's Mayor Julian Castro in combating obesity, visit www.sabalance.org.

The efforts being made by each of these communities were made possible with funding from the federally funded Communities Putting Prevention to Work Initiative.

Source: Reproduced from the Centers for Disease Control and Prevention (2011). Success Stories. Division of Adult and Community Health, National Center for Chronic Disease Prevention and Health Promotion. http://www.cdc.gov/communitiesputtingpreventiontowork/. Accessed July 13, 2012. Last updated March 27, 2012.

The CTG program goal was to support community efforts to reduce chronic disease by promoting healthy lifestyles in population groups that have the greatest burden of chronic disease. The CDC hoped these community grants would not only improve health but also reduce cost and reduce health disparities. The community and agency leadership issues are evident in these projects.

A special assessment tool called CHANGE was developed to provide data for many of these community projects. The purpose of CHANGE was to develop an assessment tool and strategies that enable a community through the community planning process to structure its activities around a common purpose and to prioritize its needs.[27] There are five stages to the community change process, as seen in **Figure 10-4**. The purpose of the CHANGE tool is to help community leaders and stakeholders survey and identify community strengths and areas that need improvement, which includes the areas of policy, systems change, and environmental change strategies. **Figure 10-5** shows the eight action steps in carrying out the CHANGE tool process.

After the CHANGE tool is completed, community leaders and stakeholders can build the community action plan. **Table 10-3** presents an example of a community action plan.

FIGURE 10-4 Community Change Process. *Source*: Reproduced from Centers for Disease Control and Prevention, Community Health Assessment and Group Evaluation (CHANGE) Action Guide. Atlanta: HHS, 2010. Public Domain. http://www.cdc.gov/healthycommunitiesprogram/tools/change.htm. Accessed July 13, 2012. Last updated February 7, 2012.

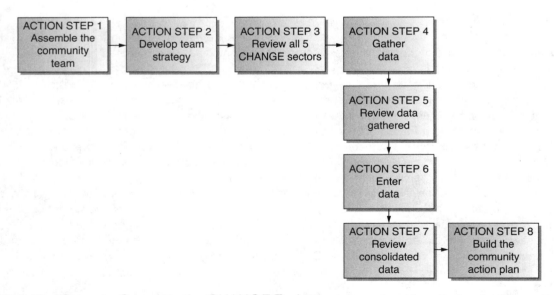

FIGURE 10-5 Action Steps to Complete the CHANGE Tool. *Source*: Reproduced from Centers for Disease Control and Prevention, Community Health Assessment and Group Evaluation (CHANGE) Action Guide. Atlanta: HHS, 2010. Public Domain. http://www.cdc.gov/healthycommunitiesprogram/tools/change.htm. Accessed July 13, 2012. Last updated February 7, 2012.

TABLE 10-3 Example of a Community Action Plan

Project Period Objective	Description of the Objective	Priority Area
By Year 3, increase the percentage of total miles of physical infrastructure for walking by 30%.	Very few neighborhoods and community common areas have sidewalks, trails, or walking paths that can support residents' need for active transporation to school and work and the ability to be physically active in the majority of the community.	Obesity and Physical Inactivity
Annual Objective	**Description of the Objective**	**Sector**
At the end of 12 months, increase percentage of developments (e.g., housing, schools and commercial) with paved sidewalks to 100%.	Current sidewalk ordinance does not require sidewalks to be paved for new housing developments with less than 120 homes; schools and commercial developments can receive a waiver if building in rural areas (designated by certain zip codes). Ordinance must be evaluated, revised, and approved to exclude such exceptions and begin developing stronger sidewalk networks.	Community-At-Large

Number of People Reached 167,000 |
Activities	**Activity Title**	**Description**
	Gap analysis on existing ordinance	Review sidewalk ordinance for policy language and language gaps
	Meeting with county architecture board	Meet with county architecture board about sidewalk development and share draft of revised ordinance language for new developments
	City Council meeting	Attend city council meeting to inquire about stance on sidewalks for future developments and current budget for developing sidewalk network
	Town hall meetings	Hold town hall meetings with neighborhood home owners associations to build local support for revised ordinace

Source: Reproduced from Centers for Disease Control and Prevention, Community Health Assessment and Group Evaluation (CHANGE) Action Guide. Atlanta: HHS, 2010. Public Domain. http://www.cdc.gov/healthycommunitiesprogram/tools/change.htm. Accessed July 13, 2012. Last updated February 7, 2012.

OTHER ASSESSMENT APPROACHES

Assessment is one of the major responsibilities of public health. The public health system is organized to provide needed programs and services, and public health leaders therefore constantly look for innovative assessment techniques that can help gauge community health status. This section discusses several assessment techniques that can be used in conjunction with the methodologies described above.

Since the mid-1980s, telephone surveys have been conducted in the United States as a means of estimating the prevalence of specific behaviors associated with health problems.[28] For example, telephone survey data have been collected on cigarette smoking, dietary fat intake, level of physical activity and exercise, seatbelt use, and screening tests for early detection of disease. The information obtained has then been used by states to develop state and local health interventions.[29,30]

For instance, a San Francisco study used the behavior risk factor survey to evaluate differences between Latino and non-Latino white adults.[31] Telephone interviews were done with 652 Latinos and 584 non-Latino whites selected by random-digit dialing. The researchers found that Latino men and women were less likely to consume alcoholic beverages and consumed fewer drinks per week than non-Latinos. The Latinos were more likely to be sedentary. Latino women were less likely to smoke and to have had a Pap smear or a clinical breast examination than their non-Latino counterparts. The researchers argued that the data showed that health programs targeted at Latinos would be beneficial. They also stressed the importance of providing information in Spanish.

In recent years, the value of community health report cards that provide an overall picture of community health status has been debated. Their advantages are clear. Community health report cards can help public health leaders monitor the overall health of the community in a straightforward way, and if they are written in easy-to-understand language, they provide a means of informing the community of its health status over time.

One type of report card can be created using Comprehensive Assessment for Tracking Community Health (CATCH), a system developed at the University of South Florida School of Public Health.[32] CATCH was used to produce a ranking of community health problems in 11 Florida counties by combining information on more than 200 indicators that was drawn from multiple data sources. The system allows public health agencies to compare their health indicator scores with those of other agencies. Trends over time can be identified so that an agency can check its progress in improving community health.

Leadership Tip

Use the essential public health services model to drive action.

The report card approach has been explored by managed care systems. Both managed care and public health use population-based approaches to health.[33] Both are concerned with the cost of health care. Managed care organizations (MCOs) use population-based assessments of their membership groups to deliver the most cost-effective quality care at the lowest price. Public health professionals are taking leadership roles in the managed care sector, for they have long supported a population-based approach to community health improvement.

The survival of MCOs depends on their evaluating the health needs of their membership. The Health Care Financing Administration and private health care systems use the Health Plan Employer Data and Information Set (HEDIS) to compare the quality of care delivered by health maintenance organizations. HEDIS, which monitors the effectiveness of care provided, is essentially an assessment tool. Some MCOs use a life care plan model oriented toward helping members increase their health potential by stressing prevention, wellness, better management of chronic conditions, and increased personal responsibility for health.[34] MCOs also conduct market research to determine whether their services are perceived to be of high quality, and they assess their programs to see if the programs reflect their mission.

MCOs and public health agencies both engage in some of the same monitoring and assessment activities.[35] They both do health risk assessments, community health assessments, health policy assessments, health systems assessments, and comparative analyses of populations and systems; they both also monitor adherence to quality standards, health outcomes, planning effectiveness, and cost effectiveness. Leadership is critical in all of these activities. Leaders from the public and private sectors need to develop partnerships to create integrated systems of assessment and care in communities.

Attempts have been made to build leadership activities directly into the assessment process. The Healthy Communities approach is an example. The goal is to foster healthy lifestyle choices by community residents from birth to death and to share the responsibility for community health among residents, public health practitioners, and community leaders.[36] The community as a whole explores health issues in detail, and the dialogues between community residents and public health practitioners are part of an overall community assessment. Communities that have implemented the Health Communities approach may use any of the assessment techniques discussed previously.

In assessing the health status of a community, public health leaders:

- use national databases when appropriate
- coordinate the use of assessment techniques in the public and private health care sectors
- explore the pluses and minuses of regularly released community report cards
- explain community health report cards to the community
- work to integrate HEDIS with public health assessment techniques so as to better identify the needs of the community

PUBLIC HEALTH INFORMATICS

Assessment depends on data collection and the use of information system techniques, and therefore public health leaders need to know how to design data collection activities, employ the latest information technologies, interpret data, translate data into useful information, and build data systems that utilize an evidence-based approach. Public health informatics is a new specialty designed to give leaders the necessary knowledge to perform these tasks.[37]

Public health informatics uses analytical tools such as meta-analysis, risk assessment, economic evaluation, public health surveillance, expert panels, and consensus conferences. It also uses tools associated with geographic information systems (GISs). GISs are user-friendly data representations (in the form of spatial maps) that provide leaders with information on health risks, underlying causes of disease transmission, and the effectiveness of public health interventions and can demonstrate needed structural changes in the health system at the community level.[38]

Data are the raw facts of public health. Collected according to objective criteria, they tend to be quantitative in nature, although there is increasing support for collecting qualitative information, which can sometimes provide especially deep insights into public health issues. Information is processed data.[39] The translation of usable quantitative data into useful information involves computer-related information technology.[40] Qualitative information may also be computer analyzed, but such information often takes the form of stories, focus group findings, or anthropologic field materials. Public health leaders use information to inform and educate the public, make decisions, develop policy, and implement appropriate public health interventions.

Following are six principles that pertain to the use of information systems by public health leaders:[41]

- Public health leaders need to use data from two different data systems. One data system reports on the delivery of direct services and on program encounters (e.g., a case management meeting or a home visit). The second system collects population-based data.
- Public health leaders need to remember that people are complex, integrated beings but that programs are fragmentary (i.e., each program focuses on just one part of the whole person).
- Leaders need to advocate for information that integrates different types of data so that they can better understand the health concerns of community residents.
- Public health consumers must get something back from data collectors. They need to know why data are being collected and must be given feedback.
- Data systems need to be flexible and should be designed to meet the needs of local health leaders as they monitor the health of community residents.
- Information systems need to be compatible so that leaders can access different data sources using just one computer. (The Internet is becoming a very useful data source for public health leaders because all the data on websites are accessible by anyone with Internet software.)
- Public health leaders need to respect confidentiality. The public wants to be assured that personal information will be kept private.

Because public health draws data from multiple sources, including sources from different disciplines, public health leaders need to understand the different perspectives of the various professions and learn how to synthesize data from different sources. Information science, computer science, and computer technology are advancing, and public health leaders need to keep up with the changes. Leaders may not be personally responsible for data collection, but they must be able to define the data they need to make effective policy decisions. They must also be involved in the development and design of the information system.

An interesting example of cooperative sharing of information is the community health status indicators project supported by NACCHO, the Association of State and Territorial Health Officials, and the Public Health Foundation. The goal of the project has been to regularly provide community-specific public health data reports to local public health leaders in counties across the United States. The reports have included information on actual causes of death, risk factors for premature death, access to care, preventive services use, and county demographics. They also summarize health measures and compare data from counties with similar demographics. The profiles were removed from the Health Resources and Services Administration website in October 2002, but were available from the Public Health Foundation for a couple of years.[42]

The County Health Ranking Project, which has been a collaboration of the Robert Wood Johnson Foundation and the University of Wisconsin Population Health Institute, is an apparent extension of the community health statuses project discussed above. Beginning in 2010, an annual ranking of county health departments was released.[43] The rankings were based on a number of indicators that affect health, including health mortality and morbidity variables, health behavior indicators, clinical care, social and economic factors, and environmental factors.[44] The rankings of counties can be found on the Internet.[45] These data are extremely useful to public health leaders and their stakeholders in community health planning activities.

Another example was the CDC's Information Network for Public Health Officials (INPHO). INPHO had several goals, including improving communication among public health leaders throughout the United States, increasing the accessibility of information, and utilizing information technology to expedite the exchange of information.[46] INPHO was tied to a vision of using telecommunication technology to help build public health infrastructure through increased connectivity, increased access to information, and data exchange.[47] The CDC funded several INPHO projects to create networks and investigate the barriers to access in present data systems. During the first decade of the 21st century, partially as a reaction to the events of September 11, 2001, INPHO was replaced by the Public Health Information Network (PHIN) with the redefined mission of being a national network facilitated by the CDC to improve the capacity of the national public health network to use and exchange information electronically. PHIN has standards and technical requirements for information systems based on best practice.[48]

Illinois is one state that has struggled with the issue of how to create useful and integrated information systems. Case Study 10-C, a review of the early history of the development of the Illinois Cornerstone project, describes the development of an integrated system for providing information on maternal and child health (MCH) to health professionals. Public health leaders need information if they are to positively affect the communities they serve. To ensure they receive the necessary information, they should:

- take training courses in informatics
- learn techniques for the collection of health status indicators
- learn how to interpret data and turn them into useful information
- learn how to access information on the Internet
- explore different analytical tools for better understanding data
- utilize quantitative and qualitative information
- become involved in the development of information systems
- integrate conflicting data systems

Case Study 10-C

Cornerstone: Illinois's Approach to Service Integration
James R. Nelson

Background

As federal and state governmental agencies became more involved in community health services, funding was increasingly offered through grants for specific diseases and other public health issues. Over a 20-year period, this funding approach resulted in numerous discrete, single-purpose programs, each with its own reporting requirements and information system. Unintended consequences of this phenomenon were fragmented, episodic, and incomplete service delivery; repetitive registration processes; redundant data collection and reporting; nonstandard assessments; incomplete understanding of clients' service history; and inconsistent documentation of services. Fundamentally, the core functions of public health—assessment, policy development, and assurance—were undermined by the continued proliferation of discrete and separate services.

Recognizing the significance and extent of discrete service delivery, the Illinois Department of Public Health, and now the Illinois Department of Human Services, moved to integrate the services of several health programs. At the heart of the issue was the need for a mechanism that would facilitate and encourage service integration and, ultimately, improve the health outcomes of Illinois residents. After considerable research and development, as well as the active participation of a diverse group of health care and human service providers, the department implemented a package of tools that redesigned community service delivery into an integrated system of care. That package of tools was Cornerstone.

At the beginning of the process, in 1992, the department offered several different MCH programs. These included Women, Infants, and Children (WIC); Healthy Moms/Healthy Kids; EPSDT; pediatric primary care; immunizations; Families with a Future; Drug Free Families with a Future; Parents Too Soon, a teen pregnancy program; and a prenatal smoking cessation program. Statewide, 173 WIC clinics, 104 Healthy Moms/Healthy Kids agencies, 115 immunization sites, and 91 primary pediatric care programs offered services. At that time, several data systems supported the information needs of many of these programs, including the following:

A statewide WIC system developed in 1989. This system operated on a personal computer (PC)–based network, using a mainframe for support. The system automated the nutritional risk assessment and food coupon issuance functions of the WIC program.

A case management information system (CMIS) originally developed for the Medicaid-eligible client population. The CMIS was a PC-based, batch-oriented system for which data were entered locally and submitted for update on disk via mail.

An HM/HK case management system. The system had limited functionality and insufficient hardware resources.

Distributed immunization databases. As an enhancement to the WIC system, several screens specific to immunization history and current status were created. The immunization data were collected locally and not compiled into a central registry.

The selection of Chicago as a federal Healthy Start Infant Mortality Reduction project site provided an opportunity for Illinois to initiate an integrated information system to support greater coordination, standardization, and sharing of information among community health programs. The requirement of the Healthy Start project to design an information system for collecting evaluation data was also viewed as a way to integrate MCH-related information systems that were not integrated with respect to clients or front-line practitioners and thus led to duplicative intake processes and information collection.

The development of the integrated information system was approached from several key philosophical points of reference. First, to the extent that potential system users were invested in the system from its inception, they would be more likely to use it. Second, to the extent that system developers understood program service delivery, they would better be able to customize it to provider needs. To facilitate this understanding, an individual with a social sciences background served as a liaison between service providers and technical staff during the design process.

An executive steering committee was formed to facilitate planning and ensure diverse representation and contributions to the project. The committee included representatives from the then state Departments of Public Health; Alcohol and Substance Abuse; Public Aid; Mental Health and Developmental Disabilities; and Children and Family Services as well as advocates and members of the provider community. The committee met frequently, and several subcommittees and standing committees were responsible for addressing specific areas, such as legal issues, local implementation, program implementation, system support, and funding. As many as 40 individuals participated in the committee work and reviewed the project design.

Cornerstone

One result of these efforts was Cornerstone. A management information system, Cornerstone supported a case management framework that ensures delivery of prenatal care, well-child visits, nutrition products and education, and immunizations in more than 300 separate locations across the state. Its design capitalized on the original WIC service delivery and information system. Cornerstone's features included combined registration, standardized risk assessment, automated care plan development, and consolidated referral and scheduling. Demographic and eligibility information specific to a client was captured once and shared with all other service providers that used the system when caring for the client. The system also provided a client's service history to the various providers responsible for that client. Following is a brief overview of the systems features from the perspective of a system user.

Registration

When registering a client, a case manager checked the client's enrollment status by searching a locally based statewide index. In this checking process, the case manager could have used the client's identification numbers

(Continues)

assigned through Medicaid, WIC, or other community health programs. Potential matches were pulled into the local system and displayed. If no match was found, the case manager enrolled the client and created a Cornerstone participant identification number. During the matching process, the case manager also obtained critical client information through the system (e.g., previously identified medical problems, MCH program status, and contact information).

Assessment

During an assessment interview, case managers accessed a table of standardized questions designed to assess a client's medical and/or psychological/social risk and prompt either "yes" or "no" or numeric responses. The system compared the responses to a table of normative values for that assessment type, generating a list of goals and recommended services. For example, a "yes" response to the question "Are you pregnant?" automatically generated the goal of adequate prenatal care and a list of recommended services (i.e., prenatal care, prenatal education, WIC, and prepared childbirth education).

Goals

The risk factors were linked to a set of goals associated with specific services and outlined a recommended care plan. The case manager reviewed the goals and services for appropriateness and had the option, based on professional judgment, to modify these recommendations. The care plan highlighted two dimensions: (1) adult/child services that incorporated MCH elements, prenatal care, well-child care, and injury prevention and (2) a risk assessment that included information on transportation, child care needs, and other requirements.

Activities and Services

Based on the care plan, a tickler file generated a list of activities and services requiring follow-up or monitoring. To facilitate the referral process, the system offered a localized provider database organized by type of service. The case manager could have selected services based on provider address, volume, or client preference. Provider selection was linked to the client record and documented in the care plan, reminding case managers to follow up to ensure receipt of services.

Referral and Scheduling

Scheduling within a clinic consisted of matching the client's service needs with the available internal and external providers. The case manager accessed the family's schedule to coordinate all appointments.

Cornerstone technical architecture was based on a PC local area network (LAN) that supported activities in the community health services clinic. The activities, particularly the ones that relied on information sharing between various program providers, were supported by a technical architecture consisting of LANs, wide area networks (WANs), and the state's central computing operation. The LANs supported 2 to 30 workstations (one for each case manager) per service location. Locally collected client information was transmitted to the state nightly for central processing. The WAN enabled local agencies to share appropriate data about clients among themselves. Access to WAN data was accomplished through a "read-only" mode; it can be read but not modified. Access was available on an as-needed basis and was accomplished by a function (or "hot") key built into specific screens. This protocol ensured the autonomy of agency operations in the event of a WAN failure.

As designed, the system consisted of approximately 150 screens and generated as many pre-established reports. It was written in FoxPro, a DOS-based software language, and utilized pull-down menus.

The development and design work was completed in 1995. In May of that year, the long process of installing the system in 300 service locations began. The Healthy Start agencies served as pilot sites where the software and installation processes were tested, reviewed, and documented. The enormousness of deploying Cornerstone across the state—which entailed supplying, installing, and maintaining equipment; providing training on system procedures; and encouraging local program providers unaccustomed to the intricacies of an integrated computer system to accept the new system—prompted a partnership with the Illinois Primary Health Care Association (IPHCA). The association was uniquely qualified for this partnership role because of its widely recognized role as advocate for community health services in Illinois. For the next two years, until December 1997, IPHCA worked side by side with state staff to install more than 3,000 computer workstations in 300 locations.

The development of Cornerstone represented an effective response to a situation that was weakening the core functions of public health. Community-based programs provided in a discreet fashion were making uniform assessment, systemwide policy development, and accurate assurance nearly impossible. Underlying Cornerstone's development was a series of guiding principles that in the end ensured the system's successful deployment. These principles included the desirability of listening to diverse viewpoints through a process of inclusion; the benefits of forging partnerships among those involved in service delivery; the interrelatedness of health care problems and social service needs; the necessity of comprehensive solutions rather than "bandage" remedies; and the need to promote service integration wherever possible. By adhering to such principles and by incorporating modern technology, the department has operationalized a model that strengthens community health management through efficient and optimal use of available information.

As of 2012, Cornerstone, which is now housed in the Illinois Department of Human Services, is installed in more than 3,000 workstations in more than 380 sites throughout Illinois. Cornerstone coordinates the delivery of integrated services to more than 3,500,000 people. The Cornerstone system is now completely computerized. It is composed of about 150 screens with pull-down menus. More than 200 reports are generated. The immunization system is now incorporated into the Cornerstone system. This system is the largest distributed health information system in the United States and has won numerous awards for its innovations.

SUMMARY

This chapter discussed the key elements of the core function of assessment. It began by describing the assessment process and then went on to consider six assessment methodologies, APEX*PH*, MAPP, PACE-EH, PATCH, the now-dated model standards approach, and emerging community assessment approaches. These various methodologies, though they overlap, are not mutually exclusive, and elements from all can be combined. Other assessment methodologies were then discussed, but not in as much detail. Finally, the chapter considered public health informatics, which involves the collection of data and the use of information system techniques to turn the data into information.

DISCUSSION QUESTIONS

1. What is the relationship among the assessment core function, organizational practices, essential public health services, and performance indicators?
2. What leadership skills are needed for community assessment activities?
3. Why does assessment start the change process?
4. What are the three parts of the APEX*PH* process?
5. Compare and contrast APEX*PH* and MAPP.
6. What is PACE-EH?
7. What are the five phases of the PATCH process?
8. How is CHANGE different from the other approaches to assessment?
9. What role can model standards play in evaluation?
10. What are community health report cards?
11. What is public health informatics?

EXERCISE 10-1: The Trainerville Gang

Purpose: to assess a potential community health problem utilizing community groups

Key concepts: assessment, board of health, community advisory board, data protocols

Procedure: Trainerville is a small city of 100,000 on the Mentor River in the northwestern United States. There are 10,000 children under the age of 10. There are also 10,000 young people between the ages of 11 and 18. Citizens have reported that there is a gang presence in the community. Data on gangs are not currently available unless a gang member gets arrested.

Mayor John Snow asked the Trainerville Health Department to develop strategies for getting data on gangs in the community. The director of the health department convenes a community health advisory group to work with him on the mayor's request. The charge to the group is to assess the extent of the gang problem in Trainerville.

Divide into groups of 5 to 10. Each group will develop strategies for determining the extent of the problem in the community. Each group will then present its assessment protocol to the Trainerville Board of Health. The Board of Health includes a representative from each of the groups. The board will then select the protocol that they think will best assess the gang problem. Because the open meetings act is operative, all group members can attend the deliberations and offer citizen comments.

REFERENCES

1. J. McKnight, *The Careless Society* (New York: Basic Books, 1995).
2. McKnight, *The Careless Society*.
3. J. P. Kretzmann and J. L. McKnight, *Discovering Community Power: A Guide to Mobilizing Local Assets and Your Organizational Capacity* (Evanston, IL: Assets-Based Community Development Institute of Northwestern University, 2005).
4. J. McKnight and P. Block, *The Abundant Community* (San Francisco: Berrett-Kohler, 2010).
5. K. G. Keppel and M. A. Freedman, "What Is Assessment?" *Journal of Public Health Management and Practice* 1, no. 2 (1995): 1–7.
6. L. Novick, "Public Health Assessment in a New Context," *Journal of Public Health Management and Practice* 1, no. 2 (1995): v.
7. P. C. Nasca, "Public Health Assessment in the 1990s," *Journal of Public Health Management and Practice* 1, no. 2 (1995): vii–viii.
8. Institute of Medicine, *For the Public's Health: The Role of Measurement in Action and Accountability* (Washington, DC: National Academy of Sciences, 2010).
9. Keppel and Freedman, "What Is Assessment?"
10. Keppel and Freedman, "What Is Assessment?"
11. B. J. Turnock et al., "Implementing and Assessing Organizational Practice in Public Health," *Public Health Reports* 109, no. 4 (1994): 478–484.
12. *Assessment Protocol for Excellence in Public Health* (Atlanta: Centers for Disease Control and Prevention and National Association of County and City Health Officials, 1991).
13. http://mapp.naccho.org
14. http://mapp.naccho.org
15. M. W. Kreuter, "PATCH: Its Origin, Basic Concepts, and Links to Contemporary Public Health Policy," *Journal of Health Education* 23, no. 3 (1992): 135–139.
16. Centers for Disease Control and Prevention, "PATCH: Planned Approach to Community Health," draft (Atlanta: Centers for Disease Control and Prevention, 1994).
17. Centers for Disease Control and Prevention, "PATCH: Planned Approach to Community Health."
18. A. Steckler et al., "Summary of a Formative Evaluation of PATCH," *Journal of Health Education* 23, no. 3 (1992): 174–178.
19. American Public Health Association, *Healthy Communities 2000: Model Standards*, 3rd ed. (Washington, DC: American Public Health Association, 1991).
20. American Public Health Association, *Healthy Communities 2000: Model Standards*.
21. American Public Health Association, *Healthy Communities 2000: Model Standards*.
22. American Public Health Association, *The Guide to Implemented Model Standards* (Washington, DC: American Public Health Association, 1993).
23. American Public Health Association, *The Guide to Implemented Model Standards*.
24. S. Randolph and J. Ford, *Community Strategies for Health: Fitting in the Pieces* (Washington, DC: American Public Health Association, 1994).
25. Randolph and Ford, *Community Strategies for Health*.
26. http://www.cdc.gov/communitiesputtingpreventiontowork. Accessed November 29, 2011.
27. Centers for Disease Control and Prevention, *Community Assessment and Group Evaluation* (CHANGE) (Atlanta: CDC, 2010).
28. L. M. Anderson et al., "Design and Use of the Behavioral Risk Factor Surveillance System," *Illinois Morbidity and Mortality Quarterly* 1, no. 3 (1994): 16–23.
29. J. M. Bacon et al., "A Consortium Approach to Local Behavioral Risk Factor Assessment," *Illinois Morbidity and Mortality Quarterly* 1, no. 3 (1994): 1–3.
30. J. I. Staff and J. Zimmerman, "Adams County Behavioral Risk Factor Survey Project," *Illinois Morbidity and Mortality Quarterly* 1, no. 3 (1994): 9–11.
31. E. Prez-Stable et al., "Behavioral Risk Factors: A Comparison of Latinos and Non-Latino Whites in San Francisco," *American Journal of Public Health* 84, no. 6 (1994): 971–976.
32. J. Studinicki et al., "A Community Health Report Card: Comprehensive Assessment for Tracking Community Health (CATCH)," *Best Practices and Benchmarking in Healthcare* 2, no. 5 (1997): 196–207.
33. L. Potts et al., *The Growth of Managed Care* (Washington, DC: Association of Schools of Public Health, 1998).
34. K. Jennings et al., *Changing Health Care* (Santa Monica, CA: Knowledge Exchange, 1997).
35. Potts et al., *The Growth of Managed Care*.
36. T. Norris and L. Howell, *Healthy People in Healthy Communities: A Dialogue Guide* (Chicago: Coalition for Healthy Cities and Communities, 1998).
37. A. Friede et al., "Public Health Informatics: How Information Age Technology Can Strengthen Public Health," *Annual Review of Public Health* 16 (1995): 239–252.
38. W. L. Roper and G. P. Mays, "GIS and Public Health Policy: A New Frontier for Improving Community Health," *Journal of Public Health Management and Practice* 5, no. 2 (1999): vi–vii.
39. J. K. H. Tan, *Health Management Information Systems* (Gaithersburg, MD: Aspen Publishers, 1995).
40. Friede et al., "Public Health Informatics."
41. J. R. Lumpkin, "Six Principles of Public Health Information," *Journal of Public Health Management and Practice* 1, no. 1 (1995): 40–41.
42. http://phf.org/research.htm
43. http://rwjf.org
44. http://countyhealthrankings.org/ourapproach
45. http://countyhealthrankings.org
46. E. L. Baker et al., "CDC's Information Network for Public Health Officials (INPHO): A Framework for Integrated Public Health Information and Practice," *Journal of Public Health Management and Practice* 1, no. 1 (1995): 43–47.
47. E. L. Baker and J. Porter, "Practicing Management and Leadership: Creating the Information Network for Public Health Officials," *Journal of Public Health Management and Practice* 11, no. 5 (2005): 469–473.
48. http:/www.cdc.gov/phin

CHAPTER 11

Leadership and Policy Development

Leaders are willing to take the blame.

—William Foege, speech to Public
Health Leadership Society

Through assessment activities, public health leaders evaluate the community's health status and identify health problems and risks that need to be addressed. The task they next face is to determine how to deal with the identified problems and risks. The activity of devising effective courses of action (or plans) for problem resolution and risk reduction is known as "policy development," and it constitutes the second core function of public health. The final task is to implement the policies that have been designed. This task is known as "assurance," because by implementing effective policies and enforcing laws and regulations, public health leaders help to ensure the health of community residents.

All state health departments are involved with policy formulation at some level. State health department activities related to policy development include health planning; policy analysis; and the setting of regulations, standards, health objectives, and disaster and emergency public health procedures. Peripheral activities include building coalitions, empowering community organizations, and determining health priorities.

In his 1991 presidential address to the American Public Health Association (APHA), William Keck argued that the public health community must change its thinking about policy if it is ever to meet the health needs of the American public.[1] The public health community has tended to let market forces and political expediency shape American public health policy rather than look for techniques for maximizing health status. Keck also claimed that American political leaders have a responsibility to develop sound public health policies for the nation. When they fail in their responsibility, they must be held accountable. Methods must be found for getting our leaders to move in different directions. Finally, Keck emphasized the importance of creating linkages between academics, practitioners, and the public in order to empower communities to assess their health status and set health priorities and in order to foster community-based demands for humane decision making.

In her 1992 APHA presidential address, Joyce Lashof stated that public health has made its greatest advances through its commitment to the common good and its strong support for the principles of social justice.[2] Despite these commitments, progress has been erratic, and there continue to be disparities in the health status of socioeconomically, racially, and ethnically diverse communities. The American economic policies of the 1980s and early 1990s have made these disparities worse. Lashof also said that health reform is needed in our society to improve its record in the areas of health promotion, health protection, and disease prevention.

In order to put the issue of policy formulation in perspective, we can observe policy from the vantage point of agenda setting. **Figure 11-1** (The Policy Development Wheel) graphically shows that the policy-making process begins with the fact that a policy agenda grows out of the agenda-setting activities of public health agencies and their external partners.[3] Out of this collaboration comes an awareness that policy is needed to back up the public health agenda. The policy agenda leads to the necessity of formulating policy. Data are needed to support the proposed policy. It is useful to develop alternative scenarios in order to test public and political reactions to proposed policies. A determination must be made about the need to have politicians create the policy or whether the policy can be made by the public health leader and the public health agency without political intervention. Once the policy is created, it is necessary to develop goals and objectives for the policy. If you think of the new policy as a variation of a vision statement, then the steps involved in the Policy Development Wheel will be followed. Except for the government intervention step, if necessary, in policy development, the Policy Development Wheel and the policy-making process are quite similar in that both involve strategic planning and action planning activities.

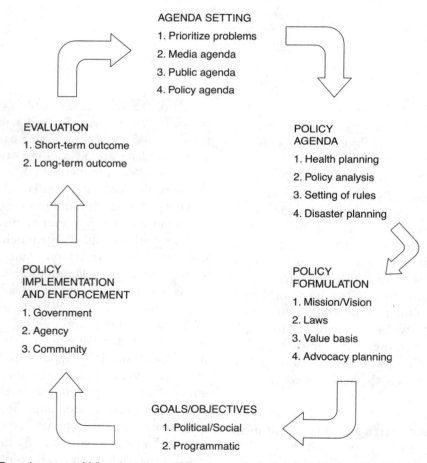

FIGURE 11-1 Policy Development Wheel. *Source*: Adapted from G. Anderson and P. S. Hussey, "Influencing Government Policy: A Framework," in D. Pencheon et al. (eds.), *Oxford Handbook of Public Health Practice* (London: Oxford University Press, 2001).

In 2010, the Washington State Department of Health addressed the issues in policy development and created a toolkit for policy makers.[4] In the report, the authors developed a policy systems and environmental framework for policy development that was updated in 2011 (**Figure 11-2**).[5] There are seven stages in the policy development framework:

1. Background (policy tied to all three core functions)
2. Partnerships and Collaborations
3. Identify a Policy Issue
4. Determine Policy Options
5. Review Feasibility Variables
6. Develop an Advocacy Plan
7. Implementation and Adaptation

An eighth step on evaluation and analysis can be added.

Exercise 11-1 is an experiment in policy development. It concerns an issue that a local health department and the county board may both have an interest in trying to resolve through the creation of a new policy. Public health departments often recognize potential problems before they become fully mature, giving public health and community leaders the opportunity to deal with the problems before they become unmanageable.

It would be possible for most public health leaders to create a list of the critical policy issues that will face public health over the next 10 years. **Table 11-1** lists some of these policy concerns. Social justice and health equity concerns seem always to be critical issues in public health. We fight vigorously to protect the health of the public. Many local health departments struggle with the general issue of access to care and the role of public health in making sure that all residents get the medical care they need. All discussions related to universal health care address access-to-care issues. In order to improve the quality of work of our public health agencies, many discussions are under way about the accreditation of public health agencies. The importance of health issues tied to public health preparedness and response have major policy considerations. How the United States will implement the new International Health Regulations will also affect policy development because the agreement for following these regulations will require state legislation for states not on the oceans, which are covered under federal support for the international regulations. Certification of public health workers is also a policy concern for the future. The final three issues in the list are also being addressed.

PARTNERSHIPS & COLLABORATION	PRIORITIZING PSE CHOICES			ADVOCACY	PSE IMPLEMENTATION	
	Identify an Issue	**Determine PSE Options**	**Review Feasibility Variables**	**Develop an Advocacy Plan**	**Implementation and Enforcement**	**Evaluation**
Who Is Involved & How?	**Should Something Be Done?**	**What Should Be Done?**	**Can It Be Done?**	**How to Get the Idea into Policy?**	**Hot to Make the PSE Idea Come Alive?**	**What Happened and What Difference Did It Make?**
Stage 1	Stage 2	Stage 3	Stage 4	Stage 5	Stage 6	Stage 7
Partnerships are core to **all stages** of PSE development Community identification Shared goal Coalition building • Leadership development • Engaging the Community Wheel • Role clarity in advocacy and lobbying	Is there a problem? What are the contributing factors? Are the data compelling (burden of the problem)? Urgency and timing What happens if it is not addressed? (societal costs) Assessing health equity (does it unequally affect the population)?	Chose type/level of PSE needed: • Federal • State • Local • Institutional Collection of proven PSE change ideas • Evidence-based • Cost-benefit (ROI) • How expensive to implement? Check biases and assumptions of key partners	Prioritize your PSE options based on the criteria below: Political • Assess political climate and readiness Programmatic • Level of complexity? • Who will implement? • Enforcement: who/how? • Can effects be measured? Social • Connection to community values • Magnitude of effect on the community • Unintended consequences	Know your authorizing environment: • Capacity and resources • Lobbying vs. advocacy Choose your PSE pathways Refine PSE Action Statement Smart Advocacy • Frame your message • Create a movement • Develop your pitch • Deploy champions	Implementation Planning: • Ensure adequate resources • Deploy media to educate about policy • Collect baseline data • Counteract obstacles and constraints • Re-deploy media to shape new norms Enforcement • Create prioritization with enforcement • Ensure adequate and sustained enforcement	Short-term outcomes: • Degree of implementation? • Magnitude of PSE enforcement? • Foundation built for PSE modification? • Funds dedicated to implementation? Long-term outcomes: • Was there any measureable change in behavior (norms)? • Answer the question: What difference did the PSE change make it the lives of the people affected? Coalition Cohesiveness **Policy Modification**

FIGURE 11-2 Policy, Systems, Environmental (PSE) Development Framework. *Source*: The "Policy Development Framework" has been developed by Uncommon Solutions, Inc., and is adapted in part from work developed at the Washington State Department of Health.

TABLE 11-1   Selected Public Health Policy Issues

Social justice
Access to care
Health disparities
Accreditation of health department
Public health preparedness and response
International health regulations
Certification
Global warming/Environmental health
Mental health/Substance abuse
Public health systems research

INSTITUTE OF MEDICINE POLICY DEVELOPMENT RECOMMENDATIONS

In 1988, the Institute of Medicine issued its report *The Future of Public Health.*[6] The report, which listed recommendations regarding policy development, emphasized that public health agencies, in constructing policies, need to balance political realities and professional practice concerns and should always try to serve the interests of community constituents. Agencies also need to provide leadership in policy development, promote the use of scientific knowledge in decision making, and use a strategic planning approach based on the democratic principles. Specific recommendations contained in the report include the following:

1. Public health leaders need to develop relationships and positive partnerships with legislators. They also need to inform politicians and other public officials of the community assessment results. The education of public officials should include an explanation of the strategies being employed by the health department to address health priorities.
2. Agency personnel need to learn the skills of constituency building as well as citizen participation techniques. Citizen involvement in program development needs to be encouraged.
3. It is important to create partnerships between the public health agency leaders, the medical community, and other private sector health entities.
4. Agencies need to cultivate relationships with other professional and citizen groups involved with public health. Such groups might include voluntary health

organizations, groups concerned with improving social services, environmental organizations, and economic development organizations.
5. Public health agencies must educate the public on public health issues.
6. Public health agencies need to ensure that the quality of their contacts with grassroots organizations and community residents is cooperative in nature as well as productive.

The follow-up report on the future of public health pointed to the importance of states taking the lead in policy development.[7] States will need to support the collection of data to better plan for public health programs. States will also need to ensure that there are appropriate laws and regulations on the books to support public health programs and activities. State health objectives and workforce development strategies also need to be developed. States need to support the 10 essential public health services throughout their jurisdictions. Local governments also need to carry out the core functions and essential public health services. In a 2011 Institute of Medicine report, it is argued that the states and federal government create and implement a Health in All Policies (HIAP) model that would involve a consideration of the health effects of major legislation, rules and regulations, and other policies that might affect the health of the public.[8]

ESSENTIAL PUBLIC HEALTH SERVICES

Three essential public health services are associated with the policy development core function. The first involves informing, educating, and empowering people about health issues. Some potential performance indicators for this service might include the following (adapted from Turnock and his colleagues):[9]

1. The local health department develops social marketing and health communication strategies.
2. The local health department disseminates information to the local media on a regular basis.
3. The local health department provides health information to the residents of its jurisdiction on a regular basis.
4. The local health department informs the public of state and local laws, rules, and regulations.
5. The local health department works with its partners on the development of health education programs.

The second essential service relates to the mobilization of community partnerships. The performance indicators for this essential service include (adapted from Turnock and colleagues):[10]

6. The local health department builds coalitions with community groups.
7. The local health department meets regularly with health-related organizations.
8. The local health department mission is given a public review every five years or less.

The third essential service is the development of policy and plans that support individual and community health efforts. Ten possible performance indicators include the following (adapted and extended from Turnock and colleagues):[11]

9. States need to support leadership development at all levels of the public health system.
10. The local health department prioritizes community health needs based on the size and severity of the needs.
11. The local health department prioritizes needs based on the possible interventions.
12. The local health department takes into account community input when prioritizing needs.
13. States and localities need to track health trends.
14. Consistent policies need to be followed in the development of laws, regulations, and protocols.
15. The local health department develops action plans to address priority health needs.
16. The local health department fosters public participation in the development of the action plans.
17. The local health department incorporates policy analysis into the development of the action plans.
18. The local health department develops a long-range strategic plan that is linked to community action plans.

Policy development guidelines for public health leaders include the following:

- Stress the importance of governance and its implications for the effectiveness of the public health system
- Develop policies that build the core functions and essential services of public health into a community-based public health system
- Learn to share power
- Put policies into action

THE POLITICS OF PUBLIC HEALTH POLICY

Policy development is a complex process in which the participants consider alternatives for action and decide which alternatives to implement. It is a team process, and many individuals and organizations can be involved, including state and local boards of health, elected officials, community groups, public health professionals, healthcare providers, and private citizens. Factors that the participants typically need to take into account in their decision making include budgetary considerations; federal, state, and local regulations; and program and organizational operating procedures.

The infrastructure of public health is currently at risk because of the general attack on social and public health programs in Congress and in state legislatures throughout the United States. The discontent with social programs in the United States can be traced back to the 1960s, when many of them were created. Since then, the American public seems to have grown increasingly disenchanted with such programs, largely because of the supposed negative effects of the welfare state as well as doubts about the effectiveness of current programs.[12] There is evidence that the public will no longer tolerate increases in taxation to support health and social programs, including public health programs, and indeed from the mid-1990s and into the 21st century, public health programs appear to have come under special assault.

Part of the discontent with federally operated social programs is based on skepticism regarding the competency of the federal government. "Decentralization" was a watchword of the 1990s, and state and local governments took over many programs that had been run by the federal government. However, part of the discontent is probably based on the idea that social programs act as replacements for traditional groups devoted to problem solving and helping people live better lives.[13] Furthermore, so goes the thinking, social programs, by weakening the authority of traditional

Leadership Tip

Because most of your work will occur outside the agency with community residents and external stakeholders, make sure you have good managers running the agency.

groups and encouraging people to become dependent on the government for help, create a demand for more social programs, which foster a higher level of dependency, and on and on in a vicious cycle.

It is easy to see the appeal of the view that communities should redefine themselves, reestablish traditional values, and become less dependent on government. Yet it is also easy to see that public health programs are importantly different from other programs. Whereas individuals arguably should assume more responsibility for protecting their own health, surely some type of public health system is necessary to assess the effects of terrorism and disasters on health, control health hazards, educate the public about these hazards, and provide population-based services designed to help individuals shed harmful behaviors. Public health leaders need to become advocates for their own agencies and for a population-based approach to health promotion and disease prevention. They also need to distinguish public health programs from other types of social programs and make a strong case that public health programs should be supported no matter what other programs the public chooses to dispense with.

According to one definition, politics is the process of putting the moral consensus of the community into practice.[14] In democratic politics at its best, interested parties discuss the issues face to face, reach a consensus, and develop and implement policies. Yet in this country conflict always enters the picture, because the ideology of self-interest (the American ethic of individualism and search for personal success) is at odds with the strong concern Americans have for promoting and protecting the community. The ideology of self-interest leads to the development of special-interest coalitions, and one of the challenges faced by public health leaders is to find ways to promote the community and satisfy special-interest groups at the same time.

Among the strategies that can be used to meet this challenge are the following:[15]

- Community leaders and organizations and special-interest groups should be involved in policy development.
- The policies developed and implemented should include some that tie together medical care and public health activities. Health promotion is a shared responsibility and calls for interagency collaboration in the pursuit of population-based goals.
- The policies should also include some that will help build a community-oriented continuum of

care. Primary prevention programs clearly need to be community based. Examples include programs to reduce the prevalence of lead paint, provide acquired immune deficiency syndrome (AIDS) education, and get people to stop smoking.

Some guidelines related to the politics of public health policy development include:

- Consider national health and social policy trends when developing local policies.
- Make a case for the importance of having a governmental public health presence in the community. Moore has called this the process of creating public value.[16]
- Use special public health interest groups in public health policy development.
- Develop integrated and interdependent health and social policies for the community.
- Partner with elected officials to promote public health programs.

POLICY TRENDS

Policy development, far from being a modern invention, is a universal requirement of community living, and it is affected by the historical circumstances in which it occurs. Many social science theorists have looked at historical trends and studied the social and cultural principles tied to these trends. Indeed, with the coming of the new millennium, there has been increasing interest in understanding where we are and where we are headed.

Alvin Toffler claimed that civilization has undergone three major periods of change, which he referred to as three waves.[17] Assuming that this is a defensible way of looking at human history, the third wave (the information age) will probably be followed by a fourth wave, which, according to Maynard and Mehrtens, will be a period in which humans will attempt to integrate all aspects of life and show an increased concern and sense of responsibility for the whole.[18] People will also attempt to tap into their full range of perceptual and cognitive abilities. The concepts of global stewardship and cultural diversity will grow in importance. Organizations will become strongly oriented toward service, they will become collaborative systems in which power is shared by everyone, and partnership development will be the key to organizational success.[19]

Toffler's theories became extremely influential in the mid-1990s. In early 1995, Newt Gingrich, speaker of the House of Representatives, assigned the book *Creating a New Civilization*[20] by Alvin Toffler and Heidi Toffler to newly elected congressional representatives. This book appeared to influence congressional agendas over the next few years, although the prestige of the Toffler model and futures planning seem to have waned in recent years.

In the preface to *Creating a New Civilization*, Gingrich stated that the current structure of the federal government is tied too closely to the industrialism of the past. The government needs to redefine itself in light of third-wave changes. In his own book, *To Renew America*, Gingrich said that the United States needs to move forward into the information age and to recognize how technology has changed our lives.[21] If the United States does not change the way it does its work, the standard of living of the American people will deteriorate. Whether or not everyone agrees with Toffler's theory of historical waves, no one can escape from the fact that change is a constant, as evidenced by the major economic downturn starting in 2008.

Furthermore, the way problems are handled changes as the rules of the game change. This means that the field of public health will need to change as well. In all likelihood, the relationship between personal healthcare issues and population-based services will be expanded and redefined. Some local health departments will become managed care entities. Most public health activities will be team based. The horizontal organization will become a reality, and the old vertical bureaucracies will continue to break down. Community health coalitions will encompass all stakeholders. Public–private partnerships will increase in number, and privatization will become more prevalent. Public health responsibilities will become increasingly decentralized. Public health will be viewed as the community's business, and different groups will take responsibility for different activities. Governance will finally become community-wide, not just limited to the few stakeholders or politicians at the top.

Public health leaders, besides acting as protectors of community values, will need to help the community redefine its values and generate new values that reflect current realities. Political structures will change as more people become involved in political activities. Public health leaders will work in the community more and be less agency-bound than in the past. The community will become stronger and its residents more empowered. Universal access to a multitude of services will be the rule rather than the exception. The quality of life for most people will improve.

In order to increase their understanding of social and economic trends, public health leaders will need to learn the techniques of forecasting. Public health leaders are seen as experts on the health issues of their communities, and public health agency governing boards look to them for guidance on what the future is likely to hold and how to prepare for future developments.

Quantitative forecasting involves applying a set of statistical techniques to present data sets. Statisticians usually do the actual manipulation of numbers. Quantitative forecasting techniques include regression and time series analysis, which can be used to predict public health trends over a period of time and into the future.[22] A regression model mathematically predicts the effect of change in one factor on other factors. For example, immunization compliance for children under two years of age increased during the 1990s. A regression model could help determine the effect of immunization compliance on other health status indicators. Finally, econometric techniques can be used to forecast future program costs.

Qualitative forecasting uses experts to make predictions.[23] One qualitative forecasting method is to survey a number of experts (a so-called opinion jury) and analyze their responses statistically. Another method is to survey clients and evaluate their responses. Reviewing similar case studies to identify trends is a third method. As an example of qualitative forecasting, imagine that a local health department in a rural area is concerned about the potential effect of a new community health center. The health department administrator might hire a consulting organization with expertise in working with primary care organizations and the effects that the entry of a federally qualified health center is likely to have on existing health care, the local public health agency, and social service providers in the community.

Futurists are experts in predicting the future, or at least experts in painting pictures of different possible futures, and considering the scenarios they devise can be helpful for "testing" alternative policies. Public health leaders can see what will be the overall outcome if one policy is chosen and one scenario occurs, if the same policy is chosen and a second scenario occurs, and so on. Together with estimations of the likelihood of the various scenarios, this type of review of different outcomes can help public health leaders make rational decisions as to which policies to implement.

In order to make good policy decisions, public health leaders need to:

- study their community's past from a systems perspective
- understand how local and state public health agencies have affected health outcomes over time
- learn forecasting techniques
- explore national trends and compare them with local and state trends
- apply forecasting techniques in a rational way to best reflect social and economic realities
- develop policies that take cost as well as community values into account
- modify forecasts or develop new ones if new information becomes available

ADVOCACY AND EMPOWERMENT

During the 1970s and 1980s, public health advocacy was viewed as an important tool for social change. The assumption was that people with all types of problems benefited from having professionals speak for them and protect their rights. Public health leaders took on the responsibility of protecting the health of community residents and pushing for the appropriate interventions to be made available to residents facing health problems or health risks. In recent years, the advocacy movement has been criticized for being too paternalistic. Community leaders have argued that they understand their communities better than the health professionals who work there (partly because the latter often live elsewhere). Advocacy without personal community involvement leads to credibility loss in the population supposedly being protected.

Public health leaders have reduced their advocacy efforts not only because they have become frustrated by their inability to gain acceptance in the communities they serve but also because advocacy has been confused with lobbying.[24] Lobbying is an activity pursued by special interests—usually an organization or group of related organizations—in order to influence the enactment or administration of laws. Advocacy is much broader in scope. Advocacy in support of public policy change involves research, policy statement development, action planning, implementation, and evaluation.

Advocacy activities are also to be distinguished from the enforcement of rules and regulations. Advocacy focuses on policy changes necessary to improve the health of the public, not the administration of existing policies. Public health leaders thus need to balance their advocacy efforts, in which there is room for passion, and their enforcement efforts, which should be dispassionate. If they have been successful in building trust and credibility in the local community, they will be able to involve the community in both health regulation and advocacy. One requisite for engaging the community in advocacy for policy changes is to communicate the reasons the changes are necessary.

One disadvantage of advocacy by professionals is that they tend to be oriented toward the weaknesses of the community rather than its strengths.[25] Emphasizing the negatives often leads to fragmented problem solving and partial solutions. In addition, the community's culture, which is typically intertwined with its problems and will have an effect on attempted solutions, is often neglected. Thus, there is a strong argument that people need to become self-advocates and not rely on third parties to protect their interests. Additional support for this conclusion is that policies developed and implemented without community involvement have historically failed. Therefore, at the very least, professional advocacy and community self-advocacy need to be combined. Each group—the professionals and the community residents—brings different strengths to the partnership and contributes to the total effect of the advocacy.

Becoming an effective advocate for health not only protects the health of the advocate, but can also affect the health of others.

There are five steps to being a successful health advocate:[26]

1. It is necessary to clearly identify whom you want to persuade.
2. It is critical that you know the facts of the issue.
3. It is important to lay the groundwork for advocacy through letters, faxes, or e-mail.
4. It is important to meet the individual you want to persuade—make an appointment.
5. Plan to follow up on your face-to-face meeting.

In a leadership exercise called the 30-second elevator speech, you have to deliver your message in a concise manner and do it before the elevator reaches the floor where the person you are trying to influence leaves the elevator.

In their efforts to empower community residents to become self-advocates, public health leaders need to understand that empowerment will not work if it is treated as a fad.[27] Empowerment means that someone will have to give up power and dominance. Public health leaders, by virtue of their skills and their leadership positions in public health organizations, tend to have more prestige as public health advocates and more control than community residents. They need to give up some of their power if empowerment is to occur. Furthermore, empowerment should be systemwide and not restricted to the community leadership. The object is to give all residents in the community a sense that they have some say over public health policy.

There are four aspects to personal empowerment. First, each individual must have a vision for him- or herself and for the local community. Second, the individual needs to identify and manage the other constituencies with which the individual has a relationship. Third, the individual needs to give up a personal wish for dependency on others (this is exceedingly important). Finally, the individual has to have the courage to make the community vision come to life. In empowerment, there is a belief that change is possible and that, through strength, problems will be solved. Empowered people believe they can make a difference and affect policy decisions.

Public health leaders should also consider taking on a mentoring role in the community. The people they are trying to empower have not, for the most part, exercised power before, at least in the public health area, and they will need guidance as they learn new behaviors.

People to be empowered need to be given authority equal to the responsibilities that they have accepted or that have been assigned to them.[28] Next, they need to learn the appropriate standards of excellence and the skills they must have to meet these standards. Mediocrity is not the goal. Public health professionals and community residents can clearly work together to improve the quality of life, but the residents need information on healthy lifestyles and the skills to bring these healthy lifestyles into reality.

Public health leaders must provide community residents with feedback on the progress they have made toward meeting their goals. They could, for instance, develop a community report card or some other mechanism to report to residents any public health successes and failures. They should also recognize the community's successes in some special way. If the teenage pregnancy rate were to drop significantly in a community, this should be publicized or otherwise specially noted.

The issue of trust plays an important role in community empowerment. Not only must community residents be given the power to make decisions on their own behalf, but they must be trusted to make good decisions. Community leaders often have difficulty recognizing that all residents are entitled to trust. Residents are also entitled to make mistakes. Life includes good decisions as well as bad. Finally, residents have the right to be respected and to be able to maintain their dignity in the community. Public health agencies sometimes struggle to respect these citizen rights fully, especially in situations where cultural diversity is present. Building trust is critical for leaders whether they function from an organizational perspective or from the vantage point of a community. Covey has discussed the five waves of trust: self-trust, the trust of relationships, trust in organizations, trust in the marketplace, and finally trust at a societal level.[29]

Social and behavioral scientists often wince at the softness of the issues being raised here. A better reaction would be for them to study the advocacy and empowerment process and determine whether empowerment increases the chance of attaining health objectives in a community. They could also investigate whether people with severe mental and physical disabilities, immigrants who do not speak English, homebound individuals, high-risk mothers, chronically ill individuals, persons with AIDS, alcohol or substance abusers, suicide- or homicide-prone individuals, abusive families, or the homeless can become successful self-advocates. These issues need to be studied in order to understand the complexities of empowerment.

Following are advocacy guidelines for public health leaders:

- Build trust and credibility with community constituents.
- Empower others to be advocates.
- Do background research on health issues and draft policy statements in the form of legislative bills.
- Work with elected or appointed officials on the enactment of appropriate legislation.

COLLABORATION

Citizen and community empowerment lays the groundwork for collaboration among organizations, constituencies, and individuals to influence the policy development process. Collaboration can take many forms, and collaborative groups come in many types. Cohen and colleagues identified five.[30] Advisory committees offer suggestions and provide technical assistance to leaders, programs, or organizations. Commissions are usually composed of citizens appointed by official bodies. (The problem with commissions is that the appointments are often political.) Consortia (or alliances) are semi-official in nature. They tend to have broad policy-oriented goals and may cover large geographic areas. A single consortium may include several coalitions. Networks, which are fairly loose in organization, are created for the purpose of resource or information sharing. Finally, task forces are short-lived groups created to address a specific issue.

To put the discussion on collaboration in a structural context, **Figure 11-3** portrays collaboration as a continuum. There are several dimensions to the continuum. First, there is the internal organization type of working together that is represented by the team. This type of working together can be collaborative, or it can be like a committee or task force in which the chair of the group guides the process. From a collaborative perspective, the second dimension shows the team model to be weak from a community collaboration approach. Teams are used in many ways, and leaders argue that they can be extremely effective in sharing leadership and responsibility.

External to the single organization, collaboration takes three major forms. First, there is the coalition, which is created for information sharing and to bring together different community leaders and organizations to map out strategies for community change. Alliances are groups of health, health care, and public health organizations that combine forces to address key community or public health issues. These alliances, which are quite common, often develop informal contractual agreements to provide more comprehensive types of programs and services to their communities. Alliances may also add or delete members as programmatic needs change. The most structured organizational model is one based on written contracts, with all details of the collaboration worked out in minute detail with possible legal consequences. These collaborations

are called partnerships. With a continuum perspective like the one presented in Figure 11-3, variations of the three major models are possible. Each major type of collaborative group is discussed below.

Coalitions

A coalition is the coming together of people and organizations to influence outcomes related to a specific problem or set of problems.[31] The synergism of joint action allows a coalition to accomplish a broader array of goals than could the participants acting on their own. (Coalitions are also important for the assessment core function.)

The collaborative relationship that sometimes forms among a public health agency, other health and human service–related organizations, and various community constituencies is typically coalition-like.[32] Such coalitions are created to get the organizations and constituencies involved in addressing community health needs and issues. They tend to be less structured than other types of collaborative groupings, and participants move in and out of the coalition as situations and priorities change.

To establish a coalition, a public health agency must make use of a number of strategies, including the following three.[33] First, it needs to establish a dialogue on health service delivery and policy with possible partners. Second, it needs to create a pool of groups willing to collaborate on the resolution of public health issues. This pool might include:

- at-risk groups affected by the health issues
- allies with whom the agency shares common interests
- experts knowledgeable about the issues
- associates that the agency works with on a day-to-day basis

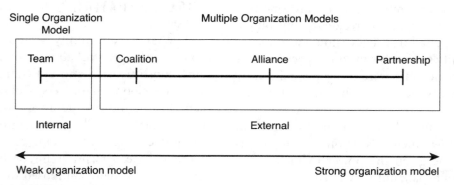

FIGURE 11-3 Models of Collaboration.

- opposition groups that may challenge agency positions on the issues
- third-party groups indirectly affected by the issues
- state and local government officials who have influence on public policy
- media organizations

Third, the agency needs to establish a communication network for the purpose of exchanging information. Communication is essential for promoting the coalition and mobilizing the members to take action to meet the community's health needs, which is, after all, the whole purpose of creating the coalition.

Coalitions have several significant advantages:[34]

- A coalition can conserve resources, because the participants cooperate in promoting the coalition's agenda and avoid duplication of efforts.
- A coalition is an excellent communication tool, because its member organizations can send out its message to many more people than any single organization can.
- A coalition, through synergy, can achieve more objectives than could the participant organizations acting alone. For example, it possesses greater power to influence political decision makers.
- A coalition has a credibility advantage over its individual members. There is clearly strength in numbers.
- A coalition provides a mechanism for sharing information. For instance, one coalition member can provide information to others not able to attend a meeting, and the entire coalition or individual members can develop releases to provide to the media.
- A coalition typically has a lead agency that most of the coalition members provide with advice, guidance, and direction. In the case of public health coalitions, the lead agency is usually the local health department or public health agency.
- A coalition helps the representatives from member organizations by improving their self-esteem, giving them personal satisfaction, and developing their understanding of their organizations' roles in improving the health of the public.
- Finally, a coalition can foster cooperation among the members and can strengthen the community by concentrating on the community's strengths.

On the downside, a public health coalition takes some effort to sustain. Over time, the community and the community's health needs will change, and the coalition must change in concert. In addition, conflicts over turf occasionally occur, and schisms within the coalition can make it more difficult to deal with public health issues than if the coalition did not exist.

Alliances

A community health alliance is a group of healthcare and public health organizations that have combined forces to address key public health risks and problems for the population of a specific geographic area.[35] Although the participating organizations may benefit from the alliance, the purpose of the alliance is to meet the needs of the community residents. A community health alliance might include the local public health agency, healthcare providers, payers, purchasers of services, advocacy groups, community social service agencies, and neighborhood groups.

Alliances can be divided into three types.[36] An opportunistic alliance is created to increase the knowledge and expertise of organizations in a new field of operation. This new information may be used to develop a new type of program in a community. For example, a local public health agency may collaborate with a number of health maintenance organizations to learn how their managed care programs work and then use this information to develop a Medicaid managed care program of its own.

A resource dependency alliance is created to provide a needed service or resource for multiple healthcare organizations. For example, a local health department may agree to immunize all children less than two years of age in the community, preventing other healthcare organizations from having to develop immunization programs.

A stakeholder alliance is developed by organizations willing to work together to achieve a common objective. For example, the alliance members may jointly develop a trauma registry to better document trauma-related problems in the community.

Partnerships

In the early 1990s, partnership became a favored type of collaborative relationship. The partnering process requires each partner to show respect for the other partners and put personal or organizational agendas aside. The partners, whether from the public or private sectors, treat each other as equals. That means that all partners engage as equals in the decision-making process. In an effective partnership, the partners share a vision, are committed to the integrity of the partnership, agree on specific goals, and develop a plan of action to accomplish the goals. A partnership may have a partnering agreement, which is like a contract, to guide its activities.

AN EXAMPLE

Case Study 11-A looks at a coalition created to develop a policy on leaf burning. Parents of asthmatic children, county public officials, and concerned citizens wanted an ordinance passed that would restrict leaf burning in the county, and by working together they were able to achieve their goal, although not all members of the coalition were perfectly happy with the regulations resulting from their efforts.

To promote the public health agenda, public health leaders should:

- identify potential collaborators among community organizations
- engage in discussion with potential collaborators to determine whether enough commonality of interest exists to justify creating a coalition, alliance, or partnership
- for each collaborative relationship, establish goals that all parties in the relationship are committed to achieving
- use the type of collaborative relationship that is most appropriate for addressing the issues of concern
- show respect for the other members of a collaborative relationship

---

Case Study 11-A

Leaf-Burning Policy
Helene Gottesmann and Michael Tryon

Background

Previous leaf-burning legislation in Acorn state had been neither enforced properly nor validated by the courts. In 1974, the Tree County board approved the Nuisance Section of the County Public Health Ordinance, which limited open burning only when adverse health effects could be demonstrated. This was hard to enforce. The state of Acorn also had an open-burning law for counties over 400,000, which was challenged in the courts in 1986, after which any municipality could burn. The state environmental protection agency's stance was that open burning was a local decision. Until January 1995, one could burn any kind of landscape anywhere in the unincorporated areas of Tree County as close as 25 feet from neighboring houses.

Health Effects of Leaf Burning

The ban on the disposal of yard waste in landfills in 1990, the subsequent increasing costs of solid waste disposal, and an increase in the county population have all contributed to the increased air pollution in Tree County. Air pollution accounts for as many as 60,000 deaths a year. Open leaf burning has been established as a significant source of air pollution and causes a significant increase in carbon monoxide levels, hydrocarbons, and total suspended particulates, which are injurious to the population.

Open leaf burning represents a significant health hazard for asthmatics and other high-risk groups—newborn infants, children, the elderly, and people with chronic respiratory, cardiovascular, and allergy problems. In 1986 and 1987, in Tree County, respiratory diseases, such as emphysema, bronchitis, and asthma, became the third leading cause of death, whereas they were the fourth leading cause of death in the United States. Bronchitis and asthma were the second leading causes of hospitalization in the 0–14 age group in Tree County during the same time period.

In the fall of 1991, a 14-year-old girl died as a result of an allergic reaction to leaf burning. The following February, another young girl died of asthma when moldy yard waste from the previous fall was being burned. During this same season, another child almost died of an asthmatic attack after being exposed to the smoke from burning leaves and had to live with relatives in another town until the air cleared. With support and facts from other parents of asthmatic children in neighboring towns with leaf-burning bans, parents attended several Smokey village board meetings to express their worries about the health hazards of open burning. As a result, in the fall of 1992 a total burn ban was passed by one vote after it was vetoed by the village president. Simultaneously, another parent with an asthmatic child in the neighboring town of Ashes went to her village board with a packet of information concerning the health hazards of leaf burning. The board decided to form a committee to investigate the issue. Not taking no for an answer, mothers continued attending village meetings, networking, and educating the community about the health hazards of leaf burning. Parents also received television and news coverage.

Coalition Building

Frustrated by the lack of action by the village board, in the spring of 1992 the concerned parents from Ashes and neighboring towns formed a coalition. In October, the Ashes village board said they wanted to wait 5 to 10 years to investigate and decide the matter.

In response to this, the coalition circulated a petition and wanted a burning ban by the state pollution control board. "Please don't burn your leaves" fliers were distributed. In November 1992, the burning ban failed. The coalition grew larger, began publishing a newsletter, and called a meeting to devise a plan of action. Individuals from the local and state lung associations and councils, public health workers, emergency department nurses, state and local environmental groups, and lawyers joined forces. The parents received some support from the board of health, which was willing to write letters on their behalf, but it was not known whether the county board members supported the ban and how they stood on the leaf-burning matter.

Lobbying on the State Level

The coalition felt a policy or law banning leaf burning was needed at the state level because villages and towns with leaf-burning bans were being affected by smoke from unincorporated areas and municipalities without bans. A former state pollution control board member who had received yearly complaints about leaf burning instructed the coalition on how to introduce a state bill. In the spring of 1993, the senate and house introduced a bill against leaf burning that included the 17 counties in Acorn. Dedicated coalition members actively lobbied their senators and representatives. Opponents of the bill tried to kill the legislation, but it finally passed. However, the governor vetoed it in December 1993, claiming it was an "unfunded mandate."

County-Level Involvement

Simultaneously, in 1993, leaf-burning ban activists expressed their concerns not only to local and state officials but also to Tree County board representatives, members of the county board public health services committee, and members of the county board of health. County board members decided not to impose an open-burning restriction on municipalities and the rural areas. Both the board of health and the public health services committee planned to address the leaf-burning issue in the future. The president of the board of health thought the county should launch a massive education effort about the health hazards of leaf burning and alternative disposal methods and start encouraging residents to voluntarily stop burning leaves. The Tree County public health services committee was scheduled to consider a "voluntary ban," but the politicians said the proposal would be ineffective because it had no enforcement measures. In November 1993, the Tree County public health services committee tabled the issue because the general assembly was considering this legislation. (In the fall of 1993, while parents were in the midst of lobbying the state for a leaf-burning ban, the village of Ashes finally voted to ban leaf burning.)

In January 1994, in response to the governor's veto of the leaf-burning bill in December 1993, lobbyists pressured the county board of health to consider a countywide ban on open burning. In the spring of 1994, the county board of health sought a voluntary burning ban; however, lobbyists against leaf burning continued to pressure board members to oppose it.

Policy Controversies

In developing a policy (or ordinance) for leaf burning, the chair of the public health services committee of the county board acted as a bridge between the county board of health and the county board, the legislative body. His main objectives were to build a consensus around the various opinions of the county representatives and develop a balanced policy. In order to develop a balanced policy, the committee needed to consider the following issues: (1) Should grass and other yard waste be included with leaves? (2) What months or days can individuals burn leaves? (3) What educational efforts are needed? (4) What are enforcement alternatives? In addition, the chair wanted to communicate and share his vision of the challenges of a rapidly growing community: "Tree County is the fastest-growing county in the state and the issue of open burning will not go away. As the county continues to grow, the issue of open burning will become more serious" (minutes of May 11, 1994, committee meeting).

Policy development and consensus building were done gradually and methodically. The chair of the public health services committee was very specific about steps he had to pursue to accomplish his goal. His first objective was to listen to all conflicting points of view concerning leaf burning before a policy was drafted. For this purpose, the public health services committee held open meetings in the spring and summer of 1994 to obtain the public's input as well as that of the various county officials. In addition, the chair tried to determine what type of ordinance

(Continues)

could be passed by the county board by personally talking to every county board member and other significant individuals.

The public health administrator of Tree County health department provided assistance to the public health services committee chair in developing a leaf-burning policy. One goal of the board of health was to reduce respiratory diseases in the county by addressing the issue of open burning. The public health administrator participated in the public meetings held by the public health services committee and presented morbidity and mortality statistics regarding respiratory diseases in the county. He pointed out that the board of health is "an organization that exists in most counties throughout the state for the primary purpose of preventing diseases in the county by addressing the issue of open burning. The board of health had as one of its goals to reduce respiratory disease and disability and improve the health status of the community. In this role, the board of health needs to know what the disease problems are" (minutes of May 11, 1994, committee meeting). In view of this, the provision of epidemiological data becomes critical in policy development.

Public Meetings on Leaf Burning

The following section briefly summarizes opposing viewpoints shared at the Tree County board public health services committee public meetings on leaf burning. Developing a policy based on these opposing views was a challenge for the chair of the health services committee and required effective leadership skills.

Opponents to the Ban

The following are issues raised by those opposed to the leaf-burning ban.

Big Government Versus Individual Freedom

Being one of the most politically conservative counties in the nation, Tree County citizens did not want the government interfering in their lives. They felt that the leaf-burning ban was an "unfunded mandate." The main issue was their right to burn leaves.

Local Versus State Government

If there had to be a ban, individuals felt that it should be imposed locally and not by the county or the state.

High- Versus Low-Density Areas

Individuals felt that the committee needed to differentiate between high- and low-density areas. People were opposed to banning leaf burning in the rural areas or the country because the smoke dissipated before it reached any of the neighbors. Also, unincorporated areas do not have the same waste disposal options as city residents.

Incorporated Versus Unincorporated Areas

The ordinance should not include incorporated areas, only unincorporated areas. Municipalities wanted to decide for themselves.

Expense of Waste Disposal

Opponents were against the additional cost for waste disposal if leaf burning was banned. Some cities include leaf pickup at no additional cost.

No Adverse Health Effects

Some opponents did not believe that the smoke from leaf burning had any ill effect. One individual noted that other allergens (such as ragweed) had not been eradicated.

Proponents of the Ban

The following are issues raised by proponents of the leaf-burning ban.

Individual Property Rights Versus Right to Breathe

Opponents of leaf burning expressed the need to act on behalf of one's fellow humans—and the right to breathe. It was pointed out that the constitution of Acorn state requires the government to protect the health, safety, and welfare of the citizens and provide a healthful environment. Therefore, leaf burning, a health hazard, should not be allowed.

Adverse Health Effects Versus No Effect

Citizens with asthma and parents of asthmatic children testified as to the adverse health effects leaf burning had had on their lives and their children's lives. Some opponents of the ban did not believe leaf burning caused asthma and wanted "proof." Medical personnel reported the increasing number of children and adults they treated with respiratory diseases and concluded that a ban on leaf burning would save medical costs as well as lives. It must be noted that some opponents of the ban and their children also had asthma, but apparently they did not feel a ban was necessary.

County or State Legislation Versus a Local Piecemeal Solution

Proponents felt a countywide solution was needed. Though some towns have burning ordinances, people live along borders where leaf burning is allowed. Children may live in one village with a ban but go to a school in a town with leaf burning and are exposed to the air pollution.

Education or Referendum Versus Legislation

Proponents of the leaf-burning ban felt education was extremely important but not a substitute for legislation. They were also against holding a referendum, for they felt people would vote according to their emotions and not the facts.

Other Burning Issues

The following are some additional concerns expressed at the public meetings on leaf burning: What kind of waste disposal would there be? How much would it cost and how much responsibility would the county take for doing it? How much would bagging leaves cost? Citizens wanted to be provided with alternatives such as composting, vacuuming of leaves, or collecting leaves for farmers. High schoolers reported that they picked up leaves for free and delivered them to farmers. People wanted to know how the county would respond to complaint calls (the fire department would respond to the calls) and who would enforce the ban. They also wanted to know whether overnight campfires and bonfires would be prohibited.

In May 1994, another open-burning meeting was held by the public health and human services committee of the Tree County board to discover how individual communities and fire districts felt about open-burning regulations. Invited were representatives of the 27 municipalities, 17 townships, and 16 fire districts. The issues brought up were similar to those that had been discussed at the April meeting: assurance of leaf disposal before a ban was enacted and methods of enforcement. Individuals felt that the leaf-burning problem should be resolved by local units of government.

Consensus Building: Drafting a Balanced Policy

In June 1994, county board members met to discuss and then vote on whether to draft a leaf-burning ordinance. The chair of the public health services committee felt he needed the board to reach a consensus in order to devote staff time and energy to drafting an ordinance. County board members said they wanted options, facts, and documentation of the health effects of leaf burning and of large composting sites. One of the members wanted it stated that the right to clean air had precedence over the right to burn leaves. Another member felt people should be more sensitive to the needs of their neighbors. Some individuals supported extensive educational efforts. A county ban may give locals more control if and when the state passes legislation. County board members voted 19 to 5 for the public health committee staff to draft a balanced policy regulating leaf burning.

At this point, the board was far from a consensus on how to regulate leaf burning. Some board members wanted a total ban, others a partial ban only in the unincorporated areas, and others regulation rather than a ban. They did not want to adopt legislation for municipalities that already had an ordinance. They felt the county could not enforce a ban anyway.

The chair felt he had to resolve the clash of conflicting opinions by means of a compromise. He knew he did not have the votes for a total ban. The committee used a conservative approach in formulating the proposal (a "balanced" policy). In order to develop a balanced, integrated policy, the staff addressed the following issues: (1) density (distance between homes), (2) type of waste, (3) disposal alternatives, (4) enforcement, and (5) time of day and year.

In January 1995, the committee presented the following ordinance to the county board for a vote (it passed 13 to 10). It would restrict burning to assigned weekends. The burning ordinance is an amendment of the National Fire

(Continues)

Prevention Code, Building Officials and Code Administrators (BOCA) Ordinance. The amendment limits burning of yard waste to weekends between dawn and dusk during the months of October, November, April, and May. Open fires would not be allowed within 30 feet of a structure or within 500 feet of a neighbor's home. The ordinance excluded municipalities.

The leaf-burning policy is an example of governance sharing and collaborative policy development, for three different departments were involved: the health department, the fire department, and the building department. Assurance or enforcement of the BOCA amendment would be provided by all three departments, with the fire department taking the lead. The health department would educate citizens on alternatives to leaf burning and already had a burning ordinance that could ban leaf and yard waste burning if it affected the health of the citizens. The building department would also be responsible for enforcing a fire and safety code that would include the leaf-burning regulation.

The BOCA amendment had a good chance to pass the county board because it is a regulation, not a ban. It provides a mechanism to let people know when the burning is occurring so they can take precautions and adjust their schedules accordingly. The BOCA amendment also exempts municipalities, whereas a public health ordinance would not. A leaf ban would not have passed because the county had no mechanism for leaf pickup. If the chair had submitted a pickup cost of $75,000, the ordinance would never have passed.

Conclusion

In 1993, after the leaf-burning ban was vetoed by the governor, concerned parents and citizens went to the Tree County board and board of health for a countywide ban. The public health services committee of the Tree County board held two open meetings to allow the public to air their opinions on this matter. After receiving the "go ahead" from the county board, the public health services committee researched the matter and developed what it considered a "balanced" policy on leaf burning.

The parent activists have mixed feelings about this ordinance because it still allows leaf burning on weekends in the fall and spring in densely populated areas. They feel that the regulation should be a health ordinance rather than an amendment to the BOCA (fire) ordinance. The proposed ban treats burning as a fire hazard, not a health hazard. Burning supporters say it was a compromise. The chair says that the BOCA compromise "is the best way of protecting the public by reducing fire hazards without also denying individual property rights." He feels that this is an effective ordinance, because it limits the amount of days leaf burning is permitted.

The coalition has introduced a bill to the state legislature that would give the state pollution control board authority over open burning in the state. Parents say they will continue to try to get stricter measures passed. Concerned citizens have noted the approach used by parents in the Quad Cities, where they plan to argue that local governments that allow leaf burning discriminate against residents with breathing ailments and thus infringe on the Americans with Disabilities Act.

PRIORITY SETTING

The community assessment process ends with the setting of priorities. In fact, priority setting is a link between assessment and policy development, because which policy issues are chosen to be worked on is determined by the priority-setting process.[37]

Setting local public health priorities should be a community-wide activity.[38] The process should include major health agencies, community organizations, key community constituencies, and individuals. Elected and appointed officials will need to put their stamp of approval on the chosen list of priorities, and they might demand changes in the list. For example, public health leaders concerned about an increase in teenage pregnancy in the community may recommend the distribution of condoms in high school clinics. If the community is politically conservative, the condom distribution recommendation may be overridden by elected or school officials.

According to Dever, those engaged in priority setting should follow these eight guidelines:[39]

1. Set realistic goals to maintain credibility.
2. Formulate the goals in understandable terms for the public at large.
3. Set goals that combine process and outcome.
4. Set quantitative and qualitative goals that are able to be evaluated.
5. Evaluate progress toward the achievement of health goals at regular intervals.
6. Set goals that can be pursued in compatible ways across geographic boundaries.

7. Develop techniques to handle data constraints.
8. Set goals that reflect the concerns of all interested parties.

Three other guidelines are worth considering. First, those who are establishing the priorities must determine the magnitude of each problem and the ability of the public health agency to address the problem given the existing staff and budgetary constraints. Second, they must estimate the seriousness of the consequences if the problem is not addressed or only partially addressed. Third, they must decide whether it is feasible to resolve the problem at all.

In the priority-setting process, public health leaders have the responsibility to:

• work with coalitions, alliances, or partnerships
• set health priorities that will be acceptable to elected and appointed officials
• set realistic goals and objectives
• make goals and objectives measurable
• tie action plans to the budget

LEADERSHIP CHALLENGES

Researchers who have investigated the advances in clinical medicine over the past 60 years estimate that only 5 of the 30 years of increase in life expectancy (now almost 80 years) can be tied to clinical breakthroughs.[40] Most of the increase in life expectancy instead is due to changes in public health policy. The last half of the 20th century saw the virtual elimination of polio, the elimination of smallpox, declines in dental decay due to fluoridation in water supplies, and reductions in childhood blood lead levels. If society continues to invest in the public health system, substantial financial savings will accrue, assuming past history is any guide. It is the public health system that prevents epidemics; protects the environment, workplaces, housing, food, and water; promotes healthy behaviors; monitors the health status of the population; mobilizes communities to take remedial action; responds to disasters; ensures the quality, accessibility, and accountability of medical care; reaches out to link high-risk and hard-to-reach people to needed services; performs research to develop new insights and innovative solutions; and leads the development of sound health policy and planning.[41]

Despite the impressive record of achievement by the public health system, financial support for public health programs has recently declined.[42] The result is likely to be an increase in disease and injury—and an increase in healthcare costs. Major public health problems, including human immunodeficiency virus (HIV), AIDS, cancer, cardiovascular diseases and stroke, diabetes, teenage pregnancy, substance abuse, and community violence, remain to be dealt with. Following are several examples of the effect that public health agencies, in collaboration with other organizations, can have on public health issues.

Leadership Tip

Keep a leadership journal where you record your personal notes on work-related events. Take notes on articles and books as well.

Public health professionals have consistently argued that tobacco use is the greatest single preventable cause of premature mortality in the United States.[43] With the harmful effects of tobacco use in mind, the *Healthy People 2000* objectives, reinforced in *Healthy People 2010,* called for the development, enactment, and enforcement of laws prohibiting the sale of tobacco products to adolescents. [44,45] Furthermore, the report stated that in order to reduce access to tobacco by adolescents, vending machine sales should not be allowed.

The tobacco industry fought the *Healthy People 2000* proposals and came up with a proposal for requiring electronic locking devices. In 1990, Forster and colleagues drew a random sample of vending machine locations in St. Paul, Minnesota, where a law mandating the use of locking devices on cigarette vending machines had been passed.[46] The researchers found that the rate of noncompliance by merchants was 34% after three months and 30% after one year. For sites in which a locking device was installed, the purchase rate of cigarette packages from the machines dropped from 86% before the law went into effect to 30% after three months. However, the rate rose again to 48% after one year. The effectiveness of the law deteriorated in all types of businesses over the course of the year. The researchers demonstrated that banning cigarette vending machines, together with other methods to improve compliance, will be necessary in the future. If businesspeople are not committed to a change in policy, its level of effectiveness will be low.

In a second example, a local health advisory board in a small Illinois city decided in 1997 that it was no longer willing to tolerate cigarette vending machines near the local high school. The board recommended a bill to the local city council, which not only agreed with the board but passed a more comprehensive anti-smoking law. This story indicates how leadership can be required in different places if a policy is to be developed and put into action. It was first needed in the health department (which addressed the question of how to reduce access to tobacco by adolescents), then on the board (which took action on a potentially volatile issue), and then on the city council (which passed a bill that had the potential to be unpopular). In 2006, this town passed a bill to outlaw smoking in restaurants and bars. In January 2008, the entire state of Illinois went smoke-free.

The challenge for public health leaders is to bring different groups in a community together when a critical public health issue needs to be addressed. There are clearly risks involved in trying to influence the political process. The public health community and local, state, and federal governments may have conflicting agendas. Special-interest groups often try to undermine the public health agenda through contributions to the political parties as well as by lobbying to prevent a bill from getting passed.

In cases where public health leaders have been instrumental in passing a bill, they need to monitor the effects of the legislation. In 1989, a cigarette tax increase of 25 cents per package went into effect in California, partly because of a public health campaign.[47] Flewelling and colleagues evaluated the effect of this increase one year after its implementation.[48] Comparing adult per capita consumption data from 1980 to 1989 in California and the United States, they showed that a sharp decline in cigarette consumption in California had occurred at the same time as the tax increase. They concluded that a 5% to 7% decline in consumption was attributable to the tax increase.

The long-term effect of the legislation is, of course, hard to determine. Undoubtedly, educational strategies and other policy mechanisms will be required if further reductions in tobacco use are to occur. Public health leaders must continue to take an active role in the antismoking movement. The battle against tobacco use will not get any easier because the tobacco industry has more money to spend on promoting smoking than public health agencies have to spend on antismoking activities. However, the public is getting the message, and antismoking legislation is becoming more acceptable.

Another example of public health–driven policy development consists of the efforts to deal with the HIV/AIDS epidemic of the 1980s and 1990s. Reducing HIV transmission is still entirely a matter of changing behavior because no vaccine or cure is yet available. Because changing behavior is such a difficult process, the challenges for public health are significant. Although the public health community has been criticized for what it has done and when it has done it, public health practitioners have been on the front lines in the public's education about HIV and AIDS. The only other critical advocacy group has been made up of people with AIDS.

The Ryan White Act stands as a premier example of what legislation can do. However, mustering the resources to deal with the mounting crisis has not been easy. During the 1980s, many policy makers, for political reasons, tried to downplay the AIDS epidemic. For example, the evidence is strong that budget considerations were put before the health needs of the American public and that research scientists were sometimes more concerned with their personal reputations than with saving lives.[49]

Public health leaders at the local, state, and federal levels have taken leadership roles in promoting better methods of AIDS surveillance, creating policies to help the afflicted, raising concerns about the cost and accessibility of new treatments, and promoting an increasing number of programs to prevent the disease from spreading. Public health leaders took a strong position in favor of confronting the crisis head on, even when it was not popular to do so. The result is that the quality of life of many people with AIDS has improved substantially.

Success sometimes creates political enemies. Public health leaders need to take risks for the important health issues they think need to be addressed. The consequences for them could include political retaliation, budget cuts, and loss of leadership positions. Public health leaders may also find themselves in conflict with community leaders. To reduce the risk of conflict, they need to work with community leaders, lobbyists, and special-interest groups on common agendas. At the same time, they need to realize that deal making has its own risks, because collaboration with lobbyists and special-interest groups in particular may compromise their community oversight activities.

Community leaders have a strong voice in community affairs. They usually have a vision of what the community should be like and want others to share it. They may, therefore, be unwilling to accept the public health leaders' view of the community, especially its health priorities. Yet without the support of community leaders, public health leaders may find it impossible to implement the health policies they think are needed. As much as possible, health policies should emanate directly from community groups. When community leaders with credibility join forces, they are usually able to convince most community residents that there is a problem that must be addressed immediately.[50] Unless the community leadership, the public health leadership, and the political leadership come together and work collaboratively, change will not be possible.

Public health leaders are often in a situation in which they have to increase their own knowledge as a prerequisite to policy development. Case Study 11-B describes a possible biological disaster and the community politics and coalition building that were necessary to avert it. All individuals involved needed to learn new things to better understand the nature of disaster planning. The interesting issue in this case is that it predates the events of September 11, 2001.

Judicial decisions have increasingly played a major role in the area of health policy. Public health leaders have found themselves as witnesses in trials or proponents of health policies being evaluated by the courts. Because courts must interpret the law, the outcomes are not always predictable. During the 1990s, class action suits were brought against tobacco companies, and the courts have ruled that these companies must pay enormous damages to the states. How to use the tobacco settlement money has become a new issue. The public health leaders want the money used to prevent smoking and promote smoking-cessation programs, but many states see this tobacco money as a windfall and want to spend large amounts of it on other state priorities. Dealing with the courts and even the happy results of court decisions thus constitutes another challenge faced by public health leadership.

In the area of policy development, public health leaders must:

- collaborate with managed care organizations and community health centers
- collaborate with state legislatures and the U.S. Congress
- create policy agendas in conjunction with community leaders
- work to implement policies even if they are opposed by special-interest groups
- understand the relationship between politics and policy
- encourage cooperation between local, state, and federal health organizations
- prepare for retaliation when pushing unpopular issues
- incorporate judicial decisions into policy development

Case Study 11-B

A Department of Health Learns about Its Role in Emergency Public Health
Linda Young Landesman

In the spring of 1995, the commissioner of health of a large metropolis was informed by federal officials that massive amounts of biological chemicals might be released somewhere in his community. This agent was highly toxic and had the potential to cause high levels of morbidity and mortality among those exposed. Although the Smithtown Department of Health had a disaster plan, the plan was inadequate to meet the needs that would follow such a release. Furthermore, there was a range of interest among the leadership in the department regarding the need to prepare for and respond to disasters.

Background

Tom Asher, MD, MPH, commissioner of health in Smithtown for five years, hung up the phone and closed his eyes to think. He wasn't sure if he had heard correctly. There were stockpiles of biological chemicals here in Smithtown. Millions could be killed if there was an accidental release. As health officer, he was responsible for protecting the public's health. Protecting public health against a hidden enemy was not an easy task, especially in this time of shrinking resources.

Smithtown was a large metropolis in the northern section of the country. It was a hub of activity, and millions of people came in and out of the city every day. They came in to work, to shop, to play. Controlling egress within the city was difficult on a good day. There were hundreds of transportation routes involving bridges, trains, buses, ferries, and airplanes. It was an international port of entry by land, sea, and air. A terrorist could slip through easily.

John Thompkins had been elected mayor of Smithtown by a slim margin the year before. His vocal constituency was demanding cutbacks in government service. The mayor was particularly sensitive to this message, because his political adversaries were eager to see his tenure limited to one term. Betsy Reardon, his predecessor, had been

(Continues)

a popular mayor. She had served three terms as head of Smithtown, and the local "spin doctors" felt that she lost the election because the city had been paralyzed by a major winter storm the previous December. It didn't matter that the citizens of Smithtown had voted down the last two transportation bond issues or that it was a 100-year storm. Betsy was blamed because it took almost a week for transportation to move smoothly again. The situation was made worse because the storm occurred the week before the Christmas holiday. Retailers suffered throughout the city. But Betsy was still a political heavyweight in the region. And she and Thompkins had never been friends.

The impetus to "do more with less" came at a time when the state and federal governments were also retrenching and reducing support for government programs. The department of health had already been hit hard. When Tom and his deputies met six months earlier to review the implications of the cuts, they realized that they had to eliminate 10% of their staff and programs. Most of these reductions had already taken place, so resources in the department were scarce.

The health commissioner believed that he was fortunate in other ways. During their mayor–commissioner get-togethers, Tom felt that the mayor was responsive to his message. In these meetings, Tom highlighted how public health professionals were really part of the public safety network. In this city, where public officials were used to dealing with the "crisis of the week," there had even been a recent opportunity for the commissioner of health to educate the mayor about the importance of vigilance against biological agents.

A strain of the bubonic plague had erupted in India. Villagers, fearful of getting sick and trying to avoid the illness, moved from one village to another. It was days before the public health officials there issued a quarantine. As a result, it was very difficult to contain the epidemic. Thousands of people had died. Indian officials suspected that exposed villagers had boarded planes and traveled abroad. Health officers around the world went on alert. When Tom learned about the possibility of plague being brought to the United States by an international traveler, he met with the mayor to discuss what should be done to protect Smithtown.

"This is the end of the 20th century. What do you mean we could have an outbreak of bubonic plague in Smithtown?" asked the mayor.

"We both realize that Smithtown is an international port," Tom said. "We have visitors coming here from countries where the public health laws are not as vigorous as ours. We need to take a defensive stand by increasing surveillance at all ports of entry and by alerting hospitals and clinics around the region. If we learn of any patients with plague, we'll jump on it immediately."

Mayor Thompkins was insistent: "Do whatever it takes. We cannot have an outbreak happen here."

Tom Asher left that meeting feeling relieved that he had administrative support for an all-out effort to contain an outbreak of the plague if it appeared necessary. At the time, he didn't realize that he'd be calling on that support so soon.

Solutions

The next day, Tom returned to his office and was hoping to spend the morning responding to correspondence and returning phone calls when he received the call about the biological agents stockpiled in Smithtown.

"Get Jayne, Jack, and Sid on the phone stat," Tom ordered. "Tell them that I need them in my office in 30 minutes." His secretary, Glen Oaks, ran into the room.

"Only Sid is in the building. What's up?" Glen asked.

"We may have a potential terrorist situation on our hands. We've got to come up with a plan as soon as possible."

"Jayne's at a meeting at the chancellor's office downtown," Glen reported. "Jack took a few hours' leave to take his daughter to the dentist. It may be a while before they can get back."

"Beep them. Tell them to get back here now!"

Glen hurried back to his desk and hoped that Jayne and Jack could get back soon. Jack was at least two hours away if he traveled by public transportation. It would be prohibitively costly for him to take a taxi back to the office. Besides, there was a city rule that travel by taxi was strictly forbidden except in a municipal emergency. Glen wasn't sure that this qualified as an emergency. He was used to the commissioner calling these types of meetings with his deputies. Last month there was that tuberculosis scare. The month before the media reported that the water wasn't safe to drink because of a death due to *Cryptosporidium*. It turned out that the patient was immunosuppressed and had been living in Milwaukee during the outbreak in that city. He had just come home to die. But the resources of the department sure rallied around until the facts were clear.

So how important was this threat? Glen couldn't tell from the commissioner's demeanor, but he felt that he had to do his best to bring the deputies back to the office. And he was in luck: both were on their way and able to meet with the commissioner within the hour.

Tom started the meeting by asking if there was anybody in the department who knew about disaster planning for biologicals. The deputies looked at each other and shook their heads. They knew about monitoring for infectious disease in shelters and guaranteeing the safety of the water supply, but they knew nothing about preparing for biologicals.

The department had a disaster plan, as required by law, but they all knew that it hadn't been tested in the types of events happening around the country. Perhaps more importantly, Jayne, the deputy commissioner for environmental affairs, had come to realize that the health department should be more involved in planning with other agencies in the city than it currently was. Emergency medical services (EMS) had a lock on responding to disasters. Yet EMS didn't have the expertise that was needed to assess and respond to public health issues. They couldn't identify hazardous materials. They couldn't identify infectious agents. They didn't have the skills to conduct surveillance or monitor the safety of those who responded to an event. With EMS as the lead health agency, there were lots of limitations in the current city plan. It was clear to Jayne that EMS was not the agency that should have lead responsibility. She had told Tom that this was a potential problem for the department. But federal dollars for disaster preparedness and response seemed to be flowing to EMS. And so the commissioner and his deputies planned the best that they could and tried to increase their influence in the system.

"What are we dealing with?" Sid asked.

"I received a call from the chief medical officer of the Office of Foreign Disaster Assistance. Remember him? We met him at the public health annual meeting last November. He called to say that he'd just returned from investigating the sarin release in the subway in Japan. While investigating the extent of the cache of chemicals over there, the U.S. team learned that there is a stockpile of hundreds of gallons of sarin somewhere in the Smithtown metropolitan area. There could be a release at any time."

"That would be disastrous," exclaimed Sid, the deputy for infectious disease. "How can we get ready for a Bhopal-type accident? All of our available staff are working around the clock as it is, just trying to keep up. Besides, what do we know about planning for these things?"

"I think that we should call Dan Nickels, chief of EMS. They have the manpower and the resources to respond to this thing," Jack insisted. Jack, deputy director for maternal and child health, could be depended on to support only those efforts that affected mothers and infants. He felt that with shrinking resources, he had to fight to ensure that services weren't diverted from this group.

"That's not a bad idea," Sid agreed.

"Wait a minute. Why should we shove this thing over to EMS?" Jayne asked. "We all know that they can't do the job that is needed to guarantee public health. Besides, if we don't know how to prepare for this thing, there must be people across the country that we can use as resources. This can't be the first time any health department in the country has had to deal with this. Besides, I don't think we should work in isolation. We should be sitting at the table where the interagency response is discussed."

Jack used this as an opportunity to complain about his current staffing. "I don't have enough staff to monitor the child health stations. We can't get newborns in for their first checkup until they are 10 weeks old, and you are talking about using staff to scrounge around the country for someone who knows something about preparing for a Bhopal here in Smithtown. I say call Dan Nickels. If you don't want to call him, then call the CDC. But let's not get over our heads."

"Jack's got a point. If we let another agency do it, it's their problem if something goes wrong," echoed Sid.

"I'm not sure I agree," said the commissioner. "I think that our responsibility is very clear. EMS doesn't have the capability to handle the public health issues. And if this thing blows, it will be our necks out there. It happens that I met with the mayor about the plague threat just yesterday. He was very clear. He wants the city prepared, and that means us. If we need to be prepared for plague, we need to be prepared for biologicals."

Jack asked, "Who's going to do it? I don't have anyone to spare."

Sid and Jayne agreed that there was no one on their staff who could be released from current responsibilities to develop a disaster plan for biologicals.

Conclusion

Tom looked around the room and pondered what to do. He knew that Jayne would find the time to supervise someone so that the department could better prepare for this thing. But how could he make this happen? More importantly, should he use valuable resources—resources that could be used to meet other public health responsibilities—to become an active player in citywide disaster preparedness?

SUMMARY

Policy development is the core function that, in a sense, follows assessment, for only after public health problems have been identified can policies be created to deal with them. Yet in the normal course of agency operations, assessment and policy development are occurring continually and often simultaneously.

The chapter first presented policy development recommendations publicized by the Institute of Medicine in its 1988 and 2003 reports. It then discussed essential public health services associated with policy development and listed performance indicators for each practice. Additional topics covered included policy trends, advocacy and empowerment, and collaboration. Finally, the chapter discussed leadership challenges related to policy development, including the challenge of bringing diverse groups together to address significant public health risks and the challenge of preparing for retaliation when pushing unpopular positions.

DISCUSSION QUESTIONS

1. What are the two essential public health services associated with policy development?
2. What leadership skills are required for developing policies?
3. What is the difference between politics and policy development?
4. In what ways can politics influence policy development?
5. What is a futurist, and why should public health leaders pay attention to what futurists say?
6. How do advocacy and collaboration contribute to empowerment?
7. What are the similarities and differences among the three main types of collaborative relationships?
8. What are the main advantages of a collaborative relationship?
9. What is the role of priority setting in policy development?

EXERCISE 11-1: Tattooing in Mid-America

Purpose: to explore how policy development occurs and how a policy can affect the relationship between a local public health agency and the county health board

Key concepts: board of health, policy development, strategic planning

Procedure: The number of tattoo parlors in Tolbert County has grown. Tolbert High School Superintendent Violet Davis calls Tolbert Health Department Director Doris Martinez about the significant increase in tattoos among high school students—an increase that has understandably upset the students' parents. Martinez researches the subject and comes up with similar findings. There is no law in the county related to tattooing.

The class should divide into teams of 8 to 10 members. Half the members of each team will act the role of Tolbert County Health Department professionals and stakeholders. The other half will act the role of members of the Tolbert County Board of Health. The health department members, as a way of addressing the issue of tattooing, develop a proposed anti-tattooing law and devise a strategy for convincing the board of health to support the proposed law. The board members invite the health department representatives to a board meeting to present their arguments favoring the proposed law, and the two groups debate the merits and limitations of the proposal, ultimately focusing on whether it should be enacted.

REFERENCES

1. W. Keck, "Creating a Healthy Public," *American Journal of Public Health* 82, no. 9 (1992): 1206–1209.
2. J. C. Lashof, "Commitment to the Common Good," *American Journal of Public Health* 83, no. 9 (1993): 1222–1225.
3. G. Anderson and P. S. Hussey, "Influencing Government Policy: A Framework," in *Oxford Handbook of Public Health Practice*, ed. D. Pencheon, C. Guest, D. Melzer, and J. A. Muir Gray (London: Oxford University Press, 2001).
4. J. Peterson, V. Colman, and R. K. Norman, *Policymaker Outreach Toolkit* (Seattle: Washington State Department of Health, 2010).
5. V. Colman and R. K. Norman (Uncommon Solutions), *Policymaker Outreach Toolkit* (Seattle: Washington State Department of Health, 2011).
6. Institute of Medicine, *The Future of Public Health* (Washington, DC: National Academies Press, 1988).
7. Institute of Medicine, *The Future of the Public's Health* (Washington, DC: National Academies Press, 2003).
8. Institute of Medicine, *For the Public's Health: Revitalizing Law and Policy to Meet New Challenges* (Washington, DC: National Academies Press, 2011).
9. B. J. Turnock et al., "Implementing and Assessing Organizational Practices," *Public Health Reports* 109, no. 4 (1994): 478–484.

10. Turnock et al., "Implementing and Assessing Organizational Practices."
11. Turnock et al., "Implementing and Assessing Organizational Practices."
12. N. Glaser, *The Limits of Social Policy* (Cambridge, MA: Harvard University Press, 1988).
13. L. A. Aday, *At Risk in America* (San Francisco: Jossey-Bass, 1993).
14. R. N. Bellah, "The Quest for the Self," in P. Rubinow and W. M. Sullivan (eds.), *Interpretive Social Science* (Berkeley: University of California Press, 1987).
15. M. H. Moore, *Creating Public Value* (Cambridge, MA: Harvard University Press, 1995).
16. Moore, *Creating Public Value.*
17. A. Toffler, *The Third Wave* (New York: Bantam, 1980).
18. H. B. Maynard Jr. and S. E. Mehrtens, *The Fourth Wave: Business in the 21st Century* (San Francisco: Berrett-Koehler, 1993).
19. J. L. Marrioti, *The Power of Partnerships* (Cambridge, MA: Blackwell, 1996).
20. A. Toffler and H. Toffler, *Creating a New Civilization* (Atlanta: Turner Publishing, 1994).
21. N. Gingrich, *To Renew America* (New York: HarperCollins, 1995).
22. S. P. Robbins and M. Coulter, *Management,* 11th ed. (Upper Saddle River, NJ: Prentice Hall, 2011).
23. Robbins and Coulter, *Management.*
24. M. Siegel and L. Doner, *Marketing Public Health: Strategies to Promote Social Change* (Gaithersburg, MD: Aspen Publishers, 1998).
25. J. P. Kretzmann and J. L. McKnight, *Building Communities from the Inside Out* (Evanston, IL: Northwestern University Center for Urban Affairs and Policy Research, 1993).
26. Trust for America's Health, *You, Too, Can Be an Effective Health Advocate* (Washington, DC: TFAH, 2004).
27. P. Block, *The Empowered Manager* (San Francisco: Jossey-Bass, 1987).
28. D. Tracy, *Ten Steps to Empowerment* (New York: Morrow, 1990).
29. S. M. R. Covey, *The Speed of Trust* (New York: Free Press, 2006).
30. L. Cohen et al., *Developing Effective Coalitions: An Eight Step Guide* (Pleasant Hill, CA: Contra Costa County Health Services Department Prevention Program, 1994).
31. Cohen et al., *Developing Effective Coalitions.*
32. M. T. Hatcher and J. K. McDonald, *The Constituency Development Practice in Public Health Agencies* (Atlanta: Centers for Disease Control and Prevention, 1994).
33. Hatcher and McDonald, *The Constituency Development Practice in Public Health Agencies.*
34. Cohen et al., *Developing Effective Coalitions.*
35. G. P. Mays et al., "Collaboration to Improve Community Health: Trends and Alternative Models," *Joint Commission Journal of Qualitative Improvement* 25, no. 10 (1998): 518–565.
36. Mays et al., "Collaboration to Improve Community Health."
37. Public Health Service, *Healthy People 2000* (Washington, DC: U.S. Department of Health and Human Services, 1991).
38. Public Health Service, *Healthy People 2000.*
39. G. E. A. Dever, *Community Health Analysis* (Gaithersburg, MD: Aspen Publishers, 1991).
40. Public Health Service, *For a Healthy Nation: Returns on Investment in Public Health* (Washington, DC: U.S. Department of Health and Human Services, 1994).
41. Public Health Service, *For a Healthy Nation.*
42. H. Tilson and B. Berkowitz, "The Public Health Enterprise: Examining Our Twenty-First Century Policy Challenges," *Health Affairs* 25, no. 4 (2006), 900–910.
43. Centers for Disease Control, *Reducing the Health Consequences of Smoking: 25 Years of Progress, Report of the Surgeon General* (Washington, DC: U.S. Department of Health and Human Services, 1989).
44. Public Health Service, *Healthy People 2000.*
45. Public Health Service, *Healthy People 2010* (Washington, DC: U.S. Department of Health and Human Services, 2000).
46. J. L. Forster et al., "Locking Devices on Cigarette Vending Machines: Evaluation of a City Ordinance," *American Journal of Public Health* 82, no. 9 (1992): 1217–1219.
47. M. Siegel and L. Doner, *Marketing Public Health: Strategies to Promote Social Change* (Gaithersburg, MD: Aspen Publishers, 1998).
48. R. L. Flewelling et al., "First Year Impact of the 1989 California Cigarette Tax Increase on Cigarette Consumption," *American Journal of Public Health* 82, no. 6 (1992): 867–869.
49. R. Shilts, *And the Band Played On* (New York: St. Martin's Press, 1987).
50. D. D. Chrislip and C. Larsen, *Collaborative Leadership* (San Francisco: Jossey-Bass, 1994).

CHAPTER 12

Public Health Law and Ethics

One of the chief organizing forces for public health lies in the system of law.

—Bernard J. Turnock

Norms, values, and laws give structure to our personal and social lives. Laws define what we can do and what we are not supposed to do. In the United States, the Declaration of Independence and the Constitution define the structure and parameters of our way of life. The Founding Fathers were visionary and created documents that were flexible enough to adapt to the changes that time and events have brought. The public health leader must understand the context in which he or she lives and works. The laws become tools to define public action and process. Our society and way of life have been under attack for the past several years. It is now critical for leaders to develop competencies related to understanding the law and how to use it. This does not mean that all prepared public health leaders need to become lawyers, but it does mean that lawyers and political scientists may need to be consulted when our understanding of the law and legal process is limited. This chapter will look at the law and what the public health leader needs to know.

On a personal note, I would like to put the following discussion in context. As a young man, I went to law school for a year. I struggled that year because I could not make the study of law real for me. It was too abstract. As I have gotten older, I have discovered the importance of understanding law in a social or work-related context. Law requires an ecological context to become real. As a public health professional, I have learned about the need to see public health in the social fabric of our society. Norms, values, law, political structure, and community context all become integrated, and thus change will occur at the intersection of all these social and political processes. Thus, public health in the United States does not look like public health structures in Africa or Asia. The public health leader needs to know the territory in which he or she works. Knowing about the law and the effect of laws on our daily lives needs to be part of a lifelong learning agenda for the leader. It is important to study the effects of the laws and the unique forms that laws take in different local jurisdictions.

THE MEANING OF THE LAW

The word *law* relates to the legal system, the legal process, the profession of lawyers and their partners, and finally to legal knowledge and experience and training.[1] The functions of laws and regulations are to regulate behavior, protect the rights of individuals and their property rights, define the duties and responsibilities of government and individuals, guide the judiciary, and provide strong ethical standards for the residents of the jurisdiction and the country as a whole. The law comes in several flavors: constitutionally based law, statutory law, regulatory law, and common law. It is also important to see the differences in types of law. For example, statutory law is legislatively based, and regulatory law is more administratively based.

It is an inherent responsibility of the state to promote the health and well-being of the population.[2] The state needs to ensure the right conditions for people to be healthy. The state does this through the identification, prevention, and amelioration of the risk factors to good health in the community.

Gostin believed in the limitation of the state to "constrain the autonomy, privacy, liberty, proprietary, or other legally protected interests of individuals for protection or promotion of community health."[3] Public health law is based, then, on the role of the government in promoting the health of its citizens, the importance of population-based approaches to health, the important relationships between the state and its citizens, evidence-based services and scientific methodologies, and the legal concerns related to coercion. There is an important ethical issue related to coercion: how much can the state ensure conformance with health and safety standards without the use of some coercion?

The major controversy, then, relates to the issue of personal rights of citizens and how much the government can do to affect these rights. Much discussion relates to the issue of police powers. A review of the U.S. Constitution does not mention the term "police powers." Police powers are inferred from the powers that governments have to protect the health, safety, welfare, and general quality of life of the citizens of a jurisdiction.[4] It also seems that police powers are associated with the authority of a state. States can give local governments the authority to exercise police powers. How police powers can be enacted differs in the various states. In the public health context, police powers involved with jurisdictional variations involves all laws and regulations that have been enacted to improve morbidity and mortality in a given population).[5]

Police powers have been used at various times to promote and preserve public health in activities ranging from preventing injury and disease to improving air and water quality. Police powers have also been used in vaccination, isolation and quarantine, inspection of residential and commercial premises for many health- and injury-related issues, concerns about unsanitary conditions such as rodents in restaurants, health nuisances of various kinds, air and water contamination, closing of beaches with *E. coli* problems, pure food and drinking water contamination, fluoridation issues, and licensure of health professionals.[6]

Much discussion has been raised in recent years about the relationship between police powers and personal freedoms. This is a complex issue that cannot be fully discussed here. However, the issue becomes critical during emergency situations. Leaders need to be cognizant of the concerns of Americans about their civil rights. In utilizing police powers, they must also recognize how people will react to the loss of their personal rights when balanced against the need to protect the community as a whole. Exercising police powers carries a strong trust of the government concern with it.[7] There are issues in public health law between volunteerism and coercion. Leaders will struggle to gain compliance with public health protocols in communities with a volunteer approach or a police powers approach.

To better prepare public health leaders for the legal issues of public health, a new training program was developed for state and local health professional staff.[8] This new training program was developed in collaboration with Dr. Richard Goodman, formerly of the Public Health Law Program of the Centers for Disease Control and Prevention (CDC). The fundamental principles behind this course are basic sources and authorities, ethics, and administrative law. The course was to be rolled out during 2005 but was delayed until 2009, and includes nine study modules in Public Health Law 101, including the following:[9]

1. Key Concepts of U.S. Law in Public Health Practice
2. Ethics and the Law
3. Administrative Law
4. Roles of Legal Counsel for Public Health Agencies
5. Law of Public Health Surveillance, Investigations, and Emergencies
6. Privacy and Confidentiality
7. Infectious Diseases
8. Environmental Public Health, Health, and Injuries
9. Obesity Prevention and Controls

The series of nine units is also offered as well in a one- to one-and-a-half-day public health law conference. Other formats will also be possible.

The Public Health Training Network course by Neuberger and Christoffel is a more advanced 10-module course with a well-developed coordinator guide.[10] This course includes the following modules:

1. Introduction
2. Data Collection and Surveillance
3. Service Delivery
4. Licensing
5. Inspections
6. Enforcement
7. Policy Development
8. Negotiation
9. Communication
10. Responsibility and Liability

This legal basis of public health course has exercises associated with each of the modules. To put some of the thinking of this course and others on the law, Exercise 12-1 will require you to do a little homework. Divide your class or training group into groups of six to eight people. Find the answers to the questions delineated in the exercise. This exercise is included in the first module of the course. If you feel that you would like to review module 1 of the course, you can download it from the CDC website for the Public Health Training Network (www.cdc.gov/phtn).

PUBLIC HEALTH LAW COMPETENCIES

The major question a public health leader asks is related to how much a nonlawyer working in public health needs to know. As in other parts of public health, the issue of core competencies gets raised when the law is discussed. The Center for Law and the Public's Health at Johns Hopkins and Georgetown Universities has reviewed this issue and developed a framework of core competencies for public health professionals. Input into the development of the core legal competencies document was accomplished using a multidisciplinary group of lawyers and other public health professionals who were brought together in June 2001. Prior to that meeting, further input was received from multiple respondents in a national electronic survey conducted by the Public Health Foundation in Washington, D.C., along with feedback from several national public health and public policy organizations, including the Association of State and Territorial Health Officials, the National Association of County and City Health Officials, the American Public Health Association, the National Association of Local Boards of Health, and the National Council of State Legislatures.

The final list of core legal competencies is linked to the set of core public health competencies developed by the Council on Linkages Between Academia and Public Health Practice of the Public Health Foundation in 2001.

Second, the competency list was stratified for three different levels of public health professionals—frontline professional staff (F), senior-level professional staff (S), and supervisory and management staff (M). The framework adds a fourth group of health officials and governance boards (O). **Table 12-1** reproduces the list of core legal competencies.[11] As can be seen, seven competency areas are designated:

1. Public Health Powers
2. Regulatory Authority/Administrative Law

TABLE 12-1   Public Health Law Competencies

I. Public Health Powers—Generally	Level(s)
A. Describes the basic legal framework for public health; roles of federal, state, and local governments; and the relationship between legislatures, executive agencies, and the courts	F
B. Describes the meaning, source of, and scope of states' powers to protect the public's health, safety, and general welfare (i.e., police powers) and to protect the individual from identifiable harm (i.e., parens patriae powers)	M, O
C. Identifies and applies basic provisions of the governmental unit's health code and regulations within the particular area of practice (e.g., communicable disease control, environmental health, public health nursing)	M, O

(Continues)

TABLE 12-1 Public Health Law Competencies (*Continued*)

I. Public Health Powers–Generally	Level(s)
D. Describes the scope of statutory and regulatory provisions for emergency powers	O
E. Distinguishes public health agency powers and responsibilities from those of other governmental agencies, executive offices, police, legislatures, and courts	O
II. Regulatory Authority/Administrative Law	**Level(s)**
A. Describes basic legal processes, such as how legislatures create and amend laws, how executive officials enforce laws, and how courts make and interpret laws	O
B. Determines procedures for promulgating administrative regulations	O
C. Determines procedures for obtaining mandatory or prohibitory injunctions from a court	O
D. Follows administrative procedure laws for conducting investigations, holding hearings, promulgating regulations, and provisions concerning open public records	M, O
E. Weighs options and applies, when necessary, processes to address public health problems through criminal charges for specific behaviors and civil suits for damages	O
III. Ascertaining Authority/Obtaining Legal Advice	**Level(s)**
A. Identifies legal issues for which legal advice should be sought and knows what action to take where legal issues arise, including contacting legal advisors	M, O
B. Provides factual assistance and states basic legal issues to legal advisors	M, O
C. Reads and comprehends basic statutory and administrative laws	M, O
D. Recognizes that legal rules do not always specify a course of conduct	M, O
E. Effectively integrates legal information into the exercise of professional public health judgment	M, O
F. Develops enforcement strategies consistent with the law and in the interest of protecting the public's health	M, O
IV. Law and Public Health Services and Functions	**Level(s)**
A. Describes how law and legal practices contribute to the current health status of the population	O
B. Determines how the law can be used as a tool in promoting and protecting the public's health	M, O
C. Identifies the mechanisms through which law can deter, encourage, or compel health-related behaviors	M, O
D. Identifies and exercises legal authorities, responsibilities, and restrictions to ensure or provide healthcare services to populations	M, O
E. Identifies and exercises legal authority over the quality, delivery, and evaluation of healthcare services within the agency's jurisdictions	M, O
F. Applies ethical principles to the development, interpretation, and enforcement of laws	F, M, O
V. Legal Actions	**Level(s)**
A. Describes how and under what circumstances legal searches of private premises can be performed	S, M, O
B. Knows how and under what circumstances legal seizures of private property for public health purposes can take place	S, M, O

C. Describes the limits of authority for legally closing private premises	S, M, O
D. Identifies legal authority for compelling medical treatment or instituting mandatory screening programs	S, M, O
E. Knows legal authority for imposing quarantine, isolation, or other restrictions on the movement or placement of persons	S, M, O
F. Identifies provisions for the issuance, revocation, or suspension of licenses, and decides what actions to take to protect the public's health	S, M, O
G. Adheres to confidentiality laws in the collection, maintenance, and release of data	S, F, M, O
VI. Legal Limitations	**Level(s)**
A. Recognizes prominent constitutional rights implicated through the practice of public health (e.g., freedom of speech, right to assemble, freedom from unreasonable searches and seizures, right to privacy, due process, equal protection) and the analytic techniques courts use in enforcing these rights	S, M, O
B. Recognizes federal, state, and local statutes or ordinances and major federal or state cases granting rights to individuals and limiting public health authority	S, M, O
C. Describes legal protections regarding minors and incompetent persons	S, M, O
D. Acknowledges the sources of potential civil and criminal liability of public health workers	S, M, O
VII. Personnel/Contracts Law	**Level(s)**
A. Implements practices to legally hire, discharge, and discipline employees	M, O
B. Applies essential tenets of antidiscrimination laws, such as the Americans with Disabilities Act (ADA) affecting employment practices and the delivery of services	F, M, O
C. Develops contractual terms when contracting for the delivery of essential public health services that serve to protect the public's health	M, O
D. Negotiates, develops, complies with, and terminates contracts with other persons, organizations, and agencies for the provision of essential public health services	M, O

F = frontline professional staff; S = senior-level professional staff; M = supervisory and management staff; O = health officials and governance boards

Source: Reproduced from the Center for Law and the Public's Health, Johns Hopkins and Georgetown Universities (2001). *Core Legal Competencies for Public Health Professionals*. http://www.publichealthlaw.net/Training/TrainingPDFs/PHLCompetencies.pdf. Accessed July 13, 2012.

3. Ascertaining Authority/Obtaining Legal Advice
4. Law and Public Health Services and Functions
5. Legal Actions
6. Legal Limitations
7. Personnel/Contracts Law

Case Study 12-A presents an interesting mix of legal issues in which the courts, state legislatures, public health departments, and other interested parties came together on a controversial set of issues related to the Master Tobacco Settlement Agreement. The case writers presented several interesting questions as part of the case; these are included for your discussion. To these questions, it is possible to add the question of what legal competencies were necessary on the part of the public health leaders in this case.

Master Tobacco Settlement Agreement: A Three-State Comparison of the Allocation of Funds

Case Study in Policy Development; *Red, White, and Glue Year 10 Team*; Jo Ambrose; Karen Kunsemiller; Emil Makar; Phyllis Pelt; Charlene Stevens; Laura Thomas

Tobacco use is the single most preventable cause of death and disease in our society. Cigarette smoking causes heart disease, several kinds of cancer (lung, larynx, esophagus, pharynx, mouth, and bladder), and chronic lung disease. Cigarette smoking also contributes to cancer of the pancreas, kidney, and cervix. Smoking during pregnancy can cause spontaneous abortions, low birth weight, and sudden infant death syndrome. Annually, tobacco use causes more than 430,000 deaths and costs the nation between $50 billion and $73 billion in medical expenses alone. These expenses have increasingly become a critical responsibility for the states to attempt to address.

In November 1998, 46 states, the District of Columbia, and five U.S. territories settled their Medicaid lawsuits against five of the largest tobacco manufacturers (Phlegm Balls Inc., Money Suckers Group, Breath Rotters, Cancerettes, and Malignant Tumors). The industry committed to pay the states approximately $206 billion over the next 25 years for recovery of their tobacco-related healthcare costs. The tobacco settlement, known as the Master Settlement Agreement (MSA), presented the states with an opportunity to reduce the terrible burden exacted by tobacco on the states' economies. In the MSA, there was no obligation for the states to spend this money on tobacco control programs, which would ultimately lead to a reduced death toll from tobacco. However, most states promised to use a significant portion of the settlement funds to attack the public health problem posed by tobacco in the United States.

The Centers for Disease Control and Prevention (CDC) recommended that states establish tobacco control programs that were comprehensive, sustainable, and accountable. The four main goals were to prevent the initiation of tobacco use by young people, promote cessation among adults, eliminate nonsmokers' exposure to secondhand smoke, and eliminate disparities related to tobacco among various population groups. To reduce smoking rates considerably, each state needed to invest a substantial amount in new or expanded integrated tobacco control initiatives. Specific funding ranges and programmatic recommendations were provided for each state. Approximate annual costs to implement all of the recommended program components were estimated to range from $6 to $17 per capita in medium-sized states.

Each state legislature had the opportunity to make the decision regarding how to spend the money that was received from the MSA. The decisions made by three of the states will be presented. These states were State of Confusion, State Wanna Be, and Exemplary State. These are medium-sized states with comparable populations. State of Confusion received $300 million for year 2000–2001, State Wanna Be received $304 million, and Exemplary State received $306 million. For each of the three states, the final decisions made by the state legislatures for the 2000–2001 fiscal year regarding the MSA moneys will be presented as well as how these allocation decisions were reached.

State of Confusion

For five years prior to the MSA, State of Confusion was spending approximately $8 million annually on tobacco prevention and control programs such as prevention of youth initiation, smoking cessation, and prevention of secondhand smoke exposure. Since establishing these programs, there was no substantial decrease in the use of tobacco and no significant reduction in the number of deaths due to tobacco. The Centers for Disease Control and Prevention's recommended range of funding for tobacco prevention and control programs for the State of Confusion was $65 million to $181 million annually.

In March 2000, the General Assembly of the State of Confusion met to discuss how to distribute the $300 million the state had received. The meeting was limited to members of the General Assembly. No members of outside groups, such as the public health department, smoking prevention advocate groups, healthcare providers such as hospitals, and managed care organizations, were allowed to witness the proceedings. Representative Upfore Reelection was the first speaker. He started the discussion by stating that most of the settlement money if not all of it should go back to the taxpayers. It belongs to them because they already paid and continue to pay for the tobacco-related healthcare costs. This money is a payback to them for what they already spent and continue to spend. It does not mean we should add more dollars to prevent smoking because this money was not given to the state for that reason. "I recommend we allocate the money to be used as a tax credit and urge you to support this decision," said Representative Upfore Reelection. Representative Veri Sensible, a school of public health graduate, objected to her colleague's opinion. She stated that spending extra dollars on smoking prevention would save the taxpayers a tremendous amount of money in the future. The conclusive evidence is that comprehensive state tobacco prevention and control programs can reduce tobacco use and the economic burden of tobacco-related diseases. This type of heated discussion continued until July 2000.

During the discussions, the State of Confusion did not include any of the essential public health services to determine how to allocate the money. No tobacco experts were consulted to determine how the funds should be divided. The legislators made all of the decisions.

Distribution of Dollars State of Confusion	
Tobacco Settlement Funds (TSF) received 2000–2001:	$300 million
CDC recommendation for tobacco prevention and control:	$65–181 million

Programs that have a direct effect on tobacco prevention and control	
Amount Allocated ($ millions)	Description
5	Youth Prevention
5	Adult Cessation
3	Eliminate Secondhand Smoke Exposure
TOTAL	$13 million
% of TSF	4.3
% of CDC minimum	20.0

Programs that have an effect on public health	
Amount Allocated ($ millions)	Description
12	HIV/AIDS Research
20	Diabetes Research
25	Gang Prevention
TOTAL	$57 million
% of TSF	19.0

Programs that do not have an effect on tobacco prevention and control or public health	
Amount Allocated ($ millions)	Description
40	Rainy Day Fund
40	State Prisons
50	State Tobacco Farmers
100	Tax Credit
TOTAL	$230 million
% of TSF	77.0%

State Wanna Be

State Wanna Be was an industrial state and had suffered recently from a slowing economy, which led to a significant increase in the number of people with incomes below poverty level. According to *Healthy People 2010*, individuals who are poor are significantly more likely to smoke than individuals of middle or high income (34% compared with 21%). Before the MSA, State Wanna Be was spending about $20 million annually on tobacco prevention and control programs. A major source of funding was a cigarette excise tax. Data from *Healthy People 2010* indicated that (1) increasing excise taxes on cigarettes is one of the most cost-effective short-term strategies to reduce tobacco consumption among adults and to prevent initiation among youth and (2) the ability to sustain lower consumption increases when the tax increase is combined with an antismoking campaign. Since establishing

(Continues)

these programs, the rate of tobacco use had been slightly decreasing steadily. The Centers for Disease Control and Prevention's recommended range of funding for tobacco prevention and control programs for State Wanna Be was $63 million to $177 million annually.

In April 2000, the General Assembly of State Wanna Be met to discuss how to distribute the $304 million the state had received through the MSA. The initial meetings were limited to members of the General Assembly. However, the Master Settlement Agreement State Committee had several public meetings in order to listen to various groups' points of view and how the groups thought the money should be spent. Represented at the hearings were members of the public health department, nonprofit health organizations, the highway safety and control commission, police and fire departments, state and private universities, and students and administrators from grade schools, junior highs, and high schools across the state. Mr. Keepa Low Profile, director of the State Wanna Be Public Health Department, was unable to completely express how he thought the money should be divided due to the fact that this topic was a very political issue. His proposal was very similar to the one the governor was promoting. The nonprofit health organizations pushed for the money to follow the CDC's recommended guidelines for "best practices." The highway safety and control commission articulated that there was a real need for the highways of the state to be repaired. Policemen and firemen thought the money should be used for new patrol cars with the latest technology and new fire trucks. They felt this would keep the residents of State Wanna Be safe. The state and private universities suggested a new scholarship fund be set up for the residents, who would otherwise be unable to attend college. The reasoning was that this would allow those individuals that were poor to receive an education and therefore be less likely to smoke. Students spoke on how they were the targets of the tobacco industry and said they would like to see the money spent on youth prevention and cessation.

Two hearings were held, one in May and the other in June. The legislators took into account what the members of their state said; however, in the long run the ultimate decision still rested on the legislators. The final allocations were decided in July 2000. State Wanna Be, through the assistance of the nonprofit health organizations, used the essential public health service of evaluating the effectiveness, accessibility, and quality of personal and population-based health services. In addition, from the students' recommendations, the state developed policies and plans that supported community health efforts.

Distribution of Dollars State Wanna Be	
Tobacco Settlement Funds (TSF) received 2000–2001:	$304 million
CDC recommendation for tobacco prevention and control:	$63–177 million

Programs that have a direct effect on tobacco prevention and control	
Amount Allocated ($ millions)	Description
13	Youth Prevention
9	Adult Cessation
7	Eliminate Secondhand Smoke Exposure
11	Eliminate Disparities Related to Tobacco
TOTAL	$40 million
% of TSF	13.0
% of CDC minimum	63.0

Programs that have an effect on public health	
Amount Allocated ($ millions)	Description
5	Dental Research
15	Diabetes Research
25	Cardiovascular Disease Prevention
50	Improvement of Healthcare System for Low SES Individuals
TOTAL	$95 million
% of TSF	31.0

Programs that do not have an effect on tobacco prevention and control or public health	
Amount Allocated ($ millions)	**Description**
35	Restructuring of Selected Golf Courses State Highway Safety and Control
34	Commission
100	College Scholarship Fund
TOTAL	$169 million
% of TSF	56.0

Exemplary State

Exemplary State had relatively no experience or knowledge concerning the state's tobacco problem. Before the MSA, Exemplary State was indirectly spending money on tobacco prevention but no true dollar amount could be calculated. The Centers for Disease Control and Prevention's recommended range of funding for tobacco prevention and control programs for Exemplary State was $64 million to $176 million annually.

In February 2000, the General Assembly of Exemplary State met to discuss how to distribute the $306 million the state had received through the MSA. The initial meetings were limited to members of the General Assembly; however, a few concerned senators and representatives investigated and consulted with national, state, and local tobacco authorities. Senator Pre Vention stated that an initial assessment needed to be done to ascertain where and which programs were needed. Statistics on current cigarette use by youth and adults and the average annual deaths related to smoking were gathered for each county. Next, Representative Breathe Easy spoke about the need to develop policies and plans. This would ensure that the money that was received over the next 25 years would be put to the best possible use. One of the policies he felt strongly about was eliminating exposure to secondhand smoke in workplaces, restaurants, and homes. After doing some of his own investigating, Representative Elimi Nate Cancer thought that focusing on adult cessation would ultimately lead to youth prevention. Senator Oso Smart agreed with her colleagues and added that there was a definite need for a competent tobacco prevention workforce. This workforce should be not only in the community offering direct services but also mobilizing the community to sustain the comprehensive tobacco prevention and control efforts once the tobacco workforce had left the community. After these initial discoveries, the state held three hearings that were open to the public, and many members of the state attended. The final decision of how to spend the $306 million was decided in June 2000.

Exemplary State decided to follow the CDC recommended guidelines for how to spend their money. Because the state is an exemplary state, it followed several of the essential public health services. Representative Pre Vention ensured that the health problems of the community were identified and diagnosed. She had her staff members research the effect that tobacco has had on the state. Representative Breathe Easy made certain there were policies and plans in place that supported individual and community tobacco efforts. A competent public health workforce was put in place due to Senator Oso Smart's insight.

Distribution of Dollars Exemplary State	
Tobacco Settlement Funds (TSF) Received 2000–2001:	$306 million
CDC Recommendation for Tobacco Prev. and Control:	$64–176 million
Programs that have a direct effect on tobacco prevention and control	
Amount Allocated ($ millions)	**Description**
20	Community Programs to Reduce Tobacco Use
5	Chronic Disease Programs to Reduce Burden of Tobacco-Related Diseases
13	School Programs
10	Enforcement

(*Continues*)

Programs that have a direct effect on tobacco prevention and control	
Amount Allocated ($ millions)	**Description**
10	Statewide Programs
21	Countermarketing
47	Cessation Programs
16	Surveillance and Evaluation
8	Administration and Management
TOTAL	$150 million
% of TSF	49.0
% of CDC minimum	234.0
Programs that have an effect on public health	
Amount Allocated ($ millions)	**Description**
11	Prescription Drugs for the Elderly
20	Cancer Research
25	Cardiovascular Disease Prevention
50	Health Insurance Improvements
TOTAL	$106 million
% of TSF	35.0
Programs that do not have an effect on tobacco prevention and control or public health	
Amount Allocated ($ millions)	**Description**
20	College Scholarship Fund
30	Trust Fund
TOTAL	$50 million
% of TSF	16.0

These three states along with the other 43 states have the task of deciding how the money should be spent for the next 24 years. Every year the state legislatures will decide how the money will be allocated. Various organizations will lobby the legislators to vote in their favor for funding. With such large amounts of money to be spent and no obligations to spend it on tobacco, the states have an extremely important role in deciding their future responsibilities: the state's economy, and tobacco's toll on themselves and their residents.

CASE STUDY Questions

Master Tobacco Settlement Agreement: A Three-State Comparison of the Allocation of Funds

The intent of the Master Tobacco Settlement Agreement was to enable states and other participants to recover money that had been spent for the treatment of tobacco-related health problems. To this end, states will receive approximately $206 billion over the next 25 years. However, every year each state will determine how the money is allocated. This case study presents a comparison of the allocation of first-year tobacco settlement dollars by three states receiving similar awards.

1. **The core public health function of policy development involves advocating for public health, building community constituencies, and identifying resources in the community to meet identified needs. Discuss the policy development activities, or lack thereof, of the three states presented in this case study. What are the strengths and weaknesses of each approach?**

2. Additional policy development activities include setting priorities and developing plans to address the health needs of the community. Using the allocation tables in the case study, discuss evidence of these activities in each state's decision-making process.

3. Discuss all factors that could influence the prioritization process and allocation of tobacco settlement dollars. In what ways do you think the tobacco industry influences the decision-making process?

4. What influence should the CDC guidelines have on the prioritization and allocation process?

5. What can public health advocates, including taxpayers, do to influence decisions regarding the use of tobacco settlement dollars in future years? What strategies should be developed now to sustain tobacco prevention efforts beyond 25 years and protect future generations?

6. Tobacco settlement dollars are intended to replace money used for tobacco-related health problems and to influence future tobacco use. However, other lobbyists can argue that many worthy state projects did not get funded because of tobacco-related expenses and, therefore, should be considered when doling out settlement funds. As a public health advocate, how would you respond to this argument?

STATE REVIEW OF PUBLIC HEALTH LAWS

A notable resolution was adopted by the National Association of Attorneys General in December 2003, urging states to review their public health laws because of all the changes in public health and the American society since September 11, 2001. The resolution can be seen in **Figure 12-1**. It was strongly believed that many of the state's public health laws were outdated. The Centers for Disease Control and Prevention had named public health law reform to be one of its 10 priorities for building public health infrastructure and improving public health outcomes.[12] In recent years, a number of states have been updating or revising their public health laws. One interesting example of this is

Adopted
National Association of Attorneys General
December 2–6, 2003
Williamsburg, Virginia

WHEREAS, every state (territory) has enacted laws to allow for proper response by health officials to public health conditions; and

WHEREAS, the majority of those statutes were passed several decades ago, and, fortunately, have been seldom needed and therefore seldom used, and so are little known; and

WHEREAS, given changes in medical and public health circumstances, the status quo is no longer satisfactory; and

WHEREAS, with the ever increasing mobility of persons, animals and products between towns, states and nations, we have been increasing levels of concern regarding contagion and increasing numbers of public health incidents, such as those involving SARS and *Monkeypox* disease; and

WHEREAS, many of those statutes address limited and previously known health conditions, but are not flexible to address present medical and disease circumstances;

NOW, THEREFORE, be it resolved that the National Association of Attorneys General;

1) encourages states to undertake a review of their public health laws and the *Model State Public Health Act*, and to update those laws to reflect present circumstances; and

2) encourages the education of public health authorities and their counsel on the constitutional and statutory laws related to public health response to assure the best response and preparedness in an emergency; and

3) authorizes its Executive Director to transmit these views.

FIGURE 12-1 A National Resolution on Public Health Laws. *Source*: Courtesy of Lawrence Gostin, Stephen Teret, and James G. Hodge of publichealthlaw.net.

discussed below in the Illinois experience. However, the updating and revision of these laws has not been a consistent enterprise across the country.[13]

States have defined public health in different ways in their laws and statutes. **Table 12-2** presents some of these statutory definitions of public health to demonstrate the diversity in definitions.[14] The other important finding from their survey can be seen in **Table 12-3** pointing to the different models various states have used to carry out their public health functions. A survey of state public health deputy directors was undertaken in which 24 states responded.[15] Some of their findings include the following:

1. More than 70% of the respondents reported that public health infrastructure bills were introduced in their state legislatures, although three respondents said the bill had failed to pass.
2. Forty-six percent of the deputy directors reported that their states had not developed comprehensive public health reforms.
3. Hot topics for legislative action as seen by the deputy directors included such topics as tobacco control, HIV/AIDS, minority health issues, bioterrorism, emerging infections, immunization

rates and registries, cancer prevention, oral health, privacy issues, West Nile virus, and children's healthcare coverage.
4. State legislatures have considered a variety of comprehensive or limited public health laws since the early 1990s.

The survey concluded by noting the complexity of the public health laws in America. This diversity was a reflection of the variations in the society as a whole. However, the diversity in the laws also complicates the political process. The public health leader needs to learn the laws of his or her jurisdiction at both the local and state levels. The differences in laws are also demonstrated in the different forms that the public health system takes in different areas of the country. The reform of the state and eventually the local public health system will involve not only the modernization of the legal bases of public health practice, but innovative ways to implement any changes proposed in a rather fragmented healthcare system. A proposal was presented for the development of a model state public health act within a national public health system. This model act is discussed in the next section of this chapter.

TABLE 12-2   Statutory Definitions of Public Health in Select States

ST	Stat. Cite	Statutory Definition of Public Health
AL	Ala. Code § 22-21-311; § 22-11A-1; § 22-2-8 (1982).	Public health includes: care of sick, injured, physically disabled or handicapped, mentally ill, retarded or disturbed persons; the prevention of sickness and disease; care, treatment and rehabilitation of alcoholics; and care of elderly persons. Public health includes protection from diseases and health conditions of epidemic potential.
AK	Alaska Stat. § 18.05.010 (2000).	The Department of Health and Social Services shall administer the laws and regulations relating to the promotion and protection of the public health, control of communicable diseases, programs for the improvement of maternal and child health, care of crippled children, and hospitalization of the tuberculous and shall discharge other duties provided by law.
AZ	Ariz. Rev. Stat. § 36-104 (1993)	Public health support services include: (i) Consumer health protection programs, including the functions of community water supplies, general sanitation, vector control and food and drugs; (ii) Epidemiology and disease control programs, including the functions of chronic disease, accident and injury control, communicable diseases, tuberculosis, venereal disease and others; (iii) Laboratory services programs; (iv) Health education and training programs; and (v) Disposition of human bodies program.
CA	Cal. Gov't Code § 855.4 (1995).	Public health of the community includes preventing disease or controlling the communication of disease.

ST	Stat. Cite	Statutory Definition of Public Health
CO	Col. Rev. Stat. § 25- 1-107	The department has, in addition to all other powers and duties imposed upon it by law, the following powers and duties: (a) (I) To investigate and control the causes of epidemic and communicable diseases affecting the public health. (II) For the purposes of this paragraph (a), the board shall determine, by rule and regulation, those epidemic and communicable diseases and conditions that are dangerous to the public health.
DE	Del. Code Ann. tit. 29, § 7904(b) (2000).	"Public health and preventative services" are defined as activities that protect people from diseases and injury. They include activities that: (i) prevent and control communicable disease epidemics; (ii) promote healthy behaviors to control chronic disease; (iii) monitor the health of the population through data analysis and epidemiological studies; (iv) result in policies to promote the health of the public; (v) assure quality health services and systems for the population; (vi) result in the setting of standards for the protection of the public's health; (vii) provide assistance during disasters; (viii) assess environmental health risks; and (ix) offer health protection strategies to environmental control agencies.
GA	Ga. Code Ann. § 31-2-1 (2000).	In order to safeguard and promote the health of the people of this state the department is empowered to: (1) Provide epidemiological investigations and laboratory facilities and services in the detection and control of disease, disorders, and disabilities and to provide research, conduct investigations, and disseminate information concerning reduction in the incidence and proper control of disease, disorders, and disabilities; (2) Forestall and correct physical, chemical, and biological conditions that, if left to run their course, could be injurious to health; (3) Regulate and require the use of sanitary facilities at construction sites and places of public assembly and to regulate persons, firms, and corporations engaged in the rental and service of portable chemical toilets; (4) Isolate and treat persons afflicted with a communicable disease; (5) Manufacture drugs and biologicals which are not readily available on the market and not manufactured for commercial purposes; (6) Promote health aspects of civil defense; (7) Detect and relieve physical defects and deformities and provide treatment for mental and emotional disorders and infirmities; (8) Protect dental health; (9) Determine the presence of disease and conditions deleterious to health; and (10) Provide education and treatment in order to prevent unwanted pregnancy.
KY	Ky. Rev. Stat. Ann. § 211.180 (2000).	Matters of public health include detection, prevention, and control of communicable, chronic and occupational diseases; the control of vectors of disease; the safe handling of food and food products; the safety of cosmetics; the control of narcotics, barbiturates, and other drugs as provided by law; the sanitation of public and semipublic buildings and areas; the licensure of hospitals; protection and improvement of the health of expectant mothers, infants, preschool, and school-age children; the practice of midwifery, including the issuance of permits to and supervision of women who practice midwifery; and protection and improvement of the health of the people through better nutrition.
MA	Mass. Gen. Laws ch. 111, § 5 (1996).	The department shall take cognizance of the interests of life, health, comfort and convenience among the citizens of the commonwealth; shall conduct sanitary investigations and investigations as to the causes of disease, and especially of epidemics, and the sale of food and drugs and adulterations thereof; and shall disseminate such information relating thereto as it considers proper. It shall advise the government concerning the location and other sanitary condition of any public institution. It may produce and distribute immunological, diagnostic and therapeutic agents as it may deem advisable.

(Continues)

TABLE 12-2 Statutory Definitions of Public Health in Select States (*Continued*)

ST	Stat. Cite	Statutory Definition of Public Health
MI	Mich. Comp. Laws § 333.2221 (1992).	The department shall continually and diligently endeavor to prevent disease, prolong life, and promote the public health through organized programs, including prevention and control of environmental health hazards; prevention and control of diseases; prevention and control of health problems of particularly vulnerable population groups; development of healthcare facilities and agencies and health services delivery systems; and regulation of healthcare facilities and agencies and health services delivery systems to the extent provided by law.
MO	Mo. Rev. Stat. § 192.011 (1996).	The department shall monitor the adverse health effects of the environment and prepare population risk assessments regarding environmental hazards including but not limited to those relating to water, air, toxic waste, solid waste, sewage disposal and others. The department shall make recommendations to the department of natural resources for improvement of public health as related to the environment.... The department of health shall develop a comprehensive disease prevention plan to expand existing and to develop new programs.
NE	Neb. Rev. Stat. §§ 71-7504, 71-7508 (1992).	Community public health services shall mean services designed to protect and improve the health of persons within a geographically defined community by (1) emphasizing services to prevent illness, disease, and disability, (2) promoting effective coordination and use of community resources, and (3) extending health services into the community. Such services shall include, but not be limited to, community nursing services, home health services, disease prevention and control services, public health education, and public health environmental services. Disease prevention and control services shall mean epidemiology, immunization, case finding and follow-up, continuing surveillance and detection, and prevention of communicable and chronic diseases.
NH	N.H. Rev. Stat. Ann. §§ 125:9, 126-A:4[I] (1995).	The commissioner of the Department of Health and Human Services shall: I. Take cognizance of the interests of health and life among the people; II. Make investigations and inquiries concerning the causes of epidemics and other diseases, the sources of morbidity and mortality, and the effects of localities, employments, conditions, circumstances, and the environment on the public health. The Department shall "... provide a comprehensive and coordinated system of health and human services as needed to promote and protect the health, safety, and well-being of the citizens of New Hampshire."
NJ	N.J. Stat. Ann. § 59:6-3 (1992).	Promoting the public health of the community includes preventing disease or controlling the communication of disease within the community.
NY	N.Y. Pub. Health § 602 (1990).	Services that promote the public health (including enhancing or sustaining the public health, protecting the public from the threats of disease and illness, or preventing premature death) include (1) family health services; (2) disease control, which shall include activities to control and mitigate the extent of non-infectious diseases, particularly those of a chronic, degenerative nature, and infectious diseases; (3) health education and guidance, which shall include the use of information and education to modify or strengthen practices that will promote the public health and prevent illness; (4) community health assessment; and (5) environmental health, which shall include activities that promote health and prevent illness by ensuring sanitary conditions in water supplies, food service establishments, and other permit sites, and by abating public health nuisances.
OK	Okla. Stat. tit. 63, § 1-206 (1996).	1. Maintain programs for disease prevention and control, health education, guidance, maternal and child health, including school health services, health in the working environment, nutrition and other matters affecting the public health; 2. Provide preventive services to the chronically ill and aged; 3. Maintain vital records and statistics.

ST	Stat. Cite	Statutory Definition of Public Health
OR	Or. Rev. Stat. § 431.416 (1999).	Local public health authorities or health district shall assure activities necessary for the preservation of health or prevention of disease in the area under its jurisdiction … including: (a) Epidemiology and control of preventable diseases and disorders; (b) Parent and child health services, including family planning clinics; (c) Collection and reporting of health statistics; (d) Health information and referral services; and (e) Environmental health services.
SC	S.C. Code Ann. § 44-1-140 (1988).	The Department may adopt rules and regulations requiring and providing: sanitation of public places; regulation of milk and milk products; sanitation of meat markets and bottling plants; sanitation in handling mollusks, finfish, and crustaceans; control of disease-bearing insects; control of industrial plants; care and isolation of people having a communicable disease; regulation of disposition of garbage and sewage; thorough investigation and prevention of all diseases; education to prevent disease.
TX	Tex. Health & Safety § 12.031 (1992).	"Public health services" means: (1) personal health promotion, maintenance, and treatment services; (2) infectious disease control and prevention services; (3) environmental and consumer health protection services; (4) laboratory services; (5) health facility architectural plan review; (6) public health planning, information, and statistical services; (7) public health education and information services; and (8) administration services.
WI	Wis. Stat. § 160.05 (1998).	Public health concerns. (a) The department shall designate which of the substances in each category are of public health concern and which are of public welfare concern. (b) In determining whether a substance is of public health concern, the department shall take into account the degree to which the substance may: 1. Cause or contribute to an increase in mortality; 2. Cause or contribute to an increase in illness or incapacity, whether chronic or acute; 3. Pose a substantial present or potential hazard to human health because of its physical, chemical or infectious characteristics; or 4. Cause or contribute to other adverse human health effects or changes of a chronic or subchronic nature even if not associated with illness or incapacity. (c) In determining whether a substance is of public health concern, the department may consider other effects not specified under par. (d) if those effects are reasonably related to public health.

Source: Courtesy of Lawrence Gostin, Stephen Teret, and James G. Hodge of publichealthlaw.net.

TABLE 12-3 Classification of State and Local Distribution of Public Health Functions

Distributional Approach	Brief Description	States	Total
Centralized (top-down) Approach	The state public health agency either performs directly or regulates the level and extent of public health services provided at the local county or city levels.	AR, FL, LA, MS, NM, SC, VA	7
Decentralized (bottom-up) Approach	The authority and direct responsibility for many public health functions lies at the local county or city level of government.	AZ, CO, CT, ID, IN, IA, ME, MO, MT, NE, NV, NJ, ND, OR, UT, WA, WI	17
Hybrid Approach	The direct responsibility for public health functions are shared between state and local governments.	AL, AK, CA, GA, IL, KS, KY, MD, MA, MI, MN, NH, NC, NY, OH, OK, PA, SD, TN, TX, WV, WY	22

Source: Courtesy of Lawrence Gostin, Stephen Teret, and James G. Hodge of publichealthlaw.net.

MODEL STATE PUBLIC HEALTH ACT

To clarify the role of public health in the 21st century and to better understand the diversity of laws defining state and local public health requirements, the Turning Point Public Health Statute Modernization National Collaborative (funded by the Robert Wood Johnson Foundation) undertook the development of a model state public health act. The purpose of the model act was to create an act based on modern constitutional, statutory, and case-based law at the national and state levels. The act was also to reflect current scientific and ethical principles that are the foundation of contemporary public health practice. The model act has nine articles with numerous subsections. The act builds on the organization and provision of the core public health functions and the essential public health services. **Table 12-4** is an outline of the model act and its many subsections. The topics of this act range from public health infrastructure concerns to the general orientation to emergency preparedness and response. By August 2007, variations of this model act were introduced in 133 bills in 33 states; 48 of the bills passed.[16]

The second major model act relates to state emergency health powers. The reason for such an act is to address the issue of public health powers (including police powers) for state and local public health authorities to make sure there are strong and effective emergency prevention, preparedness, and response mechanisms in place. The model act addresses the issue of the public health role in emergencies as well as the issue of rights of the public and how these rights can be respected. This model state emergency health powers act (see **Table 12-5** for an outline of the model act) was developed by the Center for Law and the Public's Health with support from the Alfred P. Sloan Foundation.[17] The model act has as a requirement the development of a plan to provide a coordinated response to a public health emergency. The model act itself recommended the reporting and collection of information, the immediate investigation of a threat by giving investigators access to an individual's health information under specified circumstances, the appropriation of property or other resources that may be necessary for the care, treatment, and housing of patients, and the allowance of public health authorities to provide care, test, and vaccinate residents who are ill or who have been exposed to a contagious disease, and to quarantine people when necessary. The model act has already been used by a number of state and local legislators as a guide for addressing public health reforms.

The model has already been introduced in whole or in part in over 40 states. Hodge has reviewed the progress of the states in this endeavor in a report available from the Center for Law and the Public's Health.[18] By July 2006, the act had been introduced in 171 bills of resolution in whole or partially in 44 states and Washington, DC; 66 bills were passed between 2001 and 2006.[19] To look at the process of developing a state act, Munson in Case Study 12-B presents a view of the Illinois experience.

Before leaving this section, it is interesting to note the development of a "memorandum of understanding"

TABLE 12-4   Outline of the Model State Public Health Act

Article I. Purposes and Definitions
Section 1-101. Legislative Purposes
1-102. Definitions
Article II. Mission and Functions
Section 2-101. Mission Statement
2-102. Essential Public Health Services and Functions
2-103. Roles and Responsibilities
2-104. Public Health Powers—In General
Article III. Public Health Infrastructure
Section 3-101. Public Health Infrastructure
3-102. Public Health Workforce

3-103. Performance Management

3-104. Accreditation of State or Local Public Health Agencies

3-105. Incentives and Evaluations

3-106. Public Health Planning and Priority Setting

3-107. Public Health Advisory Council

Article IV. Collaboration and Relationships with Public and Private Sector Partners

Section 4-101. Relationships Among Federal, Tribal, State, or Local Public Health Agencies

4-102. Relationships Among Public and Private Sector Partners

4-103. Relationships Among Participants in the Healthcare System

Article V. Public Health Authorities/Powers

Section 5-101. Prevention and Control of Conditions of Public Health Importance

5-102. Surveillance Activities—Sources of Information

5-103. Reporting

5-104. Epidemiologic Investigation

5-105. Counseling and Referral Services for Persons Exposed to Contagious Diseases

5-106. Testing, Examination, and Screening

5-107. Compulsory Medical Treatment

5-108. Quarantine and Isolation

5-109. Vaccination

5-110. Licenses

5-111. Public Health Nuisances

5-112. Administrative Searches and Inspections

Source: Turning Point. *Model State Public Health Act.* Seattle, WA. Author, 2003.

TABLE 12-5 Model State Emergency Health Powers Act

Article I   Title, Findings, Purposes and Definitions

Section 101—Short Title—Model State Emergency Health Powers Act

Section 102—Legislative Findings

Section 103—Purposes

Section 104—Definitions

Article II   Planning for a Public Health Emergency

Section 201—Public Health Emergency Planning Commission

Section 202—Public Health Emergency Plan

Article III   Measures to Detect and Track Public Health Emergencies

Section 301—Reporting

Section 302—Tracking

Section 303—Information Sharing

(*Continues*)

TABLE 12-5 Model State Emergency Health Powers Act (*Continued*)

Article IV Declaring a State of Public Health Emergency
Section 401—Declaration
Section 402—Content of Declaration
Section 403—Effect of Declaration
Section 404—Enforcement
Section 405—Termination of Declaration
Article V Special Powers During a State of Public Health Emergency—Management of Property
Section 501—Emergency Measures Concerning Facilities and Materials
Section 502—Access to and Control of Facilities and Property Generally
Section 503—Safe Disposal of Infectious Waste
Section 504—Safe Disposal of Human Remains
Section 505—Control of Healthcare Supplies
Section 506—Compensation
Section 507—Destruction of Property
Article VI Special Powers During a State of Public Health Emergency—Protection of Persons
Section 601—Protection of Persons
Section 602—Medical Examination and Testing
Section 603—Vaccination and Treatment
Section 604—Isolation and Quarantine
Section 605—Procedures for Isolation and Quarantine
Section 606—Collection of Laboratory Specimens—Performance of Tests
Section 607—Access to and Disclosure of Protected Health Information
Section 608—Licensing and Appointment of Health Personnel
Article VII Public Information Regarding Public Health Emergency
Section 701—Discrimination of Information
Section 702—Access to Mental Health Support Personnel
Article VIII Miscellaneous
Section 801—Titles
Section 802—Rules and Regulations
Section 803—Financing and Expenses
Section 804—Liability
Section 805—Compensation
Section 806—Severability
Section 807—Repeals
Section 808—Saving Clause
Section 809—Conflicting Laws
Section 810—Effective Date

Source: Courtesy of Lawrence Gostin, Stephen Teret, and James G. Hodge of publichealthlaw.net.

Case Study 12-B

Cloaking Public Health Leaders with Authority to Respond to Bioterrorism Threats or Events: One State's Struggle

By Judith W. Munson

Introduction

When the anthrax attacks occurred in the fall of 2001 immediately after the terrorist attacks of September 11, public health found itself in the unrelenting glare of the national media spotlight. It did not do well. Public health agencies, responding to the anthrax victims and determined to prevent further spread of the infecting bacteria, found that they were working with new and unfamiliar partners, most notably the private medical community, postal authorities, and law enforcement agencies at every level: local, state, and national. They scrambled for answers to questions about the behavior of the anthrax spores and sought confirmation in laboratory after laboratory that this was, in fact, *Bacillus anthracis* they were confronting. At first, assuming it was naturally occurring, they searched for the sites where *B. anthracis* could have been contracted. They were stunned to discover that it came through the mail and that it escaped through the pores of envelopes. Then, they were amazed to learn that it was dispersed throughout the post office by the sorting machines and the high-pressure cleaning devices used to maintain them.

Public health agency directors all around the nation watched the events as they unfolded; first in Florida, then in Washington, then in New York, and finally, in Connecticut. After it had finally played out, there were 18 confirmed cases of anthrax (11 inhalational, seven cutaneous), five deaths, and more than 30,000 individuals on prophylaxis.

Public health professionals, including agency directors, physicians, epidemiologists, environmental health practitioners, public health nurses, and many others, were horrified by what they and the nation were witnessing. They faced difficult questions. If it happened within their jurisdictions, did they have the legal authority to act? Did they have any emergency powers? Would they be able to act immediately to close a building contaminated by anthrax? Did they have the authority to detain everyone in the building for testing? Did they have the legal authority to require each exposed individual to be vaccinated? Or to command the administration of antibiotics? Or to isolate those infected and to quarantine those exposed? Suddenly, the newly hired chief counsel at the State Department of Public Health in Upper Midwestern State was bombarded by so many questions that he didn't know where to start. He had just moved into his new office on September 4, 2001, the day after Labor Day—one week before September 11—and now this.

The legal foundational authority of public health officials and public health agencies shot to the top of the national agenda. The nascent Public Health Law Program at the Centers for Disease Control and Prevention (CDC) in Atlanta became the fulcrum for this national initiative. By grant to Georgetown University Law Center and Johns Hopkins School of Public Health, the Center for Law and the Public's Health, a legally focused academic think tank, sprang into action. Within a few short weeks after the terrorist attacks on the World Trade Center and the Pentagon—and the anthrax attacks up and down the East Coast, now identified as incidents of bioterrorism—a model state emergency health powers act was drafted, vetted, revised, and circulated. Its provisions were responsive to the needs of public health agency directors to act authoritatively and with expanded powers within their jurisdictions in the event of a bioterrorism threat or event. The final version was ready for deployment in late December 2001. Within approximately six months, by June 2002, it was estimated that 34 states had introduced bills based on the provisions of this model act.

In Upper Midwestern State (UMS), the response to this model act was immediate: a high-profile senator sponsored a bill introducing the legislation in the state senate, and a highly respected state representative, a champion of public health legislation over the years, introduced it in the House of Representatives. Virtually duplicate bills, they were immediately criticized as threats to civil liberties. In addition to opposition from the group called Another Conscientious Legal Undercover Agent (ACLUA), other groups posted summaries of provisions they found objectionable in the bills. Their objections included most elements of the model act. Here is a sampling of their objections:

(The bills) create the Upper Midwestern State Emergency Health Powers Act and each of them

Authorizes $50,000,000 for expenses, approved by the governor, for any fiscal year

Allows the governor, by executive order, to declare a public health emergency if specific conditions are met

Gives the governor broad, unilateral emergency powers, including financial powers

Designates the state public health department as the public health authority and the department of state police as the public safety authority;

Provides for detecting, reporting, and tracking public health emergencies, and for disseminating information

Authorizes special powers over persons including medical exams, diagnostic tests, vaccinations, isolation and quarantine, and access to patients' health records

(*Continues*)

Provides for penalties and for trial courts to review quarantine orders and refusals to submit to vaccinations

Authorizes special powers for licensing and appointing health personnel

Provides for immunity from liability

Provides that the act overrules conflicting laws and regulations

Preempts home rule powers

Exempts actions from the reimbursement requirements of the State Mandate Act

Amends the code of civil procedure to authorize quick-take powers of eminent domain

Becomes effective immediately upon passage of law

Not only were civil liberty concerns driving the opposition to these bills, but turf issues were heightened when the UMS Emergency Management Agency perceived encroachment into the "emergency responsibility" arena by the UMS Department of Public Health. Public health was new to frontline response. Statutorily grounded emergency responders were unaccustomed to even having public health at the table, let alone in charge. The 2001 anthrax attacks had changed forever the nature of public health agencies, but other vested interests were not ready to yield authority—not just yet.

The end result was that, despite the five deaths and the 18 confirmed cases of anthrax on the East Coast, the model act was not going anywhere in Upper Midwestern State. The Senate bill was permanently stalled in the Senate rules committee, and the House bill ultimately suffered the same fate as well.

BTGAME

Upper Midwestern State was designated as a BTGAME site for the 2002–2003 bioterrorism simulation cycle. Congressionally funded, the exercise was designed to involve the heads of agencies at the federal, state, county, and municipal levels at two sites. BTGAME was designed as a five-day exercise involving a weapons of mass destruction (WMD) incident in Major Metro City in Upper Midwestern State and an explosion of radioactive material (a "dirty bomb") in a West Coast venue. Both sites involved governmental entities at multijurisdictional levels, including border issues with another country.

The BTGAME scenario in UMS featured the simultaneous release of a biological agent—pneumonic plague (*Yersinia pestis*)—at three locations in the Major Metro City area: the Big Game Center, the Major International Airport, and the Downtown Train Station. The attack would take place on Mother's Day, Sunday, May 11, 2003. The exercise would then play out over the next week, May 12–16, 2003. The planning for the events of that week began almost a year in advance. During the course of the yearlong planning process, Upper Midwestern State would experience a changeover in the governorship of the state—from Republican to Democratic—the first such changeover in 25 years, and an entirely new federal department would be created and come into being. The U.S. Department of Homeland Security was created in November 2002 and activated on January 24, 2003. It was the largest governmental reorganization in 50 years and would be an oversight agency for many of the activities in the BTGAME drill. By the time it became operational, the planning year was already half over.

The BTGAME exercise was preplanned. There were to be no surprises. The federal, state, county, and municipal levels of governmental agencies (e.g., public health, emergency management, and law enforcement)—as well as the participating private entities (e.g., hospitals)—were given scripts in advance. Some referred to BTGAME as an "open book" exam.

One important element of the exercise surfaced early because of the participation of the UMS Department of Public Health's chief counsel. He was concerned about the legal authority of the participating agencies: Did they have the authority to do what they were scripted to do? Did the legal foundations exist? For example, was the statute, or rule, or ordinance, or attorney general opinion, or judicial decision in place for the agencies to engage in a particular activity without exceeding legal bounds? If yes, then no problem; if no, then gaps needed to be identified and a legal bypass would be required, such as the drafting of executive orders for the governor to sign. The chief counsel could readily find the answers to these questions for the agency he advised—the UMS Department of Public Health—but were the legal counsels to the other agencies asking the same questions? These questions were considered to be of such importance that he decided to take action.

In an effort to address these issues and to be prepared to respond quickly when questions of legal authority were posited during the course of the exercise, the chief counsel convened a BTGAME legal team. The BTGAME legal team consisted of attorneys who provide legal counsel and services to the federal, state, county and municipal governmental agencies involved in the drill, as well as attorneys for private healthcare providers, professional associations, and academic institutions. It also included attorneys representing the interests of border state agencies. Nearly 30 agencies were invited to send their attorneys to attend the legal team meetings.

At the first BTGAME legal team meeting, the participants voted to meet monthly and quickly established sub-committees to address legal issues pertinent to

1. Emergency management/public health issues
2. Law enforcement issues
3. Border issues

Work proceeded continuously from September 2002 through April 2003. It was in April, the month before the exercise was to take place, that the result of all these efforts was produced in the form of a four-inch binder.

But during the course of the BTGAME legal team's early deliberations, much was going on in the General Assembly and the governor's office of Upper Midwestern State. In December 2002, the state representative who had always championed public health issues introduced HB 6. It was ready for first reading in January when the new General Assembly began its deliberations. After taking into consideration the many voices in disaster preparedness and response in UMS, the bill passed both houses and was signed into law in July 2003. Basically, the bill defined "public health emergency" and put the UMS Department of Public Health into the playing field for emergency response in the state, but that was all. No new powers for public health were included.

Another bill—introduced in the Senate in February 2003 by a leading senator and cosponsored by the president of the Senate—suffered a different outcome. This bill, SB 1742, initially simply a "shell" bill, was amended to allow the UMS Department of Public Health to isolate or quarantine without the prior consent of the individual or without a prior court order. Although the bill, as amended, was adopted in the House on May 31, 2003 (barely two weeks after the BTGAME exercise was concluded), it was referred to the Senate rules committee on the same day and did not resurface before the legislative session ended on July 1. No agreement on enhanced public health powers could be reached. It was dead.

On January 13, 2003, the new governor was sworn in. The first female attorney general of UMS took office on the same day. She was the former senator who was the first to introduce the State Emergency Health Powers Act into the Senate in November 2001—just a year earlier.

The BTGAME legal team binder contained the federal and state constitutions and all statutes, rules, regulations, court decisions, and opinions of the attorney general that had been identified for relevancy. For each of the items, a digest of the pertinent provisions was prepared and included as the first information sheet under each tab in the notebook. In the front cover pocket of the notebook, the BTGAME legal team emergency contact list was placed. By agency, it listed the name; title; phone, fax, cell, or pager numbers; and e-mail addresses of each participating member—in other words, all the attorneys for all the agencies taking part in the exercise. The notebook was titled *BTGAME Legal Team Handbook, April 2003.*

Compiling and assembling the *BTGAME Legal Team Handbook, April 2003*, was a monumental effort. It involved months of work on the part of the many attorneys participating in the legal team. It became the most valuable resource during the exercise—not only for the legal resources and analyses it contained, but for the ability to contact any other legal team member on a moment's notice. In addition, because of the meetings, they had met and were acquainted with the person they would be calling. They knew each other's names and recognized one another's faces.

But the notebook took on an importance in another context: by its comprehensiveness, it clearly identified where no law existed and where coverage was essential if Upper Midwestern State was to be prepared to respond instantly and effectively to a real-life bioterrorism threat or event. It highlighted the gaps of the present statutory scheme. It made the inadequacies of the public health legal authorities self-evident. It became the *raison d'etre* for revisiting the legal foundations of public health authority in Upper Midwestern State.

Still, with a new governor in the state capital, revisiting, updating, and reinforcing public health's legal authority was not high on the agenda. The BTGAME exercise took place. Public health laws remained the same. The gaps remained, except for the passage of HB 6, which defined public health emergency and made the UMS Department of Public Health a player in the emergency response capability of the State.

Monkeypox

The BTGAME exercise was barely concluded—the report on how well the Upper Midwestern State had performed would not be forthcoming for months—when a real and immediate threat surfaced. Unusual illnesses were being reported in the state. The illnesses signaled the emergence of a zoonotic infectious disease—in other words, a disease and infection that is transmitted between animals and humans. It was a rare viral disease. It had a name: monkeypox.

Monkeypox had never been seen in this country until it emerged in late May and early June 2003, in three nearby states (later, other states would report cases within their borders as well). Before June 2003, monkeypox was known as the cause of the smallpox-like human illnesses found only in Africa—and that was in 1970—more than 30 years earlier.

Upper Midwestern State's Department of Public Health provided the following description of monkeypox on its website:

> In humans, the signs and symptoms of monkeypox are similar to smallpox, but usually milder. About 12 days after people are infected with the virus, they may get a fever, headache, muscle aches and backache, swollen lymph nodes, and a general feeling of discomfort and exhaustion. Within one to three days after development of a fever, they will get a rash. The rash typically develops into raised bumps filled with fluid. It often starts on the face and spreads to other parts of the body, but can originate on other areas of the body. The bumps go through several stages before they get crusty, scab over, and fall off. A person is considered to be infectious to others until their lesions are crusted. The illness usually lasts for two to four weeks. If an exposed person does not develop signs or symptoms by the 21st day after the last exposure, they are unlikely to develop monkeypox.

In June 2003, monkeypox was traced to prairie dogs that were being sold by an exotic pet dealer in a suburb of Major Metro City. The disease was also linked to imported Gambian rats and other exotic animals. Monkeypox, closely akin to smallpox, required public health to act—and to act quickly. There was one major impediment: the UMS Department of Public Health had no authority over animals. UMS, and its sister states facing the same dilemma, looked to the federal level for help.

Federal Legal Action

The Secretary of the U.S. Department of Health and Human Services had authority over the introduction of communicable diseases from foreign countries and their spread from one state to another. Consequently, the CDC and the Food and Drug Administration (FDA) promulgated an interim final rule in November 2003 superseding a previous order issued by the agencies in June 2003.

The rule (paraphrased here) contains the following general prohibitions: It prohibits the importing of any rodents, whether dead or alive, obtained from Africa, or whose native habitat is Africa, plus any products derived from such rodents or any other animal whose importation has been prohibited by order, plus any products derived from such animals. The rule's import prohibition is intended to make clear that it covers any rodents (or other prohibited animals) that were caught in Africa and then shipped directly to the United States or shipped to other countries before being imported to the United States. The prohibition also applies to rodents whose native habitat is in Africa, even if those rodents were born elsewhere. This would apply to a Gambian giant pouched rat, for example, even if that animal was born outside Africa.

But the (now) well-seasoned chief counsel to the UMS Department of Public Health took the initiative on the state level as well.

State Legal Action

On June 7, 2003, the governor of Upper Midwestern State issued an executive order. Prepared by, and submitted to the governor by, the UMS Department of Public Health chief counsel, it identified the source of the orthopox (the family of viruses that includes monkeypox) virus as prairie dogs that had been in close proximity with Gambian rats, and it gave to the UMS Department of Public Health the lead responsibility in developing and implementing a plan for handling animals infected with or exposed to the orthopox virus. This included possible isolation or quarantine until the threat to the public's health had passed.

In addition, the executive order provided that

> Effective immediately, the following is prohibited in Upper Midwestern State with respect to prairie dogs or Gambian rats until the UMS Department of Public Health determines that the threat to the public health no longer exists: importation, sale or distribution, public display, or any other activity that could result in unnecessary human contact.

The executive order also gave the UMS Department of Public Health the responsibility for evaluating the presence of the virus in places that housed the infected animals and implementing a plan for their disposition. In addition, the UMS Department of Public Health was to immediately undertake all appropriate epidemiological investigations and communicable disease precautions to protect the public. UMS Department of Public Health was to consult with the UMS Department of Agriculture, and all other state agencies were directed to assist in the implementation of the order.

At no time during the outbreak was there any evidence of person-to-person transmission of the disease. In all cases, the infected individual had contact with an infected prairie dog. At the time of the order, there was one human case of monkeypox in Upper Midwestern State; there were 12 cases in the state bordering on the north. There were no deaths due to monkeypox at any time during or after the outbreak.

The executive order was an unusual step for the governor to take—to give the state public health agency all of these powers. Still, no legislation was introduced that would provide the UMS Department of Public Health with the ongoing authority to act in circumstances such as these, where an emerging infectious zoonotic disease—never before seen in the Unified States—was threatening the health of the people of the state.

SARS

Severe acute respiratory syndrome (SARS) made its public debut on the world stage in February 2003. It later developed that cases had been occurring in China's Guangdong Province since November 2002. The World Health Organization (WHO) stated that it was to be the "first severe and readily transmissible new disease to emerge in the 21st century." SARS emerged as an atypical pneumonia, baffling doctors and public health experts. Symptoms included high fever, dry cough, myalgia, and mild sore throat. These are not high-alert symptoms. It was when these symptoms quickly developed into bilateral pneumonia and then into acute respiratory distress—followed by death, in some cases—that alarms went off. Cases were being diagnosed in Hong Kong and Vietnam. According to WHO:

> SARS was carried out of Guangdong Province on 21 February by an infected medical doctor who had treated patients in his home town. He brought the virus to the ninth floor of a four-star hotel in Hong Kong. Days later, guests and visitors to the hotel's ninth floor had seeded outbreaks of cases in the hospital systems of Hong Kong, Vietnam, and Singapore. Simultaneously, the disease began spreading around the world along international air travel routes as guests at the hotel flew home to Trendy City, Canada, and elsewhere, and as other medical doctors who had treated the earliest cases in Vietnam and Singapore traveled internationally for medical or other reasons.

In March 2003, the disease broke out among healthcare workers in hospitals in Hong Kong and Hanoi. These developments prompted the first WHO global alert on March 12, 2003. Within days, the new disease had spread around the world, from Hong Kong to Vietnam to Singapore and to Trendy City. When it became obvious that SARS was being spread by air travel, the WHO issued a heightened global health alert, including a rare "emergency travel advisory."

SARS, its virulence and its transmissibility, were being watched by public health professionals around the world, including those at the UMS Department of Public Health. SARS was new, and it was deadly. There was no vaccine to prevent it, and there was no known medicine that would cure it. No one was yet sure they knew all the ways in which transmission occurred. No one was yet sure what caused the disease. What was known almost immediately, however, was that the healthcare workers treating patients in the hospitals were at great risk. Infection control measures and the control tools dating back to the earliest days of empirical microbiology—isolation and quarantine—were pressed back into service.

The WHO worked tirelessly to combat this new disease: electronically interconnecting public health professionals and laboratories; establishing electronic reporting of new cases and deaths on a daily basis; deploying teams expert in infection control to hot spots; and at the end of March, recommending airport screening.

But for Upper Midwestern State, it was the news on March 14 that had the most immediate significance: the Canadian government reported that "there were four cases of atypical pneumonia within a single family in Trendy City that had resulted in two deaths." Not only was SARS now in North America, it was just north of the border of a nearby state. If it could get there, it could get anywhere—even to Upper Midwestern State.

SARS in Trendy City, Canada

The news from north of the border was alarming:

- On April 23, 2003, the WHO recommended persons planning to travel to Trendy City consider postponing all but essential travel. The warning was lifted a week later, but the damage to the city's tourism industry was devastating. Canadian Broadcasting System (CBS) News reported that "preliminary estimates put initial losses for hotels and restaurants at tens of millions of dollars."
- On May 31, 2003, Trendy City went back on the WHO list of areas with local transmission for the second time. Canada reported 26 suspected and eight probable cases of the disease linked to four Trendy City hospitals.
- On July 2, 2003, WHO again removed Trendy City from its list of areas with recent local transmission.

(Continues)

But the total assessment of the economic damage that SARS inflicted upon Trendy City was yet to come. In August 2003, it was reported that:

> The provincial conservative government is being forced to withdraw $1 billion from its reserve and contingency funds because of the economic impact of SARS.

This was sobering news, especially to Upper Midwestern State, where the Major Metro City area attracts close to 30 million visitors each year, and those visitors spend nearly $9 billion annually. This produces $500 million in tax revenue for UMS and the greater Major Metro City area. The possibility of a Trendy City-type economic setback on Upper Midwestern State and Major Metro City was highly disturbing.

Legal Responses to SARS

The final tally of SARS cases and deaths around the globe was relatively small: on September 26, 2003, the WHO reported a total of 8,098 cases with a total of 774 deaths from SARS for the period November 2002 to July 31, 2003. By contrast, it is generally known that an average of 36,000 people die of influenza-related complications each year in the United States. Nonetheless, public health scrambled to contain and defeat an epidemic of a newly emerging disease with legal authorities that were outdated, outmoded, obsolete, and inadequate. This was true at all intervention levels: international, national, state or province, and local.

The International Front

The WHO, at the time of the SARS epidemic, found its own International Health Regulations (IHR) to be in urgent need of revision and updating. The last major revision was in 1969. This new undertaking is of such importance that the first European Union (EU) Commissioner of Health and Consumer Protection has been appointed special envoy for the WHO for the revision of the IHR. Final revisions are expected to be presented to the World Health Assembly at its meeting in May 2005. Working toward the goal of containing the international spread of disease, the IHR revisions will improve upon early detection of threats, the response and management of the threats through global cooperation and collaboration, and the communication among institutions and member states and the WHO office. The need for these improvements came from the SARS experience.

The National Front

In the United States, on the national level, the president issued an executive order on April 4, 2003, that added Severe Acute Respiratory Syndrome (SARS) to the list of quarantinable communicable diseases under the National Public Health Act. Although the WHO's tally of SARS cases globally reflected that, in the United States, there were 29 cases and no deaths due to SARS as of July 31, 2003, others counted far fewer, claiming there were only eight laboratory-confirmed cases of SARS corona virus, with all the patients recovering. Nonetheless, the listing of diseases for which quarantine was legally provided was updated. Months later, on Tuesday, January 13, 2004, the Secretary of the U.S. Department of HHS announced the immediate embargo on the importation of civets (the animals suspected of transmitting SARS to humans) to the United States.

In Canada, where the total number of SARS cases as of the end of July 2003 was 251, with 43 deaths, legal action was more immediate and definitive. The first action was to designate SARS a communicable, virulent, and reportable disease. Without this designation, the Ministry of Health had no authority to quarantine people or to require reports to be submitted. A second change was to amend the Public Health Protection Act to permit a judge to order an individual quarantined in a facility other than a hospital.

The State Front

At the state level, legal actions took a variety of turns.

In the provinces of Canada, the provincial chief medical officers for health have been granted greater independence. No longer appointed by the minister of health, they are appointed by the lieutenant governor. The chief medical officers can now take action when presented with a public health emergency.

In Upper Midwestern State, the governor's office asked the chief counsel of the UMS Department of Public Health to reconvene the BTGAME legal team and to work with the state representative who championed public health causes to get needed legislation through the General Assembly.

UMS Department of Public Health's chief counsel responded quickly. For this particular task, the reconvened BTGAME team would take on a new name. The bioterrorism exercise was over, and now it was time to address the realistic threat posed by the SARS experience around the globe. The group became the Public Health Emergency Preparedness Legal Team. A legislative subcommittee was established to craft a bill that would give public health the legal authorities needed to address not only bioterrorism threats or events but newly emerging and zoonotic infectious diseases as well.

The legislative subcommittee, greatly encouraged by the unprecedented participation of the state representative who had initially introduced the Model State Emergency Health Powers Act into the House, went right to work. Seeking to maximize the potential for enacting enhanced public health emergency powers, the subcommittee invited those early detractors to participate this time. For example, the group called Another Conscientious Legal Undercover Agent (ACLUA), so vocal in opposition in the past, was a willing participant this time around. Also invited were representatives from the associations of private medical practitioners and trial lawyers. From time to time, the group was joined by the chief legislative assistant to the Speaker of the House. In UMS, this was truly unprecedented. It signaled a level of importance in the deliberations that was felt throughout the room.

Established in October 2003, the subcommittee met often: sometimes fortnightly, sometimes monthly; sometimes in person, sometimes via teleconference, and sometimes by video conference. The subcommittee was chaired by the chief counsel to the UMS Department of Public Health.

The subcommittee drafted a 47-page bill that was introduced into the House by the state representative in January 2004. It established the following new public health powers:

- To order a person or a group of persons to be quarantined or a place to be closed and made off limits to the public on an immediate basis without prior notice or prior consent or court order if, in the reasonable judgment of the department, immediate action is required to protect the public from a dangerously contagious or infectious disease
- To order physical examinations, tests, vaccinations, collection of laboratory specimens, medications, or observation and monitoring
- To examine, test, disinfect, seize, or destroy animals or other related property believed to be sources of infection in order to prevent the spread of a dangerously contagious or infectious disease in the human population
- To gain emergency access to medical records
- To develop a statewide system for syndromic data collection
- To share information with law enforcement
- To modify the scope of practice for licensed or certified professionals

At every stage, care and attention was directed to due process concerns and protecting the civil liberties of the citizens of UMS. Other interests represented in the deliberations were heard as well. Whenever someone insisted upon a particular position and tensions were heightened in the room, the state representative reminded everyone of the specter of the public health threat that was the motivating energy behind this effort. The chief counsel, as chair, would initiate a move toward the positions of the detractors. When the meetings were concluded, there was consensus around the table.

The state representative introduced the bill hammered out in this deliberative process. Because potential voices of organized opposition had been heard in the meetings, there were no objections raised during the deliberations in the General Assembly. The bill passed the House unanimously. When it arrived in the Senate, it was sponsored by a rising star on the national stage and, once again, no opposition emerged. That meant it passed in the Senate unanimously as well. It went to the governor. It was signed into law on July 28, 2004, and it became effective immediately.

Conclusion

The Upper Midwestern State (UMS) Department of Public Health finally has the statutory authority it needs. The statutes now provide that it can respond quickly and authoritatively to bioterrorism threats or events and to "dangerously contagious or infectious disease(s)" whether from an animal or human source. But it took three years to do it. Why so long? Was it the specter of an anthrax attack that was the motivation behind these new authorities? Or was it the threat of another bioterrorism pathogen, e.g., pneumonic plague, as in the BTGAME exercise? Or was it the possibility of an outbreak of another zoonotic disease never before seen on this continent (e.g., monkeypox) directly within its own borders—right in its own front yard? Or was it directly in response to a newly emerging infectious disease of global implications (SARS) that prompted these enhancements to public health's legal foundational authorities? Possibly not; possibly none of them was enough, by itself, to provide the motivation for these changes.

Looking at the sequence of public health emergencies in UMS since 9/11, and the fits and starts of legislative initiatives designed to address them, it appears that it was the economic devastation that SARS brought to Trendy City, Canada, that ultimately accomplished what all the other dramatic events could not. SARS was barely even in this country and certainly not in UMS at all. So the disease itself was not, by itself, the motivator. Possibly, just possibly, it was the economic meltdown of Trendy City's tourism industry—the impact of SARS on all those businesses and all those jobs closely associated with them—that provided the impetus to make the necessary changes in the laws of UMS. Whatever the ultimate motivating factor might have been, the conclusion has now been written: the governor's office, the state representative, the legislative assistant to the Speaker of the House, the rising star of the Senate, and the entire General Assembly backed the efforts of the chief counsel of the UMS Department of Public Health. They all acted swiftly, thoroughly, and definitively. Now, at last, Upper Midwestern State is legally prepared for any foreseen (and, it is hoped, for any unforeseen) public health emergency.

model that is available in some states to develop a local public health mutual aid and assistance system. The goal of this approach is to have local governmental public health entities work together as partners during an emergency event. What these memoranda do is establish a statewide system. Depending on the plan, the personnel, equipment, supplies, and services of a local health entity from another community than the one in which the crisis occurs will come into the jurisdiction of another local public health department to help them during the emergency.

HEALTH INSURANCE PORTABILITY AND ACCOUNTABILITY ACT OF 1996 (HIPAA)

The issue of privacy of records and the protection of individual rights leads to a brief discussion of HIPAA. The public health leader must always be aware of the issue of privacy and the protection of individual rights. Today, there is increasing concern about the government or other entities being able to access the health records of individuals without their express approval. At least 20% of Americans believe that a healthcare provider, insurance company or plan, government agency, or employer has accessed personal health information in an improper manner.[20] What people are concerned about is how this information is used. It has become easier to access information in the modern computer age.[21] To this must be added the "collect more" phenomenon. There has also been an increase in the collection of person-specific data where earlier data were collected more in an aggregated form. However, data are not always readily released. They are released in a limited way to a more widely distributed audience. It is possible to think of data release on a continuum from limited to no-restrictions release.

Another issue relates to the identification of data and the anonymity of individuals.[22] There is also the availability of personal information on the Internet to

consider. The critical issue thus becomes how data can be protected. Sweeney discussed several different methods.[23] A few examples are the following:

1. Scrambling information
2. Encryption (scrambling data and hiding the key to unscrambling it)
3. Utilization of partial identifying information, such as using a birth year but not the birth date
4. Datafly (replacement of a Social Security number with a one-way encryption, for example, so that longitudinal data can be collected but specific identifiers are hidden)
5. Safe Harbor (list of data fields that cannot be released)

There are many different approaches to protecting data.

HIPAA was an attempt to deal with the issue of confidentiality. Public health leaders are clearly caretakers of personal information. There need to be guidelines for the protection of the rights of individuals and their personal information. The primary purpose of HIPAA initially was to make sure that individuals could maintain insurance coverage even in those circumstances where they needed to change jobs.[24] The act (Health Insurance Portability and Accountability Act—PL 104-191) includes provisions to administratively simplify and streamline the health services contacts that an individual has and the method of payment of these services. The act also provides for the establishment of privacy and security standards that were adjudged necessary to protect health information about individuals. A privacy rule was published by the U.S. Department of Health and Human Services in December 2000. The privacy rule mandated that security methods must be in place to protect health information by April 14, 2003.

The important concern for the public health leader is the need to know the details of HIPAA and how to address these privacy and security issues. The concerns over emergency preparedness and response also require a look at these same issues when police powers are implemented to address a crisis. The release of certain types of information may be critical during a terrorist act when people are injured and it is necessary to gain access to personal health information that can affect the treatment plan of the injured.

LAW AND HEALTH OUTCOMES

Laws, rules, and regulations are meant to be living documents. In public health, we look to them to determine how these laws, rules, and regulations help to prevent injury, disease, and death. We also want to determine if health outcomes improve as a result of these laws and regulations. The Institute of Medicine studied these issues in 2010–2011.[25] These issues are important as we look at the effects of economic crisis, health reform, shrinking governmental funds for public health and preparedness activities, and changing public health legislation. The IOM study committee came up with several policy recommendations for the future:

1. All public health laws need to be reviewed and modernized if necessary
2. States and local jurisdictions need to enact legislation with appropriate funding to fulfill legislative mandates
3. Laws should be revised to require that state and local health departments get accredited
4. All health departments should have access to a public health legal counsel

5. Throughout the public health system, minimum standards need to be set to further protect the health and safety of the public
6. Enforcement approaches need to occur regardless of who is responsible for carrying them out

PUBLIC HEALTH ETHICS

In recent years, there has been much discussion about the importance of ethical standards and their importance for every civilized society. The difficulty of developing an ethics code for public health is partially related to the population-based focus of the field. It is difficult to make the jump from the ethical behavior of a person to the ethical behavior of the population as a whole.[26] The ethics of public health professionals should not be perceived as different from the ethical behavior of any other governmental official or any other health professional. The place to look for an existing set of ethical principles is the Universal Declaration of Human Rights, adopted by the United Nations in 1948. The declaration is summarized in **Figure 12-2**. In addition, there is a need for a public health ethics statement.[27] The values of public health can serve as the foundation for such a set of ethical principles. However, the development of such a set of ethical principles would not be an easy task. The way to address ethics in public health is to not stress the abstractions of codes and principles, but rather to look at the way professionals practice public health for the knowledge of the real ethical principles that guide our work.[28]

1. People are born to be free with equal rights for all.
2. All people have the right of life, liberty, and personal security.
3. No person should be held in servitude or subjected to torture.
4. All people are equal and have recognition rights before the law and fair judicial remedies.
5. People charged with a felony should be considered innocent until proven guilty.
6. All people have the right to a nationality.
7. All have the right to marry and have a family.
8. People can own property.
9. People have the right to freedom of thought, opinion, and expression.
10. The right to freedom of assembly exists for all.
11. All can participate in government or elect representatives and all have the right to equal access for public services.
12. Social security is a right, as is the right to work for equal pay for equal work.
13. All people have the right to rest and recreation.
14. All have the right to a good standard of living with housing, food, and good medical care.
15. All have the right to a good education.
16. All have the right to participate in community life.

FIGURE 12-2 **Summary of Universal Declaration of Human Rights.** *Source*: Adapted from United Nations General Assembly (1948). The Universal Declaration of Human Rights. http://www.un.org/en/documents/udhr/. Accessed July 13, 2012.

In examining the issue of public health ethics, there are a number of moral considerations that need to be made.[29] There is first the question of the benefits of the public health services to be provided to the public. Public health professionals have to be careful to avoid or prevent harmful activities from happening. There is clearly the additional consideration of public health equity and the provision of services and programs to all people in the community regardless of background. Public health professionals need to remain cognizant that people have choices and the freedom to make them. The privacy and confidentiality of the service population also needs to be guaranteed. It is important also to keep our promises and commitments to the public and to our partners in health. Public health professionals must always be truthful and work to maintain the trust of our constituents.

An interesting experiment was undertaken by the Public Health Leadership Society (PHLS), an organization made up of alumni of the national Public Health Leadership Institute. The society has developed a set of ethical principles for public health.[30] There were some underlying assumptions to the 12 ethical principles in the code. The developers believed that people are interdependent and this interdependence is the critical element in the growth of communities. Public health needs to see this relationship between people and their communities. Health of the public is tied to their life in the community. It was also stated that the code was intended for governmental public health and related agencies in the United States. **Table 12-6** lists the 12 Principles for the Ethical Practice of Public Health. These principles are based on the following 11 values and beliefs of American society:[31]

1. Humans have a right to the resources necessary for health.
2. Humans are inherently social and interdependent.
3. The effectiveness of institutions depends heavily on the public's trust.
4. Collaboration is a key element of public health.
5. People and their physical environment are interdependent.
6. Each person in a community should have an opportunity to contribute to the public discourse.
7. Identifying and promoting the fundamental requirements for health in a community are of primary concern to public health.
8. Knowledge is important and powerful.

TABLE 12-6 Principles of the Ethical Practice of Public Health

1. Public health should address principally the fundamental causes of disease and requirements for health, aiming to prevent adverse health outcomes.
2. Public health should achieve community health in a way that respects the rights of individuals in the community.
3. Public health policies, programs, and priorities should be developed and evaluated through processes that ensure an opportunity for input from community members.
4. Public health should advocate and work for the empowerment of disenfranchised community members, aiming to ensure that the basic resources and conditions necessary for health are accessible to all.
5. Public health should seek the information needed to implement effective policies and programs that protect and promote health.
6. Public health institutions should provide communities with the information they have that is needed for decisions on policies or programs and should obtain the community's consent for their implementation.
7. Public health institutions should act in a timely manner on the information they have within the resources and the mandate given to them by the public.
8. Public health programs and policies should incorporate a variety of approaches that anticipate and respect diverse values, beliefs, and cultures in the community.
9. Public health programs and policies should be implemented in a manner that most enhances the physical and social environment.
10. Public health institutions should protect the confidentiality of information that can bring harm to an individual or community if made public. Exceptions must be justified on the basis of the high likelihood of significant harm to the individual or others.
11. Public health institutions should ensure the professional competence of their employees.
12. Public health institutions and their employees should engage in collaborations and affiliations in ways that build the public's trust and the institution's effectiveness.

Source: Reproduced from Public Health Leadership Society (2002). *Principles of the Ethical Practice of Public Health*. New Orleans, PHLS.

9. Science is the basis for much of our public health knowledge.
10. People are responsible to act on the basis of their personal knowledge.
11. Action is not based on information alone.

A BRIEF REVIEW ON ADVOCACY

An important responsibility for the prepared public health leader is to not only advocate for public health, but also be a spokesperson for the role of public health during crises. The Trust for America's Health has defined the advocate as an individual who defends and fights for the cause or petitions of others.[32] If you as a leader want to be an effective advocate, it is important to follow these five steps:

1. Identify whom you want to persuade.
2. Know the facts and do your homework.
3. Start to communicate with policy makers.
4. Begin to advocate this very day.
5. Always follow up.

Foundations have pointed out that it is important to evaluate the effectiveness of advocacy activities. In a report from the Annie E. Casey Foundation, it is argued that advocacy and policy change activities need to be evaluated for effect.[33] Although the outcomes are numerous, leaders need to determine such issues as whether the advocacy effort led to an increased awareness of the issue, more knowledge among elected officials of the severity of the issue or problem, clear determination of the actions to take to address the issue, salience of the issue, changes in the support of the issue, changes in voting on the issue, and passage of new legislation.

SUMMARY

This chapter has pointed to the critical concern that knowledge of the law involves an important set of competencies for the prepared public health leader. The legal competencies were reviewed as well as model public health practice statutes. The concern over the loss of personal rights is an important issue. How a state and local health agency exercises its police powers during emergencies is also a concern. A discussion of HIPAA was also presented. Legal recommendations for the future were mentioned, and this was followed by a discussion of public health ethics and the ethics code developed by the Public Health Leadership Society. Finally, the issue of advocacy was briefly presented.

DISCUSSION QUESTIONS

1. What is the relationship between law and policy?
2. Why do we need public health laws?
3. Compare the state public health act in your state with the model act.
4. What is HIPAA?
5. What are the ethical standards for public health, and how do we use them?

EXERCISE 12-1: Legal Research

Purpose: to use the Internet or library to learn about legal terminology

Key concepts: public health law, statutes, ordinance

Procedures: Use the Internet or library to answer the questions.

1. Where, in your jurisdiction, can you find the actual text of the following:
   State statutes
   State regulations
   Local municipal codes
   State judicial opinions
2. Have you ever used a law library to find such material? How would you describe the experience?
3. What do the following citations mean?
   Fla. Stat. § 828, 12 (1987)
   40 CFR Subpart A, § 46.101
   Ordinance 87–40
   494 U.S. 829 (1989)?
4. How would you go about determining if certain physical conditions amount to a "public nuisance"? Would you look to statute/code or the common law? Whom could you contact to get this information?

REFERENCES

1. B. Neuberger and T. Christoffel, *The Legal Basis of Public Health* (Atlanta: CDC Public Health Training Network, 2002).
2. L. O. Gostin, *Public Health Law* (Berkeley: University of California Press, 2008).
3. Gostin, *Public Health Law.*
4. Neuberger and Christoffel, *The Legal Basis of Public Health.*
5. Gostin, *Public Health Law.*
6. Gostin, *Public Health Law.*
7. Gostin, *Public Health Law.*
8. J. W. Munson, *The Public Health Law 101 Series* (introductory workshop) (Chicago: University of Illinois at Chicago Summer Institute, 2004).
9. Public Health Law Program, *Public Health Law 101* (Atlanta: CDC, 2004).
10. Neuberger and Christoffel, *The Legal Basis of Public Health* (Atlanta: CDC, 2002).
11. Center for Law and the Public's Health, *Core Legal Competencies for Public Health Professionals* (Baltimore: Johns Hopkins University, 2001).
12. Centers for Disease Control and Prevention, *Public Health's Infrastructure: A Status Report* (Atlanta: CDC, 2001).
13. L. O. Gostin and J. G. Hodge Jr., *State Public Health Law: Assessment Report* (Baltimore: Center for Law and the Public's Health, 2002).
14. Gostin and Hodge, *State Public Health Law: Assessment Report.*
15. Gostin and Hodge, *State Public Health Law: Assessment Report.*
16. www.publichealthlaw.net/ModelLaws/MSPHA.php. Accessed December 3, 2011.
17. Center for Law and the Public's Health, *Model State Emergency Health Powers Act* (Baltimore: Johns Hopkins University, 2001).
18. J. G. Hodge Jr., *The Model State Emergency Powers Act: State Legislative Activity* (Baltimore: Center for Law and the Public's Health, 2004).
19. www.publichealthlaw.net/ModelLaws/MSEHPA.php. Accessed December 3, 2011.
20. J. Lumpkin, "HIPAA in Context," *Leadership in Public Health* 4, no. 4 (2002), 3–12.
21. L. Sweeney, "Sharing Data Under HIPAA," *Leadership in Public Health* 4, no. 4 (2002), 13–27.
22. Sweeney, "Sharing Data Under HIPAA."
23. Sweeney, "Sharing Data Under HIPAA."
24. D. Mool, "Overview of the HIPAA Colloquium: Implementation in Illinois," *Leadership in Public Health* 4, no. 4 (2002), 1–2.
25. Institute of Medicine, *For the Public's Health: Revitalizing Law and Policy to Meet New Challenges* (Washington, DC: National Academies Press, 2011).
26. W. K. Mariner, "The Search for Public Health Ethics," *Leadership in Public Health* 5, no. 3 (2000), 3–13.
27. Mariner, "The Search for Public Health Ethics."
28. D. Swartzman, "Finding Ethics in Public Health," *Leadership in Public Health* 5, no. 3 (2000), 14–15.
29. J. F. Childress, R. D. Gaare, L. O. Gostin, J. Kahn, R. J. Bonnie, N. E. Kass, et al. "Public Health Ethics: Mapping the Terrain." *Journal of Law, Medicine, and Ethics* 30 (2002), 170–178.
30. Public Health Leadership Society, *Principles of the Ethical Practice of Public Health* (New Orleans: PHLS, 2002).
31. PHLS, *Principles of the Ethical Practice of Public Health.*
32. Trust for America's Health, *You, Too, Can Be an Effective Public Health Advocate* (Washington, DC: TFAH, 2003).
33. J. Reisman, A. Gienapp, and S. Stachowiak, *A Guide to Measuring Advocacy and Policy* (Baltimore: Annie E. Casey Foundation, 2007).

CHAPTER 13

Leadership and Assurance

Be sure it's done well by you or others.

K. Gebbie, Speech to the Illinois Public
Health—Leadership Institute

The core functions of public health, for the sake of explanation, can be viewed as a series of interactive steps. First comes assessment—the evaluation of the health status of a community, including the health risks it is facing. Next comes policy development—the creation of plans to deal with the community's health problems, or at least those that are given a high priority because they have serious consequences and can be dealt with effectively. Finally comes assurance, which largely consists of the implementation of the plans developed during the second stage. Assurance, in a phrase, involves ensuring that the public's health is protected and, hopefully, even improved.

Of course, these three core functions are all ongoing, interactive, and overlapping. Changes occur in a community and new problems arise, so evaluations of the community's health status must occur regularly. Newly uncovered problems call for new solutions, so

policies must be developed continually as well. And assurance is obviously a continuous function, for it involves the development, implementation, and maintenance of public health programs. Because assurance is a community-wide set of activities, public health leadership is needed to coordinate it.

OVERVIEW

Prevention

Assurance activities focus on disease prevention and health promotion. Primary prevention involves creating an environment in which disease will not come into being—the ultimate public health goal. Secondary prevention involves intervening when problems occur and implementing major initiatives to prevent the consequences from becoming worse. Tertiary prevention involves stopping the progression of a disease or disability in order to prevent dependency. As one writer put it, prevention of health problems is essentially equivalent to public health.[1]

The three levels of prevention are usually presented linearly, but a circular representation would seem to be more appropriate (**Figure 13-1**), because an intervention initiated at one level will affect activities at the other two levels. For example, the discovery of a new vaccine to prevent a childhood disease will lead to an immunization strategy at the primary prevention level. If the strategy is successful, the disease will become less prevalent, making secondary and tertiary strategies for dealing with the disease less critical, perhaps to the point where they can be abandoned. A new treatment for a disease (secondary prevention) may lead to the discovery of a vaccine to prevent the disease (primary prevention) as well as reduce the long-term harmful effects of the disease, lessening the need for rehabilitation (tertiary prevention). The virtual eradication of polio shows how scientific research, leadership, and prevention can work together creatively.

INFRASTRUCTURE

Public health agencies provide services to their communities on a regular basis, but they also are responsible for maintaining the capacity to respond to critical situations and emergencies. The term "capacity" is used extensively in public health. In 1994, the Washington State Department of Health's Public Health Improvement Plan defined capacity as the ability to perform the core functions of assessment, policy development, and assurance on a continuous, consistent basis, made possible by maintenance of the basic infrastructure of the public health system, including human, capital, and technology resources.[2]

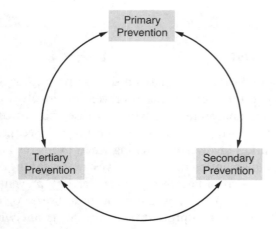

FIGURE 13-1 The Cycle of Prevention.

A public health charter was presented in a 1990 report that laid out an agenda for strengthening the infrastructure of public health in Illinois. Two articles of the charter[3] are relevant to the assurance function:

Article III: Categories of Public Health Services to Be Assured

Public health workers in Illinois have established five categories of public health services that further the mission of public health and are appropriate to the governmental role in public health. These are: Health Promotion; Primary Care; Environmental Health; Infectious Disease Control; and Health Care Regulation.

Article IV: Guiding Principles for Restructuring the Public Health System in Illinois

The following principles should guide the restructuring of governmental public health responsibilities in Illinois. The principles enumerated below are predicated on the belief that most services to public health clients are most efficiently and effectively provided at the local level by local health units:

1. The delivery of public health services in the State of Illinois should be improved.
2. The societal benefits derived from public health services should be more effectively communicated.
3. The quality of public health services provided in Illinois should be improved and standardized.
4. The funding of public health services should be increased.

The implementation of these principles has required leadership to drive their implementation. There was a clear shift in these principles from a program-oriented model to the core functions approach. Leadership is also required to keep the principles in force and to enhance the state requirements for local health department certification with the new national voluntary accreditation program.[4]

BARRIERS

An Institute of Medicine report on public health described a number of barriers to carrying out the assurance function.[5] To begin with, the roles of the state and local health departments vary from state to state, and the patterns of assurance activities performed by these departments differ as well. Four states did not even have official local health departments (Delaware, Hawaii, Rhode Island, and Vermont).[6] In seven states, the state health department operates all the local health departments (Arkansas, Florida, Louisiana, Mississippi, New Mexico, South Carolina, and Virginia), whereas the remaining states either possess completely decentralized systems or use a mixed approach.

Differences in funding sources also contribute to the variation in the types of assurance activities performed.[7] One result of the variation in assurance activities is that universal access to services is not a reality for many segments of the population. Even in the case of population-based initiatives, such as communicable disease control, the benefits are inequitably distributed.

Public health agencies and their leaders need to be proactive rather than reactive in the area of assurance. Public health leaders often seem to sit on their hands and allow other entities to decide what the role of public health agencies is to be. One difficulty they face is that, in the United States at least, public health and politics are so intertwined that it is often impossible to know which is which. Nonetheless, they need to make certain that the communities they serve receive the services that are needed to attain agreed health objectives,[8] either by having the public health agencies provide the services or ensuring, through regulation, that they are provided by other public or private health organizations. Assurance of adequate services is guaranteed by social contract. Living up to the guarantee can be difficult, for it often requires subsidization or direct provision of personal health services for those who cannot afford them.

At the federal level, assurance involves making services available that are needed to deal with nationwide problems, such as human immunodeficiency virus (HIV) transmission, and at the state level, it involves providing public health services that are needed statewide. Local public health agencies have the responsibility of ensuring "that high quality services, including personal health services, needed for the protection of public health in the community are available and accessible to all persons; that the community receives proper consideration in the allocation of federal and state as well as local resources for public health, and that the community is informed about how to obtain public health, including personal health, services, or how to comply with public health requirements."[9(p.143)] These same points are reiterated in the 2003 Institute of Medicine report on public health.[10]

Public health leaders must:

- ensure the development of priority public health programs
- explore multiple public and private funding sources for programs
- stress population-based and evidence-based program development
- start programs with a primary prevention focus
- use governance to support prevention activities
- encourage capacity-building activities in local health departments
- build community partnerships to support programs

THE ROLE OF LEADERSHIP IN ASSURANCE

There are four essential public health services associated with the assurance core function. A fifth essential service, the research dimension, is a systems integrating service but also can be considered part of the assurance function. It will be included under assurance in order to complete our discussion of the three core functions.

The first essential service is related to the enforcement of laws and regulations that protect health and ensure safety; it has important leadership implications. This essential service is also an interface between the core functions of policy development and assurance. This essential service includes the following three performance indicators.[11]

1. The local public health system reviews existing laws and regulations related to public health in the community.
2. The local public health system is involved in the improvement of laws, regulations, and ordinances.
3. The local public health system recognizes the necessity of enforcement of laws, regulations, and ordinances.

The second essential service involves connecting people in the community to needed personal health services and the necessity of ensuring that necessary services are provided. The leaders in the system need to coordinate their efforts in searching for new resources and restructuring the public health agency and the public health system to better meet community health needs. Utilizing the two performance indicators in the National Public Health Performance Standards Program[12] with the two performance standards discussed by Turnock and colleagues on organizational practices,[13] the multidimensional aspect of this essential service can be seen:

1. The local public health system is able to identify the personal health needs of the local population.
2. The local public health system is able to ensure the linkage to needed community services.
3. The local public health system addresses its programs.
4. The local public health system provides services to meet priority health needs.

The third essential service relates to the important issue of ensuring that there is a competent public health and health services workforce to serve the needs of people in the community. There are four performance standards enumerated in the National Public Health Performance Standards instrument for local public health systems.[14] To this list of four must be added the additional standard discussed by Turnock and his colleagues on professional and regulatory standards.[15] The five performance indicators are:

1. There is a need to do workforce assessments at the national, state, and local levels and then plan for recruiting new professionals into public health.
2. The local public health system needs to demonstrate compliance with professional and regulatory standards.
3. The local public health system will develop and maintain public health workforce standards required at the local level.
4. The local public health system will require public health professionals to get any special training necessary to carry out their jobs. They will support a lifelong learning model.
5. Public health professionals will get management and leadership training.

The fourth essential public health service related to assurance involves evaluation to measure effectiveness of programs, accessibility to these programs, and the quality of population-based services. Feedback data are gathered and looked at to determine if programs need to be revised or resources redirected in order to deal with problems that have arisen during implementation. The behavioral and social sciences have developed many methodological techniques for evaluating public agencies. Public health leaders need to support program evaluation, be involved in evaluating data, and adopt a system of performance monitoring. All

these activities will strengthen the functioning of the local agency. There are four program indicators for this essential service:[16]

1. The local public health system evaluates population-based services and programs.
2. The local public health system evaluates personal health services and programs.
3. The local public health system evaluates the system.
4. If changes in programs are necessary, the agency revises programs based on evaluation and quality assurance activities.

The final essential service involves research related to new insights and innovations for addressing public health challenges. This final essential service can be seen as an assurance function as well as a systems integrating function. There are three performance indicators for this essential service:[17]

1. Fosters innovation.
2. Linkage with institutions of higher education and with researchers.
3. Determination of the capacity to initiate or participate in research activities.

Whether a public health agency engages in the assurance essential services described here indicates whether it is meeting its public mandate. Of course, it can be questioned whether the essential services are comprehensive and properly defined and whether the performance indicators are a good gauge of the extent to which the practices are being adhered to. For one thing, the essential services seem to overlap, in the sense that some of the activities associated with a given essential service are associated with others as well.[18]

Furthermore, because program implementation demands more than two-thirds of the resources of local public health agencies, it might be beneficial to subdivide the essential service and local health agency organizational practices in order to take account of the diversity of programs provided. Another issue is the allocation of staff time to the activities associated with each essential service and organizational practice.[19] For example, not much staff time and not many financial resources are devoted to the practices associated with assessment or policy development, and the role of technical assistance is not clearly defined in the core function practices model. These issues need to be addressed if the model is to be workable over the long run. Many of these criticisms are also applicable to the organizational practices approach.

In a national sample of local health departments, Turnock and colleagues investigated the rate of use for the 10 organizational practices.[20] The overall rate was 50% (this figure was calculated using weighted responses from 208 local health departments). The rate of use was highest for the practices associated with assurance and lowest for practices related to policy development. The researchers also found that about 40% of the U.S. population was being served by health departments utilizing the core functions approach to public health during 1993. The rate of use for the essential services model is currently unknown except in the states and localities using the Mobilizing for Action through Planning and Partnerships process or National Public Health Performance Standards.

Illinois has been so committed to the core function practices model that the Illinois administrative code was changed in 1993 to reflect the new commitment.[21–23] **Table 13-1** shows the activities required for the certification of local health departments before and after adoption of the 10 essential public health services as part of the administrative code. This move to a core function–based system meant that all local health departments, and by extension the local public health system, would be held to the same standards and a more consistent approach to community-based public health.[24]

Case Study 13-A shows the benefits of creating community partnerships—including a partnership between the local state university and the community—as a way to enhance the implementation of community health activities. (Note that the neighborhood health advisors program described in the case study is oriented toward leadership development, an added plus.)

TABLE 13-1 Activities Required for Certification of Local Health Departments in Illinois, Before and After July 1993

Before July 1993
1. Food sanitation
2. Potable water
3. Maternal health and family planning
4. Child health
5. Communicable disease control
6. Private sewage
7. Solid waste
8. Nuisance control
9. Chronic disease
10. Administration

July 1993 and later
1. Assess the health needs of the community
2. Investigate health effects and hazards
3. Advocate and build constituencies
4. Develop plans and policies to address needs (includes analyzing for determinants and setting priorities)
5. Manage resources
6. Implement programs
7. Evaluate and provide quality assurance
8. Inform and educate the public

Source: Reproduced from Illinois Administrative Code, Title 55, Sec. 600, 1993, State of Illinois.

Case Study 13-A

Big City Neighborhood Health Advisors

Adam B. Becker, Barbara A. Israel, Rose Hollis, Yolanda Hill Ashford, and Murlisa Lockett

In today's context of decreasing budgets and increasing disparities in health status among U.S. population groups, health departments are faced with a serious challenge in trying to ensure the delivery of adequate and appropriate services to communities. Given the complex needs of communities and the differences between professional and lay experiences and perceptions, health department services often fail to be as relevant to community issues as they could be. To create more relevant services, some health departments are finding creative ways to involve community members in meeting the diverse needs in the community.

The Big City Health Department (BCHD) developed the Big City Neighborhood Health Advisor (BCNHA) project with the assistance of a local community-based organization (CBO) and a nearby school of public health. The project was funded for four years under the umbrella of a larger, multisite project aimed at increasing the capacity of communities, bringing stronger community influence into the practice of public health, and changing the public health curriculum in universities to strengthen the community focus. Developing the BCNHA project was one strategy adopted by the BCHD to meet community needs and ensure that appropriate quality services were available locally.

(*Continues*)

About Big City: The Project Setting

Big City is one of the largest cities in the United States and has a population well over 1,000,000. Among the 77 U.S. cities with populations above 200,000, Big City has at times been ranked first in the percentage of people below the poverty level (as high as 32%). Big City has also been ranked first in unemployment rate (as high as 13% overall). In certain sections of the city, the unemployment rate is as high as 36%. Within Big City, 19% of all households are female headed, and 55% of these live below the poverty level. In addition, more than 40% of all children under the age of 18 live below the poverty level.

There is an increasing amount of racial and ethnic segregation in Big City, with extreme differences in health and income status between European Americans and people of color. Racial and economic segregation in Big City is linked to decreasing access to social and structural supports within the local communities, as jobs, stores, and other community institutions relocate to suburban areas and as the city's major industries downsize or disappear altogether.

"Big City Health Department: Your Partner in Good Health"

As federal, state, and local budgets for health and human services decline, the BCHD finds it more and more difficult to ensure that quality services are available to the residents. Many residents are not aware of the services that are available, or how to access them. Those services that are available, because they are fewer in number and spread out, are often hard to reach for those who need the services the most.

In attempting to fulfill the three core functions of public health as defined by the Institute of Medicine (assessment, assurance, and policy development), the BCHD made an intensive effort to form partnerships with the communities it serves. The BCNHA project was one means by which the BCHD formed such partnerships. This kind of relationship with the communities was not new for the BCHD, nor was the BCNHA project the only example of a project it had implemented. The health department's openness to such partnerships was one of the factors that contributed to the success of the BCNHA program. This openness is evident in the BCHD's motto—"Big City Health Department, Your Partner in Good Health"—and its mission statement: "The overall role of the department is to prevent disease, promote health, and protect the environment. This is accomplished through partnerships and other types of collaboration with schools, hospitals, churches, physicians, health insurers, businesses, and other community-based agencies."

When university faculty, members of a major community-based organization, and staff of the BCHD sat down to determine the role of the health department in the umbrella project in which they were all engaged and the project activities it would take on, the BCNHA project seemed a natural fit for the BCHD. The BCNHA project would help the BCHD achieve its mission by strengthening and expanding the role of Big City community members in the delivery of services aimed at meeting community needs.

Developing the Big City Neighborhood Health Advisors Project

The first step in developing the BCNHA project was to establish a steering committee to oversee the project. This committee consisted of university faculty and students, community members, and staff from the CBO partner and the health department. The committee developed criteria for identifying and recruiting neighborhood health advisors (NHAs), established goals and approaches for training NHAs, and determined the relationship of the NHAs to the health department.

The steering committee based the BCNHA project on the lay health advisor concept. Within communities, there have always been people who are trusted and respected and whom others rely upon for care, advice, and support. The support given is often informal, spontaneous, and so much a part of everyday life that it may go unrecognized. In most cases, the informal support is given by one person to another within a preexisting relationship: friend to friend, coworker to coworker, neighbor to neighbor, or family member to family member. These special community members are knowledgeable about their community and well respected by friends, family, and neighbors. Others frequently turn to them for advice and assistance, and they are responsive to the strengths and needs of others. The NHA Steering Committee established these characteristics as the criteria for identifying potential NHAs.

In determining the relationship between the NHAs and the BCHD, the steering committee wanted to differentiate the roles of the NHAs from the roles that community members played in other BCHD projects. Health departments and other types of health and human service agencies often rely on members of their target populations to assist in the provision of services. Community members may provide information and education to others with similar backgrounds and life experiences (e.g., peer educators), extend the agency's access into the community and increase community awareness of agencies and services available to them (e.g., community outreach workers), or provide agencies with input into the types and quality of health services available (e.g., community advisory boards). These roles are extremely helpful in improving services and breaking down barriers to care.

The steering committee felt that the NHA role should be broad enough that the NHAs could provide services to their communities in some or all of the capacities mentioned above. The distinction made between NHAs and other community members in BCHD projects was that NHAs would be identified, not created; would work with the BCHD and according to their own perceptions of priorities within their communities and not for the BCHD and according to its objectives; would not be paid employees of the health department; and would live or work in the settings in which they would provide help and assistance, perhaps facing issues similar to those faced by the people who would receive their support.

The Role of the Big City Health Department

Although the NHAs would not be employees of the BCHD, the steering committee decided that the BCNHA project headquarters should be housed at the health department. The health department's role, therefore, would be to hire a program coordinator and provide support and resources wherever possible. The BCHD hired Sue Siloh as the program coordinator. At first, Ms. Siloh felt out of place at the BCHD. The characteristics that made her a perfect fit for the job of coordinator meant that she was a unique health department employee. Ms. Siloh lived in the community served by the BCNHA project, had spent some time living in public housing, and did not have public health training. Initially, Ms. Siloh often felt that others did not take her or her program seriously.

The BCHD's deputy director, who was a strong supporter of both the BCNHA project and Ms. Siloh, saw that something needed to be done to create a support system for the project within the health department. Ms. Siloh was made a member of the administrative team of the BCHD, which had traditionally consisted only of the director, deputy director, and division heads. As a result of her inclusion on the team, Ms. Siloh was able to develop personal relationships with all the division heads, and they in turn learned more about the BCNHA project, how they could help support the project, and how the project could help the community and thus strengthen the department's relationship with the community, benefiting all of BCHD's programs. As needs arose for training or delivery of services (e.g., satellite immunization clinics, health screenings in community centers or churches), Ms. Siloh could now personally contact those in the BCHD who could help her to meet those needs.

The Role of the Coordinator: Recruiting, Training, and Supporting NHAs

Sue Siloh's official title was community health coordinator. As coordinator of the BCNHA project, she was given many responsibilities. Ms. Siloh was responsible for recruiting and selecting NHAs, training new NHAs (she coordinated the eight-week training programs and additional in-service trainings and also served as a trainer for some sessions), supporting the trained NHAs (she coordinated monthly meetings, assisted NHAs with special projects, and maintained contact with each individual NHA), and starting up new NHA projects in other target areas of the city as requested (she assisted several CBOs in developing similar projects). In addition, Ms. Siloh presented the BCNHA project at professional meetings and conferences, advised other agencies in the development of NHA projects, and worked with members of the university on publications about the BCNHA project. Ms. Siloh also participated in grant-writing activities to bring in new money to sustain the project.

Recruiting NHAs

The recruiting process for NHAs was somewhat informal and combined several strategies. The coordinator contacted local block clubs, churches, and other community groups in order to spread the word about the project. Flyers were posted throughout the community. Ms. Siloh also contacted community members she knew from her work as a community organizer and advocate. For subsequent cohorts, previously trained NHAs played a recruiting role by bringing in interesting friends and neighbors. As for qualifications, NHAs were expected to have the trust and respect of people in the community, an interest in learning about the community, and an eagerness to work to improve the health and quality of life of community members.

Training the NHAs

Once the NHAs were identified, they participated in eight sessions of "core" training. This initial training covered three broad areas: health education, community resources and referrals, and community problem solving and

(Continues)

organizing. Health department staff provided most of the training in health education (topics included diabetes, high blood pressure, and HIV/acquired immune deficiency syndrome [AIDS]). Representatives from local agencies provided information about the resources available to the NHAs and their neighbors, and faculty from the university provided the community problem-solving and organizing training.

Once trained, NHAs also participated in training subsequent cohorts. They worked in teams with trainers to give the NHA perspective on the training topic and to provide "real-life" examples of how NHAs could put their skills to work.

Although the initial training content was, for the most part, determined by the steering committee, the trainees determined the training schedule as a group to fit their needs. They also had opportunities to select priority areas on which to focus during the core training. After the core training, NHAs had opportunities to go on to specialized training in areas they selected, such as cardiopulmonary resuscitation, organizing block clubs, substance abuse, and parenting. More than 40 NHAs participated in three core trainings.

Neighborhood Health Advisors at Work

Once they graduated from the training program, NHAs had increased skills to continue the help they were providing in their communities. NHAs became involved on a daily basis with individuals and groups in their own neighborhoods—helping friends and family to access needed services, assisting block clubs to organize and address community issues, providing day care to families, transporting neighbors to appointments, and providing education on health issues to church and community organizations and businesses.

Health was not the only human service sector with which BCNHAs were involved. Several NHAs began to work with a local police precinct through the Safe and Healthy Neighborhoods Program to educate neighborhood residents about crime and safety and to assist police in learning to work with community members in a way that would foster trust and cooperation.

In addition to these helping roles, NHAs developed some dynamic programs in their neighborhoods. Examples include the Community Cupboard, a neighborhood food and clothing pantry; Together We Can, a grief support group for those experiencing loss; and Facing the Challenge, a parenting program that builds skills and provides support for pregnant women. In addition to these programs, NHAs participated in other ongoing programs, such as the Peterson Clinic Advisory Council, a community board that assisted a local health clinic in developing programs for the community, and the Violence Task Force, a group that worked to provide alternative activities for youths at risk. NHAs participated in these projects according to their interests and the needs in their neighborhoods. In addition to these projects, the NHAs distributed a monthly newsletter to more than 5,000 individuals and families in Big City. The newsletter included information about health issues and services, local business news, and community events.

Special Program Issues

Recognition and Reimbursement

Given the number of activities in which NHAs were involved and the limited resources available to the program, the question of reimbursement was one that continued to arise for the BCNHA project. Many of the NHAs had full- or part-time jobs. Some did not want to be paid because they considered helping friends and family as part of their responsibility to the community or to God or as part of being a member of a family and community. There were other NHAs who wanted to have a full- or part-time job, and their hope was that the training and activities they did in conjunction with this program would lead them to a job. Regardless of whether NHAs wished to be paid, their work needed to be recognized. Whenever possible, portions of new grant monies brought in to sustain the NHA project were designated for reimbursement for travel (e.g., gas and mileage), reimbursement for meals (e.g., dinner during training sessions), to provide incentives (each NHA received a printed cloth carrying bag with the NHA logo), or as stipends for hourly work on special neighborhood projects. For most of the NHAs, these forms of compensation were enough to support and encourage them as they engaged in their work.

In a few cases, NHAs were hired by the BCHD or affiliated organizations for full- or part-time positions. Although employment was welcomed by these NHAs, formalizing their work as NHAs was not without challenges. Along with a salary came an obligation to the paying agency. Some of the NHAs who received jobs found that they had less time to work with groups in their own neighborhoods. Others found that they were limited in the scope of health issues with which they could work, because their training was specialized to fit their new jobs.

To some extent, those who became employed through their work as NHAs lost a modicum of the community's trust when they became agency employees. They were seen by some as "part of the system" rather than part of the community, and their loyalties became suspect. Because an open, trusting relationship between an NHA and the local community was essential to the work of the NHA, employment actually decreased the ability of some to provide individualized support and assistance.

Though the steering committee and the program coordinator had varying opinions on the subject of compensating NHAs, decisions about paying stipends to BCNHAs or hiring them into agencies followed two basic principles: (1) the work of NHAs had to be recognized and compensated in some way, and (2) NHAs themselves had to be involved in the decision regarding their compensation.

Evaluating the Work of the NHAs

Assurance of service delivery and the quality of those services requires public health departments to evaluate programs to determine whether they are meeting community needs appropriately and sufficiently. Several challenges faced the BCNHA program when it came to evaluation. First, designing an evaluation plan for such a diverse set of activities was extremely difficult. Some NHAs worked more with individuals and others more with groups, some worked with certain agencies and others worked independently, some participated in all monthly meetings and others attended only when they needed materials or to meet with the coordinator. In addition, all NHAs possessed unique styles of helping. Given the diversity, could an evaluation plan be developed that would be appropriate for all NHAs?

Second, collecting data on BCNHA activities was a challenge. The often spontaneous and informal nature of the work of NHAs made observation by evaluators difficult if not impossible. Likewise, NHAs found it difficult to keep records of their activities because they took place during a phone call from a friend or a chance meeting in the grocery store. Much of the "helping work" done by NHAs was seen by project staff and evaluators as program-related work. NHAs, however, saw their work as part of daily life and therefore not appropriate for documenting. Confidentiality and trust issues, as well as the sheer number of people in contact with NHAs, made "client" interviewing a challenge as well.

Given the above challenges, the steering committee, the coordinator, the evaluator, and the NHAs themselves knew that whatever evaluation methods were used would not be able to capture an entire picture of the BCNHA project. Talking with NHA "clients" who were willing to be interviewed helped the program evaluators form an idea of how the NHAs were interacting with other community members and what that interaction meant for the community. Community members were less likely, however, to talk about weaknesses of the program because of the relationships they had with the NHAs.

Looking at community outcomes was also extremely difficult. Could NHAs be credited with a drop in infant mortality rates or a decrease in visits to the emergency department? Could they be held accountable for a rise in criminal activity or incomplete immunization rates? With so many other activities going on in Big City, how would evaluators determine what changes were effects of the project? The steering committee felt that using communities without NHAs as comparisons was also a problematic strategy. The ethical responsibility of the BCHD to all the communities in which it works, the difficulty of matching diverse communities, and a shortage of resources were among the reasons why the project chose not to implement a quasi-experimental evaluation design.

The effects of participation on the NHAs themselves were, however, assessed through the evaluation. NHAs completed a profile form when they joined the program. They were asked to indicate employment status, education level, skills and talents, interest in and commitment to empowering their neighborhoods, organizational affiliations, and availability. Changes in these items for each NHA were assessed either through having the NHA complete a profile form after a certain amount of time or through an interview.

In addition, documentation gave those involved with the project a good idea of how program activities were being carried out. The program coordinator used several strategies to encourage NHAs to document their work. NHAs were given documentation forms to keep track of activities, needs, challenges, and ideas for priority projects in the community. Once a month, the NHAs jointly met with the coordinator to discuss project ideas and challenges, to learn about new resources in the community, to give each other support, and sometimes to receive additional training. The first portion of these meetings was devoted to discussing and providing assistance in completing the documentation forms.

(*Continues*)

The NHAs and Assurance

The BCHD takes very seriously its responsibility to the community. In order to fulfill part of the assurance function, the BCHD implemented and supported the BCNHA project. The project helped the BCHD to carry out assurance activities in several ways:

- by disseminating information throughout the target area regarding health issues, resources, and services available
- by strengthening the connection between the health department and the community and expanding the role that community members play in the delivery of health services
- by providing training to community members that strengthened their ability to solve problems, gain access to resources, voice their needs and concerns, and transfer these skills to other community members

This program is an excellent example of how one health department approached the function of ensuring the delivery of quality services to the community in a time of decreasing budgets and increasing needs for services.

Postscript (2012)

The BCHD sustained the BCNHA office for a number of years beyond the funding of the initial intervention under which it was established. When Ms. Siloh left the BCHD, a new director was hired and an assistant director position was established. NHAs were deployed in initiatives to address diabetes, blood pressure control, environmental health, and asthma control. New funders provided support to the program and training continued for several years. As leadership changed at the highest levels, however, and public funding streams got tighter, the program was eventually phased out. The program's methodology for training outreach workers and for conducting community outreach were incorporated in the WIC program, HIV prevention, immunizations, and other department units with community outreach or health workers. The city's overall fiscal situation also influenced the program's longevity. As robust public health budgets and grant-funded programs were increasingly seen as a means to address the declining general funds of the city, grant-funded programs and non-union employees became more vulnerable. The unions, who would have ordinarily advocated for such employees, found themselves having to focus their advocacy solely on their members. Staffs of programs like the BCNHA were unable to advocate on their own behalf. The combination of these conditions ultimately led to the demise of the BCNHA. The program no longer exists but does provide an example of what a community outreach program based in a health department can do to extend the assurance functions of departments. Critical questions are raised by the example of this case study. What issues do health departments with significant grant funding face in addressing sustainability of those programs? How does the financial state of the city itself shape these issues? Since many programs seem to die with the loss of funding, what can be done to sustain them?

Source: Courtesy of the Mid-America Regional Public Health Leadership Institute.

Public health leadership activities tied to assurance include:

- building a strong agency managerial team
- delegating authority for programmatic decisions
- restructuring agency activities to address health priority needs
- encouraging feedback to all constituents
- supporting program evaluation on an ongoing basis
- mentoring and training staff
- developing a technical assistance team
- working with external partners on community-wide population-based public health programs
- promoting a systems orientation to public health

POPULATION-BASED SERVICES AND PERSONAL HEALTH SERVICES

Public health leaders and their professional colleagues are often confronted with the question of how public health differs from health care. The usual answer is that public health practitioners provide services oriented toward the population at large and do not routinely provide personal or direct services to individuals. Population-based services are programs intended to promote health and prevent disease in a community or a larger geographic entity. Public health practitioners are concerned about the factors that affect health. Some of these factors are in the control of each person in a community and some are not.

The major determinants of health are biology, environment, lifestyle, degree of wealth, and health organizational matters.[25] All of these key determinants have psychosocial components, such as social status; ties among people (e.g., family ties), between social networks, and to voluntary organizations; and relationships to the neighborhood or community.[26]

The relationship between the provision of population-based services and the provision of direct health services is complicated. The medical care system in the United States reserves the right to provide personal health- and illness-based direct services, and the medical care infrastructure has been built up to support this medical care approach. Yet, although the public health system often takes a back seat to the medical

care system in the United States, many people who need help cannot get services, even when government financial support is available, and as a consequence, public health agencies sometimes act as service providers of last resort.[27]

Table 13-2 shows some of the population-based services that local public health agencies provide, such as surveillance, environmental health and control, communicable disease control, aging programs, and maternal and child health programs. Personal health services include community health clinical services, primary health care, case management services, dental health services, and clinical counseling programs. Some services mix elements of both, such as immunization, health screening, and dental sealant programs.

TABLE 13-2 Examples of Assurance Activities in State and Local Health Departments and Leadership

Population Based	Mixed	Personal Health Based	Leadership Activities
Public health surveillance	Community health nursing	Community health clinical services	Delegation of programmatic responsibilities to others Evaluation of collected data for decision making
Environmental health and control (air and water quality, waste disposal, toxic substances control, etc.)	Health screening programs	Clinical services for children with lead toxicity	Program oversight Translation of environmental health goals into action
Occupational health and safety	Immunization Substance abuse screening Accidents	Clinical services for workers	Development of treatment partnerships with other health providers
Injury control	Infant car seat laws Violence prevention Teen peer support	Deliver donated car seats to people who cannot afford them	Education of the public Enforcement of laws and regulations
HIV/AIDS surveillance	Screening programs Reporting laws	AIDS counseling	Enforcement of laws and regulations Use of data for decision making
Communicable disease control	Immunization programs	Primary health care	Monitoring of health issues in the community Study of global health trends Education of the public
Family planning	Statistical monitoring of lack of prenatal care by pregnant teens	School clinics	Education of the public Development of partnerships with the community

(Continues)

TABLE 13-2 Examples of Assurance Activities in State and Local Health Departments and Leadership (*Continued*)

Population Based	Mixed	Personal Health Based	Leadership Activities
Maternal and child health programs	Metabolic/genetic screening programs Women, Infants, and Children (WIC) eligibility	Case management services	Enforcement of laws and regulations
Aging programs	Medicaid eligibility	Long-term care	Collaboration with other agencies that serve older populations
Nutrition programs	WIC eligibility	Nutrition counseling	Placement of emphasis on innovation Program oversight
Disaster preparedness	Community disaster plans	Disaster clinics (emergency public health)	Advocacy of a role for public health in disasters Creation of disaster teams
Health promotion and disease prevention	Educational programs	Clinical counseling	Creation of a vision and mission based on primary prevention Development of goals Translation of goals into action Development of academic linkages
Dental health	Dental sealant programs	Dental health clinics	Delegation of responsibility to dentists Program oversight
Vector/animal control	Observation of community health standards	Maintenance of animal shelters	Enforcement of laws and regulations Delegation of responsibility to other professional staff
Restaurant inspection	Monitoring of food-borne health problems	Community health clinic services	Enforcement of laws and regulations Creation of partnership with local restaurant association
Health hazard appraisal	Evaluation of community health hazards	Community health clinic services	Placement of emphasis on innovative program development Support and evaluation of data collected
Train and educate the workforce	Leadership development programs	Application of learning to clinical programs	Mentoring and training Health communication Social marketing
Population-based managed care	Development of managed care model(s) for all community residents	Running of public health maintenance organization by a local health department	Development of partnerships with local health providers
Laboratory activities	Privatization of some laboratory activities	Personal testing for problems	Support for laboratory directors' involvement in public health decision making

Regardless of the changes that occur in the health-care field in the future, population-based programs will probably still be mainly a public health responsibility. The configuration of personal health services constantly changes in response to changes in health policy. The mixed services may remain unchanged or become reconfigured in some way. Assurance is interconnected with the whole public health system, so it causes changes and also responds to changes in other parts of the system. Currently, the three major areas of assurance arguably are personal health service provision, environmental control, and behavior modification,[28] but undoubtedly a new list will be needed for the 21st century because local public health agencies will probably be less involved in the direct delivery of personal health services.

Public health surveillance is a marriage between the core functions of assessment and assurance, and epidemiology serves as the minister who joins these two functions together.[29] In turn, surveillance connects research to service needs and monitors the linkage routinely.[30] Public health surveillance involves the collection, interpretation, and use of data (for purposes of policy development and decision making). Thacker listed 11 reasons for surveillance:[31]

1. health planning
2. monitoring changes in public health practice
3. quantitatively estimating the extensiveness of a health problem in a community
4. determining the natural history of a disease
5. detecting epidemics and disasters
6. determining the spread of disease in a population
7. facilitating epidemiological and laboratory investigations
8. hypothesis testing
9. evaluating assurance activities
10. monitoring changes in infectious agents
11. monitoring isolation activities

It is imperative to link the population-based health objectives to the assurance activities of the local public health agency at the community level.[32] Assurance of vital services is a governmental function. However, the community needs to define its own process for tying goals to services.

The state of Washington tied the population-based assurance activities of local health agencies to capacity standards that identified what the agencies and their governmental and community partners needed to do on a regular basis to protect and promote health and prevent disease.[33] Appendix 13-A presents the list of health promotion, health protection, and quality assurance activities contained in the Washington State Public Health Improvement Plan during the early 1990s.[34] Quality assurance is defined in the plan as monitoring and maintaining the quality of public health programs and services. Quality assurance includes licensing and training health professionals, licensing health facilities, and enforcing standards and regulations. Quality assurance is discussed in detail in the next section. Although this specific classification is no longer used in Washington in its original form, it still provides us with a useful classification of assurance capacity indicators.

In recent years, the Washington State Department of Health has continued its Public Health Improvement Partnerships (PHIP).[35] The core functions of public health continue to guide the process. Partnerships have expanded. As of August 2011, public health standards and exemplary practices are utilized to measure public health performance using quality improvement methods, information on public health activities has been collected since 2007, local public health indicators are measured to help determine the best utilization of limited resources, public health finance decisions are tied to core public health activities, and communication tools have been developed to help public health professionals talk about their work.

Public health leaders must:

- utilize creative techniques to maintain population-based programs during a downsizing period
- provide clinical services that are not accessible to segments of the population for lack of insurance or other reasons
- tie public health issues to personal health issues
- learn to relate surveillance to program development
- support quality assurance and quality improvement approaches
- integrate public health preparedness activities into the assurance activities of the local public health system

QUALITY ASSURANCE

The U.S. General Accounting Office (GAO) was asked in 1989 to review the issue of quality assurance in health care.[36] In a briefing report to the chair of the U.S. Bipartisan Commission on Comprehensive Health Care, the GAO pointed out the multidimensional factors associated with quality measures. Part of the difficulty in quality assurance is that quality means different things to different people and organizations. For the individual, health improvement is the measure of quality. If the improvement can be tied to a particular treatment intervention, then quality is implied in the techniques used. For healthcare leaders and providers, such factors as accurate diagnosis and treatment, the clinical content of care, and technical skill are viewed as related to quality. Purchasers tie quality to factors such as cost effectiveness, the appropriateness of the care setting, and the frequency and duration of services. For the public health leadership, quality can be tied to meeting health objectives, declines in rates of disease and infant mortality, and increases in healthy behaviors.

The GAO report also argued that quality assessment and quality assurance are sometimes confused with each other:

> Quality assessment involves the use of measures of quality, based on either explicit or implicit criteria, to assess the structure, process, and outcomes of care and to monitor levels of quality over time. Quality assurance goes beyond the simple assessment of quality to include its improvement. This requires identifying and confirming problems in the quality of medical care, planning interventions to lessen or eliminate the problems, monitoring the effectiveness of the interventions, and instituting additional changes and monitoring where warranted. . . . Quality assessment is a prerequisite to quality assurance.[37(p.7)]

Because quality assurance is an important part of the core function of assurance, developing a national strategy to address concerns about quality assurance may be required. The GAO report raised the issue of equity and people's need to gain access to services that are able to improve their well-being. Equitable access to services depends to a degree on how services get reimbursed. It is also related to the different health needs of different subpopulations. Older people, for example, have different concerns than young mothers with sick children. A national strategy may also be required to deal with the issue of comprehensiveness of healthcare services.[38] The services available in a community are partially determined by the service models in use in the community.

A comprehensive national strategy for quality assurance would likely include:

- national practice guidelines and standards of care
- enhanced data to support quality assurance activities
- improved approaches to quality assessment and assurance at the local level
- a national focus for developing, implementing, and monitoring a national system[39]

Quality of care is affected by a number of factors, including demographic factors, such as the age, gender, race or ethnicity, socioeconomic status, education, and occupation of those who use the services. Poor people, for instance, tend to be sicker and have more trouble getting the services they need. Economic factors, of course, play a role in determining the quality of care as well. It is common to hear that there is not enough money to provide universal access to services, keep the quality of care at a high level, or hire enough health professionals to provide the needed services. Finally, politics, including the political orientation of the party in office, can have an effect on the quality of the healthcare system. Indeed, the direction of healthcare policy may be largely determined by the lobbying of powerful groups such as the American Medical Association or the various managed care organizations (MCOs).

One of the keys to quality assurance is the accreditation process, in which special review organizations, most notably The Joint Commission, evaluate the care provided by healthcare organizations. One problem with present accreditation procedures is that the focus is on structural and staff performance requirements rather than treatment outcomes. Moreover, healthcare organizations, in order to improve their services, must be motivated by more than a desire to receive accreditation; they must be motivated to engage in improvement efforts out of an inner need to offer the public the best care they are capable of providing.

Public health agencies may undergo an accreditation review for some of their clinical programs, such as home care or ambulatory care services. A voluntary public health accreditation program for local public health agencies will be implemented in 2011. Also, state and federal money is given to local agencies to provide certain mandated programs, and sanctions, including

Leadership Tip

Recognize your direct reports for work well done, but fit the type of recognition to the desires of the people recognized.

loss of funds, are applied if the mandated programs are not implemented, although the use of sanctions is inconsistent.

There is a built-in quality assurance process related to health objectives. If one of a local public health agency's objectives is to increase the immunization rate to the point where 90% of children under a certain age are receiving immunizations, the agency, by developing indicators of success, can determine the extent to which the objective is being achieved and also which segments of the population are being reached effectively. Partnerships with academia are useful in evaluating progress toward the attainment of objectives, and business techniques associated with continuous quality improvement or total quality management can be applied to uncover the reasons for the failure to meet objectives. Also, publicizing the success of community programs can strengthen the local public health infrastructure by demonstrating to residents that the public health agency is an effective social service organization.

Public health agencies need to monitor community assurance activities. The fear among public health professionals is that MCOs will take over the assurance function from local agencies. Public health leaders need to make sure that all public health agency and private health organization programs are of high quality.

Public health and mental health agencies have become program partners in many communities. Quality assurance is an important issue for mental health agencies as well, and it is likely to become even more important with the likely continued growth in third-party payers, governmental regulations, and national organization involvement.[40] Quality assurance methods need to be used not only in program operations but also in the training of public health and mental health professionals. Agency leaders need to support the training of the public health and mental health workforce in innovative approaches to solving problems and making decisions.

In the area of quality assurance, public health leaders must:

- develop local guidelines for practice
- promote high-quality programs
- meet or surpass proposed health objectives
- increase access to care for underinsured and underserved populations
- engage in quality assurance activities, such as those necessary to gain accreditation
- support continuous quality improvement procedures
- promote a consumer- and community-driven public health system
- train the public health workforce in quality techniques
- work to integrate public health and mental health quality assurance activities

THE GREATEST LEADERSHIP CHALLENGE

The greatest challenge for public health leaders in the coming years will be to work out a viable relationship between governmental public health agencies and MCOs. Public health leaders have become defensive on the issue of partnering with MCOs and in fact have tended to ignore the MCOs in their communities under the mistaken assumption that they will eventually disappear.[41] As pointed out above, public health leaders are concerned that MCOs will take over many of the assurance responsibilities that currently belong to health departments. They are also concerned that MCOs will increase their community penetration by serving more and more community residents, with the result that public health agencies will suffer a reduction in operating funds for mandated services and core function activities.

It is important to point out that the assurance activities of government public health agencies will not diminish but will rather expand, especially in light of the increased emergency preparedness and response activities now required of health departments.[42] These agencies also will continue to have the responsibility of ensuring that necessary programs and services are available to all residents of the community. Each local public health agency will need to come up with unique solutions for meeting this responsibility. For example, an agency in some cases may be the managed care provider for certain segments of its community. Case Study 13-B presents an interview conducted in 1995 with Dr. Jean Malecki, a former director of a Florida public health unit that helped to develop a unique managed care program for her county. This interview shows the importance of creativity in leadership and how a local health unit can benefit from collaborating with local service providers. The interview now includes a postscript public health quiz where Dr. Malecki brings her perceptions up to date.

Case Study 13-B

A Practice Quiz with Jean M. Malecki
Louis Rowitz

Jean M. Malecki, MD, MPH, is the director of the HRS/Palm Beach County Health Unit. She holds a doctor of medicine degree from New York Medical College and a master of public health degree from the University of Miami. Dr. Malecki is also a graduate of the Public Health Leadership Institute in California. She has been one of the leaders in the development of unique models for public health service at the county level and talks about these programs during the interview, which occurred on February 17, 1995.

How have you helped your health unit reinvent public health for the county?

We have begun a countywide total quality improvement project where we initially used APEX as our tool and then brought in outside consultants on visioning and team building for all staff. In so doing, we decided as a health department that we would continue to do traditional public health, but that would be the foundation for a major effort in prevention and primary care in the managed care arena. Currently, we are putting in an application for a commercial health maintenance organization (HMO), which would use only public dollars—both Medicaid and tax dollars. The HMO will be called Healthy Palm Beaches. It will be housed in the health department. We currently have a Medicaid HMO. We are thus applying for a commercial HMO so that we can use some of the same tax dollars that are currently received to a taxing entity to provide the same level of care to the working poor that we provide to the Medicaid clients. It will be a single payer. Any willing provider can be part of the system. This proposed program provides a healthy competition environment.

Are the three core functions still relevant in a reinvention environment?

The core functions are even more relevant in a reinvention environment. You have to have the core functions in place whether the health department directly provides the care or not. The health department has to oversee healthy outcomes. It is necessary to ensure that any healthcare reform that takes place achieves what it is supposed to. In Florida, what we are seeing, unfortunately, is that the cost factor is number one to policy makers. Costs—and not quality—are driving the system. Having the core functions is extremely important if we are going to work out what we need to on the local level. Both the new model of essential public health services and the model of core functions are needed. They need to be integrated. The critical issue relates to a continuum of services and functions that need to be applied in a rational manner.

Where is public health going during the next five years?

The answer to your question depends on how rapidly and influentially we can educate our policy makers. We got a reprieve last year [1994] when national and state healthcare reform legislation was not passed. We need to intensively educate our public because education was neglected at the national and state levels. First, we need to educate our policy makers one on one in terms of what public health is. The idea of core functions is not part of the message to policy makers because the terms are misleading. It is necessary to be very concrete rather than abstract with policy makers. The arguments need to not only be concrete, but also the messages given must be very simple and strong. For example, we might say that the mission of public health is to prevent epidemics and the spread of disease, protect against environmental hazards, prevent injury, promote and encourage healthy behaviors, respond to disasters and assist communities in recovery, and ensure the quality and accessibility of health services. Specific local examples will strengthen the arguments. The important message to give is that the health reform plans will not work unless we have a strong public health foundation.

How do we do more with less money?

This depends on the decisions of the organization. In Florida, health departments are doing three things. First, they are downsizing completely and doing nothing except traditional public health activities totally out of the prevention/primary care arena. Other health departments are downsizing but are doing things in the contractual arena with local HMOs to provide some prevention and some primary care. There are other departments like us that are competitive, are entrepreneurial, and will compete for the primary care dollar in just as businesslike a manner as the private entrepreneur. The money that we get and save goes into public health. There may be less money through categorical funding, block grant funding, or whatever, but there is a way to make money to fund public health. We chose the latter road.

How do we become more entrepreneurial?

Public health professionals need to learn how to be more creative. They need to learn how to create a vision that defines what public health should be. This needs to be done by working with the community as well as other colleagues in the health department. Then, it is necessary for the public health department to market itself. You first create the vision. To achieve it, you must become more businesslike and accountable. You don't market yourself only to get more business, but market in terms of health promotion activities and successes. Thus, you need to market yourself to the community and all the way up to the policy makers. I can tell you what we did to attract the attention of our entire legislative delegation. They are impressed with our mobile clinics that go to migrant camps, as well as the fact that we serve clients at night and on weekends. We are not always as good at tooting our horns as we should be. That is a mindset that hasn't been in public health.

What is public health's role in managed care?

I look at it three ways. Number one is you are doing it yourself. Number two is that you are participating with other managed care groups. Third, if you are not in the business yourself or participating with other managed care entities, you do have to oversee the assurance piece. If you are in the business, you are going to have to monitor assurance anyhow. Assurance of the managed care activities in your jurisdiction is a critical public health activity for the health department whether the department is doing the managed care or not.

What aspects of healthcare reform will pass Congress in the near future?

I don't think anything is going to pass soon. If anything does pass, it will probably be something related to insurance reform. It will be tough because the insurance lobby is strong. With a great amount of discussion now on welfare reform, we are more likely to see action here that might relate to the tightening up of Medicaid benefits. I don't see that much change is going to occur in Florida either.

What is the relationship between strong leadership and restructuring the field of public health?

It's everything. We can't stress this more. How come we don't have a public health political action committee? Everybody else does. Public health professionals don't seem to fight for public health like other special interest groups do. Leadership development should not be separated out from professional education. It should be part of the educational experience of our public health students. Leadership training should also be available for residency training directors. Leadership training is clearly important for preventive medicine residents. Fellowship training is good, but leadership development needs to occur earlier in the educational process.

Postscript: Comments from Dr. Jean Malecki (February 2008)

Since 1995, the most critical question public health faces today is, how do we champion an assurance role in the area of healthcare access when the existing healthcare delivery system is in disarray and imploding right in front of us? A system does not exist for the delivery of appropriate, acceptable, and integrated care that incorporates prevention, early intervention, and primary and specialty care as a continuum for the individual patient. The disease-based model that is procedure driven and promotes the hospital/emergency department as the "hub" of clinical care remains the status quo. This model is antiquated and wasteful and will continue to provide no potential future health improvements for all Americans. Other critical issues that face public health today include the ability to rapidly respond to emerging health threats and recognizing the aging and neglected critical public health infrastructures that have been the primary success of public health for the past 100 years, such as water treatment facilities and wastewater plants. The globe is warming, disparities continue, and our behaviors are out of control. A third of school children in Palm Beach County are either obese or overweight. The plate of local public health is full!

The first Medicaid HMO in the state of Florida was created by the Palm Beach County Health Department. It continues to exist and is called Healthy Palm Beaches. It is now run by the Health Care District of Palm Beach County, which is the public health funder for trauma, indigent care, and public health programs. As the director of the local health department, I am a member of the Health Care District Board. This model, an HMO housed in a governmental entity, is both productive and efficient. Its focus is on prevention and early intervention. I propose that national healthcare reform consider Public Health Managed Care as its central doctrine.

Emergency preparedness and response initiatives are now part of everyday behavior of local public health agencies. Our mission statement now includes four "P's": Prevention, Promotion, Protection, and Preparedness. Fortunately, the money we receive funds core public health such as epidemiology, risk communication, and active disease surveillance. These had "unfunded mandates" in the past. We have used those dollars at the local level to test response capabilities utilizing real-life scenarios, such as distribution and provision of Flumist to up to 30 schools, more than 1,000 children within a one-week period of time. The coalition of "preparedness and response partners" has proven to be very effective. Again, public health is all about sustained relationships and a shared commitment to the public's health and well-being. Public health is everyone's business in a society that cares about its community.

Managed care can be defined as "a system of administrative controls intended to reduce costs through managing the utilization of services. Managed care can also mean an integrated system of health insurance, financing, and service delivery that focuses on the appropriate and cost-effective use of health services delivered through defined networks of providers and with allocation of financial risk."[43(p.371)] This definition does not mean that public health agencies will be without a direct service role in the future. Strong partnerships between public and private sector organizations will provide a synergy that could well lead to more effective public health initiatives at the community level—with more citizens being served as a result of the collaboration.

Strong leadership on both sides is necessary if improvement in the community's health is to occur, and everyone involved with improvement efforts needs to be aware that public health leaders, managed care leaders, and legislators have different priorities.[44] The highest priority for managed care leaders and legislators is to keep costs down. The highest priority for public health leaders is to increase access to services, the next highest is to ensure that the services are of high quality, and third in rank is keeping costs low. Managed care leaders put quality second and access third. Legislators put access before quality. Thus, partnership is sometimes difficult because of the differences in priorities.

One thing that public health leaders and managed care leaders can agree on is the importance of prevention, for preventive activities are essential for keeping the demand for managed care services low (which of course keeps MCO costs low). Novick[45] reported on an interesting partnership between the public health agency in Onondaga County, New York, and the four Medicaid MCOs that were providing services to county residents. The partners:

- set up a system for monitoring the delivery of preventive services in the MCOs and in the community at large
- created linkages between managed care clinical services and population-based prevention services

(e.g., programs to reduce the prevalence of sexually transmitted diseases, tuberculosis, and HIV infection)
- worked together to facilitate disease surveillance, health-promotion and disease-prevention programs, and behavioral and environmental interventions

The relationship between public health agencies and MCOs can take many forms. It can range from complete independence through various levels of interaction to complete integration. In my study of public health leaders, most of the leaders believed that governmental public health agencies need to remain independent if they are to serve their communities well, perhaps because it is not possible to delegate responsibility for program oversight to nongovernment organizations.

Whatever the relationship between a public health agency and local MCOs (except for complete independence), public health leaders need to create a process for creating and maintaining it. One such process, developed by Leviss and Hurtig, encompasses the following 10 steps:[46]

1. Conduct assessments of both the inside and outside of the organization.
2. Evaluate and redefine the mission and vision of the agency in order to create viable assurance activities.
3. Review partnership models and start implementation.
4. Create collaborative relationships with MCOs.
5. Develop formal structures to undergird the collaboration.
6. Create new policies and regulations to support the collaboration.
7. Market materials to demonstrate the partnership.
8. Build an infrastructure to support the partnership.
9. Not only choose models of collaboration, but implement the models.
10. Evaluate the process.

The Institute of Medicine report on healthy communities discusses the evolving relationship between government public health agencies and the MCOs.[47] Three recommendations from the report are relevant to the present discussion:

1. Local public health agencies should ensure that there are high-quality services and programs available in their jurisdiction, including personal health services, and that these are accessible to all residents.
2. The leadership of local public health agencies, MCOs, and other stakeholder organizations must agree on their proper roles and responsibilities.
3. Public health agencies need to increase the level of their oversight of the health services system in their jurisdiction. For purposes of oversight, they need to collaborate with insurance regulators and state Medicaid agencies. If they perform their oversight activities effectively, they will have the opportunity to define the integrated healthcare system of the future.

The evolving relationships between public health agencies and MCOs will continue to present formidable challenges. Whether public health leaders like it or not, managed care will not go away. Furthermore, putting your head in the sand is never a good strategy. It is clear that managed care will be part of any comprehensive system of health services.

Public health leaders must:

- make public health promotion the number one community action priority
- work proactively with MCOs and not ignore them
- redefine the healthcare delivery system to include primary prevention programs
- reorganize local public health agencies (e.g., by creating new programs and revising current ones)
- develop a public health leadership toolkit

Public health leaders need to take an active role in developing assurance programs and services. Exercise 13-1 is based on a leadership credo exercise discussed by Kouzes and Posner.[48] Discuss your credo in relation to the percentage of time that you allocate to each of the three core public health functions.

2008-2010 ECONOMIC RECESSION

Before we leave the discussion of assurance, it is important to look briefly at the effect of the 2008–2010 recession on public health. Novick has stated that the recession led to a significant reduction in the ability and capacity of local health departments to provide vital services to their constituencies throughout the country.[49] In three Web-based surveys conducted between 2008 and 2010, it was found that nationally, more than 50% of local health departments reported cuts to their core funding.[50] More than 23,000 jobs were lost. All areas that provided assurance functions were affected by the cuts, and many programs were cut altogether. In an interesting case study of an Illinois health department, the authors reported that the health department had to restructure itself to prepare for accreditation at the same time that it had to deal with a declining budget.[51] To address these economic issues, the department transferred three personal services programs to community health centers.

In a 10-year retrospective case study, Richardson and his colleagues saw not only a shift in personal health services to other community agencies, but also a rise in public health preparedness programs.[52] Funding was clearly affected by changing federal mandates. In addition, budget cuts are also affecting information technology. Local public health departments have difficulty in the current economic times in playing a significant role in information integration and exchange.[53] The message is clear: the recession has had an overall negative effect on public health. When we add the potential effect of health reform, it is clear that public health leaders will have to redefine our public health mission in new and creative ways.

SUMMARY

Finding out what problems exist (assessment) and figuring out what to do about them (policy development planning) would be pointless without the final step: doing what needs to be done (assurance). In public health, the overall goal of assurance is to prevent disease and promote health in the community. This chapter began with a discussion of disease prevention and the barriers to carrying out the assurance function. It then went on to discuss the essential public health services associated with this core function.

Oddly, even though managed care may become more prevalent and take over the provision of direct services in most communities, the assurance activities of government public health agencies will expand rather than diminish. These agencies will continue to have oversight duties and will need to come up with new ways of meeting their responsibility to ensure that necessary programs and services are available to every community resident. Indeed, working out a viable relationship between public health agencies and MCOs will be one of the main challenges for public health leaders in the early part of the new century. One important lesson of the past decade is that all health system programs and services are subject to change. If public health constantly changes, then we can expect that MCO models will also change as political and social changes occur. A universal healthcare model will further change public health and the health delivery system. The chapter concludes with a discussion of the effect of the 2008–2010 economic recession.

DISCUSSION QUESTIONS

1. What are the differences between primary, secondary, and tertiary prevention?

2. What are the program responsibilities of public health agencies in primary, secondary, and tertiary prevention?

3. What are some of the main barriers that public health leaders face in meeting their assurance responsibilities?

4. What are the five essential public health services of assurance?

5. Are the assurance activities of government public health agencies likely to diminish or increase? Explain why.

6. How do public health agencies benefit from creating community partnerships?

7. What are the differences between population-based services and personal health services?

8. What are some factors that affect quality of care?

9. The greatest challenge that public health leaders will face in the immediate future is dealing with the growing prevalence of managed care. How can public health leaders meet this challenge?

10. Why is prevention likely to play a large role in the relationship between public health agencies and MCOs?

EXERCISE 13-1:   Leadership Credo

Purpose: to develop a set of guidelines for agency staff that reflects the agency leader's beliefs, values, and concerns

Key concepts: core public health functions, delegation of responsibility, leadership credo, leadership values

Procedure: Each student is to pretend that he or she is the head of a public health agency and has been given a six-month leave of absence to luxuriate on a tropical island that lacks all modern means of communication, including mail service. Before departing, the leader of the agency must give general guidance to the staff. The staff needs to know the leader's values and beliefs—in short, the leader's credo. The leader must write a one-page memorandum that expresses that credo. After the credos are written, they are read to and discussed by the entire class.

REFERENCES

1. B. J. Turnock, *Public Health: What It Is and How It Works*, 5th ed. (Burlington, MA: Jones & Bartlett Learning, 2012).

2. Washington State Department of Health, *Public Health Improvement Plan: A Progress Report* (Olympia: State of Washington Department of Health, 1994).

3. Roadmap Implementation Task Force, *The Road to Better Health for All of Illinois* (Springfield: State of Illinois, 1990).

4. E. J. Bassler, B. J. Turnock, and L. Landrum, "Sustaining Leadership in Public Health Improvement in Illinois over Five Decades," *Leadership in Public Health* 7 (2007): 2–5.

5. Institute of Medicine, *The Future of Public Health* (Washington, DC: National Academies Press, 1988).

6. G. Pickett and J. J. Hanlon, *Public Health: Administration and Practice*, 9th ed. (St. Louis: Times Mirror and Mosby College Publishing, 1990).

7. Institute of Medicine, *The Future of Public Health*.

8. Institute of Medicine, *The Future of Public Health*.

9. Institute of Medicine, *The Future of Public Health*.

10. Institute of Medicine, *The Future of the Public's Health* (Washington, DC: National Academies Press, 2003).

11. Centers for Disease Control and Prevention, *National Public Health Performance Standards Program: Local Public Health System Performance Assessment Instrument*, Version 2.0 (Washington, DC: U.S. Department of Health and Human Services, 2007).

12. Centers for Disease Control and Prevention, *Local Public Health System Performance Assessment Instrument*, Version 2.0.

13. B. J. Turnock et al., "Implementing and Assessing Organizational Practices in Local Health Departments," *Public Health Reports* 109, no. 4 (1994): 478–484.

14. Centers for Disease Control and Prevention, *Local Public Health System Performance Assessment Instrument*, Version 2.0.

15. Turnock et al., "Implementing and Assessing Organizational Practices in Local Health Departments."

16. Centers for Disease Control and Prevention, *Local Public Health System Performance Assessment Instrument*, Version 2.0.

17. Centers for Disease Control and Prevention, *Local Public Health System Performance Assessment Instrument*, Version 2.0.

18. J. Studinicki et al., "Analyzing Organizational Practices in Local Health Departments," *Public Health Reports* 109, no. 4 (1994): 485–490.

19. Studinicki et al., "Analyzing Organizational Practices in Local Health Departments."

20. B. J. Turnock et al., "Local Health Department Effectiveness in Addressing the Core Functions of Public Health," *Public Health Reports* 109, no. 5 (1994): 653–658.

21. Illinois Administrative Code, title 77, sec. 600.

22. Turnock et al., "Implementing and Assessing Organizational Practices in Local Health Departments."

23. Turnock et al., "Local Health Department Effectiveness in Addressing the Core Functions of Public Health."

24. Bassler, Turnock, and Landrum, "Sustaining Leadership in Public Health Improvement in Illinois over Five Decades."

25. Pickett and Hanlon, *Public Health*, 9th ed.

26. L. A. Aday, *At Risk in America* (San Francisco: Jossey-Bass, 1993).

27. L. Breslow et al., "Preface," in *Annual Review of Public Health* 1, ed. L. Breslow et al. (Palo Alto, CA: Annual Reviews, Inc., 1980).

28. Breslow et al., "Preface."

29. K. Gebbie, *Redefining the Assurance Function* (speech) (Chicago: Illinois Public Health Leadership Institute, 1995).

30. S. B. Thacker, "Historical Development," in *Principles and Practice of Public Health Surveillance*, ed. S. M. Teutsch and R. E. Churchill (New York: Oxford University Press, 1994).

31. Thacker, "Historical Development."

32. American Public Health Association, *Healthy Communities 2000: Model Standards* (Washington, DC: American Public Health Association, 1991).

33. Washington State Core Government Public Health Functions Task Force, *Core Public Health Functions* (Olympia: State of Washington Department of Health, 1993).

34. Washington State Department of Health, *Public Health Improvement Plan: A Progress Report* (Olympia: State of Washington Department of Health, 1994).

35. Washington State Department of Health, *Public Health Improvement Partnership* (Olympia: Washington State Department of Health, 2011).

36. U.S. General Accounting Office, *Quality Assurance: A Comprehensive National Strategy for Health Care Is Needed* (Gaithersburg, MD: U.S. General Accounting Office, 1990).

37. U.S. General Accounting Office, *Quality Assurance*.

38. U.S. General Accounting Office, *Quality Assurance*.

39. U.S. General Accounting Office, *Quality Assurance*.

40. J. Zusman, "Quality Assurance in Mental Health Care," *Hospital and Community Psychiatry* 39, no. 12 (1988): 1286–1290.

41. G. P. Mays et al., "Managed Care, Public Health, and Privatization: A Typology of Interorganizational Arrangements," in *Managed Care and Public Health*, ed. P. K. Halverson et al. (Gaithersburg, MD: Aspen Publishers, 1998).

42. L. Rowitz, *Public Health in the 21st Century: The Prepared Leader* (Sudbury, MA: Jones & Bartlett, 2006).

43. Turnock, *Public Health*.

44. C. P. McLaughlin, "Managed Care and Its Relationship to Public Health: Barriers and Opportunities," in *Managed Care and Public Health*, ed. P. K. Halverson et al. (Gaithersburg, MD: Aspen Publishers, 1998).

45. L. P. Novick, "Managed Care and Public Health," *Journal of Public Health Management and Practice* 4, no. 1 (1998): vi.

46. P. S. Leviss and L. Hurtig, "The Role of Local Health Units in a Managed Care Environment: A Case Study of New York City," *Journal of Public Health Management and Practice* 4, no. 1 (1998): 12–20.

47. M. A. Stoto et al., eds., *Healthy Communities: New Partnerships for the Future of Public Health* (Washington, DC: National Academies Press, 1996).

48. J. M. Kouzes and B. Z. Posner, *Credibility* (San Francisco: Jossey-Bass, 2011).

49. L. P. Novick, "Local Health Departments: Time of Challenge and Change," *Journal of Public Health Management and Practice* 18, no. 2 (2012): 103–105.

50. R. Willard, G. H. Shah, C. Leep, and K. Leighton, "Impact of the 2008–2010 Economic Recession on Local Health Departments," *Journal of Public Health Management and Practice* 18, no. 2 (2012): 106–114.

51. P. L. Kuehnert and K. S. McConnaughay, "Tough Choices in Tough Times: Enhancing Public Health Value in an Era of Declining Resources," *Journal of Public Health Management and Practice* 18, no. 2 (2012): 115–125.

52. J. M. Richardson, J. Pierce Jr., and N. Lackan, "Attempts by One Local Health Department to Provide Only Essential Public Health Services: A 10-Year Retrospective Case Study," *Journal of Public Health Management and Practice* 18, no. 2 (2012): 126–131.

53. J. R. Vest, N. Menachemi, and E. W. Ford, "Governance's Role in Local Health Departments' Information System and Technology Usage," *Journal of Public Health Management and Practice* 18, no. 2 (2012): 160–168.

State of Washington Assurance Capacity Standards

HEALTH PROMOTION CAPACITY STANDARDS

All public health jurisdictions, both state and local, must:

- Bring about needed changes in laws, regulations, ordinances, and policies.
- Develop health promotion programs that are culturally and linguistically appropriate for the community.
- Provide education about and intervention to prevent specific infectious and noninfectious diseases such as dental caries, vaccine-preventable diseases, hypertension, cancer, and heart disease.
- Provide education about and intervention to address specific personal and environmental risk factors such as substance abuse and hazardous materials in the home.
- Provide assessment data to the community about the incidence and causes of intentional and unintentional injury.

- Provide education in the community to help create healthy living environments.
- Provide public and professional education and other interventions to reduce intentional and unintentional injury.
- Provide services and education that enhance the formation of healthy family relationships, promote normal child growth and development, and foster appropriate child healthcare practices.
- Provide education about reproductive health and family planning methods and strategies.
- Provide education about noninfectious disease to affected individuals and their families, especially regarding disease progression, treatment, and support services.
- Provide publications, presentations, programs, and media releases on a routine basis that inform and educate the public on the health status of the community, relevant health issues, and positive health behavior.

Each local public health jurisdiction must:

- Address prioritized public health risk factors in the community through a planning process, developed in collaboration with the community, that identifies appropriate intervention strategies for specific issues and populations.
- Maintain an information and referral system concerning available health facilities, resources, and services.
- Give community members access to information and training regarding appropriate actions that enhance their living, working, school, and recreational environments.

The state must:

- Help agencies develop education strategies, including media releases and hotlines, aimed at reducing behavioral and environmental public health risk factors.
- Provide staff and technical expertise and support where local-level resources are temporarily or permanently unavailable to ensure that health promotion plans and programs addressing health risk factors are fully implemented statewide.
- Serve as the lead agency for coordinating public health activities during emergencies.
- Develop intervention strategies, education materials, and classes for specific needs of caregivers, health professionals, and other public and private partners on a statewide basis.
- Design model health education and related organizational, environmental, and economic interventions to address public health risk factors.
- Help develop public health curricula in K–12 school health education.
- Develop or provide information and referral mechanisms, including hotlines, for statewide services (for example, oral health, mental health, and environmental health issues).
- Coordinate with local health agencies and other state organizations to draft and promote statewide legislation aimed at reducing public health risk factors and promoting healthy behaviors.
- Work with the higher education system to ensure that health education/promotion personnel and training are available to address health promotion needs in local and state agencies.

HEALTH PROTECTION CAPACITY STANDARDS

All public health jurisdictions, both state and local, must:

- Maintain appropriate monitoring, inspection, intervention, and enforcement activities that eliminate or reduce the exposure of citizens to communicable disease, environmental health, and emergency hazards.
- Coordinate protection efforts with many other local, state, and federal agencies and groups.
- Develop protection programs, in accordance with federal guidelines and scientifically identified risk factors that address prioritized health risk factors.
- Ensure that communicable disease contact, investigation, and follow-up are done in a timely and appropriate manner, in adherence to guidelines of the federal Centers for Disease Control and Prevention.
- Ensure that persons with communicable diseases are identified; treated in a timely, appropriate manner; and given information regarding treatment protocols and appropriate behavior to reduce the spread of disease.
- Take appropriate legal or other action if treatment protocols or behavior changes are not followed through.
- Ensure that individuals, especially children, are immunized according to recommended public health schedules.
- Provide surveillance, diagnosis, and treatment of infectious diseases of public health significance.
- Analyze and interpret data regarding environmental and personal risk factors.
- Provide maternity services such as outreach, case management, and support services.
- Provide nutrition intervention services for children and childbearing women that include education and provision of specific foods.
- Regularly screen and assess children who are at risk or who live in high-risk families.

Each local public health jurisdiction must:

- Conduct ongoing inspections and provide oversight consistent with state and local board of health rules and regulations.

- Respond to concerns expressed by the public regarding health problems.
- Conduct surveillance and manage the data generated so that program efforts can address community needs and problems.
- Enforce compliance with public health regulations whenever a voluntary compliance strategy is not effective or appropriate.
- Train operators of facilities (for example, water treatment plants and food service establishments) in order to ensure that facilities are properly operated and maintained on a day-to-day basis.
- Identify and control small animal, insect, and rodent populations that present potential and actual hazards to public health.
- Determine the nature and effect of public health emergencies and mobilize resources to control or prevent additional illness, injury, or death.
- Provide public health information services on a 24-hour basis to inform and help coordinate responses of local, state, and federal organizations to public health emergencies.
- Maintain an inventory of local medical and health personnel, medical equipment, facilities, and other resources that might be needed during emergencies, noting availability and response criteria.
- Provide or have access to laboratory services that can, during emergencies, support the local detection, identification, and analysis of hazardous substances that may present threats to public health.
- Maintain required potability and quality of domestic water supplies affected by emergencies.
- Provide for the public health concerns of rescue workers and care providers in emergency situations, including needs for shelter, food, and sanitation equipment.
- Provide ongoing public health staff training in emergency response plans, including participation in practice exercises on a routine basis.

The state must:

- Facilitate and provide periodic training to local health agency staff and operators of facilities (for example, hotels, hospitals, restaurants, water treatment plants, public swimming pools, sewage disposal plants) on new and emerging issues.
- Routinely coordinate with federal rule-making agencies and Congress to ensure that they take into account the effects of federal rules and statutes on the health risks, protection needs, and resources of Washington State.

- Develop, in cooperation with local health agencies, consistent uniform statewide regulations and policies that guide the public health activities of direct service providers, the local public health jurisdictions, and state agencies.
- Support the day-to-day efforts and provide assistance in the crisis response efforts of local agencies.
- Carry out the direct regulatory responsibilities over the largest public water supplies and certain community on-site sewage disposal systems.
- Assume appropriate service, consultative, and coordination responsibilities for emergency response efforts.
- Serve as the lead agency for coordinating all public health activities during emergencies in the State Emergency Operations Center.
- Provide public information support to the Office of the Governor and to other state or federal emergency management agencies during emergency and disaster recovery operations.
- Support local health agencies in the provision of laboratory services, food and water inspection, radiological assessment, and disease identification and testing during emergencies.
- Help coordinate and incorporate local emergency response plans into a statewide plan.
- Help coordinate the transfer of needed personnel, resources, and equipment to emergency sites.

QUALITY ASSURANCE CAPACITY STANDARDS

Each local public health jurisdiction must:

- Ensure that communicable diseases are being appropriately treated in the community.
- Ensure that prevention and intervention efforts for communicable diseases are being appropriately implemented, including tracking the immunization status of children in the community.
- Evaluate the health status of populations who receive public health services and the effect of those services on their health status.
- Recognize and respond to unmet community needs, especially those related to high-risk conditions or behaviors.
- Gain access to data systems to provide long-term trend analyses, including being a participant in the Health Services Information System.
- Monitor and ensure the competence of people such as food handlers whose activities can affect

the health of the public and who are not otherwise licensed or monitored by the state.

- Develop strategies to ensure that individuals and families can be linked with needed providers.
- Help inform providers regarding public health interventions, areas of concern, and recommended standards of care.
- Evaluate access to personal health services, especially for low-income and special populations. Where applicable, the evaluation should include a measure of the cultural appropriateness of services.
- Educate providers about specific public health interventions or areas of concern and recommended standards of care.
- Support strategies to ensure linkages between providers, families, and individuals.
- Evaluate the efficacy, costs, and benefits of prevention services as compared to medical treatment.
- Recognize the need for and establish criteria for competency assessment and assurance of health professionals.

- Design, implement, and evaluate licensing and certification programs and methods for health professionals and facilities and providers of other public services.
- Ensure compliance with appropriate regulations and standards in healthcare sites and facilities.
- Periodically review local health agency and community programs to ensure compliance with state standards.
- Assess and monitor state-funded public health programs for outcome results.
- Conduct quality assurance activities and operate state-mandated regulatory programs necessary to ensure that all laboratories produce high-quality outcomes. Work with agencies to correct deficiencies and provide appropriate training programs.
- Ensure that laboratories that provide data for public health purposes are linked through a common information management system that ensures consistent laboratory performance and ready access to analytical and diagnostic data.

CHAPTER 14

Leadership and Accreditation

The tool [for] accreditation standards . . . are tools of and for public health leadership.

—Bernard Turnock

Over the past twenty years, public health leaders have argued about the value of utilizing the core functions and essential services of public health. With our partners, we have used this paradigm to create tools to help us make our agencies and communities work more effectively and efficiently to address the public health needs of the people in our communities, counties, regions, and states. We have developed assessment tools like MAPP (Mobilizing for Action through Planning and Partnerships), and we have developed policies, laws, rules, and regulations to help us in our efforts to promote health and prevent illness. We have struggled with tools to measure performance, tools to improve the quality of our activities, and research to create an evidence base for our work. Despite our innovations, not every health department utilizes the core functions and essential services paradigm, and many health departments do not regularly do community assessments. Many of our public health administrators have

little or no training on management and leadership or even public health. Our advocacy efforts on behalf of the public health of our respective populations are often failures. The public often does not understand what we do. All these limits create a leadership dilemma for us. This chapter is about credibility and one approach to making our work more understandable to others. This approach is about setting standards for public health that are high and not low.

In 2003, the Institute of Medicine (IOM) noted that performance measurement is important in public health.[1] This has led to the development of tools such as the National Public Health Performance Standards (NPHPSP) for state and local health departments and a governance tool for boards of health (see **Table 14-1**).[2] These tools have become essential in quality improvement activities that hold agencies accountable for meeting the specific responsibilities related to the public health core functions and essential services. As I write this chapter, version 3.0 of the NPHPSP is being implemented. The IOM report argued that this movement to create a performance standards system of tools also increased the interest in accreditation.[3] It further stated

TABLE 14-1 Crosswalk of Model Standards and Key Points within the Three NPHPSP Instruments

Essential Services	State Public Health System Assessment	Local Public Health System Assessment	Local Public Health Governance Assessment
1. Monitor health status to identify community health problems.	**1.1 Planning and Implementation** 1.1.1 Surveillance and monitoring programs 1.1.2 Health data products accessible to data users 1.1.3 State health profile 1.1.4 Disease reporting system 1.1.5 Protection of personal health information **1.2 State–Local Relationships** 1.2.1 Assistance in interpretation and use of health data 1.2.2 Uniform set of timely community-level health data 1.2.3 Assistance with local information and monitoring systems **1.3 Performance Management and Quality Improvement** 1.3.1 Review effectiveness in monitoring efforts 1.3.2 Active performance management **1.4 Public Health Capacity and Resources** 1.4.1 Commit financial resources 1.4.2 Coordinate systemwide organizational efforts 1.4.3 Workforce expertise	**1.1 Population-Based Community Health Profile** 1.1.1 Community health assessment 1.1.2 Community health profile (CHP) 1.1.3 Community-wide use of community health assessment or CHP data **1.2 Current Technology to Manage and Communicate Population Health Data** 1.2.1 State-of-the-art technology to support health profile databases 1.2.2 Access to geocoded health data 1.2.3 Use of computer-generated graphics **1.3 Registries** 1.3.1 Maintenance of and/or contribution to population health registries 1.3.2 Use of information from population health registries	**1.1 Oversight for Community Health Status Monitoring** 1.1.1 Assessment of resources for community health status monitoring 1.1.2 Promotion of community participation in collecting, analyzing, and disseminating community health status data 1.1.3 Support activities for effective health status monitoring from population health registries

2. Diagnose and investigate health problems and health hazards in the community.

2.1 Planning and Implementation

2.1.1 Broad scope of surveillance programs

2.1.2 Enhanced surveillance capability

2.1.3 Statewide public health laboratory system

2.1.4 Laboratory analysis capabilities

2.1.5 Investigations of health problems

2.2 State–Local Relationships

2.2.1 Assistance with epidemiologic analysis

2.2.2 Assistance in using laboratory services

2.2.3 Guidance in handling public health problems and threats

2.2.4 Capability to deploy response teams to local areas, when needed

2.3 Performance Management and Quality Improvement

2.3.1 Review surveillance and investigation procedures

2.3.2 Active performance management

2.4 Public Health Capacity and Resources

2.4.1 Commit financial resources

2.4.2 Coordinate systemwide organizational efforts

2.4.3 Workforce expertise

2.1 Identification and Surveillance of Health Threats

2.1.1 Surveillance system(s) to monitor health problems and identify health threats

2.1.2 Submission of reportable disease information in a timely manner

2.1.3 Resources to support surveillance and investigation activities

2.2 Investigation and Response to Public Health Threats and Emergencies

2.2.1 Written protocols for case finding, contact tracing, source identification, and containment

2.2.2 Current epidemiological case investigation protocols

2.2.3 Designated Emergency Response Coordinator

2.2.4 Rapid response of personnel in emergencies/disasters

2.2.5 Evaluation of public health emergency response

2.3 Laboratory Support for Investigation of Health Threat

2.3.1 Ready access to laboratories for routine diagnostic and surveillance needs

2.3.2 Ready access to laboratories for public health threats, hazards, and emergencies

2.3.3 Licensed and/or credentialed laboratories

2.3.4 Maintenance of guidelines or protocols for handling laboratory samples

2.1 Oversight for Public Health Surveillance

2.1.1 Assessment of resources for diagnosis and investigation of health threats

2.1.2 Policies that support diagnosis and investigation of health threats

2.1.3 Promote collaboration regarding issues of diagnosis and investigation of health threats

2.1.4 Review of laboratory services, infectious disease epidemiologic programs, and public health surveillance and response capacity

(Continues)

TABLE 14-1 Crosswalk of Model Standards and Key Points within the Three NPHPSP Instruments (*Continued*)

Essential Services	State Public Health System Assessment	Local Public Health System Assessment	Local Public Health Governance Assessment
3. Inform, educate, and empower people about health issues.	**3.1 Planning and Implementation**	**3.1 Health Education and Promotion**	**3.1 Oversight of Public Health Information, Education, and Empowerment Activities**
	3.1.1 Health education and promotion programs	3.1.1 Provision of community health information	3.1.1 Assessment of resources for community health education and promotion programs
	3.1.2 Health communication programs	3.1.2 Health education and/or health promotion campaigns	3.1.2 Policies in support of health education and promotion programs
	3.1.3 Emergency communications capacity	3.1.3 Collaboration on health education and promotion activities	3.1.3 Review of public health education and promotion activities
	3.2 State–Local Relationships	**3.2 Health Communication**	
	3.2.1 Assistance with health communication and health education/promotion programs	3.2.1 Development of health communication plans	
	3.2.2 Assistance in developing local emergency communication capabilities	3.2.2 Relationships with media	
		3.2.3 Designation of public information officers	
	3.3 Performance Management and Quality Improvement	**3.3 Risk Communication**	
	3.3.1 Review effectiveness of health communication and health education/promotion efforts	3.3.1 Emergency communications plan(s)	
	3.3.2 Active performance management	3.3.2 Resources for rapid communications response	
	3.4 Public Health Capacity and Resources	3.3.3 Crisis and emergency communications training	
	3.4.1 Commit financial resources	3.3.4 Policies and procedures for public information officer response	
	3.4.2 Coordinate systemwide organizational efforts		
	3.4.3 Workforce expertise		

4. Mobilize community partnerships to identify and solve health problems.

4.1 Planning and Implementation
4.1.1 Building statewide support for public health
4.1.2 Partnership organization and development

4.2 State–Local Relationships
4.2.1 Assistance in building collaborative skills
4.2.2 Incentives for local partnerships

4.3 Performance Management and Quality Improvement
4.3.1 Review effectiveness of partnerships
4.3.2 Active performance management

4.4 Public Health Capacity and Resources
4.4.1 Commit financial resources
4.4.2 Coordinate systemwide organizational efforts
4.4.3 Workforce expertise

4.1 Constituency Development
4.1.1 Identification of key constituents or stakeholders
4.1.2 Participation of constituents in improving community health
4.1.3 Directory of organizations that comprise the LPHS
4.1.4 Communications strategies to build awareness of public health

4.2 Community Partnerships
4.2.1 Partnerships for public health improvement activities
4.2.2 Community health improvement committee
4.2.3 Review of community partnerships and strategic alliances

4.1 Oversight for Constituency Development and Partnership Building
4.1.1 Assessment of resources for constituency development and partnership building
4.1.2 Policies in support of public health constituency development or partnership building
4.1.3 Recognition/encouragement of community participation
4.1.4 Review of public health constituency development and partnership building activities

5. Develop policies and plans that support individual and community health efforts.

5.1 Planning and Implementation
5.1.1 Convene collaborative planning processes
5.1.2 State health improvement plan
5.1.3 State all-hazards preparedness plan and emergency response capacity
5.1.4 Policy development activities

5.1 Governmental Presence at the Local Level
5.1.1 Governmental local public health presence
5.1.2 Resources for the local health department
5.1.3 Local board of health or other governing entity (not scored)
5.1.4 LHD work with the state public health agency and other state partners

5.1 Oversight of Public Health Planning and Policy Development
5.1.1 Documentation of legal authority
5.1.2 Mission statement
5.1.3 Assessment of resources and organizational support for public health plans and policies
5.1.4 Support of a community health improvement process
5.1.5 Support establishment of all-hazards emergency response plan

(Continues)

TABLE 14-1 Crosswalk of Model Standards and Key Points within the Three NPHPSP Instruments (*Continued*)

Essential Services	State Public Health System Assessment	Local Public Health System Assessment	Local Public Health Governance Assessment
	5.2 State–Local Relationships	**5.2 Public Health Policy Development**	
	5.2.1 Assistance and training for local planning	5.2.1 Contribution to development of public health policies	
	5.2.2 Assistance in integrating statewide strategies in community health improvement plans	5.2.2 Alert policymakers/public of public health effects from policies	
	5.2.3 Assistance in development of local preparedness plans	5.2.3 Review of public health policies	
	5.2.4 Assistance in local policy development		
	5.3 Performance Management and Quality Improvement	**5.3 Community Health Improvement Process and Strategic Planning**	
	5.3.1 Monitor progress in health improvement	5.3.1 Community health improvement process	
	5.3.2 Review policies for public health effect	5.3.2 Strategies to address community health objectives	
	5.3.3 Exercises and drills to test preparedness plans	5.3.3 Local health department (LHD) strategic planning process	
	5.3.4 Active performance management		
	5.4 Public Health Capacity and Resources	**5.4 Plan for Public Health Emergencies**	
	5.4.1 Commit financial resources	5.4.1 Community task force or coalition for emergency preparedness and response plans	
	5.4.2 Coordinate systemwide organizational efforts	5.4.2 All-hazards emergency preparedness and response plan	
	5.4.3 Workforce expertise in planning and policy development	5.4.3 Review and revision of the all-hazards plan	

6. Enforce laws and regulations that protect health and ensure safety.

6.1 Planning and Implementation
6.1.1 Review of public health laws
6.1.2 Emergency powers
6.1.3 Cooperative relationships to support compliance
6.1.4 Customer-centered administrative processes

6.2 State–Local Relationships
6.2.1 Assistance on enforcement of laws
6.2.2 Assistance to local governing bodies in developing local laws

6.3 Performance Management and Quality Improvement
6.3.1 Review effectiveness of regulatory activities
6.3.2 Active performance management

6.4 Public Health Capacity and Resources
6.4.1 Commit financial resources
6.4.2 Coordinate systemwide organizational efforts
6.4.3 Workforce expertise

6.1 Review and Evaluation of Laws, Regulations, and Ordinances
6.1.1 Identification of public health issues to be addressed through laws, regulations, and ordinances
6.1.2 Knowledge of laws, regulations, and ordinances
6.1.3 Review of laws, regulations, and ordinances
6.1.4 Access to legal counsel

6.2 Involvement in the Improvement of Laws, Regulations, and Ordinances
6.2.1 Identification of public health issues not addressed through existing laws
6.2.2 Development or modification of laws for public health issues
6.2.3 Technical assistance for drafting proposed legislation, regulations, or ordinances

6.3 Enforcement of Laws, Regulations, and Ordinances
6.3.1 Authority to enforce laws, regulations, or ordinances
6.3.2 Public health emergency powers
6.3.3 Enforcement in accordance with applicable laws, regulations, and ordinances
6.3.4 Provision of information about compliance
6.3.5 Assessment of compliance

6.1 Oversight of Enforcement of Public Health Laws and Regulations
6.1.1 Know source(s) of authority regarding laws, rules, and regulations
6.1.2 Statutory authority to enact laws, rules, and regulations
6.1.3 Assessment of resources for inspection and enforcement activities
6.1.4 Advocacy for laws and regulations that protect health and ensure safety
6.1.5 Review of laws, rules, and regulations designed to protect health

(Continues)

TABLE 14-1 Crosswalk of Model Standards and Key Points within the Three NPHPSP Instruments (*Continued*)

Essential Services	State Public Health System Assessment	Local Public Health System Assessment	Local Public Health Governance Assessment
7. Link people to needed personal health services and ensure the provision of health care when otherwise unavailable.	**7.1 Planning and Implementation**	**7.1 Identification of Personal Health Service Needs of Populations**	**7.1 Oversight for Public Health Outreach and Linkage to Personal Health Services**
	7.1.1 Assessment of access to care	7.1.1 Identification of populations who experience barriers to care	7.1.1 Identification of responsible agencies for coordination, outreach, and linkage
	7.1.2 Delivery of services and programs to improve access	7.1.2 Identification of personal health service needs of populations	7.1.2 Assessment of resources to facilitate access to services
	7.1.3 SPHS entity responsible for monitoring and coordination	7.1.3 Assessment of personal health services available to populations who experience barriers to care	7.1.3 Policies supporting resources for outreach and linkage to personal health services
	7.1.4 Mobilizes to reduce health disparities, including during emergency events		7.1.4 Review of outreach efforts and linkage to personal health services
	7.2 State–Local Relationships	**7.2 Ensuring the Linkage of People to Personal Health Services**	
	7.2.1 Assistance in assessment and service delivery	7.2.1 Link populations to needed personal health services	
	7.2.2 Assistance for providers serving underserved populations	7.2.2 Assistance to vulnerable populations in accessing needed health services	
	7.3 Performance Management and Quality Improvement	7.2.3 Initiatives for enrolling eligible individuals in public benefit programs	
	7.3.1 Review effectiveness of programs in improving access, appropriateness of personal health care, and health care quality	7.2.4 Coordination of personal health and social services	
	7.3.2 Active performance management		
	7.4 Public Health Capacity and Resources		
	7.4.1 Commit financial resources		
	7.4.2 Coordinate systemwide organizational efforts		
	7.4.3 Workforce expertise		

8. Ensure a competent public health and personal health care workforce.

8.1 Planning and Implementation
8.1.1 Assessment of population-based and personal health care workforce needs
8.1.2 Statewide workforce development plan
8.1.3 Programs to enhance workforce skills
8.1.4 Ensure excellence in professional practice of workforce members
8.1.5 Incentives for lifelong learning

8.2 State–Local Relationships
8.2.1 Assistance with workforce assessment
8.2.2 Assistance with workforce development
8.2.3 Education and training to enhance local workforce skills

8.3 Performance Management and Quality Improvement
8.3.1 Review workforce development efforts
8.3.2 Review whether academic–practice partnerships are effective in preparing the workforce
8.3.3 Active performance management

8.4 Public Health Capacity and Resources
8.4.1 Commit financial resources
8.4.2 Coordinate systemwide organizational efforts
8.4.3 Workforce expertise

8.1 Workforce Assessment, Planning, and Development
8.1.1 Assessment of the LPHS workforce
8.1.2 Identification of shortfalls and/or gaps in the LPHS workforce
8.1.3 Dissemination of results of the workforce assessment/gap analysis

8.2 Public Health Workforce Standards
8.2.1 Awareness of guidelines and/or licensure/certification requirements
8.2.2 Written job standards and/or position descriptions
8.2.3 Annual performance evaluations
8.2.4 LHD-written job standards and/or position descriptions
8.2.5 LHD performance evaluations

8.3 Lifelong Learning through Continuing Education, Training, and Mentoring
8.3.1 Identification of education and training needs for workforce development
8.3.2 Opportunities for developing core public health competencies
8.3.3 Educational and training incentives
8.3.4 Interaction between personnel from LPHS and academic organizations

8.4 Public Health Leadership Development
8.4.1 Development of leadership skills
8.4.2 Collaborative leadership
8.4.3 Leadership opportunities for individuals and/or organizations
8.4.4 Recruitment and retention of new and diverse leaders

8.1 Oversight of Public Health Workforce Issues
8.1.1 Compliance with licensure and credentialing requirements
8.1.2 Policies supporting public health workforce
8.1.3 Assessment of resources for workforce training, leadership development, or continuing education
8.1.4 Access to continuing training and education for board members
8.1.5 Review efforts to strengthen the public health workforce

(Continues)

TABLE 14-1 Crosswalk of Model Standards and Key Points within the Three NPHPSP Instruments (*Continued*)

Essential Services	State Public Health System Assessment	Local Public Health System Assessment	Local Public Health Governance Assessment
9. Evaluate the effectiveness, accessibility, and quality of personal and population-based health services.	**9.1 Planning and Implementation**	**9.1 Evaluation of Population-Based Services**	**9.1 Oversight and Evaluation for Personal and Population-Based Health Services**
	9.1.1 Evaluate population-based health programs	9.1.1 Evaluation of population-based health services	9.1.1 Assessment of resources to support evaluation
	9.1.2 Evaluate personal health care services	9.1.2 Assessment of community satisfaction with population-based health services	9.1.2 Evaluation plan for personal and population-based services
	9.1.3 Assess the performance of the public health system	9.1.3 Identification of gaps in the provision of population-based health services	9.1.3 Policies supporting evaluation activities
	9.2 State–Local Relationships	9.1.4 Use of population-based health services evaluation	9.1.4 Promote participation in evaluation activities
	9.2.1 Assistance on evaluation		9.1.5 Review evaluation findings
	9.2.2 Share state evaluation results to assist local planning	**9.2 Evaluation of Personal Health Services**	
	9.3 Performance Management and Quality Improvement	9.2.1 Personal health services evaluation	
	9.3.1 Review the effectiveness of evaluation activities	9.2.2 Evaluation of personal health services against established standards	
	9.3.2 Active performance management	9.2.3 Assessment of client satisfaction with personal health services	
	9.4 Public Health Capacity and Resources	9.2.4 Information technology to ensure quality of personal health services	
	9.4.1 Commit financial resources	9.2.5 Use of personal health services evaluation	
	9.4.2 Coordinate systemwide organizational efforts	**9.3 Evaluation of Local Public Health System**	
	9.4.3 Workforce expertise	9.3.1 Identification of community organizations or entities that contribute to the LPHS	
		9.3.2 Periodic evaluation of LPHS	
		9.3.3 Evaluation of partnership within the LPHS	
		9.3.4 Use of LPHS evaluation to guide community health improvements	

10. Research for new insights and innovative solutions to health problems.

10.1 Planning and Implementation
- 10.1.1 Academic–practice collaboration to disseminate and use research findings in practice
- 10.1.2 Public health research agenda
- 10.1.3 Conduct and participate in research

10.2 State–Local Relationships
- 10.2.1 Assistance in research activities, including community-based participatory research
- 10.2.2 Assistance in using research findings

10.3 Performance Management and Quality Improvement
- 10.3.1 Review research activities for relevance and appropriateness
- 10.3.2 Active performance management

10.4 Public Health Capacity and Resources
- 10.4.1 Commit financial resources
- 10.4.2 Coordinate systemwide organizational efforts
- 10.4.3 Workforce expertise

10.1 Fostering Innovation
- 10.1.1 Encouragement of new solutions to health problems
- 10.1.2 Proposal of public health issues for inclusion in research agenda
- 10.1.3 Identification and monitoring of best practices
- 10.1.4 Encouragement of community participation in research

10.2 Linkage with Institutions of Higher Learning or Research
- 10.2.1 Relationships with institutions of higher learning and/or research organizations
- 10.2.2 Partnerships to conduct research
- 10.2.3 Collaboration between the academic and practice communities

10.3 Capacity to Initiate or Participate in Research
- 10.3.1 Access to researchers
- 10.3.2 Access to resources to facilitate research
- 10.3.3 Dissemination of research findings
- 10.3.4 Evaluation of research activities

10.1 Oversight of Public Health Innovation and Research
- 10.1.1 Policies to foster and reward innovation
- 10.1.2 Encourage collaboration for community-based research
- 10.1.3 Assessment of resources for research and identification of best practices
- 10.1.4 Encourage use of research findings and best practices

Source: Reproduced from Centers for Disease Control and Prevention (2010). National Public Health Performance Standards Program (NPHPSP): 10 Essential Public Health Services, Additional Resources. http://www.cdc.gov/nphpsp/essentialservices.html. Last updated December 9, 2010. Accessed May 7, 2012.

that accreditation creates a useful set of tools to establish standards for public health and to evaluate performance against these standards. The IOM recommended that the Secretary of Health and Human Services appoint a national commission to discuss the feasibility of a public health accreditation system. It argued that representatives on the commission should include leaders from national public health professional organizations as well as nongovernmental organizations.

Late in December 2004, the Robert Wood Johnson Foundation convened stakeholders interested in the process to examine the accreditation issue.[4] Two background papers were commissioned for the meeting. In the first paper, Thielen pointed out that local public health agencies are closer and more supportive of accreditation than state public health agencies.[5] Leadership at the local level is critical. Leadership at the state level is about providing resources, support, and coordination. State funding is a driver in discretionary funding to aid in accreditation activities and the setting of standards. State efforts have influenced accountability based on the core functions and essential services of public health. In the second background paper, Mays stated that accreditation has the potential to improve the public health service system.[6] Better service can lead to better health outcomes. On the negative side, the process of accreditation is expensive and needs to be balanced against feasibility and overall value. The costs of accreditation need to be financed carefully. The incentives for accreditation need to be examined at the state and local levels. Governance is a community concern that requires input from many stakeholders. Accreditation should lead to more evidence-based public health practice. These papers and the conference led to the Exploring Accreditation Project.[7] This project recommended creation of a voluntary national accreditation model that would be built on a foundation of high performance and continuous quality improvement. The expectation was that health departments would also be accountable to both the public and policy makers. In fact, many of the accreditation expectations correlated closely with both the National Public Health Performance Standards Program and the National Association of County and City Health Officials' operational definition of a functional local health department.[8]

Next, the Robert Wood Johnson Foundation funded the MLC (Multistate Learning Collaborative) to bring a number of states together to share information and to strengthen the performance assessment process.[9] Lenaway, Corso, and Bailey argued that the Centers for Disease Control and Prevention (CDC) needed to participate as a funder in a voluntary national system for accreditation.[10] In 2005, a Steering Committee was put together with membership from public health at the federal, state, and local levels as well as from many public health professional organizations. A proposal was ready by spring of 2006.[11] In 2007, Joly and her colleagues pointed to the necessity of linking accreditation to health outcomes.[12] **Figure 14-1** shows a logic model that attempts to link accreditation to outcome and provides an important tool to leaders to show the relationship of the two. Nolan and colleagues explored the finance issue.[13] **Table 14-2** shows the cost variables that may interfere with the undertaking of accreditation under a voluntary system.

PUBLIC HEALTH ACCREDITATION BOARD

The Public Health Accreditation Board (PHAB) was formed as a nonprofit organization in 2007. According to the PHAB website, a Standards Development Workgroup that included representatives of state and local public health leaders, representatives from states with accreditation programs, members of other national accreditation programs, and other experts developed the accreditation process.[14] In 2009, PHAB released the initial process document. The program was to be implemented in 2011, and that has occurred. **Figure 14-2** presents the PHAB Standards for 2011–2012.[15] Case Study 14-A presents a practice quiz with Kaye Bender, the president and chief executive director of PHAB. The quiz uses the "five whys" perspective, which asks "Why?" five times, starting with "Why accreditation?"[16]

HEALTH DEPARTMENT PERSPECTIVE

From the health department perspective, there are many questions to answer. The most important one is probably "Are we ready?" I recently had a conversation with a local health department about this question. The telephone conference also included the health department director in addition to the chair of the local board of health. The director told me he was undertaking a strategic plan for the agency. His agency, board, and community had carried out the MAPP community assessment process with the local performance standards evaluation as

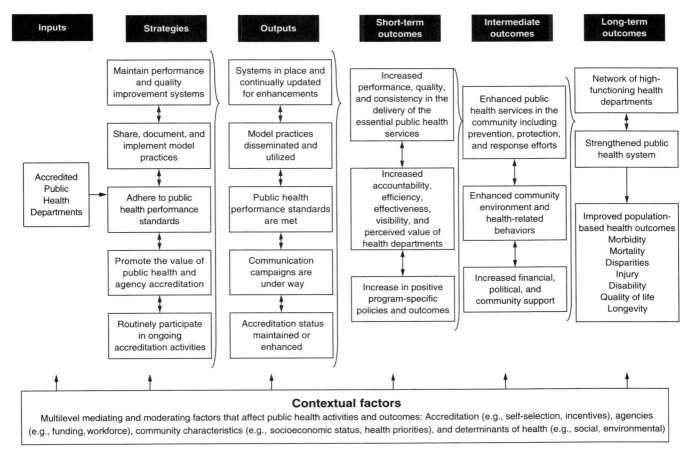

FIGURE 14-1 Linking Public Health Accreditation and Outcomes. *Source:* Reproduced from Joly et al., Linking Accreditation and Public Health Outcomes, *Journal of Public Health Management and Practice, 13*(2001)4, 349–356, Figure 1.

TABLE 14-2 Cost Variables

Governance
Board compensation
Number of meetings
Committee meetings
Sponsors—number and capital vs. operations
Implementation length
(development and pilot testing)
Appeals
Geography
Administration/management
Marketing budget
Market size/penetration over 5 years

(Continues)

TABLE 14-2 Cost Variables (*Continued*)

Size of staff/growth

Contractors/outsource

In-kind/sponsorships

    Fixed costs

    Capital costs

Data management

Preimplementation phasing/number of pilots

Standards and measurements

Number and complexity of standards

Development process

    Methods

    Interaction with stakeholders

    Timeline

Revision cycle

Conformity assessment

Cycle length

Site visit team size

Length of visit

Cost and who pays

Training site visitors

Standardizing

Volunteer vs. paid

Technical assistance/training for applicants

Benchmarking applicant activities

Web site development

Data collection

Self-assessment process

Vendors

"Surveillance" between surveys

Evaluation

Timeline

Internal/external staff

Scope

    Operation evaluation

    Impact/research

Source: Reproduced from P. Nolan, R. Bialris, M. I. Kushion, et al. "Financing and Creating Incentives for a Voluntary National Accreditation System for Public Health," *Journal of Public Health Management and Practice*, 13(2007)41, 378–382, Table 1.

ASSESS

DOMAIN 1: Conduct and disseminate assessments focused on population health status and public health issues facing the community

Standard 1.1: Participate in or Conduct a Collaborative Process Resulting in a Comprehensive Community Health Assessment

Standard 1.2: Collect and Maintain Reliable, Comparable, and Valid Data that Provide Information on Conditions of Public Health Importance and on the Health Status of the Population

Standard 1.3: Analyze Public Health Data to Identify Trends in Health Problems, Environmental Public Health Hazards, and Social and Economic Factors that Affect the Public's Health

Standard 1.4: Provide and Use the Results of Health Data Analysis to Develop Recommendations Regarding Public Health Policy, Processes, Programs, or Interventions

INVESTIGATE

DOMAIN 2: Investigate health problems and environmental public health hazards to protect the community

Standard 2.1: Conduct Timely Investigations of Health Problems and Environmental Public Health Hazards

Standard 2.2: Contain/Mitigate Health Problems and Environmental Public Health Hazards

Standard 2.3: Ensure Access to Laboratory and Epidemiologic/Environmental Public Health Expertise and Capacity to Investigate and Contain/Mitigate Public Health Problems and Environmental Public Health Hazards

Standard 2.4: Maintain a Plan with Policies and Procedures for Urgent and Non-Urgent Communications

INFORM & EDUCATE

DOMAIN 3: Inform and educate about public health issues and functions

Standard 3.1: Provide Health Education and Health Promotion Policies, Programs, Processes, and Interventions to Support Prevention and Wellness

Standard 3.2: Provide Information on Public Health Issues and Public Health Functions through Multiple Methods to a Variety of Audiences

COMMUNITY ENGAGEMENT

DOMAIN 4: Engage with the community to identify and address health problems

Standard 4.1: Engage with the Public Health System and the Community in Identifying and Addressing Health Problems through Collaborative Processes

Standard 4.2: Promote the Community's Understanding of and Support for Policies and Strategies that Will Improve the Public's Health

POLICIES & PLANS

DOMAIN 5: Develop public health policies and plans

Standard 5.1: Serve as a Primary and Expert Resource for Establishing and Maintaining Public Health Policies, Practices, and Capacity

Standard 5.2: Conduct a Comprehensive Planning Process Resulting in a Tribal/State/Community Health Improvement Plan

Standard 5.3: Develop and Implement a Health Department Organizational Strategic Plan

Standard 5.4: Maintain an All-Hazards Emergency Operations Plan

PUBLIC HEALTH LAWS

DOMAIN 6: Enforce public health laws

Standard 6.1: Review Existing Laws and Work with Governing Entities and Elected/Appointed Officials to Update as Needed

Standard 6.2: Educate Individuals and Organizations on the Meaning, Purpose, and Benefit of Public Health Laws and How to Comply

Standard 6.3: Conduct and Monitor Public Health Enforcement Activities and Coordinate Notification of Violations among Appropriate Agencies

FIGURE 14-2 PHAB Standards Overview.

(*Continues*)

ACCESS TO CARE

DOMAIN 7: Promote strategies to improve access to healthcare services

Standard 7.1: Assess Healthcare Capacity and Access to Healthcare Services

Standard 7.2: Identify and Implement Strategies to Improve Access to Healthcare Services

WORKFORCE

DOMAIN 8: Maintain a competent public health workforce

Standard 8.1: Encourage the Development of a Sufficient Number of Qualified Public Health Workers

Standard 8.2: Assess Staff Competencies and Address Gaps by Enabling Organizational and Individual Training and Development

QUALITY IMPROVEMENT

DOMAIN 9: Evaluate and continuously improve processes, programs, and interventions

Standard 9.1: Use a Performance Management System to Improve Organizational Practice, Processes, Programs, and Interventions

Standard 9.2: Develop and Implement Quality Improvement Processes Integrated into Organizational Practice, Programs, Processes, and Interventions

EVIDENCE-BASED PRACTICES

DOMAIN 10: Contribute to and apply the evidence base of public health

Standard 10.1: Identify and Use the Best Available Evidence for Making Informed Public Health Practice Decisions

Standard 10.2: Promote Understanding and Use of Research Results, Evaluations, and Evidence-Based Practices with Appropriate Audiences

ADMINISTRATION & MANAGEMENT

DOMAIN 11: Maintain administrative and management capacity

Standard 11.1: Develop and Maintain an Operational Infrastructure to Support the Performance of Public Health Functions

Standard 11.2: Establish Effective Financial Management Systems

GOVERNANCE

DOMAIN 12: Maintain capacity to engage the public health governing entity

Standard 12.1: Maintain Current Operational Definitions and Statements of the Public Health Roles, Responsibilities, and Authorities

Standard 12.2: Provide Information to the Governing Entity Regarding Public Health and the Official Responsibilities of the Health Department and of the Governing Entity

Standard 12.3: Encourage the Governing Entity's Engagement in the Public Health Department's Overall Obligations and Responsibilities

The **PHAB STANDARDS** apply to all health departments—tribal, state, local, and territorial. Standards are the required level of achievement that a health department is expected to meet. Domains are groups of standards that pertain to a broad group of public health services. The focus of the PHAB standards is "what" the health department provides in services and activities, irrespective of "how" they are provided or through what organizational structure. Please refer to the **PHAB Standards and Measures** Version 1.0 document, available at www.phaboard.org, for the full official standards, measures, required documentation, and guidance.

FIGURE 14-2 PHAB Standards Overview. (*Continued*) *Source:* Reprinted with permission of Kaye Bender and PHAB.

Case Study 14-A

A Practice Quiz with Kaye Bender

Kaye Bender, PhD, RN, FAAN, is president and CEO of the Public Health Accreditation Board, the organization charged with administering the first national accreditation program for public health. Dr. Bender has more than 30 years' experience in public health practice at the local and state levels in Mississippi. She also served as dean of the School of Nursing and associate vice chancellor for nursing at the University of Mississippi Medical Center. She served on two Institute of Medicine study committees, *The Future of the Public's Health in the 21st Century* and *Who Will Keep the Public Healthy?* She is a graduate of the Public Health Leadership Institute in California. She chaired the Exploring Accreditation Steering Committee, the exploratory precursor study that led to the development of the Public Health Accreditation Board.

What is public health department accreditation, and why is it an important goal for public health department leaders to consider?

Public health department accreditation is the measurement of a health department's performance against a nationally recognized set of practice-focused, evidence-based standards. The national public health accreditation program administered by the Public Health Accreditation Board has been developed on principles of quality improvement. Accreditation is a means by which health departments can demonstrate their interest in being transparent and accountable in their operations. In today's political environment, health department leaders have to consider their image to the public. There is an increased emphasis on "good government." Accreditation is one way to demonstrate that a health department is willing to open its performance for national-level peer review.

Why has the national accreditation program for public health departments been launched now?

Two Institute of Medicine studies on public health, one in 1988 and another in 2003, both described the governmental public health system as the backbone for coordinating and ensuring a focus on population health for a given community. However, those same studies described that governmental infrastructure as being in disarray, as not being consistent in its approaches across the country, and as not being consistently funded to carry out its mission. The national public health accreditation program was developed to assist health departments with focus and with a nationally accepted framework and process for carrying out its mission. Accreditation focuses on what a health department should do, either alone or in partnership with others. The health department then decides, based on the needs of the community it serves, how it will carry out those activities.

Why do you believe that achieving national public health department accreditation is beneficial for a health department?

Public health leaders have to balance the provision of core public health functions with the essential services needed to promote a healthy jurisdiction that they serve. Health departments who are using the accreditation standards and measures have told us that it has been very helpful to have national consensus about what a health department's specific and unique role in the community is. Even though we have had the 10 Essential Public Health Services framework and the three core functions of public health for a while, health departments tell us that having accreditation standards puts it all together for them in such a way that they have a good road map to guide their work. I believe that public health is a specialty, so why would we not have a standardized framework within which to operate, and why wouldn't public health leaders want to have their health departments reviewed for accreditation? It's a good opportunity to assure the community they serve that they are doing the best job they can to protect and promote that community's health.

What are the challenges that public health leaders face in considering whether to apply for accreditation?

The first challenge is usually to convince their governing entity that it's a good idea. This is new for public health but not so for other governmental entities like schools, universities, fire departments, child care centers, police departments, and the like. So one might think that elected officials and policy makers would naturally embrace the idea of accreditation. However, these are tough economic times, and adding any new activity can be met with resistance. Public health leaders who have engaged their governing entities early in the process and who have focused on quality improvement as the rationale for embarking upon the accreditation process have been successful in obtaining governance support for their accreditation application. The second challenge is often just getting started. A commitment to performance and quality improvement involves a different way of doing business for the long term. It involves a level of intrusion and transparency that embraces a willingness to take the health department operations apart and look at every aspect. That's a threat to many leaders. What if their health department fails? What if something major is found during the review? That level of transparency involves being willing to take those risks. Public health leaders who do so, however, are moving public health into a realm of credibility that mirrors that of the healthcare system and other businesses. There is an increased level of respect for a leader who can pull that off. Finally, another challenge lies in the engagement of the health department staff. Working on accreditation in public health requires that staff at all levels understand their health department in a more detailed way than perhaps they have before. It involves knowing how their work fits into the core functions and essential services. It also involves seeing quality improvement and the "new norm" way of doing business and not as a separate public health program. That can be a real challenge for some health department leaders.

(Continues)

What do you see as future incentives for a health department to be accredited?

As health departments become accredited and share their experiences, I believe that the opportunity for national-level peer review will emerge as the greatest incentive. There is no other organized structure for that type of review to occur. The marketing opportunity for health departments to promote their services once they have been accredited is also an incentive. Think about how many times we have read in the headlines that a school or fire department achieved national accreditation—met national standards, as determined by an independent reviewer. That has never been the case for the health department until now. PHAB is also working with various public health program funders at the national and state levels to consider providing funding opportunities for accredited health departments. For example, if an accredited health department is applying for a competitive grant, that health department would get additional credit in that competitive process because they are accredited. The rationale for this policy is that accredited health departments have been assessed for their infrastructure soundness. Public health programs can be assured that an accredited health department can implement that public health program within a strong governmental public health system. Finally, and certainly more long term in nature, PHAB hopes that funders will eventually become comfortable enough with accreditation that they will accept the certificate of accreditation in lieu of the first section of reporting for most grants, and therefore accredited health departments would have a reduced reporting burden for most program grants.

Why does PHAB support a voluntary approach to accreditation rather than a mandate?

You really can't mandate a culture of quality improvement. When PHAB was being formed and our accreditation process was being developed, we did a lot of research into the history of other accrediting programs. Mandated programs often become routine and more regulatory in philosophy. Quality improvement, by its very nature, is about embracing a culture of routinely assessing what an agency is doing, with an eye toward doing it better. Accreditation is one important step on the journey of adopting quality improvement as a health department operating principle. Mandating that seems counterintuitive to its rationale.

Why is accreditation linked to transforming public health for the future?

In many communities, the health department is almost invisible to the public. That "out of sight, out of mind" image has, for some, created opportunities for funding cuts that create great difficulties for the health department. Accreditation as a process has been shown to help other industries define who they are and then to involve their community of interest in assessing their work. It has also been shown to help entities set priorities and focus on the most significant parts of their industry. PHAB has already heard of health departments that are preparing for accreditation that have used this window of opportunity to do the same for public health. And then, once a health department is accredited, who is going to actively participate in reducing resources that might jeopardize that accreditation?

What is your hope for public health leadership and accreditation?

Public health accreditation has been developed by more than 400 practitioners, academicians, and researchers from the specialty. The accreditation process and the standards and measures are designed to reflect the existing evidence base as well as to stretch our practice. When I was working in public health practice, it was always my hope to leave the health department better than I found it. There are many ways to do that, and some public health leaders have to spend a lot of their precious time identifying what those ways are. Accreditation is already developed and will improve considerably over time as we gain experience. Public health leaders today can partner with us to assess their health department against national standards; celebrate their accomplishment of being recognized as meeting those standards; and identify ways to move their performance to a higher level. In the world of public health leadership, it doesn't get any better than that!

Source: Reprinted with permission of Kaye Bender and PHAB.

part of the process. They had collected data on the health of the county population as well as data on the social determinants of health. They had collected and involved their community stakeholders in these activities. Half of their local board of health as well as a representative of the county board were involved. They contacted their state public health training center to be involved and help them with the strategic planning process. The lingering question after the evaluation was "Are we ready?" for accreditation. They even addressed the "Health Department Readiness Checklist." At the local level, the process is clearly complex on the road to accreditation. It can be costly. Yet the local health department director felt the process was worthwhile. The questions for each health department may be similar, but the answers may vary. Although Exercise 14-1 can be difficult to do, it is worthwhile. In the exercise, several students will be asked to help a health department determine its readiness for the process of accreditation.

The PHAB's Health Department Readiness Checklist has three sections:[17]

1. Preliminary questions to determine eligibility
2. Readiness of the agency to determine if key organizational and administrative elements are in place
3. Determination of whether the health department is ready to submit an application

Specifically, the instrument raises questions like those below:

1. Is the health department eligible for PHAB accreditation?
2. Does the appointing authority (e.g., local board of health) for the health director support accreditation for the agency?
3. Is there a staff member who will be the accreditation coordinator?
4. Is there an accreditation team in place?
5. Has a statement of intent been submitted?
6. Are key documents ready?
7. Have PHAB standards based on essential public health services been reviewed?
8. Have costs been considered?
9. Does the health department know the difference between a community health assessment and a community health improvement plan?

It should be obvious by now that support for accreditation without leadership from the head of the local health department, the local board of health, and the partners will undermine the process. It is imperative to remember that accreditation is not just an expensive exercise, but an investment in public health at a community, a county, and a state level.[18] Even though shrinking resources are the business reality of today, the investment in public health is critical. Health departments have to be strategic and entrepreneurial in finding funding from public and private sources. Accreditation is about quality, a marketing tool to get funds, and program accountability. With PHAB accreditation on

a five-year cycle, accreditation becomes a motivational device by which a local health department can compete against itself by showing performance improvements over time. Accreditation will strengthen the public health infrastructure in all accredited jurisdictions.

Matthews and Baker promote the goal and the challenge to accredit all health departments in the country by 2020.[19] The authors see positive support for public health and accreditation in the Patient Protection and Affordable Care Act (P.L. 111-148). The economic realities of our time may prevent communities from being able to afford accreditation. A recommendation would be for both government and foundations to set aside a small percentage of money from their public health initiatives over the next 10 years to help support the accreditation effort. If the Patient Protection and Affordable Care Act survives and continues to be funded, it may be able to support accreditation to promote and to build the capacity of the state and local public health system to protect the public's health.

CREDENTIALING PUBLIC HEALTH ADMINISTRATORS

Although accreditation is about agencies, credentialing tends to be about individuals. It seems to me that the credentialing of public health administrators would help the accreditation process. Because most public health administrators come to their administrative roles without much background in management and leadership and some without public health training, it would be beneficial to support training programs for these administrators. The Survive and Thrive Program of the National Association of County and City Health officials is an example of such a program for administrators with less than two years of agency experience.[20] Public health leadership institutes are another example of programs that train administrators as well as their staffs.[21] As of 2012, these institutes have lost most of their federal funding.

Credentialing programs are also complex in nature. Funding is an issue related to not only evidence of training experiences but also evidence of successful administration. A portfolio model could be put forth for each candidate for a leadership or management credential rather than an examination. A portfolio would include examples of administrative success, competency-based training experiences, peer-reviewed articles, and so on. A credential should last for five years and then be renewed.

SUMMARY

This chapter introduces the importance of accreditation for state and local health departments. Leadership must drive the process. The development of a national voluntary public health accreditation process and the value of such a system were discussed. The chapter ended with an argument for the credentialing of public health administrators, which would be an important asset for the public health agency in its accreditation activities.

DISCUSSION QUESTIONS

1. What is the relationship between the public health core functions and essential public health services in the accreditation of state and local health departments?
2. Why is leadership important in the accreditation process?
3. Describe the history leading up to the PHAB board.
4. What is involved in applying for accreditation?
5. What is the difference between accreditation and credentialing?
6. Make an argument for the certification of public health administrators.

EXERCISE 14-1: To Be or Not to Be Accredited: Analyzing Health Department Readiness

Purpose: to explore the elements of public health department accreditation and their relationship to organizational performance and quality improvement

Key concepts: accreditation, peer review, core functions, essential public health services, organizational performance management, quality improvement

Procedure: The class should divide into three groups of 5–10 students each. Each group will be working on a different but related aspect of the activities that a health department has to undertake in order to consider seeking public health accreditation.

Because one of the requirements of the accreditation application is a support letter from the health department's governing entity, one group is assigned the task of convincing its board of health that their health department should pursue national voluntary public health department accreditation. Salient points should include the benefits of accreditation (including perceived benefits from other industries such as education or health care); the perceived return on investment for the time and effort spent in preparing for accreditation; and the potential long-term effect of instituting a peer review process leading to quality improvement for the entire organization. Students should consider the board of health's role in guiding the health department and in making a commitment to external review of their agency. Students should also consider counterpoints that board members might make in responding to this new and somewhat intrusive process.

The second group is assigned the task of convincing the internal leadership staff to consider making a commitment to prepare for accreditation. Using the accreditation readiness checklists, students should design strategies for assessing the health department's overall status in terms of readiness to apply for accreditation. Each of the four readiness checklists addresses a different component of accreditation and asks key questions related to those components. Students should seek ways to elicit an accurate picture of the health department's rationale for engaging in accreditation preparation and of their perception of the amount and type of work involved. Students should consider counterpoints that staff working in a health department might make as they are asked to support these efforts.

The third group is assigned the task of assessing the health department's organizational shift toward establishing a culture of quality improvement. Some assessment of the health department team's knowledge of core functions and essential services should be included, as well as the health department team's knowledge of the national accreditation program process and standards and measures. Finally, discussion of an appropriate framework for the health department to deploy as they translate the findings from the accreditation review into a performance and quality improvement system is required.

The three groups should have an opportunity to report back to each other so that the interconnectedness between making the decision to seek accreditation, assessing the health department's readiness to undergo accreditation, and preparing to use the results in meaningful ways to improve performance can be identified.

References

Public Health Accreditation Board. *Guide to Accreditation*, Version 1.0, 2011, www.phaboard.org.
Public Health Accreditation Board. *Accreditation Standards and Measures*, Version 1.0, 2011, www.phaboard.org.
Public Health Accreditation Board. *Accreditation Readiness Checklists for Health Departments*, 2011, www.phaboard.org.

REFERENCES

1. Institute of Medicine, *The Future of the Public's Health in the 21st Century* (Washington, DC: National Academies Press, 2003).

2. Available at http://www.cdc.gov/nphpsp/essentialservices .html. Accessed December 12, 2011.

3. Institute of Medicine, *The Future of the Public's Health.*

4. P. Russo, "Accreditation of Public Health Agencies: A Means, Not an End," *Journal of Public Health Management and Practice*, 13, no. 4 (2007): 329–331.

5. L. Thielen, *Exploring Public Health Experience with Standards and Accreditation* (Princeton, NJ: Robert Wood Johnson Foundation, 2004).

6. G. P. Mays, *Can Accreditation Work in Public Health? Lessons from Other Service Industries* (Princeton, NJ: Robert Wood Johnson Foundation, 2004).

7. http://www.exploringaccreditation.org. Accessed December 8, 2011.

8. National Association of County and City Health Officials, *Operational Definition of a Functional Local Health Department* (Washington, DC: NACCHO, 2005).

9. L. M. Beitsch, G. Mays, L. Corso, C. Chang, and R. Brewer, "States Gathering Momentum: Promising Strategies for Accreditation and Assessment Activities in Multistate Learning Collaborative Applicant States," *Journal of Public Health Management and Practice* 13, no. 4 (2007): 364–373.

10. D. Lenaway, L. Corso, and S. Bailey, "Accreditation as an Opportunity to Strengthen Public Health: CDC's Perspective," 13, no. 4 (2007): 332–333.

11. K. Bender, G. Benjamin, M. Fallon, P. E. Jarris, and P. M. Libby, "Exploring Accreditation: Striving for a Consensus Model," *Journal of Public Health Management and Practice* 13, no. 4 (2007): 334–336.

12. B. M. Joly, G. Polyak, M. V. Davis, J. Brewster, B. Tremain, C. Raevsky, and L. M. Beitsch, "Linking Accreditation and Public Health Outcomes: A Logic Model Approach," *Journal of Public Health Management and Practice* 13, no. 4 (2007): 349–356.

13. P. Nolan, R. Bialik, M. L. Kushion, D. Lenaway, and M. S. Hamm, "Financing and Creating Incentives for a Voluntary National Accreditation System for Public Health," *Journal of Public Health Management and Practice* 13, no. 4 (2007): 378–382.

14. Public Health Accreditation Board website, http://www .phaboard.org. Accessed December 5, 2011.

15. Public Health Accreditation Board, *Standards: An Overview*, Version 1.0 (Washington, DC: PHAB, 2011).

16. P. M. Senge, C. Roberts, R. B. Ross, B. J. Smith, and A. Kleiner, *The Fifth Discipline Fieldbook* (New York: Doubleday, 1994).

17. Public Health Accreditation Board, *National Public Health Department Accreditation Readiness Checklists*, Version 1.0 (Washington, DC: PHAB, 2011).

18. P. Verma, "Making the Case for Accreditation," *Journal of Public Health Management and Practice*, 17, no. 6 (2011): 569–570.

19. G. Matthews and E. Baker, "Looking Back from the Future: Connecting Accreditation, Health Reform, and Political Opportunities," *Journal of Public Health Management and Practice*, 16, no. 4 (2010): 367–369.

20. National Association of County and City Health Officials website, www.NACCHO.org. Accessed December 10, 2011.

21. National Public Health Leadership Development Network website, www.heartlandcenters.slu.edu/nln. Accessed December 10, 2011.

Leadership and Preparedness

CHAPTER 15

Traditional and Crisis Public Health Leaders

Crisis leadership [is] planning for the unthinkable.

—Ian Mitroff

September 11, 2001, changed our perspective on public health because it changed many of our views of life in America in the 21st century. Being a leader today is quite different than it was just a few short years ago. However, leadership is a complex process. Leaders need to learn many things, but most of all they need to commit themselves to lifelong learning. To be a successful leader, leaders need to master a number of leadership tools and techniques. Crisis leaders need to master an additional set of tools and techniques. Traditional public health leaders have worked well in environments that have some emergencies occur, but the emergencies and crises of the first decade of the 21st century and beyond have put new demands on our public health leaders. We now live in a public health environment that emphasizes preparedness and our ability as leaders to address any crisis that may occur, from a natural disaster like Hurricane Katrina or the Joplin tornado to terrorist acts and economic crises that affect our ability to do our work in an effective and efficient manner. In addition, emergency events require that public health leaders work directly with new partners like the police, fire departments, the Federal Bureau of Investigation (FBI), and of course politicians. Kahn has stated that all crises are basically political in nature.[1] Public health and political leaders become strange bedfellows in that it becomes critical that they coordinate their decision-making responses to disasters and other crises. In this chapter, we will look at some of these issues.

TRANSITION FROM TRADITIONAL TO COMMUNITY-BASED ORGANIZATIONS

Public health leaders have led their agencies from a traditional agency-based linear approach to public health to a systems-based community focus. **Table 15-1** presents some of these changes, from starting with a traditional organization in a fairly stable environment to some form of community or societal disruption that affects the agency directly. During this chaos phase, many leadership tools and techniques are utilized to restore some equilibrium in the agency. However, the changes brought about through the period of disruption push the organization into a transition phase.

For the organization in transition, the core functions and essential public health services provide a foundation on which to create change as the organization moves to a more community-based approach to public health. This transition phase is often short-lived, and the organization enters into another period of disruption. Leaders will need to use systems thinking skills, collaboration, public–private connections, culture competency learning, and performance measurement techniques to move to the organization's next level of development. Eventually, the agency will be much more community based and will use many new skills to relate to its community. In natural and human-made crises, leaders will also use these tools and techniques to aid their agencies to deal with the disruption and needed adaptation due to these emergency events.

Clearly, different skills as well as the utilization of traditional leadership skills tied to the severity of the change in the environment are required by leaders in different phases of organizational change. Exercise 15-1 presents a chance to look at the skills needed to maintain an organization internally in a traditional day-to-day organization pattern, externally in a noncrisis-affected organization, and finally in crisis situations.

THE CRISIS CYCLE

Since September 11, 2001, public health leaders have been involved in developing emergency preparedness and response activities in their communities. This model of preparedness appears to affect the overall orientation of public health leaders to the work of public health in a crisis-oriented society. Public health leaders must understand that the effectiveness and efficiency of the work they do depends on the organization of the public health system and on the strong foundation of principles guided by public health practice. These practice principles are critical in addressing all types of public health issues. It is imperative for public health leaders to integrate their knowledge of public health with the changing environment in which they work.

Since the disaster caused by Hurricane Katrina in the summer of 2005, there has been a renewed interest in public health and natural disasters. Between 1953 and the end of 2011, there was an average of 34 declared disasters per year.[2] The Federal Emergency Management Agency (FEMA) data in **Table 15-2** show the number of declared disasters for each of these years and the total for each state during this period. Note that the years since 1989 have shown above-average designated disasters, with major increases since 2000.

TABLE 15-1 A Systems Approach to Public Health Organizational Change

Traditional Organization	Chaos I	Organization Transition	Chaos II	Community Organization
1. Organizational planning	1. Evaluation	1. Core functions (system)	1. Systems thinking (transition to outside the agency)	1. Community building
2. Organizing	2. Communication	2. Essential services		2. Preparedness and response
3. Heading internally	3. Strategic planning	3. Public health law	2. Collaboration	3. Community engagement
4. Motivating staff	4. Continuous Quality Improvement (CQI)	4. Health communication	3. Public/private	4. Tipping awareness
5. Controlling activities	5. Re-engineering	5. Complexity	4. Partnerships	5. Learning organization
6. Organizational practices	6. Reinvention		5. Cultural competency	6. Meta-leadership
7. Budgeting	7. Turnaround		6. Performance measurement	
8. Development	8. Goal realignment			
9. Cultural diversity	9. Problem solving			
10. Mentoring/ coaching	10. Decision making			
11. Linear thinking	11. Conflict resolution			
	12. Negotiation			
	13. Emotional intelligence			
	14. Risk communication			
	15. Change			

TABLE 15-2 Declared Disasters by Year or State

Year	Major Disaster Declarations	Emergency Declarations	Fire Management Assistance Declarations
2012	12	0	3
2011	99	29	114
2010	81	9	18
2009	59	7	49
2008	75	17	51
2007	63	13	60
2006	52	5	86
2005	48	68	39
2004	69	7	43
2003	56	19	48
2002	49	0	70
2001	45	11	44
2000	45	6	63
1999	50	20	40
1998	65	9	54
1997	44	0	3
1996	75	8	75
1995	32	2	4
1994	36	1	20
1993	32	19	7
1992	45	2	6
1991	43	0	2
1990	38	0	5
1989	31	0	1
1988	11	0	5
1987	23	1	7
1986	28	0	1
1985	27	0	9
1984	34	4	4
1983	21	1	2
1982	24	3	0
1981	15	0	3
1980	23	6	2
1979	42	10	7
1978	25	14	2
1977	22	34	5

(*Continues*)

TABLE 15-2   Declared Disasters by Year or State (*Continued*)

Year	Major Disaster Declarations	Emergency Declarations	Fire Management Assistance Declarations
1976	30	8	7
1975	38	6	1
1974	46	5	2
1973	46	0	9
1972	48	0	0
1971	17	0	3
1970	17	0	2
1969	29	0	0
1968	19	0	0
1967	11	0	0
1966	11	0	0
1965	25	0	0
1964	25	0	0
1963	20	0	0
1962	22	0	0
1961	12	0	0
1960	12	0	0
1959	7	0	0
1958	7	0	0
1957	16	0	0
1956	16	0	0
1955	18	0	0
1954	17	0	0
1953	13	0	0

By State			
	State	Major Disaster Declarations	Emergency Declarations	Fire Management Assistance Declarations
---	---	---	---	---
1	Alabama	56	11	9
2	Alaska	37	0	15
3	American Samoa	11	0	0
4	Arizona	24	3	46
5	Arkansas	53	9	0
6	California	78	8	122
7	Colorado	16	4	53
8	Connecticut	17	9	0
9	Delaware	14	4	0
10	District of Columbia	11	5	0

	State	By State		
		Major Disaster Declarations	Emergency Declarations	Fire Management Assistance Declarations
11	Federated States of Micronesia	24	2	0
12	Florida	63	12	57
13	Georgia	36	7	10
14	Guam	12	0	1
15	Hawaii	26	1	18
16	Idaho	23	2	6
17	Illinois	51	7	0
18	Indiana	40	7	0
19	Iowa	48	4	0
20	Kansas	47	4	2
21	Kentucky	56	4	6
22	Louisiana	58	9	1
23	Maine	39	14	2
24	Marshall Islands	7	0	0
25	Maryland	22	4	0
26	Massachusetts	27	15	1
27	Michigan	25	7	1
28	Minnesota	48	5	9
29	Mississippi	50	11	0
30	Missouri	53	8	1
31	Montana	20	2	34
32	Nebraska	47	3	4
33	Nevada	17	4	52
34	New Hampshire	28	12	0
35	New Jersey	33	11	2
36	New Mexico	24	4	43
37	New York	65	21	2
38	North Carolina	40	9	3
39	North Dakota	42	8	0
40	Northern Mariana Islands	14	0	0
41	Ohio	45	6	0
42	Oklahoma	70	10	78
43	Oregon	28	2	49
44	Palau	1	0	0
45	Pennsylvania	47	7	0

(Continues)

TABLE 15-2 Declared Disasters by Year or State (*Continued*)

	State	By State		
		Major Disaster Declarations	Emergency Declarations	Fire Management Assistance Declarations
46	Puerto Rico	26	6	0
47	Rhode Island	9	9	0
48	South Carolina	15	3	3
49	South Dakota	39	2	19
50	Tennessee	51	3	6
51	Texas	86	12	234
52	U.S. Virgin Islands	17	4	0
53	Utah	10	3	12
54	Vermont	33	3	0
55	Virginia	45	6	7
56	Washington	45	4	54
57	West Virginia	48	5	2
58	Wisconsin	35	7	1
59	Wyoming	9	2	11
By State		Major Disaster Declarations	Emergency Declarations	Fire Management Assistance Declarations
Total Disaster Declarations		2,061	344	976
Average		34	6	16

Source: FEMA (2012). Declared Disasters by Year or State. http://www.fema.gov/news/disaster_totals_annual.fema. Last updated May 4, 2012. Last Accessed May 7, 2012.

FIGURE 15-1 Crisis Cycle.

Since 2001, much discussion and deliberation have occurred about natural and human-made disasters and the importance of public health response in many of these disasters. Crisis can best be seen in terms of a cycle approach. **Figure 15-1** shows one model of a crisis cycle.

First, we ask public health agencies and their partners to do a risk or crisis audit to determine their disaster history and what they have learned from them. For the audit, it is important to tie crisis planning and traditional strategic planning together.[3] Collaboration becomes an

Leadership Tip

The best time to return telephone calls is before lunch or at the end of the day. The calls will be shorter.

important second step in that different stakeholders will see crisis events differently. Third, a SWOT (strengths, weaknesses, opportunities, and threats) analysis is a very useful tool. Next, it is helpful to focus on the top four or five crisis areas, and finally narrow the crisis list to the most likely types of crises that can occur. The risk audit also addresses the concern of probability of similar events in the future. This knowledge requires the use of this information to mitigate the occurrence of future events or to lessen the effect of these events in the future.

The above knowledge will affect the preparedness planning activities of the public health agency or community partners working together on a community-wide emergency preparedness plan. When the local community emergency preparedness plan was printed in our local newspaper, I undertook an unscientific survey of my neighbors and found that many were not even aware our community had an emergency plan.

Once a plan is developed and before a disaster or emergency occurs, mitigation issues once again become important. Local crisis management teams will want to explore ways to avoid various categories of crisis or

to lessen the effects of one if it occurs. Another issue involves whether the plan's operational aspects are clear. When and if a crisis occurs, it is important to move to the response phase as quickly as possible to lessen the effects of the event. Mitigation strategies are once again important. If the response is immediate and effective, recovery will occur more quickly. After-action planning activities and mitigation strategies are once again critical to the recovery phase. Even though recovery may take time depending on the severity of the crisis event, the cycle will begin again with another risk audit.

Mitigation actions involve four types of measures.[4] First, there are engineering and construction issues related to whether buildings are constructed to prevent damage and whether there are appropriate building codes. The second set of mitigation actions relates to physical planning, which is affected by the understanding of the physical environments where people live and land use issues. The third category of mitigation measures relates to the economic factor. Strong economies seem to respond better to disasters than poor economies. The final set of mitigation actions is related to the society or community as a whole. Public awareness is an important factor. If people know what to do if a disaster will soon occur or if one does occur, this will help in response and speed up recovery. Exercises and drills are important here as well.

From a public health perspective, leaders will utilize many skills and techniques to manage and lead in a crisis situation. **Figure 15-2** graphically shows that

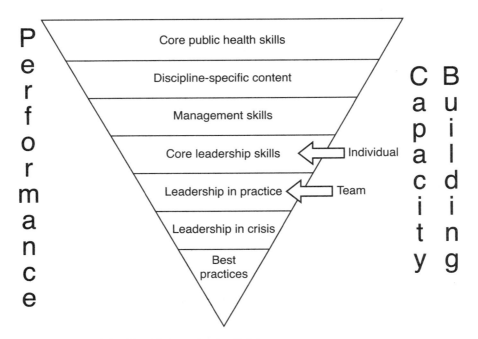

FIGURE 15-2 The Skills of the Public Health Leader in Crisis. *Source:* Reproduced from M. Lichtveld, L. Rowitz, and J. Cioffi, "The Leadership Pyramid." *Leadership in Public Health* 6(4), 3–8.

some of the leadership skills necessary in preparedness activities are different from the skills developed at other levels of the pyramid. By strengthening the public health system and its infrastructure, we can better respond to a disaster when it occurs.

THE SYSTEMS PERSPECTIVE

Public health leaders have found that the management-oriented approach to emergency preparedness and response provides only a limited understanding of how crises occur and work in the context of a community system. The assumptions that underlie a management approach to crisis will differ from the assumptions that affect a leader-based systems orientation. The management assumptions do in fact create a complex system at the same time that the assumptions seem to deny that the system they are trying to manage is complex.[5] Leaders will challenge the key assumptions. Using a systems perspective, leaders will determine the critical assumptions to be made for a given crisis or set of crises. Individual assumptions will be certain or uncertain and important or unimportant. The assumption analysis methodology will help the leader and his or her partners to better understand how emergencies of various kinds and severity affect the system as a whole.

This section will present systems approaches to crisis and the new types of information that begin to become available and to expand the leader's understanding of these emergency events. Case Study 15-A shows the use of meta-leadership principles in the analysis of two floods in two different parts of the world. This case study also explores the policy implications related to these two flood events. The case was prepared by a team of leadership fellows in the Mid-America Regional Public Health Leadership Institute from two countries, the business sector, the faith community, and the governmental sector.

Case Study 15-A

A Tale of Two Floods
Applying Multisector Cooperation to Emergency Preparedness and Response in Illinois and the Czech Republic

Case Study developed by the Meta-Balconeers Team, Mid-America Regional Public Health Leadership Institute, Class 18, 2009–2010, Victoria Sharp, Mentor; Diane Logsdon, Daryl Jackson, Jeannette Tandex, Mary Casey-Lockyer, Peter Eckart, Kaja Rihova, Lisa Ardaugh, Rev. Janette Wilson

Opening

The following case study operates on two levels. At its core, this case study is a comparison and contrast between institutional responses to recent catastrophic flooding in Illinois and the Czech Republic. However, the perspective of this study is the particular lens of "meta-leadership," an emerging model of leadership development with particular value for emergency preparedness and recovery.

Applying meta-leadership to these particular floods is no accident. The authors of this study were gathered together by the Mid-America Regional Public Health Leadership Institute (MARPHLI), and represent leadership from public health, private business, healthcare delivery, and nongovernmental organizations in Illinois, as well as a single public health leader from the Czech Republic. In addition to the regular leadership development curriculum that characterizes MARPHLI's yearlong fellowships, the federal Centers for Disease Control and Prevention asked this group to focus on meta-leadership. Therefore, this case study includes a presentation of the principles of meta-leadership and their application to two natural disasters.

We will present a fuller description of the principles of meta-leadership below, but it is most important to understand the common-sense idea behind it: problems are better solved by leaders and institutions who know each other and each other's capabilities before a crisis, and the responses and solutions to problems are better addressed by multiple stakeholders from a variety of sectors and affected institutions. Meta-leadership offers a structure of understanding and analysis of this basic idea, with particular emphasis on disaster prevention, response, and recovery.

In August 2002, heavy rain fell in central Europe for three weeks, triggering sequential flood waves across two major river systems (Smith, 2003). The Czech Republic suffered three billion euros in damage, a third of which was concentrated in Prague, where massive flooding affected both residential and commercial properties. More recently, in August 2007, six counties in Illinois were declared federal disaster areas (FEMA, 2003) after severe storms and flooding caused millions dollars of damage, and were approved for both individual and institutional assistance.

In each case, there were existing institutional disaster response plans in place, and swift action by designated agencies mitigated the potential for greater damage and loss of life. However, for the most part, the institutional response was dictated by a fairly rigid structure of predetermined roles. Traditional public and governmental actors in disaster response were present, but many other potential stakeholders—from other levels of government, business, and non-profit sectors—were not.

Meta-leadership gives us a way to understand how much more effective the preparation and planning of disaster recovery could have been, with its emphasis on multisector relationship building before a disaster and non-hierarchical cooperation during the recovery. Even without knowing the principles of meta-leadership, leaders and institutions exhibited some of the five principles of meta-leadership. However, the principles were not articulated as such, were not fully present, and the response and recovery to the disasters was not as effective as possible.

An Overview of Meta-Leadership

Meta-leadership is a new structure for leadership development that evolved from realizations that contemporary conceptions of disaster preparedness were limited and the resulting preparations not as effective as possible. Leonard Marcus, Barry Dorn, and Joseph Henderson collaborated in 2005 to articulate a new brand of leadership that challenges individuals to think and act cooperatively across organizations and sectors (Meta-Leadership Summit, 2009). This new structure is housed within the Meta-Leadership Summit for Preparedness, a joint effort of the Centers for Disease Control and Prevention, the CDC Foundation, the Robert Wood Johnson Foundation, and the National Preparedness Leadership Initiative—Harvard School of Public Health and the Kennedy School of Government.

Meta-leadership is a strategy to overcome traditional silo thinking:

> Thinking and operating beyond their immediate scope of authority, meta-leaders provide guidance, direction, and momentum across organization lines that develop into a shared course of action and a commonality of purpose among people and agencies that are doing what may appear to be very different work. Meta-leaders are able to imaginatively and effectively leverage system assets, information, and capacities, a particularly critical function for organizations with emergency preparedness (Marcus, Dorn, and Henderson, 2006).

Meta-leadership could operate across a number of distinct sectors to improve any cooperative enterprise. In the practice of disaster preparedness, response, and recovery, however, meta-leadership is principally concerned with effective coordination across government, business, and nonprofit sectors. We should note that the non-profit sector encompasses a broad range sub-sectors itself, including higher and secondary education, faith communities, and many healthcare providers, among others. Though meta-leadership is concerned with cross-sector coordination, it starts with the individual leaders within these institutions. A key element of meta-leadership recognizes that leadership is not solely or even necessarily hierarchical.

Meta-leadership reframes the process and practice of leaders. It has three functions: (1) a comprehensive organizing reference to understand and integrate the many facets of readership; (2) a strategy to engage collaborative activity; and (3) a cause and purpose to improve community functioning and performance. There are five dimensions to the learning and practice of meta-leadership (Marcus, et al. 2009):

The Person of the meta-leader: Meta-leaders tend to be systems thinkers who possess the qualities to direct large or complex initiatives: self-awareness, self-regulation, motivation, empathy, and social skills. The meta-leadership model is built upon rapidly expanding research of brain function under stress. Meta-Leaders possess the mental strength to move beyond the natural tendency to "fly, freeze, or fight," and instead move to higher-order functioning to maintain focus on the overall situation (Marcus, Dorn, and Henderson, 2006).

The Situation: That bigger picture, however, is constantly shifting during a crisis, and so meta-leaders must constantly adapt. This is especially difficult when information is incomplete, as it is in the early stages of a disaster or emergency. The connectivity that defines the rest of the meta-leadership model becomes the leading tool of the meta-leader, who uses a dynamic web of vertical and horizontal relationships to fill in the gaps and react quickly as situations change (Marcus, Dorn, and Henderson, 2006).

Lead the Silo: The meta-leader is likely to occupy a traditional leadership role as well, and is expected to activate direct reports and resources. Meta-leadership recognizes that these subordinates are likely to be more effective in a crisis if the meta-leader has already built a culture of trust and accountability among them beforehand (Marcus, Dorn, and Henderson, 2006).

(*Continues*)

Lead Up: Of course, meta-leaders are found at all levels in participating organizations, and will just as likely lead up as lead down. A meta-leader will be able to fulfill their hierarchical responsibilities while simultaneously attending to the larger systems surrounding the work to be completed. Being able to accomplish tasks on behalf of others is also the key to the fifth principle of meta-leadership (Marcus, Dorn, and Henderson, 2006).

Leading Cross-Institution Connectivity: Meta-leaders strategically and intentionally are able to make connections beyond their own institutions that leverage expertise, resources, and information across multiple public and private sectors, integrating effort and maximizing efficiency and reach. Meta-leadership further specifies that these relationships must be established before a crisis, so that institutions can discuss what they will bring to bear in a crisis ("gives"), what they will need at that time ("gets"), and how they can work together to fill the "gaps" between them (Marcus, Dorn, and Henderson, 2006).

Meta-leadership is a valid extension of traditional public health practice. In 1994, the Public Health Functions Steering Committee adopted the "10 Essential Public Health Services," the fourth of which is "Mobilize community partnerships to identify and solve health problems" (CDC, 2008). Public health has long been a governmental leader in disaster response, and is thus concerned with new approaches to leadership development. Meta-leadership is a model and method to integrate personal and institutional leadership in a systematic and relevant way.

The expression of the 10 essential services places service #4 in the Core Public Health Function of "Policy Development" (Institute Media, 1988). The core function of Policy Development reflects that how we organize ourselves and how we pay for our services is at the core of our effectiveness and reflects our priorities for public health leadership. Meta-leadership is both a new model for leadership development and an urgent call to expand the number and types of people and organizations involved in disaster preparedness, response, and recovery.

The 2007 Floods in Six Illinois Counties

On August 18, 2007, a warm front became stationary in Illinois. Additional thunderstorms formed over northwest Illinois on Sunday, August 19, exacerbating flooding. The stationary front then extended eastward through Illinois on August 19 and August 20.

Runoff from the heavy rain caused river flooding on the Des Plaines, Fox, Illinois, and Rock rivers. Moderate flooding was also reported on the Mississippi River. DeKalb County reported 4.85 inches of rain on August 23 and 24. Flooding across northern Illinois was widespread in the aftermath of the storms.

On September 25, the Federal Emergency Management Agency (FEMA) announced that federal disaster aid was available for the state of Illinois. The federal funding made individual assistance available to flood victims in Lake, Will, and Gundy counties, and individual and public assistance available to those in DeKalb, Kane, and LaSalle counties (FEMA, 2008).

Of the six counties that received federal disaster aid, only three are considered in this case study. For purposes of anonymity, the three counties will not be specifically identified.

In each of the three counties studied, the Emergency Management Agency (EMA) is the reporting agency. The information contained in this case study was collected via telephone interviews conducted on February 26 and March 1 with the EMA Coordinator. Two of the three agencies in the study had EMA Coordinators that had been on staff with some experience prior to the flood. The third County Coordinator had recently been hired and had only just moved to the Midwest.

In each case, the county health departments are involved as partners in the planning for response to disasters. However, in flood scenarios, their actual deployment is limited in scope. Mission assignments for health staff included tetanus clinics, mosquito abatement, well and septic inspection, and building inspection. Although not heavily involved in the response, each health department responded along the tasks of the essential public health services.

Each of the counties has a population base of rural and urbanized areas, as evidenced in the need for well and septic inspections. These are communities that are settled on the river, which places them in a flood hazard zone. In two of three counties, the county nursing home was inside the flood zone and needed to be evacuated. In one county, the hospital had to be diked to protect the property from floodwaters. The diking of the hospital led to a proposal for a new sandbagging program that would improve response, which the Emergency Management Oversight Committee approved at the end of February 2010 (Lutz, 2010).

In one of the nursing home settings, there were 97 residents to be protected. The county left one egress area open. Although the county had a contract with a private company to provide sandbags, the timing of the flood and the sudden onset of the flooding meant that the company did not fulfill its contract. The EMA Coordinator and a local fire chief led the efforts of many volunteers, and the county engineer and a surveyor projected the flood event to ensure that the sandbagging efforts would be sufficient. The nursing home was successfully evacuated and all patient care continued throughout the operation (Jobst, 2010).

In one of the three counties, a large wetlands project slowed the flood crest and lessened the effect of the flood due to mitigation from prior floods. This meant that the majority of the flooding was more of a nuisance than a severe danger (McKenzie, 2010).

In each of the counties in the study, the EMA Coordinator expressed the belief that, due to effective communications with their superiors, they had the full support of local politicians and experienced no concerns with decision making. In each of the counties, the staff reported to the County Board Chairman during a declared disaster. So, even in the county where the EMA Coordinator was new to the position, there was support for the work being conducted. The support for the EMA Coordinator and the mission assignment may be attributed to existing relationships or to the reality that flooding is expected on rivers and the individuals who live on the river understand the risks there.

In each of the counties, the EMA Coordinator is responsible during day-to-day operations as well as in disasters for the meta-leadership concepts of "Lead the Silo," "Lead Up," and "Lead Across." According to the Illinois Emergency Management Act, "The Coordinator shall have direct responsibility for the organization, administration, training, and operation of the emergency services and disaster agency, subject to the direction and control of that principal executive officer. Each emergency services and disaster agency shall coordinate and may perform emergency management functions within the territorial limits of the political subdivision" (20 ILCS 3305). In other words, the Coordinator brings together all community partners to plan for and respond to disasters.

In each of the counties in this study, there are good examples of systemic leadership in the areas where traditional emergency responders already had regular interaction. Because the individual and institution participation does not extend beyond the traditional disaster preparedness and response communities, it is difficult to characterize them as meta-leaders. Still, they exhibit some of the traits of meta-leadership. In each case, the Coordinator acts as a "Leader Up" in the interaction with the County Board Chairman. Additionally, each county must lead up when dealing with the Illinois Emergency Management Agency. While not all counties had subordinates, each paid staff positions, and each "Led the Silo" through staff, community members, or volunteer programs. Each county also had opportunities to "Lead Across" with community-based and volunteer organizations, including the American Red Cross. In some cases, "Leading Across" was accomplished with other emergency responders such as the local health department, fire chief, and state department of transportation.

In each of the counties, there was a dearth of media information. Press releases included information regarding the disaster declaration process, but reported very little information regarding the overall incident. There was no electronic information available regarding public safety or community updates regarding public health concerns. Additionally, the little information that was available on internet news sites dealt more with the lack of public knowledge or information regarding the assistance process and timeframes. However, two of three counties reported in our interviews that they held daily briefings and supplied public health and safety information to the media and the general public in multiple formats at many times during the flood event. It is therefore a possibility that the lack of information on the public domains following the event is a result of a lack of perceived importance on the part of the media. Another opportunity to apply meta-leadership concepts may be in the partnership with local news outlets.

In all counties, agreements were in place between and among organizations to provide services, information, or resources to enhance damage assessment, flood forecasting, mitigation of flooding, and transportation. And in some cases, new relationships were formed due to the flood and have been continued since the incidents. One case in point is a new and very effective relationship with the Fox Waterway Agency, in which the information regarding flood forecasting is shared with the emergency management organizations.

In some cases, the responding staff disregarded plans to provide integrated services during the emergency; they were unable to open an Emergency Operations Center at the onset, did not use standard Incident Action Planning, followed no formalized Incident Command System structure, and exhibited tunnel vision regarding accessing additional resources. Additionally, there seemed to be a lack of planning in some jurisdictions regarding flood mitigation and building zoning or codes. In most cases, these challenges are not the purview of the county EMA Coordinator, and so they are caught in a "catch 22" where they may make recommendations to local communities but have no authority over that community.

(*Continues*)

In every community, a disaster is an unfunded mandate, usually with no reserve fund for disaster response. Because of this fact, the EMA Coordinator has no authority over other departments where staff ought to be held over and paid overtime to support the operations. In some communities, there is no policy that states whether non-sworn personnel can be held over to support a disaster or emergency. In at least one of the counties, there was concern with multiple departments regarding the cost of overtime pay for staff.

In every community, meta-leader principles offer a shared, community solution to the lack of available resources during a disaster. In one case, a private company agreed to provide filled sandbags for community mitigation efforts, but could not meet a delivery deadline. In meta-leadership, identification of a gap, such as sandbagging capabilities (FEMA, 2008), results in discussions regarding timeliness, availability, accessibility, and barriers to service provision. Meta-leaders should ensure that community partners are involved in the local exercise programs to ensure that the agreement is plausible in different scenarios.

Another concern in some areas included the inability of residents to get to work due to flooding and whether they would be able to access unemployment benefits. The economic impact of a disaster on a community can include job loss or reduction in work, and immediate and continuing losses to private businesses. These factors are crucial to the community's economic resiliency. Meta-leaders in the community may identify opportunities to strengthen relationships with key employers to improve future response and create operational continuity plans.

Each county responded well to the floods, and processes and policies have been improved since that time. But each community also had good leaders in place who did not necessarily act as meta-leaders, especially regarding the inclusion of private industry. An example would be working with large employers to ensure that they are open for business and that their employees are earning their pay as soon as possible following the incidents. Another example would be identifying private partnerships to work to restore the community to pre-disaster status as quickly as possible, such as partnerships with businesses and agencies to conduct damage assessment services.

It should be noted that although some programs discussed in this study are in place today, they were not in place at the time of the 2007 flood incident and so they are not discussed herein.

The 2002 Floods in the Czech Republic

The Czech Republic is geographically known as the "Roof of Europe" because water from a relatively small area flows into three seas: the Vita va river and Labe river (Elbe) flow to the Northern Sea through Germany, the Odra river flows to the Baltic Sea through Poland, and the Morava river flows to Donau (i.e., to the Black Sea) through Slovakia, Hungary, and Romania (Disaster Charter, 2006).

The flooding of the year of 2002 was a significant test for the inhabitants of the affected areas of Bohemia, and of the new crisis management system of the Czech Republic—the integrated emergency system and the services and institutions necessary for the successful control of the larger disaster (Rihova, 2010).

Since the catastrophic flood in 1997, new rules were instituted in the Czech Republic with respect to floods prevention and reaction:

1. The Czech government adopted the document "Strategy for Prevention Against Floods in the Czech Republic" and enacted new regulations regarding crisis management and integrated rescue system that helped during the floods in 2002.
2. The state-controlled enterprise "Povodi" (Basins) was given responsibility for the river system in the country and the obligation to work out the plans for the anti-flooding measurements.
3. The Czech Republic adopted a new information system called "Voda" (Water) for state administration, public administration, and citizens to share up-to-date information about the status of river levels, translated into six languages because of neighboring countries.
4. The country's non-governmental organizations (NGOs) were invited to take part in the process of Environmental Impact Assessment (EIA), and their opinions are now included in the framework of programs of flood prevention. In the case of rapid response to the floods, NGOs can offer psychological and other relief services.
5. The Rescue and Fire Brigade of the Czech Republic was given supreme command of the flood control management, according to the laws regulating crisis management and the integrated rescue system (Rihova, 2010).

The Parliament of the Czech Republic enacted the Water Act (#254/2000), the Act of Integrated Rescue System (#239/2000), the Act of Crisis Management (#240/2000), and the Act of Economic Measures for Crisis Situations (#241/2000). These acts defined the obligations of the state, regional, and local institutions, together with private companies, landowners, and individuals. The integrated rescue system included the fire brigade, ambulance, and the state police. The main crisis operation center is located in Prague, with 14 operation centers in appropriate regions. The sophisticated, up-to-date warning system was created after the 1997 flood using the computer system called ALADIN modeling the weather development. It supplies appropriate information to the main crisis operation center, TV and radio, and the internet (Rihova, 2010). This system proved to be an effective instrument in performing emergency rescue operations during the floods of 2002 (Pokorny and Storek, 2000, cited in Kumar, 2005).

One key part of such services is the hydro-meteorological services, represented by the Czech Hydro-Meteorological Institute (CHMU). The activity of the Institute and its Forecast and Warning Services (PVS) is very important during flooding and other crisis situations resulting from natural disasters. According to Czech law 254/2001, the CHMU ensures that the Ministry of Environment will provide flooding forecast services in the Czech Republic in cooperation with the state enterprise Povodi, in the Ministry of Agriculture. Cooperation between the CHMU and the management of the river basins is very important, especially on dammed rivers; during the 2002 flooding, the manipulation of the Vlatva River Cascade was vitally important.

After the catastrophic flooding in 1997, the CHMU re-evaluated its overall response and instituted large-scale measures that led to the improvement of their response capabilities. Beginning in 2000, the CHMU improved its interconnection with systems of crisis management both nationally and regionally. Although the Czech Republic's response to the 2002 flood dramatically improved over 1997, the still-catastrophic dimension of the 2002 flooding presented the necessity to continue improvement of the flooding service and the system of the crisis management overall (Rihova, 2010).

The governmental structure of the Czech Republic includes a Ministry of Health with a centralized office, including the Department of Public Health Promotion and Protection. The organization and understanding of the term "public health" is different in the Czech Republic and other central European countries. Public health is equivalent to hygiene and epidemiology. The Ministry of Health is funded by governmental budgets. There exist 14 regional public health departments. Chief Public Health Officer of the Czech Republic Michael Vit and his team performed the leadership in public health during and after the 2002 flood.

Flooding was widespread during the late summer of 2002 in Germany, the Czech Republic, Hungary, and Austria. In the Czech Republic, flooding was the result of five to ten inches of rainfall between August 6th and 7th (Smith, 2003). Czech Republic reservoirs were unable to contain the flood run-off. In addition, a cyclone was generated from the north Adriatic Sea toward Poland (Smith, 2003). The cyclone was slow moving with warmer than usual water temperatures in the Adriatic and Mediterranean downpours in the previously defined areas. The Czech Republic suffered severe flooding in the Sumava mountain area and in south Bohemia. The flood wave moved from the south of the Czech Republic through Prague (Smith, 2003).

The economic impact of the flooding was estimated at more than 11 billion euros. Damage was incurred by both historic sites such as the Old Town area of Prague and the country's infrastructure including transportation. The age of the Czech Republic infrastructure contributed to the extent of the damage (Smith, 2003). In addition to the public infrastructure impact, the local residents did not have a history of wanting or needing flood insurance. This resulted in the federal government's supplying much of the recovery funds (Smith, 2003). Public transit was rendered unusable along with more than 120 bridges. Agricultural losses were estimated at 50% of the normal harvest, and livestock were not able to be fed (Willis, 2002).

Nongovernmental organizations (NGOs) sprang into action. The Czech Republic, Slovakia, and Romania Red Cross immediately mobilized to provide shelter, food, and other basic needs to those affected. Basic living supplies were distributed including food, flashlights, and hygiene items to help stem the spread of disease after the disaster. This coordination was coordinated with the federal government. In addition to the immediate response, consideration was given to the replenishment of supplies for further disaster occurrences (International Federation of the Red Cross, 2003).

Both central and regional and local authorities welcome voluntary cooperation with NGOs, but the key response role belongs to the state institutions in central, regional, and local government. During the 1997 flood, this was explained as the "national nature feature" which expresses itself by the will of the people to help their neighbors and other people. Citizens assist "the brothers and sisters in need" without any duties and any preliminary organization or given legal obligations.

(*Continues*)

During a flood, the public health department of the Ministry of Health controls the regional offices. They check the quality of drinking water supplies, food, sanitary facilities, the need of a vaccination, etc. The public health department and subject regional offices help the regional and local governments to provide the larvicides to fight mosquitoes post flood. After the 2002 flood, the U.S. government helped the Czech Republic by donation of the larvicide.

NGO Cooperation and Meta-Leadership in the Czech Floods

In his analysis of nongovernmental organization coordination in the 2002 Czech floods, Pankaj Kumar analyzed the nature and level of coordination of four Czech humanitarian NGOs to better understand the challenges and incentives for NGO coordination during the 2002 floods. While his analysis ultimately reveals an ineffective level of coordination, it does address elements of meta-leadership that could be addressed to improve future disaster responses. Kumar provides some insight into the presence or absence of meta-leadership, without employing a meta-leadership analysis; meta-leadership had not been articulated yet when he wrote his analysis in 2005 (Kumar, 2005).

Kumar identifies six obstacles to operations coordination: competition for funds, different mandates of NGOs, coordination that slows down the response, coordination that increases the bureaucracy, the costs of coordination, and coordination that reduces financial accountability (Kumar, 2005). These obstacles are well known to any institutions that seek to coordinate any activities, but they highlight a key element of the meta-leadership model: the necessity to build relationships and alliances *before* a disaster strikes. So much of what Kumar identifies as barriers could be reduced by honest conversations and negotiation before a crisis. For example, in the aftermath of the floods, the People in Need Foundation (PINF) took the initiative to try to divide the recovery work among the four leading relief organizations (Kumar, 2005). However, because they were negotiating this coordination during the crisis, lack of a common framework and understanding of each other's capabilities led to days of negotiations and delays, after which no agreements were made.

Kumar identifies two other significant barriers that have meta-leadership implications. He identifies "lack of managerial experience as an obstacle to coordination" (Kumar, 2005). Meta-leadership recognizes that the response starts with the person of the leader. If the leader is inexperienced, he may not have the individual strength or emotional maturity to respond well in a crisis. Lack of managerial experience in a disaster may also result in an inability to react quickly to the shifting nature of the crisis. This reality only highlights the need for experienced managers to "lead down" to their less experienced counterparts and build an organizational culture that connects to other institutions before and during a crisis.

Kumar identifies differing organization values as a second barrier to coordination. This issue is common to many social improvement organizations, for there is no shortage of different opinions as to how to go about it. Kumar highlights differences between secular and religious NGOs, and between groups focused in urban and rural areas, and the north and the south of the country. Certainly, there may be true differences in process, orientation, and work style. But meta-leadership is based on the principle that problems can be solved faster, better, and more efficiently by making connections between diverse institutions. In the meta-leadership model, the differences between institutions become part of what they offer to the community of leaders and actors, rather than barriers to participation. By leading across silos, meta-leaders are more efficient at serving their own constituency, and bring additional resources to bear from institutions that would not have previously supported them. This mutual self-interest ends up creating a community good that could not have been created otherwise.

In closing his paper, Kumar makes recommendations that are consistent with system improvement and offer a glimpse into meta-leadership (Kumar, 2005). For example, he proposes to improve coordination by harmonizing standards and approaches, rather than make connections between institutions with differing approaches. This might be effective if all of the NGOs are under the control of a single entity, but they are not. By definition, they are different organizations and thus requiring them to change will not necessarily encourage their participation.

Kumar makes two recommendations that are foundational for meta-leadership. In the first, he proposes that coordination planning is a fundamental component of disaster management, and goes on to suggest that it is essential to initiate this planning before the onset of an emergency. He goes on to suggest that the application of a "strategic planning approach" would be of great benefit to NGO coordination, suggesting by this language that this application of strategic planning is unfamiliar to the Czech audience.

In the second, he gets at the heart of the Czech Republic's structural deficiency and makes recommendations that look a lot like meta-leadership, but that are unable to be addressed under current Czech law. The overall Czech response to disaster and emergencies is framed by the law that defines the responsibility for disaster preparedness and response. But Kumar addressed the fact that there seems to be almost no coordination or connections between the government that has responsibilities for the disaster response and the NGOs who take responsibility for the relief efforts (Kumar, 2005). He makes what appears to be a radical suggestion that the NGO sector will tremendously benefit from coordinating their operations with other organizations that are involved in disaster preparedness or response. However, this suggestion contradicts established law in the Czech Republic (Rihova, 2010). In the Czech Republic legal system, the government cannot transfer any level of responsibility to the NGOs. The Czech constitution guarantees that every citizen has the right to be protected in the case of crisis. This is the obligation of the state and it is impossible to delegate this obligation to any other subject, even voluntary NGOs! Of course, this does not suggest that the government is uninterested in cooperation with NGOs, but just that it lacks a framework for this cooperation; the government cannot appear to be abrogating its responsibilities.

Kumar closes by citing the following list of skills identified in 1995 by the International Committee of the Red Cross to develop better organizational management and coordination in the NGO sector (International Federal of the Red Cross, 2003).

- facilitation skills ("person of the meta-leader")
- consensus building ("person of the meta-leader")
- preparation of memoranda of understanding (preparation beforehand, "gives, gets, and gaps")
- identification of each organization's comparative strengths and mandates in order ("gives, gets, and gaps")
- to establish a division of labor ("leading up and down")
- maintenance of a "communications loop" ("connectivity")
- participator decision making ("leading across silos")
- provision of personnel incentives to coordinate ("leading up and down"), and
- improved communication ("connectivity").

Perhaps meta-leadership isn't such a new idea after all.

Comparison and Contrast

After reviewing the Illinois and Czech floods, it is apparent there were instances where the themes of meta-leadership were demonstrated and other instances where the principles were not utilized in the response and recovery efforts. In each case, the responsible parties gained additional insight into areas that could have made the response to the disaster more effective. Had meta-leadership principles been utilized, the response would have been based on the criticality of cross-sector coordination. Meta-leaders would have recognized the importance of key principles including "situational awareness," the ability to effectively manage their silo, "leading up," and the importance of "cross-agency connectivity" (Meta-Leadership Summit, 2009).

In both the Illinois and the Czech floods, there were cases where meta-leaders did emerge; however, the need for improvement in both cases was apparent after the disaster. The criticality of the "situational awareness" that occurred during both floods was addressed differently based on key governing roles and responsibilities of key designated leaders. In the case of the Czech floods, the laws in place determined leadership roles; however, meta-leaders were not placed in those roles in all cases (Rihova, 2010). During the Illinois floods, the EMA officials had the responsibility per se to manage as meta-leaders, but did not have the ability to look at the bigger picture to prevail in every instance.

In the case of the Illinois floods, although previous cross-sector planning had occurred prior to the disaster, the cross-agency connectivity planning had not been tested sufficiently. In the instance where the contract was in place for sandbagging to mitigate loss, the vendor was unable to fulfill the contract. This would have become apparent if tests to the plan had been done to ensure there were no perceived gaps. Meta-leaders did emerge when the EMC Coordinator, fire chief, and others began "leading up" and focused on "leading cross-agency connectivity." Conversely, in the case of the Czech floods, one of the key lessons learned was that the CHMU needed to focus efforts on improved interconnectivity with NGOs and other organizations while planning for future disasters.

In both cases, the understanding of the "gets," "gaps," and "gives" was not apparent during the response efforts to a great extent. The basic needs for sheltering, feeding, and assisting impacted individuals and families and was met; however, if the meta-leadership model had been in place and applied during these two incidents, the response effort and the cross-agency response could have been more effective to assist citizens. Based on interviews, the private sector was not engaged to assist, nor had they planned effectively to provide input to employees on post disaster information.

(Continues)

After both flooding incidents, it was apparent to all parties that more could be done in the overall planning, response, and recovery aspects of future disasters. This is where the importance of the meta-leadership structure and model can be impactful for future planning in both the Czech Republic and the state of Illinois to whereby emerging meta-leaders can improve on their ability to leverage system assets, information, and capabilities to drive a collaborative and effective response.

Closing

It's clear from these two case examples that wildly divergent disasters—an international European flood and a mild six-county flood in Illinois—can still illustrate some stark truths about the state of disaster preparedness, response, and recovery. While both the Czech Republic and county-level efforts were effective and represented an improvement over past crisis responses, there is still additional improvements to be realized. Meta-leadership offers a model for the leadership development in times of crisis, and that model is making some headway both in the Czech Republic and in Illinois.

Illinois meta-leadership progress is measured in initiatives both small and large. In 2008 and 2009, Illinois hosted multiple events to promote meta-leadership, including a meta-leadership summit, and post-summit evaluation that brought together more than 100 leaders from a variety of governmental, nonprofit, and business institutions. One outgrowth of that summit was the intention to form a statewide institute for meta-leadership in Illinois, the first of its kind in the nation. The planning for this institute is housed at the University of Illinois School of Public Health, and this case study is the first tangible evidence that meta-leadership may become institutionalized in Illinois.

The Lake Cook Regional Critical Incident Partnership (LCRCIP) is a local program that exemplifies meta-leadership in preparedness and response to disasters. As it exists today, the LCRCIP is an outgrowth of the Critical Incident Protocol (CIP) program from Michigan State University. The Village of Libertyville, Volkswagen Credit, and Motorola brought the CIP to Libertyville in 2006. The CIP involved three facilitated meetings, the last being a large exercise. For a variety of reasons, the CIP group in Libertyville wasn't able to keep the momentum and continue with regular meetings. Discover Financial learned about the CIP program and invited a number of people from nearby businesses and jurisdictions to a kick-off meeting in July 2007. Following that meeting, in October 2007, an even larger stakeholder group met at Takeda Pharmaceuticals in Deerfield and elected a steering committee to plan for the future of the group. That steering committee met often (monthly or more often) throughout 2008 to plan a number of other meetings of the full group, and to develop formal bylaws for the group. At a meeting in February 2009, the full membership approved the organization's bylaws and late in the spring of 2009, LCRCIP incorporation was completed. Some additional information is on the LCRCIP website at http://www.lcrcip.org/default.aspx (McKenzie, 2010). Members of the LCRCIP also participated in the Illinois meta-leadership summit in 2009.

In the Czech Republic, the penetration of meta-leadership is minor. The Republic was able to send one ranking public health official to the United States to participate in the Mid-America Regional Public Health Leadership Institute, with a focus on meta-leadership. In March 2010, nationally recognized leaders on meta-leadership Professor Lou Rowitz of the University of Illinois at Chicago and the Director of the State Illinois Department of Public Health, Damon Arnold, did travel to the Czech Republic to present on meta-leadership and begin to cultivate interest in the model. While the Czech Republic is more institutionally constrained by its disaster responsibility law that limits cross-sector connectivity and silo-busting, even the small amount of interest in meta-leadership is heartening.

"Meta-leadership" as a brand is not used in the Czech Republic, but there are regular official meetings between the Security Council of the State, the Central Crisis Staff, and the regional crisis offices to get to know each other and update their flood plans (Rihova, 2010). The principles of meta-leadership suggest that these efforts will enable the participants to be more effective in times of crisis, but they will not be fully effective until their connections expand to include stakeholders from nonprofits and business. In this final respect, Czech officials are very much like their colleagues in Illinois.

Questions from the Case Study

1. **Who should have accountability and responsibility to establish policy and procedural guidelines for meta-leadership principles? Does this vary by state within agencies, institutions, and/or governments?**

2. The case study discusses private and nonprofit organizations that may be integrated into the community in a similar disaster. What specific types of public health issues could private industry address in response or recovery?

3. Of the three primary sectors identified for inter-sector coordination within the meta-leadership model, which sector is most likely to willingly participate? Which sector is least likely?

4. At the time of the Illinois floods, the economy was robust. Three years later, in the midst of an economic recession, governmental, nonprofit, and private business budgets have been substantially cut. What positive or negative impacts could meta-leadership have on the response to a similar catastrophe, even during an economic recession?

5. What are the barriers to addressing improvements outlined in the "Corrective Action Plans" instituted after the flooding in Illinois?

6. What political pressures were present during either incident? How did the leaders in this case study address these challenges?

7. Both case studies depict examples of good leadership but without the cross-sector systemic coordination exhibited by meta-leaders. Can you provide examples of ways meta-leadership could have been exemplified?

8. How are the barriers to institutionalizing meta-leadership different in Illinois and in the Czech Republic?

9. How does the meta-leadership differ from the International Red Cross's 1995 skills outlined to develop better organizational management and NGO coordination?

References

British Broadcasting Corporation. 2002. Europe's flood lessons. *BBC.com.uk*, August 19. http://news.bbc.co.uk/2/hi/europe/2203152.stm.

Cable News Network. 2002. Huge cost of Czech floods. *CNN.com*, August 2. http://edition.cnn.com/2002/WORLD/europe/08/15/floods.tourists/index.html.

CDC. *See* Centers for Disease Control and Prevention.

Center for Slavic, Eurasian, and East European Studies. 2005. *Environmental policy planning in the Czech Republic.* http://web.mit.edu/jcarmin/www/policylearning/UNCPresention.pdf.

Centers for Disease Control and Prevention. 2008. *10 Essential public health services.* http://www.cdc.gov/od/ocphp/nphpsp/EssentialPHServices.htm.

Daily (IL) Herald. 2007. Loans available for storm victims. September 2.

Disaster Charter. 2006. *Flood Dynamics, East of Prague.* http://www.disasterscharter.org/image/journal/article.jpg?img_id=30946&t=1240078885610.

Durbin, R. 2007. *Durbin, Obama: Disaster declaration for six Illinois counties will help severe storm recovery.* September 26. http://www.durbin.senate.gov.

Earth Times. 2009. Eight die amid floods in Czech Republic. June 25.

Euro-Atlantic Disaster Response Coordination Center. 2003. *Fighting floods in the Czech Republic.* January 15. http://www.nato.int/eadrcc/floods_czech_republic/index.htm.

Federal Emergency Management Agency. 2008. *Designated counties: Illinois severe storms and flooding.* http://www.fema.gov/vi/disaster/1800/affected-counties.

FEMA. *See* Federal Emergency Management Agency.

Hubalek, Z. et al. 2005. Mosquitoborne viruses, Czech Republic, 2002. *Emerging Infectious Diseases* 1.

Illinois Channel. 2007. LaSalle and Grundy counties declared disaster areas. August 27. http://illinoischannel.spaces.live.com/default.aspx.

Illinois Department of Commerce and Economic Opportunity. 2009. *State of Illinois Action Plan.* Supplemental CDBG Disaster Recovery 1800 (Ike) Funding from the Supplemental Appropriations Act Public Law 110-329, 2008, September.

(Continues)

Illinois Emergency Management (20 ILCS 3305). http://www.ilga.gov/legislation/ilcs/ilcs3
.asp?ActID=368&ChapterID=5.

Illinois Government News Network. 2007. Governor Blagojevich announces disaster unemployment assistance.
October 1.

International Federation of Red Cross and Red Crescent Societies. 2003. *Central Europe: Floods appeal no.
25/2002 final report*. October 2003.

Jobst, M. 2010. *Interview conducted by author in Oak Park, IL*. February 26.

Journal & Topics (IL) Newspapers. 2008. Gov: This place is a mess. September 24.

Kumar, P. 2005. *NGO coordination in humanitarian action: The case of the Czech floods of August 2002*. http://
dspace.mit.edu/handle/1721.1/33056.

Lutz, J. 2010. Interview conducted by author in Chicago, IL. March 1.

Marcus, L. J., Dorn, B. C., and Henderson, J. M. 2006. Meta-leadership and national emergency preparedness: a
model to build government connectivity. *Biosecurity and bioterrorism: Biodefense strategy, practice, and science*,
4(2):128–134.

Marcus, L. J., Dorn, B. C., and Henderson, J. M. (2005). *Meta-leadership and national emergency preparedness:
Strategies to build government connectivity*. Working paper, Center for Public Leadership.

Marcus, L. J., Ashkenazi, I., Dorn, B. C., and Henderson, J. M. 2009. *National preparedness and the five dimensions
of meta-leadership*. https://www.medicalreservecorps.gov/File/Promising_Practices_Toolkit/Guidance_Docu-
ments/Emergency_Preparedness_Response/Meta_Leadership_One_page_primer_March_2007.pdf.

McKenzie, K. 2010. Interview conducted by author in Wonder Lake, IL. February 26.

Meta-Leadership Summit. 2009. *Meta Leadership*. http://www.cdcfoundation.org/meta-leadership.

Ministry of Agriculture. 2003. *Report on the state of water management in the Czech Republic 2002*.

Moore, M., et al. 2009. Learning from exemplary practices in international disaster management: A fresh avenue
to inform U.S. policy? *Journal of Homeland Security and Emergency Management* 6(1). http://www.bepress
.com/jhsem/vol6/iss1/35.

Obrusnik, I. 2005. *National report of the Czech Republic towards the WCDR in Kobe, 2005*. Czech
Hydrometerological Institute.

The Prague flood of August 2002. http://www.livingprague.com/flood.htm.

Prochazkova, D. *August 2002 flood in the Czech Republic*. http://www.gadr.giees.uncc.edu/hzeventdetails.cfm?ID=5.

Quiggle, Z. 2007. Disaster recovery cneters open after president's declaration. *Northern (IL) Star online*. October 2.

Quiggle, Z. 2007. Residents unemployed due to flood may be eligible for federal aid. *Northern (IL) Star online*.
October 24.

Rihova, K. 2010. Email exchanges with author. March 1–11.

Schanze, J., et al. n.d. *Evaluation of effectiveness and efficiency of non-structural measures*. 4th International
Symposium on Flood Defense, 6–8 May, Toronto. http://www.flood-era.ioer.de

Sercl, P., and Stehlik, J. 2003. *The August 2002 flood in the Czech Republic*. EGS-AGU-EUG Joint Assembly,
abstract 12404. April.

Smith, S. 2003. Central Europe flooding, August 2002. *Risk Management Solutions*. http://www.rms.com/
publications/Central%Europe%20Floods%20Whitepaper_final.pdf.

Soukalova, E. 2002. Flood forecasting system in the Czech Republic. *Danube Watch*, 2/2002. http://www.icpdr
.org/icpdr/static/dw2002_2/dw0202p10.htm.

Sparrow, J. 2002. Europe's troubled waters. *The Magazine of the International Red Cross and Red Crescent Movement.*

Sparrow, J. 2002. *Flood horror surfaces*. August. http://www.ifrc.org/es/news-and-media/news-stories/europe-
central-asia/czech-republic/czech-republic-flood-horror-surfaces/.

St. Clair, S., and Malone, T. 2007. Weeks later, families still wait on government flood help. *Daily (IL) Herald*,
September 20.

Stich, M. 2003. *The Prague flood*. May. http://www.attitudetravel.com/czech/articles/ms_pragueflood.html.

United Nations Office for the Coordination of Humanitarian Affairs. 2010. *Czech Republic-Floods-August 2002*.
http://reliefweb.int/disaster/fl-2002-0479-cze?sl=environment-term_listing%252Ctaxonomy_index_tid_
source-1503%252Ctaxonomy_index_tid_content_format-10.

Velasquez, A. 2008. Letter to the editor. *Daily (IL) Herald*, March 19.

Willis Limited. 2002. *Central European flood report: August 2002*.

Source: Courtesy of the Mid-America Regional Public Health Leadership Institute.

High-risk accidents have not only enhanced and changed our lives, they are increasing with each passing year. Many of these technologies have the potential for being catastrophic over time. Perrow argued in the 1990s that these new technologies often lead to inevitable events that he called normal accidents.[6] Many new technologies, like nuclear power, can be seen as a system that can eventually have a normal accident occur. Failures do occur. Perrow called an accident that is isolated a discrete failure. If a subsystem has a failure, there may be a redundant subsystem that can handle the failure. Complexity occurs when a discrete and a redundant subsystem interact in a way that causes a failure. Perrow gave the example of the Three Mile Island accident in 1979, which involved four distinct failures. Perrow's work is interesting in the sense that systems work on crises leads to the conclusion that crises will inevitably occur as our high-risk technologies continue to expand.

In August of each year, my wife and I go to see several plays in Stratford, Ontario. There is a Canadian version of the Avon River in which there are many ducks and white swans. In the midst of all these white swans, we see a rare black swan. The event is always a surprise, and we discuss this unusual occurrence on each of these rare events. Taleb refers to almost all major events from scientific discoveries to historical events as black swan events.[7] Most crises and disasters are black swan events because we can predict that these events will possibly occur, but we cannot predict time or place or severity. Taleb presents an interesting argument by looking at the normal distribution in statistics (Mediocristan) and criticizes statisticians and others for overanalyzing events and trying to fit these events into the normal distribution. He argues that these unusual events occur primarily in the tails of the distribution and need to be analyzed differently as a result (Extremistan).

Black swans are outliers.[8] These events have have major effects on communities and their people. Taleb argues that we try to explain these black swans after the fact as something we can explain and also predict.[9] Because black swan events will occur even though we cannot predict them with great accuracy or when and how they will occur, planning needs to occur to handle positive and negative events if and when they do occur.

Next we come to the sand pile experiment.[9,10] Imagine that you are on a beach and decide to build a sand pile. You continue to build the sand pile and eventually it will collapse. However, you cannot predict when the collapse will occur or how severe the collapse will be. Self-organized criticality (SOC) is the point at which the collapse occurs. Lewis defines the SOC phenomenon as a characteristic of complex systems that self-organize and lead to chain reactions that disrupt the system and its operation. Change is a property inherent in all systems. In normal times, if change occurs it is very slow, but once SOC is reached, change is spontaneous and fast. Thus, if reality is measured by the change, then Lewis argues that punctuated reality is a defining component of the change process. Calm with little change is followed by crisis and then change, which is the punctuated reality between change events.

Lewis attempts to put the pieces of SOC, normal accidents, and black swans together.[11] As systems develop, criticality becomes an issue because systems are dynamic and in a constant state of change. Black swans are outliers and fairly rare. When they appear, the change is generally radical. Lewis believes that black swans represent abnormal accidents rather than the normal accidents described by Perrow. Normal accidents lead to small adaptations, and black swans lead to major change and adaptation. Lewis uses Bak's theory to argue that tipping points[12] are critical points that pull a system in some specified direction. Once the SOC is reached and a collapse occurs, then there will be an adjustment and adaptation until the next collapse and more change occurs. It is collapse that leads to societal change that Lewis calls the "Bak paradox." An important lesson here is that the public health leader must understand crisis and emergencies because the next health crisis will affect the health of the public and lead to adjustments and adaptations in the role and practice of public health.

SUMMARY

Public health leaders need to function in normal and not-so-normal times. This chapter explored the move from traditional organizations to community-based approaches to public health practice. The crises cycle was reviewed and then followed by a discussion of some of the systems and complexity issues in dealing with public health crises and emergencies.

DISCUSSION QUESTIONS

1. Describe the crisis cycle and how different types of crises and their aftermath fit the cycle.

2. What effect does the operational definition of a local health department have on understanding how public health responds to a disaster?

3. Why are mitigation strategies important in crisis?

4. How would you develop a global public health leadership development initiative?

5. Differentiate and integrate the approaches of Perrow, Taleb, and Lewis.

EXERCISE 15-1: Traditional and Crisis Leadership

Purpose: to explore the skills necessary for traditional public health leaders inside and outside their agency with crisis leadership skills to determine similarities and differences in the skills necessary to be an effective public health leader

Key concepts: traditional leadership skills, crisis leadership skills

Procedure: Divide your class or training group into groups of 8 to 10 people. One-third of the groups will create a traditional (day-to-day) inside-the-agency set of skills. Have them put the list on a flip chart sheet of paper. Another third of the groups will create a skill list for a traditional leader with external partners and constituents. The final third will create a list of crisis leadership skills. Each group will present its list, and then all participants will discuss what they discovered.

REFERENCES

1. L. H. Kahn, *Who's in Charge* (Santa Barbara, CA: Praeger Security International, 2009).
2. Federal Emergency Management Agency, *Declared Disasters by Year and State*, http://www.fema.gov.
3. *Leading Through a Crisis* (Boston: Harvard Business Press, 2009).
4. W. Coburn, R. J. S. Spence, and A. Pomonis, *Disaster Mitigation*, 2nd ed. (Geneva: United Nations Disaster Management Training Programme, 1994).
5. I. A. Mitroff and K. A. Linstone, *The Unbounded Mind* (New York: Oxford University Press, 1993).
6. C. Perrow, *Normal Accidents* (Princeton, NJ: Princeton University Press, 1999).
7. N. N. Taleb, *The Black Swan*, 2nd ed. (New York: Penguin Books, 2010).
8. M. Gladwell, *Outliers* (New York: Little, Brown and Co., 2008).
9. N. N. Taleb, *The Black Swan*.
10. T. G. Lewis, *Bak's Sand Pile* (Williams, CA: Agile Press, 2011).
11. Lewis, *Bak's Sand Pile*.
12. M. Gladwell, *The Tipping Point* (Boston: Little, Brown and Co., 2000).

CHAPTER 16

The Social Capital Perspective

I have erected a monument more lasting than bronze.

—Edna Miller, a Chicago high school Latin teacher, 1955

In the years since the 1970s, Putnam has reported extensively that social ties and strong community identifications have declined.[1] The reasons for the decline have been due to changes in social, economic, and technological factors. The American people just seem to be less involved with each other than they were in the past. Some of us live in suburban bedroom communities far from our places of work or our daily activities. Our social life also seems to take place out of our residential communities. We often do not know our neighbors even though we may have lived in our homes and apartments for several years. We do not get involved in many local activities unless our real estate taxes go up too high or our schools threaten to cut services and programs for our children. In fact, many of our citizens do not even vote. Our children spend much of their time before television sets or computer screens. It is for these reasons and many others that our level of community involvement has shown a measurable decline.

Thus, Putnam and others who view the American landscape talk about this decline in our social capital. This chapter discusses social capital and the importance of it for a renewed American perspective. The public health leader needs to understand the ramifications of building social capital in order to address critical issues in emergency preparedness and response as well as all other community-based concerns of the public health system.

Klann made distinctions between management and leadership in a crisis-prone environment.[2] Crisis management relates mainly to operational issues. It involves the management of an organization during a crisis and the development and testing of crisis plans. Since September 11, 2001, public health agency administrators have become preoccupied with emergency preparedness and response activities. However, crisis leadership is a more expansive set of activities involving the human response to a crisis. Crisis leadership involves three major sets of activities. These three sets of activities include communication, clarity of vision and values, and caring relationships. Caring relationships involve the display of true sincerity and authenticity, development of strong and viable community relationships, strong relationships strengthened by sharing experiences with each other, and solving problems together. It is these latter activities that build social capital. Leaders need time to reflect on their actions and examine the emotional effects of these activities and events on them personally.

DEFINITION OF SOCIAL CAPITAL

To successfully address the issues of bioterrorism and other threats as well as all public health concerns, it is clear that the secret to success lies in our collaborative efforts. None of the above challenges can be solved unless it is done with other partners. Collaboration is all about building social capital in our communities. Social capital refers to the synergistic effects of working together to strengthen communities and especially the public health system. Social capital refers to the value-added effect of working together to create positive change in our communities. Social capital comes into being through the combination of the following:

- The institutions, relationships, and cultural context in which such relationships are built
- The values and norms that affect these relationships
- The influence of our leaders
- The social networks that evolve through teams, coalitions, alliances, and partnerships

Social capital comes into being through action. Social capital is the glue that strengthens our communities so that they can survive any crisis that may befall them.

Social capital can be distinguished from physical capital and human capital.[3] Physical capital simply refers to physical objects, and human capital refers to the properties of individuals. Physical and human capital involve the process of being trained to use tools and learning skills that enhance individual productivity. For example, a physical capital object might be a hammer that allows a carpenter to do his work. A college education or a bioterrorism preparedness workshop can increase individual productivity (human capital). If individuals work collectively to improve the communities in which they work, we are beginning to build social capital. Thus:

$$\text{Social capital} = \text{physical capital} + \text{human capital} + \text{collaboration}$$

Exercise 16-1 will allow you to experiment with some of these principles by constructing a team flag.

Social capital involves both vertical and horizontal associations between organizations and people. At a horizontal level, people develop identification with others. At this level, personal ties are strong, and there is often both a common purpose to the interactions with relationships and roles that are clearly delineated. Vertical ties cross organizations and community diversity. These bridging relationships require extensive negotiation to learn how to work together when different roles and relationships define these different cultural groups and organizations (business as well as human service agencies). These vertical and horizontal associations must also be seen relative to the political environment of the local, state, national, and international levels. Actions at all levels of the political spectrum can affect local social capital formation and relationships. This latter issue is especially relevant in the arena of emergency preparedness and response.

Social capital is a productive resource that affects the productivity of all other resources in a community.[4] Social capital takes three forms. The first form involves information sharing that uses social relationships to gather information to address personal as well as organizational issues. The second form is built on the important consideration of trust. Trust gets built through positive social relations and may lead to reciprocal relationships as a positive norm within the community. If an individual is in crisis or is fearful, he or she will get the help they need. The third form builds on the cultural norms and values of the community. Tradition plays a critical part in this form. The norms of cooperation and social expectation can be found in all the major institutions in the community, and the values and norms of cooperation are passed on in families, churches and faith-based agencies, schools, and other social entities of the community. All three forms of social capital are reinforced through social support, social networks, honors and awards, and community celebrations of various kinds. Those who do not go along with the accepted standards of behavior relative to collaboration are punished or ostracized.

There is much confusion over the definition of social capital.[5] There are five major themes in the definitions. First, social capital is most usually defined by its function. Second, the term is sometimes seen as relationship based. It is not a property of individuals, but rather is a property of the way the individual relates to others. The third theme involves actions to pursue shared objectives within the structure of the relationship that is created through collaboration. The fourth theme involves the creation of networks with norms and rules and regulations that allow the participants to work together in an effective manner. Trust building and reciprocity are critical components in this theme. The fifth theme involves the ability of the network to garner and command scarce resources.

Ultimately, the critical decision in the use of such a concept as social capital relates to the issue of why it seems to work. There are at least four reasons for this.[6] First, the flow of information seems smoother in organizations and communities with high levels of social capital. It is through communication and interaction that social relationships develop and grow. First responders during a crisis must know how and to whom to communicate what they see. Second, these social ties seem to influence the individuals who make decisions about everything from hiring a particular person to passing a critical piece of legislation. Developing social ties between the public health leader and his and her partners opens the channel of communication during a crisis. Working together is easier with people with whom you have developed social ties than with people with whom you have little connection. Third, these social ties are seen by organizations and their representatives as evidence of the social credentials of the individual, which in turn tie that individual to other community organizations and networks.

In other words, the public health leader needs to develop relationships with other community leaders and organizations in order to gain trust and credibility. The role of public health during a crisis needs to be negotiated with these partners. If these things are done early, then social capital is built and emergency response activities run more smoothly with an awareness of the critical role of public health during a crisis. The fourth reason for why social capital works is that it reinforces the roles of each participant and organization in normal and not-so-normal community events. Not only are these relationships reinforced, they also gain recognition.

BUILDING SOCIAL CAPITAL

Although it is imperative that the public health leader builds social capital with other leaders in the community, if biological or other threats are to be addressed in an efficient manner, it is not so simple a matter to do.

There are conflicting agendas at play between people, organizations, political entities, communities, states, and so on. These conflicts and tensions often work against collaboration and infrastructure development. Building social capital can be a very difficult process in which many interconnecting relationships significantly affect the outcome of normal and not-so-normal events. The public health leader needs to understand how his or her community functions. Most communities are diverse. Diversity here has a wide meaning. It refers not only to its traditional meanings related to age, racial–ethnic groupings, gender differences, and educational differences; it now also refers to nontraditional family relationships, transorganizational relationships, and relationships with new partners such as the police, FBI, and fire departments. The differences are demonstrated in many ways such as language, cultural differences, values, norms, and relationships during crisis.

Social capital can be seen as working at the two levels of sociocultural context (the ecological level and the institutional infrastructure level). At the sociocultural level, bonding social capital relates to those factors that affect group, neighborhood, or community solidarity. People who are similar in values and other demographic characteristics such as race and ethnicity seem to bond more readily than those who differ in these demographic characteristics.[7] Bridging social capital refers to creating social capital among those individuals or organizations that differ in their values and characteristics. The social distance between people with different values and goals makes bridging social capital a more complex endeavor.[8] Social capital in the bridging situation does not occur automatically. The public health leader needs to know how to collaborate, be resilient in adapting to change, have strong people skills, have strong public health credentials, and be knowledgeable about critical elements of bioterrorism preparedness and response. Bridging social capital is a critical activity for the prepared public health leader.

Hofstede and Hofstede presented a model that should help the public health leader better understand how these various relationships become defined.[9] There are five dimensions that demonstrate the reasons for cultural variability. The first dimension is power–distance relationships. Power–distance refers to whether individuals or organizations see power as distributed unequally. This dimension also relates to how individuals think about their ability to influence decision-making activities. If certain groups or organizations feel distant from the power structure of the community, they may disengage from the process and become reactive to the decisions made. In fact, it appears that the level of inequality in a society may be unconsciously endorsed by the followers as well as the leaders. If individuals act as different and as unequal to other individuals or groups, this inequality gets reinforced in the fabric of the community and sometimes the society as a whole. Arguments abound that in a democratic society, all individuals can become involved in decision making regardless of the diversity of their group or organization. The public health leader will probably see both of the above reactions to the use of power and authority in the communities they serve. The public health leader must practice the skills of cultural competence if he or she is to address the diverse parts of the community.

The second dimension in the model relates to masculinity–femininity. Every society and every community acts in terms of expected gender roles. Masculine societies have strong concepts of the male and female roles. Males tend to be assertive and dominant in these cultures and women more submissive. To be successful in these societies, women have become more assertive and dominant as well. Societies that are defined by feminine concepts tend to be more nurturing and more relationship oriented. These societies often blur gender roles. With the diversity in culture, we often find major differences in the gender role orientation of different groups that the public health leader serves. Some occupations have a strong masculine orientation, such as the military, the police, and fire professionals. Public health professionals and many social agency professionals take a more cooperative and nurturing approach that fits more under the concept of femininity. The public health leader must relate to many individuals and groups with different orientations. An important issue for the prepared leader is how to push a caregiving agenda in a community that is more masculine in orientation.

Individualism–collectivism is the third dimension. This is a critical dimension in public health. Public health has argued strongly for the importance of working with others to accomplish tasks. Teams, coalitions, alliances, and partnership structures are utilized. The level of commitment of the group members is stressed. Leadership development programs teach collaborative skills and argue for the importance of shared leadership to accomplish our mission. Concerns about

bioterrorism preparedness and response emphasize the importance of collaboration if our communities are to remain safe. On the other hand, we live in a society in which the ties between individuals are loose. We stress individualism and competition. Trust is a trait that is hard to maintain. Social capital declines in this environment. Thus, there is an inherent tug-of-war in American society between our strong individualistic heritage and the critical need to emphasize collectivism and cooperation to address the problems of today and the terrorist threats that seem to dominate our political agendas.

The fourth dimension involves what the Hofstedes call uncertainty avoidance. Societies and communities differ in their tolerance for ambiguity and uncertainty. Cultures that rank low on this dimension are cultures in which people feel comfortable with the unknown. High-uncertainty cultures are those in which formal rules guide action and in which uncertainty expresses itself in high anxiety and often fear. Americans today seem to be more anxious and fearful than before September 11, 2001. Our tolerance for uncertainty is clearly in decline. The high fear factor in many of our communities affects the ability of the public health leader to address concerns of the people in the community. Mental health concerns as well as bioterrorism preparedness and response issues are now predominant in our public health planning activities. A key issue for many of our community residents is how to keep their families safe in this uncertain environment.

The final dimension involves short-term and long-term consequences. The long-term orientation involves virtues related to waiting for rewards in the future, such as perseverance and thrift, whereas short-term orientation involves values and virtues related to the past and present, such as the respect for tradition, the fulfillment of social obligations, and preserving face.

Building social capital as a means to address our present concern with terrorism threats means that it is necessary to address methods for working together to solve our community's concerns. Keeping in mind the Hofstedes' model and Putnam's arguments about the critical nature of social capital building, review the Hickernoodle City case study and see the issues that arise when a terrorist act occurs and how one community might handle it (Case Study 16-A). Determine the role of a public health leader in the scenario. What might have been done differently?

A Haze over Hickernoodle City: Biodefense Readiness in a Community
Margaret Beaman, RN, PhD; Peg Dublin, RN, BSN; Amy Lay, MPH; Jack Morgan, PhD; Gage Rosti, BS;
Ellen Vonderheide, MBA

Case Study 16-A

Chemical terrorism has recently surfaced as a major threat as terrorist groups have become more sophisticated in their methods. An attack of this nature can result in many casualties and severely strain the emergency response and healthcare system, as well as disrupt the normal operations of a city. Public health departments and their communities must be prepared for such disasters. One of the three core functions of public health is the assurance of the public's health and safety (Institute of Medicine 1988). Disaster preparation also addresses the *Healthy People 2010* Goal 23 to ensure that federal, tribal, state, and local health agencies have the infrastructure to provide essential public health services effectively.

This case study is a fictional account of the November 16, 2001, release of poisonous gas in the subways of Hickernoodle City, with a population of 1.4 million. The case is based on the facts of the sarin poisoning on the Tokyo subway (Ohbu et al. 1997). Hickernoodle City, like many communities, has collaborated with its state agency to develop a biodefense plan for combating terrorist acts of biological, chemical, and irradiation destruction. A release of sarin gas in the Hickernoodle subway system in November 2001 tested the functionality of the city's disaster plan. As a result of two simultaneous releases of the poisonous gas in two trains during rush hour, more than 5,000 persons were exposed and became symptomatic. Because of the magnitude of the problem, the state Emergency Management Agency became involved to assist the Hickernoodle City emergency respondents to activate the Emergency Operations Center (EOC). The effectiveness of this community's response to disaster unfolds through analysis of this fictitious, yet conceivable, scenario. This case study reflects the diagnosis and investigation of health hazards in the community, one of 10 essential public health services. The assessment focuses on identifying health, fiscal, administrative, legal, social, and political barriers that impede the community's ability to successfully handle mass disasters. The critical analysis of the health delivery system includes an evaluation of system capacity; public health leadership; and collaborations, strategic planning, and imperative local roles in disaster preparedness. This assurance exercise aims to achieve the *Healthy People 2010* Goal 23 of ensuring that federal, tribal, state, and local health agencies have the infrastructure to provide essential public health services effectively.

Hickernoodle City is a major metropolitan city in the Midwest. It has a mass transit system consisting of about 20 major passenger rail lines serving the distant city and suburbs that feed into five train stations near the downtown area. More than 100,000 passengers use this system daily. Each of these stations is connected to an extensive subway system serving the city. The rail stations are large, partially enclosed buildings that interconnect rail and subway lines.

The Facts

On Thursday, November 16, 2001, the Metro Commuter Southline train that served Hickernoodle City was unusually crowded due to the arrival of the Dalai Lama, who was scheduled to appear at a 10 a.m. rally in the city center. The train was filled with families and college students anxious to be in the presence of such a revered spiritual leader. At approximately 7:35 a.m., people in the third car noticed that a paper bag had been left behind by an exiting passenger. Several people were later able to recall seeing an oily substance seeping from the bag. Within seconds, all of the 65 or 70 people on that car began coughing; their eyes were tearing, and many were gasping for air. When the train stopped at the Southside Rail Station eight minutes later, two dozen people had lost consciousness and were lying on the floor of the car; others piled out onto the platform and collapsed. Most of the victims were vomiting and in a daze. Over the next minutes, fumes from the third railcar seeped into adjacent train cars, and soon several hundred people were coughing, their eyes were watering, and they were complaining of pain in their eyes.

As people streamed out of the cars at the station, panic began to set in among the crowd of 3,000 passengers in the rail station; many people were screaming. The stationmaster ordered the entire train evacuated and called for emergency personnel to arrive on the scene. Before emergency personnel could arrive, security guards at the station pulled 45 people out of the cars and placed the victims on the train platform. Those who could walk found their way outside, and many collapsed on the sidewalk. Those who could speak described feeling intense pain in their eyes and everything looking dark, as if they were wearing sunglasses. Some described a sudden pain when taking a breath, as if they had been shot. Because of the large numbers of children on the train, there were a disproportionate number of children among those who had lost consciousness. Parents were frantically trying to find help for their children while they experienced breathing difficulty themselves.

(Continues)

By the time the paramedics and firefighters arrived at 7:55 a.m., there had been four fatalities, three of whom were children under the age of five. Emergency personnel found persons losing consciousness, foaming at the mouth, convulsing, stumbling, and exhibiting respiratory problems. They quickly determined that some form of chemical emission had occurred on the train. To reduce continued exposure, emergency workers put on protective masks as they removed persons from the train. The immediate area was ordered evacuated and a hazardous material (HazMat) team assembled to enter the site.

Meanwhile, first respondents began treating others who were unable to evacuate the area by applying mask-valve-ventilator devices and providing oxygen. Atropine injections were prepared for those convulsing and nearing unconsciousness. However, many of the respondents were not certified paramedics and, under law, were not allowed to administer the prophylaxes; they were only able to provide protective masks and oxygen, until those supplies began to dwindle. Some personnel, without knowing the exact cause and venue of contamination, were afraid to provide mouth-to-mouth resuscitation for fear of receiving secondhand exposure. A number of the victims had to remain struggling for air.

Emergency Operations Center

Thirty minutes after the incident began at the Southside Station, a similar incident involving a chemical emission began to unfold on the Northwest line at the Westside Station about five miles away. When that train arrived at the Westside Station, dozens of dazed passengers stumbled from the train coughing and gasping for air. At least 10 people had lost consciousness in the railcar.

This time the Emergency Medical System (EMS) director was notified, and he quickly called the Hickernoodle Emergency Operations Center (HEOC) into action. The HEOC, upon realization that a terrorist-related incident may have occurred, notified the State Department of Health emergency officer, who arranged for the EMS chief to come to duty. The chief of EMS and Highway Services began notifying the point of departure (POD) designated disaster hospitals. Because the incident occurred in two EMS regions of Hickernoodle City, two POD disaster hospitals (I and II) were notified and warned of a possible influx of patients. As required by protocol, POD Hospital I, which had already begun receiving patients, contacted all participating and resource hospitals to assess emergency department (ED) availability, number of beds, units of blood, and inventory of ventilators and other supplies.

The area hospitals took inventory and began faxing the required forms to the POD hospitals, which would forward the information on to the state department, which would coordinate resources for the remaining disaster time. The POD hospitals' fax lines could not handle the influx of reports. Emergency personnel at POD Hospital II, confused about which health department was to receive their inventory and resource information, began faxing their information to the local health department. The EMS chief, upon receiving some faxes from POD Hospital I, started rerouting ambulances according to the hospital information faxes. Many hospitals had recorded limited supplies and shortages of staff, yet the ambulances kept coming because the EMS chief had not yet received their list of inventory. Before long, emergency rooms began running out of ventilators, oxygen, antidotes, and beds. One by one they started going on bypass, refusing to take any patients that arrived via ambulance.

Meanwhile, back at the scene, Hickernoodle City Mayor Edgar M. Weekly ordered all rail and subway trains to stop at the next station until further notice and for trains and stations to be evacuated. The media arrived and began interrogating anyone willing to report on the situation. The state health department director notified the state and federal bureaus of investigation of the event. The mayor contacted his director of communications to coordinate communication responses that could calm the public. Fact sheets were obtained from the local health department on the likely agent of distress, and messages on avoiding secondary contamination were prepared. Hospitals were ordered to redirect the media to the state health department emergency director, who would provide updated reports on casualties, patient conditions, and so forth.

The local health commissioner was disgruntled as she heard from an inside source that hospitals were simultaneously going on bypass and sending ambulances way out of their transport area. The city was running out of participating ambulances. The EMS director asked the fire chief to locate private ambulances in the area. However, the private ambulances refused service because a contract or payment couldn't be provided up front. As hundreds of patients arrived at emergency departments, hospitals continued to go on bypass. The local commissioner called the POD hospitals to order that no hospitals remain on or resort to bypass status. As emergency rooms became saddled with patients for whom no supplies, beds, or nurses to perform triage were available, the chief of EMS was notified. Appalled and angered by the commissioner's order, she contacted the emergency services medical director and they began calling hospitals to assess their conditions. Those lacking supplies and manpower were allowed to redirect ambulances. Some hospitals called other hospitals in their region and asked to borrow supplies in order to treat current ED patients. However, because no regulations mandate the sharing of supplies, even in a time of crisis, hospitals were hesitant to lend equipment they might need themselves.

About five hours after the initial incident was reported, FBI agents specially trained in chemical and biological terrorism began investigating the scenes at the train stations. Air and fabric samples from the rail cars were collected as well as remaining passenger items. Of particular interest was a backpack from the Southside Station and an open package from the Westside Station; both contained canisters capable of delivering gases. Neither the city nor state laboratories were capable of analyzing chemical warfare agents. Therefore, military planes out of O'Ryan International Airport were used to transport the samples to the FBI crime lab in Maryland for analysis. A medical alert was sent out to regional healthcare agencies and local health departments to report any cases showing symptoms of nerve agents. As media began reporting the incident to the public, hospitals also began receiving the "worried well." In addition, persons at the stations or on trains where the crisis had occurred began paying attention to their breathing difficulties, tightness of chest, or other mild symptoms that had previously been attributed to being in an excited or panicked state. They began worrying about the extent of their exposure.

The following day, the FBI lab reported that traces of sarin gas had been found in the rail cars and in the blood of victims. The canisters in the backpack and package were believed to be the means of dispersal. All rail and subway lines remained closed for three and a half days. Sample collection at the attacked stations and adjoining tunnels and stations began on Friday, November 17, for clearance testing of the affected structures. On Saturday, November 18, Mayor Weekly announced that limited rail service would be available on Monday, November 20. Those stations and lines directly affected by the attack would remain closed until they were determined to be safe for use. Increased security would be implemented by all public transportation agencies, and a long-range security plan would be developed.

As questions about inappropriate ambulance transport times, numbers of hospitals on bypass, inadequate supply of ambulances, and other issues arose, the commissioner, anxious to pinpoint blame for the crisis, announced that a Senate hearing would take place to investigate the disaster response.

Human Toll

Seven hundred and fifty people from both trains were taken to area hospitals the day of the attack. Symptoms of the victims included headache, shortness of breath, severe pain when breathing, uncontrollable shaking, watery eyes, and foaming at the mouth. Many of the victims who had lost consciousness remained unconscious for 24 to 48 hours. During second wave, 250 people were seen in area emergency departments (EDs) over the next three days with similar symptoms as well as severe anxiety. Complaints of panic attacks, insomnia, and intense nervousness were reported. In all, there were seven fatalities, three of whom were young children. Although most of those seen at area hospitals were released, 46 people remained hospitalized for up to 10 days.

In the days, weeks, and months following the incident, many persons present or near the incidents complained of nervousness, jitters, excessive dreaming, insomnia, increased tension, restlessness, some gastrointestinal effects, and trouble concentrating.

Over the next six months, many of the victims took advantage of mental health services offered in the community. Mental health workers reported that many of the victims had persistent sleeping problems including waking after only two to three hours and nightmares. Other symptoms included difficulty concentrating, hyperexcitability, and fear of being in confined spaces. Area mental health professionals reported symptoms of post-traumatic stress among a significant number of people seeking services, including panic attacks, recurring flashbacks (of the incident), inability to enter the subway, obsessive thoughts about the possibility of another terrorist attack, and inability to experience pleasure. In addition to victims experiencing psychological effects of the attack, many of the emergency personnel and hospital staff who had attended the victims were experiencing anxiety symptoms. The demand for mental health services exceeded the availability of services, and officials needed to request assistance from other cities. Area businesses experienced unusually high rates of absenteeism and loss of productivity among employees affected by the attack.

Public Relations

On Friday, November 17, articles appeared in three of Hickernoodle's major papers. The *Hickernoodle Sun Times'* headline read "Chemical War Zone at Southside Station." The *Sun Times* had a reporter at the Southside Rail Station who wrote a very descriptive account of the victims and the scene inside the Southside Station. The reporter described the scene as a "chemical war zone," with rescue workers appearing in moon suits to treat victims. He also mentioned that some of the rescue personnel were refusing to provide mouth-to-mouth resuscitation to some of the victims for fear of exposure.

The *Hickernoodle Tribune*'s headline read "Passengers Attacked with Nerve Gas." The reporter for the *Tribune* managed to interview victims at one of the hospitals, along with the hospital personnel. The personnel at the hospital mentioned that the victims had been attacked with nerve gas. However, at the time, they could not determine exactly which kind. The *Tribune*'s article also mentioned the confusion between the hospitals and the state and local health departments as to who was to receive inventory and resource lists. With this confusion, many victims were being rerouted to different hospitals or to hospitals that were already at capacity. "These victims were spending far more time riding around in an ambulance than they should have."

The headline for the *Hickernoodle Daily* read, "City Transportation Paralyzed by Terrorist Attacks." The *Daily* not only gave detailed descriptions of the victims and overcrowding of the hospitals, but also took the angle of the major public transportation system being shut down. The *Daily*'s reporter spoke with passengers stranded at both the Southside and Westside stations. The state of panic led to bigger traffic problems, with taxis, press, and emergency vehicles all trying to get to the stations.

Three local news networks were broadcasting live from the scene of the attacks. The reporters were talking to anyone they could—both victims and witnesses. Each of the networks also interviewed patients and emergency room personnel. One station spoke with an ambulance driver who had been rerouted to three different hospitals. One of the other networks picked up on the packages and blood being flown out of state to be tested.

Each of the newspapers and the television stations reported that a nerve gas or agent had been released in the two stations. Fact sheets were obtained from the local health department on the signs and symptoms to watch for and how to avoid secondary contamination. The biggest communication problem was incomplete information being publicized. The FBI, the city of Hickernoodle, and the local and state health departments simply did not have enough information to share with the public.

Hickernoodle City, the local and state health departments, and the FBI called a joint press conference on the afternoon of the 16th. The press conference was the first to confirm there was some form of terrorist attack on two morning trains. It was not yet known if the attack was of domestic or international origin. The chemical agents used in the attacks had not yet been identified. The second issue emphasized during the press conference was the frozen train service for the Southside and Westside stations for at least 24 hours.

Effect on Structural Systems

The attack caused great strain on the medical providers, both public and private, as well as taxing the transportation system, police, fire, and communications personnel. Although Hickernoodle City had practiced disaster preparedness, they had never dealt with a disaster of this magnitude.

The timing of the disaster, at the height of rush hour, tended to compound problems related to getting to the attack site, as did the lack of knowledge as to the agent used in the attack. Other confounding problems became apparent as the amount of devastation and the human toll mounted. A lack of trained medical professionals, both in the public health sector and in the private sector, to effectively handle the volume of injured and dying soon became apparent. A lack of available hospital beds for use in overnight observation and intensive care and the lack of a plan to evacuate the city in an orderly fashion all contributed to the confusion and hysteria.

With the shutdown of the rail system, the routes into and out of the city on surface streets soon became gridlocked. As the news of the attack spread throughout the city, people poured out of their offices into the streets in an attempt to leave. This increased the difficulties in moving the victims from the triage site to the hospitals and transporting replacement medical personal into the triage areas. The Office of Emergency Management was activated to deal with some of the transportation issues. They were able to secure air transportation for the serious victims and bus transportation for the less serious victims and medical staff. The police were assigned the task of crowd control. They were also empowered to clear the roads to and from area health facilities.

Communication among the emergency personnel, government officials, and the public was the greatest problem. The government officials, not wanting to cause mass hysteria, withheld vital information on the treatment of the victims. By doing this, they not only delayed the administration of the proper reagent, but also caused secondary exposure to some of the first responders. Transportation agencies, not wanting to be closed for an extended period of time, were slow in divulging the extent of the damage caused by the attack. Lastly, the sheer volume of the disaster pressed the communications system to its limits.

The number of people affected in the attack exceeded the bed capacity for the city's hospitals, requiring transportation to outlying facilities. Budgetary constraints imposed by the elected officials earlier in the quarter caused a reduction in the medical staff used to tend to the needy. The staff reductions, in turn, increased the time it took for the victims to be seen. This in turn caused the milder cases to progress into more severe cases, which in turn increased the price of treatment.

The lack of knowledge as to the causative agent used in the attack increased the number of secondary exposure illnesses. A failure to communicate to the first responders the nature of the substance they were encountering at the attack site caused them to be ill prepared. Of the emergency personnel who responded in the first wave, 50% became ill with sarin poisoning symptoms. The lack of decontamination facilities caused the spread of sarin poison from the attack site to the medical facilities. Members of the medical team that had had no contact with the attack site, other than treating the victims, were reporting mild symptoms.

To stem the cost of providing services, the mayor of the city requested the governor to declare a state of disaster. Once this was done, the Federal Emergency Management Agency became involved. This allowed the city to receive funding to pay for medical services, transportation services, improvement of communications, and cleanup activities. It also expanded the range of professionals available to provide assistance in dealing with the problems associated with the attack.

Because this was an act of terrorism, the FBI became involved. Their investigation slowed the return to normal by keeping the subway system closed. Their actions caused increased congestion and gridlock conditions as people looked for other means of transportation.

Post-traumatic stress symptoms were evident in many of the victims in the weeks following the attack. Cases that were followed cited a fear of the underground transit system. In addition to the nightmares, they reported fears of being trapped underground. Revenues from the subway operations also fell off dramatically following the attack.

Closing

Although this is a fictional account, the majority of the events could be realized in an actual community. The community had a disaster plan, but it was not detailed enough to account for a disaster of this magnitude, a bioterrorist attack with chemicals, or potential problems at any point in the sequence of events. This disaster demonstrated the need for increased training at the worst-case scenario level. Any disaster planning must include all potential agencies involved, including the media. A strong communication system is vital to keep everyone informed at the appropriate level, to prevent panic, and to increase cooperation. Strong disaster plans are a vital component of a sound public health infrastructure.

References

Agency for Toxic Substances and Disease Registry. (2002). *Managing Hazardous Material Incidents.* http://www.atsdr.cdc.gov/mhmi/index.asp. Accessed April 4, 2002.

Centers for Disease Control and Prevention. (2002). *Public Health Preparedness and Response.* Atlanta: CDC. Retrieved April 4, 2002, from http://www.bt.cdc.gov/. Includes information on many biological and chemical agents.

Centers for Disease Control and Prevention. (2002). *The Public Health Response to Biological and Chemical Terrorism: Interim Planning Guidance for State Public Health Officials.* Atlanta: CDC.

Federal Emergency Management Agency. (2002). *Preparedness.* Washington, DC: FEMA, 2002. Retrieved April 4, 2002, from http://www.fema.gov/pte/gaheop.htm. Information for planning a response.

Institute of Medicine, Committee on the Future of Public Health. (1988). *The Future of Public Health.* Washington, DC: National Academies Press.

Novick, L. F., and Marr, J. S. (Eds.). (2001). *Public Health Issues in Disaster Preparedness: Focus on Bioterrorism.* Gaithersburg, MD: Aspen.

Ohbu, I., Yamashine, A., Takasu, N., Yamaguchi, T., Nakano, K., Matsui, Y., et al. (1997). *Sarin Poisoning on Tokyo Subway* [electronic version]. In *Southern Medical Journal.* Retrieved from http://www.sma.org/smj/97june3.htm.

Tucker, J. (1997). National Health and Medical Services Responses to Incidents of Chemical and Biological Terrorism. *Journal of the American Medical Association*, 278, 362–368.

(Continues)

U.S. Department of Defense. (1997). *Fact Sheet on Exposure Limits of Sarin (GB)*. Washington, DC: U.S. Department of Defense.

Websites

Environmental Protection Agency, http://www.epa.gov/. Lists the chemical emergency preparedness sites.

U.S. Department of Health and Human Services, http://www.bt.cdc.gov/documents/planning/planningguidance.pdf.

PATTERNS OF SOCIAL CAPITAL

The prepared public health leader is one who is able to integrate conceptual as well as research findings into a practical application. Some of the lessons that we can learn from the social capital thinkers include the following:

1. Social capital involves the development of social networks, reciprocities that grow out of these networks, and the values that accrue from the achievement of mutual goals.[10]
2. Communities work more effectively when residents trust their neighbors and their leaders, when residents become involved in community work and strive for common community goals, and when people share a civic culture oriented toward cooperation and service.[11]
3. Societies and communities that have a high level of social involvement that translates into social capital can function at higher levels than societies and communities where residents are not socially involved.[12]
4. To build social capital, it is necessary to see and meet the individuals with whom you will work in many different settings and groups. Trust builds up from this "redundancy of contact."[13]
5. People who live in communities with high social capital tend to be healthier than people who live in communities with less social capital.[14]
6. Social capital increases when it is used. The more social capital is used, the more it gets produced.[15]
7. After September 11, 2001, people showed an increasing interest in public affairs. Trust in the government grew. Television viewing also increased. Still, evidence is that more involvement in organizations did not significantly increase.[16]

It should be clear that communities work best when they use their resources effectively and efficiently and when social capital gets built. When one individual does work or engages in any solo activity, the primary beneficiary is that individual. There may be indirect effects on the physical and human capital of the community. If we want to see an effect on social capital, then two or more people have to be involved. When a young man and a young woman meet, they test each other and try to discover each other's traits. This dating process may or may not lead to a more permanent relationship. If it does, it may lead to marriage, which is a form of social capital building in which the two people decide to create a mutual household where resources will be shared. A marriage creates synergy in which the relationship generally becomes enriched and enhanced as the social ties increase. Social capital increases and will continue to do so if the couple has children. As this family unit reaches out to other family members, friends, and neighbors, social capital begins to expand and increase. As paths cross and interconnect with other neighborhood and community groups, more social capital is generated. Thus, social capital can be an ongoing process, although it may not always be a smooth one.

As in the above example, the public health leader needs to develop social ties throughout the community. These ties and relationships will be with individuals and organizations. The new public health environment requires that relationships develop not only with traditional health professionals and health organizations, but also with nontraditional partners such as businesses and the chamber of commerce, local FBI agents, police and fire department professionals, local emergency preparedness officials and agencies, elected officials, the media, and grassroots organizations. The more partners we have, the more complex the relationships and the greater the potential for building social capital. The public health leader should be spending much of his or her time in community-based activities and should delegate more managerial responsibility in the local public health agency to others.

Building social capital can occur at all levels of the community:

- The personal level, such as families
- Grassroots organizations promoting community interests and values

- Transorganizational networks made up of public health as well as other health and social service agencies
- Emergency preparedness and response collaborations
- Community-wide networks

It is through social capital that we build the infrastructure of our communities generally and the public health infrastructure specifically.

An interesting variation on this was discussed by Marcus.[17] He pointed out that the challenge for public health leaders in this new age of preparedness is as much about developing relationships prior to a terrorist event as it is about working with new organizational partners after a terrorist event. He has called these new working relationships "connectivity." Connectivity involves interdependent agencies and organizations and their leaders working to explicitly map out and coordinate linkages during the preparedness phase of planning to ensure that they can work together during and after a crisis. This connectivity model is a practice approach to building social capital that builds on the need to develop relationships that will work during a terrorist event. It is necessary to break down silos if collaboration is to work. To train leaders to connect better, Marcus developed a program called Walk in the Woods that uses negotiation strategies to resolve conflict, shape solutions, and build constructive relationships.

SOCIAL CAPITAL AND HEALTH PROJECTS

Four interesting projects were funded through the Special Interest Projects of the Prevention Research Centers funded by the Centers for Disease Control and Prevention. The four projects were undertaken in 2001 and 2002 to determine the indicators of social capital for different racial and ethnic communities. Researchers from the Prevention Research Center at Tulane University took the lead in coordinating a multisite project to identify these indicators of social capital and capacity-building processes. The investigators at each of the four sites tested the indicators with different population groups. The four teams have developed a large-scale survey that community agencies and state health departments can use to measure community capacity and social capital that will help in health promotion and health improvement programs for community residents.

Illinois researchers were studying urban ethnic groups. They specifically tried to identify the char-

acteristics of community-based health promotion campaigns that defined the processes among community residents and organizations in four Chicago neighborhoods that may have enhanced the ability of the community to reach its health goals. The assessment of social capital in this study was limited to community grassroots organizations in these four neighborhoods. One interesting neighborhood project involved the development of community trust and social participation in community programs in Puerto Rican communities affected by HIV/AIDS.[18] A collaboration developed between the University of Illinois at Chicago Prevention Research Center, the Puerto Rican Cultural Center, and its Vida/SIDA (AIDS and Life) program. The mission of the Vida/SIDA program was to decrease the incidence of HIV infection in the Puerto Rican community and also to enhance the quality of life of those who are already diagnosed with the disease. Community programs of all kinds work to bring the community together. Another goal of the program was to promote the arts, history, and culture of the Puerto Rican community. The researchers tested whether an understanding of local social capital concepts of trust, social ties and connections, and the role of community-based organizations can affect the health status of community residents.

Tulane University, in partnership with Xavier University, studied inner-city African American communities. St. Louis University researchers are working with rural African American communities. The final project involved the study of social capital in Native American tribal communities in the southwest United States. Communities that promote strong involvement of their members as a community help to build the social capital of that community.

COLLABORATION IN ACTION

The public health leader knows that the secret to effective public health is involving community partners in carrying out the mission of public health to promote health, prevent disease, and build social capital. No leader can perform public health activities alone. In reviewing the Institute of Medicine reports on the future of public health, the new public health needs to be seen in a new context.[19] Throughout the 20th century, public health was seen primarily as a responsibility of government. Over the past several years, there has been a shift from an organizational to a community focus for public health. There has been increasing engagement of nongovernmental partners in the public health agenda for the 21st century. Utilizing the IOM reports, it seems evident that the protection of the public's health cannot be ensured by one governmental agency, but rather needs to involve many important community entities such as healthcare institutions, community organizations and grassroots leaders, businesses, the media, and academic partners.[20] To ensure that these critical partnerships are developed, the federal government needs to take a leadership role and ensure that all residents of the United States receive the healthcare coverage they require. Both the federal and state levels of government support community-led public health efforts that help strengthen the collaborations that have been mentioned and build social capital. Finally, it is necessary to build incentives into the system for the various partners, such as changes in the tax code to encourage the private sector to stay involved in the community-wide health promotion efforts. It was also recommended that the time devoted to public service announcements be increased to better inform the public of good and healthy behaviors. Finally, academic institutions need to be involved in these activities by providing real-life experiences for students as well as public health practice research activities.

Sometimes it is money that triggers collaboration. It is clear that there need to be some incentives for individuals or organizations to collaborate with other individuals or organizations. Bioterrorism and other terrorist activities were issues of concern to public health and governmental agencies prior to September 11, 2001. Public health leaders have known that preparedness is critical to carrying out the agenda of public health as well as the unintended health threats that occur and need to be addressed quickly by public health agencies and their various community partners. Public health leaders have known for many years that the level of preparedness in their communities was affected by many factors, including shrinking public budgets, health access issues, concerns about prescription drug costs for seniors, limited interest in public health issues by the public, and competition for resources by other community agencies. In 1999, the Local Public Health Centers for Public Health Preparedness Project was initiated to link state and local public health agencies, schools of public health, and other community health partners to improve public health preparedness through training the public health workforce to improve competence and increase collaborations with other community partners.

To initiate the project, the Centers for Disease Control and Prevention selected three public health agencies to serve as Local Centers for Public Health Preparedness: DeKalb County (Georgia) Board of Health, Denver Health (Denver County, Colorado), and Monroe County (New York) Health Department. Between 1999 and 2001, the following lessons were learned by these projects.[21]

1. Improvements in the infrastructure for public health bioterrorism preparedness and response capacity of the local Centers not only improved preparedness capacity but also improved routine public health functions and services.
2. The critical determination related to the implementation of new technologies tended to be administrative concerns as well as cultural acceptance concerns with less emphasis on the availability of these new technologies.
3. When new communication and information systems are introduced, it is important to determine how these new systems will be sustained over time.
4. The key to success for these preparedness programs is related to the development and maintenance of community partnerships.
5. Education of first responders and the medical community on the important role of public health is critical.
6. Money builds infrastructure, and these local Centers found that their local agencies administratively improved as preparedness programs were implemented.
7. Drills and tabletop exercises aid significantly in the development of bioterrorism plans. These exercises and drills also help measure local preparedness capacity.

The partnership activities of these local Centers to build social capital have been critical to their success. They have expanded their relationships with agencies at the local, state, and federal levels. Specifically, the three model sites developed strong partnerships with the Federal Emergency Management Agency, the Environmental Protection Agency, the Federal Bureau of Investigation, and the Department of Justice. At the state level, they have developed partnerships with their state health departments and/or state offices of emergency management. At the local level, they developed partnerships with hospitals, neighboring local health departments, municipal and county emergency medical services, police and fire departments, and other county and local agencies. These local Centers recognized the importance of having prepared public health leaders as well as the critical need for partnership in emergency preparedness and response.

In a 2002 report of the National Association of County and City Health Officials (NACCHO), a number of local resource tools were reviewed from the local Centers projects that were believed to be of use to other local public health agencies and partners who also are involved in improving their local emergency preparedness and response capacity.[22] These projects clearly serve as best practice examples for public health preparedness. In December 2003, five sites were named by NACCHO and the CDC as Advanced Practice Centers. These sites, which include the original DeKalb, Georgia, site, were funded by the CDC to serve as learning laboratories to design and test creative and innovative ways to improve the emergency preparedness and response capacity of the United States. These five sites were given resources to develop their public health emergency preparedness infrastructure and to provide technical assistance to other local health departments to develop and test innovative resources and technologies. These five sites include Georgia East Central Health District, Santa Clara County (California) Public Health Department, Seattle and King County (Washington) Department of Public Health, Tarrant County (Texas) Public Health Department, and DeKalb County. They serve as formal demonstration and training sites for other local health departments and the CDC. The specific areas of focus for these five programs are:

1. Partnerships and collaboration with first responders
2. Preparedness planning and readiness assessment
3. Workforce development and training
4. Risk communication and public education
5. Integrated communications and information systems

These tools have continued to be developed by the present twelve centers. **Table 16-1** provides a summary list of tools and products for all the Centers as of August 2012. Partnership will be a critical element in all these projects. Leaders will need to be better prepared in the future if all the new critical concerns of public health are to be addressed.

TABLE 16-1 National Association of County and City Health Officials Advanced Practice Centers Summary List of Tools and Products (as of August 2012)

Cambridge, MA Advanced Practice Center	Epi Essentials for Public Health Practitioners
	Incident Management Team Training
	Mass Care Communication Tools
	Pictographic Product Recalls
	Point of Distribution Staff Training Series
	Public Health Mutual Aid Agreements
	Signs for Mass Decontamination
DeKalb County, GA Advanced Practice Center	Conducting a BT Tabletop: A How-To Guide
	Emergency Preparedness Policies & Procedures Guide: A Resource Tool for Local Health Departments
	Local Heroes
Mesa County, CO Advanced Practice Center	Blueprint for the Use of Volunteers in Hospitals and Rural Medical Centers
	Decision Making in the Field During Disasters
	Emergency Handbook for Food Managers
	Emergency Readiness for Food Workers — Trainer Guide
	Environmental Health Emergency Response Guide

(*Continues*)

TABLE 16-1 National Association of County and City Health Officials Advanced Practice Centers Summary List of Tools and Products (as of August 2012) (*Continued*)

Montgomery County, MD Advanced Practice Center	Alternative Care Site Computer Model (Beta Version)
	America for Emergencies
	Bio-Pack Toolkit
	Building a Continuity of Operations Plan: Identifying & Prioritizing Critical Health Services
	Clinic Planning Model Generator Continuity of Operations Plan (COOP) Training for Child Care Providers
	eMedCheck for Blackberry/iPhone/iPad/Palm PDA
	Emergency Preparedness Checklist for Case Management and Home Care Services
	Emergency Preparedness Checklist for Nursing Homes, Assisted Living Facilities, and Group Homes
	Emergency Preparedness Training Curriculum for Latino Health Promoters
	Emergency Response Planning for Child Care Providers
	Flu Prevention and Care Guide
	How to Create a Partnership Between Your Public Health Agency and Area Hospitals
	How to Create a Partnership Between Your Public Health Agency and the Child Care Community
	Monitoring Community Health Status for Emergency Preparedness
	Notes from the Field: A Collection of Emergency Preparedness Exercise and Evaluation Reviews
	Online Training – Module I: Introduction to Computer Planning Models
	Pan Flu & Us: A Toolkit for Developing a Pandemic Flu Preparedness Workshop
	PDA Model – eMedCheck
	Personal Protective Equipment Toolkit
	Plan to Be Safe Campaign Toolkit
	Plan to Be Safe – Training Modules for Emergency Operations of Dispensing & Vaccination Clinics
	Preparation for Pandemic Flu: A Health Promoter Training Module (PDF)
	Preparing for Outbreak Investigations: How to Plan Your Operation and Prepare Your Staff
	A Prescription for Preparedness: An Online Community for Local Health Departments and Pharmacists to Help Ready
	Special Needs Shelter Just in Time Training for NonMedical Personnel
	Stop the Spread! A Toolkit for Preventing the Spread of Germs in Clinics and Office Settings
	Strengthening the Strengtheners
Multnomah County, OR Advanced Practice Center	Emergency Dispensing Site Signage & Materials
	Enhancing Training During Public Health Emergencies: An Inclusive Just-in-Time Training (JITT) Approach
	Inclusive Just-in-Time Training for Mass Prophylaxis/POD Operations
	Inclusive Just-in-Time Training for Public Health Investigations (PHI)
	Orientation to Inclusive Just-in-Time Training (I-JITT): An online course
	Staff Allocation Decision Guide

San Francisco Bay Area, CA **Advanced Practice Center**	CERT Pandemic H1N1 Influenza Train-the-Trainer Toolkit Closed POD Partnerships Infectious Disease Emergency Response (IDER) Toolkit Seasonal and Pandemic Influenza Vaccination Assessment Toolkit
Santa Clara County, CA **Advanced Practice Center**	Emergency Dark Site: A toolkit on how to build, use, and maintain a dark site for public health emergencies Hospital Surge Capacity Toolkit Local Health Department Guide to Pandemic Influenza Planning Managing Mass Fatalities: A Toolkit for Planning Medical Mass Care During an Influenza Pandemic: Guide & Toolkit for Establishing Care Centers Pandemic Influenza School Planning Toolkit Preparing for Pandemic Flu Pocket Guide Risk Communication and Public Education Tool Kit
Seattle & King County, WA **Advanced Practice Center**	Building Preparedness: Proven Tools for Your Health Department Creating and Operating a Family Assistance Center: A Toolkit for Public Health Developing Effective and Sustainable Medication Dispensing Strategies Emergency Risk Communication for Public Health Professionals Get Ready for Call Center Surge: A Toolkit for Local Health Departments Isolation and Quarantine Toolkit Managing Surge Response and Workforce Activation Meeting the Needs of Vulnerable Populations: Equity in Emergency Preparedness No Ordinary Flu Risk Communication and Public Education Tool Kit Speak First: Communicating Effectively in Times of Crisis and Uncertainty Strengthening Emergency Response through a Healthcare Coalition Toolkit Survivor Tales: In Deep Water, Aftershocks, Eye of Houston Sustaining Critical Services: Continuity of Operations A Toolkit for Public Health
South Carolina Region 7 **Advanced Practice Center**	On the Safe Side: A Security Planning Toolkit for Public Health Emergencies
Tarrant County, TX **Advanced Practice Center**	Building a Public Health Community of Practice – A Biosurveillance Resource Compendium Core Training for Medical Reserve Corps Volunteers Designing, Implementing, and Evaluating a Public Health Exercise – A Dirty Bomb Disaster Mass Triage Interactive Training – A Short Course Master the Disaster!/LIVE Pandemic Readiness and Response Toolkit Planning and Implementing a Public Health Exercise for Radiological Events: An Exercise Guide PPE, Decontamination, and Mass Triage – A Short Course

(Continues)

TABLE 16-1 National Association of County and City Health Officials Advanced Practice Centers Summary List of Tools and Products (as of August 2012) (*Continued*)

	Preparar Su Negocio Para Emergencias Naturales y Causadas por el Hombre
	Preparing Your Business for Emergencies, Natural and Man-Made Disasters
	PsychoSocial/Behavioral Response to Radiological and Nuclear Disasters
	Public Health 101: An Introduction for Stakeholders
	Responding to Chemical and Radiological Disasters – A Self-Paced Training Course
	Syndromic Surveillance for Epidemiological Investigation
	Using ESSENCE IV – A Self-Paced Training Course
Toledo-Lucas County, OH Advanced Practice Center	Emergency Preparedness and Response Fundamentals: Training for Environmental Health Professionals
Twin Cities Metro, MN Advanced Practice Center	Disaster Strikes – EH Responds: Stories from the Field
	Emergency Preparedness Response and Recovery Resources
	Environmental Health Resource Compendium for Emergency Response
	Equipment and Supplies List for Food Service
	Food Protection Self-Audit Picture Guide and Poster Set
	Food Safety & Security Self Audit Checklist
	Food Safety Self-Inspection Checklist
	In an Emergency: Food Service Fact Sheets
	Trainer Guide: Emergency Preparedness and Response for Environmental Health Professionals

Source: Reprinted with permission NACCHO, *Local Center for Public Health Preparedness*, Washington, DC: 2012

COLLABORATION IN REALITY

Before starting a discussion of collaboration and its benefits, it is important to present a few cautionary comments. First, it is critical to decide whether collaboration is the best direction to follow. There are situations in which an individual or an organization can accomplish more by going it alone. Second, collaboration should be used only in those situations in which working together has a synergistic effect. The issues of power, power relationships, and shared leadership often complicate any collaborative endeavor. Third, collaboration is often about the relationships between organizations, and the people relationships need to be kept in perspective. Fourth, collaboration may occur within organizations and not between organizations, and vice versa. Fifth, collaboration is more about the commitment of the members of the collaboration and less about the structure of the collaboration.

With these cautions in mind, collaboration can be defined as a mutually beneficial set of relationships that are well defined and that are entered into by two or more organizations in order to achieve some common goals.[23] The individuals who represent these collaborating organizations tend to be called members or partners. An important reason to collaborate is to achieve results that are more likely to happen when people work together than in situations where people or a specific organization would work alone.[24] Working together also creates further collaboration opportunities and builds social capital. In most circumstances, collaboration becomes a continuing set of circumstances that provides a wide range of outcomes that empower people, organizations, and systems to change. Keeping collaborations active is not an easy task. Many collaborations have to struggle with such issues as unproductive meetings, shifting members from organizations, making the same decisions over and over again, lack of accountability, difficulty of maintaining a collaboration when funding ends, and difficulty of getting agencies to implement best practices throughout the system.[25]

Ray developed a model called the nimble collaboration to orient collaborative activity toward results by emphasizing the premise of the collaboration, its promise, mission, vision, outcomes, evaluation criteria, and work plan. Another interesting approach has been called collaboration math, which creates a structure for the collaboration based on the participants in the collaboration.[26] Collaboration math requires a common set of definitions and categories that each partner to the collaboration fills out. A matrix is created based on the definition of the problem, key issues, available or needed data, funding issues, training needs, outside partners, and the results anticipated.

There are many reasons to collaborate.[27] Some of these reasons include a shared concern for an issue or community challenge and a strong belief that working together can address the challenge most effectively. A second reason is to pool power so the combined effect of several groups or agencies working together can have a substantial effect on the outcome. Third, when gridlock exists, working together will help the community or a specific agency get unstuck. Fourth, bringing several groups or agencies to work together increases the chances for diversity issues to be addressed. Several

agencies working together can also increase the ability of the various members to handle complex community issues. Exercise 16-2, which was developed by the Turning Point Leadership Collaborative, is an excellent way to explore the issue of collaboration.

Collaboration needs to be seen in relation to three other strategies for working together.[28] These three other strategies are networking, coordination, and cooperation. Time and circumstances will affect which of these strategies will be used. **Table 16-2** shows the Himmelman matrix of strategies. Collaboration was defined as the exchange of information, or altering the way activities get done, a possible sharing of resources, and enhancing the capacity of the various partners to achieve the goals defined by working together. This latter point of mutual benefit is critical to any collaboration. Networking is the most informal of the four strategies and relates primarily to the sharing of information. Many coalitions have this networking strategy as a primary goal for getting together. The coordination strategy incorporates the major goal of networking with the additional goal of altering activities. It is hoped that this strategy will reduce barriers for those seeking to access specific services. The last strategy

TABLE 16-2   Matrix of Strategies for Working Together

Definition	Networking	Coordinating	Cooperating	Collaborating
	Exchanging information for mutual benefit	Exchanging information for mutual benefit, and altering activities to achieve a common purpose	Exchanging information for mutual benefit, and altering activities to achieve a common purpose	Exchanging information for mutual benefit, altering activities, and sharing resources to achieve a common purpose
Relationship	Informal	Formal	Formal	Formal
Characteristics	Minimal time commitments, limited levels of trust, and no necessity to share turf; information exchange is the primary focus	Moderate time commitments, moderate levels of trust, and no necessity to share turf; making access to services or resources more user-friendly is the primary focus	Substantial time commitments, high levels of trust, and significant access to each other's turf; sharing of resources to achieve a common purpose is the primary focus	Extensive time commitments, very high levels of trust, and extensive areas of common turf; enhancing each other's capacity to achieve a common purpose is the primary focus
Resources	No mutual sharing of resources necessary	No or minimal mutual sharing of resources necessary	Moderate to extensive mutual sharing of resources and some sharing of risks, responsibilities, and rewards	Full sharing of resources, and full sharing of risks, responsibilities, and rewards

Source: Reprinted with permission of Arthur H. Himmelman, Collaboration for a Change, Minneapolis, MN: Himmelman Consulting.

relates to cooperation that incorporates the strategies of networking and coordination and adds the sharing of resources for mutual benefit. The major difference in cooperation and collaboration is the willingness of organizations to enhance the capacity of the various partners for the mutual benefit of all partners and to increase the chances of meeting the goals and purposes of the relationship.

The Center for Civic Partnerships has also looked at the issue of collaboration.[29] A distinction was made between collaborative actions covering such dimensions as connectivity, continuous assessment and planning, communication, capacity building, coordination of services, and collaborative initiatives and the collaborative attitudes encompassing the six Cs:

- Commitment
- Consensus building
- Community outreach and involvement
- Conflict resolution
- Cooperation
- Change

Table 16-3 presents the details of these 12 activities. They are especially interesting when compared with the four strategies of Himmelman that are incorporated into these 12 actions and attitudes.

TABLE 16-3   Collaborative Functions: The 12 Cs of a Collaborative

Collaborative Actions:

Connection—Serving as the convener of its members to promote information sharing and networking.

Continuous Assessment and Planning—Coordinating needs and resource assessments to provide current information on service delivery gaps, existing needs, and available community resources. Another collaborative function may be to convene and facilitate ongoing strategic planning activities.

Communication—Acting as a clearinghouse for information exchange and dissemination for its members and with the media.

Capacity Building—Building the knowledge and skills of individuals and organizations through training, providing information, etc.

Coordination of Services—Coordinating services in the community to improve service delivery and availability, reduce duplication, and address service gaps.

Collaboration—Participating in joint grant proposals and collaborative projects, pooled funding, shared resources and staff, and colocated services. Organizations and community members share risks, responsibilities, and rewards by working as partners. This requires a high level of trust and commitment to the collaborative process by decision makers and collaborative members.

Important Collaborative Attitudes:

Commitment—Collaboration requires an ongoing commitment from all members.

Consensus Building—Members agree on a shared vision and participate in the development, implementation, and achievement of the collaborative's goals.

Community Outreach and Involvement—A successful collaborative stays in frequent contact with the community it serves and involves community members in planning, decision making, and other collaborative activities.

Conflict Resolution—Conflict is a natural occurrence in the collaborative process. Issues should be resolved immediately through a conflict resolution process developed and approved by collaborative members.

Cooperation—Collaborative activities promote a more cooperative approach in decision making and service delivery and enhance relationships between individual agencies and community. Information and expertise are shared, but agency resources and authority are usually separately maintained and risks are minimal.

Change—Change is both a prerequisite and a result of successful collaboration! True collaboration requires organizations and the community to think differently about how they do business and usually requires change in their current systems to achieve collaborative goals.

Source: Center for Civic Partnerships, Collaborative Functions: The 12 C's of a Collaborative. (Sacramento, CA: Center for Civic Leadership, 2002).

It is important to evaluate whether a group of individuals or organizations in a community is ready to work together. To this community readiness issue must be added the concern or evaluation of the community's capacity to change. Thurman has utilized community readiness theory to explore how communities can implement successful prevention programs using a step-by-step process.[30] Communities can be defined in terms of nine stages of readiness (see **Table 16-4**). Once a collaborative group can define the stage in which a community can be located in the model, they can then develop the strategies to address ways to move a community to a higher level of readiness. Community readiness is only part of the evaluation that is necessary. It is important to determine individual, team, and organizational readiness levels as well.[31]

There is the additional issue of a collaborative or a community's capacity to work together to build social capital and to create change.[32] First, it is necessary to clearly define the issues or the problems to be addressed. Second, the issue of leadership and who will lead the change effort is critical. It is here that power sharing and turf issues become prominent. The identification of appropriate stakeholders and partners with whom to address the issues is important. It is necessary to make sure that all key organizations and community leaders are represented in the collaborative activity. The assessment of agreement between the stakeholders must also be evaluated. All possible solutions also need to be explored. Both the issue of the community's readiness to change and the capacity of the community to change are important. In the arena of emergency preparedness and response, it is important to recognize that change will occur whether a community or collaborative feels it is ready for the change or not. If community readiness issues and community capacity for change can be addressed as part of the planning and preparedness activities of the community, some of the response events will be easier to predict.

Not all leadership is collaborative. Although all leaders need followers, all leaders do not feel that they need to share power or their decision-making authority. Collaborative leadership involves a leader who believes in engaging other leaders in working together for the common good.[33] Collaborative leaders work together, convene appropriate stakeholders in the cause for which the group is brought together, and facilitate and find methods for sustaining their activities and interactions. Collaborative leaders also facilitate mutual enhancement of each other's activities.[34] Collaborative leaders have strong values and are clear in stating them. Collaborative leaders also see commonalities and try to find common interests that bind them to their partners.[35] These leaders are also expert in creating and refining their visions and in mobilizing others to work with them. They are also excellent mentors who work toward the development of others.

Himmelman has summarized some of the major characteristics of collaborative leaders.[36] These characteristics can be found in **Table 16-5**. These 10 characteristics can also be seen as a framework for a set of competencies for collaborative leaders. All sorts of skills are involved, such as the use of values to drive action, persuasion, mentoring and training, risk taking, information sharing through telling stories and

TABLE 16-4 The Community Readiness Model Identifies Nine Stages of Readiness

No knowledge (formerly community tolerance) stage suggests that the behavior is normative and accepted.

Denial stage involves the belief that the problem does not exist or that change is impossible.

Vague awareness stage involves recognition of the problem, but no motivation for action.

Preplanning stage indicates recognition of a problem and agreement that something needs to be done.

Preparation stage involves active planning.

Initiation stage involves implementation of a program.

Stabilization (formerly institutionalization) stage indicates that one or two programs are operating and are stable.

Confirmation/expansion stage involves recognition of limitations and attempts to improve existing programs.

Professionalization stage is marked by sophistication, training, and effective evaluation.

Source: Reprinted with permission of P. Thurman (2001), *Community Readiness: A Promising Model for Community Healing*, Center on Child Abuse and Neglect, Oklahoma City: University of Oklahoma Health Sciences Center, 2001.

TABLE 16-5   Some Collaborative Leadership Characteristics

1. A commitment to improve common circumstances based on values, beliefs, and a vision for change that is communicated both by "talking it and walking it"

2. An ability to persuade people to conduct themselves within ground rules that provide the basis for mutual trust, respect, and accountability

3. An ability to respectfully educate others about the relationship of processes to products and outcomes about the relationship of organizational structure to effective action

4. An ability to draw out ideas and information in ways that contribute to effective problem solving rather than ineffective restatements of problems

5. A willingness to actively encourage partners to share risks, responsibilities, resources, and rewards and to offer acknowledgments of those making contributions

6. An ability to balance the need for discussion, information sharing, and storytelling with timely problem solving and keeping focused on responding to action-oriented expectations of those engaged in common efforts

7. An understanding of the role of community organizing as the basis for developing and expanding collaborative power

8. A commitment to and active engagement in leadership development activities, both informal and formal, that can take the collaborative process to higher levels of inclusiveness and effectiveness

9. An ability to communicate in ways that invite comments and suggestions that address problems without attacking people and, when appropriate, draws upon conflict resolution and win-win negotiating to resolve differences

10. A very good sense of humor, especially whenever collaborative processes get ugly or boring or both

Source: Reprinted with permission of Arthur H. Himmelman, Collaboration for a Change, Minneapolis, MN: Himmelman Consulting.

other techniques, community-organizing skills, training other leaders, communication skills, and an ability to use humor in stressful situations. All of these competencies and characteristics are useful for all leaders. All collaboration is used for community betterment and also for the empowerment of others. Collaboration strategies are used to produce policy change and to make improvements in the local delivery of programs and services.

Ayre and a panel of public health department leaders in 2002, as part of the Turning Point Leadership Development National Excellence Collaborative, discussed the topic of building understanding and information sharing. The panel believed these skills would help address the challenges to building collaborative leadership in public health. Several key themes emerged:[37]

1. Collaboration and its leadership aspects can be seen best at a local level where there seems to be greater accountability.
2. Collaboration is vital to the work of public health, which is a population-based activity.
3. Individuals define collaboration differently. Federal, state, and foundations funders also may

define it differently from local leaders who practice collaboration on a daily basis.

4. Because different leadership styles are required for different situations, collaboration may not be the best approach in every circumstance.
5. If collaborations are beneficial, it becomes critical to nurture them over time by supporting the various members when they need it.
6. Collaboration can be unpredictable in that different members may have different agendas that take precedence to the collaborative activity, or unexpected happenings may occur.
7. It is important to deal with collaboration skeptics.
8. Collaboration skill development needs to be included as a key competency for leadership development programs.

LEADERSHIP IN CRISIS

Most discussions of collaboration are presented as a continuous process that begins small and expands over time. These discussions have not been oriented toward crisis events such as those that occurred in the United

States on September 11, 2001. Collaborations in public health occurred between public health agencies and leaders and community partners who also had strong health and healthcare agendas. Terrorist and bioterrorist events occurred, and public health leaders now find they have new partners in Federal Bureau of Investigation officials, federal and state emergency preparedness personnel, police, fire professionals, bomb experts, elected officials, and many others. It is almost like the biblical story of the Tower of Babel, in which everyone speaks a different language and there is chaos. New types of collaboration are necessary for preparedness planning and for individuals to become prepared public health leaders. The purpose of collaboration in the emergency preparedness phase of activity often relates to presenting a rationale for why public health should be at the table if a crisis occurs. Whereas the personal relationships appear to be as important as the institutional ones when collaboration occurs in fairly normal times, the institutional relationships are a critical component of emergency preparedness.

When a crisis or other emergency occurs, collaboration ends. As **Figure 16-1** shows, the issue during the crisis relates to who is in charge. In a bioterrorism or disaster event, the incident command system or the unified command system is a management system in which all roles and responsibilities have been defined prior to the event. The leadership style required is a command-and-control one. The crisis must be handled and contained. Relationships between individuals change, and it is critical that each individual in the chain of command follows orders and protocols. Once the response is made and the crisis is over, then the

various partners to the original collaborative come back together, review the events, and refine the system for the next possible crisis. Thus, there has been a change in our views of collaboration in crisis from a continuous process of growth and decline in normal times to a form of collaboration that is broken during a crisis event and reestablishes itself after the event. Prepared public health leaders need to be flexible and adaptable to changes in circumstances. It is possible that leaders during a crisis will not be the same individuals who are leaders in normal times. It is possible that vertical collaboration will occur if a governmental official from higher up in the food chain sees a need for some change in the response plan like an increase in the surge capacity of the response that leadership can modify the management protocols that are in place.

It is clear that the models of collaboration during crisis are changing.[38] The issues are less about conflicting agendas than they are about sharing work to address a problem of concern to the whole community. Of course, we are well aware that there are many global connections, but the connections at the local level are also extensive. There should be respect for diverse views without letting these views prevent necessary action from taking place. Leadership may need to be shared for success. Relationships are important, and relational dialogue skills will be required. The way that relational dialogue works is for those people who share the work to create new leadership approaches based on new methods for constructing the direction of the work, the commitments that are needed, and adaptive approaches to the challenges that the crisis or emergency presents.[39]

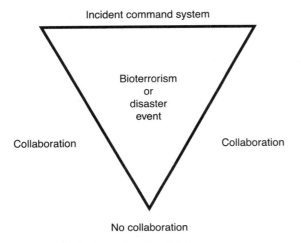

FIGURE 16-1 Collaboration in Crisis.

SUMMARY

It has been the purpose of this chapter to present a perspective that can be used in emergency preparedness and response initiatives. To understand the context in which first responders will act, it is necessary to know the human, physical, and social capital resources of the community. To successfully respond to a crisis of whatever type, the public health leader must know how his or her community functions. The leader must know how to work in an ecological context because different communities respond differently to crisis. The social capital model is a useful one for this exercise. The concept of collaboration as a mechanism for building social capital was then explored.

DISCUSSION QUESTIONS

1. What are the differences between physical capital, human capital, and social capital?
2. What is the relationship between bonding and building social capital?

3. Discuss collaboration as a mechanism for building social capital.
4. Present three scenarios where the Incident Command System response to a local disaster can be modified by a federal government official.

EXERCISE 16-1:   The Flag

Purpose: to understand how working in teams or other collaborative groups begins to build social capital

Key concepts: social capital, team building, collaboration, and coalition

Procedures: Divide the class or training group into groups of eight people. Give each group construction paper of one color (purple, orange, or green). Have each group discuss (for 10 minutes) how to build a flag with their one color. Discuss the difficulties of doing this with the group as a whole.

Put together three groups: a purple group, an orange group, and a green group. There may be several of each group in the larger group.

1. Have each new combined team name their country or community.
2. Each team then determines five major values that will serve as the foundation for their country or community.
3. The teams design and build a flag with construction paper and tape that includes the major color and two other colors from a package of different colors.
4. Each team should discuss how the new combined coalition built the flag and how it demonstrates social capital formation.
5. Discuss the process and social capital concepts in the group as a whole.

EXERCISE 16-2:   Reasons for Collaboration

Purpose: to learn the benefits of collaborative leadership techniques

Key concepts: collaborative leadership, cultural diversity

Procedures: Roseland: Reasons for Collaboration

Roseland had always been a tranquil, quiet town. To the outside observer, Roseland might be described as quaint. Most people in town knew each other, it was safe for children to play outside all over town, and town leaders were well meaning and eager to work on behalf of the town. There were not many entertainment options in Roseland: the diner, riding the local strip on weekends, hanging out at the new book/video and coffee store on Main Street, or riding 30 minutes to the next town for a movie. Oddly enough, sleepy little Roseland sat in the shadow of an intersection of two major interstates. Town people often talked of their amazement, and gratefulness, that the town did not take off in a boom of growth when the new interstates were built.

Early in spring 2001, people in Roseland began to notice a change in their sleepy little community. Several of the town teenagers were becoming involved in drugs. These were not new kids in town; they were children of families who had lived in Roseland for several generations. Teachers and school administrators were talking about the change in the students. The local high school in Roseland had five drug arrests on campus in the previous year, as well as a more than 50% increase in violence in the schools in the past two years. The police were hinting at the presence of gangs in the community, and community members were shocked to see graffiti that looked much like what they saw on television as gang tagging. Usually business owners did not mind teenagers hanging out on Main Street around their businesses, but lately there had been an increase in fighting and disturbing the customers. Community members in Roseland knew that times were different now than they were 10 or 15 years ago, and that teenagers were exposed to more temptations. However, they suspected that the change in Roseland was due to something more than just "changing times." These changes became the topic of many conversations around town and dominated many community meetings.

One day, a group of high school teachers were talking in the teachers' lounge, discussing the changes. They decided two things: (1) their children needed help, and (2) it was going to take more than just the school to accomplish the needed changes. These teachers went to their principal and talked about their idea. With the principal's blessing (and involvement), they then solicited the health department, police department, parents, churches, business leaders, a social service agency representative, and several youths to participate in a Saturday morning meeting.

The first meeting went well. They came to a general consensus that there was an issue regarding the youth. They agreed to work on the problem collaboratively, and they appointed people to tasks such as getting others involved, doing an assessment to understand the underlying issues at hand and their effects, and making a commitment to always actively include teenagers in their group. The group became known as the Saturday Morning Breakfast Club. Over the course of the next year, the Saturday Morning Breakfast Club conducted an assessment that discovered drugs were making their way into Roseland through the interstates and several businesses located at the interstate exits. This assessment was also able to document the change in Roseland youth and the effects these changes were having on youth performance in school, health, and crime rates. The collaboration used this information to apply for funding to begin a program they called Roseland Cares (RC). This is a collaborative effort to provide fun, safe, and affirming activities for teenagers in Roseland. It is based on a service model in which the teenagers get involved in service projects around Roseland. The program has been in operation for only six months. However, to date, more than 150 students are participating in the service projects.

1. Why did the people of Roseland initially collaborate?
2. What are your impressions of how or if the people in Roseland pooled power?
3. Discuss the collaboration's diversity.
4. Rate the complexity of Roseland's problem on a scale of 1 (not complex) to 10 (most complex), and discuss why people and organizations collaborate when issues are more complex.

REFERENCES

1. R. D. Putnam, *Bowling Alone* (New York: Simon and Schuster, 2000).
2. G. Klann, *Crisis Leadership* (Greensboro, NC: Center for Creative Leadership, 2003).
3. Putnam, *Bowling Alone.*
4. P. Mattesich and B. Monsey, *Community-Building: What Makes It Work* (Saint Paul, MN: Amherst H. Wilder Foundation, 1997).
5. M. Kreuter and N. Lezin, "Social Capital Theory," in *Emerging Theories in Health Promotion Practice and Research*, ed. R. J. DiClemente, R. A. Crosby, and M. C. Kepler (San Francisco: Jossey-Bass, 2002).
6. N. Lin, *Social Capital: A Theory of Social Structure and Action* (New York: Cambridge University Press, 2001).
7. Kreuter and Lezin, "Social Capital Theory."
8. R. D. Putnam and L. M. Feldstein, *Being Together* (New York: Simon and Schuster, 2003).
9. G. Hofstede and G. J. Hofstede, *Cultures and Organizations* (New York: McGraw-Hill, 2005).
10. T. Schuller, S. Baron, and J. Field, "Social Capital: A Review and Critique," in *Social Capital: Critical Perspectives* ed. S. Baron, J. Field, and T. Schuller (New York: Oxford University Press, 2000).
11. R. I. Rotberg, *Patterns of Social Capital* (New York: Cambridge University Press, 2001).
12. Rotberg, *Patterns of Social Capital.*
13. Putnam and Feldstein, *Being Together.*
14. Putnam, *Bowling Alone.*
15. E. Cox, *A Truly Civil Society* (Sydney, Australia: Australian Broadcasting, 1995).
16. Putnam, R. D. (2002). *Bowling Together: The American Prospect* 13, no. 3 (2002). Retrieved from http://prospect.org/article/bowling-together-0.
17. L. J. Marcus, *Connectivity and National Preparedness: Resolving Conflicts and Building Collaboration to Enhance System Readiness*, Unpublished.
18. M. Kelley, A. Molina, and J. Concha, "The Chicago Puerto Rican Community Responds to the HIV/AIDS Crisis," *The Acosa Update* 17, no. 4 (2003): 13–14.
19. L. O. Gostin, J. I. Boufford, and R. M. Martinez, "The Future of the Public's Health: Vision, Values, and Strategies," *Health Affairs* 23, no. 4 (2004): 96–107.
20. Gostin, Boufford, and Martinez, "The Future of the Public's Health."
21. National Association of County and City Health Officials (NACCHO), *Local Centers for Public Halth Peparedness: Models for Strengthening Public Health Capacity (Year 2 Report)* (Washington, DC: NACCHO, 2001).
22. National Association of County and City Health Officials (NACCHO), *Local Centers for Public Health Preparedness: A Resource Catalog for Bioterrorism and Emergency Preparedness* (Washington, DC: NACCHO, 2002).
23. P. W. Mattesich, M. Murray-Close, and B. R. Monsey, *Collaboration: What Makes It Work*, 2nd ed. (St. Paul, MN: Amherst H. Wilder Foundation, 2001).
24. M. Winer and K. Ray, *Collaboration Handbook* (St. Paul, MN: Amherst H. Wilder Foundation, 1997).
25. K. Ray, *The Nimble Collaboration* (St. Paul, MN: Amherst H. Wilder Foundation, 2002).
26. L. Cohen, M. J. Aboelata, T. Gantz, and J. Van Wert, *Collaboration Math* (Oakland, CA: Prevention Institute, 2003).
27. Turning Point, *Collaborative Leadership: Collaborative Leadership Learning Modules* (Seattle, WA: Turning Point, 2004).
28. A. Himmelman, *Collaboration for a Change* (Minneapolis, MN: Himmelman Consulting, 2002).
29. Center for Civic Partnerships, *Collaborative Functions: The 12 C's of a Collaborative* (Sacramento, CA: Center for Civic Partnerships, 2002).

30. P. Thurman, *Community Readiness: A Promising Model for Community Healing* (Oklahoma City: University of Oklahoma Health Sciences Center, Center on Child Abuse and Neglect, 2001).

31. D. Ayre, G. Clough, and T. Norris, *Facilitating Community Change* (Boulder, CO: Community Initiatives, 2000).

32. D. Chrislip and C. Larsen, *Collaborative Leadership* (San Francisco: Jossey-Bass, 1994).

33. Turning Point, *Academics and Practitioners on Collaborative Leadership* (Seattle, WA: Turning Point, 2002).

34. Himmelman, *Collaboration for a Change*.

35. Turning Point, *Academics and Practitioners on Collaborative Leadership*.

36. Himmelman, *Collaboration for a Change*.

37. Turning Point, *Academics and Practitioners on Collaborative Leadership*.

38. W. Drath, *The Deep Blue Sea* (San Francisco: Jossey-Bass, 2001).

39. Drath, *The Deep Blue Sea*.

CHAPTER 17

Public Health Preparedness and Response

We are life's way of getting things done. There is always something that needs doing right here and now. So do it.

—Rabbi Rami Shapiro, Congregation Beth Or,
Miami, Florida

Since September 11, 2001, it seems like most of our conversation in public health relates to bioterrorism, emergency preparedness, and our response to it. There is also conversation about the critical role of public health during any crisis. Public health preparedness is all about the need to be ready for any health crisis that a community may face. The major responsibility of public health in a crisis or other emergency that includes terrorism events similar to those of September 11, 2001, or the anthrax letters bioterrorism events in the months following, must be seen in the context of the overall mission of public health to promote and protect the health of the public. If this is the case, then emergency preparedness is to be seen as an extension of the public health mission and integral to public health.

A crisis is a disruption in the normal activities that guide the daily work of public health. Crisis is an abnormal event or series of disruptive events that threatens the total operation of an organization or threatens the functioning of a community or country. Thus, crisis and its aftermath are examples of system failure. It is the crisis event that triggers community emergency response activities. I will use the words *crisis*, *disaster*, *emergency*, and *hazard* interchangeably, although the meanings of these terms do show subtle differences, as discussed below. An excellent example of the role of public health in a crisis can be seen in the train derailment case discussed in Case Study 17-A. The case study takes place in a small rural county in the Midwest. The case study also includes a number of supporting documents in a series of short appendices attached to the case.

In terms of other relevant definitions, the World Health Organization and Pan African Emergency Training Centre made a distinction between a disaster and an emergency.[1] A disaster refers to the occurrence of an event that disrupts the normal conditions of existence and causes a level of suffering that exceeds the

Case Study 17-A

Emergency Response of Public Health to a Train Derailment and Evacuation

Barbara Black, MSN; Herb Bostrom; Jean Durch, RN, MPH; Holly Matucheski, BSN; and Jane Peterson, RN, MSN, MA, RS

Introduction

Government leaders at all levels are increasingly turning their attention toward emergency preparedness efforts. According to this state's public health statutes, health departments, as part of local government, are obligated to provide emergency management in the areas of mitigation, preparedness, response, and recovery. Communities have suffered devastating fires, floods, storms, hazardous spills, and terrorism. Because of health departments' direct experience responding to these disasters, they have had to translate concepts and plans into concrete practices. They have generally accomplished this while collaborating with other entities such as the Department of Natural Resources (DNR), the American Red Cross, hospitals, police and fire departments, National Guard units, and the U.S. Department of Agriculture.

This case study looks at operationalizing the abstract function of assurance into the public health practices needed when confronted with a train derailment and evacuation of more than 1,900 residents of a small community and the surrounding area. It studies the assurance role of a local health department in a complex emergency involving multiple agencies and levels of response.

For the purpose of this study, the assurance function is divided into four practices:

- Manage resources and develop organizational structure through the acquisition, allocation, and control of human, physical, and fiscal resources, and maximize the operational functions of the local public health system through coordination of community agencies' efforts and avoidance of duplication of services.
- Implement programs and other arrangements ensuring or providing direct services for priority health needs identified in the community by taking actions that translate plans and policies into services.
- Evaluate programs and provide quality assurance in accordance with applicable professional and regulatory standards to ensure that programs are consistent with plans and policies, and provide feedback on inadequacies and changes needed to redirect programs and resources.
- Inform and educate the public on health issues of concern in the community, promoting an awareness about public health services availability and promoting health education initiatives that contribute to individual and collective changes in health knowledge, attitudes, and practices toward a healthier community.

As you consider this case study, try to determine how successfully the local health department carried out these practices. What practices are illustrated? What practices are missing? What else could the department have done to ensure a healthy community?

Community and Health Department Background

Moogaritaville is a small Midwestern village with a population of 1,700. It is situated in the heart of rural Past-Your-Eyes County, which has a population of 48,000. Agriculture and related services are the major industries of Moogaritaville and the surrounding area. The Udder Express Train runs daily through the heart of the village and serves the industries. Located near the banks of the Meandering River, Moogaritaville prides itself on its strong economy and pristine environment.

The Past-Your-Eyes County Health and Human Services Department (PCHHSD) is located 10 miles from Moogaritaville in the city of Silage, the county seat. The health officer, who also leads the Health Services Division (HSD) of the department, serves on many community committees, including the Local Emergency Planning Committee (LEPC). The conservative Past-Your-Eyes County Board of Supervisors has not been willing to approve a position of environmental sanitarian, even though the health officer has requested it annually since 1990. Although they do not have a formal environmental health service, the HSD does work closely with the State Health Department on environmental health issues. The organizational chart for the PCHHSD and HSD is included in Appendix A.

The PCHHSD has adopted a community health plan that incorporates some of the principles of the *Healthy People* national health promotion and disease prevention objectives. Reducing human exposure to toxic agents is one of the objectives of the community plan. The plan does not include objectives for the emergency response system.

Derailment Events

Monday, March 4, 1996

5:55 a.m.   The Udder Express Train derailed in the middle of the village of Moogaritaville (see map, Appendix B, for location). A total of 36 railroad cars were derailed, which included 14 tanker cars loaded with liquid propane and two tanker cars loaded with sodium hydroxide. Two of the propane tanks ruptured, exploded, and began burning as a result of the derailment. The fire quickly spread to a feed mill adjacent to the tracks. The tankers loaded with sodium peroxide also ruptured.

6:00 a.m.   Residents' calls began flooding 911, and the local volunteer fire department responded and attempted to put out the fire. At the same time, the sheriff directed the dispatcher to notify the management of the Udder Express Train. Realizing the magnitude of the problem, the dispatcher was contacted by the fire captain, who had set up an Incident Command (IC) and notified the key personnel listed in the LEPC's Emergency Response Plan.

7:00 a.m.   Local Udder Express personnel arrived at the scene. The initial plan of the IC was to put out structural fires and let the two propane tankers burn out. After learning more about the contents of the cars and the nature of the fire, the fire department and Udder Express personnel were concerned that a catastrophic explosion known as a BLEVE (boiling liquid expanding vapor explosion) would occur. This would result in a massive explosion, hurling fire and debris over a large area. Therefore, the fire captain, with the support of Udder Express, halted firefighting efforts and moved his crew and the IC to a safer distance at a business outside of Moogaritaville. Simultaneously, law enforcement at the scene began an evacuation of the public. The American Red Cross was contacted to set up a shelter.

8:00 a.m.   Law enforcement officials completely evacuated residents who lived within a half-mile radius of the wreck, a total of 399 ambulatory individuals. The key personnel on the LEPC roster began to arrive at the IC site. The health officer also arrived after having heard the announcement on the local radio station while on her way to work. A decision was made to establish an Emergency Operations Center (EOC) at the same location as the IC.

10:00 a.m.   Because the threat of explosion continued with the ongoing burning of the ruptured cars, all residents within a two-mile radius were completely evacuated. The 1,900 residents evacuated included residents of one nursing home and three community-based residential facilities (CBRFs). Of the 85 total residents from these facilities, one-third were chronically mentally ill, one-third were developmentally delayed, and one-third were elderly. The residents were taken to the Sheltered Workshop in Silage, which was county owned. Even though there were few beds, the site was chosen because many of the residents knew it, and administration believed the residents would be returning to their facility within hours. Ambulances from adjacent communities and buses from the Sheltered Workshop assisted in the evacuation. Nursing home and shelter staff accompanied the residents and remained with them.

Udder Express officials directed residents to find rooms at motels in surrounding towns, assuring them that their expenses would be covered. Only a few residents showed up at the Red Cross shelter, but those who did received assistance with food, shelter, and other needs. Because Udder Express officials appeared very knowledgeable about the burning contents and were offering financial resources and assistance, they assumed command of the IC.

11:00 a.m.   Two additional tankers caught fire. Also, as the volume of propane decreased in each tanker, the risk of a BLEVE increased. Therefore, the decision was made to wait and let all tankers burn out.

12:00 Noon   A decision was made to move the EOC to the courthouse in Silage, primarily because of the cramped quarters at the combined site. A meeting of key personnel in the EOC was held to brief members on the events so far. The derailment had captured media attention, and reporters began to show up at the IC and the EOC,

(Continues)

asking about events at Moogaritaville. A primary media contact was designated at the EOC by the Emergency Government Director. The fire captain talked to media at the IC. The health officer called the HSD staff to the EOC to assist in manning telephones and to locate residents who had been dispersed to motels in a 35-mile radius. Home care nurses contacted evacuated patients and made arrangements for visits, special equipment, or other medical needs. Other residents who had marginally managed in their homes prior to the evacuation now needed assistance. Home care nurses provided assessments and planned for care.

2:00 p.m.   Evacuees expected to return to their homes within hours and left without taking medications, pets, or changes of clothing. With the fire still burning, individuals began to report needing their medications. The primary physician for many of the Moogaritaville residents was the one physician in private practice in the village. In addition, the prescriptions had been filled in the one local pharmacy. Because all had been evacuated, no records were available. The HSD personnel tracked down the evacuated physician and the local pharmacist to assist in ensuring that prescriptions were correctly refilled at Silage pharmacies.

5:00 p.m.   Another tanker caught on fire. It became evident that nursing home and CBRF residents would not be returning to their facilities. The HSD helped secure cots and other needed equipment and supplies for the night. Farmers who owned farms in the evacuation zone expressed concern to the fire captain and sheriff that their cows needed to be fed and milked. As long as they agreed to only do what had to be done and return immediately, the IC permitted the farmers to enter the evacuation zone and feed and milk the cows. This decision was neither communicated to the EOC nor the public, and the farmers continued to tend to cows twice a day throughout the event.

The IC at the scene of the derailment continued surveillance and kept out other evacuees throughout the night. The EOC stayed open throughout the night in the courthouse to handle arising issues, including media releases.

Tuesday, March 5, 1996

The IC established daily briefings for the evacuees by the railroad and cleanup personnel in one location. The HSD, with the assistance of the State Health Department, prepared a press release on the health effects of propane and sodium hydroxide to allay the fears of the residents about long-term effects (see Appendix C). The HSD also prepared a letter to healthcare providers in the area to inform them about substances involved in the incident (see Appendix D).

Because few residents were coming to the Red Cross shelter, HSD staff accompanied railroad personnel to the area motels to talk with evacuees and determine unmet needs. Surveillance and response continued at the IC and EOC.

It became evident that nursing home and CBRF residents would not be returning home soon. Space was available to house residents in a state-owned veterans home. The HSD contacted the State Nursing Home Regulators to get permission and a waiver to transport and house the residents at the veterans home. Community volunteers solicited by the HSD first cleaned the rooms in the vacant wing prior to their occupancy.

The dietitian of the HSD's WIC program consulted the State Health Department and arranged to give out early WIC drafts to evacuees who had left all their possessions at home and were in need of food assistance.

Wednesday, March 6, 1996

Poor reception was frequently experienced with wireless communication systems. The EOC was moved to Moogaritaville to be colocated with the IC to improve communication and utilize personnel efficiently.

The EOC began to plan for reentry. Subzero temperatures were expected later in the week, and electric and gas remained shut off to homes. Officials predicted that if the evacuation continued, with fluctuations in temperature, water damage would occur to houses, resulting from freezing and rupture of pipes and from accumulated pet waste. They planned accordingly. The HSD and State Health Department developed a section of the reentry packet to be distributed to all evacuees at the time of reentry. This included the Health and Safety

Recommendations for Reoccupying Your Home as well as a Household Public Health Profile (see Appendices E and F).

The PCHHSD director convened a group of professionals, including the health officer and evacuees, who met to assess the needs and attempt to solve problems. Called the Disaster Committee, the group included representatives from the HSD, social services, mental health, Salvation Army, Red Cross, Moogaritaville, and Past-Your-Eyes officials and evacuees. The goal was to respond to needs while preventing duplication of efforts. As a result of the first meeting, a one-stop information and service center was set up before the weekend.

The Red Cross established a hotline to take calls at its shelter, fielding incoming inquiries about residents and taking pressure off the HSD at the EOC. Because the HSD had no environmental staff, the sanitarian from the State Health Department arrived at the shelter to ensure proper handling of food. The sanitarian observed that a lot of food had been donated, and because there was limited storage space, some of the food was being stored in boxes outdoors. This was discouraged by the sanitarian, but the shelter staff did not see the problem. The health officer intervened, and the food was eventually moved indoors under protest.

Thursday, March 7, 1996

A controlled pet rescue was done. Pet owners entered the area in armored personnel carriers, dressed in protective clothing. Many pets were rescued, and in other cases where pets did not recognize their owners in the protective clothing, food was left in the home. The rescue seemed to have a calming effect on the evacuees and helped them cope with other inconveniences.

The Disaster Committee learned that evacuees at outlying motels were requesting more detailed information about the progress of the derailment response. Minutes of the IC briefings, and later videotapes, were faxed or sent to outlying sites for evacuees to view.

The shelter became a community center for evacuees with meals served and briefings occurring at the site. Public health nurses came at key times to talk to residents to determine if their needs were being met. Twenty-four-hour coverage was provided via a home care on-call system. Surveillance and response continued at the IC and EOC.

Friday, March 8, 1996

The IC observed that more tanker cars ignited and continued to burn for several days.

Saturday, March 9, 1996

The State Department of Natural Resources (DNR) representatives were a part of the IC and EOC teams. They monitored the effect of the derailment on the environment. An estimated 9,000 gallons of sodium hydroxide leaked from the derailed tankers, flowed into the drainage ditch, and entered the Meandering River. By the end of this day, HazMat teams applied 4.5 tons of citric acid to the spill and affected area. DNR staff monitored surface water conditions of the Meandering River one mile downstream. They were concerned about the effect to the ecosystem if pH exceeded 9.5. The pH never reached that level; most readings were well below 9.5.

Sunday, March 10, 1996

The HazMat team entered the site and tapped into three intact tankers to remove propane contents and begin controlled burning. The team purged the now-empty tanker cars with nitrogen. Other tankers continued burning. Throughout the week, other controlled releases of propane occurred. The IC and EOC continued surveillance and response throughout the week.

Sunday, March 17, 1996

Only two tankers remained containing propane. They were in an unstable condition, and technicians were uncertain of the amount of propane they contained. A demolition expert was hired to place two sets of explosives

(Continues)

on each car. The detonation of the first set of charges released pressure in each tank; the second, which was detonated 35 seconds later, created an opening in the base of each that allowed the propane to flow into a ditch, ignite, and burn.

Monday, March 18, 1996

The area was declared safe, and cleanup at the site began. Approximately 13% of the homes were badly damaged. Building experts from the County Housing Authority accompanied evacuees to assist in inspecting their homes.

The reentry packet was distributed to all evacuees. The completed Household Public Health Profile was returned to the HSD following the incident (see Appendix F). All who requested follow-up, a total of 30 households, received a contact from the HSD.

Tetanus immunizations were offered to workers and evacuees to protect them as they began cleanup following the incident. The HSD and Solid Waste Division assisted the community in disposal of solid waste, including household, animal, and construction waste.

Tuesday, March 19, 1996

The State Health Department sanitarians inspected the restaurants, delis, grocery stores, cheese factory, bakeries, and other public establishments. The goal was to reopen these establishments as soon as possible without compromising the safety of the public.

The State Health Department personnel also conducted sampling of selected residential walls and surfaces to ensure that there was no air deposition of hazardous substances released by the fires. The wall and surface tests were negative for hazardous substances.

The State Agriculture Department ordered that cows that had been in the hot zone be destroyed.

The village water plant was brought online. Residents were notified through the local media to boil their water until further notice, given the length of time the system was out of service.

The DNR performed residential soil sampling for inorganic metals and polyaromatic hydrocarbons. The soil test results were negative for these substances.

Following the Incident

Two months after the event, the LEPC convened a meeting of all the key participants in the derailment for the debriefing. Lessons learned were shared and documented. A report of the incident was developed and discussed at subsequent meetings in order to plan for the next community emergency.

Many months passed before recovery was complete. Frequent contacts were made to residents regarding home repairs, water quality, and health issues. Several homes had to be razed and rebuilt due to the degree of damage. No ill health was reportedly caused by the incident.

Conclusion

This case study illustrates how a local health department fulfilled the assurance function in a complex, long-term emergency involving many other agencies. The four assurance functions examined include resource management, program implementation, evaluation, and public education. Both strengths and weaknesses of the local response were revealed.

Although beyond the scope of this study, it should be noted that the ongoing recovery process is as important as the initial response. Recovery from a disaster such as the train derailment described above is a long-term process that involves not only the responding agencies but the entire community. Resumption of previous day-to-day activities, as well as coping with the aftermath of the disaster, presents an ongoing challenge to both agencies and citizens.

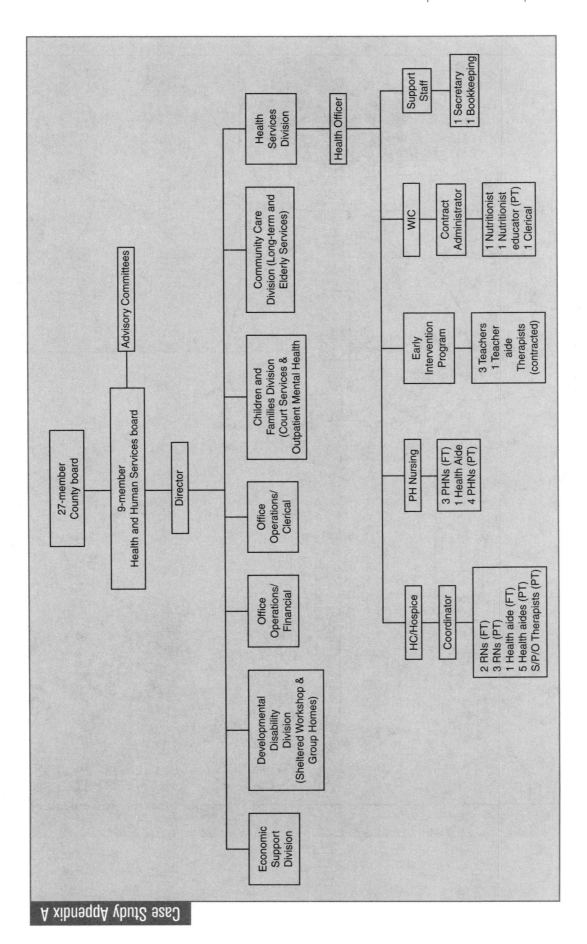

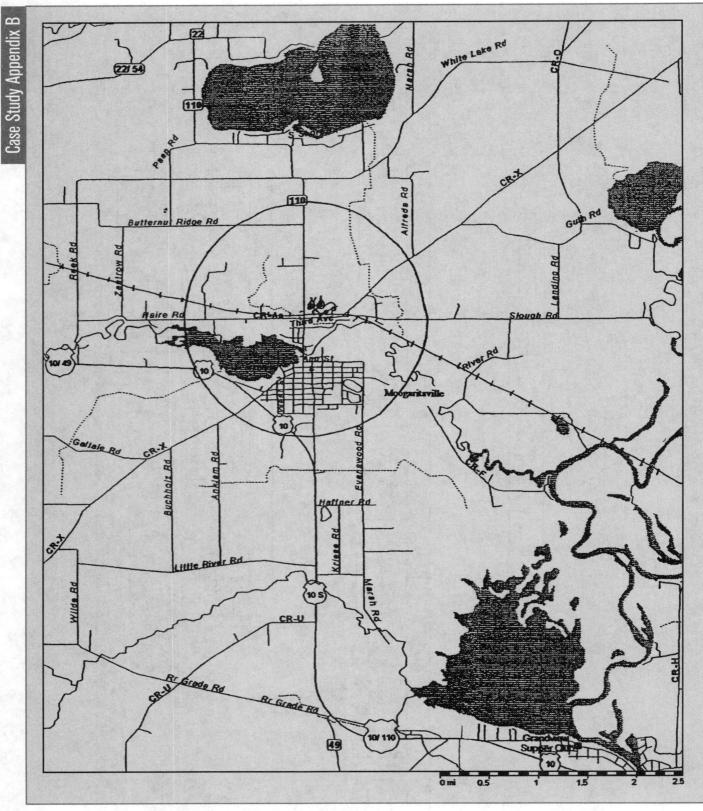

Case Study Appendix B

Moogaritaville Train Derailment

Case Study Appendix C

On March 4, 1996, a train derailed in the village of Moogaritaville. Because of the threat of explosion and the possibility that tank cars containing sodium hydroxide (lye) might be damaged by burning propane, people were evacuated from their homes. The fire at the derailment resulted from explosions of propane gas and the burning of wood.

As you return to your home, you may see ash and soot. These materials are not hazardous; however, they are messy and can be a nuisance to clean up.

As you return, you may smell smoke. As with any fire, people who are sensitive to smoke or people who have respiratory problems may experience some lung irritation. The smell of smoke will continue to be a nuisance, but we do not expect people to experience health effects from exposure to smoke.

If you do experience health effects that you believe are related to the fire, please contact your family physician. At your request, we will speak with your physician and provide information about the public health concerns associated with the emergency. Past-Your-Eyes County Health and Human Services is working closely with the State Bureau of Public Health to provide health information and assistance to concerned citizens.

Health Officer
Past-Your-Eyes County Health and
 Human Services
811 Harding St.
Silage, IW 94981-2087

Emergency Coordinator
State Bureau of Public Health
4141 Lincoln Ave., Room 96
Jefferson, IW 35703-3044
(806) 662-7089

(715) 258-6385 (Moogaritaville Office)
(715) 258-4472 (Past-Your-Eyes Emergency Operations Center)

Past-Your-Eyes County Department of Health and Human Services

Case Study Appendix D

811 Harding Street
Silage, IW 94981-2087
(517) 258-6300
TDD (517) 258-6302
FAX (517) 258-6409

March 13, 1996
Dear Healthcare Provider:
As you are aware, an Udder Express train derailed in Moogaritaville at 6:00 a.m. on Monday, March 4, 1996. The derailment involved railroad cars of liquid propane (LP) and liquid sodium hydroxide (50%). Area citizens were evacuated for an extended period of time. There is no evidence that any toxic chemicals were involved in this incident.

Naturally, this situation has caused a great deal of anxiety among area residents. You may already be receiving questions about medical testing or examinations to evaluate health effects. At this time, we are not recommending any special testing. We are not aware that any unusual situations exist in any Moogaritaville area homes.

As these residents return to their homes, they may encounter potential health hazards from food; drinking water; mold, mildew, and spores caused by moisture; smoke particulate; lead-based paint; asbestos; household chemicals; electrical and physical hazards; and other public health concerns. Patients with asthma, allergies, or other respiratory disorders may manifest symptoms some time after initially returning to their residences.

The Past-Your-Eyes County Department of Health and Human Services and the State Department of Health and Social Services are committed to helping you help your patients. Andy Henderson, MD, the Chief Medical Officer of the State Bureau of Public Health, is available at (806) 662-1253 for direct consultation on any health effects or concerns that may come to your attention that may be related to this incident.

If you notice the onset of any unusual illnesses or infectious diseases that may be related to this incident, please call me directly.

I have enclosed for your information two public information notices that were given to area residents. Also enclosed are two reference sheets designed to help you quickly access the information you may need.

(*Continues*)

I hope this information is helpful. Please feel free to call me at (517) 258-6385 if you have any other questions or needs related to this incident.

Sincerely,
Health Officer
Past-Your-Eyes County Department of Health and Human Services

Moogaritaville Train Derailment Evacuees
Residential and Commercial Reentry Plan
March 13, 1996

Objective: To conduct a door-to-door analysis of hazardous conditions and remedial measures needed to allow reentry of the general public. This process may take several days.

Before you return to your home, a team of experts, contracted by Land Construction Co., will inspect your house or business with you or your designated representative. This assessment will determine whether there are unsafe conditions to prevent you from returning to your home. If you are able to return to your home, it is because your home has been determined to be safe.

This assessment will be conducted by 20 individual teams that will be assigned sections. Each team will consist of:

1. Building owner or designee
2. Renter or lessee if a rental unit
3. Land Construction team leader
4. State gas representative
5. Plumbing subcontractor
6. Electrical subcontractor
7. HVAC subcontractor
8. Law enforcement

State Central Ltd. (WC) has retained Land Construction to act as the general contractor for repairs that may be required once the evacuated residents, merchants, and business owners of Moogaritaville return to their homes and businesses. Land has the size, experience, manpower, and equipment necessary to perform the job in the most timely and efficient manner, minimizing any further disruption to the residents and their families. Given the magnitude of the job, Land will engage all available qualified craftsmen in the area as subcontractors.

Hiring a single general contractor, which will bill WC directly for all repairs, to coordinate all the different craft work required will minimize the administrative and financial burden on the residents of Moogaritaville. *No money will be required of the residents*, as all financial arrangements will be addressed directly between Land and WC.

To enable all residents to return to their homes and businesses as soon as possible, Land plans to do the repairs in two stages. First, all residences and businesses will be repaired to the extent necessary to make them habitable and functional. In the case of residences, this will mean heat, water, and one working bathroom. After the initial repairs are completed on all structures, workers will return and entirely repair all affected homes and businesses.

WC anticipates that once the repairs are complete, residents of Moogaritaville will be satisfied with the quality and extent of the work done on their homes and businesses. All work performed by Land and its subcontractors is guaranteed by WC and Land. If you are unsatisfied with the quality or extent of the repairs performed, these disputes will be resolved by arbitration through the American Arbitration Association.

Because the extent of damage is unknown, WC and Land are unable at this time to give any estimate as to how long the first and second stages of repairs will take. As soon as the determinations are made, residents will be notified promptly. All repairs will be performed on the most expedited basis possible.

You may choose to retain a contractor of your own to perform any repairs necessitated by the derailment. Ultimately, you or your insurer will be reimbursed by WC for the reasonable and customary costs associated with necessary repairs performed by contractors other than Land. WC cannot, however, guarantee any work not performed by Land and its subcontractors. In the event you choose your own contractor, you should inform Land Construction of your decision and, furthermore, check with the appropriate consumer protection or licensing agency to ensure the contractor is reputable.

General Procedure

Assemble the evacuees at a designated location for a systematic reentry into town. Only one member or designated representative of each household or business will be allowed to join the inspection team. In the case of rental properties, the building owner and renter/lessee will be allowed to join the inspection. The elderly can be accompanied by a relative or friend. Transportation will be arranged for evacuees to their homes from the assembly area for the inspection process.

Prior to team inspections, State Gas and State Electric have preparatory work that must be done. State Gas must first close all gas meters and purge the system. State Electric must restore power in the area of the train derailment. This preparatory work is estimated to take four to eight hours.

Once safe entry has been secured, the remaining team members will be prepared to enter the building and make assessments of damage repairs. Each structure will be categorized on the amount of work needed for occupancy to the following levels:

Level 1—No damage (green tag)
Level 2—Minimal damage, 4 hrs or less for repairs (blue tag)
Level 3—Intermediate damage, 16 hrs or less for repairs (orange tag)
Level 4—Major damage, 16 hrs plus for repairs (red tag)
Level 5—Uninhabitable (black tag)

Upon completion of the initial inspection, the home or business entrances will be tagged at one of the levels listed above. When the building is ready for occupancy, it will be tagged as such. This process will depend on an onsite agreement between owner, renter, and contractor as to the schedule of repairs.

Health and Safety Recommendations for Reoccupying Your Home

1. Moogaritaville's municipal water supply is under a boil water notice. Water should be used only for bathing and flushing toilets. To ensure your personal safety, you should take the following precautions:

    a. Boil all water used for drinking, cooking, or washing. Eating utensils should be boiled at a rolling boil for at least five minutes. Bottled water can also be used for drinking and food preparation purposes.

    b. Ice and beverages prepared with unboiled tap water should be discarded.

    c. You should follow these precautions until you receive notice that the water supply has returned to a safe condition.

2. Before you reenter your home, the pilot light of all gas appliances will be relit. Appliances not safe for relighting will be tagged as **DO NOT USE** and will be replaced at a later date. If the pilot has gone out for some reason, call the Land representative. Hotline: **411-644-2296**.

3. If you use your fireplace or wood burning unit for heating, be sure the flue is open and operating correctly. *Do not overload your fireplace. Do not burn fresh cut, treated, or painted wood.*

4. If you decide to use electric heaters, be careful to place them away from items that can burn. Because of possible fire hazards, do not leave heaters unattended.

5. Food may have been damaged by extreme temperatures. Evaluate all food closely according to the following criteria. Remember that illness-causing bacteria may not be detectable by smell, taste, or appearance. *When in doubt, throw it out.*

    Frozen foods—Discard if not hard or solid. Check the food in the doors and upper levels of your freezer first. If these foods are leaky, food in lower levels may need to be discarded.
    Refrigerated foods—Discard outdated foods, foods that show decomposition or discoloration, and foods with a bad odor.
    Bottled or canned foods at room temperature—Discard if container is bulging, leaky, or rusted.
    Dry packaged foods—Discard if damaged by water or other liquids, or if color or texture has changed.
    Fruits and vegetables at room temperatures—Discard.

6. Because you may sustain a cut or puncture wound while cleaning your home, you should be protected against tetanus. Tetanus shots (Td) are recommended every 10 years and are available through the Past-Your-Eyes County Health and Human Services. The contacts for this service or any other health-related questions are:

Health Officer, Past-Your-Eyes County Health and Human Services: (517) 258-6385

(Continues)

Emergency Operations Center: (517) 258-4472
Dentin Highbred of State Bureau of Public Health: (114) 448-5232

7. If there is a hazard or a situation that you are unsure of, or if you have any questions or problems concerning the above information, please contact Land Construction at (411) 644-2296.

Keep records of all items you discard so that you can be compensated for those items.

LAND RESIDENT HOTLINE
(411) 644-2296
(24 Hours)

The Past-Your-Eyes County Health and Human Services Department wants to ensure that your health and safety concerns are addressed during and after your return home. To address those needs, we are asking that you take a couple of minutes to complete the attached Moogaritaville Household Public Health Profile. The information that you provide will assist our agency in focusing our resources to better meet your needs.

If you do experience health effects that you believe are environmentally related, please contact your physician. At your request, we will speak with your physician and provide any necessary information. Past-Your-Eyes County Health and Human Services is working closely with the State Bureau of Public Health to provide health information and assistance to the citizens of Moogaritaville. Should you have any questions, please feel free to contact the following individuals:

Health Officer
Past-Your-Eyes County Health and Human Services
811 Harding St.
Past-Your-Eyes, IW 54981-2087

T. A. Johnson
State Bureau of Public Health
4141 Lincoln Ave., Room 96
Jefferson, IW 35703-3044
(806) 662-7089

(517) 258-6385 (Past-Your-Eyes Office)
(517) 258-4472 (Past-Your-Eyes Emergency Operations Center)
Date _____/_____/____

Moogaritaville Household Public Health Profile

Name
Head of Household
Person Completing This Questionnaire (If other than head of household)
Address
Moogaritaville Home Phone
Best time to contact?

1. How many individuals live at this address? _____
2. How many are children under the age of 7? _____
3. Does anyone in this household have:
   asthma? Yes   No allergies? Yes   No
4. Does anyone in your household have a disability or other health condition that requires special assistance?
   Yes   No
   If yes, please list the conditions:
5. Does anyone in your household have a disability that you feel may be aggravated by returning to your home?
   Yes   No
   If yes, please list type of disability:
6. Would you like someone from Past-Your-Eyes County Health to call you?
   Yes   No

Case Study Appendix F

Source: Courtesy of the Mid-America Regional Public Health Leadership Institute.

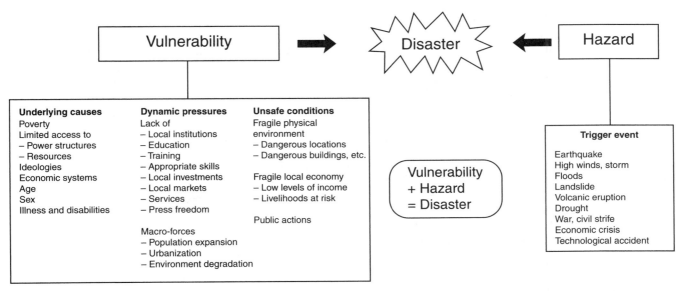

FIGURE 17-1 Factors that Affect a Disaster. *Source*: Reproduced from the World Health Organization and Pan African Emergency Training Centre: Addis Ababa (2002). *Disasters and Emergencies*: *Definitions*. Geneva, Switzerland. http://www.who.int/disasters/repo/7656.pdf. Accessed July 13, 2012.

capacity of adjustment that is usual for a given community. It is important to remember that people are the most affected by a disaster, although structural damage may also occur. WHO defined an emergency as a time in which normal procedures for dealing with events are suspended and extraordinary measures need to be taken to avert further disastrous events. WHO further distinguished between a hazard that is a natural or human event that threatens to adversely affect human life, property, or activities to such an extent that a disaster occurs, and vulnerabilities in a population or community that may make a crisis event more severe. Vulnerabilities then refer to predispositions to suffer damage in a population or community from external events. As **Figure 17-1** demonstrates, a disaster occurs when hazards and vulnerabilities meet.

The United Nations has used the following definition to refer to disaster preparedness:[2]

> Disaster preparedness minimizes the adverse effects of a hazard through effective precautionary actions, rehabilitation and recovery to ensure the timely, appropriate and effective organization and delivery of relief and assistance following a disaster.

TYPES OF CRISIS

In two excellent books on crisis and crisis management, the discussion of crisis and its aftermath is seen as related to the type of crisis that is involved.[3,4]

Bioterrorism events relate to only one type of crisis situation. Crisis falls into several different groups. Each major type of crisis requires different response patterns. **Table 17-1** reviews a typology of crisis developed by Mitroff, who noted that there are at least seven different classes of crisis.[5] The first group of crises is economic in nature and includes such things as labor strikes. In public health, an economic crisis relates to cutbacks in budget or loss of staff without an ability to hire replacements. Although there have been increases in funding for emergency preparedness and response activities, other programs in public health have suffered from budget cuts and budget shortfalls.

The second group of crises is informational in nature. These crises deal with things such as tampering with public records, computer viruses that affect an entire agency's computer system, false information in files, privacy issues, and so forth. The potential informational crises in public health are numerous and complex. Sharing information across agencies is a problem. Different methods for collecting data as well as different data classification schemes all add to the potential for informational crises in the governmental public health sector. Federal and state guidelines related to the sharing or disclosure of health information to outside parties also create data problems. Misinterpretation of data is also important because it can create an inadvertent series of reactions to the report that can have crisis consequences.

Next, there are physical crises that involve the loss of property or key equipment through breakdowns or

TABLE 17-1 Major Crisis Types/Risks

Economic	Informational	Physical (loss of key plants and facilities)	Human Resource	Reputational	Psychopathic Acts	Natural Disasters
Labor strikes	Loss of proprietary and confidential information	Loss of key equipment, plants, and material supplies	Loss of key executives	Slander	Product tampering	Earthquake
Labor unrest			Loss of key personnel	Gossip	Kidnapping	Fire
Labor shortage	False information	Breakdowns of key equipment, plants, etc.	Rise in absenteeism	Sick jokes	Hostage taking	Floods
Major decline in stock price and fluctuations	Tampering with computer records		Rise in vandalism and accidents	Rumors	Terrorism	Explosions
Market crash		Loss of key facilities		Damage to corporate reputation	Workplace violence	Typhoons
Decline in major earnings	Loss of key computer information with regard to customers, suppliers, etc. (Y2K)	Major plant disruptions	Workplace violence	Tampering with corporate logos		Hurricanes

Source: Reproduced from I. Mitroff, *Managing Crises Before They Happen*, New York: Amacom, 2001.

theft. This can lead to disruption in the normal flow of operations in an organization. Many universities report the loss of computers and laptops out of staff offices, for example. A power outage can affect activities. A lack of flu vaccine, as occurred during the fall of 2004, for people waiting for these immunizations during a potential influenza outbreak in a community is another crisis possibility. Public health agencies often struggle with a shortage of physical resources to carry out their work. The fourth group of crises relates to the human resources needs of organizations. These are the crises that occur when there is a sudden budget cut in programs, and programs and staff need to be eliminated or cut on short notice. These types of crises occur when a health administrator resigns or takes ill and the organization flounders because of a lack of competent leadership. A crisis occurs if there is a flu epidemic in the community that leads to a rise in absenteeism in the agency because the primary program staff are out sick.

Many people ignore reputational crises, but they can severely cripple an organization or community. Here we are dealing with the effects of gossip, slander, misinformation during a crisis, rumors, and so forth. This is in many ways an extremely important group of potential crisis events. They cannot be ignored. For example, a rumor that a health administrator may be leaving when this is not true can create agency problems. One health department in the Midwest had to deal with the effects of a staff member giving birth control devices to a teenage girl who, it turned out, was sent to the health department by her teacher/lover. Even though the staff member acted in the best interests of the girl, who was trying to avoid pregnancy, the image of the health department was eventually affected. The county board decided to not accept state family planning dollars for the agency as a result. Thus, it is possible that a reputational crisis can occur even when the public health agency is operating to protect the rights of the public. Crises and their occurrence are unexpected happenings.

Most of our discussions in public health in recent years have been related to psychopathic crises, which include bioterrorism events, hostage taking in domestic and foreign places, workplace rage and violence, product tampering that affects the health of the public, foreign substances in the mail, and so-called weapons of mass destruction (biological warfare). The importance of the present typology is that psychopathic crises are only one group of crises, although much of the attention of public health is turned toward this class of abnormal events. The funding that public health agencies is receiving today is tied to this class. Public health preparedness models build on the military preparedness model related to these types of events. Preparedness models do not need to be limited to psychopathic crises, but rather can be expanded and applied to all the crisis categories discussed in this section.

Public health has been most comfortable with the natural disaster form of crisis. We have dealt with these events on many occasions and have developed effective emergency preparedness and response plans for dealing with these natural disasters. For example, during the Florida hurricanes of 2004, the way agencies worked together to address the aftermath of one hurricane after another reaching landfall in Florida and other affected areas of the South is an excellent example of agencies working together. Following the earthquake and tsunami in southeast Asia during Christmas week of 2004, the emergency response was slow at first, but eventually involved worldwide response to the events.

Although public health agencies have worked well with fire departments and other emergency response groups during natural disasters, these relationships have tended to be jurisdictional in nature. Difficulties still exist when federal, state, and local entities need to work together. The situation becomes even more complex when the relationships cross state or national boundaries or have to involve federal agencies and international organizations, entities, and personnel as partners.

In the past, most disasters were caused by wars or natural events. Disasters in modern times have been natural as well as human-made. Mitroff reviewed many of these crises over time and noted that most of these modern-day crisis events occurred outside the United States.[6] Beginning with the Three Mile Island crisis in 1979 and the Tylenol poisonings in 1982, we have seen an increase in the number of crisis-related events in the United States as well as around the world. The events of September 11, 2001, changed the landscape of terrorism in that new forms of terrorism could now be waged against the United States by small terrorist groups. **Table 17-2** shows some of these crises of modern times at a glance.[7] The table describes each of these major crises, from the Three Mile Island nuclear plant disaster in 1979 to a number of other crises in 2003. The table also shows injuries, deaths, and damage due to each of these events. All of these events had important public health implications for the population in the communities in which these crises happened.

It is unfortunate that events from 2004 and onward must now be added to the list, including the flu vaccine shortages in the fall of 2004, the Sudan holocaust-like crisis, the Florida hurricanes during the summer and fall of 2004, the Iraq terrorism activities of 2004 and 2005, the southeast Asia natural disasters in late 2004, Hurricane Katrina in 2005, the Joplin tornado of 2011, wildfires in the southwest United States almost every year, and the severe winter in western Europe in 2012. Public health leaders must be able to work with their community partners to address any future crises that may occur. It seems clear that these crises have been increasing and that they will continue to increase in the future. Organizations as well as communities need to be prepared. The additional issue of international terrorism adds new dimensions to the preparedness formula because not all countries of the world are equally prepared for crisis or emergency events.

LEVEL OF PUBLIC HEALTH PREPAREDNESS TODAY

There is growing evidence that public health and its leadership are still not prepared to manage a large-scale emergency. In 2002, Congress enacted legislation as a response to the events of September 11, 2001, and the anthrax attacks that occurred later that year. The Public Health Security and Bioterrorism Response Act of 2002 was passed. This act was intended to provide guidance to public health officials at the federal, state, and local levels through cooperative agreement funding mechanisms to increase the ability of public health agencies to be prepared for potential bioterrorism activities through strengthening the public health system in the areas of emergency preparedness and response. State and local governments, including municipal health departments, were given funding to develop bioterrorism and other emergency response plans; purchase and upgrade equipment, supplies, and staff to manage national drug stockpiles necessary to enhance preparedness and response activities; conduct exercises and drills to test emergency response capabilities; improve surveillance methods; and train personnel in the use of early warning and surveillance networks to provide early detection.

Trust for America's Health reviewed our state of readiness at the end of fiscal year 2003[8] and for a second time in 2004.[9] The Trust noted progress in the

TABLE 17-2   Major Crises at a Glance

Crisis	Date	Description	Injuries/Deaths/Damage
Three Mile Island	March 28, 1979	Malfunction at a nuclear power plant near Middletown, PA, caused the core of the reactor to overheat.	No injuries or deaths, but it was the most serious accident in U.S. commercial nuclear power plant operating history.
Tylenol poisonings	September 29 to October 1, 1982	Product tampering involving cyanide being inserted into Tylenol Extra Strength capsules.	Seven people in the Chicago area died. No one has ever been charged in this case.
Bhopal disaster	December 3, 1984	Industrial accident that killed thousands of people in the Indian city of Bhopal in Madhya Pradesh, following the accidental release of forty tons of methyl isocyanate (MIC) from a Union Carbide chemical plant located in the heart of the city.	The Bhopal accident killed more than 2,000 people outright and injured anywhere from 150,000 to 600,000 others, some 6,000 of whom later died from their injuries.
Space shuttle *Challenger* explosion	January 28, 1986	Space Shuttle *Challenger* explodes on take-off from the NASA Kennedy Space Center in Florida. The cause is later determined to be failure of an "O" ring due to extremely cold weather conditions.	All seven astronauts aboard the *Challenger* died.
Chernobyl disaster	April 25–26, 1986	One of the world's worst nuclear power accidents. The Chernobyl nuclear power plant, located 80 miles north of Kiev in the former Soviet Union (now Ukraine), went out of control, resulting in explosions and a fireball that blew off the reactor's heavy steel and concrete lid.	The Chernobyl accident killed more than 30 people immediately; and as a result of the high radiation levels in the surrounding 20-mile radius, 135,000 people had to be evacuated.
Mad cow disease	1986 to present	Mad cow disease, or its scientific name bovine spongiform encephalopathy (BSE), is a fatal brain-wasting disease in cattle that was first identified in the United Kingdom (UK) in 1986. The disease can be passed from infected meat to humans, also causing brain damage and, eventually, death.	153 human cases reported worldwide; of these, approximately 100 people have died. Millions of cattle were slaughtered in an effort to eliminate the disease.

Pan Am flight 103	December 21, 1988	Pam Am flight 103 was blown out of the sky over Lockerbie, Scotland. Two Libyan citizens were later convicted of masterminding the bombing.	Deaths: 259 people on the plane and 11 on the ground
Exxon Valdez oil spill	March 24, 1989	The Exxon Valdez, an oil tanker, crashed into rocks in Prince William Sound, Alaska. Millions of gallons of oil contaminated the fragile ecosystem.	Animal deaths: 3,000 sea otters, 250,000 sea birds, 300 harbor seals, 250 bald eagles, 22 orcas (killer whales), and billions of fish and small sea creatures.\n\nMore than $2 billion was spent on the cleanup, which was not completed until 1992.
Chilean grape scare	April 1989	Chilean grapes were banned in the United States because of a terrorist threat and the finding of traces of a little cyanide on two grapes.	None.
LAPD–Rodney King beating	March 3, 1991	After a high-speed car chase in the San Fernando Valley, Rodney King, who was black, was beaten by white LAPD officers, as a sergeant directed from nearby. King sustained approximately 56 baton strokes, was kicked in the head and body, and stunned with a Taser stun gun. Some of the beating was captured on an amateur photographer's videotape, which was eventually viewed around the world.	None immediately (see the L.A. riots below)
L.A. riots	April 29 to May 4, 1992	The April 29, 1992, state court acquittal of the four officers involved in the Rodney King beating led to rioting that lasted six days. Thousands of people participated in the riots, and the violence and looting spread to other parts of Los Angeles County. Federal troops and the California National Guard were called in; the officers were subsequently tried on federal criminal civil rights charges. Sergeant Koon and Officer Powell were convicted of violating Rodney King's civil rights and sentenced to 30 months imprisonment.	54 people were killed, 2,383 injured (221 critically), and 13,212 arrested. Property damage was estimated at more than $700 million for the county.

(Continues)

TABLE 17-2 Major Crises at a Glance (*Continued*)

Crisis	Date	Description	Injuries/Deaths/Damage
World Trade Center bombing	February 26, 1993	A bomb exploded in a basement garage of the World Trade Center. In 1995, militant Islamist Sheik Omar Abdel Rahman and nine others were convicted of conspiracy charges, and in 1998, Ramzi Yousef, believed to have been the mastermind, was convicted of the bombing. Al-Qaeda involvement is suspected.	6 deaths and 1,040/933 injuries.
Waco, Texas, standoff	February 28 to April 19, 1993	Agents of the Bureau of Alcohol, Tobacco and Firearms raided the Branch Davidian compound to serve arrest and search warrants as part of an investigation into illegal possession of firearms and explosives there. Gunfire erupted and a 51-day siege ensued, which culminated on April 19, 1993.	Deaths of four ATF agents, and injuries to 16, on February 28; the resulting fire in the compound at the end of the siege on April 19 killed 80 Branch Davidians, including 22 children.
Syringes in cans of Pepsi	June 10–17, 1993	Two reports in the Seattle–Tacoma area of Washington State that consumers found syringes in cans of Diet Pepsi led to a regional FDA warning; within 24 hours, reports of syringes in Diet Pepsi cans came in from disparate locations, resulting in widespread media coverage. With no reasonable explanation from a manufacturing standpoint, the FDA recommended a course of no recall.	No injuries were reported; Pepsi incurred $25 million in lost sales revenue.
Somalia	October 3–4, 1993	Battle of Mogadishu in Somalia: A deadly shootout developed into the largest fire-fight since the Vietnam War after two Black Hawk helicopters were shot down during a mission to capture two lieutenants of the Somalian warlord General Mohamed Farrah Aidid.	The battle ended with the eventual deaths of 18 of America's most elite soldiers, and the wounding of 75 others. Estimates of Somali deaths varied between 500 and 1,500.
Texaco racism scandal	August 1994 to November 1996	A senior personnel manager in Texaco's finance department taped an August 1994 meeting at which he and three other executives disparaged black workers and discussed hiding and destroying documents that were vital to a pending discrimination case. This tape set off a racial scandal at Texaco.	Texaco settled the case for an estimated $176 million in cash and other considerations—the largest such settlement on record.

Orange County bankruptcy	December 6, 1994	Orange County, California, became the largest municipality in U.S. history to declare bankruptcy after the county treasurer lost $1.7 billion of taxpayer money through investments in risky Wall Street securities.	No deaths or injuries
Kobe earthquake	January 17, 1995	Earthquake measuring 7.2 on the Richter scale struck Kobe, Japan.	5,100 deaths; 300,000 people left homeless. The cost to restore the basic infrastructure of the city was about $150 billion.
Barron's crisis	1995	Financial crisis at Barron's Bank brought about by risky Japanese investments that failed after the Kobe earthquake.	No deaths or injuries
Tokyo subway attacks	March 20, 1995	Act of domestic terrorism perpetrated by members of AUM Shinrikyo. In five coordinated attacks, AUM members released sarin gas on several lines of the Tokyo subway. This was the most serious terrorist attack in Japan's modern history.	12 deaths and 6,000 injuries
Oklahoma City bombing	April 19, 1995	Domestic terrorist attack on the Alfred P. Murrah Federal Building in Oklahoma City, OK. The attack was in retaliation for the deaths in 1993 at the Branch Davidian compound in Waco, Texas.	168 people, including 19 children, died in the explosion. Timothy McVeigh was later convicted of the bombing and executed by the federal government.
Crash of ValuJet flight 592	May 11, 1996	Airplane disaster aboard a Miami-to-Atlanta flight. The plane crashed into the Florida Everglades shortly after takeoff; it was later determined that the crash was due to a cargo fire caused by oxygen canisters that were mistakenly labeled and improperly packed in the cargo hold.	All 110 people aboard the plane perished. As a result of the crisis, ValuJet was forced into bankruptcy. It was later reorganized as a new low-cost airline.
TWA flight 800	July 17, 1996	TWA Flight 800, a Boeing 747 bound for Paris, exploded shortly after takeoff from New York's Long Island. The FAA ruled that the explosion was caused by a spark of unknown origin in the fuel tank; there was much speculation that the plane was brought down by a shoulder-fired missile after 270 people provided the FBI with accounts of an unknown object that streaked up from the horizon and arced toward TWA flight 800 in the seconds before it exploded.	All 230 people on board the plane perished.

(*Continues*)

TABLE 17-2 Major Crises at a Glance (*Continued*)

Crisis	Date	Description	Injuries/Deaths/Damage
US Army sexual harassment scandal	April to September 1996	Sexual harassment scandal involving 12 officers at the U.S. Army's Aberdeen Proving Grounds near Baltimore, MD. The officers were accused of sexual abuses against females under their command, which included charges of rape, sodomy, and assault.	An Army hotline set up in November 1996 to field complaints of sexual harassment was flooded with about 5,000 calls, resulting in 325 investigations of misconduct at Army installations around the world.
Nazi gold	September 1996	Discovery of a paper trail linking gold in Switzerland to that which was looted by the Nazis between 1939 and 1945. The gold included bullion bars, trinkets from jeweler's shops, and gold from the teeth of those who died in the death camps. Calls issued to make restitution to the Holocaust survivors and/or their descendants.	The gold was worth around $400 million when it was looted ($3.9 billion in today's values). About three-quarters of the money was kept in the Swiss National Bank, and the remainder went to accounts in other countries.
LAPD Rampart scandal	May 1998 to November 2000	A special task force was set up to investigate misconduct by more than 70 officers at LAPD's Rampart Station Antigang unit. The officers were investigated for either committing crimes (routinely engaging in illegal shootings, beatings, perjury, false arrests, witness intimidation, and other misconduct) or knowing about them and helping to cover them up.	L.A. City Attorney's office estimated that total Rampart-related settlement costs would total $125 million; the LAPD's elite antigang unit CRASH was disbanded, and court-ordered injunctions against gang members were suspended.
Attacks on US embassies	August 7, 1998	Near-simultaneous terrorist attacks on the U.S. embassies in Nairobi, Kenya, and Dar es Salaam, Tanzania. Seventeen individuals, including Osama Bin Laden, are charged with the crimes.	Kenya: 12 American diplomats, 34 Kenyan U.S. embassy employees, and 167 citizens of Nairobi near the embassy at the time were killed, making a total of 213 dead. Tanzania: 10 deaths and 70 injuries.
Clinton–Lewinsky affair	August 1998	President Clinton, after nine months of near silence, admitted that he did have an affair with ex-White House intern Monica Lewinsky. The President was later impeached by the Senate, but was acquitted on the charges of perjury before the grand jury and obstruction of justice.	N/A

Turkey earthquake	August 17, 1999	An earthquake measuring between 7.4 and 7.9 on the Richter Scale occurs near Izmit, an industrial city about 55 miles east of Istanbul on the Sea of Marmara. At least 300 aftershocks followed in the first 48 hours.	More than 14,000 dead and 200,000 left homeless. Contractors were convicted of constructing shoddy buildings that were responsible for the deaths and injuries.
Ford–Firestone Tire Crisis	May to August 2000	Firestone tire recall is the most deadly auto safety crisis in American history. Most of the deaths occurred in accidents involving the Ford Explorer, which tends to roll over when one of the tires blows out and/or the tread separates.	More than 200 deaths and 800 injuries were linked to defective Firestone tires. The recall cost Ford $500 million in lost production. Both companies were the targets of a large number of lawsuits that likely will take years—and millions, if not billions—to settle.
California energy crisis	May 2000 to May 2001	By the early 1990s, electricity rates in California were on average 50% higher than in the rest of the United States. The three major privately held utility companies (Southern California Edison, Pacific Gas & Electric, and San Diego Gas & Electric) spent $4.3 million on lobbyists and $1 million on political campaigns in their efforts to encourage deregulation. In 1995, the state legislature unanimously passed a bill to open the industry to competition, but consumers ended up paying almost twice the rate they did before deregulation, and suffering rolling blackouts.	Nearly 60 companies were allegedly involved in a price-fixing scam that precipitated California's 2000–2001 energy crisis. A coalition including the CPUC and the state's attorney general demanded $7.5 billion in consumer refunds and almost $9 billion to cover the cost of emergency energy purchases.
Concorde crash	July 25, 2000	Concorde jet bound for New York crashed shortly after taking off from the Paris airport. It was eventually determined that the plane hit a metal strip on the runway, causing debris to burst underwing fuel tanks and start the fire that brought the plane down.	Deaths: 109 people on the plane, and 4 on the ground
USS Cole attack	October 12, 2000	Terrorist bomb attack against the *USS Cole* while it refueled in the Yemeni port of Aden.	17 sailors killed and 39 injured
9/11	September 11, 2001	Terrorist attacks carried out against the World Trade Center in New York and the Pentagon in Washington, DC. Three buildings were struck by commercial airliners that had been highjacked by Al-Qaeda terrorists. A fourth airplane crashed into a field in Pennsylvania.	Death toll in the attacks: 2,749 in the World Trade Center 189 in the Pentagon 44 in the plane crash near Shanksville, PA Total deaths: 2,982

(Continues)

TABLE 17-2 Major Crises at a Glance (*Continued*)

Crisis	Date	Description	Injuries/Deaths/Damage
Anthrax attacks	September–October 2001	Bioterrorist attacks involving the mailing of anthrax spores through the U.S. Post Office. Several attacks at various locations around the country resulted in numerous exposures, infections, and fatalities. Thousands were tested and 10,000 people in the United States took a two-month course of antibiotics after possible exposure.	19 infections and 5 fatalities
Enron/Andersen	December 2001	Houston-based Enron went bankrupt in December 2001 amid revelations of hidden debt, inflated profits, and accounting tricks. Enron's auditor (Arthur Andersen) was convicted of obstruction of justice, fined the maximum amount allowable by law ($500,000), and was given five years probation.	The bankruptcy is one of the most expensive in history, generating more than $665 million in fees for lawyers, accountants, consultants, and examiners (according to the Texas Attorney General's Office). The bankruptcy plan proposes to pay most creditors about one-fifth of the nearly $70 billion they are owed in cash and stock.
Martha Stewart insider trading scandal	December 27, 2001	Martha Stewart was found guilty of conspiracy, obstruction, and two counts of lying to investigators for covering up the circumstances surrounding her Dec. 27, 2001, stock trade of biotech company ImClone. Stewart is a good friend of ImClone's former CEO, and she sold $228,000 worth of ImClone stock the day before the Food and Drug Administration rejected the company's promising new cancer drug.	Martha Stewart was sentenced to 5 months in prison, 5 months house arrest, and was fined $30,000 in July 2004.
Pedophilia crisis in the Catholic church	2002	A national study of Catholic church records found that about 4% of U.S. priests ministering from 1950 to 2002 were accused of sex abuse with a minor. The church hierarchy is also accused of systematically covering up the problem: roughly two-thirds of top U.S. Catholic leaders have allowed priests accused of sexual abuse to keep working.	4,392 clergymen—almost all priests—were accused of abusing 10,667 people, with 75% of the incidents taking place between 1960 and 1984. Sex abuse–related costs totaled $573 million as of 2002, but the overall dollar figure is much higher than reported because 14% of the dioceses and religious communities did not provide financial data, and the total did not include settlements made after 2002, such as the $85 million agreed to by the Boston Archdiocese.

WorldCom	June 25, 2002	WorldCom, the second largest long-distance provider in the United States, announced it had filed bankruptcy. As a result of an internal audit, $4 billion in expenses had been improperly categorized as capital expenditures rather than as operating expenses. The effect was to overstate cash flow and profitability. Arthur Andersen was WorldCom's accounting firm.	17,000 WorldCom employees were laid off.
SARS	November 2002 to July 2003	Severe acute respiratory syndrome (SARS) is a viral respiratory illness caused by a coronavirus. SARS was first reported in Asia in February 2003. Over the next few months, the illness spread to more than two dozen countries in North America, South America, Europe, and Asia before the SARS global outbreak of 2003 was contained.	8,098 people worldwide became sick with SARS during the 2003 outbreak. Of these, 774 died.
Columbia disaster	February 1, 2003	The Space Shuttle *Columbia* broke apart over western Texas on reentry to the earth's atmosphere. The accident was triggered by the incredible heat generated from atmospheric friction entering the interior of the left wing, causing it to melt from within until it failed and broke free. When this occurred, the shuttle spun out of control and disintegrated.	All seven astronauts aboard the shuttle died in the accident.
East Coast power outages	August 14–15, 2003	A massive power blackout that spread through the northeastern United States and southern Canada. It was the biggest power outage in U.S. history, and within three minutes, 21 power plants in the United States had shut down. At its peak, the outage reportedly affected more than 50 million people.	Three deaths were tied to the outage, and it cost New York City alone over a half billion dollars in lost revenue.

(Continues)

TABLE 17-2 Major Crises at a Glance (*Continued*)

Crisis	Date	Description	Injuries/Deaths/Damage
New York Stock Exchange crisis	August to September 2003	Problems with the corporate governance structure of the NYSE came to light when it was disclosed that Richard Grasso, NYSE president and chief operating officer, was going to receive a retirement package totaling $187.5 million. Many of the NYSE traders were angered that Grasso had extracted such a big pay package at the same time that their own paychecks were shrinking. The Securities and Exchange Commission began an inquiry and, after much pressure, Grasso resigned on September 17, 2003.	N/A
Mutual funds	October to November 2003	Putnam, the fifth biggest mutual fund in the United States, was charged with improper trading by the Securities and Exchange Commission (SEC) and Massachusetts financial regulators. The SEC was criticized for slackness in overseeing the $7 trillion mutual funds industry, resulting in calls for a crackdown on some industry practices. Of specific concern are "market timing" practices, which involve profiting from short-term trading in mutual fund shares, but can damage the value of the fund for long-term investors.	N/A
US mad cow scare	December 2003	Mad cow disease was discovered in a cow in Washington state, prompting federal officials to recall more than 10,000 pounds of meat. The meat had been shipped to eight states and Guam. The diseased cow was determined to have originally come to the United States from Canada. A number of nations banned U.S. beef imports once the case was announced.	N/A

Source: Reproduced from I. Mitroff, *Why Some Companies Emerge Stronger and Better from a Crisis*, New York: Amacom, 2005.

area of completed bioterrorism planning documents, improvements in laboratory capabilities and upgrades, and improvements in communication systems. However, the Trust felt that there were many concerns with our progress in improving our public health preparedness activities. Their concerns related to such factors as increasing state deficits and budget declines for public health, unspent federal aid, lack of preparation for pharmaceutical stockpiles, local health departments often left out of decision-making activities, and an increasing public health workforce crisis. In fiscal year 2010, the Trust presented a state preparedness evaluation process using the following 10 indicators:[10]

1. Increased or maintained level of funding for public health over previous fiscal year.
2. Sends and receives currently electronic data information.
3. Has an electronic syndromic surveillance system that can send and receive information.
4. Has the ability to activate an emergency response team within one hour.
5. Was able to activate its Emergency Operations Center at least twice in the previous fiscal year.
6. Developed at least two after-action reports from exercises or events in the previous fiscal year.
7. Requires childcare facilities to have a multihazard written emergency plan.
8. Able to identify foodborne illnesses and submit results within four days.
9. Has necessary laboratory workforce to work five 12-hour days.
10. Increased Laboratory Response Network for chemical events.

Table 17-3 shows which states meet the indicator criteria for fiscal year 2010. As can be seen, some states miss a number of criteria. Clearly a major success has been in the improvement in laboratory capability. Half the states did not meet the childcare facility requirement of a multihazard written evacuation and relocation plan. **Table 17-4** shows how many of the criteria were met by each state in fiscal year 2010—from Iowa and Montana, which only met half the criteria, to Arkansas, North Dakota, and Washington, which met all ten.

Clearly, the Trust report indicated the importance of strengthening the public health system in the United States. Strong public health leadership is required to make this happen. By the 2011 report, much deterioration in readiness was noted.[11] Key programs related to our disaster and emergency preparedness were in jeopardy of major cuts in federal and state funding.

Specifically, 51 of the 72 cities that had received Cities Readiness funds were slated for elimination. These funds had been allocated to distribute and administer vaccines and medications during emergencies. All 10 states with laboratories with high-level chemical testing status may lose their status, leaving only the laboratory at the Centers for Disease Control and Prevention (CDC) with this Level 1 funding. CDC may have difficulty responding comprehensively to nuclear, radiological, and chemical threats due to these funding cuts. Twenty-four states were also in jeopardy of losing their career epidemiology field officers. It is possible to maintain a core and basic level of preparedness and response, but our public health leadership must develop strategies to make sure this core response coverage is developed and maintained even in the shrinking economic environment.

MANAGING A CRISIS

As discussed earlier in this chapter, a crisis is an unstable time. Normal activities are disrupted. The outcomes are unpredictable. Usual agency or organizational processes are affected. Much of the writing about crisis and its effects relates to the effects of crisis on an organization and its levels of functioning. The rationale is somewhat easy to explain. Whether we are discussing the effects of a natural disaster such as a hurricane or a terrorist event, it is the various governmental, nonprofit organizations, and other community organizations that are called upon to handle these events. Thus, the management of the crisis becomes critical to its amelioration or solution. Being a prepared public health leader may also mean being an effective manager as well.

Most discussions on management of a crisis see crisis management techniques as being different during each stage of a crisis. Crisis planning has a precrisis stage; a stage in which the crisis or disaster, either natural or human-made, occurs; a recovery phase; and some return to a new level of normality phase, which can start the entire planning and reaction cycle again. In discussing some of these issues, the time between crises seems to be shortening.[12] There seem to be many more crises today than in former times. In addition, crises sometimes overlap, or sometimes one crisis leads to another crisis. Thus, multiple crises may be occurring simultaneously. Fink saw crisis management in the context of a four-stage cyclical model.[13] Stage 1 is the prodromal crisis phase, which is basically a warning or precrisis phase. The important question to be answered is

TABLE 17-3 State Preparedness Scores

States	(1) State increased or maintained level of funding for public health services from FY 2008-09 to FY 2009-10.	(2) State can currently send and receive electronic health information with health care providers.	(3) State health department has an electronic syndromic surveillance system that can report and exchange information.	(4) State health department has the ability to convene an emergency response team within 60 minutes at least twice during 2007-08.	(5) State public health department activated its EOC as part of a drill, exercise, or real incident a minimum of two times in 2007-08.	(6) State developed at least two After-Action Report/Improvement Plans (AAR/IPs) after an exercise or real incident during 2007-08.	(7) State requires all licensed childcare facilities to have a multi-hazard written evacuation and relocation plan.	(8) State is able to rapidly identify disease-causing E.coli O157:H7 and submit results by PulseNet within four working days 90% of the time during 2007-08.	(9) State has the necessary lab workforce staffing to work 12-hour days for six to eight weeks in response to an infectious disease outbreak, such as novel influenza A H1N1.	(10) State increased Laboratory Response Network for Chemical Treat (LRN-C) capability.	2010 Total Score
Alabama	✓	✓	✓	✓	✓	✓	✓	✓	✓	✓	9
Alaska	✓	✓	✓	✓	✓	✓		✓	✓	✓	8
Arizona		✓	✓	✓	✓	✓		✓	✓	✓	8
Arkansas	✓	✓	✓	✓	✓	✓	✓	✓	✓	✓	10
California		✓	✓	✓	✓	✓	✓	✓	✓	✓	9
Colorado		✓	✓	✓	✓	✓		✓	✓	✓	8
Connecticut		✓	✓	✓	✓	✓			✓	✓	8
Delaware		✓	✓	✓	✓	✓	✓	✓	✓	✓	8
DC		✓	✓	✓	✓	✓	✓		✓	✓	7
Florida		✓	✓	✓	✓	✓		✓	✓	✓	8
Georgia		✓	✓	✓	✓	✓			✓	✓	7
Hawaii	✓	✓	✓	✓		✓	✓		✓	✓	7
Idaho		✓		✓	✓	✓			✓	✓	6
Illinois		✓		✓	✓	✓		✓	✓	✓	6
Indiana	✓	✓	✓	✓	✓	✓			✓	✓	8
Iowa		✓		✓	✓	✓				✓	5
Kansas		✓		✓	✓	✓			✓	✓	6
Kentucky	✓	✓	✓	✓	✓	✓		✓	✓	✓	9
Louisiana	✓	✓	✓	✓	✓	✓		✓	✓	✓	9
Maine	✓	✓	✓	✓		✓			✓	✓	7
Maryland		✓	✓	✓	✓	✓	✓	✓	✓	✓	9
Massachusetts		✓	✓			✓	✓		✓	✓	6

State											
Michigan		✓	✓	✓	✓	✓		✓	✓	✓	8
Minnesota		✓	✓	✓	✓	✓		✓	✓	✓	8
Mississippi		✓	✓	✓	✓	✓	✓	✓	✓	✓	9
Missouri		✓	✓	✓	✓	✓			✓	✓	7
Montana	✓	✓		✓		✓				✓	5
Nebraska		✓	✓	✓	✓	✓			✓	✓	8
Nevada			✓	✓	✓	✓	✓			✓	6
New Hampshire	✓	✓	✓	✓		✓	✓		✓	✓	8
New Jersey		✓	✓	✓	✓	✓		✓	✓	✓	8
New Mexico			✓	✓	✓	✓	✓	✓		✓	6
New York		✓	✓	✓		✓	✓	✓	✓	✓	8
North Carolina		✓	✓	✓	✓	✓	✓		✓	✓	8
North Dakota	✓	✓	✓	✓	✓	✓	✓	✓	✓	✓	10
Ohio	✓	✓	✓	✓		✓	✓	✓	✓	✓	9
Oklahoma		✓	✓	✓	✓	✓		✓	✓	✓	8
Oregon		✓	✓	✓		✓	✓		✓	✓	7
Pennsylvania		✓	✓	✓	✓	✓	✓		✓	✓	8
Rhode Island		✓	✓		✓	✓			✓	✓	6
South Carolina			✓	✓	✓	✓	✓			✓	6
South Dakota	✓	✓		✓		✓			✓	✓	6
Tennessee		✓	✓	✓		✓		✓	✓	✓	7
Texas	✓	✓		✓		✓		✓	✓	✓	7
Utah		✓	✓	✓	✓	✓	✓	✓	✓	✓	9
Vermont		✓	✓	✓		✓	✓	✓	✓	✓	8
Virginia		✓	✓	✓	✓	✓	✓	✓	✓	✓	9
Washington	✓	✓	✓	✓	✓	✓	✓	✓	✓	✓	10
West Virginia	✓	✓	✓	✓		✓	✓	✓		✓	9
Wisconsin		✓	✓	✓	✓	✓	✓	✓	✓	✓	9
Wyoming	✓	✓	✓	✓		✓		✓	✓	✓	8
Total	17	43 + D.C.	40 + D.C.	44 + D.C.	44 + D.C.	48 + D.C.	25 + D.C.	29	47	49 + D.C.	

Source: Courtesy of the Trust for America's Health.

TABLE 17-4   Number of Indicators by State

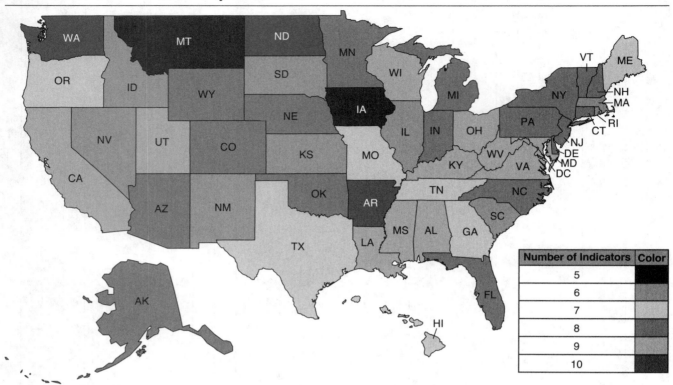

Number of Indicators	Color
5	
6	
7	
8	
9	
10	

SCORES BY STATE					
10 (3 states)	**9** (11 states)	**8** (18 states)	**7** (7 states & D.C.)	**6** (9 states)	**5** (2 states)
Arkansas	Alabama	Alaska	D.C.	Idaho	Iowa
North Dakota	California	Arizona	Georgia	Illinois	Montana
Washington	Kentucky	Colorado	Hawaii	Kansas	
	Louisiana	Connecticut	Maine	Massachusetts	
	Maryland	Delaware	Missouri	Nevada	
	Mississippi	Florida	Oregon	New Mexico	
	Ohio	Indiana	Tennessee	Rhode Island	
	Utah	Michigan	Texas	South Carolina	
	Virginia	Minnesota		South Dakota	
	West Virginia	Nebraska			
	Wisconsin	New Hampshire			
		New Jersey			
		New York			
		North Carolina			
		Oklahoma			
		Pennsylvania			
		Vermont			
		Wyoming			

Source: Courtesy of the Trust for America's Health.

whether clues to a potential crisis exist. The events of September 11, 2001, have put Americans on constant alert for the possibility of an impending human-made disaster. The increases in crises since 1979 probably mean that we need to be constantly on the lookout for warning signals.[14] Signal detection may be one of the most important components of crisis management. If public health leaders and their partners are vigilant in their signal detection efforts, many crises may be preventable.

The second stage is the acute crisis stage.[15] At this stage, the crisis has occurred. The major concern at this stage is how to control the crisis. It is at this stage that fear levels increase. Deaths may occur. Organizational structures collapse. It is here that the incident command system or its variations come into play to handle the crisis. This system is simply the model for the command, control, and coordination of a response to a community emergency that provides a well-defined structure for the coordination of the activities of community agencies and partners for dealing with the crisis.[16] These partners often include Federal Bureau of Investigation agents, local and state police, fire departments, local governmental agencies, public health leaders and their staffs, emergency medical system personnel, and many other community groups. The critical point here is that this system is basically a quasi-military model that is management based. Each participant knows his or her place in the system and his or her responsibilities in it.

The third phase in the model is the chronic crisis phase.[17] Crises do not end abruptly. They have both short-term and long-term effects. This is also the phase in which the crisis management team tries to lessen the long-term effects of the crisis. With September 11, 2001, and the anthrax letters in our background, this phase is also one in which major preparedness planning occurs to try to prevent future crises. In fact, it almost seems that there is a feedback loop at play here with the management strategies of the prodromal phase of activity. Fink talked about the importance of recovery and the need for people to get back to normal activities. An additional concern in this stage is the possible legal action that may occur as a result, which lengthens the time required for any final resolution of the crisis. An important example of the activities at this phase of a crisis included a law passed by the U.S. Congress in 2002 to establish the National Commission on Terrorist Attacks Upon the United States. President George W. Bush appointed the commission, which held hearings in 2003–2004 and presented the final 9/11 Commission Report in 2004 with recommendations for changing the way the United States handles potential terrorist activities.[18] (The recommendations were controversial and led to a number of changes in the U.S. national security system.)

The fourth and final stage in the model is the crisis resolution phase. It is hoped that the crisis is eventually resolved and life returns to some semblance of normality. However, the reality is that things are never quite the same. All crises leave some scars. New levels of adaptation must occur. Crisis resolution may actually trigger a new prodromal phase of awareness in which there is a need to prepare for other potential crisis or emergency events.

Fink also presented a model for crisis forecasting that is useful for evaluating crisis events.[19] The tool that he used is called the crisis impact scale. For any category of crisis, it should be possible to determine the potential for the crisis to escalate in intensity, the media or governmental scrutiny of the event, the effect of the event or potential event on the operation of agencies or organizations or the community, the effect of the crisis (if it is an organizational one) on the image of the organization, and the financial effect of the crisis. To develop a crisis impact scale, a score is determined for each of these variables or any others that are determined to be relevant from 0 (the lowest impact) to 10 (the highest). The scores are then added together and divided by the number of variables included in the index. The final score from 1 to 10 gives a rough index of the impact of the crisis or the potential crisis on the agency or community.

Fink took this scale and tied it to a probability scale to create something he called a crisis barometer.[20] For each crisis or potential crisis, it should be possible to tie the crisis impact score with a probability of occurrence score. The combination of these two scales can give an indication of the severity of the crisis or potential crisis. For example, a crisis such as a terrorist event would probably fall in the red zone, which would be a high score on crisis impact and probability. It could also fall in the amber zone if the probability is lowered due to good preparedness activities. Although the barometer can be a useful tool, there are some cautions to keep in mind. It is important to plan for at least one potential crisis in each of the major crisis categories presented in Table 17-1, regardless of the low probability of that crisis category leading to a disaster in the near future.[21] The public health leader can learn much about disaster preparedness from simply being ready for any possible set of circumstances coming into being.

Although a predication or the potential for a specific disaster may be useful to know, most disasters are unpredictable in terms of the time they will occur. For this reason, the crisis severity index may be more useful in that it looks at Mitroff's major crisis types presented

SEVERITY LEVELS

MAJOR CRISIS TYPES	1	2	3	4	5	6	7	8	9	10
Economic										
Informational										
Physical										
Human resource										
Reputational										
Psychopathic										
Natural disasters										

<u>Directions</u>

1. Classify specific disaster type
2. Rate specific disaster by severity level

FIGURE 17-2 Crisis Severity Matrix. *Source*: Adapted from I. Mitroff, *Managing Crises before They Happen* (New York, NY: Amacom, 2001).

in Table 17-1 and adds a severity score (see **Figure 17-2**). It is useful to develop a series of scenarios for each type of crisis at different severity levels. Then communities will be prepared for more crisis types at different severity levels. Exercise 17-1 will give you the opportunity to experiment with the crisis severity index.

TWO MODELS OF DISASTER PREPAREDNESS

To understand the management concerns related to a crisis, an exploration of the preparedness or planning phase will be made, followed by a discussion of some of the management activities related to recovery. There are many different approaches to disaster preparedness. Many of these approaches take an organizational management perspective to demonstrate the factors and procedures that need to be taken into account in preparing an agency or company for a possible crisis of whatever type. Other approaches take a more systemic view of disaster. Whatever perspective is taken, there are clearly overlaps in the approaches. This section will view an approach taken by an organizational consultant and a second approach utilized by the Disaster Management Training Programme of the United Nations.

In preparing for a possible disaster, Blythe discussed how organizations plan for potential disruptive

events in their organizations.[22] One important distinction that was made involved the need to create two different crisis teams to address different aspects of a disaster. The first is a crisis management team for which seven steps were enumerated in putting this team together. The team needs to be multidisciplinary so that it represents all aspects of the organization. As a team, they need to develop team decision-making strategies. As an organization sets up this special team, it is important to first decide the parameters by which the team will do its work. This becomes the scope of work. Second, the team needs two types of leaders—a senior-level supporter of the team's work and also a logistical person who can lead the team through the planning process in an orderly manner. The selection of members is an important third step because the team needs to represent all interests of the organization. Fourth, a planning agenda needs to be created, followed by a planning budget for the team. An important limitation related to local planning activities in health departments is that there are often no specific budgets for the agency's planning activities. For example, some local health departments have told me about the difficulty of getting local funding bodies to financially support the critical activities related to carrying out community health assessment activities. The sixth step in planning the work of the crisis planning team is establishing a schedule of regular meetings and also a schedule of how these meetings are to be run.

The crisis planning team may need to be restructured when the crisis management team has been designated. A crisis command center must be set up. Procedures for handling the crisis are included in crisis plans and crisis procedure manuals. If the crisis is primarily one that the organization handles, procedures differ from a crisis that has strong community effects. More will be said about these issues when we discuss crisis response. There is a critical need for an organization to consider the development of a humanitarian response team.[23] The crisis management team often does not have the time during a crisis to deal with all the issues related to working directly with the families of victims or injured people during a crisis. Thus, the creation of this humanitarian team is an important consideration in crisis planning and response activities.

Blythe presented a six-step preparedness process that he named the "A,E,I,O,U, and Sometimes Y" approach.[24] The A step involves the analysis of vulnerabilities. One of the tools for this activity could be the Fink crisis barometer discussed previously. This step is concerned with the determination of foreseeable risks. If a crisis type has occurred previously, procedures and strategies may already be in place for dealing with them. Reality tells us that some crises or disasters are not predictable, and a process needs to be developed to address these events. There are ways to handle different crisis types.[25–27] Even though the crisis itself is unique, certain strategies can be developed to handle a new crisis event that has not happened before. In determining vulnerabilities, all crises involve people, finances, and reputation.[28] Reputation involves the issue of blame and how the organization will be viewed relative to the way it handles these unexpected happenings.

The E step involves the evaluation of existing procedures for crisis management. A four-dimension evaluation strategy for a crisis was suggested.[29] First, there would be a determination of the foreseeable risks of a particular event. Second, a determination would be made of the types of controls that are already in place for handling this special type of risk. Third, it would then be necessary for the crisis planning team to determine if these controls could be enhanced in any way. Finally, a determination could be made of any new or additional types of controls that might be needed. Relative to the issue of controls and new methods that might be required, an organization needs to consider the issues of time needed to become prepared, money needed to implement the controls and other strategies, and the effort that these activities may require. One important strategy that is often used today to check these controls and strategies involves the use of exercises, drills, and other simulations.

The I step refers to the identification of new primary and secondary prevention preparedness procedures. This step involves a determination of types of possible incidents. For example, it is possible to use Table 17-1 as a guide. Next, ways and strategies to prevent these events are determined (primary prevention). A good example of this relates to airport security measures. Because it is possible to screen all passengers for airlines prior to entering a plane, the chances of an explosion in the air due to a passenger carrying explosives on his or her person is greatly diminished. Secondary prevention activities involve the creation of strategies for what happens if a crisis occurs so that further damage is prevented. If we take the anthrax letter example, primary prevention activities would entail the screening of all mail in the mailroom before it is delivered to the staff of the organization. Secondary prevention techniques might be to give all staff biobags if a suspected letter is delivered to a staff member.

Next, it is important for the crisis planning committee to "organize" the plan (the O step). The issue of the relationship between the culture and values of an organization and the ways that the various controls fit that culture is an important consideration.[30] It is with this step that the issue of educating and training the staff of the agency becomes critical. The additional concern of the implementation of controls as well as the person who will be responsible for monitoring that implementation needs to be determined. The importance of values clarification in an organization is a necessary early step in the process. The values clarification activity can be used by organization leaders to work with staff to modify the organizational structure to accommodate these new crises protocols. It may well be necessary to modify the mission and vision of the organization to accommodate these changes. For example, a simple change in vision might be made. If the vision of the local health department is "Healthy people in healthy communities," it can be changed to "Healthy people in healthy and safe communities."

The U in the preparedness process refers to utilization of the plan. Utilization involves the creation or change of the crisis planning team into a crisis management team. It is here that the use of all those drills and tabletop exercises becomes important as a way to determine readiness. The debriefing and the lessons learned activities are important here. As it is not possible to determine when and if a disaster will occur, these drills and exercises need to become a routine part of the activities of the agency or organization. Crisis leaders may be different people from those who lead in non-crisis times. Some leaders handle stress better than others. It is important to determine who the right leaders may be. Leadership is a complex phenomenon in that some leaders shine in crisis yet seem to be less effective in other times. An interesting example can be taken from Rudolph Giuliani, who was mayor of New York City during the crisis of September 2001.[31] Although there had been criticism of Giuliani as an effective mayor prior to September 11, 2001, most people agree that he became effective as a crisis leader during and after the terrorist events of September 2001.

The final planning step in the Blythe model refers to the need to scrutinize "yourselves," the Y step. This involves the need to check at regular internals how well prepared the organization is for a potential crisis. It seems that the further away an organization is in time, the less the organization seems to be concerned about a potential crisis. What September 11, 2001, taught us is that a crisis can occur at any time. It is always necessary to monitor our organizations to determine preparedness and readiness. This approach needs to become a critical part of the culture of the organization. The top management of our organizations need to support these preparedness activities if they are to occur. Without this support, the plans will remain on the shelf, and preparedness will not become a reality.

A second disaster preparedness model that relates more to communities and countries was developed by the Disaster Management Training Programme (DMTP) in 1991 as a joint management effort of the United Nations Department of Humanitarian Affairs and the United Nations Development Programme with the aid of the Disaster Management Program of the University of Wisconsin.[32] The purpose of the training module was to provide a framework for various countries and institutions to obtain the means to increase their capacity in emergency management in a development context. The model that was developed provides an excellent contrasting model to the Blythe model just presented. The framework on which the disaster preparedness approach is built contains nine components, as can be seen in **Figure 17-3**. Disaster preparedness was defined in the training program as a methodology to minimize the adverse effects of a hazard or crisis event through the utilization of effective precautionary actions, rehabilitation strategies, and

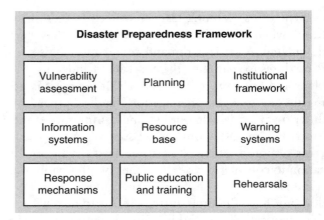

FIGURE 17-3 Disease Management Framework.
Source: Reproduced from *United Nations Disaster Management Training Programme, Disaster Preparedness,* 2nd ed. New York: Author.

recovery approaches that ensure a timely, appropriate, and effective organizational structure for the delivery of relief and assistance following a disaster.

Before exploring this model, it is useful to put it in a public health perspective. In 2001, the CDC enumerated the key elements of a public health preparedness program. These elements included:[33]

- An emergency preparedness plan to be in place prior to the emergency
- A hazards analysis of the types of events that might occur in a given community
- A plan of emergency activities in advance to ensure a coordinated response to the consequences of a potentially credible event
- A foundation and capability necessary for effective response to potentially credible emergencies
- The development of health surveillance, epidemiological investigation methods, laboratory capability, and diagnostic procedures to evaluate an emergency when it occurs
- The ability to implement the planned response quickly and effectively (consequence management)
- The stage of recovery from the emergency incident

Leadership is clearly required to develop this state of readiness.

The first of the nine components of the DMTP disaster preparedness framework involves the need for vulnerability assessment and analysis.[34] Blythe also pointed out that this is an important preparedness component.[35] Vulnerability is a determination of the probability of certain types of risks. It is a hazards analysis in the rubric of public health. It requires a continuous effort by public health professionals and other community leaders to assess the risks and hazards that a community faces in order to determine how these potential hazards and risks should be handled. Clearly, it is important to link vulnerability assessments with development or response interventions. These assessments will help community, state, and national leaders understand the utility of a national or local approach to given categories of emergencies. Although local decision makers are pretty aware of the types of crises most probable in their local jurisdiction, they may not be aware of terrorist or biological threats that could affect their communities from an outside source. Bioterrorism and other unexpected events will often require state, national, or even international approaches to preparedness and response. At a local level, vulnerability assessments often provide clues to the types of disaster plans that need to be developed.

The planning component of the framework is also common to all disaster preparedness models. It should be clear that written plans are necessary to be successfully prepared. People need to not only know the rules, but also know how to act during a potential emergency. Their roles and activities during an emergency need to be well defined. The written plan needs a set of clearly stated objectives; it should reflect the systematic sequence of activities that will occur during a response to a crisis, the assignment of specific tasks and responsibilities, and an implementation strategy to ensure that the objectives of the plan are met during an emergency. **Table 17-5** shows the typical outline of a disaster plan. If the plan is to be a community-based one, then the planners need to include representatives from all the collaborating organizations that will be involved in the response phase of the emergency. If we follow Mitroff's advice from earlier in this chapter, it is necessary to keep in mind that multiple plans may be needed for different types of crises and emergencies. Different collaborators may be involved in different types of disaster-planning activities. All plans need to be revisited after an emergency and recovery. In addition, the plans should be tested using exercises and drills that are based on the plan, and the plans should be revisited on a regular basis to determine if relevance still exists.

The third component of the model relates to the institutional framework that is put in place to respond to a crisis. A company or agency will probably develop a crisis management team model to respond to the emergency. There is also a need for a humanitarian response team to work with the families of the injured or deceased. At a country level, there are, of course, different institutional arrangements that are created. In the United States, the general model used is the incident command system. This model will be discussed in the next section of this chapter. However, the model does vary from state to state, and different names may be used for the institutional arrangements that are created. Suffice it to say at this point that, senior levels of government at the local, state, or national level need to sanction whatever response model is selected. A focal point needs to be determined to ensure effective emergency preparedness and responses as well as to guarantee that response activities are coordinated. Whatever institutional arrangement is generated, roles and responsibilities need to reflect the expertise needed to address the emergency, the roles and responsibilities of all crisis management personnel must be clearly defined, and these roles and responsibilities have to be appropriate for the crisis being addressed. To create a more uniform system, the National Incident Management System (NIMS) was announced in 2004 to develop the nation's first standardized management approach to coordinate federal, state, and local lines of government for incident response.

The next component is an important one for public health and is always a part of any public health activity. It is information that drives the public health agenda. Information systems are based on community assessment methods, scientific research epidemiologic surveillance, laboratory diagnosis, demographics, and so on. The core function of assessment is clearly one function that public health leaders must carry out on a day-to-day basis even during emergency situations. Assessment techniques related to hazards and risk analysis, crisis monitoring, and so on are all critical to public health preparedness. The development of early warning systems and leadership skills related to signal detection strategies are also important information mechanisms. Another important dimension of information is the need to share it in a disaster situation with other community partners.[36] There are complexities related to this information sharing, and there is a need to work out methods and strategies to expedite the process.

The fifth dimension of the disaster preparedness framework relates to the resource base. It is always important to determine the resources necessary to handle terrorism, in terms of organizational capacity issues or as a community or country planning a disaster preparedness program. A number of factors need to be considered. First, what are the costs of a potential crisis for the organization, community, or country? At a community level, it is important to develop some type of crisis or disaster relief funding. The issue of how to access pharmaceutical stockpiles needs to be addressed. Costs of these drugs

TABLE 17-5   Typical Structure of a Disaster Plan

Introduction	Legislative authority
	Related documents
The aim, definitions, and abbreviations	Topography
The country (region, state)	
	Climate
	Demography
	Industry
	Government organization
The threat	History
	Natural events (by type)
	Industrial accidents (by type)
Command and coordination	Powers and responsibilities at each level
	Command authorities and posts
	Description and role of emergency service
Planning groups	Arrangements for sectoral planning (such as medical, transport, and communications)
External assistance	Arrangements and authority for requesting assistance from outside the planning area
Emergency operations centers	
Activation of organizations	Warning systems
	Receipt and dissemination of warnings
Operational information	
Counterdisaster organizations	Government departments
	Defense ministry
	Local government
	Voluntary organizations
	Arrangements for liaison
Administration, financial procedures, supply	Emergency purchasing procedures
	Powers for requisitioning
Public information	Announcements (requiring action)
	Information releases
	Emergency broadcasting
	Multilanguage broadcasts
Subplans	Communications, police, fire services, medical, rescue, welfare, housing, public works, transport, power, registration, and tracing service

Source: Reproduced from *United Nations Disaster Management Training Programme, Disaster Preparedness*, 2nd ed. New York: Author.

need to be considered as well. The question of insurance coverage is another possible issue in disaster relief. In fact, the whole process of public health preparedness has both apparent and hidden costs. Similar to the issue of stockpiling is the issue of stockpiling food reserves as well as drug reserves. You can undertake a simple experiment with your community disaster partners if you are currently involved in such an effort by having your crisis team determine whether your community has a resource base strategy for a potential disaster.

The UN's Disaster Management Training Programme course next examines the dimension of whether warning systems are in place. The critical issue here relates to whether a command center has been set up with telephones, cell phones, computers, fax machines, backup electrical generators, televisions, and battery-operated radios. Is there a community-wide communications system? Are first responders trained? Are automobiles, trucks, ambulances, and other vehicles designated to work during the crisis immediately accessible? How will the public be warned? Has a surge capacity protocol been developed in case more hospital or medical services are needed for a given crisis? It is important to have alternate communications systems available for the police, fire department, military, Federal Bureau of Investigation, and any other critical governmental network support. There is also the need for redundancy in the provision of communication technologies in case of failures in a given system and the overall vulnerability of public communication networks.[37] There should always be a concern that a terrorist group might attack and immobilize the communication systems first.

The seventh dimension of the disaster preparedness framework relates to response mechanisms. Response is covered in more detail in the next section of this chapter. For now, it is enough to point out that response mechanisms need to be developed for a variety of hazards and need to include at a minimum the following mechanisms:

1. Evacuation procedures
2. Search and rescue procedures
3. Security procedures for affected geographic areas
4. Assessment and crisis management teams
5. Activation of public health and emergency medicine procedures
6. Activation of the various distribution systems (e.g., food and drugs)
7. Preparation of emergency reception centers and shelters
8. Activation of emergency programs for airports and other public transportation systems

The next dimension of the model relates to the importance of public education and training. Not only does the public health workforce need to be trained, but the public also needs to be prepared. There are many different approaches to the issue of education and training. For example, there are many computer-based training courses on emergency preparedness

and response available for the public health workforce today. Face-to-face training and continuing education opportunities are available for public health and other health professionals. For example, the state of Illinois Department of Public Health holds an annual bioterrorism summit each summer to present cutting-edge speakers discussing emergency preparedness and response. The summit also has breakout sessions to teach the participants about new program strategies as well as new preparedness tools and techniques. Public education of children in schools is one way to train the public. Offering extension programs through colleges and universities is another approach to distributing important information. Public service announcements can also be used to educate the public.

The final dimension of the framework relates to rehearsals, which are important to prepare the organization for potential disasters. Systemwide drills and exercises are also critical. An important national exercise was conducted in May 2003. The exercise, called TOPOFF 2 (acronym for Top Officials), was a five-day national exercise with Canadian partners to measure and analyze a response to terrorist attacks on Seattle and Chicago. Specifically, the exercise created a simulation based on a radiological device explosion in Seattle and a covert biological attack in Chicago. Twenty-five federal agencies in partnership with the American Red Cross were involved in the exercise. Some conclusions from the exercise were reported in a press release from the United States Department of Homeland Security in December 2003. One conclusion related to the necessity of improving communications, coordination, and connectivity during the response phase to a mass casualty incident. The need to collect information and the need to coordinate medical information placed a heavy burden on state and local authorities. A major positive finding was the ability of Chicago hospitals to carry out the requirements of the exercise on such a wide scale. Another finding of the exercise was the difficulty in disseminating a unified message during a crisis. Clearly, there is a need to improve communication systems. The exercise also helped agencies explore better ways to work together. Finally, the exercise pointed to difficulties related to resource allocation among federal, state, and local entities.

These two disaster preparedness frameworks provide excellent approaches to dealing with emergency preparedness concerns at the organization or agency level as well as at the community, state, or national level.

PUBLIC HEALTH RESPONSE

When an emergency occurs, planning activities have hopefully been completed. Public health response is about management strategies and addressing the emergency in a constructive way. Blythe discussed the immediate aftermath phase of a crisis.[38] The effects have to be determined quickly. It is best to imagine that the worst has happened and then figure out what needs to be done. The crisis management team and the crisis structure have to be called into action. Plans have to be implemented to handle the events over the first 72 hours. This has to occur even prior to receiving the information on what happened specifically, how bad the event or events were, what has been done and what needs to be done, and the ultimate question of whether the crisis can escalate.

Ten immediate actions need to be taken in any crisis:[39]

1. Evaluation of potential for continuing danger
2. Verification of the availability and quantity of emergency vehicles
3. Availability of information to determine the severity of the emergency
4. The cordoning off of the incident area and its perimeter, if appropriate
5. Implementation of a notification process for the families of the wounded or deceased
6. Implementation of strategies to prevent escalation of the crisis
7. Following of protocol for notification of individuals to assist in the emergency
8. Implementation of communication procedures for the media
9. Determination of the legal and regulatory compliance process
10. Contact of any specialists that may be required

When a crisis occurs, it is important to contain the crisis as soon as possible. In an organization, this involves the activation of the crisis management team and a crisis command center. At a community level, the activation of the incident command system is comparable to what occurs at the organization level. The community response activity will be discussed further later. What the crisis management group should do is determine and accurately document the emerging facts of the event. The development of a log of evolving facts itemizes what the emerging fact is, the time each fact was seen and verified, and the person who discovered it. The crisis team should also prioritize its activities with the determination of who takes the lead on addressing

any priority. There should also be a determination of an end time for a priority to be carried out. The goal of all response activities is to restore order as soon as possible.

Whereas preparedness is a planning and proactive stance, response is about reaction. Public health's involvement in response has often been tied to the issues of emerging infections and bioterrorism. Landesman discussed nine specific roles for public health in response situations:[40]

1. Developing and utilizing of multidisciplinary protocols for collaborative activities between public health agencies and their community and health agency partners
2. Determining the specific symptoms of various emerging infections and activating public health surveillance systems
3. Increasing laboratory capacity, upgrading public health laboratories, and developing communication criteria for a laboratory response capability that distributes information on suspected bioterrorism agents to the appropriate sources
4. Developing methods to deliver diagnostic and bioterrorism treatment protocols to the medical service community
5. Making sure response protocols are in place to reduce morbidity and mortality from a crisis event by stockpiling antibiotics and other drugs, using quarantine procedures if necessary, delivering medical services as necessary with surge capacity procedures available, using humanitarian notification procedures, and implementing a well-considered crisis communication network
6. Developing, testing, expanding, and implementing the Health Alert Network (national network to link state and local public health agencies and community and governmental partners through the Internet to get information on crisis events quickly)
7. Implementing procedures for handling victims
8. Developing training programs for the public health workforce
9. Implementing procedures for the resolution of public health legal issues relating to disasters

In the United States, the major process for response is tied to the activation of an incident command system or a number of variations of it. The models are built on a military approach to the handling of a crisis. A number of online courses are available to managers and leaders on the incident command system from the Department of Homeland Security and the Federal

Emergency Management Agency, or FEMA.[41] The following comments on the system come from the Basic ICS course offered online. The incident command system is an organizational structure utilizing command, control, and coordination approaches to response. The ICS model provides a means to coordinate the efforts of individual agencies (for our purpose, public health agencies as well) as the system works toward the primary goal of stabilizing the incident and protecting life, property, and the environment. The ICS has proved over time to be effective in the response to hazardous materials (HazMat) incidents, planned events, natural hazards response, law enforcement incidents such as potential riots outside a political convention facility, lack of a comprehensive resource management strategy, fires, multiple casualty incidents, multijurisdictional and multiagency incidents, air, water, and ground transportation incidents, search and rescue missions, pest eradication programs, and private sector emergency management programs.

As can be seen in **Figure 17-4**, the basic structure of the ICS system has five components. The command function is directed by the incident commander, whose job it is to manage the response to the crisis event. For many incidents, the commander is the senior first responder to the event. Because ICS is a management system with the roles and responsibilities of all participants well determined, it is worthwhile to list 12 of the management process activities involved in the system:

1. Establishment of command structures and procedures
2. Assurance of responder safety
3. Assessment of incident priorities
4. Determination of operational objectives
5. Development and implementation of an incident action plan
6. Development of an organizational structure appropriate to the incident

7. Maintenance of a manageable span of control for all levels of the system
8. Management of incident resources
9. Coordination of overall emergency activities
10. Coordination of partnership activities
11. Authorization and management of the communication of information
12. Maintainence of cost and financial records for the incident

The second component of the basic ICS is the planning section, which collects, evaluates, disseminates, and utilizes the information about the development of the incident and the status of resources. This section may also develop the incident action plan that lays out the response activities and the utilization of resources for a specified time period. The third component is the operations section, which has the responsibility for carrying out the response activities described in the incident action plan. This section also directs and coordinates all ICS operations, assists the incident commander in the development of response goals for the incident, requests needed resources from the commander, and keeps the commander informed about the state of the response operation and the use of resources.

The next component in the basic structure is the logistics section, which has the responsibility for providing facilities, services, personnel, and materials to operate the requested equipment for the incident. The logistics section often has a medical unit to provide care for any incident responder who is injured. The final component of the system is the finance/administration section, which is responsible for tracking incident costs and reimbursement accounting. The five components of the ICS can be and often are expanded with the appropriate delegation of authority.

There is much discussion these days about an expanded model of ICS called *unified command*. This system brings together the incident commanders from

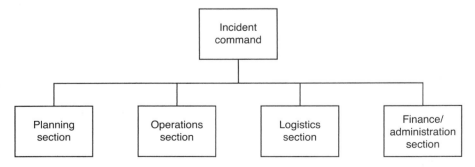

FIGURE 17-4 Incident Command System Organization.

all major organizations in the community or the state for the purpose of coordinating the response to a crisis event. This coordination does not preclude separate ICS activities related to specific jurisdictions. The unified command links the various ICS activities and allows the commanders to make consensual decisions. The unified command becomes responsible for the overall response and the overall management of the event.

A PERSPECTIVE ON FAMILIES

Even though it often appears that the public has little respect for elected officials or the people who work for governmental agencies, during a crisis the public immediately turns to these people who serve the public.

Crises of all types disrupt both family and community life activities. Especially since September 11, 2001, families keep asking public health and other officials about how to keep their families safe. Public health leaders now find themselves addressing not only health and safety issues but also issues related to mental health and distress. A critical second set of questions that the prepared public health leader has to address is the set of concerns related to community and family preparedness for emergencies. This section will address some of these issues, as they are critical to promoting the health and welfare of all residents of our communities. Case Study 17-B presents the observations of Linda Landesman, a public health leader who worked in New York City and dealt with these critical public health issues on a day-to-day basis.

A Public Health Practice Quiz for Linda Landesman

Case Study 17-B

1. What is unique about the public health orientation to the psychological consequences of terrorism in contrast to the mental health orientation to these problems?

Public health interventions are aimed at protecting or intervening with the community, while mental health is interested in improving the community by focusing on the clinical picture that the individual, family, or group presents. Public health actions often follow a careful look at data or science to determine the best intervention. Only in the most recent years has the mental health profession moved toward a population-based approach. This has been driven, in part, by broadening their management practice because of the interface with managed care companies who examine mental health costs by monitoring data.

With sophisticated data systems, it is possible to identify cohorts of patients and predict what their response to terrorism might be. With inherently elevated levels of depression in the U.S. population, we know those who were depressed before the event and who develop anxiety after a terrorism event. Clinicians have learned from the public health approach and can now plan better by looking at such data. The combined use of the World Trade Center Health Registry (Registry) is a good example. The Registry, organized by the New York City Department of Health and Mental Hygiene (NYCDOHMH), tracks 70,000 people: NYC residents near the Trade Center site, those present when the Twin Towers collapsed, and emergency responders to the disaster. With continued financial support, NYCDOHMH will monitor this group over the next two decades. When analyzing the data collected through the registry, NYCDOHMH found that these residents and emergency workers reported "symptoms of psychological distress" at a level 60% higher than the New York City average.[1] These data will be used by both the public health and mental health communities to determine the type and number of interventions needed. Mental health practitioners will organize and deliver the identified clinical services.

2. How can mental health and public health leaders work together to provide a more unified approach to mental health issues in terrorism?

As a practicing clinician, I found that the gap between hospital and prehospital mental health services was what initially interested me in emergency preparedness. In the early 1980s, with the formation of ASTM Committee F-30, the first national EMS consensus standards development activity, Blanche Newhall and I fought to have a single paragraph requiring mental health services included in the EMS standard for disasters. We were part of a small voice that understood the need for public health and mental health professionals to be integrated within the team that prepared for and responded to emergencies. Since then, many U.S. disasters and considerable research have demonstrated that major emergencies have long-term mental health impacts. Yet it wasn't until terrorism struck on American shores that there was a true societal interest in intervening in more than a cursory, time-limited way. Even so, mental health is often an afterthought.

In some states, mental health is organized as a human services agency; in other states, it is part of the department of health; and in others, public health is a stand-alone agency. As a result, mental health and public health are often not well integrated into emergency response until there is a disaster and the community understands the need to include these disciplines in the response and recovery. Dedicated effort is needed for a unified approach to mental health issues in terrorism. By partnering in their planning efforts, mental health and public health leaders can enhance their effectiveness. This might be accomplished by including each other in the organizational structure of response activities. As an example, mental health could be asked to provide behavioral services when a point of dispensing site is established for mass prophylaxis. Public health could be asked to participate in the organization of victim assistance centers established following a community emergency. By working together and building upon established relationships, the human service elements of a response can be strengthened.

3. How closely are public health agencies working with mental health agencies on emergency preparedness and response activities?

There are a variety of models that exist in practice. Some communities, such as New York City, have merged their public health and mental health departments. This organizational structure facilitates a close working relationship, including mental health as a component of the health department's incident command structure and as a full partner in the DOHMH-based emergency operations center. This integration and the community's ability to organize and provide services are enhanced by the wealth of mental health providers in the metropolitan New York City region. In contrast, many areas of the country have an insufficient number of mental health providers, even for commonly occurring problems. So these communities are dependent on outside resources following emergencies.

Despite the deluge of external resources that occurs to stricken communities, it is best if the planning process calls for the provision of emergency mental health services solely by local mental health providers. Following the events of September 11, 2001, mental health and public health professionals in the metropolitan region of New York City saw that many who sought service in the early days of that response were best served by providers who had an extensive understanding of local resources. Despite a plethora of providers who came to New York to help, providers and administrators didn't have the time to provide training or credentialing for those coming from outside the region. Many of the early needs following a disaster are for concrete services, so providers need to know which agencies provide which services and whom to call to make nonfrustrating, helpful referrals. The first task of a social worker new to an agency is to organize a list of resources and contacts. Even if that list is prepared in advance, how does an outsider tell a victim how to get there if landmarks are destroyed?

However, many areas in the country do not have enough mental health providers. Without local capacity to provide even core mental health services, communities are dependent on outside personnel to meet postcrisis demand and need. In all states, the American Red Cross has mental health units trained to conduct assessments of the mental health needs of a community following a disaster. Plans in these regions should include coordination with these groups.

4. What are the political ramifications of family involvement in community emergency planning activities?

Family involvement can only improve a community's preparedness efforts. Recent surveys suggest that citizens do not believe that their government will take care of them following an emergency. If citizens are more knowledgeable about the efforts that are in place and understand what various responding agencies will do in an emergency and what, as individuals, they should do to protect themselves and their families, then citizens are likely to feel more confident and to be more cooperative with government officials. Furthermore, community preparedness can be enhanced when responsive government adapts or expands plans so they map with community expectations and needs. None of this, however, is easy. It requires all to listen carefully and to be open to changing behavior and to taking on new tasks. Some communities will be more successful at cooperative planning than others.

The randomness of disasters makes any of us a potential victim. It is only human nature to want to protect one's family during these times, and families are a natural support system for each other following a disaster. Having a family disaster plan in place can provide peace of mind, enabling public health professionals to report to and remain at work for long shifts if necessary. At a minimum, family disaster plans should include all members knowing where to go, having an out-of-state contact to call, having adequate emergency supplies, and ensuring that elderly or infirm relatives have redundant supports who will look after them in the event of an emergency. As a collaborative, public health and the emergency management community should encourage the development of a personal/family disaster plan.

(*Continues*)

5. Should we train community volunteers to work in community crisis response activities?

When a crisis happens, there is always a spontaneous arrival of volunteers who want to help. By definition, disasters are emergencies that can't be managed with routine resources, so planning for what is known as "surge capacity" will improve a community's response. It is beneficial to have an advance structure in place that organizes that effort both to maximize the volunteer resource and to provide the volunteers with meaningful and constructive opportunities to assist their communities.

Once a crisis has begun, no one has time to train volunteers on how to be helpful. Furthermore, a procedure is needed to manage all who arrive on the scene. Without oversight, multiple problems can complicate a response, ranging from injured volunteers to looting, such as that which occurred in the shops under the World Trade Center and in the surrounding restaurants and stores that were abandoned during the collapse. It is often referred to as a "disaster within a disaster."

The Federal Emergency Management Agency (FEMA) and National Voluntary Organizations Active in Disaster (NVOAD), a membership group of national nonprofit organizations, have worked to formalize management training for disaster volunteers. Organizations such as the Volunteer Center National Network connect unaffiliated volunteers with the needs of a stricken community.

One of the initiatives through the U.S. Department of Homeland Security has been the recruitment and training of volunteers at all levels. Through collaborative planning, the Citizens Corps mobilizes local citizens to help their communities respond and recover from disasters. The Medical Reserve Corps (MRC) was established to recruit local medical providers who can augment local public health capacity during large-scale emergencies. The MRC has attracted practicing and retired physicians, nurses, and other health professionals as well as other citizens interested in health issues.

Local community leaders develop their own MRC units and identify the duties of the MRC volunteers according to specific community needs. For example, MRC volunteers may deliver necessary public health services during a crisis, assist emergency response teams with patients, and provide care directly to those with less serious injuries and other health-related issues. MRC volunteers may also assist with ongoing public health needs (e.g., immunizations, screenings, health and nutrition education, and volunteering in community health centers and local hospitals).

The decision to strengthen the response system through volunteers is not without complications. If the expectation is that a community will always look to volunteers to meet its health and safety needs in emergencies, it is easier for governments to maintain a staffing level at or below that needed to provide daily services. The trend toward smaller government could translate into never providing sufficient personnel to meet a community's needs. Without core capacity, organizations cannot provide surge capacity in times of emergency. Furthermore, citizen volunteer groups attract many of the same folks—the medical personnel in disaster medical assistance teams and emergency medicine or the staff of emergency medical services, the fire services, and the National Guard are often the same people. While redundancy is desired in disaster preparedness, this type of redundancy is a game of musical chairs. If a call-up is needed, someone will be shorthanded when the same volunteers are listed for more than one organization. While this is more likely to occur in smaller communities, an examination of the MRC volunteers in our biggest cities will also demonstrate this inherent risk.

Linda Young Landesman, DrPH, MSW
New York, New York

References

1. M. Santora, "Thousands Near 9/11 Attack Reported Ill Effect, US Says." *New York Times*, Nov. 23, 2004.

In a press release from the Columbia University National Center for Disaster Preparedness at the Mailman School of Public Health in 2004, the researchers reported a crisis of confidence in the federal government's ability to protect Americans.[42] The study was commissioned in July 2004. Specifically, about three-quarters of Americans are concerned that another terrorist attack is coming and think that the federal government will not be able to protect local areas from these attacks (a drop to 53% confidence in 2004 from 62% confidence in 2003). Only 39% of Americans think that the healthcare system is ready to respond to a biological, chemical, or nuclear attack. In addition to this lower confidence, 63% of families in the United States do not have a basic emergency plan. An interesting finding in this study was related to the U.S. transportation systems. There is more confidence in security at airports than there is at other types of transportation sites. It was also found that 59% of the population will not evacuate immediately during, or preparatory to, a crisis even if told to do so by officials. A large percentage of parents (48%) said that they were not aware of the emergency preparedness plans at the schools of their children. In fact, only 21% of residents of the United States seem to know about the emergency preparedness and response plans that exist in their communities.

There is growing concern about the psychological effect of crises of all kinds. When lives are disrupted, stress of all kinds occurs. Some people are more resilient and seem able to deal with unusual events better than others. Leaders clearly need to show this resilience.[43] The role of public health in addressing these psychological issues is to help restore order so that people can function at a psychologically and socially acceptable level as quickly as possible.[44] Public health leaders are also critical in the reduction of the occurrence and severity of adverse mental health outcomes caused by natural and human-made disasters. The methodology for doing this is complex because of the separation of mental and physical health domains in our society in the past. It has become increasingly clear that public health leaders and mental health professionals need to work together to address these critical concerns for community health. Another important public health role related to aiding the community toward speedy recovery and prevention of long-term problems is through health education about normal stress reactions to crisis and how to handle this stress.[45]

In late October 2001, a group of disaster mental health experts from six countries were brought together in Virginia to address the effect of early psychological interventions within four weeks of a disaster event to define best practices in understanding and working with the people affected by mass violence or disaster.[46] Early intervention strategies were defined as preparation, planning, education, training, and service provision evaluation. The conference participants agreed that the best efforts to carry out early mental health assessment and intervention should be conducted relative to the hierarchy of needs related to survival, safety, security, food, shelter, health concerns, mental health triage for emergencies, orientation to emergency services available in the local area, humanitarian communication concerns, and other psychological first aid methods. Psychological first aid includes such techniques as protecting survivors from further harm, reducing physiological arousal, mobilizing support for those most in need, keeping families together, providing information, and using risk communication techniques.

Some of the best practice concerns for mental health include the following:

- Early, brief, and focused psychotherapeutic intervention
- Cognitive behavioral approaches to reduce stress
- Early intervention in the form of one-on-one discussion of events that have occurred (may have limited effect over time)

It is clear that this whole area of psychological intervention needs to be further explored and developed. There are questions related to the effectiveness of many techniques that are currently used. This evolving area needs testing and further development. **Table 17-6**, from the report of the conference, is a good guide to timing of early interventions on the basis of our present state of knowledge. The table looks at interventions from the preincident phase to the return-to-life phase (two weeks to two years after the event).

CAPABILITIES AND COMPETENCIES

Leaders search for tools and strategies to help them in their crisis preparedness, response, and recovery activities. The CDC has provided funding to state, local, and territorial public health departments through the Public Health Emergency Preparedness Cooperative Agreement (PHEP). Despite this funding, threats seem to be expanding and funding is limited. Because of these major challenges, the new PHEP cooperative agreement, which took effect in August 2011, implemented a process for the definition of a set of preparedness capabilities to assist health departments in their preparedness strategic planning.[47] Fifteen preparedness capabilities were defined in six domains.

Domain 1—Community Resilience
    Capability 1—Community Preparedness
    Capability 2—Community Recovery
Domain 2—Incident Management
    Capability 3—Emergency Operations Coordination
Domain 3—Information Management
    Capability 4—Emergency Public Information and Warning
    Capability 5—Information Sharing
Domain 4—Surge Management
    Capability 6—Facility Management
    Capability 7—Mass Care
    Capability 8—Medical Surge
    Capability 9—Volunteer Management
Domain 5—Countermeasures and Mitigation
    Capability 10—Medical Countermeasure Dispensing

TABLE 17-6 Guidance for Timing of Early Interventions

Phase	Preincident	Impact (0–48 hours)	Rescue (0–1 week)	Recovery (1–4 weeks)	Return to Life (2 weeks–2 years)
Goals	Preparation, improve coping	Survival communication	Adjustment	Appraisal and planning	Reintegration
Behavior	Preparation vs. denial	Fight/flight, freeze, surrender, etc.	Resilience vs. exhaustion	Grief, reappraisal, intrusive memories, narrative formation	Adjustment vs. phobias, PTSD, avoidance, depression, etc.
Role of All Helpers	Prepare, train, gain knowledge	Rescue, protect	Orient, provide for needs	Respond with sensitivity	Continue assistance
Role of Mental Health Professionals	**Prepare** Train Gain knowledge Collaborate Inform and influence policy Set structures for rapid assistance	**Basic Needs** Establish safety, security, survival Ensure food and shelter Provide orientation Facilitate communication with family, friends, and community Assess the environment for ongoing threat/toxin	**Needs Assessment** Assess current status, how well needs are being addressed Recovery environment What additional interventions are needed for: • Group • Population • Individual	**Monitor the Recovery Environment** Observe and listen to those most affected Monitor the environment for toxins Monitor past and ongoing threats Monitor services that are being provided	**Treatment** Reduce or ameliorate symptoms or improve functioning via • Individual, family, and group psychotherapy • Pharmacotherapy • Short-term or long-term hospitalization

Role of Mental Health Professionals

Psychological First Aid

Support and be a "presence" for those who are most distressed

Keep families together, and facilitate reunion with loved ones

Provide information and education (i.e., services), foster communication

Protect survivors from further harm

Reduce physiological arousal

Monitoring the Impact on Environment

Observe and listen to those most affected

Monitor the environment for stressors

Technical Assistance, Consultation, and Training

Improve capacity of organizations and caregivers to provide what is needed to reestablish community structure, foster family recovery and resilience, and safeguard the community

Provide services to:

- Relevant organizations
- Other caregivers and responders
- Leaders

Triage

Clinical assessment

Refer when indicated

Identify vulnerable, high-risk individuals and groups

Emergency hospitalization or outpatient treatment

Outreach and Information Dissemination

Make contact with and identify people who have not requested services (i.e., "therapy by walking around")

Outreach and Information Dissemination

Inform people about different services, coping, recovery process, etc. (e.g., by using established community structures, fliers, Web sites)

Fostering Resilience and Recovery

Social interactions

Coping skills training

Education about stress response, traumatic reminders, coping, normal vs. abnormal functioning, risk factors, services

Group and family support

Foster natural social support

Look after the bereaved

Repair organizational fabric

Operational debriefings, when this is standing procedure in responder organizations

Spiritual support

Source: Reproduced from National Institute of Mental Health, *Mental Health and Mass Violence*, NIH Pub 02-5138 (Washington, DC: Government Printing Office).

Capability 11—Medical Material Management and Distribution

Capability 12—Non-Pharmaceutical Interventions

Capability 13—Responder Safety and Health

Domain 6—Biosurveillance

Capability 14—Public Health Laboratory Testing

Capability 15—Public Health Surveillance and Epidemiological Surveillance

These six domains and capabilities are to be aligned with the 10 essential public health services as well as capability targets determined by the Department of Homeland Security.

The second stream of recent thinking on preparedness relates to the issue of competencies for middle-level public health workers. The Association of Schools of Public Health and the CDC tackled this issue and developed through a modified Delphi technique a core competency model for preparedness and response.[48] **Figure 17-5** shows the model that was developed with the four competency domains of model leadership, communicate and manage information, plan for and improve practice, and protect worker health and safety.

It is important to create a crosswalk between the capabilities paradigm and the core competencies framework. Papke of the Mid-America Center for Public Health Practice at the University of Illinois at Chicago School of Public Health developed a crosswalk.[49] **Table 17-7** shows the crosswalk between the two models. This table demonstrates clearly the strong relationship between capabilities and individual core competencies.

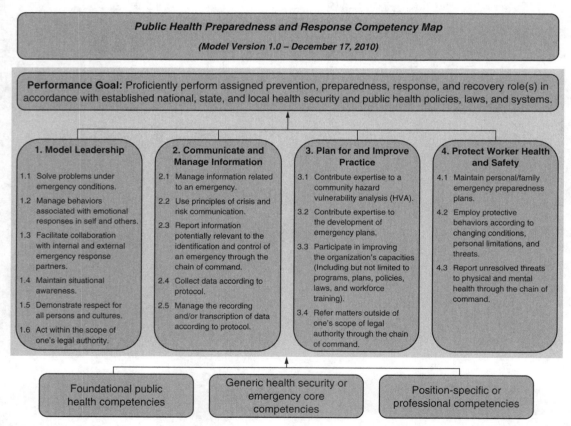

FIGURE 17-5 Public Health Preparedness and Response Competency Map. *Source:* Courtesy of the Association of Schools of Public Health.

TABLE 17-7 Crosswalk of PHEP Capabilities and Public Health Preparedness & Response Core Competencies

PHEP Capability	Preparedness & Response Core Competencies*
Capability 1: **Community** **Preparedness**	1.3 Facilitate collaboration with internal/external emergency response partners.
	1.4 Maintain situational awareness.
	1.5 Demonstrate respect for all persons and cultures.
	2.2 Use principles of crisis and risk communication.
	3.1 Contribute expertise to a community hazard vulnerability analysis.
	3.2 Contribute expertise to the development of emergency plans.
	3.3 Participate in improving the organization's capacities.
Capability 2: **Community** **Recovery**	1.1 Solve problems under emergency conditions.
	1.2 Manage behaviors associated with emotional responses.
	1.3 Facilitate collaboration with internal/external emergency response partners.
	1.4 Maintain situational awareness.
	1.5 Demonstrate respect for all persons and cultures.
	1.6 Act within the scope of one's legal authority.
	2.1 Manage information related to an emergency.
	2.2 Use principles of crisis and risk communication.
	2.4 Collect data according to protocol.
	2.5 Manage the recording and/or transcription of data according to protocol.
	3.3 Participate in improving the organization's capacities.
	3.4 Refer matters outside of one's scope of legal authority through the chain of command.
	4.1 Maintain personal/family emergency preparedness plans.
	4.2 Employ protective behaviors according to changing conditions, personal limitations, and threats.
	4.3 Report unresolved threats to physical and mental health through the chain of command.

*Version 1.0 (12/17/10)

(Continues)

TABLE 17-7 Crosswalk of PHEP Capabilities and Public Health Preparedness & Response Core Competencies (*Continued*)

PHEP Capability	Preparedness & Response Core Competencies
Capability 3: Emergency Operations Coordination	1.3 Facilitate collaboration with internal/external emergency response partners.
	1.4 Maintain situational awareness.
	2.1 Manage information related to an emergency.
	2.2 Use principles of crisis and risk management.
	2.3 Report information potentially relevant to the identification and control of an emergency through the chain of command.
	2.4 Collect data according to protocol.
	2.5 Manage the recording and/or transcription of data according to protocol.
	3.2 Contribute expertise to the development of emergency plans.
	3.3 Participate in improving the organization's capacities.
	4.1 Maintain personal/family emergency preparedness plans.
	4.2 Employ protective behaviors according to changing conditions, personal limitations, and threats.
	4.3 Report unresolved threats to physical and mental health through the chain of command.
Capability 4: Emergency Public Information and Warning	1.1 Solve problems under emergency conditions.
	1.3 Facilitate collaboration with internal/external emergency response partners.
	1.4 Maintain situational awareness.
	1.5 Demonstrate respect for all persons and cultures.
	1.6 Act within the scope of one's legal authority.
	2.1 Manage information related to an emergency
	2.2 Use principles of crisis and risk communication.
	2.3 Report information potentially relevant to the identification and control of an emergency through the chain of command.
Capability 5: Fatality Management	1.1 Solve problems under emergency conditions.
	1.2 Manage behaviors associated with emotional responses in self and others.
	1.3 Facilitate collaboration with internal/external emergency response partners.
	1.4 Maintain situational awareness.
	2.1 Manage information related to an emergency.
	2.4 Collect data according to protocol.
	2.5 Manage the recording and/or transcription of data according to protocol.
	3.2 Contribute expertise to the development of emergency plans.
	3.4 Refer matters outside of one's scope of legal authority through the chain of command.

	4.1 Maintain personal/family emergency preparedness plans.
	4.2 Employ protective behaviors according to changing conditions, personal limitations, and threats.
	4.3 Report unresolved threats to physical and mental health through the chain of command.
Capability 6: Information Sharing	1.1 Solve problems under emergency conditions.
	1.3 Facilitate collaboration with internal/external emergency response partners.
	1.4 Maintain situational awareness.
	1.5 Demonstrate respect for all persons and cultures.
	1.6 Act within the scope of one's legal authority.
	2.1 Manage information related to an emergency
	2.2 Use principles of crisis and risk communication.
	2.3 Report information potentially relevant to the identification and control of an emergency through the chain of command.
Capability 7: Mass Care	1.1 Solve problems under emergency conditions.
	1.2 Manage behaviors associated with emotional responses in self and others.
	1.3 Facilitate collaboration with internal/external emergency response partners.
	1.4 Maintain situational awareness.
	1.5 Demonstrate respect for all persons and cultures.
	1.6 Act within the scope of one's legal authority.
	2.1 Manage information related to an emergency.
	2.3 Report information potentially relevant to the identification and control of an emergency through the chain of command.
	2.4 Collect data according to protocol.
	2.5 Manage the recording and/or transcription of data according to protocol.
	3.1 Contribute expertise to a community hazard vulnerability analysis.
	3.2 Contribute expertise to the development of emergency plans.
	3.4 Refer matters outside of one's scope of legal authority through the chain of command.
	4.1 Maintain personal/family emergency preparedness plans.
	4.2 Employ protective behaviors according to changing conditions, personal limitations, and threats.
	4.3 Report unresolved threats to physical and mental health through the chain of command.

(Continues)

TABLE 17-7   Crosswalk of PHEP Capabilities and Public Health Preparedness & Response Core Competencies (*Continued*)

PHEP Capability	Preparedness & Response Core Competencies*
Capability 8: Medical Countermeasure Dispensing	1.1 Solve problems under emergency conditions.
	1.2 Manage behaviors associated with emotional responses in self and others.
	1.3 Facilitate collaboration with internal/external emergency response partners.
	1.4 Maintain situational awareness.
	1.5 Demonstrate respect for all persons and cultures.
	1.6 Act within the scope of one's legal authority.
	2.1 Manage information related to an emergency
	2.2 Use principles of crisis and risk communication.
	2.3 Report information potentially relevant to the identification and control of an emergency through the chain of command.
	2.4 Collect data according to protocol.
	4.2 Employ protective behaviors according to changing conditions, personal limitations, and threats.
Capability 9: Medical Material Management and Distribution	1.1 Solve problems under emergency conditions.
	1.2 Manage behaviors associated with emotional responses in self and others.
	1.3 Facilitate collaboration with internal/external emergency response partners.
	1.4 Maintain situational awareness.
	1.5 Demonstrate respect for all persons and cultures.
	2.1 Manage information related to an emergency.
	2.2 Use principles of crisis and risk communication.
	2.3 Report information potentially relevant to the identification and control of an emergency through the chain of command.
	2.4 Collect data according to protocol.
	2.5 Manage the recording and/or transcription of data according to protocol.
	3.3 Participate in improving the organization's capacities.
	4.1 Maintain personal/family emergency preparedness plans.
	4.2 Employ protective behaviors according to changing conditions, personal limitations, and threats.
	4.3 Report unresolved threats to physical and mental health through the chain of command.
Capability 10: Medical Surge	1.1 Solve problems under emergency conditions.
	1.2 Manage behaviors associated with emotional responses in self and others.
	1.3 Facilitate collaboration with internal/external emergency response partners.

	1.4 Maintain situational awareness.
	1.5 Demonstrate respect for all persons and cultures.
	1.6 Act within the scope of one's legal authority.
	2.1 Manage information related to an emergency
	2.2 Use principles of crisis and risk communication.
	2.3 Report information potentially relevant to the identification and control of an emergency through the chain of command.
	2.4 Collect data according to protocol.
	3.3 Participate in improving the organization's capacities.
	4.2 Employ protective behaviors according to changing conditions, personal limitations, and threats.
	4.3 Report unresolved threats to physical and mental health through the chain of command.
Capability 11: Non-Pharmaceutical Interventions	1.1 Solve problems under emergency conditions.
	1.3 Facilitate collaboration with internal/external emergency response partners.
	1.4 Maintain situational awareness.
	1.5 Demonstrate respect for all persons and cultures.
	1.6 Act within the scope of one's legal authority.
	2.1 Manage information related to an emergency
	2.2 Use principles of crisis and risk communication.
	2.3 Report information potentially relevant to the identification and control of an emergency through the chain of command.
	2.4 Collect data according to protocol.
	2.5 Manage the recording and/or transcription of data according to protocol.
	4.2 Employ protective behaviors according to changing conditions, personal limitations, and threats.
Capability 12: Public Health Laboratory Testing	1.1 Solve problems under emergency conditions.
	1.3 Facilitate collaboration with internal/external emergency response partners.
	1.4 Maintain situational awareness.
	2.1 Manage information related to an emergency
	2.3 Report information potentially relevant to the identification and control of an emergency through the chain of command.
	2.4 Collect data according to protocol.
	2.5 Manage the recording and/or transcription of data according to protocol.
	3.2 Contribute expertise to the development of emergency plans.
	3.3 Participate in improving the organization's capacities.

(Continues)

TABLE 17-7   Crosswalk of PHEP Capabilities and Public Health Preparedness & Response Core Competencies (*Continued*)

PHEP Capability	Preparedness & Response Core Competencies
Capability 13: Public Health Surveillance and Epidemiological Investigation	1.1 Solve problems under emergency conditions.
	1.3 Facilitate collaboration with internal/external emergency response partners.
	1.4 Maintain situational awareness.
	2.1 Manage information related to an emergency
	2.3 Report information potentially relevant to the identification and control of an emergency through the chain of command.
	2.4 Collect data according to protocol.
	2.5 Manage the recording and/or transcription of data according to protocol.
	3.3 Participate in improving the organization's capacities.
Capability 14: Responder Safety and Health	1.1 Solve problems under emergency conditions.
	1.2 Manage behaviors associated with emotional responses in self and others.
	1.3 Facilitate collaboration with internal/external emergency response partners.
	1.4 Maintain situational awareness.
	1.5 Demonstrate respect for all persons and cultures.
	2.1 Manage information related to an emergency
	2.2 Use principles of crisis and risk communication.
	2.3 Report information potentially relevant to the identification and control of an emergency through the chain of command.
	2.4 Collect data according to protocol.
	3.3 Participate in improving the organization's capacities.
	4.1 Maintain personal/family emergency preparedness plans.
	4.2 Employ protective behaviors according to changing conditions, personal limitations, and threats.
	4.3 Report unresolved threats to physical and mental health through the chain of command.
Capability 15: Volunteer Management	1.1 Solve problems under emergency conditions.
	1.3 Facilitate collaboration with internal/external emergency response partners.
	1.4 Maintain situational awareness.
	1.5 Demonstrate respect for all persons and cultures.
	2.1 Manage information related to an emergency
	2.3 Report information potentially relevant to the identification and control of an emergency through the chain of command.
	2.4 Collect data according to protocol.
	3.3 Participate in improving the organization's capacities.
	4.2 Employ protective behaviors according to changing conditions, personal limitations, and threats.
	4.3 Report unresolved threats to physical and mental health through the chain of command.

Source: Courtesy of the Mid-America Regional Public Health Leadership Institute.

SUMMARY

It has been a major purpose of this chapter to give an overview to the whole field of emergency preparedness and response. As a field of practice, public health has many new responsibilities. Although much discussion of emergency preparedness and response has been about terrorist acts, the issues in a crisis are more complex. Types of crises have been reviewed and commentary given about the need to plan for different classes of crises. The planning-and-response approaches differ depending on the type of crisis. The one sure fact is that crisis and disaster events seem to be increasing. Readiness is clearly an important area of concern for the prepared public health leader. Crises go through a series of stages in which different activities occur. Discussions of the preparedness phase were viewed from the vantage point of an organization as well as from the perspective of a community or country. The discussion of response was viewed from both an organizational perspective and a community one. The incident command system basic model and its extension into a unified command model was discussed as a model that is utilized in the United States. It does seem clear that many approaches to emergency preparedness and response fit into traditional management perspectives. The leadership issues are also clearly important. A discussion of some of the mental health issues in crisis were presented. Finally, there was a discussion of the public health and emergency preparedness capabilities and core competencies at the individual level.

DISCUSSION QUESTIONS

1. Discuss Mitroff's crisis types and different approaches to addressing each type of crisis.
2. What happened to U.S. readiness between 2003 and 2012?
3. Describe the stages of a crisis.
4. Why is it important to have a separate humanitarian response team during a crisis?
5. Differentiate the Blythe preparedness model from the DMTP model.

EXERCISE 17-1: Crisis Severity Matrix

Purpose: to learn how to use the Crisis Severity Matrix to make an initial evaluation of the severity of a potential crisis

Key concepts: crisis, crisis matrix, crisis impact, flu pandemic, terrorism, SARS

Procedures: With the Crisis Severity Matrix from Figure 17-2, divide the class or training group into smaller groups of about ten people. With your group, plot the following crisis events by type and severity, and discuss your reasons for plotting them the way your group did. What types of considerations need to occur for a crisis of this magnitude? What would be different if the crisis were more or less severe?

1. Thirty percent decrease in the budget of your agency
2. Flu pandemic this winter
3. Terrorist attack on a nuclear reactor plant
4. Appearance of a SARS case in New York City
5. Contamination of the water supply in a small rural community

---

REFERENCES

1. World Health Organization and Pan African Emergency Training Centre, Addis Ababa, *Disasters and Emergencies: Definitions* (Geneva, Switzerland: World Health Organization, 2002).
2. United Nations Disaster Management Training Programme, *Disaster Preparedness*, 2nd ed. (New York: UN Disaster Management Training Programme, 1994).
3. I. Mitroff, *Managing Crises Before They Happen* (New York: Amacom, 2001).
4. I. Mitroff, *Crisis Leadership: Planning for the Inevitable* (New York: John Wiley and Sons, 2004).
5. Mitroff, *Managing Crises Before They Happen*.
6. Mitroff, *Crisis Leadership*.
7. I. Mitroff, *Why Some Companies Emerge Stronger and Better from a Crisis* (New York: Amacom, 2005).
8. Trust for America's Health, *Ready or Not? Protecting the Public's Health in the Age of Terrorism* (Washington, DC: Trust for America's Health, 2003).
9. Trust for America's Health, *Ready or Not? Protecting the Public's Health in the Age of Terrorism* (Washington, DC: Trust for America's Health, 2004).

10. Trust for America's Health, *Ready or Not?*, 2004.

11. Trust for America's Health, *Ready or Not? Protecting the Public from Diseases, Disasters, and Bioterrorism* (Washington, DC: Trust for America's Health, 2011).

12. Mitroff, *Crisis Leadership.*

13. S. Fink, *Crisis Management: Planning for the Inevitable* (Lincoln, NE: Authors Guild, Backinprint.com, 2002)

14. Mitroff, *Managing Crises Before They Happen.*

15. Fink, *Crisis Management.*

16. B. Turnock, *Public Health: What It Is and How It Works* (Burlington, MA: Jones & Bartlett Learning, 2012).

17. Fink, *Crisis Management.*

18. National Commission on Terrorist Attacks Upon the United States, *The 9/11 Commission Report* (New York: W. W. Norton and Co., 2004).

19. Fink, *Crisis Management.*

20. Fink, *Crisis Management.*

21. Mitroff, *Managing Crises Before They Begin.*

22. B. T. Blythe, *Blindsided* (New York: Portfolio Penguin Putnam, 2002).

23. Blythe, *Blindsided.*

24. Blythe, *Blindsided.*

25. Mitroff, *Managing Crises Before They Happen.*

26. Mitroff, *Crisis Management.*

27. C. M. Alpaslan and I. I. Mitroff, *Swans, Swine, and Swindlers* (Stanford, CA: Stanford Business Books, 2011).

28. Blythe, *Blindsided.*

29. Blythe, *Blindsided.*

30. Blythe, *Blindsided.*

31. R. W. Giuliani, *Leadership* (New York: Hyperion Books, 2002).

32. UN Disaster Management Training Programme, *Disaster Preparedness.*

33. Centers for Disease Control and Prevention, *The Public Health Response to Biological and Chemical Terrorism Interim Planning Guidance for State Public Health Officials* (Atlanta: CDC, 2001). Retrieved from http://www.bt.cdc.gov/documents/planning/planningguidance.pdf.

34. UN Disaster Management Training Programme, *Disaster Preparedness.*

35. Blythe, *Blindsided.*

36. L. Y. Landesman, *Public Health Management of Disasters,* 3rd ed. (Washington, DC: American Public Health Association, 2011).

37. Landesman, *Public Health Management of Disasters.*

38. Blythe, *Blindsided.*

39. Blythe, *Blindsided.*

40. Landesman, *Public Health Management of Disasters.*

41. Department of Homeland Security, FEMA, *Basic Incident Command System* (IS 195) (Emmitsburg, MD: Department of Homeland Security, 2004).

42. Columbia University National Center for Disaster Preparedness, *Crisis of Confidence* [Press Release] (New York: Columbia University, 2004).

43. D. P. Connor, *Managing at the Speed of Change* (New York: Villard, 2002).

44. Landesman, *Public Health Management of Disasters.*

45. Landesman, *Public Health Management of Disasters.*

46. National Institute of Mental Health, *Mental Health and Mass Violence* (NIH Publication No. 02-5138) (Washington, DC: U.S. Government Printing Office, 2002).

47. Centers for Disease Control and Prevention, *Public Health Preparedness Capabilities* (Atlanta: CDC, 2011).

48. www.asph.org, accessed February 27, 2012.

49. www.midamericacphp.com, accessed February 27, 2012.

Leadership Skills and Competencies

CHAPTER 18

Leadership and Communication

There was an inimitable cadence, an emphasis on certain words, an exaggeration of certain phrases, a kind of intoning here and there which made his telling unforgettable.

—A. Thirkell on Rudyard Kipling, *Three Houses*

There are many tools and skills that leaders need to apply in carrying out their responsibilities. This chapter is concerned with communication skills. Leading, after all, is an interactive process involving leaders and followers, and good communication among all participants in the process is absolutely essential.

Communication is the transfer of information and meaning,[1] and it has become even more important over the past decades—the start of the so-called information age—than it was previously. Information makes situations orderly, promotes change and growth, and defines reality. Meaning and how the messages are perceived and processed by the recipient of the message are extremely important. Communication plays an important part in the leadership process, as does the transfer of information in all the various forms that such communication takes, from face-to-face conversation to electronic transfer of data. In learning organizations, it is communication that drives the process. Leaders are teachers as well as learners. Their personal experiences lead the way into their vision of the future. Tichy and Cohen stated that ideas, values, and energy drive the learning and teaching process.[2] These three skills give leaders an edge in solving problems and making decisions. This energy and passion gets communicated through many mechanisms that are discussed in this chapter.

THE COMMUNICATION PROCESS

It may be difficult to communicate effectively, but it is impossible not to communicate at all.[3] Each person's life is based on developing and using language to interact with other people.

A communicative act involves the transmission of two messages. The first message is about the topic of the communication. The second message concerns the hidden or real agenda of the parties to the communicative act. Communication is an ongoing process throughout our personal and professional lives. It does not solve all our problems itself but must be accompanied by action.[4]

Barriers to Communication

There are many barriers to effective communication.[5] Communication can be blocked by forces within the participants as well as external forces. Nonverbal behavior—in the form of facial and hand gestures—can influence how a message is received, as can conscious and unconscious thoughts and distractions such as noise and motion. In addition, men and women have different conversational styles that can either enhance communication or create barriers to communication.

The intended recipient's state of mind can be a major barrier to receiving a message. How many of us have found ourselves daydreaming in a public health agency staff meeting when the agency director or our supervisor asks our opinion on an issue? Other reasons for not listening to a conversation include anxiety about talking, lack of interest in the topic, thinking about what to say, confusion from trying to make sense of overly complicated discourse, lack of understanding of the professional lexicon, dislike of the speaker and his or her principles, and a desire to be somewhere else.[6] Lencioni has warned of the problems of boring and uninteresting meetings.[7] We need to be wary of death by meeting.

Sometimes a person says things in order to upset the listener, and the message does not completely reflect the ideas of the sender.[8] This type of behavior can create tensions in a marriage—or an agency. Suppose the director of a program says to a staff member, "John, I need further infant mortality data from the state. Please call the state epidemiologist and get me the infant mortality data for the last five years for our county. Would you also ask her to evaluate the data for us?"

The true message might be this: "I don't trust John's interpretation of the data. John probably did it wrong." John may understand the underlying message, and his response—"I'll do it immediately"—might have as its underlying message, "Why doesn't he do it himself? I did the analysis correctly."

Other barriers include injecting into the communicative process a judgment that discredits the other party to the process and avoiding the concerns of the other party.[9]

An Interactionist Model of Communication

Hulett[10,11] built a communication model based on the symbolic interactionist approach used by some social scientists, including Robert Sears, who had developed a model of communication as a dyadic action system.[12] According to Sears, each individual brings a personal history to each communicative interaction. Hulett, who thought that most communication models were simplistic, claimed that communication needs to be seen as a natural social process that encompasses what takes place within each participant as well as what takes place between the participants and that every act of communication occurs in a multilevel social system that it influences and by which it is influenced.

Hulett analyzed an act of communication into a number of steps, which he called the "instigation action sequence." Each step involves one of five types of act or event: a motivating stimulus, a covert rehearsal, an instrumental act, an environmental event, or a goal response (**Figure 18-1**). Each participant in a communicative act brings to it a cognitive map that

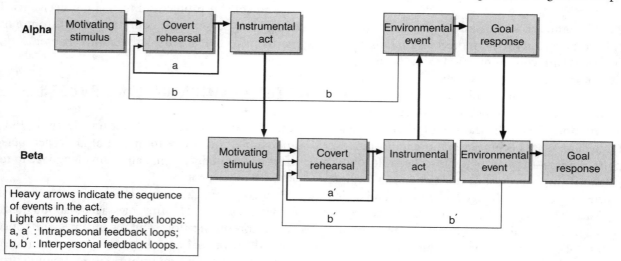

FIGURE 18-1 Block Diagram of a Social Act Between Two Interacting Individuals, According to Symbolic Interactionist Principles. *Source:* Reprinted with permission from J. R. Hulett Jr., A Symbolic Interactionist Model of Human Communication Part I, *AV Communication Review*, Vol. 14, No. 1, p. 18, © 1966, AECT.

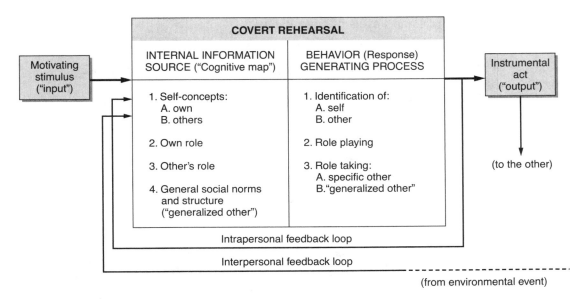

FIGURE 18-2 The Covert Rehearsal of Either Participant in a Social Act, According to Symbolic Interactionist Principles. *Source*: Reprinted with permission from J. R. Hulett Jr., A Symbolic Interactionist Model of Human Communication Part I, *AV Communication Review*, Vol. 14, No. 1, p. 18, © 1966, AECT.

affects the motivating stimulus. The initiator of the act evaluates the stimulus and mentally rehearses the proposed communication (covert rehearsal; see **Figure 18-2**). The initiator then performs some action or says something (instrumental act) that triggers the motivating stimulus for the recipient of the interaction, who then mentally goes through the covert rehearsal phase. The recipient performs an instrumental act (answers the sender), which becomes the environmental act for the initiator. If the initiator is satisfied, then the goal response will be positive. If the recipient sees the response as positive, the interaction is complete. Feedback loops in the process allow the initiator and the sender to clarify issues and then finish the process.

According to Hulett, the covert rehearsal is the stage at which the individual role-plays his or her actions and tries to determine how the other person will respond. The self-concept of each participant, the values that guide each person, and the person's perceptions of the other's role influence the communicative process. For example, a public health leader will approach communication differently depending on whether the intended recipient is an agency staff member, the leader of another agency, a client, or the president of the board of health. Furthermore, a public health leader from a middle-class, suburban background will likely have different expectations when dealing with the residents of a working-class community than would a public health leader from a working-class background.

The model devised by Hulett concerns personal communication between two people. However, leadership also occurs at the team, agency, community, and professional levels, and the communicative process at each of these levels is complicated by the fact that a multitude of individuals are involved, each of whom comes to the process with a unique agenda and a unique interpretation of the same set of facts. A public health leader addressing a coalition, for instance, must discuss the issues with each coalition member individually at another time to ensure that the communication of ideas or information is successful.

Communication Skills

Table 18-1 lists the communication skills needed by leaders at the five levels of leadership. A public health leader requires at least 20 communication skills. To be effective communicators, public health leaders must:

- fully develop their communication skills as part of their lifelong learning agendas
- respect the different agendas that coalition members or partners bring to the table
- use the core functions and essential services of public health to guide communication with others
- use their communication skills to guide the transfer and management of knowledge
- be on the lookout for barriers to communication

TABLE 18-1 Communication Skills and Levels of Leadership

Skill Categories	Personal Leadership	Team Leadership	Agency Leadership	Community Leadership	Professional Leadership
Interpersonal communication	X	X	X	X	X
Active listening	X	X	X	X	X
Public speaking	X	–	X	X	X
Interviewing	X	X	X	X	X
Written communication	X	X	X	X	X
Computer skills	X	X	X	X	X
Media advocacy	X	X	X	X	X
Cultural sensitively	X	X	X	X	X
Feedback	X	X	X	X	X
Delegation	X	X	X	X	X
Framing	X	X	X	X	X
Dialogue, discussion, and debate	X	X	X	X	X
Meeting skills	X	X	X	X	X
Health communications	X	X	X	X	X
Social marketing	X	X	X	X	X
Coaching, mentoring, and facilitation	X	X	X	X	X
Conflict resolution	X	X	X	X	X
Negotiation	X	X	X	X	X
Storytelling	X	X	X	X	X
Journaling	X	–	–	–	–

INTERPERSONAL COMMUNICATION

According to Hulett, interaction between two individuals is the basic unit of communication. In the workplace, critical communicative interactions include giving instructions, asking and answering questions, listening to the concerns of others, and, especially in the case of leaders, publicizing the organization's mission and vision.[13]

There are advantages to oral communication.[14] First, talking is the quickest form of communication. Ideas and thoughts can be relayed in a simple form that others can understand. Quick feedback is also possible. An important disadvantage is that the potential for distortion is great. Even with the best of intentions, community leaders may misinterpret the statements of public health agency leaders. Communication will have to be continuous if agreement on goals and programmatic interventions is to occur.

Communication Styles

Different conversational styles exist, and the differences in style can have social ramifications.[15] It is not uncommon for residents in a nursing home to be called by their first names by the staff, but this kind of informality may disturb some older residents, who might see the use of first names as indicative of a lack of respect. Also, major differences in conversational style exist between men and women and different cultural groups, shown by the fact that men and women and different cultural groups often seem to talk at cross-purposes. In addition, although the public health workforce is mostly female, most of the agency heads are men, and this may have something to do with the fact that women have different public speaking styles than men. Women must speak without the appearance of submission or of lack of a strong position. Women tend to not be overly aggressive,[16] but they will need to face conflict squarely in order to convince others of the truth of their beliefs.

In general, leaders need to avoid being too submissive or too aggressive in their communications.[17] Assertiveness is the most effective strategy. Assertive leaders fight for their beliefs and thus gain the respect of others without antagonizing them by being aggressive. Many public health leaders believe that they possess finely honed interpersonal skills, but in fact observation shows that these leaders frequently have trouble communicating with their staff and with community partners. Learning interpersonal skills is a lifelong process.

Types of Formal Communication

There are three types of formal communication within an organization.[18] The first type is downward communication, from a superior to a subordinate. Among its benefits, it allows a supervisor to correct problems, and it keeps communication channels open, which tends to increase employee satisfaction. The second is upward communication, in which a subordinate initiates a conversation with someone at a higher level. This type of communication has the potential of preventing problems as well as solving existing problems. The final type of communication is horizontal or lateral, as occurs when colleagues at the same level communicate among themselves. The benefits include cooperation across sections of the organization. Cooperation between public health leaders and community leaders involves the last type of communication.

Informal communication networks are based on personal friendships, similar personal interests, shared career interests, and the closeness of working together in the same organization.[19] Informal communication networks focused on community health issues can be built on love of community and a desire to help the community by strengthening the infrastructure of public health.

Interpersonal Communication Guidelines

Effective interpersonal communication requires talking to people in a way that will be meaningful and about topics that will be meaningful for them. For example, public health leaders might talk to agency staff about the importance of the core functions of public health. In talking to a community group, however, they might discuss putting on a health fair or implementing a Healthy Communities 2020 program.

Leaders need to be careful not to let hostile feelings interfere with their judgment. Expertise should drive their conversation, not their organization titles. And they should always respect those with whom they are talking. Each conversation needs to be based on mutual trust. Judgment is critical to effective leadership. According to Tichy and Bennis, judgments relate to people, strategy, and reactions to crisis events.[20] There are three stages to judgment, from a preparation stage, to the judgment call itself, and then to execution. Communication is critical during all three stages.

Leaders should use language that is understandable to their audience, which in many cases means forsaking the specialized language of public health. They should speak from the heart and take a positive perspective. Credibility is important to communication, which may fail without it. Sometimes the maintenance of credibility requires a leader to abandon his or her own agenda and replace it with an agenda favored by others.[21]

To ensure that their interpersonal communication is effective, public health leaders should:

- converse with other people in a meaningful way and on meaningful topics
- be assertive, not aggressive
- control hostile feelings
- allow their expertise, not their titles, to be the basis for paying attention to what they say
- make judgments carefully
- be open to new ideas
- respect the agendas of others and know when to abandon their own agendas
- use understandable language, speak from the heart, and take a positive perspective

Personal communication is the most important means of sharing a mission and vision with others. In the 21st century, it will be impossible for leaders without personal communication skills to sustain their credibility with colleagues, teams, agency staff, and community stakeholders.

ACTIVE LISTENING

Public health leaders must be not only proficient speakers but also active listeners. Active listening takes concentration. The goal is to understand what the other person is saying and what it entails. In his memoir on his life in leadership, Bennis states that listening is an art.[22] To listen intently is to put your ego on hold. You need to stop performing and attend to another person. Bennis refers to the whole listening process as creative listening. Four critical skills are needed for active listening:

1. intensity of involvement in the interaction
2. empathy for the other's message and meaning
3. acceptance of the other person's message without judgment until the other person finishes talking
4. willingness to get all the information needed to make a decision[23]

Passive listening is listening without much involvement.[24] Passive listening is sometimes the appropriate listening style at a public presentation, for example. How many of us have taken courses or attended conferences where we were talked at rather than with. Passive listening may be interrupted by questions from the audience.[25]

The classification of listening styles into active and passive is somewhat simplistic. Alessandra and Hunsaker divide listeners into four types.[26] First comes the nonlistener, who does not pay attention to the message being sent. The second type is the listener who only marginally listens to the message. This listener is always rehearsing what to say or is preoccupied with other thoughts. The evaluative listener, the third type, listens to the entire message but misses the intent. The final type is the active listener. Scharmer has discussed four types of listening.[27] First, downloading is where confirmation is made of previous information, judgments, and decisions. Second, factual listening is where we listen for new facts or information that goes against previous decisions or judgments. Third, empathic listening is where we are trying to understand the feelings of others; this is closely allied to the concepts of emotional intelligence.[28] Finally, generative listening is when we relate to systems issues and a view of the world that is more expansive than our usual view.

To be an active listener, a person must ask good questions that will clarify both the content and the intent of the message.[29] Open-ended questions allow the respondent to go into detail about the meaning and intent of the message, whereas close-ended questions are meant to elicit short answers that will illuminate specific comments. One strategy, the so-called funnel technique, involves starting with global, open-ended questions and then gradually moving toward focused, close-ended questions.[30]

Consider this example: A new health department administrator is asked by the local board of health to explain the core functions and essential services of public health and why they are important. The administrator gives a 15-minute informal presentation on the topic. Board members start with broad questions, indicating that they still do not understand the core functions model, or why the administrator favors this model. The administrator answers these broad questions as best as he or she can. As he or she clarifies his or her position, the board members narrow in on specific details by asking close-ended questions.

A listener can use questions to offer advice or attack the speaker for holding a position contrary to the listener's. In addition, the listener, in asking questions, may have a hidden agenda of which the speaker is unaware. The questions asked should be sincere and intended to elicit information the questioner truly needs in order to understand the speaker's meaning.

Walton listed five rules governing conversational etiquette:

1. Don't hog the floor.
2. Don't change the subject.
3. Don't step on the sentences of others.
4. Do hold your tongue.
5. Don't forget—there's always tomorrow.[31]

In active listening, the listener should make eye contact with the speaker and pay close attention to the speaker's words as well as any nonverbal message the speaker is conveying. Active listening is intense and requires an expenditure of energy. The speaker expects the listener to pay attention and not do distracting things, like answering the telephone or shuffling papers. When the speaker is finished, the listener should ask questions that show that attention was paid to the speaker's comments. The questions, however, should be as brief and to the point as possible. The author has been to talks in which an audience member got up and gave a 10-minute exegesis on his or her personal views—hardly a sign of active listening.

Active listeners:

- make eye contact and listen with all their senses
- avoid distracting actions, like answering the telephone or shuffling papers
- ask questions
- do not interrupt
- do not talk too much
- use positive gestures as part of their listening behavior

PUBLIC SPEAKING

Oral communication [handwritten annotation]

Public health leaders may have a clear vision of the future, but the effort they spent developing the vision will be all for naught unless they can publicize their vision and inspire others to share it. One of the best ways of publicizing it is to speak in different public venues, from local PTA meetings to national conferences, such as the annual meeting of the American Public Health Association. And to speak effectively, no matter what the venue, additional skills are needed beyond those required for effective personal communication.

At some state universities, public speaking is a university curriculum requirement. But even in these institutions, students tend not to understand the benefits to be gained by acquiring public speaking skills. Public speaking helps teach the individual not only how to conceptualize an issue concisely but also how to integrate words with gestures to make a more effective argument in support of a particular point of view. Furthermore, the more a person speaks in public forums, the easier public speaking tends to become.

Leaders know how to use language that strengthens the message given. Leaders tell stories, as is discussed later in this chapter. President Ronald Reagan always added inspirational stories to his talks, and presidents after Reagan have done the same. Leaders also use analogies and metaphors in their talks. A public health leader might say, for example, "We must be careful not to let the ship of public health flounder in the stormy debate over proposed cuts in federal programs." Body language is important. Holding on to the podium, for instance, does not communicate confidence. A speaker's nonverbal language should correspond with the speaker's words. In addition, the speaker should be aware of the pitch of his or her voice, especially when using a microphone.

Speakers should tailor each speech to the needs of the audience.[32] If the members of the audience cannot identify with the issues raised, they will tune out or forget the message fairly quickly. Speakers need to have a message that is realistic and focused. Unfocused presentations confuse the audience. Speakers also need to include supporting information.

Speakers need to appear credible to the audience.[33] They can maximize their acceptance by proving they are competent to discuss the chosen topic. They also need to earn the trust of the audience, which they can do partly by impressing the audience with the fact that they and the audience are basically alike and partly by appearing sincere. Also, using names of people in the audience sometimes increases the degree of acceptance of both the speaker and the speech.

Speakers are often viewed as mentors or teachers[34] and as entertainers. It has been suggested that public speaking is 25% knowledge and 75% charisma. Consequently, a speaker may find it worthwhile to rehearse the presentation ahead of time.[35] Dressing appropriately is important as well. A speaker in blue jeans does not go over well when the audience is in suits and dresses. If possible, speakers should leave time for questions, which is a good strategy for appearing human before the audience and gaining its acceptance. Of course, in some cases acceptance is hard to obtain, and so speakers should develop the skills necessary for dealing with a hostile audience. Humor usually helps when confronting hostility—and in most other cases as well.

Speakers need to know their audience but also be flexible enough to modify the prepared text if it is not appropriate for a particular audience. They also need to take note of the layout of the room because it can have an effect on the acceptance of the message.

Public health leaders who are required to do a lot of public speaking should familiarize themselves with the speaker aids that are currently available. Overhead projectors or liquid crystal display devices, for instance, allow speakers to present information concisely. One danger with overheads and slides is that they often contain so much information in such small type that they cannot be read beyond the second row or in a reasonable amount of time. (The so-called six-second rule is that every overhead or slide should be able to be read by the audience in six seconds.) Another danger is that when many overheads or slides are displayed, the audience may become frustrated trying to keep up with the overheads and slides by taking notes on what they contain. A good solution is to provide copies of the overheads and slides to the audience in order to lessen the information overload. Slides and computer-based slide presentations tend to be better in large groups, at least if the remote control switch works. Handouts can be used in conjunction with slides to good effect, for they help the audience to remember the information after the talk is over. Running a short video may enhance a presentation. New computer presentation software and new projection devices can be useful, though renting the necessary equipment at meeting sites can be costly. Furthermore, because this equipment may break down, it is important to have a backup set of slides.

Which are the best speaker aids to use in a given situation depends to a degree on the speaker's speaking technique. If the speaker reads from a prepared draft, slides can be easily coordinated with the words. When using an LCD projector, the speaker may have to leave the podium in order to see the slides. This kind of interruption can lend the presentation an informality that some audiences seem to prefer, but it can also act as an irritant.

Case Study 18-A is a public health practice quiz with Toni Rowitz. Ms. Rowitz taught public speaking at Oakton Community College in Illinois for more than 40 years and had more than 11,000 students. She looks at public speaking as a critical set of skills for an effective leader.

Case Study 18-A

Public Health Practice Quiz for Toni G. Rowitz

1. Why do leaders need to be good public speakers?

In their roles as advocates for good public health, leaders need to be effective speakers for a variety of reasons. First, though it's called "public" health, the concerns are with the well-being of individuals: vaccinations for children, mammograms for women, awareness of the propensity for high blood pressure in African American men, crisis management in catastrophic situations, etc. Second, most public speeches are "one-shot deals." They need to be clear, thorough, and open to minimal misinterpretation. Even assuming that information is valid and current, the discussion needs to be interesting so that people will listen. Unfortunately, listening skills are poor; we tend to listen in 15- to 20-minute attention spans. Most persons listen at only 25% efficiency, and most of what is remembered is distorted or inaccurate. Third, a speaker needs to be committed and focused on the specific needs of the audience(s). Speeches need to be "tailored" to make a good fit with the listeners. Finally, and perhaps most relevant, the credibility and commitment of a speaker carry more weight with audiences than the actual content. How the audience perceives a speaker will make all the difference. If you are a good speaker, you're a good leader because the information gets out where it needs to be.

2. What are the major types of public speeches?

The basic types of public speeches most likely to be used by a public health leader are information, demonstration, and persuasion. Of course, all speeches are informational; the difference is the kind of information, the way it's used, and the speaker's intention. There may be overlapping of types, but it's easier to organize a presentation, and more important, it's easier for an audience to listen intelligently if there is basic grounding.

The first question a good leader asks is, "What is the purpose of this speech?" There are two sides to this question; the speaker's purpose in delivering the presentation has to coincide with the listeners' reasons for being there. A good leader puts a great deal of consideration into achieving the goals of the audience; they are always the primary component in any speaking situation.

Information speeches "tell," making the words primary in communicating the content; visual aids are helpful in delivering the message. The demonstration speech "shows" what it looks like, how it functions, how the parts connect, etc. Visual materials are primary in developing the content; however, there needs to be a fairly steady running dialogue as well for clarification and connection. These two speeches require the audience to listen, understand, and possibly offer feedback or participate in question/answer afterward. What they do with the information may not be directly communicated to the speaker.

The most challenging of the speeches is the persuasion. Its purpose is to encourage the making of different choices in behavior and practice. Sometimes, a member of the audience is in a "show me" frame of mind and asks questions beginning with "I may not be the expert here but . . . ." In other instances, though they listen to the speaker ostensibly to examine and evaluate present programs and practices, as well as to seek expert advice, listeners may be limited by legitimate questions of money or facilities or personnel. A speaker can't do anything about those circumstances. Unfortunately, sometimes it's personalities that interfere: a speaker will have some say in this area. Energy and good will, as well as preparedness and expertise, are necessary for successful presentations, as well as for effective leadership.

3. What techniques can engage an audience?

We've all listened to speakers who were learned and well meaning and so boring we wanted to jump-start their motors. Remember the teachers who practically put you to sleep, or the ones who were so disorganized that you never knew quite where you were? There are no guarantees for audience engagement, but there are some basics that can help to shape a successful presentation, for both speaker and audience.

First, being prepared is absolutely essential. The preparation does not only include materials, notes, etc. It's necessary to view a speech in terms of before, during, and after. Speakers are speakers before they ever get up to the lectern. Personal interactions in the hallway or at receptions create impressions that will positively affect how listeners perceive and react to a speaker.

Intelligent listeners are better listeners. It's hard to listen intelligently if a speaker is disorganized, uneven, or unclear about the direction of the presentation. Initial engagement starts with the comments that capture the audience's attention and put them in the "ballpark"; an organized development of the topic makes listening easy and prevents confusion and subsequent inattention or dissatisfaction. During the speech, a smooth-flowing, natural delivery style does much to engage an audience. Eye contact, appropriate tonal variations, and response to feedback are all behaviors that encourage an audience to listen and to participate. To account for differences in learning styles and attention spans, use various support materials to increase interest and comprehension and to help listeners stay on track. Encourage active listening by assigning group or individual tasks or exercises (not busywork) that coincide with the topic. It is important to include a summary of the discussion, either on slides or hard copy, and take questions from the audience.

In short, the adept speaker/leader is confident in his or her expertise, respects the audience, is well prepared for all parts of the presentation, and makes a deliberate effort to communicate with, not talk at, the audience. At no time does a good speaker/leader get caught up in arguing or posturing. A confident, well-intentioned approach is maintained, and in cases of disrespect or deliberate misunderstanding, keeping one's cool is imperative. After the presentation, speakers need to be available for a reasonable length of time to answer questions, provide referrals, clarify concepts, etc. Presentations don't necessarily end according to the clock; leadership never does.

4. How can speakers use slide presentations to enhance their speeches?

We are living in an age of visual stimulation; it's fast, in color, and so much a part of every aspect of life—entertainment, education, communication, and advertisement—that it's expected during presentations. In fact, a presentation devoid of PowerPoint or slides or videos is often regarded as less than excellent. One picture may represent more than a thousand words, but the words have to be there as well as the person speaking them. The term used to be "visual aid," with the operative word being "aid," as in assistance or support. Now, in many instances, the speaker has become the mechanic who works the equipment.

Several mistakes are consistently made in the use of slides or other visual aids. Most predominant is the mostly "absent" speaker, or the mechanic, who just turns on the projector, steps aside, and reads the slides to the audience. It's not interesting or engaging and, worse, does not fulfill one essential requirement of effective speaking—the speaker as focal point.

That's not to say that visual materials cannot contribute to an excellent delivery style. The first secret of successful slide presentations is having hard copies for listeners, so that they can make notes as the speaker discusses—*not reads*—the slides. Pictures, diagrams, and enhanced imagery need to be interesting and pertinent, and presented on the screen in an outlined or bulleted or numbered format. The details and information that flesh out the outline are presented as the speaker weaves in and out, using the visual materials to explain or reinforce the spoken commentary, sometimes when the slide is on, sometimes in between slides. The speaker always remains the focal point, in direct contact with the listeners. Any time that a slide isn't being used or referred to, the screen should be blank. If images remain on the screen, a listener is torn among watching the screen, looking at the speaker, and writing notes; it becomes a visual triangulation that breaks concentration and disconnects speaker from audience. Keep the informative slides simple and succinct. In between, for fun or interest or as attention-getters, use the "fancy" slides. Don't combine them—it diminishes effectiveness of both the slides and the discussion objectives. Keep in mind the original term, "visual aid"; it was never "visual crutch."

5. What kind of clothes makes a difference in different types of speaking venues?

Dress is a matter of taste and common sense ... good taste and uncommon sense, in considering fashion, etiquette, special circumstances. All the information about the effect of first impressions and about your appearance shaping a person's perception of you is true. The crucial point is that speakers don't want to diminish their ethos and effect because an audience is distracted by the way they look; no speaker wants listeners to pay more attention to appearance than to presentation. Because most speeches are delivered at conferences or other professional meetings, it would be in order to ask a couple of questions: Where are you going to be speaking? Who will be there? What are you talking about?

(*Continues*)

On one hand, the safest assumption to make is that any speaker is a professional person and is expected to dress as such. For men, that means suit or jacket and slacks, and tie … no jazzy jacket or hat or reeking aftershave. Common sense—maybe a great tie is an asset. Women need to wear a dress or skirt (not a "mini") with jacket or tailored blouse. A tailored pantsuit may also be acceptable … no wild-print scarf or glitzy jewelry or heavy cologne. Common sense—a small scarf or understated piece of jewelry can work.

On the other hand, there is what's appropriate for a particular venue. Usually, no hats are worn at the lectern. Of course, if you are talking to a group of Little League baseball coaches about regional funding, and they give you a baseball hat with a logo on it, you should probably wear it, at least for a little while. Perhaps, instead of a dress with black pumps, a gaily colored lab coat and sneakers may be worn if the objective of the discussion is to effect a change in the way nurses dress in pediatric wards. Cultural and traditional apparel is always appropriate.

There are always alternatives to the "basic" dress. Sandals might be appropriate—thongs never. Jacket off may be okay, but t-shirt is out. Sleeveless blouse could be okay—tank top, not okay. Perhaps your best guide is to imagine yourself as speaker. As hard as it is, try to see yourself as others will see you … and go from there.

6. Because leaders often need to be able to communicate with audiences from other cultures, are there special techniques needed for multicultural presentations?

Multicultural presentations present an array of variables with which to deal, including language, acceptable/not acceptable body behavior, goal and style of presentation, appearance, time, behavior when not speaking, etc. There are so many cultural variations that the best advice is to get a good book, one that deals with "how to do it—don't do it" in other countries, such as Joseph DeVito's *Messages: Building Interpersonal Communications* (6th edition, Longman). Additionally, for a real-life personal perspective, if you know someone from the particular country, ask questions, especially about speaking situations. When I am up there, what is an appropriate address to my audience? Is humor a good idea? If so, what kind? Do I get straight to the point or do I have to dance around it for a while? Do I open the floor for questions or do I lead the questioning by targeting specific areas?

Do not make any assumption about another culture based on what you've been told or have been led to expect. A classic example is the situation explained to me by a Japanese colleague, whose husband is Caucasian. Whenever they dined out, the waitperson would discuss after-dinner beverage preferences, asking her if she would like tea and if her husband would like coffee. As a matter of fact, he is the tea drinker and she drinks coffee. That's minor, but a speaker cannot afford to err in any direction. Something as small as a hand gesture, or looking into the eyes of someone whose culture determines that to be disrespectful, or a casual remark that is offensive, or a mannerism that is improper, will affect an audience's perceptions to the point of making the entire presentation an exercise in disrespect. Above all, the words and phrases used will carry the most weight—be careful to be able to correctly pronounce names, places, and terms. (I shudder when somebody pronounces it "Illinoiz.")

The special technique in the area of multicultural presentations is simple and precise: recognize that you have to be diligent in the tedious, but absolutely imperative, exploration of how a leader/speaker would perform and behave in a country not his or her own.

[1]J. Daly and I. Engleberg, *Presentations in Everyday Life: Strategies for Effective Speaking* (Boston, MA: Houghton Mifflin, 2005).

In preparing a speech and giving it in front of an audience (Exercise 18-1), a public health leader should:

- become extremely knowledgeable about the topic of the speech
- find out the nature of the audience
- make the speech informative, persuasive, and entertaining
- integrate feelings and facts
- be candid and tell stories
- harmonize the verbal message and the message conveyed by body language
- blend theory and practice

INTERVIEWING

Interviewing skills are used by public health leaders when interviewing job seekers, agency staff for membership on self-directed work teams, and representatives of community organizations for partnership development.

As regards job recruitment, public health leaders must develop not only protocols for recruitment but also strategies for helping selected candidates keep their jobs.[36] Those responsible for job interviewing need to specify the qualifications for each job and follow a schedule in interviewing candidates so that all candidates are evaluated objectively.

A distinction can be made between direct and indirect recruiting. Direct recruitment is tied to defined positions that are currently vacant. Indirect recruitment is aimed at expanding the pool of potential job candidates through internships, school presentations, community health promotion programs, community lectures, and so on. Bennis has argued that the successful interviewer is one who knows many people in many different professions.[37] This type of interviewer can then draw potential candidates from many different places through friendships and acquaintances in all these places.

When interviewing a job candidate, the interviewer should cover a range of topics, from the job description to the way the candidate might fit into the agency. **Table 18-2** lists 12 topics that should be explored in an interview.[38]

The interview format can be structured or open-ended. In a structured interview, the interviewer works from a set of standardized questions. The problem with this strategy is that the set of questions lacks application beyond the selection of a candidate for the particular job. An open-ended interview uses a general outline and allows the interviewee to structure his or her responses. The two format types can be combined to create an instrument that includes some of the best features of each.

Where the interview is conducted is also important. Interview questions asked from behind a desk will elicit different responses than questions asked in a conference room or a more casual setting. In conducting the interview, the interviewer needs to establish rapport with the interviewee and control the direction of the conversation so that the necessary topics are covered.[39] The interviewer should urge the interviewee to give concise and thoughtful answers and make clear what his or her goals are. In addition, the interviewer should indicate to the interviewee the basis on which he or she will be evaluated.

The interviewer should either take notes during the interview or, if the interviewee agrees, audiotape the interview.[40] Computer programs are now available for recording voices and typing what is said into a computer document.

Checking the candidate's references is essential, because not all résumés are accurate and not all letters of recommendation are truthful.[41] Telephone reference checks are especially useful if done after the interview because they then allow the interviewer to delve into issues raised during the interview. In fact, the author has found telephone conversations with references to be more useful than letters of recommendation. Candidates sometimes develop fears about reference checks, whether or not those fears are legitimate. They also can be concerned about keeping their current employers from finding out that they are applying for other jobs.

Public health leaders, though usually acting as the interviewer, do occasionally take the role of interviewee, such as when applying for a job as administrator at another agency and being questioned by the

TABLE 18-2 Issues in Interviewing Job Applicants

1. Job requirements and expectations
2. Department and institution characteristics (including patient and staff demographics)
3. Department and institution strengths
4. Management's unique vision of healthcare delivery
5. Mission of the institution
6. Applicant's technical level of skill
7. Opportunities for advancement within the department and institution
8. Applicant's career goals
9. Salary expectations
10. Applicant's personal and professional assets and liabilities as they relate to the worker role
11. "Fit" between the institution and the individual
12. Benefits

Source: Reproduced from J. G. Liebler and C. R. McConnell, *Management Principles for Health Professionals*, 4th edition, pp. 235–236. © 2004, Jones & Bartlett Publishers.

agency's governing board.[42] In interviews for leadership positions, the board must define the relationship between the administrator and the board as well as the boundaries of the administrator's authority. A candidate should not accept a position if convinced that he or she will not be able to function within the parameters set by the board.

One cautionary note: board members rotate off the board, and some of today's members may not be on the board in a year. A candidate for a position as administrator should try to identify the challenges that exist and determine whether it is worth accepting the appointment on the chance that things will improve in the future.

Interviewers need to follow these guidelines:

- Prepare a series of questions ahead of time.
- Select the appropriate interview structure.
- Arrange the setting for the interview.
- Learn different interviewing techniques and when each is appropriate.
- Maintain high ethical standards.
- Keep each job candidate informed about the process of selection.

WRITTEN COMMUNICATION

Leaders need to be masters of all types of communication. The written word can have a major effect on readers. Leaders sometimes use the words of others to guide their vision and actions. The Declaration of Independence and the U.S. Constitution, both written more than 200 years ago, still provide the framework for political and social life in the United States.

Written communication in a modern organization encompasses, among other things, memoranda, letters, periodicals and books, e-mail, electronic bulletin boards, blogging, websites, personal notes, grants, contracts, statistical and technical reports, informational slides, and performance appraisals. One of the major advantages of written communication is that it contributes to the creation of a permanent tangible record[43] and thus allows verification of past activities and events. Another advantage is that the written word is often clearer than the spoken word, largely because it can be reviewed and revised until the author is satisfied.

On the negative side, good written communication takes time. A telephone call takes but a moment and the feedback is immediate, whereas a letter takes time

to write and reception of the response can be delayed for days or weeks. Of course, a telephone call leaves no permanent record unless it is followed up with a memo or letter. One-day mail delivery service and facsimile transmission do speed up the process of getting written feedback more quickly, but the process still lasts many times longer than a phone conversation.

Successful written communication demands preparation. The writer needs to plan the communication by organizing the underlying facts and developing the message prior to putting down words. If the organizing step is left out, the communication will almost certainly fail to be clear, specific, accurate, and concise.

Some writers find outlining to be a useful technique. Some can do this mentally. Wycoff suggested using a technique called "mindmapping."[44] This technique, in which possible approaches to an issue are diagrammed, can clarify the purpose of a written communication and provide a focus (a focus is important for the reader).

In the actual writing, choosing the right words is of the utmost importance. The use of jargon may undermine the effectiveness of the written communication and obscure the information to be disseminated. The promotion of health among community residents through written materials requires language that the residents understand. The writer should always keep in mind the recipients and how the message may be received. It is also important to follow up on the effect of the written materials over time.

Writers usually possess more facts than they are able to use. Part of the task of writing is to winnow out those facts that are unnecessary and focus on those that are critical to the intended message. The written product should of course be grammatically correct and contain no typographical errors—an attainable goal now that virtually all word processing programs have a spelling checker. The importance of writing coherently cannot be overemphasized, and it is a good idea to have a peer check the writing for clarity. The reviewer should point out places where the writing is obscure or confusing and should offer any other advice he or she thinks might be helpful.

Public health leaders engaged in producing written health promotion materials or any other kind of writing should pay attention to the following guidelines:

- Use proper English and restrict yourself to a vocabulary that the intended audience understands.
- Master different writing techniques and use the appropriate technique for each piece of writing.

- Create an outline for a piece of writing prior to writing it.
- Check spelling and correct typographical errors.
- Avoid the incorporation of extraneous material into written materials.
- Write in the same way you talk, although choose your words more carefully.

COMPUTER COMMUNICATION SKILLS

The personal computer, cell phones, and tablets have added some new wrinkles to communication and the transfer of information. Now we trade e-mail or social network messages rather than letters. One advantage is that send-and-respond times are appreciably reduced. Furthermore, although most e-mail messages are short, informal, and limited in scope, e-mail programs allow the sender of a message to attach large document files, such as for a report or research paper.[45] Personal computers can also be used to do research on the Internet, by using search engines or by tapping into various databases.

One of the latest trends in high technology is the integration of personal computers, fax machines, cellular phones, and pagers.[46] The integration of computer technology and communications technology is allowing organizations to become even more interconnected. For example, any person connected to the Internet can create a network of colleagues around the world devoted to discussing topics of common interest. One way this communication occurs is through blogging. Blogs are websites where people with common interests can communicate with each other in a narrative fashion.[47] Blogging has become a major tool of businesses, and it appears to be spreading to people working in public health. To this must be added the increase in social networking sites like Facebook, Twitter, and LinkedIn.

The new technologies have some negative consequences, however.[48] One problem is the difficulty of ensuring the security of the messages that are sent. Another is e-mail overload and the decrease in responsiveness that sometimes results. Many of us go on a one-day business-related trip to come back to 100 or more e-mail messages. All of them have to be at least perused to see which are worthwhile reading and which need a response—a time-consuming process. Reviewing and answering messages on a daily basis can eat into valuable work time, as can listening to and answering phone messages. The transfer of e-mail or phone messages over the phone lines occurs virtually instantaneously, yet it is still the same old sluggish human brain that has to interpret each message and figure what to do in response. Shipley and Schwalbe pointed to the need to be careful about e-mails being unclear in their content, inadvertently insulting, possibly criminal, cowardly, inappropriate, too casual, or sarcastic.[49]

Public health agencies are struggling to acquire the technology necessary to enter the information age. Small rural health departments with limited budgets may not be able to purchase more than one or two personal computers, which will need to be shared. Even when computers are available, public health professionals complain that the necessary training is not. Public health leaders need to convince their governing boards of the importance of computer technology, including new advances.

One recommended strategy is to chart communication activities in order to determine how much time is spent talking, listening, reading, and sending e-mail messages.[50] Public health leaders may find it necessary to reorganize their communication activities so as not to impair their ability to carry out their main responsibilities. Leaders need to remember that computers are tools for dealing with problems, not complete solutions to them. And something else they should remember is that computer communication systems are not substitutes for personal communication.

Any important new tool brings with it a need to redefine work. The advent of computer and communications technology has made it necessary, for instance, to change interorganizational and intraorganizational structures,[51] and changes in technology will continue to affect the field of public health and the way public health leaders go about doing their jobs. To keep pace with the computer and communications revolution, public health leaders must:

- learn how to use e-mail and the Internet to increase effectiveness
- understand the advantages and disadvantages of e-mail as compared with other forms of communication
- learn e-mail etiquette
- master the art of blogging and the use of social networking sites
- monitor advances in computer hardware and software
- train staff in the use of personal computers and the Internet

MEDIA ADVOCACY

Since the 1980s and early 1990s, public health leaders had to learn how to talk to the media. They had to learn, for instance, how to condense a message into a 20-second sound bite, how to use letter-writing campaigns, and how to dress for television—all with the goal of promoting the goals and objectives of public health by using the media to bring pressure on policy makers in order to influence policy.[52] Public health leaders are the leaders most likely to view public health issues from a systems perspective, taking into account social, cultural, psychological, economic, and political dimensions, and they have a duty to use media advocacy to get the message out.[53] Media advocacy can be viewed as a form of empowerment in which public health leaders galvanize community residents to fight for policies that will directly benefit them.

Major planning efforts need to be undertaken to create a coordinated approach to using the media to help solve community health problems. Public health leaders, in publicizing a public health concern, should urge the importance of developing a policy to deal with it and should involve community partners in any publicizing and policy development activities. In promoting a given policy, public health leaders must make sure the facts are researched and verified and must get key stakeholders to support the policy.[54] One of the tasks required for media advocacy is to foster good relationships with media representatives so that channels are open for important public health messages to get out to the community.[55] In developing support for public health initiatives, the use of each of the various media should at least be considered.

There are important differences between traditional public education and media advocacy (**Table 18-3**).[56] In traditional health promotion programs, the individual is the target, and the goal is to alter the individual's behavior. In media advocacy, the individual becomes empowered by becoming involved in the push for health policy changes. Advocacy is aimed at policy makers, and the goal of advocacy is to get beneficial policies legislated and put into action. The advocates, besides public health practitioners, are people who are affected by the health problem at hand and are willing to fight to ensure that the necessary changes are made.[57]

Media advocacy is most effective when it is community based. At its best it includes collaborative efforts at framing issues, setting agendas, developing talking (or writing) points, and monitoring the progress of policy proposals. Those collaborating in the media advocacy process must also keep the general public up to date on the various happenings.

A caution regarding media advocacy needs to be raised here. According to Fallows, the media often undermine the American political system by generating a sense of hopelessness about the future.[58] He stated that the media need to become more public spirited, support the American political system, and empower the public to influence policy. Those who use the media must recognize their limitations and the difficulty of controlling media reactions to local health problems. Case Study 18-B describes a situation in which the press overreacted to a potential private well contamination problem. It shows how the media need to be handled in the context of public health surveillance activities and how public health leaders should communicate these activities to policy makers and the public.

TABLE 18-3   Comparison of Media Advocacy and Public Education

Media Advocacy	Public Education
Individual as advocate	Individual as audience
Advances healthy public policies	Develops health messages
Decentralized and opportunistic	Problem and approach fixed
Changes the environment	Changes the individual
News and paid advertising	Relies on public service
Target is person with power to make change	Target is person with problem or at risk
Addresses the power gap	Addresses the information gap

Source: Reproduced from L. Wallack and L. Dorfman, Media Advocacy: A Strategy for Advancing Policy and Promoting Health, *Health Education and Behavior*, Vol. 23, No. 3, pp. 293–317, copyright © 1996 by Sage Publications, Inc. Reprinted by permission of Sage Publications, Inc.

Leadership Opportunities in Private Well Contamination with Volatile Organic Compounds

Lillian Mood

Introduction

One of the emerging public health problems of our time is the actual or perceived risk of disease, particularly cancer, as a result of exposure to toxins in the environment. Two factors make protecting the health of the public from the dangers of environmental toxins particularly difficult. One is that the science of acceptable risk is still young; standards are developed as chemical compounds are identified as being harmful or potentially harmful to human health. The second factor is that the period of time between exposure and illness is measured in years and sometimes decades rather than the few hours to several days that has been the norm for communicable diseases.

The whole concept of "acceptable risk" is a dilemma in itself. Persons who willingly take risks, such as not wearing a seat belt, exceeding the speed limit, living a sedentary life, and even smoking, want and expect their environment to be free of any contamination from sources outside their own home. To them, any chemical that can be detected at any level is harmful and must be eliminated; many insist on limits for chemical compounds in air, water, and soil that are below detectable levels. The assessments are made in parts per billion, a quantity hard for the average citizen to conceptualize. Making the acceptance of reasonable risk even more complicated is the feeling people have about risks over which they have no control. The thoughts are something like this: "I can choose to eat a diet filled with foods that increase my risk of heart disease, but I have a horrible fear of and outrage about what that industry down the road is putting into the air or into the nearby river. Someone may be doing something to harm me that I can't see or feel, and I'm not at all sure that I can trust the government to protect me."

This is the general climate in which the state health department works toward its goals of minimizing health risks, preserving the quality and safety of the environment, and being responsive to citizens' concerns.

Case Chronology

In early September 1990, a resident of the Regal Oaks community contacted Al Brown, director of the Midlands Environmental Quality Control (EQC) District of the state health department, to register a complaint about his water. The resident, Mr. Bell, was experiencing itching and a skin rash that he was sure was due to contamination of his well from a nearby industry. Because Regal Oaks is not on Capital City's public water system, groundwater is the source of water from the private wells in the neighborhood.

Surveillance (Assessment)

Because contaminated groundwater could affect the quality of water in the Regal Oaks' wells, on September 12, 1990, scientists from the Midlands EQC District took groundwater samples in response to the resident's complaint. Samples were taken from the complainant's home on the 700 block of Fore Avenue and at another home on the 200 block of Fore Avenue. They were analyzed for volatile organic compounds (VOCs), pesticides and herbicides, drinking water metals, and general water chemistry.

Analytical data received September 14 indicated the presence of three VOCs, including tetrachloroethene (PERC), trichloroethene (TCE), and cis-1,2-dichloroethene from one well in the 200 block of Fore Avenue. The level of PERC was 5.04 parts per billion (ppb), exceeding the maximum contaminant level (MCL) of 5.0 ppb that has been proposed for this compound and is in the process of negotiation by the federal Environmental Protection Agency (EPA).

The sample from the 700 block of Fore Avenue, Mr. Bell's home, was clean. More samples were taken from the 200 block of Fore Avenue and four other homes upgradient of that location. Analytical results from these samples confirmed VOCs above MCLs on the 200 block of Fore Avenue and identified detectable levels on the 100 block of Fore Avenue. A detectable level does not necessarily mean that levels are unsafe but shows the need for more testing. For this reason, the staff began an ongoing sampling program at Regal Oaks to determine the extent and source of the groundwater contamination and the resulting risk to the resident population.

On September 17, 1990, confirmatory sampling for VOCs was conducted at the previously sampled private well in the 200 block of Fore Avenue and four wells that appeared to be upgradient of the contaminated well. Analytical data received September 26, 1990, confirmed previous sampling results of PERC at 5.09 ppb and identified these same VOCs below established or proposed MCLs at a second well. The other wells sampled were free of contamination.

(Continues)

Political Inquiry

Meanwhile, Lee Steele, the deputy commissioner for environmental quality control at the state health department, received a letter from the Reed County Council chair, Jim Moore, dated September 18, 1990. Mr. Moore asked for an assessment of the air and water in Regal Oaks because residents were complaining to him that "the drinking water was often green in color and that an unpleasant smell can be frequently found in the air." The residents suspected that the air and water were being contaminated by the Woodbranch Subdivision's wastewater treatment plant, which was adjacent to Regal Oaks. Mr. Steele's response of September 25 indicated that inspectors had found problems at the treatment plant that accounted for the odors, and corrective action was being taken with the operator. Bacterial analyses of the groundwater, however, did not show contamination indicative of the presence of sewage. He also updated Mr. Moore on the status of the sampling for the VOCs.

Surveillance Follow-Up

On October 3, 1990, department personnel obtained groundwater samples for VOC analysis from 17 additional wells. Analytical data received October 19, 1990, found three additional wells with the identified VOCs above the MCLs. Two other wells had detectable levels of VOCs but below the MCLs.

When the results were received for each sampling, each resident received a letter giving the analytical data for his or her well. If an MCL was exceeded, the resident was advised not to use the water for drinking or cooking.

Between September 1990 and February 1991, concurrent with the private well samplings, EQC personnel pursued identification of a potential source, or sources, of the identified contamination. Activities included review of project files and monitoring data, site inspections and interviews with staff personnel, and review of tax maps and property records. Review of the file for Diamond Board, Inc. (formerly Wheeler Trace, Inc.), indicated that Mitchell Jones, state health officer, had responded on September 19 to an August inquiry from Mr. Moore on behalf of his constituents in Regal Oaks.

The residents were concerned that an industry (Wheeler Trace, Inc.), formerly located adjacent to the subdivision, was believed to have used or disposed of hazardous chemicals at its site, and if this were true, those chemicals may have contaminated the environment. The state health officer's reply indicated that a consent order in January 1990 required the present industry on the site (Diamond Board, Inc.) to install two groundwater monitoring wells. Two rounds of samples from these wells allowed department staff to determine that groundwater was not adversely affected by the historical discharge of wastewater.

Media Response

A local newspaper reported the investigations on November 1, 1990. The options for well owners with water problems included digging new wells, treating their existing wells, using bottled water for drinking, or tapping into the city lines. Some residents had begun using bottled water, and Mr. Moore had approached city officials about extending the city's water system to the area. The city's estimate of the cost at that time was approximately $1 million; the cost to each resident would be slightly over $3,000 for the tap-in fee.

On November 2, 1990, two existing monitoring wells located on the former Roberts and Mixon facility property were sampled for VOCs, general water chemistry, and drinking water metals. Analytical data received December 7, 1990, revealed no detectable levels of VOCs from these wells.

On February 28, 1991, EQC personnel installed a temporary well on the property at 10260 Two Notch Road located apparently upgradient of private wells previously identified as being contaminated. Sampling results received April 18, 1991, revealed no detectable levels of VOCs.

On April 25, 1991, a news article reported the status of the investigation to the public.

Department Action

A May 10, 1991, internal department memo to the managers of the Facilities Compliance Section and the Assessment and Development Section of the Bureau of Drinking Water Protection from Pat Bissell, Midlands District hydrologist, summarized the activities and findings of the investigation and requested additional sampling between residences #144 and #224 along Fore Avenue. It was Mr. Bissell's opinion that, given the configuration of the affected wells, if a single source of contamination existed, it should manifest itself in that area.

On July 3, 1991, two additional private wells were sampled for VOCs (161 Fore Avenue and 232 Wynnette Way). Analytical data received August 8, 1991, indicated both wells had detectable levels of the identified compounds, with one well exceeding the MCL for PERC (11 ppb).

On August 22, 1991, an EQC district memorandum to the Bureau of Drinking Water Protection summarized the analytical data obtained to date: "Groundwater contamination appears to approximate an elongate plume which has (or is) emanating from an unidentified point south-southwest of the subdivision. Currently, the apparent contaminate plume is undefined both in vertical and lateral extent, which indicates additional receptors may be utilizing impacted groundwater at this subdivision."

Mr. Bissell urged a meeting as soon as possible to discuss actions necessary to resolve the matter expeditiously. On August 27, 1991, Mr. Bissell met with the director of the Division of Drinking Water Quality and Enforcement, three staff members from the Groundwater Protection Division, and a representative of the Enforcement Section of the Bureau of Drinking Water Protection. The staff agreed to continue efforts to identify the source of contamination and to extend the sampling to additional wells to determine if they were affected. The division director agreed to contact the state health department's legislative liaison to discuss funding alternatives for city water in this subdivision.

On August 29, 1991, a site discovery form listing the Regal Oaks subdivision was sent from the Bureau of Drinking Water Protection to the manager of site screening at the Bureau of Solid and Hazardous Waste. The Site Screening Section is funded by the EPA to conduct investigations at sites that may potentially qualify for the National Priorities List (NPL) for federal "Superfund" action. If the Regal Oaks site qualified for the NPL, federal monies might be available to assist in remediation of the plume.

In September and October 1991, additional water samples were collected from individual wells in an effort to identify all potential receptors of affected groundwater; 19 samples were obtained on September 4, 1991; 7 samples on September 12, 1991; 19 samples on September 30, 1991; and 8 confirmation samples on October 8, 1991. Analytical results indicated that 7 samples exceeded the MCL for PERC or the MCL for TCE.

On October 22, 1991, seeking more information about potential sources of the groundwater contamination, EQC personnel sampled the sanitary septic tank (sludge bottom) at Diamond Board for VOCs. Analytical data identified three VOCs normally associated with petroleum products. None of the VOCs found in groundwater in Regal Oaks were detected by this sampling. In another attempt to locate a possible source, on October 23 Midlands EQC District hydrogeologists met with university agricultural experiment station employees to explore the history of use of the station property. Experimental station employees of many years (15 and 32 years) were not aware of any spills, landfills, or landfilling activities on the station property during their tenure.

On October 25, 1991, health department staff met with state, county, and city officials to discuss the necessity for an alternative water source for the subdivision. In addition to providing an update on the status of the investigation, department personnel informed attending officials that the department has no funding, nor does it know of any funding source, to assist in the development of an alternative water supply.

On November 15, 1991, EQC staff installed and sampled three temporary wells, two on property directly across Two Notch Road from the subdivision and one on the corner of Two Notch Road and Fore Avenue. Detectable levels of two VOCs were identified in the two wells across Two Notch Road, but the compounds and levels needed to be substantiated through additional sampling. No VOCs were found in the sample collected from the corner of Two Notch Road and Fore Avenue.

Legal Interest

On December 3, 1991, Pat Bissell wrote a letter to Jim Moore updating him on the status of the well sampling and enclosed maps of the area. Mr. Bissell also wrote a letter to the Perdy law firm in response to a Freedom of Information Act request for information on the investigation. The Perdy law firm was also referenced in a letter sent by a resident of Regal Oaks to other residents on January 17, 1992. The law firm had been retained for a class action suit. Other citizen initiatives to get action on their concerns were described.

Informally, citizens reported that persons indicating they represented a law firm were knocking on doors in the neighborhood and asking if residents were experiencing health problems and needed legal assistance.

Funding for a Public Water Supply

On January 30, 1992, EPA officials informed the health department that no source of funding was available to assist in providing a public water system for the Regal Oaks subdivision.

On January 31, 1992, department personnel met again with state, county, and city officials to provide additional information in an effort to assist in obtaining grants to fund a public water source for the affected area of Regal Oaks.

(*Continues*)

On February 5, 1992, 15 additional water samples were collected from individual wells in an effort to track the location of the suspected contaminant plume. As of February 12, 1992, the department had collected 94 samples from 73 water supply wells in the Regal Oaks subdivision. Also, the department had installed and sampled four temporary monitoring wells and sampled four existing monitoring wells at two facilities in the immediate area. Of the 73 wells sampled, data indicated that 30 wells exhibited detectable levels of VOCs, principally PERC and TCE. Twelve of the wells exceeded the established and/or proposed maximum contaminant levels for PERC and/or TCE, which are 5.0 ppb.

Communication with Residents

Each time sampling was done, a copy of the results and a letter of explanation were provided to each resident whose well was sampled. Residents were invited by the Midlands EQC District director and the Reed County Council chair to a public meeting on February 12, 1992. A large number of Regal Oaks residents attended. Al Brown, EQC District director, welcomed the group, introduced the others who would be speaking, and explained a number of the terms (e.g., ppb, VOC, and TCE) in a fact sheet furnished to each attendee. Overhead projections of maps were used to show exactly the area affected and the points beyond which no contamination had been found.

Pat Bissell, hydrologist, described the patterns of groundwater migration in the area, which provided the basis for ruling out certain industries as potential sources of the contamination.

Mac Monroe, division director of the Drinking Water Protection Bureau, explained how standards for MCLs are reached and the boundaries of authority of the drinking water program. Bill Marks, MD, director of Health Hazard Evaluation, talked about what is known and not known about exposures to VOCs and what people can do to minimize their risk of exposure.

There were a number of questions from residents about health symptoms ranging from itching to rashes and about some residents' impression that the neighborhood had too many cases of cancer. Information was given on the usual effects of toxic doses of the VOCs identified. Liver damage and tumors of the liver occurred but only after long exposure to high concentrations. Well samples had been taken from the residences of persons with health complaints and no VOCs were found.

Jim Moore, county council chair, spoke of the efforts of elected officials to find funding to provide city water to Regal Oaks. He explained the availability of funds from the governor's office if the subdivision qualified. Because qualifying was dependent on the income levels of residents, attendees were given forms to fill out documenting their income. They were assured that the confidentiality of the information provided would be maintained.

The Media Turn Up the Volume

The meeting and some of the residents' reactions were reported in the local newspaper. A letter to the editor dated February 20, 1992, cited the Regal Oaks investigation as an example of "Power Failure," a term coined by the newspaper to support the governor's initiative to restructure state government into a cabinet organization of state agencies. One part of the proposal was to separate the health and governmental protection functions into two separate departments.

A March 25 letter to the editor from the district EQC director attempted to clear up some misunderstandings of the department's actions.

Interim Measures

On March 30, 1992, residents with contaminated wells were notified that money had been made available through the Superfund program to install granular activated charcoal filters in their homes as a temporary measure. The filters would allow residents to use their well water safely until the city water system was extended to the subdivision. The filters would then be removed by the health department staff.

Obtaining a filter was voluntary; residents were told how to request a filter. After some follow-up, seven of the 11 residents contacted requested filters, one said he would give permission for additional monitoring, and one declined the filter. No reply was received from two residents.

About the same time, Reed County provided a single tap into the city water system with a faucet so residents would have access to safe water, making it no longer necessary for them to either buy bottled water or go outside the area to fill bottles of water.

On May 14, 1992, a letter was sent to all Regal Oaks residents giving them current information, and on August 6, 1992, a news article reported the status as of that date.

Current Status

The last sampling by Midlands EQC District staff occurred in March 1992. Sampling by the state Superfund staff is scheduled to begin on September 22, 1992.

Funding for the public water supply is progressing. A public hearing on funding through the community block grant is scheduled for September 23, 1992. A meeting with county officials is scheduled in order to pursue the local matching funds required by the block grant.

There has been no further word on the class action suit. The resident who made reference to the suit in her letter to other residents has sold her property in Regal Oaks and moved out of the neighborhood.

The news media has been relatively silent on the issue recently. There was one recent TV news spot that presented a very negative view of the situation. The emphasis of the story was on funding a public water supply, and the implication was that people were suffering severe health problems. The health department was not contacted by the TV news prior to or for comment on the story. The spot generated only one follow-up call to the department from a citizen.

Jim Moore was defeated in his primary bid for reelection to the Reed County Council in August 1992. He had served on the council since 1984 and as its chair for one year.

TABLE 18-4   Seven Cardinal Rules of Risk Communication

1. Accept and involve the public as a partner. Your goal is to produce an informed public, not to defuse public concerns or replace actions.
2. Plan carefully and evaluate your efforts. Different goals, audiences, and media require different actions.
3. Listen to the public's specific concerns. People often care more about trust, credibility, competence, fairness, and empathy than about statistics and details.
4. Be honest, frank, and open. Trust and credibility are difficult to obtain; once lost, they are almost impossible to regain.
5. Work with other credible sources. Conflicts and disagreements among organizations make communication with the public much more difficult.
6. Meet the needs of the media. The media are usually more interested in politics than risk, simplicity than complexity, danger than safety.
7. Speak clearly and with compassion. Never let your efforts prevent your acknowledging the tragedy of an illness, injury, or death. People can understand risk information, but they may still not agree with you; some people will not be satisfied.

Source: Reproduced from V. Covello and F. Allen, *Seven Cardinal Rules of Risk Communication*, 1988, Office of Policy Analysis, U.S. Environmental Protection Agency.

One media advocacy issue is how to publicize health risks. Public health leaders should involve key stakeholders in discussions of the technical aspects of health risks. For one thing, a given risk must be evaluated from social, psychological, economic, and political perspectives.[59]

In publicizing a health risk, public health leaders should explore the various media options and choose a presentation format appropriate to the level of concern. All the media should be used to inform the community about a health risk. See **Table 18-4** for a list of risk communication rules.

When we talk about risk, we are often talking about it from a perspective of a type of event we or others have experienced in the past. Our perceptions of these emergency events give us clues to how we might handle the occurrence of a similar event in the future. Thus, our past gives us clues to potential events in the future. In addition to this awareness of a past event and its consequences, anger or discontent enters the picture over the potentiality of another similar event. If the hazard or emergency event of the past was a serious one, then a sense of outrage occurs if a second event ensues. People also feel their personal space has been invaded. One interesting example of this is the feelings that go along with the effects of a hurricane when a person's house and all of his or her belongings are destroyed. Upset and outrage were also demonstrated by the families of victims of September 11, 2001. There is also the emotional factor of vulnerability that people feel as a result of these crisis events. Our feelings of risk are thus affected by several factors:

> Risk sensitivity = memory of past emergencies + vulnerability + outrage

The above formula is clearly an oversimplification of a very complex process. Our level of risk sensitivity is affected not only by our personal reactions to a potential hazardous event, but also by how this potential risk is communicated to us. The issue of how much we trust the communicator also becomes part of the formula. Specifically, the National Research Council described risk communication as an interactive process in which information and opinions are exchanged among individuals, groups, and institutions.[60] Risk communication also involves the relaying of multiple messages about the nature and severity of the risk and nonrisk messages that address the concerns of the public, opinions, or reactions to the risk messages. There are four major risk communication theories described by Covello, Peters, Wojtecki, and Hyde.[61] All the theories need to be seen in the context of big concern situations.

The trust determination theorists point to the fact that people who are upset tend to distrust the messenger.[62] It is critical that professionals responsible for risk communication build trust with their publics over time. Trust must be built if the effects of high-concern situations are to be lessened. The communicator needs critical skills related to active listening because people with high risk sensitivity do not believe that the communicator is listening to their concerns. Building trust requires many of the skills of emotional intelligence. Covello has demonstrated that the four factors of empathy and caring, competence and expertise, honesty and openness, and dedication and commitment are associated with the public assessment of trust in the communicator.[63,64] Crisis situations are often seen to be examples of high-concern and low-trust situations. To gain some clarity of the issue of concern and trust, look at **Figure 18-3**, which is a graphic contingency table related to concern and trust. Exercise 18-2 asks you to develop four scenarios demonstrating each of the four possible combinations of trust and concern.

Theorists who support a mental noise model discovered that people under stress who are upset have difficulty in hearing and understanding the messages being sent by a communicator.[65] This theory posits the sending of no more than three key messages at a time, keeping messages to 10 seconds or no more than 30 words,

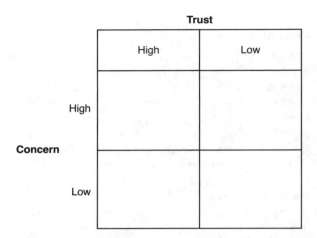

FIGURE 18-3 Trust and Concern in Risk Situations.
Source: Reprinted with permission from *Health and Environmental Digest* (1992), V. T. Covello, Risk Communication, Trust, and Credibility, 6, 1, 1-4.

repeating the messages, and using visuals when possible. Mental noise situations are greatest in high-concern situations.[66] Body language may negate a verbal message.[67] The emotional reaction to the high-concern event generates strong feelings, from fear to anger to rage, that creates the mental noise that then affects the ability of the individual to engage in rational conversations.

The negative dominance theorists have stated that when people are under stress, they tend to see the world in negative ways. This mirrors Covello's statement that one negative statement is equal to three positive statements (1N = 3P).[68] People who are communicating with the public need to be careful not to use too many negative words in their messages because stressed people in high-concern situations will increase the real value of these negative words. Communicators need to present their messages in terms of what is being done rather than what is not being done.[69]

The fourth model has been called risk perception, which relates to how risks are perceived by people. Covello and his colleagues looked at risk perception in the context of high-concern situations and stated that the level of concern tends to be strongest when people define the situation as involuntary, not equitable, not beneficial, out of a person's immediate control, associated with adverse potential or real outcomes, and, as shown above in trust determination arguments, as being associated with untrustworthy individuals or organizations.[70] It seems clear that the issue of risk perception is an important aspect of risk communication strategies. In fact, all four theories are really interrelated and cover slightly different perspectives on the issue of trust and concern as well as the important relationship between the communicator and the recipient of the communication message.[71]

These discussions often simplify what in many ways may be a more complex set of reactions. Fischoff and his colleagues studied how people's reactions to the magnitude of a risk are affected by many factors. [72] If a risk is seen as something that a person or group can control voluntarily, the risk may be more acceptable than a risk that is out of the control of the individual or group. Second, if a person feels that he or she can control the risk, then he or she will handle it. Risks that are seen as beneficial are more acceptable than risks that seem to not be so. Individuals also react more fairly when they perceive that a risk is evenly distributed among a population then when a risk is unfairly distributed. This might be labeled the "why me" phenomenon.

Risks or crises that are natural in origin are often more acceptable than human-made risks. We respond strongly to both, but more strongly to such things as terrorist events. If a risk is generated by a trusted person or resource, then people tend to be more accepting of it than when the risk comes from an untrusted person or source. Risks perceived to be familiar, such as a tornado or hurricane in a place where these natural events often occur, are more acceptable than risks that are more unusual. We also react more strongly to risks that affect children than to risks that affect adults.

It is important to see risk from a reaction perspective as well as from the individual who will be most affected by the risk. Perhaps it is possible to rate the reaction through the following formula:

Risk reaction indicator = Actual risk + rumor + level of concern + emotional reaction ÷ 4

Rate each factor in the formula from 1 to 100 and then divide by 4 to get the risk reaction indicator. This rating will help the prepared public health leader who is responsible for working and communicating with an individual or group gauge the audience that he or she is addressing. It may also affect the message that is to be given. The emotional reaction to the potential risk is also affected by whom the risk is seen to impact the most. A risk to a given person is seen in a different light than a risk to other family members. A work risk is different from a risk at home. A community risk is also different from personal or family risks. Finally, a risk to a society or to national security is different again from other types of risk.

Many myths stand in the way of the development of effective risk communication programs.[73] It is important to address these myths with action to improve communication strategies. **Table 18-5** presents some of these myths and action steps.

Chess and his colleagues have also pointed out the critical nature of community input into the risk communication process.[74] It is important to involve the community earlier and to involve community organizations and leaders in the decision-making process. The decisions to be made will affect the lives of people living in the community. It should be clear by now that people affected by the risk situation will respond differently than those who are not directly affected. In other words, the audiences for a risk message may each have different reactions and needs. The prepared public health leader needs to develop different messages for different audiences. In this case, one size does not fit all. As pointed out above, people's values and feelings are important. The trustful leader will understand this and acknowledge these realities.

Keeping in mind the above discussion, it is now useful to discuss the issue of the message. The public health leader as communicator has to craft a message or series of messages that in essence takes the crisis reaction out of the emergency situation. In a talk at the annual American Public Health Association meeting in 2004, Vanderford discussed messages in terms of three elements.[75] First, there is the content element, which relates to presenting explicit information. Second, there is the relational element, which involves such concerns as respect and caring for the recipients of the message. It also involves the implicit statements related to the power of the person giving the message. The third element is the contextual element, which looks for other competing messages and what associations are made with the message being given.

A useful tool for public health leaders in their roles as risk communicators involves the use of message-mapping techniques. All of the previous discussion concerned the critical issue of how the public perceives a risk and how the communicator tells the public about the risk and what to expect. It should be clear that an informed public will be better able to listen to the message than an uninformed public. If you were to conduct a simple nonrandom survey of your neighborhood, apartment building, workplace, or residence at a university and ask people, first, what they know about potential natural or human-made crises that might occur in their jurisdiction, and second, what their community and residence have done to prepare for these

TABLE 18-5   Risk Communication: Myths and Actions

Belief in some common myths often interferes with development of an effective risk communication program. Consider the myths and actions you can take.

Myth: We don't have enough time and resources to have a risk communication program.
Action: Train all your staff to communicate more effectively. Plan projects to include time to involve the public.

Myth: Telling the public about a risk is more likely to unduly alarm people than keeping quiet.
Action: Decrease potential for alarm by giving people a chance to express their concerns.

Myth: Communication is less important than education. If people knew the true risks, they would accept them.
Action: Pay as much attention to your process for dealing with people as you do to explaining the data.

Myth: We shouldn't go to the public until we have solutions to environmental health programs.
Action: Release and discuss information about risk management options and involve communities in strategies in which they have a stake.

Myth: These issues are too difficult for the public to understand.
Action: Separate public disagreement with your policies from misunderstanding of the highly technical issues.

Myth: Technical decisions should be left in the hands of technical people.
Action: Provide the public with information. Listen to community concerns. Involve staff with diverse backgrounds in developing policy.

Myth: Risk communication is not my job.
Action: As a public servant, you have a responsibility to the public. Learn to integrate communication into your job and help others do the same.

Myth: If we give them an inch, they'll take a mile.
Action: If you listen to people when they are asking for inches, they are less likely to demand miles. Avoid the battleground. Involve people early and often.

Myth: If we listen to the public, we will devote scarce resources to issues that are not a great threat to public health.
Action: Listen early to avoid controversy and the potential for disproportionate attention to lesser issues.

Myth: Activist groups are responsible for stirring up unwarranted concerns.
Action: Activists help to focus public anger. Many environmental groups are reasonable and responsible. Work with groups rather than against them.

Source: Reproduced from C. Chess, B. J. Hance, and P. M. Sandman, *Improving Dialogue with Communities: A Short Guide to Government Risk Communication* (Trenton, NJ: New Jersey Department of Environmental Protection (1988)).

possible crises, what would you discover? I would guess that most of our families, friends, and colleagues are not very well informed about these potential risks.

An informed public will change the message. In fact, the involvement of community people in risk assessment and communication as a partnership can have benefits. An Agency for Toxic Substances and Disease Registry (ATSDR) report for citizens discussed how community input can help in the identification of local facts that might clarify the risk determination process.[76] Community input might also improve the determination of how great the risk will be for the community. Community involvement may also simplify the planning process and communication strategies in that an informed community may well be better able to understand the risks. This process may mean that different communication issues can be addressed that go far beyond the messages needed when people are uninformed. Community involvement may also help gain acceptance and support for the emergency response activities because they know what will happen during an emergency. For example, if police powers are required, the public will understand the reasons more readily.

The interesting missing link in this discussion relates to the public health leader who often serves as the voice of his or her community. The public health leader often has the responsibility or delegates the responsibility for relaying information about an emergency to the public as well as to the media. Here it becomes evident that the leader has to read his or her own personal emotions and perceptions, as well as the emotions and perceptions of the people who work in the agency, the community that is served, the elected community officials, and finally, the concerns of the media to report the latest news. Covello and his colleagues from the Center for Risk Communication have come up with a list of the 77 questions most frequently asked of the person who relays the latest information about the crisis.[77] These questions, reproduced in **Table 18-6**, are extensions of the traditional journalist questions of who, what, when, where, why, and how. These questions are intended to find out about the causes and extent of the crisis as well as its effect on the population and community. These questions as well as the early discussion on trust and concern all guide the message-mapping process. The other element of importance that prepared public health leaders need to recognize is that the skills of conflict management are also important in any discussion of crisis management.

There are eight goals related to the use of message maps in risk communication.[78]

1. Determine who the key stakeholders are early in the process.
2. Attempt to forecast the questions and concerns of stakeholders before they verbalize them.
3. Integrate thought and feeling processes to more accurately develop prepared questions related to stakeholder fears, perceptions, and concerns.
4. As clearly and concisely as possible, assemble supporting information to go with the key messages.
5. Create an open environment for dialogue and discussion both within the agency and outside it.
6. Devise user-friendly approaches for key communicators in your organization if you are not going to be the spokesperson.
7. Guarantee that the messages to be given are consistent and trustworthy.
8. Always have your agency speak with one voice.

Message mapping provides a process for understanding communication in high-risk situations. There are seven steps in the construction of message maps.[79]

1. Identify the key stakeholders.
2. Determine a complete list of specific concerns (SCs) of each stakeholder group that is identified.
3. Analyze the list of SCs to determine the underlying general concerns (GCs) of each stakeholder group.
4. Develop three key messages of less than three seconds or less than nine words for each key message related to what most stakeholders need to know, want to know, or are most concerned about relative to both SCs and GCs.
5. Provide or discover supporting facts for each key message.
6. Undertake systematic testing of the message utilizing standardized procedures.
7. Present the prepared message maps through various communication channels.

Covello's template for message mapping can be found in **Figure 18-4**.[80] Exercise 18-3 gives you the chance to experiment with message mapping for three stakeholder groups concerned about a terrorist attack in Los Angeles in the next year.

In recent years, there has been increasing interest in logic models. The logic model approach would be an interesting variation on the message-mapping approach. In logic models, you create a chart divided into five portions.[81] In the first column, you list the inputs, including information about the crisis, specific concerns, and general concerns (see **Figure 18-5**). In the second column, you list the activities to be carried out, including the structure of the message, the various media to be contacted, and any other stakeholder activities. The third column shows the outputs that are the products of the previous column. The fourth column allows the analysis of the outcomes of the communication activities, and the final column determines the impact of all the activities done on the various stakeholders and the community as a whole. The major advantage of the logic model approach is that it can be used for all sorts of problem analysis by the prepared public health leader. You can contrast this logic model approach with the message-mapping model approach by redoing Exercise 18-3.

TABLE 18-6 77 Questions Commonly Asked by Journalists During a Crisis

What is your name and title?

What are your job responsibilities?

What are your qualifications?

Can you tell us what happened?

When did it happen?

Where did it happen?

Who was harmed?

How many people were harmed?

Are those who were harmed getting help?

How certain are you about this information?

How are those who were harmed getting help?

Is the situation under control?

How certain are you that the situation is under control?

Is there any immediate danger?

What is being done in response to what happened?

Who is in charge?

What can we expect next?

What are you advising people to do?

How long will it be before the situation returns to normal?

What help has been requested or offered from others?

What responses have you received?

Can you be specific about the types of harm that occurred?

What are the names of those who were harmed?

Can we talk to them?

How much damage occurred?

What other damage may have occurred?

How certain are you about damages?

How much damage do you expect?

What are you doing now?

Who else is involved in the response?

Why did this happen?

What was the cause?

Did you have any forewarning that this might happen?

Why wasn't this prevented from happening?

What else can go wrong?

If you are not sure of the cause, what is your best guess?

Who caused this to happen?

Who is to blame?

Could this have been avoided?

Do you think those involved handled the situation well enough?

When did your response to this begin?

When were you notified that something had happened?

Who is conducting the investigation? What are you going to do after the investigation?

What have you found out so far?

Why was more not done to prevent this from happening?

What is your personal opinion?

What are you telling your own family?

Are all those involved in agreement?

Are people overreacting?

Which laws are applicable?

Has anyone broken the law?

How certain are you about the laws?

Has anyone made mistakes?

How certain are you about mistakes?

Have you told us everything you know?

What are you not telling us?

What effects will this have on the people involved?

What precautionary measures were taken?

Do you accept responsibility for what happened?

Has this ever happened before?

Can this happen elsewhere?

What is the worst-case scenario?

What lessons were learned?

Were those lessons implemented?

What can be done to prevent this from happening again?

What would you like to say to those who have been harmed and to their families?

Is there any continuing danger?

Are people out of danger? Are people safe?

Will there be inconvenience to employees or to the public?

How much will all this cost?

Are you able and willing to pay the costs?

Who else will pay the costs?

When will we find out more?

What steps are being taken to avoid a similar event?

What lessons have you learned?

What does this all mean?

Source: Reproduced from V. T. Covello, J. G. Wojtecki, and R. Peters, *77 Questions Asked by Journalists During a Crisis* (New York: Center for Risk Communications, n.d.).

Stakeholder: Question or concern:		
Key message 1	Key message 2	Key message 3
Supporting fact 1-1	Supporting fact 2-1	Supporting fact 3-1
Supporting fact 1-2	Supporting fact 2-2	Supporting fact 3-2
Supporting fact 1-3	Supporting fact 2-3	Supporting fact 3-3

FIGURE 18-4 **Message Map Template.** *Source*: Reproduced from V. T. Covello, *Message Mapping: World Health Organization Workshop on Bioterrorism and Risk Communication* (Geneva, Switzerland: WHO, 2002).

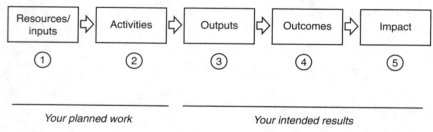

FIGURE 18-5 **Logic Model Example.** *Source*: With the permission of the W. K. Kellogg Foundation.

In summary, public health leaders should:

- use their media advocacy skills to influence policy makers
- include key stakeholders in the media advocacy process
- follow the seven cardinal rules of risk communication
- write a letter on a public health issue to the local newspaper twice a month
- dress conservatively for television events
- learn to present messages concisely
- select appropriate communication channels for advocacy and risk communication
- rehearse before doing any oral presentations of advocacy positions
- make sure they are the appropriate spokesperson for a media interview

COMMUNICATION AND CULTURAL SENSITIVITY

American society has always been diverse, ethnically and racially as well as in other ways, but it is becoming even more so. For example, women and minorities are increasingly assuming leadership roles in the workplace. Because protection against health risks is a right of all citizens, the makeup of public health programs should reflect the makeup of the larger society. This means that public health leaders need to be students of culture and develop the interpersonal skills needed for relating to staff and community residents of different social and cultural backgrounds.[82]

A culture is a type of social system that encompasses a shared language, shared values, and a shared set of behaviors. A person's culture to a large extent determines how the person acts and reacts, and thus public health leaders need to understand the cultures of the community they serve and eliminate their prejudices if they want to work for the good of the community.

Diversity can be an obstacle to communication and cooperation among agency staff or with community partners.[83] Fortunately, public health leaders can use a number of techniques to evaluate how an agency is responding to the issue of diversity. First, they need to study how the agency treats job applicants from different backgrounds as well as clients or community partners from different backgrounds. They also need to explore the power relationships that exist between staff from diverse backgrounds and to read all printed materials related to the organization in order to determine if the messages given are discriminatory. They should walk around the agency to see how people from diverse backgrounds are treated by staff and interview staff about instances of mistreatment that may have occurred or patterns of discrimination that may have developed. Finally, they should build a "web of inclusion."[84] As a prerequisite, they need to ensure that a system of open communication is in place and that information flows freely throughout the organization, allowing, among other things, power relationships to become realigned.

With regard to gender differences, the increase of women in the workplace has led to an increase in sexual harassment laws and new approaches to affirmative action.[85] In the late 1990s, there was a backlash against affirmative action laws and regulations that will affect organizations well into the 21st century. The legality of these affirmative action programs is being debated in the courts. One thing to keep in mind is that many Americans believe that the only way to create change is through opposition. As one author put it, ours is an "argument culture."[86] Yet it is best to move away from debate to more of a dialogue between equal partners. Equality and dialogue are critical if we are to understand each person, no matter what gender, race, or ethnicity, and be able to listen to him or her with an open mind.

Public health leaders will need to become multicultural in the 21st century,[87] which is to say that they will need the skills to communicate effectively with diverse social groups. In general, they will need to increase their cultural sensitivity by investigating the reasons diverse groups act in certain ways. Cultural sensitivity leads to mutual respect and to the empowerment of previously marginalized groups. It also allows public health leaders to find innovative ways to increase the health literacy of people from different backgrounds.[88]

Culturally sensitive public health leaders:

- remain objective
- learn to control gender, racial, and ethnic prejudices by clarifying values
- understand the different expectations that men and women bring to leadership
- learn the spoken and gestural languages and behavior patterns of different racial and ethnic groups
- adjust the way in which they convey messages in light of the culture of the audience and the situation

- build a web of inclusion
- become familiar with sexual harassment laws, affirmative action laws, and other laws and regulations relevant to the issue of diversity

FEEDBACK

Completion of an act of communication requires feedback from the respondent, whether in the form of a spoken statement, printed data, graphics, or a videotape. Communication strategies, including strategies for giving feedback, change to reflect the expansion of technology,[89] but certain principles remain unaltered. For example, feedback may be positive or negative, but most people seem to respond better to positive messages than to negative ones.[90] Negative feedback, however, can lead to positive results when there is potential resistance. The response is affected by the credibility of the person giving the feedback and the ability of the person receiving the feedback to evaluate what has been said objectively.

In the case of a group, such as a team or even a whole organization, the receivers of a message can engage in a conspiracy of silence in which they subvert the message without informing the sender. Leaders need to become expert at determining whether lack of feedback is a reflection of acquiescence or silent resistance.

The solicitation of feedback should be planned and not left to chance.[91] In fact, leaders need to develop continuous feedback loops between themselves and staff and organizational and community stakeholders.[92]

Feedback can be divided into various types.[93] Verbal feedback is extremely interactive, and it often affects the total process of communication. Nonverbal feedback involves the use of body language and facial gestures. Fact-based feedback presents relevant information for dealing with a specific situation. In a fourth variety of feedback, the receiver of the message expresses his or her feelings, sometimes nonverbally, about the message. Public health leaders need to be empathetic and pay attention to the feelings of those they are communicating with.

The symbolic interactionist model developed by Hulett (see Figure 18-1) includes feedback control.[94] The person initiating a communicative process performs an instrumental act that motivates the other person to become involved in the communicative process and eventually perform his or her own instrumental act, which can be viewed as a response to the message (or as feedback). The person receiving the return message may then go through the covert rehearsal phase for a second time in order to clarify the message received and perform another instrumental act, leading to further feedback. Hulett identified two feedback loops: an intrapersonal loop (part of the covert rehearsal stage) and an interpersonal loop. The interpersonal feedback loop is used to relay information from the receiver of a message back to the sender.

In performance evaluations, feedback on specific behaviors is preferable to feedback on general behaviors.[95] Specificity makes the feedback seem more personal, as if the individual giving the feedback took an active interest in the individual receiving the feedback. At the same time, the feedback should be objective. It should not consist of criticisms of the person, but of an evaluation of job-related behaviors. If the evaluator must give criticism (negative feedback), the critique needs to focus on behaviors that the individual can change. Feedback on performance should be oriented toward the goal of improving the person's performance and achieving desired outcomes, which of course means that the message must be understandable to the receiver. The timing of feedback is important as well. It should be given to an individual as soon as possible after the occurrence of the behaviors being evaluated.

In giving feedback, including feedback on a person's work performance, public health leaders should:

- accentuate the positive but point out ways in which performance could be improved
- concentrate on specific rather than general behaviors
- be objective and goal oriented (aim at improving work performance)
- provide the feedback in a timely fashion
- offer negative feedback only in regard to behavior that is controllable
- create ongoing feedback loops

DELEGATION OF AUTHORITY

To delegate is to give others, including individuals and teams, both the responsibility for certain actions and the power to ensure that the actions are performed. There is a strong communication component in delegation, and the delegators need to be cognizant of the communication factors that can enhance the delegation of responsibility and the factors that can obstruct its delegation. One way to look at delegation is that

it is a shift in the power to make decisions and to act from one level to a lower level of the organizational hierarchy.[96] Delegation is not shared decision making. Rather, if decision-making authority is truly delegated, the decision made by the delegatee will be put into force. This means that the boundaries of the delegated authority must be made clear to the delegatee, which of course requires good communication between the delegator and the delegatee.

When responsibility is delegated, the delegator must nonetheless act as an overseer to ensure that the delegatees are moving in the right direction. If the delegator loses confidence in the ability of the delegatees to carry out their assigned responsibilities, the delegator may accept their recommendations while taking back final decision-making authority.

Because a public health agency usually has many specialized public health programs, the agency leaders tend to delegate responsibility for these programs. Sharing power can increase agency effectiveness and can generate trust and credibility.[97] Among the best activities to delegate are those that a leader has done over and over but that are still needed for the smooth functioning of the organization.[98] Because the leader has extensive experience with these tasks, he or she can give detailed instructions to staff members on how to perform them. Also, because a leader cannot attain expertise in all areas under his or her purview, he or she would do well to delegate certain specialty areas to the appropriate experts. In the information age, the need for delegating responsibilities will increase in line with the expansion of technology, including information processing technology.

Leaders should not delegate the responsibility for attending meetings that require their presence, or responsibility for activities related to personnel or other confidential matters. They need to control the policy-making function, and although delegatees may influence policy development, the leaders need to make the final policy recommendations. All organizations occasionally face crises, and the leaders need to monitor any mounting crisis and maintain tight control over the efforts to resolve it.

All leaders struggle with the issue of too much responsibility and too little time. Each new task that a leader accepts brings with it new duties and often a new set of constituents. As the number of tasks grows, the leader experiences role overload.[99] On the other hand, staff members sometimes feel that they do not have enough to do—an example of role underload. Thus, delegation can lead to interesting results.

If assignments are delegated to public health practitioners lower in the organization, those staff members will experience a reduction in role underload. Conversely, the leader should feel relief because pressure is being removed. The leader, however, might also feel insecure as a result of the transfer of responsibility. Hopefully, the leader will gradually become more secure as he or she sees the positive results of the delegation of activities. Delegation involves a balance between trust and control.

Hersey and colleagues treat delegation as one of four leadership styles.[100] The ability of a leader to delegate authority is determined by the abilities and backgrounds of others in the organization. New employees may need specific instructions on how to perform tasks as well as supervision during the learning process. Gradually the leader moves from discussing decisions with the staff to delegating decision-making authority. During this process, the leader should provide continual feedback.[101] Empowered staff members need information on how they are doing, and good performance should always be recognized.

As mentioned earlier, the delegator of an activity needs to make the assignment clear to the delegatees. The best strategy is to be as specific as possible and yet leave room for the delegatees to use their creativity to address the problems presented by the assignment. If a whole task is not within the realm of authority of delegatees, they need to know the limits of their authority. Furthermore, the delegator should inform others in the organization or community about the delegation of responsibility. This is another place where communication plays an essential role in delegation.

In delegating authority and responsibility for activities and outcomes, public health leaders must:

- define the dimensions of the assignment
- specify how much freedom the delegatees possess to do the task
- delegate the whole task to an individual or a team
- include potential delegatees in the whole decision process
- let other staff or partners know about the delegation
- set up feedback channels

FRAMING

A paradigm is a set of rules that define boundaries and act as guidelines for action.[102] Followers of a professional paradigm are generally accepted by other professionals in their field. Given that science and practice continue to change, paradigms do not last forever. If a paradigm reaches its operational limits, then a new paradigm will evolve to take its place.

There is a strong communication component in paradigm building. Once the new paradigm has been constructed, the leader has to communicate it to the various public health stakeholders. Their response to it is a form of test. Following is a set of guidelines for creating a new paradigm for public health:

- Create a mission and vision or adopt existing ones.
- In developing the paradigm, take into account the perspective of key stakeholders.
- Promote individual leadership development.
- Promote organizational change on the basis of core functions and essential public health services using a strategic planning and action planning approach.
- Develop public health coalitions built on a team-based model and a community-defined agenda.
- Improve transorganizational relationships (meta-leadership).
- Move toward an integrated community-wide model with strong prevention components.
- Increase interaction among local governmental boards, local agencies, state health and health-related agencies, and the local health department.

According to Goffman, framing consists of a series of acts that integrate primary frameworks (or paradigms) and actions.[103] Primary frameworks, which create a culture of understanding in teams, organizations, and communities, include such things as values and beliefs. Communication is the mechanism for monitoring the framing process. In addition, communication, as well as new perceptions, can add new information to past experience and thus clarify a current framework or require a reframing.[104]

A framework is a tool, and like any tool it can be used well or poorly.[105] If the right framework is used in a given situation, the framework will be supported or extended. If the wrong framework is used, it may become undermined.

If a crisis occurs, mechanisms must be found for renewing the organization.[106] The leaders of an organization might even precipitate a crisis in order to break down the frameworks that do not work. Because the leadership role includes acting as a change agent, leaders need to master transformational change methodologies, people management skills, and framing skills.

It is through framing that reality gets defined.[107] Framing creates an action language that serves as an aid to understanding situations. This language helps in classifying information in the context of the framework used. Leaders tend to be more effective when they recognize framing opportunities and take advantage of them to create frameworks for self-guidance and the guidance of others. **Table 18-7** identifies several types of framework, describes their functions, indicates when to use them and when not to use them, and gives examples of each.[108]

Public health leaders need to:

- develop or adopt frameworks (paradigms) to guide action
- become familiar with the frameworks of those with whom they interact
- learn reframing techniques

- coordinate their vision and their primary frameworks (governing paradigms)
- learn how to use metaphors, jargon, contrast, spin, and stories for purposes of framing

DIALOGUE, DISCUSSION, AND DEBATE

Imagine that several public health leaders come into a room and take chairs organized in a circle. All preconceived notions and professional credentials are left at the door. The rules governing the ensuing conversation are that each person gets to talk without interruption and that no one should be concerned about the output of the group process. The kind of discussion that will result—if the leaders talk freely—is what has been called dialogue. It can be a means of uncovering hidden values and agendas[109] and exploring the way

TABLE 18-7   Framing Techniques

	Metaphors	Jargon/ Catchphrases	Contrast	Spin	Stories
Function	They show a subject's likeness with something else.	They frame a subject in familiar terms.	It describes a subject in terms of its opposite.	It puts a subject in a positive or negative light.	They frame a subject by example.
Use it because	You want a subject to take on new meaning.	Familiar references can enhance meaning. Jargon and catchphrases help communicate a vision's "god" and "devil" terms.	It is sometimes easier to define what your subject is not than state what it is.	It can reveal your subject's strengths or weaknesses.	Stories attract attention and can build rapport.
Avoid it when	They mask important alternative meanings.	A word or phrase is in danger of overuse.	Meaning can be skewed by a poor contrast.	The ratio of spin to reality is excessive.	They mask important alternative meanings.
Example	"I feel our relationship is formal, like punching a ticket."	"We've got to break the squares today."	"It's a choice between raising my hand for the teacher to ask if it's okay or just telling it like it is."	"Which Ray will show up? The one who's cooperative and generous, or the egotist who constantly reminds others of his successes and what is due him?"	"In my first three or four years here, I was a lot like you. I thought. . . ."

Source: Reprinted with permission from G. T. Fairhurst and R. A. Starr, *The Art of Framing*, p. 101. © 1996, Jossey-Bass, Inc., Publishers.

these values and agendas control the behavior of the participants. Furthermore, it can change the way people work because it diffuses information throughout the dialogue group and eventually throughout the organization and community.[110]

Dialogue, because of the group's synergism, is a communication process in which everyone can win.[111] The participants often find out things they were unaware of, such as the fact that they share patterns of thought. They might also identify shared areas of concern, common causes of conflict, ways to heal fragmented perspectives, and new approaches to personal and organizational development.[112] However, a dialogue group might find itself struggling because of the lack of objectives, even to the point where emotions flare up. Therefore, a facilitator is often used to guide the dialogue process. The goal is to prevent participants from getting angry at each other and instead get them to feel enthusiasm for the process.

The first step in holding a dialogue session is to contact potential invitees to gauge their willingness to attend a session. The invitees should be apprised of the guidelines for the session. For example, in order for the dialogue process to be effective, the participants must actively listen to what others are saying and must observe themselves as well as the other participants. In addition, the participants should suspend assumptions and judgments for the period set aside for the dialogue (usually two hours). One recommendation to give participants is that they should try to provide concrete examples of what they are talking about. Concrete examples clarify abstract language and aid in coming to a shared understanding.[113]

Following a dialogue session, the participants can begin discussing ways to implement ideas coming out of the session. Discussion is perhaps the primary mechanism for problem solving and decision making. One of the dangers of discussion is that personal agendas can undermine the activity.[114] Another is that the participants might not listen respectfully (or at all) to the opinions of others and might tend to interrupt each other. If a dialogue session is held first, the participants would have a better chance of using discussion to develop and implement action plans because their different perspectives would have already been addressed. Furthermore, discussion is the form of discourse in which attempts are made to come to agreement on the issues, whereas dialogue is intended to be only exploratory.

We live in a society full of turmoil and change.[115] There are arguments and stresses related to all our communication. A debate allows extreme views to be presented and evaluated in a controlled forum, reducing the chance of emotional flare-ups. A good example of a debating forum would be if the dueling supporters of the two U.S. political parties were on CNN, with both sides presenting their views. A debate can help to clarify positions and change opinions, but despite its value, debating as a technique for acquiring information is often ignored in organizations.

As an example of the appropriate use of debate, imagine that a group of community residents comes to a county board meeting to convince the board to do something about the contaminated water supply. Their testimony might be followed by the testimony of a local chemical company claiming that it cannot clean up the local river because of the high expense. The board thus hears both sides of the story and is in a better position to make a rational decision as to what to do.

Table 18-8 contrasts dialogue with discussion and debate. All three types of discourse are valuable if used appropriately.[116]

Public health leaders should:

- engage in dialogue rather than discussion or debate at the first level of interaction whenever possible
- be open to changing their views as a result of dialogue, discussion, or debate

TABLE 18-8 The Conversation Continuum

Dialogue	Discussion/Debate
Seeing the whole among the parts	Breaking issues/problems into parts
Seeing the connections between the parts	Seeing distinctions between the parts
Inquiring into assumptions	Justifying/defending assumptions
Learning through inquiry and disclosure	Persuading, selling, telling
Treating shared meaning among many	Gaining agreement on one meaning

Source: Reproduced from L. Ellinor and G. Gerard, eds., *Dialogue*. Copyright © 1998, John Wiley & Sons. Reprinted by permission of authors. All rights reserved.

- invite, not force, potential participants to come to a dialogue session
- use dialogue to strengthen relationships
- use discussion to problem solve
- use debate to explore both sides of an issue

MEETING SKILLS

Public health leaders spend a large amount of their time in meetings. When I held a university administrative position, more than 30 committees required my time. It is amazing how little time 30 committee assignments leave to get noncommittee work done.

Most public health leaders attend internal staff committee meetings, team meetings, board meetings (which are often open meetings), community meetings, partnership and coalition meetings, and professional meetings, among others. One way they can increase their effectiveness as leaders is to cut down the number of meetings they attend, and they can do this by delegating committee assignments to staff members who exhibit leadership ability.

For a meeting that a leader has to attend, the goal is to run the meeting as efficiently as possible. A good strategy for preparing for a meeting is to review the results of the previous meeting as soon as possible after it occurs.[117] Review successes as well as failures in order to judge whether improvements need to be made.

Problems that arise need to be addressed from a systems perspective.[118] For example, one problem may be that there are too many meetings. If so, consolidation or elimination of some committees needs to occur. Another problem may be that attendees are seldom prepared, forcing those who are prepared to educate those who are not, thereby wasting valuable meeting time. Still another common problem is the tendency of a small number of attendees to try to take over meetings. And another is the tendency of meetings to drag on past the scheduled time. It is important to set an end time and stick to it.

Each meeting should have, besides a chairperson, a facilitator (to help the group to maintain its focus) and a recorder (who should remain objective so as to record what happens accurately). This means that the recorder often does not participate in discussion and may not have a vote or an official membership role on the committee. The other participants should be actively engaged in what is going on. The regular chair may decide to delegate the role if it will lead to a more successful outcome or if he or she prefers to take an active part in the discussion of issues. It is the chair's responsibility to create a sociable climate in which sharing of thoughts can occur and objective decisions can be made. Good minutes will remind members of where the group is in dealing with the issues before it. Members may find that a review of several months of minutes will provide insights into the meeting process as well as the specific issues. Participation by all members is important. Passive members may silently disagree with decisions that are made and subvert these decisions in the normal course of their work.

The purpose of an official meeting is to solve problems, make decisions, and meet organizational challenges. Thus, the facilitator must keep the meeting on track while encouraging members to present all sides of an issue and argue in favor of the positions they sincerely hold. The facilitator's other main task, of course, is to get the members to reach a decision on each issue (even if the decision is merely to continue consideration of the issue at the next meeting).

Not all meetings are the same, and public health leaders need to adjust their roles accordingly. Organizational meetings deal with issues related to the running of the agency and its programs, and they should cover the diversity of activities in which the agency is engaged. In a team meeting, the agency director may transfer the role of chair to a staff member who is expert in the issues under examination. In a meeting of the governing board, the agency director may collaborate with the board chair in running the meeting. At a community meeting (or any open meeting), the director will have the task of listening carefully to issues raised by community residents.

In carrying out their meeting-related responsibilities, public health leaders should follow these guidelines:

- Keep committee meetings to a minimum.
- Make community and other extraorganizational meetings as information based as possible.
- Use communication skills appropriate to the meeting format.
- Hold extraorganizational meetings in a neutral place if possible.
- Use round tables to increase interaction, and do not assign seats.
- Keep the number of attendees to fewer than 15 if possible.
- Plan the agenda carefully.
- Encourage both dialogue (exploratory discourse) and discussion (problem-solving discourse) in meetings.
- Start and end meetings on time.

- Allow a few minutes for socializing.
- Then keep meetings focused on the issues.
- Serve refreshments.

HEALTH COMMUNICATION

Specific skills must be learned to translate health information into understandable messages. Not only must these messages be developed, but they must also be marketed. There is controversy over the relationship between health communications and social marketing. In an interview with media expert Robert Howard, Shirley Randolph explored some of these issues (Case Study 18-C).[119] Howard said that the concepts of health communication and social marketing are closely related. In health communication, the target audience is typically the community or population at risk, and the long-term goal is to help people in this population increase control over and improve their health.

Case Study 18-C

A Leadership Interview with Robert Howard
Shirley F. Randolph

Robert Howard was the director of public information at the Centers for Disease Control and Prevention (CDC), Atlanta, at the time of the interview. He is now a private consultant on disaster communication models who has presented health communications workshops at the Mid-America Regional Public Health Leadership Institute over the past 20 years. Dr. Howard brings a wealth of experience to his presentations about effective health communications. Prior to joining the CDC, he was a career Navy officer assigned to public and media relations in a variety of settings. This interview took place immediately following a workshop conducted by Dr. Howard in September 1995.

1. "Communications" and "marketing" are words that are frequently used interchangeably. What is the difference between health communications and health marketing?

I think that health communications and marketing are almost interchangeable. Marketing is a management tool whereby you determine exactly what your market is, whom the message is directed toward, who the audience is, whom the communication is to go to. First, identify what your communication point is … your single overriding communication objective … your SOCO. Then go back and carefully examine whom you are delivering this message to; whom you are marketing this information to … what works with this audience … what works with this market. Then, decide how to deliver the health message to the audience to which it is directed. I think, to a great extent, "communications" and "marketing" are interchangeable. They cannot be separated. You cannot have good marketing without having good communication … and vice versa. If you come up with a health message, you really do have to think about whom you are communicating this message to.

2. Many public health practitioners have never had training or developed skills relative to working with the media. Can you speak to how the "average Jane" and the "average Joe," working day to day in a local health department, can improve their media relations skills?

The very first thing you have to do is know who your local media representatives are. I think that as the local health officer or health administrator, it is important for you to get out and know these people. If you haven't already done it, you need to visit with your local media folks and introduce yourself. You need to find out who they are; they need to know who you are. It's important to know the individuals on the editorial boards of the local newspapers. You should also know the local assignment editor at the newspaper and the local television station and the news directors of the local radio stations. Let them know what use you can be to them and when they can call you. Let them know whom they should call at the health department if there is an issue dealing with public health. Let them know what resources are available to them within public health. You do that by going around and getting to meet these people. There is nothing wrong with calling a reporter who covers a health beat consistently and does it very well and saying, "You did a really great job covering that story. We really appreciate your effort." Everybody likes an occasional stroke, and it's important to say, "You did a super job on that story." At the same time, if a reporter gets something wrong, gently help that reporter get it right! Understand, the newspapers and radio stations are a medium through which you can market your communication message. It's important that you develop a relationship with them. The most important thing that a local public health official can do is to establish that base relationship with his or her media. Get to know them and discern and understand what works. Understand how you can best deliver your

(Continues)

information locally. Public health workers at the local level are truly the core of public health practice. You are where the rubber meets the road. You are out there on a day-to-day basis dealing with issues locally. You are the ones that Dr. David Satcher, director of the Centers for Disease Control and Prevention, has been pointing to and saying, "We need your help to get a better understanding of the issues and problems that face local public health."

3. Many of the local health departments in Illinois, as well as in the nation, have small staffs and do not have a media expert or a public relations expert. Do you think that it is important to have one person in the agency designated as the media contact?

I think that it is very important for the media to have a single number that they can call or a single person they can contact if they have questions. There ought to be a single or central clearinghouse or clearing point that the media can go to. It is very important that you, in your agency or office, have a policy that tells the staff this is the procedure that you need to follow in responding to media inquiries. If you don't have a plan or a policy in place, develop one quickly to establish what should happen if you're not available. Designate the person who should respond to media inquiries in your absence. Your staff won't know what to do if there is not a policy. You need to develop a policy that works, that is unique to your specific area and your specific situation ... develop that policy; identify that person. And, most important, make sure that everybody in the agency understands what the policy is. Go over it occasionally; share it and make sure that people don't violate it.

4. How can public health practitioners who use public health "lingo" on a daily basis translate our "language" in order to better "sell" our products to the media and the community?

I found that what works best at CDC is that the decisions about developing appropriate health messages are best not made in a vacuum. You need to put together a team of people in your office. Even if you have only four or five people on your staff, you will usually have one or two people who are pretty good at communication. It might be a nurse practitioner or somebody who is out there on a daily basis dealing with the public and who understands the best way to communicate with them. The public is not going to understand "risk" or "needs assessment," they're not going to understand "acute" and "chronic," or they're not going to understand "immunization schedules." Look to get your people who are working with the public to be a part of your communications team. Develop a team concept. Use the team to develop messages that the public will understand. These decisions cannot be made and communications messages cannot be developed in a vacuum by one person. It has to be a team approach.

5. What are the most important factors to keep in mind when preparing for an interview with someone from the media?

First, any time you give an interview, you ought to know why you are doing the interview, and you ought to know exactly who your target audience is. You ought to remember to tell yourself, "These are the people who brought me to this dance. These are the folks I'm representing, and I need to direct my message to them. I need to remember that they are the reason why I'm here, and I'm representing this agency or this office." You need to develop that communication point ... your SOCO ... your single, overriding communication message. What is the "take-home" message for people when your public turns off the television that night? What is the "take-home" message ... the thing that you want them to remember from having seen your message? You can only develop that message if you sit down ahead of time and plan. You can't get from Chicago to Indianapolis without knowing the route; you have to plan your trip and plan your route; and you do that by sitting down with a map and thinking about how you're going to get there. You do the same thing when you're trying to market or communicate a message.

6. Sometimes media interviews become somewhat hostile. Is there any way to prepare for that? How do you deal with a hostile reporter?

If a reporter becomes hostile, I take that opportunity to absolutely "stay within my zone" as much as I can. You really do need to remember that if a media person becomes hostile, it does not mean that you have to become hostile. As soon as you become angry, remember that you're the person being quoted ... you're the person being seen on camera. If you lose your cool, if you fall off the beam, that is all that will be seen ... not the fact that the reporter became hostile. It is really important that you keep your focus and that you remember that your body language, your image, what you project, is going to be seen by people. If you are seen as hostile, that is what is going to be portrayed; so just stay within your zone. If a reporter asks you a hostile question or creates a hostile situation, don't buy into it. Keep your cool! If the question is inappropriate or improper, just say, "I'm not the person to address that issue" or "I don't share your feelings on that one" or "That's not what this agency represents." Keep your cool! Don't terminate an interview. Don't rip off a microphone and throw it down or storm out of the room. There is no quicker way to guarantee that you will see yourself on television than to do one of those things. The moment that you lose your cool, the moment that you lose control, is the moment I can guarantee that you will be quoted.

7. Is there any way to anticipate all or a majority of the questions that you might be asked to address during an interview?

No. You cannot anticipate all of the questions, but you can anticipate many of them by knowing local issues, by knowing local sensitivities, and by sitting down ahead of time with that communications team and developing some questions and answers and thinking about where the interview might go. For instance, what does the community really think about this issue? What are some of the sideline issues that might impact on this? You can't think of every question, but you can sure think of most of them. There will be an occasional surprise question. Occasionally a reporter will surprise you, but you need to handle surprises as best you can. I find that generally you can predict around 80% of the questions you are going to get. Generally, the ones that you don't predict are relatively simple questions. If a reporter is coming to your shop to do an interview, there is probably some local tie-in or local issue to be explored. Try to keep your focus local. Try not to look at everything from a global or national perspective. Remember, once again, who brought you to the dance … who am I directing this interview to? Am I talking to doctors? Am I talking to nurses? Am I talking to teachers or to public health practitioners? Am I talking to the Hispanic community? Who is my audience? Factor your audience into all of your answers.

8. What should you do when the reporter keeps asking you the same question(s) over and over or tries to lead you down a path that you really don't want to go?

That is a frequent technique used by reporters. The most important thing to remember is the right answer is the right answer the first time and it's the right answer the tenth time. Don't change your answer just because you are asked the question again or asked the same question a little differently. If the reporter keeps doing it and becomes incessant, there is nothing wrong with saying, "I've already answered that question, but I'll be happy to answer it for you again." Then, if it gets to be too much, say, "I would really ask that we move on to something else. I've answered that question and I think I've answered it fairly, and I would like to move on to something else." But don't lose your cool!

9. What should you do if the reporter won't accept that answer? Do you just repeat, "I've answered that question … we've talked about this issue … we need to move on"?

That's exactly what you do. It doesn't matter if you're asked that question 20 times. And, finally, when you've reached the allotted time you have established in advance for the interview, you say something like, "If you don't have any other questions, I have another appointment. I have something else I really have to get on to and it is time for me to go now, and I have answered your questions." When you agree to an interview, you should establish the parameters, including the amount of time you have available, where the interview is to be held, what the background is going to be, what subject(s) will be discussed, and the area(s) of questions. You establish those parameters at the beginning of the interview. You get the reporter to buy in to that. You say, "I have about 30 to 45 minutes to spend with you; is that all right?" When you reach the time period you have established, it's okay to say, "I really do have something else I need to attend to."

10. What can or should a public health practitioner do if a media representative just shows up on the doorstep to do an interview? Something is happening in the community, and a reporter is sent to the public health department to "get a story" or a statement and says, "This is the situation … do you have a comment?" Is it better to go ahead and "get it over with," even if you're not prepared, or are there other strategies that are effective in such situations?

If a reporter just shows up, the very first thing you need to do is to make sure you are the right person to talk to the reporter on the subject she or he wishes to discuss. First, have a policy in place as to who will comment on issues as they arise. Get in touch with that person, make sure the person is briefed on the situation, get a handle on what's going on locally that would cause that reporter to show up on your doorstep. Why is this reporter here unannounced? What has brought the reporter here? Sit down with that reporter and make a determination about what it is the reporter wants to talk about. Buy yourself as much time as you possibly can to think about your comments before you go on camera or begin a taped interview. If the cameras are already rolling, if they catch you and "ambush" you, then it's very important for you to say, "The public health concerns of this issue are of great importance to us … it's important to us that we get the right message and the right information to people. You have just 'shown up on our doorstep' and I have not had an opportunity to take a look at this issue yet. We're going to do that, and as soon as I find out what the situation is, we will get back to you immediately."

11. What should you do if the media tries to "pit" you against other levels of government, such as a local health official against a state health official, or a state health official against a federal health official, or vice versa?

Remember that you should only address issues that are appropriate for you to address and that you ought to be addressing. It is appropriate to say, "I don't have those specifics in front of me and I cannot address a subject for which I do not have the specifics. I didn't know we would be doing this interview." Don't hesitate, particularly in a live situation, to let the public know you have been blindsided and to let the people on the other end of the camera or microphone know that this is the first time you have seen or heard this information. Let the public know that this is not a prepared interview. Don't hesitate to say, "You caught me without my information available. I didn't know we would be chatting today. I would like very much to address this issue or get you to the right person to get this issue addressed."

12. If you had to write the three top rules to follow when preparing for an interview, what would they be?

The very first thing to do is to establish a team within your public health department. You need to have a communications team—people who will sit together and discuss and review the issues prior to the interview. It's the difference between fire prevention and firefighting. Everything should not be a firefighting situation. You shouldn't have to break out the hoses every time something goes wrong. It's a lot better to have that smoke detector in place. It's what your communication team is … it's your smoke detector. It's your team that smells the smoke and gets together to determine what you're going to do. Have a communications team in place. Make sure everyone knows what to do when something goes bad.

Number two: on any given issue, develop your communication point … your SOCO … your single overriding communication objective. Sit down, communicate, identify who your market or media segment is, whom you are delivering this message to within the population. Share this information within your agency. Make sure that everybody within your office understands what the SOCO, the single overriding communication objective, is. Finally, write that down and take it with you when you do the interview. I mean take it with you physically and mentally. Be thinking about the SOCO during the interview. Think about delivering that message over and over. And always, particularly when you're dealing with broadcast media, think visually. What can we do to best communicate this through the visual media? What can we best do to communicate this in the way of background video, or how can we portray this best, either in a picture or on camera? Try to think, what do the broadcasters want? Try to think that this is what they're going to want … they'll want a laboratory shot or they'll want an immunization shot. Then make sure that your people in those clinics or in those areas look appropriate and appear appropriate and they know about the SOCO and the press visit. It's all part of that process of your communications team sharing that information internally and externally.

Finally, deliver your message. That always sounds so simple, but on more occasions than I can count I have seen people prepare for interviews, write the SOCO down, take the SOCO with them, and go to the interview. But because they get so caught up in the excitement or the nervousness of the interview, they fail to deliver the message. They never take the opportunity to grab hold of that interview and say, "I'm here today to say. . . ." It is really good to frame your answers with those kinds of attention-grabbing devices. And, most importantly, use what works for you. Everyone is an individual; not everything works for everybody.

Finally, practice, practice, practice! You only get good at these things by practicing. Good communication does not come naturally to anybody. You get good at communicating because you work at it and you do it a lot. You need to practice.

Source: Reproduced from S. Randolph, "A Leadership Interview with Robert Howard," *Leadership in Public Health* 3, no. 4 (1995): 7–11.

Social marketing, which is discussed in the next section, is aimed at increasing the acceptability of an idea, social practice, or social cause among the target audience. The desired goal of public health–oriented social marketing is to induce the public and policy makers to support disease prevention and health promotion concepts and programs.

The CDC perspective on health communication is that it "is the crafting and delivery of messages and strategies, based on consumer research, to promote the health of individuals and communities. . . . Effective health communication activities will be an integral component of all programs designed to promote health, improve quality of life, and foster healthful environments."[120(p.2)] The CDC developed 10 guidelines for increasing the effectiveness of health communication. They are as follows:

1. Review background information. (What is out there?)
2. Set communication objectives. (What do we want to accomplish?)
3. Analyze and segment target audiences. (Whom do we want to reach?)
4. Develop and pretest message concepts. (What do we want to say?)
5. Select communication channels. (Where do we want to say it?)
6. Create and pretest messages and products. (How do we want to say it?)
7. Develop promotion plan/production. (How do we get it used?)
8. Implement communication strategies and conduct process evaluation. (Let's do it!)
9. Conduct outcome and impact evaluation. (How well did we do?)
10. Provide feedback to improve communication. (Where do we go from here?)[121(pp.2-4)]

These 10 guidelines can be applied in Exercise 18-4, which concerns the development of a team-based health communication strategy.

Despite the fact that more than 500,000 individuals are employed in public health programs nationally, the public health system is not routinely promoted as an essential provider of health-related services of importance to all constituencies. As a result, public health practitioners are at a disadvantage in getting funds for programs in the highly competitive health services arena. It is almost as if they do not want to talk to the various media and broadcast their accomplishments.

Because of the restructuring in health service delivery and financing, the future role and functions of public health are now uncertain. The uncertainty is not necessarily to be decried. New opportunities for public health agencies to address community health issues are becoming apparent. Primary among these are opportunities to promote healthy behavior through health communication initiatives. The first step in creating an initiative is to build a coalition of equal partners for the purpose of defining, planning, operationalizing, and evaluating health communication (and social marketing) strategies. The second step is to acknowledge existing barriers to full operationalization of the coalition, including the difficulty of creating a coalition in which no one partner controls the components of the process or its outcomes.

Figure 18-6 shows the essential components and partners in any action partnership for health.[122] Each partner has a vested interest in ensuring that the health communication initiatives will succeed. In addition, each partner brings unique resources and expertise to the coalition. Once the action partnership is established and the responsibilities of the partners are negotiated, the first order of business should be to achieve a consensus on the initiatives to be pursued and to develop action plans for implementing the initiatives at the community level.

Creating action partnerships for health is one of the best ways available to public health agencies of addressing community health issues. Furthermore, by establishing such coalitions, public health agencies can maintain an important leadership role. On the other hand, if they fail to work with community partners, they may face a future of lost opportunities.

Public health leaders must:

- build coalitions of equal partners capable of defining, planning, operationalizing, and developing health communication strategies
- set communication objectives, select communication channels, and determine how to use programs
- identify the single overriding communication objectives
- identify and respond to barriers to full operationalization of coalitions

Sometimes it is difficult to evaluate a potential crisis because nothing like it has happened before. Perhaps the crisis occurs unexpectedly and it must be addressed. Crisis communication strategies, a subspecialty of

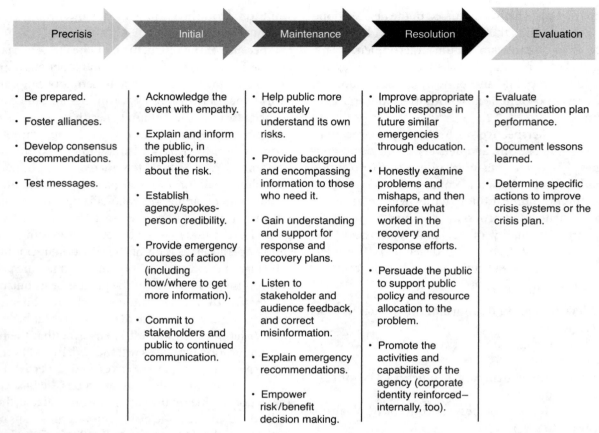

Precrisis	Initial	Maintenance	Resolution	Evaluation
• Be prepared. • Foster alliances. • Develop consensus recommendations. • Test messages.	• Acknowledge the event with empathy. • Explain and inform the public, in simplest forms, about the risk. • Establish agency/spokesperson credibility. • Provide emergency courses of action (including how/where to get more information). • Commit to stakeholders and public to continued communication.	• Help public more accurately understand its own risks. • Provide background and encompassing information to those who need it. • Gain understanding and support for response and recovery plans. • Listen to stakeholder and audience feedback, and correct misinformation. • Explain emergency recommendations. • Empower risk/benefit decision making.	• Improve appropriate public response in future similar emergencies through education. • Honestly examine problems and mishaps, and then reinforce what worked in the recovery and response efforts. • Persuade the public to support public policy and resource allocation to the problem. • Promote the activities and capabilities of the agency (corporate identity reinforced—internally, too).	• Evaluate communication plan performance. • Document lessons learned. • Determine specific actions to improve crisis systems or the crisis plan.

FIGURE 18-6 Coalition Components and Partners. *Source*: Reproduced from L. Potts and L. Rowitz, "Social Marketing/ Health Communications: Leadership Opportunities for the 1990s," *Journal of Public Health Management and Practice*, 2, 4, p. 75.

health communications, have been developed for these types of events. Crisis communication has been defined first to describe how an agency or organization faces a crisis and has to communicate to various stakeholders about the event.[123] Underlying the definition just given is an awareness that the organization, and by inference the community, is facing a crisis that requires, and in fact demands, a response. The agency that is required to respond may also feel a lack of control relative to the crisis situation. Because crises go through phases, it is critical for the communicator to understand these phases, as the response will change depending on the stage of the crisis. **Figure 18-7** demonstrates this through the crisis communication life cycle with key communication points related to each stage. Reynolds's work is an excellent resource for all aspects of crisis communication with detailed charts and evaluation techniques related to the skills necessary to carry out a well-developed crisis communication plan.[124]

All crises have some things in common.[125] There is always confusion and chaos at the occurrence of the event. There needs to be immediate response to the

media and the public when a crisis occurs. Crisis events seem to escalate in intensity during the early hours and days after the event. Information tends to be limited and sometimes misleading. The public is interested at the outset but often loses interest if they are reassured that the event is being controlled and handled well. The influence of the media and its needs to monitor the crisis can increase and exacerbate the concern by the public and all other stakeholders. It should be possible to plan for these unanticipated events. A crisis communication plan is important, and the creation of a crisis communications team is also critical.[126] It is possible to follow a seven-step communications response plan. The seven steps, reworded for clarification, are described in the following sections.

Create and Appoint the Crisis Communications Team

The development of a multiprofessional team made up of individuals from throughout an organization is important if the team is to be representative of the organization as a whole. The team may include external

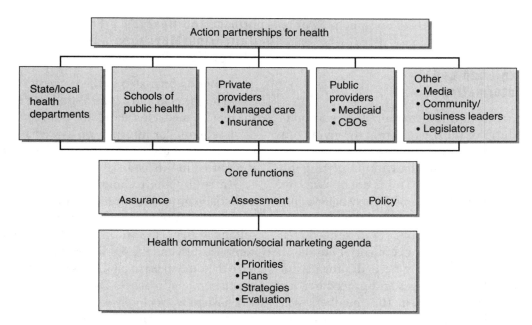

FIGURE 18-7 Crisis Communication Life Cycle. *Source*: Reproduced from B. Reynolds. *Crisis and Emerging Risk Communication*. Atlanta: CDC (2002).

stakeholders as well. A team leader and spokesperson needs to be determined. The team leader will have multiple responsibilities to the senior leadership of the organization as well as to external stakeholder groups and residents of the community. The team leader will lead the effort of developing the crisis communication plan. The crisis communication team (CCT) will activate this plan in concert with the organization's emergency preparedness and response plan.

Collect and Validate Critical Information about the Crisis

It is within the first day of the emergency that an organization will discover its credibility and trust level with internal and external stakeholders. The CCT needs to establish liaisons outside the organization to gather factual information. Some research will be needed as well as a general monitoring of the media. The information needs to be sorted, analyzed, and evaluated relative to the public health impact of the emergency.

Determine the Seriousness of the Crisis Event

The seriousness of the emergency also needs to be determined in consultation with external liaisons. It is important to carry out a situational assessment to make certain that all parties addressing the emergency are doing it from the same set of facts.

Identify the Key Stakeholders

The major reason it is important to define the key stakeholders is that differently worded messages may be necessary for different audiences. The order of informing stakeholders may also be important if there are casualties. Families need to be informed before the media. Families should not receive bad news from the media. The humanitarian response team needs to be working with families early.

Develop, Design, and Implement a Communications Strategy for the Local Jurisdiction

Fernandez and Merzer stated that the CCT needs to learn to balance the needs of the organization with all of its external communications.[127] If a crisis has community-wide implications, it may be necessary to create a crisis communications center or, as it is sometimes called, a joint information center (JIC). The JIC will usually be under the supervision of the incident commander. However, the lead agency will designate who will speak for the JIC. The key messages need to work toward allaying the fears of the public. The messages need to take a positive tone. There are two types of messages. Position key messages give the organization or the JIC a view of the nature of the incident and the response that is being given to the event. Instructional key messages direct stakeholders to do something or to take a specific action.

Develop Background and Supporting Information

Some of the background information relates to policies and procedures of the organization for giving out information. For example, many universities will not allow faculty to talk to the media without getting the approval of the administration. This is not as clear-cut as it may first appear because some faculty believe this approval process is not appropriate and is an infringement of academic freedom policy and procedures. This small example raises the concern about how conflicting policies can affect getting needed information out to the public. When messages and procedures for delivering them are determined, JIC members will need to get supporting documentation to back up their messages.

Inform and Develop a Protocol for Delivering Messages and Reacting to Stakeholder Concerns

The obvious final step is the delivery of the message based on the plan and protocol worked out in the rest of the plan. A media log should be utilized to keep abreast of all requests for information as well as the responses to these requests and who gave it. The way the message is reported in the media also needs to be monitored.

In reality, the techniques of risk communication and crisis communication overlap. Some of these overlaps are discussed by media advocacy expert and consultant Robert Howard in Case Study 18-D. This is a complex area, and the public health leader will often not have the time to learn all the ins and outs of these communication approaches. The communication specialist will have to work closely with these leaders and coordinate their preparedness and response activities as well as the noncrisis activities in a coordinated way.

Case study 18-D

A Public Health Practice Quiz: Robert Howard Redux 2006

1. How are risk communications and crisis communications related and different?

The best example that comes to mind is the people who live along the Mississippi flood plain and continue to do so year after year despite multiple years of having their homes and belongings swept away, and yet they remain in these homes. For years, government and service agencies have sought to instruct these fine people that their existence along this plain puts them at a distinct risk. This risk, of course, becomes a crisis when the flood waters begin to rise, as spring and summer rains inevitably cause the water levels to rise, and these people, their homes, farms, businesses, and livelihoods are literally swept downstream. During those times, there is a significant outreach and increase in the effort to reach these persons and warn them of the impending, potentially deadly crisis they face due to rising waters. Upstream and downstream, literally every possible means of communications are employed to inform these persons of the looming threat and risk they face from this crisis. Efforts range from sophisticated media campaigns to the practically biblical form of shouting at people from high-water marks, including helicopters, to leave the area of risk. Many dry off and stay until the next year ... and the next flood.

We inform people in virtually every possible way on a daily basis of the risks of smoking, including writing on the packages of the very products they buy that the product will undoubtedly be harmful to them. We even inform them of the genuine national crisis we face of losing tens of thousands of citizens through continued use of these products, but it does not mean they will act on the messages in a casual or critical atmosphere. It seems that legislation has the best possibility of actually getting people to act on or against risk with any regularity. This was certainly the case with seat belts when the industry and government combined over a period of time to make the nonuse of seat belts so financially and socially unacceptable that now many Americans have been driven into using these unquestionably life-saving devices. It wasn't until public safety, government, and industry came together with public health and advertising to inform, educate, legislate, and change behaviors.

This principle applies across the board to any number of habits, practices, and behaviors including drug use, HIV/AIDS and other STDs, handgun ownership, obesity, and high blood pressure. The mere fact that you have identified both a risk and the point at which it becomes a "crisis" or critical public health event *does not mean* that you have successfully reached into the minds of those impacted and changed their behavior. For each person, that trip switch is something different. It is through a *broad use of all possible media*, informed spokespersons who will affect all races, sexes, and nationalities, combined with intelligent and broadly dispersed repetition of the message, targeting the message at especially high-risk groups and varying the delivery of the message through clever and eye-catching techniques that cause the person at risk or in crisis to understand the outcome of continuing their usual behaviors. Even then, it is extraordinarily helpful to have the aid and support of legislation to assist.

Of course, laws do not always make or change behavior patterns, as we see each year with deaths due to drunk driving, speeding, and certain forms of drug use. Society can, however, make a determination that a particular risk or behavior is so unacceptable that lawmakers must take innovative and broad-reaching measures that employ multiple layers of risk communications at all levels to impact change in that risk behavior—the ultimate aim being to lower that risk bar to a level where it is no longer possible of creating or rising to a crisis level. We have seen this work in areas of risk including child labor, alcohol sales to minors, seat belt "click-it-or-ticket" campaigns, and some food safety issues such as homogenization of milk and chlorination of water.

I believe, in the end, unless laws tell them otherwise, people will determine what is too risky for them and what constitutes a life-changing or crisis environment for them and their lifestyles, tastes, and families. And yet in spite of those daunting challenges and slim likelihood of the actions of politicians, we in public health have an *absolute moral obligation* to *stand atop the high ground and shout out* to those at risk in both times of high risk and low risk that there is risk involved and options are available.

2. How is recovery possible when mental health issues remain even after the last communication message is given?

We have to get beyond the concept that we will, in any critical event, achieve a level of complete and absolute mental health recovery. The makeup of each of our own personal histories is so complex that no level of expert can predict what impact an event or crisis may have on us in a given situation.

We must instead move toward a program of *recovery and recognition.* We must recover and resume our lives as best we can with the support of community and family following a crisis. Some person will "bootstrap" wonderfully and recover with little or no assistance, while others will need a vast range of both physical and emotional support in getting through a crisis. As an example, a family of seven who recovers from a horrific tornado with all family members intact but loses a beloved family pet will certainly mourn the loss of that pet, but have the strength and support of the family unit to get through the crisis of losing the animal. On the other hand, an 80-year-old woman who loses her pet of 20 years that served as her only physical and emotional manifestation of love and caring may be devastated. Have we recognized the impact that loss has on her, and how can we get her through that event?

In public health, we must look for ways to aid, identify, and help these families, *each* get through this crisis. Let there be no mistake that the walking wounded with the thousand-yard stare, but no apparent physical injury, may well turn out to be as much a health risk in both the short and long term as the person with a fractured leg.

The emotional scars left behind in each of us from past events are the platform from which we dive into each event in our life, especially crises where life-changing events occur. It is incumbent that we recognize how the past shapes the future. This underscores the need for each of us to support and understand the mental health programs in our community and the level of mental health of those we love, care for, employ, and neighbor with, and how changes with life experiences, age, events, and illness can result in a need to shape our message of risk communication and risk recovery. We must additionally understand that there must be a constant and ongoing effort to understand which media entities our community and family employ. Have we developed a way to use not just billboards and TV in a critical event, but radio, flyers, bulletin boards, the Internet, and community meetings? This must be an ongoing campaign to stay aware of the aging of our community, the influx of new peoples, and the social and economic factors in our hometowns. Who do we go to when we want to reach everyone in our community? How do we best use all of this media for not just the quick impact, but the long-running communications efforts in understanding that all persons heal in a unique fashion?

This question goes to the core of every disaster, critical event, or crisis, and that is that there is always some level of mental or emotional impact, and in some cases that impact is life changing. In public health, we must be alert to that fact and train all of our workers, volunteers, and administrators to recognize it not only in the victims but in the workers. It is important to remember that both in the Oklahoma City explosion and in the World Trade Center disaster, 70% of the volunteers ultimately developed emotional problems that required some level of treatment. If *volunteers* are impacted, then we must expect some level of harm to the *victim* and be attuned and prepared to deal with the way and manners in which these behaviors manifest themselves. With that in mind, we must develop systems and plans and *sensitive communications* to deal with them in both the long and short term.

(*Continues*)

3. How is communication affected by community literacy concern?

It isn't the community literacy concern I have, but the community literacy reality. The fact that your community is literate does not mean they read in the conventional manner, or are impacted by messages the way we of some 50 years ago received data in public service announcements and brochures. What are those in my community who are most at risk going to most benefit from, and how can I best reach them with print and broadcast material? If I am dealing with low literacy in the local community, I may well want to go to the use of comic books or other graphic media that have a simple theme with easy-to-read language and illustrations.

Is it really worth my while to publish messages in the *Wall Street Journal* to young boys and girls with no regular interest in this publication's content? We must understand the level of literacy in the audience we are trying to reach, and the reality of the media that reaches into the homes, glove boxes, purses, and nightstands of these people I want to understand and touch. When I know the reality of the literacy range and which media are being listened to, watched, or read, I know that I am at least halfway on my way to getting into that audience. If you are managing a publicity or awareness campaign to reduce morbidity and mortality in your community, you better quickly find out what the *most at risk* are reading, listening to, and taking home.

By the way, this should include the often overlooked media of public gatherings such as churches, community meetings, and public events. These are legitimate and truly literate moments to reach and teach.

4. How important is message mapping?

Message mapping is as *critical as ring vaccination was to the smallpox effort.* This is not an overstatement or hyperbole. When you immunize a person with intelligent and lasting information, they will take that message home. It will have the same impact as herd immunity. What is vital is the important and frequent "booster shot" of data and information that reminds and underscores the original message. A grid method of reaching your community in which you seek to reach all persons within a given area is an intelligent and appropriate approach. It also recognizes the realities of the ethnic and racial makeup of neighborhoods and communities and gives you a chance to plan a strategy prior to going into that community and attempting the communications equivalent of "carpet bombing" where messages just fall everywhere and have no focus or target and we just hope they are picked up.

Message mapping makes you ask, "Where are my most at-risk communities? What media do they most often use or listen to?" Message mapping also forces you to *track, maintain, and monitor* those to whom you have reached out.

Effective public health campaigns in the year 2005 simply cannot be done without smart, targeted message mapping. In this day and age of precious and few healthcare resource dollars, we do not have the benefit of shotgunning information out and hoping it lands in the right spot. We must map, must target, and must deliver a smart, clever, and understandable SOCO (single overriding communication objective).

5. What are the most common mistakes in health communications?

One word—hubris. Far too many public health professionals clad in our Birkenstocks and jeans feel that we have seen it all and heard it all. We have failed to understand that there is a primal and basic reason we were given one mouth and two ears. We need to listen twice as much as we speak. We fail to understand the power and emergence of new forms of communications such as urban contemporary radio, blogging, and 15-second advertising. We have published papers, run programs, and dug into our data like ticks, often never poking our heads up to see what is really new, effective, and appropriate. We have forgotten our listening skills because we have initials after our names.

On more occasions than I can count, I have been in the back of a room where a presenter is describing a "new and innovative program to reach young people" only to have those very same young people in the back of the room saying, "Who is this guy and who has he been talking to?" In most cases, he or she has been listening to those members of his or her staff who tell them what they want to hear (after all, they do sign the paychecks), what a right-wing or left-wing predisposed position dictates, and have shaped a program around that. The effort is invariably a failure, and the official is rarely held accountable or led to understand by means of savvy and articulate critique where he or she went wrong.

We *must not and cannot rely* on a political appointee who completely lacks in any level of health expertise to deliver health messages to an American public desperate for critical, accurate, and timely data, as was the case in the post-9/11 anthrax attacks. People want their health information in those critical moments from a doctor, nurse, or healthcare professional, and it is only hubris that allowed a politician to decide that he was the best person to deliver that data and then handle difficult and complex questions from the highly articulate and well-educated medical media on hand. Where was the Surgeon General in the early days of that event, and why was he not used? Our initial messages were so confusing and disjointed that many Americans were calling anthrax a virus and were convinced that the initial patient had acquired the illness by drinking water from a stream in North Carolina, as stated by the Secretary of Health and Human Services. To this day, as an epidemiologist, I have sought out the conditions where a person can contract "inhaled" anthrax by drinking water. The Secretary must have access to data the rest of the scientific world lacks. Or he simply possessed such hubris that he was unable to simply defer to a qualified healthcare expert who could have assisted him.

Hubris stops us and blocks us from opening our minds to the idea that there may well be someone else in our stable of experts or healthcare professionals who is better equipped to deliver this message. Many appointed officials have true healthcare thoroughbreds at their disposal, but overlook them because of hubris and the love of the sound of their own voice and seeing their own face on TV or in a newspaper.

Hubris stops us from reaching out and seeking out experts and professionals who may rightly and accurately tell us that the way we are doing business at that moment is off-center, but can be corrected with adjustments and assistance. Hubris stops us from asking for and accepting assistance.

Hubris is the enemy of effective communication at all levels and must be actively sought out in ourselves and our colleagues and addressed in an aggressive yet sensitive manner. Hubris blocks millions of healthcare communications dollars from going where they need to go and in the end is, quite simply, a killer.

SOCIAL MARKETING

Social marketing has been defined as "the application of commercial marketing technologies to the analysis, planning, execution, and evaluation of programs designed to influence the voluntary behavior of target audiences in order to improve their personal welfare and that of their society."[128(p.7)] The purpose of public health–oriented social marketing is to increase the general acceptance of certain health practices so as to induce the public and policy makers to support health promotion and disease prevention concepts and programs. This kind of social marketing depends on mass communication, because mass communication is the easiest and surest means of informing the public of the behavior changes that are necessary to improve the health status of the community.[129]

A social marketing campaign, according to Winett and Wallack, has seven essential characteristics:[130]

1. It possesses a consumer orientation geared toward meeting the needs and values of the target audience.
2. It places an emphasis on the audience's voluntary exchange of resources for products.
3. It rests on a strong research base, including audience analyses and market segmentation studies that indicate the needs, preferences, and values of various target populations.
4. It uses formative research to test the audience's acceptance of messages, concepts, campaign design, and products prior to full implementation.

5. It seeks an optimum balance among the four P's of marketing (product, price, place, and promotion).
6. It uses channel analyses to test the appropriateness and effectiveness of the campaign delivery systems.
7. It evaluates campaign components using built-in feedback systems in order to discover how to modify them during implementation (if necessary).

To understand how the four P's of marketing apply to social marketing, consider a situation in which public health practitioners are trying to promote dietary changes to reduce fat intake.[131] *Product* encompasses the foods the public will have to give up or consume in a different form. If people are addicted to pizza, they might have to give up pizza altogether or convince the local pizzerias to offer low-fat varieties. *Price* relates to the cost to the public of making the necessary changes. Will people be willing to pay three dollars extra for a low-fat pizza and put up with the loss in flavor? *Place* is where the activities occur. Perhaps the only place to get low-fat pizza is at the supermarket, so that reducing fat intake means eating at home. *Promotion* involves activities intended to convince the public to accept the message and alter their behavior. (Note that social marketing has a fifth P, *politics*. Part of a social marketing campaign may be devoted to convincing politicians to pass or revise a law.)

Case Study 18-E is intended to clarify the relationship between health communication and social marketing. Note that it is possible to have a health communication success and a marketing failure. It will be hard, for instance, to convince pizza lovers to give up the high-fat food. Public health issues tend to

HIV Prevention: Communications Success, Marketing Failure

Fred Kroger

Case Study 18-E

"America Responds to AIDS" is the campaign banner for the federal government's campaign to inform the American public about human immunodeficiency virus (HIV) and acquired immune deficiency syndrome (AIDS). Campaign planners have employed marketing techniques that have resulted in its messages being seen or heard by more Americans and with greater frequency (e.g., more than 7 billion audience impressions estimated for 1993) than for any government-sponsored public service health campaign to date. Yet its CDC sponsors consider it more a health communications program than a social marketing effort.

In 1993, a panel of health communications experts external to the CDC was asked to assess its national efforts to promote HIV prevention and to recommend strategies for improvement. The principal elements of the effort have been a national media campaign, national toll-free hotline services, a national clearinghouse for distributing materials and managing databases on HIV services and programs, grant programs for national partnership development, grant programs to support state and local information activities, and communications research and evaluation.

The panel gave favorable marks for the program's marketing efforts to media gatekeepers and for its success in nurturing effective collaborations among its many and diverse national partnerships. Aggressive, sustained interaction with national and local public service directors helped place HIV prevention high on their list of concerns. The national partners advised CDC on its "product" development processes but also became its sales force in delivering materials and programs to constituencies at organizational and community levels. The communications program was recognized as an integrated system that allows information to flow bidirectionally, and that had mass, institutional, community, and individual elements to it.

Its shortcomings, however, fell within two dimensions that most social marketing practitioners consider essential— audience segmentation and product definition. Undergirding these two deficiencies, the fifth P of government-based marketing programs, *politics*, was described as the major impediment to effective marketing in HIV prevention.

Audience Segmentation

Congress had been clear in designating the general public as the primary audience for the CDC's mass communication efforts on AIDS. An informed and supportive population is recognized by behavioral scientists to be an important ingredient for causing healthy behaviors to be initiated and sustained. The "America Responds to AIDS" campaign was criticized by the AIDS Action Council, the Gay Men's Health Crisis in New York City, by other AIDS advocacy groups, and by the review panel for not meeting the needs of high-risk audiences, such as gay men, by not providing sexually explicit behavioral messages.

Product

"America Responds to AIDS," though viewed by some as a public service advertising and pamphlet distribution campaign, was designed to be a sophisticated communications system that includes online computer databases; toll-free, live telephone hotline services; and a network of national organizations to mediate and deliver education programs and materials. The product was seen by campaign planners as value-free, technically accurate information. AIDS activists called for condoms promotion as the principal product. Congress and media critics expected proof of prevention effects. In assessing this confusion over product specificity, the review panel called for a more behaviorally focused product—for example, "health information with an attitude." Disease-preventing behaviors, including condom use, should be aggressively promoted.

Evaluation efforts have been undertaken to position the HIV prevention "product" in more consumer-relevant terms. Just as athletic footwear is sold as aids to "soar-through-the-air, slam-dunk, in-your-face" feats of athleticism rather than as canvas covers for the feet, such prevention products as condoms, monogamy, or abstinence still lack similar consumer-oriented positioning.

The awareness task has been judged by experts to be complete. It has been accomplished primarily through communication tools. Can the adoption of risk-reducing behaviors now be sold to persons at highest risk, and will the body politic be supportive? This more challenging goal will require better application of core marketing principles. Will the second decade of HIV prevention marketing improve upon the first? Stay tuned. Kotler and Roberto developed a hierarchy-of-effects model (**Figure 18-8**) that takes into account that not all of the target audience will accept the message of a social marketing campaign.[132] It is important, therefore, to provide reinforcement for people who have made a commitment to change or have assimilated the new knowledge gained from the campaign.

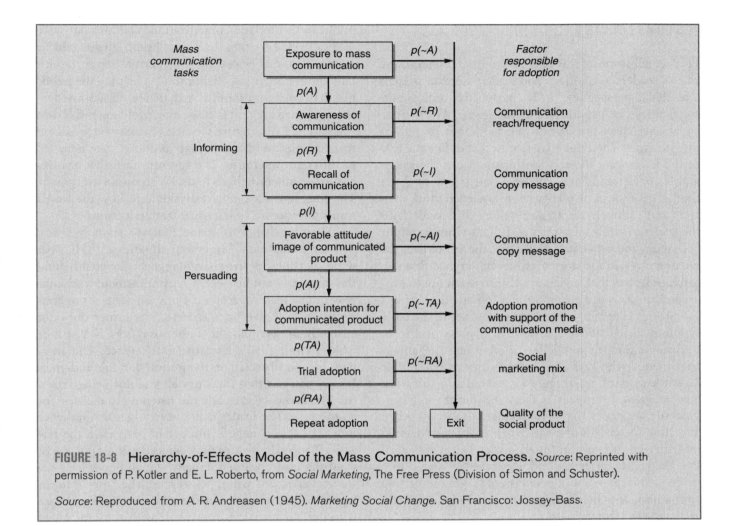

FIGURE 18-8 Hierarchy-of-Effects Model of the Mass Communication Process. *Source*: Reprinted with permission of P. Kotler and E. L. Roberto, from *Social Marketing*, The Free Press (Division of Simon and Schuster).

Source: Reproduced from A. R. Andreasen (1945). *Marketing Social Change*. San Francisco: Jossey-Bass.

be controversial, and people's views are closely related to the values they hold dear. Think of the pipe smoker who believes that smoking a pipe is safer than smoking cigarettes. Also, people do not see the results of lifestyle change for years and do not project forward their increased risk for disease as a result of present activities. Another social marketing challenge is that priorities differ in different segments of our communities, such as among the affluent and the poor. And still another is that local public health agency leaders have limited budgets for social marketing and must choose their battles carefully.

Public health leaders need to know how to develop health communication programs and monitor the effectiveness of these programs. Creating effective programs is complicated by the fact that many communities want to maintain the status quo or at least contain community groups hostile to the message of such programs.[133] In order to market public health information

more effectively, public health leaders need to conduct surveys on consumer health knowledge, investigate different behavior change strategies, target programs at appropriate population segments, and modify programs as necessary.

Public health leaders should:

- use social marketing as a process to increase the acceptance of an idea, social practice, or social cause among a specific audience
- develop strategies for encouraging health promotion and disease prevention initiatives in the community
- learn techniques for fostering behavioral change
- identify the various population segments within the overall population
- conduct research on the use of different strategies and their outcomes
- create innovative funding mechanisms for health communication and social marketing campaigns

STORYTELLING

Leaders tell stories. Tichy and Cohen have discussed the role of leaders as teachers, and leaders need to present a teachable perspective.[134] This perspective utilizes personal stories or experiences of the leader. At the basic story level, there are stories that tell about the life of the presenter. Then there are stories that define the role of the leader and the relationships between the leader and his or her audience. The final type is a story about the future. Stories also engage an audience more than facts and numbers do. In storytelling, it is critical for the leader to know the audience. It is also important for colleagues and other staff to see that the leader lives the life portrayed in the story. Gardner has argued that it is through stories that leaders are able to reach out to others and affect them at an emotional and practical level.[135]

Stories take many different approaches to the basic typology listed above. However, people working in business and in the public sector often react negatively to someone who says they have a story to tell. Public health leaders often struggle to show that a story can have as great an impact as facts and numbers. I suppose the answer is that a leader needs to know when and how to tell a story and when to present factual information. It is useful to tell stories, but it is critical that the right stories get told. Denning has stated that leadership is often about persuasion. It is about getting your audience to buy in to the lessons or plans that you are trying to create.

Narrative patterns are quite diverse. Denning presents a rationale for eight different narrative patterns.[136] First, there is the springboard pattern that is used to mobilize and motivate others to action. These stories use an example of a change that occurred in the past in an organization or a community and how that experience is relevant to a challenge of today. The past serves as a springboard to the future. The second narrative pattern is about building trust. The leader tells a story about his or her personal life in terms of strengths or vulnerabilities. The third story narrative is used to build trust in your organization. You are creating a brand narrative to show how effective your organization is or has been in promoting the health of the public. The fourth narrative involves stories that demonstrate the values of

public health for your organization. The fifth narrative is about collaboration. In public health, this would be a story that you or one of your partner organizations tells about how your collaboration is helping the public health of your community. Next, there is the knowledge-sharing narrative that focuses on a problem and how it was handled. Alternative scenarios can also be presented to demonstrate how different solutions may have led to different outcomes. The seventh narrative involves humor or other methods to deal with rumor and gossip. The final narrative involves vision and how the leader wants to move his or her organization forward.

Denning has also stated that stories are critical in transformational leadership situations.[137] He does warn that these stories have dangers. The goal behind the story may not be clear. The commitment to change may not be readily accepted. Body language is not consistent with the verbal narrative. The leader does not correctly understand the audience. There is a lack of what Denning calls narrative intelligence. The story may be too abstract or theoretical for the audience. It may be clear that the storyteller is not being truthful. The audience is clearly not listening to the story or its message. The leader is not able to get the audience to accept that change is important or is even the real issue. The leader's story may get a reaction opposite of what the leader wanted. Finally, the audience feels the storyteller is not willing to discuss the story. Monologues create boredom for the audience. Telling stories is useful and provides the leader with a useful set of skills for mobilizing others.

Public health leaders need to:

- learn the art of storytelling
- utilize different types of stories for different reasons or for different audiences

JOURNALING

About 20 years ago, I was at one of my first meetings at the Centers for Disease Control and Prevention. I noticed that almost every CDC public health professional was carrying a green book. Throughout the meeting, each CDC person opened this green book and took notes or wrote comments on the proceedings. These green books were journals. Since that time, I have observed many public health professionals carry these leadership journals. Today, many of these individuals carry a computer or tablet (e.g., an iPad) in which they write their commentaries. I started carrying a journal a couple of decades back, and now I, too, am entering

> **Leadership Tip**
>
> *Be prepared for any crisis that your agency may encounter.*

the second decade of the 21st century carrying an iPad, which I use to jot down my thoughts and ideas. In the public health leadership institute that I have been running for 20 years, we have started to give all participants journals. This one tool has become an essential for many managers and leaders.

Our lives are so busy. Ideas seem to come at breakneck speed. As leaders, we need to keep our eyes and ears focused on many things and issues in the course of a working day. Our journals prevent us from losing many of these high-speed ideas. There are a number of benefits to journaling. First, you can go back at the end of each week and make a new entry that prioritizes the ideas of the previous week. Then you can give each idea a score from 1 to 3, with 1 being an idea to continue to develop and 3 being an idea that is interesting but not of high priority at the present time. Write a few lines on the issues ranked 1 and what the next steps are in developing these ideas. Each month, look back at the high-scoring ideas and determine your progress in addressing them. Should some be dropped because a dead end has been reached?

A leadership journal needs to be a living document. Share your ideas with other leaders and have them share their ideas with you, so that idea sharing becomes a collaborative activity. It will be in the process of working with others that some of your ideas and the ideas of others will lead to new programs and policies. Don't lose your ideas. Make your ideas live by making them come to life.

SUMMARY

Communication is central to leadership. For example, the leader of an organization may be able to develop a compelling organizational vision, but if that leader is unable to communicate the vision to others in the organization in a way that inspires them, the work of visioning will have been all for naught.

This chapter began with a discussion of the nature of the communication process and the barriers to communication, which include the fact that people in a communicative situation can have different communication styles. As was pointed out, one means of getting around the barriers that exist, at least in the case of oral communication, is to engage in active listening. Of course, not all communication is oral, and the chapter presented the advantages and disadvantages of oral communication and those of written communication.

Advancements in communication technology bring new communication skills that need to be learned.

The most obvious example is the widespread use of computers for the transfer of data and for sending messages in a timely fashion and the corresponding need to master computer skills. Technological advancements also typically bring new problems, such as the e-mail overload that public health leaders frequently experience.

Public health leaders must communicate not only with their colleagues but also with the public, for part of their responsibility is to educate the public about public health issues and act as advocates for public health. In short, they need to publicize pertinent information and promote the public health agenda. The only way to do the latter is to communicate the agenda to policy makers who have a direct say in whether the agenda gets implemented. Therefore, among the communication skills that public health leaders need are media advocacy skills, including skills in risk communication. They also need to learn the various skills associated with health communication, crisis communication, and social marketing. Finally, storytelling and journaling as useful approaches to communicating with others and communicating with yourself were presented.

DISCUSSION QUESTIONS

1. As a public health leader, how would you develop a health education program to increase the health literacy of the people in your service area?
2. What are the barriers to successful communication, and how have you personally overcome them?
3. What would be a workable communication strategy to get more funds for an expanded childhood immunization program?
4. What strategies might you use to increase your interpersonal communication skills?
5. What are the advantages and disadvantages of oral communication as opposed to written communication?
6. What are the characteristics of active listening?
7. What are Walton's five rules of conversational etiquette?
8. What speaker aids can be used to enhance a public talk, and what are their advantages and disadvantages?
9. What are some guidelines for interviewing job candidates?
10. What are the differences between media advocacy, risk communications, and public education?
11. What are the advantages of engaging in dialogue before engaging in discussion or debate?
12. What are the differences between health communication, crisis communications, and social marketing?
13. Why is storytelling important? Describe the different types of stories.
14. What are the advantages of journaling as a communication strategy?

EXERCISE 18-1:   Using Persuasion

Purpose: to learn how to use public speaking for purposes of persuasion

Key concepts: persuasion, public speaking, strategic planning, team consensus

Procedure: The class should divide into teams of 8 to 10 members. Each team has the task of preparing a speech intended to persuade community residents of the benefits of a particular project. It seems likely that federal funds will become available to the community for the development of a teen clinic at Margaret Sanger High School. The team, during 30 minutes of discussion, should first identify a strategy for convincing an audience made up of community residents that the teen clinic will benefit the community and should then develop a speech based on that strategy. After the speech is completed, the team selects a spokesperson to give a five-minute presentation at a community meeting in support of the teen clinic.

EXERCISE 18-2:   Developing Scenarios on Trust and Concern

Purpose: to explore risk communication issues related to trust and concern

Key concepts: risk communication, trust, concern, scenario building

Procedures: Divide the class or training group into groups of 10. Utilizing Figure 18-3, develop four scenarios demonstrating:

1.   High trust and high concern
2.   Low trust and high concern
3.   High trust and low concern
4.   Low trust and low concern

EXERCISE 18-3:   The Risk of Terrorism in Los Angeles

Purpose: to utilize message-mapping techniques to examine the possibility of a terrorist event in a large metropolitan area

Key concepts: risk communication, message mapping

Procedures: Divide the class or training group into groups of 10. Then divide each group into the following three stakeholder groups: the community, elected officials, and the media. Each team is to develop a message map (see Figure 18-4) on the risk of a terrorist attack in Los Angeles in the next five years. Before undertaking the mapping process, have team members develop a specific and general concerns list to guide them in the process. Have each team present their findings to the entire group.

EXERCISE 18-4:   Creating a Health Communication Strategy

Purpose: to understand the process of developing a health communication strategy to address a local health problem

Key concepts: epidemiology, health communication

Procedure: A group of children eat hamburgers and drink milkshakes at a local fast-food restaurant, Old Mother Hubbard Eatery, and become seriously ill. The health department calls in the state epidemiologist, who investigates the problem and determines that a salmonella outbreak has occurred. The epidemiologist also finds evidence of *E. coli* contamination. The local health department is called in to develop a health communication strategy to get the word out to the public. Divide the class into teams of 8 to 10 to develop the communication strategy. Following the CDC guidelines, each team should draft a brief document that outlines this strategy, including the communication skills to be used by each team member during the process.

REFERENCES

1. S. P. Robbins and M. Coulter, *Management*, 11th ed. (Upper Saddle River, NJ: Prentice Hall, 2011).
2. N. M. Tichy and E. Cohen, *The Leadership Engine* (New York, Harper Business, 1997).
3. R. B. Adler and J. M. Elmhorst, *Communicating at Work*, 5th ed. (New York: McGraw-Hill, 1996).
4. Adler and Elmhorst, *Communicating at Work*.
5. J. G. Liebler and C. R. McConnell, *Management Principles for Health Professionals*, 4th ed. (Sudbury, MA: Jones & Bartlett, 2004).
6. D. Walton, *Are You Communicating?* (New York: McGraw-Hill, 1989).
7. P. Lencioni, *Death by Meeting* (San Francisco: Jossey-Bass, 2004).
8. D. Tannen, *That's Not What I Meant* (New York: Ballantine, 1986).
9. R. Bolton, *People Skills* (New York: Simon & Schuster, 1979).
10. J. E. Hulett Jr., "A Symbolic Interactionist Model of Human Communication. Part 1: The General Model of Social Behavior; the Message Generating Process," *AV Communication Review* 14, no. 1 (1966): 5–33.
11. J. E. Hulett Jr., "A Symbolic Interactionist Model of Human Communication. Part 2: The Receiver's Function; Pathology of Communication; Non-Communication," *AV Communication Review* 14, no. 2 (1966): 203–220.
12. R. R. Sears, "A Theoretical Framework for Personality and Social Behavior," *American Psychologist* 6 (1951): 476–482.
13. N. L. Frigon Sr. and H. K. Jackson Jr., *The Leader* (New York: AMACON [American Management Association], 1996).
14. Robbins and Coulter, *Management*, 11th ed.
15. Tannen, *That's Not What I Meant*.
16. D. Tannen, *The Argument Culture* (New York: Random House, 1998).
17. Bolton, *People Skills*.
18. Adler and Elmhorst, *Communicating at Work*.
19. Adler and Elmhorst, *Communicating at Work*.
20. N. M. Tichy and W. G. Bennis, *Judgment* (New York: Penguin Portfolio, 2007).
21. R. Pitino, *Success Is a Choice* (New York: Broadway Books, 1997).
22. W. Bennis, *Still Surprised* (San Francisco: Jossey-Bass, 2010).
23. Robbins and Coulter, *Management*, 11th ed.
24. Robbins and Coulter, *Management*, 11th ed.
25. Adler and Elmhorst, *Communicating at Work*.
26. T. Alessandra and P. Hunsaker, *Communicating at Work* (New York: Simon & Schuster, 1993).
27. C. O. Scharmer, "Uncovering the Blind Spot of Leadership," *Leader to Leader* 47 (2008): 52–59.
28. D. Goleman, *Emotional Intelligence* (New York: Bantam Books, 1995).
29. P. R. Scholtes, *The Leader's Handbook* (New York: McGraw-Hill, 1998).
30. Alessandra and Hunsaker, *Communicating at Work*.
31. Walton, *Are You Communicating?*
32. Adler and Elmhorst, *Communicating at Work*.
33. Adler and Elmhorst, *Communicating at Work*.
34. Walton, *Are You Communicating?*
35. Alessandra and Hunsaker, *Communicating at Work*.
36. J. G. Liebler and C. R. McConnell, *Management Principles for Health Professionals*, 6th ed. (Sudbury, MA: Jones & Bartlett, 2011).
37. Bennis, *Still Surprised*.
38. Liebler and McConnell, *Management Principles for Health Professionals*, 6th ed.
39. Liebler and McConnell, *Management Principles for Health Professionals*, 6th ed.
40. B. D. Smart, *The Smart Interviewer* (New York: Wiley, 1989).
41. Smart, *The Smart Interviewer*.
42. J. Carver, *Boards That Make a Difference*, 3rd ed. (San Francisco: Jossey-Bass, 2006).
43. Robbins and Coulter, *Management*, 11th ed.
44. J. Wycoff, *Mindmapping: Your Personal Guide to Exploring Creativity and Problem-Solving* (New York: Berkeley Books, 1995).
45. Adler and Elmhorst, *Communicating at Work*.
46. B. Nelson and P. Economy, *Managing for Dummies* (Foster City, CA: IDG Books Worldwide, Inc., 2010).
47. R. S. Scobel and S. Israel, *Naked Conversations* (Hoboken, NJ: John Wiley & Sons, 2006).
48. Robbins and Coulter, *Management*, 11th ed.
49. D. Shipley and W. Schwalbe, *Send* (New York: Alfred A. Knopf, 2007).
50. Walton, *Are You Communicating?*
51. S. M. Shortell et al., *Remaking Health Care in America* (San Francisco: Jossey-Bass, 1996).
52. L. Wallack and L. Dorfman, "Media Advocacy: A Strategy for Advancing Policy and Promoting Health," *Health Education Quarterly* 23, no. 3 (1996): 293–317.
53. L. B. Winett and L. Wallack, "Advancing Public Health Goals Through the Mass Media," *Journal of Health Communications* 1 (1996): 173–196.
54. S. Iyengar, *Is Anyone Responsible? How Television Frames Political Issues* (Chicago: University of Chicago Press, 1989).
55. M. Siegel and L. Doner, *Marketing Public Health*, 2nd ed. (Sudbury, MA: Jones & Bartlett, 2007).
56. Wallack and Dorfman, "Media Advocacy."
57. Wallack and Dorfman, "Media Advocacy."
58. J. Fallows, *Breaking the News* (New York: Pantheon Books, 1996).
59. M. R. Lum and T. L. Tinker, eds., *A Primer on Health Risk Communication: Principles and Practices* (Washington, DC: U.S. Department of Health and Human Services, Public Health Service, 1994).
60. National Research Council, *Improving Risk Communications* (Washington, DC: National Academies Press, 1989).
61. V. T. Covello, R. G. Peters, J. G. Wojtecki, and R. C. Hyde, "Risk Communication, The West Nile Virus Epidemic, and Bioterrorism," *Journal of Urban Health: Bulletin of the New Academy of Medicine* 78 (2001): 382–391.

62. Association of State and Territorial Health Officials, *Communication in Risk Situations* (Washington, DC: ASTHO, 2002).

63. V. T. Covello, "Risk Communication, Trust, and Credibility," *Health and Environmental Digest* 6 (1992), 1–4.

64. V. T. Covello, "Risk Communication, Trust, and Credibility," *Journal of Occupational Medicine* 35 (1993): 18–19.

65. ASTHO, *Communication in Risk Situations*.

66. Covello et al., "Risk Communication, the West Nile Virus Epidemic, and Bioterrorism."

67. ASTHO, *Communications in Risk Situations*.

68. V. T. Covello, Keynote Address, St. Louis: National Public Health Leadership Development Network Annual Meeting, 2003.

69. Covello et al., "Risk Communication, the West Nile Virus Epidemic, and Bioterrorism."

70. Covello et al., "Risk Communication, the West Nile Virus Epidemic, and Bioterrorism."

71. Covello et al., "Risk Communication, the West Nile Virus Epidemic, and Bioterrorism."

72. B. Fischoff, S. Lichtenstein, P. Slovik, and D. Keeney, *Acceptable Risk* (Cambridge: Cambridge University Press, 1981).

73. C. Chess, B. J. Hance, and P. M. Sandman, *Improving Dialogue with Communities: A Short Guide to Government Risk Communication* (Trenton: New Jersey Department of Environmental Protection (1988).

74. Chess et al., *Improving Dialogue with Communities*.

75. M. Vanderford, *Leading Through Crisis: New Threats, New Leadership Skills*, American Public Health Association Annual Meeting, Washington, DC, 2004.

76. Agency for Toxic Substances and Disease Registry, *Citizen's Guide to Risk Assessment for Public Health Assessments* (Atlanta, GA: CDC, 2004).

77. V. T. Covello, J. G. Wojtecki, and R. Peters, *77 Questions Asked by Journalists During a Crisis* (New York: Center for Risk Communications, n.d.).

78. V. T. Covello, *Message Mapping*, World Health Organization Workshop, Switzerland, 2002.

79. Covello, *Message Mapping*.

80. Covello, *Message Mapping*.

81. W. K. Kellogg Foundation, *Logic Model Development Guide* (Battle Creek, MI: Kellogg, 2000).

82. Robbins and Coulter, *Management*, 11th ed.

83. Adler and Elmhorst, *Communicating at Work*.

84. S. Helgesen, *The Web of Inclusion* (New York: Doubleday, 1995).

85. D. J. Breckon, *Managing Health Promotion Programs* (Gaithersburg, MD: Aspen Publishers, 1997).

86. Tannen, *The Argument Culture*.

87. A. J. DuBrin, *The Complete Idiot's Guide to Leadership* (New York: Alpha Books [MacMillan Reference USA], 2000).

88. DuBrin, *The Complete Idiot's Guide to Leadership*.

89. L. M. Harris, "Differences That Make a Difference," in *Health and the New Media*, ed. L. M. Harris (Mahwah, NJ: Lawrence Erlbaum Associates, 1995).

90. Robbins and Coulter, *Management*, 11th ed.

91. Liebler and McConnell, *Management Principles for Health Professionals*, 6th ed.

92. P. R. Scholtes, *The Leader's Handbook* (New York: McGraw-Hill, 1998).

93. Alessandra and Hunsaker, *Communicating at Work*.

94. Hulett, "A Symbolic Interactionist Model of Human Communication, Part 1."

95. Robbins and Coulter, *Management*, 11th ed.

96. Robbins and Coulter, *Management*, 11th ed.

97. M. DePree, *Leading Without Power* (San Francisco: Jossey-Bass, 1997).

98. C. L. Brown, *Techniques of Successful Delegation* (Shawnee Mission, KS: National Press Publications, 1988).

99. C. Handy, *Understanding Organizations* (New York: Oxford University Press, 1993).

100. P. Hersey et al., *Management of Organizational Behavior*, 9th ed. (Upper Saddle River, NJ: Prentice Hall, 2007).

101. DuBrin, *The Complete Idiot's Guide to Leadership*.

102. J. A. Barker, *Future Edge* (New York: Morrow, 1992).

103. E. Goffman, *Frame Analysis* (Cambridge, MA: Harvard University Press, 1974).

104. D. Tannen, *Talking from 9 to 5* (New York: Morrow, 1994).

105. L. G. Bolman and T. E. Deal, *Reframing Organizations*, 4th ed. (San Francisco: Jossey-Bass, 2008).

106. D. K. Hurst, *Crisis and Renewal* (Boston: Harvard Business School Press, 1995).

107. G. T. Fairhurst and R. A. Starr, *The Art of Framing* (San Francisco: Jossey-Bass, 1996).

108. Fairhurst and Starr, *The Art of Framing*.

109. D. Bohm et al., *Dialogue—A Proposal* (Gloucester, England: Dialogue, 1991).

110. L. Ellinor and G. Gerard, eds., *Dialogue* (New York: Wiley, 1998).

111. D. Bohm, *On Dialogue* (Ojai, CA: David Bohm Seminars, 1989).

112. J. C. Lammers, "Building Learning Communities to Expand Public Health Resources and Effectiveness," paper presented at Association of State and Territorial Directors of Health, Promotion and Public Health Annual Meeting, Washington, DC, April 27, 1996.

113. M. R. Weisbord and S. Janoff, *Future Search* (San Francisco: Jossey-Bass, 1995).

114. Bohm, *On Dialogue*.

115. Tannen, *The Argument Culture*.

116. Ellinor and Gerard, *Dialogue*.

117. M. Doyle and D. Straus, *How to Make Meetings Work* (New York: Jove Publications, 1982).

118. Nelson and Economy, *Managing for Dummies*.

119. S. Randolph, "A Leadership Interview with Robert Howard," *Leadership in Public Health* 3, no. 4 (1995): 7–11.

120. K. S. Lord, "Issues in Health Communications," *Leadership in Public Health* 3, no. 4 (1995): 1–4.

121. Lord, "Issues in Health Communications."

122. L. Potts and L. Rowitz, "Social Marketing/Health Communications: Leadership Opportunities for the 1990s," *Journal of Public Health Management and Practice* 2, no. 4 (1996): 75.

123. B. Reynolds, *Crisis and Emergency Risk Communication* (Atlanta, GA: CDC, 2002).

124. B. Reynolds, *Crisis and Emergency Risk Communication* (Atlanta, GA: CDC, 2002).

125. L. Fernandez and M. Merzer, *Jane's Crisis Communications Handbook* (Alexandria, VA: Jane's Information Group, 2003).

126. Fernandez and Merzer, *Jane's Crisis Communications Handbook.*

127. Fernandez and Merzer, *Jane's Crisis Communications Handbook.*

128. A. R. Andreasen, *Marketing Social Change* (San Francisco: Jossey-Bass, 1995).

129. Winett and Wallack, "Advancing Public Health Goals Through the Mass Media."

130. Winett and Wallack, "Advancing Public Health Goals Through the Mass Media."

131. Winett and Wallack, "Advancing Public Health Goals Through the Mass Media."

132. P. Kotler and E. L. Roberto, *Social Marketing* (New York: The Free Press, 1989).

133. Siegel and Doner, *Marketing Public Health.*

134. Tichy and Cohen, *The Leadership Engine.*

135. H. Gardner, *Leading Minds* (New York: Basic Books, 1995).

136. S. Denning, *The Leader's Guide to Storytelling* (San Francisco: Jossey-Bass, 2005).

137. S. Denning, *The Secret Language of Leadership* (San Francisco: Jossey-Bass, 2007).

CHAPTER 19

Leadership and People Development

Really great people make you feel that you too can become great.

—Mark Twain

Leadership is all about people, institutions, and communities. In discussing the leadership of the future, it can be stated that the legacy of the successful leader is the creation and sustainability of valued institutions that can survive the test of time.[1] This does not mean that stresses will not enter the system, but rather that a strong institutional structure will survive onslaughts such as the events of September 11, 2001, and the anthrax letters that followed. Leaders are also committed to the growth and nurturance of people. These people include all members of a community, whether they work directly in an organization in which the leader resides or in the surrounding community. All public health leaders need to be committed to promoting healthy communities. This chapter is concerned with the skills the leader needs to work with people, organizations, and communities.

To put the content of this chapter in perspective, I want to tell you a personal story about a very special person who affected my life. I know that it is unusual for an author of a text like this one to personalize the content, but sometimes it is important to waive the rules. This chapter is about personal things and feelings. The man about whom I am going to tell you was a man who changed the direction of my professional life. His effect on me goes back almost 50 years, even before people were talking about the importance of emotions in leadership. It was the first week of my several years as a graduate student in sociology. I remember visiting the department offices in an old university building, where I discovered that not all the department's professors were in this building. I also found to my amazement that I had received a graduate teaching assistantship in what was at that time an innovative two-semester course on the relationship between society and culture. All the lectures had been taped and were to be broadcast over the university public television station several times a week at different times. This course was one of the first attempts at distance education before distance education was popular. The lectures were given by Professor Robert Janes of the Sociology Department. Sometimes Professor Janes had televised discussions with other well-known campus faculty as part of the program. I was to run three discussion sections each semester. Professor Janes was one of the brightest, most insightful teachers I have ever known. However, if his intelligence was all that he had to offer, my story would be over.

Professor Janes's office was in an old, converted house several blocks from the departmental main offices. I remember walking to his office on a beautiful fall day. He was seated behind a big desk with books and papers strewn all over the place. As soon as I introduced myself, he concentrated on me. He listened intently and seemed to immediately understand my nervousness and uncertainties about being a graduate student. Bob always listened intently and always seemed to understand what my fellow graduate colleagues were going through. He was always available and willing to talk about anything. It wasn't just his intelligence, it was his ability to understand all of us. We graduate students all got his attention. He mentored us, coached us, and guided us through all the complexities of graduate school. He invited us often to his home, and his wife Jean always offered us her friendship as well as snacks for starving students. I married about a year into my graduate work, and Bob and Jean were always warm to us and invited my wife and me to their home many times.

About halfway through my graduate work, Professor Janes accepted a position at another university several hundred miles away. I thought that was the end of his mentoring of me. I was wrong. He remained my mentor and friend until the end of his life. In fact, he offered me my first teaching job, which I did not take for a number of reasons. He and Jean still remained my friends. I visited with him whenever I was in his city. We discussed the world, and he always asked how my wife and children were. He was always interested in me as a person. Here was a man who clearly had great intelligence as well as strong people skills. I only hope that each of my readers experiences the impact of a Bob Janes. It can change a life.

INTRODUCTION

At its essence, leadership is about the building of relationships. Leadership is about more than the personality of the person seen as a leader; it is about the behavior of that person.[2] In discussing the five practices of a leader, Kouzes and Posner stated that leaders guide others by being role models, inspire others to follow and share their vision, challenge the way things get done, empower and enable others to behave in positive ways, and encourage and reward others for their work. We can find leaders everywhere. Leaders garner trust and respect in the people they encounter. However, leadership has to be more than "follow the leader." Williams has pointed out that real leadership requires leaders to face reality in their activities.[3] Leaders help their colleagues and followers to understand situations by developing strategies to address challenges and problems and learning how to take advantage of opportunities.

Many of the activities to be discussed in this chapter involve the necessity of understanding who we are as people and as leaders. Leaders have to develop their personal leadership talents and abilities. This level of leadership requires an understanding of what self leadership means. A leader needs to accept responsibility for his or her actions rather than blaming others. Blanchard and his colleagues have stated that empowerment gives a person the responsibility to make things work.[4] Mind reading is not realistic, and it is very often incorrect. It is often our own perceptions that limit our activities. Blanchard and his colleagues call this "assumed constraints." These constraints are really the ways in which we let our mental models limit our choices. These constraints are also about the barriers we put up that limit our choices. DeBono discussed the importance of the way we let our attention limit our perceptions.[5] A paradigm limits our attention by setting up boundaries to what we observe. Freedom is exploring all the possible ways that a challenge can be addressed, and a lack of freedom is letting our personal views of the world limit our choices.

The related concepts of legacy and sustainability are an important aspect of the perception factor. Leaders want to believe that their work makes a difference and will affect public health beyond their tenure in a particular public health organization. Some of these issues can be explored in Exercise 19-1, which has been adapted from an article by Laur and Schlag.[6] This exercise looks backward, then forward, and finally to the present and how our perceptions affect our mental models and our concerns related to sustainability.

In discussing power, Blanchard and colleagues argued that it is necessary for a leader to define the different "points of power" that affect our personal leadership.[7] They discussed five major categories of power. First, there is personal power in which a leader can influence the work of others in a positive manner by encouraging them and keeping them involved in work activities. This is different from position power, where a leader uses position to guide others. In other words, I am doing this because my supervisor says I have to. Knowledge power comes from expertise on a subject. Task power is power that comes from the ability to do specific types of work. The fifth type of power that is critical to the subject matter of this chapter is relationship power, which involves the ability to work with others. An important aspect of building relationships is the ability to collaborate.

When we talk about relationships, it is important to look for guideposts. First, it is important to develop relationships with intelligent people. Robbins stated that this is controversial, although most evidence points to intelligence as being critical for leaders and the people with whom they relate.[8] Second, it is easier to relate to people with a positive perspective than those that tend to be negative. Third, past experience with others is often a good indicator of relationships in the future, though it is important to compare differences related to the past situation and contrast it to potential differences in the new job or collaborative relationship. Fourth, leaders know when to use different forms of communication that will expedite action. Fifth, the ability to develop solid relationships with others can help the leader to influence many areas of his or her life.[9] It is important to develop credibility with others. Regardless of the structure of the interactions from individual relationships to group situations, it is always critical to interact with people on an individual level. Relationships are thus built on mutual respect, common experiences that are shared, mutual trust, reciprocity (transactional leadership relationships), the ability to enjoy the relationship, and humor.

Many of us would argue that our agencies do good work. This important issue is how to move our agencies forward from being just good to being a great agency. Collins has stated that Level 5 leadership makes the difference.[10] Level 5 leaders blend knowledge, talents, and skills as well as good work habits (Level 1), contribute and work well in teams (Level 2), manage people well (Level 3), and are effective leaders (Level 4). Level 5 leaders are humble and put their organizations and communities ahead of their personal egos. They are experts in relationship building and are concerned about the needs of the people with whom they work. All leaders need to be committed to promoting healthy communities.[11] This chapter will explore the importance of building relationships with our agency staff, our community residents, and our external stakeholders. **Figure 19-1** shows these relationships as interactive. The dimensions of this figure will be explored through the rest of this chapter. However, we will first explore the importance of emotional intelligence in leadership.

EMOTIONALLY INTELLIGENT LEADERSHIP

Although intelligence and the intelligence quotient (IQ) seemed to be the critical requirements for leadership during the previous century, leaders of the 21st century need to have emotional intelligence as well.

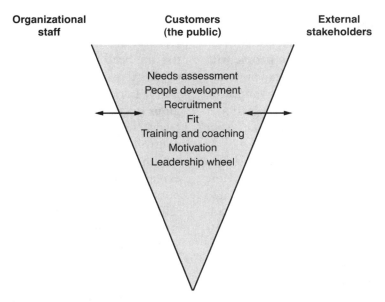

FIGURE 19-1 Relationship-Developing Interaction Model.

Today, leaders need to develop an ability and capacity to recognize their personal feelings and the feelings and emotional reactions of others.[12] In addition to developing this emotional awareness, leaders need to become motivated to manage their emotions and feelings in their relationships with others as well. In his classic book on leadership, Burns said that a critical activity for leaders is to help others become aware of their feelings, feel these needs in a strong way, understand their values and how they emotionally respond to these values, and then become involved in meaningful actions based on these emotional realities.[13] Mayer and Salovey coined the concept of emotional intelligence to refer to these important leadership skills.[14] Effective leadership thus occurs in the context of emotional intelligence.[15] You can experiment with your view of yourself as a leader who recognizes personal feelings by doing Exercise 19- 2 using a mirror.

Emotional intelligence is critical to effective leadership.[16] In reviewing extensive research, Goleman pointed out that it may be technical and cognitive skills that get a person a leadership position, but it is emotional intelligence that helps leaders keep their jobs. It is also interesting to note that leaders have to rely on these emotional skills more and more as they move up in the organization. These leaders promote the development of technical skills for those individuals who work in the more technical positions in the organization. It is also clear that leaders will have to be proficient in emotional intelligence as they expand their activities outside the organization in collaborative groups or other community-based activities. Emotional intelligence distinguishes the outstanding leaders and is clearly an important indicator of strong and effective performance.[17] This finding was strongly supported by Mayer and Salovey to explain how two people with similar general intelligence and technical expertise can end up in entirely different parts of an organization and at different leadership levels in the organization.[18] Exercise 19-3 will give you a chance to evaluate your leadership traits.

There is a need to become aware that the relationship between technical skills, cognitive skills including IQ, and emotional intelligence needs to be evaluated further. If we were to create a recipe for successful leadership, it would be necessary to determine the percentage of these three ingredients for different types of professional work. Although it seems clear that emotional intelligence increases in importance as leaders work more with others, it also seems apparent that the relationship of the three ingredients will fluctuate over time and place. Thus, the formula for effective leadership becomes:

Technical skills (__%) + cognitive skills (__%) + emotional intelligence (__%) = successful leadership (100%)

An interesting set of issues relates to the question of whether emotional intelligence can be learned. Intelligence and emotional intelligence are separate sets of competencies.[19] Having a high intelligence quotient is not a guarantee of strong social skills or high emotional intelligence. General intelligence is less flexible than emotional intelligence.[20] People do not generally increase their general intelligence over time, but emotional intelligence does increase as people become more adept at personal relationships. Emotional intelligence is not fixed at birth due to genetics.[21] It can grow over time. In making the argument that emotional intelligence can grow and be learned, there is evidence that emotional intelligence increases with age.[22] Emotional intelligence is related to neurotransmitters in the limbic system of the brain, which is tied to feelings, impulses, and drives. It will be important in the future for training programs to orient their activities to changing behavioral patterns that are associated with the limbic system. Increasing the motivation to make these changes must be a goal of training. Learning to be empathic is a critical part of the development of emotional intelligence.

It has become clear in the past several years that emotional intelligence skills for leaders are important for the individual leaders but also for the leader's relationships with others. This is not to denigrate the importance of technical and cognitive skills. The real concern is related to balance. The leader needs to use the head as well as the heart. An interesting view of this issue is found in an inspirational writing by Rabbi Lori Forman.[23] She was responding to a religious document called the Midrash in which ancient Jewish scholars defined the wicked as those who are controlled by their hearts and the righteous as those who have their hearts under control. Rabbi Forman explained this passage in terms of balance. It is not possible to separate our rational self from our feeling self. Our thoughts guide our feelings and vice versa. It is through the combination of thoughts and feelings that humankind addresses the world. Self-control is important because feelings without control can lead to chaos. It is important for the leader to realize that the mind skills and the heart skills all need to be developed if successful leadership is to occur.

Many writers have come up with frameworks for determining the important components and competencies of emotional intelligence. Three of these frameworks are discussed here. All three involve the development of personal skills as well as skills involved in dealing with others. All three models also have assessment tools tied to them that the reader can access. **Table 19-1** gives a summary of the three models. The first model relates to the structure defined by Goleman.[24–27] Goleman and his colleagues in the Consortium for Research on Emotional Intelligence in Organizations have been working with this model for a number of years. The framework now has four components, with 20 subcompetencies associated with each of the four categories. Two of the dimensions (self-awareness and self-management) involve personal competencies, and two of the dimensions (social awareness and relationship management) involve social competencies.

The self-awareness domain includes emotional self-awareness, accurate self-assessment, and self-confidence. The competencies involved here include an ability on the part of the individual to understand and recognize moods, feelings, and drives. Specifically, emotional self-awareness includes the ability to recognize moods and emotions and how it affects personal behavior. People with this competence not only understand their moods but also understand why they are feeling as they do.[28] These people also recognize the link between thoughts and feelings. They also know that their performance is often affected by these feelings and thoughts. Competency in accurate self-assessment includes the knowledge of one's strengths and limitations. This skill clearly involves learning from

experience. These people also are willing to accept feedback on their behavior. The third competency in self-awareness involves self-confidence. These people are willing to take a stand. They are often the risk takers. Exercise 19-4 will give you the chance to describe your risk-taking experiences.

The second component of the Goleman model involves self-management, which has several subcompetencies associated with it. This component includes the ability not only to understand one's feelings and moods, but also to use these feelings and moods to guide oneself toward personal goals and objectives. There is a strong motivational factor here in that the leader not only is aware of personal moods and feelings, but needs to stay flexible and positive in directing these moods and feelings into change.[29] The first subcomponent is emotional self-control, which means that the leaders know or learn how to control feelings and emotions. People strong in this competency have also mastered the ability to stay focused. Being trustworthy is an important part of self-management. Action in an ethical manner is a critical leadership responsibility. People strong in this competency also work vigorously to build trust. They also admit their mistakes and address unethical behavior in others. It is important to remember that trust takes time to build, and it can be destroyed in a moment. Part of trust is carrying through on promises, which is also involved in the competency of conscientiousness. Thus, these leaders keep their promises. Do Exercise 19-5 on building trust.

The next competency related to self-management involves the skills related to adaptability, involving flexibility in managing change. Leaders are always oriented toward the future and the changes necessary to get there. They look for new approaches and new methods for attaining goals. They are innovative and want to generate new ideas. Leaders are excellent multitaskers, and they can handle shifting priorities. They are flexible. The next competency of leaders having an achievement drive is closely tied to the competency of adaptability and innovation. These people are results and outcome based. They also take calculated risks to achieve the ends they seek. These people would be concerned with the tools of performance measurement. They would also want to create performance standards and then surpass them. The final competency for self-management involves initiative, which is a readiness and ability to act on opportunities whenever they present themselves. Optimism is part of this competency because leaders are positive in addressing challenges.[30] If you are to seize opportunities, then a

TABLE 19-1 Frameworks for Emotional Intelligence

Goleman (2001)	Cooper and Sawaf (1996)	Feldman (1999)
Self-awareness	Emotional literacy	Knowing yourself
Self-management	Emotional fitness	Maintaining control
Social awareness	Emotional depth	Reading others
Relationship management	Emotional alchemy	Perceiving accurately
_____	_____	Communicating with flexibility

positive perspective helps. Leaders create visions and then surpass them. They will do whatever is necessary to get the job done, although they will always practice ethical standards in doing so. These people are wonderful in inspiring others to follow their lead.

The next dimension of the Goleman model addresses the issue of social awareness.[31] An important ability of leaders is to be able to recognize and read the emotions, feelings, and reactions of others.[32] The interesting challenge here is to do this when you might feel differently than other people about a situation. Three competencies are tied to this dimension of emotional intelligence. The first critical set of skills is empathy or understanding others. Empathy requires the ability to be an active listener who is able to pick up emotional cues from other people. Empathy includes sensitivity to the needs of other people. Mentors and executive coaches need to be strong in this competency. If we as leaders are to enable others to act, then we must learn to empower others. One way to do this is to show others that we understand their needs and desires. Good leaders make others feel strong and capable.[33] In doing this, those who follow often exceed their own expectations.

The second competency area is service orientation. This competency is familiar to those who are proponents of continuous quality improvement methods. This competency involves the development of skills to anticipate, recognize, and meet the needs of others, whether they are the clients of a public health agency, the residents of a community, or our community partners. Leaders competent in this area are concerned about how others react to public health decisions. Public health leaders have a strong concern for others, which is tied to the belief that all people are entitled to the best that health and public health have to offer. Social justice concerns drive the public health agenda, and yet political and budgetary decision sometimes lead to health inequities.

The final competency in the social awareness cluster involves organizational awareness. This competency can be defined as an ability to increase awareness of the emotions and political realities of those with whom the leader works.[34] This competency involves the skills of networking, collaboration, influence building, and systems thinking. The leader with this competency must understand the interdependencies of groups and how feeling and emotions affect outcomes. Almost all leadership skills require this competency to be well developed.

The fourth dimension of the emotional competency model of Goleman involves the critical sets of skills related to relationship management. In fact, the skills discussed above on social awareness are closely allied to this cluster of eight competencies. Such skills as strategic planning, conflict resolution, problem solving, decision making, and other traditional leadership and management tools are subsumed under this component of emotional intelligence. The value-added piece of the current discussion relates to the effect of emotions and feelings on these traditional leadership activities. A major competency involves the development of others, which appears closely allied to the empathy competency discussed previously. Leaders need to be concerned about the future and the issue of succession planning. It is important to recognize the skills and potential of others. Leaders need to be realistic. No leadership position is forever.

The ability to be influential is another competency related to relationship management. Influence and skill in persuasion are tied together. The leader has to become skillful in getting others to buy in to his or her message. This means that complex strategies need to be developed to build consensus and support for the issues that the leader considers to be important. Successful leaders are able to put the pieces together in effective ways. They make their point and convince others of the validity of their position. It is important that the enthusiasm and positivity of the leader be contagious for others to follow.

The next competency involves the ability of the leader to listen with an open mind, monitor personal emotions and feelings, and be able to send effective messages in a number of different ways. Leaders emphasize the importance of communication in all its aspects. Communication is more than interpersonal in nature and covers many things, including written communication strategies and public discussion and dialogue. People who are strong in this competency excel at reading emotional cues in others.[35] These leaders are also effective in addressing complex issues in a straightforward manner. They are good listeners and seek to understand what is said to them at both a verbal and an emotional level. They foster communication, and they try to listen to information about good and bad events. Collaboration not only improves performance, it creates a strong level of trust.[36]

The next competency in relationship management involves conflict management. People strong in this competency know how to handle difficult people in tense situations.[37] This ability involves the use of tact and diplomacy. These leaders know how to diffuse tension and move from conflict to collaboration. They do this by addressing conflict in an open manner and encourage the voicing of diverse views. These leaders want to create win–win situations. The leader really needs to be able to spot trouble before it explodes in a major crisis situation. The leader also needs to determine when an objective negotiator needs to be brought in to resolve conflicts because the emotions are overtaking rational decision making.

The assumption in this chapter has been that all these competencies are important for leaders. The competencies of visionary leadership and catalyzing change are clearly competencies of leaders. Leaders need to be able to create a vision with an awareness that emotional factors will guide the vision process. To attain the vision, the leader needs to convince others to go along with the steps necessary to bring about change. Leaders are catalysts for change and need to not only recognize that change is necessary, but also challenge the status quo and remove the barriers to change.[38] Leaders will have to get others to emotionally invest in the change process and be part of the vision that the leader has.

The next relationship management competency addresses the building of bonds between people. Building networks between people is important if strong relationships are to be built. In informal discussions with the directors of 19 state and regional public health leadership institutes around the United States, these directors have stated that one of the hidden functions of leadership development is fostering the connections and friendships that develop among the trainees. These leaders think that one of the benefits of training relates to the leadership networks that this training generates. These relationships that evolve through training or through building bonds between people in other arenas often create trust and goodwill. Strong leaders build bonds. When these bonds develop, social capital increases.

The final competency in the Goleman framework involves the competencies of teamwork and collaboration. At the emotional intelligence level, this competency involves the creation of a balance between the work or task to be performed and the relationships necessary to carry out the work.[39] Collaboration has emotional components. The sharing of information and future plans or resources can lessen stress in many situations, although not in all of them. Feelings of competition have strong emotional reactions. The goal of leaders strong in collaboration is to build positive working and personal environments. These leaders want to nurture teamwork and collaboration in coalitions, alliances, and partnerships.

Goleman has put together the emotional intelligence competencies with leadership style, effect on climate (or social context), objective of the leadership style orientation, and its effect on organizational effectiveness.[40] **Table 19-2** shows these relationships. The important thing to note in the table is the specific competencies that seem to predominate in each leadership style. Which is your predominant style? Are you competent in the areas listed for that style? If you go through the list of the 20 Goleman competencies, which competencies would you say are your strong ones, and which do you want to develop competence in for the future?

The second approach to emotional intelligence, as seen in Table 19-1, is built on something called the four cornerstone model.[41] As will be seen in the following discussion, the four cornerstone model overlaps with the Goleman model just discussed, and yet there are some different perspectives that the authors give that can enrich the skills of the prepared public health leader. High-level executives with a strong emotional quotient (EQ) as well as a strong IQ (intelligence quotient) tend to make the best decisions and run the most dynamic and creative organizations.[42] These leaders also report that they are living very satisfying lives. The following discussion will involve a look at the four cornerstone model and the competencies associated with each of the cornerstones.

The first cornerstone relates to emotional literacy, which relates to the emotional center of all our activities. It is emotional literacy that affects our energy and motivation. This cornerstone, as well as each of the other three, has four competencies associated with it—emotional honesty, emotional energy, emotional feedback, and practical intuition. Many of our emotional reactions are tied to the first competency of honesty. Being true to yourself and others undergirds much of the Goleman discussion above. The way the leader is seen by others is important here. The honest leader needs to judge him- or herself in an honest manner as well. Whenever a leader is asked to evaluate personal skills on a leadership assessment tool, it is assumed that the leader will be honest in filling out the form and not answer the questions in such a way that the leader thinks the tester will evaluate so that their skills are seen in a more favorable light. One little exercise that you can try to evaluate this honesty dimension is to evaluate your energy level, openness, and level of focus on a scale from 1 to 10 for each dimension before and after a meeting that you have to attend.[43] Your honesty in rating yourself on this scale from 3 to 30 will give you insights into

TABLE 19-2 Leadership Style, Emotional Intelligence, and Organizational Effectiveness

Leadership Style	Emotional Intelligence Competencies	Effect on Climate	Objective	When Appropriate
Visionary	Self-confidence, empathy, change catalyst, visionary clear leadership	Most strongly positive	Mobilize others to follow a vision	When change requires a new vision or when clear direction is needed
Affiliative	Empathy, building bonds, conflict management	Highly positive	Create harmony	To heal rifts in a team or to motivate during stressful times
Democratic	Teamwork and collaboration, communication	Highly positive	Build commitment through participation	To build buy-on or consensus or to get valuable input from employees
Coaching	Developing others empathy, emotional self-awareness	Highly positive	Build strengths for the future	To help an employee improve performance or develop long-term strengths
Coercive	Achievement drive, initiative, emotional self-control	Strongly negative	Immediate compliance	In a crisis, to kick-start a turn around, or with problem employees
Pacesetting	Conscientiousness, achievement drive, initiative	Highly negative	Perform tasks to a high standard	To get quick results from a highly motivated and competent team

Source: Reproduced from D. Goleman, "Emotional Intelligence: Issues in Paradigm Building," in C. Cherniss and D. Goleman (eds.), *The Emotionally Intelligent Workplace* (San Francisco: Jossey-Bass, 2001).

your ability to address issues. If you have trouble being motivated during the meeting, evaluate the strategies that would help you become more involved.

The second competency in this first cornerstone is emotional energy. People do better when they have the energy to address tasks and develop people relationships. There are two major components to this competency. The first relates to the level of tension that the individual feels, and the second component is the level of energy itself. If the tension is high and the energy is high, the authors call this tense-energy. This pattern occurs when you push yourself to extremes and leave your personal needs at the doorstep. This pattern may lead to burnout. If you have low tension and high energy, you have calm-energy, which can lead to some very productive work. The unfortunate part is that leaders do not feel this state very often. When we feel calm-energy, it is more possible to be proactive than in the previous state, where behavior tends to be more reactive.

The third energy pattern is high tension with low energy, which can be called tense-tiredness. This is how we often feel after we get home from a busy day and a difficult freeway drive. The stress is high and the tiredness is great. In this state, individuals need to be careful to not overreact to the demands of family members or colleagues who need help in some matter. The final state is low tension with low energy, which is the state of calm-tiredness. This is the good state of just feeling content and relaxed. Leaders need to understand their energy levels and how to react to them.

The third competency involves the skills related to understanding emotional feedback. Leaders need to realize that every feeling or emotion is sending a message. Leaders who understand this will become adept at managing emotional impulsivity. This competency is similar to the competencies discussed by Goleman in the area of self-awareness and self-management. The leader needs to take responsibility for his or her actions. An interesting exercise that you can do for better understanding this competency is to ask yourself, "If you were to take responsibility for a specific feeling you have, such as anger, what would happen?"

The fourth competency relates to emotional literacy and the development of intuitive skills. Intuition is closely tied to the empathy competency in the Goleman model. The empathic individual is one who can read the feelings beneath the words that are spoken. Sometimes our gut reactions to a situation should guide our behavior rather than our rational thoughts. Trust is also important here in that relationships built on trust allow others to say and show their authentic reactions

to events. Exercise 19-6 on intuition will give you the chance to explore your use of intuition for making decisions.

The second cornerstone in the Cooper and Sawaf model involves emotional fitness, which includes the four competencies of authenticity, trust radius, constructive discontent, and resilience and renewal. Authentic power includes the issue of personal power. Authentic presence is affected by the factors of showing attentiveness to others (another aspect of empathy and building bonds), concern for others (also a part of empathy), your agenda and motives to get people involved in your vision, and the complex issue of entitlement that is affected by your organizational position or personal relationship to the other person. Authenticity also involves convincing others that you are taking discussion and dialogues seriously. The authentic leader is also one who admits to mistakes and is willing to forgive him- or herself and others. The second competency, which also exists in the Goleman model, relates to the importance of building trust. The new wrinkle in the present model is the connection between trust and believability. In addition, there is a trust radius that answers the question of how far the leader is willing to extend his or her trust network. Trust relationships take time to build, and a leader must struggle to be sociable to strangers where the trust is not yet apparent.

The third competency related to emotional fitness is constructive discontent. As a facilitator, the leader may have to create conflict in a group and get group members to address an issue in a different way than they may have in the past. Creating discontent can have positive effects even though the stress and tension levels will increase significantly. Goleman would have included this competency under conflict management. Some of the specifics in this constructive discontent include the process of increasing awareness, exposing problems in the group, using empathy to explore diverse views, promoting the development of trust in a group, understanding and promoting inclusion and participation when values and goals are in conflict, collaboration for creative solutions to problems, developing learning organizations with your colleagues in order to learn in action, creating an environment that promotes the enjoyment of the process, and a belief that constructive discontent leads to real problem solving and decision making.

The final competency for this cornerstone relates to resilience and renewal. The resilience factor is critical to creating change. It is important to point out that resilience is tied to adaptability and the ability to adjust to change. Resilient people have great curiosity. The issue of renewal is important as well. Leaders need to renew themselves. Renewal may involve taking a new job in a new place. It may be a walk on the beach or sitting in a favorite chair and reading a new book. Each of us will have different ways to address renewal. The important message is that leaders need to allow time for this sabbatical experience if they are to remain effective. We spend time taking courses or going to training workshops to expand our leadership skills, and we need to spend time on expanding our emotional intelligence skills as well.

The third cornerstone involves the critical concerns related to emotional depth.[44] This cornerstone is involved with the issue of character and how individuals over their lifetimes become more and more adept at people relationships. How we practice the skills of emotional intelligence becomes a critical indicator of emotional depth. You can experiment with some of the issues involved in this cornerstone by exploring the technical and emotional aspects of the real purpose of leading by walking around. Why do leaders walk around their organizations and communities? What is the real meaning of this activity? The four competencies of this third cornerstone include unique potential and purpose, commitment, applied integrity, and influence without authority.

The competency related to unique potential relates to the individual who is adept at analyzing personal strengths and weaknesses. Leaders need to have a purpose—a personal vision. The ability to engage in some self-analysis often gives us insights into who we are. Here are some possible questions for you to consider:

1. What are my five greatest strengths?
2. Who are the five most important people in my life?
3. What are the five major accomplishments I have achieved in the past year?
4. What are the five personal things I want to do for myself in the next year?
5. What are the five work products I want to produce in the next year?
6. When I die, what are the five things I want people to say about me?

As you answer the above questions, ask yourself why the five things you discuss are important. What feelings are created as a result?

Commitment is another competency involved in emotional depth. When you add purpose to your level of commitment and your need to be accountable for your actions, you also need to be aware that you may

have some resistance to the changes required to carry out your vision.[45] Underlying the discussion of commitment is the need to also abide by ethical standards of behavior. Accountability involves the practice of ethical behavior in a committed way. For Goleman, commitment is significantly associated with leadership.[46] The third competency of integrity is closely tied to the commitment and accountability competence. Integrity is also a part of trustworthiness. Integrity involves the recognition of the difference between right and wrong. Cooper and Sawaf called this discernment and said that discernment needs to be tied to personal actions and the way words are used to explain action.[47] Thus both the competency of commitment and the competency of integrity speak to the importance of ethical standards and how they affect thoughts and feelings. Integrity really gets to the heart of the question of what the leader represents to those who follow.

The final competency related to emotional depth is influence without authority. Influence must occur without manipulation and without authority. Influence involves perception, relationships, innovations, setting priorities, empathy, and taking account of emotional reasons for actions and not just the logical analyses. Successful leaders have influence regardless of the positions they occupy. People who are influential seem to have high energy and the ability to motivate others. They respond to the show of emotion in an understanding and nonthreatening manner. For Goleman, influence serves as the core of the relationship management component of his model.[48] One way to demonstrate this is through the use of leadership stories.[49] When you read a story of someone you consider to be a leader, look specifically for the role of the influence competency in their demonstration of leadership.

The final cornerstone in this model of emotional intelligence is emotional alchemy. Emotional intelligence is about synergy and how to use your emotions to create more value in the things you do. The four competencies tied to this final cornerstone include intuitive flow, reflective time shifting, creating the future, and opportunity sensing. In discussing the idea of flow, Csikszentmihalyi defined flow as related to the positive aspects of life and human experience.[50] Flow is demonstrated through such emotional processes as joy, creativity, total immersion in actions and all of life's experiences. Flow indicates a total concentration and involvement in what you are doing. Flow can be controlled and not left to chance. Intuitive flow is tied to strong feelings of self-worth and personal satisfaction.[51] The ability to experience intuitive flow is almost like an ability to see the real meaning of things, even when they seem obscured by rational thought. Leaders with this competency learn to use the intuition they have in more effective ways.

The next competency expands the concept of self-reflection to address the issue of shifting time. People sense time in unique ways. Some of us notice changing daylight patterns. Some of us check our wrist or pocket watches on a regular basis. Some of us let another staff member or family member remind us of where we are supposed to be. With the skill of reflective time shifting, the emotionally competent leader can picture events in the past, the present, and the future. Shifting time also requires shifting perspectives on events. This competency allows the leader to learn to shift reactions and feeling states to a given situation at a moment's notice. Cooper and Sawaf called this feeling yourself in time.[52] This set of competencies is critical in visioning activities. The next two competencies are related to visioning as well. The first is the competency of opportunity sensing. Leaders need to sense things and to push traditional sensory limits. This can be called an extension of the opportunity horizon. Leaders work to expand their awareness and to explore the larger field of possibilities. This is sometimes referred to as thinking (and sensing things) outside the box. The final competency relates to creating the future with a vision to guide the process. Goleman subsumed these three competencies within the general competency of visionary leadership.[53]

The third framework listed in Table 19-1 is somewhat different from the first two discussed frameworks. The Feldman framework is very practical and built on words that are less technical than the categories discussed above.[54] The Feldman model is also clearly based on the emotional intelligence competencies for leaders. This model integrates many of the above competencies into five core skills:

- Knowing yourself
- Maintaining control
- Reading others
- Perceiving accurately
- Communicating with flexibility

It is necessary for a leader to learn these basic skills before he or she goes on to develop higher-level skills such as learning to take responsibility, learning to generate different choices, developing and embracing a vision, having courage, and demonstrating resolve. This model is of interest because it tries to distinguish different levels of emotional intelligence. If you take the lifelong perspective on leadership, it seems obvious that different skills and competencies are needed at different points in a leader's career. If emotional intelligence skills expand over time, then it is clear that leaders should hone these skills as they go through life.

The first Feldman competency of knowing yourself is an obvious component in all emotional intelligence frameworks. It entails the recognition of personal emotional reactions, the ability to understand how emotions affect action, and also how to differentiate an emotion such as anger and how it is perceived in different social situations. My anger on a freeway shows itself in interesting ways, whereas my anger at a coworker is displayed in entirely different ways. Look at a leadership challenge you face and the emotions you display. How does your decision-making process change when you learn to control your emotional reaction to the challenge?

This first core competency affects the second competency of controlling emotions (maintaining control). The important concern for the public health leader is how the leader controls emotions during an emergency situation. Others will respond to the leader in terms of the emotions they see displayed. Others expect their leaders to appear calm during a crisis. In fact, maintaining control is all about remaining calm when chaos reigns.[55] If a leader feels that his or her emotions are getting out of control, the leader needs to briefly step back from a chaotic situation and take a deep breath. The leader in stressful situations needs to think of positive outcomes.

The third competency of reading others is in many ways similar to the empathy competency in the other two frameworks. It involves not only an awareness of the emotions of other people, but also the appreciation of the emotions of others as well as excitement involved in the diversity of other perspectives. Leaders increase their effect when they better understand the reactions of others to crisis as well as noncrisis situations. This competency also requires active listening. Respect needs to be shown to others as well. The fourth competency of accurate perception is related to this third competency. Leaders need to develop skills in assessing different types of situations. They also need to be guided by a vision as pointed out in the first two framework models. Leaders as systems thinkers need to keep their view on the big picture and try to maintain their objectivity if at all possible.

The final core competency is the importance of learning to be flexible when communicating with others. Flexibility is all about bringing our verbal and nonverbal words and actions into alignment. The messages that we send need to be clear. Others will listen to our words, but will also pay attention to our actions. Leaders need to be aware that not everyone will react to them in the same way. There are many ramifications of our words and deeds.

In this section, three frameworks of emotional intelligence have been presented. The first two frameworks have assessment tools tied to the frameworks. The third is a more practical one, with guidelines for developing each of the competencies discussed. If you would like to experiment more with emotional intelligence models, look at the Bradberry and Greaves book, which is close to the Goleman framework, and then take the online version of the emotional intelligence assessment tool developed by the authors.[56] Both the Goleman and the Cooper and Sawaf models also have assessment tools associated with them.

Kravitz and Schubert reviewed the various models of emotional intelligence and believed that this field needs to be tied to an applied perspective that they designated people-smart strategies.[57] People need to learn how to make choices in their lives. These choices extend to all the things you say and do. People-smart strategies mean you have to not only think smart but act smart. There is a need for working smart. To think smart is to understand how you function as a person, to learn self-awareness skills, to practice optimistic thinking by thinking positively, to value the work you do, to develop a support network, and to learn the skills related to caring. The three aspects of being smart involve the learning of communication skills to effectively talk to others, learning to control emotions, and developing flexibility to change. People-smart strategies are adaptive emotional intelligence that translate into the following activities:

1. Showing flexibility in communication
2. Managing personal stress
3. Helping others who express pessimism about the future
4. Showing respect for others
5. Managing work rage
6. Becoming a servant leader

ORGANIZATIONAL STAFF RELATIONSHIPS

The field of human resource management has developed over the years to address the issue of management of the people who work in our organizations and agencies. As staff and as managers and leaders, our responsibility is to put our strengths to work.[58] The role of managers is to help people find the right fit for their talents. Nurturing and supporting our work colleagues is critical. In public health, our agency colleagues need to be seen as partners in the public health enterprise. Robbins and Coulter saw human resource management as tied to improving the knowledge, skills, and abilities of staff through education and training; working to motivate people so that work is a positive experience; dealing with difficult or nonproductive colleagues; and increasing retention rates for excellent staff.[59]

Large businesses and agencies tend to have human resources departments. These departments are in charge of recruitment, interviewing, hiring, firing, performance evaluations, probationary decisions, maintaining civil service requirements in the public sector, and supporting an agency environment oriented toward retention. In addition, they protect confidentiality, provide advice when relationships with supervisors are contentious, react to problems, and deal with job-related harassment situations.[60] Human resource professionals need behavioral science training as well as training in sound business practices. An important set of concerns arises when it appears that the human resources techniques and protocols interfere with the work of the agency. These departments need to be cognizant of the culture and practices of the agency and not superimpose different human resource concepts on the staff of the agency. It sometimes appears that the human resources specialist takes authority away from the direct management staff of the agency or organization. This is a danger in that the management and leadership individuals work with both internal staff and community customers. They know when interactive situations are working well and when they are not. Human resources specialists often do not.

In small agencies, managers take on the responsibility for human resource issues related to their direct reports. This has the advantage of having managers and their direct reports in sync with the goals and objectives of the agency as a whole. The Gallup Organization has pointed out that it takes an engaged manager to help develop engaged employees.[61] Who better than an excellent manager to best fit the talents of an employee to the jobs that need to be done and the people they will serve in the community?

However, talent without application is not advantageous to an agency. According to Maxwell, talented people have to believe in their talent.[62] Engaged employees need to have passion for their work and the work of their agency. Passion helps to energize people to use their talents in a positive way. Talented people need to take the initiative to make their talents work for them. Focus is also important. Maxwell also discusses the importance of preparation. Without preparation and practice, it is hard to put your talents to work. It is easy to get discouraged. It is important to persevere. Taking risks requires courage. Teaching others also provides a way to verbalize how we use our talents. Our relationships also reinforce our strengths.

Although talent alone does not make an employee engaged, personality alone does not either. In reviewing many studies on personality factors in success at work, Robbins pointed to the conscientious employee as one who would be most likely to succeed in the workplace.[63] He also stated that extraversion is a good personality trait for managers, and I would add leaders. These are the people with high emotional intelligence. Low emotional stability may prevent a person from getting a job in the first place. Thus, engaged employees are excited by the opportunities to learn and develop friendships in the agency, are encouraged to develop their talents and skills by their supervisors, and feel that they have the resources necessary to carry out their jobs in an effective manner.[64]

Figure 19-1 lists several dimensions of better understanding and improving our relationships with our organizational colleagues. The V figure also points to the fact that our relationships inside and outside our agencies are based on a set of similar issues. It is also important to recognize that our agency staff are interacting with both our community customers and our external stakeholders in many different initiatives. If a staff member lives in the service area of the public health agency, he or she may be both employee and customer. Public health is mostly about people. When a local agency looks at the issues related to the public health workforce, its managers and leaders need to determine not only what types of workers it will need, but also the scarcity of certain categories of workers in today's environment. For example, we read about nursing shortages. The collection of data related to need is important. The question of what incentives need to be given to encourage people to enter public health or to work in public health is critical. We clearly have to distinguish need from want here. We need certain types of workers but may want to expand our staff into new areas if financial resources become available.

People development, which for the agency involves public health education and training, needs to keep the agency staff up to date on cutting-edge issues related to the health of the public. The agency needs to have a

commitment to lifelong learning for its staff. Because public health is always changing, this is a requirement. Educating and training are requirements for staff from the top leadership, managers, public health professionals, and the nonprofessional staff. There are many places to get this knowledge, from online to face-to-face training opportunities. Graduate education in public health should also be encouraged.

Whether the agency is guided by civil service or not, recruitment is an important issue. Present recruitment processes are not the most effective. People tend to be hired on the basis of their credentials and not on the basis of whether they have the talent, knowledge, and skills to carry out the responsibilities of the job. The credibility of the manager who is hiring a staff member is affected by poor selections.[65] It is the job of the recruiter to select talented people, successfully recruit people who will be high-level performers, address potential performance issues in a timely manner, develop appropriate training opportunities that will improve performance, and retain the excellent employees. If a staff member does not wake up in the morning excited about going to work, it is going to be difficult to retain this worker. Work has to be more than just work.

Many people have difficulty in defining their own strengths. Buckingham used the acronym SIGN to help individuals define their personal strengths.[66] The "S" refers to an awareness of those times when we are aware of our successful experiences as one clue to our personal strengths. Instinct ("I") is another factor in that we seem drawn toward certain types of activities. The "G," or growth indicator, is evidence that we seem to get better at doing certain types of things than others. The "N" stands for need. We find that sometimes we need to engage in certain types of activities. People need to put their strengths to work. When we do, we seem to get great satisfaction. Managers and leaders love what they do.

All of these activities of managers and their direct reports relate to creating a good fit between an individual and the organization's culture and subcultures, values, activities, and overall direction. Thus, it is not technical skills alone that create the fit; it is personality, talent, knowledge, skills, emotional intelligence and

Leadership Tip

Be a role model to your staff and show good ways to balance work and home.

reactions, vision of the leader, administrative skills of the manager, organizational culture, community relationships, social justice, and commitment to improving health and preventing disease that combine within a systems framework to make the fit work.[67] Coaching and mentoring help in this process and create teachable moments for managers and their direct reports. With this in mind, it is important to recognize that people will fit some organizations and agencies and not others.[68] In looking at the perspective of staff members and how they evaluate their activities in an agency, there are three signs of a miserable job.[69] First, there is the concern with being seen as a contributing person in the agency by managers and supervisors (anonymity factor). Second, performance measures have to be clear. Staff who think they are not being measured appropriately will evaluate their jobs negatively. Finally, people need to see their jobs as relevant to the mission and vision of the agency.

It should be clear by now that motivation of colleagues is critical to making the job worthwhile and reinforcing the fit of the employee to the organization. It is also clear that many of us are in public health because of our strong beliefs in social justice and not primarily for the salaries that we receive. It is not that salary is an unimportant factor, but it is not the most important. Motivation is about the activities and the processes that affect our commitment to public health and its mission to promote health and prevent disease in our communities and about the factors that guide us to work hard to reach the goals of our agencies and our community relative to our mission. The critical relationship in the workplace is the one between a supervisor and the direct report. Motivation is personal and is derived from this critical relationship. If this relationship is not built on trust and collegiality, then motivational techniques will often not work. Leaders and managers all need to strive for these solid relationships if we want to engage staff members in our agencies.

Performance level is not the same as motivation, although motivation can increase performance. Ramundo and Shelly pointed out that motivated people want to do their work, and leadership is inspiring others to want to work to help the agency reach its organizational goals.[70] Managers and leaders need to be careful not to be pessimistic, stifle creativity, gossip, be uncommunicative, discourage friendships and teamwork, and criticize staff in front of others. These behaviors and other negative behaviors will stifle and decrease motivation in others. Motivation is an emotional thing that affects the individual at a personal level. Ramundo

TABLE 19-3   Top Ten Ways to Motivate Employees

1. Coaching
2. Rewards/Recognition
3. Training and Conference Opportunities
4. Career Ladder Possibilities
5. Open Communications
6. Career Counseling(Mentoring)
7. Insurance Benefits
8. Listening to New and Innovative ideas
9. Discipline that Encourages
10. No Gossip

Source: Adapted from M. Ramundo and S. Shelly, *The Complete Idiot's Guide to Motivating People* (Indianapolis, IN: Alpha Books, 2000). Used by permission of Alpha Books, an imprint of Penguin Group (USA) Inc.

and Shelly have created a list of 25 ways to motivate an employee.[71] As can be seen in **Table 19-3**, these motivational tips are also relevant to our community residents and our external stakeholders.

It is also important for our agency colleagues to support the core functions and essential public health services. This does not mean that every employee is involved in all the functions or all the essential services. We need to collaborate with our community to make the public health functions work.

COMMUNITY RELATIONSHIPS

If organizational staff are not engaged in their agency work and do not feel motivated by managers and leaders, work with community clients and residents will be adversely affected. The external environment is also critical in defining the service community for human services agencies. If public health is all about the system, the public health agency is embedded in its community and needs to be seen relative to its customers (residents of the community), its agency competitors (other community stakeholders), public pressure groups (also community stakeholders as well as elected officials), and suppliers (public health technology and public health experts external to the community).[72] The specific community is also strongly influenced by its neighbors, the state, the federal government, and the global public health community. Broad economic, political, social, legal, and technological concerns affect the local community.

For public health agencies, the relationship with community customers is a primary relationship. The concept of Human Sigma has been formulated to show the importance of this relationship.[73] There are five key components or rules that define the Human Sigma model. The first rule requires good management of public health agency staff by local administrators and good relationships with community clients and all community residents. Staff and customers need to be seen in terms of the relationships that are generated between them. In fact, these relationships need to be seen as primary to the work of public health. If the agency staff are not engaged in their work, then the community clients will also be affected. This rule and the other three rules work synergistically in that staff and customer interactions are affected by the positive and negative consequences that come from the interaction as well as customer feedback. It is often impossible to predict these synergistic outcomes, but it is possible to learn from them to help in future encounters.

If I take my child to the public health agency to be immunized and my child and I are kept waiting for several hours for the nurse, then I will be upset. If the nurse is patronizing, my negative experience gets compounded. I will complain and I may also tell others in the community about my negative experience. The second rule of Human Sigma is the necessity of paying attention to the emotions aroused in an encounter between an agency staff member and a community resident. Emotions become facts in relationships.[74] The third rule addresses the issue of thinking globally and acting locally. Public health is a local phenomenon but is clearly affected by health issues in other parts of the world. If staff and customer interactions are mostly positive, then the chances increase that these positive occurrences can affect future budgeting considerations. The fourth rule points out that successful staff and customer relationships will affect the financial bottom line of the organization. These solid relationships will lead to the better utilization of the finances of the agency. The final rule states that intentions are not enough. Action will be the criterion for success. Despite these rules, all people have good and bad days. Exercise 19-7 explores this dimension.

There are many factors that can help to build customer loyalty. In addition to building good relationships between agency staff and community residents, leaders look for such things as consistency in services that are provided, caring and helpfulness, authenticity, positive attitude, professionalism, orientation to detail, responsiveness to complaints, good communication and follow-up, knowledge of other service providers to address special needs of clients, humor when appropriate, and community health days to celebrate improvements in the health of the community.[75] Good customer relationships are affected by always knowing why and for whom you are doing your work, treating your clients the way you want to be treated, supporting staff as discussed above, and providing leadership in support of the public health enterprise.[76]

As shown in Figure 19-1, part of the responsibility of the local public health agency is to monitor the health needs of the public and provide the technology and programs necessary to address those needs. Sometimes, things do not work out as expected. Case Study 19-A explores a situation of unanticipated events or anticipated events that are ignored when there is not enough influenza vaccine to go around. In addition to the needs assessment process, public health agencies have to determine how to help community residents understand public health and how their behavior affects their health. Education and training of the public is one way to increase knowledge of the public about public health. Recruitment of community residents to serve as volunteers in public health is also a useful process. Another interesting approach used by business is to use satisfied customers as spokespeople for successful public health programs. The development of the Medical Reserve Corps to address a community crisis is another example.

The issue of "fit" requires that there be a solid relationship between the engaged staff member and an engaged community resident. Not all residents choose to go to a public health agency for service. It is necessary to point out that the public health agency is only one partner in the public health enterprise. Fit needs to be expanded to all the community agency and hospital resources. The goal is to strive to find appropriate access to service for every resident somewhere in the community and to even extend the service option to other agencies outside the community when necessary. In many ways, public health is about education. People need to learn how to help make themselves more healthy. Public health leaders need to use their skills to create teachable moments. Community residents need motivation and support for their health. The motivation tips listed in Table 19-3 clearly fit here as well. Finally, strategic and action planning require that the public be involved in public health activities. Their needs and concerns must be addressed as part of all planning activities.

Facing the Long Shot: Out of Vaccine, Out of Time

Steven Curatti; Devon "Tony" Dede; Troy C. Hedrick; Veronica Halloway; Gwendolyn Mitchell; Tom Szpyrka; and Jerrod Welch

Introduction

Emerald County lies along the shores of the Ohio River, and its borders encompass plentiful farm fields and orchards, as well as multiple communities, including the rapidly growing city of Thumbsville, with a population of just over 125,000. The county's ideal location along the river has created a busy riverfront with high-volume barge traffic to ship goods from a growing manufacturing base and grains from large agricultural farms. This strong economic base has drawn many young urbanite professional families, as well as many Hispanic families. Combined with the pre-boom farming community population, this has led to a diverse county demographic. The majority of the county's Spanish-speaking population lives in the town of Greensboro, which is typically considered a part of Thumbsville, but has its own borders and government.

The Emerald County Health Department (ECHD) was established as a certified local public health department in the 1950s. Its structure is similar to that of many county health departments in that it has a governing board, a public health administrator, and multiple divisions with division directors reporting to the administrator. With the population boom Emerald County has experienced in recent years, election to the Board of Health has become very competitive because it is a prestigious post and a springboard for future political ambitions. Despite this, the board displays remarkable knowledge and flexibility and maintains a strong relationship with the administrator and most of the health department's staff.

ECHD is by all accounts highly effective in protecting the public's health through its various programs. The board, the administrator, and the department staff all take pride in ECHD's reputation for quality and effective service to all residents of Emerald County. Residents of the county rely heavily on many of these services and, in recent years, have come to know ECHD as "the" provider of flu vaccine each influenza season. ECHD's clinics have always run early in October, and the philosophy of Ima Lamduk, the longtime director of nursing (DON), has been that protection of the public from seasonal influenza is much more important than making money on seasonal clinics. This view is shared by the Board of Health, and in recent years the cost of adult and pediatric flu shots has remained stable even as surrounding providers have increased their prices regularly.

This fall, it was expected that vaccine would arrive during the first week of October, as it always had. Ima had placed her vaccine order in March, and the Centers for Disease Control and Prevention (CDC) reported throughout the spring, summer, and early fall that more doses would be available this year than ever before. There was no reason for concern that ECHD would be short on doses; it never had been before, and after all, it was a public agency and a participant in a statewide ordering group that would lobby on its behalf should vaccine distribution bog down. Advertisements for the first clinic had been placed in both of Thumbsville's major newspapers, as well as in the Greensboro Spanish-language newspaper. Radio and television ads and public service announcements were running daily, and Ima was confident that the community was receiving the message and that it would be no problem giving most of the 18,000 doses of Flu-Goo that had been ordered. Staff were actively promoting clinics, as were community advocates such as Diego Verde, the director of the Hispanic Cultural Center of Greensboro and a prominent and influential member of the Spanish-speaking community. Clinics would be held periodically throughout October and November, beginning October 10 at the Emerald County Courthouse.

The Call—October 1 and Beyond

In the mid-morning of Thursday, October 1, Ima had just met with her administrator, Guy Newman, in a regularly scheduled biweekly update meeting. Among the topics they had discussed were the bioterrorism grant budget, the implementation of a new continuing education policy, and final details of the seasonal flu kickoff clinic at the courthouse. Mr. Newman had been through only one previous flu season as ECHD's administrator, and it had gone very smoothly. Ima reported that everything was in order and they were waiting on the arrival of Flu-Goo, which they expected any day. There was no reason for concern, just business as usual.

The meeting ended and Ima headed back to her office. She noticed her phone message light was blinking but had a few e-mails to read before checking the message. Nitus Flourengale, Ima's immunizations coordinator, dropped in to chat, and before Ima knew it, lunchtime had arrived. She grabbed her jacket and was just about to head out the door when she remembered the phone message. Though she could feel her stomach growling, she decided to listen to the call just to make sure it was nothing urgent.

"Ms. Lamduk. This is Mordy Lemmas from the SVOC (Statewide Vaccine Ordering Consortium). I wanted to touch base with all of our members about some vaccine distribution problems we are experiencing. It seems that there have been some problems with the vaccine distribution chain and we aren't going to be receiving all doses of Flu-Goo until at least late October. We are going to make every effort to get at least some doses out to all consortium members before next Friday, but right now we just aren't sure if that is feasible. I'm sorry for the inconvenience, and please don't hesitate to call me if you have any concerns. Thanks, and talk to you later."

It took a moment for Ima to register what she had just heard, and all of the possible fallout from the news. Her first reaction was to call the SVOC and tell them that ECHD already had clinics scheduled and needed priority. After thinking about it for a second, she reconsidered, knowing that many other health departments were also scheduling or had scheduled clinics for the second and third weeks of October. It would do no good to make that call, though Ima decided to write a letter later on to voice her frustration and concern. Now, she thought, was the time to think through the implications of having a limited and undefined vaccine supply.

The first thing that came to mind was her conversation just hours ago with Mr. Newman. "Everything is going as planned," she had told her boss. Now what would she tell him? That was really the least of her concerns considering all of the problems this would cause with the Board of Health during an election year, with the media and public trust in ECHD, and especially with the impact on general public health during what was predicted to be one of the worst flu seasons in recent years. She knew action was needed quickly to get this information out, but she wanted to get her thoughts in order before discussing this with Mr. Newman and her staff. She began to write down these thoughts.

Public Health: Who will be affected most?

1. *CDC says young will be especially vulnerable this year, as will the elderly.*
2. *We also need to keep medical and first-responder personnel protected so they can report to work to assist others.*

Who else provides in the county?

County General (NFP)   *Who has vaccine?*
Eastside Medical Center (NFP)   *Priority groups?*
Greensboro Medical Group (private)   *Can we purchase?*
Green-Wall Pharmacy (private)   *Can we coordinate?*

Who have we told about our clinics?

We'll have to get the word out that they are either postponed or that we may not have enough vaccine.

Staff and Board of Health
Volunteer nurses planning to show
Courthouse staff
Media: get the public notified quickly
Senior population and schools
_____ *who else???*

PR and Damage Control: *Message must be consistent, up to date, and honest. We need to give viable alternatives to the clinics we planned (e.g., refer to other providers). Set up phone line and website for updated info.*

Ima thought that she had covered most immediate concerns in her written thoughts, though she felt like she was missing something. She just couldn't remember what. Well, she thought, it would come to her once she started talking things out with Mr. Newman and her staff.

Early that afternoon, Mr. Newman returned from lunch to find a hastily written e-mail from Ima telling him they needed to meet ASAP about flu vaccine delivery. He was curious, but not overly concerned, and wanted to get settled in and check his other messages before calling Ima. In the meantime, Ima had decided lunch was not all that important, and that she would get in touch with other providers in the community to assess their current supply and distribution plans. She found that County General had received 500 doses, which they were planning to give to CDC-defined high-risk individuals and key staff. Eastside Medical Center, the area's federally qualified health clinic, had received 2,000 doses of the 5,000 they had ordered. The clinic's 2,000 doses were Flu-Squirt, the inhaled version of the seasonal flu vaccine, and they were earmarked for distribution to pediatric populations to

(Continues)

avoid giving kids injections. Eastside was happy to work with ECHD, though, and would take any recommendations to better serve the community. Vaccine price varied based on ability to pay, but most individuals were asked to pay $20 per dose. Greensboro Medical Group, the large private-practice clinic in the area, had received its full order, 1,500 doses of Flu-Goo and 500 doses of Flu-Squirt. Though the director of patient services said to Ima that they would help in any way they could, she could detect that their plan was to preserve the vaccine for their own staff and patients. They planned to charge $35 per dose for either vaccine and did not take the state medical card. Ima spoke with the pharmacy manager at Green-Wall, the chain pharmacy in Thumbsville, but couldn't get any useful information about the plans Green-Wall had for its vaccine (nor how much had been ordered, because that was proprietary information). Through the grapevine, Ima heard from one of her nurses who knew a Green-Wall pharmacist that the business had received 7,000 doses of Flu-Goo and 2,500 of Flu-Squirt and would be charging $18.50 per dose and would accept some Medicare. It seemed to Ima that Green-Wall was trying to undercut other providers, either to pick up a larger chunk of customers or as a political maneuver. Ima knew that the owner of the Green-Wall store in Thumbsville was currently running against a Board of Health incumbent for a seat at the board table, and it would look good politically to be able to tout this public service in his campaign.

By the time Mr. Newman called Ima, it was 2:00 PM, and Ima was starving. She had a little bit of hypoglycemia and was shaking slightly. As she broke the news that ECHD's order would be delayed, Mr. Newman noted her shaking and perceived it to mean she was very worried and nervous about the developments. As Ima went over her thoughts on the delay, he mentally registered what she was saying, but also began thinking about the major political ramifications for the Board of Health and how that might affect him. Board members, already touting the reputation of ECHD in delivering reliable and broad flu vaccine coverage to the county, had begun e-mailing him to inquire about the arrival of the vaccine. He had assured them it was scheduled to arrive on time. He also thought about the February board meeting, where he had proposed that ECHD continue to order through the consortium to save money, even though Ima had recommended that for an additional 20 cents per dose, they could order directly from the manufacturer and receive a guaranteed delivery. This was never really a consideration, though, because never before had there been a problem with arrival of vaccine in plenty of time for the first public clinic. As Ima finished her summary, Mr. Newman voiced these concerns. It was decided to notify the chairman of the Board of Health of this situation, and to begin an active effort to notify the media that vaccine would not arrive on time and that clinics were postponed until further notice. Mr. Newman was to talk to the chairman, and Ima was to talk with her staff and begin drafting a press release that would notify county residents. She would also have to pull all advertising immediately.

By the end of the day on October 1, Ima had contacted all local media and made sure that all advertising for ECHD's public clinics was pulled. She asked the Supportive Services Division to be prepared to change the phone message to reflect information that she would provide them in a press release. She also asked that they designate one phone line, (123) 444-5678, to play the pre-recorded message in English and Spanish, with the option of being transferred to the switchboard once the message was completed. She contacted Mordy Lemmas at SVOC to see if anything else was known at present, but Mordy could only tell her that from what he understood, the manufacturer of Flu-Goo had all the vaccine produced, but there was a problem with the packaging. Mordy also felt that there would be a partial shipment by Tuesday, October 6, and that ECHD could consider keeping the first clinic scheduled. Ima asked how sure Mordy was about this, and he said, "Off the record, 100%. I can get you 1,800 doses, shipped Monday by FedEx." Ima discussed this with Mr. Newman and the chairman of the board on a conference call, and together they decided that ECHD would keep the October 10 clinic scheduled, but "postpone" all other clinics. With that information at hand, Ima had Nitus Flourengale draft a press release to fax (Appendix A).

October 2 turned out to be a much busier Friday than ECHD staff and management had hoped for. Ima's entire staff was busy contacting churches, schools, nursing homes, and other groups that had made arrangements to receive flu shots through ECHD. Ima and Mr. Newman were busy fielding calls from the media, from concerned citizens, and from various board members who wanted to be kept directly informed of the situation. One staff member was assigned the duty of monitoring television and radio media for misinformation. At one point, conflicting statements were discovered between information on Channel 10 and Channel 12. Ima suspected that Mr. Newman might have misspoken to the Channel 12 newscaster that the clinic would run extended hours to accommodate schoolchildren (after all, it was on a Saturday). Ima quickly ensured that the information was corrected and suggested to Mr. Newman that she be the public information officer to ensure a consistent message. He quickly agreed, relieved to be able to focus on the Board of Health concerns.

By late afternoon on Friday, Ima had been asked a number of times by various individuals and media why there appeared to be no vaccine supply problems at Green-Wall or Greensboro Medical Group, the two private providers in the area, but that all of the public providers were without their full vaccine orders. She had no strong answer and alluded to the type of vaccine ordered and the fact that vaccine supplies, especially flu vaccine supplies, were always vulnerable to manufacturing and distribution problems. Green-Wall had stepped up its media advertising campaign, stating that it had plenty of vaccine, plenty of staff ("average wait times are shorter than a fast-food drive through," the ad stated), and an affordable price. Ima and Mr. Newman discussed partnering with Green-Wall by offering staff and a location but elected not to because it may have stepped on the toes of the current board members facing re-election. Instead, Ima contacted the chief medical officer at County General and the director of nursing at Eastside Medical Center to form a "County Emergency Flu Response Strategy." The goal of the group was to assess the current countywide situation and determine level of coverage for vulnerable populations, medical personnel, and community first responders and how best to utilize the available combined vaccine (currently approximately 4,300 doses, including the promised shipment from SVOC). The group was to meet Tuesday, October 6. Ima didn't call Greensboro Medical Group for this planning committee, because she had already decided that its administration would not cooperate.

Monday, October 5, was much like the previous Friday, with Ima's staff busy fielding calls and making last-minute plans for the October 10 clinic. All supplies were ready, and if Flu-Goo arrived as promised by SVOC, there would be just enough doses to cover the clinic unless the media coverage had caused a panic. Ima made a mental note to ask Eastside's director of nursing if it would provide vaccine should ECHD run out at the clinic. In the afternoon, the sheriff's office called Mr. Newman to inquire about security at the clinic. Sheriff Andy Fife had concerns that long lines and possible shortages may have led to some level of civil unrest. He was up for re-election and didn't need a black mark on his record fresh in voter's minds. Mr. Newman agreed that security was not a bad idea, but asked that officers carry their weapons concealed so as not to create an atmosphere of fear, especially in any Hispanic individuals who already distrusted county and city police. Sheriff Fife thought this request was ridiculous and the issue was left unresolved, though two officers were committed to attend the clinic. Late in the day, Ima and Mr. Newman met to make sure everything was proceeding well. They discussed how the media had been handled, the prospect of receiving their 1,800 doses of Flu-Goo the next day, and various other issues. Ima reported that staff had handled all of the public inquiries admirably, and that there didn't appear to be an air of panic in the community. Mr. Newman thought that the Board of Health would be as satisfied as it could be with the situation as it had been handled.

The next morning, the three-member flu response strategy committee met. The Eastside DON agreed to provide up to 500 doses for the October 10 ECHD clinic, as well as three nurses and one support staff. Her only caveat was that Ima make every effort to give Eastside's doses to individuals aged 4 to 18 years, to which Ima agreed. County's chief medical officer stated that he was concerned that there was unrest in the Spanish-speaking community about receipt of timely information related to the current flu vaccine issue. Suddenly Ima had a sinking feeling in her stomach: "Oh no, I didn't call Diego."

"Hello Mr. Verde, this is Ima at the health department. I know you have already heard on the news that we are having some problems with the delivery of vaccine. I wanted to touch base though, and give you an update on where things stand at this point. We are still running our October 10 clinic and appreciate your help in promoting it. Right now, our other clinics are postponed, including the one planned on October 14 at St. Mary's Cathedral. We do hope to be rescheduling later in October and early November, and hope that the church will be available at some point during that time."

"Ima, I must be honest. I have already been telling others that the clinics are canceled, but I am very concerned that we as a community are not being fully informed of the situation. You know, many of us in Greensboro won't be able to have transportation to the courthouse in Thumbsville. We have been banking on the clinic at St. Mary's. In fact, I have been assuring others that there will certainly be a clinic here because I hadn't heard from you yet. I truly appreciate all your department does for our community, but I see a real issue here, and I plan to point it out. Also, I have been told that you have a Spanish-language message on your question line, but that if additional information is needed, no person at the health department speaks Spanish fluently enough to help. I think we have multiple problems that the Board of Health should be addressing in the future if this is indeed a county health department."

After the uncomfortable conversation with Mr. Verde, Ima checked in with Nitus, who was happy to report that 1,800 doses of Flu-Goo had arrived. She also reported that in pre-filling syringes, it seemed that nurses could get about 10.75 doses per vial instead of 10, which would yield as much as 1,935 doses. Ima agreed that this was good news indeed and reported the same to Mr. Newman. In the meantime, he had received a call from County Judge

(Continues)

Roy Bean (the main man in Emerald County by all accounts), who felt that his family was at high risk for flu and would be coming down on Thursday to receive their shots. Ima was proud that Mr. Newman had told Judge Bean that no exceptions could be made and he should arrive early on Saturday to avoid any delays in receiving vaccine.

On Wednesday, Green-Wall began running daily clinics on a walk-in basis. They appeared to be running smoothly despite reports that some retired nurses volunteering at the clinics might have been working under expired licenses (or, as they stated, working under the license of the pharmacy director). Green-Wall even went as far as to rent a bus to travel back and forth from Greensboro to ensure access for the Hispanic population, a move praised mightily by local media (though one political analyst questioned whether the move was mainly political in nature).

The rest of the week went relatively smoothly for ECHD, and by Friday afternoon everyone was ready to get Saturday going. People began lining up at 8:30 AM, and Ima made the decision to begin service at 10:00 instead of 11:00 so that an 11:00 rush would not further add to the line lengths. She assumed that she would hear some negative feedback on this move but felt it was the right thing to do. With the additional Eastside nurses helping, things still ran relatively smoothly. The courthouse had been the site of a "kickoff" clinic for many years, and the layout and flow was well known to staff and patrons. However, at 2:00 PM, Nitus found Ima and reported her concern that the vaccine supply was running low and might not last until 3:00. Ima reminded Nitus that Eastside would give an additional 500 doses, but cringed when Nitus reported that she had included that in her calculations. The clinic had already distributed 2,200 doses and only 250 remained. The nurses were beginning to panic. "Nitus," Ima said, "we've done all we can do. I will go count out the line and at 250 will cut it off. I'm just going to direct the rest of these folks to Green-Wall."

The clinic ended and only about 25 individuals had to be redirected. Everyone breathed a sigh of relief. They had come through without too many problems. Of course they faced the rest of the flu season with the prospect of no additional vaccine unless SVOC came through.

The Aftermath: Post 10/10

After the Saturday clinic, Ima felt that ECHD had handled the flu vaccine crisis as well as could be expected. Public health had remained her highest priority despite the various pressures from the media, the board, other political factions, and the public in general. She contacted SVOC the next Monday, October 12. Mordy Lemmas had bad news; vaccine would not be available until late November. ECHD would give no more vaccine that flu season, because demand would be nonexistent after Thanksgiving. Green-Wall had already successfully purchased an additional 7,500 doses from another regional provider who had ordered excess and would by default be the primary provider of flu vaccine that season, effectively privatizing this vital public health service.

Flu season did not strike as hard this year as the CDC said it would. Ima and all of the ECHD breathed a sigh of relief at that. The community as a whole had received fairly adequate coverage, only about 5% down from the previous five-year average. Though a small blow to the ECHD's reputation of being a "premier" public health department in the state, the whole incident quickly died down in the media and the general populace seemed to forget there was ever concern. By February, ECHD had rapidly and effectively handled a small local outbreak of salmonella and had launched a new after-school program for at-risk youth, and the media had raved at these successes. However, Ima's mind still mulled over the problem-riddled flu season. She decided that this could not happen again and wanted to make sure that multiple stakeholders considered what had occurred and how to plan for the expected and unexpected in future flu seasons. In late February and just before flu vaccine orders would be due through the SVOC, Ima called representatives from her staff, the previously organized "Emergency Flu Strategy" group, the Board of Health (including the two newly elected members, neither of which was the Green-Wall owner), schools, the senior center, and the cultural center (Mr. Verde was definitely remembered this time) together for a planning meeting. The meeting was well attended, and everyone was very appreciative to be included in the process. At the meeting, the following questions and issues arose.

February 23 Flu Planning Group Meeting: Critical Questions and Issues

1. What thoughts and facts discussed during the assessment of the situation would lead the coalition to decide who would receive the first doses of vaccines?
2. What information should be included in the assessment process as the group develops a plan for next year?
3. Should there be more than one source to purchase vaccine? Should the vaccine be purchased through a competitive bid process involving several manufacturers/providers? Why?
4. What would be the advantages and disadvantages to public health relinquishing the administration of the vaccines to the private sector? Does it really matter who gives the vaccine?

5. How can the Hispanic community be better included and informed in this scenario?
6. Where in the assessment process did Ima go wrong in developing her response to the shortage?
7. Are there other groups that could/should be included in the collaborative assessment of this year's project and in the planning for the coming year's effort?
8. In Ima's assessment of stakeholders, who else could she have included?
9. What role does the assessment of political interests have in the delivery of public health services?

Case Study Appendix A

Nitus Flourengale's October 2 Press Release

Emerald County Health Department—For Information Contact: (123) 456-7890

Press Release—For Immediate Release—October 2, 2006

Updated Information on Emerald County Health Department Seasonal Influenza Clinics

Emerald County Health Department (ECHD) was notified today that shipments of seasonal flu vaccine have been delayed. ECHD orders seasonal flu vaccine through a consortium representing multiple local health departments in the state. According to the distributor, it is anticipated that distribution of vaccine to all consortium members will be completed by late October. As a result of the delay in receipt of flu vaccine, changes to ECHD's seasonal flu clinics will occur as follows:

- ECHD's previously scheduled flu clinic at the Emerald County Courthouse on Saturday, October 10, will proceed as scheduled from 11:00 AM to 3:00 PM.
- All other flu clinics previously scheduled are postponed and will be rescheduled upon ECHD's receipt of flu vaccine.
- The United States Centers for Disease Control and Prevention have indicated that seasonal flu this year may be most severe in young children and the elderly. At this time, ECHD will not limit the distribution of vaccine to these target groups but does ask that healthy adults consider waiting to receive their flu shot until more supply arrives.
- A question line has been set up, and anyone with concerns or questions may call (123) 444-5678 and an ECHD representative will address their concern. In Emerald County, influenza typically does not circulate in the community until February - March. Therefore, at this time, a short delay in vaccine delivery does not present a public health concern to Emerald County. Individuals who have specific concerns regarding receipt of an adult flu shot prior to public clinics should call their primary care provider to discuss their concerns. As always, individuals should practice good personal hygiene to minimize their risks from flu and other illnesses. These practices include:
  - Cover your mouth and nose with a tissue when you cough or sneeze. Discard the used tissue and thoroughly wash your hands with soap and warm water. If no tissue is available, sneeze into your sleeve instead of your hand.
  - To minimize the spread of germs, stay home when you are sick and avoid close contact with others who are sick.
  - Parents should ensure that their children wash hands frequently.
  - Practice other good health habits, including getting plenty of rest, eating nutritious food, being physically active, and avoiding stress. ECHD will continue to provide updated information to the community regarding rescheduling of seasonal flu clinics as information on vaccine delivery becomes available.

References

Centers for Disease Control and Prevention, "Notice to Readers: Updated Recommendations from the Advisory Committee on Immunization Practices in Response to Delays in Supply of Influenza Vaccine for the 2000–01 Season," *MMWR* 49, no. MM39 (October 6, 2000): 888.

Centers for Disease Control and Prevention, "Experiences with Obtaining Influenza Vaccination Among Persons in Priority Groups During a Vaccine Shortage—United States, October–November, 2004," *MMWR* 53, no. MM49 (December 17, 2004): 1153.

(*Continues*)

Centers for Disease Control and Prevention, "Influenza Vaccine Prebooking and Distribution Strategies for the 2005–06 Influenza Season," *MMWR* 54, no. MM12 (April 1, 2005): 307.

Centers for Disease Control and Prevention, "Prevention and Control of Influenza," *MMWR* 55, no. RR10 (July 13, 2005): 1.

Centers for Disease Control and Prevention, "Influenza Vaccination of Health-Care Personnel," *MMWR* 55, no. RR2 (February 24, 2006): 1.

Henrich, Janet, *Testimony Before the Subcommittee on Health and the Subcommittee on Oversight and Investigations, Committee on Energy and Commerce, House of Representatives: Flu Vaccine: Recent Supply Shortages Underscore Ongoing Challenges*, November 18, 2004 (Washington, DC: U.S. Government Accountability Office, 2004).

Johnson, Cheryl, Executive Director/Public Health Administrator, Kendall County Health Department, Personal interview, January 4, 2007.

National Association of Community Health Centers, www.NACHC.org (various topics).

National Association of County and City Health Officials (NACCHO). "Local Public Health Agency—Federally Qualified Health Center Collaboration to Improve Health Services Delivery," *Issue Brief* 4, no. 1 (April 2004).

National Association of County and City Health Officials (NACCHO). *Web-based Influenza Vaccine Distribution Survey*, October 2006, found at: http://www.naccho.org/topics/infectious/documents/InfluenzaSurveyresults10-10-061_000.doc

National Association of County and City Health Officials (NACCHO), "Important Issues for Smooth Financing of a Community Health Center in a Local Health Department," audio conference, available from naccho.org.

National Association of County and City Health Officials (NACCHO), "Local Health Departments That Have Collaborated with a Federally Qualified Health Center," audio conference, available from naccho.org.

National Association of County and City Health Officials (NACCHO), "Local Health Departments That Have Received Community Health Center Funding and the Community Health Center Governance Structure," audio conference, available from naccho.org.

National Association of County and City Health Officials (NACCHO), "Making Strategic Decisions about Service/Delivery Partnerships Project." Available by naccho.org.

Sandman, Peter, *Crisis Communication: A Very Quick Introduction*, April 15, 2004. http://www.psandman.com/col/pandemic.htm

World Health Organization (WHO), "Global Pandemic Influenza Action Plan to Increase Vaccine Supply," publication WHO/IVB/06.13, available at http://www.who.int/csr/resources/publications/influenza/WHO_CDS_EPR_GIP_2006_1/en/index.html

Source: Courtesy of the Mid-America Regional Public Health Leadership Institute.

COMMUNITY STAKEHOLDERS

Public health leaders know that they have to work with other community partners if the public health enterprise is to work. These decision makers outside the public health agency will need to be involved in the overall public health planning and agenda if there is to be successful implementation of public health programs and services.[77] These stakeholders will have to make a commitment and also provide financial resources to the enterprise.

Public health leaders also need to view the community with a systems thinking orientation. The public health system includes the local public health agency and the population of the community; it also includes many stakeholders such as other health and social agencies from the private, public, not-for-profit, and volunteer sectors who will work with the local public health agency in carrying out the essential services.

Figure 19-2 views the public health system as a network of interacting partners that includes public health agencies, healthcare providers, public safety agencies, human service and charity organizations, education and youth development organizations, recreation and arts-related organizations, economic and philanthropic organizations, and environmental agencies and organizations.[78] Community residents have many relationships with these organizations and influence policy through these relationships with community stakeholders.

In strategic planning, stakeholder analysis is one of the techniques involved. Public health leaders need to study stakeholders to see what the local public health system is like and to determine if gaps exist in the service system. There are three steps in stakeholder analysis.[79] The first step involves a determination of the services available. This step involves an enumeration not only of resources, but also of what each stakeholder resource

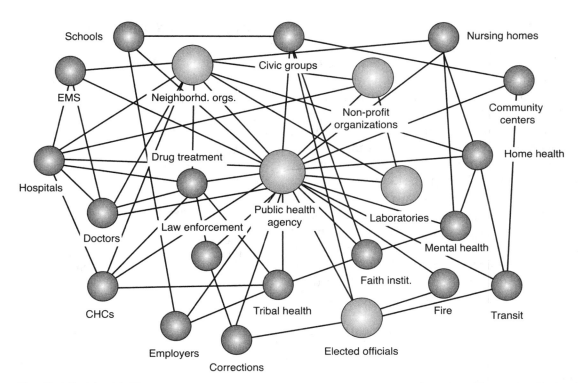

FIGURE 19-2 **The Public Health System.** *Source*: Reproduced from Centers for Disease Control and Prevention, *National Public Health Performance Standards Program Users Guide*, Version 2.0 (Washington, DC: U.S. Department of Health and Human Services, 2007).

can contribute to the overall public health enterprise. Second, a determination needs to be made about the level of organizational performance by potential public health partners. Finally, public health leaders need to determine how public health stakeholders will perform relative to the goals and objectives for public health in a given community.

One important dimension that is often ignored is the necessity of stakeholder development. Stakeholders do not always understand what public health does. They need training in public health and need to develop a virtual public health stakeholder learning community if a face-to-face community is difficult to sustain. Public health leaders also need to be on the lookout for new or emerging resources as they develop. Partners from outside the service community are also important. At the transactional leadership level, recruitment of new stakeholders will address reciprocity concerns.

Fit is clearly important as well. A few years ago, a small local health department in a Midwest state applied for a state grant to develop a special maternal and child health program. A local community agency

also applied for the same grant. The directors of the two agencies were extremely competitive and did not work well together. The state gave the grant to the community agency, requiring the two agencies to work together on the program. The staff of the two agencies tried to collaborate, but the fit was not a good one. Many conflicts ensued.

Because leaders are often dealing with leaders in stakeholder situations, motivation strategies still remain important. Relationships need to be on a person-to-person level. If the relationships are always or mostly position to position, these relationships tend to be conflictual. There have to be both transactional and transformational gains if collaboration is to succeed. Decisions will need to be made about carrying out the 10 essential public health services. Whenever strategic planning activities occur or the public health assessment process is undertaken, community partners need to be involved in the process. Public health planning both strategically and in terms of action requires a partnership among the local public health agency, its customers, and its partners.

SUMMARY

This chapter has presented the subject of relationships in public health. First, leadership in terms of emotional intelligence was discussed. Next, these relationships involve the staff of the local public health agency, its community customers, and its community partners. Public health practice requires a systems view of the community. Public health leaders and managers must strive for good relationships with their staff inside the agency. Public health agency staff need to develop good relationships with their clientele in the community. Good relationships inside the agency often mean that relationships outside the agency have a better chance at success. Public health leaders also need to nurture and develop good relationships with their community stakeholders and bring them together as partners in the public health enterprise.

DISCUSSION QUESTIONS

1. What is the relationship between emotional intelligence and leadership?
2. What are the key factors in recruiting new employees into the local public health agency?
3. Why is the relationship between the public health manager or supervisor so important?
4. What are the best methods for motivating agency staff?
5. How does the Human Sigma model apply to public health?
6. What are the factors that increase chances for more solid relationships with the public?
7. Who are public health's partners?
8. What is the relationship between public health customers and the network of public health partners?
9. Why is a systems perspective more viable than an agency-based perspective in public health?

EXERCISE 19-1: Journey Through Time

Purpose: to see the effect of perception on sustainability

Key concepts: perception, sustainability, mental models, visioning

Procedure: This exercise will help you to explore how your impact on your agency over the years will be affected by your personal mental models. Divide the class or training group into small groups of four or five people. Each group should answer the journey questions:

1. Go back 100 years and describe the world of your ancestors. What was their world like, and what were their mental models about health and the environment? What would your ancestors want you to learn from their world?

2. Go forward 100 years and describe the world of your descendants. How has the present affected their lives? What is their mental model about health and the environment? What messages do they want to relay to you?

3. Go forward 10 years and describe yourself and your family and co-workers. What did you learn from the you of today about health and the environment? What would you have done differently?

4. Reflect on what you have learned. What do you want to do differently at work and in your community? What must we do to improve the ways we make public health more effective?

Source: Adapted from J. Laur and S. Schlag, "A Journey in Time," in P. Senge, J. Laur, S. Schlag, and B. Smith (eds.), *Learning for Sustainability* (Cambridge, MA: Society for Organizational Learning, 2006).

EXERCISE 19-2: The Mirror

Purpose: to understand some of the characteristics that define you as a leader

Key concepts: leadership, emotional intelligence

Procedures: Hold up a hand mirror or look into a wall mirror.

1. Do you see a leader?
2. How do you feel as you view this person?
3. Is this person successful?
4. What do you think holds the person in the mirror back?
5. What are five things you can do in the next six months to increase your success?

EXERCISE 19-3: What Makes a Leader?

Purpose: to understand the traits of a successful leader

Key concepts: leadership, emotional intelligence

Procedures:

1. Write down the 10 traits of a successful leader.
2. How many of these 10 traits do you have?
3. How many of these traits relate to emotional intelligence?
4. What do you have to do to demonstrate more of these traits?

EXERCISE 19-4: Risk Taking

Purpose: to understand how taking risks affects emotions

Key concepts: emotional intelligence, risk taking, leadership

Procedures: Divide the class or training group into groups of 10. Each group will discuss the following:

1. Think back over the past year and see if you took a risk in some work or social situation.
2. How did you feel?
3. What was the reaction of other people?
4. Discuss with your group your risk-taking experience and have other members of the group tell you about their experience.

EXERCISE 19-5: Building Trust

Purpose: to explore the issue of building trust in collaborative leadership

Key concepts: trust, collaborative leadership

Procedures: Divide the class or training group into smaller groups and have each participant fill out the self-assessment tool on trust. Score your results, and have the group answer the questions at the end of the assessment tool.

Collaborative Leadership
Building Trust
Self-Assessment Exercise

For each item, circle one rating under the Behavior Frequency column indicating your view of how often you exhibit that behavior. Your responses to this questionnaire are for your own use. You will not be asked to share your scores after you have answered. You will be asked to use your score and your responses to help you develop a personal learning plan.

	Behaviors	Behavior Frequency						
1	I build communication processes that make it safe for people to say what is on their minds.	1	2	3	4	5	6	7
2	I refuse to engage in "rigged" processes.	1	2	3	4	5	6	7
3	I protect the group from those who would wield personal power over the collaborative process.	1	2	3	4	5	6	7
4	I create credible processes for collaborating.	1	2	3	4	5	6	7
5	I ensure that processes for exercising collaborative leadership are open to all stakeholders.	1	2	3	4	5	6	7

6	I ensure that the processes for collaborative leadership are transparent to all stakeholders.	1	2	3	4	5	6	7
7	During the first stage of creating collaborative relationships, I establish the common ground among the stakeholders.	1	2	3	4	5	6	7
8	I approach collaboration by relying heavily on building trust among stakeholders.	1	2	3	4	5	6	7
9	I "walk the talk," i.e., I do what I say I will do.	1	2	3	4	5	6	7
10	I demonstrate to my peers that I believe that trust is the foundation for successful collaboration.	1	2	3	4	5	6	7

Your score: Add all the circled behavior frequencies.
Write the number in the box.

70–61 Excellent score	40–21 Opportunities for growth
60–41 Stronger score	20–1 Important to change behavior

Written comments:

What do you think are your strengths in building trust as a collaborative leader?

What do you think are your most important areas for improvement in building trust?

EXERCISE 19-6: Intuition

Purpose: to see the relationship between intuition and decision making

Key concepts: intuition, leadership, decision making, emotional intelligence

Procedures: Divide the class or training group into groups of 10.

1. Can you think of a situation in which your intuition was correct but your decision was wrong?
2. Can you think of a situation in which your intuition and your decision were aligned?
3. Discuss your experiences with your team.

EXERCISE 19-7: Good Days and Bad Days

Purpose: to explore our relationships with the public and determine the factors that lead to both positive and negative experiences

Key concepts: engaged public health workers, engaged customers, motivation

Procedure: Divide the group into dyads. Each person will describe a good day with the community and the factors that made it so. How much of the good day related back to the agency, and how much of it was affected by the encounter with the community? Share the experiences with your dyad partner. Repeat the discussion for an example of a bad day in the community. What are the differences in the two types of day? What would you have changed? Return to the large group and report on the things that make a good day and what makes a day not so good. For the large group, have a recorder list the good day and bad day factors.

REFERENCES

1. J. M. Kouzes and B. Z. Posner, *The Leadership Challenge*, 4th ed. (San Francisco: Jossey-Bass, 2007).
2. Kouzes and Posner, *The Leadership Challenge*, 4th ed.
3. D. Williams, *Real Leadership* (San Francisco: Berrett-Kohler, 2005).
4. K. Blanchard, S. Fowler, and L. Hawkins, *Self Leadership and the One Minute Manager* (New York: William Morrow, 2005).
5. E. De Bono, *Free or Unfree* (Beverly Hills, CA: Phoenix Books, 2007).
6. J. Laur and S. Schlag, "A Journey in Time," in P. Senge, J. Laur, S. Schlag, and B. Smith (eds.), *Learning for Sustainability* (Cambridge, MA: Society for Organizational Learning, 2006).
7. Blanchard, Fowler, and Hawkins, *Self Leadership and the One Minute Manager.*
8. S. P. Robbins, *The Truth About Managing People* (Upper Saddle River, NJ: Prentice-Hall, 2002).
9. J. C. Maxwell, *Relationships 101* (Nashville, TN: Thomas Nelson, 2003).
10. J. Collins, *Good to Great* (New York: Harper Business, 2001).
11. L. Rowitz, *Public Health in the 21st Century: The Prepared Leader* (Sudbury, MA: Jones & Bartlett, 2006).
12. D. Goleman, "Who Makes a Leader," *Harvard Business Review* 76, no. 6 (1998): 94–102.
13. J. M. Burns, *Leadership* (New York: Harper and Row, 1978).
14. J. D. Mayer and P. S. Salovey, "The Intelligence of Emotional Intelligence," *Intelligence* 17, no. 4 (1993): 433–442.
15. D. A. Feldman, *The Handbook of Emotionally Intelligent Leadership* (Falls Church, VA: Performance Solutions Press, 1999).
16. D. Goleman, *Working with Emotional Intelligence* (New York: Bantam Books, 1998).
17. Goleman, *Working with Emotional Intelligence.*
18. Mayer and Salovey, "The Intelligence of Emotional Intelligence."
19. D. Goleman, *Emotional Intelligence* (New York: Bantam Books, 2006).
20. T. Bradberry and J. Greaves, *Emotional Intelligence 2.0* (San Diego, CA: Talent Smart, 2009).
21. Goleman, *Working with Emotional Intelligence.*
22. Goleman, *Working with Emotional Intelligence.*
23. L. Forman, "Directing the Heart," In K. M. Ovitsky and L. Forman, eds., *Sacred Intentions* (Woodstock, VT: Jewish Lights, 1999).
24. Goleman, *Emotional Intelligence.*
25. Goleman, "Who Makes a Leader."
26. Goleman, *Working with Emotional Intelligence.*
27. D. Goleman, "Emotional Intelligence: Issues in Paradigm Building," in *The Emotionally Intelligent Workplace*, ed. C. Cherniss and D. Goleman (San Francisco: Jossey-Bass, 2001).
28. Goleman, *Working with Emotional Intelligence.*
29. Bradberry and Greaves, *Emotional Intelligence 2.0.*
30. Goleman, *Working with Emotional Intelligence.*
31. Goleman, "Emotional Intelligence: Issues in Paradigm Building."
32. Bradberry and Greaves, *Emotional Intelligence 2.0.*
33. Kouzes and Posner, *The Leadership Challenge*, 4th ed.
34. Goleman, "Emotional Intelligence: Issues in Paradigm Building."
35. Goleman, *Working with Emotional Intelligence.*
36. Kouzes and Posner, *The Leadership Challenge*, 4th ed.
37. Goleman, *Working with Emotional Intelligence.*
38. Goleman, "Emotional Intelligence: Issues in Paradigm Building."
39. Goleman, *Working with Emotional Intelligence.*
40. Goleman, "Emotional Intelligence: Issues in Paradigm Building."
41. R. K. Cooper and A. Sawaf, *Executive EQ* (New York: Perigee Books, 1996).
42. Cooper and Sawaf, *Executive EQ.*
43. Cooper and Sawaf, *Executive EQ.*
44. Cooper and Sawaf, *Executive EQ.*
45. Cooper and Sawaf, *Executive EQ.*
46. Goleman, "Emotional Intelligence: Issues in Paradigm Building."
47. Cooper and Sawaf, *Executive EQ.*
48. Goleman, "Emotional Intelligence: Issues in Paradigm Building."
49. Cooper and Sawaf, *Executive EQ.*
50. M. Csikszentmihalyi, *Flow* (New York: Harper Perennial, 1990).
51. Cooper and Sawaf, *Executive EQ.*
52. Cooper and Sawaf, *Executive EQ.*
53. Goleman, "Emotional Intelligence: Issues in Paradigm Building."
54. Feldman, *The Handbook of Emotionmally Intelligent Leadership.*
55. Feldman, *The Handbook of Emotionally Intelligent Leadership.*
56. Bradberry and Greaves, *Emotional Intelligence 2.0.*
57. S. M. Kravitz and J. D. Schubert, *Emotional Intelligence Works* (Menlo Park, CA: Crisp Learning, 2000).
58. M. Buckingham, *Go Put Your Strengths to Work* (New York: Free Press, 2007).
59. S. P. Robbins and M. Coulter, *Management*, 11th ed. (Upper Saddle River, NJ: Prentice-Hall, 2011).
60. H. E. Chambers, *Finding, Hiring, and Keeping Peak Performers* (Cambridge, MA: Perseus, 2001).
61. C. Coffman and G. Gonzalex-Molina, *Follow This Path* (New York: Warner Books, 2002).
62. J. C. Maxwell, *Talent Is Never Enough* (Nashville, TN: Thomas Nelson, 2007).
63. Robbins, *The Truth About Managing People.*
64. J. H. Fleming and J. Asplund, *Human Sigma* (New York: Gallup Press, 2007).
65. Chambers, *Finding, Hiring, and Keeping Peak Performers.*
66. Buckingham, *Go Put Your Strengths to Work.*
67. Fleming and Asplund, *Human Sigma.*
68. Robbins, *The Truth About Managing People.*
69. P. Lencioni, *The Three Signs of a Miserable Job* (San Francisco: Jossey-Bass, 2007).

70. M. Ramundo and S. Shelly, *The Complete Idiot's Guide to Motivating People* (Indianapolis, IN: Alpha Books, 2000).

71. Ramundo and Shelly, *The Complete Idiot's Guide to Motivating People*.

72. Robbins and Coulter, *Management*.

73. Fleming and Asplund, *Human Sigma*.

74. Fleming and Asplund, *Human Sigma*.

75. J. Brandi, *Building Customer Loyalty* (Dallas, TX: Walk the Talk, 2001).

76. K. Blanchard, J. Ballard, and F. Finch, *Customer Mania* (New York: Free Press, 2004).

77. J. M Bryson, *Strategic Planning for Public and Nonprofit Organizations*, 3rd ed. (San Francisco: Jossey-Bass, 2004).

78. Centers for Disease Control and Prevention, *National Public Health Performance Standards Program Users Guide*, Version 2.0 (Washington, DC: U.S. Department of Health and Human Services, 2007).

79. Bryson, *Strategic Planning for Public and Nonprofit Organizations*.

CHAPTER 20

Leadership and the Planning Process

We live in a world where no one is "in charge." No one organization or institution has the legitimacy, power, authority, or intelligence to act alone on important public issues and still make substantial headway against the problems that threaten us all.

—J. M. Bryson and B. C. Crosby, *Leadership for the Common Good*

No matter what changes occur in the world of public health, planning activities will continue to occupy much of the work time of public health leaders. Because preparing for the future is part of their mandate, public health leaders must devote substantial energy to strategic thinking, which is basically thinking devoted to the resolution of problems and the achievement of desired goals. Strategic thinking is essential for all varieties of planning, such as working out the details of strategic planning, a continuous quality improvement (CQI) program, a Six Sigma program, a reengineering project, or a community partnership scheme. This chapter covers the skills that public health leaders need in order to do the full range of planning they will be responsible for over the next few decades.

COMMUNITY HEALTH PLANNING

As noted, public health leaders work at many different levels, including the community level. Community health planning involves the development of public health goals and objectives and the ordering of the actions necessary to accomplish these. In this type of planning, it is important, first, to use an approach that is able to generate innovative public health strategies and, second, to keep in mind the core functions and essential services of public health for guidance.

Planning is a form of rational decision making.[1] The first step in the process is to decide on goals and objectives. The next step is to determine the constraints on the planning process and the likely changes in the environment that may affect how easy the goals and objectives are to achieve. The third step is to figure out what actions, policies, and programs to implement. A good strategy at this stage is to develop a series of outcome scenarios so that those engaged in the planning have several options to choose from.[2] Note that even if a plan is a good one—that is, its implementation will lead to the achievement of the desired goals and objectives—leaders must remain constantly aware of factors that may undermine the implementation process and sometimes will have to modify their activities as a result of unexpected happenings.

Planning is often viewed as a routine task and something that managers do rather than leaders. It has routine aspects to it, but planning, especially strategic planning, must ultimately be driven by the big picture and strategic thinking that leads to the leaders' vision of the future. Therefore, leaders need to remain intimately involved in the planning process because the planning process will be an important set of techniques to help leaders realize their visions.

The planning process can be formal or informal. Formal planning leaves a paper trail, because all critical decisions are documented, whereas informal planning is less organized and more guided by social interaction.

Planning, although time consuming, is almost never a waste of time. It gives structure to the activities that are directed toward achieving desired goals and may also save money by encouraging the monitoring of these activities. Planning does not eliminate change but rather fosters change. It can also foster flexibility in the implementation process, although it has the potential, if done poorly, to act in the opposite way and hinder flexibility.

In public health, planning was not common until the 1920s.[3] The increase in the funds devoted to public health over the years has created a need to plan for and be accountable for the expenditure of the funds. In the mid-1960s, Congress passed a comprehensive health planning act (P.L. 89-749) that required states and local areas to be involved in planning activities. The reasoning was that public health is the responsibility of state and local entities. The act did not work as well as expected. The development of health service agencies (HSAs) led to a duplication of activity. Many local health department leaders, even those involved in HSA activities, believed that the local public health agency should be doing the health planning. With the end of federal funding for HSAs in the 1980s, state and local public health agencies re-absorbed planning into their program portfolios.

Community health planning is key to the promotion of public health services.[4] Planning activities should use epidemiological data and be community based in the sense that they integrate public and private interests for the benefit of the residents. Public health leaders should include community partners in the planning process, and the plans developed should encompass all segments of the community.

Rohrer describes three planning models that are typically used in the field of public health.[5] The rational planning model encompasses "fact finding, problem definition, goal setting, implementation, monitoring, feedback, and evaluation." This model is generally applied to planning directed toward reforming the internal operations of an agency. The community development model is empowerment oriented and promotes local citizen participation in planning activities. Decisions are reached by consensus. The activist model is applicable when community groups threatened by a particular public health danger become mobilized. These models are limited in value. The strategic planning approach discussed in the next section has the advantage that it applies to both organizational reform and community health planning.

Assessment is a prerequisite for planning, although assessment and planning activities are typically ongoing. The gathering of assessment data informs public health leaders about community needs that should be addressed immediately, and they can thus direct their planning activities at developing policies and programs to respond to these needs. Once the programs and policies are in place, their effectiveness should be evaluated, and if they are found to be less effective than expected, the leaders could then engage in further planning in order to improve them.[6]

Public health leaders must:

- use the core functions and essential services of public health as a foundation for community health planning
- learn how to use the different planning methodologies and how to choose the appropriate model for a given initiative
- determine the actions necessary to achieve desired community health goals and objectives
- use planning and scenario building to discover innovative public health strategies
- be involved in formal planning activities
- create community partnerships to carry out planning activities

Figure 20-1 presents a view of the issue related to community health planning as it relates to different community assessment measures. Underlying many of these assessment approaches is the core functions and essential services paradigm. The approaches taken are a critical public health leadership concern because they affect everything from the decisions related to community health priorities to the issues of whether to go for national accreditation.

Model	Essential steps in community health assessment and health improvement planning							
	Assess health of the community					Get results, take action		
	Develop plan	Gather input	Review data	Public health system	SWOT analysis	Prioritize	Set goals	Action plan
PATCH (planned approach to community health) CDC, 1985		Mobilizing the community	Collecting data			Choosing health priorities		Developing a plan evaluating PATCH
PACE EH (protocol for assessing community excellence in environmental health) NACCHO, 2000	Task 1 – determine community capacity Task 2 – define community Task 3 – assemble team	Task 4 – define goals, objectives, scope Task 5 – generate list of community-specific environmental health issues	Task 6 – analyze issues within system framework Task 7 – develop locally appropriate indicators Task 8 – select standards			Task 9 – create issue profiles Task 10 – rank issues Task 11 – set priorities		Task 12 – develop action plan Task 13 – evaluate progress and plan for future
APEX PH (assessment protocol for excellence in public health) NACCHO, 1991		Part II: community process (identify health problems, set health status goals; programmatic objectives and identify resources)		Part I: organizational capacity assessment (self-assessment of local health dept.)		Part III: completing the cycle (implement action plan and community health plan, review policy development and assurance functions of local health department)		
MAPP (mobilizing for action through planning and partnerships) NACCHO, 2000	Organize for success, partnership building, visioning	Community themes and strengths assessment	Community health status assessment	Local public health system assessment	Forces of change assessment	Identify strategic issues	Formulate goals and strategies	Action cycle, evaluation, celebrate success
Healthy people in healthy communities (HP2010) CDC, 2001		Mobilize key individuals and organizations	Assess community needs, strengths, and resources		Assess community needs, strengths, and resources	Plan for action		Implement action plan, track progress and outcomes
CHANGE tool (community health assessment and group evaluation) CDC, 2010	Action steps 1, 2 – assemble team, develop strategy (focus on physical activity, nutrition, tobacco use, chronic disease management, leadership)	Action step 3 – review CHANGE sectors	Action steps 4–7 – gather, review, enter, consolidate data					Action step 8 – build community action plan

FIGURE 20-1 Community Health Assessment and Health Improvement Planning Models Matrix*. *Source:* Reproduced from Florida Department of Health, COMPASS, Partnerships for improving community health web conference series, 2009. http://www.doh.state.fl.us/COMPASS/partnerships_training.htm. Accessed September 21, 2012.

*Terminology for steps matches language in each model.

STRATEGIC PLANNING

The relationship between strategies and tactics is similar to that between goals and objectives. Both goals and objectives are ends or desired states of affairs. One difference is that goals tend to be broad in scope and objectives relatively less so. Another is that objectives are ends that are sought largely because they lead to the achievement of goals. Improving the level of health in a community is a good example of a goal. Relative to this goal, testing the community's water supply might be one objective. Note that it is relatively narrower in scope and would be one step on the way to achieving the goal.

Strategies are plans or methods that are relatively broad in scope, are often long term in nature, and often involve a significant expenditure of resources. Tactics are methods that are relatively narrow in scope and use relatively few resources. Roughly speaking, strategies are likely to be used in attaining goals, whereas tactics are likely to be used in attaining objectives. (Be warned that there is some looseness in the use of these terms and that many people employ "goal" and "objective" as synonyms and "strategy" and "tactic" as near synonyms.)

Strategic planning is directed at the achievement of goals—significant or even ultimate ends. As such, it is an extremely important task and falls largely on the shoulders of the leadership. A list of strategic planning guidelines and a 10-step strategic planning model follow. As in the case of any major task, those responsible for completing the task should remain upbeat in order to motivate others involved to do their share. First, the guidelines:

1. Strategic planning is a team process in which the team members need to share the leader's vision. The team members also need to be carefully selected and represent all parts of the organization. The leader needs to be clear about the responsibilities of the team and may want to convene a community advisory board to discuss how the plan meets the health needs of the community.
2. The team needs to set a timeline for the planning process. The process should be short enough to devise a plan and implement it before events have rendered it irrelevant.
3. The team needs to consider how to get the plan accepted after the planning process.
4. The team needs to create a schedule for the planning process.

5. The team must disseminate the results of the process—the plan—following its completion. The team must carefully determine what will be disseminated, but it is generally better to disseminate more rather than less.
6. The team must decide on the techniques that will be used to evaluate the process.[7]

Bryson developed a 10-step procedure for strategic planning (see also **Table 20-1**).[8] The first step could be called the "planning to plan" stage.[9] According to Bryson, the leader needs to be clear on the reasons that strategic planning was chosen rather than some other technique. A readiness assessment occurs. The leader also needs to communicate with potential stakeholders and to lay the groundwork for a shared vision. The partners will want to know what they are "buying" and how long the planning and implementation process will take. Bryson suggested that partners might do well to start the process by going on a retreat. Strategic planning can be an expensive process, and funds will be needed to carry it out.

Step 2 involves the clarification of organizational mandates. Public health practitioners are constantly bombarded with formal mandates that take substantial time to abide by. Not only that, public health agencies are legally mandated to perform certain functions and are given funds to carry out these functions but might not be funded to implement other public health initiatives closer to the mission of public health as defined by the local health department and the community stakeholders. Stakeholders are persons or organizations that have an interest in public health programs and how they are implemented. They include concerned citizens, government representatives, other health and social service representatives, governing board members, church representatives, and members of professional associations.

It is critical to include the appropriate stakeholders in strategic planning. For example, major community employers, unions, regulatory or licensing agencies, bankers, and neighbors of the agency are often excluded from community coalitions despite the fact that they can prevent decisions from being implemented.[10] In general, stakeholders expect the agency and its leadership to be responsive to their needs and can even issue what might be called informal mandates. If the agency does not respond to these informal mandates, the stakeholders will look elsewhere for support. The local public health agency must determine whether the formal mandates prevent addressing the informal

TABLE 20-1 Bryson Strategic Planning Model Applied to Public Health

Bryson Model	Public Core Functions	Organizational Practices	Essential Services	System Activities
Initiation and agreement on a strategic planning process	Policy development	Constituency building	Mobilization of community partnerships to identify and solve health problems	Coalition building and values clarification
Identification and clarification of the nature/meaning of externally imposed formal and informal mandates	Policy development and assurance	Evaluation of programs in accordance with plans and policies	Enforcement of laws and regulations that protect health and ensure safety	Values clarification
Clarification of organizational mission and values	Policy development	Not applicable	Not applicable	Values clarification and mission and vision development
Assessment of the organization's external and internal environments to identify strengths, weaknesses, opportunities, and threats	Assessment	Assessment of health needs of the community Investigation of the occurrence of health effects and health hazards	Monitoring of health status to identify community health problems Diagnosis and investigation of health problems and health hazards in the community	Vision and goals and objectives development (based on assessment data)
Identification of the strategic issues facing the organization	Policy development and assessment	Analysis of the determinants of identified health needs Setting of priorities among health needs	Development of policies and plans that support individual and community health efforts	Development of goals and objectives and action plans
Formulation of strategies to manage these issues	Policy development	Development of plans and policies to address priority health needs	Development of policies and plans that support individual and community health efforts	Action planning
Review and adoption of the strategic plan or plans	Policy development	Management of resources and development of organizational structure	Not applicable	Action planning
Establishment of an effective organizational vision	Policy development	Not applicable	Not applicable	Vision development
Development of an effective implementation process	Assurance	Management of resources and development of organizational structure Education of the public	Linkage of people to needed personal health services and assurance of the provision of health care when otherwise unavailable	Action plan development and implementation
Reassessment of strategies and the strategic planning process	Assessment, policy development, and assurance	Evaluation of programs and performance of quality assurance activities	Evaluation of the effectiveness, accessibility, and quality of personal and population-based health services	Evaluation using the systems perspective

Source: Adapted with permission from J. M. Bryson, *Strategic Planning for Public and Nonprofit Organizations* (3rd edition). © 2004, Jossey-Bass, Inc, Publishers.

mandates. Several local public health administrators interviewed by the author said that responding to the formal mandates in their state took almost 90% of their agency's time. Creating innovative programs became virtually impossible because of the lack of time.

In step 3, agency leaders begin to investigate the values that will govern the agency and the agency's community relationships. The agency's mission should refer to its role in the community. By going through the values clarification process and developing a mission, the agency will be in a better position to monitor the strategic planning process. This step might include the performance of a stakeholder analysis, which will clarify who the stakeholders are, what their values are, what their goals and objectives are, what issues are likely to affect them, and what their degree of commitment is to the status quo.

The fourth step involves the assessment of the internal and external environments in order to identify the opportunities and the challenges arising from the change process.[11] This has been referred to as a SWOT analysis, for it focuses on strengths, weaknesses, opportunities, and threats. The external assessment looks at forces that may affect agency programs, whether at the local, state, federal, or global level. For example, diseases or disease-causing agents that originate in one portion of the globe may eventually spread to all other parts, as did the human immunodeficiency virus (HIV).[12] The analysis should include key stakeholders who have an agenda that they wish to see implemented and major competitors, such as local managed care organizations (which may want to take over public health roles and responsibilities). Assessing external forces should be an ongoing activity and not be limited to one step in the strategic planning process.[13]

The internal assessment looks at the agency's resources, the process of carrying out the agency activities, and the performance outputs. Part 1 of the Assessment Protocol for Excellence in Public Health (APEX-PH) is an assessment of an organization's internal capacity. This organizational component is not visibly present in the Mobilizing for Action through Planning and Partnerships (MAPP) assessment process, which is a system-based assessment. However, there is nothing that prevents a public health agency from doing an internal capacity assessment.

The collection of information, the clarification of values, the development of a mission, and the assessment of the agency and its environment provide the foundation for the rest of the strategic planning process. Step 5 is the identification of the issues to be addressed by the plan. In this stage, the stakeholders typically come together to define the issues, utilizing a group process approach. The stakeholders need not only to identify the critical issues but also explain why these issues are critical and to describe what the consequences of not addressing these issues will be.

Another approach to completing this step is to define goals and objectives and then develop issues based on the goals and objectives. Still another approach is for the partners in the strategic planning process to devise ideal scenarios (descriptions of the way they would like the world to be) and present them to each other and try to come to a consensus. One problem with scenario building is that it is a complex process and requires the participants to be trained in how to create scenarios.[14] Without proper training, the participants may not be able to get results that are valid. In a fourth approach, the strategic planning team tries to facilitate the formulation of issues by slowly guiding the stakeholders through the process.

Step 6 involves the development of strategies to address the issues delineated in step 5. In short, it is during this step that the strategic plan is actually devised. Possible strategies include the setting of new policies or new rules and regulations, the development of new programs and services, and changes in the allocation of resources. The stakeholders need to determine how the chosen strategies interrelate and thus how the whole system works. Some strategies might involve both the agency and the community, some might involve just the agency or just agency subdivisions, and some might involve agency programs and services.

In step 7, the stakeholders review, modify, and adopt the strategic plan developed in step 6. Here, as in steps 5 and 6, they must consider the actions that will be necessary to carry out the plan. The plan in a sense consists of actions that are intended to achieve the goals and objectives identified by the stakeholders early in the planning process.

Step 8 is the creation or revision of the organizational vision. Strategic planning may lead to changes that affect the vision, and thus visioning is tied to each step of the strategic planning process. In point of fact, the vision need not be fully determined early on but can be left to evolve during several cycles of this process.[15] The vision should grow out of an integration of past accomplishments and perceptions of the future. The vision also needs to provide inspiration to other stakeholders. However, the agency's mission tends to drive the strategic planning process more than the vision does.[16]

Step 9 is the implementation of the plan. In prior steps, while developing the plan, the stakeholders need to define their roles in the implementation process. They also should try to ensure that accomplishments, even if small ones, will occur early in the process. Success tends to foster success, because the stakeholders will remain motivated and undiscouraged if they see progress. The stakeholders need to allocate the necessary resources before the implementation process begins. As changes are made, the agency and the other stakeholders need to adjust accordingly and monitor the effects of the changes over time.

Step 10 involves monitoring the implementation and making necessary midcourse corrections.

Each of the 10 steps of the Bryson model is related to one of the three core public health functions (assessment, policy development, and assurance). The model is in fact compatible with the systems approach to public health leadership (leadership wheel), and all of the activities in this approach, which is based on the core functions of public health, are included in the Bryson model. The relationships between the model and the organizational practices and essential services of public health are more cloudy. For example, visioning is not included in typical lists of such practices and services. Montgomery has noted that the strategic process should move beyond being a distinctive set of strategies toward being a dynamic evolving process.[17] The dynamic approach to strategic planning should create an interactive model that ties changes in the community to changes and adaptations within the agency.

As regards strategic planning, public health leaders must:

- learn the benefits of such planning
- determine the readiness of the agency to undertake the strategic planning process
- perform a stakeholder analysis
- expand the strategic planning process to include stakeholders in the community
- remain optimistic during the strategic planning process as a means of motivating other participants
- do the necessary homework to prepare for each successive step of the strategic planning process
- be realistic about what is possible
- perform an assessment of organizational capacity

Exercise 20-1 is intended to give you a chance to use or develop your strategic planning skills. The task is to use strategic thinking in the planning of a community education program designed to inform the public of the advantages of empowerment and community coalitions. An additional perspective can be seen in Case Study 20-A, which explores the issues raised in border health disputes when strategic processes vary in two different countries.

Case Study 20-A

Health Issues at the United States–Cannico Republic Border
Bailus Walker

Introduction

One of the tasks of public health is to ensure that services necessary to achieve agreed-upon goals are provided. The assurance function does not always entail the direct supervision of needed services but rather their identification and development, their coordination, and oversight of their accessibility and quality.

As the governmental presence in health, public health has the responsibility for ensuring (1) that every community is adequately served by an emergency health services system, by adequate hospitals with prenatal care, and by appropriate environmental health services and (2) that community residents are properly immunized and are provided with services designed to prevent the transmission of infectious diseases and the occurrence or progression of noninfectious diseases and dysfunction as well.

The assurance function today requires that state and local health agencies not only merge the pursuit of comprehensive health services with social and economic goals within state or local boundaries but also recognize the transboundary dimensions of public health challenges and opportunities. Massive amounts of goods, services, and capital and large numbers of people flow across international boundaries each day. At the same time, certain human activities continuously increase the risk of disease, dysfunction, and premature death and create unprecedented demands on the health services system.

(Continues)

For example, along the 2,000-mile border between the United States and Cannico, U.S. hospitals report that a third of the emergency admissions are Cannico nationals who cannot afford treatment or other personal health services. The health, social, and economic conditions in one border community raise critical issues for policy makers and health service specialists, administrators, and program managers dedicated to making sure their community is adequately served by a comprehensive public health service system.

Bingo County

Bingo County is in the southwest section of the state of Pennsylcola. It is on the United States–Cannico border. Bingo City has been the county seat since 1871. The chief employment opportunity in the county is manufacturing. Farm production, timbering, tourism, and military installations are major sources of employment.

Bingo County, which is larger than Massachusetts and Rhode Island combined, covers 9,266 square miles, of which 25% are rural. The county includes a population estimated in a special 1990 census to be 1.2 million. Within the county are five incorporated cities: Bingo City (population 669,000), Randolph (101,000), Pickett (94,000), Thompson (78,000), and Edgar (67,000). There are 14 other incorporated towns of smaller size (with populations ranging from 2,000 to 20,000) and 163,000 people living in unincorporated areas of the county. In the 1990 census, 93.4% of the residents were considered urban.

According to the same census, 80.9% of the county's population was white, 14.6% Hispanic, 3.4% black, and 1.1% Native American.

Estimates furnished by the Pennsylcola Department of Economic Security in 1990 placed the median family income at approximately $12,100, with 15.8% of the population falling below the poverty line. Of the population over age 25, 49.7% had completed high school. In December 1990, 9.3% of the workforce was unemployed.

Cannico

Within the past five years, the country of Cannico restructured its government, moving from a communist system toward democratization of all aspects of its society, including more liberal migration policies. In the process of this change, Cannico experienced severe social and economic problems. Prices rose and wages fell because the industries no longer received huge allotments of cash from the government for their payroll. Food shortages were pervasive and health services were described by some analysts as "substandard" by U.S. criteria.

There is very little information on demographics and health resources of Cannico because during the upheaval that led to the change in government, many valuable records and databases were destroyed. What is clear is that the border with Bingo County has become a favored place of entry for Cannico nationals desiring to get into the United States. This development has been fueled by growth in Cannico's population and shifts in the country's economy.

Bingo County Health Resources and Services

There are an estimated 900 primary physicians in Bingo County, and several health maintenance organizations (HMOs) serve the county. The state of Pennsylcola has eight programs for Medicaid enrollment, each with its own criteria for eligibility. There are 10 privately owned acute-care hospitals with a combined bed capacity of 3,228. Several of the hospitals in the area provide extensive outpatient services, drawing clientele from the entire region. Five hospitals are tertiary care centers.

The mission of the Bingo County Department of Public Health reads as follows: "To provide for the health care of the people and to protect and promote the health of all persons in the county in a professional and effective manner."

The Bingo County Department of Public Health provides a range of services, including disease control, sanitation, food inspection and licensure, screening, and health education. The department provides direct personal health services, including maternal and child health services; nutrition services, including a Women, Infants, and Children supplemental feeding program; and categorical programs to cope with alcohol and drug abuse. All of the varied activities of the agency are ultimately accountable to the Bingo County health officer, who has statutory responsibility for leadership of the department.

The County Government

Bingo County operates under an executive commission nonpartisan form of government. The executive is entrusted with broad powers and appoints most of the administrative officials and department heads, including the head of the local board of health and the county director of public health.

In the state of Pennsylcola, the local health department operates with decentralized authority in relation to the state department of health. The state's guidance and support are regarded as "moderate."

It is the view of the state policy makers that the Bingo County Department of Public Health has three responsibilities: (1) promotion of personal and community health, (2) maintenance of a healthful environment, and (3) prevention of disease and disability.

Bingo County Department of Public Health Personnel and Services

In 1990, the Bingo County Department of Public Health had a staff of approximately 1,000 people who provided medical care, social services, environmental health services, and nursing, among other services. Of the 20.5 full-time equivalent (FTE) physician employees, 10 were full time. Three of these employees had administrative positions. The other 10.5 FTE physicians were part-time physicians engaged in private practice.

The majority of personal health services are delivered through the department's family primary healthcare program, which operates three health centers. These clinics provide the following services for all age groups:

- promotion and maintenance of health
- prevention of illness and disability
- basic care during acute and chronic phases of illness
- guidance and counseling of individuals and families
- referral to other healthcare providers and community resources

The department also provides dental services. The head of dental services for the Bingo County Department of Public Health, Dr. Bush, DDS, told the Centers for Disease Control and Prevention (CDC), "By definition our department is the provider of last resort in dental care."

Limited laboratory services are provided for water and food analysis and to support efforts in infection control.

Environmental health services include regulatory services in food sanitation, sanitary nuisances, water quality monitoring, housing and recreational sanitation (e.g., swimming pools and air pollution monitoring). The department also participates in land use planning, including the approval of community development (e.g., housing construction).

The department makes modest use of nurse practitioners; they are classified as public health nurse clinicians. Other personnel include family planning specialists, laboratorians, dentists, environmental health specialists, and veterinarians.

The Bingo County Department of Public Health employs approximately 15 community health services assistants. These workers are from disadvantaged backgrounds, lack formal education, and serve as patient advocates, helping consumers interact with other agencies (e.g., social services) and enroll in appropriate programs (e.g., food stamps).

Because the department has a number of categorical programs, staff members are generally employed by specific programs. This practice constrains, to some extent, staff mobility and departmental flexibility.

Encounter data for a number of the department's major activities are shown in **Table 20-A-1**.

TABLE 20-A-1 Service Encounters (1989–1990)

Program	Number of Encounters
Communicable Disease	52,172
Immunizations	10,966
Venereal Disease	15,229
Chronic Disease	2,000
Multiphasic Screening	1,109
Well-Child Conference	5,063
Prenatal Classes Attended	6,784
Family Planning	21,000
Environmental Health Inspection	19,000

(Continues)

The total budget for fiscal year 1989 was $26,652,351 (**Exhibit 20-A-1**). The budget is made up of 12 different state contributions or allocations (each representing separate state laws), federal grant programs, numerous fees, and different local actions. From the revenue of $21,283,954, Bingo budgeted a wide variety of services, shown under public health control and regulatory programs.

EXHIBIT 20-A-1 Bingo County Department of Public Health Budget

General Revenue Funds (State)	
General	$6,330,294
AIDS Patient Care	379,000
School Health	205,198
Improved Pregnancy Outcome	667,513
Federal Funds	
Family Planning	$240,136
Child Health	33,610
AIDS	129,199
Hypertension	37,041
Nutrition Program Administration	250,000
EPA Grants	128,300
Child Health Improvement Program	50,000
Sterilization	11,337
AIDS Testing and Counseling	31,891
Fees	
For Enforcement	$361,784
Personal Fees	87,280
For Primary Medical Care	623,475
Other Sources	
Interest on Trust Fund	$100,000
Primary Care	3,000,000
Sexually Transmitted Diseases	198,675
State Lab Revenue	561,459
Tuberculosis Control	95,851
Immunizations	48,947
Supplemental Food Supplies	1,763,703
Pharmacy	452,929
County Support	
General Appropriation	$5,611,055
Fees	1,618,556

Building Rental	1,595,148
Maintenance of Buildings	481,134
School Board	55,000
County Air Pollution	398,308
County Toxic Substance Control	83,102
Epilepsy Foundation	18,000
Primary Care Grant	716,898
Headstart Dental Program	1,700
Sabal Palm (Private Grant)	27,398
Robert Wood Johnson (Grant)	87,879
Communications	170,551
Total	$26,652,351
Expenditures	
Control and Regulatory Programs	
Immunizations	$536,163
Sexually Transmitted Diseases	353,082
AIDS	111,156
Tuberculosis Control	405,393
Private Water Systems	32,693
Public Water Systems	379,237
Bottled Water	26,154
Swimming Pools	307,313
Individual Sewage Disposal	496,931
Public Sewage System	235,388
Solid Waste Disposal	170,003
Water Pollution Control	268,081
Food Hygiene	1,013,478
Group Care Facilities	379,237
Migrant Labor Camps	104,617
Housing Safety and Sanitation	130,771
Mobile Home Parks	32,693
Occupational Health	26,154
Consumer Product Safety	26,154
Sanitary Nuisances	241,927
Air Pollution Control	536,163
Radiologic Health	19,616
Toxic Substances	111,156

(*Continues*)

Rabies Control	13,077
Arbovirus Surveillance	13,077
Emergency Medical Services	13,077
Vital Records	268,081
Personal Health Services	
Chronic Disease Services	$286,327
Nutrition Services	805,293
Family Planning	702,313
Improved Pregnancy Outcome	3,684,791
School Health	2,113,801
Dental Health Services	1,355,180
Comprehensive Child Health	2,765,493
Comprehensive Adult Health	3,032,187
Total	$21,283,954

Other Economic Considerations

The undocumented immigrant population (from Cannico) of Bingo County costs nearly $172 million a year in local government services.

A two-year study conducted by private consultants for the Pennsylcola state auditor general examined the impact of the city's 200,000 illegal immigrants on schools, law enforcement, health care, and social services. Some groups have criticized the report. They suggest that any discussion of the impact of immigrants must include the fact that this population provides a cheap, flexible labor pool that stimulates the creation of new businesses and helps preserve labor-intensive ones in Bingo County and the surrounding region.

The findings also indicate that HIV-related health care provided through the Pennsylcola Medicaid program costs about $2,800 per month per person. The data used to calculate this statistic were from a fixed period and included many persons who were still in the early stages of infection at the end of the data collection period.

Although in theory Cannico has a national health system, in fact there are major gaps in access and quality. Persons with a large income have access to private facilities and practitioners at home and abroad. The middle class, which includes government workers and residents of certain agricultural communities, generally have access only to government clinics and hospitals.

Utilization by Canniconians of health services in the United States takes place on the following levels. First, there are the wealthy, who pay in full or on a fee-for-service basis for their physician and hospital care. Second, there are those who seek care in the United States because of their desire to have a child who is a U.S. citizen, because they hope to find adequate services, or because they are responding to an emergency. In urban areas of Cannico, the Health and Welfare Ministry maintains health clinics and hospitals often staffed by recent medical school graduates. Rural areas of Cannico are likely to be served only by a nurse. Hospital access for those who are poor and not covered by the Health and Welfare Ministry programs is often limited to civil hospitals, which are not well staffed or funded.

Community Health Assessment

In November 1989, Frank Daly was appointed county executive. When the county health officer retired soon afterward, Daly appointed James Verdon Reed, MD, MPH, to fill the position. Concerned about the health problems of Bingo County, Dr. Reed asked the CDC to conduct a community health assessment.

This community health analysis provided indicators of how citizens, activities, and services on one side of the border relate to and influence those of the other side and ultimately both nations. The CDC report suggests that it is unlikely that any other bi-national border has such variety in health status and healthcare utilization. What follows are relevant findings of the CDC analysis.

General

While most residents of Bingo are eligible for public assistance, relatively few physicians are willing to accept Medicaid payment and the tangle of paperwork that goes with it. People seeking Medicaid assistance in Bingo County also must go through a complicated set of procedures. The state of Pennsylcola has eight programs for Medicaid enrollment, each with its own eligibility criteria. An indigent, mentally disabled person must negotiate up to 13 different application procedures for federal and state benefits. Many of these programs, the CDC team reports, have periodic review procedures with provisions for termination of benefits for those who do not complete the necessary paperwork. It is not uncommon for persons who are functioning marginally and miss filing deadlines for review of their disability benefits to learn that their benefits have been terminated.

In the county, an estimated 13,000 women are eligible for Medicaid maternity benefits, but only 50 doctors are willing to treat them under the state aid program—a patient–doctor ratio that CDC representatives call far too high.

In Bingo County, there are nine nonprofit community health centers, which charge fees based on the patients' ability to pay. The centers served approximately 8,000 patients—in 1989, 44% of them children. But many more were turned away because of excessive patient loads. As many as 3,000 people, from both Bingo County and Cannico, are typically on waiting lists for the tight-budgeted health centers. In Bingo County, last winter, amid a heavy viral respiratory outbreak, there were waiting periods up to 36 hours for pediatric care.

The effects of the lack of care are various, according to the CDC report. Pregnant women who have received no prenatal care often suffer severe complications, and many babies are born underweight, contributing to the infant mortality rate of 19 per 1,000 live births (for the past three years) in Bingo County. A separate CDC study of five counties in Pennsylcola, including Bingo County, showed that the chance of a bad pregnancy outcome was 35% greater for women without health insurance, even when income, race, and other factors were controlled for.

A study prepared by the Bingo Chamber of Commerce reported that in 1989, 19.9% of the city's residents had no insurance coverage, largely because their employers did not provide it and their wages were so low that they could not buy a policy. The results of the lack of insurance can be seen every day in hospitals along the Bingo–Cannico border, where patients whose medical problems might have been prevented or easily treated in the early stages have waited until their conditions have become acute.

The CDC reports that childbirth itself is an issue in Bingo County. Many pregnant Cannico women show up at hospital emergency departments in Bingo County at the last minute, so far along in labor that they cannot be turned away. The children they bear are American citizens eligible for immediate medical and nutritional aid as well as other long-term benefits.

According to the CDC analysis, the Lamplight Medical Center, a private hospital, receives the largest share of what are known as "disproportionate funds" from the state to help compensate for care given to patients from both sides of the United States–Cannico border.

In one lower socioeconomic section of Bingo County, there is only one pediatrician for a population of 170,000 people, and only six physicians in the area accept Medicaid. Of the 900 physicians in the county, only 20 have offices or clinics south of Burlington Highway, the line of demarcation between the poor and middle-class neighborhoods and the entry point for most Canniconians.

These health service problems are developing at a time when rapid population growth shifts have severely taxed the infrastructure of Bingo County. Lured by the possibility of jobs in the United States, hundreds of impoverished Canniconians from the interior of the country have made their way to the border neighborhoods near Bingo.

During the past several years, as the Cannico economy has weakened, the border population has ballooned from 36,000 to more than 500,000, and most of the growth has occurred in the past two years. Shantytowns, without sewers or running water, have become part of the border landscape.

Cholera

The CDC report indicates that the Pennsylcola–Cannico border is an ideal setting for an outbreak of cholera that has taken an estimated 5,000 lives in 14 states of Cannico. At least one cholera case has been confirmed recently in Bingo County. A woman contracted the disease from eating contaminated shrimp while on a trip to Borisville, the southernmost city of Cannico.

Rubella

From January through June 1989, an outbreak of rubella occurred among Bingo County residents. It was part of a widespread outbreak reported among lower socioeconomic groups in three states in Cannico and the state of Pennsylcola on the U.S. side.

(*Continues*)

The Bingo County Department of Public Health, in cooperation with the CDC, conducted an investigation to document cases of rubella among pregnant women in Bingo County.

The health department and the CDC identified 89 women from Bingo County and Cannico as having rubella-like illness during pregnancy. Vaccination histories were available for 25 of these women. One (from Bingo County) had a history of prior rubella vaccination. Of the 89 women, 18 (20%) had laboratory-confirmed acute rubella; 31 specimens were insufficient for analysis, and no specimens were obtained from the remaining 40.

Based on the findings for a five-month study period, the rate of congenital rubella infection was 83 per 1,000 live births in the lower socioeconomic groups of Bingo County. The CDC notes that the risk of congenital rubella syndrome is greatest when maternal infection occurs early in pregnancy. When infection occurs during the first trimester, congenital rubella syndrome occurs in up to 85% of births.

Dengue Fever

Another problem on the Pennsylcola–Cannico border is dengue fever. Indigenous dengue transmission was documented in southern Cannico in the 1980s, where of 63 reported cases at least 27 cases were identified in patients who had traveled outside that country before the onset of the disease. In Bingo County, 10 cases were reported as imported cases. Persistent large-scale outbreaks of dengue fever in Cannico make this area more at risk, but a widespread outbreak could occur in the United States, because the *Aedes aegypti* mosquito is now in the Bingo County region and on the Pennsylcola–Cannico border. There is no eradication program at this time.

Tuberculosis and AIDS

A review of 2,205 clinical charts for 1985–1989 at the four largest hospitals in Bingo County for patients who had *Mycobacterium* tuberculosis isolated from spinal fluid revealed that 455 patients (21%) also had an HIV infection. Of the 37 HIV-infected patients with tuberculosis meningitis for whom records were available, 24 (65%) had clinical radiological evidence of extrameningeal tuberculosis at the time of admission.

Local officials believe that in recent years, men from Cannico have brought acquired immune deficiency syndrome (AIDS) to Bingo County. Doctors and epidemiologists report that official statistics on AIDS in Cannico describe only the tip of the phenomenon, which remains submerged in denial and social taboos.

The nurse in charge of AIDS treatment at a Cannico hospital, having carefully traced the sexual partners of her patients, concludes that a score of local people in Cannico are probably infected. Few of them wanted to be tested for the virus. National health officials in Cannico emphasize that, even when suspicious cases are added to those in which AIDS infection can be clearly traced to the victim's migration to Bingo County, the connection still accounts for only a small fraction of the 9,000 cases of the disease reported in Cannico.

Given the hundreds of Canniconians who cross legally and illegally into Bingo County each year, the number of those who come to Bingo County with AIDS and those who return to Cannico with AIDS appears to be small. But as the epidemic in Cannico has begun to level off among homosexual men and victims of a blood supply that was still poorly screened and badly contaminated less than five years ago, the spread of AIDS among migrants has become a growing concern on both sides of the border.

The concern is fueled by the difficult lives of undocumented workers from Cannico and the different sexual mores of two neighboring societies. While Cannico migration patterns have more women and families joining the flow of male job seekers, it is the archetypal lonely young men who are at highest risk. Almost everywhere these young men land, activities that put them at risk of infection tend to be more available than affordable health care, AIDS prevention programs, or information in the Canniconian language. Moreover, sexually transmitted disease on the border has long been a problem, not only because of the cross-border use of red light districts but also because contact tracing is much more difficult.

Measles

During the past three years, measles cases and deaths have risen sharply in Bingo County. In 1989, more than 500 cases and nine deaths were reported, the largest number of deaths in two decades. The epidemic intensified during 1990, with more than 700 cases and more than 11 deaths. The principal cause of the measles epidemic was failure to provide vaccine to children at the recommended age.

According to the CDC, many families in Bingo County have no ongoing relationship with a healthcare provider. The low immunization rate reflects, in part, inadequate access to health services. The CDC's analysis also showed that many opportunities to provide the needed vaccines were missed. Two types of missed opportunities were particularly noticeable in Bingo County: (1) a child brought to a center for immunization is not vaccinated because of inappropriate contraindications, such as minor illness, or only one of two vaccines is given when, in fact, others are also needed and should be given, and (2) a child in need of vaccination has contact with a healthcare provider for other reasons but his or her immunization status is not assessed and immunizations are not offered.

Reproductive and Developmental Problems

From 1986 to 1989, 102 women in Bingo County gave birth to babies without brains. The rate occurrence in the county of this rare congenital defect, known as anencephaly, is 10 times the national average. No cause has been identified, but some longtime residents of Bingo County suspect toxic emissions from factories above the border in Cannico. Other residents suspect the nuclear power plant accident that occurred inside Cannico several years ago.

On the Cannico side of the border, the infant mortality rate is significantly higher than in Bingo County and in the United States as a whole, although it is beginning to decline. In Cannico, the infant mortality rate has declined from an estimated 59 deaths per 1,000 live births during 1967–71 to 47 during 1982–87.

In Bingo County, the infant mortality rate for the period between 1982 and 1987 was 18 per 1,000 live births. Bronchitis and pneumonia, noninfectious gastroenteritis, and intestinal infection disease accounted for 220 deaths in the postneonatal period in Bingo County from 1982 to 1989.

Chronic Disease

In 1989, the overall mortality rate for coronary heart disease, stroke, lung cancer, cervical cancer, cirrhosis, and diabetes in Bingo County (age adjusted) was 75.8 per 100,000 population. Of the five risk factors examined—cigarette smoking, hypertension, obesity, alcohol consumption, and "never use Pap screening"—cigarette smoking made the largest contribution to deaths from the six diseases (30%). Examined one at a time, other risk factors also contributed to deaths due to these diseases: obesity (25%), high cholesterol level (15%), hypertension (15%), and diabetes (10%).

Environmental Health

Sanitation in Cannico (i.e., water supply, waste water disposal, and solid waste collection and disposal) is far below U.S. standards. There is no evidence of regulatory control of environmental quality—broadly defined—in Cannico. Daily, 12 million gallons of raw sewage flow into the Kopa River, which flows into the Bingo County area from Cannico. Users of well water in the rural areas in Bingo County have noted increased contamination.

Air pollution in the Bingo–Cannico area has been a continuing problem, and discharges from the smelters on the Bingo side have been cited as a cause of high blood lead levels in both Cannico and Bingo County. More recently, Bingo County has exceeded the Environmental Protection Agency's ozone and carbon monoxide standards, largely because of older vehicular fleets in Cannico, the lack of emission controls, and the poor quality of gasoline used. Depending on wind speed and wind direction, air pollutants discharged in Cannico can add to the pollution load in Bingo County. Emissions in Bingo County may also affect atmospheric conditions in Cannico.

CONTINUOUS QUALITY IMPROVEMENT

Whereas strategic planning is a process that can be analyzed into a number of specific steps, CQI involves accepting a whole new philosophy of doing business or providing services. Public health organizations have been slow to adopt CQI methods, and where they have done so, they have not had great success.[18] Part of the explanation for the lack of success is that public health leaders have not kept up with the developments in the field of CQI. In studying public health clinics in California, Scutchfield and his colleagues found that less than 20% of the agencies performed CQI activities.[19] They also found that public health leaders were often unclear when it was appropriate to use specific tools.

Public health agencies have a reputation for providing mediocre service. One problem obstructing the improvement of service is that federal and state funding for new public health programs has been shrinking. Another is that government rules and regulations, as well as union rules, put obstacles in the way of delivering services in a timely fashion. A third problem is that public health leaders often misinterpret quality assurance as a type of CQI. Improving quality is more than an assurance issue, and it depends on viewing the public health consumer as entitled to the best that public health professionals have to offer. It requires, in other words, a whole change in philosophy.

The focus of CQI activities in a public health agency is on improving service provision and enhancing relationships with external stakeholders.[20] These activities are based on information about the public health issues to be addressed, the strengths and weaknesses of the public health agency, and stakeholder concerns.

To improve service provision, public health leaders need to utilize a systems perspective, promote a client orientation,[21] and engage in strategic thinking. Some public health leaders have found that they can integrate strategic planning approaches and CQI, especially if one of the strategic goals of the agency is to improve the quality of service. Quality needs to be a personal issue as well as an agency or systems issue.[22] Each public health staff person has to be personally committed to high quality. A commitment to quality will improve performance. Having talent, knowledge, and skills to do public health's work will go nowhere without a personal commitment to do the best work possible with strong positive relationships with the public and with external stakeholders.

CQI is closely related to another management methodology called "total quality management" (TQM), and in fact the terms "continuous quality improvement" and "total quality management" are often used interchangeably.[23] They will be treated as synonymous here, and the term that appears in each instance below will be the term used by the particular author (or authors) under discussion.

TQM is based on the philosophy of total quality control, first promoted by Feigenbaum.[24] According to Sashkin and Kiser, TQM uses an evolving methodologic toolkit that includes all sorts of ways of measuring quality. The two main principles are that the focus of the organization must be on the customer and that everybody in the organization, not just the leadership, must be committed to quality. In their words, "TQM means that the organization's culture is defined by and supports the constant attainment of customer satisfaction through an integrated system of tools, techniques, and training. This involves the continuous improvement of organizational processes, resulting in high quality products and services."[25(p.39)]

CQI Models

Five names are traditionally tied to the CQI movement: Shewhart, Deming, Crosby, Juran, and Feigenbaum. Shewhart demonstrated that statistical control is critical in CQI activities.[26] Deming, the best known of the CQI theorists, in the 1950s had to go to Japan to test his ideas about quality. To publicize his ideas, he devised a 14-point set of principles (**Table 20-2**).[27] The focus of these principles is on training the workforce and fostering a total commitment to quality. As Deming was aware, each customer wants high-quality products and services and evaluates the quality of products and services received. Deming also developed the planning, doing, checking, acting cycle.[28]

Crosby argued that the only way to improve quality is to demand zero defects and refuse to accept anything less.[29] After all, customers define quality, and in the business world, dissatisfied consumers will stop buying defective products. The public health customer, however, has limited service choices and will grudgingly accept less than the best, so it is up to public health leaders to empower their communities and make sure that high-quality standards are maintained. Public health leaders also need to gain support for the CQI approach from both internal and external stakeholders and must be prepared to cope with resistance. Deciding to apply for accreditation may help in this process.

CQI requires total commitment and involvement.[30] Crosby outlined a 14-step process for implementing TQM in organizations.[31,32] The process starts with a commitment by the leadership to the pursuit of quality and all that this entails. Most of the steps involve the core functions of policy development and assurance. There is only one step in which assessment plays the major role.

The Crosby model applies to intraorganizational change, whereas the kind of assessment public health agencies must perform encompasses both internal operations and community needs. The focus on intraorganizational change is a characteristic of the Deming model as well (Table 20-2). Note, however, that in the case of a public health agency, an assessment of community needs provides critical data for determining what intraorganizational changes are required and for integrating complex systems of health care in order to provide high-quality programming.

The fourth theoretician in the quality revolution is Joseph M. Juran. Juran pointed out that quality does not occur by chance.[33] It requires a planned process that encompasses planning, quality control, and quality

TABLE 20-2   Deming's 14 Points

1. Create constancy of purpose toward improvement of product and service with the aim to become competitive and to stay in business and to provide jobs.

2. Adopt the new philosophy. We are in a new economic age. Western management must awaken to the challenge, must learn their responsibilities, and take on leadership for change.

3. Cease dependence on inspection to achieve quality. Eliminate the need for inspection on a mass basis by building quality into the product or service in the first place.

4. End the practice of awarding business on the basis of price tag. Instead, minimize total costs. Move toward a single supplier for any one item on a long-term relationship of loyalty and trust.

5. Improve constantly and forever the system of production and service to improve quality and productivity and thus decrease costs.

6. Institute training on the job.

7. Institute leadership. The aim of leadership should be to help people and machines and gadgets to do a better job. Leadership of management is in need of overhaul as well as leadership of production workers.

8. Drive out fear so that everyone may work effectively for the company.

9. Break down barriers between departments. People in research, design, sales, and production must work as a team to foresee problems of production and use that may be encountered with the product or service.

10. Eliminate slogans, exhortations, and targets for the workforce asking for zero defects and new levels of production.

11. Eliminate work standards (quotas) in the organization. Eliminate management by objectives. Eliminate management by numbers, numeric goals. Substitute leadership.

12. Remove barriers that rob the hourly worker of rights to pride of workmanship. The responsibility of supervisors must be changed from sheer numbers to quality. Remove barriers that rob people in management and engineering of their right to pride of workmanship. Abolish annual or merit rating and management by objective (MBO).

13. Institute a vigorous program of education and self-improvement.

14. Put everybody to work to accomplish the transformation.

Source: Reproduced from *Out of the Crisis* by W. Edwards Deming. Copyright 1986 by the W. Edwards Deming Institute.

improvement (known as the Juran trilogy). Juran also believed that leaders need to organize information for the purpose of monitoring the process. Finally, Feigenbaum held that quality is involved in every activity of an organization, from direct service activities to marketing and finance, and that an organization must determine the cost of quality improvement programs before embarking on them.[34]

Building on the work of the founders of the TQM approach, Creech identified what he called the five pillars of TQM: product (service), process, organization, leadership, and commitment.[35] According to Creech, TQM has been more effective in Japan than in the United States because Japanese businesses seem to accept the concept of quality more readily than American businesses do. Creech has further pointed out that TQM is an organizational philosophy and cannot deliver full benefits without complete

organizational acceptance. In order to put the five pillars into perspective, Creech formulated 16 guidelines for the TQM process (**Table 20-3**).

Figure 20-2 shows that organization is the central pillar of the five. How the organization is perceived and what its cultural orientation is will have an effect on the implementation and consequences of TQM. Also, whereas centralization has been the traditional management approach, decentralization appears to be better suited to TQM. Consequently, multidisciplinary teams play an important role. As Figure 20-2 shows, one of the pillars is leadership. As indicated by the comment about decentralization, the leaders of the organization must be willing to share their power.

Organizational commitment to quality needs to occur at the border between the organization and its environment. If the frontline workers do not buy the quality message, TQM will be doomed to failure. In

TABLE 20-3 Creech Guidelines for Five-Pillars TQM

1. Build your TQM approach, and its principles, on five system pillars.
2. Firmly establish the character and culture of your organization.
3. Use a decentralized, interactive system that integrates all levels.
4. Organization is the central pillar—it influences everything else.
5. Base the structural building blocks on small teams and not big functions.
6. Orient employees' focus and activity to their product, not their job.
7. Place the prime leadership focus on the outputs, not the inputs.
8. Keep score, assess, and provide timely feedback to one and all.
9. Know your marketplace inside out and create strong customer linkage.
10. Provide a climate of quality that promotes pride and professionalism.
11. Base any and all decisions on the inseparability of cost and value.
12. Provide detailed, focused training to employees at every level.
13. Give high priority and pay great attention to the communication flow.
14. Work unceasingly to instill common purpose from the bottom to the top.
15. Build the commitment through genuine ownership and shared success.
16. Build your TQM on all five pillars.

Source: Adapted from *The Five Pillars of TQM* by Bill Creech. Copyright © 1994 by W. L. Creech.

The Five Pillars of TQM

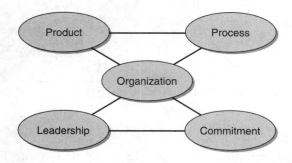

FIGURE 20-2 TQM: The Need, the Issues, the Shape It Must Take. *Source:* Reproduced from *The Five Pillars of TQM* by Bill Creech. Copyright © 1994 by W. L. Creech. Used by permission of Dutton, a division of Penguin Putnam Inc.

fact, everyone in the organization needs to make a commitment to quality.

The CQI Toolkit

CQI makes use of a number of tools, including various kinds of charts and diagrams. Traditional tools include:

- control charts (for showing the results of statistical process activities)
- Pareto charts (for graphically showing defects or problems over time)
- fishbone diagrams (for tracing cause-and-effect relationships)
- run charts (for displaying trends over time)
- histograms (for showing service patterns at given time periods)
- scatter diagrams (for showing relationships between two factors)
- flowcharts (for showing input-output relationships)[36]

Seven new tools of use in CQI are shown in **Figure 20-3** and described below.[37] The first is the affinity diagram, which allows a team to organize ideas and problems into general categories. The team would first sort the items into categories, then list the items in each category in a separate column. Affinity diagrams could be used for clarifying values; for constructing the organization's vision, mission, and goals and objectives; and for action and strategic planning. The affinity diagram process, like any group process, is affected by how well the team members get along.

The interrelationship digraph shows the interconnection between ideas, problems, actions, or other types of items. The arrows between the items show the direction of their relationship (e.g., cause to effect). Once a digraph is developed, it can be reworked to show new ways to relate the items. The team will want to simplify the digraph by looking for converging or diverging clusters of arrows. Constructing a digraph is especially useful for deciding on goals and objectives and during the action planning phase.

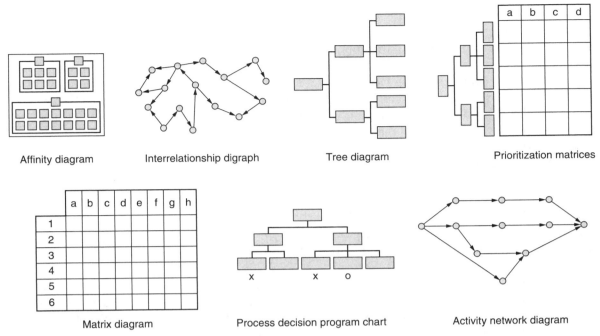

Affinity diagram   Interrelationship digraph   Tree diagram   Prioritization matrices

Matrix diagram   Process decision program chart   Activity network diagram

FIGURE 20-3 Seven Management and Planning Tools. *Source*: Reprinted with permission from M. Brassard, *The Memory Jogger*, © 1989, Goal and QPC.

The third tool, the tree diagram, can be used in many leadership activities. For instance, a tree diagram could be used by the leadership team of a public health agency to map out how the agency's mission is to be fulfilled. The team might start by stating the mission, which, say, is to promote the health of the public and prevent disease. The next step would be to determine the goals and objectives needed to fulfill this mission, and the third step would be to decide on the tasks that must be performed to achieve the chosen goals and objectives. In CQI, the leadership team might use tree diagrams in developing quality improvement plans. In general, the process of creating a tree diagram begins with stating an overall goal (e.g., the agency's mission or an important subsidiary goal) and then breaking the process of achieving the goal into individual steps or tasks.

Prioritization matrices allow the leadership team to prioritize tasks, service activities, community activities, and so on. A prioritization matrix can be used in conjunction with a tree diagram to rank the tasks and responsibilities identified during the tree diagram process. If six activities are projected, the diagram allows the team to see what will happen if any two activities occur together. The team is able to calculate a score for each cell, and where the score falls in relation to the other scores determines the degree of importance of the conjunction of activities.

Brassard suggested that the prioritization process should encompass three steps.[38] The first step is to list and then rank the criteria that will be used in prioritizing the items (e.g., activities). Such criteria might include the speed of possible implementation, the likely degree of acceptance by staff, the effect on other parts of the agency, the cost, and the technology needed. Once the criteria are chosen, each should be assigned a percentage that reflects its perceived importance (the total of percentages should, of course, equal 100%). In step 2, each item is given a score in relation to each criterion. Finally, the total scores for all the items are calculated, and the results determine the priority ranking of the items.

The fifth tool is the matrix diagram, which allows the leadership team to compare two or more sets of items and explore the strength of the relationship between them.

Process decision program charts allow the leadership team to show probable events and contingencies that might occur as the action plan is implemented. For example, suppose the public health agency director wants to plan how the community will perform health assessment activities. The director might create a chart that shows how the community advisory board is to be selected, when the various activities will occur and how much time they will take, and how they will be carried out. Process decision program charts, like the other tools described here, can also be used to explore options.

The last tool, the activity network diagram, exhibits the schedule for the completion of tasks. This tool is also known as an arrow diagram. Exercise 20-2 provides an opportunity to practice applying the seven CQI tools just described.

There has been increasing awareness of the importance of utilizing quality improvement tools and methodology for public health agencies. These techniques have been recognized for their value in performance measurement and also as critical to accreditation of public health agencies. However, most of the tools of quality improvement, including the fishbone diagram, are limited in their application to community-wide quality improvement activities. Exercise 20-3 will allow agencies and public health coalitions to experiment with a variation of the fishbone that I call the fan. The advantage of the fan is that it will allow us to recognize the potential of multiple factors or causes for quality change in a community or systems context. You can add multiple ribs to the fan depending on the number of causes or factors that you find critical. Increase the number of ribs of the fan to allow for this. The ribs are connected by the material of the fan, which demonstrates the interconnectedness of all the factors or ribs necessary to improve quality. A simple matrix will also help in this process.

CQI requires a total commitment by public health leaders and all their constituencies if it is to be successful. The professional staff of the public health agency must buy in to the total quality approach. To get staff to do this, public health leaders must:

- develop a commitment to quality and best practices
- incorporate CQI into a systems framework
- become educated about CQI
- master the seven CQI tools
- educate the public about CQI
- inspire staff and others to see the value of the CQI approach
- train the public health workforce
- integrate strategic planning techniques and CQI techniques

Six Sigma

Many businesses interested in quality improvement methodologies have explored the new techniques of Six Sigma, which was developed and trademarked by Motorola. Six Sigma involves continuous process improvement methods that are oriented to improving the work processes of an organization to near perfect.[39] The issue of variation and monitoring the effects of variation are part of the methodology. The issue of variation is also applied to not only what goes on inside the organization but to the variance issues associated with customers outside the organization. The overall goal of Six Sigma is to cut the variation as much as possible. Data drive the process in that managers and leaders will use the data to make better decisions. Five stages define the process, which has the acronym DMAIC:[40]

1. Define the problem.
2. Measure defects in the process.
3. Analyze data to determine causes of problems.
4. Improve work processes to remove the causes of problems.
5. Control events so that the causes of problems do not recur.

A leadership dimension is part of Six Sigma, which involves training.[41] There is a Black Belt training for project managers that takes several weeks. Master Black Belts are generally leaders who are responsible for the training and coaching of others. Green Belts are people who are trained for specific roles in the process and also carry out other roles in the organization. Yellow Belts are individuals involved in the process but did not go through specific training.[42] Other partners include the Executive Sponsor, who makes sure that the process is followed.[43] This person does not run the Six Sigma protocols but supports the activities related to the process. This may be the head of the organization. There will also be Department or Project Champions.

There have been many variations to the Six Sigma approach. Tools from inductive statistics, systems tools, CQI tools, and many other techniques have been adapted for use in Six Sigma. Although many of these tools are also used in public health, the application of Six Sigma methodology to public health has been limited. The development of the National Public Health Performance Standards, which utilize both a systems and a CQI approach, does begin to look at the way public health professionals work to carry out the essential public health services. The effect of performance improvement has yet to be tied to health outcomes.

Jacquescoley believes that Six Sigma may provide useful tools and methods to public health.[44] The Six Sigma framework does explore the effect of defects or program limitations on the process, operation, and practice of public health work. The definition of defects in public health is less clear. Are these defects specific health issues or lack of understanding of how to address these issues that are the relevant factors? How to transfer the idea of process in a business to process in the human services arena is a major challenge to the use of Six Sigma approaches. As leaders, we look at all possible methods and tools to better improve the way we work in public health.

Reengineering

Sometimes an organization cannot be fixed in its present form. If this is the case, the organization must be restructured so that it can make use of new approaches to problem solving and decision making. The restructuring of an organization is often referred to as reengineering. Manganelli and Klein defined reengineering as "the rapid and radical redesign of strategic, value-added business processes—and the systems, policies, and organizational structures that support them—to optimize the work flows and productivity in an organization."[45(pp.7–8)]

Imagine that a public health agency wants to incorporate bioterrorism interventions into the range of services it is capable of providing. If no new funding is currently available for the project, the agency leadership will look for methods to reorganize the agency and reassign staff to carry out the project. The leaders might not only phase out programs of less relevance but also reeducate the staff to work in different organizational units. This is not as easy a task as it might seem. Barriers to public health reengineering include objections to the changes by a public employee union or by the board of health.

As Drucker pointed out, knowledge-intensive organizations require continual reengineering.[46] Therefore, because the 21st century, like the 20th, will undoubtedly be a century of technological advances and new public health concerns, public health agencies will have to redefine and reengineer themselves on an ongoing basis. Public health leaders will play an essential role in reengineering projects because, as pointed out repeatedly, they define their organization's vision and motivate others to share the vision.

To get stakeholders, including governing board members, involved in and committed to reengineering, leaders must win their trust. Staff members are often wedded to the status quo and will have to be reassured that they will not lose their jobs as a result of the reorganization.[47] Another way to build trust is to include people from all parts of the organization on the reengineering team. In the case of a local health department, the leaders might recruit community leaders and members of the local board of health to be on the team.

Several additional guidelines should be kept in mind when considering embarking on a reengineering project. First, the leaders of an agency need to determine the agency's mission and how the reengineering will increase its chances of fulfilling its mission.[48] If a local public health department is committed to the promotion of health but its activities are hindered by a cumbersome bureaucracy, it should explore reengineering. Again, unless the legislature, city council, and board of health buy in to the process, it will likely be unsuccessful.

Second, the leaders must recognize that the reengineering process changes the culture as well as the job responsibilities of the staff. Third, they will need to develop new measures to evaluate staff performance and monitor the change process. Fourth, they should mobilize the staff for change and provide staff members with the tools they will need to carry out their reengineering responsibilities. Fifth, they should define the goals and objectives of reengineering. Sixth, they should ensure that communication channels exist between all those involved in the reengineering process.

The leaders who are best qualified to oversee reengineering projects tend to have a process orientation and a holistic perspective (**Table 20-4**) and to be comfortable with strategic thinking.[49] They are also creative, find the status quo boring, tend to be enthusiastic and able to motivate others, are persistent and tactful, and are excellent communicators who support teamwork and good interpersonal relations. In reviewing the best practices of organizations that underwent

TABLE 20-4 Profile of a Reengineering Leader—Top Ten Traits

1. Systems Thinker
2. Design and Implementation Ability
3. Change Agent
4. Resilient
5. Transparent
6. Optimistic
7. Persistent
8. Collaborative
9. Team Player
10. Trustworthy

Source: Adapted from Michael Hammer, *The Reengineering Revolution*, New York: HarperCollins, 1995.

reengineering, Carr and Johansson searched for the lessons to be learned.[50] The rules they discovered are listed in **Table 20-5**.

Manganelli and Klein presented a five-stage model for rapid reengineering (**Figure 20-4**).[51] In the first stage, the leaders recognize that there is a need for organizational change, foster a consensus among staff that such a need exists, clarify the mission of the organization, select and train a reengineering team, and develop a plan to guide the reengineering process (action plan). In stage 2, the leaders create a consumer-focused model for the organization, determine who the stakeholders are, and involve them in the reengineering process. In stage 3, the leaders develop a realistic vision based on current process performance activities and on projections of where the organization is headed. In stage 4, a reengineering plan tied to the vision is developed. Technical design issues are addressed in the first part (stage 4A), and social design issues are addressed in the second (stage 4B). Finally, the implementation of the new organizational model occurs during stage 5.

Public health leaders must be committed to restructuring the agency if substantial changes are necessary for it to carry out its mission. They must, therefore:

- learn to distinguish reengineering, strategic planning, continuous quality improvement, and Six Sigma methodologies
- master new approaches to organizational improvement
- improve relationships with key stakeholders
- work closely with the reengineering team
- master the five-stage rapid reengineering model

TABLE 20-5 Reengineering Principles

1. Recognize and articulate an "extremely compelling" need to change.
2. Start with and maintain executive-level support.
3. Understand the organization's "readiness to change."
4. Communicate effectively to create buy-in. Then communicate more.
5. Instill in the organization a "readiness and commitment" to sustained change.
6. Stay actively involved.
7. Create top-notch teams.
8. Use a structure framework.
9. Use consultants effectively.
10. Pay attention to what has worked.
11. Link goals to corporate strategy.
12. Listen to the "voice of the customer."
13. Select the right processes for reengineering.
14. Maintain focus: don't try to reengineer too many processes.
15. Create an explicit vision of each process to be reengineered.
16. Maintain teams as the key vehicle for change.
17. Quickly come to an as-is understanding of the processes to be reengineered.
18. Choose and use the right metrics.
19. Create an environment conducive to creativity and innovation.
20. Take advantage of modeling and simulation tools.
21. Understand the risks and develop contingency plans.
22. Have plans for continuous improvement.
23. Align the infrastructure.
24. Position IT as an enabler, even if the extent of the IT change necessary is great.

Source: Reprinted with permission from D. K. Carr and H. J. Johansson, *Best Practices in Reengineering*, pp. 209–210. © 1995, McGraw Hill, Inc.

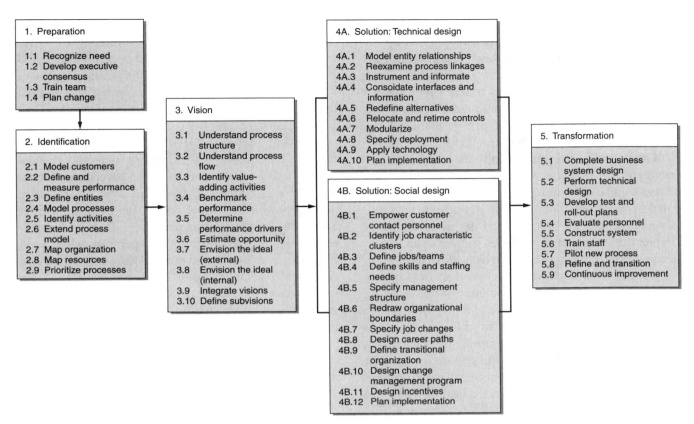

FIGURE 20-4 **Reengineering: Stages and Tasks.** *Source*: Reproduced from *The Reengineering Handbook*. Copyright © 1994 Raymont L. Manganelli et al. Reprinted from AMACOM, a division of American Management Association International, New York, NY. All rights reserved. http://www.amanet.org

REINVENTING GOVERNMENT

Since the 1990s, we have seen an increase in public discussions about the structure and function of government. Some have argued that the old ways of governing do not work any longer[52] and that the public sector must keep open the option of employing entrepreneurial techniques from the business sector. "Reinvention" is the term used to describe the use of entrepreneurial techniques by those in the public sector. Osborne and Plastrik defined reinvention as "the fundamental transformation of public systems and organizations to create dramatic increases in their effectiveness, efficiency, adaptability, and capacity to innovate. This transformation is accomplished by changing their purpose, incentives, accountability, power structure, and culture."[53(pp.13–14)]

Reinvention of government became more common during the 1990s and was seen as less radical than originally believed.[54] Reinventing government involves strategies such as tying rewards to performance, listening to and being accountable to community consumers, making organizations less hierarchical and more

decentralized, and empowering staff to make decisions and influence work processes. Discussions on reinventing government have been quieter since the terrorist events of September 11, 2001.

For reinvention to work, it needs to be seen as more than a patching operation. It must involve a significant restructuring of organizations, a rethinking of the activities and mission of the organization, and an abandonment of old models that no longer work. Also necessary is the reformation of the relationship between government entities and community-based organizations.[55] For one thing, bureaucracy seems to get in the way of reinvention activities.

As for reinvention in the public health arena, we have seen this happen since September 11, 2001, where the preparedness model has been superimposed on public health's core functions and essential public health services paradigm. This new orientation with many new community partners has led to the development of innovative programs capable of being funded. Funding itself is an issue that may motivate reinvention efforts. The decrease in money available for local public health agencies for nonpreparedness activities means that the agencies have to become more efficient. Public health agencies also seem to be struggling with their identity. The general public and many public health professionals think that public health programs are only for the poor, and traditional public health activities are being taken over by the private managed care sector or community health center sector.

Other traditional public health activities are being transferred to other types of agencies. For example, most maternal and child health programs in Indiana have been outsourced through grants and contracts to local hospitals and agencies and out of local health departments. Despite these types of happenings, public health leaders seem reticent to lobby for the public health agenda.

Public health leaders must act as advocates for public health in the debate over the appropriate roles for government agencies. They have the responsibility to ensure that public health is practiced in schools, managed care organizations, community health centers, and other venues in the public and private sectors. The real goal of public health reinvention should be to create in each community an integrated healthcare system that increases access to health-related services so that no one is prevented from getting needed services.

Leadership Tip

Live your values.

According to Bacon, reinvention of government should encompass capacity building, workforce training, performance monitoring, and public and private collaboration.[56] **Table 20-6** contains lists of recommended ingredients for reinvented government culled from three sources (the fourth list is a synthesis of the other three lists).

During the early 1990s, Vice President Gore headed a national performance review whose mission was to find out how to make government agencies more effective and less expensive. Every office and agency of the federal government was examined. **Table 20-7** presents the principles that guided the review.[57] The goals were to cut spending while serving customers better and empowering employees and communities. The means to achieve these goals, listed in the second part of the table, included creating a clear sense of mission, delegating authority and responsibility, replacing regulations with incentives, and fostering competition. Although performance reviews still occur, they have played a much more minor role in recent years.

Local public health departments, too, need to be creative in their utilization of resources. For example, some local agencies, required to perform state nursing home inspections, have been burdened with additional responsibilities. A reinvention process could address the drain on resources caused by inspections through innovative techniques and collaboration among agencies.

TABLE 20-6 Recommended Ingredients for More Effective and Efficient Government

Osborne/Gaebler	NCSLPS	Thompson	Synthesis
Catalytic	Strong executive leadership	Leadership	Capacity building
Community owned	Lean, responsive	Productive workforce	High performance
Competitive	High-performance workforce	Information management	Leadership
Mission driven	Citizen involvement	Public/private networks	Public/private cooperation
Results oriented	Fiscal stability	Fiscal reform	Fiscal stability
Enterprising			
Anticipatory			
Decentralized			
Market oriented			

Source: Data from D. Osborne and T. Gaebler, *Reinventing Government* (Reading, MA: Addison-Wesley, 1992); The National Commission on the State and Local Public Service, *Hard Truths/Tough Choices* (Albany, NY: Nelson A. Rockefeller Institute of Government, 1993); and F. J. Thompson, ed., *Revitalizing State and Local Public Service* (San Francisco: Jossey-Bass, 1993).

TABLE 20-7 Principles of the National Performance Review

We will invent a government that puts people first, by:
- Cutting unnecessary spending.
- Serving its customers.
- Empowering its employees.
- Helping communities solve their own problems.
- Fostering excellence.

Here's how. We will:
- Create a clear sense of mission.
- Steer more, row less.
- Delegate authority and responsibility.
- Replace regulations with incentives.
- Develop budgets based on outcomes.
- Expose federal operations to competition.
- Search for market, not administrative, solutions.
- Measure our success by customer satisfaction.

Source: Reprinted from A. Gore, *The Report of the National Performance Review*, 1993, Government Printing Office.

TABLE 20-8 The Five C's: Changing Government's DNA

Lever	Strategy	Approaches
Purpose	Core strategy	Clarity of purpose
		Clarity of role
		Clarity of direction
Incentives	Consequences strategy	Managed competition
		Enterprise management
		Performance management
Accountability	Customer strategy	Customer choice
		Competitive choice
		Customer quality assurance
Power	Control strategy	Organizational empowerment
		Employee empowerment
		Community empowerment
Culture	Culture strategy	Breaking habits
		Touching hearts
		Winning minds

Source: Reprinted with permission from *Banishing Bureaucracy: The Five Strategies for Reinventing Government* by David Osborne and Peter Plastrik.

Reinvention should not be confused with internal reform or downsizing.[58] Its goal is change in the social and organizational fabric of a community, and its methods are entrepreneurial and self-renewing. Osborne and Plastrik likened the changes brought about by reinvention to changes in the DNA of government. They suggested there were five key strategies to reinventing government, the five C's, as they called them: the core strategy, the consequences strategy, the customer strategy, the control strategy, and the culture strategy (**Table 20-8**).[59] Note that a cookbook approach to reinvention is not really possible because each community and each government agency is different.

It is increasingly clear that traditional concepts of community are no longer relevant. As a consequence, community must be reinvented. In any actual community, community values must be clarified and redefined, key community stakeholders must be identified and empowered, and social structures and organizations that are consistent with the new values must be put into place. Once a community knows its values and its assets, it can tackle its problems, and thus a community assessment directed toward documenting community assets is another essential element of the reinvention process.

Public health agencies are not the only organizations that will address the public health needs of the community. Community reinvention should include creation of a partnership among all health care and public health stakeholders—a partnership in which all players are equal. In addition, the partners must work with other community stakeholders to ensure that public health needs are met. Thus, reinvention demands strategy and communication at many levels if it is to work.

Reinvention calls for new concepts of leadership. First, leadership must be shared among members of community teams. Second, community stakeholders must be empowered. With empowerment, people become free to influence their own future. Yet for empowerment to occur, people need to be informed about their options and be provided with the skills needed to exercise these options. In particular, community stakeholders need to be educated about public health and have their leadership skills developed through continuous learning opportunities.

There is more to reinventing community and government than meets the eye. Reinvention provides an opportunity to make constructive changes. The danger is that it can be used to justify funding cuts and downsizing rather than as a means of strengthening the community and the public health system. Strategic planning and CQI methods can be combined with reinvention techniques as a way of improving the reinvention process and increasing the chance of success. In a sense, reinvention is a form of strategy, because it involves major medium- and long-term changes in the structure of the community for the improvement of community life.

Public health leaders must:

- be prepared to move from a traditional hierarchical organizational structure to an entrepreneurial one (which may still be hierarchical in form)

- use public funds and grants in new ways that increase productivity and efficiency
- create coalitions that support change
- understand the realities of the information age and how they can affect organizational change
- utilize reinvention techniques not only for organizational change but for system change as well
- see reinvention as necessary at the local, state, and federal levels
- empower staff and community partners to share leadership and responsibility for changes that occur
- practice the five C's strategy

PUBLIC-PRIVATE PARTNERSHIPS

A public health agency, although it must lead the way, cannot carry out all the public health activities needed to protect and improve the health of a community. Consequently, it must foster new types of alliances and partnerships, including joint ventures, research sharing, community-based projects and programs, and semi-structured alliances.[60] For example, a local public health agency might contract with a local federally qualified health center to provide childhood immunizations at a price that the local health department cannot match—an interesting example of what the business community calls outsourcing.

Because trust is a critical component of any partnership, the public health agency must know both its agenda and the agendas of its partners, whether from the public or private sector. Possible partners include businesses, hospitals and managed care organizations, community health centers, private healthcare providers, local community organizations, local community clubs, churches and synagogues, schools, and police and firefighter groups, among others.

A local health leader told the author that a good way to involve the private sector in public health is for public health leaders to become involved in local organizations, such as the Kiwanis or the local chamber of commerce, which will create opportunities for them to network with other leaders on community issues. Public health leaders need to become known in the community if they are to gain credibility. Their goal should be to create an integrated system of care that will provide every resident of the community with the care they need and at the same time promote a healthy lifestyle among the residents in order to prevent disease.

Public health leaders must:

- develop public and private relationships to improve the local community public health system
- share power and responsibility with other community members who have an interest in improving the community's health
- become involved in the activities of the community
- join local community groups and organizations
- act to gain the trust of the community

overlap, public health leaders can create a customized planning methodology that includes pieces from all of them.

Public and private alliances and partnerships are needed at the planning stage as well as at the implementation stage. Developing and maintaining collaborative relationships require leadership skills, and public health leaders must master these skills and the planning skills necessary to formulate strategies for improving the community's health.

SUMMARY

The needs of the public are constantly changing, and public health agencies need to respond to the changes. The first step in responding adequately is to develop a plan of action, which is the subject of this chapter.

Leaders learn that creating a vision is not enough; the vision will remain just that without a strategy for making it a reality. Strategic planning, CQI, Six Sigma, reengineering, and reinventing government are all useful, individually or jointly, for turning a vision into programs and services. For example, the tools of CQI can be used to monitor the strategic planning process, and the CQI goal of improved customer service could be a guiding principle. Also, because the methods

DISCUSSION QUESTIONS

1. What is strategic planning?
2. What is the relationship between strategies and tactics?
3. What is the relationship between strategies and goals?
4. What roles do an organization's mission and vision play in strategic planning?
5. What are the five pillars of TQM?
6. What is Six Sigma, and can it be utilized in public health?
7. What steps are necessary for implementing a CQI process in a local health agency?
8. What are some of the tools used in TQM?
9. What distinguishes reengineering from other forms of organizational reform?
10. What are the principles of reinventing government?
11. What are some ways to open the door to public–private partnerships?

EXERCISE 20-1:   Training Course Development

Purpose: to use strategic thinking in developing a community education program and in creating an environment conducive to putting together a public health coalition

Key concepts: coalition building, community education plan, empowerment, leadership style, strategic thinking

Procedure: As a homework assignment, each student is given the task of devising a 10-step plan for implementing a community education program. The student is to imagine that he or she has been hired as a consultant by the Burchfield County Health Department. The health department has struggled unsuccessfully to create a coalition to promote public health in the county, which has few residents but many health-related problems. The head of the department, Dr. Hanson, has hired the consultant to devise a 10-step plan for implementing a program intended to educate the public on the advantages of community coalitions and empowerment.

All the students bring in the homework assignment on a designated day. The class is divided into groups of 8 to 10 members. One group member is assigned the role of the consultant; another, the role of Dr. Hanson, director of the county health department; a third, the role of Professor Alexander, a faculty member at the local university who has applied for a grant to train county residents in the techniques of empowerment; and a fourth, the role of Dr. Cassidy, prospective head of a wellness institute with a strong community education component that Western Health Alliance, an HMO servicing the county, plans to locate in the county. Dr. Hanson invites the consultant, Professor Alexander, and Dr. Cassidy to a 30-minute staff meeting to present and defend the community education plan the consultant has developed. The students playing Dr. Hanson, Professor Alexander, and Dr. Cassidy, because they have all created their own 10-step plans, should be able to offer insightful criticisms of the consultant's plan or make helpful recommendations to improve it. Following the review of the plan, the group should discuss strategic thinking and its role in devising the plan.

EXERCISE 20-2: Planning Tools in Action

Purpose: to explore ways to combine strategic planning tools and continuous quality improvement tools

Key concepts: activity network diagram, affinity diagram, continuous quality improvement, interrelationship diagraph, matrix diagram, prioritization matrix, process decision, progress chart, strategic planning, tree diagram

Procedure: Each team should reexamine the community education plan developed in Exercise 20-1, identifying areas where one or more of the seven planning tools discussed in this chapter could be used to enhance the plan and its acceptance by the community. Discuss the relative advantages and disadvantages of using each planning tool in the creation of the plan. After 30 minutes of discussion, each team should reach consensus on the specific tools to be used in improving the plan and on how these tools are to be applied. A representative from each team should present the rationale and conclusions reached to the full class.

EXERCISE 20-3: The Fan (Systems Quality Improvement)

Purpose: to determine the causes or factors affecting quality improvement at the community level (systems level). This exercise does not specifically address quality improvement strategies as much as the underlying issues related to community patterns and systems issues that will eventually lead to the quality improvement strategies.

Key Concepts: quality improvement, community, systems-level thinking, fan, matrix

Procedure: Divide the training group into groups of five to eight people. Each group draws a wedge-shaped fan with five ribs to start with on a piece of newsprint. Your community is struggling with a influenza pandemic like H1N1. In each fan rib, write a cause or factor necessary for determining whether your community is addressing the critical areas necessary for addressing the problem. Add fan ribs if more factors are involved. Determine how the fan helps measure performance, determines major factors or causes of a challenge, clarifies the interrelationships of causes relative to a specific community context, and begins a process of quality improvement. Draw a matrix with the causes or factors along both axes. Check the boxes that clearly demonstrate a relationship between factors. Discuss the importance of the fan material between the ribs that demonstrates how the rib factors (the data) are interconnected. Discuss how these data increase the understanding of how the community context affects the interrelationships. Debrief the exercise with the entire training group. Discuss the different fans and matrices developed by different groups.

REFERENCES

1. B. J. Turnock, *Public Health: What It Is and How It Works*, 5th ed. (Sudbury, MA: Jones & Bartlett, 2012).
2. B. C. Crosby and J. M. Bryson, *Leadership for the Common Good* (San Francisco: Jossey-Bass, 2005).
3. G. Pickett and J. J. Hanlon, *Public Health: Administration and Practice*, 9th ed. (St. Louis: Times Mirror and Mosby College Publishing, 1990).
4. J. E. Rohrer, *Planning for Community-Oriented Health Systems* (Washington, DC: American Public Health Association, 1996).
5. Rohrer, *Planning for Community-Oriented Health Systems*.
6. Rohrer, *Planning for Community-Oriented Health Systems*.
7. A. Ross, *Cornerstones of Leadership for Health Services Executives* (Ann Arbor, MI: American College of Healthcare Executives, 1992).
8. J. M. Bryson, *Strategic Planning for Public and Nonprofit Organizations*, 3rd ed. (San Francisco: Jossey-Bass, 2004).
9. L. Goodstein et al., *Applied Strategic Planning: A Comprehensive Guide* (New York: McGraw-Hill, 1993).
10. P. R. Scholtes, *The Leader's Handbook* (New York: McGraw-Hill, 1998).
11. Bryson, *Strategic Planning for Public and Nonprofit Organizations*.
12. Bryson, *Strategic Planning for Public and Nonprofit Organizations*.
13. Goodstein et al., *Applied Strategic Planning*.
14. H. Mintzberg, *The Rise and Fall of Strategic Planning* (Englewood Cliffs, NJ: Pearson, 2000).
15. Bryson, *Strategic Planning for Public and Nonprofit Organizations*.
16. Goodstein et al., *Applied Strategic Planning*.
17. C. A. Montgomery, "Putting Leadership Back into Strategy," *Harvard Business Review* 86, no. 1 (2008): 54–60.
18. E. A. Scutchfield et al., "The Presence of Total Quality Management and Continuous Quality Improvement Processes in California Public Health Clinics," *Journal of Public Health Management and Practice* 3, no. 3 (1997): 57–60.
19. Scutchfield et al., "The Presence of Total Quality Management and Continuous Quality Improvement Processes in California Public Health Clinics."

20. G. P. Mays et al., "CQI in Public Health Organizations," in *Continuous Quality Improvement in Health Care*, 2nd ed., ed. C. P. McLaughlin and A. D. Kaluzny (Gaithersburg, MD: Aspen Publishers, 1999).

21. C. P. McLaughlin and A. D. Kaluzny, "Defining Quality Improvement: Past, Present, and Future," in *Continuous Quality Improvement in Health Care*, 2nd ed., ed. C. P. McLaughlin and A. D. Kaluzny (Gaithersburg, MD: Aspen Publishers, 1999).

22. H. V. Roberts and B. F. Sergesketter, *Quality Is Personal* (New York: Free Press, 1993).

23. McLaughlin and Kaluzny, "Defining Quality Improvement."

24. A. V. Feigenbaum, *Total Quality Control* (New York: McGraw-Hill, 1961).

25. M. Sashkin and K. J. Kiser, *Putting Total Quality Management to Work* (San Francisco: Berrett-Koehler, 1993).

26. W. A. Shewhart, *Statistical Method from the Viewpoint of Quality Control* (Mineola, NY: Dover, 1986).

27. W. E. Deming, *Out of the Crisis* (Cambridge, MA: Massachusetts Institute of Technology, 1986).

28. M. Walton, *Deming Management at Work* (New York: Pedigree Books, 1991).

29. P. B. Crosby, *Quality Without Tears* (New York: Penguin Plume, 1984).

30. P. B. Crosby, *Completeness* (New York: Penguin Dutton, 1992).

31. P. B. Crosby, *Quality Is Free* (New York: McGraw-Hill, 1989).

32. P. B. Crosby, *Let's Talk Quality* (New York: Penguin Plume, 1990).

33. J. M. Juran, *Juran on Leadership for Quality: An Executive Handbook* (New York: The Free Press, 2003).

34. Feigenbaum, *Total Quality Control*.

35. B. Creech, *The Five Pillars of TQM* (New York: Truman Talley Books and Dutton, 1994).

36. Sashkin and Kiser, *Putting Total Quality Management to Work*.

37. M. Brassard, D. Ritter, F. Oddo, and J. MacCausland, *The Memory Jogger II* (Methuen, MA: Goal and QPC, 2010).

38. M. Brassard, *The Memory Jogger Plus* (Methuen, MA: Goal and QPC, 1996).

39. M. D. Nichols and R. D. Collins, "Six Sigma," in *The Executive Guide to Improvement and Change*, ed. G. D. Beecroft, G. L. Duffy, and J. W. Moran (Milwaukee, WI: ASQ Quality Press, 2003).

40. P. S. Pandi, R. P. Neuman, and R. R. Cavanagh, *The Six Sigma Way: Team Fieldbook* (New York: McGraw Hill, 2002).

41. Nichols and Collins, "Six Sigma."

42. http://en.wikipedia.org/wiki/SixSigma

43. Nichols and Collins, "Six Sigma."

44. E. Jacquescoley, "Can Six Sigma Methods Meet the Demanding Rigors of Local Public Health Practice," *Helium*, http://www.helium.com/items/200858-six-sigma-methods-meet-public-health-practices.

45. R. L. Manganelli and M. M. Klein, *The Reengineering Handbook* (New York: AMACOM [American Management Association], 1994).

46. P. P. Drucker, "Really Reinventing Government," *Atlantic Monthly* 275, no. 2 (1995): 49–61.

47. S. P. Robbins and M. Coulter, Management, 11th ed. (Upper Saddle River, NJ: Prentice-Hall, 2011).

48. J. Champy, *Reengineering Management* (New York: Harper Business, 1995).

49. M. Hammer, *The Reengineering Revolution* (New York: HarperCollins, 1995).

50. D. K. Carr and H. J. Johansson, *Best Practices in Reengineering* (New York: McGraw-Hill, 1995).

51. Manganelli and Klein, *The Reengineering Handbook*.

52. D. Osborne and T. Gaebler, *Reinventing Government: How the Entrepreneurial Spirit Is Transforming the Public Sector* (Reading, MA: Addison-Wesley, 1992).

53. D. Osborne and P. Plastrik, *Banishing Bureaucracy* (Reading, MA: Addison-Wesley, 1997).

54. D. Osborne, "The State of the Revolution: An Interview," *Leader to Leader* 6 (1997): 43–49.

55. Osborne, "The State of the Revolution."

56. J. M. Bacon, "Reinventing Government for Public Health Improvement," *Leadership in Public Health* 3, no. 3 (1994): 1–5.

57. A. Gore, *The Report of the National Performance Review* (Washington, DC: Government Printing Office, 1993).

58. Osborne and Plastrik, *Banishing Bureaucracy*.

59. Osborne and Plastrik, *Banishing Bureaucracy*.

60. P. P. Drucker, *Managing in a Time of Great Change* (Boston: Harvard Business School Press, 2006).

CHAPTER 21

Leadership and Decision Making

Once a decision was made, I did not worry about it afterward.

—Harry S. Truman, *Memoirs*

Leading involves decision making, and decision making involves taking risks. Public health leaders often confront disagreement or discontent with their decisions. They need to be aware of this possibility and that leadership and risk go together.[1] Risk taking is a prerequisite for "challenging the process" and being innovative.[2] As part of the decision-making process, public health leaders need to evaluate the costs and benefits of their decisions—the expenditures necessary to carry out their decisions and the consequences, good and bad, for the functioning of the public health agency—and also consider the ethical implications of their decisions.

Public health leaders, like all decision makers, will make mistakes and will learn from their mistakes.[3] Taking risks, after all, means opening oneself to the possibility of making mistakes. One way public health leaders can reduce the burden of the bad consequences of their decisions is to develop power-sharing arrangements with community partners. If different partners take responsibility for different pieces of a project, for example, the costs associated with problems that occur (or even the failure of the project) will be borne by more than one entity.

Our mental models will create boundaries for the way we view situations. This "bounded awareness" means that leaders will ignore information that does not fit into their conceptual orientations.[4] Leaders will need to expand their views of the world in order to increase their decision choices and decision-making accuracy. It becomes critical that leaders increase their perceptions not only by looking for information as if they were outsiders. They also need to look for information that is contradictory. Using information of different kinds for decision making is also important. Finally, sharing information with others may expand the information available to guide decisions.

Decisions will come about through other skills as well. Consequently, leaders will need to develop, in addition to decision-making skills, conflict resolution skills and negotiation skills. Although problem solving requires specialized skills, decision making as discussed below is different and requires different skills. Problem solving involves the resolution of conflicts and negotiation activities. Decision making is the end of the problem-solving process. This chapter discusses what can be done when decision making gets complicated by conflict. As should be obvious in decision making by leaders and managers, conflict resolution, negotiation, and communication skills are absolutely essential to ensure that all voices are heard before a decision is made. A decision can also become a tipping point. Case Study 21-A demonstrates a complex combination of relationships at different levels of the public health system that relate to problem solving, communication, conflict, and decision making.

Case Study 21-A

Lumps in the System: A Mumps Outbreak Story

Diane Christen, Kelli Jones, Jan Klawitter, Debbie Konitzer, Jackie Ove, Kitty Rahl, and RoAnn Warden

Abstract

In December 2005, two college students in the Midwest were diagnosed with mumps—the first two cases in what would become the largest mumps outbreak in the United States since 1991. By October 2006, 45 states and the District of Columbia reported 5,783 cases of mumps, with 54% of cases classified as confirmed, 45% as probable, and 1% unknown (*MMWR Weekly*, Oct. 27, 2006 [55(42);1152–1153]).

The mumps virus spread from its epicenter in the Midwest state of Maize to surrounding states, including the state of Fromage, which had its first confirmed mumps case on March 20, 2006. By mid-May 2006, the Fromage State Health Laboratory (FSHL) would suspend its serological mumps testing because of concern about testing accuracy.

This factual and fictional case study examines the evolution of the mumps outbreak in the state of Fromage in the context of the core function of assessment and its essential public health services of "monitoring health status to identify community health problems" and "diagnosing and investigating health problems and health hazards in the community." The case study will focus primarily on the March–May 2006 period, which saw the highest level of mumps activity in Fromage. It will focus on how decisions made and information distributed at the state level both helped and hindered the ability of local health departments around the state of Fromage to serve their communities. And it will tell the story of what happens when a disease that's rarely seen shows up in a highly vaccinated population and needs to be diagnosed by a test that's rarely performed.

Case Study

Background

In December 2005, two students at Northeastern Maize State University went to the student health center complaining of fever, head and muscle aches, and general malaise. The chief physician at the health center also noticed that the students had swelling in their parotid salivary glands causing their cheeks to swell near their jawlines. The physician collected parotid duct swab samples from the students and sent the samples off to the Maize Public Health Laboratory for viral culture. Test results came back positive for mumps virus. Little did the physician know that an outbreak had begun.

Since 2001, the United States has averaged a reported 265 mumps cases a year (range: 231–293) (*MMWR Dispatch*, March 30, 2006 [55(13);366–368]). College campuses are a perfect breeding ground for viruses such as mumps, which are easily spread, by respiratory and oral secretions, due to the communal living, dining, studying, and recreational areas. As college students mix with community members, travel home, visit friends at other schools, and so on, the virus can spread far beyond the site of the original infection.

The vaccination requirements of colleges and universities vary. One dose of the MMR (measles-mumps-rubella) vaccine can prevent approximately 80% of mumps cases, while two doses can prevent about 90% of cases (CDC National Immunization Program Mumps website: http://www.cdc.gov/vaccines/vpd-vac/mumps/default.htm). So even if a school requires two doses of the MMR vaccine, the virus can still occur and spread—just not as widely. This is true in the general population as well. It's also speculated that the vaccine might be less effective in preventing asymptomatic infection than the classic parotitis mumps. Persons with asymptomatic mumps are capable of spreading the infection to others (*MMWR Dispatch*, May 18, 2006 [55(Dispatch);1–5]).

Adding to the difficulty of tracking and containing mumps outbreaks is the fact that the disease is so rarely seen. Many physicians, nurses, and public health professionals have never seen a case of mumps and might dismiss the diagnosis in a vaccinated person. Also, up to 30% of persons infected with mumps never show signs of parotitis and can have nonspecific symptoms similar to those of many other respiratory infections. Laboratory serological testing for a disease in a highly vaccinated population like the United States is also problematic. A vaccinated person may not produce antibodies that indicate a recent mumps infection even though he or she has the disease. Hence, serological mumps testing cannot be used to rule out a case of mumps. It's clear that the health care and public health sectors have their work cut out for them.

The Outbreak in Fromage

Although the mumps outbreak was beginning to ramp up in Maize, it didn't really hit Fromage until March 2006. Staff at local health departments had been following the outbreak in Maize via the news media. Some sent alerts to their local healthcare providers offering information on mumps from the Maize State Health Department website. On March 20, 2006, the FSHL would report the first positive test result for mumps.

In early April 2006, the Fromage State Health Department (which is separate from the FSHL) sent local health departments a mumps frequently asked questions (FAQ) sheet along with information on collecting patient blood for IgM serologic testing at the FSHL. Wanting to err on the side of not missing cases and realizing that only 30% of mumps cases actually have the characteristic swelling, the Fromage State Health Department defined a suspect case as anyone with an upper respiratory infection. This meant that healthcare providers sent a large number of specimens to the FSHL for testing and many of these patients did not have mumps. This resulted in the probability of obtaining a "true" positive test result to be much less.

In late April, the State Health Department issued a news release about the mumps situation in Fromage and recommended vaccinations for those unvaccinated for mumps. In early May, the State Health Department updated the FAQ and continued to post to its website information related to Fromage's outbreak with national recommendations.

It became clear that there were four major issue areas in the Fromage mumps outbreak: laboratory testing, schools/daycare centers, physicians/infection control practitioners, and the media.

Laboratory Testing

Just as mumps is a disease rarely seen by healthcare providers, the mumps IgM test is rarely performed by laboratories. Also, there is no standard mumps serological test that has been well validated, so different state laboratories use different test kits. The National Public Health Laboratory performs a test created in-house by its scientists. This lack of test uniformity and validation, combined with the lack of baseline data on the true prevalence of mumps in the population because it is so rarely seen, makes it difficult to track outbreaks and determine true case numbers.

FSHL began receiving specimens for mumps testing in March 2006, with its first positive mumps result on March 20, 2006. The initial testing algorithm called for healthcare providers to submit urine specimens and buccal (inside cheek) swabs for culture testing. Although culture is the gold standard for mumps testing, its diagnostic sensitivity is only 30%.

For this reason, healthcare providers were encouraged to also submit blood serum specimens for IgM and IgG testing. In mid-April 2006, FSHL brought online a DNA-based real-time PCR (polymerase chain reaction) test for mumps. This molecular test provides results in hours rather than days. PCR testing is more sensitive than either culture or IgM testing. The downside is that it's a more expensive test to perform. However, the rapid results and increased sensitivity allow for better control and management of outbreaks.

Many healthcare providers submitted specimens for culture/PCR and IgM testing for each patient. In the first week of May 2006, Fromage State Lab scientists noticed a worrisome trend in the test data. Of specimens from patients submitted, only three patients were positive for mumps by culture/PCR testing, but 177 patients were positive by IgM testing. Because the culture/PCR testing combination should be detecting more than 30% of infected individuals, the scientists were worried that more people were being called "positive" for mumps than actually were. They asked the Fromage State Health Department to correlate the IgM results with patients' clinical data received from the patients' physicians. The positive IgM test results and the clinical data *appeared* to correlate based on the information the State Health Department was receiving. However, FSHL scientists still had their suspicions.

Also during the first week of May, the FSHL received calls from a few physicians suggesting there might have been false positive IgM test results reported for their elderly patients because the patients had no symptoms of and no exposure to mumps.

FSHL began an investigation. Scientists tested 30 serum specimens collected during the summer of 2005 (when no mumps was present in Fromage) from patients suspected of having a mosquito-borne virus. Nineteen of the 30 specimens tested positive for mumps by IgM testing. It was clear—the IgM test could not be trusted. The FSHL also contacted the National Public Health Laboratory to alert them to the issue and ask for assistance in the investigation.

The FSHL consulted with the State Health Department, and scientific leaders at the two agencies agreed that the State Lab should suspend its IgM serology testing due to a concern about false positive test results. The State Health Department sent a memo to all local health officers and infection-control practitioners explaining that the Fromage State Lab was suspending IgM serology testing for mumps, but that patient specimens should still be submitted for PCR and culture testing, which are reliable test methods. The State Lab also sent the memo to all hospital and clinic laboratories in the state. The memo was also posted on Fromage's password-protected Health Alert website.

In their conversations with mumps experts at the National Public Health Laboratory, scientists from the Fromage State Lab were told that the National Lab was hearing from other state labs that they were also seeing false positive tests results from their IgM testing (although no state other than Fromage had suspended this form of testing yet). After deciding to suspend the IgM testing, FSHL sent a number of its IgM-positive mumps specimens to the National Lab for further testing. The National Lab found that less than half of the Fromage specimens were positive for mumps by the National Lab's in-house test method. The National Lab was also conducting follow-up testing on specimens from other states that had expressed concerns about false positive test results. The National Lab verbally acknowledged that there were discrepancies between the number of positive test results derived from those states' test methods and the National Lab's method. The problem in Fromage was being experienced in other states, too.

Schools/Daycare Centers

With the first positively diagnosed case of mumps in Fromage, the local public health departments responded by assessing the at-risk populations of daycare and school attendees and staff. The impact that this vaccine-preventable disease could have on a daycare or school is great given the incubation period, the communicability of the disease, and the fact that 30% of the population can be infected and be asymptomatic. Thus, not only were local health departments concerned with the vaccinated population, but of greater concern were those that had not been vaccinated at all or had not been adequately vaccinated, because isolation and quarantine could occur up to 25 days post exposure.

Public health nurses assessed vaccination records of daycare attendees and students of public and parochial schools. Staff at these facilities were asked to report history of disease or vaccination status also. In accordance with Fromage Administrative Code HFS 145, Control of Communicable Disease, a letter was drafted and sent home with attendees and staff of all daycares and schools explaining the disease, the incubation period, signs and symptoms, and especially the need for vaccination of susceptibles if the child or adult had been previously unvaccinated. This letter also explained the procedure for isolation and quarantine if persons not adequately protected were exposed to a suspect, probable, or confirmed case, and for close contacts to a case.

Local health department staff reinforced to key personnel, school attendance secretaries, school principals, and daycare directors the importance of reporting suspected or possible cases to the health department.

Physicians/Infection Control Practitioners

As medical and infection control practitioners became aware that mumps was in the neighboring state of Maize during March 2006, the assessment process began in the local communities. Individuals who were coming into the clinics and emergency departments with signs and symptoms of mumps were being tested for mumps with IgM and IgG serological tests and instructed by their healthcare providers to remain isolated. In addition, they were told that someone from their local health department would be contacting them with more information. Infection control practitioners (ICPs) and healthcare providers started collecting the necessary patient information for the mumps worksheet or communicable disease reporting form and then forwarded this information to the health departments. Local health departments proceeded to follow up on the suspect mumps cases reported.

As new information was coming from the Fromage State Health Department in late April and May 2006 regarding mumps testing recommendations, isolation/quarantine, and revaccinating, it was passed on to the local healthcare providers. Many ICPs and physicians were invited and tuned into the mumps teleconference updates put on by the Fromage State Health Department. Local health officers routinely forwarded to local healthcare providers and ICPs the e-mails and correspondence from the state health department and checked the Health Alert website for new information that covered the mumps outbreak. Physicians primarily wanted to know what tests they should run and where they should send the samples for the testing. ICPs relied on the state and local health departments to get this needed information out to their physicians and facilities.

ICPs and physicians were not as confident in their understanding of the state's and the National Public Health Department's recommendations on who should be vaccinated or revaccinated for healthcare workers and teachers. The recommendations from the national level were different from those of the Fromage State Health Department. In the past, ICPs could accept the employee's word if the individual knew whether he or she had ever had mumps. Now employees were being required to have lab work done to determine their immune status for mumps if they were not adequately immunized or if they were born before 1957.

On May 11, 2006, the Fromage State Health Department announced that the FSHL was suspending the IgM and IgG serology testing for mumps because of concern over testing accuracy. The announcement came with very clear and concise recommendations for healthcare providers and ICPs to follow.

Billing issues also arose in some areas because some insurance companies would not cover the cost of specimen collection for patients who were being screened for mumps. Patients were being billed for the uncovered charges even though the laboratory testing was being done on the recommendation of the State Health Department.

Media

Within five days of receiving the initial notice of the Maize outbreak, Clear Water County in west central Fromage received its first media inquiry about local mumps status and implications for the community. The health officer provided a television news interview on April 11, 2006, to report there had been no cases of mumps locally and to provide information about mumps disease, signs and symptoms, and vaccination as a preventive measure.

Nine days later, the Southern Big City Health Department recommended that all colleges and universities in the Southern Big City metro area set up special mumps vaccination clinics to update vaccinations for all college students. The action was reported in the *Southern Big City Gazette*. This was followed a day later by a Fromage State Health Department news release regarding the Midwest mumps outbreak.

In Clear Water County, these stories raised concerns among students at the University of Fromage–Clear Water campus. A campus newspaper reporter contacted the local health department for information. The health officer provided information about the disease, signs and symptoms, and the importance of updated vaccination and referred the reporter also to the director of the local student health services. The story headlines were "Mumps Mayhem in Midwest: Disease Is Making Appearances Even Among Vaccinated." The health officer and the student health services director coordinated media messages on an ongoing basis.

By May 5, 2006, Clear Water County received reports of two laboratory-confirmed cases of mumps in the county. The health officer provided interviews to television and newspaper reporters. The local newspaper's front-page headline that evening boldly stated, "Mumps Confirmed: Infectious Disease Spreads to Clear Water County." The media messages emphasized and accurately reported were that (1) the cases were not related and their sources of exposure were unknown; (2) the county health department was working closely with all healthcare providers; and (3) up-to-date immunization is an important protection.

On May 6, 2006, a campus newspaper reporter again approached the health department for information for a follow-up story to educate concerned students. The published article was titled "Experts Say Mumps No Reason for Alarm: Viral Disease Reaches Area for First Time Since '90s." The article identified the emergence of mumps as a concern but not a reason for alarm. Key points included the importance of vaccination, respiratory hygiene, and seeking medical care if symptomatic.

Community and media interest subsided when case counts remained at two over a two-week period. No further cases were identified in Clear Water County. The local media did not pursue stories about suspension of mumps IgM testing.

Conclusions/Areas for Improvement

Based on the experiences related in this case study:

1. The identification and required reporting of communicable disease is a very effective assessment/ surveillance system when healthcare providers and ICPs are informed in a timely manner with up-to-date recommendations and guidelines from the health departments (state and local). In order for

(Continues)

public health professionals to do their job of assessment and "monitor health status to identify community health problems" and "diagnose and investigate health problems and health hazards in the community," it is critical that they have a good partnership/relationship with their clinics and ICPs. Having an established contact person, like an ICP, within the clinics and hospitals who can act as a conduit for the sharing of information back and forth was very effective during this mumps outbreak.

2. Local health departments need clarification for payer source for specimen collection if the testing is being done for screening/epidemiological purposes. Testing can be done at the State Laboratory fee-exempt, but who covers the costs of specimen collection? As noted in *Healthiest Fromage 2010*, one of the core principles and values that support the transformation of Fromage's public health system is "All Fromage residents deserve a basic level of health services. Improved individual and community health will happen when basic health services are affordable for all and access does not depend on race, cultural heritage, or geographic location."

3. The authority for the control of communicable disease comes from Fromage Administrative Code HFS 145, Control of Communicable Disease; however, there is confusion surrounding the health officer's ability to isolate and quarantine an unvaccinated or inadequately vaccinated individual. A clear answer as to the authority to follow through on that process was never established from the State Health Department and continues to be an unanswered question for local health officers.

4. Local health departments rely on the State Health Department to provide clear, consistent, and timely information about the situation. Delay on the part of the state can force local health departments to take independent action and release their messages and intervention recommendations before the state.

5. When it became clear that other states were also experiencing problems with their mumps IgM testing, federal-level leadership was needed to address the issue.

Source: Courtesy of the Mid-America Regional Public Health Leadership Institute.

DECISION MAKING

Any organization's vision and mission need to be tied to the real world.[5] A vision without substance is pointless. The challenge for the leaders of an organization is to figure out what strategies will be most effective in realizing its vision, make the hard decisions required to implement these strategies, and get others in the organization to accept the decisions and commit themselves to carrying out the strategies.[6] Decisions involve the making of choices from alternative possible solutions. Decision making is also about the taking of risks by the decision maker. Leaders need to be aware that a decision itself does not change an organization; rather, the actions resulting from the decision are what bring about change.[7]

Decision making is an essential outcome step in problem solving. Leaders need to address problems as they arise and modify operations in light of the factors introduced by the problems. One strategy is to appoint a task force to develop potential solutions to a problem and then decide what to do based on recommendations of the task force or the information provided by it. For example, a public health administrator in a suburb adjoining an urban neighborhood with a high crime rate might appoint a community task force consisting of professionals from the health department and the police department to determine how the community could prevent gang violence.

Problem solving can sometimes assume a cyclic form.[8] Suppose the leaders of an organization discover a serious problem that demands action. They determine the nature of the problem, come up with solutions, and begin to implement them. The problem, as it begins to be addressed, becomes less serious and of less concern to the leaders and others in the organization. One result might well be that the implementation of the solutions is not carried through to its conclusion, allowing the problem to intensify again and eventually causing the leaders to restart the problem-solving process. Organizations that concentrate on putting out fires do not advance much but instead struggle constantly with maintaining the status quo. **Figure 21-1** graphically shows this process.

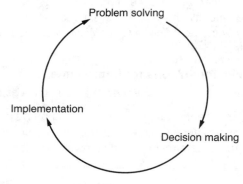

FIGURE 21-1 Decision-Making Cycle.

Leadership style, leadership practices, and governing paradigms affect the process of making decisions and the outcomes of the decisions. Also affecting the process and outcomes are the kind and quality of the information that is available. In particular, public health leaders depend on epidemiological assessment data, among other types of information, for making decisions about community health programs. The Cynefin framework addresses the important issue of context as a critical dimension of decisions.[9] Contexts can be simple, complicated, complex, or chaotic. Leaders need to learn to shift their decision-making strategies to address the public health context in which the decision needs to be made. **Table 21-1** presents a guide on these four contexts for leaders.

TABLE 21-1   Decisions in Multiple Contexts: A Leader's Guide

	The Context's Characteristics	The Leader's Job	Danger Signals	Response to Danger Signals
Simple	Repeating patterns and consistent events Clear cause-and-effect relationships evident to everyone; right answer exists Known knowns Fact-based management	Sense, categorize, respond Ensure that proper processes are in place Delegate Use best practices Communicate in clear, direct ways Understand that extensive interactive communication may not be necessary Sense, analyze, respond Create panels of experts Listen to conflicting advice	Complacency and comfort Desire to make complex problems simple Entrained thinking No challenge of received wisdom Overreliance on best practice if context shifts	Create communication channels to challenge orthodoxy Stay connected without micromanaging Don't assume things are simple Recognize both the value and the limitations of best practice
Complicated	Expert diagnosis required Cause-and-effect relationships discoverable but not immediately apparent to everyone; more than one right answer possible Known unknowns Fact-based management Flux and unpredictability No right answers; emergent instructive patterns Unknown unknowns Many competing ideas A need for creative and innovative approaches Pattern-based leadership	Probe, sense, respond Create environments and experiments that allow patterns to emerge Increase levels of interaction and communication Use methods that can help generate ideas: open up discussion (as through large group methods); set barriers; stimulate attractors; encourage dissent and diversity; and manage starting conditions and monitor for emergence Act, sense, respond Look for what works instead of seeking right answers Take immediate action to reestablish order (command and control) Provide clear, direct communication	Experts overconfident in their own solutions or in the efficacy of past solutions Analysis paralysis Expert panels Viewpoints of nonexperts excluded	Encourage external and internal stakeholders to challenge expert opinions to combat entrained thinking Use experiments and games to force people to think outside the familiar

(Continues)

TABLE 21-1   Decisions in Multiple Contexts: A Leader's Guide (*Continued*)

	The Context's Characteristics	The Leader's Job	Danger Signals	Response to Danger Signals
Complex	High turbulence No clear cause-and-effect relationships, so no point in looking for right answers Unknowables Many decisions to make and no time to think High tension Pattern-based leadership		Temptation to fall back into habitual, command-and-control mode Temptation to look for facts rather than allowing patterns to emerge Desire for accelerated resolution of problems or exploitation of opportunities	Be patient and allow time for reflection Use approaches that encourage interaction so patterns can emerge
Chaotic			Applying a command-and-control approach longer than needed "Cult of the leader" Missed opportunity for innovation Chaos unabated	Set up mechanisms (such as parallel teams) to take advantage of opportunities afforded by a chaotic environment Encourage advisers to challenge your point of view once the crisis has abated Work to shift the context from chaotic to complex

Source: Reproduced from D. J. Snowden and M. E. Boone, "A Leader's Framework for Decision Making," *Harvard Business Review* 85, no. 11 (2007): 68–76.

Decision-Making Roles and Styles

Mintzberg identified four decisional roles that leaders assume.[10] First, leaders take on an entrepreneurial role when making decisions that expand the parameters of the organization. As pointed out previously, leaders of public health agencies need to look for resources from the private and public sectors if they want to fulfill the overall public health mission—improving health and preventing disease.[11] Approaching businesses for funds to support public health programs is a form of entrepreneurism. Second, leaders are occasionally confronted with work disturbances that require administrative decisions for their resolution.[12] Third, leaders must act as resource allocators and determine where the limited human and financial resources of the agency could best be applied to implement or operate agency programs. Finally, leaders must occasionally act as negotiators.

There are three conditions that affect the decision-making style of a leader.[13] If all the potential outcomes are known, this brings some evidence of certainty and accuracy to the decision. Fear of risk is one of the main barriers to the making of rational decisions. Effective leaders constantly take risks and do not avoid them. A strategy of incremental change will weaken an organization if substantial reforms are necessary. By giving in to caution, leaders pass up the chance of being creative. Such leaders also tend to ignore negative feedback, which can lead to disaster. The third condition is one of almost complete uncertainty and the possibility that the decision will not be applicable. These conditions will clearly affect the decision and be affected by the decision style of the leader.

In contrast to Mintzberg, Robbins and Coulter have a four-category model for decision styles.[14] Decision making can be rational or intuitive, and it can also exhibit a high or low degree of tolerance for ambiguity.[15,16] As shown in **Figure 21-2**, an analytical style of decision making is rational and exhibits a high degree of tolerance for ambiguity. Analytical decision makers base their decisions on information. A directive style is characterized by a high degree of rationality but a low degree of tolerance for ambiguity. Directive decision makers are logical and tend to make decisions quickly and for the short term. Directive decision making is a style favored by managers. Conceptual decision making is intuitive and exhibits a low degree of tolerance for ambiguity. Conceptual decision makers tend to concentrate on the future and its possibilities, and they also tend to be creative. The behavioral style of decision making is intuitive and shows a low degree of tolerance for ambiguity. Decision makers who use this style concentrate on people relationships and tend to accept information from other staff before making a decision. Exercise 21-1 will give you a chance to test the two decision-making style models as they relate to you and others.

Decisions require implementation, and the implementation process is often complex and hard to complete.[17] Leaders must determine the sequence of implementation steps and the interactions that are likely to occur at each step. Furthermore, they must understand that the implementation proc more ess has important decision points—places where critical decisions must be made. At these decision points, the leaders review the implementation process in order to determine if modifications are necessary and if the objectives of the implementation are being achieved.

Shared Decision Making

Decision making may be a shared activity. Much public health work occurs in teams, coalitions, and other groups, and if power is shared, decision making would likely be shared as well. There are at least four advantages to shared decision making.[18] First, each party brings to the group new information, a diversity of experience, different professional credentials, and a different perspective. Second, a group is likely to come up with more options than an individual. Third, there is likely to be more acceptance of a decision if more people are involved in making the decision. A group-made decision is a decision with a ready-made consensus. Finally, the involvement of others increases the legitimacy of the decision.

There are also four disadvantages to shared decision making, whether in a team, coalition, or other group.[19] First, the process can consume a great amount of time. In decision making, reaching a quick decision is often critical, and delays can prevent a solution from being fully effective. Second, a strong minority will sometimes try to dominate the whole process—and will sometimes succeed. Third, the appearance of agreement or consensus may disguise the fact that there really is no agreement. Finally, shared decision making and the shared sense of responsibility that goes with it can lead to a situation where no one feels responsible for negative outcomes related to the decisions.

Decision-Making Models

Table 21-2 presents an outline of three decision-making models. As can be seen, the basic decision-making process is similar in all three. Each model starts with a problem, utilizes information to evaluate the problem, and eventually leads to a decision.

In the first model, designed by Liebler and McConnell, the first step is to set an agenda, which includes recognizing that a problem or challenge to the status quo has arisen and collecting information to validate the problem or challenge.[20] Searching for alternative solutions is the second step. The leaders need to be objective and to listen to possible scenarios presented by their colleagues. The third step is the evaluation of the alternative solutions to determine which one is the most promising. The task in the fourth stage is to get a commitment to the chosen solution from participants in the decision-making process. The solution is then pilot tested, and if the results are positive,

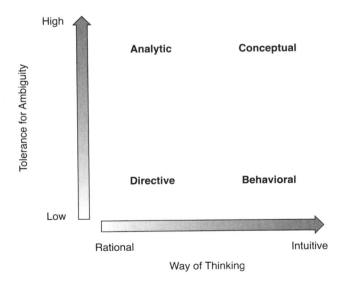

FIGURE 21-2 Decision-Making Styles by Ways of Thinking and Tolerance for Ambiguity. *Source*: Robbins, Stephen P., Decenzo, David A., Wolter, Robert, *Supervision Today!*, 6th Edition, © 2010. Printed and electronically reproduced by permission of Pearson Education, Inc., Upper Saddle River, New Jersey.

TABLE 21-2 Three Contrasting Approaches to Decision Making

Liebler and McConnell*	Robbins and Coulter†	Systems Approach
Build agenda	Identify problems	Set goals and objectives
Search for alternatives	Identify decision criteria	Engage in action planning
Evaluate alternatives	Allocate weights to criteria	Implement action plans
Commit to chosen alternatives	Develop alternatives	Evaluate implementation of plans
Continually assess decisions	Select alternative	
	Implement alternative	
	Evaluate effectiveness of implementation	

Source: *Data from J. G. Liebler and C. R. McConnell, *Management Principles for Health Professionals*, 4th ed., pp. 235–236. © 2004, Jones & Bartlett Publishers.

†S. P. Robbins and M. Coulter, *Management*, 8th ed. (New York: Prentice Hall, 2005).

the leaders devise an implementation plan. The final step involves assessing the results of the chosen solution during the implementation, including the results of decisions made as part of the implementation process.

The second model, designed by Robbins and Coulter, begins with roughly the same first step as the model described above—that is, problem identification.[21] The problem identified might be related to legal mandates, budget restrictions, lack of information, or lack of support from the local board or from community constituencies. The next two steps are to identify decision criteria and attach weights to them (so that relatively unimportant criteria do not influence the decision to the same degree as important criteria). Then alternative solutions are developed and analyzed. The best solution (or the one that seems the best) is chosen and implemented. Finally, as in the preceding model, the results of the implementation are evaluated.

In the third model, the first step is to identify goals and objectives based on the organization's mission and vision. The next step is to embark on the task of devis-

ing action plans to achieve the goals and objectives. The plans are then implemented and the implementation process is evaluated, as in the other two models. This model follows the Leadership Wheel paradigm.

To be effective decision makers, public health leaders must:

- learn that making decisions involves risk taking
- learn the differences between problem solving and decision making
- build decision-making strategies into implementation plans
- empower employees and community partners to take an active role in decision making
- identify their style of leadership and understand how to use it in decision making
- tie decisions to the goals and objectives of the organization

CONFLICT RESOLUTION

The Dangers of Conflict

Life and leadership are full of twists and turns, and there are always individuals who disagree with any position taken on an issue. This is partially explained by the multicultural nature of our society and partially by the wide spectrum of political positions held by policy makers.

Conflict over a decision needs to be resolved if the decision is to be effective. As pointed out above, decision making does not occur in a vacuum and is usually a group process. Even when conflict appears to be absent or to have been resolved, there is no guarantee of full acceptance of the solution.[22] Moreover, the main disagreement may be not over the solution, but over how to implement the solution.[23]

Conflict, although based in the facts of a given situation, is often partly the result of differences in ideology,[24] and there are typically mythologies that support the positions of the partners to a conflict. Ideology, information, and key players change over time, and thus the techniques needed to resolve conflicts also change.

Conflict is the reverse of cooperation.[25] When it permeates an entire organization, it needs to be addressed immediately. Conflict entails negativity and opposition to decisions.[26] In addition, people fear conflict and suffer stress as a result of it, another serious consequence of a situation in which conflict remains rampant.[27]

Yet life without conflict is not a possibility, especially in our complex society.[28,29] In fact, conflict has, if anything, become more prevalent in the 21st century. Therefore, leaders must learn how to handle conflict. Exercise 21-2 allows students to explore the meaning of conflict and to experience ways in which conflict may be resolved.

Conflict within an organization can have diverse causes, including the culture and atmosphere of the organization, its structure, the needs of the leadership and the organization, and the solutions to past conflict.[30] Major sources of conflict and obstacles to conflict resolution include the following:[31]

- Conflict arises when different leaders assert their authority and engage in a power struggle. In the U.S. Congress, power struggles are common causes of gridlock (the inability to pass major legislation).
- The assignment of the wrong people to a team or task force can lead to conflict. It is unfortunately common to see an executive appointed to a major task force either not attend most of the meetings or send as a proxy someone without the power to make decisions.
- Conflict will naturally arise in a meeting run by someone who lacks respect for the attendees, communicates poorly, or hides the reason for the meeting.

Having a clear mission and vision and basing the discussion of issues on these is essential for conflict avoidance. Conflict will inevitably occur in a team, for example, if the members are unclear as to the team's mission.

It is important not to spend time revisiting conflicts that have been resolved unless the solutions did not win real agreement. Some groups continually return to conflicts that have already been worked out, thereby wasting time and often generating frustration.

Conflict resolution by a group requires that the group be given full authority to resolve the conflict. If the group doesn't have adequate authority, it will spend fruitless hours discussing issues that are beyond its power to do anything about.

Conflicts use up much of the leader's time. For example, if a public health leader is spending 20% or more of the workday resolving conflicts, he or she should look at ways to reduce that amount. And time is not the only issue. As noted above, conflict creates stress, and the leader must not allow his or her personal health to be jeopardized as a result of managing conflict.

A third danger is the potential for sabotage by employees who have become disaffected because of the prevalence of conflict.[32] Conflict can also increase workplace violence. For example, if employees who are members of a union come in conflict with employees who are not members, the difference in perspective between these two groups could lead to a buildup of tension and eventually to actual violence.

Dealing with Conflict

A preliminary step in resolving conflict is to select an appropriate strategy or style. Which conflict resolution style is best will depend on the nature of the conflict and the situation in which the conflict occurs.[33] Rahim defined five styles that a leader might use to deal with conflict between him- or herself and other parties.[34] He arranged these styles based on the degree of concern for self and degree of concern for others exhibited by the leader. The integrating style, which involves collecting pertinent facts as part of the conflict resolution process, is oriented toward finding an innovative solution that satisfies both parties. The leader who uses this style exhibits a concern for both self and others.

An obliging style would be typical of a leader who showed great concern for others but little concern for self. The leader would tend to go along with whatever the other party to the conflict wanted, perhaps out of a worry that he or she lacked the expertise necessary to resolve the conflict in any other way. This style is diametrically opposite to the dominating style, in which the leader exhibits great concern for self but little for others. The leader acts in an authoritarian manner and basically lays down what the resolution is going to be.

One way to deal with conflict is to avoid it, and the avoiding style is often used by leaders who exhibit a low degree of concern for self and for others. The goal is to protect the status quo, and the conflict-avoiding leader stays in the background and lets others deal with the conflict and its ramifications.

The compromising style is the middle-of-the-road style, and the compromising leader shows average concern for self and others. Compromise involves reciprocity, which means that each party to the conflict gets something. This style is useful for resolving conflict between individuals engaged in a partnership, because the partners are treated as they expect to be—with equal respect. Collaboration is difficult, if not impossible, if conflict exists or is not resolved. The major advantage of resolving conflict is that each

Intergroup Styles	Intragroup Styles
1. Avoidance	1. Avoidance
2. Competition	2. Integrating
3. Accommodation	3. Obligation
4. Compromise	4. Compromise
5. Collaboration	5. Domination

FIGURE 21-3 Conflict Styles for Intergroup and Intragroup Relationships. *Source*: Adapted from A. Rahim, *Organizational Conflict Inventories*, Palo Alto, CA: Consulting Psychologists Press, 1983, and S. P. Robbins and M. Coulter, *Management* (10th ed.), Upper Saddle River, NJ: Pearson Educational, 2009, p. 243.

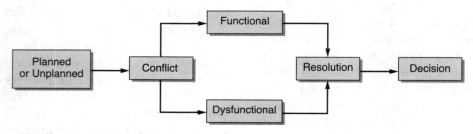

FIGURE 21-4 Elements of Resolution of Conflict.

party to the discussion has his or her position stated, and the resolution will often create the buy-in to the eventual decision. **Figure 21-3** looks at style from the perspective of intergroup and intragroup relationships.

Conflict may be planned or unplanned (**Figure 21-4**). Conflict stimulation is sometimes needed if change is to occur. It can be a method of ending gridlock and breaking through barriers protecting the status quo. Leaders need to know not only when to stimulate conflict for the good of the organization but also how to deal with it once it occurs.

Robbins and Coulter make a distinction between functional and dysfunctional conflicts.[35] Functional conflicts contribute to the attainment of goals and objectives, whereas dysfunctional conflicts hinder their achievement. The former, of course, are conflicts of the kind that leaders would want to stimulate if they were not occurring in the natural order of things.

The end result of all these activities is a regimen of activities that leads to the favorable or unfavorable resolution of the conflict. The resolution of the conflict is not sufficient. The leader still needs to make a decision and put the solution into action.

A Conflict Resolution Process

Weeks devised a process for dealing with conflict.[36] The steps are as follows:

1. Create an effective atmosphere.
2. Clarify perceptions.
3. Focus on individual and shared needs.
4. Build shared positive power.
5. Lead to the future, then learn from the past.
6. Generate options.
7. Develop doables.
8. Make mutually beneficial agreements.

There are at least two sides to every conflict. Each party enters the conflict situation with an agenda based on personal, organizational, or community concerns and values and possibly goals and objectives. Emotions get involved. Out of this mix, a consensus of some kind needs to be forged. To achieve a consensus, the leader needs to create an environment conducive to working on a resolution to the conflict (step 1 in the conflict resolution process outlined above). For instance, the leader must try to create the right atmosphere for meetings between the parties and make sure that the times and locations of meetings are agreeable to everyone. A neutral meeting place is often the best choice. The leader, in preparation for the first meeting, might develop several possible scenarios for starting the conflict resolution process. The choice of the right scenario might have to happen at a moment's notice.

People's perceptions are affected by many factors, including past experiences as well as present realities. In step 2, the leader needs to determine whether the conflict is tied to personal, organizational, community, or professional concerns. Is the conflict related to values or needs? Are goals and objectives driving the process? Finally, the leader must examine the components of the conflict and develop strategies based on his or her analysis.

In step 3, each party to the conflict identifies his or her personal needs. The leader then helps the parties to identify needs that they share. The process of looking at their needs often helps the parties to discover needs, values, and perceptions they unknowingly possess.

The goal in step 4 is to develop the power (means) to resolve the conflict and get the parties to share in this power. For power sharing to occur, the parties must come to share a clear mission and vision, be willing to settle for realistic goals and objectives, and view resolution of the conflict as in everyone's best interest.

Step 5 requires the leader to evaluate how past decisions influence the present conflict and prepare the way for a less conflictive future. The parties need to be careful not to let past experiences keep them from building a better future.

In step 6, the parties identify and explore options for resolving the conflict. These options can help the parties to see the issues more clearly and be less governed by previous perspectives. This step requires the parties to be creative and to use imaging techniques to examine the likely consequences of the various options. The use of the dialogue technique might be beneficial here. Dialogue allows each party to present his or her position and possible solutions to the conflict without interruption and comment. When the parties move into the discussion phase, the agenda of each party will be helpfully on the table.

Leadership Tip

Fit your personal talents, knowledge, and skills to the tasks to be accomplished.

In step 7, the parties need to develop a set of "doables," which are small actions that are easy to complete and which will improve the relationship between the parties.

As their relationship improves, they will be better able, in step 8, to agree on a final resolution to the conflict. This resolution, like the doables, must be realistic and mutually beneficial. Otherwise the process will fail.

Conflict resolution is best achieved through a fairly flexible series of activities that are modified to address the unique issues associated with the particular conflict. The model presented above allows flexibility in each of the eight steps so that the different perspectives of the parties can be accommodated. Guidelines for conflict resolution are listed below. To reduce the number and intensity of conflicts and resolve them when they occur, public health leaders must:

- utilize conflict resolution techniques to define disagreements between colleagues or external partners
- define whether a conflict enhances or hinders the ability of the organization to fulfill its mission, vision, goals, and objectives
- monitor power struggles between colleagues or external partners
- decrease (if possible) the percentage of time allocated to conflict resolution
- select the best method of conflict resolution to use based on their personal leadership styles and the core functions of public health
- implement a protocol that colleagues or partners agree upon in order to resolve conflicts
- put solutions to conflict into action as quickly as possible after a decision is made
- identify the mutual benefits to be obtained by conflict resolution

NEGOTIATION

Conflict can be resolved through coercion (the threat or exercise of physical force), adjudication (legal proceedings), mediation, arbitration, or negotiation.[37] Negotiation, the topic of this section, is also used in bargaining (e.g., when two parties are engaged in working out an exchange of goods and services) and in forming partnerships and other types of alliances.

In negotiation, two or more parties are involved in trying to reach an agreement (or resolve a conflict); each is represented by a negotiator, whose role is to help make the agreement satisfactory to all parties.

Mediation occurs when a neutral third party takes on the role of honest broker and tries to get the interested parties to reach an agreement. Both negotiation and mediation are covered in this section.

Every person is continually involved in informal negotiations throughout life.[38] Negotiation skills can be used to resolve personal, organizational, community, and professional issues and problems. Most people use what might be called soft negotiation techniques. In soft negotiation, each party wants a decision reached or a problem resolved with as little fuss as possible and without antagonizing the other parties. Hard negotiation is favored by those who love the challenge of the negotiation game and tend to shoot for more than they can easily get.

Principled negotiation occurs when the parties attempt to resolve a conflict based on merit rather than on their personal agendas.[39] In a sense, the relationship between the parties becomes more important than the conflict. In some cases, this type of negotiation is not applicable, because objective criteria needed to reach a "fair" or defensible resolution may be lacking. Each party simply possesses a given agenda, the agendas are inconsistent with each other, and there is no right or wrong conclusion to the process.

Table 21-3 lists 16 skills and abilities that a leader-negotiator (or leader-mediator) needs in order to be successful.[40] Negotiation skills are applicable to a range of types of negotiation, from union negotiations to bargaining over salary and position title to negotiations with the local health board regarding the distribution of funds for specific activities.

Negotiation is both an art and a science.[41] It is a science inasmuch as negotiation models exist that lay out procedures for reaching agreements and resolving conflicts. It is an art inasmuch as effective negotiations require flexibility and an intuitive ability to choose the appropriate skills and apply them expertly and at the right time.

Prenegotiation

Negotiators must deal with a number of issues before the actual negotiations begin.[42] First, they must determine how many individuals or group representatives will be involved in the process. The more might not be the merrier. They must also consider whether the organizations being represented are monolithic or made up of diverse components, each with its own perspective. In a complex, multiperspective

TABLE 21-3 Interpersonal Skills for the Negotiator

1. Being in control of oneself
2. The ability to elicit the needs, interests, and goals of those on whose behalf the negotiator is acting
3. The ability to properly counsel those persons regarding the realities of the situation
4. Obtaining clear authority from the appropriate decision maker
5. Understanding and being able to utilize the full range of effective strategies and tactics
6. Planning efficiently
7. Being credible
8. Perceptively analyzing the other party and its negotiator
9. Being able to tolerate conflict and ambiguity
10. Knowing or learning the relevant market factors
11. Disclosing information selectively and persuasively
12. Obtaining necessary information
13. Listening to and perceiving the real information being conveyed
14. Making changes in strategy and tactics or counseling those for whom the negotiator is acting regarding terms, as appropriate during the negotiation
15. Being both patient and tireless
16. Knowing when and how to either close the negotiation with an agreement or to terminate it because a desirable agreement cannot be reached

Source: Reprinted with permission from M. K. Schoenfield and R. M. Schoenfield, *The McGraw-Hill 36-Hour Negotiating Course*, p. 10, © 1991.

organization, an agreement reached through the efforts of a single representative might not be perceived as acceptable by certain components within the organization.

The negotiator for each organization should find out if the other organizations involved in the negotiations spend large amounts of time in bargaining situations. If they do, the process may become more important than the outcome, and the negotiator should be forewarned of this possibility.

Another issue is whether there is a connection between the outcome of the negotiations at hand and the outcomes of other negotiations. If there is, this will complicate the current negotiations. Other issues include whether an agreement must be reached, whether ratification is required, and whether agreement between the parties creates a binding contract. The negotiators need to know if there are any internal or external threats to the negotiation process. They also need to determine whether the negotiations are to be open or closed.

Negotiation Barriers

Negotiations, like any human activity, face many obstacles in the way of their completion.[43] First, the process might become more expensive, in time and money, than expected. Second, people are often resistant to change and will fight for maintenance of the status quo. Third, negotiators sometimes view the issues at stake in the negotiations as making up a "fixed pie" and assume that their role is to ensure that their slice is as big as or bigger than it was before. They seem not to realize that negotiations can result in a bigger piece of pie for everyone.

Another obstacle is that negotiators occasionally hold on to old opinions or keep bringing up issues that were settled early in the negotiations. In addition, they may present information to the other negotiators in a way that leads to the disintegration of the whole process. A sixth obstacle is that important information is sometimes unavailable, and an agreement reached on the basis of partial information may not be the best agreement for one or more of the parties.

There is also the "winner's curse."[44] The "winner" in a negotiation may wish that the process would continue and may be depressed about its closure. Furthermore, the negotiators must not allow overconfidence to thwart the process, nor should they make the mistake of treating disagreement among the parties as more important than the relationship that is being forged between them.[45]

Negotiation has unique characteristics that differentiate it from other types of conflict resolution. Two processes, with feedback loops connecting them, are going on at the same time: the planning process and the actual negotiations. Public health leaders in negotiations receive feedback from the community, they receive feedback from colleagues in the public health agency, and they and the other negotiating parties give and receive feedback from each other.

Getting to Yes

There are many approaches to prenegotiation and negotiation activities. We will look at two of them. First, Fisher and colleagues developed the "Getting to Yes" model.[46] This model, which is intended to be user friendly, allows great flexibility. The steps are as follows:

1. Determine interests.
2. Identify options.
3. Determine alternatives.
4. Review the legitimacy of the process.
5. Choose appropriate communication strategies.
6. Strengthen relationships.
7. Promote commitment.

The first step is to determine the interests of the parties to the negotiation. These interests are more important than the official position held by each party. The negotiators must try to clarify the issues involved. The second step is to identify options for resolving the conflict. The parties should be aware that they all could gain from the resolution of the conflict although no party is likely to get everything desired.[47] The third step is to determine alternatives. The fourth step is to review the legitimacy of the process. Because complete agreement between the parties is not likely to occur, they must accept the legitimacy of the process and its outcome. The fifth step is to choose an appropriate communication strategy. Two-way communication is essential if the negotiations are to proceed smoothly. For one thing, the reframing of issues may be a continuous activity. In step 6, the negotiators try to strengthen their relationship. It is important in this step to separate substance from relationship. The promotion of commitment to the agreed solution occurs in the final step. This commitment is critical to the success of the whole process.

The "Getting to Yes" model has been criticized as unrealistic.[48] Nonetheless, the model seems to work and has been used successfully in teacher–college administration contract negotiations. Public health leaders may find the model easier to use if the proper coalition development has occurred, because then the parties to the negotiations will have already established a working relationship.

The Schoenfield and Schoenfield Negotiation Model

Schoenfield and Schoenfield developed a 14-step model that incorporates major steps from other negotiation models.[49] The model comprises both prenegotiation and negotiation steps.

Prenegotiation:

1. gathering prenegotiation information
2. determining goals

3. identifying issues
4. analyzing the market
5. assessing strengths and weaknesses
6. estimating the other party's bottom line and opening position
7. considering win-win outcomes

Negotiation:

8. setting the opening position
9. setting the bottom line
10. choosing strategies and tactics
11. considering concessions and trade-offs
12. determining an agenda
13. analyzing timing
14. choosing the modes of communication

The first seven steps of this model overlap the steps of the "Getting to Yes" model, although the Schoenfield and Schoenfield model is more specific. Its higher degree of specificity can be both an advantage (because it provides detailed guidance) and a disadvantage (because it decreases flexibility and increases the burden placed on the negotiators). One of its faults is that it does not take into account the feedback loops that need to exist if the negotiations are to be as effective as possible and lead to agreements that the parties can commit to.

In the first step, each negotiator collects needed data. For public health issues, data from community assessments will have to be gathered. The parties should identify information gaps and make plans to search for the missing data or knowingly proceed with the negotiations under the current data limitations. (Note that public health negotiations often involve more than two parties,[50] but for ease of exposition this account of the model assumes there are just two parties.)

Step 2 involves setting goals for the planning process. These goals will include short- and long-term goals and also essential and merely desirable goals. The last task in this step is to prioritize the goals.

In step 3, the parties identify the issues that will be the focus of the negotiations and begin to discuss concessions and trade-offs.

The purpose of step 4 is to look at the market (or the community, in the case of public health) and identify the market factors that might influence the negotiations. Public health leaders, in their negotiations, must keep in mind that the public might have an agenda that diverges from the agenda of each negotiating party. They should also review the culture and norms of the specific population that will be directly affected by the

outcome of the negotiations. In general, they have an obligation to look after the needs of the community during the negotiation process.

In planning step 5, each party looks at its own strengths and weaknesses and, to the extent possible, those of the other party. The problem here is that each party assesses strengths and weaknesses based on its own worldview. During this step, each party also considers settlement alternatives and determines what, in its view, would be the "best alternative to a negotiated agreement" (BATNA).[51]

In step 6, each party estimates the other party's bottom line and likely opening position. This step aids in identifying areas of agreement as well as difference. The negotiators also need to determine if personal values could interfere with the process.

The final step in the prenegotiation phase is the consideration of win-win scenarios—outcomes that represent net gains for each of the negotiating parties. This step is essential, because win-win outcomes are the ones that both parties are liable to accept eventually. Each party should understand going into the negotiations that it is not going to get everything it wants but can get some of what it wants if it is willing to compromise and allow the other party to win something as well.

The eighth step is the opening step in the negotiations themselves. Here the parties put forth their opening positions. In the ninth step, each party sets the bottom line—the minimum it will accept. In other words, each party lets the other know what its particular BATNA is. The discussion in this step helps to determine if a negotiated agreement is possible or not.

At any stage in the negotiation process, one or both parties may return to an earlier step and redo it in the interests of arriving at a better outcome. For example, the negotiators may want to re-evaluate information collected earlier in order to determine whether their current bottom line is justified or needs to be revised.

Negotiation strategies and tactics are chosen in step 10. The negotiators might use the strategy of expressing up front their desire to achieve a win-win outcome, or they might take a no-concessions stance. Each strategy has several tactics associated with it. Examples of tactics include the setting of deadlines and methods for dealing with a deadlock.

In step 11, the negotiators consider concessions and possible trade-offs. Planned concessions and trade-offs are needed for a successful outcome.[52] Negotiations in which there are more than two parties provide extra opportunities for trade-offs, because deals can be struck between some of the parties but not all. During this step especially, the parties need to make an effort to act respectfully toward each other and build trust among themselves. The best strategy is to focus on the issues at the heart of the negotiations and not on the personalities of the people at the table.

Also, the beginning positions set forth by the negotiators need to be open to revision. If they are not, the result will be inaction and a breakdown in the negotiations. The best strategy is to focus on the interests that lie behind the stated positions rather than the positions themselves. In addition, the development of options should be separated from the decision making, and objective criteria should be used in the decision-making process, because they provide the parties with a template for action and make concessions and trade-offs easier to navigate.

Agenda setting occurs in step 12. The main task is to determine the actions that have to be completed, such as the identification of issues and the making of concessions. The parties need to agree on the agenda, and if they are unable to reach an agreement, they may have to return to an earlier step and work through the process again.

The agenda identifies the actions; the schedule, to be devised in step 13, lays down timeframes in which the actions are to occur. The task of creating a schedule is complicated by the fact that the parties to a negotiation often have hidden agendas (and even hidden deadlines) that only become apparent over time.

The model's final step is to choose the modes of communication that are most appropriate to the situation. Of course, resolution of the negotiation issues and obtainment of an agreement are yet to come, and they might be considered to compose the fifteenth step.

Negotiation Strategies

The two models of negotiation described above cover the major steps that parties to a negotiation need to go through. A separate issue is the strategies that are available for use during these steps. Following is a list of strategies that negotiators can use to reach an outcome satisfactory to them (strategies 1–9 are described in Fuller,[53] and 10–16 are described in Schoenfield and Schoenfield):[54]

1. win-win
2. stonewalling
3. good Samaritan
4. finessing the process
5. splitting the difference
6. nickel-and-dime tactics
7. controlling the action
8. ambiguity
9. defensive techniques
10. no concessions
11. deadlock-breaking techniques
12. high realistic expectations with small systematic concessions
13. concede first
14. problem solving
15. extraneous goals
16. closure strategies

Several of these strategies can undermine the negotiation process. Therefore, they must be used cautiously. Also, note that for every strategy, there is a counterstrategy.

As pointed out, each party to a negotiation wants to gain something as a result of the negotiation. A commitment to try to win and let the other party win too—the essence of a win-win strategy—increases the chances that the negotiation will continue until a final agreement is reached. A win-win strategy, although it seems to make good sense, is not always easy to follow, because negotiators tend to be protective of their interests and do not want to lose anything. For some negotiators, the goal is to prevent losses rather than accumulate gains, and this goal is usually inconsistent with a win-win strategy, because it is rare that both parties can win without cost.

Stonewalling is used to slow down the negotiation process. Some negotiators look for bargain solutions and practice stonewalling to wait for the bargains to appear. Negotiators need to learn how to break through stone walls and get the negotiation process moving again. One useful tactic is to set deadlines for decisions.

Some negotiators present themselves as good Samaritans and try to convince the other parties of their beneficent motives. This kind of behavior should send up a warning signal. Most "good Samaritan" negotiators are dishonest and their protestations of good intentions are a sham. To counteract this strategy, the other parties need to refocus on the facts and get away from considering motives.

A good example of finessing the process is to engage in a form of brinkmanship and confront the other parties with a stark choice: accept the terms of agreement currently on offer or watch the negotiation process disintegrate. This strategy can sometime scare parties into accepting terms they otherwise wouldn't have agreed to, but it runs the risk of causing a lose-lose situation—that is, if the negotiations really end without an agreement.

Some negotiators and partners are committed to compromise and are willing to split the differences in order to come to a solution. The negative side of this strategy may be a half win-win situation with losses involved for all partners. The selection of this strategy must be weighed carefully to determine its relevance to a specific set of negotiations.

There are also strategies that micromanage the process and are so detail based that very little seems to be done. The nickel-and-dime strategy is a slow one where each element is evaluated piece by piece. The advantage of this strategy is that it lessens the disagreements of the parties to the negotiation. On the negative side, it often seems that a final agreement is not reached.

Most people feel more secure on their own turf, and negotiators who demand that the negotiation talks take place in their work environment are trying to control the action. If any of the negotiators feel uncomfortable with a potential meeting location, neutral territory should be found.

Language is not a perfect tool, and there is likely to be some unclarity of meaning and some vagueness to any agreement no matter how long and carefully the negotiators work on it. What have to be watched for are cases of intentional ambiguity, where one of the negotiators tries to keep the language so loose that the agreement doesn't adequately resolve the pertinent issues but merely seems to. Of course, the negotiators may allow some loose ends to remain untied in order to permit flexibility in the interpretation of the agreement, but they should do this with their eyes open and not be fooled into doing it.

Because some negotiating strategies are deceitful, negotiators need to learn defensive techniques to combat these strategies. Public health leaders acting as negotiators must thoroughly understand the negotiation process and the major impediments to a successful completion of the process.

Sometimes a negotiator will decide that a point in the negotiations has been reached beyond which no further concessions will even be entertained.[55] Though dangerous, because it can cause the negotiations to break down entirely, this strategy has the potential to force the parties to come to some kind of agreement.

Some strategies, including stonewalling and the no-concessions strategy just mentioned, can cause negotiations to become deadlocked. Because a deadlock is an impasse, negotiators should have on hand strategies to break deadlocks. One strategy is a return to one of the prenegotiation steps in order to clarify issues and goals and thereby get the negotiations back on track.

The twelfth strategy listed is abbreviated as HRESSC (high realistic expectations with small systematic concessions).[56] Negotiators who use this strategy maintain expectations that are high but can be met. They also realize they will have to make some concessions in order to keep the negotiation process headed toward completion. Because the expectations are high, the concessions and trade-offs tend to be small.

Some negotiators start the negotiating process by making concessions immediately. This strategy can disarm the other party and actually lead to a better outcome for the party using the strategy. It is best employed from a position of strength. If the party doing the conceding is perceived as weak, the other party will view the strategy as a further sign of weakness and may try to push its own agenda as far as it can, defeating the purpose of the strategy.

The next strategy involves a focus on problem solving. The strategy demonstrates that there is confusion between conflict resolution strategies oriented to the long term and problem solving, which tends to be more short-term in effect. Many factors and interests enter into negotiation.

One delaying tactic used by negotiators is to direct attention to goals or issues that are peripheral to the main goals or issues. This may seem to be a counterproductive strategy, but in some situations it can in fact clarify the major interests involved, prevent a breakdown in the negotiation process, allow important information to be discovered, and influence the other parties to come to a resolution more quickly.

Finally, negotiators make use of closure strategies to get an agreement written and accepted by all parties. Once this is done, closure can occur. However, a decision may be made to review progress in a specified period of time.

Every negotiation is unique, and negotiators often combine standard strategies or create new ones to deal with the specifics of the individual case. Exercise 21-3, adapted from a case study by Jurkowski and Neuberger,[57] presents a scenario in which the students have the opportunity to carry out a negotiation regarding a critical public health problem. The students can either use some of the strategies described above or create their own strategies.

Negotiation is a complex type of process that has many potential pitfalls. It is related to the other types of process described in this chapter, and indeed decision making, problem solving, and conflict resolution can all play a role in typical negotiations. Public health leaders must:

- learn to resolve conflict through negotiation, adjudication, mediation, and arbitration
- learn various methods for carrying out negotiations
- use well-trained and experienced negotiators for negotiating with other parties
- make sure the negotiators have skills and abilities described in this section
- learn to use the "Getting to Yes" and the Schoenfield and Schoenfield negotiation models
- master the steps of the negotiation process
- learn the standard negotiation strategies and tactics

TIPPING POINT AWARENESS

The decisions we make and the problems we solve as well as events outside our control may create tipping points that move us in unexpected ways and directions. Many defining events in our society can be looked at in a similar fashion to epidemics.[58] For example, there have been terrorist acts around the world for a long time, but at some point these acts create major reactions related to controlling these events more overtly. Gladwell described terrorism as being like a growing virus that reached an epidemic status on September 11, 2001, and gave an example of a yawn in comparison to a virus. One person yawns, and it seems to become contagious, as many other people nearby then yawn as well. I have noticed this phenomenon as well at concerts or plays when one person coughs—within minutes, many people are coughing.

With regard to terrorist activities, it sometimes seems that one terrorist event triggers many more such events. This phenomenon is seen as each day brings new terrorist activities in Iraq and in the Middle East. However, it seems that September 11, 2001, created a tipping point where terrorism became clearly seen as a worldwide threat that needs to be controlled in a systematic way. An important consideration is that a tipping point may be interpreted in different ways by different groups. Terrorist groups might see the event as justification for further terrorist activities. The targeted group will see the event as a need to protect themselves and institute security measures as well as strategies for finding the terrorists. A vicious cycle is created when terrorist attacks lead to further security

measures, hunts for the terrorists that lead to further terrorist attacks, and on and on.

Epidemics have three characteristics: (1) the level of contagiousness, (2) small facts or events that have large and long-lasting consequences, and (3) changes that can occur suddenly or at a dramatic moment like September 11, 2001. The interesting issue is related to the question of why certain events create epidemics and other events do not. It does appear that leaders need to constantly look in their communities or, in fact, elsewhere on this planet for clues to events that may trigger an epidemic. The public health leader needs such skills to put many factors together to determine the chances for certain events happening.

Epidemics are seen in terms of the following triad:

- Agent—person who spreads infectious agents
- Host—the infectious agent itself
- Environment

The tipping point then relates to the event that triggers the crisis. It becomes a disruption of the equilibrium. When scientists began to note the occurrence of dead birds at the start of the West Nile virus epidemic, the concern was not great, but a point was reached when the Centers for Disease Control and Prevention and other federal agencies thought that there was a crisis—in other words, a tipping point. Gladwell defined the three rules of a tipping point: the "Law of the Few" (the agent), the "Stickiness Factor" (the host), and the "Power of Context" (the environment).[59]

The Law of the Few points to the fact that it is often a few exceptional people who lead the way to potential epidemics or change. It becomes important for the public health leader to find these people. The interesting factor is that there are really only a small number of these people. In the terrorist arena, Osama Bin Laden was one of these. The nature of the messenger is important. The messages that he or she gives are often contagious. Gladwell described three types of agents: Connectors, Mavens, and Salespeople.[60] Connectors are people who seem to know many important people and also know how to bring them together. They are extremely social in that they are socially aware, have high emotional intelligence, and are very intuitive about people. They also are good at remembering names and places. They know people in many different areas of endeavor. They would meet you, talk to you for a few minutes, and then say, "There is someone that you need to meet." They also are excellent at spreading messages that are true as well as false.

One way to determine if you are a connector is to answer the next few questions:

1. If you see a good movie, how many people do you recommend to go see it?
2. If you read a good book, do you recommend it to others?
3. Do you bring friends with similar interests together, or do you keep your friends isolated from one another?

If everyone you recommend a movie or book to goes to the movie or buys and reads the book and they recommend it to others, you may have helped create a high-grossing film or a best seller even when the reviews were not so good.

Mavens are information specialists. They seem to know everything and are willing to share the information. They like to help others solve their problems. They mainly want to teach and help others by introducing them to new information. They also want to get information in return so that they can give that information to others. In some situations, Mavens appear arrogant to others. They also love to see the reaction of others to their supposed expertise. Some Mavens are also Connectors, although this is not always the case. Mavens tend not to be persuaders like Salespeople are. Salespeople are wonderful at convincing us to buy the message that they are delivering. They strongly believe that small things can make as large a difference as bigger things.

The Stickiness Factor refers to the host in the epidemiologic triad and is the second rule of the tipping point.[61] The question here is: What makes a specific message catch on with some people, but not with others? The message and its presentation may affect how great the effect or stickiness is. Tinkering with the message may change its effect, although the general content of the message may not have changed. Finding the best way to transmit the information is critical. Exploring factors that create stickiness are critical in the long run. If you think about the recent flurry of activity related to the harmful effects of secondhand smoke in the workplace and the attempt to convince people of this fact, what are five ways to create a sticky message related to this? Write a public announcement to create such a message, and then present it to a group to determine who is influenced enough by your message to support a change in a local ordinance related to outlawing smoking in all workplaces in your community.

The final tipping point rule relates to the Power of Context. Epidemics are strongly affected by local conditions in a community or neighborhood. Sometimes it seems like a small incident or factor affects the outcome. Such factors as the demographic characteristics of the area, urban and rural differences, level of family life in terms of whether areas are predominantly family based or not, socioeconomic factors, streetlighting, transportation hubs, values, cultural issues, and so on can affect the spread of an epidemic. Some of the environmental tipping points can be changed. For example, if there is no streetlighting, adding streetlighting can affect the incidence of crime. Creating a block club in an inner city can also change social relationships in a community. Case Study 21-B is a question-and-answer session written by Gladwell to explain his interpretation of why the tipping point approach is so important. To give you a chance to experiment with these three tipping point rules, Exercise 21-4 on the Broccoli Diet presents an example of such an experiment.

An Interview with Malcolm Gladwell

What is *The Tipping Point* about?

It's about change. In particular, it's an idea that presents a new way of understanding why change so often happens as quickly and as unexpectedly as it does. For example, why did crime drop so dramatically in New York City in the mid-1990s? How does a novel written by an unknown author end up as national bestseller? Why do teens smoke in greater and greater numbers when every single person in the country knows that cigarettes kill? Why is word-of-mouth so powerful? What makes TV shows like *Sesame Street* so good at teaching kids how to read? I think the answer to all those questions is the same. It's that ideas and behavior and messages and products sometimes behave just like outbreaks of infectious disease. They are social epidemics. *The Tipping Point* is an examination of the social epidemics that surround us.

What does it mean to think about life as an epidemic? Why does thinking in terms of epidemics change the way we view the world?

Because epidemics behave in a very unusual and counterintuitive way. Think, for a moment, about an epidemic of measles in a kindergarten class. One child brings in the virus. It spreads to every other child in the class in a matter of days. And then, within a week or so, it completely dies out and none of the children will ever get measles again. That's typical behavior for epidemics; they can blow up and then die out really quickly, and even the smallest change—like one child with a virus—can get them started. My argument is that it is also the way that change often happens in the rest of the world. Things can happen all at once, and little changes can make a huge difference. That's a little bit counterintuitive. As human beings, we always expect everyday change to happen slowly and steadily, and for there to be some relationship between cause and effect. And when there isn't—when crime drops dramatically in New York for no apparent reason, or when a movie made on a shoestring budget ends up making hundreds of millions of dollars—we're surprised. I'm saying, don't be surprised. This is the way social epidemics work.

Where did you get the idea for the book?

Before I went to work for *The New Yorker*, I was a reporter for the *Washington Post* and I covered the AIDS epidemic. And one of the things that struck me as I learned more and more about HIV was how strange epidemics were. If you talk to the people who study epidemics—epidemiologists—you realize that they have a strikingly different way of looking at the world. They don't share the assumptions the rest of us have about how and why change happens. The term *tipping point*, for example, comes from the world of epidemiology. It's the name given to that moment in an epidemic when a virus reaches critical mass. It's the boiling point. It's the moment on the graph when the line starts to shoot straight upward. AIDS tipped in 1982, when it went from a rare disease affecting a few gay men to a worldwide epidemic. Crime in New York City tipped in the mid-1990s, when the murder rate suddenly plummeted. When I heard that phrase for the first time, I remember thinking—wow. What if everything has a tipping point? Wouldn't it be cool to try to look for tipping points in business, in social policy, in advertising, or in any number of other nonmedical areas?

Why do you think the epidemic example is so relevant for other kinds of change? Is it just that it's an unusual and interesting way to think about the world?

No. I think it's much more than that, because once you start to understand this pattern, you start to see it everywhere. I'm convinced that ideas and behaviors and new products move through a population very much like a disease does. This isn't just a metaphor, in other words. I'm talking about a very literal analogy. One of the things I explore in the book is that ideas can be contagious in exactly the same way that a virus is. One chapter, for example, deals with the very strange epidemic of teenage suicide in the South Pacific islands of Micronesia. In the 1970s and 1980s, Micronesia had teen suicide rates 10 times higher than anywhere else in the world. Teenagers were literally being infected with the suicide bug, and one after another they were killing themselves in exactly the same way under exactly the same circumstances. We like to use words like *contagiousness* and *infectiousness* just to apply to the medical realm. But I assure you that after you read about what happened in Micronesia, you'll be convinced that behavior can be transmitted from one person to another as easily as the flu or the measles can. In fact, I don't think you have to go to Micronesia to see this pattern in action. Isn't this the explanation for the current epidemic of teen smoking in this country? And what about the rash of mass shootings we're facing at the moment—from Columbine through the Atlanta stockbroker through the neo-Nazi in Los Angeles?

Are you talking about the idea of memes, which has become so popular in academic circles recently?

It's very similar. A meme is an idea that behaves like a virus—that moves through a population, taking hold in each person it infects. I must say, though, that I don't much like that term. The thing that bothers me about the discussion of memes is that no one ever tries to define exactly what they are and what makes a meme so contagious. I mean, you can put a virus under a microscope and point to all the genes on its surface that are responsible for making it so dangerous. So what happens when you look at an infectious idea under a microscope? I have a chapter where I try to do that. I use the example of children's television shows like *Sesame Street* and the Nickelodeon program *Blues Clues*. Both of those are examples of shows that started learning epidemics in preschoolers, that turned kids onto reading and "infected" them with literacy. We sometimes think of *Sesame Street* as purely the result of the creative genius of people like Jim Henson and Frank Oz. But the truth is that it is carefully and painstakingly engineered, down to the smallest details. There's a wonderful story, in fact, about the particular scientific reason for the creation of Big Bird. It's very funny. But I won't spoil it for you.

How would you classify *The Tipping Point*? Is it a science book?

I like to think of it as an intellectual adventure story. It draws from psychology and sociology and epidemiology, and uses examples from the worlds of business and education and fashion and media. If I had to draw an analogy

(*Continues*)

to another book, I'd say it was like Daniel Goleman's *Emotional Intelligence*, in the sense that it takes theories and ideas from the social sciences and shows how they can have real relevance to our lives. There's a whole section of the book devoted to explaining the phenomenon of word of mouth, for example. I think that word of mouth is something created by three very rare and special psychological types, whom I call Connectors, Mavens, and Salesmen. I profile three people who I think embody those types, and then I use the example of Paul Revere and his midnight ride to point out the subtle characteristics of this kind of social epidemic. So just in that chapter, there is a little bit of sociology, a little psychology, and a little bit of history, all in aid of explaining a very common but mysterious phenomenon that we deal with every day. I guess what I'm saying is that I'm not sure that this book fits into any one category. That's why I call it an adventure story. I think it will appeal to anyone who wants to understand the world around them in a different way. I think it can give the reader an advantage—a new set of tools. Of course, I also think they'll be in for a very fun ride.

What do you hope readers will take away from the idea of the tipping point?

One of the things I'd like to do is to show people how to start "positive" epidemics of their own. The virtue of an epidemic, after all, is that just a little input is enough to get it started, and it can spread very, very quickly. That makes it something of obvious and enormous interest to everyone from educators trying to reach students, to businesses trying to spread the word about their product, or for that matter to anyone who's trying to create a change with limited resources. The book has a number of case studies of people who have successfully started epidemics—an advertising agency, for example, and a breast cancer activist. I think they are really fascinating. I also take a pressing social issue, teenage smoking, and break it down and analyze what an epidemic approach to solving that problem would look like. The point is that by the end of the book I think the reader will have a clear idea of what starting an epidemic actually takes. This is not an abstract, academic book. It's very practical. And it's very hopeful. It's brain software.

Beyond that, I think that *The Tipping Point* is a way of making sense of the world, because I'm not sure that the world always makes as much sense to us as we would like. I spend a great deal of time in the book talking about the way our minds work—and the peculiar and sometimes problematic ways in which our brains process information. Our intuitions, as humans, aren't always very good. Changes that happen really suddenly, on the strength of the most minor of input, can be deeply confusing. People who understand *The Tipping Point*, I think, have a way of decoding the world around them.

Figure 21-5 looks at the issue of complexity and the tipping point in public health from the leadership perspective. If we imagine the tipping point as the balancing part of a seesaw, it is first necessary to realize that the foundation for change is always in the context of the community in which it occurs. If a particular event is to become sticky, then an understanding of external events that are labeled *societal* in the figure needs to be balanced against strategic public health concerns that affect the given community. From a slightly different perspective, **Figure 21-6** examines the public health response to a crisis from the external pressures on a community from the larger state or national perspectives, the community crisis itself, and the relationship of this crisis to the priorities of the community—such as health and safety concerns, national agenda issues that emergency responders need to act within, and those strategic challenges discussed below that affect the messages that get developed.

Societal pressures are all those factors in the culture of the community that affect such things as its power structure, its social capital infrastructure, its organizational structure, its views of public health, its concerns about personal rights and freedoms, its fear level related to a disruption in the quality of community life as perceived by its residents, and so on. There are many strategic challenges facing public health in the 21st century. The creation of human services superagencies was a major activity in the 1990s and is still being discussed in the 21st century. As we look at the strategic challenges after September 2001, the challenge related to emergency preparedness and response clearly rises to the top of a potential list. In addition, the issue of health disparities is also key in this new century. All these strategic challenges affect the public health system and how it is influenced by specific events. With regard to new and reemerging diseases, we now have West Nile virus, SARS, monkeypox, H1N1, and the reemergence of pertussis to contend with.

The national public health agenda and new initiatives are also a factor in public health response. **Table 21-4** lists some of these national agenda concerns. There are many discussions occurring about the certification of public health professionals and the accreditation of

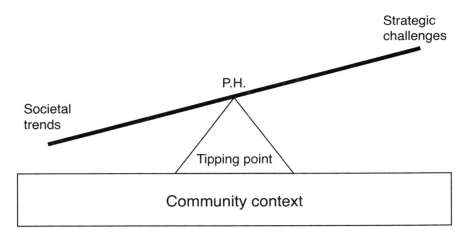

FIGURE 21-5 Public Health Complexity Issues: Leadership Demands.

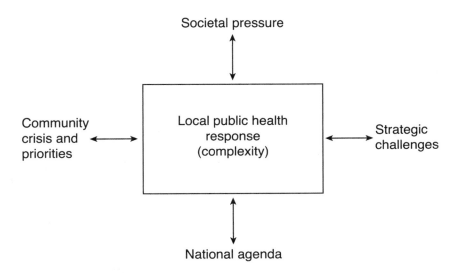

FIGURE 21-6 Public Health Response.

TABLE 21-4 National Agenda Concerns

Public health credentialing and accreditation
• Health Alert Network
• Public health leadership
• Essential public health services
• Workforce development
• Public health infrastructure
• National performance standards
• Public health informatics
• MAPP assessment
• Evidence-based public health
• Homeland security

public health agencies. These discussions involve the factors to be considered in the development of these certification programs. Getting agreement on all the factors to be considered is not an easy process. Increasing concern with management and leadership development programs has become a reality. The Health Alert Network and its rapid dissemination of information and homeland security concerns are major parts of the agenda, as is increasing emphasis on evidence-based public health practice. There is also emphasis on workforce development. New tools for community assessment are being developed, such as MAPP (Mobilizing for Action through Planning and Partnership) and the National Public Health Performance Standards program, which is based on performance tied to the 10 essential public health services.

The public health leader is always looking for clues based on the above factors that might tip the scales and move public health in new directions. It thus becomes a question as to whether it is possible to develop an awareness to potential shifts that certain types of events may cause. We now know that a terrorist act or potential terrorist or bioterrorist act is one of these events. We also know that a judicial decision at the Supreme Court level may also create such a tipping point. Exercise 21-5 will give you the chance to interpret American history, tipping points, and the effects of these events.

Gladwell has now added to this discussion with *Blink*.[62] Sometimes, leaders have to make decisions so rapidly that the emotional component does not seem to affect the decision. Rapid cognition refers to the kind of decisions that are made on the spot as a situation occurs. It is only after the event and the blink that emotions and other reactions enter the picture. Each individual carries a cognitive map of all his or her previous life experiences into each new situation. Each new situation builds on previous ones. Thus, an important question relates to this cognitive historical map we carry around with us and its relationship to a rapid cognition decision. Finally, Gladwell discusses outliers, who are people who make decisions and create change, but are people you would not expect to do these things.[63]

SUMMARY

This chapter has presented new tools to add to the public health leadership toolkit. Public health leadership, like other kinds of leadership, encompasses the essential activities of decision making, conflict resolution, and negotiation. Public health leaders who lack the skills needed to perform these activities will fail, at least partially, to live up to their responsibility as leaders. This chapter also presented the beginning of a discussion of a set of skills for the public health leader related to tipping point awareness, which builds on public health's epidemiological tradition and shows how the skills of epidemiology may be useful in better predicting and understanding the relationship between emergency and crisis events, their causes, outcomes, and effects on the community of these often unanticipated events.

Furthermore, to develop these skills, they must open up the public health leadership toolkit and work with the tools, even if they are less adept at using them than more experienced colleagues.

Learning new skills is difficult and requires dedication and a willingness to take risks. Leaders who put in the time and effort, however, will soon master the skills and become expert at making decisions, resolving conflicts, negotiating agreements, and increasing tipping point awareness.

DISCUSSION QUESTIONS

1. Why is risk taking an important part of public health leadership?
2. What are three examples in which you have taken a leadership risk during the past year?
3. What are the differences and similarities between decision making and problem solving?
4. What are some effective conflict resolution strategies?
5. Is intraorganizational conflict always to be avoided? Explain.
6. What are some usual obstacles to successful negotiation?
7. What is the difference between mediation and negotiation?
8. What are the key elements in the prenegotiation phase and the negotiation phase?
9. What are some common negotiation strategies?
10. What is the relationship between tipping points and decision making?

EXERCISE 21-1: Decision-Making Styles

Purpose: to explore two models of decision-making styles

Key concepts: decision-making styles

Procedures: Divide the class or training group into groups of five to seven people. Each group discusses what is involved in being a good decision maker. Discuss your personal experience in making decisions with your group. For example, how did you make a decision to take this class or come to this training workshop? Pick a decision that you made at work and one you made at home. Did your style shift in the two different situations? Using the Mintzberg and the Robbins and Coulter models of decision-making styles, do you fit in one or more categories in the two models? Compare and contrast the two models. Does your style change in a team situation where you are the sole decision maker? What are the leadership issues in your decision-making style?

EXERCISE 21-2:   The Meaning of Conflict

Purpose: to recognize the causes of conflict and how to resolve conflict

Key concepts: conflict, conflict resolution

Procedures: The class should break into groups of 8 to 10 members. First, each group member offers one word in reaction to the term "conflict." The words are put on a large sheet of paper and discussed by the group. The group then divides into two subgroups, one of which assumes the role of a team from the local health department, the second of which assumes the role of a management team from a local health maintenance organization (HMO). The HMO wants to build a major new medical center on land owned by the city, but the public health department wants the land for a new substance abuse clinic. Each team explains its position, and together they try to resolve the conflict between them.

EXERCISE 21-3:   Negotiation and HIV Prevention Case

Purpose: to explore the use of negotiation techniques to address a major community health problem

Key concepts: coalition building, negotiation, prenegotiation, win-win strategy

Scenario: The Benton County HIV Prevention Council has experienced internal disagreements about how to allocate federal funds for human immunodeficiency virus (HIV)/acquired immune deficiency syndrome (AIDS) community programs. Some members of the council adamantly reject needle exchange programs, whereas others are strongly in favor of them. Because the conflict between the council representatives has lasted more than two years, the council has agreed to implement a negotiation process to build an agenda and protocol to guide the allocation of financial resources for HIV/AIDS prevention and treatment. The key players include a variety of stakeholders and constituency groups from the local department of health (located in Hamilton, the largest city in the county), the Benton County Health Department, and the community at large. Substance abuse is a major problem in Hamilton, and the number of reported HIV/AIDS cases has doubled in the past five years. HIV/AIDS cases are also increasing in the rural areas of the county. The Benton County Board of Health has hired a professional negotiator to work with the Benton County HIV Prevention Council. The county has also been informed that it will receive a million dollars from the federal government to fund the protocol that is developed.

Procedures: The class should divide into groups of eight. Seven people from each group act as members of the Benton County HIV/AIDS Prevention Council, taking a specific role and position as discussed in the group before starting the exercise. For example, one person can be a conservative minister. One individual becomes the negotiator. The group should spend an hour negotiating an end to the conflict using the Fisher et al model and another hour using the 14 steps of the Schoenfield and Schoenfield model, if possible. If both models are used, the group should discuss the similarities and differences between the two models. Once all groups have completed their comparison of the two models, a representative from each group should present a five-minute talk to other groups about the negotiation process, and then all groups should engage in a discussion about the negotiation strategies that were used.

Benton County Cast of Characters	
Connie Sultan	Professional Negotiator
I. M. Leader	Director of the Benton County Health Department
Rev. Smith	Minister of the Benton County Methodist Church
Sally Justice	Social Worker, Hamilton AIDS Foundation
Tom Driver	Chief Executive Officer of Benton County Admiral Motors Company
Guy Brown	President, Benton County Gay and Lesbian Alliance
Vera Straight	President, Hamilton Parent Teachers Assembly
Berry Organized	Hamilton City Manager

Source: Adapted from E. Jurkowski and B. Neuberger, *Negotiation Skills for Community Resource Planning*, 1995, the Centers for Disease Control and Prevention, Illinois Public Health Leadership Institute.

EXERCISE 21-4: The Broccoli Diet

Purpose: to understand the tipping point model utilizing the three Gladwell laws

Key concepts: tipping point, Law of the Few, Stickiness Factor, Law of Context

Procedures: Dr. I. M. Green has conducted major research on the effects of eating specific vegetables as a method for losing weight. After 15 years, he has discovered the weight-loss effect of eating broccoli as part of each meal. As a result of his research, he has created the Broccoli Diet and a new recipe book for using broccoli in many recipes. He has created an entire line of spices that include powdered broccoli as part of the spice mixture.

Divide the class or training group into groups of 10. Using the three Gladwell laws, discuss how quickly the Broccoli Diet will become the predominant diet plan in America. How will your group know that the tipping point has been reached?

EXERCISE 21-5: Historical Tipping Points

Purpose: to understand the tipping points of history

Key concepts: tipping point

Procedures: Divide the class or training group into groups of 10. Utilizing the chart below, have each person list five American historical events that they feel were tipping point occurrences. Two of the five should be public health tipping points. Each small group will look at each member's list and come up with a list of 10 events, of which five relate to public health tipping points. Explain with notes on the chart below why each event is a tipping point. Present your list to the class or training group as a whole.

Historical Event	Tipping Point	Explanation

REFERENCES

1. M. DePree, "The Leaders Legacy," in *Leader to Leader*, ed. F. Hesselbein and P. M. Cohen (San Francisco: Jossey-Bass, 1999).
2. J. M. Kouzes and B. Z. Posner, *The Leadership Challenge*, 4th ed. (San Francisco: Jossey-Bass, 2007).
3. N. L. Frigon and J. K. Jackson Jr., *The Leader* (New York: AMACOM [American Management Association], 1996).
4. M. H. Bazerman and D. Chugh, "Decisions Without Blinders," *Harvard Business Review* 84, no. 1 (2006): 88–97.
5. R. Fritz, *Corporate Tides* (San Francisco: Berrett-Koehler, 1996).
6. P. Hersey et al., *Management of Organizational Behavior*, 9th ed. (Upper Saddle River, NJ: Prentice Hall, 2007).
7. J. Pfeffer, *Managing with Power* (Boston: Harvard Business School Press, 1992).
8. Fritz, *Corporate Tides*.
9. D. J. Snowden and M. E. Boone, "A Leader's Framework for Decision Making," *Harvard Business Review* 85, no. 11 (2007): 68–76.
10. H. Mintzberg, *Mintzberg on Management* (New York: The Free Press, 1989).
11. D. Osborne and T. Gaebler, *Reinventing Government: How the Entrepreneurial Spirit Is Transforming the Public Sector* (Reading, MA: Addison-Wesley, 1992).
12. Mintzberg, *Mintzberg on Management*.
13. S. P. Robbins and M. Coulter, *Management*, 11th ed. (Upper Saddle River, NJ: Prentice Hall, 2011).
14. Robbins and Coulter, *Management*.
15. S. P. Robbins, D. A. DeCenzo, and R. Wolter, *Supervision Today*, 6th ed. (Upper Saddle River, NJ: Prentice Hall, 2009).
16. Robbins and Coulter, *Management*.
17. J. L. Pressman and A. Wildavsky, *Implementation*, 3rd ed. (Berkeley, CA: University of California Press, 1984).

18. Robbins and Coulter, *Management*.
19. Robbins and Coulter, *Management*.
20. J. G. Liebler and C. R. McConnell, *Management Principles for Health Professionals*, 4th ed. (Sudbury, MA: Jones & Bartlett, 2004).
21. Robbins and Coulter, *Management*.
22. B. Wall et al., *The Visionary Leader* (Rocklin, CA: Prima Publishing & Communication, 1992).
23. A. J. DuBrin, *The Complete Idiot's Guide to Leadership* (New York: Alpha Books, 2000).
24. J. A. Schellenberg, *Conflict Resolution: Theory, Research, and Practice* (Albany, NY: State University of New York Press, 1996).
25. Liebler and McConnell, *Management Principles for Health Professionals*.
26. Robbins and Coulter, *Management*.
27. P. C. Nutt, *Making Tough Choices* (San Francisco: Jossey-Bass, 1989).
28. W. Hendricks, *How to Manage Conflict* (Shawnee Mission, KS: National Press Publications, 1991).
29. D. Weeks, *The Eight Essential Steps to Conflict Resolution* (New York: Jeremy P. Tarcher and Putnam Books, 1994).
30. Liebler and McConnell, *Management Principles for Health Professionals*.
31. M. Winer and K. Ray, *Collaboration Handbook* (St. Paul, MN: Amherst H. Wilder Foundation, 1994).
32. DuBrin, *The Complete Idiot's Guide to Leadership*.
33. Robbins and Coulter, *Management*.
34. A. Rahim, *Organizational Conflict Inventories* (Palo Alto, CA: Consulting Psychologists Press, 1983).
35. Robbins and Coulter, *Management*.
36. Weeks, *The Eight Essential Steps to Conflict Resolution*.
37. Schellenberg, *Conflict Resolution*.
38. R. Fisher et al., *Getting to Yes*, 2nd ed. (New York: Penguin Books, 1991).
39. F. E. Jandt, *Win-Win Negotiating* (New York: Wiley and Paul Gillett Books, 1985).
40. M. K. Schoenfield and R. M. Schoenfield, *The McGraw-Hill 36-Hour Negotiating Course* (New York: McGraw-Hill, 1991).
41. H. Raiffa, *The Art and Science of Negotiation* (Cambridge, MA: Harvard University Press, 1982).
42. Raiffa, *The Art and Science of Negotiation*.
43. Robbins and Coulter, *Management*.
44. Robbins and Coulter, *Management*.
45. Jandt, *Win-Win Negotiating*.
46. Fisher et al., *Getting to Yes*.
47. Jandt, *Win-Win Negotiating*.
48. Jandt, *Win-Win Negotiating*.
49. Schoenfield and Schoenfield, *The McGraw-Hill 36-Hour Negotiating Course*.
50. E. Jurkowski and B. Neuberger, *Negotiation Skills for Community Resource Planning* (Chicago: Illinois Public Health Leadership Institute, 1995).
51. R. Fisher and D. Ertel, *Getting Ready to Negotiate* (New York: Penguin Books, 1995).
52. Schoenfield and Schoenfield, *The McGraw-Hill 36-Hour Negotiating Course*.
53. G. Fuller, *The Negotiator's Handbook* (Paramus, NJ: Prentice Hall, 1991).
54. Schoenfield and Schoenfield, *The McGraw-Hill 36-Hour Negotiating Course*.
55. Schoenfield and Schoenfield, *The McGraw-Hill 36-Hour Negotiating Course*.
56. Schoenfield and Schoenfield, *The McGraw-Hill 36-Hour Negotiating Course*.
57. Jurkowski and Neuberger, *Negotiation Skills for Community Resource Planning*.
58. M. Gladwell, *The Tipping Point* (Boston: Little Brown, 2000).
59. Gladwell, *The Tipping Point*.
60. Gladwell, *The Tipping Point*.
61. Gladwell, *The Tipping Point*.
62. M. Gladwell, *Blink* (Boston: Little Brown, 2005).
63. M. Gladwell, *Outliers* (Boston: Little Brown, 2008).

Leadership and Community Engagement

The pursuit of happiness is never ending—the happiness lies in the pursuit.

—Saul Alinsky, political activist

The public health leader spends more of his or her time in the community he or she serves than inside the agency he or she leads. Public health today is about community and community relationships. It is also about building social capital, and about new partnerships. The positive orientation of the leader will serve as a guide through the good times and also through the times of crisis. In a book of reflections on his leadership experiences told as short vignettes, Magee, who is a physician, stated that positive leaders stand on principle, and these principles then have a visible effect on all those with whom they interact.[1] Positive leadership is clearly needed in times of crisis. Leaders need to see beyond the crisis to recognize the lessons to be learned and the important tasks related to healing. The goal of leadership is to learn the skills necessary to make our communities safe and to always respect every individual who lives in

these communities. This chapter will look at additional skills that are needed by leaders as they face the challenges of public health in the 21st century in a positive way.[2]

OVERVIEW OF COMMUNITY BUILDING

There has been much discussion in recent years about the importance of building community. It is believed that a strong community is one that can address any attack on its infrastructure. There has also been discussion about the concern that our communities are disintegrating because people who live within a jurisdiction do not relate to that community in anything other than a superficial manner. It is clear that communities grow when there is collaboration with and commitment to that community. The public health leader needs to work with all community groups to create an environment for positive social change through collaboration. Mattessich and Monsey have enumerated 15 factors that can help the process of community growth and development:[3]

1. It is important to get widespread community involvement and participation.
2. Good, if not great, communication skills are critical to successful community building.
3. Collaboration to support community development is better than competition.
4. It is important to develop a community identity and agreement on community priorities.
5. Community residents need to see and feel that they are benefiting from any changes that occur.
6. Community development is tied to building relationships with others and offers events and accomplishments that support relationship-building activities.
7. Communities that succeed have relationships with organizations and communities other than themselves.
8. Community growth begins small and simple and becomes bigger and more complex over time.
9. It is important to monitor changing needs of community residents and any other gauge of community reaction or concern.
10. Community residents and leaders need to be offered training and informational meetings so they can learn and better understand what is occurring.
11. Community organizations with long tenure in the community need to be involved in any community-building activity.
12. Technical assistance and consultation should be utilized to expedite change and to help residents to better understand why changes and growth are necessary.
13. It is important for communities on the move to grow new leaders.
14. Residents and their trustee community leaders need to be able to control any decisions that need to be made.
15. There needs to be a balance between internal and external resources to promote community growth.

COMMUNITY LEADERS

As public health leaders extend their work into the community, the involvement of residents becomes more and more important. Most leaders with positional authority are not willing or lack understanding of the ways to interact with community people in a collaborative way. Part of the challenge relates to that abstract phenomenon referred to as *sharing power*. Because many community people lack leadership training, it is important for the public health leader to work with the community in developing leaders who will become trustees in the sense that they will represent other community residents. Empowering the community to train its representatives as leaders involves working with people rather than doing the work for them.[4] These grassroots leaders will often be part of a community-based coalition or organization. They also need to see themselves as community trustees.

A trustee becomes involved in what has been called community ownership. Community ownership involves taking responsibility for the challenges that a community needs to face. Community leaders will thus define the issues of concern for community health. Not only will they help to define the issues, but these grassroots leaders, in collaboration with public health leaders, will help to define and implement the solutions and strategies for carrying them out. These leaders need the training and tools necessary to make these solutions work. Trust can easily erode when community leaders are not involved in the implementation of the strategies or when the professionals take over and disenfranchise the community leaders.

Leaders in the community come from several places.[5] Formal community leaders include elected or appointed officials, heads of community agencies, direct service providers, and civic leaders. These leaders often represent specific constituents in the community and have the power to speak for a group or groups of residents. A second key group of leaders are volunteers. These leaders are community residents with grassroots constituencies. They clearly have the trust of their constituencies, where formal leaders may not have the same level of community trust. The third group of community leaders are informal leaders. This often includes people with high community respect but without an active constituency. They include those people who know the history of the community, people who will always give advice when you have a problem, and the person who will just listen to you and not give advice.

All communities have organized sectors with people who are seen as leaders in those sectors. It is possible to create a list of these organized sectors in a specific community. These sectors include leaders from police and fire departments, elected offices, youth and senior centers and agencies, healthcare organizations, and so on. Because many communities are in a state of flux, there may also be developing community sectors from a variety of places, including new industry, new gangs, a new church, and so on. Exercise 22-1 will give you the opportunity to explore community sectors and some ways to increase community outreach.[6] Some community outreach strategies for the public health leader include the following:[7]

1. Identify and reach out to community leaders in all three sector groups.
2. Contact organized and developing community sector groups through public and house meetings and door-to-door contact.
3. Perform street outreach by going to the sector sites.
4. Set up information tables at community meeting sites, such as supermarkets.
5. Attend community meetings and speak at the open portion of a meeting, if possible.
6. Do community assessment or community participatory research.

Another dimension of working with community leaders relates to why a community leader may want to participate in the endeavors being supported by public health leaders. Kaye and Wolff stated that there are six reasons (the Six Rs) that people participate in all types of groups or community-based endeavors:[8]

1. People participate for *Recognition* of their leadership. Recognition can be shown through such activities as award dinners.
2. People want *Respect*, which involves the respect of their peers or neighbors. Involvement also needs to occur in nonwork hours when community people who work during the day can attend.
3. Community leaders like to have a specific, defined *Role* in a community initiative. These roles also need to have some power and authority associated with them.
4. Community leaders will become involved in community activities because they have a *Relationship* with others who are involved.
5. There need to be *Rewards* for being a member of a coalition or involved in a community-based activity that outweigh the costs of involvement.
6. Community leaders want to see *Results*. As business people will state, there needs to be a demonstrable product out of the interaction.

There are many tools available for evaluating community involvement. In addition to the two sources described in this section, Ayre, Clough, and Norris have developed a manual that examines change in communities from the vantage point of community

readiness for change, the importance of energy in team activities, the importance of building successes into the program, motivating the community, setting direction for the change that is proposed, and then implementing the change.[9]

An interesting set of issues relates to the self-determination part of community leadership. The Community Toolbox is a website that is utilized by many community leaders. Axner has studied the issue of learning how to be a community leader.[10] People who become community leaders have strong concerns about where their communities are going. They also want to improve their communities. Community leaders need to think they can make a difference. Leadership development is a growth activity, and there is not really a limit on how many leaders there can be in a community. There are several issues for potential community leaders to consider, including the following:[11]

1. It is important to create a personal vision for a community in a *big picture* way.
2. Listening skills are important because the community leader needs to know what the concerns of other community members are.
3. It is critical that the potential leader agrees to serve a community in a leadership role.
4. Leaders need to turn their vision into a set of goals.
5. Leaders need to protect the interests of other people in their community group.
6. Leaders also have to look at their collaborative in terms of what is best for the community as a whole and be able to justify their position to others.
7. Leaders guide the process of developing and proposing programs and policies.
8. Follow-through is important—the work needs to get done.
9. Leaders need to nurture the leadership potential of other community residents.

LEADERSHIP WHEEL APPLIED TO COMMUNITIES

Elsewhere, I introduced a systems approach to the tasks of leadership in organizations in a model called the *Leadership Wheel*, and it can now be expanded to include the tasks of leaders in communities. The wheel not only utilizes the activities of groups in communities but applies these activities to the core public health functions of assessment, policy development, and assurance. It is some community challenge, crisis situation, or community-building process that brings the public health leader together with community leaders and all the emergency preparedness and response officials. In a collaborative group, these leaders will form themselves into a coalition, alliance, or partnership. It is usually some community need (assessment) as defined qualitatively or quantitatively with some policy considerations that bring the collaboration into being. Skills in collaboration with a strong commitment to address the community need serve as catalysts for the leadership process required.

The wheel represents a strategic and action planning approach, with the addition of a values-clarification stage and potential for feedback at every stage of the wheel. Values clarification is often ignored as a stage in community collaboration. It is important to understand the cultural and organizational diversity that every collaboration entails. Exercise 22-2 will give you the chance to tie values to agendas in your collaboration. Try to understand the policy implications of the exercise. If your group takes the values-clarification task seriously, then the job of developing a mission and vision statement will be greatly simplified. Mission and vision are also part of the public health core function of policy development. Once the mission and vision are discussed and agreed upon, then specific goals and objectives need to be developed to make the vision a reality. Goals and objectives are the link between the mission of today and the vision of tomorrow. If the goals and objectives do not reflect this linkage, then there is a disconnect between the mission and the vision. Goals and objectives also connect the core function of policy development with the assessment function, as goals and objectives are often tied to information gleaned from the needs assessment that brought the collaborative group into being.

The steps thus far are often where strategic planning ends and action begins. It is possible to develop a series of action steps for each goal and objective. Action planning is closely related to the important considerations related to goals management, performance measurement, and performance standards. Goals management and performance measurement tell us how effective we are in tying our action steps to addressing goals and objectives. Performance standards are benchmarks to measure our progress and successes and failures. This step is often not given the time and effort it needs to create a viable implementation.[12]

Action planning requires a series of steps for the creation of an action plan. The first step is determining the underlying reasons for the plan by relating it back to both vision and overall goals and objectives. Next it is important to develop a framework based on the core functions and essential public health services. A series of design meetings can then be held to create the plan. The plan should be written down so there will be no confusion about its components. Validation will be needed not only from members of the collaborative, but also from any other affected stakeholders. Finally, the plan needs to be disseminated to the community as well as to all the agency partners.

The plan then needs to be implemented, which will bring the core function of assurance into play. Here is where the real action occurs. All activities should be evaluated as well. The next stage is for the group to begin discussions about next steps and whether the group should continue, disband, or restructure itself and start the planning and implementation process again. It is difficult to determine how long the entire cycle will take. It will vary from community to community.

MULTICULTURAL CONSIDERATIONS

It is important to consider the multicultural diversity of a community in any community-building process. Multicultural representatives should be part of any community-based activity. It is important to have different social and cultural groups involved in shaping a community collaboration, making decisions that will affect the community in which these groups live, and making sure the collective interest is supported and nurtured.[13] If public health leaders want to build effective community coalitions, alliances, and partnerships, several steps need to be followed:[14]

1. Create a vision for any collaborative activity, taking into account that trust needs to be built through values clarification.

2. Be as inclusive as possible in membership recruitment—making a conscious effort to do this is critical.

3. Respect cultural differences and create rules for the collaboration that do not undermine these differences. A safe and nurturing environment is required.

4. Ensure that whatever structure is created for the collaboration reinforces social and cultural equity.

5. Develop communication rules that reflect language differences as well as cultural etiquette so people do not feel threatened.

6. Create leadership opportunities for every member of the collaboration regardless of gender, race, or ethnic identity.

7. Make sure all action plans and program implementation strategies are culturally sensitive.

ASSETS-PLANNING MODEL

Especially in this age of fear of terrorism or bioterrorism, the prepared public health leader needs to better understand the strengths of our communities and how to use these strengths in confronting all types of crises. Public health leaders have traditionally taken a problem focus in their data collection activities. A negative approach slows the process of effecting change. In working with communities, it is important to build on the strengths and resources of the community. If these resources are mobilized effectively, then all sorts of community challenges can be addressed.

There are differences between a problem-oriented focus and an assets-based focus.[15] If we were to map the problems in a community, we would have to consider such things as unemployment, school truancy, rates of literacy, lead paint in old buildings, school dropouts, gang activity, adult crime, domestic and child abuse, broken families, the number of people on welfare, and on and on. Each of these problems creates a community need for a solution. If we were to determine the assets of the community in terms of individuals, community collaborative efforts, associations, and public and private organizations, it would be possible to determine an interesting balance of resources against needs. On the assets side, we would create a map of resources such as schools, churches, libraries, parks, businesses, community colleges, healthcare resources, local health departments, citizen organizations, cultural groups, artists, and so on. To these assets can be added the personal gifts of community people, in terms of talent or money, and special gifts of people in different age groups.[16] It is important not only to recognize the assets of the community, but also to mobilize the resources in such a way that community growth becomes more possible.

There are five steps involved in assets planning.[17] First, it is necessary to create an assets map of the community that delineates the capacities and gifts of individuals in the community, citizens' organizations and other entities, and local institutions (see sample map in **Figure 22-1**). Once this mapping process is tentatively completed, the next step involves the building of new community relationships between local assets in order to better develop strategies and programs to address community needs. In reality, assets maps are constantly changing as the community changes. It is important to mobilize these assets for community-building activities. The third step in the process is to expand mobilization activities for economic and social development. It is also important to increase information-sharing activities with all community assets. Fourth, community leaders need to convene a group of people from all assets categories to build a community vision and plan for community growth and development. Finally, it is important to leverage internal community resources with likely external resources, possibly through grants, contracts, and gifts to support the assets-based planning and development activities.

Communities need to develop a toolbox of techniques for community-building activities.[18] There are several tools to help in carrying out assets-planning and development activities. First is the assets map just discussed, with the addition of a capacity inventory of information about the given assets and ways that different individuals and groups can better work together. The important question is whether a given community has enough assets and capacity to address all the needs that exist in that community. A second set of tools is based on self-help techniques similar to the 12-step program of Alcoholics Anonymous, where peer groups form to address needs using some self-help model. A third tool employs something called a circle of support that is used in Canada to help people in need find support in difficult times. A fourth tool is also an expansion of the map to discover any small associations or groups in the community that were not caught in the mapping process but are groups that can address community needs. Finally, a business inventory is useful for helping community residents address employment issues in the community. Ayre and his colleagues would add some sort of civic index process that would specifically pull together the preferred vision for the community, governance factors, strategies for collaboration, and information needed to help the community to better address community needs.[19]

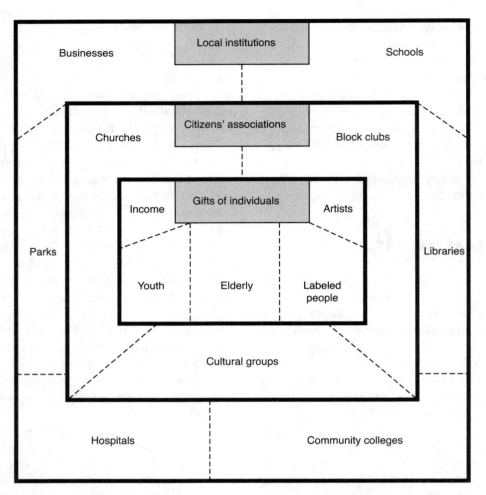

FIGURE 22-1 **Community Assets Map.** *Source:* Reproduced from J. P. Kretzmann and J. L. McNight (1993). *Building Communities from the Inside Out.* Evanston, IL: Northwestern University, ABCD Institute.

NATIONAL PUBLIC HEALTH PERFORMANCE STANDARDS

To bring the above discussion back to public health, it is useful to briefly review a program that was developed to determine how well communities are addressing public health issues.[20] First, the standards assume that public health is the community's business and not just the work of a local public health agency. The larger view is clearly a systems perspective, and all the standards are built on a systems foundation. This means that a community collaborative of some kind representing the major groups and organizations undertakes the process of evaluating the performance of that community relative to the public health performance standards. The entire system of standards is built on how well the system is carrying out the core functions and essential public health services. Next, the program assumes that public health needs to be customer focused and

community focused, which means the goals are quality and accountability. Thus, the program assumes a continuous quality improvement orientation will occur. Finally, public health practice at all levels must be built on a science base. This goal has been expanded upon in the recent acceptance of evidence-based practice considerations.

The National Public Health Performance Standards are based on three instruments. The first instrument is the state public health system assessment tool, which is oriented to state public health agencies and other partners who contribute to public health services at the state level. These state partners, which will vary from state to state, establish the parameters for public health in the state, set directions for public health practice, and implement the core functions and essential public health services for their respective states. Each of the 10 essential services has a number of indicators. For example, all the essential services in the state instrument have four indicators associated with them. These indicators are planning and implementation, technical assistance and support, evaluation and quality improvement, and resources. Under each indicator are a number of questions that the performance standards team discusses and then scores. For example, **Table 22-1** shows the questions for Essential Service 1 on monitoring health status to identify health problems and Indicator 1.1 related to planning and implementation. Once the entire form is filled out, the state can transmit the instrument electronically to the Centers for Disease Control and Prevention (CDC), which will analyze the data and return a report for the state. The state can then use the form for all types of statewide planning activities. It is clear that the state tool provides the public health leader and his or her partners with all sorts of data that can clearly influence public health practice in the state. It will also be possible to determine how the state is performing relative to each of the 10 essential public health services. In addition, state-by-state comparisons become possible.

TABLE 22-1 Example of Performance Standards for a State Public Health System

Essential Service #1: Monitor Health Status to Identify Health Problems

This service includes:

Assessment of statewide health status and its determinants, including the identification of health threats and the determination of health service needs.

Attention to the vital statistics and health status of specific groups that are at higher risk for health threats than the general population.

Identification of community assets and resources that support the SPHS in promoting health and improving quality of life.

Utilization of technology and other methods of interpreting and communicating health information to diverse audiences in different sectors.

Collaboration in integrating and managing public health-related information systems.

Indicator 1.1 Planning and Implementation.

SPHS Model Standard:

The SPHS measures, analyzes, and reports on the health status of the state. The state's health status is monitored through data describing critical indicators of health, illness, and health resources that are collected in collaboration with local public health systems and other state partners.

To accomplish this, the SPHS:

Develops and maintains population-based program that collect health-related data to measure the state's health status.

Organizes health-related data into a state health profile that reports trends in health status, risk factors, and resource consumption.

Tracks the state's health-related data and compares them to national health objectives and other benchmarks

Compiles and analyzes data for local, state, and national health surveillance efforts.

Collaborates with data-reporting entities such as local health departments, hospitals, physicians, and laboratories to assure the timely collection, analysis, and dissemination of data.

Develops and manages a uniform set of health status indicators that are derived from a variety of sources (e.g., hospitals, managed care organizations, health departments, universities) and accommodates state and local health-related data needs.

Protects personal health information by instituting security and confidentiality policies that define protocols for health information access and integrity.

Please answer the following questions related to Indicator 1.1:

1.1.1 Has the SPHS developed any surveillance programs for measuring the state's health status?

(*Continues*)

TABLE 22-1   Example of Performance Standards for a State Public Health System (*Continued*)

If so, do these programs:

    1.1.1.1 Identify the data elements required for monitoring health status?

If so, do these data include:

        1.1.1.1.1   Demographic characteristics?

        1.1.1.1.2   Socioeconomic characteristics?

        1.1.1.1.3   Mortality?

        1.1.1.1.4   Natality?

        1.1.1.1.5   Infectious disease incidence?

        1.1.1.1.6   Chronic disease prevalence?

        1.1.1.1.7   Injuries?

        1.1.1.1.8   Mental health and substance abuse?

        1.1.1.1.9   Behavioral risk factors?

        1.1.1.1.10 Environmental risks?

        1.1.1.1.11 Occupational risks?

        1.1.1.1.12 Availability of personal healthcare services?

        1.1.1.1.13 Utilization of personal healthcare services?

        1.1.1.1.14 Availability of population-based public health services?

        1.1.1.1.15 Utilization of population-based public health services?

        1.1.1.1.16 Barriers to health services?

        1.1.1.1.17 Health insurance coverage?

        1.1.1.1.18 *Healthy People 2010* leading health indicators?

    1.1.1.2 Identify the methods for data collection and storage?

    1.1.1.3 Identify the roles of state and local governmental agencies and relevant nongovernmental agencies in the collection of health data?

    1.1.1.4 Facilitate access to the health-related data among state and local public health and constituent groups?

1.1.2 Does the SPHS organize health-related data into a state health profile?

If so, is the profile used to:

    1.1.2.1 Identify emerging health problems?

    1.1.2.2 Report trends in health status?

    1.1.2.3 Report changes in the prevalence of health risk factors?

    1.1.2.4 Report changes in health resource consumption?

1.1.3 Does the SPHS track the state's health-related data over time?

If so, are state data compared to:

    1.1.3.1 National health objectives?

    1.1.3.2 Benchmarks from previous state health profiles?

1.1.4 Does the SPHS compile and provide locally collected data to organizations conducting local, state, and national health surveillance?

If so, does the SPHS operate:

    1.1.4.1 A data warehousing capacity that links data from diverse sources (e.g., universities, hospitals, managed care organizations, and health departments)?

    1.1.4.2 Protocols that meet the standards for compiling vital statistics and vital records?

    1.1.4.3 Geographic information systems (GIS) to analyze geocoded health data?

    1.1.4.4 Population health registries?

1.1.5 Does the SPHS collaborate with organizations or individuals that report health information to help assure the timely collection, analysis, and dissemination of data?

If so, does the SPHS collaborate with:

    1.1.5.1 Local health departments?

    1.1.5.2 Hospitals?

    1.1.5.3 Ambulatory care sites?

    1.1.5.4 Laboratories?

    1.1.5.5 Professional health organizations (e.g., state medical and nursing societies, state hospital associations)?

1.1.6 Does the SPHS develop a uniform set of health indicators to describe the health of the state's population?

If so,

    1.1.6.1 Do these indicators provide data specific to local jurisdictions?

    1.1.6.2 Are these indicators compiled from a variety of sources?

1.1.7 Does the SPHS enforce established laws and the use of protocols to protect personal health information and other data with personal identifiers?

If so, do these protocols include procedures to:

    1.1.7.1 Protect personal identifiers?

    1.1.7.2 Specify access for confidential and nonconfidential health information?

1.1.8 How much of this SPHS Model Standard is achieved by the state public health system collectively?

    0–25%   26–50%   51–75%   76–100%

    1.1.8.1 What percent of the answer reported in question 1.1.8 is the direct contribution of the state public health agency?

        0–25%   26–50%   51–75%   76–100%

Source: Reproduced from Centers for Disease Control and Prevention, 2003, National Public Health Performance Standards Program, Atlanta: CDC.

The local public health system assessment instrument brings together the local public health department and its community and health partners to contribute to the delivery of the core functions and essential public health services at the local level. It is evident that the local public health department will have a key role in the process, but there is no reason why some other entity may not be the lead agency. In many ways, it is true that public health is carried out mostly in local communities. As can be seen in **Table 22-2**, the indicators tied to each essential service are quite detailed and cover many activities not seen in the state instrument previously shown. Because the issue of local emergency preparedness and response is an important underlying theme, **Table 22-3** shows how the performance standards address the issue of planning for public health emergencies.

TABLE 22-2 Indicators for the Local Public Health System Performance Standards Instrument

Essential Service 1—Monitor health status to identify community health problems
Indicator 1.1—Population-based community health profile
Indicator 1.2—Access to and utilization of current technology to manage, display, analyze, and communicate population health data
Indicator 1.3—Maintenance of population health registries
Essential Service 2—Diagnose and investigate health problems and health hazards in the community
Indicator 2.1—Identification and surveillance of health threats
Indicator 2.2—Plan for public health emergencies
Indicator 2.3—Investigate and respond to public health emergencies
Indicator 2.4—Laboratory support for investigation of health threats
Essential Service 3—Inform, educate, and empower people about health issues
Indicator 3.1—Health education
Indicator 3.2—Health promotion activities to facilitate healthy living in healthy communities
Essential Service 4—Mobilize community partnerships to identify and solve health problems
Indicator 4.1—Constituency development
Indicator 4.2—Community partnerships
Essential Service 5—Develop policies and plans that support individual and community health efforts
Indicator 5.1—Governmental presence at the local level
Indicator 5.2—Public health policy development
Indicator 5.3—Community health improvement process
Indicator 5.4—Strategic planning and alignment with the community health improvement process
Essential Service 6—Enforce laws and regulations that protect health and ensure safety
Indicator 6.1—Review and evaluate laws, regulations, and ordinances
Indicator 6.2—Involvement in the improvement of laws, regulations, and ordinances
Indicator 6.3—Enforce laws, regulations, and ordinances
Essential Service 7—Link people to needed personal health services and assure the provision of health care when otherwise unavailable
Indicator 7.1—Identification of populations with barriers to personal health services
Indicator 7.2—Identifying personal health services needs of populations
Indicator 7.3—Assuring the linkage of people to personal health services
Essential Service 8—Assure a competent public and personal healthcare workforce
Indicator 8.1—Workforce assessment
Indicator 8.2—Public health workforce standards
Indicator 8.3—Lifelong learning through continuing education, training, and mentoring
Indicator 8.4—Public health leadership development
Essential Service 9—Evaluate effectiveness, accessibility, and quality of personal and population-based health services
Indicator 9.1—Evaluation of population-based health services

Indicator 9.2—Evaluation of personal health services

Indicator 9.3—Evaluation of the local public health system

Essential Service 10—Research for new insights and innovative solutions to health problems

Indicator 10.1—Fostering innovation

Indicator 10.2—Linkage with institutions of higher learning and/or research

Indicator 10.3—Capacity to initiate or participate in timely epidemiological, health policy, and health systems research

Source: Reproduced from Centers for Disease Control and Prevention, 2003, National Public Health Performance Standards Program, Atlanta: CDC.

TABLE 22-3 Example of Performance Standards for a Local Public Health System

Essential Service #2 Diagnose and Investigate Health Problems and Health Hazards in the Community

Indicator 2.2 Plan for Public Health Emergencies

LPHS Model Standard:

An emergency preparedness and response plan describes the roles, function, and responsibilities of LPHS entities in the event of one or more types of public health emergencies. Careful planning and mobilization of resources and partners prior to an event is crucial to a prompt and effective response. LPHS entities, including the local public health agency, law enforcement, fire departments, healthcare providers, and other partners work collaboratively to formulate emergency response plans and procedures. The plan should create a dual-use response infrastructure, in that it outlines the capacity of the LPHS to respond to all public health emergencies (including natural disasters), while taking into account the unique and complex challenges presented by chemical hazards or bioterrorism.

To plan for public health emergencies, the LPHS:

Defines and describes public health disasters and emergencies that might trigger implementation of the LPHS emergency response plan

Develops a plan that defines organizational responsibilities, establishes communication and information networks, and clearly outlines alert and evacuation protocols

Tests the plan each year through the staging of one or more mock events

Revises its emergency response plan at least every two years

Please answer the following questions related to Indicator 2.2:

2.2.1 Has the LPHS identified public health disasters and emergencies that might trigger implementation of the LPHS emergency response plan?

2.2.2 Does the LPHS have an emergency preparedness and response plan?

If so,

2.2.2.1 Is the emergency preparedness and response plan in written form?

2.2.2.2 Is there an established chain-of-command among plan participants?

Does the plan:

2.2.2.3 Describe the organizational responsibilities and roles of all plan participants?

2.2.2.4 Identify community assets that could be mobilized by plan participants to respond to an emergency?

(Continues)

TABLE 22-3   Example of Performance Standards for a Local Public Health System (*Continued*)

2.2.2.5   Describe LPHS communications and information networks?

2.2.2.6   Connect, where possible, to the state emergency response and preparedness plan?

2.2.2.7   Clearly outline protocols for emergency response?

If so, does the plan:

       2.2.2.7.1   Build on existing plans, protocols, and procedures within the community?

       2.2.2.7.2   Include written alert protocols to implement an emergency program of source and contact tracing for communicable diseases and toxic exposures?

       2.2.2.7.3   Include protocols to alert affected populations?

       2.2.2.7.4   Include an evacuation plan?

       2.2.2.7.5   Include procedures for coordinating public health responsibilities with law enforcement responsibilities?

2.2.3   Has any part of the plan been tested through simulations of one or more mock events within the past year?

2.2.4   Has the plan been reviewed or revised within the past two years?

2.2.5   How much of this LPHS Model Standard is achieved by the local public health system collectively?

    0–25%   26–50%   51–75%   76–100%

    2.2.5.1   What percent of the answer reported in question 2.2.5 is the direct contribution of the local public health agency?

       0–25%   26–50%   51–75%   76–100%

Source: Reproduced from Centers for Disease Control and Prevention, 2003, National Public Health Performance Standards Program, Atlanta: CDC.

The local public health governance performance instrument concentrates on the governing body responsible for oversight of the 10 essential services at the local level. It is the governing board that is accountable for promoting the public's health at the local level. The performance standards related to governance are based on ensuring legal authority, resources, policy making, accountability through continuous quality improvement and evaluation, and collaboration. Each of the 10 essential services in the governance instrument is charged with an oversight function, as can be seen in **Table 22-4**. **Table 22-5** gives an example of the indicator for Essential Service 4 with the accompanying questions.

It is important to recognize that these tools need to lead to a statewide coordinated approach to performance standards. As can be seen in **Figure 22-2**, the state performance standards will clearly be affected by the level of performance in every local jurisdiction. Local jurisdictions provide feedback to the state on emerging trends and challenges. The federal government influences the performance standards of the state through the funding and policy mechanism. This relationship affects state priorities as well. The state will work to implement both federal and state mandates at the local level. There needs to be a close working relationship between the local governing body and the local public health system. Governance is tied to oversight by the governing body. The relationship between the local governing body and the state through its elected officials, state agencies, or the state board of health (if there is one) can also be important for coordinating and developing statewide relationships.

The performance standards tools can give the public health leader much information to guide planning and future action. These standards will also help in building community infrastructure. There also needs to be a connection between these standards and performance standards related to emergency preparedness and response. First, it is necessary for the emergency preparedness and response system to begin to build its programs on the core functions and essential public health services model using the instruments developed so far or by developing a special performance standards instrument for emergency preparedness. Emergency preparedness programs need to be based on the same principles that guide the performance standards programs. Assessment is part

TABLE 22-4 Indicators for Local Health Governance

Essential Service 1—Monitor health status to identify community health problems
Indicator G1—Oversight to assure community health status monitoring
Essential Service 2—Diagnose and investigate health problems and health hazards in the community
Indicator G2—Oversight to assure public health surveillance and response
Essential Service 3—Inform, educate, and empower people about health issues
Indicator G3—Oversight of public health information, education, and empowerment activities
Essential Service 4—Mobilize community partnerships to identify and solve health problems
Indicator G4—Oversight to assure constituency building and partnership development
Essential Service 5—Develop policies and plans that support individual and community health efforts
Indicator G5—Oversight of public health policy making and planning
Essential Service 6—Enforce laws and regulations that protect health and ensure safety
Indicator G6—Oversight of public health legal and regulatory affairs
Essential Service 7—Link people to needed personal health services and assure the provision of health care when otherwise unavailable
Indicator G7—Oversight to assure public health outreach and enabling services
Essential Service 8—Assure a competent public and personal healthcare workforce
Indicator G8—Oversight of public health workforce issues
Essential Service 9—Evaluate effectiveness, accessibility, and quality of personal and population-based health services
Indicator G9—Oversight of public health service evaluation
Essential Service 10—Research for new insights and innovative solutions to health problems
Indicator G10—Oversight to assure public health innovation and research

Source: Reproduced from Centers for Disease Control and Prevention, 2003, National Public Health Performance Standards Program, Atlanta: CDC.

TABLE 22-5 Example of Governance Standards

Essential Service #4 Mobilize Community Partnerships to Identify and Solve Health Problems
This service includes:
Identifying potential stakeholders who contribute to or benefit from public health and increasing their awareness of the value of public health
Building coalitions to draw upon the full range of potential human and material resources to improve community health
Convening and facilitating partnerships among groups and associations (including those not typically considered to be health related) in undertaking defined health improvement projects, including preventive, screening, rehabilitation, and support programs
Indicator G4   Oversight to Assure Constituency Building and Partnership Activity
Governance Model Standard:
The board of health or other governing body is responsible for creating a supportive environment that assures traditional and nontraditional partnerships are nurtured in order to draw on the full range of potential human and material resources in the cause of community health.
For effective constituency building and partnership development, the board of health or other governing body:
Assures constituency building, partnership activities, and resource development partners to identify and solve health problems

(*Continues*)

TABLE 22-5   Example of Governance Standards (*Continued*)

Assures the development, implementation, and review of policies articulating commitment to these activities

Conducts annual evaluations of these activities and provides relevant feedback to its constituents and the community at large

Implements strategies to enhance participation among current and potential constituents

Please answer the following questions related to Essential Service #4:

G4.1:   Does the board of health or other governing body periodically identify the individuals, agencies, or organizations providing public health leadership in constituency building and partnership activities within the community?

G4.2:   Does the board of health or other governing body assure access to national, state, or local resources that could be used for constituency building or partnership activities?

G4.3:   Does the board of health or other governing body assure the coordination of resources in the community to enhance partnerships and collaboration to achieve public health objectives?

G4.4:   Does the board of health or other governing body periodically assure the development, implementation, and/or review of written policies in support of public health constituency building or partnership activities?

G4.5:   Does the board of health or other governing body annually assure that an evaluation of public health constituency and partnership activities is performed?

If so, does the board of health or other governing body:

G.4.5.1:   Annually assure that feedback is provided directly to LPHS partners on community mobilization around health issues?

G.4.5.2:   Assure recognition of LPHS partners for their commitment and role in addressing public health goals and objectives?

G4.6:   Does the board of health or other governing body periodically implement strategies to enhance participation among current and potential constituents? (This could include activities designed to acknowledge and reward participants.)

Source: Reproduced from Centers for Disease Control and Prevention, 2003, National Public Health Performance Standards Program, Atlanta: CDC.

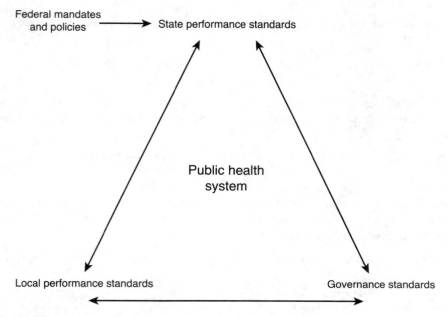

FIGURE 22-2 Building the Public Health System through Collaboration.

of emergency preparedness, as are policy development and assurance functions. It follows that the paradigm of essential public health services would also enhance the emergency preparedness initiatives. These performance standards have undergone revisions over the years. Version 3 will be released during 2012.

Paul Halverson, the father of the national public health performance standards program and who is now a professor at the College of Public Health at the University of Arkansas for Medical Sciences and Director of the Arkansas Department of Health, has addressed some of these issues in detail in Case Study 22-A.

Case Study 22-A

A Public Health Practice Quiz for Paul Halverson

1. How can performance standards help us in the community-building process?

First of all, the National Public Health Performance Standards have been designed around the concept of the *public health system*. The public health system is broadly defined to include all stakeholders in the health of the public, including the governmental public health organization and health department, as well as any other organization, governmental or private, that has an interest, or stake, in the health of a population group. This definition is meant to be very inclusive and does, for example, specifically include the contribution made by other governmental organizations, such as the departments of social services and the departments of mental health. It is also meant to include the contributions made by hospitals, physicians, and other voluntary organizations, such as United Way, the Red Cross, and the American Heart Association, as well as more informal, community-based organizations that have a compelling interest in the health of the community. This includes neighborhood associations, as well as the contributions of employers and others.

This public health system is a critically important construct of the performance standards, and it is this broad context in which the performance standards were developed. Using the active participation and input of all these organizations and individuals with an interest in the health of the community, the performance standards provide the opportunity for an objective look at the degree to which the community is served by an effective public health system.

The performance standards were developed by individuals in practice and are representative of the optimal standards of practice using the 10 essential services of public health as the organizing framework. The 10 essential services provide us with a clear idea of the breadth of public health and build upon the work of the consensus of many different national public health organizations. The 10 essential services are not perfect, and there may be other frameworks that better describe public health. However, the decision was made in the beginning that the effort should focus on the development of specific examples of good practice in public health, rather than in developing yet another framework for providing the conceptual overview of public health.

So, in essence, the performance standards build upon a broad, inclusive definition of public health and the system in which it operates. Second, the performance standards provide for an objective, consensus-based assessment of the current state of affairs in a particular community. And, third, given the results of the assessment, the standards provide an avenue for discussion and prioritization of community asset building.

The process itself is often reported by communities as critically important because it opens the dialogue between all the various players and partners in the community who have been engaged in public health, and in some cases were even unaware of the efforts of others who have similar goals. In addition, it provides a context by which a community can assess its strengths and weaknesses and commit publicly to specific improvement strategies. This public and community consensus-building exercise is a critical component of the use of the performance standards program and is seen as a major benefit.

Another aspect of the community-building process is to provide comparative information by which community leaders, as well as public health professionals, can reach consensus on what is "good." For many people who are involved in public health, the concepts and goals related to public health have been diffuse and it is sometimes hard to gain a common understanding around specific measures of success. The performance standards attempt to provide specificity and a comparative level of performance for communities to judge how well they are able to achieve the optimal standards. Frequently, public policy decisions are based upon comparative information, which can be an important component of the performance standards program. Especially when the standards process is completed on a statewide basis, individual counties may then compare their results to neighboring and what are frequently seen as "competing" jurisdictions for evaluative purposes. Likewise, communities as well as the state taken as a whole can review their data and more objectively define their areas most in need of development in a more scientific and data-based way, rather than simply choosing areas that may or may not have the greatest need.

(Continues)

Lastly, the performance standards program is imbedded within the MAPP (Mobilizing Action for Partnership and Planning) process. This is a very comprehensive, inclusive methodology that was developed around community health improvement and the performance standards as one of four community assessment measurements that are included. The designers of the National Public Health Performance Standards Program are committed to community building as a major reason for the conduct of the performance standards.

2. What is the relationship between performance standards and action planning?

Again, the assessment of the public health system is the first step in building a strong capacity within that jurisdiction's public health system. Once the assessments are completed and scores are derived, the leadership of the public health system can begin a dialogue within the context of the public health system and define the highest priority for action. This priority-setting process is critically important and lends itself toward specific assignment of action steps. In many communities, the priorities that are chosen by the community public health system are then assigned leadership responsibility, and leaders within the community commit to specific action steps as part of the leadership for the community. An important indicator of the seriousness of the commitment of building a strong public health system can often be found in the degree to which community organization leaders are willing to take on leadership responsibility for solving a public health system area and including it in their organization's strategic plan. For example, if an important goal for a public health system relates to improving the health status measurement of the community and if the hospital president chooses to take on this leadership role with the public health system, the degree to which he or she is able to incorporate this health status measurement goal within the context of his or her personal performance plan and similarly includes it within the hospital strategic plan is an important clue as to the seriousness of the commitment made for improving the public health system. In other words, the action planning is a critical next step after the completion of the performance standards and should be seen as a commitment by the community to use the information obtained from the performance standards to make a difference for the community. Additionally, communities should not consider doing the performance standards unless they are willing to commit to a multiple-year strategy that includes the initial measurement, prioritizing and action planning, and then the subsequent implementation of improvement, followed by measurement and then repeating of the performance standards process. This entire process is very consistent with the quality improvement processes used throughout health care and other industries and provides an important linkage to system change.

3. Why is there so much resistance to implementing the National Public Health Performance Standards Program at the local level?

Actually, their resistance to implementing the performance standards program has steadily decreased over the years. First, the National Public Health Performance Standards Program was developed principally by practitioners from a variety of practice settings. The local standards, for example, were developed as part of the effort led by the National Association of County and City Health Officials (NACCHO) to develop the MAPP process and to include the performance standards as one of the four assessments within MAPP. The NACCHO-led group consisted of public health officers from large and small jurisdictions in both urban and rural settings. In addition, the performance standards were subject to extensive field testing and were subsequently improved and changed based upon reports from the field testing activities. The performance standards program then represents a practice-based and practice-led effort by the National Public Health Partners to improve the practice of public health.

Additionally, CDC reports that now nearly half of the states in the country have committed to or completed a statewide implementation of the National Public Health Performance Standards Program. This implementation is good news and, frankly, speaks less to resistance and more toward fairly optimistic and enthusiastic adoption.

Accountability within public health is frequently seen by practitioners as inviting the opportunity to be beat up or punished. The fact of the matter is that accountability really needs to be seen as the opportunity to celebrate success and get credit for good things that have been accomplished, rather than seeing accountability as the opportunity to be punished for poor performance. We have much to celebrate in public health in terms of our success, and the performance standards provide us with the opportunity to clearly demonstrate this using nationally adopted consensus standards. That being said, however, there is pause given by all of us as it relates to the idea of being measured in terms of performance. The performance standards were not developed to be used as a "report card," but rather as an instrument for quality improvement. However, there are still individuals that see public health as the sole domain of the public health department, and anything negative that might surface as somehow being equivalent to pointing a finger at the health officer.

Encouraging news from the field is that more and more health officers see the performance standards as an important way to celebrate success and are voluntarily leading the way toward implementation. So, in summary, we don't see major opposition by local communities in using the performance standards, but rather a very positive movement toward using the performance standards as a way to celebrate success.

4. What are the next steps in implementing the National Public Health Performance Standards Program?

The next steps in implementation relate to the continuation of efforts by the national associations, principally the Association of State and Territorial Health Officers (ASTHO), the National Association of County and City Health Officers (NACCHO), the National Association of Local Boards of Health (NALBOH), the National Network of Public Health Institutes (NNPHI), and the American Public Health Association (APHA)/Public Health Foundation (PHF). These organizations are working together to provide technical assistance and support the state and local public health agencies and their boards who are interested in implementation. The CDC continues to play a leadership role in providing resources to these associations to facilitate this work.

One of the important next steps is the updating of the performance standards to meet the office of Management and Budget Guidance for Modernization. The commitment made by the CDC at the inception of the program was that these standards would be continually updated to reflect the optimal practice of public health. This is a continuing obligation that is important for the field to acknowledge. The performance standards, should they fail to remain contemporary, would in fact be seen as a way to hold back progress and to not support growth and expansion within public health. So, the expansion and modernization of the performance standards is a critical next step, which will be led by the CDC and the National Partners.

In addition, an important next step would be the use of the National Public Health Performance Standards as the basis for the development of an accreditation program. With nearly half of the state and local health departments in the country having used the performance standards, and many others interested in utilizing the instruments, it is critical for us to maintain the momentum of the standards program, while at the same time beginning to commit to accreditation activities. The 10 essential standards and the performance standards provide an important basis for the development of the accreditation instruments. The performance standards provide a national consensus on the optimal public health practice at the public health system level. The accreditation process should be based upon the performance of the governmental public health agency and would, in its nature, include minimum standards or minimum levels of achievement as a basis for granting an accreditation to the agency. Therefore, the performance standards have a continuing and important role in providing the beacon of optimal performance for the system and the basis for accreditation. The accreditation instruments, while providing differing levels of standards for achievement in the accreditation process, must include a minimum level of achievement and, therefore, are different from the performance standards program. Both the performance standards for optimal practice of public health within a system context and agency-based minimum standards for accreditation are critical components of system-building activities.

Indeed, one suggestion that I would have for those crafting the certification standards would be to have, as a minimum requirement, all organizations being considered for accreditation demonstrate their use of the performance standards as part of their quality improvement process. Therefore, the performance standards in the accreditation process can be tightly linked, and both can be better because of a complementary set of standards.

An area that has frequently received attention in the interaction between accreditation and the use of the standards is the role of the agency in the building and maintaining of an appropriate and effective public health system. I can't think of a more important role for the governmental public health agency than in the development, maintenance, and continuous improvement of a vibrant and robust public health system. Indeed, it's my belief that an effective public health system is an absolute prerequisite to an effective governmental public health organization. Any health officer today who believes that the governmental public health agency can solely, within its own authority and budget, perform all those services necessary for the community is clearly not seeing the same picture of public health that most see in the importance of engaging the community in the practice of public health. Sustained community involvement is a critical component to the success of public health, and the public health officer's primary responsibility is to build and maintain those relationships that will enable effective system work.

(Continues)

5. Why don't our emergency preparedness and response leaders recognize the utility of the public health core functions and essential public health services?

In large part, the failure of emergency preparedness and response leaders to recognize the core functions and essential services lies with our inability as public health leaders to effectively communicate and utilize important examples with others in explaining public health. I am confident that communities who engage in the use of the National Public Health Performance Standards Program and complete the assessment as a community-wide organization, including emergency preparedness and response leaders in the process, would have much less difficulty gaining acceptance of the essential services framework than those who simply expect the emergency response people to know this framework without significant exposure. It would be similar to the lack of understanding by many public health officials of the framework for evaluation of corrections or fire control activities. We need to expose emergency response leaders to the 10 essential services framework and engage these leaders in helping to build an effective public health system. We need to listen carefully to the contributions they make and help them understand the role they play in building a strong and effective public health system.

It is critical that we acknowledge that emergency preparedness and response are critical components of any effective public health system. It is, therefore, incumbent upon public health leaders to ensure that the full array of stakeholders engage in the public health system-building processes engendered by the National Public Health Performance Standards Program.

COMMUNITY ENGAGEMENT

As we enter the second decade of the 21st century, there is once again belief that the community working together is best qualified for promoting the health of the public. Community engagement approaches and strategies are being pursued for these renewed activities. Community engagement has been defined as a process in which individuals and community organizations promote programs that will benefit the community.[21] With a community benefit philosophy, community engagement through collaboration is the goal, with a common vision of health promotion and disease prevention. Specifically, community benefits refer to programs and services that are designed to improve health in a community and to also increase access to a comprehensive array of community services.[22] The definition of community will vary depending on the type of jurisdiction covered.

Table 22-6 is the CDC's list of principles to guide community engagement.[23] The first two principles are to be considered before a community engagement process occurs. The second two principles refer to what needs to occur as part of the engagement process. The final four principles relate to what makes the community engagement process successful. Leadership is critical for successful community engagement. It is through our leaders that community engagement creates change that supports health improvement. It is possible to use the skills of meta-leadership to increase the chances for success

TABLE 22-6 Principles of Community Engagement

Before Starting a Community Engagement Effort . . .
1. Be clear about the purposes or goals of the engagement effort, and the populations and/or communities you want to engage.
2. Become knowledgeable about the community in terms of its economic conditions, political structures, norms and values, demographic trends, history, and experience with engagement efforts. Learn about the community's perceptions of those initiating the engagement activities.
For Engagement to Occur, It Is Necessary to . . .
3. Go into the community, establish relationships, build trust, work with the formal and informal leadership, and seek commitment from community organizations and leaders to create processes for mobilizing the community.
4. Remember and accept that community self-determination is the responsibility and right of all people who comprise a community. No external entity should assume it can bestow to a community the power to act in its own self-interest.
For Engagement to Succeed . . .
5. Partnering with the community is necessary to create change and improve health.
6. All aspects of community engagement must recognize and respect community diversity. Awareness of the various cultures of a community and other factors of diversity must be paramount in designing and implementing community engagement approaches

7. Community engagement can only be sustained by identifying and mobilizing community assets, and by developing capacities and resources for community health decisions and action.

8. An engaging organization or individual change agent must be prepared to release control of actions or interventions to the community, and be flexible enough to meet the changing needs of the community.

9. Community collaboration requires long-term commitment by the engaging organization and its partners.

Source: Reproduced from Centers for Disease Control and Prevention (1997). Principles of Community Engagement. Public Health Practice Program Office, Atlanta, GA. http://www.cdc.gov/phppo/pce/. Accessed July 31, 2012.

in our endeavors. Two major initiatives to promote community engagement and transformation have been funded by the Centers for Disease Control and Prevention during the latter part of the first decade of the 21st century and into the second decade—the Communities Putting Prevention to Work (CPPW) initiative and later the Community Transformation Grant (CTG) program.

SUMMARY

This chapter presented a number of techniques related to building the community and improving our community engagement activities. Public health leaders are often not aware of many of these skills. The issue of developing and working with community leaders was discussed, as was the importance of assets planning. Multicultural considerations were also discussed. The Leadership Wheel was used to show the various activities leaders need to use in working in collaborative relationships. The importance of utilizing performance standards was also discussed by reviewing the three instruments developed for the National Public Health Performance Standards Program.

DISCUSSION QUESTIONS

1. What are the factors involved in community growth, and how might these factors contribute to that growth?
2. How does the assets-planning model change how community challenges are handled?
3. How do the three performance standards measures help to give a comprehensive view of the work of public health?
4. Describe the relationship between community engagement and community benefit.

EXERCISE 22-1: Community Sectors

Purpose: to identify community resources for building communities

Key concepts: community sectors, community building

Procedures: Look at your home community and identify the community sectors. Determine how you can increase community outreach. What are the outcomes that you would like to obtain? If you are a member of a community collaborative, the collaborative can do this exercise.

Community Sectors	Possible Outreach Activities	Potential Outcomes

---

EXERCISE 22-2: Cascading Values

Purpose: to utilize values as a framework for collaboration

Key concepts: values, collaboration, agenda setting

Procedures: This exercise has been developed for you in your work with a community group.

Have each member of your collaborative group, whether it be a coalition, alliance, or a partnership, write down on an index card three values that each member sees as related to his or her involvement in such a community activity. Write all the values on a large sheet of paper (flip chart). Discuss each value with the group as a whole to see how the group sees the collaboration. On a second index card, write three statements that reflect how each member sees the agenda for the group. Write the agenda items on a large sheet of paper, as you did for the values. Match the values to the agenda items. Discuss the results. Create a value statement and a six-month agenda protocol for the collaborative as a whole.

REFERENCES

1. M. Magee, *Positive Leadership* (New York: Spencer Books, 2000).
2. Magee, *Positive Leadership*.
3. P. Mattessich and B. Monsey, *Community Building: What Makes It Work?* (St. Paul, MN: Amherst H. Wilder Foundation, 1997).
4. W. K. Kellogg Foundation, *Sustaining Community-Based Initiatives: Developing Community Capacities* (Battle Creek, MI: Author, 1995).
5. Kellogg, *Sustaining Community-Based Initiatives*.
6. Kellogg, *Sustaining Community-Based Initiatives*.
7. Kellogg, *Sustaining Community-Based Initiatives*.
8. G. Kaye and T. Wolff, *From the Ground Up* (Amherst, MA: AHEC Community Partners, 1997).
9. D. Ayre, G. Clough, and T. Norris, *Facilitating Community Change* (San Francisco: Grove Consultants International, 2000).
10. M. Axner, *Developing a Plan for Building Leadership, Community Toolbox*. Accessed from http://ctb.ku.edu/en/tablecontents/sub_section_main_1119.aspx, September 2005.
11. Axner, *Developing a Plan for Building Leadership*.
12. K. Johnson, W. Grossman, and A. Cassidy, eds., *Collaborating to Improve Community Health* (San Francisco: Jossey-Bass, 1996).
13. Kaye and Wolff, *From the Ground Up*.
14. Kaye and Wolff, *From the Ground Up*.
15. J. P. Kretzmann and J. L. McKnight, *Building Communities from the Inside Out* (Evanston, IL: Northwestern University ABCD Institute, 1993).
16. Kretzmann and McKnight, *Building Communities from the Inside Out*.
17. Kretzmann and Mc Knight, *Building Communities from the Inside Out*.
18. J. P. Kretzmann and M. B. Green, *Building the Bridge from Client to Citizen: A Community Toolbox for Welfare Reform* (Evanston, IL: Northwestern University ABCD Institute, 1998).
19. Ayre, Clough, and Norris, *Facilitating Community Change*.
20. Centers for Disease Control and Prevention, *National Public Health Performance Standard* (Atlanta, GA: Author, 2003).
21. www.cdc.gov/phppo, accessed December 2011.
22. www.chausa.org/communitybenefits, accessed December 2011.
23. www.cdc.gov/nphpsp, accessed December 2011.

CHAPTER 23

Cultural Competency

Only by venturing into the unknown do we enable new ideas to take shape, and those shapes are different for each voyager.

—Margaret Wheatley, *Leadership and the New Science*

By the year 2050, racial and ethnic minorities are expected to total 30% of the U.S. population (**Table 23-1**), up from 25% at the start of the new century.[1] In 2010, African Americans represented about 12.7% of the population, Hispanic or Latino about 16%, Asians about 3.8%, and other groups about 3%.[2] As a result, the professions, like the general population, will include a steadily increasing percentage of ethnically diverse populations as members. The growth in minority representation will bring both challenge and promise.

A federal report on the public health workforce in the 21st century released at the end of the previous century stated that it would be in the best interests of the American public to be served by a workforce that is ethnically and culturally diverse.[3] Furthermore, a study of middle-class Americans found that these Americans generally support multiculturalism.[4] However, they also generally believe that all immigrants should learn English and become integrated into American society—a point of view referred to as "benign multiculturalism."[5] Many immigrants and native-born people think that the emphasis on integration into the mainstream is a form of disrespect toward and denigration of the cultural values of the diverse minority groups that make up a large portion of the U.S. population. In short, it seems as if recent attempts to value the full range of diverse population groups have been a failure.[6] Some of these issues are explored in Case Study 23-A, which

TABLE 23-1 Population by Race and Hispanic Origin for the United States 2009–2050

Race	2009	2050
White	79.5%	74%
Black	12.7%	13%
Asian	3.8%	7.8%
Hispanic	16.0%	30.2%
Other	3.0%	5.2%

Source: Adapted from L. B. Shresta and E. Heisler, *The Changing Demographic Profile of the United States* (Washington, DC: Congressional Research Service, 2011).

Racism: A Mental Health Issue

D. Clemons, J. A. Janssen, K. Pakieser-Reed, J. Pitzer, and S. Strachniak

Background

A Mexican American male (father of two children, married, intact family) was accused of molesting a young "white" girl. The incident occurred in Harvest City. The allegation was publicized in the local paper. A group of Anglo males gathered outside the Mexican American's home and stoned it. Two Anglos were arrested for ethnic intimidation. The charge against the Mexican American male was dropped as a false charge, without publicity.

The local newspaper's editorial declared the incident was racist in nature and stated that the community cannot "sweep [it] under the carpet." Local church leaders offered (1) to facilitate the process of cultural awareness by the majority population of the minority population, (2) to increase awareness of racism in the community, and (3) to increase understanding among people.

The Harvest City Council established a human relations committee in the fall of 1991 and hired Mr. George as a consultant to help define the committee's role. As a result of Mr. George's actions, the city forwarded a survey to the local schools for distribution to all parents and high school seniors. The survey focused on identifying the perceived community needs as determined by the parents and seniors. The committee's actions would then be directed by the survey results. In the spring of 1992, tension continued to grow, and some fighting occurred between Anglos and Hispanics in the Harvest community.

The human relations committee sponsored "Fiesta Days" to increase cultural awareness in a fun atmosphere in the summer of 1992. The celebration was a success!

Case Study Chronology

Fall 1992

Tension increased between Anglo and Hispanic students at Harvest High School. The Harvest City Council Human Relations Committee met with the dean of students to discuss the problem. They determined that this was not a gang problem but did have some "ganglike" aspects. The school hired Mr. George to serve as a consultant and to develop plans to deflate the racial tension. The Harvest police chief said that the problems were the responsibility of the parents and that the parents needed to be involved in the solutions.

Fistfights broke out among the Anglo and Hispanic students at Harvest High School and Junior High School. Both Anglo and Hispanic students were suspended. School officials believed that the fights were racially motivated. (About 10% of the high school students were Hispanic.) Additional fights between Anglos and Hispanics were reported at various locations in the community.

The Temporary Farmers Association approached the Macmillian County Mental Health Board with a request for funding a mental health advocate position (Hispanic liaison) that would be "bilingual and bicultural and dedicated to improving the accessibility and quality of mental health and social services for the Hispanic residents of Macmillian County." The association stated that a growing number of residents in the county were Hispanic, spoke only Spanish, and were becoming an "at-risk" population due to little or no access to services that would improve their lives. The board denied the request and recommended formation of a task force to study the issue.

In a separate request, the Temporary Farmers Association requested funding from the Macmillian County Mental Health Board for a six-month study of racism in the county and its effects on the mental health of Hispanic residents. This project was funded.

As a result of the Mental Health Board's recommendation, a Hispanic connection task force was developed, primarily through the efforts of the association. The task force represented almost all of the social service, law enforcement, and religious organizations in the county. In its first meeting, the task force discussed the difficulties of providing services to the Hispanic population. The task force concluded that each member organization would benefit from the services of a countywide Hispanic liaison. They also decided that a "needs assessment should be done to determine county resources and needs regarding Hispanics."

The task force met a second time to design the needs assessment survey and to identify who should receive it. The task force also discussed the Hispanic liaison position: what should be the focus, where would the position be "housed," and how would it be funded? The members agreed that the position should be within the Temporary Farmers Association because the association was the "only agency within the county that has an ongoing and committed relationship with the county's Hispanic population." They also agreed that it must be apparent that all of the task force's member agencies endorsed and supported the liaison role and that the task force would actively support and coach the person chosen as liaison.

In an unrelated action, the Harvest City Council Human Relations Committee requested from the Macmillian County Mental Health Board funding for and/or assistance with the creation of workplace cultural diversity training programs to build bridges between people (Anglos and Hispanics). The project was not funded because it did not directly relate to the provision of mental health services.

Winter 1992–1993

The Hispanic Connection Task Force forwarded a survey to social service and mental health agencies to "better assess available county resources and needs related to our Hispanic population."

A second survey, one for the Hispanic community, was developed by the Hispanic Connection Task Force and distributed to the population through member agencies of the task force. Survey results were slow coming in, partially due to the length of the survey. The task force extended the time for the survey to receive sufficient responses to make a conclusion.

After summarizing results from both needs assessments, the task force developed and forwarded a resolution to government and social service agencies countywide. The resolution acknowledged the value of ethnic and cultural diversity and showed the organizations' support of the Hispanic liaison position. Sixty organizations signed the resolution, including churches, libraries, and mental health and health organizations as well as the county board.

The Macmillian County Board voted 19–2 in support of the liaison position. However, some board members felt that all non-English-speaking residents should have liaison services available to them and that the position as proposed was providing Hispanics with special status. No funding decision was made with this vote.

Following the passing of the resolution, the Macmillian County Mental Health Board approved partial funding for a Hispanic liaison position as presented by the Temporary Farmers Association. They forwarded information about the position and a request for the second half of the salary (up to $20,000) to the Macmillian County Mental Health Board and Human Services Committee. The mental health board felt that the liaison position would help the Hispanic population of 11,000 people access mental health, school, social service, and government programs and enhance their functioning in the county as a whole. The mental health board felt that prevention and lessening of barriers would decrease the likelihood of more intensive (and expensive) mental health interventions in the future. The liaison would also be responsible for community coordination between Latino and non-Latino organizations.

Spring 1993

Two agencies that did not originally sign the resolution altered their positions to a more positive stance regarding the liaison position. The All Faith Church wrote a letter to the Macmillian County Mental Health Board in full support of the liaison position. Charitable Services signed the resolution with qualifications noted.

The Macmillian County Board and Human Services Committee voted in favor of funding the liaison position to "bridge the cultural gap between Hispanics and county officials in delivering services." Prior to the vote, one member of the committee raised the question of the appropriateness of mental health funds being allocated for a Hispanic liaison position that was developed in response to racist actions. Members of the committee who voted for the position felt that racism was a mental health issue. The committee forwarded the position and funding request to the Macmillian County Board Finance Committee for final recommendation to the county board.

A week after the health and human services committee voted in favor of the liaison position, Charitable Services stated that it had been providing liaison services for the past three and a half years in Harvest and Stone Lake. The county board chairperson, Ms. Ace, stated that she would investigate to see if the new liaison services were needed and would determine if it was appropriate for the county board to fund the position. The mental health board president, Mr. Jones, stated that the proposed liaison position was much broader in scope than the newly discovered social service position.

The county board chairperson decided to not recommend funding to the finance committee of the county board for the proposed liaison position until the Temporary Farmers Association and Charitable Services met, discussed the proposed position, and resolved funding issues. (By now, both groups wanted to be considered for the total of $40,000 salary funds.) The groups agreed to meet with the mental health board executive director, Mr. Jones, and come to a resolution.

(Continues)

Mr. Jones and Ms. Hope, Temporary Farmers Association director, kept a scheduled meeting with the Macmillian County Board Finance Committee to discuss the position. The committee then voted 4–3 against funding the position but agreed to discuss the position again in two months after further study.

The Charitable Services and Temporary Farmers Association directors met and clarified the roles of the two liaison positions. A letter was sent to the county board chairperson noting the clarification and joint support of the new position as proposed.

In the meantime, the mental health board voted to fund the proposed liaison position on a full-time basis for six months. The board felt that the issue was too important to wait for a final funding vote by the county board. The Temporary Farmers Association had to make a decision whether to take the risk and hire a full-time liaison or wait for the county board's funding decision.

The Temporary Farmers Association filled the position; Mr. George gave up his SASS position to become the liaison through November with the hope that additional funds would be approved by the county board.

Two months later, after a positive recommendation from Ms. Ace, the Macmillian County Board Finance Committee met again and unanimously recommended funding of the position through FY 93. The next month, the finance committee's recommendation for funding went to the full county board. The vote was 20–4 in favor of funding the position.

Since 1993, the position has continued to be funded jointly by the county board and the mental health board and has been responsible for the development of five community human relations councils and hundreds of interventions with the Latino and non-Latino communities on individual and organizational levels.

Conclusion

Racism is a topic that many people would rather not address, as evidenced by the population described at the beginning of the case study. When racism finally reaches a level that cannot easily be ignored, ownership of the resolution process can be difficult to determine.

Racism can be evidenced by property and personal damages. Wouldn't the proper "owner of the problem" be the legal and law enforcement authorities? When the symptoms lead to physical harm that requires medical attention, then wouldn't the "owner" be the healthcare institution? If the symptoms are acts of disregard for the human spirit, then isn't the rightful "owner" the church membership? What symptoms need to be exhibited for the problem of racism to fall under the ownership of mental health?

Using the core values of public health as a guideline, answers to these questions can be achieved, as well as a perspective on how racism becomes a public health problem falling within the purview of mental health.

---

explores the issue of racism in a small, rural city undergoing demographic change.

Public health leaders, to function effectively in a more culturally diverse environment, will have to confront their personal prejudices and stereotypes and take measures to overcome them. They also should try to understand the nature of the challenges presented by increased cultural diversity at the organizational and community levels.[7] First, many people want to maintain things as they are because they feel comfortable with the familiar. Second, some people are prejudiced against certain racial or ethnic groups because of how they were raised. Third, organizations often use impersonal hiring methods and favor people who fit the organizational mode, which usually means people like those who are already organizational members.

Affirmative action programs were instituted to address the fact that the makeup of many organizations did not reflect the makeup of the general population.

Their goal is not to obliterate differences but rather to create an environment in which cultural diversity becomes a strength: having employees with a range of different backgrounds and cultural values can create synergy and allow them to lead with greater effectiveness. A synergistic system is not one in which individual differences are obliterated but rather one in which the parts work together harmoniously. Therefore, if public health leaders are to be successful in the 21st century, they need to deal with the issue of cultural diversity today and learn to appreciate the diversity that exists in our society.[8] In the past, leaders expected people to adjust to the existing organizational culture and suppress their unique characteristics. This expectation has ceased to be a reasonable one.

Moreover, no public health agency operates independently of other organizations, the community in which it is located, or, for that matter, other parts of the globe. Global health issues have a way of affecting local communities. Thus, local public health leaders may find themselves dealing with an extremely diverse range of colleagues from around the world, one more reason for these leaders to work at becoming culturally competent.

MULTICULTURALISM

Multiculturalism is tied to what has been called the "politics of recognition."[9] Each cultural group in an organization, community, or country strives for acceptance. If not accepted, the group feels demeaned or looked down upon. The politics of recognition are not new in the United States. Different cultural groups have repeatedly fought for public recognition.

The nature and degree of the public's commitment to multiculturalism are not easy to determine.[10] For instance, public health leaders and others argue in support of "multiculturalism" but typically expect different cultural groups to accept the dominant Western European culture. Public health organizations need to review, restudy, rethink, and reorganize their structure in order to become truly multicultural.[11] Differences based on culture and language should enhance the profession of the public health community rather than create divisions within it. Yet divisiveness seems to be increasing.

Culturally competent leaders have the skills and attitudes needed to relate to people with different backgrounds and with different characteristics, including people of different races, genders, ages, sexual orientations, social classes, and lifestyles (see **Table 23-2**).[12] One way to develop these skills is to walk around the workplace and the community and talk to people regularly. Furthermore, talking directly to individuals defuses friction caused by cultural differences. The development of others is an important role for leaders and managers. There are a number of multicultural principles to keep in mind when working with people with different backgrounds:[13]

1. Understand your own cultural background and respect the backgrounds of others.
2. Lessen individualism and promote the value of teams and working together.

TABLE 23-2 Categories of Diversity

Race
Sex
Religion
Age (young, middle-aged, old)
Ethnicity (country of origin)
Education
Job-relevant abilities
Mental disabilities (attention deficit disorder)
Physical disabilities (hearing impairment, wheelchair use)
Values and motivation
Sexual orientation (heterosexual, homosexual, bisexual)
Marital status (married, single, cohabiting, widow, widower)
Family status (children, no children, two-parent family, single parent, grandparent)
Personality traits (introverted, extroverted, conscientious)
Functional background (area of specialization)
Technology interest (high-tech, low-tech, technophobe)
Weight (average, obese, underweight, anorexic)
Hair (full head of hair, bald, wild hair, tame hair, long hair, short hair)
Tobacco use (smoker versus nonsmoker, chewer versus nonchewer)
Gum use (chewer versus nonchewer)
Styles of clothing and appearance (dress up, dress down, professional appearance, casual appearance)

Source: Reprinted with the permission of Alpha Books, an imprint of Macmillan USA, a division of Pearson Education, from *The Complete Idiot's Guide to Leadership*, by Andrew Dubrin. Copyright © 1998.

3. Demonstrate empathy for others.
4. Share leadership.
5. Promote social justice and health equity.
6. Make servant leadership your goal.
7. Develop a shared vision with the community.
8. Utilize culturally appropriate language.
9. Treat people like family.
10. Promote "gratitude, hope, and forgiveness."

Public health leaders must get to know not only their workforce but also their community. Getting out of the office and meeting with different cultural groups helps leaders define the public health needs of the community better and also presents the public health agency in a better light. The agency might hold an open house to allow the community to get a better sense of what a public health agency does. An agency leader might invite residents from a range of backgrounds to his or her home for a party. By eating at local ethnic restaurants, leaders can learn about different cultural groups and reach out to those groups at the same time. Public health practitioners in general should be encouraged to learn languages, because being able to speak the native language of a community group will enhance the public health agency's credibility.

Although most cross-border alliances are business related, public health leaders may be involved in the creation of a cross-border alliance or partnership, in which case they need to engage in assessing and understanding the cultural differences that exist as one of the preliminary steps.[14] Furthermore, they must continue to address cultural factors even when they seem to have become less important. Management of cultural differences should be a part of any cross-cultural relationship.

To increase their cultural competency and act with cultural sensitivity, leaders need to:

- be aware of their own strengths and weaknesses as well as their own prejudices. Without this kind of self-awareness, they will not be able to address effectively the cultural issues that arise in their organizations.
- be alert for opportunities to receive feedback. Feedback, in this area as well as others, is an important information source.
- become lifelong learners, always on the lookout for new knowledge and skill development opportunities.
- integrate work life with personal life and maintain a multicultural perspective in both.
- learn to respect the differences between people. Out of existing differences can come strength.

Multicultural issues need to be addressed early in the formulation of a multicultural team, coalition, or partnership.[15] Exercise 23-1 was developed by Rosenthal to gauge the effectiveness of a group in addressing multicultural issues. To deal with multicultural issues, public health leaders must:

- learn how to analyze demographic data
- study social, economic, and political trends
- increase the number of minority public health staff so that the agency's makeup reflects the community's makeup
- consult with community leaders with different cultural backgrounds to guarantee that the programs developed fit the needs of the relevant cultural groups
- use feedback to monitor communication with cultural groups
- evaluate the workplace using the inclusivity checklist (see Exercise 23-1)

CULTURAL DIVERSITY

Cultural diversity programs are distinct from affirmative action programs. Affirmative action programs are generally intended to guarantee access to jobs by minority groups. Cultural diversity programs address the differences between people and try to ensure that people from different cultural backgrounds respect each other and are able to work together in harmony. They teach people to look beyond race, gender, and sexual orientation, for example, and treat each individual with the full respect due a human being. Diversity issues need to be incorporated into the strategic thinking activities of leaders. One interesting program was developed at IBM, where it was thought that different groups might require different approaches.[16] With diversity as a strategic goal, IBM developed eight task forces to deal with these issues, focusing on Asian issues, African American issues, issues of people with disabilities, white male issues, women issues, issues related to sexual orientation, Hispanic and Latino concerns, and issues of Native Americans. In Exercise 23-2, students explore the cultural diversity that exists among themselves with the purpose of gaining greater cultural understanding.

It is imperative that leaders view multicultural differences from a positive perspective rather than a negative one. Negativism undermines the communication process and obstructs the positive effects of building community partnerships. It is worth pointing out here the essential role that communication plays in dealing with cultural diversity. Little progress can be made unless everyone understands each other. Note that communication encompasses vocal inflections, hand gestures, and other types of nonverbal communication.

The two major ways in which diversity has been viewed in the workplace are limiting in perspective.[17] The first diversity paradigm has been defined as the discrimination and fairness model. With an awareness that discrimination and segregation are a reality, this model posits the negative aspects of discrimination, and fairness is required in recruitment, hiring, and retention of employees from different gender, racial, and ethnic groups. The second model is an access and legitimacy model. Here agencies will attempt to hire people who fit the demographic profile of the community that is being served. Thomas and Ely find this model lacking in that people hired under this model feel marginalized.[18] A third paradigm is emerging in which the values and perspectives of diverse people are incorporated into the mission, vision, and work of the organization. In order to shift to this new paradigm, leaders in the organization must understand the value of diversity as well as the learning opportunities that become available. High performance standards will be required of all staff. Training programs are important as well.

Leadership Tip

Having friends at work keeps you more committed to your organization.

Public health leaders must keep track of trends that have the potential to affect the extent and nature of the cultural diversity confronting them, such as the globalization of business, changing community demographics, and the ways of dealing with cultural diversity, such as new types of programs. Public health leaders must be devoted to promoting the health of everyone in the community, including members of diverse minority populations. The special health needs of these populations and their lack of access to programs and services must be addressed. Noncommonality of language is sometimes an obstacle in the way of residents receiving needed services, and public health leaders need to ensure that individuals who do not speak English will still get the care or services they require.

A report of the President's Initiative on Race cited major health findings regarding culturally diverse populations.[19] For example, the infant mortality rate is two and a half times higher for African Americans and one and a half times higher for Native Americans than for whites. In 1995, the age-adjusted rate of death attributable to heart disease for African Americans was 147 deaths per 100,000 people, compared with 105 deaths per 100,000 for whites and 108 deaths per 100,000 overall. The number of new acquired immune deficiency syndrome cases among African Americans is now greater than the number of new cases among whites. The prevalence of diabetes is 70% higher among African Americans than among whites, and the prevalence among Hispanics is nearly double the prevalence among whites. As for national immunization rates, 79% of white children less than two years of age have the full series of vaccinations, whereas only 74% of African American youngsters and 71% of Hispanic youngsters do. There are inequities in access to health care as well. For example, minority mothers are less likely than white mothers to get prenatal care. Access seems to be directly related to income level, which partly explains why certain minority groups have low rates of service use. Another access-related issue is whether a cultural group favors using traditional healers rather than medical school–trained physicians.

Figure 23-1 presents an interactionist model showing how diversity influences the careers of leaders and the effectiveness of their organizations.[20] As can be seen in column one, cultural diversity can have an effect at the individual, team, and agency levels (and, as noted above, it can also influence relations between a public health agency and the community in which it is located). The next two columns list possible effects on the individual and the organization. To get a fix on the diversity climate in an agency or a community, agency leaders can answer the questions in **Table 23-3**.

If you are trying to develop diversity training and coaching programs, it is necessary to include several dimensions in the content. Some of these dimensions are:[21]

- developing skills and acquisition of information to work with people of diverse backgrounds
- using surveys and personal interviews to address any potential problems
- promoting of accountability that the agency's diversity goals are being implemented throughout the organization

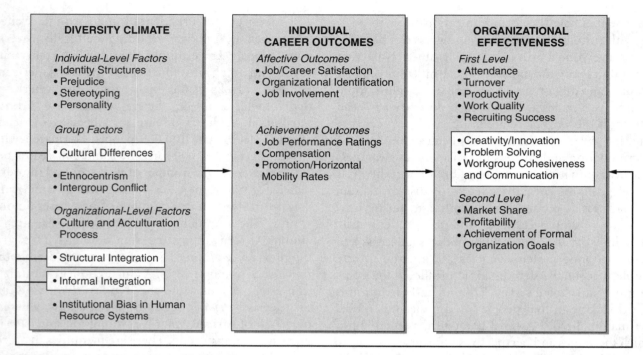

FIGURE 23-1 An International Model of the Effect of Diversity on Individual Career Outcomes and Organizational Effectiveness. *Source:* Reprinted with permission of the publisher. From *Cultural Diversity in Organizations,* copyright © 1993 by T. Cox Jr., Berrett-Koehler Publishers, Inc., San Francisco, CA. All rights reserved. 1-800-929-2929.

TABLE 23-3 Diversity Climate Index

1. Identify personal stereotypes and prejudices.
2. Do these stereotypes affect my job performance?
3. Does the staff in my agency judge others by standards different from community standards?
4. How is intergroup conflict resolved?
5. Within the agency, does the composition of the workforce reflect the community diversity?
6. Are culturally diverse people in the upper echelons of the organization?
7. How do agency personnel interact with the community?
8. How does the community relate to the agency?
9. Does the agency address the key health issues of concern to the community?
10. Have community partnerships been developed?

Source: Reprinted with permission of the publisher. From *Cultural Diversity in Organizations,* copyright © 1993 by T. Cox Jr., Berrett-Koehler Publishers, Inc., San Francisco, CA. All rights reserved. 1-800-929-2929.

- working with employees and work teams to make sure these groups are diverse
- providing of assistance when special needs are apparent

- implementing communication strategies related to the organization's commitment to diversity
- mentoring and coaching of employees

People with different backgrounds need to be involved in the planning related to any training initiative. It is also important that top leadership and management in the agency support these activities.

The road from merely managing diversity to creating a culturally competent organization has many steps.[22] First comes awareness and understanding of cultural diversity; action plans are then developed. **Figure 23-2** presents one model for developing cultural competency.[23] Note the importance given to integrating diversity issues into planning activities. As in any extended process, regular feedback is essential, and revisiting the issue of cultural awareness and understanding may be beneficial after the implementation of certain action steps.

Leaders must be sensitive to the needs of cultural groups in the community and in the agency. They should monitor these needs using epidemiological data. To be fully culturally competent, public health leaders must:

- directly address the issue of cultural diversity in the workplace
- concentrate on understanding the cultural values and norms of community partners

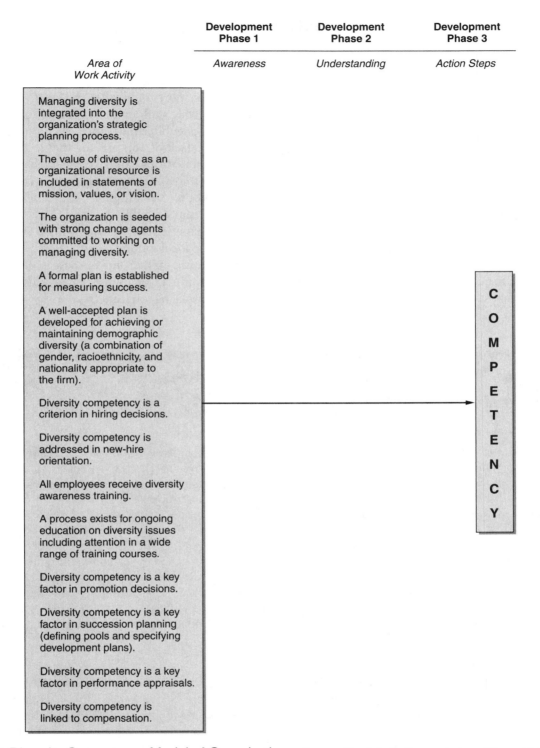

	Development Phase 1	Development Phase 2	Development Phase 3
Area of Work Activity	*Awareness*	*Understanding*	*Action Steps*

Managing diversity is integrated into the organization's strategic planning process.

The value of diversity as an organizational resource is included in statements of mission, values, or vision.

The organization is seeded with strong change agents committed to working on managing diversity.

A formal plan is established for measuring success.

A well-accepted plan is developed for achieving or maintaining demographic diversity (a combination of gender, racioethnicity, and nationality appropriate to the firm).

Diversity competency is a criterion in hiring decisions.

Diversity competency is addressed in new-hire orientation.

All employees receive diversity awareness training.

A process exists for ongoing education on diversity issues including attention in a wide range of training courses.

Diversity competency is a key factor in promotion decisions.

Diversity competency is a key factor in succession planning (defining pools and specifying development plans).

Diversity competency is a key factor in performance appraisals.

Diversity competency is linked to compensation.

COMPETENCY

FIGURE 23-2 **Diversity Competency Model of Organizations.** *Source:* Reprinted with permission of the publisher. From *Developing Competency to Manage Diversity*, © 1997 by T. Cox Jr. and R. L. Beale, Berrett-Koehler Publishers, Inc., San Francisco, CA. All rights reserved. 1-800-929-2929.

- learn to face personal stereotypes and prejudices in order to remove barriers due to cultural differences
- learn to be culturally sensitive and empathic to those they interact with

- evaluate the work environment to determine the positive and negative effects of a diverse workforce
- learn epidemiological techniques for analyzing the health needs of the community

- analyze diversity issues at each step in the leadership process
- develop a cultural diversity training program for all employees
- develop a workplace policy statement on cultural differences

Exercise 23-3 provides an opportunity to explore the way in which cultural diversity affects public leadership activities.

CULTURAL COMPETENCY SKILLS

Cultural competency includes the willingness and ability to develop programs and services for people of different cultures. As the report of the President's Initiative on Race states, "By understanding, valuing,

and incorporating the cultural differences of America's diverse population and examining one's own health-related values and beliefs, health providers deliver more effective and cost-efficient care."[24(p.17)]

Furthermore, public health leaders need to ensure that all agency staff act in a culturally sensitive way by setting and publicizing appropriate policies and procedures. A lack of concern for the needs of culturally diverse populations can have legal consequences. Case Study 23-B involves a discrimination complaint made to an Office for Civil Rights. (This case study was written by a team of public health leaders based on their personal experiences.) Another important set of issues involves a local public health agency and undocumented immigrants. Some of these issues are discussed in Case Study 23-C. (This case was also written by a team of public health leaders.)

Case Study 23-B

Gold County Health Department: A Case of Discrimination Requiring Assessment, Policy Development, and Assurance Practices

Nancy Bluhm, Valerie L. Webb, Ann Rodriguez, Robert Brewster, and Dale W. Galassie

Introduction

The Gold County Health Department received a discrimination complaint from the Office for Civil Rights (OCR) necessitating identification (assessment practices), development of policies and plans (policy development practices), and management of organizational resources (assurance practices) to adequately address the complaint, which claimed a lack of adequate interpreter services. Approximately 46% of this large urban health department's budget was funded by grants or reimbursables now placed at risk due to the discrimination complaint.

The landmark document *Healthy People 2000: National Health Promotion and Disease Prevention Objectives* noted that by the year 2000, the racial and ethnic composition of the American population would differ significantly. Whites will decline in population from 76% to 72% of the population. The Hispanic population could rise from 8% to 11.3%. Blacks could increase their proportion from 12.4% to 13.1%. In addition, other groups are projected to increase from 3.4% to 4.3%. The coloring of the American workforce is clearly evident by these statistics. That information further grounded the need for the Gold County Health Department to offer adequate interpreter services to meet the needs of its constituency.

Statement of Facts

The OCR received a complaint filed against the Gold County Health Department on October 8, 1992. The complainant, Mr. Peter Citizen, who filed on behalf of himself and non-English- and limited-English-speaking people, alleged a violation of Title VI of the Civil Rights Act of 1964 and its implementing regulation, 45 CFR Part 80. Specifically, the complainant alleged that the Gold County Health Department discriminated against non-English- and limited-English-speaking people on the basis of national origin by denying and delaying services, requiring them to provide their own interpreters, and treating them in a discriminatory manner, as evidenced by negative comments and a hostile attitude and by assigning them to Spanish-speaking clinics.

The behavior cited in the allegation would constitute a violation of Title VI and its implementing regulation. OCR has jurisdiction over complaints alleging discrimination on the basis of race, color, and national origin by recipients of federal financial assistance. The Gold County Health Department is a recipient of substantial federal financial assistance and is, therefore, subject to the provisions of Title VI, which prohibits such discrimination. The millions of federal dollars received by the agency are for the Alcohol, Drug Abuse, and Mental Health Block Grant, Medicare, and Medicaid programs.

A prompt investigation to determine whether a violation occurred was scheduled by OCR (within 30 days). During the course of the investigation, the OCR representatives advised they would investigate all allegations in the complaint, interview the complainant, contact and develop information from the Gold County Health Department, and interview any witnesses having information or material relevant to the alleged discrimination.

If a violation had occurred, OCR would attempt to bring the affected institution into voluntary compliance through negotiations. If such corrective action was not secured, OCR would initiate formal enforcement action and perhaps freeze future funding.

The OCR office notified the Gold County Health Department of the following request prior to the investigation scheduled for November 20, 1992:

1. Copies of policies and procedures relating to the provision of translators for people who are non-English- or limited-English-speaking and how this information is disseminated to staff, persons seeking services, and relevant community organizations
2. A description of staff training on how and when to offer and use a translator
3. A list of bilingual staff (or other translators available to the recipient) showing:
   a. Name
   b. Position, unit in which employed or name of outside organization, if appropriate, and telephone number
   c. Language spoken and level of fluency
   d. Hours of availability
   e. For each outside organization used, a copy of any agreement or a description of the nature of the arrangement
4. Copies of brochures, forms, and other information in each language in which they are available
5. An explanation of how written information, policies, consents for treatments, etc., are provided to persons not fluent in English
6. A copy of the complainant's job description
7. Copies of the complainant's past and current work evaluations

Background

Racial, cultural, and linguistic minorities compose a rapidly increasing percentage of the county population. The number of Hispanics, for example, increased by 83.1% since 1980.

EXHIBIT 23-B-1 **Gold County 1990 Census**

	Total	Hispanic
County population	516,418	38,570
White	450,666	20,100
Black	34,771	1,035
Asian and Pacific Islander	12,588	453
American Indian	1,198	189
Other	17,195	16,793

Hispanic Population 1980–90 Change			
1980	1990	Number	Percentage
21,064	38,570	117,506	183.1

Hispanic Origins (1990)		
Mexican	27,220	5.3%
Puerto Rican	4,829	0.9%
Cuban	539	0.1%
Other Hispanics	5,976	1.2%
Hispanic origin	38,570	7.5% of county population

(*Continues*)

The Gold County Health Department, as a major provider of preventive and primary health and mental health services, experienced serious difficulties in meeting the needs of non-English-speaking clients. During 1992, for example, the ambulatory primary healthcare clinics alone delivered 23,649 patient visits. Hispanics account for nearly 30% of the visits, with nearly half requiring assistance from bilingual staff.

TABLE 23-B-1   Language Spoken at Home (Gold County Census Data)

Language	Number of Persons
Spanish	30,759
German	5,000
Polish	3,348
Italian	3,041
French	2,599
Tagalog	2,402
Chinese	1,635
Indic	1,397
Korean	1,248
Slavic	1,050
Greek	1,028

Other linguistic minorities are also served. In Gold County, the number of major languages spoken at home is representative of the challenges faced by federally funded primary care providers throughout the country.

Despite Gold County Health Department's having spent considerable resources to meet multicultural needs through the development of Hispanic clinics, bilingual brochures, and recruitment of minority staff, the OCR investigation directly advised the Gold County Health Department that, effective immediately, Hispanic clinics must be abolished and clients must be served in their primary language.

OCR requested that Gold County Health Department compile and forward the requested information to its office within 20 days of the date of the written request. These data would be retained by the reviewer as partial documentation of the findings.

The Gold County Health Department was in the midst of an administrative transition as well. The executive officer had resigned only two and a half months earlier, and the health board appointed an interim director. The recruitment process for the executive officer occurred at the same time as the complaint investigation.

The breadth of the discrimination complaint required that all clinic facilities countywide be audited for multicultural sensitivity and the ability to meet non-English-speaking clients' needs. In addition, the health board had recently approved a hiring freeze to be implemented on December 1, which would inhibit increasing the current staff to address the need for interpreters.

An on-site investigation was scheduled for November 20, 1992.

Source: Courtesy of the Mid-America Regional Public Health Leadership Institute.

Two Countries/Two Names/Broken Policies

Lisa Crane, RN, BSN; Laura M. Hurt, RN, BSN; Nohora Keener, BA; Beth Morris, LCSW, MSW; Mary Ellen Nelson, BA; and Petra Shepard, PhD
2005–2006 Mid-America Regional Public Health Leadership Institute

Introduction

The increasing diversity in many areas of the United States has posed both challenges and opportunities for healthcare providers. These challenges can be especially salient in rural areas that have been largely homogeneous until the past five to eight years, and that may not have the dual-language support materials, people, and processes in place to respond to an influx of non-English speakers.

Maria Guadalupe Gom, age 22 and married, was five months pregnant with her first baby in January 2006 when she walked into Clinica Medica, the Hispanic health clinic in a rural area of southern Indiana. She had been in the United States for five years, immigrating from near Puebla, Mexico. She and her husband were living with her sister's family, which included her sister's husband and two children. Although previously a patient at Clinica Medica, which sees only uninsured patients, she had not needed clinic services since she had become employed full-time at a local factory that provided her with health insurance benefits. Catherine Z. Jones, the registered nurse who serves as the clinic coordinator at Clinica Medica, was surprised when Maria nervously signaled her in the crowded waiting room indicating a need to speak with her. Catherine could sense, upon seeing Maria's demeanor, that her former patient was especially agitated about something.

Inviting her into a quiet corner of the exceedingly busy clinic, she inquired, "Did you need to speak with me?"

"Sí. I hope you can sign paper for me, yes?"

"Well, I am happy to help you if I can. What paper is it?"

"Just a paper for my employer so that I can have my job back after my baby is born." She presented Catherine with a Family Medical Leave Act (FMLA) form, nearly 10 pages long.

It took several minutes of conversation for Catherine to understand what Maria was asking. Maria's face and neck turned bright red and she lowered her voice as she explained. Since getting pregnant, Maria had been receiving prenatal services at a federally qualified health clinic (FQHC) in another county without telling clinic officials that she had insurance. She had chosen this route because her employer knew her by one name, the name on her purchased Social Security card. But she wanted her baby born with her name, not the false name known to her employer. She dared not tell her employer of her correct name. Nor did she want the clinic where she received prenatal care to know she was insured or she believed she would be compelled to use the false name. Not really understanding how the U.S. system worked, Maria had decided to tell her employer she would be going to Mexico to have her baby and would return following the birth. Although she actually had no intention of going to Mexico for the birth, she thought that this falsehood would explain why she was not using her insurance, should her employer ever become curious about their pregnant employee. Although not fully understanding the rules and expectations of her new home, Maria did know she wanted to keep her job at all costs following the birth of her child. She showed great anxiety and embarrassment in sharing all of this with Catherine, clearly uncomfortable with the position she was in, yet not seeing any way out that did not involve additional deception.

Maria insisted that she simply needed a signature on the form. When she presented it to Catherine, Catherine saw it was an FMLA application and knew she would not be able to complete it. She encouraged Maria to take it to the physician at the FQHC that was providing her prenatal care. However, she knew from Maria's reaction that Maria was in a very difficult situation. Should she take the FMLA form to her physician, they would know she had misrepresented her insurance status. At the same time, failing to have it signed could mean the loss of a stable income, her reason for coming to the United States in the first place. She had approached Catherine as a trusted community professional whom, she hoped, would have a solution for this dilemma. Instead, needing to follow the law as well as the ethics of the nursing profession, Catherine could only encourage Maria to take the form to the prenatal clinic for completion. It tugged at Catherine's heart to see, once again, the stress on Mexican immigrants of our failed immigration and health policies and the knotty dilemmas often faced by people like Maria, who are existing as second-class citizens in a foreign country while displaced by their own because of the lack of opportunities. How many other Marias were out there, struggling with similar issues that put them in no-win situations where a lie of one kind or another seemed to them to be the only way to cope? How many immigrants were forgoing health care so as to avoid interacting with a system they did not understand or trust? The stress of living day to day under these circumstances seemed exhausting and, in fact, Catherine had seen many symptoms of post-traumatic stress syndrome in her immigrant patients.

Case

Catherine had no crisis of conscience regarding her refusal to sign Maria's FMLA form; it would be ethical to sign such a form only if Catherine's clinic had currently been providing care for Maria and her unborn child. But Catherine was nevertheless very unsettled by the circumstances that led Maria to make such a request. Numerous times, this bicultural nurse, who was also born in Mexico, had seen her fellow countrymen arrive in this country not only for the chance to better their lives but also to meet a real economic need in her adopted country.

(Continues)

A town of 35,000, Catherine's adopted home had changed dramatically in the past six years. She had been among a handful of Latin American immigrants who had married U.S. citizens and had become naturalized themselves 20 years ago or so. This small, closely knit bicultural community ballooned in the late 1990s as economic circumstances led to labor shortages in the manufacturing and service sectors of her town (see **Figure 23-3**).

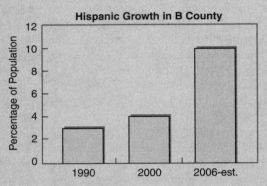

FIGURE 23-3 Hispanic Growth in B County, Indiana, from 1990 through 2006 (estimated).
Source: Courtesy of the Mid-America Regional Public Health Leadership Institute.

In fact, Catherine had heard human resources directors not only at Maria's factory but also at other local factories say that if it had not been for the Mexican laborers who came to fill jobs at the factory, they would have had to move the entire operation offshore or else close down. Undocumented immigrant labor had provided important support for economic development in the community in recent years. Employers and community leaders seemed all too willing to keep their collective heads in the sand regarding the true legal status of their workforce. As long as prospective employees presented the required Social Security card, employers appeared to have little interest in discovering the vast underground economy that had sprung up to provide false cards to willing Mexican laborers who come to this country without documents, or to understand the compounding problems that these laborers experience outside of their work environment.

As Emily Friedman recently wrote, "Projected patterns of demographic change [in the United States] are more complex than they were historically, and the implications for the healthcare system are profound. . . . Furthermore, the presence of minorities is being felt more in communities that historically have not been very diverse. Both native-born and immigrant minority Americans are moving to areas in New England and the Midwest, which traditionally were far less diverse than the South, the West, and the industrial Northeast" (Friedman, 2006).

Maria's story was truly remarkable for the persistence she had demonstrated and the strength of character she had needed to navigate from her home country to the United States. Maria was the oldest child and lived with her parents, four brothers, and three sisters in a two-room house. They had no electricity and no running water. When Maria was little, both her mother and father had to work to survive. They would leave the young children alone all day. Maria, being the oldest (eight years old at this point in time), cared for her brothers and sisters while her parents worked. On good days her mother and father would earn $10. (Dad made belts and Mom cleaned in various places.) Some days there was very little food. Maria and her brother often sold gum on the street corners to earn extra money. Other times, they would wash car windows for people stopping on the streets. Maria went to school until sixth grade. She loved school and wanted to continue, but her parents could not afford to buy the uniforms and supplies that were needed to go to school. Maria had to quit to allow the rest of her brothers and sisters to go.

When Maria was 17, her father was suffering from diabetes and needed medical care. Her mother also had various medical problems. Maria had heard that if she went "north" she would be able to earn money and send enough back to help her parents and brothers and sisters. She had a cousin, Luis, who was anxious to go, too.

Maria and Luis made plans to go to the United States. They needed a lot of money, $1,500 each, for a "coyote" who would take them across the border. They were able to collect money from many different family members and were ready to go. The coyote led them through the desert. During the day it was very, very hot. They had nothing to eat or drink. They had not been told to bring anything with them, and nothing was provided. At night they would walk through the desert not being able to see where they were going and hearing all kinds of animals. One night they were left with a group of people in a shack. It was filthy. It was evident that this place was used often. There was no place to go to the bathroom, no food or water. In the desert, it can get very cold at night. After sweating all day in the heat, they froze at night. The five people that were left in the shack had to huddle together to keep warm. They could hear real coyotes howling just outside. The coyote (person bringing them to the border) left them there for three days. They were very frightened and felt if they left the shack they would be caught by immigration. They didn't know what to do. Finally, on the third night the coyote returned to take them on their way. They finally made their way to the *frontera* (border). The scariest part of the trip was at the border. In Mexico, there are many dangerous people preying on the people leaving. It is almost like the Mafia on the border. Maria and Luis were robbed three times and beaten. There were areas that had electrical fencing to prevent people from crossing. Tunnels had been dug in the ground. They had to crawl down in the ground to get through. The holes were very small and it was very dark and scary. After six days, three days walking with blisters and swollen feet and three days spent in the shack, they crossed the border. They were terrified at not knowing what would happen next. Someone was waiting with a large van filled with other people to take them to where they were going—Indiana—where someone they knew from Mexico lived. Maria was scared, but knew there was no hope for her or her family in Mexico. She was very sad and depressed to leave all those she loved, but she had a responsibility to help and this was the only way.

Catherine knew Maria's story and dozens of others, too. Her concerns and commitment to this growing population had led her to exert leadership in the community to create a more welcoming environment for Hispanic workers. She was proud of the Hispanic clinic she had helped to form and for which she was responsible for recruiting volunteer physicians, nurses, and interpreters. No other community in southern Indiana had been as proactive in responding to and welcoming the workers who were keeping local services going. Thank goodness the faith community had also joined in these efforts, allowing Maria to get free prenatal vitamins through Mary's Chapel, a local, ecumenical food pantry with aid for prescriptions.

Closing

It is clear to Catherine and to other leaders in her community that there is a growing number of people with challenging emotional problems due to the situations they face where their behavior is at odds with their values. The anxiety, depression, and stress-related illnesses seen at Clinica Medica are seen at many other sites serving the undocumented workers who are keeping many Midwestern communities alive. It seems inhumane, yet there is no solution in sight. Interested, concerned people feel unable to help as our state and country laws become more and more strict. Growing numbers of immigrants are driving without licenses or insurance, living with the fear of being sent back to extreme poverty in their home countries, living without loved family members whom they are supporting with checks sent home, and so on. The history of first-generation immigrants in the United States is fraught with challenges and continues unabated to this day.

References

Friedman, E. Tapestry. *Hospitals and Health Networks Online,* February 9, 2006. Accessed February 27, 2006, at http://www.emilyfriedman.com/columns/2006-02-tapestry.html.

Tienda, M., and F. Mitchell, eds., *Multiple Origins, Uncertain Destinies: Hispanics and the American Future* (Washington, DC: National Academies Press, 2006).

United States Census Bureau (2005). Accessed February 8, 2006, at http://quickfacts.census.gov/qfd/states/18/18005 .html.

Source: Courtesy of the Mid-America Regional Public Health Leadership Institute.

It is through language that we express our culture and our personal needs. Words have power.[25] In American society, most people view English as the language of choice. The assumption that only English should be spoken in public venues, such as a healthcare clinic, constitutes a denigration of other languages and leads to a resistance to helping people who do not speak English or speak English peppered with words from their native language. Public health leaders and organizations have to address the issue of bilingualism or multiple languages in their community if they are to maintain credibility.

As pointed out, it is necessary to go through a series of stages—awareness, understanding, and action—before cultural competency is attained.[26] Of course, this analysis of the process of achieving cultural competency is very general, and the process can be broken down further, as in the following model:[27]

1. Cultural destructiveness occurs when cultural groups are discriminated against.

2. If the public health system is biased and culturally incompetent, it will be unable to facilitate change in health behaviors of culturally diverse groups.

3. Cultural incompetency may in part be a result of cultural blindness on the part of public health leaders, including a lack of awareness of the cultural factors in health and disease.

4. The fourth stage is reached when public health leaders and other practitioners begin to achieve cultural sensitivity. They become aware of cultural differences and attempt to develop special programs to address the needs of different cultural groups.

5. Cultural competency is achieved when the leaders develop programs tied to different cultural groups.

6. If the programs are successful in meeting the special needs of different cultural groups, the public health leaders can be said to have become culturally proficient.

Exercise 23-4, based on Case Study 23-B, allows the students to develop an action plan based on the cultural competency models presented previously.

Cultural competency must start at the individual level, but it also must be present at the organizational and community levels (**Figure 23-4**).[28] Each individual in an organization has the responsibility of becoming culturally competent, and the organization's leaders need to support cultural competency by developing a written policy on cultural competency and providing awareness training to staff. They themselves need to be trained in demographic analysis, at least to the extent of being able to understand the demographic

FIGURE 23-4 Multidisciplinary Aspects of Cultural Competency. *Source*: Adapted from T. Cox Jr. and R. L. Beale, *Developing Competency to Manage Diversity* (San Fransisco: Berrett-Koehler, 1997).

changes in the community and in the health status of culturally diverse populations.[29] The achievement of organization-wide cultural competency will likely result in changes in recruitment programs, staff orientation, performance appraisals, compensation packages, and promotion rules.

It is important to reinforce culturally competent staff behavior[30] and to recognize the value of cultural competency and the value of protecting diverse viewpoints. Public health leaders need to celebrate diversity in the community by holding, for example, an annual diversity and health fair. Leaders should also honor individuals involved in innovative diversity programs and publicize the positive results of these programs.

Cultural competency confers many benefits (**Figure 23-5**).[31] For one thing, community residents

FIGURE 23-5 Benefits of Cultural Competence in Health Care. *Source*: Adapted with permission from *Minority Managerial Programs*, © 1997, American Association of Health Plans.

want to feel that the programs of the local public health agency are oriented toward them and will be more satisfied with programs that are culturally competent. Such programs will increase access to care by culturally diverse groups. **Table 23-4** lists five benefits of cultural competency that accrue to health agencies and the recipients of their services.

Money is always an issue. Leaders will need to make choices as to how many resources to devote to creating a culturally competent organization. They will also need to ensure that the resources assigned to improving the level of cultural sensitivity are used as efficiently as possible.

Public health leaders must:

- lead the agency at all times with cultural diversity in mind
- monitor the appropriateness of programs and services for multicultural groups

TABLE 23-4 Positive Effects of Cultural Competency in Health Agencies

- It allows the provider to obtain more specific and complete information to make a more appropriate diagnosis.
- It facilitates the development of treatment plans that are followed by the patient and supported by the family.
- It reduces delays in seeking care and allows for more use of health services.
- It enhances overall communication and the clinical interaction between provider and patient.
- It enhances the compatibility between Western health practices and traditional cultural health practices.

Source: Reproduced from President's Initiative on Race, *Health Care RX: Access for All*, 1998, Health Resources and Services Administration, U.S. Department of Health and Human Services.

- put cultural diversity policies into practice and live the policies
- develop cultural awareness programs and foster intercultural understanding
- understand the stages necessary to make cultural proficiency a reality
- evaluate agency progress toward cultural competency on an ongoing basis
- celebrate the accomplishments of others in the area of cultural competency
- develop diversity and health community fairs with community partners

SUMMARY

People do not feel that many social programs work. There is a critical need to concentrate on what works rather than what does not work. It is up to the public health system and its leadership to help find solutions for problems related to our cultural diversity. The task will not be easy, and yet it is necessary. The trend toward greater cultural diversity will not stop. Public health leaders need to be at the forefront of attempts to get rid of our stereotypes, correct inaccurate cultural assumptions, build solid relationships with cultural neighbors, and empower all Americans.

DISCUSSION QUESTIONS

1. How would you as a public health leader deal with the alleged ethnic discrimination described in Case Study 23-A?
2. How would you set about helping the local high school develop a cultural diversity training program?
3. What are the guidelines for dealing with cultural diversity in the community and in the public health agency workforce?
4. What are the steps that someone needs to go through to reach cultural competency?
5. What are some strategies for creating a culturally competent staff?

EXERCISE 23-1: Rosenthal Inclusivity Checklist

Purpose: to learn how to build multicultural teams and coalitions and evaluate inclusivity issues

Key concepts: inclusivity, multiculturalism, team performance

Procedure: The class should divide into teams of seven or eight members. Each team then fills out the Rosenthal inclusivity checklist (**Table 23-5**) and discusses how the team might function in a multicultural environment. The discussion should focus on those items on the checklist that are not checked and the implications for team functioning and performance. As part of the discussion, team members should also consider the types of environments in which the team would be likely to perform well and the types of environments in which the team would perform poorly. Representatives from each team should then summarize their results and conclusions for the class as a whole.

TABLE 23-5 Inclusivity Checklist

Instructions: Use this Inclusivity Checklist to measure how prepared your coalition is for multicultural work and to identify areas for improvement. Place a check mark in the box next to each statement that applies to your group. If you cannot put a check in the box, this may indicate an area for change.
The leadership of our coalition is multiracial and multicultural. ☐
We make special efforts to cultivate new leaders, particularly women and people of color. ☐
Our mission, operations, and products reflect the contributions of diverse cultural and social groups. ☐
We are committed to fighting social oppression within the coalition and in our work with the community. ☐
Members of diverse cultural and social groups are full participants in all aspects of our coalition's work. ☐
Meetings are not dominated by speakers from any one group. ☐
All segments of our community are represented in decision making. ☐
There is sensitivity and awareness regarding different religious and cultural holidays, customs, recreation, and food preferences. ☐
We communicate clearly, and people of different cultures feel comfortable sharing their opinions and participating in meetings. ☐
We prohibit the use of stereotypes and prejudicial comments. ☐
Ethnic, racial, and sexual slurs or jokes are not welcome. ☐

Source: Reprinted with permission from T. Wolff and G. Kaye, eds., *From the Ground Up: A Workbook on Coalition Building and Community Development*, pp. 54–55, 69. © 1995 AHEC/Community Partners.

EXERCISE 23-2: Cultural Understanding

Purpose: to explore the issue of diversity and the best means of increasing cultural understanding

Key concepts: cultural diversity, cultural understanding, personal characteristics

Procedures: Each student is given a "Quest for Diversity" form and, for each category, tries to find the person in the class who best represents that category (see **Table 23-6**). When the student succeeds in identifying a person for a category, the student then talks to that person about one of his or her personal characteristics. Students should be careful to avoid cultural stereotyping and similar barriers to understanding. Students who find representatives for the most categories and for the least categories should be selected to present their findings to the class as a whole. The class should discuss the merits and limitations of each student's approach to diversity categorization.

TABLE 23-6 Quest for Diversity Form

Diversity Categories	Found People	Personal Characteristics
Professional woman/homemaker		
Oldest grandparent		
Youngest parent		
Native American background		
Asian American background		
African American background		
In public health at least 30 years		
Parent was a migrant worker		
Parent who was an immigrant		
Largest number of siblings		
First in family with college degree		
Latino background		

Diversity Categories	Found People	Personal Characteristics
Russian or Polish background		
An elected official		
Most children		
Man who is homemaker		
Rural dweller		
World traveler		
Person with a disability		
Speaks five languages		
Gay relative		
Relative in prison		

EXERCISE 23-3: Leadership and Cultural Diversity

Purpose: to explore how diversity influences the way in which public health leaders carry out their responsibilities

Key concepts: cultural diversity, leadership system activities

Procedure: The class or training group should divide into groups of seven or eight members. Each group explores the ways in which diversity affects team building; values clarification; the development of a mission, a vision, goals and objectives, and action plans; the implementation of program interventions; and the evaluation of programs. After the discussion, each group prepares a five-minute presentation based on the discussion and shares its findings with the other groups.

EXERCISE 23-4: Cultural Competency in Gold County

Purpose: to develop a personnel recruitment action plan to diversify the public health agency workforce

Key concepts: action planning, cultural competency, cultural sensitivity, personnel recruitment

Procedure: Case Study 23-B presents the demographics for Gold County. An analysis of the ethnic and racial makeup of the county health department indicates that 80% of the staff are white, 15% are African American, and 5% are Hispanic. The class should divide into teams, and each team should discuss the action steps needed to ensure that the health department is culturally competent. One area of focus should be the development of a personnel recruitment plan to ensure that the health department's workforce is capable of understanding and responding appropriately to cultural issues in the community it serves. An issue that needs to be decided is whether the best approach is to attempt to recruit a workforce that mirrors the demographic composition of the community.

REFERENCES

1. L. B. Shresta and E. Heisler, *The Changing Demographic Profile of the United States* (Washington, DC: Congressional Research Service, 2011).
2. Shresta and Heisler, *The Changing Demographic Profile of the United States.*
3. Public Health Service, *Public Health Workforce: An Agenda for the 21st Century* (Washington, DC: U.S. Department of Health and Human Services, 1997).
4. A. Wolf, *One Nation, After All* (New York: Viking Penguin Books, 1998).
5. Wolf, *One Nation, After All.*
6. T. Wicker, *Tragic Failure* (New York: Morrow, 1996).
7. W. J. Paul and A. A. Schnidman, "Valuing Differences: The Challenges of Personal Prejudice and Organizational Preference," in *The Promise of Diversity*, ed. E. Y. Cross et al. (Burr Ridge, IL: Irwin Professional Publishing, 1994).
8. A. M. Schlesinger Jr., *The Disuniting of America* (New York: Norton, 1992).

9. C. Taylor, ed., *Multiculturalism* (Princeton, NJ: Princeton University Press, 1994).

10. R. Bernstein, *Dictatorship of Virtue* (New York: Knopf, 1994).

11. E. Y. Cross et al., eds., *The Promise of Diversity* (Burr Ridge, IL: Irwin Professional Publishing, 1994).

12. A. J. DuBrin, *The Complete Idiot's Guide to Leadership* (New York: Alpha Books, 2000).

13. J. Bordas, "How Salsa, Soul, and Spirit Strengthen Leadership," *Leader to Leader* 46, no. 46 (2007): 35–41.

14. L. Segil, "Managing Culture in Cross-Cultural Alliances," *Leader to Leader* 6 (Fall 1997): 12–14.

15. B. Rosenthal, "Inclusivity Checklist," in *From the Ground Up: A Workbook on Coalition-Building and Community Development*, ed. T. Wolff and G. Kaye (Amherst, MA: AHEC Community Partners, 1995).

16. D. A. Thomas, "Diversity as Strategy," *Harvard Business Review* 82, no. 9 (2004): 88–107.

17. D. A. Thomas and R. J. Ely, "Making Differences Matter: A New Paradigm for Managing Diversity," *Harvard Business Review* 74, no. 5 (1996): 79–90.

18. Thomas and Ely, "Making Differences Matter."

19. President's Initiative on Race, *Health Care Rx: Access for All* (Washington, DC: U.S. Department of Health and Human Services, Health Resources and Services Administration, 1998).

20. T. Cox Jr., *Cultural Diversity in Organizations* (San Francisco: Berrett-Koehler, 1993).

21. C. R. O'Connell, *Umiker's Management Skills*, 5th ed. (Sudbury, MA: Jones & Bartlett, 2009).

22. T. Cox Jr. and R. L. Beale, *Developing Competency to Manage Diversity* (San Francisco: Berrett-Koehler, 1997).

23. Cox and Beale, *Developing Competency to Manage Diversity*.

24. President's Initiative on Race, *Health Care Rx: Access for All*.

25. C. Lemert, ed., *Social Theory: The Multicultural and Classic Readings* (Boulder, CO: Westview Press, 1993).

26. Cox and Beale, *Developing Competency to Manage Diversity*.

27. J. L. Rorie et al., "Primary Care for Women: Cultural Competence in Primary Care Services," *Journal of Nurse Midwifery* 41, no. 2 (1996): 92–100.

28. Cox and Beale, *Developing Competency to Manage Diversity*.

29. T. H. Cox and S. Blake, "Managing Cultural Diversity: Implications for Organizational Competitiveness," *The Executive* 5, no. 3 (1991): 45–56.

30. S. P. Robbins and M. Coulter, *Management*, 11th ed. (Upper Saddle River, NJ: Prentice Hall, 2011).

31. American Association of Health Plans, *Minority Managerial Programs* (Washington, DC: American Association of Health Plans, 1997).

CHAPTER 24

Leadership and Change

Change is the law of life. And those who look only to the past or present are certain to miss the future.

—John F. Kennedy

Every leadership book is about change. September 11, 2001, taught us that change is often unexpected. Leaders need to better understand the dynamics of change if they are to become change agents themselves. Mahatma Gandhi once said that it is important to "be the change you want to be in the world." The artist Pablo Picasso said, "I am always doing that which I cannot do, in order that I may learn how to do it." One of the best quotes on change from an unknown source is, "If nothing ever changed, there would be no butterflies." This chapter will explore change and some understanding of the process and tools of change. The Robert Wood Johnson Foundation and the W. K. Kellogg Foundation Turning Point Initiative to build public health capacity to better improve the health of the public through collaborative partnerships began in the mid-1990s. The Turning Point projects were all about change. Case Study 24-A presents one of the interesting stories from this initiative.[1]

Although it is true that change can be planned, we do live in an age where unanticipated change events such as terrorist attacks and other crises come into our lives in an unpredictable way. Most theories of change have assumed that social change is a continuous process, but the events of the past few years clearly create discontinuities in our social structure and in our personal lives. What crisis forces us to do is view these major change events in terms of explanation rather than prediction. It is necessary to trace the event backward to garner information that will allow us to prevent or better predict similar events in the future. Chaos theories show that an understanding of how to address potential crises is tied to an awareness that unanticipated events (and the changes that occur because of them) are now part of the social fabric of our lives. All crises create messes and may lead to more crises and more complex messes.[2] Systems thinking approaches are critical in addressing emergencies and the effect of change on communities. This chapter will look at the stages of change and how transition in our lives may be as important as our understanding of the process of change.

Collaborating for Community Health

Bob Cassa serves his community by developing the conditions that will keep the population healthy. In this case, his community is a nation within a nation, the San Carlos Apache Nation in Arizona. A public health educator with the Indian Health Service, he coordinates, organizes, and implements a variety of health promotion and disease prevention activities in the schools and community. He especially loves working to improve the health of kids because he remembers what it was like to be young and making life-altering decisions. One of those decisions led him to public health and back to the San Carlos Apache Nation.

Twenty-nine years ago, San Carlos tribal leaders saw the future of their nation in a promising kid and encouraged him to pursue higher education. When Bob first started at Arizona State University, his options were wide open, but he soon found himself in pursuit of a B.A. in health services. As a child, Bob recalls being a patient in the local hospital, where he remembers noticing the great number of nonnative doctors and nurses. His decision to go into the health field came in part from his awareness of the need to increase the number of native providers. After receiving his bachelor's degree, he followed up with a master's in public health from the University of Hawaii. He started his career with Indian Health Services (IHS) in 1985 in Nevada but soon found his way back home to San Carlos in 1988.

Bob had already been serving in his community for 16 years when he was asked to participate in a training program called the Academy Without Walls. Created by Arizona Turning Point and the Mel and Enid Zuckerman Arizona College of Public Health, the academy delivers training to frontline public health workers in Arizona. San Carlos was chosen as a pilot site for the academy's competency-based training in basic public health science skills, community dimensions of practice, and cultural competency. Tribal health department employees and the employees of the Indian Health Service Unit planned to participate in the academy together to strengthen communication and collaboration between the two entities.

For Bob, the experience allowed him to revisit key principles in health education and the underlying purpose of public health. For others, some or all of the information was new. The training sessions prompted Bob to identify how he could improve health education through better collaboration, communication, community assessment, and community participation. Bob recognized that although he and his colleagues valued collaboration, in the daily activities of doing their jobs, the importance of collaboration was sometimes lost.

The Academy Without Walls provided public health workers who serve the people of San Carlos with tools, resources, ideas, and the opportunity to explore collaboration. Several agencies in San Carlos had been planning programs for kids during spring break. As a result of their participation in the academy, some IHS departments and the tribal health programs collaborated with other community groups, such as the Boys and Girls Clubs, to put on a spring break event together. The larger event allowed them all to do more for the kids with the same resources. The spring break event and the lessons learned from the Academy Without Walls are living on in San Carlos. Agencies and community groups now collaborate in other ways to improve health and are moving in a new direction to achieve public health gains—together.

Change is a process of moving from what has become an obsolete present into a revitalized present with an eye on the future. Change also means that the old rules do not seem to be working anymore, and new rules and procedures need to be developed for the changing context in which we live today. The quote by President Kennedy at the beginning of this chapter reinforces these ideas. Schein clarified the issue of change and why people are often resistant to structured and unstructured change.[3] People like equilibrium in their lives. The process of coping, growth, and survival are measured against some sense of stability in their environments. Some of this stability comes from the culture, shared values, routines, and some ability

to predict how our day-to-day activities will play out. These assumptions are shared with the people with whom we interact.

Unanticipated change clearly disrupts the equilibrium of people, organizations, and their communities. We now live in an age of constant and speeded-up change. The question is how to adapt to these changes or how to live in a world of unpredictable change. When change transforms a culture or community, people need to unlearn the old rules and also learn the new rules.[4] Change can be incremental or slow and intense. This latter type of change is sometimes called deep change.[5] The good news about incremental change is that the process is so gradual that people, organizations, and communities can adapt to the changes more easily. Another advantage of incremental change is that it is possible to revert to the prechange stage more easily because the change process is so gradual. Deep change is much more profound in that it requires new ways of thinking, feeling, and behaving. It is not possible to go back. There has been a tipping point. We cannot go back to our pre–September 11, 2001, lives. Thus, deep change is a major change that breaks with the past.

Change can be seen in the context of surprises.[6] We live in a world of inevitable surprises. The things we do know are that these surprises will continue to occur, perhaps at a much faster rate than in the past. Second, we know now that surprise is inevitable, but we can plan for the things that are not expected. We can, even with some degree of accuracy, predict how certain types of crisis events will play out over time. One critical set of skills is creating different scenarios for different types of events. For example, it is possible to create scenarios about the effect of a terrorist event similar to September 11, 2001, from a number of perspectives. Exercises 24-1 and 24-2 will give you the chance to explore surprises and create some scenarios for the future.

Schwartz also explored some lessons that he believed we have learned about change and these inevitable surprises.[7] First, it is important that change agents keep looking for clarifications of a surprise event. Conversations between individuals who have been involved in similar events can often provide new information, interpretations of happenings, and new understandings of the variations in outcomes of different types of surprise events. Successful leaders also become better at prediction and timing related to surprises by watching for what factors will speed up events and which factors will slow them down or stop them in their tracks. Change agents become more aware of warning indicators and are adept at developing skills related to early detection. It is possible to discard techniques and approaches that might create environments for crisis.[8]

It is also important for leaders to be careful not to deny the potential for surprise events. It is important for leaders to understand how they judge things. Each of us has different learning and behavioral styles. Our perspectives and judgments are affected by these styles. It is worthwhile for leaders to explore these issues either through using some leadership profile instruments or through working with executive coaches who specialize in these analyses. Once again, it is important to emphasize lifelong learning for leaders. Different leadership tools and skills are required for different times and events. Leaders need to better understand how

their actions are seen in their organizations and in their communities by their partners and by community residents. It is clearly critical for the public health leader to cultivate these community connections because all traditional public health activities and emergency preparedness and response activities are community-wide efforts and not just the work of one individual.

STYLES OF CHANGE

The public health leader has to be both a catalyst for change and also a reactor to change caused by unanticipated consequences. Leaders have different change styles. Musselwhite has studied the issue of styles for a long time. His organization developed an instrument to define and test change styles.[9] From more than 10 years of research, three primary change styles have emerged.

The Conservers

Conservers are people who are able to gauge reality in a pretty accurate way. They also like structure and tend to work well within frameworks or organizations with well-defined rules and regulations. The conservers also tend to follow continuous quality improvement techniques. When they support making changes, they want to go slow and methodically. They have many strengths in that they see the details of every situation. They are steady and reliable, they honor commitments, they encourage people to follow the rules, they investigate situations thoroughly, they see all sides of the issue when change is contemplated, and they work to protect the integrity of the organization or community. On the negative side, they tend to be so conservative that opportunities for progress may be passed by.

The Pragmatists

Pragmatists are task oriented and tend to want to get things done with clear results. They are less concerned than the conservers with maintaining the structure of the organization or with things as they currently are. They tend to focus on the action plan phase of the Leadership Wheel. They want strategies for change and want to see them implemented. They also support the development of scenarios of possible outcomes. Whereas the conservers take a more evolutionary and gradual approach to change, the pragmatists react to the situation and do what needs to be done in a timely fashion. As leaders, pragmatists are very practical, open to exploring different approaches to solving problems, respect other people's opinions, build teamwork, and move teams toward making decisions. They are good facilitators who also know how to tie theory to practice. These are the people who walk the walk. However, they sometimes have trouble making decisions. They straddle the middle of the road. Their indecisiveness may lead to decisions that are not made in a timely fashion.

The Originators

Originators are the people who like to challenge the process.[10] These people like to make things happen. They are innovative and creative. They also seem to search for opportunities to create change. In many ways, these leaders are revolutionaries.[11] They tend to be navigators rather than rowers or helmsmen. They are systems thinkers who are big-picture thinkers and tend to be less concerned with the details of implementation. As leaders, the originators are clearly change agents, are enthusiastic, are visionary, tend to multitask, and are analytic, in the sense that they look for unique ways to put things and situations together. However, they do sometimes threaten their organizations and communities because they are less concerned about the status quo. This disturbs many people. Musselwhite and Jones have found that the originators make up about 25% of the population, the conservers another 25%, and the pragmatists are the most prevalent and make up the remaining 50% of the population.[12] Exercise 24-3 will give you the opportunity to experiment with the ways leaders would react to a terrorist event depending on which change style they favor.

UNDERSTANDING CHANGE

Over the years, there have been many theories and explanations about change and its meaning. In this section, there will be a review of two contemporary approaches to change that give public health leaders two influential approaches that are useful for increasing understanding of the challenges facing public health in this new century. One proposes an eight-stage approach to carry out change initiatives in organizations and communities. The second approach presents change from the perspective of resilience and the ability of people to adapt to change.

In reviewing older theories of change, Musselwhite and Jones found that most of the perspectives could be boiled down to four general stages:[13]

- The first stage involves acknowledging that a threat exists or that change is needed.
- The second stage is the reaction of people to the threat or change.
- The third stage is the need to investigate and determine the kinds of change that are needed.
- The fourth stage is the implementation phase.

The challenges that our country faces seem to be increasing. There were many threats to our way of life prior to September 11, 2001. All these societal and economic factors affect our organizations as well as our communities. In 1995, Kotter pointed to technological advances, international economic policy, expansion of global markets, maturation of markets in developing countries, and the changing of the guard in many countries, especially with the fall of most communist and many socialist regimes, as factors affecting American communities.[14] To this must also be added the increase in terrorism and the potential for bioterrorist acts around the world. People change when their behavior changes, and their behavior changes because leaders speak to the feelings of individuals.[15] It is important, when change is occurring, that the solutions are seen in terms of emotions and not just changes in people's minds. Thus, the central issue in change is not just strategy, structure, culture, or systems change, but how people see the proposed change and how it affects their feelings about the changes proposed.

Kotter and Cohen[16] looked at this perspective from the vantage point of an eight-step model (which Kotter had developed earlier) for successful large-scale change.[17] Whether a change is planned or unanticipated, a sense of urgency has to be generated before any change or adaptation to an unexpected change can occur. Crises clearly increase the sense of urgency. The second step involves the development of a team or coalition to guide the change or reaction to crisis process. This means that the selection of a group must also be representative of those who will be affected by change. Third, there needs to be a vision toward which to aim. The vision will lead to the development of goals, objectives, action plans, and implementation. Next, the change, vision, or adaptation strategy has to be communicated to all affected partners and community residents. What the public health leader needs is acceptance, participation, and commitment from all the affected parties. Fifth, it is necessary to empower people to be a part of the action necessary to bring the changes into being. Sixth, it is important to emphasize short-term wins to keep people involved in the process.

TABLE 24-1   The Eight Steps for Successful Large-Scale Change

Step	Action	New Behavior
1	Increase urgency	People start telling each other, "Let's go, we need to change things!"
2	Build the guiding team	A group powerful enough to guide a big change is formed, and they start to work together well.
3	Get the vision right	The guiding team develops the right vision and strategy for the change effort.
4	Communicate for buy-in	People begin to buy in to the change, and this shows in their behavior.
5	Empower action	More people feel able to act, and do act, on the vision.
6	Create short-term wins	Momentum builds as people try to fulfill the vision, while fewer and fewer resist change.
7	Don't let up	People make wave after wave of changes until the vision is fulfilled.
8	Make change stick	New and winning behavior continues despite the pull of tradition, turnover of change leaders, etc.

Source: Reproduced from J. P. Kotter and D. S. Cohen, *The Heart of Change* (Boston: Harvard Business School Press, 2002).

Seventh, it is important to maintain the momentum of the process by showing connections between the gains and the need to produce further changes so that the projected outcomes will occur. Finally, step eight involves making the changes stick and also fitting the changes into the cultural fabric of the community.

Table 24-1 presents the eight-stage model with the behavioral changes that occur at each stage.[18] Culture and values change last and not first. In addition, the first seven stages are easy compared with step eight. Before culture can change, behavior has to change. People need to feel that the changes are necessary for the future growth of an organization or a community. It is important for behavior to change with each step of the process. Exercise 24-4 gives you the opportunity to apply the model to a community trying to improve its security-planning activities.

Conner stated that it is not enough for leaders to recognize that change is necessary.[19] The critical issue is how individuals can adapt to change. Leaders are most effective and efficient when the process of change occurs at a speed at which the leader can absorb and assimilate the changes in a reasonable way. In this second perspective, the issue of changes involves the resilience of the leader and others to adapt to the changes occurring in their environment. The resilience factor is the most critical factor if successful change is to occur. Resilience is affected by seven support patterns. What the concept of support implies is that each support pattern will aid the leader or increase the capacity of the leader to assimilate or process changes that are needed in the organization or community. Changes in one part

of the world affect the lives and communities of all other people and places.[20]

The first support pattern involves the nature of the change. For the leader, a concern is whether the change can be controlled. There is also the issue of whether the outcome of the change event can be predicted. The level of disruption is also a part of the nature issue and is greater for unanticipated events such as terrorist or bioterrorist events. Conner stated that all changes have associated costs. Leaders need to determine their ability to assimilate the effects of change. It is possible to imagine that each person has a certain number of assimilation points and that people who are resilient have more points to use. If the change affects the individual only, this is a micro change.[21] Organizational change means each person in an organization or agency must change. Macro change is when everyone has to change whether they want to or not.

The process of change is the second support pattern. Resilient leaders see change as a process, where less resilient people see change as a yes-or-no situation, in which change is moving from one place to another over a period of time. There is a transition between these two end points. The less resilient have difficulty with the ambiguity of the change process. Resilient people accept change as a part of life and believe that it is possible to manage that process. Leaders do not worry about the ambiguity of the process. This does not mean that the resilient leader does not feel stressed at times. Some change events are unpredictable in terms of when they occur and how they will affect all those concerned. Stress is also a part of the human condition.

The third support pattern relates to the roles of change. Resilient people are aware that the roles and relationships between people change during change events. For example, during an emergency event, the incident command system, which was discussed earlier, changes traditional roles and relationships into predetermined roles and relationships required during the emergency. There are four special roles specifically discussed by Conner during change.[22] First, there is the *sponsor*. This is an individual who has to legitimize and sanction the change activities whether in reaction to an emergency event or in anticipation of an intended change. *Agents* are individuals or groups who are responsible for reacting to the event or for making the change if it is a planned activity. The *targets* of change are those who have to do the changing. The final role relates to the *advocate*. This is a person or group that supports the change or the implementation of a reaction procedure, but does not have the power to implement the process.

Resistance to change is the fourth support pattern. Leaders expect that there will be resistance to change or the effects of unanticipated change events. Open resistance is a healthy process that brings all issues related to the change out in the open. It is covert resistance that is not healthy. Resilient people see the positives in the change process. Less resilient people see only the negative. The issue of realistic expectations is also important in that there will be resistance if people feel their expectations are not being met. After September 11, 2001, many people became resistant to the many security measures that needed to be imposed. I remember seeing the resistance and anger of some individuals at airports who were upset with the increased security measures. It also seems as if some people become more resistant if they think the security precautions are permanent rather than temporary.

The next support pattern involves the issue of commitment. As mentioned earlier, change has costs. If change is to be successful, all individuals must pay those costs. Conner pointed to a number of issues that affect the level of commitment.[23] First, the commitment will increase if people put personal resources such as time, money, and energy into the change process. Second, there needs to be allegiance to the goals that the change process is to achieve. This level of commitment needs to continue even if the changes take a long time to occur or if the proposed changes increase stress or ambiguity. Although small wins are nice, the goal always needs to be on the prize at the end of the process. Next, there may be adversity, but it is important

to be steadfast. Finally, leaders know they will need to be creative, innovative, and resourceful in removing blockages to the achievement of the end changes that need to occur.

The sixth support pattern relates to the cultural dimension, which is critical in that the outcome of any change is affected by culture, shared beliefs and values, behavior, and the ecological nature of the community and how all these factors change over time. Cultural variables are hard to change. Behavior must change first. Behavioral change will affect attitudes, which in turn will affect beliefs and values, which in turn will eventually affect the culture as a whole. Leaders must understand how their organizations and communities work. They must be willing to spend the time showing their organizations why change is necessary. There still needs to be a concern about the values of the community and how they can be modified to accommodate the necessary changes that need to occur. Resilient leaders also know that not all people will react to change in the same way or in the same timeframe that the leader is proposing.

The final support relates to synergy, which can be demonstrated in terms of four steps. First, there needs to be interaction among team and community members. All parties to the change need to communicate with each other and generate trust and credibility. Second, there needs to be "appreciative understanding," which relates to the ability to use and value diversity. The third step is integration, which relates to the blending of people with diverse backgrounds and diverse perspectives on the proposed changes. The fourth step in synergy is implementation, for which there must be successful wins. The diverse views must come together and create products of the change that add value beyond the inputs to the change. Thus, the resilient leader needs to be able to make $1 + 1 = 3$ or more.

More recently, Conner pointed out that change seems to be speeding up.[24] Organizations and communities will have to become nimble. We live in a time of potential chaos and complexity that requires constant changes to adapt to these unexpected events. An organization or community must develop strategies for success in unpredictable times and environments by implementing critical changes as effectively and efficiently as possible. The ability of the organization or community to adapt to constant change is important if these entities are to become nimble and increase their chances for successful change.

In addition to the above change factors, other factors also need to be considered. As can be seen in

Change factors	Culture
	Shifting roles
	Type of change or crisis
	Process of change
	Resistance to change
	Commitment to process
	Unexpected results

Types of resilience	Moral
	Physical
	Social
	Community
	Cultural
	Political
	Ecological
	Disaster related

Response to change	Positive/negative action
	Flexible
	Organized or structured action
	Disorganized or chaotic

FIGURE 24-1 Factors That Define Resilience. *Source*: Adapted from D. R. Conner, *Managing at the Speed of Change*, New York: Villard Books, 1992.

Figure 24-1, resilience is an issues at many different levels. There is resilience in reaction to a disaster or emergency of some kind. Political resilience can be seen at the political level as politicians react to the constantly changing landscape of real-life issues such as a recession. Individuals have different levels of resilience depending on given events. Finally, the response to change may be organized and structured or disorganized and chaotic. The incident command system is often utilized in emergencies to help structure response.

CHANGE AND ADAPTATION

Much of the discussion of change in this chapter relates to the effect of intended and unintended change on an organization or community. Although change affects the lives of people in these entities, there does seem to be a difference in the ability of people to adapt to change and the change process itself. There are two interesting approaches to understanding adaptation in people. Conner discussed what he called the adaptation reflex in terms of a four-step model.[25] Initially, there is the disturbance in the equilibrium of the environment in which the individual lives or works. This disequilibrium leads to the attempt by a person to try to adjust to the changed situation to regain personal control. An individual will explore options to regain a sense of

equilibrium. The event either will appear to be strange or will appear to be somewhat familiar (conventional). Second, a decision needs to be rendered that leads to some clarification or judgment about the meaning of the event. This is followed by a response to the situation and, finally, a realignment process in which the individual develops new or modified behaviors to adjust to the change event. The response is the attempt to restore balance. The response can be adaptation with new behavior, avoidance, or assimilation of the event within the existing framework of reaction to change. In summary, the adaptation reflex involves moving from one state of equilibrium to another.

Bridges saw all adaptation as a series of transitions that occur throughout an individual's life.[26] Transitions are clearly different from the change process itself. For the individual, all change is about a loss (an ending stage), whether it be a loss of old ways of doing things or the loss of a loved one. The ending is almost like the death of someone. Endings create disengagement, sometimes a disorientation as to who the person really is, disenchantment with the way things used to be, and sometimes disorientation, or perhaps denial, and a sense that life has been changed by the event. This sense of ending is clearly exacerbated when a terrorist or bioterrorist event occurs. The sense of loss is generally followed by a period of disorientation and confusion that varies in length for each person and for each type of change event. It is important for the individual to learn that this "neutral zone" is not an abnormal one but just a time in which the individual is learning to cope with the changes in his or her life and also learning to let go of the past. Recovery can thus be a long process. This recovery period eventually leads to a new perspective that Bridges called a "new beginning." As Conner previously pointed out, individuals go through adaptation in different ways. The new beginning can be very exciting in that it offers the person new opportunities and new life possibilities.

The public health leader needs to develop the skills to understand his or her adaptation responses to different types of events and to understand the three stages of transitions. The leader must also realize that each person experiences these things in different ways. Recovery and adaptation will be different for each member of the community. Simple expectations about change, adaptation, and transitions are complex and will affect the recovery effort after any change, crisis events, and other life-modifying occurrences.

PUTTING THE PIECES TOGETHER

Although there is not a perfect fit between the theories and perspectives discussed in this chapter, it is possible to attempt this integration, although imperfect, to better understand the effects of planned and unintended changes in our society. Most of the skills and perspectives discussed come into play as part of the leadership toolbox that the public health leader who wants to be prepared puts together over his or her professional career. **Figures 24-2** and **24-3** show flowcharts for the two types of change. A cursory look at the two figures shows many similar processes at play during the change process. The figures show that changes during and after a crisis are complicated by the possible effect of activating the incident command system during the crisis.

Figure 24-2 looks at the process of planned change. The need for change in an organization or community requires the leader to respond to the need. Although many may be aware that changes are needed, it will be the leader who triggers the response. It is clear from our earlier discussion that different leaders will respond in various ways. The resilience factor comes into play in that the high-resilience leader will probably respond differently than the low-resilience leader. The high-resilience leader is more flexible and willing to change. The high-resilience leader will make a decision based on need and the facts at his or her disposal to either move slowly or move more quickly and comprehensively to create the necessary changes. This leader may move incrementally, but probably never looks back. If deep change is needed, this leader will take the risk and make it happen. Kotter's eight-stage model could then be followed to bring about the changes and create a new environment as a result of the changes. The leader is also aware that the changes will not be complete until most, if not all, of the affected individuals have been

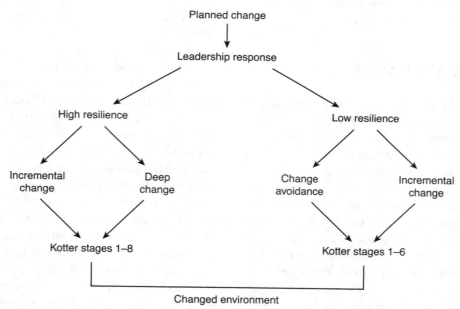

FIGURE 24-2 Integrated Model for Planned Change.

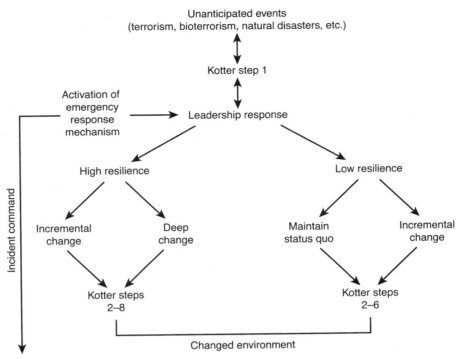

FIGURE 24-3 Integrated Model for Change During and After a Crisis.

able to adapt to the changes by seeing that a new beginning is possible.

In contrast, the low-resilience leader will probably treat similar needs for change in a different way. This leader will explore maintaining the status quo as a viable option, because change tends to be traumatic for people, and it appears that adaptation to the change will take too long to accomplish. The low-resilience leader always seems to be looking for a way out. Even if this leader decides change is necessary, he or she finds it hard to create a sense of urgency for change.[27] If change is required, the low-resilience leader will probably opt for incremental change because it allows people the chance to adapt to the change gradually. It is also possible under this model to return more easily to the starting point than it is with deep change. If change is needed, the process will begin. Using the Kotter model in Table 24-1, steps 1–6 will probably occur. The final steps of not letting up and making the changes stick will be difficult for the low-resilience leader.

Although there are many similarities in the change flowchart for change due to a crisis, there are still differences. As shown in Figure 24-3, the change event comes out of a chaos perspective when the status quo is destroyed by some generally unanticipated event. This emergency event triggers the need for not only adaptive responses, but also further changes in the organization

or community. There needs to be a response by the public health leader whether or not that leader is a high-resilience leader. The change process may need to be filtered through an overlay response that is triggered by the activation of the incident command structure of the community. However, the leaders will need to respond to guide the change process in their organizations or communities while incident command is operating. The public is already feeling a loss of the way things were, and some people will already be trying to adjust to the loss and will have entered the neutral zone that Bridges discussed.

The high-resilience leader knows that further changes are inevitable. A way of life has been altered by the emergency event. This leader will have to decide whether incremental or deep change is the best strategy. The event has had major impact. Some leaders will decide that it is necessary to slow the change process because deep change will cause further trauma. However, the nature of the event may also require deep change because incremental change will not work. The sense of urgency has already occurred with the crisis event. The high-resilience leader needs to maintain the sense of urgency as the stages of change occur. The high-resilience leader knows that it is not possible to return to the precrisis event stage. Community and organization life are forever changed.

The low-resilience leader struggles with the need for further changes as a result of the emergency event. This leader may try to maintain the status quo, even though the old status has changed. This leader may opt for no further change so as not to disrupt the lives of people too much. Sometimes, the low-resilience leader recognizes that some further change is needed even though it will be painful to bring it about. This leader will probably go for an incremental change approach without great enthusiasm. Kotter's steps 2–6 will probably occur without the final steps that will sustain the changes over time. The low-resilience leader will probably believe that it will eventually be possible to return to the way life was before the emergency.

The goal of this section has been to begin to create a perspective on change that builds on the multiple models of change that have been studied. As more is learned about change, it will be possible to add to the synergistic model presented in this section and begin to better understand how change occurs when it is planned and when it is unplanned. Axelrod believes that both the Kotter and the Conner models are part of what he calls traditional approaches to change management.[28] The new approach to change management needs to involve a major concern with engagement. First, it is important to increase your circle of involvement with both internal organizational and external stakeholders. Next, it is important to increase the connections with these stakeholders. Third, Axelrod argues for communities of action and stresses fairness in all change activities. In addition, leaders need to build their change activities honestly and with transparency and trust. In public health we often confront new crises. As an example, Case Study 24-B addresses the public health issues related to school violence and the necessity of developing new strategies tied to this issue.

Case Study 24-B

Code Red: A Public Health Approach to School Gun Violence
A Case Study in Assessment and Policy Development
Gerard Castro, MPH; Carol Coughlin, MBA, BA; Diana Derige, MPH; Tamarah Duperval, MD, MPH; Suzet M. McKinney, MPH; Anne Sobocinski, BSN

Abstract

The purpose of this case study (Code Red) is to demonstrate why school gun violence is a public health issue and to draw attention to the need for policy to address it. Traditionally, the concept of "safe schools"—addressing the global problem of violence in schools—has been managed under the auspices of the school systems, the Department of Justice, and the Department of Education, along with a number of community coalitions that have investigated youth violence. However, with the publishing of *Deadly Consequences* by Dr. Deborah Prothrow-Stith and Michaele Weissman in 1991, the challenge was issued to consider the problem as a public health issue, citing, "Public health people understand that behavior is difficult to alter and that change comes not as a result of a quick fix, but following a steady barrage of interventions that erode destructive attitudes and behavior over time." Former Surgeon General of the United States, C. Everett Koop, captures the essence of their message in the book's introduction with, "The discipline of public health possesses the solution to the mounting toll of violence in this country. The public health approach seeks to prevent tragedy; it seeks to identify and treat young males who are at risk for violence before their lives and the lives of those around them are ruined. The discipline of public health provides strategies to stop violence before it maims and kills."

Public health offers a community-based approach to health promotion and prevention of injury or disease. Utilizing a primary prevention focus, practitioners assess behavioral, environmental, and biological risk factors with the goal to educate individuals and communities and to protect them from these risks. Code Red specifically addresses the assessment core function. The ensuing team discussion details the policies integrating public health that need to be developed to address school gun violence.

This case study is a fictional account of events, based on actual events (Ramsland, Handlin, Frontline, etc.), that occurred in Redtown, Midwest, as the town struggled to deal with an incident at the local high school. The case of Kirt Kunkel, 15, occurred in Redtown in May 2001 and involved the killing of Kunkel's parents followed by a separate shooting at school. Two students died and 25 were injured in the school incident. Kirt's behavior was indicative of a very troubled child with disciplinary and learning problems over an extended period of time. Kirt had a documented history of obsession with weapons, as well as many other "early warning signs" that were missed opportunities for intervention and possible prevention.

In the previous three years, two other incidents occurred in the region that involved students who brought guns to school and shot their classmates and teachers. In May 2000, Newton Brazil, a 13-year-old student, was sent home from school, later returned with a gun, and fatally shot his English teacher. In March 1998, Marcus Johnson, 13, and Andrew Garcia, 11, were involved in an incident that resulted in the deaths of five fellow students and the wounding of 10 others, including a teacher.

The Code Red Action Team was formed to provoke thought among public health leaders surrounding the development of policies and interventions to prevent future incidents. We challenge future public health leaders to accept the charge of determining the stakeholders, defining the problem, seeking opportunities to identify risk, developing interventions, setting priorities for action, and putting their conclusions into a plan.

The Problem of School Gun Violence

In the fall of 2003, a team of public health leaders from Redtown, Midwest, were assembled to be a part of a special commission created to address the increasing problem of school gun violence perpetuated by children. In recent years, three cases of school gun violence were noted in or near Redtown. Kirt Kunkel, Newton Brazil, Marcus Johnson, and Andrew Garcia, youngsters between the ages of 11 and 15 years, all carried out violent acts at their schools. Their actions raised awareness of the problem in the community and prompted a call to action.

Given the nature of the recent tragedies and the public outcry, the mayor of Redtown declared a state of emergency in the area of school violence, and together with city and county leaders, legislators, community coalitions, and public health leaders called a "Code Red" and established the Commission for the Deterrence and Prevention of School Violence. The public health leaders served as the lead players of the commission and were commonly known as the Code Red Action Team. The commission began with an assessment of the problem, followed by an intense investigation of the events that led up to each of the three incidents.

The Tragedy of Kirt Kunkel

The first major school violence event hit Redtown in May 2001 when Kirt Kunkel, 15, was expelled from school for having a loaded pistol in his locker. Terrified as to what his parents would say and not wanting to face causing them another disappointment, Kunkel felt his only option was to kill his parents, classmates that had previously teased and belittled him, and himself. Kirt's father picked him up from the police station that day and drove him home. Kirt went to his room and retrieved a semiautomatic weapon that he had hidden there. He then shot his father to death as the father sat at the kitchen table eating a sandwich. Kirt then called a friend and talked for a while as he waited for his mother to return home from work. He allowed her to pull into the garage and park her car. As she approached the door to enter the home, he stopped her there, told her he loved her and then shot her six times. Kirt placed homemade bombs around the house, one under his mother's body, and spent the night in the home with his parent's bodies before driving his mother's car to school the next day and firing off 48 rounds of ammunition into his classmates. Kirt killed two students and injured 25 others. He was wrestled to the ground by some other kids before he could turn the gun on himself.

From the outside, Kirt's family seemed like a very functional and happy family. Kirt's parents were both well-respected teachers; his oldest sister, Louise, was a cheerleader and honor roll student. The family traveled together and were model community residents. However, from an early age Kirt displayed signs of depression and had disciplinary problems at home and at school. Below is a chronology of some key events in Kirt's life:

- Kirt was born in August 1985. He went to kindergarten in Spain for a year when his parents took a sabbatical from teaching in the United States. He was very frustrated in school, where everyone was speaking a language foreign to him.

- Kirt entered first grade in September 1991. In a report card, his teacher indicated he "lacked maturity and had slow emotional and physical development."

- In 1993, Kirt was diagnosed with learning disabilities and was placed in special education classes for reading and writing, and in gifted and talented classes for math and science.

- In 1998, Kirt showed an interest in explosives and weapons. He used the Internet to purchase a book about how to make bombs. Kirt's mother was concerned about the type of friends Kirt was spending time with.

- In 1999, Kirt was caught shoplifting a CD in a music store. His mother found a hidden gun in his room.

- In January 2000, Kirt was caught throwing rocks off of a bridge with a friend. One rock damaged a car, but there was no personal injury. He paid for damages to the victim's car and performed community services as retribution. He showed remorse for his actions. He said his friend threw the stone that actually hit the car.

(*Continues*)

- In February 2000, as a result of the rock-throwing incident, Kirt's depression, and his obsession with guns and explosives, Kirt's mother decided to send him to a psychologist for counseling. He was diagnosed with "major depressive disorder" and given a prescription for Prozac.

- In March 2000, Kirt continued to see the doctor for depression. The psychiatrist noted that his parents were "impressive parents" for wanting their son to take responsibility for the rock-throwing incident. The doctor saw nothing out of the ordinary with Kirt or his family.

- In April 2000, Kirt's psychiatrist noted that he was less depressed and handled anger better, but that he still had an interest in explosives.

- In May 2000, Kirt was suspended from school for fighting with a student in his class.

- On June 28, 2000, Kirt's father went with him to buy a gun. His psychiatrist was concerned about the gun purchase.

- Kirt's psychiatric treatment was discontinued on July 30, 2000, since he was doing well in school.

- In the summer of 2000, Kirt bought a gun from a student at school and hid it from his parents.

- Kirt entered Redtown High School in the fall of 2000. He also went off Prozac.

- September 2000: Kirt's father bought him a semiautomatic rifle, but told him that he could use it only under his father's supervision.

- In October 2000, Kirt delivered a "How to Make a Bomb" speech in public speaking class.

- On May 20, 2001, Kirt was expelled from school for having a gun in his locker. He was embarrassed about how his father would react to his expulsion. Kirt returned home from school and killed his father while he was eating at the kitchen table. Kirt waited for his mother to return home from work, told her he loved her, then killed her.

- On May 21, 2001, Kirt drove to school dressed in a trench coat with a semiautomatic rifle and a knife taped to his leg. He went on a rampage, killing two students and injuring 25 others.

After this tragic event, much research was done to better understand why Kirt Kunkel killed and if the tragedy could have been prevented. Some retrospective thoughts about this case follow.

Even after he killed their parents, Kirt's sister, Louise, still loved Kirt very much and knew that he had struggled with learning disabilities from early on in Spain. Many said he came from a "good family" and had understanding, caring parents. His mother was said to have been proactive about getting him in treatment after the rock-throwing incident. Some have speculated that he may have felt like a failure compared with Louise and never lived up to his parents' expectations. Some friends at school said he spoke of "voices in his head"; others said he told them that he would soon do something "memorable." He was voted by his classmates as the person "most likely to create World War III" and was obsessed with guns, explosives, and other weapons. He had trouble controlling his anger and had disciplinary issues both at home and at school. He was said to have had feelings of hopelessness and loneliness and to have been suicidal. Kirt was once quoted as having said "My only hope is that tomorrow will be better. When I lose hope, people die." He used the antidepressant Prozac, which has since been found to cause psychotic side effects in a small percentage of minors.

Other School Shooters

Newton Brazil, a 13-year-old student, shot and killed his English teacher on the last day of school. The shooting took place after Newton and a friend had been sent home early that day for throwing water balloons. As they were leaving, Newton told his friend he was going to get a gun and return to school to shoot the school administrator who had dismissed him. Newton arrived home and could not find his mother or grandmother to return with him to school to discuss his dismissal. Newton then took a gun and returned to the school. Newton arrived at the door of his English class and asked to speak with two friends in the hallway. The English teacher refused and sent Newton away. Newton pulled out the gun, pointed it in his English teacher's face and shot. He said he only pointed the gun to scare the teacher, but it went off accidentally.

By many accounts, Newton seemed to be a well-adjusted teenager who was doing well in school. Unique to this case is that Newton held his victim in high esteem. Newton considered this teacher one of his favorites. In addition to mentioning to a friend that he planned to return to school with a gun and shoot an administrator, Newton had shown the gun to his classmates a few weeks prior. The gun in question was stolen by Newton from a family acquaintance. Some indications also suggest that Brazil was smitten with the girl he requested to see in the English class and the shooting was a youth reaction to being denied access to her.

Marcus Johnson, 13, and Andrew Garcia, 11, are cousins raised in Jonesboro, Arkansas, who carried out a plan that resulted in the deaths of five fellow students and the wounding of 10 others, including a teacher at the Westside Middle School. Marcus, the elder cousin, was the leader in this tragedy, vowing to "kill girls who broke up with [him]" following the breakup with a girlfriend just two weeks before the incident. He was heard by classmates just the day prior saying that "he had a lot of killing to do," but no action was taken. On the morning of March 24, 1998, the two cousins took the Johnson family minivan (driven by Marcus) and headed toward the Westside Middle School armed with rifles and handguns reportedly belonging to Andrew Garcia's grandfather. On their way to school, they stopped at two or three gas stations, but no attendant would sell them gas because of their age. Somehow they made it to the school, dressed in camouflage and ready to attack. Andrew entered the school, tripped a false fire alarm to lure students outside, and then ran back to the designated position, where Marcus was waiting to open fire. As students exited the building in response to the fire alarm, the boys mowed the students down with gunfire.

Discussion of Theme—Early Warning Signs

What made these young people kill? The Code Red Action Team examined each case carefully, attempting to identify themes or early warning signs that were common to these cases. While there do not appear to be specific "events" that spawned these killing sprees, there are some relevant similarities that are evident among these three cases.

Child psychologist Jonathan Kellerman, author of *Savage Spawn: Reflections on Violent Children*, says that a good predictor of dangerousness in children is the combination of a certain temperament with a chaotic environment. In each of these three cases, the killers had some exposure to violence. However, that violence was not openly apparent to the parents, school officials, or community members who interacted with these boys on a daily basis. Kirt Kunkel used a small collection of books to educate himself about explosives and bomb making. He then began to stockpile firearms in his home and detonate homemade bombs in the woods behind his home to vent his feelings of anger and frustration. Although his parents were not violent people, we believe that his strained relationship with his parents coupled with his strong desire to please them created feelings of failure and despair in Kunkel. His lack of popularity among his peers only seemed to add to the chaos that went on in the mind of this lonely, immature boy. He was holding out for hope that his world would change. In his words, "When I lose hope, people die."

Newton Brazil witnessed physical abuse inflicted on his mother by her boyfriend. He often tried to rescue her from the abuse. What everyone outside the family saw each day was "a good student with little history of disciplinary problems." But the domestic violence was never discussed in Brazil's home. He had no outlet for his feelings and therefore kept everything inside. Eventually, it bubbled over. In the case of Andrew Garcia and Marcus Johnson, the boys had been introduced to guns and hunting at very young ages. "Killing was made a central part of their understanding of what defines manhood."

There were other commonalities among these cases. All of these boys had troubled relationships with their fathers. Sometimes, the father was absent altogether. These boys had feelings of low self-esteem and poor social skills. They were loners or outcasts. Additionally, they had all been rejected by the young girls that were the objects of their affections. So what made these young people kill? Dr. Helen Smith, a forensic psychologist in Knoxville, Tennessee, conducted a national survey of violent and nonviolent kids. She found that "Using guns and being violent toward others moves these kids from powerlessness to power, from nobodies to media celebrities."

Pointing Fingers: The Shift of Responsibility

In hindsight, the warning signs should have been obvious. Many blame the parents. Others blame violence in the media that youth are exposed to. Still others question the police, the school, and judicial or mental health systems that may have had run-ins with the perpetrators. The National School Safety Center has created a profile of the youngster most likely to commit school violence, based on the profiles of juveniles who already have. The 20-item checklist includes drug abuse, tantrums, threats, depression, truancy, cruelty to animals, and a fascination with weapons and violence that spills over into schoolwork.

Profiles, however, are problematic because they tend to apply to a lot of kids who never become violent. Using a profile gives one the tendency to stereotype and group a large number where only a very small minority will act. And there is no guarantee that the kids most likely to kill won't be missed.

(*Continues*)

Violence in movies, on television, and in video games has become pervasive in our society, and studies have shown that media violence can lead to aggressive behavior in children. By age 18, the average American child will have viewed about 200,000 acts of violence on television alone. The American Academy of Pediatrics states that violence is especially damaging to young children (under age 8) because they cannot easily tell the difference between real life and fantasy. They go on to say that media violence affects children by:

- Increasing aggressiveness and antisocial behavior

- Increasing their fear of becoming victims

- Making them less sensitive to violence and to victims of violence

- Increasing their appetite for more violence in entertainment and in real life

Additionally, media violence often fails to show the consequences of violence. This is especially true of cartoons, toy commercials, and music videos. As a result, children learn that there are few, if any, repercussions for committing violent acts.

This, however, does not explain the majority of children who are exposed to the same influences and grow up to be productive members of society. Ultimately, the media does not commit the crimes; people do.

Many have pointed to the accessibility of guns as the cause of this growing problem. Has our society taken this matter seriously? Our answer is no! The proliferation of guns in our society is startling. How many gun laws have been changed? Not enough. Even current gun laws aren't being universally enforced. Despite continued acknowledgments by school shooters that the guns they used were stolen from parents or other family members, many parents have still not disposed of their guns. Some are still traveling to the local Wal-Mart to buy rifles or guns for their children. Has every family in a school community where there has been a lethal school shooting destroyed every gun they own? Of course not, but this is a question that all community stakeholders need to consider.

Missed Opportunities

Could anything have been done to prevent the murders of Kirt Kunkel's parents, the murders of two students, and the injuries to 25 other students at the Redtown, Midwest, school? In hindsight, many of the public health leaders on Redtown's special commission on school gun violence think that there were warning signs that were missed or went unheeded in the years preceding the killings.

Kunkel exhibited many of the early warning signs at a young age: a troubled childhood, disciplinary problems, early learning disabilities, and an obsession with weapons. As a high school freshman, Kirt was caught shoplifting and had a gun hidden in his room. A year later, he was again in trouble for rock throwing and property damage. He was diagnosed with a major depressive disorder and started on an antidepressant.

Newton Brazil was a model student and overall a "good kid." He didn't have constant and recurring disciplinary problems. However, he was constantly exposed to violence in his home, and he had no outlet for his feelings. His mother did not seek help for the domestic abuse that she was suffering. Nor did she talk with her son to reinforce the basic fact that what he was seeing was not socially acceptable. His attempts to thwart the violence that he thought was wrong were unwanted and went unrecognized. On the occasion that Brazil became upset about something, violence was the only coping mechanism that he had. He simply was not aware of anything else.

Andrew Garcia and Marcus Johnson were hunters. They had been taught very early in life that normal rules don't apply to hunters, that hunters can attack fair game at any time. Although hunting is acceptable and welcomed in many parts of the country, we must question the most appropriate age at which children should be exposed to hunting. We submit that Andrew and Marcus were not mature enough to be allotted as much freedom around guns as they were. These boys thought it would be fun to see what would happen if they opened fire on a crowd of teachers and fellow classmates. To them, it was a game. Clearly, they did not have the proper education about guns and hunting that would have enabled them to know that the taking of human life is not only wrong, but very different from hunting animals for food.

We have found that there are similarities among almost all of the school shooters. There are also differences. They are not all loners. They are not all abused children. Anger is the most common thread. Access to guns is universal.

In hindsight, the warning signs come together to form a more complete portrait of potential shooters. But in the present, how do we quantify and qualify the traits and actions of these students? The warning signs were all there. Individually, as parents, friends, teachers, police, courts, doctors, and social workers, we know something about the feelings or behaviors of these young people, but how do we put it together? The answer is simple enough: we need to develop a mechanism for pooling information and sharing that information. The discipline of public health offers us a solution: surveillance and data sharing. Surveillance can be carried out on a daily basis in our basic interactions with students. A 2000 study conducted by researchers from the U.S. Secret Service offers some key insight: "In their own words, the boys who have killed in America's schools offer a simple suggestion to prevent it from happening again: 'Listen to us.'" How do we develop the wisdom to determine which child will go on to act out in violence and direct our limited resources to preventing that future action? The wisdom comes in learning how to recognize the warning signs and building on the information you have. Wisdom also comes in extending the information we have individually to our constituents, addressing the barriers to sharing it, understanding each other, and acting together for the good of the community. Data sharing, perhaps via a confidential databank, among stakeholders will continually provide more information upon which to build.

Communication is a key factor in preventing these tragedies. It is a well-known fact that many of these young killers often tell their friends of their plans prior to carrying them out. Therefore, fellow students sometimes know that something could happen. These students need teaching and support so that they will feel comfortable revealing their information to parents and authorities. Those students who come forth will also need respect, confidentiality, and appreciation. Their information must be valued and then evaluated, rather than filed away, buried, or ignored.

We need a process for tying all of these traits together without stereotyping a significant percentage of lonely high school students. Many students will have learning problems, have insecurities, and feel alone until they move through the teenage years and out of the school environment. Many will overcome the challenges of adolescence and move on to brighter lives that stereotyping could make difficult.

We can't change their ages, but we can change their environments. We need to teach students who fit the profile of potential shooters to cope in their climactic and unstable environments. For vulnerable students, spending seven hours a day, five days a week for years in a perceived hostile and nonsupportive environment can prove disastrous for these students and the communities in which they live. Even for students who don't become violent in school, environmental changes could help many to develop better self-esteem and be less prone to anger and violence in other areas of their lives.

Violence in the Nation—A Call to Public Health

Violence is not a new phenomenon in our nation. Recent examinations of community response to, social responsibility for, and societal cost of violence have allowed prevention practitioners and communities to reexamine our approach to violence. Indeed, violence is a global issue, but for the United States, violence seems epidemic. The U.S. homicide rate is three to eight times greater than that of any other Western democracy. According to the Center for the Study and Prevention of Violence, intentional violence accounts for one-third of all injuries in the United States, and intentional interpersonal violence disproportionately involves young people as predators and victims. Furthermore, homicide is the second leading cause of death for youth ages 15 to 24 years.

School violence is often at the center of discussion when examining youth violence trends. School violence is not limited to urban areas. On the contrary, in 1998, students ranging in ages from 12 to 18 years in urban, suburban, and rural locales were equally vulnerable to serious violent crime and theft at school. School violence often calls our attention to the relatively recent phenomenon known as "school shootings." And while these cases are seen as especially heinous and lend themselves well to the sensationalism of media, in examining violence in the lives of our youth, we must also keep in mind that more youth victimization happens away from school than at school. Violence is a societal issue that, like water, finds its way into all corners of our lives.

The news isn't all bad. According to the Department of Justice's Bureau of Justice and Statistics, violent crime and victimization rates have declined since 1993, reaching the lowest level ever recorded in 2000. Likewise, public health officials have taken notice. *Youth Violence: A Report of the Surgeon General* was developed by the Centers for Disease Control and prevention, the National Institutes of Health, and the Substance Abuse and Mental Health Services Administration. The report defines the problem, using surveillance processes designed to gather data that establish the nature of the problem and the trends in its incidence and prevalence; identifies potential causes through epidemiological analyses that identify risk and protective factors associated with the problem; designs, develops, and evaluates the effectiveness and generalizability of interventions; and disseminates successful models as part of a coordinated effort to educate and reach out to the public. Public health constituents have the opportunity to examine violence, and specifically youth violence, at a community health level, using both integrated models and community strategies to develop violence prevention practices.

(Continues)

Current public health antiviolence programs often limit their scope and resources to victims of domestic violence and abused children. While these prevention and intervention programs are crucial, we must begin to examine the wider scope of violence in society. Of concern in this examination is violence prevention focused on adolescent males and adult males who are both the perpetrators and victims of the majority of violent acts in the United States.

Public health methods are essential to violence prevention. Public health practice is both systematic and concerned with the discovery, examination, perpetuation, and the root cause of disease. Public health at its core can be described as "changing behavior and changing attitudes through intervention as the base of prevention." Therefore, the nature of violence that continues to permeate our communities and degrade both community health and well-being requires a systematic response.

The public health leaders of Redtown's special commission on youth violence in schools reviewed much material, interviewed many experts, and came up with many questions. Their unanimous response to these questions is that Redtown will develop public health policy to prevent violence in schools.

Study Guide Questions

1. In your group, discuss the similarities and differences in the school shooters in these three cases.

2. What are some of the missed opportunities raised in these cases?

3. Discuss the impact of the following on these cases:
   a. Parents
   b. Drugs
   c. Availability of weapons
   d. Past violent behavior/tendencies
   e. Bullying at school
   f. Exposure to violence in the home
   g. Exposure to violent video games

4. What role should public health have in school-based violence prevention programs?

5. Discuss the various jurisdictions involved and how they could work together to develop a prevention program (criminal law, the school administration, public health, parents/teachers groups, neighborhood coalitions against violence).

6. Researchers from the U.S. Secret Service studied 37 school shootings. Of the 40 school shooters interviewed, they all offered the same suggestion for prevention of school gun violence: "Listen to us." Discuss ideas for how prevention programs can provide avenues for those contemplating violence to express their feelings, free of punishment.

7. Discuss ways that public health practitioners can use tools such as surveillance and data sharing to hone in on warning signs before tragedy strikes.

References

Animal People. (1998, May). *Hunting and Trapping: Teach the Children Well*. Retrieved December 12, 2003, from http://www.animalpeoplenews.org/98/4/hunting.html

Center for Prevention of School Violence. (2003). *Parental Involvement in School Safety: What Every Parent Should Know; What Every Parent Should Say*. Retrieved September 29, 2012, from http://www.ncdjjdp.org/cpsv/pdf_files/parental_involvement.pdf

Center for the Study and Prevention of Violence. (2002). *School Violence Fact Sheets*. Retrieved October 27, 2003, from http://www.colorado.edu/cspv/publications/factsheets/scoolviolence/FS-SV02.html

Centers for Disease Control and Prevention, National Center for Injury Prevention and Control. *Youth Violence*. Retrieved December 8, 2003, from http://www.cdc.gov/ncipc/factsheets/yvfacts.htm

Chicago Department of Public Health. *A Public Health Approach to Violence Prevention*. Retrieved October 30, 2003, from http://www.cocpweb3.cityofchicago.org/health/Publications/ViolencePrevention/pub_health_ap

Children's Drugs? An Inquiry into the School Shootings in America. Retrieved November 7, 2003, from http://www.trunkerton.fsnet.co.uk/children.htm

Constitutional Rights Foundation. (n.d.). *The Challenge of School Violence*. Retrieved from http://www.crf-usa.org/violence/school.html

Court TV Online. (n.d.). *Trial Report: Nathaniel Brazill Says He's Sorry, Asks Judge for Leniency.* Retrieved December 12, 2003, from http://www.courttv.com/trials/ brazill/072601_am_ctv.html

Dedman, B. Deadly Lessons: School Shooters Tell Why. *Chicago Sun-Times.* Retrieved October 28, 2003, from http://www.suntimes.com/shoot/

Dedman, B. Examining the Psyche of an Adolescent Killer. *Chicago Sun-Times.* Retrieved December 28, 2003, from http://www.suntimes.com/shoot/shoot_15.html

ERIC Clearinghouse and Urban Education. (1996). *An Overview of Strategies to Reduce School Violence.* Retrieved October 27, 2003, from http://eric=web.tc.columbia.edu/digest/dig115.asp

Family Education Network. (2003). *When Student Writings Set Off School Alarms.* Retrieved October 27, 2003, from http://www.familyeducation.com/article/0,1120,24-21838,00.html

Fox News. (1999). *Kinkel Was on Prozac—Heard "Voices" in His Head.* Retrieved November 7, 2003, from http://www.foxnews.com/health/healthw_ap_1113_32.sml,11-15-99.

Gellert, G. A. (2002). *Confronting Violence* (Boulder, CO: Westview Press).

Keefer, Bob. 1998, May 31. Potentially Deadly Youngsters Not Common. *Eugene Register Guard.* Retrieved November 7, 2003, from http://www.oslc.org/InTheNews/youngsters.html

Malone, J. "3 Paducah Families Ask: Why, Michael?" *(Louisville) Courier-Journal.* Retrieved November 22, 2003, from http://www.courier-journal.com./cjextra/schoolshoot/SCHvictims.html

O'Toole, M. E. (1999). *The School Shooter: A Threat Assessment Perspective* (Washington, DC: Federal Bureau of Investigation).

PBS NewsHour. (1999, April 21). *Kids Who Kill.* Retrieved October 27, 2003, from http://www.pbs.org/newshour/bb/law/jan-june99/violence_4-21.html

PBS Online and WGBH/Frontline. (n.d.). *The Killer at Thurston High: Who Is Kip Kinkel? Chronology.* Retrieved November 2, 2003, from http://www.pbs.org/wgbh/pages/frontline/shows/kinkel/kip/cron.html

PBS Online and WGBH/Frontline. (n.d.). *The Killer at Thurston High: Profiling School Shooters.* Retrieved November 2, 2003, from http://www.pbs.org/wgbh/pages/frontline/shows/kinkel/profile

PBS Online and WGBH/Frontline. (n.d.). *The Killer at Thurston High: An Interview with Kristin Kinkel.* Retrieved November 2, 2003, from http://www.pbs.org/wgbh/pages/frontline/shows/kinkel/kip/kristin.html

PBS Online and WGBH/Frontline. (n.d.). *The Killer at Thurston High: 111 Years Without Parole.* Retrieved November 2, 2003, from http://www.pbs.org/wgbh/pages/frontline/shows/kinkel/trial/

PBS Online and WGBH/Frontline. (n.d.). *The Killer at Thurston High: Placing Blame.* Retrieved November 2, 2003, from http://www.pbs.org/wgbh/pages/frontline/shows/kinkel/blame/

Prothrow-Stith, P., and M. Weissman. (1991). *Deadly Consequences* (New York: HarperCollins).

Ramsland, K. (n.d.). School Killers: Copy Cats. *Court TV, Crime Library: Criminal Minds and Methods.* Retrieved September 29, 2012, from http://www.trutv.com/library/crime/serial_killers/weird/kids1/cats_4.html

Ramsland, K. (n.d.). School Killers: Kipland Kinkel. *Court TV, Crime Library: Criminal Minds and Methods.* Retrieved September 29, 2012, from http://www.trutv.com/library/crime/serial_killers/weird/kids1/kinkel_2.html

Ramsland, K. (n.d.). School Killers: The List. *Court TV, Crime Library: Criminal Minds and Methods.* Retrieved September 29, 2012, from http://www.trutv.com/library/crime/serial_killers/weird/kids1/index_1.html

Ramsland, K. (n.d.). School Killers: What the Kids Say. *Court TV, Crime Library: Criminal Minds and Methods.* Retrieved September 29, 2012, from http://www.trutv.com/library/crime/serial_killers/weird/kids1/say_5.html

Ramsland, K. (n.d.). The Young Rampage Killer. *Court TV, Crime Library: Criminal Minds and Methods.* Retrieved September 29, 2012, from http://www.trutv.com/library/crime/serial_killers/weird/kids1/killer_6.html

Ramsland, K. School Killers: School Violence and the Media. *Court TV, Crime Library: Criminal Minds and Methods.* Retrieved September 29, 2012, from http://www.trutv.com/library/crime/serial_killers/weird/kids1/media_7.html

Smith, Helen. (1998). *School Killings: Prevention and Response.* Testimony before the Arkansas House of Representatives Committee on the Judiciary. Retrieved November 7, 2003, from http://www.violentkids.com/articles/violence_article_6.html

U.S. Department of Health and Human Services, Office of Disease Prevention and Health Promotion. (2001). *Prevention Report: Youth Violence Is a Public Health Issue.* Retrieved December 2, 2003, from http://www.odphp.osophs.dhhs.gov/pubs/prevrpt/01spring/Spring2001PR.htm

U.S. Department of Health and Human Services. Youth Violence: A Report of the Surgeon General. Retrieved December 8, 2003, from http://www.surgeongeneral.gov/library/youthviolence/report.html

Violence Prevention Center. *Where'd They Get Their Guns? An Analysis of the Firearms Used in High-Profile Shootings, 1963 to 2001.* Retrieved November 21, 2003, from http://www.vpc.org/studies/wguncont.htm

Why Files. (n.d.). *When Kids Kill.* Retrieved October 27, 2003, from http://www.whyfiles.org/065school_violence/1html

Source: Courtesy of the Mid-America Regional Public Health Leadership Institute.

SUMMARY

Although much of leadership is about change, it is important for the public health leader to understand the elements of change as a process and how it works. This chapter has looked at this issue and discussed it from the viewpoint of the individual who has to adapt to the changes that are occurring in our society on a daily basis, the leaders who have to respond to the need for change or adapt to changes that are unplanned, and the need to have strategies for addressing change as a process.

DISCUSSION QUESTIONS

1. What is deep change?
2. Compare and contrast the Kotter and Conner models of change.
3. What is change management, and how does it differ from the new change management model?

EXERCISE 24-1: Surprises

Purpose: to look at change from the perspective of events that were surprises

Key concepts: change, surprises, tipping points

Procedures: Divide the class or training group into groups of 10. Have each participant list on an index card five surprise events that have occurred between September 11, 2001, and today that have had public health implications. Students should share their lists with other group members and put the events on a large sheet of paper. Have each group present the group list to the larger group and discuss the meaning of surprises. Were any of the events tipping points?

EXERCISE 24-2: Scenario Building

Purpose: to use scenarios to better understand how change is affected by terrorist events

Key concepts: scenario building, change

Procedures: Assume that a terrorist event similar to the events of September 11, 2001, is being planned by an extremist political group in the next three years. Divide the class or training group into groups of 10. Ask groups to describe the public health concerns in the following situations:

1. Scenario in which the event is prevented
2. Scenario in which the event occurs in New York City, Los Angeles, Chicago, and Washington, DC, within a 24-hour period
3. Scenario in which a "dirty bomb" is used
4. Two alternate scenarios to the above

Present the scenarios to the group as a whole. This exercise may take three to four hours to complete.

EXERCISE 24-3: Leadership and Terrorism

Purpose: to see how leaders with different styles respond to a terrorist event

Key concepts: leadership, leadership style, conservers, pragmatists, originators

Procedures: Divide the class or training group into groups of 10. Using the Florida anthrax letters of 2001 as an example, discuss how leaders who are conservers, pragmatists, and originators would address the case. Have each small group come up with five recommendations for action by the three types of leaders. Then have each group present their recommendations to the larger group.

EXERCISE 24-4:   Terrorism and Change

Purpose: to explore public health in the context of different potential terrorist planning activities

Key concepts: change, emotional intelligence, security planning

Procedures: Divide the class or training group into groups of 10. Apply the eight-stage change model of Kotter and Cohen (2002) to address the changes needed in community security planning related to potential terrorist events where some of the issues are:

1. Smallpox vaccination program

2. Enforced curfew for the entire community in high-alert situations

3. Increase in real estate taxes to fund hiring of more police and firefighters

4. Anthrax prevention program

5. Implementation of police powers during all high-alert situations

6. No local support for restrictions on personal freedom

Each group should discuss the emotional element in each stage of the group application of the model. Discuss the experience of the exercise with the group as a whole.

REFERENCES

1. Turning Point, *States of Change* (Seattle, WA: Turning Point National Office; R. W. Johnson Foundation, 2004).

2. C. M. Alpaslan and I. I. Mitroff, *Swans, Swine, and Swindlers* (Stanford, CA: Stanford University Press, 2011).

3. E. H. Schein, *Organizational Culture and Leadership*, 3rd ed. (San Francisco: Jossey-Bass, 2010).

4. Schein, *Organizational Culture and Leadership*.

5. R. E. Quinn, *Deep Change* (San Francisco: Jossey-Bass, 1996.

6. P. Schwartz, *Inevitable Surprise* (New York: Gotham Books, 2003).

7. Schwartz, *Inevitable Surprise*.

8. Schwartz, *Inevitable Surprise*.

9. C. Musselwhite and R. Jones, *Dangerous Opportunity: Making Change Work* (Philadelphia: Xlibris, 2004).

10. J. Kouzes and B. Posner, *The Leadership Challenge*, 4th ed. (San Francisco: Jossey-Bass, 2007).

11. Musselwhite and Jones, *Dangerous Opportunity*.

12. Musselwhite and Jones, *Dangerous Opportunity*.

13. Musselwhite and Jones, *Dangerous Opportunity*.

14. J. P. Kotter, *The New Rules* (New York: The Free Press, 1995).

15. J. P. Kotter and D. S. Cohen, *The Heart of Change* (Boston: Harvard Business School Press, 2002).

16. Kotter and Cohen, *The Heart of Change*.

17. J. P. Kotter, *Leading Change* (Boston: Harvard Business School Press, 1996).

18. Kotter and Cohen, *The Heart of Change*.

19. D. R. Conner, *Managing at the Speed of Change* (New York: Villard Books, 1992).

20. Conner, *Managing at the Speed of Change*.

21. Conner, *Managing at the Speed of Change*.

22. Conner, *Managing at the Speed of Change*.

23. Conner, *Managing at the Speed of Change*.

24. D. R. Conner, *Leading at the Edge of Chaos* (New York: John Wiley and Sons, 1998).

25. Conner, *Leading at the Edge of Chaos*.

26. W. Bridges, *Transitions* (Cambridge, MA: Perseus Books, 1980).

27. Kotter, *Leading Change*.

28. R. Axelrod, *Terms of Engagement* (San Francisco: Berrett-Koehler, 2010).

CHAPTER 25

Mentoring, Coaching, and Training in Public Health

My experiences as a mentor were first rate. Just say yes, if you're asked to serve as a mentor.

—S. F. Randolph

Mentoring and coaching are critical leadership activities. Leadership development depends on experienced leaders acting as role models for novice leaders. Leader-mentors and coaches need to understand leadership and promote the development of leadership skills by others.[1] Mentoring and coaching novice and experienced leaders has become even more important in the past few years than in the previous century. An important aspect of the increase of interest in mentoring, coaching, and training is the lifelong learning acceptance by leaders and managers as well as young public health professionals. As leaders, we plan our actions as a key aspect of our work and nonwork lives. We often plan life projects related to family, work, recreation, creative activities, and social action and our contributions to our social justice values.[2] Life projects give us direction and motivation.

In general, mentoring is a form of one-to-one teaching, to be contrasted with training, which involves instructing more than one person. Public health leaders do engage in training as well, such as in team building.[3] A public health leader might facilitate the team-building process by presenting guidelines to the team as a whole and also acting as a mentor for each team member. (Peer mentoring is also possible in a team situation.) Mentors generally do not give formal instruction but instead teach by example.[4] They understand how public health works and can explain the written and unwritten laws to their mentees.[5]

Some authors use the term "coaching"[6] rather than "mentoring." This has become confusing. Coaching is more about how to do a specific job more effectively, and mentoring is more about career and career choices.[7] Leadership development is important in both mentoring and coaching situations. The relationship between the mentor and the mentee or the coach and the coachee are true partnerships, and each involved individual should gain something from it (in other words, it should be a win-win relationship). It should also be contractual, which means that the needs and expectations of both parties should be addressed when the relationship is first established.

Mentors can help in the training of a team by guiding the learning of each team member in leadership. The challenge for the mentor in formal training situations is to help the team become a learning community. The mentor must be committed to the goals of the team and facilitate the learning process for the team members, including through direct one-on-one interaction related to the professional needs of a given member. It may also be beneficial to help the trainee address job-related issues, which means that a modified coaching relationship will be established in addition to the mentoring one. Thus, the boundary between mentoring and coaching becomes blurred.

The learning contract model has been utilized by both coaches and mentors to guide their development process with their protégés.[8] The learning contract has evolved from the literature on adult learning. In 1970, Knowles utilized the concept of andragogy to discuss the four assumptions of learning by adults.[9,10] The major assumption is that adult learners tend to move from a dependency model where they are passive learners to an approach that is more active and self-directed. Adult learning is also experiential in that adults incorporate their experiences into the learning process. Third, adults tend to accept that learning will be a part of all new jobs and activities in which they engage. Finally, adults learn new knowledge as required by new tasks. Leaders who accept adult learning approaches tend to become ecological leaders who tie their learning experiences to the contexts in which they work and play.

In developing a learning contract, several steps are followed:[11]

1. Diagnose personal learning needs.
2. Specify learning objectives.
3. Designate learning resources and strategies.
4. Determine target dates for completion.
5. Specify ways to determine that objectives are met.
6. Determine how evidence will be judged.
7. Review the contract personally and also with your mentor or coach.
8. Carry out the goals of the contract.
9. Monitor the process.
10. Evaluate the contract.

One way to translate these steps into a usable form is to create a chart with the objectives (step 2) on one axis and the remaining steps on the other axis as columns. Step 1 can be listed separately.

Experiment with a learning contract in Exercise 25-1.

The remainder of this chapter explores the nature of mentoring, coaching, and training, and their role in leadership development. As will be seen in the following discussion, friendship is an important element in mentoring and coaching, as is trust in a training situation. In discussing the importance of having vital friendships at work that are relationships benefitting both parties, Rath defined eight types of friendship roles: builder, champion, collaborator, companion, connector, energizer, mind opener, and navigator.[12] A friend at work may have a combination of the behaviors associated with each role. Mentors and coaches tend to be builders who are friends and who support your personal growth and are not threatened by your progress. When you appear valued by your organization, you enjoy the work more and become more committed to the work of the organization.

MENTORING

The Benefits of Mentoring

Mentoring offers a number of benefits.[13] First, mentoring young professionals in a given field expands the network of professionals working in that field. This is especially important in public health, where practitioners come from many different disciplines. The mentees also gain the knowledge and tools needed to develop leadership skills. (Note that mentors give tools to their mentees, but the tools need to be translated into action for leadership skills to begin to evolve.) In addition, mentoring usually increases the mentees' chances for promotion.[14]

If a mentor is impressed by a mentee, the mentee may be assigned more challenging tasks. The mentor helps the mentee not only solve problems but make decisions as well. The mentee can acquire cutting-edge information that will aid the mentee in providing technical assistance to others in the future. The mentor can help the mentee navigate through tough choices. The mentee learns the ropes and will know, during his or her tenure as a leader, how to change the ropes as they fray.

For the mentor, the relationship can be extremely positive. Being a role model increases the self-esteem of the mentor and adds to the mentor's legacy.[15] To be looked upon as a person who has knowledge to impart also is important for the mentor. Mentors are usually among the senior members of an organization, and having the sense of being needed by younger members is a clear benefit for them.[16] In general, mentoring is a renewal process for mentors, who may feel rejuvenated. Case Study 25-A reports on the experiences of a mentor.

Case Study 25-A

The Mentoring Experience: What Is a Mentor?

Shirley F. Randolph for University of Illinois School of Public Health, Illinois Public Health Leadership Institute (now the Mid-America Regional Public Health Leadership Institute)

The literature defines a mentor in a number of ways, none of which fulfills the mission of mentors as envisioned by the Illinois Public Health Leadership Institute. So those of us who enjoyed the privilege of being in the original group of five mentors developed a definition to fit that vision.

The definition agreed on by the mentors has two parts. Part one covered the mentors' role during the three-day conference with the initial group of 25 fellows. The mentors determined that their role for the conference would be one of facilitator and coach.

Part two of our definition of "mentor" refers to the mentoring role following the conference. The mentors defined their role for that portion of their yearlong responsibility to be one of teacher, counselor, friend, and "encourager."

The mentoring experiences that are described herein relate to part one: facilitator and coach during the three-day conference.

The most critical experience—not only for me as a mentor but also, I think, for the five fellows assigned to my group—was to be part of a small cadre of public health professionals, all of whom are leaders in their agencies, who developed a sharing, caring, and trusting relationship with all members of the group. There was plenty of "give and take" and exchange of viewpoints and information as we moved through the three-day agenda.

My responsibility as a facilitator turned out to be easily fulfilled due to the professional approach taken by each of my fellows and the fact that each had prepared by reviewing materials in advance of the conference.

The role of coach turned out to be exciting, rewarding, and fun as the conference progressed. It was a challenge to be coach to five bright, well-prepared individuals. It was also a tad scary because being a mentor to a group of public health practitioners was a role I had never performed prior to the conference.

The challenge was to direct attention to new concepts, to encourage the group to examine issues from a different perspective, and to delve into certain aspects of the issues presented in the case studies we dissected. That meant that I, as a mentor, had to stretch my personal limits in order to be an effective coach!

In my attempts to be effective as a coach, I uncovered a truism that constitutes another critical experience: mentoring is not a mystery. It goes beyond the sharing of information and guidance from a more experienced person to one with less experience, the traditional mentoring role. Mentoring is the giving of time and thought. It is caring coupled with gentle guidance.

I discovered that being a mentor also requires patience and a willingness to listen carefully. Some of the choice discussions in our group evolved from pertinent issues and personal experiences brought up and shared with the group by the fellows as opposed to discussions stimulated by the content of the more formal sessions.

One of the unexpected experiences of being a mentor occurred when I realized that maybe one of my most important contributions as a mentor could be just being available when needed, to be someone who could reinforce an idea, affirm a reaction, or lend credence to a different approach.

I experienced many other, less subtle "happenings" during the first annual conference of the Illinois Public Health Leadership Institute in 1992, such as:

- the harried feeling of being pushed to cover as much ground and to "cram in" as much information as possible in three short days
- the pressure to excel and to make the initial conference a "showpiece"
- the lack of time to relax and socialize more with the entire group of fellows
- the excitement that comes with learning something new
- the mental and physical exhaustion following an intense, 12-hour—or longer—day
- the joy of sharing time and thoughts with longtime public health colleagues
- the excitement of making new public health friends
- the eagerness and anticipation for each new session on the agenda
- the nostalgia that came with spending time on a university campus
- the satisfaction of seeing a plan come together
- the pleasure in knowing that the vision for the Institute was right on target, judging from the response of the fellows

(Continues)

- the intellectual stimulation that occurs when listening to ideas presented by noted public health leaders
- the annoyance that comes with not doing well playing parlor games

That about sums it up. Bottom line: my experiences as a mentor were first-rate. Just say yes if you're asked to serve as a mentor, whether it be for the Illinois Public Health Leadership Institute, in a more traditional role within your community, or for the agency in which you work. You will be richly rewarded!

Mentoring is increasing in many organizations as the value of mentoring and coaching becomes recognized.[17] A key factor about mentoring is that age is not the critical issue but rather knowledge, skills, and experience in the field. Mentoring is also not about forever relationships. Mentoring occurs when it is needed. Either the potential mentor or mentee can begin the relationship, which is usually a volunteer one. An important fact is that individuals need to understand when they need coaching and when they need mentoring. In addition, different mentors may be needed for different concerns. I may need a mentor to guide and help me better understand public health and a different mentor to help my leadership development. All parties to a mentoring situation gain from the relationship.

The organization also gains from mentoring.[18] Often both the mentor and the mentee become more productive as a result of their relationship. Working together, they are able to assess problems and find solutions better than when working solo. Because mentoring leads to leadership development, the mentee is soon able to take over leadership activities. The mentoring relationship may also lead to the discovery and nurturing of hidden talents possessed by the mentee and can help the mentee hone his or her rough edges. Mentored professionals tend to stay in organizations for longer periods and also move up in the organizational hierarchy more easily.[19] Mentoring can occur anywhere in the organization. What is needed is an organizational commitment to mentoring. As one author put it, professionals need "mentorcentives."[20]

Table 25-1 lists qualities that mentors should possess and roles they should play.[21] At various times in the mentoring process, different qualities and roles will predominate, partly because the influence of the mentor decreases over time as the mentee begins to develop the skills that the relationship is intended to foster.[22] Indeed, mentoring needs to be time limited; it should not result in long-term dependency.

Professionals want mentors who will give advice, support, and assistance, such as with the task of setting

TABLE 25-1   Mentor Qualities and Roles

Role Model	Trusted Counselor	Observes Confidentiality
Guide	Leader	Interested
Willing to be a mentor	Friend	Shows mutual respect
Supporter	Listener	Shows affection
Experienced	Knowledgeable	Accessible
Adviser	Shares resources	Networker

Source: Reprinted with permission from J. Carruthers, "The Principles and Practices of Mentoring," in *The Return of the Mentor: Strategies for Workplace Learning*, B. J. Caldwell and E. M. A. Carter, eds., p. 20. © 1993, The Falmer Press, Taylor & Francis, Inc.

career goals.[23] The mentee has a responsibility to allocate time and effort to improving skills and competence.[24] Because not all leaders are good mentors, mentees should be careful in choosing whom to establish a mentoring relationship with. Mentoring can be formal, with each new employee assigned to a mentor for a period of time, or informal, where professionals who want a mentor seek one who will understand their professional aspirations. In general, it is preferable for mentees to choose their own mentors.

Developing a Mentoring Relationship

Public health professionals may look for mentors outside their agency. For example, a community leader or board of health member may help a public health professional better understand how the community works. It is possible to have more than one mentor at a given time, but the more usual scenario is to have several mentors sequentially. Exercise 25-2 allows students to explore their personal mentoring history.

As mentioned above, in some organizations mentees are assigned to mentors. Whether a mentor is assigned or freely chosen, there is no guarantee mentor and mentee will be right for each other. To increase the chance that they will be, a potential mentee can go through a selection process such as the one presented in **Table 25-2**.[25] As can be seen, the mentee needs to determine the things that he or she wants to accomplish and then select at least one goal to attain. The process is complex, for the mentee must first engage in personal values clarification and develop a personal vision as steps on the way toward developing personal goals, and then determine if there is anyone in the organization who has accomplished similar goals. The best strategy is to identify several possible mentors and do research on them. **Table 25-3** presents a contrasting set of selection criteria used in the Illinois Public Health Leadership Institute.

After a mentor is selected, the mentor and mentee go through a series of steps as part of the development of the mentoring relationship. They need to set meeting goals, make appointments, and set an agenda. Early on, the mentor should tell his or her personal story, and together the mentor and mentee will discuss possible goals for the relationship and set a timetable for achieving the goals they choose. The deadlines should be flexible, however, and the timetable can be revised if both parties approve. During the entire relationship, mentor and mentee will need to negotiate with each other and discuss results on a regular basis.

For mentoring to be successful, whether in an agency or in a community, the environment must nurture the mentoring relationship. In addition, the focus should be on developing the mentee's character as well as on the sharing of information. Finally, the mentoring relationship should have as its ultimate goal independence for the mentee. Good mentoring will make the mentee feel so comfortable with change that his or her reliance on the mentor eventually disappears.

TABLE 25-2   The 21 Steps to Choosing Your Mentor

1. Brainstorm desires.
2. Set goal.
3. Identify achievers.
4. Select top candidates.
5. Research backgrounds.
6. Set goals for meeting.
7. Write letter to mentor prospect.
8. Call to set appointment.
9. Prepare 10 questions.
10. Ask to hear life story.
11. State goals, and ask questions. (See Table 25-4.)
12. Ask for suggestions.
13. End trial.
14. Send thank-you note, gift.
15. Evaluate information.
16. Take action on mentor suggestions.
17. Call mentor with activity results.
18. Evaluate prospect's response.
19. Request second appointment.
20. Propose a mentoring relationship.
21. Commit to the 16 Laws of Mentoring.

Source: Reprinted with permission from F. Wickman and T. Sjodin, *Mentoring*, p. 70. © 1996, The McGraw-Hill Companies.

TABLE 25-3   Criteria for Selection of Mentors

1. Must be an accomplished, recognized leader in the health and public health arena
2. Must be willing to work for one year as a mentor to five fellows, providing consultation and assistance as appropriate
3. Must be able to participate in orientation/training; the three-day institute; the two-day, six-month follow-up meeting; the one-day, 12-month follow-up meeting; and four to six meetings with the assigned fellows' group
4. Must have the skills to provide insights to fellows during discussion of case studies
5. Must be able to facilitate small-group discussions and guide group to consider most important factors in case studies and readings
6. Must be willing to provide ongoing support to fellows in their professional growth and implementation of successful leadership practices following the formal training program
7. Must be supported by employer (i.e., time off from regular duties to serve as mentor)
8. Must have held a leadership position in public health for at least 10 years
9. Should have national leadership credentials as well as state/local recognition
10. Must have demonstrated skills in administering and directing the three core governmental functions: needs assessment, policy development, and assurance
11. Must have considerable experience in working successfully with subordinates

Source: Courtesy of the Mid-America Regional Public Health Leadership Institute.

The mentee shares the responsibility for the relationship and its direction. The mentor and mentee are partners who together choose goals for the relationship, make plans to achieve the goals, and implement the plans. They will regularly study options and scenarios. If the mentee becomes overly dependent on the mentor, the latter may have to exhibit a little tough love. The mentoring process usually consists of a series of small changes that accumulate; massive sudden changes are rare. The relationship also carries with it some risk. A mentee can adversely affect the reputation of the mentor. In addition, the mentor's advice may not work in some situations. These caveats aside, the mentoring relationship tends to be mutually beneficial.

The mentoring relationship is mainly a working-hours relationship unless the two partners define it differently. The mentor guides the mentee in learning how to be effective on the job, not how to deal with his or her personal life. One secret of mentoring is that it should be fun as well as exciting. Another is that the best mentoring relationships are mismatches rather than pairings of similar individuals.

Mentoring and Cultural Diversity

Cultural diversity issues may affect many relationships in an organization. Mentor and mentee should respect each other as human beings and not let race, ethnicity, or gender get in the way of the relationship. Currently, men often mentor women, partly because men still predominate in the higher levels of most organizations. Cross-sex mentoring must include rules for the relationship that preclude sexual involvement of any kind, coerced or not.[26] Whereas sex can be an issue in cross-sex mentoring, the dearth of women in some organizations can cause women at the top to feel threatened by women poised to move upward, and the feeling of threat can prevent same-sex mentoring relationships from being effective. Note that women make up a large proportion of the public health workforce and that women in the upper echelons of public health often serve as mentors to both men and women.

Mentoring by women, according to one author, is "more about commitment than about chemistry. It's about personal growth and development rather than about promotions and plums. And it's more about learning than power."[27(p.188)] Many of the old approaches to mentoring have been revised by women. Female mentees tend to get mentoring from several different mentors on different issues.

Mentoring Guidelines

Figure 25-1 presents a mentoring model that includes mentoring functions and activities.[28] The mentoring relationship is based on role modeling, nurturing, and caregiving. There are many functions associated with mentoring related to teaching: sponsorship, encouragement, counseling, and friendship. The purpose of the relationship is to get the mentee to put the lessons learned into action. **Table 25-4** presents a list of 10 rules that apply to mentoring.[29]

Public health leaders should research mentoring and develop a mentoring program within their agencies. Guidance is needed if the core public health functions model, the organizational practices model, the essential services model, or some combination model is to be implemented successfully in a public health organization. Public health leaders must:

- adopt a formal agency mentoring program
- devise "mentorcentives" to increase the number of mentoring relationships
- develop a mentoring contract for use by mentors and mentees
- integrate leadership skills with core public health functions in the mentoring relationship
- support and guide the long-term personal growth of the mentee; the relationship needs to be consensual

Mentees are ultimately responsible for putting the learning into action. It is essential for mentors to maintain objectivity through the mentoring process.

COACHING

Coaching and mentoring are leadership partners. Most of the information in Tables 25-1 to 25-4 is also applicable to coaching. Coaching is about improving performance on the job.[30] The coaching process is one way to close the gap between present performance and improved performance. Executive coaching involves the hiring of a professional coach to counsel the leaders and managers in an organization.[31,32] It is important to look at performance in terms of an individual's talents, knowledge, and skills. An individual's emotional response is also a critical dimension of the coaching relationship. In structuring the coaching process, several steps are important.[33,34] The coach must:

- observe the coachee in action
- discuss issues and process with the coachee
- determine performance goals

Mentoring model

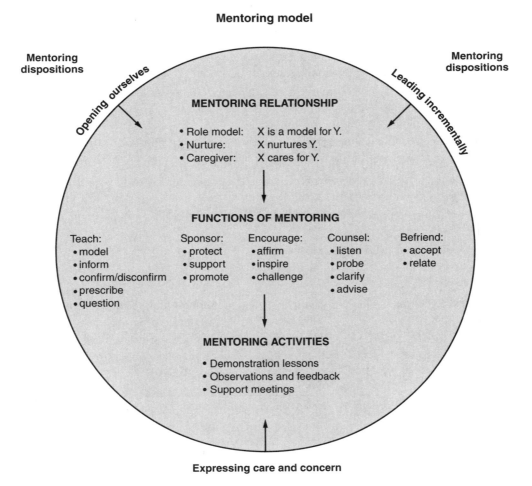

FIGURE 25-1 **Anderson and Shannon Mentoring Model.** *Source:* Reproduced from E. M. Anderson and A. L. Shannon, "Toward a Conceptualization of Mentoring," *Journal of Teacher Education* 39 (1988): 38–42. © 1988 by American Association of Colleges for Teacher Education. Reprinted by permission of Sage Publications, Inc.

- specify active coaching methodology with defined times to meet
- analyze the coachee's present performance
- define options or strategies for the coachee to reach new goals
- set a timetable for actions
- ensure implementation of actions
- provide feedback and follow-up

Coaching fosters skill development based on talents and knowledge acquisition. Coaching thus involves the learning of new information and finding its fit with preexisting information. The individual who is being coachee needs to tie the new knowledge to the vision, mission, goals, and values of the home organization. Action applications are important. A manager needs to see how his or her new skill applications fit the agency, and the leader needs to tie his or her new knowledge to work both inside and outside the agency. As seen above,

the feedback mechanism is very important in coaching. Objectivity is important, and the feedback and response will concentrate on performance improvement and the future rather than the past, be given in a timely fashion, focus on behavior and how to change it, be specific in recommendations, give criticism in a positive way, and be realistic about what is possible.[35] O'Neill has stated that coaches do have emotional reactions to what they observe but need to keep their emotions in check.

Goldsmith has argued for the use of the concept of "feedforward" rather than feedback.[36] The new concept

Leadership Tip

Act positively, even when you do not feel like it.

TABLE 25-4   The Ten Commandments of Mentoring

1. Don't be afraid to be a mentor. Many people, especially women, underestimate the amount of knowledge that they have about . . . their organization, the contacts they have, and the avenues they can use to help someone else. A person does not have to be at the absolute top of his or her profession or discipline to be a mentor.

2. Remember that you don't have to fulfill every possible function of a mentor to be effective, but let your mentees know where you are willing to help and what kind of information or support you can give that you believe will be particularly helpful.

3. Clarify your expectations about how much time and guidance you are prepared to offer.

4. Let mentees know if they are asking for too much or too little of your time.

5. Be sure to give criticism, as well as praise, when warranted, but present it with specific suggestions for improvement. Do it in a private and nonthreatening context.

6. Where appropriate, "talk up" your mentees' accomplishments to others in your department and institution, as well as at conferences and other meetings.

7. Include mentees in informal activities whenever possible.

8. Teach mentees how to seek other career help whenever possible, such as money to attend workshops or release time for special projects.

9. Work within your institution to develop formal and informal mentoring programs and to encourage social networks as well.

10. Be willing to provide support for people different from yourself. "It is far easier for women than it is for many men to cross boundaries such as race, color, ethnicity, class, and religion in working with others. But we all need to practice this skill and avoid the temptation to assist only those with whom we feel the most comfortable, those who are the closest to being clones of ourselves."

Source: Reprinted with permission from B. R. Sandler, "Women as Mentors: Myths and Commandments," *Chronicle of Higher Education*. © 1993.

emphasizes the future rather than the past. It also emphasizes the concept of progress rather than dwelling on the mistakes of the past. Successful people tend to be visionary and concentrate on where they want their organizations to go. Feedforward also creates a climate in which support comes not only from the coach but also from colleagues. This new concept tends to be oriented to the goals of the organization and less to the personality of the leader.

Successful coaching has several benefits:[37]

1. It aids in improving performance of managers and leaders.
2. It helps all employees gather new knowledge and skills based on talents.
3. Productivity improves in positive work environments.
4. Coaching increases promotion opportunities and career choices.
5. Retention rates improve.
6. Coaching shows that employees are valued.

Executive coaches need to utilize both the skills of a coach and the skills of a mentor. They need to observe on-the-job behavior both in the day-to-day activities of the leader and manager inside the agency and for the leader inside and outside the agency. Executive coaches also need to explore present job issues with the professional and long-term career goals of their clients. These two sets of skills related to job and career can affect present job performance or future effectiveness. Successful coaches will utilize their own backgrounds and work with other clients while always protecting the privacy of those other clients in order to guide their present clients.

There are a number of keys to creating a successful executive coaching relationship. The underlying dimension of coaching is that the relationship needs to be reciprocal. Both parties need to contribute to the relationship. At the meeting level, regular meetings need to be scheduled at least monthly and more often if necessary. Executive coaches will sometimes request that the client take a battery of tests. The results of these tests need to be discussed and used to explain how the client leader or manager is carrying out leadership activities in the agency or in the community. The coach will also observe the leader or manager in action. This technique, which is sometimes called shadowing, gives much relevant information to both the coach and the client. Books and journals will also be used to expand the knowledge of the leader and manager. The learning contract will be discussed and monitored throughout the coaching experience. Coaches in the guise of a mentor will examine professional goals as they relate to the future of the leader's agency. Exercise 25-3 will give you the opportunity to try shadowing.

Coaching is important for successful leadership and management of an organization. There will be times in the tenure of an individual when coaching may be needed. The leader will:

- utilize a coach when necessary
- develop a learning contract with the coach
- schedule regular meetings
- take leadership profiles to evaluate personal leadership characteristics
- read articles and books on leadership and management to expand resources and knowledge

TRAINING

Business leaders have known for a long time that an educated workforce will increase the effectiveness and efficiency of a company. They view the cost of training as low in comparison with the long-term benefits. In the government sector, in contrast, training has been seen as a luxury that often cannot be justified. The result for public health has been a learning gap that has kept public health practitioners from promoting public health in their communities in an effective manner. There is increasing fear that public health agencies may not have a future. The challenge is to train public health leaders for the 21st century. Many public health leaders lack an adequate background in public health, have had limited exposure to academic public health content, are ignorant of advanced information technology, and have had limited leadership training.

A Strategy for Training the Public Health Workforce

In a report of the Public Health Functions Project of the U.S. Department of Health and Human Services (DHHS), a five-pronged strategy was laid out for training the public health workforce for the 21st century. The report also included a series of steps for achieving training-related goals.[38]

The first prong concerns the development of a national public health leadership (**Table 25-5**).[39] The suggested federal role is to provide standards and guidelines, promote and conduct research, disseminate

TABLE 25-5 Proposed Action Steps for National Public Health Leadership

A. Organize a national forum of key stakeholders from both the public and private sectors to examine human resource allocation and trends in public health. Potential forum participants in addition to the Public Health Functions Steering Committee members include the American Association of Health Plans, Health Care and Financing Administration, state Medicaid directors, social workers, substance abuse and mental health professionals, nurses, professional organizations, and the business community in general.

B. Develop and implement modules for Leadership Training Institutes that enable public health leaders to better assess their roles in providing public health services in a changing environment.

C. Involve frontline public health practitioners from all types of organizations in the efforts to enumerate, plan for, and educate the public health workforce.

Source: Reprinted from Public Health Service, *Public Health Workforce: An Agenda for the 21st Century*, pp. 11–12, 1997, U.S. Department of Health and Human Services.

TABLE 25-6 Proposed Action Steps for State and Local Public Health Leaders

A. Ensure that workforce planning takes place in all appropriate jurisdictions. Allocation of human resources should be determined by state and local governments or on a regional basis when appropriate due to resources, geography, or other factors.

B. Within each jurisdiction, encourage the participation of medical care delivery systems and others with public health responsibilities to achieve mutual goals in workforce development.

C. Develop a partnership with states to quantify the supply and demand of personnel providing essential public health services at the state, local, and private sector levels.

Source: Reprinted from Public Health Service, *Public Health Workforce: An Agenda for the 21st Century*, p. 12, 1997, U.S. Department of Health and Human Services.

the results, guarantee equity across states, and develop priorities for the nation every 10 years.

The second prong concerns leadership at the state and local levels (**Table 25-6**).[40] Each state is different, and public health leaders, in applying any public health model, need to be guided by the unique characteristics of their state or locality. Training should include leadership development initiatives created in partnership with academia. Local and state public health leaders need to let the national leadership know about the day-to-day realities of public health practice.

The training process includes monitoring the public health workforce and acting to ensure that its composition reflects the ethnic and racial diversity of the society at large (**Table 25-7**).[41] The first step is to define the public health workforce. The DHHS report defined the workforce as all professionals who are responsible for providing essential public health services regardless of the organization for which they work. One of the next steps is to classify and count the public health professionals, and the final step is to identify and implement plans

to ensure that the workforce is ethnically and culturally diverse.

The fourth prong of the strategy is to develop a curriculum based on the competencies needed for public health practice (**Tables 25-8 and 25-9**).[42] Public health leaders need to determine the skills, abilities, and knowledge bases that the public health workforce will need in the 21st century. Included among these are the following: analytical skills, communication skills, policy and development and program planning skills, cultural competency, and basic public health sciences knowledge. Once public health leaders determine the appropriate competencies, they should help develop training initiatives to foster these competencies. Linkages between academics

---

TABLE 25-7   Proposed Action Steps Related to Workforce Composition

A. Identify a lead agency or organization to provide leadership in continuing efforts to assess the size, composition, and distribution of the workforce as related to essential services of public health.

B. Examine methods used by professional organizations such as the American Nurses Association, American Medical Association, American Psychological Association, American Dental Association, and National Environmental Health Association to classify their respective workforces and incorporate where helpful.

C. Develop a standard taxonomy based on the 10 essential public health services to qualitatively characterize the public health workforce. This classification scheme must be derived through collaboration and consensus of the entire public health community.

D. Use the SOC System of the workforce and data from the Bureau of Labor Statistics and census surveys to track shifts in the staffing mix of personnel among the governmental, private, and voluntary sectors.

E. Identify and take action steps to ensure that the public health workforce is ethnically and culturally diverse.

F. Work with the Office of Management and Budget to include appropriate public health entries in the SOC System to facilitate identification of public health worksites, such as local health departments and other organizations providing essential public health services.

Source: Reprinted from Public Health Service, *Public Health Workforce: An Agenda for the 21st Century*, p. 12, 1997, U.S. Department of Health and Human Services.

TABLE 25-8   Proposed Action Steps for Competency Development

A. Verify that identified competencies are indeed necessary for efficient and effective practice of public health. Validations of these competencies should be provided by a panel of practice-based experts who are in public health organizations, including employers.

B. Identify competencies critical to all public health practitioners and those critical to successful practice in specific organizational settings. The competencies should be viewed as "organizational" competencies, those required for the entire workforce deployed within a given public health setting. (Although all public health practitioners should be familiar with the essential services of public health, few, if any, individuals will be equally competent in all areas.) Categorizing competencies should be conducted by a review panel of experts including practitioners and employers from all practice settings.

C. Improve long-range planning. Public health competencies are evolutionary. They are affected by changes in responsibilities and the practice of public health. There must be a formal mechanism to update competencies to reflect changing demands. A mechanism for assuring current and accurate competencies may take the form of an institute, task force, or other entity supported by government, foundations, and/or the academic community. Responsibilities will include monitoring trends in the demand for public health services and interpreting those demands in terms of the skill and knowledge needed to provide the 10 essential services of public health.

Source: Reprinted from Public Health Service, *Public Health Workforce: An Agenda for the 21st Century*, p. 13, 1997, U.S. Department of Health and Human Services.

TABLE 25-9 Proposed Action Steps for Curriculum Development

A. Ensure that the practice community has a substantial role in the curriculum development process. Examine existing models that link the academic and practice communities as a first step in facilitating practitioner involvement and target efforts and resources in their replication.

B. Determine the current status of "competency" of the workforce. Develop and implement a methodology (survey, direct observation, etc.) to assess the current level of proficiency in the practice of the competencies. This research effort will include an evaluation of how the competencies have been acquired (on-the-job training, formal education, mentoring, continuing education, etc.) and the perceived adequacy of these approaches in the context of the communities being served.

C. Develop measurable performance indicators for identified competencies.

D. Survey public health training/education institutions to assess the extent to which competencies are currently being employed to structure the curriculum.

E. Conduct an analysis of the competency statements and make revisions for their most effective use in curriculum development. Education and training specialists should conduct this analysis.

F. Identify gaps between high-priority competencies that are needed and those competencies already present in the workforce. The competencies proposed by the Competency-Based Curriculum Workgroup incorporate projections of competencies needed now and in the future (five years hence). After additional review, these projections can serve as a baseline. Identification and prioritization between the actual and the needed profile of competencies may best be accomplished by a panel composed of practice association representatives, academic institutions, and federal agencies.

G. Translate competencies into discrete didactic and field-based learning experiences and activities.

H. Create a matrix of addressed and unaddressed competencies based on public health organizational needs with the results of the instructional provider survey (data collected during the needs assessment activity) by cross-referencing each element in the competency listing.

I. Support a curriculum development process that is sensitive to the needs of local communities in order to be responsive to the local priorities of each agency, state, or local community relating to the essential services of public health.

J. Recommend to the Council for Education in Public Health and other organizations within the accreditation community that competency-based approaches be incorporated into the standards for educational institution accreditation and into the standards for professional certification and/or licensure.

K. Develop criteria for identifying providers of public health training and education that are "models of excellence" and support these providers through grants and other forms of support.

L. Implement the operation of a "clearinghouse" to promote sharing of exemplary teaching approaches among institutions.

Source: Reprinted from Public Health Service, *Public Health Workforce: An Agenda for the 21st Century*, pp. 14–15, 1997, U.S. Department of Health and Human Services.

and practicing professionals are critical for ensuring the proper education of the public health workforce.

The fifth prong is to prepare for the increased use of distance learning that will occur in the new century (**Table 25-10**).[43] The point is not to demean face-to-face learning but to foster other learning options for public health professionals. Distance learning technologies are constantly evolving, and each technology will be especially effective in some applications and ineffective in others. Public health professionals seem to opt for on-site training because of the obvious fact that public health practitioners practice their craft face to face with clients. However, distance learning can be

integrated into the overall education system without reducing the ability of practitioners to handle actual encounters with clients.

Using Education and Collaboration to Heal the Division Between Public Health and Medicine

The past few decades have seen the rise of divisiveness between medicine and public health.[44] Many of the physicians chosen to head health departments whose statutes require a physician at the helm had little knowledge of public health. In fact, public health

TABLE 25-10 Proposed Action Steps for Distance Learning

A. Establish a formal structure to advocate for the integration of distance learning techniques into practice and academic entities involved in public health strategies for training, education, and communication. Actions necessary for this to proceed include:

- Evaluate previous studies that document distance learning resources among partners.
- Develop a strategy for participant registration that is compatible across agencies and that is supported by a technology that allows for orders of magnitude expansion and comparability of data.
- Establish a standard practice and methodology for stakeholder's evaluation of distance learning results.
- Institute a common practice for program promotion and marketing.
- Develop a strategy to facilitate sharing resources across organizational lines (e.g., interagency agreements, cooperative agreements, grants, memorandums of understanding).
- Initiate standards for distance learning technology that permit system integration across agencies.
- Encourage and support the use of public/private assignments to promote collaboration in training.
- Share innovative and effective procurement mechanisms for distance learning services (e.g., task order contracts and other procurement mechanisms).
- Assist in identifying and developing distance learning faculty and subject matter experts and establishing incentives for their support.
- Provide grant assistance for development of distance learning programs at regional and local levels.

B. Directly link distance learning systems and program development priorities to the information generated by the Workgroups on Workforce Composition and Competency-Based Curriculum.

C. Routinely gather input from key partners regarding training needs and technological capabilities.

D. Develop agency expertise in distance learning; participate in relevant organizations such as the United States Distance Learning Association (USDLA) and Government Alliance for Training and Education (GATE).

E. Provide access to information about public health distance learning programs and resources through mechanisms such as FedWorld Training Mall and the Public Health Training Network Web site.

F. Organize a mechanism for pooling and accessing resources and expertise on distance learning across all of public health.

Source: Reprinted from Public Health Service, *Public Health Workforce: An Agenda for the 21st Century*, p. 16, 1997, U.S. Department of Health and Human Services.

seemed artificially separated from primary care. In many countries, primary care and public health are seen as one. Several years ago, I traveled to Armenia to teach a group of public health professionals about public health leadership. The experience led me to make two important observations. First, clinical activities supported at a countrywide level define the official public health policy. Primary care is public health. Second, independent public health leadership is generally not possible in a country where the nationalized system of health care is politically controlled. Administrators have the responsibility to maintain the status quo. The 21st century will see renewed collaboration between medicine and public health in the United States. This type of collaboration has been called cross-sectoral.[45]

Four actions are necessary for the relationship between medicine and public health to improve.[46] First, both physicians and public health professionals must be educated about strategies for fostering cross-sectoral collaboration. Second, each group must legitimize the process. Third, physicians and public health professionals must develop tools to promote the collaboration approach. Finally, they must examine barriers to collaboration and program options and create policies to support collaboration. All four of these actions have a strong training component. Public health leaders need the skills to carry out collaboration and need to train staff to support collaborative efforts. In other words, they must understand both the culture of medicine and the culture of public health.

Table 25-11 presents goals and strategies (under the headings "Synergy" and "Models") for medicine–public health collaboration.[47] The use of "synergy" is intended to indicate that the results of collaboration are greater than would occur if the activities were performed separately.

TABLE 25-11 Models of Medicine and Public Health Collaboration

Synergy	Models
I. Improving health care by coordinating services for individuals	A. Bring new personnel and services to existing practice sites B. Establish "one-stop" centers C. Coordinate services provided at different sites
II. Improving access to care by establishing frameworks to provide care for the uninsured	A. Establish free clinics B. Establish referral networks C. Enhance clinical staffing at public health facilities D. Shift indigent patients to mainstream medical settings
III. Improving the quality and cost-effectiveness of care by applying a population perspective to medical practice	A. Use population-based information to enhance clinical decision making B. Use population-based strategies to "funnel" patients to medical care C. Use population-based analytic tools to enhance practice management
IV. Using clinical practice to identify and address community health problems	A. Use clinical encounters to build community-wide databases B. Use clinical opportunities to identify and address underlying causes of health problems C. Collaborate to achieve clinically oriented community health objectives
V. Strengthening health promotion and health protection by mobilizing community campaigns	A. Conduct community health assessments B. Mount health education campaigns C. Advocate health-related laws and regulations D. Engage in community-wide campaigns to achieve health promotion objectives E. Launch "Healthy Communities" initiatives
VI. Shaping the future direction of the health system by collaborating around policy, training, and research	A. Influence health system policy B. Engage in cross-sectoral education and training C. Conduct cross-sectoral research

Source: Reproduced from R. D. Lasker & the Committeee on Medicine and Public Health, *Medicine and Public Health: The Power of Collaboration* (Chicago: Health Administration Press, 1997).

Training raises important concerns for public health leaders. These leaders need to make a commitment to continuing their own education and to supporting the continued learning of others, including community partners. Training for practitioners needs to be experientially based so that the skills acquired can be put into practice. In regard to training, public health leaders must:

- be lifelong learners
- master emerging information technologies
- share information
- mentor and coach others

- support training initiatives
- train their partners
- orient training toward the future of public health
- make training programs experientially based

TRAINING THROUGH MENTORING

In public health, training can be enhanced by incorporating mentoring as one of the components. The Illinois Public Health Leadership Institute (now the Mid-America Regional Public Health Leadership Institute) used mentoring to create the foundation for leadership development in its one-year training program. Four different types of mentors were and are included in the training (**Figure 25-2**). First, a mentor advocate—a public health leader with 10 years of experience who usually has graduated from the national or a state or regional public health leadership institute—is assigned the responsibility of facilitating the training experiences of a team of public health leaders. The mentor advocate helps each team member network with an experienced public health professional, helps team members deal with concerns and questions, and assists in the development of the team's training projects. The mentor advocate is available to the trainees throughout the year.

In order to explore new skills in the work setting, each leadership trainee selects an agency mentor and coach to help solve work-related problems. Whatever the problem, the solution needs to involve the application of leadership skills and the placement of the problem in a public health core functions context. The trainee has the responsibility of giving the mentor agency advisor readings or case studies that explain or demonstrate the conceptual approaches included in the leadership development training. The trainee and advisor can also explore ways to use leadership skills in the public health agency.

The third mentor is the trainee's "buddy," a person who has gone through the leadership development program a year or more ago. The buddy offers the new trainee insights about the leadership training approaches. He or she provides friendship, helps the trainee interpret the program's readings and case studies, and strengthens the public health leadership networking activities. The buddy relationship puts the responsibility for the development of these activities firmly in the hands of the buddy and the trainee. This relationship tends to be an informal one, usually determined by the trainee and the leadership graduate.

Finally, a fourth mentor type has emerged in leadership development programs. Trainees develop mentoring relationships with their peers. A training team creates opportunities for the team members to interact, and individual members can look to other members for guidance. Peer mentoring clearly enhances the learning experiences of the trainees by enriching their understanding of readings and presentations and allowing them to get more out of experientially based projects.

The Illinois Public Health Leadership Institute, founded in 1991, was the first state leadership institute funded by the Centers for Disease Control and Prevention (CDC). In 1999, it was renamed the Mid-America Regional Public Health Leadership Institute, and it now trains public health leaders from Illinois, Indiana, Wisconsin, and Michigan. Teams have also participated from North Dakota, Arkansas, and the Canadian province of Quebec. Two participants from the Czech Republic have also participated. Public health leaders in all 50 states have had access to a state or regional public health leadership development program, although this has not continued because of major funding cuts in 2010. There has been increasing recognition of the importance of the training they provide. Owing to the expansion of leadership development programs, the CDC has encouraged the development of the National Public Health Leadership Development Network Conference to address the common concerns of public health leadership programs.

Public health leaders will be both mentees and coachee individuals and mentors and coaches at various stages in their careers. In particular, they should consider:

- volunteering to mentor a leadership development team
- serving as a mentor and coach agency advisor to public health professionals confronted with local or state public health issues
- increasing networking among graduates of public health leadership programs
- utilizing peer mentoring as a way to spread the use of effective conflict resolution and decision-making strategies
- encouraging the development of state and regional leadership programs

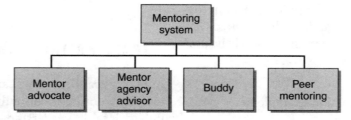

FIGURE 25-2 **Leadership Development Mentoring System.** *Source*: Adapted from S. F. Randolph, *Mentoring and the Illinois Public Health Leadership Institute*, 1993, University of Illinois School of Public Health, Illinois Public Health Leadership Institute.

A LEADERSHIP LADDER OF LEARNING

Learning needs to be a lifelong process. Public health leaders live in a constantly changing environment, and the public health agenda is partly unpredictable. As stated above, public health leaders will need different training opportunities at different times in their professional lives, but it is clear that mentoring adds to virtually any learning experience. **Figure 25-3** presents a lifelong learning agenda for leaders. As leaders move up the ladder, they begin to focus more on national or even global public health concerns rather than local ones and also begin to become aware of the abstract aspects of leadership and develop conceptual models to guide their leadership activities.

On the first step of the ladder, where public health professionals initially take on supervisory or other administrative roles, they need to learn how to utilize basic management and leadership tools. They need training in planning, organizing, monitoring, and administering.[48] They also need to learn to distinguish clinical activities from management activities and learn leadership skills that will help them advance to a more creative

leadership role in the organization. There are numerous courses and training materials available for new leader-administrators. The foundation skills are fairly concrete and less conceptual than at the higher levels of leadership.

Entry-level leadership development can occur through involvement with a profession-specific group or a multidisciplinary group. After three to five years in an organizational leadership position, leaders will benefit from training at a state or regional public health leadership institute. Such training is intended to integrate leadership concepts and public health governing paradigms.

National public health leadership institutes, such as the CDC-funded Public Health Leadership Institute, are useful for leaders in key state positions. Top-level leaders may also gain from specialized training programs that stress some major leadership functions.

At the highest step on the ladder, public health leaders can become involved in a think tank in order to explore public health issues with graduates of national leadership development programs and state and local public health leadership institutes. Public health think tanks are in the business of producing policy papers to guide public health action.

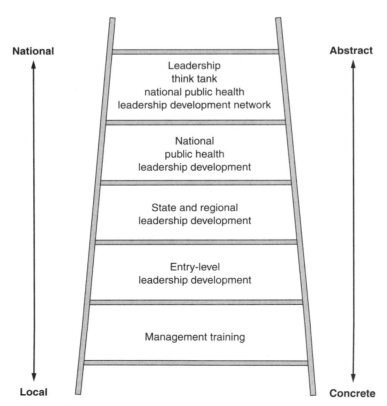

FIGURE 25-3 Leadership Ladder of Learning. *Source*: Reproduced from Public Health Program Office, 1999, the Centers for Disease Control and Prevention.

SUMMARY

This chapter has emphasized the importance of mentoring, coaching, and training public health leaders. Mentoring in all its guises enhances leadership development. A combination of mentoring, coaching, and training facilitates the learning of leadership skills. Therefore, experienced leaders must be willing to mentor novice leaders, who, of course, must be willing to be mentored. In addition, public health leaders who head agencies and health departments must find ways to foster mentoring within their organizations.

DISCUSSION QUESTIONS

1. What are the benefits of mentoring and coaching for the mentee or coachee?
2. What are the benefits for the mentor or a coach?
3. What examples of mentoring have you experienced, either as mentee or mentor?
4. How are personal mentoring and team mentoring related?
5. What skills are needed for someone to become a mentor?
6. What strategies would you propose to bring medicine and public health closer together in your community?

EXERCISE 25-1: The Learning Contract

Purpose: to utilize the learning contract to structure a training or educational experience

Key concepts: adult learning, mentoring, coaching, learning contract

Procedures: Following the general procedure for developing a learning contract, write out such a contract related to either this course or this training program. Create dyads in the class or training program. Each person in the dyad takes the role of a coach or mentor and discusses how to use this educational or training experience to guide your future or present work as a manager or leader in public health.

EXERCISE 25-2: Mentoring

Purpose: to explore both sides of a mentoring relationship and to evaluate the experience of being a mentor and a mentee

Key concepts: mentee, mentor

Procedures: As a homework assignment, each student or trainee writes two one-page stories, the first about a situation in which the student or trainee was mentored, the second about a situation in which the student or trainee acted as a mentor. The stories are read to the class or training group and discussed. (If the group is large, it should divide into smaller groups, and each group will listen to and discuss the stories of those in that particular group.)

EXERCISE 25-3: Shadowing

Purpose: to follow a leader for several hours or a day to see how a leader works in the real world

Key concepts: shadowing, leadership

Procedures: Choose a leader of your choice in government or a health organization. Arrange to follow him or her for a designated amount of time. Discuss the experience with the leader you chose. Share the experience with your class or training group.

REFERENCES

1. C. R. Bell, *Managing as Mentors*, 2nd ed. (San Francisco: Berrett-Koehler, 2002).

2. T. Fields, *Planning Life's Projects* (Tucson, AZ: Hats Off Books, 2001).

3. F. Wickman and T. Sjodin, *Mentoring* (Chicago: Irwin Professional Publishing, 1996).

4. Bell, *Managing as Mentors*.

5. B. Nelson and P. Economy, *Managing for Dummies* (Foster City, CA: IDG Books Worldwide, 2010).

6. T. Peters and N. Austin, *A Passion for Excellence* (New York: Random House, 1985).

7. Harvard Business Essentials, *Coaching and Mentoring* (Boston: Harvard Business School Press, 2004).

8. M. S. Knowles, *Using Learning Contracts* (San Francisco: Jossey-Bass, 1986).

9. M. S. Knowles, *The Modern Practice of Adult Education*, revised and updated ed. (Chicago: Follett Publishing Co., 1988).

10. M. S. Knowles, R. A. Swanson, and E. F. Horton III, *The Adult Learner*, 7th ed. (New York: Butterworth-Heinemann, 2011).

11. R. Hiemstra and B. Siseo, *Individualized Instruction for Adult Learning* (San Francisco: Jossey-Bass, 1990).

12. T. Rath, *Vital Friends* (New York: Gallup Press, 2006).

13. J. Carruthers, "The Principles and Practices of Mentoring," in *The Return of the Mentor: Strategies for Workplace Learning*, ed. B. J. Caldwell and E. M. A. Carter (London: The Falmer Press, 1993).

14. Carruthers, "The Principles and Practices of Mentoring."

15. Wickman and Sjodin, *Mentoring*.

16. Wickman and Sjodin, *Mentoring*.

17. L. Phillips-Jones, *The New Mentors and Proteges* (Grass Valley, CA: Coalition of Counseling Centers, 2001).

18. E. Alleman, "Two Planned Mentoring Programs That Worked," *Mentoring International* 3, no. 1 (1989): 6–12.

19. Alleman, "Two Planned Mentoring Programs That Worked."

20. C. Dahle, "Women's Ways of Mentoring," *Fast Company* 17 (1998): 187–195.

21. Carruthers, "The Principles and Practices of Mentoring."

22. W. A. Gray, "Situational Mentoring: Custom Designing Planned Mentoring Programs," *International Journal of Mentoring* 3, no. 1 (1989): 19–28.

23. S. P. Robbins and M. Coulter, *Management*, 11th ed. (Upper Saddle River, NJ: Prentice Hall, 2011).

24. J. G. Liebler and C. R. McConnell, *Management Principles for Health Professionals*, 6th ed. (Sudbury, MA: Jones & Bartlett, 2011).

25. Wickman and Sjodin, *Mentoring*.

26. Carruthers, "The Principles and Practices of Mentoring."

27. C. Dahle, "Women's Ways of Mentoring."

28. E. M. Anderson and A. L. Shannon, "Toward a Conceptualization of Mentoring," *Journal of Teacher Education* 39 (1988): 38–42.

29. B. R. Sandler, "Women as Mentors: Myths and Commandments," *Chronicle of Higher Education*, March 10, 1993, B3.

30. J. Eaton and R. Johnson, *Coaching Successfully* (New York: Dorling Kindersley Books, 2000).

31. Eaton and Johnson, *Coaching Successfully*.

32. M. B. O'Neill, *Executive Coaching with Backbone and Heart* (San Francisco: Jossey-Bass, 2007).

33. Eaton and Johnson, *Coaching Successfully*.

34. O'Neill, *Executive Coaching with Backbone and Heart*.

35. Harvard Business Essentials, *Coaching and Mentoring*.

36. M. Goldsmith, "Try Feedforward Instead of Feedback," in *Coaching for Leadership*, 2nd ed., ed. M. Goldsmith and L. Lyons (San Francisco: Pfeiffer, 2006).

37. Harvard Business Essentials, *Coaching and Mentoring*.

38. Public Health Service, *Public Health Workforce: An Agenda for the 21st Century* (Washington, DC: U.S. Department of Health and Human Services, 1997).

39. Public Health Service, *Public Health Workforce*.

40. Public Health Service, *Public Health Workforce*.

41. Public Health Service, *Public Health Workforce*.

42. Public Health Service, *Public Health Workforce*.

43. Public Health Service, *Public Health Workforce*.

44. R. D. Lasker, *Medicine and Public Health: The Power of Collaboration* (New York: New York Academy of Medicine, 1997).

45. Lasker, *Medicine and Public Health*.

46. Lasker, *Medicine and Public Health*.

47. Lasker, *Medicine and Public Health*.

48. Robbins and Coulter, *Management*.

Leadership, Evaluation, and Research

CHAPTER 26

Measuring the Leader

Work experience, hardship, opportunity, education, role models, and mentors all go together to craft a leader.

—J. A. Conger, *Learning to Lead*

Leadership is multidisciplinary as well as multilayered, and no single measure of leadership exists. Most quantitative evaluation instruments do not have specific public health leadership dimensions and are quite general to begin with. Case studies, interviews, and stories, of course, provide qualitative information. The quantitative and qualitative information that is available can be used to evaluate the development of leadership skills and determine whether leadership development programs lead to changes in behavior.

The purpose of this chapter is not to review all the leadership assessment instruments on the market but rather to describe several instruments currently used in various public health leadership development programs. This chapter will also explore the concept of 360-degree feedback and consider recent arguments for and against credentialing public health administrators.

A LEADERSHIP COMPETENCIES FRAMEWORK

The late 1990s saw a renewal of interest in training the public health workforce, including public health leaders. The issue of leadership training was addressed by the Public Health Functions Project, which was coordinated by the Assistant Secretary of Health and the Surgeon General.[1] **Table 26-1** presents the 10 tasks this project undertook. A project subcommittee was appointed to:

Provide a profile of the current public health workforce and make projections regarding the workforce of the 21st century. The subcommittee should also address training and education issues, including curriculum development, to ensure a competent workforce to perform the essential services of public health now and in the future. Minority representation should be analyzed and the programs to increase representation should be evaluated. Distance learning should be explored. The subcommittee should examine the financing mechanisms for curriculum development and for strengthening the training and education infrastructure.[2(p.v)]

TABLE 26-1   Public Health Functions Project

The following tasks will be undertaken as part of the Public Health Functions Project:

1. Develop a taxonomy of the essential services of public health that can be readily understood and widely accepted for use by the public health community.

2. Using the taxonomy developed, assess the public health infrastructure and document the federal, state, and local expenditures on essential services of public health.

3. Propose a mechanism to ensure accountability for outcomes related to the delivery of essential public health services at the state and local levels, in return for greater flexibility in administration of federal grants to support public health.

4. Develop a strategy for communicating to the general public and key policy makers the nature and impact of essential public health services.

5. Document and publish analyses of the health and economic returns on investments in essential public health services.

6. Identify the key categories of public health personnel necessary to carry out the essential services of public health, assess the nation's current capacity and shortfalls, and establish a mechanism for ongoing monitoring of workforce strength and capability.

7. Develop and publish a full set of evidence-based guidelines for sound public health practice.

8. Collaborate with the PHS Data Policy Committee to identify the information and data needs for the effective implementation of the essential services of public health and develop a strategy for the interface between the personal services and population-wide systems, ensuring the availability of information necessary to both.

9. Develop a process to ensure the appropriate collaboration of the public health community and adequate inclusion of public health perspectives in the development of national health goals and objectives for the year 2010.

10. Develop a strategy for regular communication among interested parties at the national, state, and local levels on progress related to these activities.

Source: Reproduced from Public Health Service, *Public Health Workforce: An Agenda for the 21st Century*, 1997, U.S. Department of Health and Human Services.

One of the subcommittee's tasks was to look at the feasibility of a competency-based curriculum. In the past, learning objectives were used to evaluate educational attainment. A competency-based system is intended to be more oriented toward outcomes. Both learning objectives and competency-based outcomes can be useful for gauging a student's or trainee's mastery of new skills and abilities. Learning objectives define the key topics of the course or curriculum in a general way, whereas competencies define what a student or trainee is supposed to master over the long run. The critical issue is how to measure progress toward achieving the competencies and objectives.

The project subcommittee reported on six priority areas for a competency-based curriculum: cultural competency, health promotion skills, leadership development, program management, data analysis, and community organization. It identified a number of action steps for acquiring the competencies.

The development of competencies is a complex process. At the 1995 annual meeting of National Public Health Leadership Development Network (then under a different name), a project was undertaken to develop a series of leadership competencies for use in the creation and evaluation of state and regional public health leadership programs. The task groups formed at the meeting named four core categories for the competency exercise: transformational leadership skills, political competencies, transorganizational skills, and team-building skills. Over the course of 1996, the framework evolved. With the advent of a concern for competencies for leaders in a public health preparedness environment, Dr. Kate Wright and the Heartland Center for Public Health Preparedness have modified the framework to include these new competencies. Appendix 26-A presents this updated framework.[3]

Transformational leadership skills are needed by public health leaders because leaders are change agents. Leaders need to have a mission and vision and need to motivate and manage change effectively. As for political competencies, leaders need to understand how the political process works, how to negotiate, how to build alliances, and how to market public health and educate the community about public health issues. Because so much public health activity occurs between organizations, public health leaders need transorganizational competencies, including an understanding of organizational dynamics, interorganizational collaboration mechanisms, and social forecasting and marketing. The team-building skills they require include the ability to develop team-oriented structures for purposes of planning and implementing objectives and evaluating progress toward the objectives, the ability to facilitate team development, and the ability to mediate when a conflict occurs.

The framework presented in Appendix 26-A provides a template for learning and for making sense of the multidimensional aspects of public health leadership. No framework should be etched in stone. It must be allowed to evolve. Data need to be collected to determine if the identified competencies can be taught and put into practice. For example, Discovery Learning has developed a 360-degree public health leadership profile based on the framework that will provide these data in the future.[4] The profile is based on evaluation of such skills as innovation, client service, mentoring, collaboration, team skills, and conflict and negotiation skills.

The main problem with most competency frameworks is that the competencies are not defined with sufficient specificity to permit their measurement. Take, for example, the competency "Identify, articulate and model professional values and ethics," which is obviously very general and difficult to gauge. The solution is to break down each competency into specific components that can be measured. Discovery Learning has attempted to do this. In addition, there must be an applied research strategy to evaluate the leadership competencies routinely and revise them as necessary. None of this is to imply that the leadership competency framework is useless. The process of refining the framework has just begun and will probably take several years to complete. The end result is hoped to be a performance standards system capable of evaluating leadership outcomes.

CREDENTIALING AND ACCREDITATION

The credentialing of public health professionals became a live issue in the 1990s. In 1971, the U.S. Department of Health, Education, and Welfare defined credentialing as "the process by which a nongovernmental agency or association grants recognition to an individual who has met certain predetermined qualifications specified by that agency or association. Such qualifications may include: (a) graduation from an accredited or approved program; (b) acceptable performance on a qualifying examination or series of examinations; and/or (c) completion of a given amount of work experience."[5]

The supporters of credentialing argue that it will increase the credibility of public health professionals in the political arena as well as with the public at large. Professional standards will be developed that will guide

public health programs. Some supporters want to tie credentialing to licensure. The critics argue that no credentialing system is possible because of the multidisciplinary background of public health professionals. Despite this criticism, a credentialing examination for graduates of accredited schools of public health and public health programs was given for the first time in the summer of 2008 and supervised by a newly created National Board of Public Health Examiners.

Schools of public health point out that they go through an accreditation process overseen by the Council on Education in Public Health. Accreditation would be prima facie evidence that graduating students have the necessary competence to practice public health, and a master's degree in public health from an accredited school of public health should preclude the necessity of further testing. In contrast, many public health practitioners have not been trained in public health and thus don't have the stamp of approval conferred by graduation from a school of public health. In addition, there is a question whether schools of public health are teaching the skills that practitioners need to have. For example, leadership courses do not exist in some schools of public health.

A report to the U.S. Health Resources and Services Administration defined accreditation as follows: "Accreditation is generally used to refer to the evaluation of academic programs which prepare individuals for professional practice and to determine whether such programs meet predetermined standards. Accreditation may be carried out by public and private agencies or associations."[6(p.9)]

Licensure, credentialing, and accreditation are related, although proponents of credentialing may argue that accreditation is not a guarantee that the credentialed public health professional has acquired the desired knowledge or the ability to translate this knowledge into practice. Credentialing proponents point out that a process of evaluating professional knowledge helps develop standards for professional performance, whereas accreditation is tied to an organization rather than a specific individual.

A report prepared for the Association of Schools of Public Health discussed factors that need to be included in any sound credentialing system.[7] First, role delineation that distinguishes between professionals who have different skills and levels of knowledge is a requisite. Because the role of public health administrators would be distinguished from that of other practitioners in the field, the credentialing of public health leaders could occur. Second, the credentialing system must specify the knowledge, skills, and attitudes (KSAs) required to carry out the duties of a credentialed professional and public health leader. Third, the system must determine the education, training, or experience necessary to generate the required competencies. Fourth, a testing procedure or other form of assessment must be devised to determine when a practitioner has achieved entry-level competency levels as well as more advanced levels of ability and knowledge. Finally, the system must include a process for recertification and require certified practitioners to undergo recertification periodically. Because leadership tools and skills change over time, the recertification process would encourage advanced training.

In the early 1990s, the American Public Health Association looked at the issue of professional credentialing.[8] The committee assigned to the task found very little information in the literature related to credentialing. To further its understanding of the issue, the committee conducted interviews with leaders in the field and with credentialing experts and also surveyed these two groups. The committee found that public health leaders generally did not support the development of a credentialing system. The leaders recognized that a credentialing system would need to be multifaceted and be able to accommodate a number of subspecialties and different education levels. The reaction of the credentialing experts was similar. The committee concluded that, despite the obvious benefits of credentialing, there was no consensus on the form credentialing should take.

One successful credentialing system was developed by the Society for Public Health Education (SOPHE) for undergraduate health educators.[9] The National Commission for Health Education Credentialing (NCHEC) was organized to carry out the certification of health educators. Since 1988, more than 2,000 individuals have become certified health education specialists. The certification process, which is based on what NCHEC has determined are necessary educational and professional experiences, is voluntary. A health educator cannot take the examination unless he or she has a college degree from an accredited institution. A candidate also must have a minimum of 25 college semester hours in health education.

At the present time, there are more than 100 sites in the United States where the examination is given twice a year. Those people who pass the certification examination are seen as having met the minimal health education requirements. New criteria were introduced in 2006.[10] A three-tiered model for credentialing was developed for health education practice at the entry level and two advanced levels. SOPHE also became concerned with leadership and developed a leadership program for its members.

Questions have been raised about the qualifications of local health officers. During the 1990s, the Health Resources and Services Administration gave a three-year grant to the School of Public Health at the University of Illinois at Chicago to develop procedures for credentialing health administrators. A voluntary credentialing program was developed. It is too early to evaluate the experiment, but the experience of public health management and leadership programs around the country indicates that public health leaders gain from the management and leadership development process. What they gain, however, is difficult to determine in other than a general way. The National Public Health Leadership Development Network will begin to discuss the issue of credentialing for public health leaders in 2013.

360-DEGREE LEADERSHIP ASSESSMENT AND FEEDBACK

We all have perceptions of ourselves that others around us may not share. Leaders are no exception. They may view themselves one way and be viewed by their colleagues in quite a different way. Therefore, the assessment of a leader needs to include a self-evaluation as well as evaluations by colleagues. In other words, it should be a 360-degree assessment.

The 360-degree assessment process involves a multilevel evaluation that focuses on whether the leader's style of leadership supports or obstructs achievement of the mission and goals of the organization. In a comprehensive 360-degree assessment, all key stakeholders have a voice in evaluating the leader and assessing the direction in which the organization is moving.[11]

Requirements of a 360-degree assessment include the following:[12] First, the leaders of the organization must determine whether sufficient enthusiasm for and commitment to the process exists in the organization and whether they are willing to institute changes based on the results of the assessment. Second, they must collect high-quality assessment data. Finally, they must identify possible responses to the results, such as the development of leadership training programs or formal mentoring programs.

There is a much-utilized 360-degree leadership assessment instrument, the Leadership Practices Inventory (LPI), which evaluates leaders based on their performance of best leadership practices.[13] The five practices in the initial LPI were selected on the basis of interviews with senior and midlevel administrators and on leadership case studies. These five practices are still the major emphasis of the LPI. The practices are (1) modeling the way, (2) inspiring a shared vision, (3) challenging the way, (4) enabling others to act, and (5) encouraging the heart.

The third edition of the LPI has 30 leadership practice items, and for each item there are 10 possible responses, from "almost never" to "almost always." (In the first edition, there were only five choices for each item, from "rarely" to "very frequent.") The score for a given practice, therefore, can range from a low of 6 to a high of 60. One version of the LPI is used for self-evaluation, and a second version is used for evaluation by observers (colleagues and stakeholders). The LPI can be used at different times to determine whether the leader has made progress in performing the five leadership practices.

Using the original LPI, data on 43,000 leaders from around the world were collected, and means, standard deviations, and internal reliability measures were computed.[14] Most of the leaders were from the business sector, but some were from academia and the public sector. The reliability rates fell between 0.81 and 0.91. Enabling others to act was seen by leaders and their observers as the most common practice, followed by challenging the process, modeling the way, encouraging the heart, and, in last place, inspiring a shared vision.

In a pilot study using the LPI, baseline leadership information was collected from 163 public health leaders selected as fellows by the Illinois Public Health Leadership Institute between 1992 and 1997. There may be a self-selection bias built into the study, because fellows are likely to have identified themselves as leaders before embarking on the leadership program and to be committed to leadership development to enhance their skills. Thus far, public health leaders have not specifically been studied. Comparisons of public health leader self-evaluations and observer evaluations have not been done thus far. Some preliminary data indicate that observers rate their leaders higher than the leaders rate themselves.

Mean scores for business leaders and public health leaders are presented in **Table 26-2**. The scores for public health leaders are consistently higher, but a confounder is the fact that the sample of business leaders includes academics and human service professionals. The scores for the two groups were not significantly different on the practice "challenging the process," an indicator of orientation to change, nor on the practice "inspiring a shared vision" (both groups scored relatively low). The public health leaders scored significantly higher than the business leaders on the other three practices, all of which are associated with the quality of work-related relationships.

One of the difficulties of using the LPI in studies of leadership is that the main purpose of the instrument is to assess individual leaders through self-evaluation and observer evaluation. The aggregation of LPI data should hide the characteristics of individual leaders, but nonetheless they need to be informed of the fact that their evaluations may be used for research. The instrument also may create biases in the responses because it is tied to a conceptual model that the developers promote. Not every leader supports this model.

TABLE 26-2 Means and Standard Deviations for Public Health and Business Leaders

Leadership Practice Item	Business Leaders (N = 543,889)		Public Health Leaders (N = 5,166)		Significant Difference
	Mean	SD	Mean	SD	
Challenging the process	22.38	4.17	23.4	3.46	None
Inspiring a shared vision	20.48	4.90	21.6	3.98	None
Enabling others to act	20.48	4.37	25.3	2.46	p # .0015
Modeling the way	22.89	4.16	23.8	3.24	p # .001
Encouraging the heart	21.89	5.22	23.6	3.59	p # .001

Note: This study was done with Elanine Jurkowski.

Another instrument used in several public health leadership programs is the Skillscope 360-degree assessment developed by the Center for Creative Leadership.[15] This instrument assesses information skills, decision-making skills, interpersonal skills, personal resources, and effective use of self. The instrument is flexible to use and can be used for individual assessments tied to coaching and a part of a structured leadership program. On a group level, the Skillscope can help to establish a group profile related to the strengths of the group and areas that need work. Another instrument developed by the Center for Creative Leadership is the 360-degree Benchmarks profile, which is one of the leadership instruments used in the National Public Health Leadership Institute.[16] Benchmarks is a comprehensive tool that measures 16 success skills and five career derailers. The 16 skills fall into the four categories of meeting job challenges, respecting yourself and others, leading people, and potential for derailment.

On the negative side, a 360-degree assessment is often expensive and time consuming.[17] Not only must the measurement instruments be bought, but staff need to be trained to interpret the results. Another issue is whether leaders are willing to reveal self-perceived weaknesses to their colleagues and whether subordinates feel comfortable rating their leaders. This issue is of special concern in smaller organizations. If anonymity is not maintained and the observer evaluations are negative, animosity may occur between leaders and their professional colleagues. Finally, there is the question whether the process will make any difference.[18]

Despite these issues, the process can result in important information. If the leadership data are linked to organizational needs, organizational efficiency and effectiveness can be improved. The results need to be communicated to the entire workforce, but with a sensitivity for the possible effect on the person who was evaluated. On the whole, the 360-degree approach offers individuals and the organization information that can improve the services provided by the organization.

QUALITATIVE LEADERSHIP ASSESSMENT

Public health programming is driven by population-based statistics, including mortality and morbidity rates. The problem is that the vitality of public health as an approach and perspective can get lost in the numbers, with the result that public health loses credibility among community residents.[19] As a consequence, public health leaders need to acquire qualitative information to help them evaluate their performance and to publicize public health as a way of enhancing their credibility.

Qualitative information often comes in the form of stories and case studies. The case studies of interest to us here describe public health practitioners in action and present conclusions about what was done right and what could have been done better. As we will use the term, "case" refers to whatever is the subject of a case study (usually a single event or a series of events).

Case studies, for our purposes, can be divided into four classes: (1) specific empirical studies, (2) general empirical studies, (3) specific theoretical studies, and (4) general theoretical studies. Empirical case studies describe actual cases, whereas theoretical case studies are constructed specifically to illustrate some point. Specific case studies have definable boundaries, and general case studies are examples already available that can be used to demonstrate a perspective.

The cases chosen for research inquiry are typically different from those chosen for training purposes. In this section, we are interested in the latter, especially their potential to clarify the application of leadership principles in the real world of public health practice. Training case studies describe how professionals handle problems and thus can serve as guides to future action. Leaders can develop their own case studies in order to analyze public health community activities and evaluate their own leadership skills.

Public health case studies are used for three main purposes.[20] First, they can be used to offer insights into how a public health agency carries out its activities. Second, they can be used to help public health leaders explore different scenarios as part of a problem-solving process. **Table 26-3**, for instance, presents a number of public health scenarios helpful for defining outcomes that might occur if a public health agency instituted a certain policy or embarked in a certain direction. Third, case studies can be used to illuminate why events unfolded in a certain way and to explore better ways to handle an emergency situation, for instance.

In regard to the last two uses, the role of leadership and the causal consequences of actions need to be interpreted carefully. It is always difficult to tease

TABLE 26-3 Public Health Scenarios Based on Schwartz Categories

Scenario 1: Winners and Losers

A health reform plan passes Congress. The plan presents a system redesign that is state based and involves local health alliances. The health plans incorporate most of the direct service functions of local health departments. Block grant funds that remain are given directly to the health alliances for distribution. This scenario initially positions the local health department as a loser.

Scenario 2: Challenge and Response

The American Public Health Association creates a strong lobbying coalition that includes representatives from all the major public health interest groups and organizations. As Congress reviews changes in the financing of health services, the public health community is able to affect legislation so that CDC and state public health agencies become responsible for collecting all data related to health care, are responsible for oversight of all health programs, become the lead agency for all government-sponsored primary prevention programs, are directly funded for health-related community programs by a block grant, and so on. Public health meets every challenge and wins.

Scenario 3: Evolution

There is a major change in the economy of the state. Several new biotechnology companies move to the state, and many new jobs are created. The state unemployment rate drops to 3%. With the increase in employment, the number of people on welfare drops significantly. With new jobs, the teenage pregnancy rate drops, as does the incidence of gang-related violence, because gang members get jobs.

Scenario 4: Revolution

Congress passes a major piece of legislation. The government decides to get out of the public health business. All public health activities are transferred to the private healthcare system.

Scenario 5: Cycle

Five years after the evolution scenario above takes place, the American economy collapses. A major depression occurs. People lose their jobs. Gang warfare increases. The teenage pregnancy rate expands significantly.

Scenario 6: Infinite Possibilities

A health reform package passes that provides universal coverage.

Scenario 7: The Lone Ranger

Through the efforts of public health professionals and researchers, a cure for AIDS is found, a chemical substance that purifies all water is discovered, and a vaccine that prevents Alzheimer's disease is developed. Because of these breakthroughs, the American public unequivocally supports all public health initiatives.

Scenario 8: My Generation

The early years of the 21st century see a major increase in births in the United States.

The above scenarios can be looked at individually or can be combined to form more complex scenarios.

Source: Adapted from *The Art of the Long View* by Peter Schwartz. Copyright © 1991 by Peter Schwartz. Used by permission of Doubleday, a division of Random House, Inc.

out the causal factors in a complex set of relationships and happenings. In addition, the events that make up a case rarely repeat themselves in exactly the same way.

Some case studies are merely free-flowing stories about examples of leadership, for instance. These stories nonetheless must have a message intended for a well-defined audience.[21] There are three main types of leadership stories. One is the "Who am I?" story. The second is the "Who are we?" story. The third is a story of the realization of a vision. It is possible to add a fourth category consisting of "What I learned on my summer vacation" stories. These stories describe what a leader learned from other leaders or from workshops on leadership.

Case study stories have plots intended to elucidate ideas or values. They should be tested before being released to the public to make sure that their messages are clear. One variant of the personal story is the biographical portrait.[22] A portrait of a historical or present-day leader, such as C. Edward Koop or Paul Farmer, can be employed for the same purposes as a personal story. Another variant is to focus on a leader whose values stand in contrast to those of a typical public health leader, such as a senator from a tobacco state.

An interview can also make up the content of a case study. Questions serve as the mechanism for getting information. For example, the author interviewed more than 130 public health leaders in four countries in order to explore their understanding of the meaning of public health, their vision of the future, and the changing characteristics of leaders. (**Table 26-4** consists of a guide for interviewing public health leaders.)

An interesting variation on the interview is the focus group, in which leaders, for example, might answer questions as a team. A conversation is another variation—a variation explored in Exercise 26-l.

A case study protocol for public health practice narratives was developed for public health practitioners in a leadership development program under the assumption that structured case studies provide trainees and other lifelong learners with models of public health practice.[23] Case studies can also be used to explore cutting-edge issues in public health that are in need of resolution. In other words, case studies can be based on completed events or on situations in progress.

Each case has a unique character.[24] For example, even similar cases will differ in historical background, setting, or economic, political, legal, social, or cultural aspects. They also can have a different slant depending on the reason they were written.

Case studies, as stories, have characters, a plot, and a setting. Their purpose is to give insight into leadership styles and practices, personality concerns, power concerns, organizational intrigues, politics in action, media involvement, and so on. They can be effective mentoring tools; the mentor can assign a case study for the mentee to read, and then the two can discuss the issues raised in the case study. A problem-based case study can present a possible vision of the future.

The best case studies are built on real experiences. Whereas ideal cases can be constructed, most people seem to relate better to real-life situations that seem real in their unfolding. That is one of the reasons that every case study in this book is factually based, although names and places have sometimes been changed to protect the actual participants.

TABLE 26-4 Interview Guide for Public Health Leaders

1. What are the reasons you decided on a career in public health?
2. How would you define public health?
3. What is your definition of leadership?
4. What are the necessary leadership practices and skills that a public health leader needs to use?
5. Are these practices and skills different from the practices and skills of business leaders?
6. What elements of public health's organizational system enhance or create barriers to leadership?
7. What is the role of public health in carrying out the core functions of assessment, policy development, and assurance?
8. What is your vision for public health in the 21st century? What are the three most important systems issues for the future, and what are the key health issues for the future?
9. How successful is the system in promoting community coalitions to address the health of the community?
10. Are public–private partnerships that address public health concerns possible? What is public health's role in managed care?
11. Does the public understand public health? If not, what can you do to change this situation?
12. Should public health be integrated into the general health sector, or should public health be maintained as part of a separate governmental office?
13. What distinguishes a practitioner, a manager, and a leader?
14. Is the mentoring of future leaders important? What type of mentoring program do you recommend?
15. What is the role of politics in public health?

Most case studies are written as narratives and have a beginning, middle, and end[25] (**Table 26-5**). The opening should present the issue that the case is intended to illustrate and describe the setting and key characters. The middle, or the body of the case study, describes the events that make up the case. If this is done properly, then the lesson of the case becomes clear. In some instances, elements of the setting and key characters may be described in more detail than was provided in the opening. Political factors that affected the outcome may be critically examined.

Many case studies include all sorts of supplemental documentation to elucidate the circumstances. The closing reviews the issue in light of the events described and analyzes the decisions made by the key characters.[26] It may explore possible options that might have led to an outcome different from the one that actually occurred. (Some case studies are intended to deal with multiple issues and use a slightly different organization to address the issues in a coherent manner.)

Case Study 26-A has the classic organization described here. It deals with the issues of privatization of laboratory services and the lack of involvement by public health laboratory directors in public health policy issues. It is also based on variations of real-life situations.

TABLE 26-5 Case Study Development Protocol

Opening (first few paragraphs)
Name and title of responsible professional
Date: month and year (fix the case in time)
Synopsis of decision required or problem setting or issues presented, keeping in the forefront the core functions of health departments
Case body (no more than four to five pages)
Department/agency history, if pertinent
Environmental setting, if pertinent
Political concerns
Expanded description of the decision or problem situation
Human interaction facts, etc.
Human element
Personality impact
Public relations factor
Presence/absence of vision/enthusiasm
Organizational relationships
Other case characters or entities
Program and process
Financial concerns, where pertinent
Closing (last paragraph or two)
Conclusion of the case
Suggested methods
Setting the scene to establish a sense of urgency about the problem or decision
Setting out a range of decision options

Source: Reprinted with permission from J. Munson, *Case Study Development: Guidelines and Protocols for Case Study Development*, 2nd ed., 2003. © 1994, University of Illinois School of Public Health, Mid-American Regional Public Health Leadership Institute.

Organization of Public Health and Clinical Laboratory Services in a Reformed Health Service Delivery System

Jon Counts

Introduction

In 2009, the U.S. Congress passed comprehensive legislation that would establish universal healthcare coverage by the year 2012. Congress mandated that each state would develop a strategic plan that would integrate and restructure the public and private healthcare programs. The commissioner of health, Dr. Strangelove, has designated you, Dr. Vision, to develop a plan to define the role of hospital, commercial, public health, and academic laboratories as part of the state of Innovation's strategy for a reformed health system.

Case Body

The result of three decades of heavy clinical laboratory utilization has been the development of a fractured, duplicative, and costly laboratory system in the state of Innovation. The laboratory network in this state fits the general description of the current health system: a patchwork of private and public programs, with goals and objectives as varied as the groups and organizations represented in the system. Clinical laboratories represent a significant component of the rapidly increasing costs of health care. The Health Care Financing Administration estimates that spending on laboratory services composes 4.5% of all national healthcare expenditures.

Clinical laboratories, like the rest of the healthcare community, have been significantly affected by the nation's health reform legislation, the Health Services Act of 1993. The primary vehicle for the implementation of the legislation is the new Health Services Commission. The Health Services Act will enable each state to control spending by:

1. shifting the state toward a system of "managed" health care
2. defining a uniform benefit package and developing standards of certified health plans through which the uniform benefits package will be provided
3. setting the maximum rate a certified health plan may charge for the uniform benefit package
4. establishing a maximum healthcare inflation rate and lowering the rate until it matches the rate of general inflation
5. setting rules for fair competition among certified health plans
6. minimizing malpractice and its costs
7. simplifying the administration of claims, billing, and information
8. promoting the use of cost-effective healthcare practices and services
9. defining the role and function of public health agencies

Dr. Vision realizes that the task ahead of him will be a challenge and very controversial.

1. First, the development of any coalition among laboratory organizations, physicians, pathologists, laboratory managers, hospital and commercial laboratories, and government will be exceedingly difficult to achieve.
   a. There will be opposition to a government agency leading the discussion about the role of laboratories in a reformed system. There will be suspicion, lack of trust, and concern about the regulatory approach that government agencies might mandate.
   b. For the most part, there has been little or no historical interaction among individuals/organizations who will be involved in the coalition; therefore, the plan must be carefully developed and staged, ensuring that a process for developing consensus has been established.
   c. The activities of the coalition will be monitored closely; therefore, there cannot be any secrecy and they must be open to the public, outside review, and scrutiny. There must be a system for dissemination of information and recommendations to the laboratory and medical community.
   d. There will be strong opposition to the possibility that the plan will lead to the re-engineering and downsizing of commercial and hospital laboratory staff.
   e. The issue of competition between public health laboratories and private sector facilities will be raised as well as the need to consider the privatization of diagnostic services provided by government laboratories. This obviously will be a contentious point because Dr. Vision will have a vested interest in the outcome.
2. The nature of health problems has changed dramatically during the 20th century; chronic conditions have become predominant as well as new and re-emerging infectious diseases.

3. The utilization of managed care plans and capitation to control costs and share the risk with providers has increased dramatically. The march of managed care, new technologies, and alternative treatment settings will prompt a 34% decrease in inpatient hospital days over the five years from 2009 to 2013. Ambulatory facilities will eliminate many surgical inpatient days, use of birthing centers will increase, mental health care will be delivered more often in residential settings such as halfway houses, and home care will be the most dramatic and fastest-growing segment of the healthcare industry. These changes will have a significant effect on diagnostic laboratory testing. Hospital laboratories will undergo significant reduction in routine and inpatient testing, vertical integration will occur, and regional delivery systems will consolidate and centralize laboratory testing. Large national commercial laboratories will capture the vast majority of testing.

4. The role of laboratory medicine will be expanded into promoting health and preventing disease. Home testing will increase, as will the need to promote direct public access to preventive and screening testing. Genetic testing obviously is going to expand. Hospital and commercial laboratories will play a much more active role in the nation's disease surveillance, promoting the need for a statewide electronic network between private clinical laboratories and the public health systems. Other anticipated changes in the future laboratory system include:

   - active management of laboratory utilization, elimination of unnecessary testing, and utilization of practice guidelines
   - standardization of lab instrumentation and testing methodology and increasing automation
   - utilization of clinical patient outcome measures of laboratory quality

Proposal Solution

The implementation of health reform makes strategic planning imperative for all components of the health system. Historically there have been few efforts to draw the clinical laboratory community together into cooperative efforts toward long-range planning except in the area of laboratory regulation and the credentialing of laboratory personnel. This initiative has been developed to assist the leadership of the clinical laboratory community in the state of Innovation in assessing the effect of health reform and in developing recommendations for integrating the diverse segments of the existing laboratory system into a more cost-effective and efficient structure. The process will include creation of a steering committee to provide recommendations to Dr. Vision for the guidance, direction, and oversight of the initiative. The steering committee may also appoint technical advisory work groups to study and develop specific recommendations on such issues as the following:

- structure and integration of delivery system
- utilization of clinical laboratories in medical decisions or development of practice parameters
- laboratory regulations
- effect of malpractice tort reform on laboratory utilization
- utilization of new technology in laboratories
- personnel resource training and credentialing
- utilization of out-of-state laboratories
- reimbursement policies
- direct billing
- laboratory information systems—collection, analysis, integration, and dissemination of data
- surveillance of emerging infectious diseases
- point-of-care testing
- home testing
- public access to laboratory testing

The steering committee will consolidate its recommendations into a report to be submitted to the commissioner of health, Dr. Strangelove, for his consideration in establishing public policy.

Dr. Vision must first establish a process to identify and appoint members from the department and community to the steering committee, individuals who are experts in laboratory science, strategic planning, public policy, development of community constituencies, and consensus building and who are representatives of medical specialties.

Next, the steering committee must establish a strategic-planning process, including identification and prioritization of major components and issues. In order to address those issues listed, it is essential that a mechanism be developed to collect and evaluate health-related data to determine the need for diagnostic laboratory services. Finally, it must be determined by the steering committee how it will solicit public input.

Exercise 26-2 provides the opportunity to write a case study. The work of researching and writing the case study, which may take several weeks, is done using teams. The case studies presented in this text can serve as models.

QUANTITATIVE LEADERSHIP ASSESSMENT TECHNIQUES

Leadership assessment comes in more than one variety. Part of the explanation is that the standard leadership assessment instruments grow out of different theories of leadership. Another part of the explanation is that there are at least five levels of leadership and different traits and behaviors that are needed for each level. Most leadership assessment techniques are oriented toward the personal level, but leadership can also be evaluated at the team, agency, community, and professional levels.

> ## Leadership Tip
>
> *Serve refreshments at meetings.*
> *It reduces absenteeism.*

Because it is usually the individual who fills out the leadership assessment instrument, most leadership assessment relates to personal traits and behavior, and these traits and behaviors, unsurprisingly, are stressed by psychometricians. One of the best-known personality assessment tools has been adopted by a number of public health leadership programs. The Myers-Briggs Type Indicator (MBTI), based on Jung's theory of psychological types, measures personality along four dimensions.[27] The first is the extroversion (E) and introversion (I) dimension. Where someone falls along this dimension is determined by whether he or she relates more to the external world or more to his or her inner world. The second dimension, defined by the contrast between sensing perceptions (S) and intuitive perceptions (N), measures whether a person focuses on the here and now or on future possibilities and abstract theory and symbols. The next dimension, defined by the contrast between thinking (T) and feeling (F), measures whether a person responds to situations rationally or emotionally. The fourth dimension, defined by the contrast between

judgment (J) and perception (P), measures whether the person tends naturally to engage in organizing, planning, and decision making or instead tends to want to keep options open.

The MBTI instrument is quite comprehensive[28] and requires the person being tested to answer numerous forced-choice questions. After completing the questionnaire, the person receives a report on his or her profile. The author, who filled out the questionnaire in order to gain a better understanding of how it is used, was found to be an ENTJ. The report said that the author tends to be decisive and frank, quick to take charge of people and projects, applies logic and analysis, prefers action to contemplation, and often pays more attention to tasks than to the people.

To discover how leaders in the public sector would score, researchers tested and compared five groups of leaders in local, state, and federal government.[29] The first group included 1,394 senior federal government administrators tested from 1983 to 1986. The next three groups, tested in the early 1980s, consisted of managers attending special government institutes at the University of North Carolina. The fifth group consisted of about 100 social service administrators from Nebraska. **Figure 26-1** shows how these groups scored on the four dimensions. The point to note is that leaders do not score in a uniform way. Different patterns emerge. Leaders with different styles engage in different leadership practices.

The Leader Behavior Analysis II instrument differs substantially from the MBTI.[30] It presents the person being tested with 20 typical job situations that involve a leader and one or more staff members. After reading each scenario, the person, putting him- or herself in the position of the leader, selects one of four possible actions. The instrument, which can be self-scored, investigates three dimensions. The first is flexibility (whether the person tends to try to be directive or supportive). There are four score categories for this dimension:

S1: high directive, low supportive behavior
S2: high directive, high supportive behavior
S3: high supportive, low directive behavior
S4: low supportive, low directive behavior

The responses to the pertinent scenarios are used to compute a style flexibility score between 0 and 30. The higher the score, the greater the flexibility. The second dimension is leadership effectiveness, and the third is diagnosis.

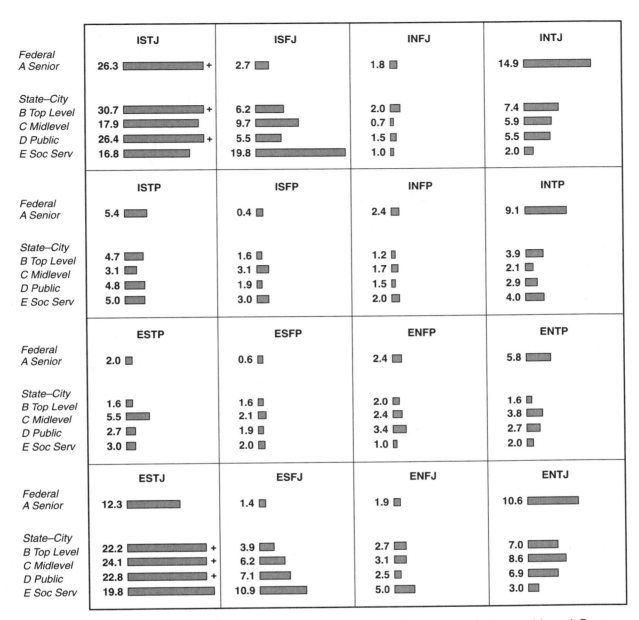

FIGURE 26-1 Myers-Briggs Type Indicator Percentages for Managers in Federal, State, and Local Government.
Source: Reprinted with permission from M. H. McCaulley, *The Myers-Briggs Type Indicator and Leadership, in Measures of Leadership*, K. E. Clark and M. B. Clark, eds., p. 389, © 1990, Leadership Library of America, Center for Creative Leadership.

Scores for these dimensions are computed in roughly the same way as for the first dimension. There is also a form for others to fill out, which allows for a 360-degree personal leadership evaluation.

A study of an earlier version of this instrument found that leadership assessment tools help leaders evaluate their leadership styles and compare their self-perceptions with the perceptions of colleagues.[31] The sample included evaluations of 20,000 leaders from 14 cultures (each evaluation comprised a self-assessment and assessments by others). About 2,000 leaders from industry and education were interviewed, and about 500 in-depth interviews were done. The situational leadership model was supported by the data collected.

There is a Team Leadership Practices Inventory that is basically similar to the LPI developed for leaders and colleagues.[32] The Team LPI is based on the same five leadership practices used in the initial version of the LPI: challenging the process, inspiring a shared vision, enabling others to act, modeling the way, and encouraging the heart. Because the use of teams has increased in most organizations, evaluating how teams function is essential. Each team member fills out the Team LPI, which has 30 items. The scores for each practice are totaled and then averaged. By using the Team LPI, a team can determine its strengths as well as the practices that need improvement. The LPI is highly correlated with the Team LPI. Both instruments are less concerned about leadership style than about the practices of leadership.

There has been growing interest in leadership skills and practices at the organizational level. In 1984, a study of effective organizational leadership was undertaken,[33] and it led to the development of the Leader Behavior Questionnaire (LBQ). The LBQ consists of 50 questions. It is intended to measure focused leadership (listening ability), communication abilities, trust leadership, respectful leadership (how leaders treat others), risk leadership, bottom-line leadership (the belief of leaders that they can make a difference), empowered leadership (sharing power), long-term leadership (visionary leadership), organizational leadership, and cultural leadership (leadership based on the values of the organization). An important underlying assumption of the LBQ is that leadership is multidimensional and that each of its dimensions must be evaluated.

An important assessment-related breakthrough occurred in the mid-1990s. The healthcare sector became more interested in the measurement of outcomes as a way of evaluating effectiveness.[34] Performance measurement encompasses the measurement of program inputs, intermediate outcomes (process issues), and end outcomes.[35] One goal of performance measurement is to determine whether changes in public health expenditures affect the outputs of public health agencies and the final outcomes for the community.

Two important new instruments give added clarity to the way talents affect leadership and also thinking and behavioral preferences. The Gallup Organization has been studying managers and leaders for more than 40 years. From its work has come an instrument called Strength Finder (now Strength Finder 2.0).[36] This instrument measures the strengths of an individual as tied to 34 talent themes. Rath has pointed out that it is important to build on individual talents to create strengths at work and not concentrate on individual weaknesses. This instrument is easy to take and is not costly. A leader buys the book, which has a unique access code to the Gallup

Organization website. The recipient will receive a profile of the top five strengths.

Leadership Tip

Use social media to expand your leadership network.

The Emergenetics instrument gives the individual a profile in color of his or her thinking preferences and behavioral attributes.[37] This instrument has also been tested on individuals throughout the world. The instrument relates to four major thinking preferences of people: analytical (blue), structural (green), conceptual (yellow), and social (red). Most individuals have profiles that show some mixture of all four preferences, but they tend to have dominance in one, two, three, or four thinking domains. The three behavioral attributes are expressiveness, assertiveness, and flexibility.

An Institute of Medicine report presented a framework for improving the health of community residents. The community health improvement process is shown in **Figure 26-2**.[38] It encompasses the identification and analysis of health issues, the development and implementation of strategies to resolve the issues, and the monitoring of the implementation process and outcomes. One of the steps is to develop an indicator set that links the implementation of strategies with their outcomes so that the effectiveness of the strategies can be determined, which is the essence of performance measurement. **Figure 26-3** presents a performance measurement model consisting of six steps.[39] Despite the existence of this model, public state and local agencies have been slow in adopting the performance measurement approach.[40] This is beginning to change, as mentioned below.

Performance monitoring is related to evidence-based public health.[41] Evidence-based public health promotes the use of traditional biostatistics measures, epidemiology, healthy communities assessment, and continuous quality improvement methods. Public health agencies and their leaders have not routinely used the tools at hand in an effective manner, nor have they routinely approached their responsibilities from a population-based perspective.

Public health leaders need to develop the competencies to carry out performance monitoring. Currently, they often assign the task of performance

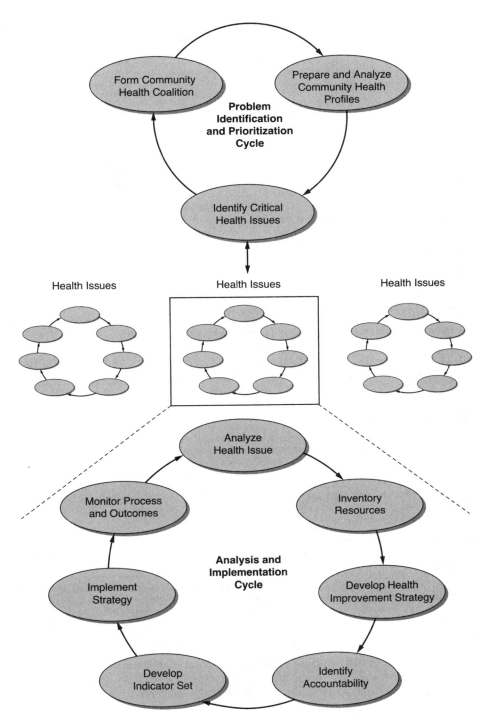

FIGURE 26-2 The Community Health Improvement Process (CHIP). *Source*: Reprinted with permission from *Improving Health in the Community: A Role for Performance Monitoring*, p. 6. © 1997 by the National Academy of Sciences. Courtesy of the National Academies Press, Washington, DC.

monitoring to other staff members. They also need to ensure that performance measurement is accepted by agency staff and that the information gained is used by the staff to improve operations. In fact, performance measures for evaluating the activities of public health leaders and their community partners utilizing a sys-

tems perspective and the essential public health services in the performance process have been developed in the National Public Health Performance Standards Program. The use of performance measurement by leaders will become more prevalent with the accreditation of local health departments, which began in 2011.

STEP 1	Relate the performance measure to an important national, state, or local priority area.
	Maryland has undertaken work related to the national health objective to reduce coronary heart disease deaths to no more than 100 per 100,000 people.

STEP 2	Measure a result that can be achieved in 5 years or less.
	Maryland has identified an achievable result that is linked scientifically to the *Healthy People 2000* Heart Disease and Stroke priority area: Increase the proportion of people who engage in light to moderate physical activity to at least 30 percent of the population.

STEP 3	Ensure that the result is meaningful to a wide audience of stakeholders.
	Target stakeholders are essentially all Marylanders, with an emphasis on school-age children and people at high risk for diseases and medical conditions associated with physical inactivity (for example, persons with hypertension and high cholesterol). Stakeholders include principals, teachers, students, parent-teacher associations, the state education department, state and local health and recreational agencies, public health and medical professionals, and others.

STEP 4	Define the strategy that will be used to reach a result.
	The State of Maryland has selected four strategies: 1. Implement a combination of strategies that include consumer education and skills development, health assessment, professional training, and environmental changes. 2. Reinforce risk reduction messages and promote programs and policies in schools, worksites, faith communities, and other settings. 3. Focus on youth and families so that healthy habits are started early and nurtured in the family. 4. Use a health promotion approach tailored to reach diverse ethnic and socioeconomic groups.

STEP 5	Define the accountable entities.
	The accountable entities depend on the strategies selected and the way in which a particular community is organized. For Maryland's Strategy 2, these entities include schools, worksites, and community centers. For example, the Cecil County Public Schools have agreed to be accountable for specific tasks related to Strategy 2 and are working in partnership with the Cecil County Health Department to offer health lifestyle programs to elementary school children. The programs, such as the **Heart Challenge Course**, bring teachers and food service workers together to promote healthy eating habits and physical fitness through educational games, classroom projects, and other activities that appeal to children.

STEP 6	Draft measures that meet statistical requirements of validity and reliability and have an existing source of data.
	In consultation with biostaticians and epidemiologists, organizations can draft measures that are statistically sound. One of Maryland's performance measures might be "Increase to 30 percent the proportion of students in each Cecil County elementary school who engage in light to moderate physical activity for 30 minutes or longer every school day by participating in school physical fitness activities."

FIGURE 26-3 Performance Measurement Step-by-Step. *Source:* Reproduced from *Improving the Nation's Health with Performance Measurement, Prevention Report,* Vol. 12, No. 1, p. 3, 1997, Office of Disease Prevention and Health Services, U.S. Department of Health and Human Services. Based on example of State of Maryland's *Healthy Maryland 2000.*

SUMMARY

Evaluation plays a multifaceted role in public health. Evaluation techniques are used for uncovering the public health problems that exist in a given community and for assessing the implementation of the programs intended to deal with such problems. They can also be used to assess the level of a leader's skills and abilities.

The chapter began with a description of the leadership competencies framework and listed some of the competencies that public health leaders need to have. It then discussed the question of whether a system should be put in place for credentialing public health leaders—a question over which public health leaders are divided.

Quantitative leadership evaluations are problematic at best. Each instrument incorporates a conceptual model on which the instrument is based. The organization in which the leader works is often conceptually different from the model used in the instrument. One alternative is to do a qualitative evaluation using case studies and other qualitative techniques and a battery of several quantitative tools. No matter what type of evaluation is done, however, the evaluation should include the opinions of both the leader being evaluated and the leader's colleagues. In short, it should be a 360-degree evaluation. Furthermore, the evaluation should cover the leader's performance at the agency level and also at the community level.

EXERCISE 26-1:   Conversations with Leaders

Purpose: to learn how peers view public health and what they think about current public health leadership issues

Key concepts: core functions, evaluation of leadership, focus group, interviewing skills, leadership skills

Procedures: It is possible to learn many things from peers. The class should divide into focus groups of six to eight members. Each group engages in a discussion of leadership using the interview questions in the text as a guide (Table 26-4). The discussion should last at least an hour, although it is not necessary to go through all the questions. The group should allow the discussion to go in any direction it naturally moves. The class can repeat the exercise several times, each time concentrating on a different set of issues.

EXERCISE 26-2:   Development of a Public Health Case Study

Purpose: to develop a public health case study to examine how leaders address public health issues

Key concepts: case study, core functions, essential services, leadership, team learning

Procedures: The class should divide into teams of five to eight members. Each team will be responsible for writing a case study using the Munson protocol (Table 26-5). Much of the work will take place outside of class. Select a facilitator to monitor each phase of the project. Identify a public health case worthy of being written about. Investigate the case and collect information for writing up the case. Analyze the case from a policy development perspective. Identify leadership issues involved in the case, and then write up the case (the study should be 5 to 10 pages). Finally, give an oral report on the case to the other teams.

DISCUSSION QUESTIONS

1. What is one of the problems with using competencies as a means of evaluating leadership?
2. What are the pros and cons of credentialing leaders?
3. What are five personal leadership lessons you learned during the past year?
4. What is a 360-degree assessment?
5. What are some difficulties associated with performing a 360-degree assessment?
6. What is a qualitative leadership assessment, and what are some techniques for performing such an assessment?

REFERENCES

1. Public Health Service, *The Public Health Workforce: An Agenda for the 21st Century* (Washington, DC: U.S. Department of Health and Human Services, 1997).
2. Public Health Service, *The Public Health Workforce.*
3. National Public Health Leadership Development Network and the Heartland Center for Public Health Preparedness (Dr. K. Wright, Director).
4. Discovery Learning, http://www.discoverylearning.com/products/profile-public-health.aspx
5. U.S. Department of Health, Education, and Welfare, *Report on Licensure and Related Health Personnel Credentialing* (Washington, DC: U.S. Department of Health, Education, and Welfare, 1971).
6. A. C. Gielen et al., *Health Education in the 21st Century: A White Paper*, report prepared for Health Resources and Services Administration (Washington, DC: Health Resources and Services Administration, 1997).
7. E. Carpenter, *Proposed Credentialing System for Public Health Professionals: What Would It Mean for Schools of Public Health* (Washington, DC: Association of Schools of Public Health, 1990).
8. W. C. Livingood et al., *Perceived Feasibility and Desirability of Public Health Credentialing: Final Report* (Washington, DC: American Public Health Association, 1993).
9. Gielen et al., *Health Education in the 21st Century.*

10. http://www.nchec.org

11. M. R. Edwards and A. J. Ewen, *360° Feedback* (New York: ANACOM, 1996).

12. R. Lepsinger and A. D. Lucia, *The Art and Science of 360° Feedback* (San Francisco: Jossey-Bass, 1997).

13. J. M. Kouzes and B. Z. Posner, *Leadership Practices Inventory (LPI): Facilitators Guide,* 3rd ed. (San Francisco: Jossey-Bass, 2003).

14. J. M. Kouzes and B. Z. Posner, *The Leadership Challenge,* 4th ed. (San Francisco: Jossey-Bass, 2007).

15. www.ccl.org

16. www.ccl.org

17. Lepsinger and Lucia, *The Art and Science of 360° Feedback.*

18. Lepsinger and Lucia, *The Art and Science of 360° Feedback.*

19. J. M. Kouzes and B. Z. Posner, *Credibility* (San Francisco: Jossey-Bass, 2011).

20. H. C. White, "Cases Are for Identity, for Explanation, or for Control," in *What Is a Case? Exploring the Foundations of Social Inquiry,* ed. C. C. Ragin and H. S. Becker (Cambridge: Cambridge University Press, 1992).

21. N. M. Tichy, *The Leadership Engine* (New York: Harper Business, 1997).

22. G. Wills, *Certain Trumpets* (New York: Simon & Schuster, 1994).

23. J. Munson, *Case Study Manual: Guidelines and Protocol for Case Study Development,* 2nd ed., Leadership in Public Health Monograph 1 (Chicago: University of Illinois School of Public Health, Mid-America Regional Public Health Leadership Institute, 2003).

24. R. E. Stake, "Case Studies," in *Handbook of Qualitative Research,* ed. N. K. Denzin and Y. S. Lincoln (Thousand Oaks, CA: Sage Publications, 1994).

25. Munson, *Case Study Manual.*

26. Munson, *Case Study Manual.*

27. M. H. McCaulley, "The Myers-Briggs Type Indicator and Leadership," in *Measures of Leadership,* ed. K. E. Clark and M. B. Clark (West Orange, NJ: Leadership Library of America, 1990).

28. K. C. Briggs and L. B. Myers, *Myers-Briggs Type Indicator Step II Booklet (Form K)* (Palo Alto, CA: Consulting Psychologists Press, 1991).

29. McCaulley, "The Myers-Briggs Type Indicator and Leadership."

30. http://www.kenblanchard.com

31. P. Hersey et al., *Management of Organizational Behavior,* 11th ed. (Upper Saddle River, NJ: Prentice Hall, 2012).

32. J. M. Kouzes and B. Z. Posner, *The Team Leadership Practices Inventory* (San Francisco: Pfeiffer and Co., 1992).

33. W. G. Bennis, "The Four Competencies of Leadership," *Training and Development Journal* 38, no. 8 (1984): 15–18.

34. G. E. A. Dever, *Improving Outcomes in Public Health Practice* (Gaithersburg, MD: Aspen Publishers, 1997).

35. K. E. Newcomer, "Using Performance Measurement to Improve Programs," *New Directions for Evaluation* 75 (1997): 8–13.

36. T. Rath, *Strength Finder 2.0* (New York: Gallup Press, 2007).

37. G. Browning, *Emergenetics* (New York: Collins, 2006).

38. National Academy of Science, *Improving the Nation's Health with Performance Measurement* (Washington, DC: National Academies Press, 1997).

39. National Academy of Science, *Improving the Nation's Health with Performance Monitoring.*

40. H. P. Hatry, "Where the Rubber Meets the Road: Performance Measurement for State and Local Public Measurement," *New Directions for Evaluation* 75 (1997): 31–44.

41. Dever, *Improving Outcomes in Public Health Practice.*

Leadership Competency Framework: Public Health Leadership Competencies for State/Regional Programs

Adapted by the Heartland Center for Public Health Preparedness, St. Louis University School of Public Health, from K. S. Wright et al., "Competency Development in Public Health Leadership," *American Journal of Public Health*, 90, no. 8 (2000): 1202–1207.

I. CORE TRANSFORMATIONAL COMPETENCIES
  A. Visionary Leadership
     1. Articulates vision and scenarios for change
     2. Facilitates development of vision
     3. Encourages others to share the vision
     4. Applies innovative methods for strategic decision making
  B. Sense of Mission
     1. Articulates and models professional values, beliefs, and ethics
     2. Facilitates development of mission and purpose
     3. Facilitates reassessment and adaptation of mission to vision
     4. Facilitates development of strategies to achieve mission

  C. Effective Change Agent
     1. Facilitates development of a learning organization
     2. Creates systems and structures for transformational change
     3. Creates evaluation systems for change strategies
     4. Facilitates strategic and tactical assessment and planning
     5. Facilitates identification of emerging and acute problems
     6. Utilizes change theories and models in strategic development
     7. Identifies emotional and rational elements in strategic planning
     8. Creates critical dynamic tension within change strategies
     9. Facilitates development of effective dialogue
    10. Utilizes methods to empower others to take action
    11. Models active learning and personal mastery

12. Models and facilitates cultural sensitivity and competence
13. Models utilization and application of systems thinking
14. Models critical thinking and analysis skills
15. Models appropriate risk-taking behaviors
16. Models group process behaviors: listening, dialoging, negotiating, encouraging, and motivating
17. Models leadership traits: integrity, credibility, enthusiasm, commitment, honesty, caring, and trust

II. POLITICAL COMPETENCIES[1]
   A. Political Processes
      1. Directs mission-driven strategic planning at policy and operational levels
      2. Articulates political processes and variables operating at federal/state/local levels
      3. Identifies and assesses critical political issues and related stakeholders
      4. Identifies policies and alternatives related to critical public health problems
      5. Develops capability for advocacy, community education, and social marketing
      6. Utilizes principles of media advocacy to support public policy change
      7. Assesses political resources to address needs of diverse and underserved communities
      8. Implements collaborative strategies to involve constituencies and stakeholders
      9. Utilizes political action models for infrastructure development and capacity building
      10. Collaborates to analyze needs and develop regulatory actions and legislative proposals
      11. Facilitates analysis and development of legislative action on public health issues
      12. Directs development of systems, programs, and services for policy implementation
   B. Negotiation and Mediation
      1. Identifies emerging public health issues and guides or mediates action to avoid crises
      2. Guides and mediates the investigation and resolution of acute public health crises
      3. Identifies key stakeholders and resources necessary for mediating, negotiating, and/or collective bargaining
   C. Ethics and Power
      1. Models use of professional values and ethics
      2. Models use of principles of integrity and high ethical standards

3. Creates collaborative systems using high ethical standards
4. Describes the role of public health law and public health practice
5. Describes the role of clinical/research ethics in public health practice
6. Develops power-based alliances with a values-based and ethical perspective
7. Utilizes transitional/conditional ethics when interpreting functions of power structures
   D. Marketing and Education
      1. Communicates with target audiences utilizing principles of social marketing and health education
      2. Communicates with target audiences regarding needs, objectives, and accomplishments

III. TRANSORGANIZATIONAL COMPETENCIES
   A. Organizational Capacity and Dynamics
      1. Utilizes models to assess environment, needs, opportunities, threats, and resources
      2. Utilizes models of new organizational development, behavior, and culture
      3. Develop structures for workforce development and organizational capacity improvement
      4. Implements structures and capability as need, opportunity, risk, or threat arises
   B. Trans-Organizational Capacity and Collaboration
      1. Identifies and includes power brokers and stakeholders in collaborative ventures
      2. Implements and evaluates collaborative and partnering strategies
      3. Facilitates networking and broad and diverse stakeholder participation
      4. Facilitates change with a balance of critical tensions within collaborative systems
      5. Develops and evaluates collaborative strategic action plans
      6. Facilitates transorganizational shared or complementary mission and vision
      7. Creates transorganizational systems with an ethical and values-based approach
   C. Social Forecasting and Marketing
      1. Utilizes social forecasting methods and interprets emerging needs and trends
      2. Creates and articulates predictions and potential scenarios

3. Communicates analysis and interpretation of information to partners and constituents

4. Utilizes social marketing for media, health and risk communications, and community relations

IV. TEAM-BUILDING COMPETENCIES
 A. Team Structures and Systems
    1. Develops structures for organizational learning and systems thinking
    2. Creates systems for team development and evaluation
    3. Creates incentive and reward systems
    4. Facilitates strategic outcomes-based team activities
    5. Develops team systems for customer service and quality improvement
    6. Facilitates collaborative leadership and entrepreneurial spirit
 B. Team Development
    1. Facilitates development of shared vision, mission, and values
    2. Facilitates development of clear goals and objectives
    3. Facilitates group process and dynamics
    4. Implements communication processes for team development
    5. Develops problem-solving, conflict resolution, and decision-making skills
    6. Communicates need to balance critical tensions for team development
    7. Facilitates empowerment and motivation to accomplish objectives
    8. Celebrates team culture and accomplishments
    9. Facilitates development of cultural sensitivity and competence
    10. Facilitates development of appropriate risk-taking behavior
    11. Develops servant leadership; selflessness, integrity, and perspective mastery
    12. Facilitates development of personal mastery and team learning
 C. Facilitation and Mediation
    1. Establishes team member roles and responsibilities
    2. Facilitates effective workgroup processes and relationships
    3. Mediates in non-productive, dissident, or demoralized team situations
    4. Facilitates problem-centered coaching

5. Utilizes negotiation to mediate disputes and resolve conflicts

V. CRISIS LEADERSHIP COMPETENCIES
 A. Planning for the Unthinkable[2]
    1. Articulates the definition of crisis levels and its elements
    2. Articulates the definition of crisis management
    3. Articulates the definition of crisis leadership
    4. Articulates the difference between crisis leadership and crisis management
    5. Articulates the role of leaders before and during crisis events
    6. Articulates the systemic nature of crisis leadership
    7. Identifies the elements of crisis anticipation and its relevance to crisis leadership
    8. Utilizes methods and processes for anticipatory thinking and "thinking the unthinkable" before and during crisis events
    9. Identifies the difference between normal/abnormal accidents/events and natural disasters
    10. Identifies the elements of crisis types and methods for signal detection
    11. Identifies and analyzes elements of multiple, inter-related or non-related and unthinkable crises events
    12. Analyzes problems that partner organizations experience during multiple crises events
    13. Articulates the full range of crises that can potentially affect the organization/system
    14. Articulates the range and scope of crisis for which the organization/system should prepare
    15. Develops the competence and capability necessary to anticipate, prepare for, respond to, and mitigate multiple crises
    16. Develops a unified planning, capability, and resource system among partner organizations
    17. Develops an emergency management/unified command system prepared for multiple crises
 B. Crisis Patterns and Key Elements[2]
    1. Utilizes the concept of technical and ethical uncertainties in a crisis event
    2. Articulates the concept of objectivity as a "turnoff" during crises events

3. Articulates the concept of the court of public opinion vs. the court of law during crisis events
4. Articulates the importance of no secrets and complete transparency during crisis events
5. Articulates the importance of the concept of lessons ignored and not learned during a crisis event
6. Identifies the six phases of crisis leadership
7. Identifies the set of different crisis types
8. Identifies the effect of different crisis mechanisms
9. Identifies the different crisis families
10. Identifies different crisis stakeholders in relation to crisis types

C. Risk Assessment[2]
1. Utilizes the four elements of the crisis framework to identify how organizations/systems responds to crisis events
2. Applies the crisis framework to human-caused crises (normal/abnormal accidents) and natural disasters
3. Recognizes the basic patterns of organizational/system response and what elements should be reinforced or changed
4. Utilizes six phases of crisis leadership to redesign effective crisis systems

D. Command Capability and Improvement
1. Develops and implements a unified chain of command for emergency response
2. Demonstrates individual functional and leadership roles/responsibilities for emergency response
3. Demonstrates ability to make critical decisions and take decisive actions during crisis events
4. Facilitates development of key values and shared vision to guide decisions and actions during crisis events
5. Implements a multiyear emergency preparedness education, training, and exercise system
6. Implements a system for performance measurement, after-action reviews, and improvement planning
7. Identifies, communicates, and retests performance and maturity levels

E. Ethics and Crisis/Emergency Response[3]
1. Articulates the role of ethics in crisis leadership

2. Utilizes methods to balance emotion and use of reason during crisis events
3. Identifies historical incidence of leaders who faced moral challenges
4. Utilizes professional ethics in the context of community and society during crisis
5. Models ethical decision-making during emergencies/crises
6. Utilizes ethical decision making to apply/alter use of emergency plan procedures
7. Describes the role of public health law during emergencies/crisis events
8. Describes ethical issues regarding public health challenges and emergency events
9. Describes principles of ethical leadership and caring competence during disasters

F. Personality and Emotional Intelligence[4]
Personality Factors and Crisis Response
1. Identifies personality styles of leaders and leadership teams during crisis events
2. Utilizes assessment methods to determine personality style/preferences and crises
3. Analyzes the relationship of personality type/preferences to functioning during crises
4. Analyzes the impact of leadership cognitive and emotional intelligence during crises
5. Recognizes and reconciles rational and emotional elements during crisis events

Emotions and Performance: Leaders
1. Identifies critical emotional intelligence competencies during crisis events
2. Analyzes how feelings affect personal performance in stressful situations
3. Describes emotions that are aroused during crises
4. Describes personal strengths and weaknesses associated with emotions and stress
5. Utilizes methods to resist acting or responding in impulses during high-stress events
6. Utilizes methods to behave calmly in stressful or emergency situations
7. Utilizes methods to stay composed and positive during crisis events
8. Utilizes methods to calm others in stressful situations and emergency events
9. Utilizes methods to change ideas and perceptions under stressful situations
10. Utilizes methods to balance emotional and rational elements for decision making and decisive action during crises

11. Utilizes methods to handle ambiguity and multiple demands associated with crises
12. Utilizes methods to chronicle individual experience for after-action analysis

Emotions and Performance: Others
1. Utilizes assessment methods to identify personality style and the relation to performance during crises
2. Utilizes methods to identify moods, feelings, and nonverbal cues of others under stress
3. Analyzes underlying causes for feelings, behavior, or concerns of others under stress
4. Utilizes factual arguments (reason or data) to persuade/influence others under stress
5. Utilizes the support of influential parties to convince others in stressful situations
6. Utilizes methods to increase perception and perspectives of others during crises
7. Utilizes methods for reducing stereotyping of and reactions to diverse populations
8. Utilizes methods for broad support for increasing persuasive effect during crises
9. Utilizes methods to promote cooperation/collaboration in stressful situations
10. Utilizes methods to reduce conflict in crisis situations
11. Utilizes methods to chronicle experience of others to prepare for after-action analysis

G. Risk and Crisis Communication[5]
1. Identifies leadership role/responsibilities to develop a crises communication plan
2. Utilizes theoretical methods for and stages of risk communication
3. Identifies primary obstacles for use of appropriate risk/crisis communication in emergency situations
4. Utilizes basic elements of the concept of risk and factors associated with determining magnitude of risk
5. Articulates the Environmental Protection Agency's seven rules of risk communication
6. Utilizes the 21 guidelines for effective communication by leaders during high-anxiety, stress, or threat situations
7. Utilizes appropriate risk/crisis communication methods during crisis events
8. Utilizes problem-solving, conflict resolution, and decision-making skills using principles and methods for risk communication

9. Utilizes communication role and methods with team members during emergency events
10. Utilizes communication role and methods with partner organizations during emergency events
11. Utilizes communication role and methods with the media during emergency events
12. Utilizes communication role and methods with the public during emergency events

H. Cultural Competence and Crisis[6]
1. Understands the difference between cultural diversity and cultural competencies
2. Describes the process for cultural competency development
3. Identifies the role of cultural, social, and behavioral factors in the delivery of public health services
4. Describes the relationship(s) between culture and health
5. Explores and describes knowledge about worldviews, mental models, values, beliefs, practices, and/or ways of other cultural groups
6. Identifies and discusses differences within cultural groups at the community level as well as across cultural groups
7. Describes the dynamic forces contributing to cultural diversity at the organizational level
8. Interacts with sensitivity and effectiveness with persons from diverse (cultural, socioeconomic, educational, racial, ethnic, professional, age, lifestyle preferences) backgrounds in the practice setting and in crisis situations
9. Actively seeks ongoing education, consultation, coaching, and/or training experience to enhance understanding and effectiveness with culturally and ethnically diverse populations in both normal and crisis situations
10. Identifies and understands one's own competence level when interacting with cultural/ethnically diverse populations in normal and crisis situations
11. Identifies own stereotyping attitudes, preconceived notions, and feelings toward members of other ethnic/cultural groups and how these dimensions affect decision making

12. Participates in cultural/ethnic groups in communities of practice and community settings
13. Develops strategies and adapts approaches to problems and emergency/crisis situations that take into account cultural differences
14. Identifies institutional barriers that prevent cultural/ethnic groups from seeking public health services and assistance in emergency or crisis situations
15. Facilitates understanding of the importance of and methods to increase diversity in the public health workforce
16. Recognizes that communication and related actions are culturally bound

I. Legal Basis for Preparedness[7]
1. Identifies the source and scope of state and federal powers to protect the public's health, safety, and welfare in the event of emergency events
2. Analyzes and applies how public health law contributes to emergency response
3. Identifies and applies the basic legal framework for public health preparation in emergency events and the roles of federal, state, and local governmental agencies
4. Identifies and applies basic provisions of the governmental unit in the health code and regulations during public health emergencies

NOTES

1. University of North Carolina School of Public Health Doctoral Program Leadership Competencies were used and adapted in part for use in this domain.
2. Competency sets were developed by the Heartland Centers in collaboration with Dr. Ian Mitroff, Comprehensive Crisis Management, Inc.
3. Competencies were developed by the Heartland Centers in collaboration with Dr. Shugg Yagel-McBay.
4. Comprehensive Crisis Management, Inc., Therese Jacobs-Stewart, M.A., and materials from the Hay Group, Dr. Daniel Goleman, Harvard University.
5. Competencies developed by the Heartland Centers in collaboration with Dr. Vincent Covello. http://centerforriskcommunication.org/.
6. Competencies developed by the Heartland Centers in collaboration with Dr. Louis Rowitz and adaptation of the Core Competencies in Public Health of the Council on Linkages Between Public Health Practice and Academia.
7. Competencies developed by the Heartland Centers in collaboration with Jason Sapsin, JD, MPH, the Johns Hopkins Center for Law and the Public's Health.

CHAPTER 27

Leadership Evaluation and Research

It requires a very unusual mind to undertake the analysis of the obvious.

—Alfred North Whitehead,
Science and the Modern World

During the 1990s, the public health community realized the importance of developing public health leaders. A national Public Health Leadership Institute (PHLI) was created by a consortium of California universities through a grant from the Centers for Disease Control and Prevention (CDC). From 2000 to 2011, the national program was housed at the University of North Carolina Institute for Public Health. In 1991, the first two state public health leadership institutes were founded in Illinois at the University of Illinois School of Public Health and in Missouri at the Saint Louis University School of Public Health. The Illinois program began with CDC support, and the Missouri program with support from the state of Missouri. Until late 2011, there were a number of public health regional and state leadership development programs covering 49 of the 50 states. Georgia (50th state) was in the process of developing a state-based program. Beginning in 2011, the

funding for a number of these institutes ended. A few have managed to survive from state and local dollars. A new model was initiated in 2011 for a national community public health institute. As leadership programs have proliferated, there has grown a concern about the effectiveness of these programs in training leaders.

Leaders need information for making decisions. Ongoing program evaluation creates an atmosphere in which effective leadership and organizational learning can flourish.[1] Leaders need to show strong support for program evaluation and include evaluation as a part of the mission and vision of their agencies. They also need to be involved in the evaluation process and work with other agency professionals to ensure that the process is successful. The organization will not achieve excellence without opportunities for continual learning provided by training and leadership development programs.

In 1999, the CDC reported on the deliberations of the CDC Evaluation Working Group regarding effective program evaluation.[2] The working group developed a framework for program evaluation in public health. The top part of **Table 27-1** lists the steps in the evaluation process, from engaging stakeholders in the process

TABLE 27-1   Narrative Steps and Standards of the CDC Evaluation Framework

Engage stakeholders

   Those involved, those affected, primary intended users

Describe the program

   Needs, expected effects, activities, resources, stage, context, logic model

Focus the evaluation design

   Purpose, users, uses, questions, methods, agreements

Gather credible evidence

   Indicators, sources, quality, quantity, logistics

Justify conclusions

   Standards, analysis/synthesis, interpretation, judgment, recommendations

Ensure use and share lessons learned

   Design, preparation, feedback, follow-up, dissemination

Utility

   Serve the information needs of intended users

Feasibility

   Be realistic, prudent, diplomatic, and frugal

Propriety

   Behave legally, ethically, and with due regard for the welfare of those involved and those affected

Accuracy

   Reveal and convey technically accurate information

Source: Reproduced from "Framework for Program Evaluation in Public Health," *Morbidity and Mortality Weekly Report*, Vol. 48, 1999, the Centers for Disease Control and Prevention.

to ensuring that the lessons learned are applied. The bottom part of the table lists the four major standards of program evaluation: utility, feasibility, propriety, and accuracy.

The term "program" has a broad meaning.[3] Indeed, the CDC Evaluation Working Group listed 12 different program categories: direct service interventions, community mobilization efforts, research initiatives, surveillance systems, policy development activities, outbreak investigations, laboratory diagnostics, communication campaigns, infrastructure building projects, training and education services, administrative systems, and other programs. In this chapter, the focus is on the evaluation of leadership development programs.

EVALUATION OF TRAINING PROGRAMS

A training program must have a reason for being. If a training program is developed but no one registers for it, it obviously does not address a need. That is why the first step in the training process is to determine whether the proposed training program is required. The program planners should investigate the needs of the target population using focus groups, surveys, and interviews. The planners themselves will also have an agenda that should be built into the needs assessment. If the purpose of the assessment is to determine the need for training in governance, then the assessment must include questions about governance.

In a study of board of health members' understanding of public health, it was found that the members believed their most important role was in the area of policy development.[4] They believed they were least effective in the area of assessment. In addition, board members thought they were not given appropriate training for their board activities and that the principles of governance were not clear. They were also concerned about the lack of funds for the running of the board, the lack of information about public health in general, and the lack of awareness of political priorities and statutory regulations. All of these findings can be translated into training objectives.

Once the training topics are determined, the program's objectives are set and the program is developed.[5] Among the things that need to be determined are procedures for the selection of participants, the times and places of the training, the best speakers for each topic, and methods for evaluating the program's outcomes.

The third step is to offer the training program itself. Measurements need to be done before or at the start of the training program and also at its conclusion in order to determine changes that occurred. Session and speaker evaluations also need to be done in order to assess the quality of the program. It is beneficial to tie the program evaluation to changes reported by the trainees. Research can be done on:

- the association between program elements and leadership change
- measurable and unmeasurable leadership competencies
- differences between new leaders and more established ones
- differences between trainees and colleagues who have not been trained

- differences between continuing education approaches and academic approaches
- 360-degree measures at the start and the conclusion of the training program

If trainees do not take new information and skills back to their agencies, the training course loses much of its effectiveness. One way to spread the benefits of training is for graduates of training, using what they learned, to develop a training workshop for colleagues who were unable to attend the training.

The last step in the training process involves following the trainees over time to determine what parts of the program work in practice. By taking the same measurements as were taken during the training, the planners can determine the changes that occurred over time and pinpoint areas in which skills deteriorated. The information gained can be used to develop follow-up programs and make the current program more effective in the future. A few public health leadership institutes have created annual update courses for graduates of their programs.

Evaluation itself can be divided into four components. First, the trainees' reactions to the program need to be assessed. There may be differences between reactions to in-house programs and reactions to programs outside the organization.

Second, the learning that occurred has to be evaluated. The hoped-for results of training include the acquiring of new skills and new knowledge.

Third, behavior changes due to the training need to be identified. The ultimate goal of all training programs is to alter the behavior of the trainees in ways that improve their effectiveness on the job. The expected behavior changes do not always occur, sometimes because leaders go to the training course with a personal agenda or believe they already know everything about leadership that they need to. In addition, trainees who are primarily managers sometimes do not understand the difference between managing and leading. Finally, trainees often face community or organizational barriers to putting their new skills into action.

Fourth, the long-term effects of the training need to be studied. One leader who attended a state-based leadership program showed very little behavior change at the end of the program but reported that he eventually (two years later) used the skills learned to improve the agency environment. This example shows the difficulty of evaluating results from a training program during the program or immediately after. Follow-up is

clearly important, as is measuring behavior change in a control group that has not been through training.

The above model has been criticized for not going far enough. Performance evaluation needs to extend into the community.[6] In addition, the work environment must be analyzed to determine whether changes in behavior will be possible. It is important to keep in mind that behavior change is affected not only by the training but also by such factors as attitude and the reaction of others to proposed changes.[7]

EVALUATION OF LEADERSHIP DEVELOPMENT PROGRAMS

The Center for Creative Leadership (CCL) undertook a study of leadership programs for school superintendents in Florida.[8] The study focused on the outcomes of training, the influence of the curriculum on the outcomes, and the influence of other factors on the outcomes. Three general outcomes were discovered to have occurred. First, leaders became committed to continuous learning and believed they had acquired continuous learning strategies and skills. Second, they acquired personal leadership skills and underwent personal changes. Third, they were able to perform their jobs more effectively.

With regard to factors affecting the outcomes, the trainees were influenced by their contact with facilitators, who appear to have taken a mentoring role. These facilitators helped the trainees to conceptualize their experientially based learning projects. The trainees also kept a journal during training, which helped document their learning experiences and contributed to the development of their leadership abilities.

The outcomes of training differ for different individuals.[9] Some leaders have much experience and use the new training to fine-tune their skills. Others struggle with self-control and self-esteem issues and have trouble maintaining flexibility. These leaders often do not benefit from leadership programs. A third group of leaders thrive in leadership programs and make substantial progress in developing their skills. For example, they often learn the importance of sharing power and how to create a better balance in their lives. Exercise 27-1 explores the expectations that students had starting the leadership program and the extent to which their expectations were met.

In their comprehensive approach to leadership program evaluation, the CCL made a distinction between leader development and leadership development.[10]

Leadership Tip

*Hold meetings at a round table.
It levels the playing field.*

Leader development evaluation refers to evaluation done on how individuals use their leadership development training to become more effective in carrying out their leadership activities. Leadership development evaluation refers to how organizations and agencies increase their capacity to carry out the agency's work and also to carry out public health's work. In other words, training enhances the performance of leaders and has an important effect on increasing the capacity of the public health organization to carry out public health work collaboratively with internal and external stakeholders and public health clients.[11]

Evaluators have discussed the importance of strategic evaluation, which relates to a determination of the values of organization-based processes and interventions to see if the values that affect an agency are maintained by the changes promoted through leadership training or whether the training increases the capacity of the agency to do its work.[12] The purpose of strategic evaluation is to use training to add value for the leaders and their leadership partners over time. There are challenges that affect the successes of strategic evaluation. Because leadership development is sometimes used as a reward for public health professionals, there is a danger that this reward will benefit the individual and not the public health system if the training opportunity is not evaluated relative to the needs of the system. Another challenge relates to the fact that leadership development may not show an immediate return on investment. This delay between leadership development and the development of strategic outcomes creates difficulties in determining the value of training programs. The costs of the training provide challenges for agencies

with limited training resources. The cost of these leadership programs is often prohibitive for public health professionals. There is also a feasibility challenge related to information. Because there are privacy protection concerns for trainees, leadership development programs cannot relate the use of leadership behavior tools to action outcomes without the specific consent of the person going through the training. Another challenge relates to the lack of funding in public health leadership development for the evaluation function. There is also a lack of understanding about what evaluation is supposed to accomplish.

Despite some of these challenges, we still learn much about the benefits of evaluation when it does occur. This chapter presents three program evaluation case studies. The first, Case Study 27-A, describes the process of developing an evaluation program for the South Central Public Health Leadership Institute in the late 1990s. One of the themes is that funding concerns can have an effect on training programs. The project team recognized the importance of evaluation and the complexity of the leadership development process, and it explored the possibility of using observers to monitor the training process. However, the team decided that the leadership trainees would not accept this technique, and so it adopted a 360-degree self-evaluation and observer feedback procedure in which confidentiality was protected. The case study includes a postscript on what has happened since the evaluation.

Case Study 27-B describes the comprehensive evaluation of the Public Health Leadership Institute from 1991 to 2006.[13] The retrospective evaluation explored what alumni were doing, what skills have been used, and what skills can be attributed to the training experience. Results from this evaluation are now available. The final case study, by Sarpy and Kaplan, is an evaluation of a program for new public health administrators carried out for the National Association of County and City Health Officials (Case Study 27-C).

Case Study 27-A

Be Careful What You Ask For—You May Get It (with 2008 Postscript)
Sheila W. Chauvin and Ann Anderson

This case study was developed based on the experiences of the South Central Public Health Leadership Institute (SCPHLI), Tulane University School of Public Health and Tropical Medicine, and the development of an objectives- and performance-based 360-degree feedback process.

Issue: How does one assess effective leadership and leadership development among public health professionals?

Time Period: May 1997–October 1999.

Professionals involved: Alata Angst, project director; Ben Thare, program coordinator; Helen Bach, evaluation consultant.

Alata sat at her desk feeling rather good about the progress of the new leadership development program. This first year had been really stressful, as is often the case with any new program. Alata had worried quite a bit about how the program would be perceived in the region, because participants were being drawn from practicing and experienced supervisors, managers, and leaders in the public health sector. She had just returned from the project team meeting for the SCPHLI, and from all indications the first year had been successful indeed. A good thing, because everyone had worked so hard. Participants in the first cohort had completed feedback forms at the end of each multiday session throughout the year, and their comments revealed high levels of satisfaction with most of the program offerings and activities. Of course, as always, there were a few negative and pessimistic comments, and there were indeed areas for improvement and expansion that the project team agreed they would need to target in the future. However, for the most part everyone thought that the first year of development and implementation was a success. Ben Thare, the project coordinator, had raised an interesting issue during the meeting: Is it sufficient to gauge the effectiveness of the institute based simply on participants' satisfaction with the sessions? Shouldn't the team base its judgments on the extent to which participants actually demonstrate new and enhanced leadership skills in everyday practice? That's the true test, isn't it? As he said, satisfaction and the "friendly factor" were not necessarily going to get people to participate in the second year.

Ben's comments were working their way to the surface as Alata sat contemplating the future of the SCPHLI. How do we really know if the institute is making a difference? Certainly this was going to be an issue, probably sooner than she or Ben or even the participants might realize. Although they had funding for the institute now, Alata knew that she would need additional extramural funding to continue and enhance the institute in the future, especially if they were going to add more states to the group of participatory states. A visual reminder lay on her desk in the form of a request for proposals from the CDC. If the team was going to seek funding for the institute from the CDC, surely they would need a stronger evaluation plan than just session feedback forms asking participants to comment on what they liked and disliked. Ben was right. Even if she wasn't seeking additional funding, sooner or later officials in the various state agencies were going to want evidence that sending their public health leaders to multiday retreats and seminars was worth their investments of time, effort, and dollars. Sooner or later, state agency directors were going to expect visible evidence back "in the trenches."

But what could they do? What kind of evidence would they need? This was clearly out of Alata's comfort zone. Public health administration and microbiology were areas in which she could hold her own, even excel, but measuring the effectiveness of educational programs was clearly not part of her expertise. Certainly Alata had statistical support available in the school, but statisticians didn't know much about evaluating educational programs or things like leadership development, change facilitation, communication, conflict resolution, coalition building, coaching and mentoring skills, and so on. Now Alata was concerned! Who could help? Maybe the institute wasn't as successful as she had thought originally. Maybe it was just fluff, as had been suggested by a few of the negative and pessimistic comments that she was now reflecting on once again. As Alata continued to think about how the team could really know whether the institute was making a difference in participants' leadership development and practices, she got up and started to walk down the hall toward Ben's office. She thought, Ben should be back from the team meeting by now. He raised the question about effectiveness and evaluation, so maybe he has some ideas as to how to proceed? Yes, that's it, ask Ben.

One Week Later

Alata and Ben walked into the office of Helen Bach. They were meeting with Helen to discuss how they might examine the extent to which the SCPHLI participants develop and use key leadership concepts and skills in everyday practice. Luckily, Ben had met Helen earlier in the year at a conference, during which he learned about Helen's background in leadership development and change process and her expertise in instrument development and program evaluation. It was lucky that Ben met her in the first place and doubly fortunate that she had the background that seemed ideally suited to meet their project needs. Alata knew about Helen and the medical education research office that she directed in the School of Medicine, but she hadn't realized that the unit might be a potential resource. In any case, they were glad the connection was made. With the CDC proposal deadlines looming near, they would not have had much time to search for an evaluation consultant, much less one with a leadership development background. As they waited in the reception area to meet with Helen, Alata and Ben reviewed the program goals and expectations that they planned to share with Helen.

(Continues)

After the Meeting

As Alata and Ben left Helen's office, they were feeling both drained and overwhelmed. They had no idea that evaluating the effectiveness of the leadership institute could be so complex. Going into the meeting, both Alata and Ben thought they could just administer some type of test or survey and have some of the staff or faculty in the biostatistics department "crunch the numbers" and give them the results. What Helen had suggested was more of a performance-based assessment. Direct observation by several trained assessors over several occasions would be an ideal approach, she had told them, but the associated costs and time constraints were formidable. In addition, potential difficulties and political and interpersonal considerations were at the top of the list for decision making. For example, who would assess, how would assessors be trained and monitored, who would own the data, and how would the data be used for programming decisions and for helping individuals improve their leadership abilities? These were some of the questions raised and scenarios discussed.

Ultimately, the results of any assessments must be used for decision making and continuous improvement. Certainly, if the participants' direct supervisors were the ones doing the assessments, there might be little potential for collaborative reflection and professional development to occur, at least at first. For example, individuals might tend to view the assessments as yet another formal job evaluation rather than an opportunity to learn and develop new abilities. In contrast, if peers were trained to do the observations, how would their assessor responsibilities affect day-to-day work relationships? Should the peer assessors be individuals who work with participants on a regular basis, or should they be brought in from some other office, agency, or region to conduct "snapshot" observations and assessment reports? In what context should the assessments be explained and occur? And then there were all the instrument development, validity, and reliability issues that Helen raised for them to consider. How were they going to accomplish this? Alata and Ben had not realized what they had asked for. What they had was a task of elephantine proportions.

Alata and Ben felt like they should run—not walk—out of Helen's office. This was way too much work and complexity for their program. Participants would never agree to be observed and rated on behaviors, and after their discussion, paper-and-pencil tests did not seem much better than session feedback forms. But they felt a ray of hope when Helen suggested that they limit the scope of work and take things one step at a time. Obviously she had noted the look of being overwhelmed on Ben and Alata's faces. She said, "Folks, this is an evolutionary process, not a revolution." Phew! Alata and Ben stayed in their seats and leaned forward with interest. Helen went on to describe several other options for their evaluation goals. She mentioned self-assessment and peer-assessment methods and told them about techniques that were currently being described as 360-degree feedback processes. Helen also discussed concepts such as self-efficacy and organizational context and explored the notion of assessment performance levels at the beginning of the institute and then again at the end (i.e., pre- and postassessments). By the end of the meeting, they had an action plan in place and a renewed sense of confidence about the tasks that lay ahead. As they left Helen's office, they thought about the last thing she said to them: "If you're going to eat an elephant, do so one bite at a time. Let's approach this as a team."

Over the next several months, Helen worked with Alata and Ben to review the goals and objectives of the SCPHLI to identify key leadership traits that were being addressed by the program. As she explained, it would be impossible to measure everything, so they should concentrate on the specifics of the program. They also began to work on a process that included pre- and postassessments and self- and peer-assessment components. Once again, ideal approaches were identified first, but then, once they figured out what their resources were, they settled for less than the ideal.

In the end, the SCPHLI had an observation-based questionnaire that included multiple descriptions of leadership behaviors grounded in the program goals and objectives. Participants completed a self-assessment form at the beginning and at the end of the institute. They identified five individuals in their work environment with whom they work regularly and who agreed to complete a confidential peer assessment form of the questionnaire, again before and after participation in the institute. A process was developed by which all data were submitted directly to Helen's office, and voluntary and confidential assurances were established. Preassessment profiles and postassessment profiles were completed by the staff in Helen's office and mailed directly to each participant, with options for confidential and individualized consultation. Only group or cohort assessment data were available to the project team, and no individually identifiable data were shared. In essence, they were able to achieve many of the 360-degree feedback features and minimize the political and interpersonal threats that are often associated with on-the-job performance assessments.

October 1999

Alata sat at her desk feeling rather good about the progress of the SCPHLI. She had just returned from the project team meeting. As another cohort containing participants from four states completed the institute, Ben shared in the meeting evidence that suggested another successful year indeed. A good thing, because everyone had worked so hard—not this year, but for the past several years. Alata thought about the first year that they implemented a pilot version of the self-assessment questionnaire and the anxiety it had raised among the participants and the large number of individuals who initially expressed their apprehension about peers completing a similar form. She remembered watching Ben manage the group discussions about the participants' concerns pertaining to confidentiality of assessment data. She thought, just hearing the word "evaluation" does tend to make the hair on the back of your neck stand on end. Now, two years later, most, if not all, participants embraced the pre- and postassessments for the 360-degree feedback process. At first, individuals thought about evaluation as being done "to them"; now it seems evaluation is being done "with them." She looked out the window and chuckled to herself: guess we do need to be careful about what we ask for—we just might get it!

Postscript: February 2008

The case study above was originally developed based on the early experiences of the SCPHLI, Tulane University School of Public Health and Tropical Medicine, and the development of an objectives- and performance-based 360-degree feedback process. Since 1999, the SCPHLI has continued and expanded. The leadership development resulting from the program and ongoing development of its project team members has contributed substantially to professional development of public health staff and formation of a strong and ever-expanding academic-practice partnership in the region. As was the case from the onset of the SCPHLI, formative and summative evaluation have been a core component and a driving force of the ongoing development of the South Central Public Health Partnership, as a regional consortium, and of the new centers and expanded curriculum and programs that have been achieved since 1999. This postscript provides a brief summary of some of the major accomplishments that have contributed to leadership development through both formal educational processes and on-the-job collaboration. In each instance, performance and overall program evaluation have been used from the onset to support ongoing monitoring, to guide midcourse adjustments, and to regularly gauge progress toward achieving important goals and value-added impact.

The continuation of the 360-degree assessment in the SCPHLI has continued to provide evidence of the effectiveness of its educational program. Statistically significant and positive gains have been observed in every year of the SCPHLI since the 360-degree assessment was implemented. The curriculum continues to offer substantial benefit, and only minor modifications have been necessary (e.g., routine updates and refinements). In 2003–2004, further validation of the 360-degree assessment was completed, and 20 of the original 24 items continue to be retained on the instrument. Today, full participation of SCPHLI fellows is common, and pre- and post-SCPHLI 360-degree profiles continue to be used to provide individual and programmatic guidance. In 2006–2007, and with modest funding from the CDC, a longitudinal and follow-up study of all SCPHLI graduates was completed using a mixed-methods research design to further examine the effect of the program on its graduates and the supporting public health agencies. Based on quantitative and qualitative results, the SCPHLI is highly regarded by leaders, graduates, and public health professionals generally throughout the region. The SCPHLI is viewed by many as a substantial source for developing future public health leaders. Enrollment in the SCPHLI continues to be strong, and individuals in the various practice partner agencies actually view participation (and then graduation) as an honor. When the region was devastated by Hurricane Katrina, the SCPHLI was interrupted, as was the case for most other things, and the opportunity for losing momentum was certainly present. However, there was strong support for resuming the program. In 2006, the SCPHLI was resumed and expanded to offer graduates additional learning opportunities through an Advanced Crisis Leadership course that has been well subscribed to for each offering. Finally, an SCPHLI Alumni Society continues to offer graduates opportunities for collaboration and ongoing professional development.

The SCPHLI has served as a foundation for additional program development, and through such efforts, individuals have developed leadership skills on the job. For example, in 1999, the SCPHLI project team decided to invite colleagues from the University of Alabama–Birmingham School of Public Health to join them. This expanded team of leaders and representatives of four public health agencies (Alabama, Arkansas, Louisiana, and Mississippi) and two academic institutions (Tulane and UAB) reorganized to form a steering committee for the regional partnership. In addition, with successful acquisition of funding from the Health Resources and Services Administration, the South Central Public Health Training Center (SCPHTC) was established in 2000 to develop and provide competency-based training courses and resources for public health professionals in the region. Grounded in the core functions and essential services endorsed for public health professions at the time, overall program evaluation (including systematic training needs assessments) was used to establish goals, provide focus and guidance, and

(Continues)

maintain forward momentum. Achieving early success with the SCPHTC, the Partnership Steering Committee (of which many members were graduates of the SCPHLI) continued to put into practice essential leadership competencies they had learned in their SCPHLI experiences (e.g., creating and sharing vision, obtaining resources, providing professional development and ongoing assistance, communicating effectively, and building coalitions).

In 2001, they sought additional resources from the CDC to establish a third center, the South Central Center for Public Health Preparedness (SCCPHP), to lead an effort in preparing the region's public health professionals in emergency and bioterrorism preparedness. Again, with a successful funding award from the CDC, the SCCPHP was established in 2002, and together with the SCPHLI and SCPHTC, a synergy of efforts and resources has continued to expand.

Since 2000, an overall program evaluation model has been used to provide formative and summative input for the regional consortium (partnership) and for each of the three centers, with particular emphasis on goal achievement, consortium effectiveness, and value added to public health professional development. Each year, the overall program evaluation activities provide opportunities for direct input from all stakeholders. Quantitative and qualitative methods have been used to answer core questions across years, including longitudinal study of innovation and change process, and to address specific issues at hand in each year. Reports of ongoing evaluation are provided at least twice each year to provide external review of progress to goals and summative assessment of goal achievement, consortium effectiveness, and value-added impact.

Leadership development has been a core component of both formal and on-the-job educational opportunities affiliated with the partnership and each of its centers. A much-expanded South Central Public Health Advisory Board has now replaced the Partnership Steering Committee and reflects a greater variety of agency and academic partners that interact with each other to support public health. Again, real-life experiences within the partnership have fostered leadership development and putting into practice the core leadership competencies that are reflected in the SCPHLI curriculum (e.g., shared visions, communication skills, coalition building, strategic planning, and change facilitation). So, as Alata reflected in the original case above, we have been careful about what we asked for, and through the ongoing collaboration and development of individual and group leadership, we have achieved quite a lot.

Case Study 27-B

Evaluation of the National Public Health Leadership Institute, 1991–2006

Karl E. Umble, Sandra J. Diehl, and Susan Haws

Background

The PHLI is a leadership development program in the United States sponsored by the CDC. The institute's mission is to strengthen the leadership competencies of senior public health leaders and to build a network of senior leaders who can work together and share knowledge on how to address public health challenges.

The CDC founded PHLI in 1990 and remains its sponsor. PHLI represented a significant CDC commitment to improve public health infrastructure following the influential 1988 Institute of Medicine report, *The Future of Public Health*, which called for major improvements in the practice of public health in the United States.

From 1991 to 2000, PHLI was offered under the continuous management of the Center for Health Leadership and Practice, which is part of the nonprofit Public Health Institute in Oakland, California. During this time, nine cohorts of about 50 scholars per year were developed. In 2000, the CDC selected a new partnership to offer PHLI, headed by the North Carolina Institute for Public Health at the University of North Carolina at Chapel Hill (UNC) School of Public Health. Other partners included the Kenan-Flagler Business School at UNC–Chapel Hill and the nonprofit Center for Creative Leadership (CCL) in Greensboro, North Carolina. This partnership developed an additional six cohorts of scholars through 2006. The total number of graduates was 806.

In 2006–2007, the CDC sponsored an evaluation of the program's first 15 years of operation. This report presents the results of that evaluation, which examined PHLI's influence on the following major domains:

Domain 1. Individual Leader Development
Domain 2. Leader Actions: Career-Related Outcomes and Voluntary Leadership Positions Taken
Domain 3. Public Health Leadership Network Development and Network Actions
Domain 4. Public Health Systems and Infrastructure Development

In addition, the evaluation examined graduate and stakeholder perspectives on PHLI and the future direction of public health leadership development in the United States, which was Domain 5.

The evaluators developed those themes on the basis of interviews with CDC staff who were involved with the evaluation; present and past PHLI staff members; a few selected graduates of the program from city, state, and federal government; previous evaluations of PHLI; and literature from evaluations of other leadership development programs. This process reflected the first step in the CDC's evaluation framework, which is to "engage stakeholders." By giving us ideas of key outcomes to measure, these interviews also greatly helped us in developing our evaluation instruments.

Methods

Evaluators used quantitative and qualitative data from an online survey sent to all program graduates and qualitative data from telephone interviews with a subset of program graduates and with key informants.

Survey

The Web-based survey sought to ascertain whether the program achieved basic objectives and focused on key areas that most interested stakeholders. It included questions related to:

- Career patterns of graduates and voluntary service in public health
- Individual leader development, including the influence of PHLI on scholars' understanding, skills, interest in leadership service, confidence, courage, sense of belonging to the national cadre of leaders in public health, self-awareness, openness to the ideas of others, networks, and overall leadership
- Individual practices, including changes in involvement in local, state, and national leadership activities
- Specific results of PHLI and improved leadership, including changes in programs, organizations, policies, and systems

We took great care while developing these instruments to be sure they would capture the data requested by the CDC and other stakeholders, and went through many drafts and item formats over a period of six intensive weeks before finalizing the instruments. This stage included pilot tests with program graduates in several locations, and with our own staff and graduate students. When the survey was ready, we uploaded it into a Web-based survey tool. Using Internet search engines and key informant referrals, we located a working (nonbouncing) e-mail address for 80% ($n = 646$) of the 806 graduates. To encourage participation, we sent a hard copy letter from the director of the North Carolina Institute for Public Health to all graduates, requesting participation in the survey, while the director of the PHLI alumni association also sent an e-mail encouraging participation. We then sent an e-mail to all graduates with a link to the survey, and approximately four additional e-mails to all graduates who had not yet responded to the survey over a period of about eight weeks. The final response rate was 61% ($n = 393$) out of those 646 for whom we had working e-mail addresses.

Interviews

We interviewed 17 graduates on how PHLI influenced their leadership knowledge, attitudes, skills, practices, positions, and involvement in voluntary work, leadership networks, and collaborations. We also asked about changes at organizational and systems levels that they could attribute at least partially to PHLI. Of the 17, eight (47%) were graduates of the California PHLI, and nine (53%) were graduates of the UNC program. We also conducted 18 interviews with key informants who had knowledge of the history, purpose, and results of PHLI. These interviews focused on national-level trends and changes that they could trace to PHLI, plus recommendations for future leadership programming and related efforts.

Quantitative survey data were analyzed using SAS (SAS Institute, Cary, North Carolina). Differences in means were analyzed using paired samples t-tests. Qualitative data from the open-ended survey questions were analyzed using content analysis methods. Interviews with program graduates and key informants were digitally recorded and transcribed. The two staff members who conducted the interviews conducted a content analysis (Patton, 1990) of the transcripts using across-case matrices derived from within-case summaries (Miles & Huberman, 1994).

(*Continues*)

Findings

Figure 27-1 summarizes study findings and their relationships to one another.

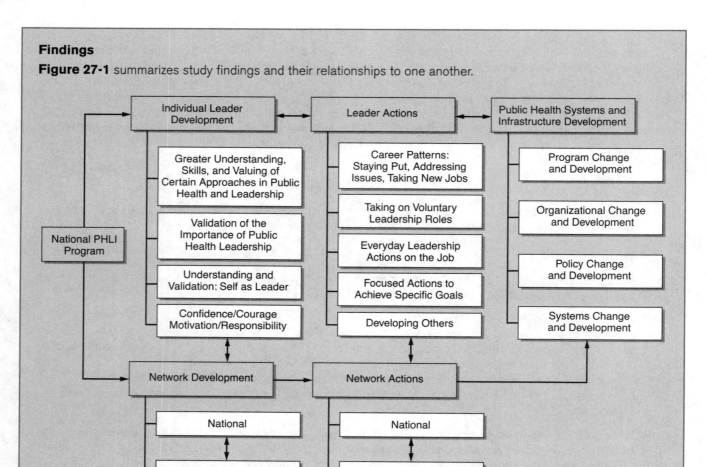

FIGURE 27-1 Model of National Outcomes.

Domain 1. Individual Leader Development

We asked graduates to rate PHLI's long-term influence on their leadership; 36% chose "large," 43% chose "moderate," 18% chose "small," and 2% chose "no influence."

The majority reported that PHLI had strengthened these constructs related to understanding and skills to a "moderate" or "large" degree:

- Understanding useful general principles of leadership (81%)
- Awareness of best practices and models for public health leadership (68%)
- Understanding of the breadth of the public health system and their role (56%)
- Openness to the ideas of others about how to address problems (75%)
- Skills in leading efforts that require the collaboration of many people or organizations (73%) and other specific leadership practices that are useful in public health (73%)

The majority reported that PHLI had strengthened their interest in the following possible involvements to a "moderate" or "great" extent:

- Interest in deepening their involvement with leadership efforts to improve their agency or community (78%)
- Interest in deepening their involvement with public health leadership efforts at the national level (59%) and at the state level (54%)
- Their commitment to staying in public health in their work (66%)

In addition, the majority reported that PHLI has strengthened these constructs to a "moderate" or "great" extent:

- Self-awareness as a leader: their strengths, liabilities, and how others view and receive their leadership (82%)

- Sense that as a public health leader, they are important and have a valuable role to play (77%) and belong to the national cadre of leaders in public health (68%)
- Professional network of people they can contact for ideas about how to handle their leadership (55%)
- Confidence to take on public health leadership responsibilities (75%)
- Courage to take the initiative and act to improve public health (75%)

Interview themes and hundreds of survey comments reinforced and explained scholars' improvements in understanding of leadership; improved understanding, skill, and valuing of collaborative leadership and systems thinking to address challenges; and other specific skills gained. Many also emphasized that PHLI connected them to a wide network of leaders with whom they could exchange valuable information. The network helped them feel that they "belonged" to a national network of public health leaders and were themselves "valid" leaders and increased their courage and confidence to "step up to the plate" and take on additional leadership responsibilities. One put it succinctly:

> PHLI helped to give me the requisite leadership skills, the support group to feel others in my position were making/could make a difference, gave me the confidence to step up to the plate, and impressed upon me the obligation to do so. PHLI was a very limited opportunity and almost all of us in it felt this privilege we had been given should be reciprocated for via active public health leadership in our respective work and personal spheres of influence.

Although some of these benefits may seem "soft" and unimportant to some readers, they are directly related to more recent and holistic concepts of competence that are widely embraced today. "Competence is not to be synonymous with skill. A competence is defined as the ability to successfully meet complex demands in a particular context. Its manifestation, competent performance, depends on the mobilization of knowledge, cognitive and practical skills, and social and behavioral components such as attitudes, emotions, values, and motivations. This holistic notion of competence is not reducible to one cognitive dimension" (Hakkarainen et al., 2004, p. 16).

Put differently, these findings about scholars' perceptions of important gains from PHLI remind us that leaders are not "machines" in need only of new practical skills, but complex personalities in search of a role and mission, vision, courage and encouragement, validation and confidence, and companions for the journey.

Domain 2. Leader Actions: Career-Related Outcomes and Voluntary Leadership Positions Taken

The great majority—87%—of survey respondents were still working in public health. Seven percent were working in another closely related field. About 20% of all PHLI graduates have now retired, but nearly all of them had remained in public health until they retired.

Using the construct of "trained leader-years"—full-time employment years after PHLI graduation—we found that graduates had invested 1,210 trained leader-years in local government, 640 years in state government, and 314 in federal government. In addition, scholars had spent 366 years in academic work, and 3 years working in health care.

Main foci for graduates' daily work after graduation included general organizational leadership in governmental agencies, community public health development, bioterrorism and preparedness, policy development and advocacy, and workforce development (both general and leadership development). Other fairly common foci included nonprofit leadership, epidemiology, chronic disease, healthcare leadership, and infectious disease.

About 52% had stayed in the same organization and position since graduation—which interviewees attributed to commitment to a place rather than any form of stagnation.

About 19% said that PHLI had helped them attain new jobs by increasing their skills, confidence, interest, and networks, or by impressing the employer that the scholar had attended. Jobs that PHLI helped scholars attain often included federal bureau or division chief and state or local health officer, deputy, or division chief.

About 81% had taken on additional "voluntary" leadership roles that were not required by their jobs, such as task forces, boards, professional associations, and informal advocacy; 54% had taken on such roles and responded that PHLI had played some role in their doing so, mainly by increasing their confidence, interest in the work, skills, and networks.

Examples of voluntary roles scholars had taken on with PHLI's influence included, at the national level, serving on boards and committees with the National Association of County and City Health Officials (NACCHO), the Association of State and Territorial Health Officials (ASTHO), the National League for Nursing (NLN), the Public Health Leadership Society (PHLS), the American Public Health Association (APHA), and other associations. At the state level, roles commonly included helping with or serving on boards with a state public health association or state association of county and city health officials. At the local level, many worked with community-level task forces and boards. The great majority of scholars responded that PHLI had made "some" or a "great" contribution to the leadership actions that they took when they assumed these voluntary roles.

(Continues)

I was appointed shortly after I graduated [from PHLI] to the board of the Massachusetts Public Health Association, the nation's largest APHA affiliate, and successfully implemented at MPHA a statewide initiative called the Coalition for Local Public Health, which is finally before the Legislature dealing with reform of a fragmented … local health structure.… Taking on a reform of local public health structure … has taken almost 10 years of steady development to arrive now at active dialogue with the state legislature. Without PHLI, I would never have conceptualized developing a statewide local public health coalition comprising five major public health associations to achieve a reorganization of the antiquated Massachusetts local health department structure.

Domain 3. Public Health Leadership Network Development and Network Actions

When asked to "explain in some detail one of the most important influences that PHLI has had on your leadership," more than 80 scholars (24% of the respondents who answered this question) cited gaining improved and valuable network connections.

The most commonly cited benefits of these connections included enhanced overall understanding of public health leadership's roles and goals; long-term professional knowledge sharing; social support for taking action—such as ideas, encouragement, and good examples set by others; and being introduced to opportunities for formal collaborative work, such as with NACCHO or a state public health association. In addition, many described how these collaborations had led to specific improvements in organizations, programs, policies, and "systems" at organizational, community, and state levels.

Forty-five percent had sought "wise counsel" from another PHLI graduate in the past two years, while 55% had collaborated with other PHLI graduates on projects or activities. Formal network activities that emerged from PHLI included the PHLS, the NLN, and state and regional PHLIs. These comments were typical about the value of network development:

Being part of a national cadre of very outstanding leaders, developing good relationships within that network, had a significant impact on me and my work. It continues to affect how I think, what I ask about, and how I approach many challenging situations.

Through PHLI, I met other public health leaders across the country and have maintained friendships with them since 1997. This network of accomplished leaders has been an invaluable source of advice, best practices, referrals, and support. I have held leadership positions at the local (health officer) and state (deputy health secretary) level for almost 12 years, and have found that a leadership network has been essential in my career.

Domain 4. Public Health Systems and Infrastructure Development

We wanted to know if PHLI had wide influences on programs, organizations, relationships, and policies. We operationalized these concepts by asking the question in this way:

- Can you think of an organizational change that PHLI graduates influenced directly or indirectly? (e.g., revised mission, process, positions, expansion, reorganization, funding, or other)
- Can you think of a program change that PHLI graduates influenced directly or indirectly? (e.g., new, expanded, improved, better-funded program)
- Can you think of a systems change that PHLI graduates influenced directly or indirectly? (e.g., a partnership, collaboration, new cross-organizational system or method for improving practice)
- Can you think of a policy (law) change that PHLI graduates influenced directly or indirectly?

For each question, the response options were "Yes," "No," and "Not sure." The results were as follows:

- 40% reported having observed a policy (law) change that PHLI graduates influenced directly or indirectly
- 60% reported having observed a program change that PHLI graduates influenced directly or indirectly
- 66% reported having observed an organizational change that PHLI graduates influenced directly or indirectly
- 67% reported having observed a systems change that PHLI graduates influenced directly or indirectly

We asked graduates to pick one such change and "(a) describe in some detail the change that was made, (b) explain how PHLI contributed to it, and (c) tell us why you view the change as important." We received nearly 300 responses, many of them extensive paragraphs, with these general themes:

- 96 described improved collaborations, partnerships, coalitions, and relationships at the national ($n = 525$), state ($n = 542$), or local ($n = 526$) levels.
- 76 described developing or implementing specific methods and tools for improving organizational and system performance, such as Essential Services, Performance Standards, accreditation systems for public

health agencies, the National Code of Ethics, Mobilizing for Action through Planning and Partnerships (MAPP), and Assessment Protocol for Excellence in Public Health (APEXPH). Others described substantial restructuring and improvements in local health services on a statewide basis, and other more specific state and local efforts in such domains as immunization and Medicaid fraud prevention.

- 31 described new policies passed at the national ($n = 4$), state ($n = 23$), and local levels ($n = 4$) in domains such as preparedness, tobacco control, injury control, public health systems funding, and health insurance for preventive care.
- 94 described organizational changes including reorganizations ($n = 26$), developing and adopting new approaches to planning for organizational or community public health improvement ($n = 15$), adopting stakeholder and community engagement as a fundamental way of leading an agency ($n = 10$), new ($n = 8$), installation of performance management and improvement tools ($n = 7$), quality improvements ($n = 6$), and other diverse improvements.
- 68 described improved or new programs at national ($n = 14$), state ($n = 39$), and local/organizational levels ($n = 15$) including workforce and leadership development, human immunodeficiency virus testing, worksite wellness, dental public health, and other diverse areas.

Many scholars described specific changes they personally had initiated, or which their team had initiated through the applied team project component of the program.

A large number of others explained that a group or critical mass of PHLI graduates had accumulated over time within a state or federal agency, jurisdiction, or association (such as NACCHO) and collaborated to shape a new initiative.

Graduates frequently collaborated with one another to lead others through a collaborative process that led to infrastructure and systems improvements—such as leading a community public health system through a MAPP process, or leading an organization through a participatory strategic planning process that engaged a wider group of stakeholders than had previously been included.

A general historical pattern emerged from the data: a group of thought leaders met at PHLI and worked together to reconceptualize how public health systems should be structured and should function, and also how public health leaders should work to improve them. This highly influential group of graduates worked with others in senior positions nationally, and through associations such as NACCHO, ASTHO, PHLS, and the National Association of Local Boards of Health, to devise and disseminate new tools to help state and local governments define and improve public health infrastructure and systems. These tools included but were not limited to the Essential Services, Performance Standards, agency accreditation systems, APEXPH and MAPP, the Code of Ethics, and state and regional public health leadership development institutes.

Many PHLI graduates working at national, state, and local levels followed the lead of the early thought leaders by further refining these tools and ideas, and leading national, state, and local implementation of them.

These quotations were typical of many we received describing these developments:

[A] reconceptualization of the public health system following [the 1988] IOM Future of Public Health report. Early graduates and subsequent graduates have been the "thought leaders" advancing the reconceptualization. [This is important because it] has helped a whole new generation of public health officials rethink their work.

Relating to "systems" change, several key PHLI graduates were directly responsible for the exploration of a new national accreditation program for state and local public health agencies. This was effective and visionary leadership at its best. PHLI contributed in two ways, first, by developing the sense of shared leadership among top public health professionals as the "standard" for how we would achieve advances in public health practice, and second, and importantly, PHLI brought public health leaders together to share experiences, become true colleagues, and create a common ideal for WHAT public health could become. I do not believe we would have pushed public health in the direction of creating a national accreditation system to assess and improve public health agencies across the nation without the efforts and vision of PHLI graduates.

[PHLI influenced] the growth of local health departments in Nebraska in 2001. Prior to a local-statewide initiative, there were 16 local health departments covering 22 counties in the state. After the intervention, there were 32 health departments covering the ENTIRE state (all 94 counties). Several PHLI alums were involved, along with public health leaders who had participated in the state-level PLHI. These folks served as change-agents and were leaders who helped guide and got the process passed. This change was HUGE in that an entire state went from part-time to full-time coverage of public health services. Health status change measures are now in place to evaluate and affirm the positive impact that local public coverage DOES make.

(Continues)

Domain 5. PHLI and the Future Direction of Public Health Leadership Development in the United States

Graduates and key informants made these observations:

- Individual leader development and network development are important synergistic efforts that have helped to create a common public health framework and a fertile ground for diffusion of innovation.
- Adequate and ongoing funding is needed in order to support innovative programming and to enhance the existing leadership development foundation.

Graduates and key informants offered these recommendations:

- Offer a continuum of "cutting-edge" or forward-looking development opportunities, including a national institute as well as continuing education and informal development activities to build a culture of lifelong learning and to sustain vibrant networks.
- Consider how to support a more integrated and coordinated system of leadership development at the national and state levels.
- Consider strategies to strengthen networks beyond the current methods, including enhanced connections to support succession planning and to facilitate opportunities to work on issues of national importance.
- Build in an ongoing evaluation system, focusing on both process and outcome measures.

Discussion

Leader Development and Network Development: Warp and Woof

In PHLI, leader and network development were simultaneous, mutually supportive, and parts of one another. We might say that they were "warp and woof," essential parts of the same woven cloth, or a virtual cycle. Either one without the other would have been less effective.

All of the personal gains that leaders made in PHLI helped them become interested, knowledgeable, skilled, and confident network members. Likewise, being part of a network of trusted colleagues at the vanguard of public health leadership promoted confidence and courage, inspired graduates to imitate their peers and network colleagues, and taught them much more than they could learn in a classroom setting.

This study's observations of the complementary but distinct roles of leader development and leadership network development reflect wider discussions in the leadership literature. For example, some writers recently have used "leader development" to refer to initiatives designed primarily to develop individual leaders' capabilities, and reserve "leadership development" for efforts to develop networks of leaders who can work together (Day, 2003). That conception of leadership development is becoming more prominent as the concepts of collaborative or shared leadership have gained favor for use in complex multiparty settings (Chrislip & Larson, 1994).

This understanding of leader and network development as warp and woof also fits very closely with models of collective expertise being discussed in scientific literature about networks (Cross & Cummings, 2004), competence, expertise, professional development and communities of practice (Wenger, McDermott, & Snyder, 2002), and professional performance. "The expertise needed in the knowledge society cannot be understood by referring only to a sum of individual cognitive competencies, but also to joint or shared competence manifest in the dynamic functioning of communities and networks of experts and professionals as well as supporting tools and instruments" (Hakkarainen et al., 2004, p. 8).

Visions for the Future Direction of Public Health Leadership Development in the United States

The data and recommendations from graduates and key informants summarized above endorse the program's historic emphases on both leader and network development, and offer ways to strengthen both. Future versions of PHLI should integrate leader development and leadership network development tightly with one another and with applied leadership work on issues of importance to agencies and systems. Such applied work can be quite valuable for both leadership learning and network development during the program itself. In addition, the long-term collaborations that emerge from PHLI can and should be nurtured. This study found that they can have significant effects.

Evaluation Case Study Summary

This study benefited from sufficient resources to hire a lead program evaluator and several graduate research assistants to assist with all phases. Keys to success were taking great care to design the study to meet stakeholders' information needs; spending a great deal of time developing the survey and interview guides and basing them on preliminary interviews and pilot tests with graduates; and taking several months to carefully analyze and interpret the data. We also learned to allot enough time for data analysis, and were reminded of the importance of limiting data collected to amounts that one will have time to analyze thoroughly. The full study and the instruments used are available at www.phli.org/evalreports.

Note

This Case Study was originally published as Karl E. Umble, Sandra J. Diehl, and Susan Haws (2007). *Developing Leaders, Building Networks: An Evaluation of the National Public Health Leadership Institute, 1991–2006*. Chapel Hill: North Carolina Institute for Public Health.

References

Chrislip, D. D., & Larson, C. E. (1994). *Collaborative Leadership: How Citizens and Civic Leaders Can Make a Difference*. San Francisco, CA: Jossey-Bass.

Cross, R., & Cummings, J. N. (2004). Tie and Network Correlates of Individual Performance in Knowledge-Intensive Work. *Academy of Management Journal* 47(6): 928–937.

Day, D. (2003). Leadership Development: A Review in Context. *Leadership Quarterly* 4: 581–613.

Hakkarainen, K., Palonen, T., Paavola, S., & Lehtinen, E. (2004). *Communities of Networked Expertise*. Oxford, UK: Elsevier Ltd.

Miles, M. B., & Huberman, A. M. (1994). *Qualitative Data Analysis*, 2nd ed. Thousand Oaks, CA: Sage Publications.

Patton, M. Q. (1990). *Qualitative Research and Evaluation Methods*. Thousand Oaks, CA: Sage Publications.

Wenger, E., McDermott, R., & Snyder, W. (2002). *Cultivating Communities of Practice: A Guide to Managing Knowledge*. Boston: Harvard Business School Press.

Source: Reproduced from Karl E. Umble et al. (2007). *Developing Leaders, Building Networks: An Evaluation of the National Public Health Leadership Institute—1991–2006*. Chapel Hill, NC: North Carolina Institute for Public Health. http://www.phli.org/evalreports/index.htm. Accessed August 1, 2012.

Case Study 27-C

Evaluating the Effectiveness of the Survive and Thrive Training Program for New Local Health Officials

Sue Ann Sarpy and Seth Kaplan

Background

Sarpy and Associates, LLC (Sarpy and Associates), develops and implements evaluation systems to assess the effectiveness of various types of workforce training efforts, including those directed toward the development of public health professionals. The Sarpy and Associates research team developed and implemented an evaluation to assess the effectiveness of the National Association of County and City Health Officials (NACCHO) *Survive and Thrive Training: A Roadmap for New Local Health Officials* (Survive and Thrive).

The Survive and Thrive program was designed in 2007 in response to a need for action-oriented programs that are tailored to train new local health officials—top executives who have served in their position at the local health departments (LHDs) for two years or less—effective strategies and solutions to respond to a host of local-level challenges. More specifically, the Survive and Thrive program was developed to increase the competence and skills of new local health officials (LHOs) to maintain and succeed ("survive and thrive") within the multifaceted environment of local health practice (that is, the knowledge and skills needed to build, maintain, and enhance public health capacity and infrastructure).

Survive and Thrive is a 12-month program consisting of five major program components: (1) pre-workshop preparation (i.e., two online assessments and reading assignments); (2) training modules that are presented at three workshops; (3) group participation that contributes to peer learning among fellows; (4) coaching by experienced local health officials; and (5) an individual development plan that includes individually tailored learning tasks.

(Continues)

Management and leadership skills for leaders are emphasized in the Survive and Thrive curriculum. Those LHOs completing Survive and Thrive will become more effective leaders for, and managers within, their local health departments. Specific competency expectations entail LHOs completing the program to be able to:

- Clearly describe their roles and responsibilities within their local departments (LHDs) and their LHDs' roles and responsibilities within their local public health systems to their staff and a variety of public audiences;
- Effectively engage elected officials, governing boards, and state health departments in carrying out the roles and responsibilities of their LHDs;
- Effectively manage their LHDs, which includes strategic planning and oversight of human, financial, and information resources;
- Effectively engage community partners in developing local public health systems for community health improvement and community preparedness initiatives;
- Rapidly access peer and coaching resources that may assist in developing leadership skills needed to address and resolve problems and issues that challenge LHOs.

Development Process

Several steps were followed in developing the Sarpy and Associates Evaluation Plan of the Survive and Thrive Program. Importantly, a participatory approach was undertaken in developing the evaluation so that input from all major program stakeholders was included in each phase of the process. First, all existing information regarding the development of the Survive and Thrive program was reviewed. This included results of the brief environmental scan and notes from previous advisory workgroup meetings. Furthermore, the preliminary curriculum plan was reviewed, including documentation of major modifications made. Second, all relevant literature regarding public health leadership and top executive development programs and their evaluation efforts was gathered and reviewed. Based on this information, preliminary evaluation measures and a related logic model were designed. These measures were presented and critiqued by major project stakeholders, including advisory board members who represent new and seasoned local health officers and boards of health, curriculum designers, NACCHO Survive and Thrive program staff, and representatives from the Robert Wood Johnson Foundation (RWJ), which funded the program. Their input was incorporated into the final evaluation plan.

Survive and Thrive Logic Model

As part of the Sarpy and Associates evaluation activities, a logic model of the Survive and Thrive program was developed (see **Figure 27-2**). A logic model is a systemic way to visually present the relationships between the program inputs, activities, and changes or expected results. As such, it links the program outcomes (short, intermediate, and long term) with program activities designed to achieve these outcomes and the principles of the program. The Survive and Thrive logic model was used to clarify stakeholders' understanding of the program and help focus the evaluation activities.

The Survive and Thrive logic model follows an outcome approach in that it describes the program's anticipated outcomes or impact over time (from short-term to intermediate to long-term outcomes). The logic model visually presents and documents the relationships among the program components (that is, program activities that lead to their related outcomes). This type of logic model focuses on the early steps of program planning in an attempt to highlight the approach and expectations behind the intended results of the Survive and Thrive program. The outcome approach logic models tend to be most useful in designing effective evaluation and reporting strategies. In this way, the logic model helps to elucidate the ways in which the new Survive and Thrive program will be evaluated in terms of short-term, intermediate, and long-term outcomes. The model clarifies not only what a program expects to achieve (that is, short-term and long-term outcomes) but also how the program achieves them (that is, inputs and activities).

In other words, the logic model helps to outline the approach and expectations underlying the NACCHO Survive and Thrive program and projected outcomes. The logic model was used during various phases of the evaluation development and implementation. That is, the logic model provided the general road map of the program objective and outcomes. In this way, it is used to generate discussions that help clarify the goals and intended outcomes to align the expectations among the various program stakeholders.

The Survive and Thrive logic model contains two separate but related categories: (1) Planned Work (i.e., inputs and activities) and (2) Program Results (i.e., outputs, short-, intermediate-, long-term outcomes and effects). The

Mission: To prepare new local health officials with the necessary knowledge and skills to succeed in the multifaceted environment of local public health practice.

Inputs	Activities	Outputs	Short-Term Outcomes (1–2 yr)	Intermediate Outcomes (3–4 yr)	Long-Term Outcomes (5–6 yr)	Effect (7–10 yr)
Robert Wood Johnson Foundation support and expertise	Recruit cohort of 30 new LHOs (i.e., two years or less experience) to participate— in the 12-month S&T program.	30 qualified LHO applicants enrolled (i.e., fellows)	Fellows are satisfied with S&T program components (including relevance and usefulness of content and activities)	Contingent of trained coaches is developed	S&T program helps to build capacity of the local health departments (e.g., improved core functions; accreditation of LHDs)	S&T program graduates and program-related activities strengthen the infrastructure of public health
National Association of County and City Health Organizations expertise including program staff activities and support	Recruit seven experienced LHOs to serve as coaches and one experienced LHO to provide coaching support	Seven experienced LHOs selected and trained to serve as coaches and one experienced LHO selected and trained to provide coaching support	Fellows are more self-aware in their LHD leadership and management activities	Contingent of trained faculty is developed		
NACCHO Advisory Workgroup expertise	Coaching training module for seven seasoned LHOs serving as coaches	Coaches engage in activities	Fellows demonstrate increased competence and skills to maintain and succeed (survive and thrive) in their job (i.e., self-knowledge, interpersonal skills, systems knowledge)	Fellows apply their training-related competence and skill to improve their general on-the-job performance	Greater support for the development of new leaders is achieved	
Curriculum designer expertise	S&T Program Components: Pre-workshop preparation • self-assessments • readings	Workshop training modules are implemented and are responsive and of high quality		Fellows apply their acquired training-related competence and skill in other venues (e.g., boards, volunteer activities, networks)		
Evaluation team expertise	Workshop 1 (three days) • Six interactive, faculty-led modules including panel discussions • Fellows develop an individual learning contract with coach review • Peer learning via group and networking exercises	Supplemental trainings (e.g., webinars) are presented according to fellows' needs and evaluation results	Fellows complete their learning contracts with the assistance of their coaches	Fellows continue to use and expand their contacts and related networking activities to benefit their LHDs		
New LHOs as participants		S&T fellows and coaches attend workshops and engage in activities	Fellows apply their acquired competence and skill to improve their training-related on-the-job behaviors	Fellows and those with whom they work feel that are more effective leaders		
Seasoned LHOs serving as coaches	Fellows and coaches provide information for content of Workshop 2	S&T fellows engage in peer learning (e.g., conference calls)				
Seasoned LHOs and national experts serving as faculty	Workshop 2 (two days) • Six months after Workshop 1 • Four interactive, faculty-led modules • Topics identified by fellows • Fellows review learning contract • Peer learning via group exercises and discussion	S&T fellows engage in coaching sessions (e.g., conference calls)	Graduated fellows create action plans to put S&T experiences into action	Fellows maintain their formal ties to the S&T program through alumni participation (e.g., recruiting, serving as coaches)		
LHDs in targeted regions including supervisory and organizational support (e.g., board of health members; county commissioners)		S&T fellows and coaches participate in the 360-degree evaluation and feedback process	Fellows maintain their relationships that were developed through the S&T program			
	Workshop 3 • Two interactive/faculty-led presentations • Presentation of individual projects	S&T fellows implement and modify their independent development plans and learning contracts	Fellows present their S&T experiences and training-related activities at national conferences and forums			
	Tailored 360-degree performance evaluation and feedback process developed	S&T fellows become resources to one another and engage in networking activities				
	Refine workshops as program proceeds based on feedback from participants.					
	Webinars are presented according to S&T fellows' needs and results of workshop evaluations.					

Contextual Factors: Organizational Factors in Local Health Departments Influencing S&T Training

FIGURE 27-2 The Survive and Thrive Road Map for New Local Health Officials Program Logic Model: Pilot Phase.
Source: Reprinted with permission from Sue Ann Sarpy.

(Continues)

Planned Work portion of the Survive and Thrive logic model outlines the resources and actions needed to achieve the intended results. The Program Results section of the Survive and Thrive logic model describes the specific, measurable, action-oriented, realistic, and time outcomes associated with the program.

In interpreting the Survive and Thrive logic model, it is important to recognize the linear and columnar depiction of the program. That is, one can move from left to right in the model to gain greater insight into the underlying logical reasoning of each program phase using "if . . . then" statements. More specifically, one can assume that *if* the inputs explicated in the model are available, *then* these resources will be used to accomplish the Survive and Thrive program activities. *If* the Survive and Thrive program activities are accomplished, *then* the products and services highlighted in the Survive and Thrive program will be delivered. *If* the products and services are generated, *then* the fellows will benefit in Survive and Thrive program-specific ways. *If* the fellows benefit by attending and graduating from the program, *then* certain changes in their respective LHDs, communities, and the public health system will likely occur. The linkages among major components are indicated by the large arrows connecting each column. It should be noted that the individual program components are not separately linked due to the inextricable relationships among program components. For example, the Survive and Thrive 360-degree evaluation process is heavily dependent upon the facilitated feedback sessions with the coaches. This informational session is then used to create and modify the Learning Contracts and Independent Development Plans (IDPs). Therefore, the columns as a whole are linked rather than the individual programmatic components. This point will be further clarified in the evaluation discussion that follows.

The Survive and Thrive logic model is useful not only in providing program stakeholders with a road map of the approach and expectations behind the program and for communicating projected outcomes, but also in affording all stakeholders the opportunity to have a greater understanding of evaluation and reporting strategies. That is, the Survive and Thrive logic model guides the way in which the program can be evaluated with respect to short-, intermediate-, and long-term outcomes.

Evaluation Framework

The practice and academic literature has long recognized the need for comprehensive systematic evaluations of the effectiveness of training with respect to increasing training-related knowledge, performance, and desired outcomes. In response, the Sarpy and Associates evaluation team established a standardized process for assessing the effectiveness of training programs to assist to organizations with ongoing quality control activities. This comprehensive training evaluation framework is straightforward and provides information on trainees' satisfaction, learning, and performance, and the effect of the training on meeting the desired organizational results. The Sarpy and Associates evaluation process is consistent with the academic and practice literature and has been utilized to assess other public health workforce development and training degree programs, occupational healthy and safety training, and minority worker training programs.

More specifically, the evaluation process for assessing the effectiveness of training programs was established consistent with Kirkpatrick's training evaluation framework (Kirkpatrick, 1959; 1994). Kirkpatrick's framework includes four levels of evaluation criteria: Level 1: Reactions (evaluations of trainees' reactions to the training program and its content); Level 2: Learning (evaluations of the extent to which trainees acquired the knowledge, skills, abilities, and attitude during training); Level 3: Behavior (evaluations of the extent to which the knowledge, skills, abilities, and attitudes learned during training transfer to improved performance on the job); Level 4: Results (evaluations of the extent to which the results of the training program contribute to the objectives of the organization). Moreover, the evaluation procedures are strategically designed to assist in enhancing project-planning efforts such as revising training course objectives, modifying training system features (e.g., training delivery modalities), and attending to organizational factors (e.g., communication/coordination systems, resource availability) that may be affecting the transfer of training to the job and related outcomes. Although most training program evaluations utilize only Level 1 criteria, the Sarpy and Associates evaluation process uses Level 1, 2, 3, and 4 criteria to assess training program effectiveness. This evaluation framework was used to design the evaluation measures to assess program effectiveness of the Survive and Thrive program and to address the major goals of the evaluation (see **Table 27-2**).

TABLE 27-2 Overview of Sarpy and Associates Evaluation Plan

Focus of Evaluation	Method	Data Source	Time	Information Provided
Reactions: Measures of opinions or feelings about various aspects of training program including affective (satisfaction) and utility (relevance) judgments	Level 1 Training Module Evaluation questionnaire (fellow version)	Fellow	Following completion of each training module	Qualitative and quantitative information regarding effectiveness of training module (e.g., content, instructor, format)
	Level 1 Training Module Evaluation questionnaire (fellow version)	Faculty	Following completion of training module	Qualitative and quantitative information regarding effectiveness of logistical aspects of training (e.g., support services, facilities)
	Level 1 Workshop Evaluation questionnaire	Fellow	Following completion of each workshop	Qualitative and quantitative information regarding workshop effectiveness, learning experiences, and competency enhancement
	Level 1 Training Program Evaluation structured interview	Fellow	Following program completion (exit interview)	Qualitative and quantitative information regarding effectiveness of various program components and overall effectiveness
	Level 1 Training Program focus group	Fellow, Coach	Following completion of training for each cohort	Qualitative and quantitative information regarding various program components and overall program effectiveness
Learning: Determination of the extent to which specific competencies and skills have changed as a result of training	Level 2 Coaching Evaluation questionnaire	Coach	Following (post-test) coaching training	Qualitative and quantitative information regarding attainment of learning objectives associated with coaching training
	Level 2 Training Module Evaluation questionnaire	Fellow, Coach	Following completion of each training module (post-test)	Quantitative information regarding attainment of learning objectives and related competencies and skills
	Level 2 Mid-year Assessment of IDP	Coach	6 months following Workshop 1	Qualitative and quantitative information regarding key indicators of fellow's program commitment

(Continues)

TABLE 27-2 Overview of Sarpy and Associates Evaluation Plan *(Continued)*

Focus of Evaluation	Method	Data Source	Time	Information Provided
Behavior: Determination of the extent to which specific training-related activities are performed more frequently on the job as a result of training	Level 3 Performance Evaluation questionnaire (fellow version)	Fellow	Pre-training, directly following graduation	Qualitative and quantitative information regarding performance of training-related activities on the job
	Level 3 Performance Evaluation questionnaire (other raters version)	Immediate supervisor, Direct reports, Peers, Other organizational constituents	Pre-training, directly following graduation	Qualitative and quantitative information from LHO direct reports regarding fellows' performance of training-related activities on the job
	Level 3 Learning Contract/ Independent Development Plan Evaluation	Fellows	Following program graduation	Qualitative and quantitative information regarding the completion of Learning Contract/IDP including barriers to completion and intended future actions
	Level 3 Social Networking Among Fellows and Coaches	Fellow, Coach	Directly following Workshops 1, 2, and 3, and 3–6 months after graduation	Social network analyses to provide information regarding the change in interaction among program participants and in problem-solving capacity using peers as resources
Results: Determination of whether improved training-related performance results in valued organizational outcomes	Level 4 Outcome Evaluation	Existing LHD documentation	Pre-training, directly following graduation, 3–6 months after graduation	Quantitative information regarding the effect of the training on LHD organizational objectives (e.g., reduced turnover, higher productivity, greater community service)
	Organizational Factors Survey	Fellow, Direct reports, Immediate supervisor, Other	Pre-training, directly following graduation	Quantitative information of situations and actions that indicate organizational support for training-related competencies, skills, and behaviors

Source: Reprinted with permission from Sue Ann Sarpy.

Level 1: Reactions

Level 1 evaluations are designed to measure reactions to the training program. These evaluations assess the individual's thoughts or feelings about the training, including the perceived effectiveness of the instructor, and training content, format, and delivery method. Level 1 evaluations assess affective reactions, such as level of satisfaction and enjoyment of the training, and utility judgments, such as perceived relevance and practical value of the training for subsequent job performance. With respect to the current evaluation process, Level 1 measures include the use of Training Module Evaluation questionnaires administered to fellows, coaches, and faculty following each training module and workshop. Note that data captured from the coaches (i.e., seasoned LHOs) provide expert opinion concerning the content and delivery of the training. Furthermore, structured interviews and focus groups are held with fellows and coaches following completion of the training to gather information with respect to effectiveness of each program component as well as overall effectiveness of the program.

Level 2: Learning

Level 2 evaluations are designed to measure the extent to which the training participants acquired the principles, facts, techniques, and attitudes stated in the competency-related learning objectives of the Survive and Thrive training. Evaluation of learning gains, including case studies, behavioral role plays, and scenario-based simulated exercises, are examples of Level 2 tools used to assess learning. Level 2 measures include traditional knowledge measures (e.g., written tests) as well as measures of behavior and skill demonstration (e.g., performance-based tests). These measures, however, do not include measures of on-the-job performance, which are considered Level 3 criteria. With respect to the current training evaluation, various training module evaluations were administered to the fellows and coaches following training. Furthermore, coaches completed a mid-year assessment of fellows' progress on their IDP to monitor progress and provide relevant feedback.

Level 3: Behaviors

Level 3 evaluations are designed to assess the extent to which the acquired learning transfers to improved job performance; that is, how trainees apply the learned principles and techniques to desired on-the-job performance. Level 3 measures are designed to assess the extent to which the training-related activities and behaviors are performed more frequently in the work setting. Level 3 evaluations included a tailored 360-degree evaluation and feedback process that was administered before and after the training program. This type of evaluation and feedback system involves ratings from various sources, including direct reports, peers, supervisors, coaches, and the LHOs themselves (i.e., self-ratings), as well as other organizational constituents (e.g., state department representatives, community partners). Obtaining information from multiple sources, experiences, and perspectives imparts a more thorough and accurate analysis of the effectiveness of the fellow's training-related performance and often leads to greater self-awareness for the individual. Because the curriculum targets specific knowledge, skills, abilities, and related competencies directed at improving the new LHO's performance in their individual job setting, a tailored 360-degree performance measure was created that focused on behaviors critical to the success of a new LHO. Also, social network analysis was conducted at several points during the program to track the growth of professional relationships and networks (e.g., participants' providing and seeking resources and information to/from each other) that developed over the yearlong program.

Level 4: Results

Level 4 evaluations are designed to assess the utility of the training program in terms of its contribution to the objectives of the organization. Results of training can include outcomes such as increases in service, quality, or workforce retention. This type of evaluation provides information concerning the effect of training on the organization's bottom line. Whereas a Level 3 training evaluation effort focuses on the extent to which training leads to improved individual or team-level performance, a Level 4 evaluation examines the extent to which training is associated with outcomes that are expected from the demonstration of these behaviors. It should be noted that one cannot simply assume that because trainees (fellows) report favorable reactions to the training methods utilized by the Survive and Thrive training program that they will acquire the intended competencies and skills. Similarly, positive reactions and learning do not necessarily translate into LHOs performing the training-related behaviors in their respective LHDs. In fact, it has been demonstrated that trainee reactions, learning, behaviors, and results are often not as closely related to one another as is often assumed. A primary reason for this disconnect is the influence of contextual or organizational factors. These factors (e.g., lack of needed equipment and supplies;

(*Continues*)

poor communication and coordination) may inhibit the demonstration of appropriate training-related behaviors of the LHOs and desired results of the Survive and Thrive program. Therefore, the Survive and Thrive Organizational Factors survey was developed. This survey was administered to the fellows and their supervisors, direct reports, and various organizational constituents to gain a greater understanding of the Survive and Thrive program effectiveness.

Evaluation Methodology

The Sarpy and Associates research team established a rigorous process for objectively evaluating training program effectiveness. In the management and organizational behavioral literatures, several general recommendations have been advanced as guidelines to follow for designing effective leadership and executive development evaluations. Noteworthy, the evaluation plan generated by the Sarpy and Associates evaluation team followed each of these recommendations. More specifically, it is recommended that the program stakeholders should be engaged during the various phases of the evaluation development process to account for the multiple perspectives and differing needs among program stakeholders. The Survive and Thrive program stakeholders have been involved in each major phase of the evaluation development process and have provided feedback and suggestions on all aspects of the evaluation plan and resulting activities, including its implementation.

It is also important to design the evaluation process *before* the Survive and Thrive program is initiated. Ideally, the program design and evaluation design should be conducted in a parallel fashion, as evinced by the current Survive and Thrive project. It is also recommended that the outcomes of the program be clarified, preferably through the use of a logic model such as the one developed for the Survive and Thrive program, to delineate the types and levels of the outcomes. Furthermore, the purpose of the evaluation and its major goals should be clarified, as well as how the evaluation results should be used. The evaluation meetings with the Survive and Thrive program stakeholders were vital in this effort. Related, multiple measures and multiple sources should be used to assess the complex outcomes associated with leadership and executive development programs. The methodology utilized by the Sarpy and Associates evaluation plan incorporates the multi-method, multi-source approach and is further explained in the following section.

1. *Multi-methods.* The Sarpy and Associates evaluation process is an integrated mixed methods programmatic assessment designed to gather both quantitative and qualitative data. In this way, information can be obtained to demonstrate not only *what* effects the program has with respect to its intended goals and objectives, but also *how* and *why* the training program achieved these effects. In order to gain a comprehensive representation of whether the Survive and Thrive program goals and objectives were attained as well as the relative effectiveness of the program activities and components for achieving these program goals and objectives, a combination of both quantitative and qualitative data is collected and analyzed. Furthermore, the evaluation utilizes various methods of data collection to gather this information, including questionnaires, focus groups, and structured interviews. In order to integrate this information, content is standardized across survey methods. In addition, this standardization of measures allows for direct comparisons across respondents and LHDs.

2. *Multi-sources (multi-stakeholder).* The Sarpy and Associates evaluation process also implements a multi-source evaluation system that is associated with a 360-degree feedback system. The evaluation also includes gathering information from both coaches and fellows regarding the effectiveness of the training modules and workshops. Obtaining information from multiple sources, experiences, and perspectives imparts a more thorough and accurate analysis of the effectiveness of the program. In addition, gathering information from the various stakeholders lends greater perspective and thereby more credibility to the evaluation process, particularly regarding feedback of the results. Furthermore, these multi-source evaluations are typically associated with leadership training and executive development programs.

3. *Contextual (Organizational) Factors.* The Sarpy and Associates evaluation process is unique in that it also examines the influence of contextual (i.e., organizational) factors on training effectiveness. In understanding the effects of workforce development initiatives on building capacity of public health workers, it is crucial to consider contextual factors such as organizational features that can either positively or negatively influence the effects of training. For example, one often-asked and very important question for research and practice in public health workforce development focuses on the effect of the organization itself on the capacity to

perform training-related behaviors. These organizational factors are the conditions in the work environment that can either facilitate or inhibit the attainment of high levels of effectiveness in LHOs' performance. Once should consider these factors in examining workforce training initiatives and, in particular, their effect on workers' ability to translate the training-related knowledge, skills, abilities, and attitudes into improved performance on training-related tasks and associated outcomes. This is particularly relevant to the Survive and Thrive training initiative with respect to addressing the issue of inclusion of representatives from LHDs that vary in structure, size, resources, and so on.

4. *Evaluation Goals.* The Sarpy and Associates evaluation process is designed to assess the Survive and Thrive program with respect to five questions associated with the evaluation goals:

1. Is the curriculum achieving the stated goals and objectives of the program?
2. Are the delivery modalities being used for the curriculum most appropriate?
3. Is the coaching component of the program working as expected?
4. Are the fellows using the skills, knowledge, and abilities targeted in the curriculum?
5. What are the general recommendations for continuous quality improvement of the project?

In addressing these questions, evidence can be provided with respect to short-term outcomes of increasing competence and skills of new LHOs to maintain and succeed in their jobs (formative evaluation) to ensure continuous improvement of the curriculum. The evaluation is also designed to gather evidence of program impact (summative evaluation) to demonstrate its relative effectiveness in building LHD capacity, developing effective leadership, and strengthening the infrastructure of public health.

The evaluation goals and associated questions were identified by NACCHO and the Survive and Thrive Advisory Workgroup as critical to assessing the effectiveness of the program. In addition, the lead evaluator reviewed and discussed each of the goals in subsequent advisory committee meetings to ensure alignment of the evaluation goals with those of the major stakeholders' expectations. A matrix was developed that highlights the evaluation goals, associated questions, and methodology used to address them (see **Table 27-3**) In this way, the stakeholders are able to visualize the general purpose and expected results for each of the major goals.

TABLE 27-3 Matrix of Survive and Thrive Evaluation Goals, Related Issues, and Methodology

Evaluation Goals	Related Issues	Methods
Is the curriculum achieving the stated goals and objectives of the program? Goals: 1. Increased competence and skills to succeed in the job (short term); build capacity, develop effective leadership, and strengthen the infrastructure of public health 2. Test curriculum and implementation methods 3. Develop "esprit de corps," build network, and increase sense of pride in being an LHO	Did the fellows report learning gains in the modules? Did the fellows demonstrate incremental gains in Survive and Thrive competencies? Did fellows demonstrate incremental gains in Survive and Thrive behaviors (360-degree instrument)? Did the fellows complete IDP tasks? Were the major curriculum components implemented as planned? Were the major curriculum components implemented in the most effective manner (i.e., pre-assessments, workshops, coaching, learning contracts)? Did fellows develop relationships to create a cohesive network, develop an esprit de corps, and increase their sense of pride in being an LHO?	Training Module Evaluations (fellows, coaches) Workshop Evaluations (fellows, coaches) Final Evaluation Survey (fellows, coaches) Survive and Thrive 360 surveys (fellows, other raters) Learning Contract/IDP final completion Social Networking surveys

TABLE 27-3 Matrix of Survive and Thrive Evaluation Goals, Related Issues, and Methodology (*Continued*)

Evaluation Goals	Related Issues	Methods
Are the delivery modalities being used for the curriculum most appropriate?	Are the modules/workshops effective? Are the principles of adult learning and instructional design followed? Are the trainees, coaches, and faculty generally satisfied with the workshop content/format/instructors? Are the webinars effective? Are there differences among the fellows and coaches?	Training Module Evaluations (fellows, coaches, faculty) Workshop Evaluations (fellows, coaches) Focus Groups (fellows, coaches) Exit Interviews (fellows) Final Evaluation Survey (fellows, coaches)
Is the coaching component of the program working as expected?	Did the coaches assist the fellows in attaining their goals in the program? Were the coaches satisfied with the coaching component? Were the fellows satisfied with the coaching component?	Mid-year IDP assessments (coaches) Focus Groups (fellows, coaches) Exit interviews (fellows) Final Evaluation Survey (fellows, coaches)
Are the fellows using the skills, knowledge, and abilities targeted in the curriculum?	Did the fellows demonstrate the competencies and behaviors back on the job? Did the fellows complete the IDP tasks? Did the fellows demonstrate other examples of program effect in their LHD? What are the common and important barriers and facilitators affecting LHO performance and program effectiveness? Were the same factors identified across LHDs?	Survive and Thrive 360 surveys Organizational Factors survey Learning Contract/IDP final completion
What are the general recommendations for continuous quality improvement of the project?	What strengths and areas for improvement exist in Survive and Thrive (cross-cutting issues)? What are the best practices identified? What are the lessons learned? What are the general recommendations for improvement?	Workshop 1 evaluation report Workshop 2 presentation Overall evaluation presentation Draft Survive and Thrive Evaluation Report Final Survive and Thrive Evaluation Report

Source: Reprinted with permission from Sue Ann Sarpy.

In addressing each of the evaluation goals, specific best practices and lessons learned are identified as well as a discussion that includes general recommendations for improvement. However, the major stakeholders requested that beyond these more narrowly defined issues remained a need for the cross-cutting strengths and areas for improvement that exist in the Survive and Thrive program as a whole. Therefore, the focus of the final evaluation goal centered on the cross-cutting themes that emerge as a result of examining the four other evaluation goals. In this way, regardless of the chosen format of the program in future years (that is, greater including of distance learning methods; regional versus national approach) the primary drivers of programmatic excellence are identified and can be better incorporated to ensure program success.

Because of the participatory process used in developing and implementing the evaluation, the five evaluation goals are reflective of the key concerns and questions of the major stakeholders. That is, the goals have been developed and executed in an iterative process so that major stakeholders can utilize resulting information to assist in further program refinement and growth. More specifically, the evaluation results can be used (1) to make better-informed decisions; (2) to provide feedback to major stakeholders for continued improvement; and (3) to demonstrate achievement of desired outcomes to ensure sustainability and growth of the program. In this way, the information can be used to address the issues of potential program reach and sustainability that are key considerations for the major program stakeholders as the program transitions beyond the pilot phase to its full-scale implementation.

Conclusion

The Sarpy and Associates evaluation is designed to provide evidence of the extent to which the Survive and Thrive program meets its immediate goal of increasing the competencies and skills (i.e., self-knowledge, interpersonal skills, and systems knowledge) of new LHOs to maintain and succeed ("survive and thrive") within the multifaceted environment of local health practice. Therefore, the evaluation assesses the effectiveness of the Survive and Thrive training curriculum in achieving program goals and objectives, examines major programmatic components, provides information regarding best practices and lessons learned, and offers general recommendations for continuous quality improvement of the program curriculum. The Sarpy and Associates outcome evaluation is standardized yet responsive to any programmatic changes that occur, and, as such, is used throughout the project to evaluate all program components and provide interim feedback to enhance programmatic effectiveness. In meeting this objective, the evaluation measures the success of the NACCHO Survive and Thrive program in meeting its specific objectives associated with the content as to evaluate more broadly define goals such as helping to determine the benefits and challenges with having specific or broad requirements for selection of participants (e.g., of having a national cohort or selecting according to a specific by geography). In this way, the information can be used to address the issues of potential program reach and sustainability that are key considerations for the major program stakeholders as the program transitions beyond the current pilot phase to full-scale program implementation.

Source: Reprinted with permission from Sue Ann Sarpy.

SUMMARY

This chapter looked at the issue of evaluation of training programs, specifically leadership development programs. A number of research questions were raised for future leadership investigations. The chapter's case studies concern program evaluation at a regional and a national public health leadership institute. They document the complexity of leadership development and the concerns of trainers regarding how to assess leadership training and make it more effective.

DISCUSSION QUESTIONS

1. Why is leadership program evaluation important?
2. What is one difficulty in evaluating leadership programs?
3. How do leadership development programs differ from other training or educational programs?
4. What leadership issues do you think should be the focus of research?
5. What are some benefits to be gained by keeping a leadership journal?

EXERCISE 27-1: **Great Expectations**

Purpose: to investigate the relationship between personal expectations and training experiences

Key concepts: evaluation, leadership development, leadership expectations, lessons learned

Procedures: If you are in a leadership development program, each student or trainee should write down five expectations he or she has regarding the course. At the end of the training program, each student or trainee should review those expectations, indicate to what degree each was met, and whether he or she learned things that were not anticipated. The class or training groups should then divide into groups of 5 to 10 members and discuss the expectations and their fulfillment or lack of fulfillment.

REFERENCES

1. S. T. Gray, *Leadership Is: Evaluation with Power* (Washington, DC: Independent Sector, 1995).
2. Centers for Disease Control and Prevention, "Framework for Program Evaluation in Public Health," *MMWR* 48 (1999): RR11.
3. Centers for Disease Control and Prevention, "Framework for Program Evaluation in Public Health."
4. E. Jurkowski et al., "The Core Functions and the Role of Governance Within the Public Health Arena: A Perspective from Board of Health Members" (submitted for publication).
5. D. L. Kirkpatrick, *Evaluating Training Programs: The Four Levels*, 2nd ed. (San Francisco: Berrett-Koehler, 1998).
6. J. Hale, "Evaluation: It's Time to Go Beyond Levels 1, 2, 3, and 4," in *The 1999 ASTD Training and Performance Yearbook*, ed. J. A. Woods and J. W. Cortada (New York: McGraw-Hill, 1999).
7. M. L. Lanigan, "New Theory and Measures for Training Evaluation," in *The 1999 ASTD Training and Performance Yearbook*, ed. J. A. Woods and J. W. Cortada (New York: McGraw-Hill, 1999).
8. C. D. McCauley and M. W. Hughes-James, *An Evaluation of the Outcomes of a Leadership Development Program* (Greensboro, NC: Center for Creative Leadership, 1994).
9. McCauley and Hughes-James, *An Evaluation of the Outcomes of a Leadership Development Program.*
10. C. D. McCauley and E. Van Velsor, eds., *The Center for Creative Leadership Handbook of Leadership Development*, 2nd ed. (San Francisco: Jossey-Bass, 2004).
11. J. W. Martineau, K. M. Hannum, and C. Reinelt, "Introduction," in *The Handbook of Leadership Development Evaluation*, ed. K. M. Hannum, J. W. Martineau, and C. Reinelt (San Francisco: Jossey-Bass, 2007).
12. E. J. Davidson and J. W. Martineau, "Strategic Uses of Evaluation," in *The Handbook of Leadership Development Evaluation*, ed. K. M. Hannum, J. W. Martineeau, and C. Reinelt (San Francisco: Jossey-Bass, 2007).
13. K. E. Umble, S. J. Diehl, A. Gunn, and S. Haws, *Developing Leaders, Building Networks: An Evaluation of the National Public Health Leadership Institute—1991–2006* (Chapel Hill: North Carolina Institute for Public Health, 2007).

The Future

CHAPTER 28

The Global Public Health Leader

"When it comes to global health, there is no them… only us."

—Global Health Council

The requirements associated with successful leadership seem to present leaders with a moving target. Our world is ever changing at the same time that it appears to be flattening. As the world changes and flattens, public health leaders need to be flexible enough to adjust to these changes. Not only is public health important for building the infrastructure of public health in the United States, but leadership is important for building the infrastructure of public health around the world.[1] With the health issues of the world becoming more complex, the number of agencies addressing these issues appears to be increasing as well. Leadership is critical for this growing response to health and disease around the world. Public health leaders are needed for policy development, development and formulation of innovative public health and primary care programs, monitoring of global health issues, and evaluation. Leadership development programs similar to those in the United States are needed throughout the world. If these programs can be collaborative with the leadership development programs in the United States, coordinated global public health initiatives become more possible. As we look forward, we discover the necessity of understanding people throughout the world.

With an understanding of the importance of broadening our view of leadership and the recognition that being a leader on a global level may be different, it is worth briefly looking at the GLOBE Project (Globe Leadership and Organizational Behavior Effectiveness Research Project), begun in 1991 by Robert J. House of the Wharton School of Business. The GLOBE Project became a 62-society, 11-year study involving 170 researchers throughout the world. The respondents included more than 17,000 middle managers from about 950 organizations in the food processing, financial services, and telecommunications industries. The 62 societies were classified into 10 cultural clusters: Anglo Cultures, Latin Europe, Nordic Europe, Germanic Europe, Eastern Europe, Latin America, Sub-Saharan Africa, Arab Cultures,

Southern Asia, and Confucian Asia. The GLOBE work was guided by the Implicit Leadership Theory, which states that from childhood, people gradually develop beliefs about the characteristics and behaviors of leaders.[2] House and his colleagues reported that across all societies included in the GLOBE study, people expect their leaders to be trustworthy, just, honest, decisive, encouraging, positive, motivational, able to build confidence in others, and dynamic, and to have foresight.[3] And yet leader effectiveness is clearly contextual and may vary in its presentation in different cultures and societies. With the flattening of the world, however, our overall expectation of our leaders may coalesce across cultures.

With a shift from a domestic look at leadership to a global look, public health issues such as global warming, pandemic influenza, child survival initiatives, human immunodeficiency virus/acquired immune deficiency syndrome, and other emerging and reemerging global infections become more and more important.[4] Public health leaders need to remove the barriers between countries to work in partnership with our public health colleagues all over the world. Hesselbein has stated that the time for partnership is now.[5] A world vision related to healthy families and children, excellent schools, decent and available housing and work opportunities, and health equity is necessary for international and global public health to become a reality.

It will not be possible to attain global health equity without partnerships. Collaboration becomes critical if we are to make these partnerships productive. In order to make collaboration work, it is important to move from a business-as-usual approach to a new stage of transformation that makes collaboration lead to positive change. In real collaboration, the partners become an integrated team that dialogues and debates health challenges on a global level in order to come up with potential solutions to these challenges.[6] Rosenberg and his colleagues discuss the partnership pathway as going from its beginning or genesis through the first mile, the journey, and the last mile. In the genesis comes the realization that positive changes can occur. After the right partners come together during the first mile, a shared goal or goals are set, an appropriate structure is created, system-based strategies are created, and organizational roles are defined. During the journey, management issues predominate in which there needs to be a disciplined and flexible approach that guides the partnership. The individuals who compose the partnership will also

need to take leadership roles at an individual level to bring about change. In the last mile, there will need to be adaptation to sustain the momentum created, transfer of control in a supportive way, understanding and communicating of the lessons learned, and finally a method for dissolving the partnership when the goal or goals are reached.

A cautionary note is necessary here. Public health is not the same everywhere. It has different meanings from country to country. For example, leadership is practiced differently in countries where health service is provided at the national level. In these countries, there is a clinical focus, and almost all the leaders are physicians. Public health does not extend to social and behavioral scientists and other professions in the same way. In Asia, Africa, and some European countries, public health leaders put public health and clinical health together with a primary care focus. In the United States, we tend to separate the clinical focus from the public health focus. There are strengths and weaknesses in all of these systems. In partnerships, the cultural differences must be dealt with first before the partners can ever deal with collaboration and discover ways to work together.

There is the important question of what motivates people to become involved in these important partnerships or to become involved at an individual level in improving the health of the peoples of the world. Former President Bill Clinton explored some of these issues.[7] He pointed out the increasing involvement of private citizens in doing public good. With the end of the Cold War, Clinton believes that citizen advocacy has increased, specifically in democratic societies with elected governments. Second, he argues that the explosion of information technology and the globalization of commerce have made many individuals wealthy. Finally, charitable giving has also been democratized and has increased the number of people willing to help the rest of the world. Giving takes many forms, including the giving of money, time, things, skills, and so on. Another term for when individuals become involved in these international and global activities is *social entrepreneurship*. In spite of all the barriers that can be established to block change, social entrepreneurs make positive change and create model programs in spite of the barriers.[8]

The International Health Regulations provide a blueprint for some of this work. Case Study 28-A, by Judith Munson, executive director of the International Collaborative for Public Health Emergency Preparedness (ICPHEP), explores some of these issues.

A Public Health Practice Quiz for Judith W. Munson

1. What are the emergency preparedness leadership issues in global public health?

This is an important question, because leadership in emergency preparedness in a globalized world requires a significant broadening of our knowledge. In global public health, knowledge is required about the world we live in and about the Earth we live on. We need to be alert to where the threats are and how to contain or to prevent them. These are the most essential elements.

How to pursue this knowledge; where to start? Before embarking on this adventure, consider your own personal background and your own depth of experience. This search will guide your entrance onto the international platform. Find that one country or that one region or that area of practice that has formed your life or has informed your career path. Then pursue the issues that are connected to those countries, regions, or areas of practice.

If that exercise does not provide the necessary guidance to you, then pursue one or more of the many media outlets for information. Suggestions include:

- Select and review daily online publications of international reach, for example, the *Economist*, the *International Herald Tribune*, the *Financial Times*, the *New York Times World*, or simply Reuters and CNN International.
- Access websites devoted to public health internationally, for example, the World Health Organization (www .who.int/en/), the European Union Commission on Health and Consumer Protection (http://ec.europa.eu/ dgs/health_consumer/index_en.htm), the European Centre for Disease Prevention and Control (http:// ecdc.europa.eu/), and the Pan American Health Organization (www.paho.org/).
- Subscribe to daily e-mail updates from websites with topics of interest to you (many, if not most, are free of charge).

As you use these resources, news of public health emergencies around the globe will come into your purview. They could be disease outbreaks, natural disasters, environmental contaminants, or other phenomena such as nuclear incidents, toxic spills, or the reemergence of a highly infectious communicable disease. You will also be instantly knowledgeable about the response and recovery capabilities of the public health agencies and their practitioners wherever the incident may have occurred. You will be well informed concerning threats to public health around the globe and knowledgeable about public health leadership models that work, as well as those that do not.

2. How do we develop relationships with public health leaders in other countries?

Developing relationships with public health leaders in countries other than the United States takes time, effort, and attention. Relationships start first with a meeting and then proceed according to mutual needs and perceived benefits. To begin, it is essential to meet the other individual, at least initially, "in person." The best place to meet public health leaders from other countries is at conferences, seminars, or other professional gatherings. But even in these familiar settings, it takes an effort to make an acquaintance and to establish a rapport. It is rare for the individual from the foreign country to initiate a conversation. More typically, it is the person who is a citizen of the host country who engages others who are in attendance. This is not surprising, because one accepts the role of host and the other accepts the role as guest. If a rapport is established and a common collegial interest has been discussed and acknowledged, an exchange of calling cards signals the potential for developing a relationship.

Still rare, but more and more possible as technology provides even greater (and more cost-effective) options, the "in person" requirement can take place by other than face-to-face conventional meetings. Technological innovations have been used more and more in establishing and enhancing personal contacts internationally because of the cost savings. Some examples are participating in an online chat room, posting regularly on a blog, or actively participating in an online continuing education offering. Internet-based course offerings and conference calls initiated by international professional associations that make use of VOIP (voice over Internet protocol, also known as Internet telephony) mechanisms such as Skype (http://about.skype.com/) provide opportunities to "meet" public health leaders from other countries without leaving your office. When the conference call for the meeting uses the VOIP telephony mechanism with webcams, these audio and video conferencing mechanisms provide a close approximation of an in-person meeting or a face-to-face introduction with colleagues in foreign jurisdictions—and often the entire service is free.

(*Continues*)

Typically, however, technological enhancements are more effective after the "in-person" meeting has taken place and a baseline of interaction has been set. The conversations that take place among the participants in an Internet-based forum provide opportunities to hear a colleague express expertise on a topic of interest to you. This may prompt you to make the effort to follow up on that introductory mechanism.

But to maintain a relationship—and even to nurture it into a friendship—requires patience and understanding. E-mail is a quick and commonplace method of communicating, but there are some potential problems. Often, a name of a person e-mailing from a foreign country will incorporate accents and other diacritical marks that can throw an e-mail message or e-mail response into the spam folder, where it can sit for days or weeks without being read. The time lags occasioned by such events can often be the death knell to a developing international relationship if communication is based solely on e-mail. Making calls to a land line or to a cell phone by using the Internet (VOIP offerings) is inexpensive and can save a relationship.

3. What are the leadership and emergency preparedness issues in the application of the International Health Regulations?

The most recent version of the International Health Regulations (IHR 2005) came into force on June 15, 2007 (http://www.who.int/csr/ihr/en/). This revision represents the most important treaty to emerge from the community of nations interested in protecting the health of the world's populations. In large measure a response to the severe acute respiratory syndrome (SARS) epidemic that shook the world of public health when it circled the globe in 2003, this revision is geared toward international public health security.

The virus—which was the causative agent of the newly emerging disease—perplexed and confounded the public health practitioners and laboratory scientists around the globe because of four factors: (1) they did not know where it came from; (2) they did not know how it was transmitted; (3) they did not know how to cure it; and (4) they did not have a vaccine that could prevent it. Air travelers, exposed to the emerging virus while in Hong Kong, returned to their home countries with this new disease, which at that point did not even have a name. The name ultimately given to it described the symptoms of its victims.

The World Health Organization (WHO) and its governing body, the World Health Assembly (WHA), had been in the process of redrafting and updating the International Health Regulations (IHR 1969) even before SARS emerged. Applicable to only three diseases since 1969—cholera, plague, and yellow fever (smallpox having been declared eradicated by 1980)—the IHR (1969) were not beneficial during the SARS epidemic. Nonetheless, WHO had to step into the leadership role. It did so by issuing the first global travel alert, and shortly thereafter it issued the first emergency travel advisory. There followed a series of travel recommendations (e.g., postpone all but essential travel) until all affected destinations were removed from the list and the areas with recent transmissions were finally given the all-clear.

The SARS experience prompted more focused attention at WHO headquarters on the need to update the IHR (1969). Results came quickly. The revisions were adopted at the WHA meeting of June 2005 and came into force two years later on June 15, 2007. Instead of being applicable only to named diseases, activation of this new international framework hinges upon reporting a "public health emergency of international concern" to the National Focal Point (NFP) office. As of August 15, 2007, 179 state parties had designated an NFP office. The U.S. NFP office is located in the Department of Health and Human Services, at its operations center.

Leadership issues with regard to the implementation of the IHR (2005) abound. WHO published the IHR (2005) Areas of Work for Implementation in June 2007 (http://www.who.int/csr/ihr/area_of_work/en/index.html).

The primary leadership concern that must be addressed now is this: the need to educate our public health workforce on the provisions of the IHR and their importance to public health preparedness in every sector. This is essential. Likewise, public health faculties must make them a part of the curriculum so that the future leaders—those who are students now—graduate ready to assume their roles on the international platform.

4. Can you give an example of a successful partnership in global public health leadership?

Yes. There are several outstanding examples of successful partnering in global public health leadership. The one that is spotlighted here, however, is the "Knowledge Management for Public Health" program (also known as KM4PH) launched by WHO and its partners, including the World Federation of Public Health Associations (WFPHA), within the past couple of years (http://www.who.int/km4ph/en/).

It is an example of a working partnership between a public health agency of global reach—WHO—and its technology partner located in the heart of the American Midwest—the University of Iowa College of Public Health. The college provides the Global Public Health Campus software that allows the KM4PH's activities to be brought to public health practitioners around the globe, even countries where connectivity to the Internet is slow. The knowledge transfer opportunities and benefits are greatest under these circumstances.

KM4PH features an online discussion portal that provides an opportunity for public health practitioners, students, and academics to participate in real-time, live, Web-based conferences. Held weekly, the online conferences are conducted in several languages (different languages at different times) and can accommodate 150 participants at any one time. Those signing in are from many different countries. Participants can see the list of participants and can send e-mail messages to any one (or all) of them during the conference. The presentations are visible on the computer screen, and the voice of the presenter is heard. At times the presenter is seen as well, depending upon the availability of camera (webcam) capability. Participants can raise their hands online and be heard by using the microphone icon. Participants can even applaud!

The software the KM4PH network uses through the University of Iowa Global Campus is called Elluminate Live! It provides the online collaborative learning forum. The KM4PH program collaborates with the WFPHA, which has official relationship status with WHO. WFPHA is an organization of public health associations around the globe. It seeks to enhance international understanding among international nongovernmental, multiprofessional, and civil society organizations dedicated to developing and promoting effective global policies, all directed to improving the health of populations. WFPHA's governing members are national and regional public health associations, currently numbering more than 70. Members also include regional associations of schools of public health. The KM4PH network is an integral part of the WFPHA Strategic Plan 2007–2012.

Here in the United States, in one state, a successful organization known as ICPHEP (www.ICPHEP.org) has been mounted between and among public health and law schools in Illinois and a law school and a medical school—as well as governmental entities—in the Czech Republic. Although originating in academia, the practice community has quickly signed on, and the benefits of establishing collaborative relationships are resulting in increased interest in international affairs and its possibilities on both sides of the Atlantic. One example is the participation of the First International Fellow, the Senior Officer for Pandemic Preparedness at the Czech Ministry of Health, in the Mid-America Regional Public Health Leadership Institute at the University of Illinois, School of Public Health.

5. What are the connections between law and public health practice in a global context?

This is such an important question, because law is the foundational element of public health practice. The International Health Regulations (IHR 2005) are an excellent example of what can be achieved when the legal framework for a public health initiative has been processed, vetted, and adopted by all the members of the international community. The same can be said about the WHO Framework Convention on Tobacco Control (WHO FCTC). There are currently 168 signatories to the WHO FCTC (www.who.int/tobacco/framework/countrylist/en/index.html). These two instruments represent major strides in the practice of public health in a global context, but there are also others that are of equal importance in a regional or cross-border context.

The United States has been reaching out beyond its borders for the purpose of establishing significant relationships grounded in legal instruments or in legislative enactments. One initiative is the Early Warning Infectious Disease Surveillance (EWIDS) Program Activities on the Northern and Southern Border States (www.bt.cdc.gov/surveillance/ewids/). Another initiative consists of the four regional public health collaborations that have been established across the border areas between the United States and Canada and the United States and Mexico. Two of the many activities that are now under way are the drafting of memoranda of understanding to share data, personnel, and equipment between jurisdictions during an infectious disease public health emergency; another is expanding the Laboratory Response Network into Canada and Mexico. See Progress Areas at http://www.bt.cdc.gov/surveillance/ewids/.

Recently, the United States Senate and House of Representatives passed a joint resolution granting consent to the International Emergency Management Assistance Memorandum (IEMAMOU), which states:

> The purpose of this compact is to provide for the possibility of mutual assistance among the jurisdictions entering into this compact in managing any emergency or disaster when the affected jurisdiction or jurisdictions ask for assistance, whether arising from natural disaster, technological hazard, manmade disaster, or civil emergency aspects of resources shortages.

The IEMAMOU had been agreed upon by Connecticut, Maine, Massachusetts, New Hampshire, Rhode Island, and Vermont and the Canadian provinces of New Brunswick, Newfoundland, Nova Scotia, Prince Edward Island, and Quebec. The joint resolution can be found at http://www.ifrc.org/docs/idrl/I653EN.pdf.

GLOBAL HEALTH LEADERSHIP

Public health leaders gain from lifelong learning. Global public health cannot do its job effectively without a well-trained public health workforce. The best next step is a strong commitment to public health professionals who dedicate their lives to serving others in the international arena. It is not that leaders in the domestic arena have different leadership traits and abilities. The public health tasks of leaders domestically and globally are quite similar. According to Gundling and his associates, the differences are in the strategies used, business processes, and personal style changes related to different cultural environments.[9] The authors use a five-stage model called SCOPE. S is for seeing differences between practicing leadership in different cultures. C is for closing the gap and building intercultural relationships. O is for opening the system in order to expand the ownership and involvement in the public health enterprise. By expanding ownership and promoting approaches to health that may have been developed elsewhere, it is necessary to train future leaders from the local communities in many of these new strategies. P is for preserving balance and knowing when to change and when not to. Flexibility becomes critical. The idea of resilience becomes important, as does transparency. E is for establishing solutions and results that matter. The authors present the idea of a three-pronged process beginning with a recognition of past results, building intercultural trust, and promoting lifelong learning, leading to co-creating of solutions and then their implementation.

Global work is more than complex—it is multiplex.[10] Gundling and his colleagues argue that there are 10 traits necessary to be a successful global leader. Some of these traits are not required for domestic leadership activities. Coaching for global activities is very beneficial. The obvious first behavior is cultural self-awareness, which includes cultural issues related to health behavior. The second behavior looks for the unexpected or approaches in the environment that are unexpected for you as a new global leader. With a personal commitment to lifelong learning, there is also a strong readiness to learn new things. The third behavior relates to the skills tied to building relationships and the awareness of the importance of these relationships in building a solid public health agenda. Transactional leadership skills are the essence of this third behavior. The fourth behavior involves frame shifting. This behavior is more than paradigm busting. It involves flexibility in addressing health issues that may require leaders to change visions and directions in the way they have developed programs in the past. Expanding ownership is the next behavior. The community owns the programs and services. Agencies respond to community need with an awareness that ownership is a shared activity. The sixth behavior relates to the importance of the future development of leaders. Questions arise as to how to do this. Is it through formal training programs, mentoring and coaching, some other technique, or a combination of approaches? The seventh behavior involves the skills of adaptation and the adding of value tied to local public health practice. To do this well, leaders need to be totally self-aware and to have good judgment and perhaps restraint. These traits need to be combined with cultural and contextual awareness. The eighth set of skills involves the learning of the values of the new culture in which you work and live and the flexibility to adjust to living in the new culture and developing relationships around the values of the community. Next, global leaders have to help generate solutions to public health problems in the new country and to generate solutions across functional boundaries. By putting organizational needs and consumers up front, the final behavior involves third-way solutions, which are integration of the same behaviors discussed previously.

Exercise 28-A is based on a story of a family reunion in Moklahoma. It is Grandma and Grandpa's 60th wedding anniversary. Family have come from all over the world to attend the reunion and party. There is a big chicken dinner served with all sorts of wonderful side dishes representing the cultures of the family members. A week after the party, family members who attended the reunion come down with flu-like symptoms. Global leadership issues are involved in addressing the issue.

SUMMARY

There is increasing concern about public health challenges and practice on the global stage. This chapter has begun a discussion of leadership challenges of growing concern in the 21st century. This chapter addressed some of these issues, including the GLOBE study, international health regulations, social entrepreneurship, giving at a global level, the SCOPE model, and the 10 global leadership behaviors.

DISCUSSION QUESTIONS

1. How would you develop a global public health leadership training initiative?
2. How would you apply the International Health Regulations domestically?
3. Compare and contrast public health leadership in the United States with leadership in other places.
4. Give domestic examples of the 10 behaviors discussed by Gundling and his colleagues.

EXERCISE 28-1:   The Family Reunion: An Exercise in Global Leadership

Purpose: to explore and try to address a new foodborne virus in three countries. The virus appears in several individuals who attended a family reunion and 60th wedding anniversary in Moklahoma. Partygoers came from three different countries. One country is the United States, the second is Poland, and the third is France.

Key concepts: foodborne illness, virus, comparative health systems, global leadership behaviors

Procedures: Divide the training group into three groups representing the Centers for Disease Control and Prevention in the United States and the health ministries in France and Poland. Address the illness and its consequences and ways it will be addressed at a local level. Report back to the group as a whole.

REFERENCES

1. W. L. Roper and J. Porter, "Creating Public Health Leaders: Public Health Leadership Institutes," *Global Health Leadership and Management*, ed. W. H. Foege, N. Daulaire, R. E. Black, and C. E. Pearson (San Francisco: Jossey-Bass, 2005).
2. http://www.grovewell.com/pub-GLOBE-leadership.html, accessed March 1, 2012.
3. R. J. House, P. J. Hanges, M. Javidan, P. W. Dorfman, and V. Gupta, *Culture, Leadership, and Organizations* (Thousand Oaks, CA: Sage Publications, 2004).
4. W. H. Foege, "Preface," in Foege, Daulaire, Black, and Pearson, eds., *Global Health Leadership and Management*.
5. F. Hesselbein, "Leadership and Management for Improving Global Health," in Foege, Daulaire, Black, and Pearson, eds., *Global Health Leadership and Management*.
6. M. L. Rosenberg, E. S. Hayes, M. H. McIntyre, and N. Neill, *Real Collaboration* (Berkeley, CA: University of California Press, 2010).
7. B. Clinton, *Giving* (New York: Alfred A. Knopf, 2007).
8. D. Bornstein, *How to Change the World* (New York: Oxford University Press, 2007).
9. E. Gundling, T. Hogan, and K. Cvitkovich, *What Is Global Leadership* (Boston: Nicholas Brealey Publishing, 2011).
10. Gundling, Hogan, and Cvitkovich, *What Is Global Leadership*.

CHAPTER 29

Leadership for the 21st Century

Everyone overrates the significance of his own era. . . . Things change.

—Robert Stone, *Damascus Gate*

It is important to explore public health leadership in depth and suggest ways in which leadership knowledge can be translated into practice, especially in the coming years. American society is changing, and old leadership approaches are no longer working. Change did not stop with the new millennium, neither in society in general, nor in the area of public health. Therefore, public health leaders have to be trained to work in an environment of constant change.

American social life does not seem to be governed by natural laws.[1] Because different eras bring forth different social circumstances, different types of leaders are needed at different times. It is clear that leaders will guide social developments whatever the social climate is.

Many organizational practices now in use are out of date. Drucker identified seven organizational assumptions that no longer hold true.[2] He also identified seven realities of contemporary management. The seven realities entail that no cookie-cutter approach to

the development of organizations is feasible. People cannot all be managed in the same way. Everyone is different. Each organization has multilevel activities and services, and no one service drives the organization. New technologies, such as social networks like Facebook, Twitter, and LinkedIn, are constantly being created. Complexity rules. In addition, the command and control approaches of the past will no longer be acceptable or tolerated. Finally, global concerns will drive the organizations of the future.

LEADERSHIP CHALLENGES IN THE 21ST CENTURY

Public health leaders face 13 strategic challenges for the second decade of the 21st century (**Table 29-1**).[3] When I talked with Lenihan for the first edition of this book, the challenges were more categorical in nature. Now his challenges are systemic and more strategic in nature. Lenihan now posits that leadership challenges necessitate an adaptive response of a whole agency or an entire community and not just a technical response to a single

TABLE 29-1   Public Health Strategic Challenges: A Baker's Dozen

1. Changing scope of public health
2. Greater accountability and performance
3. Growing competition for roles and resources
4. A focus on the public health system
5. Shifting demographic composition
6. Alternative organizational arrangements
7. The chronic disease epidemic
8. Emerging and reemerging threats
9. Invisibility and search for public support
10. A strained healthcare system and growing number of uninsured
11. Stagnant revenues
12. The technology revolution: information and biological
13. Devolution of federal responsibilities to the state and local level

Source: Courtesy of D. Patrick Lenihan.

public health initiative or program. With increasing complexity in public health as in life generally, all these challenges are interrelated. With changes occurring every day in our environment, these changes cannot help but affect the daily operations of our public health agencies. In addition, public health agencies are being asked to do work on many new areas of concern and often with limited financial resources. An important consideration is a determination of whether our agencies should do the work, whether our partners should do it, or whether some form of collaboration can be developed to do it.

The first challenge relates to this changing and evolving scope of public health. In the past, public health agencies concentrated much of their work on communicable disease control. Now our agencies are involved in public health preparedness, regulation of healthcare providers, and providing of healthcare services to the poor and uninsured as providers of last resort. Those public health professionals with a strong social justice orientation seem to be unable to say no as more programs are added to our agency portfolios.

The second challenge is an expectation of greater accountability and performance. It seems that the public and our elected officials are requiring more and more service for each tax dollar spent. These expectations also require that public health leaders demonstrate how the money was spent and how the expenditures improved the health of the public. This is further complicated by local governments and agencies being more accountable for public health than state or federal agencies. Many new instruments have been developed to show how public health works and performs. For example, the Mobilizing for Action through Planning and Partnerships assessment process and the National Public Health Performance Standards are two sets of tools that have been developed to demonstrate accountability and quality improvement.

The third challenge involves the issue of growing competition for roles and resources. Competition is something that the business community understands and something that public health professionals have difficulty understanding because we are collaborative in our orientation. However, public health leaders still have difficulty in demonstrating the value of our work. We still struggle to carry out the mission of public health as our resources dwindle and our work is being done by other organizations in the healthcare sector. The boundaries between the public, private, and not-for-profit sectors in health seem to be dissolving. We see this especially in the area of emergency preparedness and response and the emphasis on meta-leadership skills and strategies.

The fourth strategic challenge involves systems thinking and the focus on the public health system. There has been a shift from a public health agency focus to a community-based public health focus. The core functions and essential public health services model emphasizes community partnerships to carry out the public health enterprise. Many of the available leadership tools provide a toolkit for leaders engaged in community and systems work. Public health leaders will need to become navigators who steer and guide public health work rather than only reacting to today's crisis. Collaboration with partners is a system-level involvement. Public health leaders need to increase their skills in policy formulation and development.

Shifting demographic composition is the next strategic challenge. Our population is aging, requiring that public health be more involved in chronic disease and aging issues. The increasing diversity of our population and the erosion of the middle class bring the potential for increasing our public health involvement in healthcare issues such as access to service and to health disparities concerns. The global economy and the increase in illegal immigration raises important policy and health service delivery issues because our health and public health system are already overburdened.

Leadership Tip

Leaders know the primary importance of family and community.

The next challenge involves alternative organizational arrangements. Over the past two decades, we have seen the reorganization of the governmental service sector. We now have superagencies trying to integrate a complex array of services and programs. We are seeing some hospital systems now running county health departments with oversight from a county board of health. Regionalization will be an issue in the future when smaller health departments need to work together and share resources. This may lead, as it has in a number of areas of the United States, to regional health departments. Thus, we seem to be more open to exploring alternative organizational arrangements than in the past.

As discussed above on the challenge of shifting demographics, the challenge of chronic disease epidemics needs to be addressed. Chronic diseases are the major cause of death (more than 70%) for the U.S. population. Although chronic diseases have been monitored and addressed by public health for many years, it seems that these diseases have taken a back seat to emergency preparedness and response agendas. Smoking bans have been one mechanism by which public health issues have been addressed by elected officials and public health professionals in recent years. The increased incidence of diabetes is also being addressed even though limited financial resources are available. Addressing coronary heart disease and stroke through preventive mechanisms such as improved nutrition and exercise has been promoted. Improved lifestyle changes are more about education than treatment.

The next challenge relates to emerging and reemerging threats and the increased concern about such infectious diseases as severe acute respiratory syndrome, pandemic influenza, drug-resistant tuberculosis, and bioterrorism. Many reports have argued that we still have low levels of readiness, although there is some evidence of improvement to address these potential health problems. We have developed critical skills related to emergency planning and response, although work needs to occur on the issues of mitigation and recovery. The challenge for public health agencies is to be in a constant state of readiness in the future. This is difficult without financial support from our elected officials or

interest from the public. An important question involves the impact of a preparedness agenda on the day-to-day activities of our local health departments.

The ninth strategic challenge involves the issue of public health's invisibility and the need for public health leaders to search for public support. Public health leaders tend not to promote their good deeds. Public health leaders monitor the health of the public, push prevention agendas, work collaboratively with their community partners, alert the public to potential health threats, give service when other health providers do not, push a preparedness agenda, and foster many other health-enhancing activities. We do not get recognition for most of these activities. We tend to be shy about our accomplishments. Perhaps we need to develop a "Brag About Public Health Week" that coincides with our annual Public Health Week. We need to make friends with our elected officials and our media representatives. Leaders need to create more public value for our activities. Part of this public health visibility is to demonstrate how a health department plays a role in these public health accomplishments.

Another strategic challenge that has been partially addressed above is the reality of a strained healthcare system and a growing uninsured population. There is a need for public health agencies to take a more visible role in community health care because the medical care system in our society is in disarray. Managed care organizations still address high costs and the difficulty of the uninsured having appropriate access to health care. Catastrophic illness has led to personalbankruptcies. Health disparities still exist. Local public health agencies no longer have the resources to provide direct healthcare services to residents. We have not figured out our relationships to community health centers or to the clinics in drugstores and large retail stores like Wal-Mart. It is critical for public health to redefine its role in the public health activities in communities.

Stagnant revenues are our next strategic challenge. Since the terrorist acts of September 11, 2001, the federal budget for domestic programs has been decreasing as our government has had to put more funds into the Iraq and Afghanistan wars, other military activities, and strengthening our military. Public health agencies received funds after 2001 for preparedness activities as funding for other programs declined. Now we are seeing the decline in preparedness funding as well. Retirements of public health professionals are occurring without people being rehired when retirees leave. The public health workforce is shrinking at a time when more demands are being made on local health departments to increase their work in new areas. Future growth of public health will not happen without investment in the enterprise.

New technologies are creating another strategic challenge. Advances in information technology and the developing field of informatics, biotechnology, and research applications tied to our increasing knowledge of genomics will greatly change the public health agency of the future. The negative issue related to these changes involves such issues as invasions of privacy of individuals and ethical concerns in public health practice. Biotechnology concerns will become visible with more concentration on genetic profiling and discrimination. These new technologies will also be expensive and difficult to fund from our present tax base.

The final strategic challenge will have significant effects on the work of public health leaders and other professionals with possible devolution of federal responsibilities to the state and local levels. This has been occurring since the 1980s. Of course, the scenario can change if political parties in the White House and Congress change their attitudes and funding priorities to strengthen the national public health system, increase support for state and local public health, pass universal healthcare programs, and continue to support training the public health workforce. The chances for this turnaround seem slight at this time, and an increasing federal role in public health does not seem on the horizon.

These strategic challenges will clearly affect the public health system of the future and increase the pressure on public health leaders to protect the health of people and the environment. Public health leaders need to be more proactive and not follow the crowd. They need, in other words, to both navigate and steer the course of public health program change rather than be among the rowers. They have the leadership skills to move public health organizations forward, and they need to apply these skills to this task. Public health leaders have an obligation to develop a set of ethical standards pertaining to public health and to use these standards for guiding the public health process.

PUBLIC HEALTH DURING THE THIRD WAVE

What Toffler has called the third wave began with the transition from industrial forms of organization (which are characteristic of the second wave) to information-based forms of organization.[4] **Table 29-2** lists 12 third-wave public health issues. The last two decades of the 20th century saw major changes in technology and the emergence of knowledge as an important commodity, a view that continues in the 21st century.

Table 29-3 compares certain elements of the second wave with corresponding elements of the third wave. Some of the changes have already occurred. For example, many alternative family approaches were already common in the 1990s, the use of educational vouchers to allow parents to select public or private schools for their children is under discussion, and some parents educate their children at home utilizing computers and educational software.

The large-organization model still prevails, however, and mergers are making big organizations bigger.

TABLE 29-2 Public Health in the Third Wave

1. Expanded models of public health
2. Team-based problem solving
3. Community health coalitions based on partnership
4. Privatization of assurance activities
5. Decentralization of responsibilities across the community
6. Community-wide governance
7. Value generation
8. A new political structure
9. Third-wave leadership
10. Integration between individuals' needs and the community's needs
11. Complete community empowerment
12. Universal access to a multitude of services to improve quality of life

TABLE 29-3 The Second and Third Waves Compared

Second-Wave Civilization	Third-Wave Civilization
Nuclear family	Alternate families
Mass education	Individual education
Giant corporations	Small specialty organizations
Centralized nation-state	New democracy
Mass trade unions	Demassification
Hand work	Mind work

Source: Data from "Products of the Third Wave," in *The Third Wave* by Alvin Toffler. Copyright © 1980 by Alvin Toffler. Reprinted by permission of HarperCollins Publishers, Inc.

It is true that there has been an increase in small specialty organizations, but this has been going on for a long time. Also, national struggles have continued to plague the world, and whether democracy will finally triumph as the one viable political system is open to question. In fact, the meaning and direction of our democratic society have come under increasing scrutiny. Trade unions have lost their strength, and many professionals are redefining the workplace. Thus, the year 2000 found American society still tied to the second wave, although clear examples of third-wave realities are disrupting society.

Table 29-4 lists 10 products that reflect the transition between the second wave and the third wave. Many of the products will have an impact on public health whether or not the third-wave theory is valid. For instance, public health leaders will require more information to do their jobs well. The human genome project is changing our understanding of how diseases work and is leading to new techniques for helping people. Innovation will be the order of the day. Strategies for running organizations will be based on the leadership model rather than the management model. The old ways and the old methods will have to be modified.

Public health leaders and their human services colleagues will have to make public health a community-based activity through partnering with community leaders and community residents generally. Citizens of the 21st century will have to assume responsibility for improving their personal health and fitness. If it appears that technology is advanced now, wait 20 years. Think of the changes that have occurred since 1980. Desktop computers became as powerful as the massive computers of the past. The Internet grew

from nothing into a whole new means of communicating, transferring information, and doing business. Now we work remotely from our offices on laptops and tablets.

The American educational system will have to change. The educational process will be different for each individual. The challenge will be to determine how to use our educational tools to meet the needs and wants of people committed to lifelong learning. The expansion of distance-learning programs will be part of the answer. Training opportunities, including mentoring opportunities, will need to grow if public health professionals are to keep up with the changes in their field.

The medical care sector is already changing. Community health centers are only one approach. One major trend will be the creation of integrated systems of care. Another will be the development of public-private partnerships. Possibilities for the development of some procedures for a universal healthcare system are increasing. New financial services will also evolve. Varying levels of health reform will occur in spite of all the political flack. Finally, national and international military protection will require the continued development and production of more advanced weapon systems.

During the third wave, leaders who integrate their leadership skills and their management skills will be the ones who are most successful. In short, leadership and management will become united.

Following are 10 key leadership issues for the information age:

1. Leaders will need strategies oriented toward growth rather than retrenchment. They will also have to engage in strategic thinking rather than merely tactical thinking.
2. Customer- and community-focused activities will become more prominent.
3. More and more knowledge sources will appear. For example, the Internet will expand the professional horizons of public health practitioners.
4. The information age is also the age of teams, coalitions, and partnerships. Networking will be the preferred method of operation.
5. Public agencies will discover that they cannot serve all segments of the population. The service sector will need to be shared by both public and private entities. An integrated healthcare system will evolve, with public health agencies as lead partners. Each partner in the integrated system will serve specific client sectors.

TABLE 29-4   **Products of the Third Wave**

1. Information and innovation
2. Management strategies
3. Culture and pop culture
4. Advanced technology
5. Software
6. Education
7. Training
8. Medical care through the private sector
9. Financial services
10. Military protection

Source: Data from "Products of the Third Wave," in *The Third Wave* by Alvin Toffler. Copyright © 1980 by Alvin Toffler. Reprinted by permission of HarperCollins Publishers, Inc.

6. Accounting systems will become more relevant to public health activities. Public health agencies will need to budget on the basis of core functions, organizational practices, and/or essential services rather than traditional public health service activities.

7. All partners in an enterprise will need to be empowered. Empowerment must be balanced against control.

8. Shared values will change. Leaders will have to review shared values regularly because changes in values have an impact on the program effectiveness of public health agencies.

9. Leaders must honor the best practices and the most effective individuals.

10. Leaders must work to transform a second-wave organization into a third-wave one.

Leaders need guidance in how to motivate and manage change to facilitate the transformation to the third wave or the modification of the present system.[5] Leadership commitment to the transformation is also a major factor. **Figure 29-1** presents a model of transformation for healthcare organizations. One critical task to address before starting a transformation is to make certain that a real need for change exists. If change is inevitable, then the leaders need to restructure teams and coalitions so as to bring about the change with as little difficulty as possible.

A successful transformation requires that all the steps shown in Figure 29-1 be followed. Leaders will need to adopt strategic planning, total quality process, re-engineering, and reinvention methods, among others, to expedite the change process. The next stage involves the commitment of all players to the idea of change and the philosophical underpinnings of the management strategies selected to help bring about the change. Next, the leaders need to encourage creativity in the workforce and promote innovation. These factors will change not only the way people work but also the way public health organizations look.

It is not necessary to accept the third-wave theory. Much more important is to accept the changes that have been occurring in our society since September 11, 2001. This is clearly a time of major change in which leaders from all segments of our society will need to address the issues that are causing the change and arising out of the change. It is clear that there may be more waves in the future. Maynard and Mehrtens have defined an emerging fourth wave.[6] The fourth wave moves beyond the collaboration approaches defined by Toffler to a more complexity-based approach that unifies us as a society and creates an environment in which we co-create our future out of our beliefs about what we want the future to be. Leadership will be different in the future, where global stewardship and a view of the world that ignores boundaries will guide our leadership

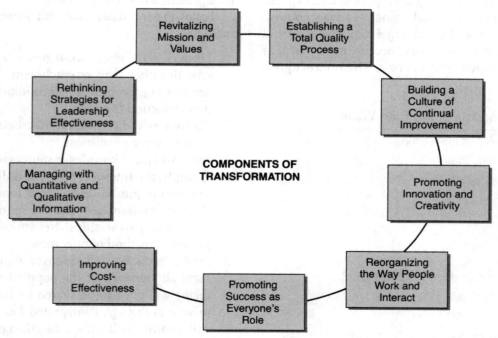

FIGURE 29-1 **Components of Transformation.** *Source*: Reprinted with permission from E. Murszalek-Gaucher and R. J. Coffey, *Transforming Healthcare Organizations*, p. 57, © 1990, Jossey-Bass Inc., Publishers.

activities. Protection of our environment and our communities will also guide our activities. Quality-of-life issues will also be a dominant factor in our thinking and work. Shechtman has viewed the fourth wave as a communication-intensive social system.[7] As he looks forward to a fifth wave, he points to a period of personal transformation where we take more responsibility for our actions. Exercise 29-1 presents an opportunity to explore wave theory from the perspective of a public health problem.

In terms of the practical applications necessary for our work today, public health leaders will need to answer the call for a new form of public health based on the following principles:

- Public health must clarify its mission, its vision, and its parameters and sell its vision to the public.
- Public health must become proactive rather than reactive.
- In a mostly private health system, public health must become the voice of the public. Public health should not be privatized.
- Public health must remain the provider of last resort (although last means last).
- Boards of health must be strengthened.
- A federal presence in public health must continue.
- Prevention must be stressed and marketed.
- Environmental health and occupational health must be treated as public health partners.
- State laboratories need to be involved in setting up the public health agenda.
- Assessment activities must be strengthened through the use of modern technology and applied epidemiological methods.
- Public health leaders need to work with their public health partners to develop a stronger infrastructure for addressing public health concerns of our communities.
- Public health professionals must become policy makers.
- Leadership development must not only be stressed but also be financially supported.
- Stronger links need to be forged between academics and practitioners. The links need to incorporate the core academic fields of public health and the core functions of public health.
- The multidisciplinary nature of public health must be strengthened at the same time that a unified perspective on public health must be promoted among public health's constituencies.
- State-level public health agencies must remain largely independent.
- The partnership between state-level health agencies and local health agencies must be strengthened.
- Public health agencies must think globally but act locally.
- Public health agencies must teach the public about public health.
- Coalitions, including public–private partnerships, must be built.
- Assurance must be redefined on a regular basis.
- Public health must sell its best practices.
- Public health leaders need to be prepared for any emergencies that may arise.
- Public health leaders should run for and hold elected office.

THE LEADERS SPEAK

In a study done by the author from 1996 to 1998, 100 American public health leaders and 30 public health leaders from England, Scotland, and Ireland were interviewed. In the American portion of the study, the leaders were asked about an agenda for public health in the 21st century. Some leaders predicted that certain potential health-related problems, such as new infectious diseases and increased resistance of microorganisms to antibiotics, might erupt and affect the overall tasks of public health agencies. Some were also concerned about the aging of the American population.

The leaders did not fully agree on what public health is and what it does. The lack of consensus was probably partly due to the multidisciplinary background of the leaders and the specific emphasis of the programs they oversaw. Although many leaders believed that the mission of public health was to promote health and prevent disease, some found this mission statement too simplistic. Without a clear mission and a well-formulated vision, it becomes difficult to talk to others about public health. Thus, public health leaders jointly should explore the governing public health paradigms and revise them as necessary, develop a consensus on a mission and a vision for public health, and sell the mission, vision, and paradigms to community constituents.

During the last few decades of the 20th century and even more since the terrorist events of 2001, public health leaders have tended to respond to health crises rather than plan public health agendas likely to prevent crises. The goal for the 21st century is for public health leaders to take charge of their destiny and devise action plans directed toward improving the health of community residents. Proactive approaches should be the order of the day and the century.

Public health leaders will continue to act as the voice of the public in matters of health. Because public health agencies perform oversight activities, complete privatization of public health will not occur, and public health agencies will need to be integrated into the healthcare system. Because the development of a national health system in the United States remains a remote possibility, oversight by public health leaders is critical.

Boards of health and local and state departments of health should act as partners rather than adversaries. Board members are community gatekeepers and have an obligation to promote the community's priorities. Because of the importance of their role, board members need training in how to do their job. If boards become strengthened, the whole infrastructure of public health will become strengthened as well. It would help if board members would network with other board members, with all boards of health in the state (if a board of health structure exists), and with the public health practitioners at the local and state levels. Public health leaders are aware of the lack of connection between the federal health agencies, the state health department (or, in some states, the human services agency), and local public health agencies. It is important to create strong links among these three levels of government, and public health leaders, among others, will have to take the initiative in forging these links. A federal presence is critical if policy is to be formulated for the nation.

Public health leaders need to push a primary prevention agenda. In many places, although prevention constitutes a major portion of the public health agenda, the public health leaders do little to promote the agenda. Public health agencies and their leaders need to address primary prevention in a strategic manner and come up with approaches for improving the health of the public through the prevention of disease.[8] Prevention includes actions that reduce susceptibility or exposure to health threats (primary prevention), detect and treat disease in early stages (secondary prevention), and alleviate the effect of disease and injury (tertiary prevention).[9]

During the late 20th century, local public health agencies concentrated their efforts on secondary and tertiary prevention programs. A shift to primary prevention initiatives, in which people become responsible for their own health, is needed.

Public health encompasses occupational health and safety as well as environmental health. Unfortunately, these disciplines tend to be neglected by public health leaders with a strong personal services orientation. Environmental health and occupational health specialists need to be given the same standing as other public health professionals. Also meriting a seat at the table are state and local laboratory directors, many of whom have been trained in a number of areas, including public health science. The professional diversity that characterizes public health is not a weakness but one of its strengths.

The public health leaders interviewed by the author recognized the importance of the community assessment process and argued that assessment techniques need to be improved. One recommendation was to train public health partners in the basics of epidemiological methods in order to combine community assessment and epidemiology. Without question, public health leaders must acquire good computer skills and become acquainted with new information technologies as they emerge. Sharing epidemiological and other types of data with public health leaders across the country will become the norm.

Public health leaders will need to become more versed in policy development. As experts, these leaders can influence elected officials and thereby promote the public health agenda at the local, state, and federal levels. In addition, public health agencies, like other human services organizations, need money to operate and carry out their mandate. Financial support is critical, and public health leaders will need to seek funding from multiple sources. State funding will cover only part of a health department budget, and so public health leaders will need to act as entrepreneurs in getting outside funding.

Public health leaders need to share ideas with their academic partners. Faculty members are often excluded from the strategic planning process, yet they bring to the table a knowledge of health-related sciences, an understanding of the core disciplines of public health, and a knowledge of emerging health problems—all of which can be extremely important for addressing the problems that public health leaders face.

As noted, public health professionals come from many different disciplines, and although the diversity in educational background is an important strength, public health leaders must create a unified perspective to present to the public. To put it one way, while speaking with many voices to each other, public health leaders must speak with a common voice when dealing with community partners.

The public health leaders interviewed were intrigued, to varying degrees, with three models for the future of public health: a situation in which independent public health agencies exist, an integrated system in which public health is one of the players, and an integrated system in which public health is the organizer of the system. Although some of the leaders liked each of the three models, they generally believed that it is necessary to maintain an independent public health presence in the community. Maintaining independent agencies will be critical if the United States does not develop a national health service.

There is a caution here. Public health leaders in other countries pointed out that public health often gets lost in a national health system. In England, public health leaders found that much of their time was spent purchasing services for their districts. American public health leaders were concerned about the possibility that the state health department would get absorbed into a state human services superagency. They believed that the state health department should be maintained as a separate entity within state government.

Public health agencies at different governmental levels must act as partners and cease to be antagonistic. Public health leadership programs are a means of creating partnerships between state and local agencies because the trainees come from all levels of government. Local public health leaders should communicate with state leaders and understand their concerns, and they should also be aware of the current activities of the World Health Organization and, where necessary,

incorporate international health concerns into their planning efforts. Local leaders also need to communicate to the proper authorities information about local health issues that may eventually have a national or international impact.

Despite the efforts to promote public health, the public still does not understand the nature of the field. Without the support of the public, public health leaders will have difficulty planning for the future. The solution is for public health leaders to develop a multi-pronged approach to both health communication and social marketing. They also need to get out into the community, forge partnerships in the public and private sectors, and educate their partners about public health.

It is through assurance activities that creative intervention strategies will be tested and evaluated. Yet assurance itself will have to be redefined regularly, as new techniques are developed and tested. Assurance in the year 2020 will be different from assurance in the year 2050.

Finally, the public health leaders interviewed by the author emphasized the importance of selling public health's best practices and not being shy about it. If public health leaders do not market themselves well, the public health field as a whole suffers. However, one thing I noticed about public health leaders was their passion and strong belief in the issues that they support. Case Study 29-A is the story of Ardell Wilson, a public health leader, and her crusade on behalf of asthmatic children.[10]

Case Study 29-A

Story of Ardell Wilson
The Faces of Public Health, Pfizer

When the *New York Times* reported in May 2003 that one in four school-age children in central Harlem had asthma, even longtime asthma researchers were surprised. This New York City neighborhood had one of the highest rates of asthma ever documented in the United States. High rates of asthma are not limited to inner-city neighborhoods like Harlem, however. Dr. Ardell A. Wilson, chief of the Bureau of Community Health at the Connecticut Department of Public Health, knows this all too well. Born and raised in New York City—and living with asthma herself—Ardell confronted the disease and made Connecticut the first state in the nation to standardize the treatment protocol for asthma for school-age children.

A graduate of Washington Irving High School in Manhattan, Ardell enrolled at Bronx Community College to earn her associate's degree. While still at Washington Irving, Ardell's guidance counselor pushed her to take college prep courses in advanced biology and advanced algebra even though she intended, like her elder sister, to stick with secretarial studies. That encouragement helped her do well at Bronx Community College. After graduating, and by this time married with a young son, she attended City College of the City University of New York part time, earning her bachelor's degree in 1976. She planned to major in elementary education but after one semester switched to biology, which she found more interesting.

(Continues)

As she completed her degree at City College, Ardell knew she wanted to work in health care. She chose dentistry because she felt it was the most stable health-related field—with a young son at home, she needed her work hours to be predictable. Ardell attended the Columbia University School of Dental and Oral Surgery for four years with the idea that she would start her own dental practice. During the last two years, she enlisted with the U.S. Public Health Service. In return for help with her tuition costs, she committed to practice in underserved areas for three years after graduation.

Upon graduation, Ardell joined the Boriken Neighborhood Health Center, a community health center in East Harlem, and spent three years there in an all-female dental service. She also worked at Columbia one day a week, teaching preventive dentistry. Ardell believed that the preventive aspects of dentistry were more critical to a population's long-term health than corrective dentistry. During her final year at Boriken, and based on positive feedback from her preventive dentistry students, Columbia recruited Ardell to join the Division of Community Health as a faculty member. She taught ethics, jurisprudence, and statistics and, at the same time, began a private practice in lower Manhattan, working there part-time with a colleague from Columbia. Her work at Columbia was fulfilling because she could make an impact teaching those who in turn would serve the underserved. She also discovered in her private practice that she preferred the community health center setting, where she served those who were truly in need.

In 1984, the Robert Wood Johnson (RWJ) Health Services Research Scholars Program awarded Ardell a fellowship to study at Harvard. The program was intended to train academics to become leaders in health services research. Dr. Howard Bailit, then at the Columbia University School of Public Health and now at the University of Connecticut, encouraged Ardell to apply for the RWJ program to broaden her perspective on healthcare delivery systems. At Harvard, she worked with mentors outside of dentistry and was especially grateful for the training she received from Dr. Laurence Branch, a specialist in geriatrics, survey research, and aging. During her fellowship, Ardell earned her master's degree in public health from the Harvard School of Public Health with a concentration in maternal child health and aging. Although she lived apart from her family for two years—her husband and son remained in New Rochelle and they saw each other only on weekends—she would gladly choose to do those two years over again. She credits her experience at Harvard for preparing her to do what she does today.

At Harvard, Ardell geared her research activities toward becoming a diplomate (specialist) of the American Board of Dental Public Health (ABDPH). She involved herself in learning everything she could about the aging of America, including health insurance and the delivery of services.

She received a certificate in geriatrics from the Harvard School of Medicine Geriatric Education Center. With her mentor, Dr. Branch, she turned her attention to the most vulnerable elderly population, those living in nursing homes. Her work in this area resulted in the documentation of the oral health problems of the elderly living in nursing homes in Massachusetts and earned her the James M. Dunning Award in Health Services Research. She also became the first African American woman diplomate of the ABDPH.

Upon completing her fellowship in 1986, Ardell returned to Columbia to direct the Division of Community Health and the joint degree program in public health and dentistry. In 1988, Connecticut recruited her to become the state's oral health director.

Ardell rose through a series of positions in Connecticut as the state restructured its government agencies numerous times. She served as the state's oral health director for only two months and then combined that position with community health programs involving school-based health centers, community health centers, maternal child health, and substance abuse. In 1991, she became deputy director of the Connecticut Drug and Alcohol Abuse Commission. She oversaw four state hospitals serving substance abusers and collaborated with community-based agencies. Her greatest contribution, she believes, was expanding services for women by creating residential facilities where the women's children could join them.

In 1993, the Alcohol and Drug Abuse Commission merged into the newly named Connecticut Department of Public Health and Addiction Services, and Ardell resumed some of her previous responsibilities in community health. In 1995, she became bureau chief of Community Health within a reconstituted Department of Public Health, a position she still holds. She supervises 150 to 200 people in a wide range of public health endeavors, including epidemiology, infectious disease, chronic disease, family health, and risk assessment for environmental and occupational health. She also oversees the State Loan Repayment Program, which encourages young health professionals (physicians, dentists, hygienists, nurses) to practice in underserved areas while the state repays their school loans. Ardell also develops relationships with funders, mostly at the federal level, a key responsibility of her position.

In 2000, Ardell turned her attention to the issue of asthma, a chronic respiratory disease that affects an estimated 10.4% of Connecticut's children under age 18, or more than 86,000 children statewide. She collaborated with the New England Regional Task Force on Asthma as well as stakeholders from Connecticut—managed care organizations, community organizations, and public health professionals—on a Pediatric Asthma Management Initiative. Those collaborations resulted in a model Asthma Action Plan for Connecticut. The Asthma Action Plan, a color-coordinated management tool, is developed in conjunction with a healthcare provider to help people manage asthma by teaching them to recognize when they are in the green zone (under control), yellow zone (need to improve control), or red zone (need immediate care). The Asthma Action Plan is available in both English and Spanish. Copies are distributed to clinical practices and managed care organizations throughout the state.

In 2001, on the heels of the Asthma Action Plan, Ardell convened a statewide Asthma Summit to publicize the extent of the asthma problem documented in the newly released "Asthma in Connecticut Report." The summit led to a Statewide Asthma Task Force charged with developing a Comprehensive Statewide Asthma Plan and Implementation Process. Numerous activities were initiated to address asthma—from public education and awareness campaigns and provider education to clinical management and surveillance activities. Because children spend a significant part of their day in school and school-related activities, a toolkit called "Managing Asthma in Schools" for school nurses (and school administrators) was developed with the help of school nurses. Shortly afterward, the Department of Public Health helped daycare providers develop their own kit, called "Managing Asthma in Childcare Facilities." The toolkits—three-ring binders with inserts that can be reproduced as needed—addressed the facts of asthma triggers, asthma management, and the administration of medications in simple and accessible terms. Although the approach and materials were low tech, they worked.

In 2003, the Connecticut Legislature responded to the advocacy efforts of Ardell and the task force and passed legislation that gave the Department of Public Health the ability to collect data from schools and implement a statewide surveillance system for schoolchildren with asthma. This added to the department's ongoing hospital inpatient and outpatient surveillance activities. As someone with asthma herself, Ardell found the calendar sent by her managed care organization, based on the Asthma Action Plan materials, to be proof of the success of this initiative. The red, yellow, and green indicators for the severity of an attack, matched to recommended interventions, are quick and handy references for anyone suffering from asthma.

The Association of State and Territorial Health Officials recognized Connecticut's Asthma Action Plan as a program of vision, the first of its kind in the nation and still leading the way. In addition to school employees, Connecticut authorized daycare personnel to administer medicine to treat asthma attacks as they occur, the first state to do so, making possible a continuum of care. The Connecticut Asthma Program distributes easy-to-use, understandable materials to all levels of the public health system—parents, school nurses, daycare providers, physicians, clinics, and hospitals. In fact, the department produced 10 educational pediatric asthma management vignettes (with an interactive website) entitled "Natalie Says," directed at young children and their parents. The vignettes (in English and Spanish) review the importance of asthma management in a child-friendly way. The comprehensive array of asthma materials standardizes asthma management protocol and helps patients and caregivers understand what makes asthma worse and how to adjust medications and physical activities accordingly. The materials lead to effective management of asthma in children and are a testament to Ardell Wilson's vision and leadership.

Ardell believes this is an excellent time for young people to go into public health. For the first time, the human genome project offers hope that the genetic causes of some diseases can be discovered and the course of those diseases altered. The issue of healthcare access has come under greater scrutiny, with workforce studies and evaluations of the fairness of insurance and delivery systems. Environmental health will continue to be at the center of public health, encouraging people to consider what they can do to make home and work environments safer. Yet another issue, public health systems that are needed to address health emergencies, has emerged front and center in the public eye.

Ardell believes that public health will be very different 10 years from now. Technologies now being perfected will make computer/Internet-based training the preferred method, replacing conferencing. A focus on the elderly population will be more pronounced, and research should advance treatment for Alzheimer's disease, falls, and other perils of old age. The growing elderly population will require big increases in healthcare delivery systems, especially nursing homes and assisted living facilities. Ardell sees a bright future for prevention and health promotion after education strategies that limit the growth of healthcare costs are recognized to work.

For Ardell Wilson, the journey from New York to Connecticut has been long but enjoyable. Along the way, she has made her mark as a dentist and public health specialist. Perhaps most significantly, she has been a literal breath of fresh air for the children and families of Connecticut. Her leadership in asthma management is a model for communities throughout the United States.

Source: Reproduced from Pfizer Public Health Group, *The Faces of Public Health* (New York: Pfizer Global Pharmaceuticals, 2004).

A VIEW OF TOMORROW

Although leaders are oriented to change, change without a vision does not take the leader very far. Leadership is as much about learning from our experiences as it is about coping with the critical events of modern times. Covey has stated that leaders for the future will be involved in developing values and cultures based on the principles that guide a society.[11] Democracy provides an excellent template for change. Our founding fathers created a system based on freedom, growth, and the ability to adapt to changing circumstances. The public health leader adopts these principles and adds his or her own spin to them. Leaders realize that the future of public health is based on preventing disease and promoting health and not just on treatment and diagnosis of the disease. Prevention is what our leaders must focus on—not just reaction. It is important for successful leaders to be pathfinders who build our society on positive visions for the future.[12] These leaders must also be expert in aligning our health issues with the culture and values that make our society strong. Leaders also need to empower people so that they share power, authority, and responsibility for the growth and change that will inevitably occur in our society.

Vision is not only about the future; it is a strong belief in possibilities. It is based on the concept of hope and an understanding that whatever unfortunate events occur, there are always possibilities of positive social change. Vision involves the leader's ability to picture what the future might look like. Leaders always see what is possible for people in terms of the projects they do and the activities in which they will become involved.[13] Vision is about the discipline necessary to bring change into being, the passion to carry it out, and a sense of doing only what is morally correct. Vision is also about building on past experiences. It is looking to the past for the positive lessons that we have learned. It is not about holding on to past grievances or blaming others for what has happened.[14] Vision is as much about the present as it is about the past. It is necessary to put the past in perspective and see the present for what it really is. One critical mistake many leaders make is to think that the answer for past mistakes is to completely reinvent the wheel. Politicians make this mistake every time there is a new election. The future is about making plans based on the perspectives of now. Vision is about planning for possible futures.

Blanchard and Miller explored the issue of what makes leaders successful. The real secret of leadership relates to a strong belief in service to the public. Leaders always need to gain credibility and trust from the people they serve.[15] The important issue relates to the true meaning of service. The definition of service embraces the following:

- See and perceive possible futures.
- Engage constituents in the process of change.
- Realize that change is inevitable.
- Accept the need to constantly reinvent the future.
- Advocate for concrete outcomes while protecting values and a way of life.
- Protect and embody society's values in everything that is done.

Normal and not-so-normal acts have a critical impact on our way of life, and we need leaders who are prepared to address any future emergencies that our society will face. Public health concerns are primary. Our leaders need to be involved in addressing the critical issues of our times. At the same time, leaders need to lead the way toward the future by investigating and understanding the possibilities that our way of life presents. This does not mean that our lives will not be affected by these unfortunate events, but rather that we are strong enough to overcome these actions, adapt in new ways, and still promote the strengths that democracy brings to the way we live. In this last section, we explore the skills of visioning in order to better prepare for our futures.

Many people talk about vision these days. However, predicting the future takes more than a crystal ball. For a vision to be useful, it needs to be realistic about the realities of today as well as certain factors that are predictable for the future.[16] A vision must also be credible in that the future that is proposed must be possible. Finally, the vision must appear to be positive for the organization or community. A vision needs to gain adherents. The credibility of the leader will clearly be a factor in this. A vision must also seem real to the people who will strive to bring it to reality. The vision needs to set a standard for high quality.[17] Visions provide a link between the present and the future.

Mission and vision are also linked. If we look again at the Leadership Wheel, we see that vision also is connected with goals and objectives. In addition, priority setting in public health and the use of performance standards can also be a useful part of visioning. The United States Federal Highway Administration viewed visioning as a way to get the public to participate in long-range planning efforts.[18] Visioning can also be seen as a mechanism for policy development. It helps in the generation of ideas and an exploration of different possible scenarios for change. Visioning is also flexible in that it can be accomplished in retreats or as part of the general process of planning. The process of vision is useful in many ways:[19]

1. It sets the stage for both short-term and long-term planning activities.
2. It can help set some new directions for policy formulation.
3. It is possible to review current policies in light of several possible futures.
4. It helps to integrate different issues in a more organized way.
5. It allows different ideas and perspectives to be applied to potential futures.
6. It gives a perspective on problem solutions.

There are four distinct phases that delineate the process of vision. A number of questions can be posed during each of these four phases.[20] Whatever questions are posed can then provide information to guide the next step of the visioning process. Nanus gives a possible list of questions for each of the four phases.[21] The important issue is that the visioning process should be systematic and carried out in a well-documented fashion.

In the first phase, a vision audit puts the need for the development of a new vision in context. This audit links vision with values, cultural factors, and mission. The context is an important characteristic of the process. History, demographic changes, health status indicators, and so on become part of the vision audit. Performance measures can be useful here as well. This audit helps to define present reality and what is possible in the context of today's realities. Some urban anthropologists would equate the process with some elements of what they call a cultural audit, although the cultural audit is more intense and takes longer. The second phase is the important discussion related to the scope of the proposed vision exercise. In the third stage, leaders put the proposed vision in context of the community or organization for the long term. Finally, a scenario-building process is undertaken to explore the impact of a potential vision on the organization or community.

Because vision is so time sensitive, it should be possible to experiment with vision statements for an organization or community at different future time points. To give you some practice with the visioning process, Exercises 29-2 and 29-3 allow you to experiment with the process of the development of a vision for a public health agency that has been affected by the terrorist events of September 11, 2001, at 5-year, 10-year, and 25-year periods post event.

A PERSPECTIVE FOR LEADERS

Talking about vision is, in many ways, more complex than it first appears. I remember a public health agency director telling me a few years ago that he had no time to develop a vision. He was too busy putting out fires. The successful public health leader knows that he or she must find the time to plan and use the vision as a mechanism for setting the course of the agency and the community. Planning and visioning should make our jobs easier over the long run. Many tools exist to help leaders to improve public health practice activities. It is not only the formal instruments required by the profession to monitor the health of the public. There are more informal tools, such as the following:

- Case studies
- Calls to experts for their views
- Stories of leaders
- Many exercises and games that help better define a problem and give added perspectives to its solution
- Site visits to other communities and agencies
- Community participation in health surveys
- Team-building tools
- Use of executive coaches to help leaders develop personal learning contracts
- Use of journals to document leadership experiences
- Mentoring of staff to take on management and leadership responsibilities
- Learning of skills from business leaders that can better structure public sector leadership activities

In other words, leaders must fill their toolboxes with all sorts of tools and gadgets to make themselves more effective.

Although our discussion has mainly focused on how public health leaders relate to other leaders, leaders of all kinds should also be aware that they need to develop their own personal visions for their professional future. Leaders need to guide their own actions as well as those of others. A leader's emotional reaction to various situations will clearly guide others.[22] In fact, the leader's reactions may stimulate similar reactions in others. When leaders are positive, others seem to become positive as a result. The reverse is also true. This leadership role of being an emotional guide to others has recently been dubbed "primal leadership."

Visions also are emotional in content. It is important to address this as visions are formed.

There are many self-help books on leadership in the marketplace. It is not necessary to repeat that extensive literature here. However, it is possible to mention a few important steps to reach peak performance for leaders.[23] In the *Catch Fire* model, leaders need to understand the mind set that guides their actions from values, cultural issues, professional background, and emotional intelligence issues. The obvious issues of eating well and exercising to keep fit not only are role model issues for the public health leader, they are healthy lifestyle issues. Leaders need to develop methods for relieving stress and fatigue if they are to work at peak levels. Leaders also need to love to work on all sorts of challenges. Change is real, and leaders need to be resilient. If they do not like to work on problems, they are in the wrong business. Humor is clearly important. Good leaders know how to use humor to ease their own stress and the stress and fears of others. The work environment needs to be livable. People need to enter a positive and pleasant workplace.

SUMMARY

This chapter reviewed the main challenges facing public health leaders in this new century. The strategies that public health leaders will need to use in order to meet these challenges are both numerous and diverse in kind. Among the most important, at least if public health leaders are themselves to be believed, is to return to public health's traditional focus on primary prevention. Another is to work at educating the public about public health, because it is clear there is general ignorance about what public health practitioners do. By pushing a prevention agenda and publicizing public health successes, along with the other strategies listed, public health leaders will go a long way toward ensuring that public health has the future it deserves and that the public deserves it to have.

Walt Disney once said that all our dreams can come true if we have the courage to pursue them. Leaders believe in this philosophy even in the face of the tragedies of the past several years. Leadership is about learning and about growth. It is usually more than a one-time event, although we have heroes who do a courageous act and then move back into the anonymity of their lives. The public health leader lives a life of community involvement with a commitment to the people that he or she serves. To carry out the critical responsibilities associated with this responsibility, the leader needs the tools, skills, and competencies necessary to carry out these tasks with high standards for success. Leaders need to learn the skills of leadership, but also must commit to learning these new skills over a lifetime. The public health leader has learned the basic skills of leadership and now adds the skills of this new age to those basic leadership skills.

In conclusion, we have looked at the new world of public health from the perspective of public health in normal and not-so-normal times. We have also looked at public health today in the context of the new dimensions of the field as outlined by the Institute of Medicine. It is by building social capital that leaders will add strength to their pursuits to working with others to improve the quality of life of all residents of the United States. The issues of emergency preparedness and response were also considered from the context of public health, mental health, community and family health preparedness, and the issue of safety. There are new tools for this new world. The importance for systems thinking and the need to understand the complexities of our world guide our actions. The importance of emotional intelligence and people-smart strategies are critical. The need for leaders to understand law and its importance for carrying out our public health work it is also important. The need to look for tipping points and how these points help us to better understand our world increase our understanding of social events. The partnerships that develop between law enforcement and public health help strengthen our public health initiatives. There is also the need to emphasize our assets and not dwell on our problems. We need to build our communities from strength rather than from weakness. Change and acceptance of it frame our ongoing agenda. Finally, it is important to plan for a positive future and create visions to guide us toward this positive future.

It is important to keep looking for strategies and tools to make ourselves more effective leaders. We need to work together to discover these new directions.

DISCUSSION QUESTIONS

1. What current public health challenges do you see as most needing the attention of public health leaders?
2. What strategies might public health leaders use to meet some or all of these challenges?
3. What are some new characteristics of public health predicted to occur in the so-called third wave?

4. Why is there a lack of consensus on what public health is, even among public health practitioners?

5. How can public health leaders promote a prevention agenda?

6. How can public health leaders support the creation of an integrated healthcare system?

7. Will government public health agencies exist in 2050? Why or why not?

EXERCISE 29-1: Infant Mortality and Wave Theory

Purpose: to examine how public health leaders would address a public health issue in five scenarios based on wave theory

Key concepts: wave theory, scenario building, leadership

Procedures: Divide the class or training group into smaller groups of five to eight people. Looking at infant mortality, develop a scenario for addressing this public health problem from the five waves of change discussed in the chapter.

> Wave 1: Hunting and gathering to an agriculture-based society
>
> Wave 2: Agriculture-based society to an industrial one
>
> Wave 3: Industrial society to an information and knowledge-based society
>
> Wave 4: Information and knowledge-based society to a complexity-based society that is communication intensive
>
> Wave 5: Complexity-based society to one based on personal transformation

---

EXERCISE 29-2: Visions over Time

Purpose: to explore the factors that affect visions over the short and long terms

Key concept: visioning

Procedures: A number of exercises have explored the terrorist acts of September 11, 2001. This exercise asks you and your partners to look at public health at different times in the future. Divide the class or training group into three smaller groups. Group 1 will develop a vision for your local health department in 5 years based on the events of September 11, 2001, and the anthrax letters. Group 2 will develop a vision for public health for the next 10 years. Group 3 will develop a vision for public health for the next 25 years. Discuss your visions in the larger group or do Exercise 29-3.

EXERCISE 29-3: Expert Reactions to the Vision

Purpose: to explore reactions to the visions developed in Exercise 29-2

Key concept: vision

Procedures: Take the three vision statements developed by the small groups and role-play the reactions of the following leaders to these statements:

1. John F. Kennedy
2. Abraham Lincoln
3. Eleanor Roosevelt
4. Martin Luther King Jr.
5. President of the American Public Health Association

REFERENCES

1. P. F. Drucker, "Management's New Paradigms," *Forbes*, October 5, 1998, 152–156.
2. Drucker, "Management's New Paradigms."
3. D. P. Lenihan, *Strategic Management in Public Health: A Leadership Approach* (Burlington, MA: Jones & Bartlett, in preparation).
4. A. Toffler, *The Third Wave* (New York: Morrow, 1980).
5. J. Kotter, *Leading Change* (Boston: Harvard Business School Press, 1996).
6. H. B. Maynard Jr. and S. E. Mehrtens, *The Fourth Wave* (San Francisco: Berrett-Kohler Publishers, 1993).
7. M. R. Shechtman, *Fifth Wave Leadership: The Internal Frontier* (Tempe, AZ: Facts on Demand Press, 2002).
8. B. J. Turnock, *Public Health: What It Is and How It Works*, 5th ed. (Burlington, MA: Jones & Bartlett Learning, 2012).
9. Turnock, *Public Health: What It Is and How It Works*.
10. Pfizer Public Health Group, *The Faces of Public Health* (New York: Pfizer Global Pharmaceuticals, 2004).
11. S. R. Covey, "Three Roles of the Leader in the New Paradigm." In F. Hesselbein, M. Goldsmith, and R. Beckhard (Eds.), *The Leader of the Future* (San Francisco: Jossey-Bass, 1996).
12. Covey, "Three Roles of the Leader in the New Paradigm."
13. S. R. Covey, *The Eighth Habit* (New York: The Free Press, 2004).
14. S. Johnson, *The Present* (New York: Doubleday, 2003).
15. K. Blanchard and M. Miller, *The Secret* (San Francisco: Berrett-Kohler, 2004).
16. B. Nanus, *Visionary Leadership* (San Francisco: Jossey-Bass, 1992).
17. Nanus, *Visionary Leadership*.
18. Federal Highway Administration, *Public Involvement Techniques for Transportation Decision Making* (Washington, DC: U.S. Department of Transportation, n.d. Retrieved from http://www.Fhwa.dot.gov/reports/pittd/vision.htm.
19. Federal Highway Administration, *Public Involvement Techniques for Transportation Decision Making*.
20. B. Nanus and S. M. Dobbs, *Leaders Who Make a Difference* (San Francisco: Jossey-Bass, 1999).
21. Nanus, *Visionary Leadership*.
22. D. Goleman, R. Boyatziz, and A. McKee, *Primal Leadership* (Cambridge, MA: Harvard Business School Press, 2002).
23. P. McLaughlin, *Catch Fire* (Denver: McLaughlin, 1998).

Glossary

Accreditation A process by which a public health agency is determined to meet national standards of performance.

Action Plan A written plan that outlines the steps necessary to make an organization's goals a programmatic reality.

AIM Leadership Model A model incorporating five building blocks of leadership, including communication, follower empowerment, key issue focus, linkage to others, and life balance.

Assessment One of the three core functions of public health related to the collection and evaluation of qualitative and quantitative data to determine the health and disease rates among a population.

Assurance One of the three core functions of public health related to the development and implementation of public health programs for a specified population.

Bak's Sand Pile The notion that crises are inevitable. As you pile sand on a pile, it will eventually collapse, but it is impossible to determine the severity of the collapse ahead of time.

Black Swan Theory (Taleb) The theory that events often deviate from what is normally expected.

Boundary-Spanning Leadership Leadership oriented to soften borders and boundaries in order to promote collaborative work to create change.

Business Plan A written plan that documents the cost of doing business.

Capacity This refers to the resources, staff, budget, and internal and external relationships that are necessary to effectively carry out the core functions and essential public health services.

Certification A process of preparation with a national or state test that determines the qualifications of an individual to work successfully in the field of public health.

Coaching Working with another person to advise him or her on job-related choices and how to do a job more effectively and efficiently.

Coalition A group of interested people or organizations interested in a particular issue and wanting to share information about that issue.

Collaboration Two or more people or organizations working together to create change that is a benefit to all parties involved.

Community Benefit Programs and services designed to improve the health of the community and to increase access to community services.

Community Engagement Process in which individuals and community organizations promote programs to benefit the community.

Competency Framework The skills that a public health professional needs to be successful.

Complexity Thinking The strategies used by individuals and organizations to understand complex events and work to integrate solutions to these events into a social system.

Conflict Resolution A strategy for resolving problems or differences in perspective between two or more parties to a disagreement.

Continuous Quality Improvement A performance management system that monitors the effectiveness of services and programs with an emphasis on positive results over time.

Core Functions The three universal activities for public health: assessment, policy development, and assurance.

Credentialing A set of criteria to determine whether an individual is ready to work in a specialized field like public health.

Crisis Cycle Emergencies and disasters tend to go through a cycle from a risk audit before an event with preparedness planning occurring next to the crisis itself, a response period, and then recovery. Mitigation occurs constantly, as leaders tend to constantly monitor and change their strategies as time goes by.

Cultural Competency The development of an understanding of the cultures of different groups in our society.

Cultural Diversity Support for persons of different races, religions, genders, sexual orientation, and so on, living and working together.

Emotional Intelligence Area of cognitive ability, leadership skills, personal traits, and social skills that impact interpersonal behavior.

Empowerment Sharing power with others.

Essential Public Health Services The 10 service activities of public health as a system; these are the specific activities that grow out of the three core functions.

Governance Administration of governmental programs by a board or governmental group of elected officials with adjustment of these programs and agencies to fit policies developed as part of the political process.

Implicit Leadership Theory The theory that people gradually develop their concepts of leadership from an early age.

Incident Command System A management system for responding to a crisis or emergency with the five components of an incident commander planning section, operations section, logistics section, and financial/administration section.

Leadership Style The way a leader provides direction to an organization.

Leadership Trait Personal characteristic that impacts leadership style.

Leadership Wheel A systems model utilized to guide and monitor how public health leaders do their work.

Learning Contract Planning document prepared by one who is coached or mentored that specifies a learning plan for the next year.

Learning Management System (LMS) Software application or Web-based system used to plan, register, implement, and assess workforce development activities; the software also tracks registrants' training activities.

Management Organizational elements tied to planning, organizing, commanding, coordinating, and controlling.

Manager An individual whose job it is to make an agency operate effectively and efficiently.

MAPP Mobilizing for Action through Planning and Partnerships. This is a set of tools and processes for community public health assessment.

Matrix Organization A horizontally based organization that tends to be program-focused rather than position-oriented.

Mentoring Advising another individual about career and career choices.

Meta-leadership Refers to leaders who work successfully to break down silo thinking in organizations and who work effectively across organizations.

Mission The purpose of an organization.

Multiculturalism A political philosophy that supports a society with representatives from different races and cultures.

National Incident Management System A standardized approach to the management of a crisis, disaster, or emergency throughout the United States.

Negotiation When a third party who is objective helps others resolve a conflict.

Performance Management Measurement of the ability of an organization to meet its goals and objectives through the performance of its workforce.

PERFORM Model Purpose, Empowerment, Relationships and communication, Flexibility, Optimal productivity, Recognition and appreciation, and Morale. This is a model for high-performance teams.

Policy Development One of the three core functions of public health related to the development of policies and laws to address health threats or problems.

Primary Prevention Public health policies or programs to prevent health problems from occurring.

Public Health Infrastructure The building blocks for an effective public health system at the community level.

Reengineering Systematically starting over and restructuring how governmental agencies work.

Reinventing Government Restructuring a government agency to work more effectively and cut costs to the taxpayers.

Resilience The ability of individuals, organizations, and communities to bounce back from emergency and crisis events quickly.

Servant Leadership Leadership activities with the primary purpose to serve the needs of others.

Shadowing Following a leader to observe how the leader works on a day-to-day basis.

Situational Leadership Adaptation of the appropriate leadership style to the context in which it is demonstrated.

Six Sigma A management approach that emphasizes setting clarifying objectives, collecting data, and analyzing results in order to cut or eliminate mistakes.

Skunkworks A team that works on specialized tasks or new program development in a neutral place away from the usual workplace.

Social Capital Strong social relationships between people built through collaboration.

Social Media Web-based sites like LinkedIn, Facebook, and Twitter that facilitate social interaction.

Social Networking Practice of expanding personal and business contacts through face-to-face meetings or through computer-based social media.

Strategic Planning A process used by agencies to determine ways and programmatic methods that the agency can employ to reach its goals and objectives.

Syndemics A form of epidemiologic analysis of two health issues that interact synergistically to contribute to an excess burden of disease in a population.

System An agency, organization, or community with interacting, interrelated, or interdependent parts.

Systems Thinking Refers to the ability of a leader to see beyond the parts of a system to the whole with its interacting parts.

Third Wave Theory The theory that our society is moving from the industrial age to the information age.

Tipping Point A critical point at which a change is inevitable.

Transactional Leadership Building relationships through reciprocity.

Transformational Leadership Leading in order to create changes in policy and program direction.

Transparency Clarity and openness by top leaders about the activities taking place inside and outside the agency.

Unified Command Response to an incident by representatives from several agencies.

Value An enduring belief that generates socially acceptable behavior.

Vision Picture of where an agency wants to go in the future.

Workforce Development Training or educational programs to bring the public health employees up to date on the skills necessary to do their jobs better or to train the next generation of public health leaders.

Index

Note: Italicized page locators indicate figures; tables are noted with *t*.